TELECOMMUNICATIONS LAW AND POLICY

TELECOMMUNICATIONS LAW AND POLICY

Stuart Minor Benjamin
UNIVERSITY OF SAN DIEGO

Douglas Gary Lichtman
UNIVERSITY OF CHICAGO

Howard A. Shelanski
UNIVERSITY OF CALIFORNIA,
BERKELEY

CAROLINA ACADEMIC PRESS
Durham, North Carolina

ISBN: 0-89089-625-9
LCCN: 2001088779

CAROLINA ACADEMIC PRESS
700 Kent Street
Durham, North Carolina 27701
Tel. (919) 489-7486
Fax (919) 493-5668
www.cap-press.com

Printed in the United States of America

For Arti, Jack and Isaac.

CONTENTS

Table of Materials   xv
Copyright Permissions   xvii
Foreword   xix
Preface   xxi

Introduction: A Regulatory Overview   3

Part One. Broadcast and Spectrum Regulation   9
Chapter 1. An Introduction to Broadcast Regulation   11
  I. Early History of Broadcast   11
  II. An Introduction to the Electromagnetic Spectrum   24
    A. The Basics: Encoding, Transmitting, Receiving   24
    B. Allocating Spectrum   29
    C. The Spectrum as a Resource   32
    D. Allocating Spectrum Use   32

Chapter 2. Why Regulate Broadcast?   35
  I. The Classic Arguments: Scarcity and Interference   35
    Coase, Why Not Use the Pricing System in the Broadcast
      Industry?   37
    Benkler & Lessig, Will Technology Make CBS Unconstitutional?   40
  II. Did Government Regulate Simply to Benefit Special Interests?   42
    Hazlett, The Rationality of U.S. Regulation of the Broadcast
      Spectrum   42
  III. Are There Market Failures That Might Justify Regulation?   49
    A. Public Goods   49
    Coase, Why Not Use the Pricing System in the Broadcast
      Industry?   50
    B. Should We Respect Consumer Preferences?   52

Chapter 3. How We Regulate Broadcast   57
  I. The FCC as an Administrative Agency   57
  II. Four Roles for the Regulator   62
  III. The Band Plan   64
    A. Finding Spectrum for PCS   64
    In re Redevelopment of Spectrum to Encourage Innovation
      in the Use of New Telecommunications Technologies   66
    B. Permitting Changing Uses   72
    In re Service Rules for the 746–764 and 776–794 MHZ Bands   73

Chapter 4. License Hearings at the FCC (1934–1998)   81
  I. Initial Assignment Hearings   82
      In re H.E. Studebaker   82
      In re Charles Henry Gunthorpe, Jr.   83
  II. Comparative Hearings   85
      A. Basic Comparative Licensing Criteria   86
         FCC Policy Statement on Comparative Broadcast Hearings   86
      B. Special Considerations for Racial Minorities and Women   90
         i. Minority Preferences (Pre-*Adarand*)   90
            Metro Broadcasting, Inc. v. FCC   90
         ii. Preferences for Women   101
         iii. *Adarand* (*Metro Broadcasting* Overruled)   102
         iv. Equal Employment Opportunity Regulations   103
            Lutheran Church-Missouri Synod v. FCC   104
  III. License Renewal for Incumbents   111
      Citizens Communications Center v. FCC   113
      Central Florida Enterprises v. FCC   116
  IV. License Transfers   122
      Changes in the Entertainment Formats of Broadcast Stations   124
      WNCN Listeners Guild v. FCC   126
      FCC v. WNCN Listeners Guild   129
  V. Licensing Case Study   132
      In re Application of Simon Geller   132

Chapter 5. The Transition from Hearings to Auctions   139
  I. Reform of the Licensing Process   140
      In re Prevention of Abuses of the Renewal Process   140
  II. Lotteries, Auctions, and Comparative Hearings   144
  III. Initial Assignment by Auction   146
      In re Implementation of Section 309(j) of the
         Communications Act   147

Chapter 6. The Licensee as Public Trustee   157
  I. The Fairness Doctrine and Related Obligations   159
      A. The Fairness Doctrine   159
         Miami Herald Publishing Co. v. Tornillo   159
         Red Lion Broadcasting Co. v. FCC   161
         Fairness Doctrine Report   168
         In re Complaint of Syracuse Peace Council   180
      B. The Personal Attack and Political Editorial Rules   187
      C. Political Broadcasting   189
         In re Request of ABC, Inc. for Declaratory Ruling   190
         In re Request for Declaratory Ruling of National
            Association of Broadcasters Regarding Section 312(a)(7)
            of the Communications Act   196
         In re Petition for Reconsideration by People for the American
            Way and Media Access Project of Declaratory Ruling
            Regarding Section 312(a)(7) of the Communications Act   199
  II. Indecent Broadcasts   204

FCC v. Pacifica Foundation   204
In re Pacifica Foundation [*Jerker*]   215
Action for Children's Television v. FCC [*Act III*]   220
III. Televised Violence   239
  Balkin, Media Filters, the V-Chip, and the Foundations of
    Broadcast Regulation   242
IV. Children's Television   254
  In re Children's Television Programming and Advertising
    Practices   255
  Policies and Rules Concerning Children's Television
    Programming (1991)   260
  Policies and Rules Concerning Children's Television
    Programming (1996)   263
V. Commercialization, Ascertainment, and Other Commission Rules 279
  In re Deregulation of Commercial Television   279

Chapter 7. Fostering Competition in Broadcasting   289
  I. The Television Networks   290
    A. Network Dominance   290
      Besen et al., Misregulating Television   291
    B. The Network/Affiliate Relationship   297
      Besen et al., Misregulating Television   298
    C. The Network/Program Supplier Relationship   302
      Schurz Communications v. FCC   304
  II. Ownership Restrictions   313
    Biennial Report, Review of the Commission's Broadcast Rules
      and Other Rules Adopted Pursuant to Section 202 of the
      Telecommunications Act of 1996   314

Chapter 8. Case Studies in Low Power FM Radio and
  Digital Television   325
  I. Low Power FM Radio   325
  II. Digital Television   332
    A. Making Room for HDTV   333
      In re Advanced Television Systems (1991)   334
    B. Choosing a Standard   340
      In re Advanced Television Systems (1996)   341
    C. Services Required and Permissible on Spectrum Given
      to Broadcasers for DTV   351
      In re Advanced Television Systems (1997)   351
    D. Public Interest Obligations   360
      Final Report of the Advisory Committee on Public Interest
        Obligations of Digital Television Broadcasters   361

Part Two. Cable Television   369
Chapter 9. Cable Basics and the Early History   371
  I. Introduction   371
  II. The Problem of Natural Monopoly   374
  III. Early Regulatory Responses to Cable   380

Besen & Crandall, The Deregulation of Cable Television   380
Home Box Office (HBO) v. FCC   391
IV. The Jurisdiction Puzzle: Who Should Regulate?   399
Group W Cable, Inc. v. City of Santa Cruz   400

Chapter 10. Rate Regulation and Local Franchise Authority   413
I. Rate Regulation   413
Rate Regulation of Cable Services   414
Note on Rate Regulation   425
II. Local Franchise Agreements   429
Time Warner Entertainment Co. v. FCC   431
Rate Regulation of Cable Service   438

Chapter 11. The Broadcast/Cable Relationship   441
I. Copyright and Compulsory Licenses   442
II. Syndicated Exclusivity and Network Nonduplication   445
United Video v. FCC   446
III. Must-Carry and Retransmission Consent   453
Turner Broadcasting System, Inc. v. FCC [*Turner I*]   456
Turner Broadcasting System, Inc. v. FCC [*Turner II*]   474

Chapter 12. Structural Limitations   499
I. Protecting Program Suppliers   500
A. Controls on Vertical Integration   501
Implementation of Section 11 of the Cable Television
Consumer Protection and Competition Act of 1992   501
B. Controls on Horizontal Concentration   508
Implementation of Section 11(c) of the Cable Television
Consumer Protection and Competition Act of 1992   508
Judicial Review   522
II. Regulation of Program Supply Contracts   525
Development of Competition and Diversity in Video
Programming Distribution and Carriage   525

Chapter 13. Direct Broadcast Satellite   541
I. The Primetime Litigation   544
CBS Broadcasting v. Primetime 24   544
II. The Satellite Home Viewer Improvement Act of 1999   550
The Satellite Television Act of 1999   551
Note on the SHVIA   553
III. Requiring Educational Programming on DBS   557
Time Warner Entertainment Co. v. FCC (1996)   558
Time Warner Entertainment Co. v. FCC (1997)   561

Chapter 14. Indecency Revisited   567
Cruz v. Ferre   567
Denver Area Educational Telecommunications Consortium,
Inc. v. FCC   570
United States v. Playboy Entertainment Group, Inc.   588

Part Three. Telephone Regulation   603

Chapter 15. An Introduction to Telephone Regulation   605
  I. Telephone System Basics   605
    A. The Early History   605
      Huber et al., Federal Telecommunications Law   607
    B. Federal Versus State Regulation   610
    C. Telephone System Vocabulary   613
  II. Telephony as a Monopoly Service   614
    Note on Ramsey Pricing   621
  III. Precursors to Divestiture   623
    A. Competition in Customer Premises Equipment   624
      Huber et al., Federal Telecommunications Law   624
    B. Competition in the Long Distance Market   628
      Robinson, The Titanic Remembered: AT&T and the Changing
        World of Telecommunications   629
    C. Communications/Computer Convergence   632
      Robinson, The Titanic Remembered: AT&T and the Changing
        World of Telecommunications   633
    D. Rate-of-Return Regulation   635
      In the Matter of Policy and Rules Concerning Rates for
        Dominant Carriers   636

Chapter 16. Breakup of the Bell Monopoly   641
  I. Introduction   641
  II. The Modification of Final Judgment (MFJ)   643
    United States v. American Telephone & Telegraph Co.   643
    Note on the Government's Theory   661
  III. Antitrust Theories Underlying the MFJ   664
    Noll & Owen, The Anticompetitive Uses of Regulation: *United
      States v. AT&T*   664

Chapter 17. Issues Post-Divestiture   681
  I. Rate Regulation in a Post-Divestiture World   682
    In re Policy & Rules Concerning Rates for Dominant Carriers   683
  II. The BOC "Line of Business" Restrictions   691
    A. An Overview of the Restrictions   691
      Robinson, The Titanic Remembered: AT&T and the Changing
        World of Telecommunications   691
    B. Judicial Review of the Restrictions   693
      i. The Consent Decree   693
        United States v. Western Electric Co. (1990)   693
        United States v. Western Electric Co. (1993)   700
      ii. FCC Rules Independent of the Decree   704
        California v. FCC [*Computer III*]   704
  III. Universal Service after Divestiture   712

Chapter 18. The Telecommunications Act of 1996   715
  I. The Local Competition Provisions   717

In re Implementation of the Local Competition Provisions
    of the Telecommunications Act Of 1996   719
AT&T Corporation v. Iowa Utilities Board   725
Note on Jurisdiction   731
In re Implementation of the Local Competition Provisions of
    the Telecommunications Act of 1996   735
Note on the Pricing of Network Elements   740
Iowa Utilities Board v. FCC   743
Note on Interconnection   749
In re Implementation of the Local Competition Provisions of
    the Telecommunications Act of 1996   751
II. BOC Line of Business Restrictions Under the Act   755
AT&T Corporation v. FCC   758
SBC Communications, Inc. v. FCC   762
III. Universal Service and Access Charge Reform   768
FCC News Release: Joint Board Adopts Universal Service
    Recommendations   771
In re Federal-State Joint Board on Universal Service   773
In re Access Charge Reform   784

Chapter 19. Mergers and Acquisitions   793
I. Background   794
II. The SBC/Ameritech Proceeding   797
In re Applications of Ameritech Corp., Transferor, and SBC
    Communications, Inc., Transferee, for Consent to Transfer
    Control of Licenses and Lines Pursuant to Sections 214 and
    310(D) of the Communications Act   797
Separate Statement of Commissioner Harold Furchtgott-Roth,
    Concurring in Part, Dissenting in Part   807
Statement of Commissioner Michael K. Powell, Concurring in
    Part, Dissenting in Part   814
III. Merger Reform   817
Statement of Chairman William E. Kennard   818
Statement of Commissioner Harold Furchtgott-Roth   820

Part Four. The Internet and Advanced Services   825

Chapter 20. The Internet and its Regulation   827
I. The History and Architecture of the Internet   828
II. Regulation of the Internet   835
A. The Principles of Internet (Un)Regulation   837
Clinton Administration, A Framework for Global Electronic
    Commerce   837
B. Content Regulation   839
i. Indecent Communication via Telephone   839
Sable Communications of California, Inc. v. FCC   839
In re Regulations Concerning Indecent Communications by
    Telephone   845
ii. Indecent Communication over the Internet   848
Reno v. ACLU   848

Chapter 21. Advanced Services and Internet Architecture 867
  I. An Introduction to Advanced Services 867
    A. The FCC's Implementation of Section 706 868
      Inquiry Concerning the Deployment of Advanced
        Telecommunications 868
    B. Regulatory Alternatives 878
  II. Unbundled Access to Telephone System Infrastructure 880
      In the Matter of Implementation of the Local Competition
        Provisions of the Telecommunications Act of 1996 881
      Notes and Questions 885
      In the Matters of Deployment of Wireline Services Offering
        Advanced Telecommunications Capability and
        Implementation of the Local Competition Provisions of the
        Telecommunications Act of 1996 886
  III. Open Access to Cable System Infrastructure 892
      AT&T v. City of Portland 895
      Inquiry Concerning High-Speed Access to the Internet over
        Cable and Other Facilities 901
      Rogerson, The Regulation of Broadband Telecommunications,
        the Principle of Regulating Narrowly Defined Input
        Bottlenecks, and Incentives for Investment and Innovation 912
  IV. Non-Regulation of the Internet Backbone: Peering and Transit
    Arrangements 915
      Kende, The Digital Handshake: Connecting Internet Backbones 916

Chapter 22. Characterizing Internet Service Providers 927
  I. Access Charges and Reciprocal Compensation 930
      In the Matter of Access Charge Reform 931
      In re Implementation of the Local Competition Provisions in
        the Telecommunications Act of 1996, Inter-Carrier
        Compensation for ISP-Bound Traffic 935
      Bell Atlantic Telephone Company v. FCC 941
  II. Internet Protocol Telephony 945
      In the Matter of the Federal-State Joint Board on Universal
        Service 946

Chapter 23. Why an FCC? 951
      A New Federal Communications Commission for the 21st
        Century 952
      Huber, Abolish the FCC and Let Common Law Rule the
        Telecosm 956
      Sunstein, The First Amendment in Cyberspace 963
      Krattenmaker & Powe, Converging First Amendment Principles
        for Converging Communications Media 969

Statutory Appendix 979

Conceptual Index and Telecommunications Glossary 1045

TABLE OF MATERIALS

Access Charge Reform, In re, 784

Access Charge Reform, In the Matter of, 931

Action for Children's Television v. FCC [*Act III*], 220

Advanced Television Systems (1991), In re, 334

Advanced Television Systems (1996), In re, 341

Advanced Television Systems (1997), In re, 351

Application of Simon Geller, In re, 132

Applications of Ameritech Corp., Transferor, and SBC Communications, Inc., Transferee, for Consent to Transfer Control of Licenses and Lines Pursuant to Sections 214 and 310(D) of the Communications Act, In re, 797

AT&T Corporation v. FCC, 758

AT&T Corporation v. Iowa Utilities Board, 725

AT&T v. City of Portland, 895

Bell Atlantic Telephone Company v. FCC, 941

Biennial Report, Review of the Commission's Broadcast Rules and Other Rules Adopted Pursuant to Section 202 of the Telecommunications Act of 1996, 314

California v. FCC [*Computer III*], 704

CBS Broadcasting v. Primetime 24, 544

Central Florida Enterprises v. FCC, 116

Children's Television Programming (1991), Policies and Rules Concerning, 260

Children's Television Programming (1996), Policies and Rules Concerning, 263

Children's Television Programming and Advertising Practices, In re, 255

Citizens Communications Center v. FCC, 113

Complaint of Syracuse Peace Council, In re, 180

Cruz v. Ferre, 567

Denver Area Educational Telecommunications Consortium, Inc. v. FCC, 570

Deployment of Wireline Services Offering Advanced Telecommunications Capability and Implementation of the Local Competition Provisions of the Telecommunications Act of 1996, In the Matters of, 886

Deregulation of Commercial Television, In re, 279

Fairness Doctrine Report, 168

FCC Policy Statement on Comparative Broadcast Hearings, 86

FCC v. Pacifica Foundation, 204

FCC v. WNCN Listeners Guild, 129

Federal-State Joint Board on Universal Service, In re, 773

Federal-State Joint Board on Universal Service, In the Matter of the, 946

Final Report of the Advisory Committee on Public Interest Obligations of Digital Television Broadcasters, 361

Group W Cable, Inc. v. City of Santa Cruz, 400

Gunthorpe, Jr., In re Charles Henry, 83

Home Box Office (HBO) v. FCC, 391

Inquiry Concerning High-Speed Access to the Internet over Cable and Other Facilities, 901

Iowa Utilities Board v. FCC, 743

Local Competition Provisions in the Telecommunications Act of 1996 (Inter-Carrier Compensation for ISP-Bound Traffic), In re Implementation of the, 935

Local Competition Provisions of the Telecommunications Act Of 1996 (Overview Excerpt, First Report & Order), In re Implementation of the, 719

Local Competition Provisions of the Telecommunications Act of 1996 (Third Report & Order), In re Implementation of the, 735

Local Competition Provisions of the Telecommunications Act of 1996 (Interconnection Issues, First Report & Order), In re Implementation of the, 751

Local Competition Provisions of the Telecommunications Act Of 1996 (Internet Infrastructure), In re Implementation of the, 881

Lutheran Church-Missouri Synod v. FCC, 104

Metro Broadcasting, Inc. v. FCC, 90

Miami Herald Publishing Co. v. Tornillo, 159

Pacifica Foundation [*Jerker*], In re, 215

Petition for Reconsideration by People for the American Way and Media Access Project of Declaratory Ruling Regarding Section 312(a)(7) of the Communications Act, In re, 199

Prevention of Abuses of the Renewal Process, In re, 140

Rates for Dominant Carriers, In re Policy & Rules Concerning, 683

Rates for Dominant Carriers, In the Matter of Policy and Rules Concerning, 636

Red Lion Broadcasting Co. v. FCC, 161

Redevelopment of Spectrum to Encourage Innovation in the Use of New Telecommunications Technologies, In re, 66

Regulations Concerning Indecent Communications by Telephone, In re, 845

Reno v. ACLU, 848

Request for Declaratory Ruling of National Association of Broadcasters Regarding Section 312(a)(7) of the Communications Act, In re, 196

Request of ABC, Inc. for Declaratory Ruling, In re, 190

Sable Communications of California, Inc. v. FCC, 839

Satellite Home Viewer Improvement Act of 1999, 550

SBC Communications, Inc. v. FCC, 762

Schurz Communications v. FCC, 304

Section 11 of the Cable Television Consumer Protection and Competition Act of 1992 (Vertical Integration), Implementation of, 501

Section 11(c) of the Cable Television Consumer Protection and Competition Act of 1992 (Horizontal Concentration), Implementation of, 508

Section 309(j) of the Communications Act, In re Implementation of, 147

Service Rules for the 746-764 and 776-794 MHZ Bands, In re, 73

Studebaker, In re H.E., 82

Time Warner Entertainment Co. v. FCC (1996), 431, 558

Time Warner Entertainment Co. v. FCC (1997), 561

Turner Broadcasting System, Inc. v. FCC [*Turner I*], 456

Turner Broadcasting System, Inc. v. FCC [*Turner II*], 474

United States v. American Telephone & Telegraph Co., 643

United States v. Playboy Entertainment Group, Inc., 588

United States v. Western Electric Co. (1990), 693

United States v. Western Electric Co. (1993), 700

United Video v. FCC, 446

WNCN Listeners Guild v. FCC, 126

COPYRIGHT PERMISSIONS

The following copyright holders have granted permission for us to reprint or excerpt copyrighted materials in this book. Our sincere thanks thus goes to:

Aspen Publishers, Inc., for permission to excerpt *Federal Telecommunications Law* by Michael K. Kellogg, John Thorne, and Peter W. Huber. Copyright 1992 by Michael K. Kellogg, John Thorne, and Peter W. Huber. All rights reserved.

Aspen Publishers, Inc., for permission to excerpt from *Federal Telecommunications Law*, Second Edition, by Michael K. Kellogg, John Thorne, and Peter W. Huber. Copyright 1999 by Michael K. Kellogg, John Thorne, and Peter W. Huber. All rights reserved.

Stanley Besen, Thomas Krattenmaker, Richard Metzger, and John Woodbury for permission to excerpt a section of their book, *Misregulating Television* (1984). All rights reserved.

The Duke University School of Law, the Duke Law Journal, and Jack Balkin for permission to excerpt J.M. Balkin, Media Filters, The V-chip, and The Foundations of Broadcast Regulation, 45 Duke L.J. 1131 (1996).

The Duke University School of Law, Law and Contemporary Problems, Stanley Besen, and Robert Crandall, for permission to reprint the article, "The Deregulation of Cable Television," 44 Law & Contemp. Probs. 77 (1981).

Thomas Krattenmaker and Lucas Powe, for permission to adapt various sections of their text, *Regulating Broadcast Progamming* (1994). All rights reserved.

The New Republic, Yochai Benkler, and Larry Lessig, for permission to excerpt the article, "Will Technology Make CBS Unconstitutional," *The New Republic* (Dec. 14, 1998), at 12-14.

Roger Noll, Bruce Owen, and Larry White, for permission to excerpt Noll & Owen's article, "The Anticompetitive Uses of Regulation: United States v. AT&T," in *The Antitrust Revolution* (J. Kwoka & L. White, eds., 1989).

Oxford University Press and Peter Huber, for permission to excerpt Peter Huber, *Law and Disorder in Cyberspace* (1997). All rights reserved.

Phillips Business Information, Inc., for permission to reprint a cartoon from PBI's collection of telecommunications cartoons.

Universal Press Syndicate, for permission to reprint a CALVIN AND HOBBES cartoon in Chapter Six. That cartoon is copyright 1993 by Bill Watterson. All rights reserved.

FOREWORD

BY THOMAS G. KRATTENMAKER

The book you are about to read is first-rate. I know this not because I had anything to do with its writing (although you may find one or two of my old jokes in here), but because I was privileged to read the full Benjamin, Lichtman, and Shelanski text in final draft form.

As many of you know, my involvement with this project actually began much earlier than that. Back in 1991, I wrote a telecommunications law textbook for Carolina Academic Press. I wrote that text for a simple and very personal reason: to help me teach the kind of course I believed beginning students of telecommunications law should have. I published it in the hopes that colleagues at other schools might be able to use those same materials to teach the kinds of courses that they, too, wanted to teach.

I am gratified to report that my book achieved success far beyond what I had imagined. And to all of you who have made it possible for me to share my enthusiasm for telecommunications law and policy so broadly, let me offer a heartfelt thank you. Through two editions and ten years, it was an incredible experience to learn from and with so many of you.

That said, a couple of years ago I decided to hand the project over to Stuart, Doug, and Howard. At first, I invited them to simply update my book, the original goal being a third edition that would incorporate some of the many technical and legal changes that had taken place since I finished the second edition back in 1997. But the project took on a life of its own, and the book in your hands now is almost entirely new.

After reviewing the final draft of this book just a few days before it went to press, we decided that it was appropriate to name the book as it now stands. This is not the third edition of Krattenmaker; it is instead the first edition of Benjamin, Lichtman, and Shelanski. I write here to say that I am proud of what Stuart, Doug, and Howard have accomplished and delighted that I helped them get started on a project that they brought to such a successful conclusion.

I wish them, and all of you, a wonderful experience with the book. As I wrote a decade ago, and can now repeat with even greater force, telecommunications is an exciting, challenging, and important field of inquiry. Welcome to it.

Tom Krattenmaker
February 2001

PREFACE

The theme of almost any law school casebook is apparent from the outset. An administrative law casebook, for example, pulls together materials about a particular style of governmental institution. A copyright text similarly considers a particular combination of exclusive rights recognized in a particular range of creative works. Thus, even though an administrative law text will consider agencies as diverse as the Environmental Protection Agency and the Federal Aviation Administration; and even though a copyright text will similarly examine works as varied as paintings, sculptures, and computer software; in each of these texts it is easy to understand why such seemingly disparate materials are bundled together into a single coherent conversation.

The implicit logic of a telecommunications text, however, may be less transparent. Why should statutes and regulations related to broadcast radio, broadcast television, cable, satellite, wireline telephony, cellular telephony, and the Internet all be considered in a single volume? Do these communication mechanisms really have that much in common? Why not divide the book into two, for example, featuring technologies used for one-to-many communication in one volume, and technologies used for one-to-one information exchanges in another? Why, in short, a book on telecommunications law writ large?

The insight, we think, is that telecommunications technologies are all to some degree substitutable, and therefore much of telecommunications law is about making sure that society uses the right resources to accomplish the right tasks. Television content, for example, can be delivered over the airwaves, but it also can be delivered by wire. Television by wire can be a pay service or an advertiser-supported service, just as broadcast television can operate in either form. Shifting television from the airwaves to wires frees up the airwaves for other uses, such as cellular telephony; and, indeed, putting television exclusively onto wire would likely lead to significant new investments in the cable television infrastructure—something that would be valuable in the short run for the delivery of television signals and in the long run perhaps for the provision of more advanced telecommunications services like, for example, Internet access.

Almost every telecommunications issue plays out exactly the way the television issue played out above: a question that starts by focusing on one telecommunications topic inevitably has implications for virtually every other. Thus, it is hard to consider any one branch of telecommunications in isolation. All telecommunications resources can be put to more than one telecommunications use; telecommunications topics are therefore hopelessly interconnected.

This same point explains why sometimes this text will dabble into discussions of media that seem utterly peripheral to the telecommunications heading,

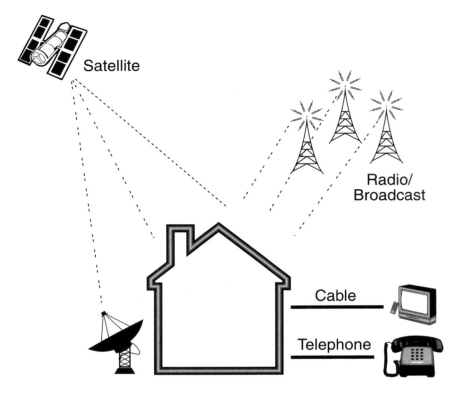

INFORMATION PIPELINES INTO THE HOME. There are many pathways into the modern home, each to one degree or another capable of delivering interactive information services.

for example the markets for videocassettes and music albums. After all, one question broadcast policy has to answer is the question of why any of the airwaves should be devoted to the delivery of music via radio given that music aficionados can purchase their favorite tunes at the local store. It might be that the airwaves could be put to better use by making possible various portable Internet services than by, instead, transmitting Mariah Carey's latest musical offering. Here again, then, no telecommunications topic can be studied in complete isolation.

There are other reasons why broadcast radio, broadcast television, cable, satellite, wireline telephony, cellular telephony, and the Internet should all be considered together. For example, in all of these markets, one of the main concerns motivating regulation is the worry that competition is either unworkable or undesirable. To give but one example, policymakers have long worried that the economics of local telephone service are such that either only one firm can survive in the long run ("competition is unworkable") or a single firm can provide a given quality of phone service at lower total cost than can multiple competitors ("competition is undesirable"). Policymakers in this area therefore continually struggle with the question of whether regulation should displace competition as the principal mechanism for ensuring good performance. Similar arguments that regulation might have advantages over competition arise in every telecommunications market.

Finally, any attempt at separating the various strands of telecommunications is inevitably confounded by the phenomenon of technological convergence. Not only are broadcast, cable, telephony, and the Internet substitutable and interconnected, but also the lines between them are blurry, and becoming more so over time. More than merely substituting for each other, televisions, telephones, and computers increasingly *are* each other. That provides yet another reason to treat them all together in one volume.

Of course, this blurring of technological lines contrasts sharply with the regulatory regime, which has long put broadcast, cable, telephony, and the Internet into separate legal categories and subjected them to quite different rules and regulations. Technologies may be converging, but the legal world is still significantly balkanized. Indeed, one way to articulate the current state of telecommunications law is to say that society is today in the middle of a transition process that will likely result in not only technological but also legal convergence; but how long that transition will take, and on whose terms the law (and the technology) will converge, remain open issues. During this period, battles will therefore erupt not only over technology but also over the guiding legal regime. And the stakes for all players, including not only the firms but also the regulators, are quite high.

All of these considerations make both organizing and writing a casebook a major challenge. We would do a disservice to our readers—particularly as many are likely to be lawyers and law students—if we let a focus on technological convergence blur the important distinctions between the legal regimes for broadcast, cable, telephony, and the Internet. At the same time, we would fail to capture important technological developments if we treated these legal categories as wholly separating each technology from the others. We have therefore sought an approach that attempts to capture the richness and complexity of the regulatory regime while emphasizing the ways that telecommunications technologies cross the lines that regulators have written in the sand. Accordingly, we have organized the book along the four main dimensions suggested here—Part One considers broadcast, Part Two cable, Part Three telephony, and Part Four the Internet and advanced services—yet, at the same time, each section offers contrasts and questions that cross these somewhat artificial boundaries and thereby begin to explain how telecommunications policy is necessarily linked from topic to topic.

A note about the project: initially, we envisioned this as a relatively modest attempt to update Tom Krattenmaker's telecommunications text, the end goal being a book that would update and revise the text that Tom had most recently published in 1997. The deal was clear at the outset, however, that we were going to revise Tom's manuscript but not rewrite it. There were parts of Tom's book that could use an overhaul, but each of us thought that any such overhaul could wait for a new edition a few years hence.

That deal lasted all of five seconds. Lichtman was first to lose any semblance of self-restraint, within the first few months going back to even the historical sections and reediting, reorganizing, and rewriting huge chunks of material. The disease turned out to be a contagious one. As we write this final entry, there is barely a paragraph from Tom's original text that has been left untouched. Throughout the text there are new questions, new materials, and new discussions of core concepts. That said, we have endeavored to maintain Tom's basic architecture. Our hope is that our revisions have been broad enough so as to make the book even stronger than it originally was, but narrow enough that faculty members who have used Tom's earlier two editions will easily be able to integrate the new text into the course they already love to teach.

Now, some acknowledgments. This text would not have been possible without Tom Krattenmaker's help and support. One of us actually used Tom's book back in law school; and, in the years since, all of us have enjoyed learning from Krattenmaker the person as well as Krattenmaker the book. Thank you, Tom, for entrusting the three of us with your manuscript. Karl Auerbach, Jack Balkin, Karl Mannheim, John Roberts, Peter Shane, Jim Speta, and Phil Weiser also have contributed significantly to this project and are owed substantial thanks. Each reviewed significant portions of the manuscript (if not the whole thing) and offered helpful suggestions that are now reflected here. Our thanks go to Stanley Besen and Lucas Powe as well. While their contributions were explicitly made to Tom's two editions, their suggestions surely continue to benefit us here as well. Lastly, sincere thanks to our research assistants: from the University of Chicago, Adam Bellack, Barry Blonien, Martha Pacold and Danny Sokol; from the University of San Diego, Joe Hughes, Dana Robinson, and Mike Whittaker; and from Boalt Hall, Madeline Burgess, Elizabeth Field, Chris Swain and Larry Trask.

One final word before we step aside: the materials included in this book have been ruthlessly edited for style, length, and clarity. To avoid clutter, we have left almost all of those changes unmarked. While we are confident that none of our edits altered the meaning of the relevant passages, we do want to warn readers that the materials have been edited so as to maximize their value in the educational setting and, thus, attorneys looking to cite materials in court documents are advised to look to the original sources before quoting any of the materials excerpted here.

With that, we welcome you to the text. We hope you find your study of telecommunications to be a rewarding one.

Stuart Benjamin, Douglas Lichtman & Howard Shelanski
February 2001

TELECOMMUNICATIONS
LAW AND POLICY

A REGULATORY OVERVIEW

The governing statute for the regulation of telecommunications in the United States is the Communications Act of 1934, 47 U.S.C. §1 et seq., and the governing agency the Act established to implement its provisions is the Federal Communications Commission. The 1934 Act brings together under one legal umbrella and one administrative body the regulation of all sectors of the telecommunications industry—from televisions to telephones, from cable to satellites, and everything in between. The Communications Act of 1934 has been amended numerous times, and several of those amendments have been sufficiently extensive that they are often referred to as Acts in and of themselves, despite their being incorporated into the 1934 Act. Principal examples of such amendments are the Cable Communications Policy Act of 1984, the Cable Television Consumer Protection and Competition Act of 1992, and the Telecommunications Act of 1996, all of which amended (among other things) scattered sections of 47 U.S.C. In this book, we will often refer to those laws by their own names, but readers should understand that, as a technical matter, they are statutory amendments to the 1934 Act.

Communications Regulation Before 1934

The 1934 Act was not the first communications statute passed in the United States. It was, however, the first statute to bring different areas of the telecommunications industry under one statutory title and one administrative agency. Before 1934, telegraph, telephone, and radio communications were governed by separate laws and separate governmental bodies. Radio, for example, was first regulated by the Radio Act of 1912. That statute required all users of the radio spectrum to obtain a license and placed licensing authority with the U.S. Secretary of Commerce.[1] The thrust of the 1912 Act was to allocate different blocks of spectrum to different users—for example the military, commercial interests, and amateur radio operators—and to prioritize their access to the airwaves. Emergency signals such as marine distress calls had first priority for transmission; military signals came next, followed by commercial uses and, finally, amateur signals.

Fifteen years later, Congress passed the Radio Act of 1927, which repealed the 1912 Act. Like its predecessor, the 1927 Act stipulated that spectrum could be used only upon grant of license; but it also formally declared the electromagnetic spectrum to be government property and moved the authority for issuing such licenses from the Secretary of Commerce to a new Federal Radio Commis-

---

1. Ch. 287, 37 Stat. 302 (1912) (repealed 1927). Congress had previously passed the Wireless Ship Act, ch. 379, 36 Stat. 629 (1910) (repealed 1954), which required all passenger ships to carry wireless sets. Both statutes are discussed in Chapter One.

sion.[2] The 1927 Act broadly defined radio communications as "any intelligence, message, signal, power, pictures, or communication of any nature transferred by electrical energy from one point to another without the aid of any wire connecting the points." 44 Stat. at 1173. Of the activities it covered, the Act particularly targeted commercial broadcasting. Importantly, this was the legislation that formally introduced the requirement that licensees serve the "public interest, convenience, or necessity" — of which there will be considerably more discussion later in the book. 44 Stat. at 1167. The Act did not in any way address wireline communications like telegraphy or telephony.

Regulation of telephone and telegraph services developed separately from regulation of radio in the early 1900s. For a time, telephone service was not regulated. The first statute to regulate telephone service was the Mann-Elkins Act of 1910,[3] passed more than fifteen years after the original Bell telephone patents had expired and well after numerous independent telephone carriers had entered into competition with the Bell system. The Mann-Elkins Act assigned regulatory jurisdiction over telephony to the Interstate Commerce Commission, which already had regulatory authority over the railroads as well as other network services. The mandate of the Act was fairly narrow by current standards. The Act categorized telephone service providers as "common carriers" — *i.e.* carriers that were "obligated to provide service on request at just and reasonable rates, without unjust discrimination or undue preference."[4] The ICC's charge was to enforce these common carrier requirements. The Mann-Elkins Act, however, neither contained any requirement that telephone carriers file tariffs (rate plans) nor authorized the ICC to implement such a requirement. The Act thus gave the agency quite limited power, and it is perhaps not surprising that the ICC held only four proceedings to investigate telephone rates in the years from 1910 to 1934.[5] While the ICC did try actively to regulate merger and acquisition behavior in the telephone industry, as an agency it was far more concerned with regulating railroads than with regulating telephones and, in the end, it played only a modest role in overseeing the performance of the telecommunications industry.

The ICC was not the only regulatory authority concerned with telecommunications, however. Unlike radio, telephony was subject not just to federal oversight, but to state regulation as well. State regulators reviewed rates, established accounting rules, and implemented service requirements related to local telephone service. As we will discuss in greater detail in Chapter Fifteen, the states' regulatory sphere was strictly limited to intrastate telephone service and related facilities. But given that the vast bulk of telephone calls have typically been "local," this limitation did not mean that state commissions were weak or insignificant regulatory forces. Indeed, even today the boundary between state and federal regulatory jurisdiction over telephone carriers continues to be an area of both important and vigorous dispute.[6]

---

2. Ch. 169, 44 Stat. 1162 (1927) (repealed 1934).

3. Mann-Elkins Act of 1910, ch. 309, 36 Stat. 539 (1910). This statute is discussed more fully in Chapter Fifteen.

4. 36 Stat. 539, Ch. 309 §§7, 12.

5. Peter W. Huber, Michael K. Kellogg & John Thorne, Federal Telecommunications Law (2d ed. 1999) at 215.

6. We address jurisdictional issues primarily in Chapters Fifteen (pre-1996 Act) and Eighteen (jurisdiction under the 1996 Act).

Regulatory Integration under the 1934 Act

The Communications Act of 1934 thus accomplished an important organizational task. It extended jurisdiction over telecommunications to an expert agency rather than assigning such jurisdiction to entities, such as the ICC or the Department of Commerce, that had other concerns. But, instead of creating separate experts for each telecommunications field, the 1934 Act would ultimately be interpreted to have created a single expert agency with broad purview.[7] The Radio Act of 1927 had created a focused agency for spectrum management (the Federal Radio Commission); the 1934 Act would now create a regulatory agency for telephony and charge that same agency with the duty to regulate the airwaves. That new agency was the Federal Communications Commission (FCC). The Act thus abolished the Federal Radio Commission, repealed the Mann-Elkins Act, and put an end to the fragmented jurisdiction that had existed until 1934:

> For the purpose of regulating interstate and foreign commerce in communication by wire and radio so as to make available, so far as possible, to all people of the United States, a rapid, efficient, Nation-wide, and world-wide wire and radio communication service with adequate facilities at reasonable charges, for the purpose of the national defense, and for the purpose of securing a more effective execution of this policy by centralizing authority hereto granted by law to several agencies and by granting additional authority with respect to interstate and foreign commerce in wire and radio communication, there is created a commission to be known as the "Federal Communications Commission," which shall be constituted as hereinafter provided, and which shall execute and enforce the provisions of this chapter.[8]

The FCC was thus responsible for promulgating regulations to implement the 1934 Act, and for interpreting the many gaps and ambiguities that appeared throughout that lengthy statute. This implementing role was of immediate and substantial importance. For while the Act incorporated many aspects of preexisting regulation (like the licensing requirements for broadcasters, and common carriage obligations for telephone companies), and the Act also preserved and even strengthened the jurisdiction of state regulators over intrastate telephony, it also markedly increased the scope of federal communications regulation. It was in the exercise of that new authority that the FCC would ultimately find its most significant powers.

The Structure of the 1934 Act

The 1934 Act is codified at Title 47 of the United States Code which, in turn, is divided into seven subchapters or "titles" of its own. Titles I, IV, V, and VII set forth general provisions that relate either to the FCC itself or to issues

---

7. This was an open question in certain settings. For example, we will see in Chapter Nine that there was considerable doubt over whether the FCC had authority to regulate cable television under the 1934 Act. The Supreme Court ultimately held that it (for the most part) did, and Congress later amended the 1934 Act to make that authority explicit.

8. 48 Stat. 1064, §1 (1934) (codified as amended at 47 U.S.C. §151). The section has been amended twice: in 1937 when the words "for the purpose of promoting safety of life and property through the use of wire and radio communication" were added, and in 1996, when the words "without discrimination on the bases of color, religion, national origin or sex" were added.

that transcend any particular industry sector or category of service. Title I, for example, sets forth general provisions pertaining to the structure, jurisdiction, and operation of the Federal Communications Commission. 47 U.S.C. §§151–161. Titles IV and V address a variety of procedural matters, with the former focusing on enforcement jurisdiction and requirements for administrative proceedings and the latter focusing on penalties and forfeitures for violation of regulations under the Act. 47 U.S.C. §§410–416, 501–510. Title VII of the Act, which is entitled "Miscellaneous Provisions," covers issues ranging from the President's emergency powers in this area to closed captioning of video programming. 47 U.S.C. §§701–714. Titles II, III, and VI—the subchapters with which this book will be primarily concerned—differ in that they prescribe distinct sets of regulation for ostensibly distinct categories of services, service providers, and technologies.

Title II of the Act governs common carriers and thus contains the principal set of substantive provisions pertaining to telephony. The provisions of Title II cover a vast number of topics—from rates, competition, and network interconnection to harassing phone calls, services for the disabled, and the regulation of payphones. 47 U.S.C. §§201–276. Although neither Title II nor any other subchapter of the Communications Act explicitly regulates the Internet, Title II contains provisions that affect network infrastructure essential to the Internet. We will examine many aspects of regulation under Title II (especially Title II as it was amended by the Telecommunications Act of 1996) in Chapters Fifteen through Eighteen of this book. The relation of Title II to the Internet will be discussed in Chapters Twenty to Twenty-Three.

Title III of the Act establishes the regulatory regime for radio spectrum and broadcast services. It, too, covers substantial ground, ranging from the licensing of spectrum and construction of radio facilities to more particular regulation of the content of broadcast communications. 47 U.S.C. §§301–399. The most important aspects of Title III for our purposes are those that involve the allocation of spectrum and those that impose restrictions and conditions on the use of that spectrum. We address the many interesting issues arising under Title III in Chapters One through Eight.

Finally, Title VI addresses "cable services" and, obviously, governs the regulation of cable television as well as many other services provided over the cable infrastructure.[9] 47 U.S.C. §§601–641. Some of the provisions here also extend either implicitly or explicitly to other multichannel video delivery systems, for example direct broadcast satellite service and video services delivered over the telephone network. 47 U.S.C. §§651–653. The current Title VI was not, of course, part of the original 1934 Act, because cable service did not then exist. It was added over time through amendments to the Act, notably in the 1984 and 1992 Cable Acts mentioned above. We examine the regulation of cable television and related multichannel video services in Chapters Nine through Fourteen.

Overall, the structure of the Act follows the deceptively simple outlines of the telecommunications industry as Congress found it in 1934. On one hand were the "natural monopolies"—the telephone and telegraph companies that

---

9. The extent to which these provisions apply to certain services—for example, Internet access over the cable network—is unclear, as we discuss in Chapter Twenty-One.

transmitted their data by wire, operated as common carriers, and should therefore, it was assumed, be subject to classic public utility regulation. This is the intuitive legislative feel behind Title II of the Act, which envisions the FCC regulating the entry, rates, and services of common carriers of telephonic
communications; auditing their books; and assuring that they provide nondiscriminatory access to all.

On the other hand, in 1934 AM radio was gaining popularity throughout
the country and radio stations were just beginning to link up into networks.
These stations broadcast through the airwaves, and so the prime danger envisioned here was that these stations would interfere with each other if not
legally constrained from doing so. Radio stations did not behave as common
carriers, but rather selected programs to appeal to listeners and then sold
commercial time to advertisers who thereby gained access to those listeners.
Title III of the Act is directed at this commercial radio phenomenon, and it
portrays a Commission particularly concerned with the licensing process — deciding who should be licensed to broadcast, on what frequencies, and in
which communities. In contrast to Title II, the Act says nothing about controlling rates or providing equal access to broadcast stations. In fact, Title III
specifically forbids the FCC from subjecting broadcasters to common carrier
obligations.

Today, of course, some firms act like broadcasters but transmit by wire
(e.g., cable television), while other firms act like common carriers but transmit
through the airwaves (e.g., mobile telephone). Different titles of the Act may
thus apply to a single service, as in the case of mobile telephony where, for example, spectrum licensing provisions from Title III and network interconnection provisions from Title II are both relevant. And a single title of the Act may
apply to multiple and very different services, as is plainly the case for Title II
which, as we just pointed out, applies both to broadcast television and to cellular telephony. More fundamentally, whether a carrier transmits by wire or over
the air is not a reliable indicator of whether it is a monopoly or of how it
should be regulated, if at all. Many of the materials in this book therefore involve regulatory issues that arise from the fact that neither "broadcaster" nor
"common carrier" has the unambiguous, objective implications assumed by
Congress in 1934.

Other Relevant Statutes and Agencies

To be sure, the Communications Act of 1934 (including its amendments) is
not the only statute relevant to the regulation of U.S. telecommunications. As we
will see, antitrust and copyright laws have also been very important. The Copyright Act of 1976 specifically created compulsory licenses that allow cable operators to retransmit copyrighted content at regulated rates. And the Satellite Home
Viewer Improvement Act of 1999 amended the Copyright Act to recognize a
comparable, but not quite identical, compulsory license in providers of direct
broadcast satellite service. These provisions of the Copyright Act are considered
in Chapters Eleven and Thirteen, respectively. Similarly, one of the most important events in the history of American telecommunications — the breakup of the
Bell Telephone System in 1984 — resulted not from anything in the 1934 Act, but
from an antitrust suit under the Sherman Antitrust Act. That suit is considered in
significant detail in Chapter Sixteen.

Just as the Communications Act is not the only law relevant for telecommunications in the United States, the FCC is not the only relevant federal agency or authority. The case that broke up Bell, for example, was brought by the Antitrust Division of the U.S. Department of Justice (although the FCC was involved).

In addition, another Executive Branch entity, the National Telecommunications and Information Administration (NTIA) located within the Department of Commerce, plays two important roles. First, NTIA and the FCC together determine what parts of the electromagnetic spectrum will be reserved for federal government use. (NTIA then manages all the spectrum assigned to the government.) In discharging these responsibilities, NTIA relies heavily on advice from the Interdepartment Radio Advisory Committee, which is composed of representatives from the various federal agencies that use spectrum extensively. Second, NTIA bears principal responsibility for determining presidential policy on telecommunication issues. To this end, NTIA has a substantial research staff and frequently submits comments on major FCC policymaking proceedings.

While it is important to note the role of other agencies and government departments in regulating telecommunications, the FCC has the overwhelming share of authority in this domain. So, while other regulatory or enforcement entities will enter into the discussions in this book, our principal focus will be on the Federal Communications Commission and its activities—a topic to which we now turn.

Part One

BROADCAST AND SPECTRUM REGULATION

Our study of telecommunications begins with a detailed look at the regulation of broadcast technologies as well as some background information on telecommunications policy more generally. Broadcast is a logical place for us to start because it in many ways is the reason we have federal telecommunications regulation today. Difficulties with broadcast technology, after all, led Congress to create the agency that would ultimately evolve into the Federal Communications Commission—the agency that today regulates not only broadcast, but also significant aspects of virtually every other telecommunications market.

Broadcast is where federal telecommunications regulation was born in a more important sense as well. By regulating broadcast, the federal government effectively committed itself to regulating the other telecommunications technologies. Cable, for example, almost *had* to be regulated at the federal level; given that cable and broadcast were to some degree substitute technologies, regulation of cable was the only way to defend the policies first set out in the broadcast context. The same argument, of course, would later lead to the regulation of satellite—defending policies established for broadcast and cable—and so on down the line, as the Introduction points out. The study of broadcast is thus integral to an understanding of how the government got into the business of regulating in the first place.

We begin in Chapter One with an introduction to the history and vocabulary of broadcast regulation. Chapter Two then turns to the question of why the federal government regulates broadcast at all—asking what, in short, differentiates broadcast from the many other goods and services that are regulated only by laws of general applicability like the antitrust statutes and tort law. Chapters Three through Six focus on particular regulatory roles, with Chapter Three looking at how the FCC allocates particular frequencies to particular uses, Chapters Four and Five considering how the FCC first assigns broadcast licenses and then approves renewals and transfers of those licenses, and Chapter Six surveying the various "public trustee" obligations the FCC has over the years imposed on broadcast licensees. Chapter Seven considers structural regulations that affect the relationships between networks, their affiliates, and independent program suppliers; the chapter also looks at structural regulations that more broadly limit consolidation in telecommunications markets. Finally, Chapter Eight concludes, reviewing all of the previous materials through two case studies: one on low power FM radio, and one on digital television.

CHAPTER ONE

AN INTRODUCTION TO BROADCAST REGULATION

The purpose of this chapter is:

- to survey some of the early history of broadcast regulation as a way of helping readers gain a better perspective on the real-world events that caused the government to get involved with broadcast regulation; and
- to introduce some basic broadcast concepts, particularly the notions of "spectrum" and "spectrum allocation."

~

I. EARLY HISTORY OF BROADCAST

There are many ways to begin the story of radio and broadcast television.[1] One approach would be to start with the work of Joseph Henry and Michael Faraday, two physicists whose work in the late 1800s showed that one device can induce electric current in another without the two sharing any physical connection. Such a story would focus on the scientific marvel at work here—something both the readers and authors of this casebook likely take for granted.

Another approach would be to start in 1899, when a young entrepreneur named Marconi showed the world that Henry's and Faraday's scientific accomplishment had significant commercial application as well. Marconi developed what modern audiences might conceptualize as a basic walkie-talkie, and on October 1, 1899, he used it to provide up-to-the-minute news coverage of the America's Cup yacht race. Marconi stationed his men on boats and had them radio information back to dry land. It was for both Marconi specifically and broadcast technology more generally a public relations coup: news coverage of the race focused more on Marconi's amazing "wireless" invention than on the race itself.[2]

---

1. Many sources recount the early history of broadcasting. Among the best: Susan Douglas, Inventing American Broadcasting 1899–1922 (1987); Erik Barnouw, A Tower in Babel (1966); Susan Smulyan, Selling Radio: The Commercialization of American Broadcasting 1920–1934 (1994).
2. Douglas, *supra* note 1, at 19.

Our approach, however, is to start not with these key scientific and entrepreneurial events, but instead to start with the event that first triggered substantial government interest in regulating the broadcast spectrum. That event was the sinking of the *Titanic* in 1912. At the time the *Titanic* went down, the only significant broadcast regulation in effect was a law passed in 1910 that required passenger ships above a certain size to carry wireless sets.[3] The theory behind that law was simple: in the event of an emergency, wireless would allow ship operators to call for help.

The *Titanic* tragedy suggested, however, that this sort of light-handed regulation was insufficient. There were two significant problems with the existing regulation. First, while the law required ships to carry wireless sets, it imposed on those ships no obligation to keep their wireless sets manned or even operational. So the *California*—a ship that was a mere twenty miles away from the *Titanic* on that fateful night—never heard the *Titanic*'s distress call. The *California* had cut its engines in order to more slowly navigate the dangerous waters that both it and the *Titanic* faced, and the wireless on board had no independent power supply.

Second, the law as it stood in 1912 focused only on wireless equipment, saying nothing about the airwaves the equipment used. This led to what might be thought of as the second tragedy of the *Titanic*: not only did the ship sink, but information about the sinking was significantly misreported in the days following the accident. In one case, for example, the question "are all *Titanic* passengers safe?" was mistakenly interpreted by an amateur wireless operator and reported in the news media to be the affirmative statement that all passengers were in fact safe.[4] In another, congested airwaves caused a message from the ship that picked up *Titanic* survivors to be combined with an unrelated message about a failed oil tanker, the result being an errant report that the *Titanic* was being safely towed to Halifax.[5] This confusion and misinformation surely added to the heartache for concerned friends and families; it also contributed to a general sense that it was time to regulate broadcast more significantly.

Not that congressional leaders were reluctant to regulate. The Navy had for some time been calling for further government intervention, its concern being that "outside unrecognized stations" (*i.e.*, amateur forerunners to radio stations) were cluttering the airwaves and drowning out official military messages. And the Navy had also by this time fallen victim to several hoaxes where one or another amateur wireless operator would impersonate a Navy official and give a ship false orders. Even before the *Titanic*, then, Navy officials had been pushing for increased regulation—even military control—of the airwaves.

The sinking of the *Titanic* provided a focal point for action, however, and so a few months after that tragedy Congress passed the Radio Act of 1912.[6] As Thomas Krattenmaker and Lucas Powe explain in the excerpt below, this would turn out to be a key piece of legislation in that it established several concepts that continue to influence broadcast policy through the present day:

---

3. 36 Stat. 629 (1910).
4. Douglas, *supra* note 1, at 227.
5. *Id.*
6. 37 Stat. 302 (1912).

First, the federal government would control broadcasting. No one could broadcast without a license. Second, the spectrum would be allocated among uses and users. Thus the military obtained excellent wavelengths. Ships were given their own block. And amateurs, those unrecognized stations, were relegated to oblivion. They could listen anywhere along the spectrum, but could transmit only on what at that time were technologically unusable short waves. Third, some communication was more important than others and the government would determine which was which. Distress calls took precedence. Then came the Navy; operators near a military installation had to reduce transmitting power to just one kilowatt. If war came, there was no doubt about military paramountcy. After the military, commercial use was next; amateur was last.[7]

A few years later, World War I would reaffirm these priorities and principles. Wireless communication was a military tool during wartime, with the Navy using wireless both to coordinate the fleet in battle and to pass timely information to the troops. Wireless played a significant propaganda role as well. German authorities used friendly wireless operators in the United States to disseminate information from the German perspective, at least until April 1917 when federal authorities seized the handful of wireless stations then in operation (approximately eighty in total) and stopped the German transmissions. Perhaps the war's most significant effect on broadcast policy, however, was the fact that many American soldiers were trained in the use of the wireless. When the war ended, those soldiers returned to civilian life and brought with them an enthusiasm for, and understanding of, wireless broadcast.

Herbert Hoover and the Early Growth of Radio[8]

All this led to the airing of the 1920 presidential election results by Westinghouse's station KDKA and the Detroit News' WWJ. Their broadcasts made the medium famous. Yet, despite these successes, there were only five new applications for station licenses during the next year.[9] Then, following the broadcast of the 1921 World Series between the Yankees and the Giants on WJZ, broadcasting as we know it took off.

One important reason for the early growth of commercial radio broadcasting was that it found a sympathetic champion in its licensor, Secretary of Commerce Herbert Hoover. Hoover remolded the Radio Act of 1912 from its original emphasis on wireless point-to-point telegraphy to a new emphasis that fostered a wider use of the emerging technology. The Radio Act had created a division among military, commercial (meaning for-profit, for example telegraphy), and amateur uses. Hoover subdivided the commercial category, creating a separate grouping called "broadcasting" to satisfy the needs of the thousands of Americans purchasing receiving sets.[10] True amateurs were forced to use undesirable

---

7. Thomas Krattenmaker & Lucas A. Powe, Jr., Regulating Broadcast Programming 6 (1994).

8. Part of this material also appears in Krattenmaker & Powe, *supra* note 7.

9. Lucas A. Powe, Jr., American Broadcasting and the First Amendment 52–54 (1987).

10. Eric Barnouw, A Tower in Babel 91 (1966).

wavelengths under 200 meters, but the "more powerful and sophisticated amateur stations" were re-licensed under this new "commercial" category and authorized to use 360 meters (833.3 kilocycles).[11] "Broadcasting" — propagating a signal for all to receive — thus became a permissible commercial venture, just as
"telegraphy" — transmitting personal messages from point to point — had been
for some time.

As both champion of the new industry and the official in charge of licensing,
Hoover now faced a problem that would plague him and the industry throughout
the early years: signal interference. The periodical *Radio Broadcast* editorialized in
both October and November of 1921 about the crowding of the air and its "resulting interference of signals between the several stations, which made listening no
pleasure."[12] The problem would only get worse as demand grew. In 1922, seventy-
seven broadcast licenses were issued in March, followed by seventy-six in April,
ninety-seven in May, seventy-two in June, and seventy-six in July. By the end of
1922, nearly six hundred stations were on the air and interference was pervasive.

Attempting to achieve both consensus and legislation, Hoover called, in
1922, what would be the first of four National Radio Conferences. Hoover
keynoted the Conference and actively participated in its deliberations, which emphasized the public good that came from this new service.

Hoover thought broadcasting used "a great national asset" (the spectrum)
and believed "it becomes of primary public interest to say who is to do the
broadcasting, under what circumstances, and with what type of material."[13]
Hoover opened the Conference by noting "this is one of the few instances where
the country is unanimous in its desire for more regulation."[14] At its end, the conferees — broadcasters, manufacturers, and a handful of other important
players — unanimously resolved: "It is the sense of the Conference that Radio
Communication is a public utility and as such should be regulated and controlled
by the Federal Government in the public interest."[15]

When Congress did not act, Hoover took action on his own. In December
1922, Hoover expanded the frequencies available for commercial broadcasting
from enough to support two stations per city to three and reassigned broadcasters to these frequencies.[16] To prevent further congestion resulting from added applications in the expanding industry, he would either deny applications or require
some form of time sharing between broadcasters. Hoover's policies, however,
were undermined two months after they were announced. In Hoover v. Intercity
Radio Co., 286 F. 1003 (D.C. Cir. 1923), the U.S. Court of Appeals for the District of Columbia Circuit held that Hoover had the discretion under the Radio
Act to select a frequency and set the hours of use, but that he lacked discretion to
deny any application for a license.

---

11. Douglas, *supra* note 1, at 301.
12. Powe, *supra* note 9, at 54–55.
13. "Speech to the First National Radio Conference," February 27, 1922. Document
No. 209 Hoover Collection, Stanford University, quoted in Daniel E. Garvey, "Secretary
Hoover and the Quest for Broadcast Regulation," 3 Journalism History No. 3 at 66, 67
(1976).
14. George Archer, History of Radio to 1926, at 249 (1938).
15. Hearings Before the Committee on the Merchant Marine and Fisheries, House of
Representatives on H.R. 11964, 67th Cong. 4th Sess. 32 (1926).
16. Phillip T. Rosen, The Modern Stentors 54 (1981).

With chaos looming again, Hoover called a second National Radio Conference. When it convened in late March 1923, Hoover had its recommendations already prepared.[17] They included invasion of the areas reserved for the government, moving maritime uses to a lower frequency than the Radio Act prescribed, and creating three different power levels for stations. Ignoring the contrary conclusion of *Intercity Radio*, the Conference declared, as Hoover had planned, that he had full authority "to regulate hours and wavelengths of operation of stations when such action is necessary to prevent interference detrimental to the public good."[18]

Following the Conference, Hoover once again reallocated broadcasters, this time squarely contrary to the express language of the Radio Act. He moved commercial users into spectrum reserved for government. The Navy was also moved from its statutory spectrum space, but voiced no objections because the move necessitated purchasing new and better equipment.[19] Broadcasters were placed between 550 and 1365 kilocycles. In an article entitled "Secretary Hoover Acts," *Radio Broadcast* noted that the broadcast interference problem had been "suddenly remedied" without passage of any legislation.[20]

The expanded band, combined with a downturn in radio revenues, allowed Hoover to give licenses to all who asked.[21] Half of the outlets were associated with either manufacturers or retailers of electrical appliances.[22] Newspaper publishers were another typical sponsor.[23] Sales of radio sets mushroomed and ten percent of the population owned one by the end of 1924.[24]

The Rise and Fall of Hoover's Policies

By the end of 1925, 578 stations were broadcasting, and the band was full again.[25] Furthermore, as the industry matured, stations began to broadcast for longer hours and with increased power, resulting in widespread interference. Hoover first addressed this problem by urging stations to work out time sharing agreements or to agree to have one station buy the other's license. Often these measures worked; sometimes they did not. In Cincinnati, two stations on the same frequency could not find a satisfactory solution and simply broadcast simultaneously for weeks.[26] When private parties could not agree, Hoover again stepped in. Sometimes he ordered time sharing. Sometimes he demonstrated how excruciatingly slow the application process could be.[27] Eventually, after the

---

17. *Id.* at 56.
18. Barnouw, *supra* note 1, at 121.
19. Rosen, *supra* note 16, at 58.
20. Quoted in *id.* at 57.
21. Powe, *supra* note 9, at 57.
22. Rosen, *supra* note 16, at 62.
23. Newspaper publishers got involved with radio in part as a way to sell newspapers. The idea: listeners might purchase newspapers in order to find out what times particular radio programs would air. A famous newspaper-backed station (WGN, or "World's Greatest Newspaper") is considered later in these materials.
24. Rosen, *supra* note 22, at 69.
25. Powe, *supra* note 9, at 58.
26. *Id.* at 59.
27. Thomas W. Hazlett, The Rationality of Broadcast Regulation, 33 J. Law & Economics 133, 146 (1990).

fourth National Radio Conference in November 1925, Hoover announced that no more applications (including those for increased power) would be granted.[28]

Hoover thus completed an administrative tour de force, creating a working policy directly contrary to the one enshrined in law—one that ignored both the Radio Act and *Intercity Radio*. But it was not to last.

Hoover's outlaw edifice came tumbling down in December 1925 when the Chicago-based Zenith Corporation jumped from 930 kHz to 910 kHz for its Chicago broadcasts. Hoover had assigned Zenith 930 kHz. But, because this was the same frequency that General Electric had previously obtained in Denver, Hoover had limited Zenith to Thursdays between 10 p.m. and midnight, and only if GE chose not to broadcast then. Finding the limitations unacceptable, Zenith bolted for clearer air at 910 kHz, a Canadian frequency, ceded by treaty.[29] When Hoover, now without options, moved against Zenith, his whole regulatory house of cards collapsed. The federal district judge read the Radio Act as the D.C. Circuit had in *Intercity Broadcasting*; Hoover's duty was to license, not to impose restrictions.[30] He could encourage time sharing, but imposing it was beyond his power.

Hoover did not appeal; instead he arranged for the acting attorney general to state that the *Zenith* opinion was correct.[31] The next day, Hoover ran up the white flag and announced that he was out of the business of regulation.[32] The result of this capitulation, which Hoover knew was inevitable, was chaos.

Louis Caldwell, the first general counsel of the Federal Radio Commission, described the six months following *Zenith*: "Nearly 200 new broadcasting stations crowded into channels already congested with about 550 stations. Existing stations 'jumped' their waves and increased their power at will; reception was practically ruined for the listening public, and anarchy reigned in the realm of radio."[33] As the Supreme Court subsequently noted, "the result was confusion and chaos. With everybody on the air, nobody could be heard."[34]

The Radio Act of 1927

The manufactured dispute between Zenith's president, Eugene McDonald, and Hoover produced what both wanted: action by a Congress heretofore unwilling to act.[35] The Radio Act of 1927, 44 Stat. 1162, enacting ideas that had been in the legislative hopper since the first National Radio Conference, replaced the statute enacted after the *Titanic* disaster and gave the nation a legal regime focused on the newly emerged commercial radio broadcasting industry.

The new Radio Act put first things first. Although the 1912 Act had required a license to use the air, it had been silent on the issue of ownership of the airwaves. The 1927 Act was not. It bluntly declared that there could be no private

---

28. Rosen, *supra* note 16, at 79–80.
29. Powe, *supra* note 9, at 59.
30. United States v. Zenith Radio Corp., 12 F.2d 614 (N.D. Ill. 1926).
31. 35 Opinions of the Attorney General 126 (1926).
32. National Broadcasting Co. v. United States, 319 U.S. 190, 212 (1943) [hereinafter *NBC*].
33. Louis Caldwell, Clearing the Ether's Traffic Jam, Nation's Business, Nov. 1929, at 34–35.
34. *NBC*, 319 U.S. at 212.
35. Rosen, *supra* note 16, at 93–95.

ownership of the airwaves; they were public and their use could only occur with the government's permission. That permission, in the form of a license, would be granted without charge, but for no more than three years.

Congress knew that these licenses could not be granted to all comers. Thus, unlike the old Radio Act, the 1927 Act had to give the licensor guidance as to which applications should prevail. Any number of standards were possible—for example, first come, first served; a lottery; or an auction. Congress, however, had determined that the license should be free, so the idea of an auction was out. Adopting the idea that Hoover had articulated at the first National Radio Conference, Congress instead required licensees to render public service in exchange for the privilege of using the now federally owned spectrum. Licenses would be granted according to the needs of the "public interest, convenience, or necessity"—a standard already in use in the public utilities and transportation areas.

The House of Representatives wanted to leave licensing power with the Secretary of Commerce. The Senate did not, instead preferring an independent regulatory commission. The Act reflected a compromise between the two. For one year, a geographically balanced five-member commission was to exercise the government's licensing function; then that function would revert to the Secretary of Commerce. Senator Clarence Dill of Washington, the Senate's expert on radio and a key figure in drafting the Act, liked the compromise because, understanding both Congress and bureaucracy, he believed "if we ever got a Commission we would never get rid of it."[36] He was right. Congress ultimately abandoned the provision to return powers to the Commerce Department, and the successor to the "one year agency," the Federal Communications Commission, remains with us.

Finally, Congress understood that it did not want to create a National Board of Censors. Thus, section 29 of the Act made plain that the licensing power did not include the power of censorship and licensing therefore could not "interfere with the right of free speech by means of radio communications."[37] Congress did not clarify how the mandate in section 29 would mesh with the equally strong mandate to award licenses in the public interest. By default that issue was left for future resolution by the Commission and the courts.

Principal Features of the 1927 Act

This background reveals that a central feature of the 1927 Radio Act was its deliberate choice to preclude private ownership of spectrum rights while licensing those rights for brief periods to private users free of charge. As we will see later in the book, nothing in the nature of broadcasting or the electromagnetic spectrum made that choice inevitable, but in fact no other alternatives were seriously considered. Senator Dill stated that "the one principle regarding radio that must always be adhered to, as basic and fundamental, is that government must always retain complete and absolute control of the right to use the air."[38] A contemporaneous analysis in the *Yale Law Journal* stated: "the idea that the 'government owns the ether' was an idée fixe in the debates of Congress."[39] Enacting this idea

---

36. Quoted in Barnouw, *supra* note 1, at 199.
37. 44 Stat. 1162, at 1171, Section 29 (1927).
38. Clarence Dill, A Traffic Cop for the Air, 75 Review of Reviews 181, 184 (1927).
39. Note, Federal Control of Radio Broadcasting, 39 Yale L. J. 244, 250 (1929).

meant that administrators would parcel out, among competing technologies, permitted uses of the spectrum. Administrators also would select, from among competing applicants, which subset would become spectrum licensees. In short, government ownership meant government control—a point probably not lost on lawmakers of the time.

Congress deferred most issues to the future, of course, choosing the relatively amorphous public interest standard as a codification of whatever standards would ultimately be applied. This was probably a welcome result from Hoover's perspective. Hoover had always understood that there would be some sort of amorphous quid pro quo for licensing: "It becomes of primary public interest to say who is to do the broadcasting, under what circumstances, and with what type of material."[40] And in broadcast—as distinct from comparable regulations applicable to transportation or public utilities—that public interest quid pro quo would determine not only the issues of the need for service and who would provide it, but also the somewhat novel issue of what the service itself would be.

The broadcast establishment, which accurately assumed that regulation would prefer its interests to those of the marginal stations and potential entrants, fully concurred in a public interest regulatory scheme. Each National Radio Conference endorsed Hoover's program. When Hoover, in 1925, stated that "we can surely agree that no one can raise a cry of deprivation of free speech if he is compelled to prove that there is something more than naked commercial selfishness in his purpose,"[41] the National Association of Broadcasters agreed: "The test of the broadcasting privilege [must] be based on the needs of the public."[42]

House sponsor Wallace White of Maine echoed the point after House passage of the Act. Under the Radio Act of 1912, an individual could "demand a license whether he will render service to the public thereunder or not." No longer. One of the "great advantages" of the 1927 Act is the requirement of service to the public.[43] As his Senate counterpart, Clarence Dill, so vigorously put it, "Of one thing I am absolutely certain. Uncle Sam should not only police this 'new beat'; he should see to it that no one uses it who does not promise to be good and well-behaved."[44]

The Federal Radio Commission

What did the public interest mean? That would be left to the Federal Radio Commission (FRC). The charm of the public interest standard, Dill noted, was its vagueness and breadth: "It covers just about everything."[45]

---

40. Speech to first National Radio Conference, quoted in Garvey, *supra* note 13, at 67.
41. Opening address to the fourth National Radio Conference, reprinted in Radio Control, Hearings Before the Senate Interstate Commerce Committee, 69th Cong. 1st Sess. 56 (1926).
42. Resolution of the National Association of Broadcasters (NAB), presented at the fourth National Radio Conference, quoted in *id.* at 59.
43. Wallace White, "Unscrambling the Ether," The Literary Digest, March 5, 1927, at 7.
44. Dill, *supra* note 38, at 181.
45. Quoted in Powe, *supra* note 9, at 61. William Mayton, The Illegitimacy of the Public Interest Standard at the FCC, 38 Emory L.J. 715 (1989), presents a contrary argument, suggesting that the Communications Act (which was based on the Radio Act) did not intend to give the FCC anything more than the powers of a traffic cop. This neglects the significance of the National Radio Conferences as well as the statements of Dill and White about control. The Commission may well have reached for even more power than it was granted, and perhaps compliant courts, especially the Supreme Court, too readily rubber-stamped the

The FRC, with but one confirmed member, no staff, and no appropriation, got off to a shaky start. But its *First Annual Report* defined the task ahead in a manner that set the regulatory agenda for decades: section 29 prohibits censorship, but "the physical facts of radio transmission compel what is, in effect, a censorship of the most extraordinary kind. There is a definite limit, and a very low one, to the number of broadcasting stations which can operate simultaneously." Consequently, some applicants must be told "there is no room for you." In making these determinations, the key policy question would be how to "measure the conflicting claims of grand opera and religious services, of market reports and direct advertising, of jazz orchestras and lectures on the diseases of hogs."[46]

The answer that unfolded over the next three years was a two-step process. In its first step, the FRC reclassified and reordered broadcast stations while refusing to expand the broadcast band. The outcome continued Hoover's policy of favoring larger, established commercial broadcasters. The second step was acknowledging that programming counted and weeding out those stations that aired the less favored types. The first step slew the weak; the second destroyed the different.

Structuring the Broadcast Industry

The initial task facing the Commission was to decide how many stations to allow on the air, where they would be located, and under what conditions they would be operated. This task was made more complex by a 1928 amendment to the Radio Act that mandated an equalization of stations across five geographical zones.[47] Offered by Congressman E.L. Davis of Tennessee, it sought to replace stations in the more populous East with newcomers in the South and West. Toward the end of the summer of 1928, the FRC issued *General Order Number 40*, which enunciated the general principles to govern the allocations of frequencies and power nationwide.

Possibly the most important decision made at this time was the decision not to increase the broadcast band.[48] Instead, the Commission simply changed the assignments of ninety-four percent of all broadcast stations, making assignments that favored applicants with superior technical equipment, adequate finances, experienced personnel, and the ability to operate without interruption. These were Hoover's policies, and they favored established commercial broadcasters.[49] The Commission knew that there would be a reaction to all the redistributions, and it "launched an educational and public relations campaign to counteract this threat. Its press releases explained that the familiar broadcasting band originally established by Secretary Hoover had been retained in order to reduce inconvenience to listeners."[50] That is, listeners would not be troubled by having to choose between retaining their old sets limited to the stations already available on them or purchasing newer ones that could receive added stations (made available by broadening the band).[51]

Commission, but the FRC understood it would have to look at programming and there was ample legislative support for just such a view.

46. Federal Radio Commission, *First Annual Report* 6 (1927).
47. 45 Stat. 373 (1928).
48. Hazlett, *supra* note 27, at 155.
49. Rosen, *supra* note 16, at 133.
50. *Id.* at 135.
51. Hazlett, *supra* note 27, at 155–56.

Defining Permissible Broadcasting

With these structural decisions made, the Commission next turned to the question of defining what would be permissible broadcast content. On this score, the Commission's position was clear; whatever section 29 might say about censorship, someone had to evaluate programming:

> Since the number of channels is limited and the number of persons desiring to broadcast is far greater than can be accommodated, the Commission must determine from among the applicants before it which of them will, if licensed, best serve the public. In a measure, perhaps, all of them give more or less adequate service. Those who give the least, however, must be sacrificed for those who give the most. The emphasis must be first and foremost on the interest, the convenience, and the necessity of the listening public, and not on the interest, convenience, or necessity of the individual broadcaster.[52]

In the summer of 1928, the Commission admonished those stations playing phonograph records, noting that such stations did not give the public anything it could not receive elsewhere in the community.[53]

Over the next year, the Commission turned on what it called "propaganda stations (a term which is here used for the sake of convenience and not in a derogatory sense)."[54] A year earlier it had warned New York socialist station WEVD (named for the socialist leader Eugene Victor Debs) to "operate with due regard for the opinions of others."[55] The Commission, relying on scarcity, asserted that stations should aim their programs at everyone. There was "not room in the broadcast band for every school of thought, religious, political, social, and economic, each to have its separate broadcasting stations, its mouth piece in the ether. If franchises are extended to some it gives them an unfair advantage over others, and results in a corresponding cutting down of general public service stations."[56] Thus when the Chicago Federation of Labor applied for an increase in power and hours for its station WCFL, arguing that it broadcast programs of particular interest to organized labor and that there were sufficient listeners to justify the increase, the Commission responded that "there is no place for a station catering to any group. All stations should cater to the general public and serve public interest against group or class interest."[57]

The Commission campaigned against what it feared would be a balkanizing of the dial. "If, therefore, all the programs transmitted are intended for, and interesting or valuable to, only a small portion of that public, the rest of the listeners are being discriminated against." Broadcasters should strive for "a well rounded program" where the needs of all potential listeners are met.[58] It did not matter whether there were several stations in the area. Each station was required to serve all potential listeners.

---

52. Statement of the Commission, August 23, 1928, reproduced as Appendix F in *Second Annual Report* 166, 170 (1928).
53. *Id.* at 168.
54. FRC, *Third Annual Report* 34 (1929) (reporting *Great Lakes Broadcasting*).
55. FRC, *Second Annual Report* 156 (1928) (reporting decisions of August 22, 1928).
56. FRC, *Third Annual Report* at 32.
57. *Id.* at 36 (reporting *Chicago Federation of Labor*).
58. *Id.* at 34.

It was also not relevant whether the station was popular. If the station was not meeting the needs of its community, then it could be replaced even if it was highly popular. Commission actions against the Reverend Bob ("Fighting Bob") Shuler[59] and the famous "goat gland doctor," John R. Brinkley,[60] illustrate this principle. Further, each case generated appellate litigation that fully vindicated the FRC, setting a judicial pattern of deference that continued over the decades.

The *Shuler* Case

In 1926 a wealthy widow from Berkeley, impressed by one of Shuler's indignant sermons, gave him $25,000 to purchase KGEF Los Angeles, a one-kilowatt station broadcasting nearly twenty-four hours a week on a shared frequency. Shuler broadcast his sermons each Sunday and took two additional weekday hours for himself. On Tuesdays he hosted the "Bob Shuler Question Hour" and on Thursdays he gave "Bob Shuler's Civic Talk."

As a rigid moralist with an intense dislike for prostitution and alcohol, Shuler found an incredible array of targets in prohibition-era Los Angeles. During his two evening hours he railed against local corruption. Over the years Shuler built such a following that commercial stations were unable to sell advertising time opposite these two programs. Question Hour was the fourth most popular show in the market, and audience surveys showed that "Fighting Bob" reached an audience of about 600,000 as he lashed out at an imperfect world.

Shuler's application for renewal in 1930 stated that KGEF had "thrown the pitiless spotlight of publicity on corrupt public officials and on agencies of immorality, thereby gladly gaining their enmity and open threats to 'get' this station's license." No lie. The FRC hit Shuler with a hearing that aired charges that he had used his station irresponsibly in attacking virtually all aspects of Los Angeles city government. The hearing lasted sixteen days, and at its end the hearing examiner ruled for Shuler.

Shuler's opponents then went to the full Commission, which reversed and ordered KGEF off the air immediately. The Commission concluded that Shuler had used his station as a forum for outrageous and unfounded attacks on public officials "which have not only been bitter and personal in their nature, but often times based upon ignorance of fact for which little effort has been made to ascertain the truth. [Shuler] has vigorously attacked by name public officials and individuals whom he has conceived to be moral enemies of society or foes of the proper enforcement of the law. He has believed it his duty to denounce by name any enterprise, organization, or individual he personally thinks is dishonest or untrustworthy. Shuler testified that it was his purpose 'to try and make it hard for the bad man to do wrong in the community.'" The finding was, in the Commission's words, that his broadcasts were "sensational rather than instructive."[61]

The *Brinkley* Case

The FRC believed "Fighting Bob" Shuler had been operating KGEF as a personal outlet, a category that the Commission had ranked even lower than propa-

59. All of the facts about Shuler are taken from Powe, *supra* note 9, at 13–18.
60. The facts about Brinkley are also taken from *id.* at 23–27.
61. Trinity Methodist Church v. FRC, 62 F.2d 850 (D.C. Cir. 1932).

ganda stations. That spelled nothing but trouble for Brinkley, the "goat gland doctor," whose KFKB was a personal outlet *par excellence*. Yet it was also the most popular station, not just in central Kansas, but in the entire United States, out-polling the runner-up by a four to one margin. KFKB blanketed the area between the Rockies and the Mississippi and beyond, and Brinkley held his audience with an astute combination of fundamentalist theology and medical information. It was with the latter that Brinkley gained notoriety.

Brinkley's initial fame had come from his efforts to rejuvenate the male sex drive by implanting the gonads of a young Ozark goat in the patient's scrotum. A public-spirited man, he even sponsored a Little League baseball team nicknamed the Brinkley Goats. Yet Brinkley understood that there was a limited future in goat gland transplants, and by the late 1920s his medical business focused on the prostate. Using both the mails and KFKB, Brinkley attempted to reach "the prostate man" and convince him that he had a problem that Brinkley could solve. "It certainly behooves a man who has an enlarged prostate to consider it, and we are indeed glad to hear from such men for we are convinced we can render [them] a real, genuine, and lasting service."

On a typical day Brinkley took to the air twice (after lunch and dinner) to speak on medical problems. The evening program would be a gland lecture, explaining the male change of life. "Our bodies are not holding up as well as those of our forefathers did. Enlargement of the prostate is on the increase." His other program was his "Medical Question Box." This grew out of his enormous daily mail. Typically he would pick up some letters on the way to the microphone, leaf through them, and choose which to read on the air. He would then quickly give his diagnosis, and prescribe the medicine required — by number, *e.g.*, "Brinkley's 2, 16, and 17. If his druggist hasn't got them, he should write and order them from the Milford Drug Company, Milford, Kansas." As this indicates, Brinkley had expanded into the pharmaceutical business.

Predictably, the "goat gland doctor" drew the ire of organized medicine which challenged both his right to broadcast and his right to practice medicine. On a single unlucky Friday the thirteenth, in June 1930, he lost both. The FRC found that Brinkley's "Medical Question Box" diagnosis "upon what symptoms may be recited by the patient in a letter addressed to him, is inimical to the public health and safety, and for that reason is not in the public interest"; furthermore, KFKB was a "mere" adjunct to his medical practice and insufficiently attuned to the needs of Kansas.[62]

The Commission and the Courts

Both Shuler and Brinkley appealed to the D.C. Circuit. Both lost. These initial appellate decisions set a tone that would be adopted by the Supreme Court a decade later.

---

62. KFKB Broadcasting v. FRC, 47 F.2d 670, 672 (D.C. Cir. 1931). *See also id.* at 671 (noting the FRC's statement that "the operation of Station KFKB is conducted only in the personal interest of Dr. John R. Brinkley. While it is to be expected that a licensee of a radio broadcasting station will receive some remuneration for serving the public with radio programs, at the same time the interest of the listening public is paramount, and may not be subordinated to the interests of the station licensee.").

The court reviewing Brinkley's appeal agreed fully with the Commission that broadcasts should have a "public character. Obviously, there is no room in the broadcast band for every school of thought."[63] Broadcasting is "impressed with the public interest," and therefore the Commission "is necessarily called upon to consider the character and quality of the service to be rendered." The court summarily dismissed Brinkley's argument that the Commission had engaged in forbidden censorship. Section 29 went exclusively to prior scrutiny. What the Commission did, by contrast, was exercise its "undoubted right" to look at past performance. The court stated that, "in considering an application for a renewal of the license, an important consideration is the past conduct of the applicant, for 'by their fruits ye shall know them.' Matthew VII:20."[64]

The court treated Shuler's appeal similarly. There was no censorship or denial of free speech, "but merely the application of the regulatory power of Congress in a field within the scope of its legislative power."[65] Shuler remained free to "inspire political distrust and civic discord"; he simply couldn't demand to use an instrumentality of interstate commerce "for such purposes."[66] The Commission was duty-bound to look at Shuler's past broadcasts, and its conclusion that the public interest would not be served by re-licensing him was hardly arbitrary and capricious.[67]

Notes and Questions

1. **Telecommunications in Context.** The evolution of telecommunication regulation is best understood in context. Real events focused public attention on the various issues that are the concern of this textbook; and those events inevitably influenced the debates that followed. The early history of broadcast crystalizes this point well. For example, did you notice how Marconi and his contemporaries used the term "wireless" instead of, say, "radio" or "broadcast"? Do you see how these terms emphasize different aspects of the technology? How that emphasis might matter when it comes time to make important policy and regulatory choices?

2. **Localism and Diversity.** The early history of broadcast regulation exposes themes that will stay with us throughout the entire text. Two themes in particular are worth special mention here. First, note the emphasis on localism, evidenced in these early materials by Congressman Davis's legislation mandating an approximate equalization of broadcast radio stations across five geographic zones. Localism in the broadcast setting (arguably) serves two goals: (1) by restricting the number of stations in large markets, it increases investment in broadcast infrastructure in smaller markets, thus ensuring that no one is left too far behind in the broadcast revolution; and (2) to the extent localism means local

---

63. *Id.* at 672. The Commission might have contrasted KFKB with a Gary, Indiana station that prevailed over a Chicago station because its programs were "musical, educational and instructive in their nature and [stressed] loyalty to the community and the Nation." FRC v. Nelson Bros. Bond & Mortgage, 289 U.S. 266, 271 (1933).

64. *KFKB*, 47 F.2d at 672.

65. *Trinity Methodist Church*, 62 F.2d at 851.

66. *Id.* at 853.

67. *Id.* at 852.

owners, localism helps to ensure that broadcasters will be part of, and thus perhaps more responsive to, the local community. Second, these early materials also emphasize the importance of diversity—phrased here as an obligation that each broadcaster strive to present a well-rounded menu of offerings that would appeal to a broad group of listeners. Diversity in all of its forms is a central theme in broadcast regulation, a point later materials will reveal.

3. *Shuler* and *Brinkley*. What are we to make of the *Shuler* and *Brinkley* decisions? If Brinkley had chosen to write a newspaper column where readers would write in for advice and he would choose some subset of the letters and respond in print, would the Commission have had any power to stop him? Would the government have acted against him? Was there something special to the case because Brinkley was using the airwaves instead of the newspaper? Would Shuler have been treated differently were he writing a newspaper column instead of giving talks on the radio?

4. The 1934 Act. The Communications Act of 1934 ultimately replaced the Radio Act of 1927 and substituted the Federal Communications Commission (FCC) for the Federal Radio Commission. The 1934 Act made only minimal changes in broadcasting law; its principal purpose and effect was to take federal regulation of interstate telephone and telegraph service away from the Interstate Commerce Commission (ICC) and lodge those powers with the FCC.

5. Fundamental Issues. It is truly remarkable how the fundamental issues concerning broadcast regulation today are the same as they were back in the early days of broadcast. The early radio acts confronted such questions as: What rules and processes should govern allocation of spectrum rights to new technologies? Should government "own" the spectrum? Give it away? On the basis of comparing the merits of various programs? Measuring "merit" by its appeal to the public generally or to specific, "deserving" segments of the public? If the issues today are the same, but they lead to different policy responses, what might explain the change? Is it a function of differences in the technology? How the technology is perceived? Are we just more experienced today than we were back in 1927?

II. AN INTRODUCTION TO THE ELECTROMAGNETIC SPECTRUM[68]

A. The Basics: Encoding, Transmitting, Receiving

In nearly every setting, people value the ability to communicate rapidly over long distances. Imagine two mountains separated by a valley ten miles wide. People situated on these mountains would surely like to be able to communicate, for example warning one another about any approaching storm clouds. The same is true for, say, airline passengers and their business colleagues back on the ground, and so on.

Centuries ago, such communication might have occurred by smoke signals.[69] Today, it might take place as a cellular telephone communication. And, although

---

68. This note is modified from Krattenmaker & Powe, *supra* note 7, at 46–57.

69. The smoke signal analogy is suggested by Don L. Cannon & Gerald Luecke, Understanding Communications Systems 1 (2d ed. 1984).

450 B.C. WIRELESS DATA
* Cartoon provided by Phillips Business Information's Wireless Data News

the cellular system seems infinitely more advanced than the smoke signal, these two communications systems have much in common: each transmits encoded information, at the speed of light, to a receiver that decodes the information. In this way, each very quickly sends a large amount of information a long way.

In short, telecommunications technology differs in detail, but not in essential concept or function, from smoke signal technology. Employing telecommunications technologies rather than smoke signals means only that people can pack more information into a second's worth of transmission and can transmit that information over a longer distance. One might understand telecommunications, then, as the latest in an evolving technology for extending the speed and reach of data (or information) transmission.

To progress from smoke signals to wireless radio transmissions required that people learn to convert information to electromagnetic radiation. This is what Marconi taught us. The radio waves he pioneered—waves that today carry sound, pictures, numbers, and other data through the air—are basically sine waves, *encoded* with information, that are generated by a power source and then *transmitted* by that power source to a device (the receiver, radio, or TV set) that searches out the sine wave and strips off the encoded information.[70] Today, a perception exists that there are almost countless telecommunications products, mar-

---

70. To "invent" broadcast radio, then, one had to discover how to encode the human voice onto energy waves and then to decode that information at a receiver. Similarly, television requires the ability to break a picture down into bits of data (millions of points of light).

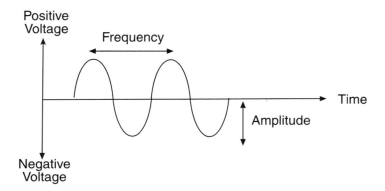

Figure 1.1. RADIO WAVES. Radio waves typically are transmitted as sine waves which is to say that they typically follow a pattern in which their energy level varies from high voltage to low voltage and back again, with the transitions accomplished in the gradual manner shown in the figure. Two significant attributes of a sine wave are its *frequency* (which measures how many times per second the wave hits its peak) and its *amplitude* (which measures the magnitude of that peak).

kets, and technologies available. Yet virtually all of them are defined simply by the encoding and transmitting process they employ. That is, telecommunications technologies, and thus telecommunications markets, are usually defined by the manner in which information is encoded and the means by which that information is later decoded.

Encoding. Information—such as pictures on a television screen or voices in a telephone conversation—can be encoded onto sine waves in either of two ways: (1) by varying the waves' amplitude (amplitude modulation, or AM) or (2) by varying their frequency (frequency modulation, or FM).

"Analog" and "digital" are terms frequently employed to describe two ways of transmitting continuous information, such as a moving picture. To transmit a moving picture by analog signal requires encoding the complete picture in each frame transmitted. Digital transmission of a moving picture requires only that one send the information that differs from one frame to the next. In digital transmissions, the information is encoded as a pattern of "0"s and "1"s. Among other benefits, this approach is particularly resistant to "noise" (misinterpreted information) because a receiver only has to distinguish between two digital possibilities as opposed to many possible analog signal levels. Most telecommunications media initially employed analog coding and transmission but more recently have begun to adopt the newer digital approach.

To retrieve information that has been encoded, of course, one needs a receiver that can decode the signal. This can create substantial problems, particularly where different firms or individuals own the encoder and decoder. For example, the benefits of owning an FM radio transmitter are slight if no one owns an FM radio receiver. In the same manner, digitally encoded television signals cannot be received by most television sets now in use.

Transmitting. For telecommunication, the medium of transmission can be a wire (*e.g.*, telegraph, wireline telephone, cable television) or the airwaves (*e.g.*,

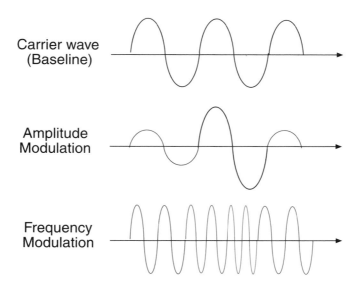

Figure 1.2. AMPLITUDE AND FREQUENCY MODULATION. Information can be encoded on sine waves by means of amplitude modulation (AM) and also by means of frequency modulation (FM). Compare the AM signal pictured here to the unmodified baseline ("carrier") signal shown above it. Can you see how the amplitude of the AM signal differs from the baseline, thereby possibly communicating information to the recipient? Similarly, can you see how the frequency of the FM signal differs from the carrier, again possibly communicating information to a recipient familiar with this method of encoding?

broadcast television, cellular telephone, satellite links) or both.[71] Today, telecommunication by wire usually employs one of two technologies. "Coaxial cable" is a braided metallic cylinder surrounding a wire. The wire carries the radio waves while the cylinder prevents signals from other wires (or from outside radiation) from interfering with the signals on the wire. The genius of coaxial cable is that the outside cylinder offers superior noise suppression while the braiding allows the cable to remain flexible. "Fiberoptic cable," a technology that entered widespread use in the 1980s, uses light traveling through a very thin glass fiber to transmit data. Fiberoptic cable forms the bulk of the long distance telephone network and the Internet backbone. It is particularly well suited for data transmitted at the highest frequencies, for transmission over very long distances, and for carrying many signals within one cable.

When information is transmitted by wire, the system may be designed so that many streams of data are in the wire and the recipient chooses one stream (*e.g.*, cable television) or so that the wire leading directly to the recipient carries less information (*e.g.*, wireline telephone). In the latter case, decisions as to what goes to the recipient are made, in part, further up the wire by specialized computers called switches and routers.

---

71. Many complicated telecommunications employ both wire and air. For example, a domestic long distance telephone call might start out over local telephone lines, move across states through over-the-air microwave transmitters, and then travel through different local telephone lines to reach its destination.

When information is transmitted through the air, the radio waves can be radiated in all directions or to only a single point. Conventional AM and FM radio stations, like lawn sprinklers, radiate in all directions; a series of microwave transmitters linked together into a 2000-mile hook-up, by contrast, each "radiate" only to a single spot. The direction and characteristic of the radiated signal is determined by the size, shape, and direction of the transmitting antenna. Transmitting through the airwaves also allows the transmitter or the receiver or both to be mobile during the dissemination or exchange of data. The cellular telephone system, for instance, employs transmission and reception through the airwaves to enable people to connect to the telephone system from moving vehicles. The same concept allows dispatchers and taxi drivers to converse via radio waves.

Whether transmission occurs through wire or air, the encoded electrical energy can be sent or radiated at varying degrees of power (compare the "transmitter" that is the portable in-home telephone handset connected to a base station in the house to the broadcast transmitter for a major metropolitan TV station). The amount of transmission power affects both the distance over which the signal can be transmitted and the signal's clarity at its reception point.

A telecommunications system can be designed so that recipients are also transmitters. Where this two-way communication occurs, the system is usually termed "interactive" or "duplex." Ordinary telephone systems are interactive because one can both receive and transmit voice data through the telephone. Conventional television broadcast systems are not interactive, but the addition of a microwave transmitter from the TV set to the broadcast station could alter that. Cable television systems typically contain a narrow "upstream" channel from the subscriber to the transmitting head-end that can be used for interactive applications.

Of course, it simplifies matters somewhat to describe telecommunication simply as encoding and electronically transmitting information, but most telecommunications technologies and markets are defined principally by these two characteristics. Thus, the difference between AM and FM radio is that one uses amplitude modulation and the other uses frequency modulation to encode the sine waves. Television is simply a mixture of both modulation schemes. The visual data (pictures) are amplitude modulated while the audio data are frequency modulated.[72] Conventional telephone communication is like AM radio in that it requires little spectrum because it transmits only voice data, but is unlike radio in that it transmits locally by wire and so it is somewhat easier to exclude people from listening in on the communication and there is less of a problem with congestion. Communications satellites are very tall transmitting and receiving antennas, and CB radios are portable AM radio stations transmitting at very low power.

Similarly, altering the technology employed in a telecommunications system can change the effects it produces. For example, the extent to which a radio signal creates potential interference with other signals is reduced if the broadcast

---

72. Of course, a television signal must convey more data than an FM radio signal, so a television broadcast requires more bandwidth in the spectrum than does an FM radio broadcast.

is not radiated in all directions, but is transmitted only from one point to another, or is radiated at less power. The amount of information that can be transmitted through a cable of a certain size can be increased by switching from coaxial to fiber optic cable. The amount of spectrum necessary to transmit a television signal can be reduced if a digital, rather than an analog, signal is employed. By increasing the power at which a satellite transmits television signals, one can reduce the size of the antenna necessary to receive those signals (and vice versa).

In almost every case, moreover, more than one telecommunications technology can accomplish a given end. Transoceanic cables can substitute for geostationary orbiting satellites. Telephone calls and television signals can be transmitted by wire or over the air. A weak broadcast signal can be strengthened by boosting the power at which it is radiated or by using a relay station to capture and retransmit the signal. In much the same way, coaxial or fiberoptic wires periodically have repeaters that strengthen the signal over long distances. Multi-channel packages of television signals can be sent to the home by cable, microwave, or satellite.

Choosing a telecommunications technology is therefore like choosing virtually any other good. One compares price and quality. There are many ways to transfer data from one place to another. For a specific task, some are cheaper, some are faster, some are more reliable. The distinct advantage of spectrum, for instance, is mobility. A particular telecommunications technology will be chosen for a specific data transmission task based on its price and quality as compared to other ways of getting the job done. Should one write, phone, email or instant message? Presumably, the choice is made by comparing the costs and benefits of each. Further, as new desires arise, new configurations of telecommunications technology will be developed to create cost-effective ways of satisfying these desires. Cable television wedded telephone and radio technology to serve the desires of viewers for more signals of greater clarity. Cellular telephone combined the same technologies to increase accessibility at some cost in clarity and in the ability to exclude unwanted listeners.

B. Allocating Spectrum

One major difference between markets for telecommunications goods and markets for other goods is that governmental regulation plays a very large role in determining what kinds and quality of telecommunications services may be offered at what costs. The central issue in telecommunications law and policy today is why telecommunications goods and markets are not treated like most other goods and markets. For most goods (books, desks, shoelaces) government subjects the relevant industry to laws of general applicability—such as antitrust, labor, and securities regulation—but does not control entry, prices, quantity or quality, and does not appoint a regulatory agency to oversee the industry's performance or enact legislation specific to that industry. The question on which all else turns, then, is this: what, if anything, justifies the different treatment accorded telecommunications service providers?

The regulation that most heavily affects the market for telecommunications services is government control over the use of the electromagnetic spectrum, an "input" into the "product" of communicating data electronically via the airwaves. In the United States, no one may broadcast through the airwaves without a license from the federal government.[73] Further, in many cases, that license will specifically limit the types of information the licensee can transmit and the technology that may be employed in transmitting it. This control over who may broadcast and what kinds of broadcasts may be offered substantially constrains the ability of the telecommunications market to adapt to consumer demand. If a faster, cheaper, or more reliable method of quickly getting data to places far away requires over-the-air transmission, one cannot offer that service without first getting the government to grant a license that permits such transmission.

Just to be concrete: no matter how highly consumers in New York City would value the ability to receive telecasts on channel eight, no one can broadcast through the airwaves on channel eight from a transmitter located in New York City because the FCC does not allow it. One cannot simply purchase on the market the right to broadcast on channel eight in New York City; the FCC will not permit such a market to exist.[74]

Once the government decides to issue a broadcast license, it in principle has several ways to decide who will obtain the license. In the case of broadcasting, the government has usually given the license away but imposed public interest requirements on licensees. We will consider the merits of this process in Chapters Three, Four, and Five; but note here that the process likely produces serious inefficiencies. One example: suppose that someone has the choice between transmitting over a wire and transmitting through the air. In some cases, sending data through the air might be more attractive not because the real cost to society is any less, but because the government does not give away wire in the way it for many years gave away broadcast licenses.

What is this "spectrum" that the government controls so tightly but, in the beginning at least, relinquished without charge? "Spectrum is the entire available range of sinusoidal signal frequencies."[75] Recall that telecommunication through the air involves the transmission of encoded sine waves. These waves can be made to vary in length, which is conventionally measured in meters. The wavelength determines the frequency of the signal. Very long waves have very low frequencies because they repeat infrequently. Short waves are high frequency because they recur more often.

The unit of measurement of frequency is called a "hertz." One hertz is a very low frequency; a one hertz wave would cycle through its sinusoid once every second. AM radio broadcasts in the United States occupy frequencies between 535 kHz (for "kilohertz," one thousand hertz, one thousand sinusoidal cycles per second) and 1605 kHz. FM radio broadcasts occur at the frequencies between 88 MHz (for "megahertz," one million hertz, one million cycles per second) and 108 MHz.

Thus, the spectrum is that range of lengths of radio waves which, to date, people have learned to encode, transmit electronically near the speed of light,

---

73. 47 U.S.C. §301.
74. Since, as observed above, a substitute is always available, one could build, or arrange to be carried on, a cable television system in New York City. Whether, however, that substitute is as cost effective in meeting consumer demand is another question.
75. Cannon & Luecke, *supra* note 19, at 87.

and decode. It follows, of course, that the spectrum—like chemistry's periodic table—has expanded substantially during the past 100 years. For example, when the FCC was established in 1934, spectrum capacity was under 300 MHz. By the end of World War II, usable spectrum had increased to 40 GHz (for "gigahertz," one billion hertz).

Different frequencies (*i.e.*, various wavelengths) of radio waves have somewhat different characteristics. Broadcasts at the very lowest frequencies require very large antennas because exceedingly long waves must be propagated. Radio waves in the medium frequency, which include AM radio broadcasts, are reflected back to earth by the ionosphere, particularly at night, thus considerably extending the reach of many of these signals.[76] Transmissions in the very high frequency (VHF) and ultra high frequency (UHF) ranges are not reflected back to earth and so can usually be captured clearly only by a receiver that is within the transmitting antenna's line of sight. Above UHF, which includes the super high and extremely high frequencies, the wavelengths are so small that they can be packed into narrow focused beams of energy, such as are employed in microwave and radar. In general, the higher the frequency (all other things held constant) the more data can be transmitted per unit of time.

The different characteristics of the various frequencies are interesting to note, but they are seldom crucial in determining where in the spectrum the signal carrying particular types of data should be located. This is particularly true for mass communications media. Television signals, for example, not only can be transmitted in both the VHF and UHF bands, but also are clearly and effectively transmitted at much higher frequencies by microwave and through satellites. Radio broadcasting, as noted, takes place all the way from 535 kHz to 108 MHz.

To generate a good quality signal, then, the particular location of that signal in the electromagnetic spectrum is not often crucial. At the very least, a rather wide range of choices will be available. An important qualification, however, is that the presence of other communications media near a particular slice of spectrum may make that slice unsuitable for a particular use. For example, given current technology, a mobile paging service within one slice of the spectrum can create spillover effects that would render a neighboring slice unsuitable for television (say, causing static) but satisfactory for some less complex or less delicate transmission.

Separate from its location in the spectrum (wavelength), the extent of the spectrum that a signal occupies (bandwidth) is also often very important. The preferred amount of bandwidth for a particular use depends on the amount and types of information that must be impressed on the radio waves. For example, much more bandwidth is required to carry a color television signal than to carry the human voice. (Indeed, since television signals contain an audio component, the point is axiomatic.) The preferred amount of bandwidth also depends on the technology being employed. The same information subjected to traditional analog encoding will require more bandwidth than if encoded digitally and compressed.

By now, it should be apparent that "the spectrum" is just a concept, somewhat like "the multiplication tables." More specifically, the spectrum is a list of

---

76. This also means that, for signals at these frequencies, the problem of interference is greater at night than during the day.

wavelengths (frequencies) at which people have learned effectively to transmit data via electrical impulses sent through the airwaves.

C. The Spectrum as a Resource

The government treats spectrum as if it were a natural resource, one to be allocated both to specific uses and to specific users. This is actually a helpful way to look at spectrum in that it reminds us that spectrum shares many basic properties with other natural resources. For example:

Spectrum can help to create both wealth and value. People are often willing to pay substantial sums for the ability to send or receive large quantities of data quickly and from far away.

Spectrum can be used in varying amounts for the same purpose. To get a television signal from a New York stage to a Los Angeles nightclub one could use no spectrum (send it via wire, door-to-door), some spectrum (wire from New York to Los Angeles, but broadcast to the nightclub), or nothing but spectrum (transmit directly from stage to satellite which transmits, in turn, directly to the nightclub).

Spectrum use is costly in that any spectrum committed to one use can no longer be employed toward a different valuable end. If one person is broadcasting a television signal on channel two in New York, that means someone else cannot use those frequencies for mobile telephony, FM stereo, or dispatching ambulances.

Lastly, while the absolute amount of available spectrum is finite, the amount of usable spectrum can be increased with appropriate investments in technology. Not only do improvements in technology add to the range of usable spectrum, but also within any existing range of usable frequencies, spectrum capacity can be increased by advances in technology. To pick one notable example, digital compression allows a broadcaster to send much more information over the same amount of spectrum that would otherwise be occupied by an uncompressed analog signal. In short: "With airwaves, as with other media, the more you spend, the more you can send: it all comes down to engineering and smart management."[77]

D. Allocating Spectrum Use

Because spectrum is a costly and productive resource that can be used in different ways and for different purposes, some mechanism had to be devised to "allocate" the spectrum—that is, to decide how much of what parts of it would go to what people for what uses. In a free market capitalist economy, the usual mechanism employed for such purposes is a pricing system. In such a system, potential users of the resource bid for it. These bids establish the value of the resource and, if it goes to the highest bidder, the resource is employed in its highest

---

77. Peter Huber, Law and Disorder in Cyberspace 75 (1995).

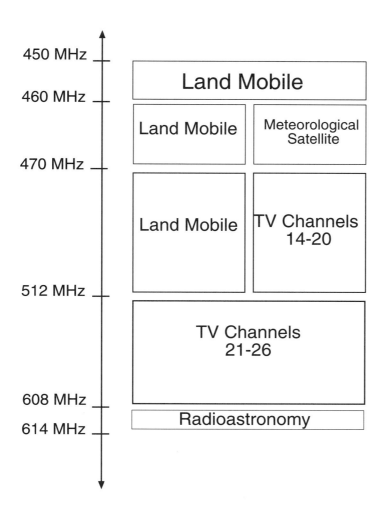

450 MHz

460 MHz

470 MHz

512 MHz

608 MHz

614 MHz

Land Mobile

Land Mobile

Meteorological Satellite

Land Mobile

TV Channels 14-20

TV Channels 21-26

Radioastronomy

Figure 1.3. SPECTRUM MANAGEMENT. This chart shows the current allocation of spectrum in the range of frequencies between 450 MHz and 614 MHz. Note that some frequencies—for example, the range between 470 MHz and 512 MHz—can be used for any of several uses, in this case both land mobile telecommunication and broadcast television. The National Telecommunications and Information Administration's Office of Spectrum Management produces a full spectrum chart, which is available from that office or at http://www.ntia.doc.gov/osmhome/allochrt.pdf.

valued use. This means that the resource is as productive as it can be given present technology, at least within the limits of the market mechanism as an evaluator of value.

At an early stage in the developing science of telecommunication, however, a very different approach was taken toward the problem of allocating spectrum. The government declared that broadcasting without a license was illegal and that only the government could convey a license. Further, licenses were handed out without charge and, although most of them could subsequently be bought and sold, these licenses were valid for only a brief period of time.

How does the process work today? For starters, radio waves do not respect geopolitical boundaries, so it is necessary for spectrum allocation in the United States to conform to rules established by the International Telecommunications Union (ITU), an organization established by treaty. Particularly for terrestrial transmission of radio waves, ITU regulations are not typically very confining. Usually, within any range of the spectrum, international standards permit a wide variety of uses. Further, international law does not restrict any spectrum usage within a country so long as that use does not radiate into other countries.

Within the broad parameters set by the ITU, spectrum allocation inside the United States is, initially, a joint effort of the FCC and the National Telecommunications and Information Administration (NTIA), located within the Commerce Department. NTIA manages those portions of the spectrum that are reserved for federal government use. The FCC manages the rest. The FCC and NTIA jointly decide which frequencies will be reserved for government use.

For those wavelengths not set aside for NTIA's management, the FCC determines permissible uses. Typically, this is accomplished through rulemaking proceedings, in which the agency announces tentatively what portions of the spectrum it will assign to what uses and then reassesses that conclusion in light of comments submitted in response to the announcement. Some tangible results of the spectrum allocation procedure discussed above are illustrated in Figure 1.3. We will look in more detail at the process that led to this particular allocation pattern in Chapter Three.

Chapter Two

WHY REGULATE BROADCAST?

The purpose of this chapter is:

- to examine and challenge the classic arguments in favor of government broadcast regulation, including the scarcity and interference rationales; and

- to gain a better understanding of the advantages and disadvantages of market transactions in the broadcast setting.

~

Chapter One introduced the basic concept of spectrum, pointing out that spectrum is in reality just a resource employed in assembling telecommunications services, much as wood pulp is a resource used in the production of newspapers and cotton fiber is a resource used in the production of shirts and socks. What Chapter One did not do is explain why the federal government is so involved in the allocation of spectrum given that—beyond establishing some basic property rules—it is not very involved at all with wood pulp or cotton fibers.

To answer that question, this chapter considers the classic arguments that have been made in favor of government regulation of the broadcast spectrum. As you consider these arguments, see if they help you to answer the following questions: Why did the federal government decide to seize the spectrum and give an administrative agency, rather than market forces, ultimate control over how producers would deliver information products over the air to consumers? Why did the government likewise give that same federal agency influence over the content of the information transmitted instead of simply allowing consumers to determine content through their viewing and purchasing decisions? Are there good reasons that we allocate spectrum to broadcasters through an administrative agency but ration their other equipment—say, antennas—through conventional markets?

I. THE CLASSIC ARGUMENTS: SCARCITY AND INTERFERENCE

It is often said that the government must regulate spectrum because spectrum is scarce. But every productive resource—labor, steel, land, investment capital—is scarce in that (a) if given away at no charge people would request more of it than is available and (b) if we could create more of it, that additional increment also could be put to productive use. To say that spectrum is scarce is quite true, then, but the statement fails to distinguish spectrum from virtually every other resource, most of which are not regulated.

Phrased another way, to say that spectrum is "scarce" is only to say that the use of spectrum must be allocated among those who desire it. Use of any scarce resource must be allocated. But in the U.S. economy this allocation usually is accomplished by prices set in open markets. It begs the question, therefore, to say that administrative allocation of spectrum is necessary because of spectrum scarcity. The real issue seems to be whether spectrum is "scarce" in some special way (unlike, say, land or iron ore) that peculiarly requires a non-market allocation mechanism.

Another common justification for broadcast regulation is that the government must control spectrum in order to prevent interference among users. Certainly, interference would destroy the utility of the spectrum resource. If two transmitters broadcast at the same time, on the same frequency, from the same location, in the same direction, and at the same power, neither of them is likely to be heard. Again, however, interference is a pervasive problem, affecting not only spectrum but also virtually every other good. To pose a trivial but illustrative example, two people cannot comfortably sit at the same time in the same desk chair, yet that fact has not led government to regulate chair use. Rather, ownership of the chair is taken to confer the authority to exclude others from sitting in it, and, with that property right in place, government regulation is deemed unnecessary. Tom Hazlett puts the point this way: "The interference problem is [rightly understood to be] one of defining separate frequency 'properties,' but it is logically unconnected to the issue of who is to harvest those frequencies. To confuse the definition of spectrum rights with the assignment of spectrum rights is to believe that, to keep intruders out of (private) backyards, the government must own (or allocate) all housing. It is a public policy *non sequitur*."[1]

A property rights approach was in fact taken early in the history of broadcast regulation. In Tribune Co. v. Oak Leaves Broadcasting,[2] the Chicago Tribune Company alleged that WGN (a radio station it owned) had been broadcasting daily for two years, had expended substantial money on equipment, and had a large and regular audience; and that the defendant, Oak Leaves, after jumping frequencies twice, had landed within 40 kilocycles of WGN's frequency. WGN asserted that Oak Leaves had moved in so close because it was an unpopular station. According to WGN, Oak Leaves' hope was that some of WGN's listeners would tune to the wrong station by accident. Oak Leaves essentially responded that the separation was ample and therefore it had not harmed WGN.

It is obvious from the opinion that the "thousands of affidavits"[3] filed by the parties allowed the trial judge to learn a considerable amount about a new and complex industry. His opinion notes the local mores whereby all the Chicago sta-

---

1. Thomas W. Hazlett, The Rationality of Broadcast Regulation, 33 J. Law & Economics 133, 138 (1990).
2. Tribune Co. v. Oak Leaves Broadcasting Station, Unreported Circuit Court of Cook County (November 17, 1926) reproduced in 68 Cong. Rec. 216 (1926).
3. *Id.* at 218.

tions went silent on a specific night so that their listeners could tune in distant stations. It also notes that the public had become educated in the use of radio and knew how to obtain the type of programming it desired. This would prove difficult, the judge concluded, unless at least a 50 kilocycle separation was maintained within a 100-mile radius.

The trial judge thus resolved the issue by defining property rights. Drawing analogies to the law of unfair competition and also the law of water rights, the judge concluded that, by reason of use and expenditure of money and effort, the plaintiff had under the common law acquired something "generally recognized" as property.[4] According to the judge, 40 kilocycles was not a sufficient separation to respect that property, and so judgment came down in favor of the plaintiff.

Of course, the property rights approach did not carry the day. The federal government today regulates the spectrum, and the main justifications put forth in support of that regulation are scarcity and interference. Thus, the question of whether something about telecommunications makes scarcity and interference unique deserves a closer look. It is to that endeavor we now turn, beginning with remarks given in 1959 before the FCC by Nobel Prize-winning economist Ronald Coase.

WHY NOT USE THE PRICING SYSTEM IN THE BROADCAST INDUSTRY?

Ronald Coase, Testimony before the FCC, December 1959
Reprinted in 4 Study of Radio & T.V. Broadcasting (No. 12782) (1959)

I appear before you with a strong conviction and a bold proposal. My conviction is that the principles under which the American economic system generally operates are fundamentally sound. My proposal is that the American broadcasting industry adopt those principles.

In presenting my case, I suffer from the disadvantage that, at the outset, I must attack a position which, although I am convinced it is erroneous, is nonetheless firmly held by many of those most knowledgeable about the broadcasting industry. Most authorities argue that the administrative assignment of radio and television frequencies by the Commission is called for by the technology of the industry. The number of frequencies, we are told, is limited, and people want to use more of them than are available.

But the situation so described is in no sense peculiar to the broadcasting industry. All resources used in the economic system are limited in amount and are scarce in that people want to use more of them than exists. This is so whether we think of labor, land, or capital. However, we do not ordinarily consider that this situation calls for government regulation. It is true that some mechanism has to be employed to decide who, out of the many claimants, should be allowed to use the scarce resources. But the usual way of handling this problem in the American

---

4. 68 Cong. Rec. at 219.

economic system is to employ the pricing mechanism, and this allocates resources to users without the need for government regulation.

This is the system under which broadcasting concerns obtain the labor, land, and capital equipment they require. There is no reason why the same system could not be adopted for radio and television frequencies. If these were disposed of by selling or leasing them to the highest bidder, there would be no need to use such criteria as proposed or past programming as a basis for the selection of broadcast station operators. Such a system would require a delimitation of the property rights acquired, and there would almost certainly also have to be some general regulation of a technical character. But such regulation would not preclude the existence of private rights in frequencies, just as zoning and other regulations do not preclude the existence of private property in houses.

Such a use of the pricing mechanisms would bring the same advantages to the radio and television industry as its use confers on the rest of the American economy. It would avoid the need for much of the costly and time-consuming procedures involved in the assignment of frequencies by the Commission. It would rule out inefficient use of frequencies by bringing any proposal for the use of such frequencies up against the test of the market, with its precise monetary measure of cost and benefit. It would avoid the threat to freedom of the press in its widest sense which is inherent in present procedures, weak though that threat may be at the moment. And it would avoid that arbitrary enrichment of private operators of radio and television stations which inevitably follows from the present system. A station operator who is granted a license to use a particular frequency in a particular place may be granted a very valuable right, one for which he would be willing to pay millions of dollars and which he would be forced to pay if others could bid for the frequency. We sometimes hear denunciations of giveaways and their corrupting influence. You, gentlemen, are administering what must be one of the biggest giveaways of all.

It has been my experience that such a suggestion as I have made horrifies my listeners. I am told that it is necessary to choose those who should operate radio and television stations to make sure that the public interest is served and that programs of the right kind are transmitted. But, put this way, the case for governmental selection of broadcast station operators represents a significant shift of position from that which justifies it on technological grounds. It is, of course, a tenable position. But if the object of the selection is, in part, directly or indirectly, to influence programming, we have to face squarely the issue of freedom of the press so far as broadcasting is concerned.

But in any case it may be doubted whether an indirect attempt to influence programming through the selection of broadcast station operators could ever be very effective. For over 30 years, the federal government has been selecting broadcast station operators on the basis, among other things, of their good character and their devotion to the public interest. By now one would expect the broadcasting industry to be a beacon of virtue, shining out in a wicked world. Such, I am afraid, is not the case.

Notes and Questions

1. Interference. Interference in the telecommunications context can be difficult to predict, in part because interference is in many cases caused by the interaction of several signals. That is, it is entirely possible that two signals will not interfere with one another if they are the only two signals in the area, but that those same signals will interfere if a third signal is added to the mix. This phenomenon is called intermodulation. Similarly, interference is also partly a function of atmospheric conditions; a signal that is perfectly clear at a given power level on a cloudy day might need to be transmitted at a higher power on a day when the sun is strong. Coase does not address technical considerations like these, but do they sufficiently distinguish spectrum from more conventional goods so as to undermine Coase's argument?

2. Defining Property Rights. In order for a market system to work, the government would need to delimit specific bundles of rights that could then be recognized in particular users. Just as land ownership includes, among other things, the right to exclude others under certain circumstances and rights with respect to the use of natural resources above and below ground level, spectrum ownership, too, would have to be articulated in terms of specific rights to use and exclude. How difficult would that articulation be? More difficult than it is in other settings? Enough to explain why we regulate broadcast but not wood pulp? (Does the current system suffer from the same difficulties, or does government involvement mean that there is less of a need for clearly delimited rights?)

Think specifically about how you would define property rights in spectrum. Perhaps in terms of inputs, with the government recognizing in a particular party the (transferable?) right to build a tower of a certain height, at a particular location, transmitting a signal at a particular frequency and power level, during particular times, and in a particular direction? Indeed, a group of scholars in 1969 proposed just such a definition of spectrum property rights based on parameters of time, geographic area, power, and wave frequency.[5] What drawbacks do you see to such a style of rights definition? Are there other approaches that might prove more workable? What further parameters would need to be articulated beyond these technical ones in order to complete the definition of property rights in radio spectrum?

3. The Coase Theorem. Coase is perhaps most famous for his work on the importance of transaction costs. Yet, might it be argued that, in his remarks before the FCC, Coase neglected the important role transaction costs play in the market for telecommunications services? Think about how many parties use spectrum on both the national and international level, both as suppliers of telecommunications services and as consumers of those services. Or how even a single radio signal at a relatively low energy level can still interfere with dozens of signals hundreds of miles away. Does Coase jump over this point too quickly? Are transaction costs a good reason for government regulation of the spectrum?

4. Zoning. Thus far, the theme of this section has been to point out that scarcity and interference are common problems to which the typical response is not to regulate but instead to define property rights and then defer to market interactions. With respect to land ownership, however, government does regulate—in the form of zoning laws, tort suits for nuisance, and so on. Does Coase's attack

---

5. Arthur S. Devan et al., A Property System for Market Allocation of the Electromagnetic Spectrum: A Legal-Economic-Engineering Study, 21 Stan. L. Rev. 1499 (1969).

call all these "regulations" into question? Conversely, does the existence of zoning law make you wonder whether Coase has missed something in his analysis of spectrum allocation?

Looked at another way, is there something special about both land and spectrum that distinguishes them from other goods? For example, the government uses land for public purposes (say, government buildings and public parks) and the government also generates significant demand for spectrum (for example, military use and police radio). Does this fact help to explain why, in telecommunications and land use, scarcity and interference have led to government regulation whereas elsewhere they have led to more market-based solutions?

5. For Further Consideration. What is lost by the use of an administrative agency instead of market forces? Are there corresponding gains? Are traditional worries about markets — say, the fear of monopoly or concerns about wealth effects — somehow more salient in the telecommunications context? Can a market work in telecommunications given that the equipment that transmits signals is typically owned by one group (broadcasters) whereas the equipment that receives those signals is typically owned by another, independent group (consumers)? Is this why we regulate? If we ask broadcasters to bid for spectrum, would they consistently underbid, on the theory that broadcasters who rely on commercial advertisements for revenue likely are willing to pay less for the right to air any given program than viewers would pay were they paying for content directly? (If that is the case, is it an argument against free broadcast and in favor of subscription television instead?) Does regulation perhaps preserve for the government more flexibility than a market regime would? Given the newness of the technology, was that a good justification for at least the early pattern of regulation?

6. A Modern Twist. Consider the following essay, written for a popular press magazine by two law professors. Knowing what you know now, is their argument convincing?

WILL TECHNOLOGY MAKE CBS UNCONSTITUTIONAL?
Yochai Benkler & Lawrence Lessig, The New
Republic (Dec. 14, 1998) at pp. 12–14

Forty years after Nobel Prize-winning economist Ronald Coase suggested privatizing the radio spectrum, the FCC has caught on. Now there's a quiet frenzy raging in Washington. Every slice of spectrum, from cellular to satellite, is being sold off to help fund the budget. Everyone seems to assume that this radio bake-off is constitutional. No doubt at one time it was. But is it constitutional anymore? Does the government have the right to auction off spectrum as if it were just another national resource?

We think the answer is probably no. Changes in technology are likely to render much of the allocation of spectrum constitutionally suspect, and it's time that the auctioneers — and the buyers — took note.

Our argument is straightforward: The FCC regulates speech. It says that, if you want to speak on 98.6 FM in Boston, you must get a license (or, now, buy one). If you speak on 98.6 without a license, you will have committed a crime. The FCC will prosecute you and seize your transmitter. All this despite the fact that the First Amendment to the Constitution says, "Congress shall make no law...abridging the freedom of speech." What gives?

The traditional rationale goes something like this: 98.6 is part of the radio spectrum; radio spectrum by its "nature" must be allocated for it to be useable. Two transmitters can't use the same channel, so someone must decide who gets which. Since 1927, the FCC has had that authority. For many years, the FCC did this by licensing. During the 1990s, it has increasingly allocated spectrum through auctions. But, whether through licensing or auctioning, the government must, the argument goes, organize and police the parceling out of the spectrum commons. We have, it is said, no other choice. Thus has "allocated spectrum" been the dominant architecture for broadcasting. This architecture in turn has justified massive involvement by government in the distribution of speech sans wires. Nature makes it so, the government says, and government must respect nature.

But what if "nature" changed? What if it were no longer true that spectrum had to be allocated? What if the spectrum could be shared by all rather than set aside for a narrow class of licensees? What if the FCC, CBS, or Bell Atlantic Mobile became unnecessary?

A growing body of research suggests exactly this. Using a variety of strategies, mostly known as spread spectrum, researchers in wireless technology have begun to demonstrate the viability of systems that allow many users to share the same slice of spectrum without interfering with one another. Just as packet-switching is replacing circuit-switched telephony, spread-spectrum techniques, these researchers argue, could replace traditional broadcasting. And just as TCP/IP protocols tell packets on the Internet where to go, and how not to get mixed up or interfere with packets carrying other people's messages, spread-spectrum technologies could use one of a number of protocols to avoid collision and congestion in wireless communication.

The implications of this change are profound. Instead of defined frequency ranges over which someone—a licensee or an owner—gets to decide who communicates what, and to whom, the government would permit anyone using certain kinds of equipment (basically a computer with a wireless modem) to send and receive whatever he or she wants, over broad swaths of spectrum. Instead of a market in spectrum, we would have a market in efficient wireless modems. Instead of the government and a small group of companies dictating how wireless communications will be used, we would have everyone deciding for her- or himself whether to use a computer to talk to a friend, watch a movie, or play an online game. In other words, instead of a few railroad companies deciding who gets to go where, and when, people would buy cars and go wherever they wanted to go.

If the engineers are right—if the efficiency of an architecture of spread-spectrum wireless technology were even roughly equivalent to the architecture of allocated spectrum—then much of the present broadcasting architecture would be rendered unconstitutional. If shared spectrum is possible, in other words, then the First Amendment would mean that allocated spectrum—whether licensed or auctioned—must go. And, if allocated spectrum must go, then so must the government's giveaways and sales to private industry. If we are right, the government can no more auction the right to broadcast in Boston than it can auction a license to print a newspaper there.

Notes and Questions

1. Scarcity. Benkler and Lessig argue that "spread spectrum" presents a new challenge to the government's authority to regulate broadcast. But is their argument really new, or is this just another round of the same old argument about scarcity, with the authors in essence saying that spectrum isn't as scarce as we thought it was? If so, does that take them very far? If not, what more are they saying?

2. Breaker, Breaker. Can you think of a service for which, today, the FCC does exactly what Benkler and Lessig advocate? Does that support or undermine their argument? (Hint: Before cellular telephony, how did truckers pass information back and forth about traffic accidents, police speed traps, and so on?)

3. Congestion. What are the authors assuming about congestion? Do they account for the fact that, as portable technology gets more affordable and reliable, there might be such a significant increase in demand that—even if spectrum is less scarce than we once thought—spectrum might end up being more congested? Hasn't that been our experience with the seemingly vast resource called the Internet?

II. DID GOVERNMENT REGULATE SIMPLY TO BENEFIT SPECIAL INTERESTS?

If scarcity and interference do not provide a convincing account for why it is that the government regulates spectrum, perhaps a more convincing account centers on the politics of government regulation. In the excerpt that follows, Thomas Hazlett offers an interpretation of the 1927 Act under which the purpose of the Act was not to reduce interference among broadcasters by asserting control over the airwaves, but rather to distribute the monetary rewards from broadcasting among certain politically dominant claimants. The 1927 Act was not, in his view, about efficiency, scarcity, or interference; it was about simple, run-of-the-mill rent seeking.

THE RATIONALITY OF U.S. REGULATION OF THE BROADCAST SPECTRUM

Thomas W. Hazlett, 33 J. Law & Econ. 133, 146–170 (1990)

[Spectrum was for many years awarded to private users on a no-fee basis, thus conferring significant economic rents on private parties at substantial opportunity cost to the fisc. Moreover, Federal Communications Commission policies openly sought, virtually throughout the agency's entire life span, to restrict the number of licensed broadcasters in any given area to something below the number technically possible. These regulations were at one time justified on theories of scarcity and interference; now, with scarcity and interference both called into question, these policies are described as if they were simple mistakes, the historical product of policymakers who failed to understand the nature of property rights to airwaves.][6]

---

6. [Ed. For clarity and brevity, we paraphrase Hazlett here, using many of his phrases. Readers interested in Hazlett's fuller articulation of these introductory points are encouraged to consult the original article.]

This article seeks to revise such thinking about the "wrongheadedness" of U.S. regulatory policy toward the broadcast spectrum. Rather than stumbling into a legal structure under erroneous pretenses, a careful examination of the early radio broadcasting market and the legislative history of the Federal Radio Act of 1927 reveals that subsequent decision making under the "public interest, convenience, or necessity" licensing standard was a compromise designed to generate significant rents for each constituency influential in the process. Most fundamentally, the nature of rights in the "ether" was precisely understood; the regulatory approach adopted chose not to reject or ignore them but to maximize their rent values as dictated by rational self-interest.

I. The Possibility of a Market for the Ether

In the early days of radio (that is, pre-1927), there existed a very lively market in broadcast properties, sold with frequency rights attached. Station licenses were known to be scarce, were commonly taken to confer exclusive rights, and were traded freely, often at prices reflecting considerable rents. Indeed, the spectrum policy problem of this era (1923–26) was that the Secretary of Commerce had been ordered to issue licenses to all comers, and the Secretary in the end relied on market transactions to solve that problem, minimizing broadcasting disruptions by engaging in the sorts of negotiations predicted by the Coase Theorem. All this is apparent in the following exchange between Judge Davis (then-Solicitor General of the Commerce Department) and Senator Smith, which took place on January 8, 1926:

> SENATOR SMITH: Now, in those licenses, do you give the total control of that wave length to the licensee? For instance, if I had a license to use a certain wave length, could I sublet it to others to use it for such time as I, or whoever had the principle use of it, might not be using it?

> MR. DAVIS: That situation is worked out somewhat similar to this, Senator. For instance, take the situation here in Washington. We have two stations, WRC and WCAP. Both operate on a single wave length. In other words, we assign one wave length to both of those stations. Then, Senator, they for themselves work out their time division.

> SENATOR SMITH: Yes; that is what I meant.

> MR. DAVIS: In other words, we do not say to one, "You go until 12 o'clock tonight." But they get together and work out the time on this wave length, the fact being that they do not both go on the same wave length at the same time.

> SENATOR WHEELER: Then suppose they do not agree, what do you do?

> MR. DAVIS: We would have authority to enforce such a time division.

> SENATOR WHEELER: How?

> MR. DAVIS: Because we would give them licenses which would allow them to operate only at certain limited times. That situation, however, has not arisen. In other words, the stations which are operating on one wave length have been able to get together and agree among themselves. And, obviously, that is what the department wanted them to do.

Not only do these passages indicate the philosophical disposition of the Commerce Department; they also more importantly illustrate that the price mechanism was the institutional tool used to allocate frequencies in the 1920s. It was understood by the regulators (who then explained it to the legislators) and it was accepted as socially efficient. Trades of spectrum rights were commonplace; the market was robust (indeed, the Washington radio band discussed above by Stephen Davis ended in Coasian optimality as WRC bought WCAP's air time). It is clear that such chaos as potentially could exist was explicitly remedied by federal establishment of property rights, followed by market trading to assign such rights to their highest valued employments.

II. An Innocent Solution Preempted

The solution to the interference problem, then, was in the 1920's being crafted not only in Washington but also in the courts. The common resource problem was clearly identified by contemporary analysts, and so was its solution: "establishing legally the priority to an established wave length," as Radio Broadcast magazine then put it.

In the fall of 1926, a simple and compelling state court decision did just that. [Hazlett here introduces Tribune Co. v. Oak Leaves Broadcasting Station, discussed earlier this chapter.] Chancellor Francis S. Wilson decided *Oak Leaves* wholly within the spirit of a property rights solution to a common resource problem. The decision found that "unless some regulatory measures are provided for by Congress or rights recognized by State courts, the situation will result in chaos and a great detriment to the advancement of an industry which is only in its infancy." It went on to analogize the right in broadcast frequencies to other long-protected propertied interests.

> While it is true that the case in question is novel in its newness, the situation is not devoid of legal equitable support. The same answer [that no rights in air space exist] might be made, as was made in the beginning, that there was no property right, or could be, in a name or sign, but there has developed a long line of cases, both in the Federal and State courts, which has recognized under the law known as the law of unfair competition, the right to obtain a property right therein, provided that by reason of their use, he has succeeded in building up a business and creating a good will which has become known to the public and to the trade and which has served as a designation of some particular output so that it has become generally recognized as the property of such person.

Using the further analogy of riparian rights, the Chancellor concluded "that a court of equity is compelled to recognize rights which have been acquired by reason of the outlay and expenditure of money and the investment of time. We are of the further opinion that, under the circumstances in this case, priority of time creates a superiority in right." Judge Wilson then issued an admonition to the respondents, pending a final hearing, for the "pirate" broadcaster to keep a distance of at least fifty kilocycles from the established WGN frequency. Owing to his fundamental understanding of radio law and the crucial nature of *Oak Leaves* to the policy outcome, I quote the magistrate's findings at length.

> So far as broadcasting stations are concerned, there has almost grown up a custom which recognizes the rights of the various broadcasters, partic-

ularly in that certain broadcasters use certain hours of the day, while the other broadcasters remain silent during that particular period of time. Again, in this particular locality, a certain night is set aside as silent night, when all local broadcasters cease broadcasting in order that radio receivers may be able to tune in on outside distant stations.

Wave lengths have been bought and sold and broadcasting stations have changed hands for a consideration. Broadcasting stations have contracted with each other so as to broadcast without conflicting and in this manner be able to present their different programs to the waiting public. The public itself has become educated to the use of its receiving sets so as to be able to obtain certain particular items of news, speeches, or programs over its own particular sets.

The theory of the bill in this case is based upon the proposition that by usage of a particular wave length for a considerable length of time and by reason of the expenditure of a considerable amount of money in developing its broadcasting station and by usage of a particular wave length educating the public to know that that particular wave length is the wave length of the complainant and by furnishing programs which have been attractive and thereby cause a great number of people to listen in to their particular programs that the said complainant has created and carved out for itself a particular right or easement in and to the use of said wave length which should be recognized in a court of equity and that outsiders should not be allowed thereafter, except for good cause shown, to deprive them of that right and to make use of a field which had been built up by the complainant at a considerable cost in money and a considerable time in pioneering.

In other words, private rights in the airwaves under common law were immediately recognized as a solution to the interference problem. *Radio Broadcast* noted in its February, 1927 issue that the case was key in "establishing legally the priority to an established wavelength," and concluded that "it establishes a most acceptable precedent." Other stations beleaguered by spectrum trespassers quickly moved to file similar claims in state courts.

It was clear that a system of excludable, transferable property rights in spectrum (1) was widely understood as necessary and desirable so as to efficiently solve the radio allocation problem and (2) could well be expected to come by way of common law, via the priority-in-use principle. A single trial court decision would in no definitive way answer the national property rights question, but the analysis—and its political implications—were clear.

III. The Agenda of The Regulators[7]

The Congress responded to *Oak Leaves* instantly. After years of debate and delay on a radio law, both houses jumped to pass a December 1926 resolution

---

7. [Ed. We have renumbered and also reordered sections of Hazlett's article so as to make it more accessible to new readers. Part III, for example, was Part VII in the original, and it came before our Part IV, which Hazlett put as Part VI. We have taken great care so as to ensure that Hazlett's argument is not in any way distorted by these changes, but readers are of course welcome to consult the original document.]

stating that no private rights to the airwaves would be recognized as valid, mandating that broadcasters immediately sign waivers relinquishing all rights and disclaiming any vested interests. The power to require such was the Interstate Commerce Clause, but the motive was that Congress was nervous that spectrum allocation would soon be a matter of private law.

Should those common-law principles apportion the spectrum to private users, the "breakdown of the law" would be remedied, but the federal government's ability to control or even influence broadcasting would vanish. Compromise legislation was quickly hammered together; a bill creating an independent five-member regulatory commission was passed by both houses, endorsed by Hoover, and signed by President Coolidge.

The policy debate was led by men who clearly understood—and articulated—that interference was not the problem, interference was the opportunity. The efficiency issues were demarcated from political-distributional questions both in their words and their actions. In 1925, Herbert Hoover explicitly separated the respective issues of rights-definition and political control over licensees thus:

> It seems to me we have in this development of governmental relations two distinct problems. First, is a question of traffic control. This must be a Federal responsibility. From an interference point of view every word broadcasted is an interstate word. Therefore radio is a 100 percent interstate question, and there is not an individual who has the most rudimentary knowledge of the art who does not realize that there must be a traffic policeman in the ether, or all service will be lost in complete chaos of interference. This is an administrative job, and for good administration must lie in a single responsibility.

> The second question is the determination of who shall use the traffic channels and under what conditions. This is a very large discretionary or a semi-judicial function which should not devolve entirely upon any single official and is, I believe, a matter in which each local community should have a large voice—should in some fashion participate in a determination of who should use the channels available for broadcasting in that locality.

Senator C.C. Dill authored the bill that finally gained passage in 1927. He was equally unconfused as to the purpose of federal licensing. "Of one thing I am absolutely certain," he declared. "Uncle Sam should not only police this 'new beat'; he should see to it that no one uses it who does not promise to be good and well-behaved."

IV. The Agenda of the Radio Broadcasting Interests

Broadcasters' agenda focused on "the non-issuance of additional broadcasting licenses, the freedom from further division of time with other broadcasters, [and] the maintenance of the present distribution of frequency channels," as the 1925 Radio Conference's resolution put it.

This agenda was artfully accomplished. When the Federal Radio Commission (FRC) was born out of the Federal Radio Act of 1927, it immediately grandfathered rights for major broadcasters, while eliminating marginal competitors and all new entry. Indeed, the FRC restored order out of chaos by ordering stations to "return to their [original Commerce Department] assignments," thus revealing much about the previous rights regime and the privatization of airwave properties achieved in "the public interest."

Still, the industry was most concerned about how the FRC would deal with "such dangerous propositions as the pressure to extend the broadcast band; the fatuous claims of the more recently licensed stations to a place in the ether; and the uneconomic proposals to split time on the air rather than eliminate excess stations wholesale," as one trade journal forthrightly summarized.

Radio men were quickly assured that the newly appointed commission was politically sensitive to their needs and aspirations. Only two months after its inception they could be relieved that the commissioners had acted wisely. "Broadening of the band was disposed of with a finality which leaves little hope for the revival of that pernicious proposition; division of time was frowned upon as uneconomical; the commissioners were convinced that less stations was the only answer."[8]

And in the official rights allocation under the Federal Radio Commission in 1927–28, the agency chose to employ the market success standard of public interest—in essence, a simulated auction, with awardees keeping rents.

> The commissioners agreed that the prevailing scarcity of channels required that those available be used economically, effectively, and as fully as possible. In practical terms, this meant that they favored the applicants with superior technical equipment, adequate financial resources, skilled personnel, and the ability to provide continuous service. According to this interpretation, established broadcasters with demonstrated ability best fulfilled the public interest standard. In most instances, priority and financial success guided the FRC in favoring one operator over another.[9]

V. The 1927 Radio Act as an Equilibrium Political Solution

Although licensing control passed into the hands of an independent commission, economic allocation was not much affected vis-a-vis the rights established in the pre-"breakdown" period. By virtually all accounts, the commission made legal what Secretary Hoover had accomplished via extralegal authority: it recognized priority-in-use rights to spectrum space, with discretionary power and time assignments favorable to those broadcasters serving larger audiences. Marginal broadcasters with irregular transmissions were expropriated altogether; nonprofit institutions were relegated to crowded spectrum "ghettos" where time was scarce and listenership difficult to attract. Many such licenses were soon withdrawn by their owners due to unsustainable financial losses.

The commission's "public interest" solution to the property right problem essentially accomplished the following:

(1) it served to establish quickly and cheaply de facto property rights to spectrum based on the priority-in-use rule;

(2) it thinned out the spectrum by failing to renew licenses of 83 broadcasters in July 1927 and gave reduced power and time assignments to nonprofit organizations;

---

8. Stabilizing the Broadcast Situation, Radio Broadcast 79 (June 1927).
9. Phillip T. Rosen, The Modern Stentors 133 (1981).

(3) it awarded enhanced power assignments (as high as 50,000 watts—up from 5,000 watts) to some fortunate large broadcasters, generally network affiliated;

(4) it established a rights-enforcement mechanism, wherein license holders were to self-police the airwaves by filing complaints against interfering broadcasters;

(5) it froze AM band width at essentially its 1924 size, using less than five percent of the then-utilizable capacity for broadcasting.

This solution represented an optimum politically because each of the influential parties was given a share of the rents created in proportion to their political influence, making each better off than they would fare in alternative nonlicensing arrangements. Such rents emanated from the allocation of spectrum rights to private users on a nonfee basis and from entry restrictions enhancing the values thereby created. In that vested rights were developing, and lengthy, costly litigation would have followed had an expropriation of major broadcast license holders occurred, an outright nationalization of airwave property was not a desirable alternative for regulators. Such a course would also have carried the opportunity cost of an immediate loss of support by major broadcasters. It was far better for regulators to award broadcasters generous rents subject to "public interest" discretion in the licensing process that could be partially apportioned by incumbent officeholders.

What was evident was that the issuance of zero-priced franchises could stimulate an effective rent-seeking competition from constituencies willing and able to pay for the broadcasting privilege. For instance, Congress immediately acted to regulate content with such incumbent protectionist devices as the equal time rule (codified in the Radio Act), and the commission very quickly found it could exercise authority over broad forms of content, such as "fairness." And, of course, pure influence peddling in the procurement of licenses could yield both legal and extralegal benefits for incumbent Congressmen.

In summary, private spectrum rights were not rejected in favor of government allocation out of "ignorance" but were actually established as part of a hybrid regulatory system that respected vested rights in broadcast spectrum and even enhanced them in value via supply restriction. Such private rights were "purchased" by broadcaster subsidies to "public interest" concerns, a tax which initially amounted to little more than nominal acquiescence to (and political support for) a federal licensing authority but would, over time, include significant payments to unprofitable local programming, "fairness doctrine" regulation, extensive proof of commitment to "community" in station renewals, and the avoidance of broadcasting content offensive to the political party in power.

Notes and Questions

1. **Counter-Evidence.** Hazlett's account is provocative and well argued. But note that there is at least some evidence suggesting that scarcity and interference were not so well understood even after 1927, let alone before. For example, in 1959, right after Coase delivered the talk excerpted earlier this chapter, the floor was opened for questions and then-FCC Commissioner Philip Cross opened the question period by asking Coase, in all seriousness, "Are you spoofing us? Is this all a

big joke?"[10] When Coase wrote up those same ideas in a paper for the Rand Corporation, one referee who reviewed the document advised Rand to kill the project entirely, and another "stated that, by definition, the spectrum was a public good and consequently a market solution was not appropriate and that the project represented a waste of Rand's resources."[11] Coase, of course, would go on to win the Nobel Prize in Economics, in part for this work that referees deemed wasteful and Hazlett suggests was fully understood by politicians decades earlier.

2. Implications. Suppose, however, that Hazlett is correct and that, in 1927, the policy debate was indeed "led by men who clearly understood—and articulated—that interference was not the problem, interference was the opportunity." Where does that leave us? Should the newly-discovered motivations of the creators of the regulatory structure raise First Amendment concerns about that structure? In short, what should we do with the historical evidence Hazlett uncovers in this research?

III. ARE THERE MARKET FAILURES THAT MIGHT JUSTIFY REGULATION?

A. Public Goods

Once a television or radio program is being broadcast in a given community, it costs nothing to allow an additional listener or viewer to receive the signal. Broadcast content, in other words, is "non-rivalrous"—what an economist would term a public good. To some commentators, the non-rivalrous nature of broadcast content implies that this content should be made available free of charge, funded either through government subsidies (think PBS) or advertiser sponsorship. Prices, these commentators argue, serve to deny certain consumers access to the content; and why should any family be denied access to broadcast content when there would be no additional cost to allowing them to listen or watch?

The response is that prices can serve two important functions in the broadcast context: they can help broadcasters better measure the intensity of consumer preferences for particular programs, and they can give broadcasters a strong incentive to satisfy those preferences. To take a specific example, advertiser-supported television is not particularly responsive to consumer preferences since, while broadcasters care that viewers watch a given program (seeing the commercials), so long as a viewer is willing to watch, broadcasters do not care how much the viewer enjoys the program. Intensity of preference, in other words, is neither very relevant to, nor very apparent in, the advertiser-supported system.

A more responsive regime might be what used to be called "subscription television" but today is more often referred to as pay-per-view. Such a regime sets

---

10. Ronald Coase, Comment on Thomas W. Hazlett: Assigning Property Rights to Radio Spectrum Users: Why Did FCC License Auctions Take 67 Years?, 41 J. Leg. Stud. 577, 579 (1998).

11. *Id.* at 580.

specific prices for specific programs and, in that way, allows consumers to register their preferences by voting with their dollars. One result is that pay-per-view stations air a different mix of programs. For example, under a pay scheme, television stations are more likely to air niche programs that attract fewer but more enthusiastic viewers. The downside to pay-per-view, of course, is that absent perfect price discrimination there is inefficient exclusion: some consumers who value a given program above its marginal cost (zero) are nevertheless unwilling to pay the market price and thus are denied access.[12]

This tension between free broadcast content and subscription systems is intractable. If viewers pay a fixed price for programs, some inefficient exclusion of those who do not pay will result. If viewers are not charged, then the programs broadcasters air may well not reflect viewer preferences. Therefore, at least in principle, it is almost always possible to argue that any change in the mix of broadcast programming (and, consequently, any change in telecommunications regulation that can affect the programming mix) is a change for the worse—and for the better.

Consider in this light the second half of the speech Ronald Coase gave before the FCC in 1959. The first half, excerpted above, argued that scarcity and interference were not good justifications for heavy-handed government broadcast regulation. The second half considers the problem of advertiser-supported television.

WHY NOT USE THE PRICING SYSTEM
IN THE BROADCAST INDUSTRY?

Ronald Coase, Testimony before the FCC, December 1959
Reprinted in 4 Study of Radio & T.V. Broadcasting (No. 12782) (1959)

The essence of a commercial broadcasting system is that the operator of a radio or television station is paid for making broadcasts or allowing them to be made. But he is not paid by those who listen to or view the programs. He is paid by those who wish listeners to receive a particular message—the advertisement, or commercial. However, simply to broadcast the commercial will not usually lead people to listen or view. A program, therefore, has to be broadcast to induce people to listen or view. In a commercial broadcasting system, the object of the program is to attract an audience for the commercials.

With such a system, what programs will be broadcast? They are the programs which maximize the difference between the profits yielded by broadcast advertising and the costs of the program. If programs were supplied in the way which is normal in the American economic system, the programs which would be broadcast would be those which maximize the difference between the amount people would pay to hear or see the programs and the cost of the programs. It is easy to see that these are completely different ways of determining what programs to transmit—and that a broadcasting system organized as other industries are (with revenue accruing directly from the consumers) would lead to a very different structure of programs. But how different and in what ways?

---

12. Readers interested in exploring these issues more rigorously should consult Jora Minasian, Television Pricing and the Theory of Public Goods, 7 J. Law & Econ. 71 (1964). Some empirical evidence is presented in Roger Noll et al., Economic Aspects of Television Regulation 129–50 (1973).

It is clear that some programs which people would be willing to pay for will have costs which are higher than the profits that would accrue from any commercials that might be associated with them and that therefore they would not be made available with the commercial system. Again, with commercial broadcasting, a program which attracts a larger audience may be chosen even though viewers or listeners in total would pay more for one which would attract a smaller audience. The result of all this is that commercial broadcasting leaves some sectors of the public with the feeling that they are not being catered for. And this is true.

I need not go into the rationale of the competitive system, which treats all money demands equally and operates in such a way as to maximize the value of output. But it will hardly come as a surprise to you that, holding these views, I urge you to do all you can to bring about the introduction of subscription television (and subscription radio, too, if possible). There may be practical difficulties standing in the way of subscription television. But I am convinced that there are no substantial objections to subscription television in principle.

Much is made of the fact that with commercial television service is free. The argument is essentially the same as that for socialism and the Welfare State. What is being attacked is the price mechanism. The factors of production used in television are not made available for nothing. They will be paid for by someone: the government out of the proceeds of taxation, the advertiser, or the consumer. What is important is that factors of production should be used where their output is most valuable, and this is most likely to happen if the use of factors of production is determined by what consumers are willing to pay. The objection to a "free" system is that it is not really "free" and it is less efficient.

It has been pointed out that, with subscription television, programs will only be seen by those who have the money to pay for them. But if reliance on ability to pay is so unfortunate when applied to television programs, how much worse it must be when applied to food or clothing or housing—or even to television sets and phonograph records.

Notes and Questions

1. Non-Rivalrous Goods. Our discussion above began by pointing out that broadcast content is non-rivalrous. Unlike, say, pizza, broadcast is a good for which one person's consumption does not diminish another person's ability to consume. Can you think of other examples of non-rivalrous goods? Are these goods provided by government, provided by private parties through unregulated market mechanisms, or provided by private parties but in markets subject to significant government regulation? Does your answer help to explain why broadcast is regulated?

2. Food, Clothing, and Housing. Coase concludes his remarks by noting that, if reliance on ability to pay is troubling in the broadcast setting, it should be all the more troubling when applied to food, clothing, or housing. Is that a fair analogy?

3. Summing Valuations. In an advertiser-supported regime, a television broadcaster might choose to air a program that fifty people each value at $1 instead of offering a program that forty-nine people each value at $10. No one who respects consumer preferences can regard that situation as maximizing consumer welfare. But what if fifty people each value a given program at $10 and ten people each value a competing option at $51? Which program would be aired under subscription television? Advertiser support? Which is the "right" result from a policy perspective?

4. Advertising Distortions. Do the distortions introduced by advertiser support go away as the number of broadcast channels increases? Do you see why they might? Do any distortions remain? Similarly, are there distortions of any sort inherent in pay systems? Under what conditions?

5. The Costs of Free Television. Advertiser support is not really free. For one thing, advertisers must recoup their costs, and presumably do so through increased prices on goods that viewers of the show are likely to purchase. Moreover, while there might be some informational and entertainment value in watching commercials, to some degree the time spent watching commercials is a cost to viewers as well. Most viewers would pay a modest sum if there were an option to do so and then receive a commercial-free television signal. Then again, advertising also benefits consumers. Some studies suggest, for example, that advertising increases the degree of competition in a given market and that the resulting competition, in turn, leads to lower prices even though the firms all incur increased advertising expenses. One such study compared eyeglass prices in markets where advertising was permitted to eyeglass prices in markets where an advertising ban was in effect. The market with advertising averaged lower prices. *See* Lee Benham, The Effect of Advertising on the Price of Eyeglasses, 15 J. L. & Econ. 337 (1972).

6. Are Advertiser Preferences Illegitimate? An implicit assumption in the above is that advertiser preferences are somehow illegitimate. Is that true? Why shouldn't broadcast content in part be determined by advertiser preferences and in part by viewer preferences, exactly as the current advertiser-supported system operates today?

7. Non-Excludable Goods. Public goods are always non-rival, but they are sometimes non-excludable as well. Non-excludable goods are goods such that, if one person consumes the good, it is impossible to prevent others from consuming that same good simultaneously. A street light is a classic example. Once a given lamp has been built and is operational, it is difficult to deny passers-by the benefit of that additional light. We say, above, that broadcast content is non-rival; is it also non-excludable? Is that important to understanding the appropriate policy response here?[13]

8. Hooray for Hollywood? Movie theaters sell tickets person-by-person. Is movie content, then, like subscription television in that we might expect it to better reflect viewer preferences than does advertiser-sponsored television?

B. Should We Respect Consumer Preferences?

Arguments in favor of subscription television (or radio equivalents) seem to presume that consumer preferences should be respected. That is, these arguments

---

13. Note that some non-excludable goods are rival. For instance, it is difficult to meter access to air, but air pollution clearly makes air a rival resource.

assume that, if consumers want their MTV, they should get it—even if that means fewer viewers are watching the nightly news or listening to congressional debates on C-SPAN. There is reason to wonder, however, whether the broadcast marketplace should, in fact, so completely respect consumer preferences.

There are two principal arguments to consider here. First, there is what might be thought of as the paternalistic argument that, when it comes to information consumption, consumers don't know what is in their own long-term best interests. Cass Sunstein has made this argument, although he seems to object to the "paternalism" label:

> What people now prefer and believe may be a product of insufficient information, limited opportunities, legal constraints, or unjust background conditions. People may think as they do simply because they have not been provided with sufficient information and opportunities. It is not paternalistic, or an illegitimate interference with competing conceptions of the good, for a democracy to promote scrutiny and testing of preferences and beliefs through deliberative processes.

> It may seem controversial or strange to say that there is a problem for the Madisonian system if people do not seek serious coverage of serious issues. Perhaps this suggestion is unacceptably paternalistic; perhaps we should take people however we find them. But the system of deliberative democracy is not supposed simply to implement existing desires. Its far more ambitious goal is to create the preconditions for a well-functioning democratic process.[14]

Second, there is an externality argument that similarly might cause us to question consumer sovereignty in broadcast markets, to wit: one person's consumption of broadcast content may affect another person's well-being. For example, some people believe that repeated exposure to television violence causes viewers to become more violent.[15] If that is true, then this is a negative externality, and because of this externality it might not be wise to allow viewers to determine for themselves how many hours of violent television they watch each week. Each viewer's choice, after all, neglects the harm that decision imposes on others.

A similar point can be made with respect to the decision to watch (and, in a subscription system, pay for) children's educational television. Educational television arguably creates a positive externality in that these programs help young viewers become more informed, and hence more productive, citizens. Because of this externality, if left to make their own decisions, children might not watch as much educational television as would be optimal from a societal perspective.[16]

Notes and Questions

1. Distinctions. Are the "paternalistic" and "externality" arguments different, or does one simply recast the other in new words? Similarly, is there really a distinction between a "positive" and a "negative" externality in this setting, or does that distinction also collapse, depending on your political perspective?

---

14. Cass R. Sunstein, Demoracy and the Problem of Free Speech 19–21 (1993).
15. We consider televised violence in Chapter Six.
16. We also consider children's television in Chapter Six.

2. Remedies. To whatever extent we find the paternalistic and externality arguments convincing, what types of responses might they justify? Consider, for example, educational television. If the FCC believes that it would benefit society to have more children watching educational television, is it a sufficient response for the government to increase the amount of educational television available — perhaps by, say, offering more funding to PBS? Must the government do more, perhaps both funding PBS and restricting the simultaneous broadcast of programs that children prefer? After all, merely having virtuous programming available will not change anything if nobody watches. Consider in this light news analyst Jeff Greenfield's remark that, "when you no longer need the skills of a safe-cracker to find PBS in most markets, you have to realize that the reason people aren't watching is that they don't want to."[17]

3. Federal Support of Noncommercial Broadcasting. The federal government supports noncommercial programming in a variety of ways. First, since 1939 for radio and 1952 for broadcast television, the FCC has reserved frequencies explicitly for noncommercial educational uses.

Second, and as alluded to above, noncommercial broadcasters receive direct government funding — most prominently through the Corporation for Public Broadcasting, a federally chartered nonprofit corporation that receives money from Congress and in turn funds various radio and television stations, including stations that are affiliated with the Public Broadcasting Service (PBS). This funding has been a source of periodic controversy, with some members of Congress suggesting that the federal government could better spend its money in other ways, and private parties at times challenging the government's relationship with noncommercial broadcasters on First Amendment grounds. One particularly notable controversy involved a statutory provision that forbade any noncommercial educational broadcasting station that received a grant from the Corporation for Public Broadcasting from "engag[ing] in editorializing."[18] A sharply divided Supreme Court found the provision violative of the First Amendment in FCC v. League of Women Voters, 468 U.S. 364 (1984). More recently, after a state-owned public television broadcaster included in a congressional debate only those candidates with substantial popular support, a candidate who had little popular support filed suit alleging that the station had violated his First Amendment rights by excluding him from the debate. The Supreme Court ruled that the debate was a nonpublic forum from which the public broadcaster could exclude the candidate because it had engaged in a viewpoint-neutral exercise of its journalistic discretion. Arkansas Educational Television Comm'n v. Forbes, 523 U.S. 666 (1998).

Third, several federal statutes give special treatment to noncommercial programming. For instance, the statute requiring cable operators to carry local broadcast stations has a separate provision requiring cable operators to carry "noncommercial educational television stations," 47 U.S.C. §535; similarly, a statute governing direct broadcast satellite (DBS) providers requires that they devote a portion of their channel capacity "exclusively for noncommercial programming of an educational or informational nature," 47 U.S.C. §335.[19]

---

17. Quoted in Krattenmaker & Powe, Regulating Broadcast Programming 314 (1994).
18. Section 399 of the Public Broadcasting Act of 1967, Pub. L. 90-129, 81 Stat. 365.
19. These provisions are discussed in Chapters Eleven and Thirteen, respectively.

4. Implications for Other Media. Neither the paternalistic argument nor the externality argument is specific to broadcast, or even to telecommunication more generally. Any form of communication (television, movies, street theater, even good old-fashioned conversation) can affect participants in ways they themselves might fail to account for and can also affect other people, even those not directly involved in the communication. As you read the remaining materials in this book, consider on what basis we might distinguish among different forms of telecommunication, and between telecommunication and communication more generally, and what sort of regulations those various distinctions might justify. Is broadcasting uniquely powerful? If so, is that an argument in favor of greater regulation, or greater freedom from regulation? Assuming that scarcity and interference do distinguish broadcasting, does that justify limiting non-meritorious programming, subsidizing meritorious programming, or both?

CHAPTER THREE

HOW WE REGULATE BROADCAST

The purpose of this chapter is:

- to introduce the FCC as an administrative agency, examining its basic powers and the scope of its discretion;
- to establish a basic framework that will, over the next four chapters, organize our consideration of the FCC's role in broadcast regulation; and
- to begin that consideration by examining how the FCC allocates particular services to particular frequencies, creating the federal band plan.

~

I. THE FCC AS AN ADMINISTRATIVE AGENCY

The previous chapter asked why the government regulates spectrum more rigorously than it regulates wood chips or cotton fibers. This and the next three chapters turn to the related question of how that regulation is accomplished.

The basic answer was first given back in 1927 when Congress created the Federal Radio Commission (FRC), the forerunner to what is today the Federal Communications Commission (FCC). This was a momentous decision, and it bears emphasizing at the outset that many other paths could have been taken. Government regulation of the spectrum could have been achieved through a number of different mechanisms — utilizing courts, legislatures, and/or agencies, on the federal or state level. Admittedly, some approaches would have been more complicated than others. For example, leaving spectrum regulation to state entities might have introduced significant coordination, compliance, and enforcement costs because, whether intentional or no, telecommunication broadcasts frequently cross state lines.[1] Even assuming a preference for regulators with a national purview, there were still a number of options on the federal level. Spectrum regulation could have been left up to Congress, for example, or to a specialized federal court with national jurisdiction (like the Court of Appeals for the

---

1. Some commentators argue that the benefits of regulation by common-law courts outweigh the costs. *See* Peter Huber, Law and Disorder in Cyberspace (1997). And it is worth reflecting on the argument about state versus national borders. Spectrum does not respect national boundaries either, and yet we are governed by a federal commission and not a global one.

Federal Circuit, which hears all patent appeals). Regulatory authority could have been vested in an agency directly controlled by the President, for that matter, rather than the more independent FCC that eventually was created.[2]

There is of course no easy answer to this question of institutional design, but the main arguments that carried the day back in 1927 were, first, that an independent administrative agency could develop relevant expertise; and, second, that using an independent agency was the only way to sufficiently insulate spectrum decisions from the political process. As to expertise, the argument was that judges are generalists with too few resources at hand, and, though Congress and the executive branch have greater resources at their disposal, they lack the narrow focus that was thought to enhance the development of sound regulation in this complicated area.[3] As for insulation, an even bigger concern than their lack of expertise was the worry that both Congress and the executive branch were too political. During the time when the FRC and later the FCC were created, there was a widespread belief that politically insulated expert administrators would do a better job of managing complex regulatory undertakings than would their masters in Congress and the White House.[4]

Why not give commissioners life tenure and the further accouterments of even greater independence? Well, perhaps that would be too much insulation. One person's insulation, after all, is another's unaccountability. So Congress settled upon a multimember commission, currently with five commissioners each serving a five-year term of office.[5] Replacements for commissioners who leave during their term serve only for the unexpired portion,[6] and there can be no more than a bare majority (three, currently) of commissioners from any one political party.[7] The President nominates commissioners and they are confirmed by the Senate, and the President designates one to serve as Chair, which means that the Chair is almost always from the President's party.[8] The vast majority of commissioners have been lawyers, many of whom knew little about the agency or the industry before their appointment. Presidents have rarely appointed to the FCC individuals with a professional working knowledge of the industry's technology (for example, electrical engineers) or its structure (economists or industry executives.)

---

2. Recall that the original plan was for the Federal Radio Commission to regulate for just one year, and then for the Secretary of Commerce to take over.

3. It is of course unclear whether a narrow focus is preferable. Do you want a regulating entity to have a broad perspective that looks at the whole economy or one that concentrates more narrowly on a given industry? Your answer may vary depending on the situation (and which answer aids your cause). What looks like admirable focus to one person may look like blinders to another. And note that, precisely because a narrowly focused agency deals with a smaller number of regulated entities than would an agency with a broader purview, the potential for capture by an interested party may be greater in the case of the narrowly focused agency.

4. Although the FRC was created before the New Deal and the FCC was created during it, one commonality between the periods was a belief in the wisdom of governance via independent regulatory commissions. *See* Joseph B. Eastman, The Place of the Independent Commission, 12 Const. Rev. 95 (1928); James M. Landis, The Administrative Process (1938).

5. 47 U.S.C. §154(a).

6. 47 U.S.C. §154(c).

7. 47 U.S.C. §154(b)(5).

8. 47 U.S.C. §154(a).

How much discretion would the agency have? The belief in the wisdom of independent expert administrators was relevant to this decision as well: Congress would refrain from binding the commissioners to specific marching orders and would instead give them broad latitude to act in the public interest. Thus section 303 of the Communications Act of 1934 stated in remarkably sweeping terms that:

> Except as otherwise provided in this Act, the Commission from time to time, as public convenience, interest, or necessity requires, shall—
>
> (a) Classify radio stations;
>
> (b) Prescribe the nature of the services to be rendered by each class of licensed stations and each station within any class;
>
> (c) Assign bands of frequencies to the various classes of stations, and assign frequencies for each individual station and determine the power which each station shall use and the time during which it may operate;
>
> (f) Make such regulations not inconsistent with law as it may deem necessary to prevent interference between stations; [and]
>
> (r) Make such rules and regulations and prescribe such restrictions and conditions, not inconsistent with law, as may be necessary to carry out the provisions of this Act, or any international radio or wire communications treaty or convention.

The catchphrase, then, was the "public convenience, interest, or necessity," a phrase lawmakers had borrowed at the last minute from a preexisting (and largely unrelated) statute. Evidence of this sloppy, last-minute scramble was in fact apparent on the face of the new law itself. Section 303, quoted above, required that the "public convenience, interest, or necessity" be served; section 309 of the very same Act inexplicably employed the slightly altered phrase "public interest, convenience, and necessity."[9] (This latter variant has been favored in more recent amendments to the Communications Act.) From these humble beginnings, the modern scheme of federal broadcast regulation was born.

The broad public interest standard does not mean that the FCC can act without any constraints. First, courts have interpreted "public interest, convenience, and necessity" as itself imposing some limitations on the FCC; indeed, they had to, as otherwise this would have been an unconstitutional delegation of the legislative power to an entity outside the legislative branch.[10] Second, Congress can, and often does, give the FCC more specific mandates in particular contexts, such as legislation enacted in the 1990s requiring that spectrum be assigned via auc-

---

9. The original language can be found at 48 Stat. 1085, c. 652, Title III, §309 (1934).

10. This issue was directly addressed in National Broadcasting Co. v. United States, 319 U.S. 190 (1943), where the Supreme Court rejected the argument that "public interest, convenience, or necessity" was unconstitutionally broad. The Court concluded that "the 'public interest, convenience, or necessity' is a criterion which is as concrete as the complicated factors for judgment in such a field of delegated authority permit," and that the terms do not convey unlimited powers to the FCC, as they indicate that the FCC should be guided by, for example, "the ability of the licensee to render the best practicable service to the community reached by his broadcasts." *Id.* at 216.

tion (a topic we consider in Chapter Five). Third, other statutes—most notably the Administrative Procedure Act[11]—impose additional constraints on agency actions and give individuals the right to sue an agency if it runs afoul of these requirements. So, for example, the FCC is required to follow certain rulemaking procedures that, among other things, give the public ample opportunity to comment on proposed regulations. Fourth and finally, the political branches can exercise control over the agency via *ad hoc* levers, such as reducing the FCC's budget, refusing to confirm newly appointed commissioners, or subjecting FCC actions to intensive public hearings and debate.

Within these guidelines, what sort of actions does the FCC take? As with all other administrative agencies, the FCC's formal actions fall primarily into one of two categories: adjudication and rulemaking. The division between the two can sometimes be murky, but the key distinguishing characteristics are generality versus specificity, and to a lesser extent prospectivity versus retrospectivity. Adjudications usually involve specific actions aimed at the past behavior of a small number of particular named parties, and rulemakings are broader orders that apply across-the-board and prospectively to a class of activities or people that are defined but not enumerated.

Adjudications are a significant part of the FCC's docket, as they include actions on possible rule violations, licensing disputes, and other proceedings focused on specific acts or actors. An example from this book is the *Order* in the *Jerker* case (excerpted in Chapter Six) that determined whether two particular broadcasts were indecent. When the FCC implements a statute, however, it usually does so via rulemaking. That is, when Congress enacts a statute and leaves some aspect of the statute's administration to the FCC, the Commission generally proceeds by launching a rulemaking process. The materials in this casebook skew heavily toward the rulemaking process, as this is the main vehicle through which telecommunications regulation is implemented.

The rulemaking process formally begins with the Commission issuing a Notice of Proposed Rulemaking (NPRM) or a Notice of Inquiry (NOI). An NPRM contains a discussion of the issues to be addressed and a proposed set of rules to address them, usually with some explanation of the basis for those proposals. The NPRM requests comments from interested parties on the proposed course of action. Of course, parties often communicate with the Commission before it issues an NPRM in the hope of influencing these proposals; but there is a statutorily mandated comment period after an NPRM is issued, so even uninvolved parties have an opportunity to comment before any regulation takes effect. An NOI, meanwhile, raises the issue to be addressed and invites comments but usually does not propose any particular rules. An NPRM generally follows an NOI. After either an NPRM or an NOI, the FCC receives comments and sifts through them, and afterwards issues a rulemaking (often called a "Report and Order") in which it responds to the comments, issues final rules, and provides a statement of the basis and purpose of those rules.

---

11. 5 U.S.C. §551 et seq. (establishing processes and standards for agency decision-making as well as standards for judicial review of agency decisions).

This sounds streamlined, but often it is not. Frequently the FCC will issue an NPRM or NOI and later (sometimes in response to comments, sometimes of its own initiative, sometimes in response to external events) decide to issue a further NPRM or NOI, which creates a new round of comments and responses but on a refined set of issues. On the back end, a final order might not resolve all outstanding issues and might instead request comment on some additional matters. The result is that many orders are final orders as to some matters and an NPRM or NOI as to others. The possibility of multiple NPRMs and multiple orders, combined with the opportunities for communications to the Commission not only during the official comment period but also before a rulemaking formally commences, make for a more fluid rulemaking process than one might imagine from merely reading the statutory provisions that govern FCC behavior.

When a final Report and Order is issued, even that is not the end of the process. A party can petition the FCC for reconsideration, but the Commission rarely grants such requests (which is not surprising, as the whole point of comments after the issuance of proposed rules is to allow parties to present their arguments before final rules are issued). But other avenues are available. First, Congress can overturn an FCC decision by legislation. For example, the FCC decision to repudiate the Fairness Doctrine (discussed in Chapter Six) triggered a congressional attempt at reinstating the Fairness Doctrine that nearly succeeded despite the Reagan Administration's support for the FCC's decision. More recently, Congress passed legislation (discussed in Chapter Eight) that gutted the FCC's plan to allow Low Power FM broadcasting.

A second, and more common, path is that an aggrieved party can file suit challenging the agency action. The rules governing suits against the FCC are, by and large, the same as those employed more generally in administrative law. This means that most agency final actions (whether rulemaking or adjudications), and some decisions not to act, can be appealed to a federal court. By statute, the United States Court of Appeals for the District of Columbia Circuit has exclusive jurisdiction to hear challenges to most licensing decisions made by the FCC.[12] Almost all other final FCC actions (including, notably, rulemaking proceedings) can be challenged in any United States Court of Appeals, though a disproportionate share are heard by the appeals court in the District of Columbia (which is where the FCC is located).[13]

Most agency findings of fact, exercises of discretion, and policy judgments are subject to "arbitrary and capricious" review, under the catch-all provision of the Administrative Procedure Act that empowers courts to "set aside agency action, findings, and conclusions found to be…arbitrary, capricious, an abuse of discretion, or otherwise not in accordance with law."[14] This is fairly lenient re-

---

12. *See* 47 U.S.C. §402(b) (setting out the exact categories of licensing decisions that can be appealed only to the D.C. Circuit).

13. *See* 47 U.S.C. §402(a) and 28 U.S.C. §2342(1), which provide that all federal courts of appeals (other than the Court of Appeals for the Federal Circuit) have jurisdiction to hear challenges to FCC final actions that are not appealable under 47 U.S.C. §402(b).

14. 5 U.S.C. §706(2)(A). There are a few provisions that create a different standard for some decisions—most notably 5 U.S.C. §706(2)(E), which provides that findings of fact in formal proceedings will be set aside if "unsupported by substantial evidence."

view, in which the court will inquire whether the agency based its decision on substantial evidence, considered arguments on the opposite side, and explained the basis of its decision. The courts do not (or at least are not supposed to) substitute their judgments on the merits for those of the agency; that would defeat the purpose of having an expert agency in the first place.

Legal interpretations made by the agency—which often loom large, as they involve what the guiding statutes actually provide—are subject to a slightly different form of review known as *Chevron* analysis, named for the case Chevron U.S.A., Inc. v. Natural Resources Defense Council, Inc., 467 U.S. 837 (1984). Under *Chevron*, the court first determines "whether Congress has directly spoken to the precise question at issue. If the intent of Congress is clear, that is the end of the matter" and there will be no deference to the agency's determination. *Id.* at 842. But "if the statute is silent or ambiguous with respect to the specific issue, the question for the court is whether the agency's answer is based on a permissible construction of the statute," which entails quite considerable deference to the agency. *Id.* at 843. Suits challenging FCC actions are nevertheless frequently filed in response to major FCC actions, and sometimes they meet with success. A sizable percentage of the judicial opinions excerpted in this book, in fact, were brought as challenges to FCC rulemakings.

Overall, the FCC operates like any other bureaucracy. It has a rather well-defined hierarchical structure and an excruciatingly detailed set of internal operating rules that account for every procedural issue the agency has ever encountered and many others that it fears (or hopes) it may confront. Substantive issues usually go to, or emerge from, one of several bureaus, for example, the Mass Media Bureau (radio, television), the Cable Services Bureau (cable television), the Wireless Telecommunications Bureau (cellular telephony), the International Bureau (satellites and international telecommunications), and the Common Carrier Bureau (conventional telephones). No particular bureau focuses exclusively on the Internet at this time.

II. FOUR ROLES FOR THE REGULATOR

The Communications Act of 1934 set up the basic system of broadcast regulation that in large part survives in the United States even today. Under the Act, the FCC allocates spectrum to particular uses and users, segregating uses by type and separating users by geography, power, and time. These various separations decrease the risk of signal interference. Licenses were originally given out at no explicit charge but were subject to an implicit fee in the form of various "public interest" obligations. The government sells most licenses today, but some of the public interest obligations nonetheless survive. Licenses were and are renewable and transferable, with both renewal and transfer subject to FCC approval.

In short, then, the FCC performs four basic regulatory functions with respect to broadcast spectrum. First, it creates the band plan, specifying exactly which frequencies will be used for which services, how those frequencies will be partitioned,[15] and, in certain cases, specifying in addition what stations will be available in which cities and at what power levels. Television, for instance, was allocated one particular portion of the spectrum; FM radio another. In both of these cases, the FCC went ahead and designated specific stations as well, so firms have long been able to seek licenses for television and FM stations without having to assert or prove that their use is technically feasible. The FCC left AM radio in a slightly less organized state; while a particular band of frequencies was allocated to AM radio, and it was further decided how much spectrum would be given out with each license, allocation of particular stations is made "on demand." Applicants for AM licenses therefore have to demonstrate that their proposed service is technically feasible before any license will issue.

Second, the FCC establishes rules for the initial assignment of broadcast licenses. The rule in the early years was that license applicants would be subject to hearings to determine whether they were suitable licensees. These hearings were sometimes uncontested, meaning that the applicant seeking the license was the only party involved in the hearing, and they were sometimes contested, meaning either that another party stepped forward either to argue against the applicant or, more often, to claim the license for itself. In more recent times, most initial assignment is done by auction.

Third, the FCC sets the rules for the transfer and renewal of already allocated licenses. Once a party is awarded its license, can it sell that license to another of its choosing? What are the criteria on which licensees will be judged come renewal time? The rules here obviously have significant practical effects. For example, too stringent a policy with respect to license transfer might end up keeping licenses in the hands of their current owners even in cases where another owner would make more efficient use of the spectrum. Too lax a policy, however, would make the FCC's initial assignment process all but irrelevant. Renewal rules, too, have significant practical effects, with a high likelihood of renewal serving to encourage broadcast licensees to invest in the long-term value of their licenses by, for example, making expensive equipment and marketing investments, and a low likelihood of renewal giving the FCC greater ability to influence licensee behavior by threatening ramifications come renewal time

Fourth and finally, the FCC establishes what, if any, public interest obligations will be imposed upon licensees. Public interest obligations were in some sense the "price" of license ownership back when licenses were distributed at no charge. A licensee would receive his license at no monetary cost but, in exchange, would assume a vague and constantly changing obligation to serve the public. This obligation would take different forms at different times, for example sometimes including a very specific commitment to air educational programs for children, almost always including the duty to provide a forum for political advertisements, and for many years including a formal (and enforced) obligation to present balanced news coverage. Public interest obligations survive today even though licenses are no longer given away at no charge, perhaps justified instead

---

15. In other words, if the Commission determines to auction 50 MHz of spectrum within a certain frequency band, it must decide whether to auction a single parcel of 50 MHz, two parcels of 25 MHz, and so on.

by the paternalistic and externality arguments presented at the end of Chapter Two.

The next section of this chapter, and the three chapters that follow, use these four functions as an organizational theme. That is, we consider in turn: the FCC's role in defining the band plan (this chapter); the various rules that have been used to make initial assignments of broadcast licenses (Chapters Four & Five); the rules regarding renewal and transfer (Chapter Four); and the public interest obligations imposed on broadcast licensees (Chapter Six).

Notes and Questions

1. **Relationships.** Consider the relationships between the four functions sketched above. For example, is it true that a lax policy with respect to transfers makes the initial assignment largely irrelevant? Do the rules with respect to initial assignment, renewal, and transfer affect the FCC's ability to devise a sensible band plan?

2. **Analogies.** The four functions have analogies in other areas of law. For example, with respect to land, local authorities in essence create a "band plan" in the form of zoning regulations. There are also rules for the initial assignment, transfer, and renewal of land, for example the rule against perpetuities and the procedure for perfecting a claim to land via adverse possession. Interestingly, can you identify "public interest requirements" of any sort in this context?

III. THE BAND PLAN

Our study of these four functions begins with some material on the FCC's role in establishing the band plan—a regulatory function also referred to as "spectrum management." Again, the FCC actually designates which range of frequencies will be used for which services. For example, 54–72 MHz is currently reserved for television channels 2 through 4, and 88–108 MHz is similarly reserved for FM radio. Of course, determining which services should be allocated to which frequencies is no easy task. There are difficult questions here about both technological requirements and, where several services could use the same band, relative importance. The readings that follow are designed to help you evaluate the FCC's current decision-making process. At the end of the day, do you have faith that the FCC can accomplish this task more effectively than could an unregulated spectrum market?

A. Finding Spectrum for PCS

In the Notice of Proposed Rulemaking that follows, the FCC seeks to "find" and then "set aside" spectrum that will be suitable for several emerging new technologies. The most important of these technologies is what the Commission refers to as personal communications services (PCS), a category of services that

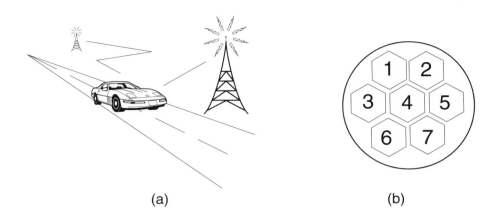

(a)   (b)

Figure 3.1. CELLULAR TELEPHONY. The panel to the left shows the basic concept: as the portable telecommunications equipment moves away from one receiver, it moves toward another and thus service is maintained. The panel to the right shows how cells are used to break up the service area into small geographic chunks. One advantage of this structure (emphasized in the text) is that cellular telephones can transmit at low power but still reach a receiver. A second advantage is that, in this picture, seven conversations can simultaneously use the same bit of spectrum without interfering with one another; if this were just one giant region, only one conversation would be able to use that bit of spectrum at any given time.

the Commission sees as a more advanced version of the modern-day cellular phone.

"Cellular telephony" takes its name from the manner through which the technology transmits and receives telephone communications. Basically, cellular telephony is a form of wireless telephone service. The relevant geographic area ("service area") is broken into discrete "cells"—hence the name—each of which is served by its own receiving and transmitting equipment. Cellular telephones, then, can transmit signals at relatively low power but, because so many cells are established, the transmissions can usually nevertheless be picked up by some nearby cell. As the cellular phone moves, its signals are picked up by the (new) nearest cell site, and so the cellular phone can move from site to site while remaining in constant contact with the telephone network. Indeed, so long as there is a cell in the vicinity, that cell will pick up the mobile telephone's transmission and relay it to its destination, be that a landline home telephone, a fax machine, or even another cellular telephone.

PCS takes this concept and extends it to smaller and lower power equipment, such as pocket-size telephones, laptop computers, and small fax machines. Like cellular telephones, these devices also transmit to scattered cell sites, but PCS requires many more such sites since that is the only way to assure that one cell is always near enough to receive these even weaker signals. To build a national PCS system capable of accommodating millions of users without substantial interference (or long delays due to cell traffic) requires a sizeable chunk of spectrum. It is this chunk of spectrum that is at issue in the document that follows.

IN RE REDEVELOPMENT OF SPECTRUM TO ENCOURAGE INNOVATION IN THE USE OF NEW TELECOMMUNICATIONS TECHNOLOGIES

7 FCC Rcd. 1542 (1992)

1. By this *Notice*, the Commission proposes to establish new areas of the spectrum to be used for emerging telecommunications technologies. These new frequency bands would be designated from 220 MHz of the spectrum between 1.85 and 2.20 GHz. We further propose to provide a regulatory framework that will enable the existing fixed microwave users in these bands to relocate to other fixed microwave bands or alternative media with minimum disruption to their operations. We believe this can best be accomplished through the use of a flexible negotiations approach that permits financial arrangements between incumbents and new service providers during an extended transition period. We also propose to permit state and local government facilities, including public safety, to continue their current operations on a fully protected basis by exempting such facilities from any mandatory transition period.

NEED FOR EMERGING TECHNOLOGIES BANDS

4. In recent years, technological advancements in digital and signal processing systems have opened possibilities for the development of a broad range of new radio communication services. These technological advances have increased the need for spectrum to foster the growth and development of new services, primarily for mobile applications. However, this has created an environment in which new services are vying with each other and with existing users for relatively small slivers of spectrum that are incapable of supporting full implementation of new service. The Commission currently has pending before it a number of requests for new services and technologies for which sufficient spectrum is unavailable. These requests include: 200 MHz for new personal communications services (PCS); 40 MHz for data PCS; 33 MHz for a generic mobile-satellite service; 70 MHz for a digital audio broadcasting service; and 33 MHz for low-Earth orbit satellites.

6. We need to develop a plan that includes specific provisions for minimizing impact on existing services. Nevertheless, we believe that establishing these emerging technologies bands is desirable and will again prove advantageous for facilitating the continuing development of new communications technologies and the growth and expansion of existing services.

7. The current lack of available spectrum tends to have a chilling effect on the incentives for manufacturers and financial institutions to develop and fund new communications research. The emerging technologies bands would help provide some of the structure, in terms of frequency of operation and operating plan, that is needed to facilitate the development of equipment. At the same time, this new concept would provide considerable flexibility with regard to the types of technologies and services that can be authorized.

SPECTRUM ISSUES

9. In the early 1970s, spectrum was available in the lower frequency bands that was only lightly used and the licensees on those frequencies could be relo-

cated relatively easily. Today there are substantial operations on virtually all of the lower frequency bands, so that establishment of emerging technologies bands will unavoidably necessitate relocation of significant numbers of existing users. The task, then, is to identify a relatively wide band of frequencies that can be made available with a minimum of impact on existing users and that also can provide suitable operating characteristics for new, primarily mobile, services.

10. The spectrum selected must meet the requirements of a broad range of possible services, including land mobile and satellite. The factors that must be considered include:

Cost of equipment—If the spectrum chosen is in a range for which state-of-the-art equipment is not available, then high costs would delay the introduction of new services.

Amount of spectrum—There must be enough spectrum available to allow substantial development and economies of scale.

Feasibility of relocation—The existing licensees must be able to relocate with a minimum of cost and disruption of service to consumers.

Non-government spectrum—In order to avoid the need for coordination and to speed the process of transition, the new bands should come entirely from spectrum regulated by the FCC.

International developments—It is desirable for the spectrum chosen to be compatible with similar international developments.

11. *Spectrum Study.* With the above considerations in mind, the Commission's staff conducted a study to examine the possibility of creating emerging technologies bands. This study identified the most suitable region of the spectrum, determined the existing users of that spectrum, explored alternatives for relocating those users to higher bands or other media with a minimum disruption of service, and examined the cost of such relocation. The study concluded that 220 MHz in the 1.85–2.20 GHz region could be designated for innovative technologies and services.

12. The study limited the consideration of candidate frequency bands to those in which mobile operations are practicable with current state-of-the-art electronic components and manufacturing capabilities. It found that while experimental mobile use is taking place at higher bands, the state-of-the-art technology for the compact, lightweight, portable electronic components expected to be used in new services generally will limit operations in those services to frequencies under 3 GHz. Thus, the study concluded that frequencies above 3 GHz would not be acceptable. It next found that the spectrum below 1 GHz generally does not appear to offer any possibilities for spectrum availability. Most of this spectrum is used for broadcasting and land mobile services that would be very difficult to relocate. These services have very large numbers of users, particularly in the major urban areas, and there are no bands with similar technical characteristics to which the existing users could be relocated. The remaining frequencies below 1 GHz are narrow, scattered bands that would not provide sufficient spectrum. [For the above reasons, the study concentrated on the spectrum between 1 and 3 GHz.]

14. The study identified three non-Government bands from this spectrum for consideration: 1.85–2.20, 2.45–2.50, and 2.50–2.65 GHz. The study found the

2.45–2.50 GHz band, which is allocated for use by Industrial, Scientific, and Medical (ISM) equipment, less desirable because it has a limited amount of spectrum (50 MHz) and because there is no replacement band that offers the same physical characteristics for the existing ISM operations in that band. The 2.50–2.60 GHz band also was eliminated because there are no other frequency allocations currently available to which services in that band could be relocated.

15. The remaining 1.85–2.20 GHz band is used for fixed private and common carrier microwave services, public land mobile service, broadcast auxiliary operations, and multipoint distribution service. Specifically, the 1.85–1.99, 2.11–2.15, and 2.16–2.20 GHz bands are used for private operational fixed and common carrier microwave operations. The private operational fixed licensees are local governments (including public safety), petroleum producers, utilities, railroads, and other business users such as the manufacturing, banking, and service industries. Systems range from a few links to very large systems that use hundreds of links. They are used as part of communications systems for local government and public safety organizations. These facilities are also used to control electric power, oil and gas pipeline and railroad systems, and to provide routine business voice, data, and video communications. The common carrier licensees are telephone, cellular telephone, and paging providers. Telephone companies use this band to provide telephone service to remote areas, cellular companies to interconnect cell sites with mobile telephone switching offices, and paging companies for control and repeater stations.

16. The 1.99–2.11 GHz band is used for broadcast auxiliary services. The licensees in this service are television broadcasters and cable television operators. Broadcast auxiliary services include studio-to-transmitter links, inner city relays, and electronic news gathering (ENG) mobile operations. These services are used to transmit video programming from remote sites to the studio and from the studio to the transmitter sites. The 2.15–2.16 GHz band is used for multipoint distribution service (MDS) and its licensees are, for the most part, wireless cable television operators. MDS is used to supply video programming to subscribers over city-wide areas and to rural areas where it is not economical to install cable service.

17. The study finds that the private and common carrier fixed microwave operations using this spectrum can be relocated to higher frequency bands that provide for similar type services and can support propagation over similar path lengths. Further, it observes that there are other reasonable alternatives for fixed microwave such as fiber, cable and satellite communications, which can utilize off-the-shelf equipment to provide these services.

18. The study also concludes that it is not practicable at this time to relocate the broadcast auxiliary and the multipoint distribution services that use spectrum in the 1.85–2.20 GHz range. It finds that currently there is heavy use of [these] bands and that the forthcoming introduction of broadcast advanced television service may result in more congestion in these bands. Since there currently are a large number of MDS applications before the Commission and the MDS service is a developing industry, the study further finds that it would not be desirable to relocate the MDS channels at 2 GHz.

19. *Proposed Reallocations.* Based on the findings of our staff study, we propose to reallocate 220 MHz of the 1.85 to 2.20 GHz band that is currently used

for private and common carrier fixed microwave services. The specific frequencies proposed to be reallocated are the 1.85–1.99, 2.11–2.15, and 2.16–2.20 GHz bands. We believe that this spectrum will meet the requirements of a significant number of new services and technologies. The private and common carrier fixed microwave services operating in these bands provide important and essential services. Accordingly, we intend to pursue this reallocation in a manner that will minimize disruption of the existing 2 GHz fixed operations.

20. In this regard, we propose to make available all fixed microwave bands above 3 GHz, both the common carrier and the private bands, for reaccommodation of fixed microwave operations currently licensed in the 1.85–2.20 GHz spectrum.[16]

22. *Transition Plan.* Our proposed transition plan would consist of three basic elements, discussed below.

23. First, we wish to ensure the availability of the existing vacant 2 GHz spectrum for the initial development of new services and to discourage possible speculative fixed service applications for this spectrum. We therefore will continue to grant applications for fixed operations in the proposed new technologies bands; however, applications for new facilities submitted after the adoption date of this *Notice* will be granted on a secondary basis only, conditioned upon the outcome of this proceeding. [For the meaning of "secondary basis," *see* ¶24.]

24. Second, except for state and local licensees, we propose to allow currently licensed 2 GHz fixed licensees to continue to occupy 2 GHz frequencies on a co-primary basis with new services for a fixed period of time, for example ten or fifteen years. Ten years could generally be expected to provide for a complete amortization of existing 2 GHz equipment. A fifteen year period would extend the relocation period through the useful life of that equipment. At the end of this transition period, these facilities could continue to operate in the band on a secondary basis. This means that if, after the transition period, new services were not able to use the spectrum because of interference from fixed microwave systems, those fixed microwave systems would be required to eliminate the interference, negotiate an arrangement for continued operation with the new service op-

---

16. We also will encourage fixed microwave operators to consider other non-radio alternative media to meet their telecommunication needs, particularly fiber optic circuits. In allocating spectrum, one of the primary considerations is whether there is a technological dependence of the service on radio rather than wire lines. Mobile communications necessarily will always require use of radio spectrum, and in the past the Commission provided large amounts of spectrum for fixed microwave because wireline alternatives often were economically prohibitive. However, in the last five years technological advancements in optical communications have resulted in fiber being very competitive with fixed microwave. Further, the capacities of fiber optic circuits greatly exceed those of fixed microwave. For these reasons, many common carrier and private communication requirements, which in the past were met by fixed microwave, are now met with fiber optic circuits. In connection with encouraging migration to other, non-radio alternative media, we ask for comment on whether we should award tax certificates to fixed microwave licensees who receive financial compensation from an entity seeking to use the spectrum for new technology as part of an agreement to surrender their license and use other, non-radio alternative media. Grant of tax certificates in such circumstances would appear to be similar to our recent decision to award tax certificates to AM broadcast licensees receiving financial compensation for surrendering their licenses for cancellation. *See* Review of Technical Assignment Criteria for the AM Broadcast Service, 6 FCC Rcd. 6273, 6472 (1991).

erator, or cease operation. This would allow some fixed microwave systems to continue operations indefinitely, particularly in rural areas where less spectrum may be required for new services.

25. We recognize that state and local government agencies would face special economic and operational considerations in relocating their 2 GHz fixed microwave operations to higher frequencies or alternative media. We are particularly sensitive to the need to avoid any disruption of police, fire, and other public safety communications. To address these concerns, we propose to exempt state and local government 2 GHz fixed microwave facilities from any mandatory transition periods. Rather, these facilities would be allowed to continue to operate at 2 GHz on a co-primary basis indefinitely, at the discretion of the state and local government licensees. These agencies would be permitted to negotiate the use of their frequencies with other parties. In this manner, transfer of state and local government operations could be arranged so as to accommodate fully any special economic or operational considerations with regard to the institutions affected.

26. To provide maximum flexibility in the relocation process, we believe it is desirable to permit parties seeking to operate new services to negotiate with the existing users for access to the 2 GHz frequencies and, conversely, to permit incumbents to negotiate with the new service providers for continued use of the spectrum. Therefore, we propose to allow providers of new services assigned spectrum allocated to the new emerging technologies bands to negotiate financial arrangements with existing licensees. This would encourage reaccommodation and underwriting of the costs of transition for the 2 GHz users. In return, the new licensees would receive earlier access to the frequencies used by the existing fixed microwave operators. Such arrangements would allow market forces to achieve a balance between the need to minimize the reaccommodation cost to existing operators and the immediate need for the spectrum to permit provision of these new services. It would also provide incumbents with a way to assure that the new licensees would not interfere with their expanded facilities or current facilities at the end of a mandatory transition period.[17]

Notes and Questions

1. Subsequent Proceedings. The FCC ultimately adopted the reallocation plan laid out in the *Notice*. *See* 7 FCC Rcd. 6886 (1992). That plan came to be known as the "broadband" PCS plan because it provided sufficient spectrum for two-way data exchanges. "Narrowband" PCS involves only enough spectrum to transmit simple one-way signals (*e.g.*, to activate a pager). Congress then directed the Commission to use competitive bidding (auctions) to choose from among mutually exclusive applications for PCS licenses within local markets and directed the agency to commence issuing PCS licenses by May, 1994. Pub. L. No. 103-66, 107 Stat. 312.

2. Valuing PCS. Why did the Commission decide to allocate any spectrum to PCS? That is, how did the FCC know that spectrum would be more valuable if

---

17. Our principal desire is to compensate existing 2 GHz users for the costs of relocation. We recognize, however, that such market-based negotiations could possibly result in windfalls for the incumbent 2 GHz licensees. [Footnote relocated.]

used for PCS than if used for other services? Conversely, why allocate only 220 MHz to PCS? If PCS is so valuable, how did the Commission know that it didn't warrant an even larger chunk of frequency?

3. Finding Frequencies. To find spectrum for PCS, the Commission first studied the physical properties of the technology and determined, within a very wide margin, which areas of the spectrum seemed best suited for PCS transmission and reception. It concluded that some ranges of the spectrum (those above 3 GHz) were technologically unsuited to PCS and thus those ranges were no longer considered. Next, the Commission identified other ranges (specifically, frequencies below 1 GHz) and determined that they were already so crowded that they, too, would not be made available for PCS. That left the range between approximately 1GHz and 3 GHz. The FCC identified services already in that range that, in the Commission's view, should be relocated to make room for PCS, and then announced a transition plan that would move those services out.

But how did the FCC make each of these determinations? Consider each step in isolation. First, the unusable frequencies. The Commission states in ¶12 that it limited its consideration of "candidate frequency bands to those in which mobile operations are practicable with current state-of-the-art electronic components and manufacturing capabilities." How confident are you that the Commission can make this sort of technical determination accurately? Besides, even if then-current PCS designs did not work in certain frequency bands, why couldn't the Commission tell PCS innovators to develop variants of the technology that would? The Commission itself reports that "experimental mobile use" was already taking place in these unusable bands. Why not encourage that innovation? In fact, if higher frequencies tend to be particularly uncrowded—something the Commission hints at early in the document—shouldn't the Commission shunt PCS to those higher frequencies, in essence encouraging new technologies to make use of underused spectrum resources?

Now, let's turn to the frequencies below 1 GHz that were ruled out because they were already in use by broadcasters and land mobile services. (Also discussed in ¶12.) How did the Commission know that these services should be left in place whereas services in the 1 GHz to 3 GHz range would ultimately be moved? Did the FCC determine, in each of these instances, that PCS was not a more valuable use for the spectrum at issue? Or was the Commission instead making a prediction about transaction costs? On what basis exactly?

Finally, consider the frequencies between 1 GHz and 3 Ghz that the Commission deemed acceptable for PCS. How did the agency determine that PCS was a more valuable use of this spectrum than the private operational fixed services and the common carrier microwave operations that were already there? If PCS is a more valuable use, why did the Commission structure a complicated transition period; won't the more valuable use (PCS) simply buy out the less valued uses? Indeed, why did the Commission not simply announce that, henceforth, any license (including those already outstanding) for the 1.85–1.99, 2.11–2.15 and 2.16–2.20 GHz bands would be interpreted so as to permit the licensee to offer PCS service, and, further, that those licenses were now freely transferable?

4. Transitions. Relatedly, if PCS is so clearly a more valuable use, why not simply revoke all existing licenses in this band and then issue PCS licenses instead? Moreover, why did the FCC adopt so many different rules with respect to the transition from preexisting uses to PCS? Some users were authorized to sell their rights to PCS newcomers. Some (especially fixed microwave) were given a fixed period of time to relocate, while others (especially state and local government services) were allowed to stay where they were indefinitely. How can all of these rules be equally in the public interest? And how did the Commission decide which licensees fall into which group?

5. A Windfall? If you were an incumbent 2 GHz licensee, how would you respond to this turn of events? Is this bad news for you, or quite the opposite? As a policy matter, should the Commission have focused more on these incumbents and the financial effect this spectrum allocation might have for them?

6. Lessons. The overriding question here is simply this: how should telecommunications policy respond to the spectrum requirements of new technologies? Can the FCC estimate and compare the likely value of competing uses? Given the large coordination problems that need to be resolved, would it be folly to just leave these issues to the marketplace? Are there intermediate steps? How would you respond if Congress were to put forward legislation conferring perpetual spectrum property rights on current licensees and then permitting those licensees to sell their rights to whomever they chose for use in whatever service the market deemed most valuable?

B. Permitting Changing Uses

The FCC's original approach to allocating spectrum was rather heavy-handed: the FCC identified which frequencies would be used for which services and then announced that licensees were under no circumstances allowed to use those frequencies for other services—even if those other uses would not cause interference problems. In the 1980s, however, the FCC's policy changed, with the newer view recognizing that a little flexibility might both give licensees good incentives to optimize their use of spectrum and give the FCC new information about how spectrum can be used and how valuable particular uses are.

To take a specific example, in 1983 the FCC authorized FM stations to use part of their spectrum for secondary uses. These licensees still had to use their spectrum primarily to provide FM stereo sound; but to the extent that there was any spectrum remaining under these licenses, they could also provide non-broadcast services such as private paging, data transmission, and dispatch services. In 1984, the FCC extended to AM stations a similar flexibility. Both of these changes had an important incentive effect. Under the old regime, stations had no reason to minimize their use of bandwidth, because no matter how efficient they were, all they were allowed to do was transmit their one broadcast signal. Under the new rules, by contrast, FM and AM station owners had a strong incentive to minimize their bandwidth consumption; there was money to be made developing and selling services that could operate in any remaining spectrum.[18]

The FCC introduced flexibility in other ways as well. For instance, in 1984 the Commission combined what previously were two separate allocations for a particular type of common carrier service, announcing that instead of licensing

---

18. Amendment of Parts 2 and 73 of the Commission's AM Broadcast Rules Concerning Use of the AM Sub-Carrier, 100 FCC 2d 5 (1984).

particular licensees to provide one or the other service, the FCC would allow market forces to determine to which service any given slice of this spectrum would be dedicated. The goal here was again to increase efficiency by deferring to the market—the assumption being that the market would better allocate this spectrum than would the FCC.[19]

By 1999, flexibility and substantial market deference were both explicit guiding principles for the Commission's spectrum management duties. As a contemporaneous FCC policy statement summarized:

> In the majority of cases, efficient spectrum markets will lead to use of spectrum for the highest value end use. Flexible allocations may result in more efficient spectrum markets. Flexibility can be permitted through the use of relaxed service rules, which would allow licensees greater freedom in determining the specific services to be offered. Another way to allow flexibility in use of the spectrum is to allow licensees to negotiate among themselves arrangements for avoiding interference rather than apply mandatory technical rules to control interference.[20]

The *Report and Order* that follows shows how these and other modern principles work in practice. At issue in this proceeding is the reallocation of spectrum in the 746–764 MHz and 776–794 MHz ranges. In what ways does the Commission allow market forces to help shape the final allocation of this spectrum? Do the arguments put forth below suggest that the FCC exercised too tight a grip for all those early years—that the market can, in fact, establish the band plan without government intervention?

IN RE SERVICE RULES FOR THE 746–764 AND 776–794 MHZ BANDS

First Report and Order, 15 FCC Rcd. 476,
15 FCC Rcd. 8634 (2000)

I. INTRODUCTION

1. By this *Report and Order* we adopt service rules for licensing the commercial use of the 746–764 MHz and 776–794 MHz bands—bands that have been reallocated, by Congressional direction, from their previous use solely for the broadcasting service. We believe that, under these rules, these bands can be used to provide a wide range of advanced wireless services. The rules we adopt today are aimed at enabling the broadest possible use of this spectrum.

2. This *Report and Order* therefore establishes a flexible, market-based approach for determining service rules in this band. Rapidly expanding demand for wireless voice and data services, as well as projections of international demand and the increased spectrum necessary to support wideband ap-

---

19. *See* D. Webbink, Radio Licenses and Frequency Spectrum Use Property Rights, 9 Communications and the Law 3, 3–5 (1987) (discussing FCC decisions authorizing both multiple and secondary spectrum use).

20. Principles for Reallocation of Spectrum to Encourage the Development of Telecommunications Technologies for the New Millennium, 14 FCC Rcd. 19868 (1999), at ¶9. This document provides an excellent overview of all the issues associated with the Commission's spectrum management responsibilities.

plications to be implemented with next generation technologies, confirm that these bands should be structured to enable their efficient and intensive use for wireless services and technologies. New broadcast-type services that can be provided within the technical parameters adopted here are also permissible in these bands.

4. We expect these service rules will enable a significant number of existing and potential wireless service providers to pursue these bands, potentially to deploy new methods of providing high speed Internet access in competition with digital subscriber loop (DSL) and cable modem operators. These bands are also suitable for new fixed wireless service in underserved areas, as well as next generation, high-speed mobile services. Because the record indicates a wide range of possible technical approaches to serving the expanding demand for wireless services, we have sought to establish an open regulatory framework with the potential to accommodate both existing and future technologies. This framework permits new broadcast-type services that are consistent with the technical rules essential to fostering efficient development of wireless services in this band, and sound spectrum management. By setting the scope of our flexible service rules to enable the most efficient and intensive use of this spectrum, we believe we have fully satisfied our statutory spectrum management responsibilities.

5. The 746–806 MHz band at issue here has historically been used exclusively by television stations (Channels 60–69). Incumbent conventional television broadcasters are permitted by statute to continue operations in this band until their markets are converted to digital television.

III. SERVICE RULES

A. In General

8. The *Notice of Proposed Rulemaking* (NPRM) [in this proceeding] sought comment both on broad spectrum management issues and on the unique technical issues raised by the reallocation of this band. In this *Report and Order*, we initially address the broad question of whether our service rules for these bands should implement flexible use at the interservice level by providing for sharing of these bands between incumbent conventional, full-power television broadcasting licensees and the range of possible broadcasting and wireless services. After this discussion, we turn to the specific service rule decisions required by this proceeding.

1. Spectrum Management Considerations

9. Background. In the NPRM, we emphasized our continued interest in the broader aspects of spectrum management, noting the potential for new technologies to blur technical and regulatory distinctions and affect the balance between licensee discretion and regulatory requirements. We also sought comment on the extent to which flexible use allocations that juxtapose such technically dissimilar services as wireless and conventional broadcasting might raise new issues.

11. Many commenters assert that renewed conventional television operations on these bands would create such a wide range of interference difficulties as to effectively preclude other, non-broadcast wireless applications. Motorola states

that it is not possible to "craft service rules that will permit efficient operation of advanced mobile systems and traditional wide area broadcast systems in the same geographic area," and warns of "unrealizable" business plans. US WEST cautions against renewed broadcast use of the band, stating that the interference caused by full-power broadcast services would deter necessary investment in new services and systems.

15. <u>Discussion</u>. After careful consideration, we will not adopt service rules that would permit the sharing of this band by conventional television and wireless services. The inherent interference difficulties presented by sharing between these dissimilar services require that we orient our service rules to one service or the other, if efficient and intensive use of this spectrum is to be realized. Based on the predominant interest in fixed and mobile wireless services expressed in the record, we will adopt service rules primarily oriented toward fulfilling the need for a variety of wireless services on these bands. The rules are not structured to establish particular service configurations. Rather, the service rules allow licensees to make determinations respecting the services provided and technologies to be used, including provision of new broadcast-type services so long as those services comply with our technical rules.

16. We have previously identified as a Commission objective the development of a variety of mechanisms to make spectrum markets more efficient, including flexible service rules and innovative assignment mechanisms. In this proceeding, we find that such flexibility cannot extend to opening these bands to both conventional television and wireless services. Establishing regulatory flexibility sufficient to accommodate conventional television broadcasting would impose disproportionate, offsetting burdens on wireless services, constraining their technical effectiveness and, consequently, their economic practicability.

17. The interference problem arises from the disparity between the two services' characteristic power levels, and between their transmitter tower heights. Any substantial disproportion between the power levels of services sharing a spectrum band creates much greater interference difficulties for the lower-power service than when sharing or adjacent-band services operate at comparable power levels. The disparity between television transmitter tower heights and those used by typical wireless providers adds to the difficulty by accentuating the power of the more powerful service. Even at considerable distance from the higher-power service's transmitter, its signal is still strong enough, due in part to the effect of tower height, to make a receiver designed for a nearer, lower-power service vulnerable to interference.

18. Establishing standards to manage the inherent interference between such dissimilar transmissions as conventional television and wireless services would create substantial spectrum inefficiencies in a band where efficiency is especially important because of the band's suitability for uses ranging from wideband mobile communications to innovative, fixed wireless Internet access services and new broadcast-type services.

19. Although we have determined to orient our technical and service rules primarily to enable the efficient and intensive use of these bands for wireless service, we will nonetheless allow any broadcast-type services consistent with the Table of Allocations that meet those rules. This approach will allow the broadest degree of flexibility possible, consistent with technical interference limits and their economic consequences here.

2. Band Plan

27. <u>Background</u>. Several commenters urge us to auction a single, 36 megahertz license. A single, 36 megahertz license would, Metricom contends, leave the details of flexible use, including management of interference between distinct services, to be determined by the licensee. AirTouch also advocates a single, 36 megahertz license, though it would designate the entire band for terrestrial mobile services, predicated on substantially expanded spectrum needs for the implementation of next generation broadband wireless services. Cisco contends that a single, 36 megahertz license would better enable use of these bands for efficient fixed wireless applications without precluding mobile services, and asserts that discrete sub-bands are not necessary to protect adjacent public safety uses.

28. Several other commenters, including AMTA, FreeSpace, Motorola, PCIA, Intek, and US WEST, support a more structured approach to band management. Some of these commenters argue for division of the band into comparatively modest spectrum segments, configured to flexibly enable a range of new and existing narrowband technologies, and propose division of the 36 megahertz into several bands with varying degrees of flexibility.

31. <u>Discussion</u>. We decline to grant a unitary, 36 megahertz license. In light of the range of technologies, services, and spectrum needs asserted by commenters, we find that the best course is to adopt a band plan that will allow bidders to pursue licenses that are less than the full 36 megahertz, but will allow bidders to aggregate a substantial portion of the band. In that way, the marketplace forces operating through the auction process, rather than regulatory fiat, will determine which of the multitude of service proposals will actually be implemented.

39. We recognize assertions by Cisco and others that establishing any sub-bands reduces spectrum efficiencies achieved by aggregation and creates more frequency boundaries between licensees that require interference management. We believe our decision here is appropriate, however. First, encouraging a variety of technologies and entrants is an important spectrum management goal. Subdividing the 36 megahertz of available spectrum will make it more likely that start-ups and companies that are not highly capitalized will have the opportunity to pursue spectrum. Second, our auction rules allow bidders to aggregate these band segments. This allows entities that believe they need to acquire a larger amount of spectrum than that available in the individual licenses to do so.

B. Licensing Rules

2. Eligibility and Use Restrictions; Spectrum Aggregation

49. We will impose no restrictions on eligibility for a license in the 747–762 MHz and 777–792 MHz bands. Thus, no prospective licensee will be barred from participation in the auction or from post-auction acquisition of a license for this spectrum based on its status as a provider of cable services, for example, or of telephone or other telecommunications services. We believe that opening this spectrum to as wide a range of applicants as possible will encourage entrepreneurial efforts to develop new technologies and services, while helping to ensure the most efficient use of the spectrum.

50. We have pursued a policy of flexible use for the 747–762 MHz and 777–792 MHz bands. We are particularly concerned that eligibility restrictions could impede efficient development of this spectrum. Were we to exclude all incumbent providers of services that could compete with services that could be provided using this spectrum, we would exclude virtually every major telecommunications service provider active today. We anticipate that use of this spectrum will offer incumbent providers of both wireline and wireless services an opportunity to augment their existing services and systems, rather than to act in an anticompetitive manner, for example, by warehousing the spectrum acquired.

3. Size of Service Areas for Geographic Area Licensing

55. The majority of commenters tended to recommend large geographic sizes for this spectrum band. Those parties advocating CMRS[21] use for the spectrum generally tended to recommend larger geographic areas. They contend that the trend in the marketplace toward the development of nationwide footprints by CMRS carriers demonstrates that CMRS is increasingly a nationwide service and should be licensed on that basis. Some companies proposing innovative technologies argued for a nationwide license divided into narrow bands at different frequencies. A larger geographic licensing area, it is argued, would also allow these new service providers to build-out over large regions reaching rural areas in a cost-effective manner by taking advantage of the long distance propagation characteristics of this UHF band. Other reasons given by commenters for larger geographic area licensing include the economies of scale needed to lower equipment costs and to deploy innovative services rapidly; advantages in facilitating interoperability and standards; the simplification of interference coordination; and lowered-cost pricing plans by minimizing roaming costs or allowing for single-rate pricing plans. A few commenters argued for much smaller geographic licensing areas in order to be affordable for rural areas, to enable reuse of existing tower sites, or to better serve smaller market areas. [The *Report and Order* goes on to establish six geographic partitions, the logic being that larger geographic areas might be too expensive for start-ups and rural-based companies to afford, but smaller areas would increase transaction and interference costs.]

Notes and Questions

1. Other Issues. Elsewhere in the *Report and Order*, the FCC establishes that licenses in this band will be valid for approximately fourteen years. The FCC also establishes performance requirements—in essence benchmarks that each licensee must satisfy as it builds out its technology over the duration of the license—and notes in particular that license renewal in this band will in part turn on whether the licensee has included rural areas in that build-out, even if the licensee has otherwise satisfied all of the enumerated benchmarks.

2. Technological Neutrality. The Commission strives in the excerpt above not to favor any particular technology or constituency. But, in light of the paragraphs

---

21. [Ed. CMRS (commercial mobile radio service) is the generic term for all mobile communications services, such as paging, cellular telephony, radio dispatching, and so on. It does not include fixed wireless services like, for example, microwave transmission of long distance telephone calls.]

you have read, can the Commission really avoid weighting the scales in favor of one use versus another in deciding on the size and geographical scope of spectrum blocks? For example, in not auctioning a single, nationwide license for all 36 MHz, wasn't the Commission effectively saying that it had decided to favor other uses over use by a new, nationwide entrant into the mobile communications market? Or was the Commission simply saying that it would not favor the latter use?

3. Fostering Innovation. Why does the Commission place such emphasis on small companies that are "not highly capitalized" in designing its band plan? Should the Commission try to foster innovation through its band plan or should it instead allow spectrum to be bought in the configuration that will bring the highest total price, leaving the market to sort out which technologies will be implemented? Are there reasons not to leave such considerations to the marketplace? How might large, incumbent firms behave strategically in their purchase and use of spectrum?

4. Transaction Costs. The Commission in the end adopted a compromise solution: it would auction twelve licenses (two blocks in each of six geographical areas) in order to allow users with distinct needs to enter the auction. But it also would allow any bidder to purchase the licenses and aggregate them into a nationwide license. What are the transaction costs involved in aggregating such licenses? If the most efficient use of the spectrum is for some kind of nationwide network using all of the spectrum at issue in this auction, has the Commission just raised the costs of such a network and created an inefficient result? Is there any reason to believe that aggregation of licenses entails fewer transaction costs than subdivision of licenses? If not, why did the Commission not go the other way and auction a single block that could (if necessary) be purchased and subdivided by a consortium of bidders desiring smaller blocks?

5. Inevitable Compromises. As the *Order* makes clear, the Commission will not be able to avoid helping some potential bidders more than others when it designs the band plan. The best the Commission can do is attempt to minimize these biases, make decisions on an informed basis, and maintain (to the extent possible) opportunities for aggregation and subdivision of frequency licenses. But it is important to consider and assess the degree to which predictive judgements will almost always play a role in band plan design.

6. Chickens and Eggs. Allocating spectrum for new technologies seems to raise a classic chicken-and-egg problem. Firms are reluctant to invest research dollars creating new equipment until they are sure that the Commission will license the new service in the designed-for band. The Commission, meanwhile, is reluctant to allocate spectrum to a technology that is unproven both as a technical matter and in terms of its desirability to consumers. How does the Commission address this problem in its spectrum decisions?

7. Ongoing Reform. Throughout this chapter we have been watching the Commission shift its perspective away from a rigid, heavy-handed view of spectrum management and toward a more flexible, market-determined alternative. That trend continues. For example, in 2000 the Commission released a major policy statement on the subject of how the Commission might "promote the operation of competitive markets for the sale and lease of spectrum usage rights by licensees, and thereby facilitate both [1] the transfer of the right to use spectrum for existing services to new, higher valued uses and [2] the availability of unused and underutilized spectrum to those who would use it for providing service."[22] The document announced four guiding principles for the new initiative:

1. Licensees should generally have clearly defined usage rights to their spectrum, including frequency bands, service areas, and license terms of sufficient length, with reasonable renewal expectancy, to encourage investment.

2. Licenses and spectrum usage rights should be easily transferable for lease or sale, divisible, or aggregatable.

3. Licensees/users should have flexibility in determining the services to be provided and the technology used for operation consistent with the other policies and rules governing the service.

4. Licensees/users have a fundamental obligation to protect against, and the right to be protected from, interference to the extent provided in the Commission's rules.[23]

The policy statement proposed several specific reforms, including (most notably) the elimination of unnecessary restrictions on the use of spectrum. According to the statement, the Commission will instead endeavor to promote "flexibility and fungibility" by—to the extent possible—authorizing licensees to make secondary use of any surplus spectrum assigned to them under preexisting licenses, and allowing licensees to use their spectrum for new, alternative uses even if those uses replace (instead of simply supplementing) the original assigned uses.[24] The policy statement thus consolidates and continues the reforms begun in the mid-1980s and discussed throughout this chapter.

---

22. Policy Statement, In re Principles for Promoting the Efficient Use of Spectrum by Encouraging the Development of Secondary Markets, FCC 00-401, 2000 WL 1760080 (2000), at ¶18.
23. *Id.* at ¶20.
24. *Id.* at ¶19.

CHAPTER FOUR

LICENSE HEARINGS AT
THE FCC (1934–1998)

The purpose of this chapter is:

- to study hearings as a mechanism for initially assigning broadcast licenses; and
- to survey the former and current rules pursuant to which the Commission oversees both license renewal and license transfer.

～

Section 301 of the 1934 Communications Act, 47 U.S.C. §301, makes it unlawful for anyone to broadcast in the United States without first obtaining a license from the Federal Communications Commission. Before being amended, the original Act empowered and indeed required the FCC to give out those licenses though a trial-like hearing process. Three main types of hearings were authorized: (1) hearings in which the FCC would assign a new license; (2) hearings in which the FCC would either renew an incumbent's license or transfer that license to a competing applicant; and (3) hearings in which the FCC would decide whether to approve a proposed license transfer from an incumbent to a new owner of the incumbent's choosing. Through these hearings the FCC directly determined who would own each broadcast license and indirectly exerted considerable influence over the content those broadcast licensees would air.

Hearings today are no longer the mechanism of choice, in large part because the hearing process turned out to be a very expensive way of accomplishing very little. The First Amendment, after all, greatly limits the FCC's discretion in choosing licensees; and, that being true, there was little left to accomplish in a hearing. Once an applicant had shown evidence of its basic technical abilities and financial backing, the FCC could not learn much in a hearing that would constitute a permissible basis for rendering an ultimate licensing decision.

Instead of hearings, then, modern law requires that almost all new licenses be assigned by open auction. The days of the free license are over; licenses today are sold to the highest bidder. Note that the change from hearings to auctions is not as significant as might at first appear since many licenses have already been distributed and the change in approach affects only as-yet unissued licenses. Then again, an important class of licenses—specifically, licenses that govern new services and licenses that affect newly usable parts of the spectrum—will almost all be distributed by auction, and to that extent the change in the assignment mechanism is significant.

This chapter offers an historical look at, and evaluation of, the hearing process as an assignment mechanism. We consider initial assignment hearings first, then expand our scope to include renewal and transfer hearings. The next chapter will contrast hearings with auctions and lotteries, considering the relative advantages and disadvantages of each approach.

I. INITIAL ASSIGNMENT HEARINGS

The simplest type of hearing was the hearing that took place if only one party stepped forward to request a particular license. If there were multiple applicants for a new license, the FCC would have to hold a comparative hearing and, within the constraints imposed by the First Amendment, attempt to grant the disputed license to the party most likely to serve the public interest. Where there was only one applicant, by contrast, initial assignment hearings could focus exclusively on the merits of the party at issue. The decisions from two of the earliest such hearings are reprinted below. Can you tell what specific criteria the FCC used in these licensing hearings? Can you explain why the first applicant below was successful, but the second one was not?

IN RE H.E. STUDEBAKER
1 FCC 191 (1934)

This is an application for a construction permit filed by H.E. Studebaker, a resident of Walla Walla, Washington, applying for authority to construct a local or 100-watt radio broadcast station at Lewiston, Idaho, to be operated on the frequency of 1420 kilocycles.

The applicant is a citizen of the United States. He has had several years' experience in the management of broadcast stations at Spokane, Washington, where he managed Station KGA, and at Walla Walla, Washington, where he is presently engaged in the broadcast business as an executive officer of KUJ, Incorporated. The evidence regarding the applicant's financial ability indicates that he is in a position to provide adequate capital for this project. His indicated net worth is $28,750, and it is clear from the evidence, which includes the testimony of representative business men of his community, that he has a good reputation for business ability and financial responsibility. In reference to technical qualifications, the applicant shows that he has engaged an engineer who has constructed transmitters for other stations and who has had experience in the operation and maintenance of stations.

No objectionable interference with the service of other stations may reasonably be expected to follow from the operation of the proposed new station as the evidence shows that all other stations assigned to the frequency of 1420 kilocycles are well beyond the geographical separation necessary to prevent interference and that the same situation obtains with respect to stations assigned to adjacent frequencies.

Lewiston, which is the community the proposed new station is intended to serve, has a population of slightly more than nine thousand. It appears, however, to be a trade center for a considerable area having several smaller communities. There is not at present a broadcast station in the community, and there are no services of dependable, high quality signal value available from outside stations. From the evidence regarding the present lack of radio broadcast facilities and from the testimony of business men, educators, ministers, and other residents of Lewiston, claiming a need for an additional avenue of expression for the cultural, educational, religious, and commercial interests of the community, it appears that there is a need for the proposed new service. In this connection, it was also shown that a broadcast station could be very useful to broadcast weather information, and particularly, frost warnings for the benefit of fruit growers.

The applicant appears to be prepared to present and arrange programs suited to local needs. The testimony clearly indicates that he will have the cooperation of local people in presenting a local broadcast service.

On consideration of the examiner's report and the evidence, the Commission is satisfied that the granting of the instant application of H.E. Studebaker would serve the public interest, convenience, and necessity, and accordingly enters an order granting the application, effective December 21, 1934.

IN RE CHARLES HENRY GUNTHORPE, JR.
1 FCC 177 (1934)

This is an application filed by Charles Henry Gunthorpe, Jr., Nacogdoches, Texas, for authority to construct a radio broadcast station to be operated on the frequency of 1420 kilocycles, the power of the station to be 100 watts and the hours of operation to be restricted to daytime hours.

The evidence shows that the applicant is a citizen of the United States and that for the past two years he has been a resident of Nacogdoches, Texas, where he conducts a radio and electrical shop. He expected to invest approximately $3,000 in apparatus for the proposed new station. By way of supporting his claim of financial ability to make this initial investment and to maintain a station, the applicant listed his total assets, including cash value of life insurance, furniture, real estate, business, and cash, as having a total value of approximately $12,400.

The proposed new station was intended to serve a community of less than 6,000 people and certain other small communities located in the same general area. Nacogdoches has a population of 5,687, and Nacogdoches County has a total population of 30,290 (U.S. Census). The community of Nacogdoches is in the eastern part of Texas, and while residents do not have broadcast service available from any stations located within or near the community, there is broadcast service of fair signal quality available from such stations as KWKH, Shreveport, Louisiana, eighty miles distant, and from WFAA and KRLD, Dallas, Texas, about one hundred fifty miles distant.

The applicant's specifications described transmitting apparatus of such design as to conform to the regulations applicable thereto. There appeared to be no likelihood that the proposed use of the frequency of 1420 kilocycles with 100 watts power and daytime hours of operation would cause objectionable interference in the reception of established stations. Programs outlined provided for a general local service. Considerable local talent was listed by the applicant as available for presentation. But the actual construction of the station and its operation and the actual presentation of the programs outlined would necessarily be dependent upon the applicant's ability to carry out his plans with his capital and the resources and commercial support available to him. In view of the applicant's showing as to his financial ability, need for broadcast service in his community, and prospects for obtaining adequate commercial support to maintain a worthwhile service, the Commission is doubtful that the project would be carried out successfully if authorized by the issuance of a construction permit. On consideration of the whole matter, the application, the evidence, the examiner's report, and the exceptions, the Commission was not satisfied that public interest, convenience, and/or necessity would be served by the granting of the application.

The application is accordingly denied.

Notes and Questions

1. Terminology. The two hearings considered in the cases above were both uncontested hearings, meaning that the only party before the Commission was the party applying for the license. Contested hearings can arise in either of two ways. A party might contest a rival's application by filing a petition to deny, in that way opposing the application but not seeking the license for itself. Or a party might itself seek either the same or a mutually exclusive license (a license that would cause undue interference with the license at issue if both were granted), in that case triggering a comparative hearing in which the two applicants would be judged relative to one another.

2. Statutory Authority. The FCC's specific authority to conduct license hearings derives from section 309 of the 1934 Communications Act, 47 U.S.C. §309, which reads in relevant part:

(a) [T]he Commission shall determine, in the case of each application filed with it...whether the public interest, convenience, and necessity will be served by the granting of such application....

(d)(1) Any party in interest may file with the Commission a petition to deny any application [even if that party does not itself seek the license]....

(e) If...a substantial and material question of fact is presented...[the Commission] shall formally designate the application for hearing....Any hearing subsequently held upon such application shall be a full hearing in which the applicant and all other parties in interest shall be permitted to participate....

Other provisions of the Act add detail to this broad authority. For example, section 312 authorizes the Commission to revoke any station license for, among other things, circumstances that would have warranted the Commission to refuse to grant the license in the first place, 47 U.S.C. §312(a)(2), and "willful or repeated failure to operate substantially as set forth in the license," §312(a)(3). A separate statutory enactment authorizes applicants to appeal licensing decisions to the D.C. Circuit. 47 U.S.C. §402(b).

3. Minimum Qualifications. Section 308(b) of the Act requires that applicants demonstrate "citizenship, character, and financial, technical, and other qualifications." 47 U.S.C. §308(b). The FCC ultimately translated this into seven specific requirements. First, an applicant has to be either a United States citizen or an entity principally owned by U.S. citizens. Second, an applicant has to pass rudimentary character qualifications which essentially mean not being a convicted felon, a past violator of FCC rules, or a past violator of federal antitrust law. Third, an applicant has to show that it has both the financial ability and (fourth) the technical experience to construct and operate the applied-for broadcast station. Fifth, if the station is not explicitly allocated in the band plan, there has to be a showing that the station would not cause undue interference with other licensed services. Sixth, an applicant has to show that there is a need for the proposed broadcast station in the community. And, seventh, an applicant has to show that it will be responsive to local community needs.

4. Studebaker and Gunthorpe. Of course, Studebaker received his license, and Gunthorpe did not. Do the above criteria explain why these two hearings, both of which took place in 1934, reached different results? Can you explain the results on some other ground?

5. Refusals on Other Grounds. If a party submitted a petition to deny under section 309(d)(1) but did not itself seek the license, should that party be allowed to object on grounds beyond those enumerated above? Looked at another way, assuming that an applicant satisfies all of the above criteria, could the FCC nevertheless deny a license on grounds that denial better served the public interest? Even though the applicant was both technically and financially capable and there was no other applicant?

II. COMPARATIVE HEARINGS

In 1944, a case arose in which the FCC had before it two mutually exclusive applications for broadcast licenses. Even though only one of the licenses could be granted, the Commission considered the applications separately. In fact, on the very same day, the FCC first granted one of the applications without a hearing and then set a hearing at which it offered to consider the other. That, this second applicant claimed, was a farce; his application was effectively precluded by the earlier grant, a grant that took place before his application was even considered. This second applicant therefore brought suit alleging that the Communications Act of 1934 required the FCC to hold comparative hearings in cases involving mutually exclusive applications. The case ultimately reached the Supreme Court as Ashbacker Radio Corp. v. FCC, 326 U.S. 327 (1945).

The FCC's position was simple: the Commission was not precluded "at a later date from taking any action which it may find will serve the public interest" and, thus, the fact that the first application was granted even before the second application was considered was not particularly momentous. *Id.* at 331.

No licensee obtains any vested interest in any frequency. The Commission for specified reasons may revoke any station license pursuant to the procedure prescribed by §312(a) and may suspend the license of any operator on the grounds and in the manner specified by §303(m). It may also modify a station license if in its judgment "such action will promote

> the public interest, convenience, and necessity, or the provisions of this chapter...will be more fully complied with." §312(b). And licenses for broadcasting stations are limited to three years,[1] the renewals being subject to the same considerations and practice which affect the granting of original applications. §307(d).

Id. at 331–32. As the Court pointed out, however, all of these remedies were available against any licensee, whether that license had been granted in peculiar circumstances like those at issue here or no. Moreover, by granting the earlier application, the Commission had placed the later applicant "under a greater burden than if its hearing had been earlier." *Id.* at 332. As the Court put it, "Legal theory is one thing. But the practicalities are different."

The Supreme Court thus held §309 of the Communications Act to require that mutually exclusive applications be considered in a single hearing. "Where two bona fide applications are mutually exclusive, the grant of one without a hearing to both deprives the loser of the opportunity which Congress chose to give him." *Id.* at 333. With that, comparative hearings became a staple Commission responsibility.

A. Basic Comparative Licensing Criteria

The criteria used in uncontested hearings were basically useless in the comparative setting. It was almost always true that both applicants were U.S. citizens, both were technically capable, and so on. Indeed, the Court of Appeals for the District of Columbia Circuit acknowledged the absence of clear standards in Johnston Broadcasting Co. v. FCC, 175 F.2d 351 (D.C. Cir. 1949), flatly stating that, in comparative hearings, "there are no established criteria by which a choice between the applicants must be made." *Id.* at 357. To weigh the comparative merits of competing applications, then, the Commission had to make findings concerning "every difference, except those which were frivolous or wholly unsubstantial, between the applicants." *Id.* Comparative hearings therefore brought a potentially limitless range of issues into contention.

On several occasions the Commission sought to add structure to the otherwise amorphous comparative hearing. The main such attempt was the Commission's 1965 *Policy Statement on Comparative Broadcast Hearings*, excerpted below. This document pulled together principles from a number of previous cases and it ultimately turned out to be the FCC's most complete statement of the standards it applied when choosing among competing applicants.

FCC POLICY STATEMENT ON
COMPARATIVE BROADCAST HEARINGS
1 FCC 2d 393 (1965)

One of the Commission's primary responsibilities is to choose among qualified new applicants for the same broadcast facilities. This commonly requires extended hearings into a number of areas of comparison. The hearing and decision

---

1. [Ed. Under current law, broadcast licenses are limited to eight years. *See* 47 U.S.C. §307(c).]

process is inherently complex, and the subject does not lend itself to precise categorization or to the clear making of precedent. The various factors cannot be assigned absolute values and the differences between applicants with respect to each factor are almost infinitely variable.

Furthermore, membership on the Commission is not static and the views of individual Commissioners on the importance of particular factors may change. For these and other reasons, the Commission is not bound to deal with all cases at all times as it has dealt in the past with some that seem comparable; and changes of viewpoint, if reasonable, are recognized as both inescapable and proper.

We believe that there are two primary objectives toward which the process of comparison should be directed. They are, first, the best practicable service to the public, and, second, a maximum diffusion of control of the media of mass communications. The value of these objectives is clear. Diversification of control is a public good in a free society, and is additionally desirable where a government licensing system limits access by the public to the use of radio and television facilities. Equally basic is a broadcast service which meets the needs of the public in the area to be served, both in terms of those general interests which all areas have in common and those special interests which areas do not share. An important element of such a service is the flexibility to change as local needs and interests change. Since independence and individuality of approach are elements of rendering good program service, the primary goals of good service and diversification of control are also fully compatible.

Several factors are significant in the two areas of comparison mentioned above, and it is important to make clear the manner in which each will be treated.

1. *Diversification of control of the media of mass communication.* Diversification is a factor of primary significance since, as set forth above, it constitutes a primary objective in the licensing scheme.

As in the past, we will consider both common control and less than controlling interests in other broadcast stations and other media of mass communications. The number of other mass communication outlets of the same type in the community proposed to be served will also affect to some extent the importance of this factor in the general comparative scale.

2. *Full-time participation in station operation by owners.* We consider this factor to be of substantial importance. It is inherently desirable that legal responsibility and day-to-day performance be closely associated. In addition, there is a likelihood of greater sensitivity to an area's changing needs, and of programming designed to serve these needs, to the extent that the station's proprietors actively participate in the day-to-day operation of the station. This factor is thus important in securing the best practicable service. It also frequently complements the objective of diversification, since concentrations of control are necessarily achieved at the expense of integrated ownership.

We are primarily interested in full-time participation. No credit will be given to the participation of any person who will not devote to the station substantial amounts of time on a daily basis. In assessing proposals, we will also look to the positions which the participating owners will occupy, in order to determine the extent of their policy functions and the likelihood of their playing important roles in management. Merely consultative positions will be given no weight.

While, for the reasons given above, integration of ownership and management is important per se, its value is increased if the participating owners are local residents and if they have experience in the field. Participation in station affairs by a local resident indicates a likelihood of continuing knowledge of changing local interests and needs. Previous broadcast experience, while not so significant as local residence, also has some value when put to use through integration of ownership and management.

Past participation in civic affairs will be considered as a part of a participating owner's local residence background, as will any other local activities indicating a knowledge of and interest in the welfare of the Community.

Since emphasis upon [previous broadcasting experience] could discourage qualified newcomers to broadcasting, and since experience generally confers only an initial advantage, it will be deemed of minor significance.

We recognize that station ownership by those who are local residents and, to a markedly lesser degree, by those who have broadcasting experience, may still be of some value even where there is not the substantial participation to which we will accord weight under this heading. Therefore, a slight credit will be given for the local residence of those persons with ownership interests who cannot be considered as actively participating in station affairs on a substantially full-time basis but who will devote some time to station affairs, and a very slight credit will similarly be given for experience not accompanied by full-time participation.

3. *Proposed program service.* The importance of program service is obvious. The feasibility of making a comparative evaluation is not so obvious. Hearings take considerable time and precisely formulated program plans may have to be changed not only in details but in substance, to take account of new conditions obtaining at the time a successful applicant commences operation. Thus, minor differences among applicants are apt to prove to be of no significance.

The applicant has the responsibility for a reasonable knowledge of the community and area, based on surveys or background, which will show that the program proposals are designed to meet the needs and interests of the public in that area. Failure to make contacts with local civic and other groups and individuals will be considered a serious deficiency.

In light of the considerations set forth above, and our experience with the similarity of the program plans of competing applicants, taken with the desirability of keeping hearing records free of immaterial clutter, no comparative issue will ordinarily be designated on program plans and policies, or on staffing plans or other program planning elements, and evidence on these matters will not be taken under the standard issues. The Commission will designate an issue where examination of the applications and other information before it makes such action appropriate.

No independent factor of likelihood of effectuation of proposals will be utilized. The Commission expects every licensee to carry out its proposals, subject to factors beyond its control, and subject to reasonable judgment that the public's needs and interests require a departure from original plans.

4. *Past broadcast record*. This factor includes past ownership interest and significant participation in a broadcast station by one with an ownership interest in the applicant. It is a factor of substantial importance upon the terms set forth below.

A past record within the bounds of average performance will be disregarded, since average future performance is expected. We are interested in records which, because either unusually good or unusually poor, give some indication of unusual performance in the future. Thus, we shall consider past records to determine whether the record shows (i) unusual attention to the public's needs and interests, such as special sensitivity to an area's changing needs through flexibility of local programs designed to meet those needs, or (ii) either a failure to meet the public's needs and interests or a significant failure to carry out representations made to the Commission.

5. *Efficient use of frequency*. In comparative cases where one of two or more competing applicants proposes an operation which, for one or more engineering reasons, would be more efficient, this fact can and should be considered in determining which of the applicants should be preferred.

6. *Character*. Significant character deficiencies may warrant disqualification, and an issue will be designated where appropriate. In the absence of a designated issue, character evidence will not be taken. Our intention here is not only to avoid unduly prolonging the hearing process, but also to avoid those situations where an applicant converts the hearing into a search for his opponents' minor blemishes, no matter how remote in the past or how insignificant.

7. *Other factors*. Our interest in the consistency and clarity of decision and in expedition of the hearing process is not intended to preclude the full examination of any relevant and substantial factor. We will thus favorably consider petitions to add issues when, but only when, they demonstrate that significant evidence will be adduced.

Notes and Questions

1. What Role for Precedent? Reread the second paragraph of the *Policy Statement*. Is it surprising? How would you respond if the Supreme Court were to include a paragraph like that at the start of the majority opinion in an important case? Is the FCC's inclusion of this paragraph different? If so, why?

2. Character. The Commission eliminated character as an issue in comparative hearings as of 1986, at least so long as any character deficiencies did not rise to the level of questioning the applicant's basic qualifications (*i.e.*, its ability to obtain an uncontested license). *Character Qualifications in Broadcast Licensing*, 102 FCC 2d 1179 (1986); *see also* 5 FCC Rcd. 3252 (1990). The main reason was that comparative hearings on character were costly, with large amounts of finger-pointing and name-calling but little payoff in terms of revealing valuable comparative information.

3. Bechtel. A significant dismantling of the comparative hearing process came in Bechtel v. FCC, 10 F.3d 875 (D.C. Cir. 1993), where the D.C. Circuit ruled that the FCC's preference for integrating ownership and management—item number two in the *Policy Statement* —was arbitrary and capricious. The FCC had justified using integration as a factor on the theory that integrated owners would probably be more active and effective when it came to running the station, for example being more likely to learn about and react to local conditions. Bechtel's response was empirical: whatever the policy argument, the fact of the matter was that integration never lasted more than one year past the FCC hearing. Integration, in other words, was a sham, done only to influence the outcome of comparative hearings.

This was more than a theoretical battle in *Bechtel*. Bechtel's rival was integrated, but Bechtel was going to invest in technical infrastructure that would allow the station to reach many more listeners. The D.C. Circuit compared the ephemeral to the actual, and held that the FCC's predictive judgment was no longer a sufficient ground for favoring integration. Said the Court: "Despite 28 years of experience with the policy, the Commission has accumulated no evidence to indicate that the policy achieves even one of the benefits that the Commission attributes to it." 10 F.3d at 880. Without evidence that integration mattered, and non-trivially, the FCC's policy could not stand.

The dispute was sent back to the Commission, which, in turn, decided not to appeal the *Bechtel* ruling and instead to simply suspend all mutually exclusive applications for commercial broadcast stations in which integration was an issue. These applications were frozen for several years, with the Commission unable to reform or delete the integration criterion. The problem was solved by the switch to auctions, discussed in Chapter Five.

B. Special Considerations for Racial Minorities and Women

The 1965 *Policy Statement* contains no explicit reference to preferences for racial minorities or women, and the FCC's initial interpretation of both that document and the Communications Act was that no preference to minority ownership was appropriate unless the record indicated that the owner's race likely would affect the content of the broadcaster's service. The Court of Appeals for the District of Columbia Circuit rejected the FCC's interpretation in TV 9, Inc. v. FCC, 495 F.2d 929 (D.C. Cir. 1973), and in 1978 the Commission created preferences for applicants who were women and also for those who were members of racial minorities. The following cases address these programs.

i. Minority Preferences (Pre-*Adarand*)

METRO BROADCASTING, INC. v. FCC
497 U.S. 547 (1990)

BRENNAN, J., delivered the opinion of the Court, in which WHITE, MARSHALL, BLACKMUN, and STEVENS, JJ., joined. STEVENS, J., filed a concurring opinion. O'CONNOR, J., filed a dissenting opinion, in which REHNQUIST, C.J., and SCALIA and KENNEDY, JJ., joined. KENNEDY, J., filed a dissenting opinion, in which SCALIA, J., joined.

JUSTICE BRENNAN delivered the opinion of the Court.

The issue in these cases is whether certain minority preference policies of the Federal Communications Commission violate the equal protection component of the Fifth Amendment. The policies in question are (1) a program awarding an enhancement for minority ownership in comparative proceedings for new licenses, and (2) the minority "distress sale" program, which permits a limited category of radio and television broadcast stations to be transferred only to minority-controlled firms. We hold that these policies do not violate equal protection principles.

I

A

Although for the past two decades minorities have constituted at least one-fifth of the United States population,[2] in 1971, minorities owned only 10 of the approximately 7,500 radio stations in the country and none of the more than 1,000 television stations; in 1978, minorities owned less than 1 percent of the Nation's radio and television stations, *see* FCC Minority Ownership Task Force, Report on Minority Ownership in Broadcasting 1 (1978) (hereinafter *Task Force Report*); and in 1986, they owned just 2.1 percent of the more than 11,000 radio and television stations in the United States. *See* National Association of Broadcasters, Minority Broadcasting Facts 6 (Sept. 1986). Moreover, these statistics fail to reflect the fact that, as late entrants who often have been able to obtain only the less valuable stations, many minority broadcasters serve geographically limited markets with relatively small audiences.

The Commission has recognized that the viewing and listening public suffers when minorities are underrepresented among owners of television and radio stations:

> "Acute underrepresentation of minorities among the owners of broadcast properties is troublesome because it is the licensee who is ultimately responsible for identifying and serving the needs and interests of his or her audience. Unless minorities are encouraged to enter the mainstream of the commercial broadcasting business, a substantial portion of our citizenry will remain underserved and the larger, non-minority audience will be deprived of the views of minorities." *Task Force Report*, at 1.

The Commission has therefore worked to encourage minority participation in the broadcast industry. The FCC began by formulating rules to prohibit licensees from discriminating against minorities in employment.

Initially, the FCC did not consider minority status as a factor in licensing decisions, maintaining as a matter of Commission policy that no preference to minority ownership was warranted where the record in a particular case did not give assurances that the owner's race likely would affect the content of the station's broadcast service to the public. The Court of Appeals for the District of Columbia Circuit, however, rejected the Commission's position that an "assurance of superior community service attributable to...Black ownership and participation" was required before a preference could be awarded. *TV 9, Inc.*, 161 U.S. App. D.C. at 358.

---

2. The FCC has defined the term "minority" to include "those of Black, Hispanic Surnamed, American Eskimo, Aleut, American Indian and Asiatic American extraction." Statement of Policy on Minority Ownership of Broadcasting Facilities, 68 FCC 2d 979, 980 n.8 (1978).

In April 1977, the FCC conducted a conference on minority ownership policies, at which participants testified that minority preferences were justified as a
means of increasing diversity of broadcast viewpoint. *See Task Force Report*, at
4–6. Building on the results of the conference, the FCC adopted in May 1978 its
Statement of Policy on Minority Ownership of Broadcasting Facilities, 68 FCC
2d 979. The FCC concluded:

> "The views of racial minorities continue to be inadequately represented
> in the broadcast media. This situation is detrimental not only to the mi-
> nority audience but to all of the viewing and listening public. Adequate
> representation of minority viewpoints in programming serves not only
> the needs and interests of the minority community but also enriches and
> educates the non-minority audience. It enhances the diversified program-
> ming which is a key objective not only of the Communications Act of
> 1934 but also of the First Amendment." *Id.*, at 980–981.

Describing its actions as only "first steps," *id.*, at 984, the FCC outlined two elements of a minority ownership policy.

First, the Commission pledged to consider minority ownership as one factor
in comparative proceedings for new licenses. When the Commission compares
mutually exclusive applications for new radio or television broadcast stations, it
looks principally at six factors: diversification of control of mass media communications, full-time participation in station operation by owners (commonly referred to as the "integration" of ownership and management), proposed program
service, past broadcast record, efficient use of the frequency, and the character of
the applicants. In the *Policy Statement on Minority Ownership*, the FCC announced that minority ownership and participation in management would be
considered in a comparative hearing as a "plus" to be weighed together with all
other relevant factors. The "plus" is awarded only to the extent that a minority
owner actively participates in the day-to-day management of the station.

Second, the FCC outlined a plan to increase minority opportunities to receive
reassigned and transferred licenses through the so-called "distress sale" policy. As a
general rule, a licensee whose qualifications to hold a broadcast license come into
question may not assign or transfer that license until the FCC has resolved its
doubts in a noncomparative hearing. The distress sale policy is an exception to that
practice, allowing a broadcaster whose license has been designated for a revocation
hearing, or whose renewal application has been designated for hearing, to assign
the license to an FCC-approved minority enterprise. The assignee must meet the
FCC's basic qualifications, and the minority ownership must exceed 50 percent or
be controlling. The purchase price must not exceed 75 percent of fair market value.

II

It is of overriding significance in these cases that the FCC's minority ownership programs have been specifically approved—indeed, mandated—by Congress. [Congress's involvement is discussed in Part II.B.2., *infra.*] We hold that
benign race-conscious measures mandated by Congress[3]—even if those measures

---

3. We fail to understand how Justice Kennedy can pretend that examples of "benign"
race-conscious measures include South African apartheid, the "separate-but-equal" law at
issue in Plessy v. Ferguson, 163 U.S. 537 (1896), and the internment of American citizens of
Japanese ancestry upheld in Korematsu v. United States, 323 U.S. 214 (1944). We are confi-

are not "remedial" in the sense of being designed to compensate victims of past governmental or societal discrimination—are constitutionally permissible to the extent that they serve important governmental objectives within the power of Congress and are substantially related to achievement of those objectives.

We hold that the FCC minority ownership policies pass muster under the test we announce today. First, we find that they serve the important governmental objective of broadcast diversity. Second, we conclude that they are substantially related to the achievement of that objective.

A

Congress found that "the effects of past inequities stemming from racial and ethnic discrimination have resulted in a severe underrepresentation of minorities in the media of mass communications." H.R. Conf. Rep. No. 97-765, p. 43 (1982). Congress and the Commission do not justify the minority ownership policies strictly as remedies for victims of this discrimination, however. Rather, Congress and the FCC have selected the minority ownership policies primarily to promote programming diversity, and they urge that such diversity is an important governmental objective that can serve as a constitutional basis for the preference policies. We agree.

We have long recognized that "because of the scarcity of [electromagnetic] frequencies, the Government is permitted to put restraints on licensees in favor of others whose views should be expressed on this unique medium." Red Lion Broadcasting Co. v. FCC, 395 U.S. 367, 390 (1969). The Government's role in distributing the limited number of broadcast licenses is not merely that of a "traffic officer," National Broadcasting Co. v. United States, 319 U.S. 190, 215 (1943); rather, it is axiomatic that broadcasting may be regulated in light of the rights of the viewing and listening audience and that "the widest possible dissemination of information from diverse and antagonistic sources is essential to the welfare of the public." Associated Press v. United States, 326 U.S. 1, 20 (1945). Safeguarding the public's right to receive a diversity of views and information over the airwaves is therefore an integral component of the FCC's mission. We have observed that the Communications Act has designated broadcasters as "fiduciaries for the public." FCC v. League of Women Voters of California, 468 U.S. 364, 377 (1984).

Just as a "diverse student body" contributing to a "'robust exchange of ideas'" is a "constitutionally permissible goal" on which a race-conscious university admissions program may be predicated, University of California Regents v. Bakke, 438 U.S. 265, 311–313 (1978) (opinion of Powell, J.), the diversity of views and information on the airwaves serves important First Amendment values. The benefits of such diversity are not limited to the members of minority groups who gain access to the broadcasting industry by virtue of the ownership policies; rather, the benefits redound to all members of the viewing and listening audience.

B

We also find that the minority ownership policies are substantially related to the achievement of the Government's interest. One component of this inquiry

---

dent that an "examination of the legislative scheme and its history," Weinberger v. Wiesenfeld, 420 U.S. 636, 648 n.16 (1975), will separate benign measures from other types of racial classifications.

concerns the relationship between expanded minority ownership and greater broadcast diversity; both the FCC and Congress have determined that such a relationship exists.

1

As the Commission observed in its 1978 Statement, "ownership of broadcasting facilities by minorities is [a] significant way of fostering the inclusion of minority views in the area of programming" and "full minority participation in the ownership and management of broadcast facilities results in a more diverse selection of programming." 68 FCC 2d, at 981. The FCC's conclusion that there is an empirical nexus between minority ownership and broadcasting diversity is a product of its expertise, and we accord its judgment deference.

Furthermore, the FCC's reasoning with respect to the minority ownership policies is consistent with longstanding practice under the Communications Act. From its inception, public regulation of broadcasting has been premised on the assumption that diversification of ownership will broaden the range of programming available to the broadcast audience.[4] The Commission has never relied on the market alone to ensure that the needs of the audience are met. Indeed, one of the FCC's elementary regulatory assumptions is that broadcast content is not purely market-driven; if it were, there would be little need for consideration in licensing decisions of such factors as integration of ownership and management, local residence, and civic participation.

2

Congress also has made clear its view that the minority ownership policies advance the goal of diverse programming. In recent years, Congress has specifically required the Commission, through appropriations legislation, to maintain the minority ownership policies without alteration. For the past two decades, Congress has consistently recognized the barriers encountered by minorities in entering the broadcast industry and has expressed emphatic support for the Commission's attempts to promote programming diversity by increasing minority ownership.

When in 1981 it ultimately authorized a lottery procedure [for awarding certain broadcast licenses], Congress established a concomitant system of minority preferences. *See* Omnibus Budget Reconciliation Act of 1981, Pub. L. 97-35, 95 Stat. 357, 736–737. The Act provided that where more than one application for an initial license or construction permit was received, the Commission could grant the license or permit to a qualified applicant "through the use of a system of random selection," 47 U.S.C. §309(i)(1) (1982 ed.), so long as the FCC adopted rules to ensure "significant preferences" in the lottery process to groups underrepresented in the ownership of telecommunications facilities. §309(i)(3)(A). After the FCC complained of the difficulty of defining "underrepresented" groups and raised other problems concerning the statute, Congress enacted a second lottery statute reaffirming its intention in unmistakable terms.

---

4. The Commission has always focused on ownership, on the theory that "ownership carries with it the power to select, to edit, and to choose the methods, manner and emphasis of presentation, all of which are a critical aspect of the Commission's concern with the public interest."

Section 115 of the Communications Amendments Act of 1982 directs that, "to further diversify the ownership of the media of mass communications, [a] significant preference [is to be given] to any applicant controlled by a member or members of a minority group." 47 U.S.C. §309(i)(3)(A) (1982 ed.). Observing that the nexus between ownership and programming "has been repeatedly recognized by both the Commission and the courts," Congress explained that it sought "to promote the diversification of media ownership and consequent diversification of programming content," a principle that "is grounded in the First Amendment." H.R. Conf. Rep. No. 97-765, p. 40 (1982). With this new mandate from Congress, the Commission adopted rules to govern the use of a lottery system to award licenses for low power television stations.

As revealed by the historical evolution of current federal policy, both Congress and the Commission have concluded that the minority ownership programs are critical means of promoting broadcast diversity. We must give great weight to their joint determination.

C

The judgment that there is a link between expanded minority ownership and broadcast diversity does not rest on impermissible stereotyping. Although all station owners are guided to some extent by market demand in their programming decisions, Congress and the Commission have determined that there may be important differences between the broadcasting practices of minority owners and those of their nonminority counterparts. This judgment—and the conclusion that there is a nexus between minority ownership and broadcasting diversity—is corroborated by a host of empirical evidence.[5] Evidence suggests that an owner's minority status influences the selection of topics for news coverage and the presentation of editorial viewpoint, especially on matters of particular concern to minorities. Minority-owned stations tend to devote more news time to topics of minority interest and to avoid racial and ethnic stereotypes in portraying minorities.[6] In addition, studies show that a minority owner is more likely to employ

---

5. For example, the Congressional Research Service (CRS) analyzed data from some 8,720 FCC-licensed radio and TV stations and found a strong correlation between minority ownership and diversity of programming. See CRS, Minority Broadcast Station Ownership and Broadcast Programming: Is There a Nexus? (June 29, 1988). While only 20 percent of stations with no Afro-American ownership responded that they attempted to direct programming at Afro-American audiences, 65 percent of stations with Afro-American ownership reported that they did so. Only 10 percent of stations without Hispanic ownership stated that they targeted programming at Hispanic audiences, while 59 percent of stations with Hispanic owners said they did.

Other surveys support the FCC's determination that there is a nexus between ownership and programming. A University of Wisconsin study found that Afro-American-owned, Afro-American-oriented radio stations have more diverse playlists than white-owned, Afro-American-oriented stations. See J. Jeter, A Comparative Analysis of the Programming Practices of Black-Owned Black-Oriented Radio Stations and White-Owned Black-Oriented Radio Stations 130, 139 (1981) (University of Wisconsin-Madison).

6. For example, a University of Massachusetts at Boston survey of 3,000 local Boston news stories found a statistically significant difference in the treatment of events, depending on the race of ownership. See K. Johnson, Media Images of Boston's Black Community 16–29 (Jan. 28, 1987) (William Monroe Trotter Institute, University of Massachusetts at Boston). A comparison between an Afro-American-owned television station and a white-owned station in Detroit concluded that "the overall mix of topic and location coverage be-

minorities in managerial and other important roles where they can have an impact on station policies.[7] While we are under no illusion that members of a particular minority group share some cohesive, collective viewpoint, we believe it a legitimate inference for Congress and the Commission to draw that, as more minorities gain ownership and policymaking roles in the media, varying perspectives will be more fairly represented on the airwaves. The policies are thus a product of "'analysis'" rather than a "'stereotyped reaction'" based on "'habit.'" *Fullilove*, 448 U.S., at 534, n.4 (Stevens, J., dissenting) (citation omitted).

D

The Commission adopted and Congress endorsed minority ownership preferences only after long study and painstaking consideration of all available alternatives. [In 1968] the Kerner Commission warned that the various elements of the media "have not communicated to whites a feeling for the difficulties and frustrations of being a Negro in the United States. They have not shown understanding or appreciation of—and thus have not communicated—a sense of Negro culture, thought, or history.... The world that television and newspapers offer to their black audience is almost totally white...." Report of the National Advisory Commission on Civil Disorders 210 (1968). In response, the FCC promulgated equal employment opportunity regulations and formal "ascertainment" rules requiring a broadcaster as a condition of license "to ascertain the problems, needs and interests of the residents of his community of license and other areas he undertakes to serve," and to specify "what broadcast matter he proposes to meet those problems, needs and interests." Primer on Ascertainment of Community Problems by Broadcast Applicants, 27 FCC 2d 650, 682 (1971). The Commission expressly included "minority and ethnic groups" as segments of the community that licensees were expected to consult. The FCC held that a broadcaster's failure to ascertain and serve the needs of sizable minority groups in its service area was, in itself, a failure of licensee responsibility. Pursuant to this policy, for example, the Commission refused to renew licenses for eight educational stations in Alabama and denied an application for a construction permit for a ninth, all on the ground that the licensee "did not take the trouble to inform itself of the needs and interests of a minority group consisting of 30 percent of the population of the State of Alabama" and that such a failure was "fundamentally irreconcilable with the obligations which the Communications Act places upon those who receive authorizations to use the airwaves."

By 1978, however, the Commission had determined that even these efforts at influencing broadcast content were not effective means of generating adequate programming diversity. As support, the Commission cited a report by the United States Commission on Civil Rights, which found that minorities "are underrepre-

---

tween the two stations is statistically different, and with its higher use of blacks in newsmaker roles and its higher coverage of issues of racial significance, [the Afro-American-owned station's] content does represent a different perspective on news than [that of the white-owned station]."

7. Afro-American-owned radio stations, for example, have hired Afro-Americans in top management and other important job categories at far higher rates than have white-owned stations, even those with Afro-American-oriented formats. The same has been true of Hispanic hiring at Hispanic-owned stations, compared to Anglo-owned stations with Spanish-language formats.

sented on network dramatic television programs and on the network news. When they do appear they are frequently seen in token or stereotyped roles." Window Dressing on the Set 3 (Aug. 1977).

In short, the FCC established minority ownership preferences only after long experience demonstrated that race-neutral means could not produce adequate broadcasting diversity.

Moreover, the considered nature of the Commission's judgment in selecting the particular minority ownership policies at issue today is illustrated by the fact that the Commission has rejected other types of minority preferences. For example, the Commission has studied but refused to implement the more expansive alternative of setting aside certain frequencies for minority broadcasters. In addition, in a ruling released the day after it adopted the comparative hearing credit and the distress sale preference, the FCC declined to adopt a plan to require 45-day advance public notice before a station could be sold, which had been advocated on the ground that it would ensure minorities a chance to bid on stations that might otherwise be sold to industry insiders without ever coming on the market. *See* 43 Fed. Reg. 24560 (1978).

Congress and the Commission have adopted a policy of minority ownership not as an end in itself, but rather as a means of achieving greater programming diversity. Such a goal carries its own natural limit, for there will be no need for further minority preferences once sufficient diversity has been achieved.

III

The Commission's minority ownership policies bear the imprimatur of long-standing congressional support and direction and are substantially related to the achievement of the important governmental objective of broadcast diversity.

[Concurring opinion of JUSTICE STEVENS is omitted.]

JUSTICE O'CONNOR, with whom CHIEF JUSTICE REHNQUIST, JUSTICE SCALIA, and JUSTICE KENNEDY join, dissenting.

I

In both the challenged policies, the FCC provides benefits to some members of our society and denies benefits to others based on race or ethnicity. The dangers of such classifications are clear. They endorse race-based reasoning and the conception of a Nation divided into racial blocs, thus contributing to an escalation of racial hostility and conflict. Such policies may embody stereotypes that treat individuals as the product of their race, evaluating their thoughts and efforts—their very worth as citizens—according to a criterion barred to the Government by history and the Constitution. Racial classifications, whether providing benefits to or burdening particular racial or ethnic groups, may stigmatize those groups singled out for different treatment and may create considerable tension with the Nation's widely shared commitment to evaluating individuals upon their individual merit.

Untethered to narrowly confined remedial notions, "benign" carries with it no independent meaning, but reflects only acceptance of the current generation's conclusion that a politically acceptable burden, imposed on particular citizens on the basis of race, is reasonable.

II

Our history reveals that the most blatant forms of discrimination have been visited upon some members of the racial and ethnic groups identified in the challenged programs. Many have lacked the opportunity to share in the Nation's wealth and to participate in its commercial enterprises. It is undisputed that minority participation in the broadcasting industry falls markedly below the demographic representation of those groups and this shortfall may be traced in part to the discrimination and the patterns of exclusion that have widely affected our society. For these reasons, we have repeatedly recognized that the Government possesses a compelling interest in remedying the effects of identified race discrimination.

Yet the policies challenged in these cases were not designed as remedial measures and are in no sense narrowly tailored to remedy identified discrimination. The FCC appropriately concedes that its policies embodied no remedial purpose, Tr. of Oral Arg. 40–42, and has disclaimed the possibility that discrimination infected the allocation of licenses.

III

Under the appropriate standard, strict scrutiny, only a compelling interest may support the Government's use of racial classifications. The interest in increasing the diversity of broadcast viewpoints is clearly not a compelling interest. It is simply too amorphous, too insubstantial, and too unrelated to any legitimate basis for employing racial classifications.

The asserted interest in this case is certainly amorphous: the FCC and the majority of this Court understandably do not suggest how one would define or measure a particular viewpoint that might be associated with race, or even how one would assess the diversity of broadcast viewpoints. A claim of insufficiently diverse broadcasting viewpoints might be used to justify unconstrained racial preferences, linked to nothing other than proportional representation of various races. And the interest would support indefinite use of racial classifications, employed first to obtain the appropriate mixture of racial views and then to ensure that the broadcasting spectrum continues to reflect that mixture.

Under the majority's holding, the FCC may also advance its asserted interest in viewpoint diversity by identifying what constitutes a "Black viewpoint," an "Asian viewpoint," an "Arab viewpoint," and so on; determining which viewpoints are underrepresented; and then using that determination to mandate particular programming or to deny licenses to those deemed by virtue of their race or ethnicity less likely to present the favored views. Indeed, the FCC has, if taken at its word, essentially pursued this course, albeit without making express its reasons for choosing to favor particular groups or for concluding that the broadcasting spectrum is insufficiently diverse.

The FCC's extension of the asserted interest in diversity of views in this case presents, at the very least, an unsettled First Amendment issue. The FCC has concluded that the American broadcasting public receives the incorrect mix of ideas and claims to have adopted the challenged policies to supplement programming content with a particular set of views. Although we have approved limited measures designed to increase information and views generally, the Court has never upheld a broadcasting measure designed to amplify a distinct set of views or the views of a particular class of speakers.

IV

The FCC's choice to employ a racial criterion embodies the related notions that a particular and distinct viewpoint inheres in certain racial groups, and that a particular applicant, by virtue of race or ethnicity alone, is more valued than other applicants because "likely to provide [that] distinct perspective." Brief for FCC in No. 89-453, p. 17. The policies directly equate race with belief and behavior, for they establish race as a necessary and sufficient condition of securing the preference. The policies impermissibly value individuals because they presume that persons think in a manner associated with their race.

Race-neutral and untried means of directly accomplishing the governmental interest are readily available. The FCC could directly advance its interest by requiring licensees to provide programming that the FCC believes would add to diversity. Yet in adopting the challenged policies, the FCC expressly disclaimed having attempted any direct efforts to achieve its asserted goal. The FCC and the Court suggest that First Amendment interests in some manner should exempt the FCC from employing this direct, race-neutral means to achieve its asserted interest. They essentially argue that we may bend our equal protection principles to avoid more readily apparent harm to our First Amendment values. But the FCC cannot have it both ways: either the First Amendment bars the FCC from seeking to accomplish indirectly what it may not accomplish directly; or the FCC may pursue the goal, but must do so in a manner that comports with equal protection principles. And if the FCC can direct programming in any fashion, it must employ that direct means before resorting to indirect race-conscious means.

Other race-neutral means also exist, and all are at least as direct as the FCC's racial classifications. The FCC could evaluate applicants upon their ability to provide and commitment to offer whatever programming the FCC believes would reflect underrepresented viewpoints. If the FCC truly seeks diverse programming rather than allocation of goods to persons of particular racial backgrounds, it has little excuse to look to racial background rather than programming to further the programming interest. Also, race-neutral means exist to allow access to the broadcasting industry for those persons excluded for financial and related reasons. The Court reasons that various minority preferences, including those reflected in the distress sale, overcome barriers of information, experience, and financing that inhibit minority ownership. Race-neutral financial and informational measures most directly reduce financial and informational barriers.

The FCC's policies assume and rely upon the existence of a tightly bound "nexus" between the owners' race and the resulting programming. [But] the market shapes programming to a tremendous extent. Members of minority groups who own licenses might be thought, like other owners, to seek to broadcast programs that will attract and retain audiences, rather than programs that reflect the owner's tastes and preferences.

JUSTICE KENNEDY, with whom JUSTICE SCALIA joins, dissenting.

Almost 100 years ago in Plessy v. Ferguson, 163 U.S. 537 (1896), this Court upheld a government-sponsored race-conscious measure, a Louisiana law that required "equal but separate accommodations" for "white" and "colored" railroad passengers. The *Plessy* Court concluded that the "race-conscious measures" it reviewed were reasonable because they served the governmental interest of increasing the riding pleasure of railroad passengers.

Today the Court grants Congress latitude to employ "benign race-conscious measures... [that] are not... designed to compensate victims of past governmental or societal discrimination," but that "serve important governmental objectives... and are substantially related to achievement of those objectives." *Ante*, at 565–565. The interest the Court accepts to uphold the Commission's race-conscious measures is "broadcast diversity." Furthering that interest, we are told, is worth the cost of discriminating among citizens on the basis of race because it will increase the listening pleasure of media audiences. In upholding this preference, the majority exhumes *Plessy*'s deferential approach to racial classifications.

Once the Government takes the step, which itself should be forbidden, of enacting into law the stereotypical assumption that the race of owners is linked to broadcast content, it follows a path that becomes ever more tortuous. It must decide which races to favor. While the Court repeatedly refers to the preferences as favoring "minorities," and purports to evaluate the burdens imposed on "nonminorities," it must be emphasized that the discriminatory policies upheld today operate to exclude the many racial and ethnic minorities that have not made the Commission's list.[8]

Policies of racial separation and preference are almost always justified as benign, even when it is clear to any sensible observer that they are not. The following statement, for example, would fit well among those offered to uphold the Commission's racial preference policy: "The policy is not based on any concept of superiority or inferiority, but merely on the fact that people differ, particularly in their group associations, loyalties, cultures, outlook, modes of life and standards of development." *See* South Africa and the Rule of Law 37 (1968) (official publication of the South African Government).

Although the majority disclaims it, the FCC policy seems based on the demeaning notion that members of the defined racial groups ascribe to certain "minority views" that must be different from those of other citizens. Special preferences also can foster the view that members of the favored groups are inherently less able to compete on their own. And, rightly or wrongly, special preference programs often are perceived as targets for exploitation by opportunists who seek to take advantage of monetary rewards without advancing the stated policy of minority inclusion.[9]

---

8. The Court fails to address the difficulties, both practical and constitutional, with the task of defining members of racial groups that its decision will require. The Commission, for example, has found it necessary to trace an applicant's family history to 1492 to conclude that the applicant was "Hispanic" for purposes of a minority tax certificate policy. *See* Storer Broadcasting Co., 87 FCC 2d 190 (1981). [Footnote relocated.]

9. The record in one of these two cases indicates that Astroline Communications Company, the beneficiary of the distress sale policy in this case, had a total capitalization of approximately $ 24,000,000. Its sole minority principal was a Hispanic-American who held

Notes and Questions

1. The Commission's Goals. Precisely what are the constitutionally permissible and substantial goals that the FCC's policies are designed to achieve? Would the reasoning of *Metro Broadcasting* also permit the Commission (or Congress) to award a "plus" to people over 65? To religious minorities?

2. And Its Assumptions. Is the FCC's position that licensees tend to air programs aimed at people just like themselves? But the WB isn't a network run by angst-ridden teenagers, yet its program offerings are widely understood to target (quite successfully) the teen audience. What, then, is the logic behind the FCC's position?

3. Promoting Diversity. Could the FCC determine that an ethnic group's views or interests were over-represented on radio or television and so assign demerits to applicants of that race? Can you logically distinguish this program from the programs the Commission endorses?

4. Testing the Results. If the FCC were to attempt to ascertain whether its minority preference and distress sale policies were working effectively, what questions should it seek to answer and what data would be relevant? If these policies cannot be adequately tested, what does that tell us about them? About the decision in *Bechtel*?

5. Race or Speech? Is this case about "race" or "speech"? Apparently, the majority and the dissenters in *Metro Broadcasting* differ in the latitude each would grant to the FCC and to Congress to employ race-specific standards. Do they not also differ in the latitude each would ascribe to the Commission in adopting regulations that are justified with reference to the content of broadcast programs? Doesn't the majority envision an FCC that is legally and practically empowered to control program content in ways that the dissenters would find legally objectionable and practically unrealistic?

6. More Direct Approaches. The dissent and majority seem to differ on the question of whether the FCC should be forced to accomplish program diversity directly (say, a regulation that explicitly requires licensees to air diverse programming) or whether, instead, the indirect approach of using ownership diversity as a proxy for program diversity is acceptable. But should the FCC be forced to develop a regulation that directly responds to its policy goal? If the FCC cannot promulgate such a regulation, doesn't that support the dissent's position that the policy goals at issue here are too amorphous and the regulation must be struck down on that ground?

ii. Preferences for Women

Preferences for women fared somewhat differently from the above-discussed minority preferences, both in their status as FCC policies and in their judicial reception. The 1978 *Statement of Policy on Minority Ownership of Broadcasting Facilities*, 68 FCC 2d 979, contained three major programs for racial minorities: the comparative hearing preference and the distress sale policy, both discussed in *Metro Broadcasting*, and a tax certificate program that gave companies prefer-

---

21% of Astroline's overall equity and 71% of its voting equity. His total cash contribution was $210. *See* App. in No. 89-700, pp. 68–69.

ential tax treatment on their capital gains if they sold broadcast facilities to minority-owned or minority-controlled entities. The FCC decided that women should benefit from some of these advantages as well, and so, in 1978, female ownership was deemed a "plus" in the comparative hearing process, albeit a smaller plus than minority ownership would be.[10] Women who were not minorities were not, however, allowed to participate in the tax certificate or distress sale programs.

Two years after the Supreme Court issued its opinion in *Metro Broadcasting*, a panel of the Court of Appeals for the D.C. Circuit decided Lamprecht v. FCC, 958 F.2d 382 (D.C. Cir. 1992). The court, dividing 2-1, struck down the FCC's policy of awarding extra credit in comparative hearing proceedings to women applicants.

In that case, Jerome Lamprecht contested the award of an FM radio station license to Barbara Marmet. Lamprecht was a 30-year-old male who had worked as an announcer, program director, station manager, and general manager at various radio stations. Marmet was a 58-year-old woman who was married to a communications lawyer and divided her residences among Bethesda, Maryland; Frederick County, Maryland; and Amelia Island, Florida. She had served on the parents' committee of the St. Albans School for Boys, was a sustaining member of the Washington Junior League, a member of the Chevy Chase Country Club, and fiscal officer of her garden club. Marmet received a decisive preference over Lamprecht because of her gender.

The majority in *Lamprecht* held that *Metro Broadcasting* required that any predictive judgments about the behavior of men and women as station owners must be sustained by meaningful evidence in order to avoid the risk that such judgments merely reflected stereotypical assumptions about men and women. The court concluded that the FCC offered no evidence that women and men were likely to program stations differently. The court also examined a study by the Congressional Research Service but concluded that the study had methodological flaws and, more importantly, failed to establish a substantial nexus between gender and the likelihood of offering women's programming.

Dissenting, Judge Mikva accused the *Lamprecht* majority of deliberately misreading *Metro Broadcasting*. Mikva argued that *Metro Broadcasting* dictated that courts should defer to Congress's conclusions about the link between ownership and programming, so long as the conclusions reflect reasoned analysis rather than archaic stereotypes.

iii. *Adarand (Metro Broadcasting* Overruled)

In Adarand Constructors, Inc., v. Pena, 515 U.S. 200 (1995), the Supreme Court struck down a federal program that granted preferential treatment to

---

10. "We hold that merit for female ownership and participation is warranted upon essentially the same basis as the merit given for black ownership and participation, but that it is a merit of lesser significance." Mid-Florida Television Corp., 70 FCC 2d 281, 326 (Rev. Bd. 1978), *set aside on other grounds*, 87 FCC 2d 203 (1981).

racial minorities in bidding on public works projects. The five justices in the *Adarand* majority were the four *Metro Broadcasting* dissenters plus the subsequently appointed Justice Thomas (the author of *Lamprecht*). With respect to *Metro Broadcasting*, the Court stated:

> We hold today that all racial classifications, imposed by whatever federal, state, or local governmental actor, must be analyzed by a reviewing court under strict scrutiny. In other words, such classifications are constitutional only if they are narrowly tailored measures that further compelling governmental interests. To the extent that *Metro Broadcasting* is inconsistent with that holding, it is overruled.

515 U.S. at 226–27.

The FCC did not respond to *Adarand* by jettisoning its programs for racial and ethnic minorities; nor is it clear that the FCC had to. The *Adarand* majority did not say that the programs at issue in *Metro Broadcasting* were unconstitutional, as those programs were not before the *Adarand* Court. The majority held only that *Metro Broadcasting* had employed too lenient a standard of review.

The minority distress sale policy thus remains in place even today. The tax certificate program and the "plus" in comparative hearings have been abolished, but those changes were the result of statutory amendments rather than FCC actions. Spurred by Viacom's planned sale of cable systems to a consortium led by an African-American businessman for $2.3 billion (creating a tax certificate that would reduce Viacom's tax liability by about $600 million), Congress in 1995 voted to repeal the tax certificate program. Act of Apr. 11, 1995, Pub. L. No. 104-7, §2(a), 109 Stat. 93, repealing 26 U.S.C. §1071; Senators Join Opposition to Tax Break, Broadcasting & Cable (Mar. 20, 1995). The "plus" in the comparative hearing process was similarly eliminated, this time by a 1997 enactment (codified as §309(j) of the Communications Act) that for all intents and purposes ended the use of comparative hearings in favor, instead, of auctions as the assignment mechanism of choice. Section 309(j) does provide, however, that the FCC should "ensure that small businesses, rural telephone companies, and businesses owned by members of minority groups and women are given the opportunity to participate in the provision of spectrum-based services, and, for such purposes, consider the use of tax certificates, bidding preferences, and other procedures," 47 U.S.C. §309(j)(4)(D). Thus, we likely have not seen the last of these sorts of preference policies.

iv. Equal Employment Opportunity Regulations

The policies at issue in *Metro Broadcasting* were relevant only during particular events, namely the initial assignment of broadcast licenses, renewal hearings, and any proposed transfer from one licensee to another. But, throughout the licensing period, licensees are subject to a related and ongoing obligation: equal employment opportunity regulations. Those regulations are considered in the case excerpted below. As you read this case, ask yourself what would happen today if the programs at issue in *Metro Broadcasting* were challenged in the D.C. Circuit.

LUTHERAN CHURCH-MISSOURI SYNOD v. FCC

141 F.3d 344 (D.C. Cir. 1998)

Opinion for the court filed by Circuit Judge SILBERMAN, in which Circuit Judges WILLIAMS and SENTELLE concur.

SILBERMAN, Circuit Judge:

Lutheran Church-Missouri Synod appeals the Federal Communication Commission's finding that it transgressed equal employment opportunity regulations through the use of religious hiring preferences and inadequate minority recruiting.

The Commission has adopted equal employment opportunity (EEO) regulations that impose two basic obligations on radio stations. Stations are forbidden to discriminate in employment against any person "because of race, color, religion, national origin, or sex." 47 C.F.R. §73.2080(a) (1997). And stations must adopt an affirmative action "EEO program" targeted to minorities and women. 47 C.F.R. §73.2080(b) & (c) (1997). Such a program must include a plan for (1) disseminating the equal opportunity program to job applicants and employees; (2) using minority and women-specific recruiting sources; (3) evaluating the station's employment profile and job turnover against the availability of minorities and women in its recruitment area; (4) offering promotions to minorities and women in a nondiscriminatory fashion; and (5) analyzing its efforts to recruit, hire, and promote minorities and women. 47 C.F.R. §73.2080(c).

II

The Church contends that the affirmative action portion of the Commission's EEO regulations is a race-based employment program in violation of the equal protection component of the Fifth Amendment.

The Commission (but not the Department of Justice (DOJ)) asserts that the Church lacks Article III standing to raise an equal protection challenge since it-as opposed to a hypothetical non-minority employee-has not suffered an equal protection injury. It is undeniable, however, that the Church has been harmed by the Commission's order finding it in violation of the EEO regulations. The order is a black mark on the Church's previously spotless licensing record and could affect its chances of license renewal down the road. And the remedial reporting conditions, which require the Church to keep extremely detailed employment records, further aggrieve the Church by increasing an already significant regulatory burden.

Independent of the order, the regulations cause the Church economic harm by increasing the expense of maintaining a license. Every broadcast station must develop a fairly elaborate EEO program and document its compliance. 47 C.F.R. §73.2080(b) & (c). Particularly for smaller stations like [the ones at issue here], this requirement can be burdensome. It involves paperwork, monitoring, and spending more money on advertisements. And if the rules do force a station to discriminate, they expose it to risk of liability under 42 U.S.C. §1983.

To the extent the Commission suggests that the personal nature of the equal protection right precludes third party standing, the Supreme Court has explicitly rejected that view. When the law makes a litigant an involuntary participant in a discriminatory scheme, the litigant may attack that scheme by raising a third party's constitutional rights.

The Church argues that under Adarand Constructors, Inc. v. Pena, 515 U.S. 200 (1995), the Commission's use of racial classifications provokes strict scrutiny, a standard the EEO program cannot survive. The FCC has identified "diversity of programming" as the interest behind its EEO regulations. The Church protests that this is an insufficient interest and that furthermore, the regulations do not serve it. The Commission, applying its *King's Garden* policy [exempting religion broadcasts from the FCC's ban on religious discrimination, but only for employees reasonably connected to the espousal of religious philosophy over the air], decided that the Church could not prefer Lutheran to non-lutheran secretaries because low-level employees would have little or no effect on the broadcast of religious views. At the same time, however, the Commission has defended its affirmative action recruiting policy by arguing that *all* employees affect programming diversity. How, the Church asks, can the FCC maintain that the religion of a secretary will not affect programming but the race of a secretary will? After all, religious affiliation, a matter of affirmative intellectual and spiritual decision, is far more likely to affect programming than skin color. Appellant contends that the FCC's convoluted reasoning undermines the suggestion that there is any kind of link between the Commission's means and end, much less a narrowly tailored one.

Neither the Commission nor the Justice Department have claimed that the Fifth Amendment is wholly inapplicable to this case. If the regulations merely required stations to implement racially neutral recruiting and hiring programs, the equal protection guarantee would not be implicated. But as the Commission itself has said, "Our broadcast EEO rules require that broadcast licensees...establish and maintain an affirmative action program for qualified minorities and women."[11] Proceeding within the equal protection framework, the Commission and DOJ argue that we should review the EEO program under rational basis rather than the more demanding strict scrutiny standard which has tested race-based government classifications since Korematsu v. United States, 323 U.S. 214, 216 (1944). Though the Supreme Court did not initially apply strict scrutiny to federal "affirmative action" programs, *see* Metro Broadcasting, Inc. v. FCC, 497 U.S. 547 (1990), it recently reversed itself to hold that strict scrutiny applies whether or not the government's motivation to aid minorities can be thought "benign." *Adarand*, 515 U.S. at 227. The Commission and DOJ, however, argue that *Adarand* does not go so far as it appears. The Commission insists that *Adarand* reaches only race-conscious "hiring decisions." Taking a slightly different approach, the Justice Department urges that it only applies to race-conscious "decision-making." But both say that because the EEO regulations stop short of establishing preferences, quotas, or setasides, rational basis is the appropriate standard.

We rather doubt that restricting *Adarand* to race-based "decision-making" — as DOJ would have us do — would save these regulations from strict scrutiny. They affect all kinds of employment decisions. For example, when deciding how to fill job vacancies, the regulations require a station to choose minority- specific

---

11. 4 FCC Rcd. 1715 (1989). The gender classification has not been challenged in this case, so we will not address it. *But see* Lamprecht v. FCC, 958 F.2d 382 (D.C. Cir.1992).

referral sources. 47 C.F.R. §73.2080(c)(2). Likewise, an employer must conduct a formal analysis of its success in recruiting women and minorities and make decisions about its selection techniques and tests accordingly. 47 C.F.R. §73.2080(c)(5).

We need not decide this question, however, because the EEO regulations before us extend beyond outreach efforts and certainly influence ultimate hiring decisions. The crucial point is not, as the Commission and DOJ argue, whether they require hiring in accordance with fixed quotas; rather, it is whether they oblige stations to grant some degree of preference to minorities in hiring. We think the regulations do just that. The entire scheme is built on the notion that stations should aspire to a workforce that attains, or at least approaches, proportional representation. The EEO program guidelines instruct the broadcaster to:

> (3) Evaluate its employment profile and job turnover against the availability of minorities and women in its recruitment area. For example, this requirement may be met by:
>
>> (i) Comparing the composition of the relevant labor area with the composition of the station's workforce;
>>
>> (ii) Where there is *underrepresentation* of either minorities and/or women, examining the company's personnel policies and practices to assure that they do not inadvertently screen out any group and take appropriate action where necessary. Data on representation of minorities and women in the available labor force are generally available on metropolitan statistical area (MSA) or county basis.

47 C.F.R. §73.2080(c) (emphasis added). The very term "underrepresentation" necessarily implies that if such a situation exists, the station is behaving in a manner that falls short of the desired outcome. The regulations pressure stations to maintain a workforce that mirrors the racial breakdown of their "metropolitan statistical area."

The Commission and DOJ nevertheless insist that the FCC's program should be regarded as if it did no more, or not significantly more, than seek non-discriminatory treatment of women and minorities. That argument-which logically suggests the government should have challenged the very applicability of the Fifth Amendment-presupposes that non-discriminatory treatment typically will result in proportional representation in a station's workforce. The Commission provides no support for this dubious proposition and has in fact disavowed it, saying that "we do not believe that fair employment practices will necessarily result in the employment of any minority group in direct proportion to its numbers in the community." *EEO Processing Guidelines for Broadcast Renewal Applicants*, 79 FCC 2d 922, ¶19 (1980).

Nor can it be said that the Commission's parity goals do not pressure license holders to engage in race-conscious hiring. In 1980, the Commission issued processing guidelines disclosing the criteria it used to select stations for in-depth EEO review when their licenses came up for renewal:

> (1) stations with less than five full-time employees will continue to be exempt from having a written EEO program;

(2) stations with five to ten full-time employees will have their EEO program reviewed if minority groups and/or women are not employed on their full-time staffs at a ratio of 50% of their workforce availability overall and 25% in the upper-four Form 395 job categories;

(3) stations with 11 or more full-time employees will have their EEO programs reviewed if minority groups and/or women are not employed full time at a ratio of 50% of their availability in the workforce overall and 50% in the upper-four job categories; and

(4) all stations with 50 or more employees will have their EEO programs reviewed.

EEO Processing Guidelines for Broadcast Renewal Applicants, 46 RR 2d 1693 (1980). It cannot seriously be argued that this screening device does not create a strong incentive to meet the numerical goals. No rational firm-particularly one holding a government-issued license-welcomes a government audit. Even DOJ argued, in comments to the Commission recommending that these guidelines be changed, that they operated as a "*de facto* hiring quota," and that "broadcasters, in order to avoid the inconvenience and expense of being subjected to further review, will treat the guidelines as 'safe-harbors.'" *Amendment of Part 73*, 2 FCCR. 3967, ¶45 (1987).

In 1987, the Commission changed its policy to de-emphasize statistics, but this new policy did not abandon the 1980 numerical processing guidelines. *Amendment of Part 73*, 2 FCCR. 3967 (1987). Instead, the Commission now looks at them along with the descriptions of the station's EEO program and policies, any EEO complaints filed against it, and any other pertinent information available. *Id.*, ¶48–50. The FCC, to be sure, has emphasized that the guidelines should not be interpreted as a quota, and its licensing decisions indicate that stations cannot achieve compliance simply by meeting the 50% of parity goal. *See, e.g., Kelly Communications, Inc.*, 1997 WL 662077 (FCC Oct. 27, 1997) (licensee who hired at 50% of parity was nevertheless sanctioned for failing to keep recruiting records). But the fact that the FCC looks at more than "numbers" does not mean that numbers are insignificant. A station would be flatly imprudent to ignore any one of the factors it knows may trigger intense review-especially if that factor, like racial breakdown, is particularly influential. As a matter of common sense, a station can assume that a hard-edged factor like statistics is bound to be one of the more noticed screening criteria. The risk lies not only in attracting the Commission's attention, but also that of third parties. "Underrepresentation" is often the impetus (as it was in this case) for the filing of a petition to deny, which in turn triggers intense EEO review. *Amendment of Part 73*, ¶48. Further, and most significant in a station's calculus, the Commission itself has given every indication that the employment profile is a serious matter. In its proposed EEO forfeiture guidelines, for example, minority underrepresentation is grounds for an upward adjustment in forfeiture amount. *Streamlining Broadcast EEO Rule and Policies*, 11 FCCR. 5154 (1996). Similarly, the EEO regulation applicable to television stations warns that the Commission will send a letter recommending "any necessary improvements" to licensees whose minority representation falls below the FCC's processing guidelines. 47 C.F.R. §73.2080(d) (1997).

We do not think it matters whether a government hiring program imposes hard quotas, soft quotas, or goals. Any one of these techniques induces an employer to hire with an eye toward meeting the numerical target. As such, they can and surely will result in individuals being granted a preference because of their race. As the Court said in *Adarand*, "*All* governmental action based on race... should be subjected to detailed judicial inquiry." *Id.* at 226, 115 S.Ct. at 2112–13 (emphasis added). Strict scrutiny applies and we turn to whether, in accordance with recognized doctrine, the regulations are narrowly tailored to serve a compelling state interest.

The Commission has unequivocally stated that its EEO regulations rest solely on its desire to foster "diverse" programming content. The Justice Department, on the other hand, argues that the FCC's policy is supported by twin governmental goals of seeking diversity of programming and preventing employment discrimination. It may be that the Commission has framed its objective more narrowly because it doubts that it has authority to promulgate regulations on an anti-discrimination rationale. As we have observed elsewhere, "the FCC is not the Equal Employment Opportunity Commission...and a license renewal proceeding is not a Title VII suit." Bilingual Bicultural Coalition on Mass Media, Inc. v. FCC, 595 F.2d 621, 628 (D.C. Cir.1978) (en banc). The only possible statutory justification for the Commission to regulate workplace discrimination would be its obligation to safeguard the "public interest," and the Supreme Court has held that an agency may pass anti-discrimination measures under its public interest authority only insofar as discrimination relates to the agency's specific statutory charge. Thus the FCC can probably only regulate discrimination that affects "communication service"—here, that means programming. 47 U.S.C. §151 (1994). But it does not really matter why the FCC has expressed the government interest differently than DOJ. As the independent agency which promulgated the regulations in question, its view of the government interest it was pursuing must be accepted.

The Commission never defines exactly what it means by "diverse programming."[12] (Any real content based definition of the term may well give rise to enormous tensions with the First Amendment. *Compare Metro Broadcasting*, 497 U.S. at 567–68 (opinion of the Court) *with id.* at 616 (O'Connor, J., dissenting)). The government's formulation of the interest seems too abstract to be meaningful. The more appropriate articulation would seem the more particular: the fostering of programming that reflects minority viewpoints or appeals to minority tastes. Still, the Supreme Court, in *Metro Broadcasting*, recognized an abstract diversity interest as "important" without being much more precise about it than the Commission. And although *Metro Broadcasting*'s adoption of intermediate scrutiny was overruled in *Adarand*, its recognition of the government interest in "diverse" programming has not been disturbed by the Court. The government thus argues that we are bound by that determination.

We do not think that proposition at all evident. Even if *Metro Broadcasting* remained good law in that respect, it held only that the diversity interest was "important." We do not think diversity can be elevated to the "compelling" level, particularly when the Court has given every indication of wanting to cut back *Metro Broadcasting*. In that case, the majority's analysis of the government's "diversity" interest seems very much tied to the more forgiving standard

---

12. It is clear, though, that the Commission is not referring to format diversity—*i.e.*, the FCC's interest in ensuring that not every station on the spectrum is devoted to news radio.

of review it adopted. It is true that the Court, denying that the supposed "link between expanded minority ownership and broadcast diversity rest[s] on impermissible stereotyping," thought the Commission and Congress had produced adequate evidence of a nexus between minority ownership and programming that reflects a minority viewpoint. *Metro Broadcasting*, 497 U.S. at 579. Yet the Court never explained why it was in the government's interest to encourage the notion that minorities have racially based views. We do not mean to suggest that race has no correlation with a person's tastes or opinions.[13] We doubt, however, that the Constitution permits the government to take account of racially based differences, much less encourage them. One might well think such an approach antithetical to our democracy.

In *Metro Broadcasting*, four Justices (who were subsequently in the *Adarand* majority) argued that the government's desire to encourage broadcast content that reflected a racial view was at odds with equal protection. Even the majority in *Metro Broadcasting* who thought the government's interest "important" must have concluded implicitly that it was not "compelling"; otherwise, it is unlikely that the majority would have adopted a wholly new equal protection standard to decide the case as it did. After carefully analyzing *Metro Broadcasting*'s opinions and considering the impact of *Adarand*, it is impossible to conclude that the government's interest, no matter how articulated, is a compelling one.

As a final point, we note the sort of diversity at stake in this case has even less force than the "important" interest at stake in *Metro Broadcasting*. While the minority ownership preferences involved in *Metro Broadcasting* rested on an *inter-station* diversity rationale, the EEO rules seek *intrastation* diversity. It is at least understandable why the Commission would seek station to station differences, but its purported goal of making a single station all things to all people makes no sense. It clashes with the reality of the radio market, where each station targets a particular segment: one pop, one country, one news radio, and so on.

Even assuming that the Commission's interest were compelling, its EEO regulations are quite obviously not narrowly tailored. The majority in *Metro Broadcasting* never suggested that low-level employees, as opposed to upper-level employees, would have any broadcast influence. Nor did the Commission introduce a single piece of evidence in this case linking low-level employees to programming content. *See Lamprecht.* Indeed, as appellant emphasizes, the FCC's *King's Garden* policy indicates that the Commission itself does not believe that there is any connection between low-level employees and programming substance. The Commission reprimanded the Church for preferring Lutheran secretaries, receptionists, business managers, and engineers precisely because it found these positions not "connected to the espousal of religious philosophy over the air." Yet it has defended its affirmative action rules on the ground that minority employees bring di-

---

13. For example, BBDO's annual television survey consistently finds that blacks and whites prefer different television shows-during the 1996–97 season, the black "top twenty" list and the white "top twenty" list had only four programs in common. But it is not simply a question of race. Among teens aged 12 to 17, 8 out of 20 programs appeared on both lists; in the over 50 age group, there were 13 crossover programs. Latino and white viewing preferences, moreover, are very similar, with 13 of the top twenty programs in common. Race, by itself, seems a rather unreliable proxy for taste.

versity to the airwaves. The FCC would thus have us believe that low-level employees manage to get their "racial viewpoint" on the air but lack the influence to convey their religious views. That contradiction makes a mockery out of the Commission's contention that its EEO program requirements are designed for broadcast diversity purposes. The regulations could not pass the substantial relation prong of intermediate scrutiny, let alone the narrow tailoring prong of strict scrutiny.

Perhaps this is illustrative as to just how much burden the term "diversity" has been asked to bear in the latter part of the 20th century in the United States. It appears to have been coined both as a permanent justification for policies seeking racial proportionality in all walks of life ("affirmative action" has only a temporary remedial connotation) and as a synonym for proportional representation itself. It has, in our view, been used by the Commission in both ways. We therefore conclude that its EEO regulations are unconstitutional and cannot serve as a basis for its decision and order in this case.

Notes and Questions

1. Standing. The opinion starts with a discussion of standing. Why exactly does the Church have standing in this case? If the only harm identified by the Church had been that "black mark on the Church's previously spotless record," would the Court nevertheless have been correct to grant the Church standing to challenge the regulations at issue?

2. Intrastation and Interstation Diversity. Note that *Lutheran Church* distinguishes sharply between interstation and intrastation diversity. Why should we distinguish between these two kinds of diversity? Does the court overstate the difference between them? Are you persuaded that the "purported goal of making a single station all things to all people makes no sense"?

3. Subsequent Events. The government filed a petition for rehearing in the D.C. Circuit shortly after the above decision came down. When that court declined to grant a rehearing, however, the FCC decided not to seek Supreme Court review, leaving the opinion excerpted above as the last word on the case. In response to *Lutheran Church*, the FCC suspended certain mandates (for example, that broadcasters file annual employment reports) pending a full order designed to comply with *Lutheran Church*. In 2000, the Commission issued that order. *First Report and Order on Review of the Commission's Broadcast and Cable Equal Employment Opportunity Rules and Policies*, 15 FCC Rcd. 2329 (2000). As the title suggests, it applies both to broadcasters and cable entities. In the *Report and Order*, the FCC mandated outreach efforts—for instance, that broadcasters and cable entities widely disseminate information about job openings—that the FCC presented as race and gender neutral. ¶¶217–220. The *Order* also reinstated the requirement that broadcasters file annual employment reports, but stated that it would no longer use the employment profile data in those reports in screening renewal applications or assessing compliance with EEO program requirements. ¶6. Separately, individual commissioners have encouraged broadcasters to implement affirmative action programs even though they are no longer required to do so in light of *Missouri Synod*. Then-Chairman Kennard, for instance, offered to support broadcasters' efforts to relax limitations on the number of telecommunications properties a single party can own if broadcasters would in exchange help to increase the number of minority-owned stations. *See* Steven A. Holmes, Broadcast-ers Vow to Keep Affirmative Action, N.Y. Times (July 30, 1998), at A12.

III. LICENSE RENEWAL FOR INCUMBENTS

Spectrum licenses are of limited duration. Commercial television and radio licenses, for example, are awarded under current law for eight-year periods.[14] Licenses for advanced wireless services in the 746–764 MHz and 776–794 MHz bands expire after fourteen years.[15] Every licensee must therefore period-ically appear before the FCC and petition that its license be renewed. This gives the FCC extraordinary power to influence licensee behavior; to wit, every decision a licensee makes throughout its tenure is a decision made in the shadow of an implicit threat of an FCC response come renewal time. This form of implicit regulation—regulation through the threat of license non-re-newal or some lesser ramification, for example renewal for a shorter-than-nor-mal period—is a prime example of what is often referred to as regulation by raised eyebrow.

The big policy debate regarding license renewal has thus been the question of how much discretion the FCC should enjoy with respect to its renewal decisions. One possibility is to give the FCC broad discretion, the logic being that the FCC is supposed to select the most promising licensees, and greater discretion to ana-lyze an incumbent's record would maximize the FCC's ability to do just that. True, this might be a little unfair to incumbents: by its nature, the comparative hearing process requires that the FCC make comparisons between would-be li-censees and yet, in this setting, the FCC really would have nothing to compare the incumbent's record to, except perhaps a challenger's promises. But the FCC could surely account for this imbalance, for example by holding challengers to the promises they make. There are two possible advantages to empowering the FCC in this way: first, if subject to broad review, poor and even average incum-bents could be identified and replaced as their licenses expire; and, second, dur-ing their terms, licensees hoping to ultimately renew their licenses would be very responsive to regulation by raised eyebrow, thus empowering the FCC to adjust its policies from time to time and in that way respond to changing conditions.

Another possibility would be to constrain the FCC such that there was a strong presumption of renewal with perhaps some small, well articulated, and relatively stable list of standards that would have to be met before that presump-tion would take hold. Such an approach would allow the agency to weed out cer-tain types of poor or average licensees, but it would leave the agency with much less power to regulate implicitly. (Regulation by raised eyebrow works, after all,

---

14. 47 U.S.C. §307(c)(1).
15. In re Service Rules for the 746–764 and 776–794 MHz Bands, First Report and Order, 15 FCC Rcd. 476, 15 FCC Rcd. 8634 (2000) (excerpted in Chapter Three). Licensees in this band must meet periodic buildout benchmarks or risk license revocation.

only to the extent that the FCC has discretion in its renewal decisions.) The prime advantage of this approach would be that licensees would likely have stronger incentives to make long-term investments related to their licenses. A broadcast licensee, for instance, would be more likely to invest in expensive equipment and marketing if it knew that, so long as it follows the various announced FCC rules and meets any articulated renewal standards, it will be allowed to keep its license and thus reap long-term benefits from those investments.

For many years, the FCC and the D.C. Circuit struggled with these and other intermediate options. The Commission's position was complicated. On the one hand, many of the Commission's policies were not expressed in rigid rules. For example, a station that airs no local programming or that broadcasts mostly commercials does not violate any explicit Commission rule. This means that the FCC relies heavily on regulation by raised eyebrow. On the other hand, the FCC never seemed to want to maximize its own discretion; quite the opposite, for many years the FCC took the view that licensees should enjoy a strong renewal expectancy, and in practice the FCC then, as now, almost always renewed the licenses of broadcasters who had not violated any explicit FCC rules. Interestingly, it was the D.C. Circuit that pushed for greater FCC discretion, arguing that the FCC's job is to evaluate licensees and grant licenses only to the best available parties.

Today, the debate has been resolved by statute. Section 204 of the Telecommunications Act of 1996, 47 U.S.C. §309(k), provides that, when an incumbent broadcaster seeks renewal of its license, the FCC must grant the application if the licensee has served the public interest, committed no "serious violations" of the Communications Act or the FCC's rules, and has not committed any other violations "which, taken together, would constitute a pattern of abuse." Only if the incumbent flunks one of those tests — and the agency has determined that some sanction short of non-renewal would be insufficient — is the Commission allowed to consider a competing application in a comparative hearing.[16] Importantly, this renewal presumption precludes the FCC from considering other licensees. Section 309(k) explicitly states that "the Commission shall not consider whether the public interest, convenience, and necessity might be served by the grant of a license to a person other than the renewal applicant."

In response to the 1996 Act, and much to the delight of incumbents, the FCC abolished comparative hearings for renewal applicants in *Broadcast License Renewal Procedures*, 11 FCC Rcd. 6363 (1996). The question that we explore in the materials below, however, is whether such a strong renewal presumption is wise, or whether instead it is simply evidence of existing broadcasters' political clout. We begin with the argument against a strong renewal presumption, as made by the D.C. Circuit in the 1971 case of Citizens Communications Center v. FCC.

---

16. Options here might include renewal for a shorter-than-normal duration, *see* 47 U.S.C. §309(k)(2), or renewal plus a fine under 47 U.S.C. §503.

CITIZENS COMMUNICATIONS CENTER v. FCC
447 F.2d 1201 (D.C. Cir. 1971)

Opinion for the court filed by Circuit Judge WRIGHT, in which Circuit Judges MacKINNON and WILKEY concur. Concurring opinion filed by Circuit Judge MacKINNON.

WRIGHT, Circuit Judge:

Petitioners challenge the legality of the "Policy Statement on Comparative Hearings Involving Regular Renewal Applicants," 22 FCC 2d 424 (1970). Briefly stated, the disputed Commission policy is that, in a hearing between an incumbent applying for renewal of his radio or television license and a mutually exclusive applicant, the incumbent shall obtain a controlling preference by demonstrating substantial past performance without serious deficiencies. Thus if the incumbent prevails on the threshold issue of the substantiality of his past record, all other applications are to be dismissed without a hearing on their own merits. We hold that the 1970 Policy Statement violates the Federal Communications Act of 1934, as interpreted by both the Supreme Court and this court.

The Communications Act itself places the incumbent in the same position as an initial applicant. Under the 1952 amendment to the Act, both initial and renewal applicants must demonstrate that the grant or continuation of a license will serve the "public interest, convenience, and necessity." The Communications Act itself says nothing about a presumption in favor of incumbent licensees at renewal hearings.

Nonetheless, the history of Commission decisions and of the decisions of this court reflected until recently an operational bias in favor of incumbent licensees. The well known *Hearst*[17] and *Wabash Valley*[18] cases were typical of the Commission's past renewal rulings in that their actual effect was to give the incumbent a virtually insuperable advantage on the basis of his past broadcast record *per se*. In *Hearst* the Commission ruled that the incumbent's unexceptional record of past programming performance, coupled with the unavoidable uncertainty whether the challenger would be able to carry out its program proposals, was sufficient to overcome the incumbent's demerits on other comparative criteria. And in *Wabash Valley* the Commission held that a newcomer seeking to oust an incumbent must make a showing of superior service and must have some preference on other comparative criteria.

Then, in the very controversial *WHDH*[19] case, the Commission for the first time in its history, in applying comparative criteria in a renewal proceeding, deposed the incumbent and awarded the frequency to a challenger. Finding that because the incumbent's programming service had been "within the bounds of the average" it was entitled to no preference, and that the incumbent was inferior on

---

17. Hearst Radio, Inc. (WBAL), 15 FCC 1149 (1951).
18. Wabash Valley Broadcasting Corp. (WTHI-TV), 35 FCC 677 (1963).
19. WHDH, Inc., 16 FCC 2d 1 (1969), *aff'd sub nom.* Greater Boston Television Corp. v. FCC, 444 F.2d 841 (1970).

the comparative criteria of diversification and integration, the Commission awarded the license to one of the challengers.

The *WHDH* decision became the immediate subject of fierce attack, provoking criticism from those who feared that it represented a radical departure from previous law and that it threatened the stability of the broadcast industry by undermining large financial investments made by prominent broadcasters in reliance upon the assumption that licenses once granted would be routinely renewed. While the Commission's decision was still on appeal to this court, a bill introduced by Senator Pastore, Chairman of the Communications Subcommittee of the Senate Commerce Committee, proposed to require a two-stage hearing wherein the renewal issue would be determined prior to and exclusive of any evaluation of challengers' applications. The bill provided that if the Commission finds the past record of the licensee to be in the public interest, it shall grant renewal. Competing applications would be permitted to be filed only if the incumbent's license is not renewed. Although more than 100 congressmen and 23 senators quickly announced their support, the bill was bitterly attacked in the Senate hearings by a number of citizens groups testifying, *inter alia*, that the bill was racist, that it would exclude minorities from access to media ownership in most large communities, and that it was inimical to community efforts at improving television programming.

The impact of such citizen opposition measurably slowed the progress of S. 2004. Then, without any formal rule making proceedings, the Commission suddenly issued its own January 15, 1970 Policy Statement, and the Senate bill was thereafter deferred in favor of the Commission's "compromise." The 1970 Policy Statement retains the single hearing approach but provides that the renewal issue must be determined first in a proceeding in which challengers are permitted to appear only for the limited purpose of calling attention to the incumbent's failings.[20] Thus, in effect, the Policy Statement administratively "enacts" what the Pastore bill sought to do.

III

Superimposed full length over the preceding historical analysis of the "full hearing" requirement of section 309(e) of the Communications Act is the towering shadow of Ashbacker Radio Corp. v. FCC, 326 U.S. 327 (1945), and its progeny. *Ashbacker* holds that under section 309(e), where two or more applications for permits or licenses are mutually exclusive, the Commission must conduct one full comparative hearing of the applications. Although *Ashbacker* involved two original applications, no one has seriously suggested that its principle does not apply to renewal proceedings as well.

To circumvent the *Ashbacker* strictures, the Policy Statement would limit the "comparative" hearing to a single issue—whether the incumbent licensee had

---

20. The Commission has in effect abolished the comparative hearing mandated by §309(a) & (e) and converted the comparative hearing into a petition to deny proceeding. The petition to deny proceeding is separately provided for in the Act under §309(d), but this section is intended to cover only those situations in which the petitioner does not seek the license himself but seeks only to prevent its award again to the incumbent.

rendered "substantial" past performance without serious deficiencies. If the examiner finds that the licensee has rendered such service, the "comparative" hearing is at an end. Challenging applicants would thus receive no hearing at all on their own applications, contrary to the express provision of section 309(e) which requires a "full hearing."

In *Ashbacker* the Commission had promised the challenging applicant a hearing on his application after the rival application was granted. The Supreme Court in *Ashbacker* said that such a promise was "an empty thing." At least the Commission here does not make any empty promises. It simply denies the competing applicants the "full hearing" promised them by section 309(e) of the Act. The proposition that the 1970 Policy Statement violates section 309(e) as interpreted in *Ashbacker* is so obvious it need not be labored.

We do not dispute, of course, that incumbent licensees should be judged primarily on their records of past performance. Insubstantial past performance should preclude renewal of a license. The licensee, having been given the chance and having failed, should be through. At the same time, superior performance should be a plus of major significance in renewal proceedings.[21] Indeed, as *Ashbacker* recognizes, in a renewal proceeding, a new applicant is under a greater burden to "make the comparative showing necessary to displace an established licensee." 326 U.S. at 332. But under section 309(e) he must be given a chance.[22]

The suggestion that the possibility of nonrenewal, however remote, might chill uninhibited, robust and wide-open speech cannot be taken lightly. But the Commission, of course, may not penalize exercise of First Amendment rights. And the statute does provide for judicial review.

---

21. The court recognizes that the public itself will suffer if incumbent licensees cannot reasonably expect renewal when they have rendered superior service. Given the incentive, an incumbent will naturally strive to achieve a level of performance which gives him a clear edge on challengers at renewal time. But if the Commission fails to articulate the standards by which to judge superior performance, and if it is thus impossible for an incumbent to be reasonably confident of renewal when he renders superior performance, then an incumbent will be under an unfortunate temptation to lapse into mediocrity, to seek the protection of the crowd by eschewing the creative and the venturesome in programming and other forms of public service. The Commission in rule making proceedings should strive to clarify in both quantitative and qualitative terms what constitutes superior service. Along with elimination of excessive and loud advertising and delivery of quality programs, one test of superior service should certainly be whether and to what extent the incumbent has reinvested the profit on his license to the service of the viewing and listening public.

22. Since one very significant aspect of the "public interest, convenience, and necessity" is the need for diverse and antagonistic sources of information, the Commission simply cannot make a valid public interest determination without considering the extent to which the ownership of the media will be concentrated or diversified by the grant of one or another of the applications before it. As new interest groups and hitherto silent minorities emerge in our society, they should be given the same stake in and chance to broadcast on our radio and television frequencies. No more than a dozen of 7,500 broadcast licenses issued are owned by racial minorities. The effect of the *1970 Policy Statement* would certainly have been to perpetuate this dismaying situation. Diversification is a factor properly to be weighed and balanced with other important factors, including the renewal applicant's past record, at a renewal hearing. [Footnote relocated.]

[Concurring opinion of Judge MacKINNON is omitted.]

Notes and Questions

1. The Commission's Error. In effect, the *Policy Statement* declared that, no matter what other advantages a challenger might offer, they would be overcome by an incumbent's demonstration of substantial past performance without serious deficiencies. Precisely what was wrong with that declaration?

(a) *Ashbacker*. The court seems to say that the *Policy Statement* conflicts with the requirements of *Ashbacker*. But the court also states that "superior performance should be a plus of major significance in renewal proceedings." Didn't the *Policy Statement* simply hold that this plus would be sufficient to cancel out any other plus that a non-incumbent challenger might prove and, therefore, once this superior performance plus was awarded, there would be no need to continue the comparative hearing? Surely, *Ashbacker* does not require a comparative hearing once an insurmountable, determinative fact has been established, does it?

(b) Regulatory Responsibility. Was the FCC's error, then, a failure to employ the license renewal process as a tool for regulating industry behavior? Does the court hold that the FCC lacks authority to renew licenses of broadcasters who emit "excessive and loud advertising" or that it must take account of an applicant's membership (or lack of it) in "new interest groups and hitherto silent minorities"?

2. Further Litigation. In the opinion that follows, the FCC and the D.C. Circuit were able to agree on a renewal expectancy standard acceptable to both institutions.

CENTRAL FLORIDA ENTERPRISES v. FCC
683 F.2d 503 (D.C. Cir. 1982) *cert. denied*, 468 U.S. 1084 (1983)

Opinion for the court filed by Circuit Judge WILKEY, in which ROBINSON, Chief Judge, and FLANNERY, District Judge, concur.

WILKEY, Circuit Judge:

The appeal before us is taken from a new decision, Cowles Broadcasting, Inc., 86 FCC 2d 993 (1981), by the Federal Communications Commission after our opinion in Central Florida Enterprises v. FCC, 598 F.2d 37 (D.C. Cir. 1978) (*Central Florida I*), vacated the Commission's earlier orders involving the present parties. The FCC had granted the renewal of incumbent's license, but we held that the Commission's fact-finding and analysis on certain issues before it were inadequate, and that its method of balancing the factors for and against renewal was faulty. On remand, while the FCC has again concluded that the license should be renewed, it has also assuaged our concerns that its analysis was too cursory and has adopted a new policy for comparative renewal proceedings which meets the criteria we set out in *Central Florida I*. Accordingly, and with certain caveats, we affirm the Commission's decision.

Central Florida Enterprises has challenged the FCC's decision to renew Cowles Broadcasting's license to operate on Channel 2 in Daytona Beach, Florida. In the case here, there were four considerations potentially cutting against Cowles: its illegal move of its main studio, the involvement of several related companies in mail fraud, its ownership of other communications media, and its relative (to Central Florida) lack of management-ownership integration. On the other hand, Cowles' past performance record was "superior," *i.e.*, "sound, favorable and substantially above a level of mediocre service which might just minimally warrant renewal." 62 FCC 2d 953, 955 (1977).

In its decision appealed in *Central Florida I* the FCC concluded that the reasons undercutting Cowles' bid for renewal did "not outweigh the substantial service Cowles rendered to the public during the last license period." *Id.* at 958. Accordingly, the license was renewed. Our reversal was rooted in a twofold finding. First, the Commission had inadequately investigated and analyzed the four factors weighing against Cowles' renewal. Second, the process by which the FCC weighed these four factors against Cowles' past record was never "even vaguely described" and, indeed, "the Commission's handling of the facts of this case [made] embarrassingly clear that the FCC [had] practically erected a presumption of renewal that is inconsistent with the full hearing requirement" of the Communications Act. 598 F.2d at 50, 51.

On remand the Commission has followed our directives and corrected, point by point, the inadequate investigation and analysis of the four factors cutting against Cowles' requested renewal. The Commission concluded that, indeed, three of the four merited an advantage for Central Florida, and on only one (the mail fraud issue) did it conclude that nothing needed to be added on the scale to Central's plan or removed from Cowles'. We cannot fault the Commission's actions here.

We are left, then, with evaluating the way in which the FCC weighed Cowles' main studio move violation and Central's superior diversification and integration, on the one hand, against Cowles' substantial record of performance on the other.

We believe that the formulation by the FCC in its latest decision is a permissible way to incorporate some renewal expectancy while still undertaking the required comparative hearing. The new policy, as we understand it, is simply this: renewal expectancy is to be a factor weighed with all the other factors, and the better the past record, the greater the renewal expectancy "weight."

> In our view [states the FCC], the strength of the expectancy depends on the merit of the past record. Where, as in this case, the incumbent rendered substantial but not superior service, the "expectancy" takes the form of a comparative preference weighed against [the] other factors.... An incumbent performing in a superior manner would receive an even stronger preference. An incumbent rendering minimal service would receive no preference.

86 FCC 2d at 1012.

The reasons given by the Commission for factoring in some degree of renewal expectancy are rooted in a concern that failure to do so would hurt broadcast *consumers*.

The justification for a renewal expectancy [states the FCC] is three-fold. (1) There is no guarantee that a challenger's paper proposals will, in fact, match the incumbent's proven performance. Thus, not only might replacing an incumbent be entirely gratuitous, but *it might even deprive the community of an acceptable service and replace it with an inferior one.* (2) Licensees should be encouraged through the likelihood of renewal to make investments *to ensure quality service. Comparative renewal proceedings cannot function as a "competitive spur" to licensees if their dedication to the community is not rewarded.* (3) Comparing incumbents and challengers as if they were both new applicants could lead to a haphazard restructuring of the broadcast industry especially considering the large number of group owners. *We cannot readily conclude that such a restructuring could serve the public interest.*

Id. at 1013 (emphasis added). We are relying, then, on the FCC's commitment that renewal expectancy will be factored in for the benefit of the public, not for incumbent broadcasters.

There is a danger of course, that the FCC's new approach could still degenerate into precisely the sort of irrebuttable presumption in favor of renewal that we have warned against. But this did not happen in the case before us today, and our reading of the Commission's decision gives us hope that if the FCC applies the standard in the same way in future cases, it will not happen in them either. The standard is new, however, and much will depend on how the Commission applies it and fleshes it out. Of particular importance will be the definition and level of service it assigns to "substantial"—and whether that definition is ever found to be "opaque to judicial review," "wholly unintelligible," or based purely on "administrative 'feel.'"[23]

In this case, however, the Commission was painstaking and explicit in its balancing. The Commission discussed in quite specific terms, for instance, the items it found impressive in Cowles' past record. It stressed and listed numerous programs demonstrating Cowles' "local community orientation" and "responsive[ness] to community needs," discussed the percentage of Cowles' programming devoted to news, public affairs, and local topics, and said it was "impressed by [Cowles'] reputation in the community. Seven community leaders and three public officials testified that [Cowles] had made outstanding contributions to the local community. Moreover, the record shows no complaints...." The Commission concluded that "Cowles' record [was] more than minimal," was in fact "'substantial,' *i.e.,* 'sound, favorable and substantially above a level of mediocre service which might just minimally warrant renewal.'"[24]

It discussed the integration and diversification disadvantages of Cowles and conceded that Central had an edge on these issues—"slight" for integration,

---

23. *Central Florida I,* 598 F.2d at 50, 59. We think it would be helpful if at some point the Commission defined and explained the distinctions, if any, among: substantial, meritorious, average, above average, not above average, not far above average, above mediocre, more than minimal, solid, sound, favorable, not superior, not exceptional, and unexceptional—all terms used by the parties to describe what the FCC found Cowles' level of performance to have been. We are especially interested to know what the standard of comparison is in each case. "Average" compared to all applicants? "Mediocre" compared to all incumbents? "Favorable" with respect to the FCC's expectations?

24. 86 FCC 2d at 1006–08.

"clear" for diversification. But it reasoned that "structural factors such as [these] — of primary importance in a new license proceeding — should have lesser weight compared with the preference arising from substantial past service."[25]

We note, however, that despite the finding that Cowles' performance was "substantial," *i.e.*, "sound, favorable and substantially above a level of mediocre service," the combination of Cowles' main studio rule violation and Central's diversification and integration advantages made this a "close and difficult case."[26] Again, we trust that this is more evidence that the Commission's weighing did not, and will not, amount to automatic renewal for incumbents.

We are somewhat reassured by a recent FCC decision granting, for the first time since at least 1961, on *comparative* grounds the application of the challenger for a radio station license and denying the renewal application of the incumbent licensee.[27] In that decision the Commission found that the *incumbent deserved no renewal expectancy* for his past program record and that his application was inferior to the challenger's on comparative grounds. Indeed, it was the *incumbent's* preferences on the diversification and integration factors which were overcome (there, by the challenger's superior programming proposals and longer broadcast week).

Finally, we must note that we are still troubled by the fact that the record remains that an incumbent *television* licensee has never been denied renewal in a comparative challenge. American television viewers will be reassured, although a trifle baffled, to learn that even the worst television stations — those which are, presumably, the ones picked out as vulnerable to a challenge — are so good that they never need replacing. We suspect that somewhere, sometime, somehow, some television licensee *should* fail in a comparative renewal challenge, but the FCC has never discovered such a licensee yet. As a court we cannot say that it must be Cowles here. Accordingly the Commission's decision is affirmed.

Notes and Questions

1. **Come Full Circle?** Does the 1996 Act take us back to where the FCC started — that a licensee who demonstrates substantial past performance without serious deficiencies has an application that cannot be beaten? If so, is there anything wrong with that?

2. **Excessive and Loud Advertising.** What has become of the D.C. Circuit's admonitions to the FCC to employ the renewal process, *inter alia*, to police against "excessive and loud advertising," to foster "quality programs," and to extend a stake in radio and television frequencies to "new interest groups and hitherto

---

25. *Id.* at 1009–10, 1015. The FCC argues that diversification and integration should not be given "heavy weight in the comparative renewal context" since "challengers could easily structure their proposals to be superior to the incumbent's," resulting in possible "substantial restructuring of the industry with possible disruptions of service" and a loss of "incentive to provide quality programming." *Id.* at 1016.

26. *Id.* at 1006, 1018.

27. In re Application of Simon Geller, FCC Docket Nos. 22104–05 (Rel. June 15, 1982). [Ed. In 1985, the FCC reversed the 1982 *Geller* decision cited here. The 1985 *Geller* order is excerpted later in this Chapter.]

silent minorities"? In particular, have the FCC, the Congress, and the D.C. Circuit now agreed that the goals of diversification and integration are less important than the goal of establishing a legally protected renewal expectancy?

3. Practical Implications. Specifically, what did Cowles show to demonstrate its "sound, favorable" past performance? If a licensee were determined to assure its renewal expectancy by compiling a similar record, how difficult or expensive would it be to do so?

4. Deregulation. As the court noted in *Cowles*, incumbents who sought renewal and had not violated express Commission rules almost always prevailed, even before the 1996 Act. One reason for this was the power of the renewal expectancy factor. Another was the fact that, during the 1980s, the FCC removed many of the requirements and prohibitions that had previously been placed on radio and television licensees. These actions had the effect of making successful challenges to renewal applications difficult. Even though a would-be rival could still look at the incumbent's track record and try to show deficiencies, deregulation by the agency meant that there were not many relevant facts that could be brought forward.

Below we survey some of the principal changes that took place in the 1980s. Note that, in almost all of these decisions, the Commission's principal rationale for changing the requirement, standard, or guideline was that the FCC was not able to outperform the marketplace in assuring that licensees served the public interest. Note, further, that all but the first two changes listed here resulted from a combination of two seminal pronouncements: *In re Deregulation of Radio*, 84 FCC 2d 968 (1981) and *In re Deregulation of Commercial Television*, 98 FCC 2d 1076 (1984).

(a) **Fraudulent Billing and Network Clipping.** The FCC deleted its rules against fraudulent billing (*e.g.*, billing twice for one ad) and network clipping (cutting out the network's commercials to insert commercials sold locally by the station) in *Elimination of Unnecessary Broadcast Regulation*, 59 Rad. Reg. 2d 1500 (1986). Violations of these rules were the principal reasons for many refusals to renew during the 1970s.

(b) **Character.** As we noted earlier in the chapter, "character" was also eliminated in the 1980s as an issue to be considered in comparative hearings, at least so long as any character deficiency did not rise to the level of questioning the applicant's basic qualifications (*i.e.*, its ability to qualify for a license in even a non-contested proceeding). *Character Qualifications in Broadcasting Licensing*, 102 FCC 2d 1179 (1986). In a subsequent adjustment to that ruling, the Commission stated that it would be concerned with (a) fraudulent representations to government units; (b) violations of antitrust law involving a medium of mass communications; and (c) any felony or "serious misdemeanor" conviction. *Character Qualifications in Broadcast Licensing*, 5 FCC Rcd. 3252 (1990).

(c) **Post Card Renewal.** Perhaps most importantly, the FCC (in the two pronouncements mentioned above) authorized commercial radio and television stations to renew their licenses simply by filling out a five-question form. This practice continues today. The form provides: (1) information concerning the licensee's equal employment opportunity program; (2) a description of the licensee's other media ownership interests; (3) a certification of compliance with the alien ownership requirements of the 1934 Act; (4) any necessary disclosures about the licensee's character; and (5) a certification that the licensee has placed all required documents in its public file. Thus, renewal forms provide scant information on which to mount a challenge to an incumbent and, similarly, scant information through which the FCC might itself monitor and evaluate licensees.

(d) **Non-Entertainment Programming.** The same pronouncements eliminated certain non-entertainment programming processing guidelines. Prior to 1981, the Commission maintained a series of processing guidelines for renewal applications from radio or VHF television stations. These guidelines specified how much non-entertainment programming (expressed as a percentage of all programming) a licensee ideally should air. The renewal application of a licensee that met or exceeded these percentage guidelines could be routinely granted, pursuant to delegated authority, by the Commission's Broadcast Bureau. The renewal application of a licensee that fell short of those guidelines had to be brought to the full Commission's attention, where it could be designated for hearing.

(e) **Commercialization.** The FCC had also specified maximum percentages of broadcast time that could be devoted to commercials without triggering full Commission review of a renewal application. These processing guidelines were eliminated for both radio and television.

(f) **Ascertainment.** All radio and television license applicants formerly were required to complete a detailed study (ascertainment) of the needs of the community in which the applicant sought to be licensed. The FCC had prescribed an intricate series of steps necessary to complete the process. (The Commission had once solemnly addressed the question of whether an ascertainment interview was insufficiently serious because it took place at a restaurant where a belly dancer performed. Doubleday Broadcasting Co., Inc., 56 FCC 2d 333 (1975).) The FCC also had specified nineteen interest groups that the applicant was required to interview. The list included the elderly, youth, and women, but the FCC refused to add homosexuals or disabled persons. In place of the deleted ascertainment rules, the Commission starting in the 1980s simply required that new applicants file programming proposals and that licensees seeking renewal determine the issues facing their community by any reasonable means. It thus became much more difficult for would-be challengers to structure a challenge around the inadequacy of the applicant's ascertainment effort and, again, much more difficult for the FCC itself to monitor and evaluate licensee behavior.

(g) **Program Logs.** Lastly, commercial radio and television licensees were excused from keeping detailed program logs. Instead, starting in the 1980s, licensees needed only to place in a public file, every three months, a list of the programs that had provided the station's most significant treatment of community issues during the past quarter. Potential challengers thus no longer had ready-made access to all of the incumbent's previous programming decisions.

5. Empirical Evidence. Denials of license renewals are rare.[28] During the 1970s, for example, the Commission revoked or denied only sixty-four radio and televi-

---

28. Even after the 1996 Act strengthened the renewal presumption, denial of renewal sometimes occurs. In 1999, by a 3-2 vote, the Commission denied the renewal application of Trinity Broadcasting of Florida, finding that Trinity had lied to the Commission in asserting that two of its stations were controlled by racial minorities. (The multiple ownership rules in effect at the time limited the number of stations in which a person could have an attribut-

sion station licenses. Moreover, a study of those denials and revocations by Weiss, Ostroff, and Clift[29] reveals that, even before *Cowles* and the deregulation orders, factors mentioned in the *Policy Statement on Comparative Broadcast Hearings* rarely accounted for license revocations or refusals to renew. Instead, the most frequent reasons given by the agency were: misrepresentations to the Commission (18); abandonment of license or failure to prosecute renewal (16); departure from promised programming (11); fraudulent billing practices (11); and unauthorized transfer of control (10). In most cases, more than one reason was given. Over-commercialization was cited once, violation of the personal attack rules twice, and fairness violations three times. Further, the authors note that, even when used, programming-related rationales "were usually part of a longer litany of charges against the licensee." The Commission, in short, was reluctant to rely on subjective factors alone when denying a renewal application.

6. Renewal Expectancies. This section began with a summary of the conventional wisdom with respect to renewal presumptions. But, having now thought about the issue from a variety of perspectives, are you convinced that the conventional wisdom is correct? For example, conventional wisdom has it that a renewal presumption increases a licensee's incentive to make long-term investments related to its license. But couldn't the incentive to make long-term investments be maintained by a system that denied incumbents any renewal expectancy but, instead, allowed rejected incumbents to auction off their licenses to the highest bidder? Any long-term investment would increase the value of the relevant license in that auction, would it not?

Relatedly, did Congress understand that it could grant a renewal expectancy and yet still seriously review incumbents' records? For instance, is there any argument against requiring that an incumbent satisfy a set of stringent criteria before being awarded a strong renewal presumption? So long as those criteria are well articulated *ex ante*, the FCC's discretion would be minimized and so licensees would still have a strong incentive to make long-term investments, right? Did Congress let incumbents off too easily, then?

IV. LICENSE TRANSFERS

Licensees have always been free to transfer their licenses to other owners. In the days when the FCC assigned licenses by hearing instead of by auction, there

---

able interest to twelve, but a person could have an interest in additional stations that were "minority-controlled.") 14 FCC Rcd. 13570 (1999). And even in that case, the FCC order did not last, because the D.C. Circuit vacated the FCC's denial of Trinity's license renewal application. Trinity Broadcasting of Florida, Inc. v. FCC, 211 F.3d 618 (D.C. Cir. 2000). The court ruled that Trinity did not have fair warning of the FCC's interpretation of "minority-controlled" as requiring not only that a majority of an applicant's board of directors be minorities, but also that an applicant demonstrate actual control by minorities. *Id.* at 631–32.

29. Frederic A. Weiss et al., Station License Revocations and Denials of Review, 1970–78, 29 Journal of Broadcasting 69 (1980).

was a brief waiting period during which the party originally awarded a license was not allowed to sell it. Specifically, between 1962 and 1982, a broadcast licensee had to wait three years from the moment it was awarded the license before it would be allowed to transfer that license to another owner;[30] and, after 1982, the waiting period was reduced to one year, and, at that, only for licensees who won their licenses in comparative hearings.[31] The reason to have any waiting period at all was that waiting periods gave the FCC's initial assignment hearings meaning. A licensee selected by the FCC had to keep its license for at least some length of time, even if the unsuccessful applicant was willing to purchase it from the successful one.

All this became moot when the FCC abandoned hearings and began to make initial assignments by auction. Today, then, licensees are free to transfer their licenses at will, subject only to the relatively limited hearings authorized by section 310(d) of the Communications Act, 47 U.S.C. §310(d). That provision reads in relevant part:

> No construction permit or station license . . . shall be transferred . . . to any person except upon application to the Commission and upon finding by the Commission that the public interest, convenience, and necessity will be served thereby. . . . [B]ut in acting thereon the Commission may not consider whether the public interest, convenience, and necessity might be served by the transfer, assignment, or disposal of the permit or license to a person other than the proposed transferee or assignee.

Notes and Questions

1. The Public Interest Standard. Section 310(d) again requires that the FCC define the "public interest, convenience, and necessity." Can you see why that question is in many ways easier here than it would be in, say, the context of a comparative hearing regarding license renewal?

2. Considering Other Possible Transferees. That said, can you defend the part of the statute that forbids the Commission from considering whether the public interest might be better served by transfer to some third party? Did Congress overlook a better approach?

3. Format Changes. The materials that follow focus on one of the few significant issues to arise in the context of transfer hearings: the question of whether (and how) the FCC should analyze transfers that would likely lead to a change in the programming mix available in a given community. That is, the materials below consider how the FCC should react if, for example, the local classical music station petitions to sell its license to a new owner who proposes to use the license to air heavy metal music all day, every day.

---

30. Amendment of Part I of the Commission's Rules Adding Section 1.365 Concerning Applications for Voluntary Assignments or Transfers of Control, 32 FCC 689 (1962).

31. Elimination of the Three Year Rule and Underlying Anti-Trafficking Policy, 52 Radio Reg. (P&F) 1081 (1982).

CHANGES IN THE ENTERTAINMENT
FORMATS OF BROADCAST STATIONS

60 FCC 2d 858 (1976) rev'd, 610 F.2d 838
(D.C. Cir. 1979) , aff'd, 450 U.S. 582 (1981)

2. This Inquiry grows out of the opinion of the Court of Appeals, en banc, in Citizens Committee to Save WEFM, Inc. v. FCC, 506 F.2d 246 (D.C. Cir. 1974), the latest in a line of cases which hold that when an application for the sale of a radio station license is before the Commission, and in connection with that sale the purchaser intends to discontinue the station's existing entertainment format, if there has been expressed a significant amount of public protest to the effect that this change of format, if completed, would deprive the public of an entertainment format not otherwise available in the market, then the Commission must hold a hearing pursuant to section 309 of the Communications Act, as amended, to determine whether the public interest would be served by a grant of the application.

11. The Commission has long been reluctant to define and enforce the "public interest" in entertainment format preservation, because of both practical considerations and our understanding of the structure and meaning of the Communications Act. The practical problems are simple to comprehend. To determine, in the context of a prospective format change, whether the public interest would be served by allowing it, we must ascertain: (1) what the station's existing format is; (2) whether there are any reasonable substitutes for that format in the station's market; (3) if there are not, whether the benefits accruing to the public from the format change outweigh the public detriment which the format abandonment would entail. Moreover, where a prospective purchaser alleged that its proposed new format would add as much program diversity to the communities in its service area as the abandonment of the old format would subtract, evidence would have to be heard on this issue as well.

14. In practical terms, "format" means program material. As Commissioner Robinson has put it: "What makes one format unique makes all formats unique.... Questions of pacing and style, the personalities of on-the-air talent (both individually and in combination with one another) all contribute to those fugitive values that radio people call a station's 'sound' and that citizens' groups (and alas, appellate judges) call format."

15. The Commission does not know, as a matter of indwelling administrative expertise, whether a particular format is "unique" or, indeed, assuming that it is, whether it has been deviated from by a licensee.

16. The evidence on this record supports the conclusion that the marketplace is the best way to allocate entertainment formats in radio, whether the hoped for result is expressed in First Amendment terms (i.e., promoting the greatest diversity of listening choices for the public) or in economic terms (i.e., maximizing the welfare of consumers of radio programs).[32] We recognize that

---

32. [Ed. Elsewhere in the Order, at ¶8, the FCC notes that "broadcasters are to compete with one another, and they must necessarily do so in the domain of program formats, because there is virtually no other form that competition among broadcasters can take."]

the market for radio advertisers is not a completely faithful mirror of the listening preferences of the public at large. But we are not required to measure any system of allocation against the standard of perfection; we find on the basis of the record before us that it is the best available means of producing the diversity to which the public is entitled. A description for the advertising trade of the radio stations in the New York and Washington, D.C. markets shows that in large markets, with many aural services and intense competition, there appears an almost bewildering array of diversity. In New York, the menu includes all-news, classical music, rhythm and blues, Jewish ethnic, Greek ethnic, Spanish, country, modern country, country and gospel, talk, easy listening, middle of the road, show tunes, beautiful music, popular standard, and one which calls itself "mellow." How these various program themes differ from one another, and how each is faithful to its own conception, are questions we need not reach to observe the variety of choices available to radio listeners in the New York market.

17. Format allocation by market forces rather than by fiat has another advantage as well. It enables consumers to give a rough expression of whether their preference for diversity within a given format outweighs the desire for diversity among different formats. As Commissioner Robinson has observed, "with respect to formats which objectively seem identical, people — radio listeners — can and do make distinctions. For example, in most large markets there are a number of formats which seem identical on any objective or quantifiable basis; yet they are far from interchangeable to their respective audiences. Indeed, if people did not distinguish among these stations, there would be no reason for them to co-exist and little economic likelihood that they would." 57 FCC 580, 594–595 (1976).

18. A recent staff study of audience ratings for major market radio stations lends further credence to this observation. The results of that investigation indicate that audience ratings for major market radio stations tend to differ nearly as much for stations programming similar types of music (e.g., middle of the road) as they do for stations programming markedly different types (e.g., progressive rock as opposed to classical). This finding strongly indicates that audiences carefully discriminate in selecting stations. There is no way to determine the relative values of two different types of programming in the abstract. This is a practical, empirical question, whose answer turns on the intensity of demand for each format. In these circumstances, there is no reason to believe that government mandated restrictions on format changes would promote the welfare of the listening public. Indeed, in view of the administrative costs involved in such a program of regulation, and in view of the chilling effect such regulations would doubtlessly have on program innovation, there is every reason to believe that government supervision of formats would be injurious to the public interest.

19. Finally, allocating entertainment formats by market forces has a precious element of flexibility which no system of regulatory supervision could possibly approximate. In our society, public tastes are subject to rapid change. The people are entitled to expect that the broadcast industry will respond to these changing tastes — and the changing needs and aspirations which they mirror — without having to endure the delay and inconvenience that would be inevitable if permission to change had to be sought from a government agency.

20. These costs, and the uncertainties that impose them, have a constitutional dimension as well. Under the threat of a hearing that could cost tens or hundreds of thousands of dollars, many licensees might consider the risks of undertaking innovative or novel programming altogether unacceptable. The existence of the obligation to continue service, we find, inevitably deprives the public of the best efforts of the broadcast industry and results in an inhibition of constitutionally protected forms of communication with no off-setting justifications, either in terms of specific First Amendment or diversity-related values or in broader public interest terms.

Dissenting Statement of Commissioner Benjamin L. Hooks

I do not disagree that the "marketplace" abhors an unfilled commercial need and that enterprise generally will hasten to satisfy unmet demands sufficiently identified and sufficiently lucrative. I dissent because, without suggesting an alternative response to minority format abandonment, the majority does not provide a mechanism to ensure service to significant minority tastes and needs if market forces do not. In this Republic, the role of regulation of commerce has been to offset and remedy errant or inefficient market forces. The Commission's role in the commercial regulatory structure is well defined.

I do not intend to imply a desire for the end of "format radio" or wish to impose a comprehensive duty on every station to proportionately serve every entertainment preference. Neither do I wish to impede program experimentation and creativity.

It could be that the courts, upon re-evaluation, will find that the present case law with respect to agency format review is overly intrusive. If they do, I strongly feel that guidance must be given as to other actions to ensure that the Commission has the flexibility to correct significant neglect of the tastes, needs and interests of substantial minority segments and to promote the diversity that is the linchpin of our regulation of public trustees. Thus, it is unquestionable that the Court of Appeals was correct in noting that a primary mission of this agency is to secure "the maximum benefits of radio to all the people of the United States," Citizens Committee to Save WEFM, Inc. v. FCC, 506 F.2d 246, 268 (D.C. Cir. 1974), and that accomplishment of that goal must not be hindered materially by absolutist orthodoxies.

WNCN LISTENERS GUILD v. FCC
610 F.2d 838 (D.C. Cir. 1979) (en banc),
rev'd, 450 U.S. 582 (1981)

Opinion for the court filed by Circuit Judge McGOWAN, in which Chief Judge WRIGHT and Circuit Judges LEVENTHAL, ROBINSON, ROBB and WILKEY concur. Concurring opinions filed by Circuit Judges BAZELON and LEVENTHAL. Dissenting opinion filed by Circuit Judge TAMM, in which Circuit Judge MacKINNON joins.

McGOWAN, Circuit Judge:

In cases culminating with Citizens Committee to Save WEFM v. FCC, 506 F.2d 246 (D.C. Cir. 1974) (en banc), this court, always in the context of the Federal Communications Commission's statutory responsibility to pass upon voluntary assignments of radio licenses, construed that responsibility as comprehending the issue of whether the proposed abandonment of a distinctive programming format was in the public interest. In particular, we said that, where a significant sector of the listening community, in opposition to the assignment, protests the loss of such a format by substantial factual allegations that it is both unique and financially viable, the statute requires that the Commission hold a hearing.

Thereafter the Commission, after notice and comment proceedings, issued a "policy statement" disagreeing with *WEFM*, arguing that the public interest in diversity of entertainment formats is best served by unregulated competition among licensees, and urging this court to repudiate the approach it has taken. Unpersuaded that our reading of the Act is wrong, we decline the Commission's invitation to announce our abandonment of it.

The basic premise of our format cases is that the Communications Act's "public interest, convenience, and necessity" standard includes a concern for diverse entertainment programming. Congress set aside the radio spectrum as a public resource and acted to secure its benefits, not only to those in the cultural mainstream, but to "all the people" of our richly pluralistic society. It "is surely in the public interest," therefore, "as that was conceived of by a Congress representative of all the people, for all major aspects of contemporary culture to be accommodated by the commonly-owned public resources whenever that is technically and economically feasible." Citizens Committee to Preserve the Voice of Arts in Atlanta v. FCC, 436 F.2d 263, 269 (D.C. Cir. 1970).

The Commission need not consider the public interest implications of format abandonment, however, when there are compelling indications that the loss in diversity is not serious or that the assignment is otherwise clearly in the public interest. For example, if notice of the change does not precipitate an outpouring of protest, the Commission may properly assume that the proposed format is acceptable. Similarly, even if a committed and vocal minority engages in significant public grumbling, no public interest issue is raised if their preferred format is the choice of a population segment too small to be accommodated by the available frequencies. Finally, no public interest issue arises if there is an adequate substitute for the endangered format within the service area. In these situations the evidence is strong that the assignment will not result in a troublesome diminution of format diversity. Further, if the format itself is shown to be economically unfeasible in the particular market—*i.e.*, if even an efficiently managed station would have no realistic prospect of economic viability—then abandonment of the existing format does not contravene the public interest.

We fully recognize that market forces do generally provide diversification of formats. The licensee's discretion over programming matters is therefore very broad while the Commission's role is correspondingly narrow. However, we also recognize—as does the Commission—that the radio market is an imperfect reflection of listener preferences. Because broadcasters earn their revenues from advertising, they tend to serve young adults with large discretionary incomes in preference to demographically less desirable groups like children, the elderly, or the poor.

Further, the Commission's obligation to consider format issues arises only when there is strong prima facie evidence that the market has in fact broken down. [In those cases] market mechanisms have not satisfied the Communications Act's mandate that radio serve the needs of all the people.

Finally, we must emphasize the narrowness of the Commission's remedial powers. It merely has the power to take a station's format into consideration in deciding whether to grant certain applications. It has no authority under *WEFM* to interfere with licensee programming choices: it cannot restrain the broadcasting of any program, dictate adoption of a new format, force retention of an existing format, or command provision of access to non-licensees.

One difficulty noted by the Commission and intervening commercial broadcasters is the alleged impossibility of classifying radio formats. They point to our statement that "we know [a format] when [we hear] it,"[33] as being overly subjective, and to some of the distinctions we have drawn between formats as being nice to the point of administrative infeasibility.[34] Yet these were the judgments of a court forced to decide the case before it by reference to the language of the Communications Act and the Congressional purpose informing it.

Indeed, the Commission used a format classification in its staff study to demonstrate the existence of broad diversity in major radio markets. There is a marked inconsistency in its endorsing the validity of a study largely premised on classifications it claims are impossible to make. In any case, the schema used in the staff study follows accepted industry usage and would appear facially rational. It is likely that the perceived administrative difficulties would be greatly reduced if the Commission were to adopt a similar approach.[35]

With regard to *WEFM*'s perceived intrusiveness, the Commission could set rigorous standards as to when petitioners to deny have established a prima facie case. It could, for example, require a relatively high level of public grumbling, could classify formats into broader rather than narrower categories, and could place the burden of demonstrating "uniqueness" on the petitioners.

None of this is to imply, however, that the Commission is free to "administer" the format cases as a dead letter. Whatever administrative means the Commission adopts must be capable of identifying and rectifying those infrequent situations in which market allocation has failed and in which the public interest would not be served by granting the assignment application.

---

33. *Atlanta, supra*, 436 F.2d at 265 n.1, quoting Jacobellis v. Ohio, 378 U.S. 184, 197 (1964) (Stewart, J., concurring).

34. *See WEFM, supra*, 506 F.2d at 265 n.28, 264–65 (suggesting distinctions between twentieth century and other classical music and between "fine arts" and "classical"); Progressive Rock, *supra*, 478 F.2d at 932 ("progressive rock" distinguished from "top forty").

35. Furthermore, the Commission is not precluded from experimenting with more innovative approaches. It might consider, for example, dispensing altogether with the need for classifying formats by simply taking the existence of significant and bona fide listener protest as sufficient evidence that the station's endangered programming has certain unique features for which there are no ready substitutes in the service area. This approach would obviate the need for "subjective" distinctions among formats and would respond, also, to the objection that listeners perceive important differences among stations programming the "same" format. And by concentrating on the existence of listener unrest, this approach would focus attention on the essentials of the format doctrine, namely, that when a significant sector of the populace is aggrieved by a planned programming change, this fact raises a legitimate question as to whether the proposed change is in the public interest.

[Concurring opinions of Judges BAZELON and LEVENTHAL, and dissenting opinion of Judge TAMM, are omitted.]

FCC v. WNCN LISTENERS GUILD
450 U.S. 582 (1981)

WHITE, J., delivered the opinion of the Court. MARSHALL, J., filed a dissenting opinion, in which BRENNAN, J., joined.

JUSTICE WHITE delivered the opinion of the Court.

Sections 309 (a) and 310 (d) of the Communications Act of 1934 empower the Federal Communications Commission to grant an application for license transfer or renewal only if it determines that "the public interest, convenience, and necessity" will be served thereby. The issue before us is whether there are circumstances in which the Commission must review past or anticipated changes in a station's entertainment programming when it rules on an application for renewal or transfer of a radio broadcast license. The Commission's present position is that it may rely on market forces to promote diversity in entertainment programming and thus serve the public interest.

The Court of Appeals and the Commission agree that in the vast majority of cases market forces provide sufficient diversity. The Court of Appeals favors Government intervention when there is evidence that market forces have deprived the public of a "unique" format, while the Commission is content to rely on the market, pointing out that in many cases when a station changes its format, other stations will change their formats to attract listeners who preferred the discontinued format. The Court of Appeals places great value on preserving diversity among formats, while the Commission emphasizes the value of intraformat as well as interformat diversity. Finally, the Court of Appeals is convinced that review of format changes would result in a broader range of formats, while the Commission believes that Government intervention is likely to deter innovative programming.

The Commission did not assert that reliance on the marketplace would achieve a perfect correlation between listener preferences and available entertainment programming. Rather, it recognized that a perfect correlation would never be achieved, and it concluded that the marketplace alone could best accommodate the varied and changing tastes of the listening public. These predictions are within the institutional competence of the Commission.

It is contended that rather than carrying out its duty to make a particularized public-interest determination on every application that comes before it, the Commission, by invariably relying on market forces, merely assumes that the public interest will be served by changes in entertainment format. Surely, it is argued, there will be some format changes that will be so detrimental to the public interest that inflexible application of the Commission's Policy Statement would be inconsistent with the Commission's duties. But radio broadcasters are not required to seek permission to make format changes.

To assess whether the elimination of a particular "unique" entertainment format would serve the public interest, the Commission would have to consider the benefit as well as the detriment that would result from the change. Necessarily, the Commission would take into consideration not only the number of listeners who favor the old and the new programming but also the intensity of their preferences. It would also consider the effect of the format change on diversity within formats as well as on diversity among formats. The Commission is convinced that its judgments in these respects would be subjective in large measure and would only approximately serve the public interest. It is also convinced that the market, although imperfect, would serve the public interest as well or better by responding quickly to changing preferences and by inviting experimentation with new types of programming. Those who would overturn the Commission's Policy Statement do not take adequate account of these considerations.

Contrary to the judgment of the Court of Appeals, we hold that the Commission's Policy Statement is not inconsistent with the Act.

JUSTICE MARSHALL, with whom JUSTICE BRENNAN joins, dissenting.

Although the Act does not define "public interest, convenience, and necessity," it is difficult to quarrel with the basic premise of the Court of Appeals' format cases that the term includes "a concern for diverse entertainment programming." 610 F.2d 838, 842 (D.C. Cir. 1979).

The Act imposes an affirmative duty on the Commission to make a particularized "public interest" determination for each application that comes before it. The Policy Statement completely forecloses any possibility that the Commission will re-examine the validity of its general policy on format changes as it applies to particular situations. Thus, even when it can be conclusively demonstrated that a particular radio market does not function in the manner predicted by the Commission, the Policy Statement indicates that the Commission will blindly assume that a proposed format change is in the "public interest." This outcome is not consistent with the Commission's statutory responsibilities.

The Commission concedes that the radio market is an imperfect reflection of listener preferences, and that listeners have programming interests that may not be reflected in the marketplace. The Commission has long recognized its obligation to examine program formats in making the "public interest" determination required by the Act. The Commission's famous "Blue Book," published in 1946, explained: "It has long been an established policy of broadcasters themselves and of the Commission that the American system of broadcasting must serve significant minorities among our population, and the less dominant needs and tastes which most listeners have from time to time."

This theme was reiterated in the Commission's 1960 Program Statement, which set forth 14 specific categories of programming that were deemed "major elements usually necessary to meet the public interest, needs and desires of the community," and which emphasized the necessity of each broadcaster's programming serving the "tastes and needs" of its local community. To ensure that licensee programming serves the needs of the community, the Commission has, for example, decreed that licensees have a special obligation to provide programs for children, even going so far as to declare that licensees must provide "a reasonable amount of [children's] programming which is designed to educate and inform—and not simply to entertain."[36]

---

36. Children's Television Report and Policy Statement, 50 FCC 2d 1, 6 (1974).

Moreover, in examining renewal applications, the Commission has considered claims that a licensee does not provide adequate children's programming, or programming for women and children, or for a substantial Spanish-American community, or that the licensee has ignored issues of significance to the Negro community, or has not provided programming of specific interest to residents of a particular area.

There is an obvious inconsistency between the Commission's recognition that the "public interest" standard requires it to consider licensee programming in the situations described above and its Policy Statement on review of entertainment program formats. Indeed, the sole instance in which the Commission will not consider listener complaints about programming is when they pertain to proposed changes in entertainment program formats.

Notes and Questions

1. The Several Opinions. What would the rule espoused by the D.C. Circuit have required the Commission to do in the event of a proposed format change? Why did the FCC reject this rule? Why was the D.C. Circuit not persuaded by the Commission's policy statement? Did the Supreme Court side with the FCC because it thought the FCC had provided the better analysis or because it thought this was a matter best left to the FCC's discretion? What should the FCC and the Supreme Court have done?

2. The Dispute. Is the dispute between the FCC and the D.C. Circuit a disagreement over what comports with the public interest or a dispute over whether it is possible, as a practical matter, to discern where the public interest lies in format cases?

3. If You Can't Measure This. Can the FCC's position that no one can measure the relative value of different formats be squared with its frequent claim that diversity in programming is a general goal of the Commission and the Communications Act? If the FCC cannot distinguish among formats, how can it measure whether its other regulations — e.g., limiting multiple ownership of broadcast facilities or encouraging minority ownership of broadcast licensees — promote diversity of programming?

4. Long Term Consistency? Recall that, in the early years of broadcasting, the Federal Radio Commission denied licenses to stations that catered to a small minority of listeners; its interpretation of its public interest mandate led it to require that all stations appeal to the general public. By the 1970s, the D.C. Circuit was interpreting the FCC's public interest obligations as protecting the rights of small groups to have a station that responded to their particular interests. Are these two positions in conflict?

5. Realistic Alternatives. Would a requirement that a licensee adhere to a format that it wished to abandon be (a) administratively enforceable and (b) constitutional?

6. Reliance on the Market. Is the Commission's reliance on marketplace forces consistent with the notion that a broadcast licensee must serve "the public interest"? In what sense is the Commission relying on market forces? Does the FCC simply conclude that, because the agency cannot compare the value of some people's loss with the value of other people's harm, the Commission will always defer to the market's choice? Since, by this reasoning, the FCC cannot evaluate the market's choice either, what basis does the Commission have for deferring to markets?

7. Subsidies. Is a better answer to the problem of changing program formats simply to have government subsidize broadcast content targeted at those populations the market (arguably) underserves? Even the dissenters think that this will be a rare occurrence, so we are not talking about a great deal of money, are we?

8. Merger Review. Note that the FCC's authority to approve or disapprove license transfers has become an issue of renewed importance in recent years given the many mergers that have taken place between large telecommunication companies. The FCC reviews many of these mergers (as does the Department of Justice), and the jurisdictional hook for FCC review is often the simple fact that one of the companies needs FCC approval to transfer its various broadcast licenses to the other. We consider FCC merger review and the debate over this jurisdictional hook in Chapter Nineteen.

V. LICENSING CASE STUDY

IN RE APPLICATION OF SIMON GELLER
102 FCC 2d 1443 (1985)

BACKGROUND

1. This proceeding involves the application of Simon Geller for renewal of his license to operate Station WVCA-FM (WVCA), Gloucester, Massachusetts, and the mutually exclusive application of Grandbanke Corporation (Grandbanke) for a construction permit. On June 15, 1982, the Commission issued a Decision denying Geller's application and granting Grandbanke's. The Commission held that Geller's past performance as a broadcaster had been minimal and, thus, undeserving of a renewal expectancy. The Commission further held that this inadequate past record diminished the comparative credit that Geller would otherwise be due for his advantages with respect to diversification of media ownership and integration of ownership into management. In the Commission's view, Grandbanke was entitled to decisive preferences for its superior proposed programming and more efficient use of frequency. However, the District of Columbia Circuit Court of Appeals remanded this proceeding to the Commission for further consideration. The Court held that the Commission had failed to explain adequately the justification for diminishing Geller's advantages for diversification and integration and thereby had given unjustified weight to Geller's past record.

GELLER'S BROADCAST RECORD — RENEWAL EXPECTANCY

9. During the 1972–75 license term at issue here, WVCA presented less than 1% nonentertainment programming and no programming in response to ascertained community needs. Virtually all of WVCA's programming was devoted to symphonic music. WVCA broadcast no news, no editorials, and no locally pro-

duced public affairs programs. The station did, however, broadcast 18 public service announcements a week.

10. In view of his failure to present substantial nonentertainment programming responsive to the needs and interests of the community, the Commission concluded that Geller's past performance was minimal and, hence, undeserving of a renewal expectancy. The Commission noted that WVCA is the only broadcast facility licensed to Gloucester and that Geller's financial shortcomings did not mitigate the inadequacy of WVCA's programming. Under Commission precedent, a renewal applicant with a substantial past record, receives a renewal expectancy in the form of a preference taken into account along with all other preferences in the overall comparative analysis. Because Geller's performance was less than substantial, he received no such preference.

11. The Court of Appeals affirmed the Commission's denial of a renewal expectancy to Geller.

PROPOSED PROGRAMMING

12. Geller proposes to continue his present format, broadcasting 99.52% symphonic music, no news, 0.24% public affairs, and 0.24% other nonentertainment programming. Grandbanke proposes to devote 16.9% of its broadcast time to news, 5.9% to public affairs, and 5.9% to other nonentertainment programming, with 55% of its news to be local and regional. Unlike Geller, Grandbanke proposes that its informational programming will be directly related to ascertained community needs and interests. Whereas Geller proposed a 44 hour 27 minute a week program schedule, Grandbanke proposes to broadcast 136 hours of programming a week.

13. The Commission concluded that Grandbanke deserved a substantial preference for proposed programming for its demonstrated superior devotion to public service. This preference arose from Grandbanke's superior attention to presenting informational programming responsive to ascertained community needs and interests and was enhanced by the significant discrepancy between the applicants' proposed hours of operation and the relative restrictiveness of Geller's programming.

14. As it did with respect to the renewal expectancy, the court affirmed the award of a substantial preference to Grandbanke for its proposed programming.

EFFICIENT USE OF FREQUENCY

15. Because of differences between their engineering proposals, Grandbanke's facilities will have greater coverage than Geller's. Grandbanke's 1 mV/m contour will cover more than 300 square miles, providing a signal to nearly 360,000 people, as opposed to Geller's 73 square miles and 43,000 people.

16. The Commission awarded Grandbanke a slight preference based on the superiority of its coverage. Only a slight preference was warranted since the areas in question are already well served by at least five other aural signals.

17. The court did not specifically address this issue. Grandbanke will therefore continue to receive a slight preference.

INTEGRATION OF OWNERSHIP INTO MANAGEMENT

18. Geller is WVCA-FM's sole owner and employee and will devote full time to the operation of the station. He has been a resident of Gloucester for 13 years.

Grandbanke proposes that its 66% owner Edward Mattar will serve as the station's general manager. Mattar has had 3 years of broadcast experience and proposes to move to Gloucester in the event Grandbanke's application is granted.

19. The Commission previously held that despite Geller's technical advantages under the integration criterion, Geller merited only a slight preference over Grandbanke. The Commission reasoned that the rationale of the integration criterion was that an integrated owner would tend to be more sensitive to an area's changing needs and that Geller's poor past broadcast record detracted from these assurances.

20. The court criticized the Commission's conclusions in this regard. In the court's view, the Commission had failed to reconcile its integration analysis in this case with past precedent. The court noted that the Commission did not make, as it usually does, an explicit analysis of the quantitative and qualitative aspects of integration. Moreover, the court noted that the Commission does not customarily reduce the merit accorded for a quantitative integration advantage unless the applicant has committed misconduct. The court speculated that the Commission may have engaged in the type of "functional analysis" of the essentially structural characteristic of integration, which was previously disapproved by the court. Considering the Commission discussion too cursory and vague, the court remanded the matter for further analysis.

21. In his Comments, Geller maintains that his integration advantage is entitled to special weight because of his commitment to Gloucester and his long and unique relationship with that community. Geller claims that he has long served as the "voice of Cape Ann" despite receiving only a meager income. Grandbanke argues that reconsideration of the integration factor should not yield a different result. According to Grandbanke, the Commission normally accords no more than a moderate preference for a quantitative disparity in proposed integration such as that found here. Grandbanke contends that Geller's past deficiencies as a licensee fail to enhance his proposed integration and in fact detract from it.

22. Having reexamined the integration aspect of this case pursuant to the court's remand, we conclude that our prior treatment of this issue constituted the type of functional analysis previously criticized by the court. We will therefore reevaluate the integration criterion using our ordinary analytical approach. This approach encompasses a weighing of the customary quantitative and qualitative factors, without attempting to factor in other considerations, such as renewal expectancy and Geller's past broadcast record.

23. Turning first to the quantitative aspect of integration, we agree with Grandbanke that, consistent with precedent, an applicant proposing 100% integration deserves a moderate preference over an applicant proposing 66% integration. Qualitatively, Geller's integration is enhanced by his long term local residence, which outweighs Grandbanke's proposal that Mattar will move to Gloucester prospectively and Mattar's limited broadcast experience. Geller will therefore receive a qualitatively enhanced moderate integration preference to be taken into account in the overall comparative analysis.

DIVERSIFICATION OF MEDIA OWNERSHIP

24. Geller owns no media interests other than WVCA. On the other hand, Grandbanke's principals have interests in other broadcast stations. Edward Mat-

tar, Grandbanke's 66% owner, has a 100% interest in station WINQ-FM, Winchendon, Massachusetts. Stockholders with a 34% interest in Grandbanke have a 100% interest in Station WNCS-FM, Montepelier, Vermont.

25. The Commission awarded Geller a moderate preference for diversification. In the Commission's view, based on the degree of media ownership alone, Geller would have been entitled to a substantial preference. However, the Commission believed that Geller's preference should be diminished because of his failure to present substantial amounts of informational programming. The Commission reasoned that the rationale of diversification was to present the public with diverse and antagonistic points of view. Since Geller had virtually abandoned his role as an information source, the Commission concluded that he did not qualify as a diverse and antagonistic voice or deserve full credit for diversification.

26. The court rejected the Commission's analysis. The court held that the crux of the diversification issue is ownership, based on the probability that diverse ownership will lead to a diversity of views. Moreover, the court held that a direct evaluation of the content of a broadcaster's views would be questionable under the First Amendment. In this vein, the court indicated that there was no basis for inferring that the amount of informational programming presented necessarily represented the broadcaster's value as a diverse voice. On remand, the court required, at minimum, that the Commission adequately explain its apparent departure from established principles.

27. In his Comments Geller urges that his diversification advantage deserves special weight because he owns no other media interests whereas Grandbanke's principals have connections with several regional interests. Grandbanke maintains that Geller deserves no more than a moderate diversification advantage based on considerations of ownership alone. Grandbanke observes that its principals' outside media interests are relatively small and not located in the service area of the proposed station.

28. Having reexamined our diversification analysis pursuant to the court's mandate, we conclude that it must be revised. As in the case of integration, we believe that our prior discussion relied on an improper functional analysis. In accordance with the court's ruling, we will not look behind the presumption that underlies the diversification criterion. Our prior conclusion that, based on considerations of media ownership alone, Geller deserves a substantial preference stands unabridged. Accordingly, Geller will receive a substantial preference for diversification.

OVERALL COMPARATIVE ANALYSIS

29. The Commission ultimately concluded that Geller's license renewal application should be denied and Grandbanke's application for a construction permit should be granted. The Commission found that Grandbanke's substantial preference for proposed programming and slight preference for efficient use of frequency outweighed Geller's slight integration advantage and moderate diversification advantage. Because the court disagreed with the manner in which the Commission considered the integration and diversification criteria, it did not reach the overall comparison between Geller and Grandbanke.

30. In his Comments, Geller maintains that once his integration and diversification preferences are given their proper weights, undiminished by "multiple

counting" of his past broadcast record, these advantages are decisive. Grand-banke, which considers Geller's integration and diversification advantages to be moderate, submits on the other hand that its advantages for proposed program-ming and efficient use of frequency are dispositive. Grandbanke continues to as-sert that Geller's failure to provide substantial amounts of informational pro-gramming responsive to local needs and interests should weigh heavily in the comparative balancing.

31. The framework for the comparative evaluation of broadcast applicants is provided by the Commission's *1965 Policy Statement on Comparative Broadcast Hearings*. There, the Commission enunciated two primary objectives: (1) best practicable service to the public, and (2) diversification of control of the media of mass communications. The former objective encompasses several factors of which those relevant here are: (1) integration of ownership into management, (2) proposed programming, and (3) efficient use of frequency. Under the best practi-cable service to the public criterion, we have concluded that Grandbanke de-serves a substantial preference for proposed programming and a slight preference for efficient use of frequency, while Geller deserves an enhanced moderate prefer-ence for integration. On balance, we believe Grandbanke should receive a mod-erate preference for best practicable service. As to diversification, the other pri-mary criterion, Geller receives a substantial preference. Thus, we are faced with a situation in which each applicant is superior to the other with respect to one of the primary objectives of the comparative process. However, the substantial pref-erence awarded to Geller for diversification clearly outweighs the moderate pref-erence awarded to Grandbanke for best practicable service. For this reason, we believe that Geller is ultimately the preferred applicant.

Notes and Questions

1. In Review. Virtually every issue raised by these licensing materials arises in this case. To understand the case, it is important to (1) see why the opinion treats this as a comparative, non-renewal proceeding even though Geller already has the li-cense, and (2) trace carefully through the calculus the FCC employs in judging each factor, assigning preferences for each, and comparing the various preferences.

2. Geller's Renewal Expectancy. Why does the Commission refuse to grant Geller a preference for renewal expectancy? Is its reasoning consistent with the First Amendment? If so, then why is it "questionable under the First Amendment" (¶26) to measure the value of diverse ownership in part by whether the owner engages in informational programming? Did Geller fail to gain a renewal ex-pectancy simply because he failed to program what the FCC thought people in Gloucester would (or should) want to hear?

3. Current Law. Under modern law regarding license renewals, it appears the FCC would have to either renew Geller's license or deny his application before considering Grandbanke's. Does this seem preferable to the approach taken in the *Geller* case by the Commission? Is it in tension with the logic of *Ashbacker*?

4. Commission Discretion. Suppose the Commissioners, for whatever reason, wanted to give Grandbanke the license. How hard would it be to write an opin-ion doing so? Consider, for example: (a) Why does the FCC equate the impor-tance of best practicable service and diversification (¶31)? If the Commission had announced that it considered service to be three times as important as diversification (perhaps, in part, because service encompasses at least three times as many factors as diversification, or because, in this case, Grandbanke would reach more than three times as many listeners as Geller) and so would award the license to Grandbanke, would the decision have been equally rational? (b) What is a "qualitatively enhanced moderate preference" (¶23)? Did the Commission give the term its precisely correct weight?

5. Coasian Bargains. Geller sold his station after receiving the renewal. Why doesn't the Commission's analysis proceed from the premise that the matter to be decided is who is to be allowed to reap the value of programming WVCA, either by operating it or by selling it as the winner chooses?

CHAPTER FIVE

THE TRANSITION FROM HEARINGS TO AUCTIONS

The purpose of this chapter is:

- to compare and contrast three approaches to the initial licensing decision: hearings, auctions, and lotteries; and

- to introduce and evaluate the modern auction approach.

~

Throughout the preceding chapter, we observed the FCC's attempts to exercise its statutory responsibility to select licensees on the basis of a "public interest" standard. Implicit in all those policy discussions was the assumption that the public interest test meant that the Commission should select, from among the applicants in front of it, the one who, as operator of the station at issue, was most likely to serve the public interest. But did the Commission make any real progress in elaborating or refining its licensing standards after those early cases in 1934? Certainly the later decisions, like *Central Florida* and *Simon Geller*, employed fancier language (and more of it) than did the 1934 decisions. But did they evince any difference in substance?

As time went on, even the FCC seemed increasingly dubious that Commission hearings could outperform the market when it came to selecting deserving licensees. Thus, as we saw at the end of last chapter, the Commission gradually jettisoned many of its guidelines and requirements. The ascertainment rules, for example, were abandoned. Post card renewal was born. At the same time, nudged along by the Supreme Court, the D.C. Circuit, and ultimately Congress itself, the FCC narrowed the scope of its reviews of both transfer and renewal applications. There was nothing to review, anyway; the FCC was for the most part out of the business of evaluating licensee programming and behavior.

Not surprisingly, this left spectrum policy in a somewhat curious state. The FCC would engage in a sometimes expensive and time-consuming hearing to select initial licensees, but those licensees were then free to turn around and sell their licenses to the highest bidder. Licensing hearings did not necessarily determine who would be allowed to program a given station; rather, they often determined who would be allowed to auction off the license that the government would for some reason not sell itself. Naturally, this state of affairs could not last.

The chapter proceeds in three steps. First, we consider some of the final adjustments the FCC made to the licensing process in the late 1980s. These adjustments help us to begin to think about the hearing process in strategic context, a useful perspective for the discussions that follow. Second, we consider the relative merits of auctions, lotteries, and hearings as mechanisms for assigning spectrum licenses. Third, we examine the current statutory provision that authorizes spectrum auctions and look at some anecdotal evidence and commentary about how the auction process has worked thus far.

I. REFORM OF THE LICENSING PROCESS

IN RE PREVENTION OF ABUSES OF THE RENEWAL PROCESS
First Report and Order, 4 FCC Rcd. 4780 (1989)

I. INTRODUCTION

2. In response to troubling allegations that some parties might be using the renewal process to obtain payments or benefits from the renewal applicant unrelated to any legitimate public interest aims, we invited public comment on this alleged abuse of the comparative renewal process. In line with virtually unanimous support from the commenters for limitations on settlement payments, we are: (1) banning all payments that can be made to competing applicants, other than to the incumbent licensee, in exchange for withdrawing an application prior to the Initial Decision stage of the comparative hearing, and thereafter, limiting payments to the legitimate and prudent expenses of the withdrawing applicant; (2) limiting payments that can be made in exchange for withdrawing petitions to deny to the legitimate and prudent expenses of the withdrawing petitioner; and (3) reviewing citizens' agreements reached in exchange for withdrawing petitions to deny on a case-by-case basis. These measures should effectively remove the economic incentive present in the renewal system to file competing applications and petitions to deny for the principal purpose of extorting settlements in exchange for dismissing these challenges.

4. In a *Report and Order* adopted concurrently with this *Report and Order*, we are amending Form 301 [required of applicants seeking permission to construct a commercial broadcast station] to require all applicants to provide more financial, ownership and integration information. In so doing, we expect, among other things, to discourage financially unqualified, sham and abusive applicants from filing competing applications in the license renewal context, and to provide the means to identify such persons who do file.

II. PAYMENT LIMITATIONS

A. Background

8. Settlements among mutually exclusive applicants in the comparative renewal context are governed by section 311(d) of the Communications Act. The statute makes it unlawful for a competing applicant to agree to withdraw an application "in exchange for the payment of money, or the transfer of assets or any other thing of value" by any other applicant "without approval of the Commission." The statute further provides that: "The Commission shall approve the

agreement only if it determines that (A) the agreement is consistent with the public interest, convenience, or necessity; and (B) no party to the agreement filed its application for the purpose of reaching or carrying out such agreement."

9. The right to file a petition to deny is provided by section 309(d) of the Communications Act. Unlike competing applications, there is no specific statutory provision that governs settlements of petitions to deny.

10. A citizens' agreement is a formal, written agreement between a citizens' group (e.g., civic association, listeners' group, consumer organization, church group or minority or civil rights protective organization) and a broadcast licensee which usually addresses some aspect of a station's programming or employment practices. Citizens' agreements can be reached in numerous contexts. Those pertinent to our discussion here are reached in exchange for the withdrawal of a petition to deny.

11. Since 1982, we have not imposed any general limits on the amount of money or other consideration competing applicants or petitioners can receive in exchange for dismissing a renewal challenge. Furthermore, as a part of our regulatory reforms, we significantly reduced the filing requirements for competing applicants. We are concerned that these reforms have had the unintended result of encouraging the filing of non bona fide applications and petitions to extort settlements rather than for the intended goals of obtaining a license or identifying deficiencies of incumbent licensees.

C. Discussion

22. *Need for Limits.* Abuse of the renewal process hurts the public interest in several ways. Incumbent licensees are required to expend considerable amounts of money to defend against and pay off challengers,[1] including those who are unfunded and have no real intention of owning or operating a station. Moreover, the staff and management of the incumbent are forced to spend considerable funds as well as time and effort opposing challenges to license renewals.[2] The expenditure of such resources that otherwise might have been devoted to programming and other services, to defend against an abusive challenge is inefficient and wasteful.

24. Respondents to a National Association of Broadcasters (NAB) survey variously reported, for example, that they have been threatened with license renewal challenges unless they contributed to the challenger's organization, that

---

1. *See, e.g.*, United Broadcasting Co. of Eastern Maryland, Inc., FCC 85R-83 (1985) ($400,000 settlement paid to opposing applicant in an FM renewal); United Broadcasting Company of New York, Inc., FCC 85R-81 (1985) ($240,000 paid to competing applicant in settlement of AM renewal); and Western Broadcasting, Inc., FCC 86M-3434 (1986) ($75,000 for dismissal and $198,000 for related civil litigation expenses paid to competing applicant).
2. According to Post-Newsweek, the cost to its Miami and Jacksonville stations and their personnel of fighting renewal challenges while trying to operate effectively to serve the public was enormous. They noted that the staff was required to review 14,000 pages of records to compile information for one interrogatory alone out of 299. Metroplex reported that defending the WHYI renewal challenge has required hundreds of hours of station and management time to review thousands of documents, respond to interrogatories and depositions, prepare written hearing testimony, oversee work of counsel and appear at the hearings.

they regularly contribute to certain groups to avoid license renewal challenges, and that they have been subjected to costly competing applications by disgruntled former employees.

25. *Competing Applications.* We are adopting a policy prohibiting all payments to competing applicants (other than the incumbent licensee) for the withdrawal of an application prior to the Initial Decision stage of a comparative hearing.[3] Thereafter, we will approve settlements that do not exceed the withdrawing party's legitimate and prudent expenses for filing and litigating the competing application.

26. This should virtually eliminate those applicants whose purpose in filing is to settle out for profit and generally assure that applications are being filed solely for their intended purpose—that of acquiring a broadcast license. An applicant that makes it through the Initial Decision stage has demonstrated that it is willing to develop a complete record on all pertinent hearing issues. For these reasons, we believe that an applicant's prosecution of its application through the Initial Decision stage is a persuasive indication of the bona fides of the application.

27. Currently, settlements most often occur at the beginning of the comparative process, when an incumbent still faces a long, expensive license renewal process, experiences the disadvantages of having a cloud over its license during that process, and has little information with which to evaluate challengers' applications.[4]

28. After the Initial Decision, however, the potential for abuse is dramatically diminished. If the Initial Decision favors the incumbent,[5] the incumbent is under far less pressure to settle. The incumbent goes into the appeal process with a decision in its favor; the expense of litigating an appeal is generally a fraction of the cost of obtaining the Initial Decision; and the incumbent knows the merits and demerits of the challenger's application. For these same reasons, a challenger generally has less leverage to force a settlement and its leverage is more consistent with the relative merits of its application.

39. *Petitions to Deny.* A person has the statutory right to file a petition to deny to challenge an incumbent licensee's renewal application on the grounds that the licensee lacks qualifications or that the grant of renewal would be inconsistent with the public interest. Petitions to deny in the comparative renewal context are often filed to achieve nonfinancial goals such as to require a licensee to cure a deficiency in its performance, to provide certain types of programming, to continue to consider issues of concern to its community of license, or to improve its employment record regarding minorities and women. Petitions to deny can be dismissed in exchange for the payment of money and/or for promises to imple-

---

3. The Initial Decision is the determination by an Administrative Law Judge, after a full hearing on the merits, as to the applicant that should be awarded the broadcast license.

4. Prior to modifications in our *Form 301 Report and Order,* adopted concurrent with this rule making, competing applicants were permitted to file applications without identifying in the application (1) a financial plan or sources of funding, (2) equity owners in the applicant who are sometimes the real parties behind the application, or (3) their plans for ownership integration.

5. If the Initial Decision favors the challenger, there is less concern about potential abuse of process. An incumbent licensee who seeks to renew its license is not in this category of potential abusers. Thus, as discussed *infra,* a challenger is free to pay an incumbent either to sell the station or to dismiss its renewal application at any time without monetary limitation.

ment some type of nonfinancial reform. Where a petition to deny is dismissed in exchange for an agreement by a licensee to implement nonfinancial reforms, such settlements are often referred to as citizens' agreements. Our policy with regard to settlements of petitions to deny depends on whether the petition is dismissed in exchange for money or for a nonfinancial promise.

40. Where a petition to deny is settled in exchange for money, we will allow such payments provided they do not exceed the petitioner's legitimate and prudent expenses in prosecuting its petition. We must not discourage the use of petitions to deny in order to further our public interest goals. Petitions to deny play a critical role in our current regulatory scheme. Members of the public, through the use of petitions to deny, serve as private attorneys general informing us of deficiencies in the performance of licensees and helping us ensure that licensees serve the public interest.

41. By prohibiting payments in excess of legitimate and prudent expenses we are removing the profit motive for filing petitions to deny.

43. *Citizens' Agreements.* A citizens' agreement is a contract in which a petitioner to deny agrees to dismiss its petition in exchange for a promise by the licensee to implement a nonfinancial reform such as a programming or an employment initiative.

44. Many of the same concerns regarding potential abuse that motivated our restrictions on money payments in exchange for the withdrawal of petitions to deny appear to be equally applicable to citizens' agreements.

46. In light of this potential for abuse, we will review all citizens' agreements reached in exchange for dismissing a petition to deny on a case by case basis to determine whether the agreement furthers the public interest. In making this determination, we will presume that any agreement with a petitioner that calls for the petitioner, or any person or organization related to the petitioner, to carry out, for a fee, any programming, employment or other "nonfinancial" initiative does not further the public interest and hence will likely be disapproved. In contrast, a licensee's agreement with a petitioner to make changes in operations or programming, either by itself or through disinterested third parties without further participation by the petitioner, will likely be approved.

49. We have also become involved in the interpretation and enforcement of citizens' agreements filed at the Commission. We have regarded promises of future performance as commitments to the agency, and we have relied upon these commitments in our decision making process. The principal area where this has present relevance concerns agreements touching on programming matters. Over the course of the last decade we have eliminated detailed programming proposals from our processes, including our renewal application. For what we believe are good and valid reasons, we no longer apply a "promise versus performance" standard to renewal applications. Accordingly, unless an action taken by the Commission is specifically conditioned on licensee representations relating to programming matters, we do not intend to enforce private contractual agreements relating to programming.

Notes and Questions

1. **Subsequent Events.** The rules adopted in the above *Report and Order* applied only to license renewal proceedings. Subsequently, however, the Commission de-

termined that it should apply these rules to petitions to deny in all proceedings, including those where a firm sought a new license and those where a firm sought to modify, assign, or transfer an existing license. The Commission therefore banned any individual or group from making or receiving monetary payments in excess of legitimate and prudent expenses in a wide array of instances, each of which had formerly been vulnerable to this same sort of strategic threat. *See Rules Concerning Abuses of the Commission's Processes*, 5 FCC Rcd. 3911 (1990).

2. Abuses Defined. In what sense are the practices regulated here "abuses" of the licensing process? Do citizens' agreements or petitions to deny that are filed only to obtain cash settlements cause any "harm" beyond transferring money from one person to another? Is such a transfer a harm to the interests of the listening and viewing public, or a benefit?

3. Other Reforms. Could the licensing process have been changed in ways more clearly and directly beneficial to listeners and viewers? Was the move to auctions necessary, or could the hearing process have been salvaged by more aggressive reforms? If auctions turn out to have significant drawbacks of their own, would you advise against returning to comparative hearings as an assignment mechanism? If so, what approach would you favor?

II. LOTTERIES, AUCTIONS, AND COMPARATIVE HEARINGS

Three primary mechanisms for the initial assignment of spectrum licenses have been used at one time or another by the FCC: the comparative hearings studied last chapter; auctions, which we will discuss later in this chapter; and lotteries, introduced immediately below.

In 1982, Congress authorized the Commission to assign licenses by random selection. The provision, codified at 47 U.S.C. §309(i)(1), provided[6] that:

> If there is more than one application for any initial license or construction permit..., then the Commission...shall have authority to grant such license or permit to a qualified applicant through the use of a system of random selection.

The FCC employed lotteries several times between 1982 and 1997 (the year Congress mandated the use of auctions for most license allocations and all but revoked the FCC's lottery authority). For example, lotteries were used to distribute certain licenses for low-power television service, *see, e.g., In re Amendment of the Commission's Rules to Allow the Selection from Among Certain Competing Applications Using Random Selection of Lotteries Instead of Comparative Hearings*, 93 F.C.C. 2d 952 (1983), and again to distribute licenses for cellular

---

6. The provision as passed in 1982 remains largely intact, except for one important substantive change: section 309(i)(5) provides that, with the exception of licenses for noncommercial educational or public broadcast stations, "the Commission shall not issue any license or permit using a system of random selection under this subsection after July 1, 1997." *Id.*

telephony in markets other than the thirty largest, *see In re Selection by Lottery for Competing Cellular Applications*, 98 F.C.C. 2d 175 (1984). In both cases, the FCC maintained its role in establishing the band plan—that is, defining exactly what the license allowed its holder to do. From there, however, the FCC simply accepted applications, screened them to make sure that applicants met basic qualification standards (like financial ability and certain technical qualifications), and then randomly awarded the licenses to some subset of the qualified applicants.

The FCC never used lotteries as a mechanism for allocating licenses for AM, FM, or conventional television stations, however. Said the Commission: "We are concerned that any potential gains in efficiency that may be achieved by use of a lottery would be outweighed by the possible reduction in quality of broadcasting licensees and service to the public. Therefore, we will seek instead to improve the efficiency and integrity of our current comparative hearing process for the grant of new broadcasting facilities." *In re Selection by Lottery for New AM, FM, and TV Stations*, 5 FCC Rcd. 4002, ¶3 (1990).

To explore the relative advantages and disadvantages of auctions, lotteries, and comparative hearings, consider the following issues:

Governmental Costs. Which approach is likely to minimize governmental costs? Hearings, of course, can be expensive to conduct, especially given the many possible layers of review. Auctions and lotteries seem likely to have lower costs, the main costs of each being paperwork costs—for example the costs of confirming that applicants meet some basic qualifications in terms of financial backing and so on. Lotteries are likely to be more expensive on this score than auctions, however, since (assuming that lotteries are inexpensive for applicants to enter) there are likely more applications to process in a lottery than there would be in a comparable auction or hearing.

Private Costs. Similarly, which approach likely minimizes private costs for applicants? Hearings are expensive for applicants, because they must pay for representation (perhaps at several formal interactions) and also must submit to a possibly expensive fact-finding process. Some of those expenses have value, of course; the ascertainment procedure, for example, is expensive for an applicant but also generates information that will be useful to the applicant should it be awarded the license at issue. Lotteries are probably the least expensive for applicants, the only real cost being the time needed to fill out a lottery application. And the primary expense involved in auctions would be the expense associated with developing a good bidding strategy, an expense that surely varies considerably across different parties and different auctions.

Efficient Allocation of Licenses. Is one of the three methods more likely to get licenses into the "best" hands? Faster? The answers here depend on how efficiently license transfer works—both in terms of how easy transfer is as a legal matter and how practical it is in terms of transaction costs, holdout problems, and the like. That said, the three techniques do differ in their odds of making a good assignment in the first instance. We have no reason to believe that lotteries, for example, will very often lead to a good initial assignment; and so lotteries are likely to be the slowest and worst mechanism in terms of efficient license allocation, since almost every license assigned by lottery will have to be resold before it is matched with its highest-valuing user.

Rewards to the Government. Will one approach better inform the FCC as to how it should design the band plan? Does one approach give the government greater revenues? Does one approach give the government greater influence over licensee behavior? Auctions surely get a plus on the first two counts here. First, auctions help the government see how much a given slice of spectrum is worth, information that might help the FCC in its spectrum management duties. Note that this information is available under hearings and lotteries, too, but only some time after the initial assignment, when licensees start to sell their licenses on the open market. Second, auctions obviously fill the government's coffers rather effectively; it is hard to imagine those same revenues being generated by hearings or lotteries. As for the third factor—the extent of the government's influence over licensee behavior—it would seem that hearings earn the nod on this criterion because, while auctions largely defer to the marketplace and lotteries defer to chance, hearings (as we've seen) to some degree force licensees to defer to the FCC and its ever-powerful eyebrow. Whether that's good or bad as a policy matter, of course, depends on your perspective.

Strategic Behavior, Monopoly, and Minorities. Lastly, does one approach impose a greater risk of strategic behavior by would-be licensees? Can that behavior be more easily avoided by appropriate regulation in one instance versus another? Is monopoly a greater concern under one of these approaches? Do the approaches have different implications for minorities, women, or low income applicants? Does that matter when the issue is the allocation of licenses for cellular telephony as opposed to broadcast television? All of these questions are implicitly answered by materials elsewhere in this chapter, but each is worth keeping in mind as you evaluate the relative advantages and disadvantages of the three mechanisms.

* * *

Overall, note that the choice between auctions, hearings, and lotteries might not be much of a choice at all. Each mechanism turns out to be an auction mechanism; all that changes is the identity of the auctioneer. Phrased another way, while in some ways the FCC's authority to conduct auctions is new, the real truth is that, while the Commission has not conducted auctions for broadcast licenses until recently, its licensees have long done so quite routinely. Given that reality, little need turn on which approach the FCC employs. Indeed the favored approach should likely be the one that is cheapest in terms of the expense of its administration and the costs involved in having spectrum sit idle between the time of its initial allocation and the moment when it finally is transferred to the party who values it most.

III. INITIAL ASSIGNMENT BY AUCTION

The Commission was first given the authority to auction licenses in 1993,[7] but at that time auction authority extended only to licenses used in common carrier and private radio services. Common carrier services are those (like telephone

---

7. Omnibus Budget Reconciliation Act of 1993, Pub. L. 13–66, August 10, 1993.

service) for which traffic is received on equal terms from all parties irrespective of its specific content. In 1997, however, Congress expanded the Commission's auction authority, requiring the use of auctions for nearly all initial licenses and construction permits. *See* 47 U.S.C. §§309(i) & (j). The statute contains a few exceptions to its auction mandate, notably excluding licenses for digital television service and excluding licenses for which the comparative hearing process had already commenced as of July 1997.[8] With respect to the latter category, the Commission was given the option to use auctions. The FCC exercised that option in the main order implementing the 1997 legislation, excerpted below.

IN RE IMPLEMENTATION OF SECTION 309(J) OF THE COMMUNICATIONS ACT—COMPETITIVE BIDDING FOR COMMERCIAL BROADCAST LICENSES
First Report and Order, 13 FCC Rcd. 15920 (1998)

II. BACKGROUND AND SUMMARY

2. As fully described in the *Notice of Proposed Rulemaking* in this proceeding, 12 FCC Rcd. 22363 (1997) (hereafter *Notice*), the Commission has traditionally used comparative hearings to decide among mutually exclusive applications to provide commercial broadcast service, and it has used a system of random selection to award certain types of broadcast licenses, such as low power television and television translator, pursuant to Section 309(i), 47 U.S.C. §309(i). For purposes of comparative hearings, the Commission has developed a variety of comparative criteria, *see* Policy Statement on Comparative Broadcast Hearings, 1 FCC 2d 393, 394 (1965), including the "integration" of ownership and management, which presumed that a station would offer better service to the extent that its owner(s) were involved in the station's day-to-day management. However, in Bechtel v. FCC, 10 F.3d 875, 878 (D.C. Cir. 1993), the United States Court of Appeals for the District of Columbia Circuit held that "continued application of the integration preference is arbitrary and capricious, and therefore unlawful." The Commission subsequently froze all ongoing comparative cases (including comparative renewal cases) pending resolution of the questions raised by *Bechtel*.

3. Subsequently, on August 5, 1997, Congress enacted the Balanced Budget Act of 1997, which expanded the Commission's auction authority under Section 309(j) of the Communications Act to include commercial broadcast applicants. Amended Section 309(j) provides that, except for licenses for certain public safety noncommercial services and for certain digital television services and noncommercial educational or public broadcast stations, "the Commission shall grant the license or permit to a qualified applicant through a system of competitive bidding...[i]f...mutually exclusive applications are accepted for any initial license or construction permit." Balanced Budget Act of 1997, §3002(a)(1), codified as 47 U.S.C. §309(j). In addition, Section 3002(a)(2), codified as 47 U.S.C. §309(i), amends Section 309(i) to terminate the Commission's authority to issue

---

8. The other exceptions to the FCC's auction authority are licenses or construction permits for public safety radio services and for noncommercial educational or public broadcast stations. 47 U.S.C. §309(j)(2).

any license through the use of a system of random selection after July 1, 1997, except for licenses or permits for stations defined by Section 397(6) of the Communications Act (*i.e.*, noncommercial educational or public broadcast stations). Finally, Section 3002(a)(3) adopts Section 309(l), codified as 47 U.S.C. §309(l), which governs the resolution of pending comparative broadcast licensing cases. Specifically, it says the Commission "shall have the authority" to resolve mutually exclusive applications for commercial radio or television stations filed before July 1, 1997 by competitive bidding procedures. It specifies further that any auction conducted under this provision must be restricted to persons filing competing applications before July 1, 1997.

4. As a result of the Budget Act, the Commission no longer has the option of resolving competing applications for commercial broadcast stations by comparative hearings except for certain applications filed before July 1, 1997, and it lacks the authority to resolve competing applications for commercial broadcast stations by a system of random selection. The Commission began this rulemaking proceeding to implement these provisions of the Budget Act.

III. DISCUSSION

7. As indicated above, the Commission's authority to award spectrum licenses is set forth in Section 309(j) of the Communications Act. Prior to the enactment of the Budget Act, Section 309(j) provided that the Commission "shall have the authority...to grant...any initial license or construction permit...through the use of a system of competitive bidding," but that authority was limited to awarding licenses for certain non-broadcast uses of the electromagnetic spectrum and required a determination by the Commission that "a system of competitive bidding will promote the objectives described in" Section 309(j)(3). By virtue of the enactment of the Budget Act, however, Section 309(j)(1) now reads:

> If, consistent with the obligations described in paragraph (6)(E) [to avoid mutual exclusivity], mutually exclusive applications are accepted for any initial license or construction permit, then, except as provided in paragraph (2), the Commission *shall* grant the license or permit to a qualified applicant through a system of competitive bidding.

(Emphasis added.)

8. Given the express language of amended Section 309(j)(1) providing that the Commission shall grant any initial license or permit through a system of competitive bidding, we tentatively concluded in the *Notice*, 12 FCC Rcd. at 22379 (¶40), that we are required to use auctions for all pending and new mutually exclusive applications to provide secondary broadcast service, such as low power television (LPTV), and FM and television translators. We also tentatively read Section 309(j)(1) as mandating that, except for certain pending licensing cases, the resolution of which is expressly governed by Section 309(l), and certain digital stations governed by Section 309(j)(2), the Commission must use competitive bidding to award authorizations for all new primary commercial broadcast stations, if mutually exclusive applications are filed.

B. Resolution of Comparative Initial Licensing Cases Involving Applications Filed Before July 1, 1997

1. Discretion to Use Auctions in Pending Cases

26. As noted above, Section 309(l) expressly governs the resolution of pending mutually exclusive applications for new commercial radio and television stations filed before July 1, 1997. We tentatively concluded in the *Notice* that this provision accords us the discretion to decide such cases either by a competitive bidding proceeding or through the comparative hearing process.

27. We continue to believe that we have discretion to resolve comparative licensing proceedings that involve pre-July 1, 1997 applications for new commercial radio and television stations by either competitive bidding procedures or through the comparative hearing process.

2. Public Interest Considerations Favoring Resolution by Competitive Bidding

34. We believe that auctions will generally be fairer and more expeditious than deciding the pending mutually exclusive applications filed before July 1, 1997 through the comparative hearing process. We conclude that auctions will generally expedite service and better serve the public interest in these cases. Based upon our long experience with the comparative process, we believe that once the competitive bidding procedures, as well as any special processing rules for these pending comparative cases are in place, auctions will result in a more expeditious resolution of each particular case, thereby expediting the initiation of new broadcast service to the public. In this regard, we note that, despite the 180-day period during which we waived our settlement rules as required by Section 309(l)(3), there are approximately 150 proceedings involving more than 600 pre-July 1, 1997 mutually exclusive applications that remain to be decided.

36. We have long noted the potential for delay inherent in the adjudicatory nature of the comparative process. In connection with a rulemaking initiated in 1989 to explore the possibility of using lotteries to award initial broadcast licenses, for example, we estimated that a routine comparative proceeding can take from three to five years or more to complete after designation of the mutually exclusive applications for hearing, and that complex cases may take much more time.[9] More recently in Orion Communications Limited v. FCC, 131 F.3d 176, 180 (D.C. Cir. 1997), the court recognized that repetitious appeals may prolong proceedings for years even after the Commission's decision.

37. Here, the potential for delay is also increased by the court's decision in *Bechtel* invalidating our central comparative criterion, integration of ownership and management, and the resulting freeze on the processing and adjudication of comparative proceedings in effect since February 1994. The commenters are divided over the ease by which the Commission may resolve the standard comparative issue if it elects not to use auctions to resolve the frozen *Bechtel* cases, and the extent to which *Bechtel* permits us to modify the existing comparative crite-

---

9. *See* Amendment of the Commission's Rules to Allow the Selection from Among Competing Applicants for New AM, FM, and Television Stations By Random Selection, 4 FCC Rcd. 2256, 2257 (1989), cataloguing various factors contributing to this delay, including the heavy use by comparative broadcast applicants of motions to enlarge issues; complex and intricate discovery procedures that materially add to the cost and length of comparative proceedings; lengthy hearings that may involve numerous witness and hearing exhibits; the 30–90 day time period for filing findings with the Administrative Law Judge; the approximately six-month period that it takes the Administrative Law Judge to issue his opinion; and the time for any administrative or judicial appeals.

ria. But none dispute our assertion in the *Notice*, 12 FCC Rcd. at 22366–67 ((¶5), that the integration criterion has been crucial in recent comparative cases, or urge that we decide these cases without regard to the court's express holding in *Bechtel*, 10 F.3d at 878, that "continued application of the integration preference is arbitrary and capricious, and therefore unlawful." Moreover, we note many other relevant factors (*e.g.*, local residence, civic participation, past broadcast experience) were "enhancements" of the integration criterion. Determining which of these criteria could best survive *Bechtel*-type scrutiny and determining how such criteria should now be weighted is a difficult process that no doubt would lead to serious challenges in the courts with the outcome unclear. Indeed, there is wide disparity in the record as to what the best approach would be. The value of developing a revised comparative system (and expending the associated administrative costs) is further attenuated by the fact that it would only be used for these pending cases (and potentially also a very small number of comparative renewal cases) and would have no future applicability. Thus, we conclude that using a system of competitive bidding rather than the comparative hearing process for competing pre-July 1, 1997 applications that are subject to Section 309(l) will avoid the difficulties and potential delays of developing and defending new or modified comparative criteria to apply in the cases that did not settle during the 180-day period that ended February 1, 1998.

38. Moreover, we are acutely aware of the delay already occasioned in all of the frozen *Bechtel* cases. Section 309(j)(3) provides that "[i]n identifying classes of licenses and permits to be issued by competitive bidding," the Commission shall seek to promote "(A) the development and *rapid* deployment of new technologies...*for the benefit of the public...without administrative or judicial delays.*" (Emphasis added.) As a more general matter, expedited service to the public is an important public interest consideration. We estimate that it would take many years for the Commission's administrative law judges to adjudicate and decide well over 100 cases. Auctions can be carried out much more quickly. And, whatever the cause of past delay in resolving these cases, we believe that minimizing further delay and now providing new service to the public as quickly as possible best serves the public interest.

39. Some commenters favoring the use of comparative hearings for these pending cases express concern that the switch to auctions will detrimentally affect the quality of broadcast service. They focus particularly on the impact that auctions will allegedly have in terms of securing service that is narrowly tailored to the needs of the small, local community. As to these more general policy concerns, however, Congress itself has made the judgment that auctions are generally preferable to comparative hearings by requiring them for commercial broadcast applications filed on or after July 1, 1997. In giving us discretion to determine whether or not to use auctions in pending cases, we believe Congress intended us to focus on any special circumstances in these cases that would tip the policy balance in favor of comparative hearings, not to revisit the general congressional determination that broadcast auctions serve the public interest. In any event, it is far from clear that a licensee that wins its license in an auction has less incentive to serve the needs and interests of the community than one who wins in a comparative hearing.

40. Moreover, auctions will have significant public interest benefits. In a 1997 report to Congress, we indicated that our experience with auctions shows

that competitive bidding is a more efficient and cost-effective method of assigning spectrum in cases of mutual exclusivity than any previously employed method, including comparative hearings. And, as we stated in the *Notice*, 12 FCC Rcd. at 22371 (¶18), we have relied on the relative advantages of auctions—which also include the public interest benefits of encouraging the efficient use of the frequency, assigning the frequency to the eligible party that values it the most and recovering for the public a portion of the value of spectrum made available for commercial use—in other contexts in which we have faced a choice of either using comparative hearings or a system of competitive bidding to resolve mutual exclusivity among license applicants. We believe many of these same benefits will apply in this context.

C. General Rules and Procedures for Competitive Bidding

4. Designated Entities

186. Section 309(j) of the Communications Act provides that the Commission "ensure that small businesses, rural telephone companies, and businesses owned by members of minority groups and women are given the opportunity to participate in the provision of spectrum-based services." 47 U.S.C. §309(j)(4)(D). To achieve this congressional goal, the statute directs the Commission to "consider the use of tax certificates, bidding preferences, and other procedures."[10] *Id.* In addition, Section 309(j)(3)(B) instructs the Commission, in establishing eligibility criteria and bidding methodologies, to promote "economic opportunity and competition...by avoiding excessive concentration of licenses and by disseminating licenses among a wide variety of applicants, including small businesses, rural telephone companies, and businesses owned by members of minority groups and women," which are collectively referred to as "designated entities." 47 U.S.C. §309(j)(3)(B). Section 309(j)(4)(A) further provides that to promote these objectives, the Commission shall consider alternative payment schedules, including lump sums or guaranteed installment payments. 47 U.S.C. §309(j)(4)(A). In addition to the statutory directive to "ensure" opportunities for designated entities in spectrum auctions, the Commission has had a long-standing commitment to promoting the diversification of ownership of broadcast facilities. Indeed, "a maximum diffusion of control of the media of mass communications" was one of the two primary objectives of the traditional comparative broadcast licensing system. Policy Statement on Comparative Broadcast Hearings, 1 FCC 2d 393, 394 (1965). Section 257 of the Telecommunications Act of 1996, moreover, directed the Commission to identify and eliminate market entry barriers for small and entrepreneurial telecommunications businesses.

187. To fulfill our obligations under Section 309(j), the *Notice*, 12 FCC Rcd. at 22397–22404 (¶¶83–97), sought comment on whether bidding credits or other special measures were necessary to encourage participation by rural telephone companies, small businesses, and minority- and women-owned businesses in the provision of broadcast services, and, if so, how eligibility for any such special measures should be established. In particular, we requested comment on how special measures for minority- and women-owned entities could be developed

---

10. Congress repealed, as of January 17, 1995, that portion of Section 1071 of the Internal Revenue Code, 26 U.S.C. §1071, under which the Commission administered the tax certificate program.

consistent with applicable constitutional standards. The *Notice* also asked for comment on the advisability of adopting bidding credits or other measures to promote diversification of ownership, and on the appropriateness of adopting rules to prevent unjust enrichment in connection with the special measures approved for designated entities.

188. Many commenters argue that the present record is insufficient to support the adoption of bidding credits for women and minorities under the standards enunciated in United States v. Virginia, 518 U.S. 515 (1996) and Adarand Constructors, Inc. v. Pena, 515 U.S. 200 (1995). Some commenters urge that we delay the adoption of competitive bidding procedures for broadcast auctions until completion of studies already in progress that may shed light on these questions. And, although a number of commenters support the adoption of bidding credits for small businesses, they have supplied relatively little information regarding the capital requirements of, or the characteristics of the expected pool of bidders for, the various broadcast services. Determining the details of any small business credit is also complicated in the broadcast context by the fact that, at least traditionally, most applicants for new broadcast stations are in fact small businesses under almost any reasonable definition, particularly in the context of radio. Pursuant to our Section 257 proceeding, we have commenced a series of studies to examine the barriers encountered by small, minority- and women-owned businesses in the secondary markets and the auctions process. We believe it is important to complete these studies and provide for an opportunity for public comment before any ultimate determination of what rules we should have for designated entities. At the same time, we believe that it is important to move forward promptly with auctions. Particularly with regard to pending cases, considerations of fairness demand that no further delays occur and that we proceed expeditiously to licensing.

189. In proceeding with auctions before determining what rules we may ultimately adopt for small, minority- or women-owned businesses, we are, of course, sensitive to our statutory obligations regarding designated entities. As a preliminary matter, we note that, based on our experience in conducting comparative hearings under the 1965 Policy Statement on Comparative Broadcast Hearings, it is likely that the vast majority of the pending pre-July 1st applicants are small businesses, and indeed likely very small businesses. With respect to specific measures that may further assist designated entities, we note that all of the commenters who addressed the question supported a bidding credit or other special measure for applicants with no or few other media interests. We conclude that, based on the record to date, adopting such a "new entrant" bidding credit would be the most appropriate way to implement the statutory provisions regarding opportunities for small, minority- and women-owned businesses before the completion of the studies mentioned above and related public comment. Providing bidding credits to entities holding no or few mass media licenses will promote opportunities by minorities and women consistent with congressional intent without implicating prematurely the constitutional issues raised in ¶188.

Notes and Questions

1. Record-Setting Revenues. If nothing else, auctions have been a financial windfall for the government. In July 1994, for example, a spectrum auction for ten nationwide narrowband PCS licenses generated $617 million for the U.S. Treasury. By April 1996, the FCC had completed six spectrum auctions that netted $20 billion in total auction revenues.[11] The three-month auction of ninety-nine PCS licenses which ended on March 13, 1995, raised more than $7.7 billion, and was at that time recognized in the *Guinness Book of World Records* as the largest auction in history.[12]

2. Strategic Considerations. Some auctions, however, have yielded revenues much lower than predicted, and there is concern that those lower revenues resulted from would-be licensees outsmarting the government when it came to auction strategy. For example, in a 1997 auction, a Texas firm seems to have "warned off" potential auction rivals by, in early auction rounds, using odd bid amounts to signal which licenses it coveted most. Thus, instead of bidding, say, $80,000, this firm would bid $80,312, indicating by the area code "312" that it was going to seriously pursue a Chicago license. The strategy could have backfired, of course, attracting rivals' attention to the desired licenses and in that way pushing bids up; but the FCC apparently believes otherwise, since in subsequent auctions the Commission has rounded reported bid amounts to thwart this strategy. *See* Learning to Play the Game, The Economist, May 1997, at 86.

These sorts of strategic considerations are important not just because they mean that the government might be short-changed, but also because they mean that the government is not getting an important quid pro quo from bidders: information as to how valuable particular bands of spectrum are in particular areas and for particular uses. Auctions, after all, were in part designed to help the government better understand spectrum value and in that way better manage the band plan. Low bids undermine this goal by keeping true market valuations hidden—although the possibility of license resale in part mitigates this problem.[13]

3. Unintended Consequences. The difficulty in crafting auction rules is troubling for yet another reason: government auction policies might have unintended consequences. Consider the minority preferences alluded to at the end of the above *Order*. Ian Ayres and Peter Crampton argue that, whatever the intended effect, minority auction preferences might increase the net revenues earned by the government in auctions where preferences are used.[14] The two studied an auction where designated bidders were, first, allowed to pay for licenses in installments over a ten year period at a favorable interest rate and, second, granted a forty percent bidding credit applicable to ten of the licenses up for auction. The combined effect of both policies, according to the authors, was that "favored bidders

---

11. FCC Wireless Telecommunications Bureau, News Release, FCC Hits $20 Billion Mark in Total Auction Revenues (1996), http://www.fcc.gov/Bureaus/wireless/News_Releases/1996/nrw16015.txt. These auctions included Nationwide & Regional Narrowband PCS, Interactive Video and Data Services, Broadband PCS (A, B, & C Blocks), Direct Broadcast Satellite, Multipoint Distribution Service, and 900 MHz Specialized Mobile Radio.

12. FCC Wireless Telecommunications Bureau, News Release, FCC Grants 99 Licenses for Broadband Personal Communications Services in Major Trading Areas (1996), http://www.fcc.gov/Bureaus/wireless/News_Releases/1995/nrw15009.txt.

13. Resale only helps, of course, if it actually happens. If the top-valuer buys the license in an auction but at an artificially low price, the extent of his true valuation might never be revealed.

14. Ian Ayres & Peter Crampton, Deficit Reduction Through Diversity: How Affirmative Action at the FCC Increased Auction Competition, 48 Stan. L. Rev. 761 (1996).

had to pay the government only 50 percent of a winning bid."[15] The authors argue that bidding preferences nevertheless increased government auction revenue. Their logic: the existence of preferences caused unsubsidized bidders to bid more, "both because they had fewer licenses for which to compete (once the substantial designated preferences effectively set aside ten of the thirty licenses) and because they had to compete against the subsidized designated bidders crossing over to bid on non-set-aside licenses."[16] Ayres and Crampton thus conclude that bidding preferences are not as costly to the government as one might at first suspect, a result that might not help these preferences satisfy *Adarand* requirements, but one that surely would make these preferences more politically acceptable.

4. Foreclosure. Auctions work only if the auctioneer holds bidders to their bid amounts, if necessary foreclosing on the auctioned property in the event of nonpayment. Yet, for obvious political reasons, the government has been reluctant to foreclose, especially as against minority and small business bidders of the sort discussed above. After an auction for 493 licenses in 1996, for example, the FCC allowed companies holding a full 47% of those licenses to restructure their payment plans and in that way avoid default. Worse, even with that relief, dozens of these licenses ended up in bankruptcy proceedings, many of which were still unresolved years later. *See* FCC Says Many Wireless Bidders, Short of Cash, to Return Licenses, The Wall Street Journal (June 18, 1998), at C1; Two Opposite Court Rulings Raise Questions About FCC's Next Move on NextWave Licenses, The Wall Street Journal (Nov. 2, 2000), at C17. All this delays the productive use of allocated spectrum.

5. Auctions in Other Settings. The federal government uses auctions as an assignment mechanism for other resources in addition to spectrum. For example, for nearly forty years the U.S. Department of the Interior has been using auctions to allocate rights in oil-rich land in the Outer Continental Shelf. In these auctions, successful bidders pay an up-front fee and then share revenues (and hence risk) with the government for the duration of the lease. The federal government similarly uses auctions to allocate federal coal leases. For discussion, *see* Kwerel & Felker, Using Auctions to Select FCC Licenses, FCC Office of Plans & Policy (May 1985).

6. Domain Name Auctions. Is there some reason why we auction some resources but fail to auction others? Think, for example, about the Internet's domain name system. Domain names are a limited resource in that there are only so many descriptive alphanumeric combinations currently in use in the English language. Why doesn't the government put all domain names up for auction, with "www.furniture.com" simply being awarded to the highest bidder?

7. The First Amendment. Should the fact that a license was auctioned, as opposed to being given out in some form of a merit-based hearing, matter at all for First Amendment analysis? For example, should a "purchaser" enjoy greater First Amendment protections than a "recipient"? And where does that leave a firm that purchased its license from another firm, the original firm having gotten the license from the government through a comparative hearing? Is this "purchaser" in any meaningful way different from the firm that purchased as part of a government-sponsored auction?

---

15. *Id.* at 763.
16. *Id.*

8. Revising the Commission's Auction Authority. Legislation since 1997 has in certain cases restricted the FCC's auction authority. For instance, §647 of the Orbit Act of 2000, Pub. Law 106-180, 114 Stat. 48, states that, "notwithstanding any other provision of law, the Commission shall *not* have the authority to assign by competitive bidding orbital locations or spectrum used for the provision of international or global satellite communications services" (emphasis added). As a practical matter, that means that if spectrum will be used for any satellite-based common carrier service, it cannot be auctioned because some subset of the transmissions carried might be international in either their origination or termination. By contrast, spectrum for satellite services whose transmission and reception is limited to the United States, such as direct broadcast satellite (DBS) video, can be auctioned.

Unable to engage in auctions for this spectrum, the FCC adopted an application procedure that divides available spectrum among all qualified applicants and then imposes on those applicants specific buildout benchmarks that each licensee must satisfy in order to retain his license. *See In re Establishment of Policies and Service Rules for the Mobile Satellite Service in the 2 GHz Band*, FCC 00-302, 2000 WL 1209424 (2000).

CHAPTER SIX

THE LICENSEE AS PUBLIC TRUSTEE

The purpose of this chapter is:

- to examine the "public trustee" obligations imposed on broadcast licensees, such as FCC requirements concerning balanced news coverage, indecent programing, violent programing, and children's fare; and

- to ask, in that process, whether the public trustee obligations continue to be a sensible form of regulation now that licenses are not given away but are instead sold at auction to the highest bidder.

In Chapter Three we explained that the FCC performs four main functions in the regulation of spectrum: the Commission establishes the band plan; assigns licenses to their original owners; determines the rules for license renewal and transfer; and imposes public interest obligations on licensees. The first three functions were considered in Chapters Three, Four, and Five; this chapter considers the fourth.

Early in its history, the FCC adopted the view that broadcast stations should operate as "public trustees" and that an important function of the Commission would be to ensure that broadcasters perform that role. "Public trustee" was and is an amorphous phrase. In general, it signifies that one has a special duty to subordinate one's own interests to those of the wider public good. For purposes of this discussion, we might say that a broadcaster acts as a "public trustee" when it sacrifices financial gain to the interests of the viewing and listening public.

In the early days of broadcasting, the public trustee notion seemed easy to justify. Broadcasters employed an essential input, use of the spectrum, that government gave them free of charge. Further, in determining who would be allowed to use that input, the government chose the most meritorious applicants, and merit was defined in large measure by public interest criteria. Thus, it seemed only natural that the government should impose upon those who won broadcast licenses a special obligation to use them to serve the public.

From the end of World War II until very recent times, radio and television broadcasters were, pursuant to this intuitive logic, subject to a wide array of regulations. These regulations included familiar requirements, such as compliance with the so-called "fairness doctrine," and more arcane rules, such as the one detailing specific steps that licensees were required to take periodically to ascertain the viewing and listening desires of people within their service areas. The public trustee model also encompassed less rigid forms of oversight, such as suggestions by the Commission that stations should broadcast certain percentages of news, public affairs, and general informational or educational programming.

In all these cases, the Commission's position was that the FCC should pressure stations to offer programs other than those licensees would broadcast were they free to follow only their own incentives. This position rested on the view, as articulated by Justice Frankfurter, that, in regulating broadcast telecommunications, the FCC was not relegated to the role of a "traffic officer, policing the wave lengths to prevent stations from interfering with each other. . . . [T]he Act does not restrict the Commission merely to supervision of the traffic. It puts upon the Commission the burden of determining the composition of that traffic." NBC v. United States, 319 U.S. 190, 215–16 (1943).

Beginning in the mid-1970s, however, and moving at a constantly accelerating pace through the 1980s, the FCC retreated from this view and came to hold, ever more tenaciously, the view that broadcast stations ought to be governed by market forces. Viewers and listeners should exercise influence over licensees by turning the dials on their receivers, not by petitioning the Commission for relief—or so the Commission seemed to say time and again. In the newly relevant words of Supreme Court language that preceded Justice Frankfurter's, the Communications Act "recognizes that the field of broadcasting is one of free competition"; "Congress intended to permit a licensee who was not interfering electrically with other broadcasters to survive or succumb according to his ability to make his programs attractive to the public." FCC v. Sanders Bros. Radio Station, 309 U.S. 470, 474, 475 (1940).

Modern use of auctions as the mechanism for initial license assignments seems only to reinforce this latter argument in favor of market deference and against public trustee obligations. The intuitive logic of public trustee regulation turned on the fact that licenses were given away at no charge and were therefore distributed in the first instance according to public interest criteria. Public interest obligations were, in this story, a natural extension to the hearing process. Licenses today, however, are awarded to the highest bidder; and so the old rationale for public trustee obligations is considerably undermined.

As you read the materials that follow, however, you should consider whether public trustee obligations might be justified for other reasons, even given the new approach to license assignment. Are there reasons to interfere with the market that are completely unrelated to the fact that broadcasters use a public resource? Are there objectives the government can accomplish through public trustee obligations that it cannot accomplish equally well through the market—for example, by selling licenses and then using that revenue to further the particular aims in question?

The materials on regulation of broadcast content begin with Miami Herald Publishing Co. v. Tornillo, a case that concerns a newspaper, not a broadcast station. The Supreme Court's opinion there makes clear that, as applied to newspaper content, the public trustee concept is utterly alien to U.S. law, in large part because of the First Amendment. In fact, *Tornillo* goes so far as to suggest that the First Amendment requires that government permit publishers to "do good by doing well"—*i.e.*, to fulfill their public functions of educating, informing, and arousing the populace by whatever means they choose in the pursuit of their own self interest, subject only to content neutral laws of general applicability. *Tornillo*

stands in sharp contrast to the case that immediately follows it in the materials —
Red Lion, a case where the Supreme Court seems to reach fully opposite conclusions about the same sort of public trustee obligations. The only difference? *Red Lion* is a case involving broadcast.

The chapter then proceeds to consider (in varying degrees of detail) all the main areas of regulation that have, at one time or another, been part of licensees' overall public trustee obligations. Each area raises the question of whether broadcasting ought to be governed by the public trustee model or, instead, by the more conventional free market approach epitomized by *Tornillo*. Specifically, the chapter considers in turn: the fairness doctrine and related obligations, indecency, televised violence, children's television, and FCC rules related to commercialization and viewer preference ascertainment.

I. THE FAIRNESS DOCTRINE
AND RELATED OBLIGATIONS

A. The Fairness Doctrine

MIAMI HERALD PUBLISHING CO. v. TORNILLO
418 U.S. 241 (1974)

BURGER, C.J., delivered the opinion of the Court. BRENNAN, J., filed a concurring opinion in which REHNQUIST, J., joined. WHITE, J., filed a concurring opinion.

CHIEF JUSTICE BURGER delivered the opinion of the Court.

In the fall of 1972, Tornillo, Executive Director of the Classroom Teachers Association, was a candidate for the Florida House of Representatives. On September 20, 1972, and again on September 29, 1972, the Miami Herald printed editorials critical of Tornillo's candidacy. In response to these editorials Tornillo demanded that the Herald print verbatim his replies. The Herald declined to print Tornillo's replies, and Tornillo brought suit based on a Florida "right of reply" statute which provides that if a candidate for nomination or election is assailed regarding his personal character or official record by any newspaper, the candidate has the right to demand that the newspaper print, free of cost to the candidate, any reply the candidate may make to the newspaper's charges. The reply must appear in as conspicuous a place and in the same kind of type as the charges which prompted the reply, provided it does not take up more space than the charges. Failure to comply with the statute constitutes a first-degree misdemeanor. The Herald contends the statute is void on its face because it purports to regulate the content of a newspaper in violation of the First Amendment.

Tornillo and supporting advocates of an enforceable right of access to the press vigorously argue that government has an obligation to ensure that a wide variety of views reach the public. Newspapers have become big business and there are far fewer of them to serve a larger literate population. Chains of newspapers, national newspapers, national wire and news services, and one-newspaper towns are the dominant features of a press that has become noncompetitive and enormously powerful and influential in its capacity to manipulate popular opinion and change the course of events. The result of these vast changes has been to place in a few hands the power to inform the American people and shape public opinion. In effect, it is claimed, the public has lost any ability to respond or to contribute in a meaningful way to the debate on issues.

The obvious solution, which was available to dissidents at an earlier time when entry into publishing was relatively inexpensive, today would be to have additional newspapers. But the same economic factors which have caused the disappearance of vast numbers of metropolitan newspapers have made entry into the marketplace of ideas served by the print media almost impossible. It is urged that the claim of newspapers to be 'surrogates for the public' carries with it a concomitant fiduciary obligation to account for that stewardship. From this premise it is reasoned that the only effective way to insure fairness and accuracy and to provide for some accountability is for government to take affirmative action. The First Amendment interest of the public in being informed is said to be in peril because the "marketplace of ideas" is today a monopoly controlled by the owners of the market.

However much validity may be found in these arguments, at each point the implementation of a remedy such as an enforceable right of access necessarily calls for some mechanism, either governmental or consensual. If it is governmental coercion, this at once brings about a confrontation with the express provisions of the First Amendment and the judicial gloss on that Amendment developed over the years.

The clear implication of our previous cases has been that any compulsion exerted by government to publish that which "reason tells newspapers should not be published" is unconstitutional. A responsible press is an undoubtedly desirable goal, but press responsibility is not mandated by the Constitution and like many other virtues it cannot be legislated.

Tornillo's argument that the Florida statute does not amount to a restriction of the Herald's right to speak because "the statute in question here has not prevented the Miami Herald from saying anything it wished" begs the core question. The Florida statute operates as a command in the same sense as a statute or regulation forbidding the Herald to publish specified matter. The Florida statute exacts a penalty on the basis of the content of a newspaper. The first phase of the penalty resulting from the compelled printing of a reply is exacted in terms of the cost in printing and composing time and materials and in taking up space that could be devoted to other material the newspaper may have preferred to print. It is correct, as Tornillo contends, that a newspaper is not subject to the finite technological limitations of time that confront a broadcaster but it is not correct to say that, as an economic reality, a newspaper can proceed to infinite expansion of its column space to accommodate the replies that a government agency determines or a statute commands the readers should have available.

Faced with the penalties that would accrue to any newspaper that published news or commentary arguably within the reach of the right-of-access statute, editors might well conclude that the safe course is to avoid controversy. Therefore, under the operation of the Florida statute, political and electoral coverage would be blunted or reduced. Government-enforced right of access inescapably "dampens the vigor and limits the variety of public debate," New York Times Co. v. Sullivan, 376 U.S. 254, 279 (1964).

Even if a newspaper would face no additional costs to comply with a compulsory access law and would not be forced to forgo publication of news or opinion by the inclusion of a reply, the Florida statute fails to clear the barriers of the First Amendment because of its intrusion into the function of editors. A newspaper is more than a passive receptacle or conduit for news, comment, and advertising. The choice of material to go into a newspaper, and the decisions made as to limitations on the size and content of the paper, and treatment of public issues and public officials—whether fair or unfair—constitute the exercise of editorial control and judgment. It has yet to be demonstrated how governmental regulation of this crucial process can be exercised consistent with First Amendment guarantees of a free press as they have evolved to this time.

[Concurring opinions of JUSTICES BRENNAN and WHITE are omitted.]

RED LION BROADCASTING CO. v. FCC
395 U.S. 367 (1969)

WHITE, J., delivered the opinion of the Court. DOUGLAS, J., took no part in the Court's decision.

JUSTICE WHITE delivered the opinion of the Court.

The Federal Communications Commission has for many years imposed on radio and television broadcasters the fairness doctrine requirement that discussion of public issues be presented on broadcast stations, and that each side of those issues must be given fair coverage. This obligation is distinct from the statutory requirement of §315 of the Communications Act that equal time be allotted all qualified candidates for public office. Two aspects of the fairness doctrine, relating to personal attacks in the context of controversial public issues and to political editorializing, were codified more precisely in the form of FCC regulations in 1967. The two cases before us now, which were decided separately below, challenge the constitutional and statutory bases of the doctrine and component rules. *Red Lion* involves the application of the fairness doctrine to a particular broadcast, and *RTNDA* arises as an action to review the FCC's 1967 promulgation of the personal attack and political editorializing regulations, which were laid down after the *Red Lion* litigation had begun.

I

The Red Lion Broadcasting Company is licensed to operate a Pennsylvania radio station, WGCB. On November 27, 1964, WGCB carried a 15-minute broadcast by the Reverend Billy James Hargis as part of a "Christian Crusade" series. A book by Fred J. Cook entitled "Goldwater—Extremist on the Right" was discussed by Hargis, who said that Cook had been fired by a newspaper for making false charges against city officials; that Cook had then worked for a Communist-affiliated publication; that he had defended Alger Hiss and attacked J. Edgar Hoover and the Central Intelligence Agency; and that he had now written a "book to smear and destroy Barry Goldwater." When Cook heard of the broadcast he concluded that he had been personally attacked and demanded free reply time, which the station refused. After an exchange of letters among Cook, Red Lion, and the FCC, the FCC declared that the Hargis broadcast constituted a personal attack on Cook; that Red Lion had failed to meet its obligation under the fairness doctrine to send a tape, transcript, or summary of the broadcast to Cook and offer him reply time; and that the station must provide reply time whether or not Cook would pay for it. On review in the Court of Appeals for the District of Columbia Circuit, the FCC's position was upheld as constitutional and otherwise proper.

Not long after the *Red Lion* litigation was begun, the FCC adopted rules making the personal attack aspect of the fairness doctrine more precise and more readily enforceable, and specifying its rules relating to political editorials. The rules were held unconstitutional in the *RTNDA* litigation by the Court of Appeals for the Seventh Circuit, on review of the rule-making proceeding, as abridging the freedoms of speech and press.

As they now stand amended, the regulations read as follows:

"Personal attacks; political editorials.

"(a) When, during the presentation of views on a controversial issue of public importance, an attack is made upon the honesty, character, integrity or like personal qualities of an identified person or group, the licensee shall, no later than 1 week after the attack, transmit to the person or group attacked (1) notification of the date, time and identification of the broadcast; (2) a script or tape (or an accurate summary if a script or tape is not available) of the attack; and (3) an offer of a reasonable opportunity to respond over the licensee's facilities.

"(b) The provisions of paragraph (a)...shall not be applicable (1) to attacks on foreign groups or foreign public figures; (2) to personal attacks which are made by legally qualified candidates...on other such candidates...and (3) to bona fide newscasts....

"(c) Where a licensee, in an editorial, (i) endorses or (ii) opposes a legally qualified candidate or candidates, the licensee shall, within 24 hours after the editorial, transmit to respectively (i) the other qualified candidate or candidates for the same office or (ii) the candidate opposed in the editorial (1) notification of the date and the time of the editorial; (2) a script or tape of the editorial; and (3) an offer of a reasonable opportunity for a candidate or a spokesman of the candidate to respond over the licensee's facilities."

II

Before 1927, the allocation of frequencies was left entirely to the private sector, and the result was chaos. It quickly became apparent that broadcast frequencies constituted a scarce resource whose use could be regulated and rationalized only by the Government. Without government control, the medium would be of little use because of the cacophony of competing voices, none of which could be clearly and predictably heard. Consequently, the Federal Radio Commission was established to allocate frequencies among competing applicants in a manner responsive to the public "convenience, interest, or necessity."

Very shortly thereafter the Commission expressed its view that the "public interest requires ample play for the free and fair competition of opposing views, and the commission believes that the principle applies to all discussions of issues of importance to the public." *Great Lakes Broadcasting Co.*, 3 F.R.C. Ann. Rep. 32, 33 (1929), *rev'd on other grounds*, 59 App. D.C. 197, *cert. dismissed*, 281 U.S. 706 (1930). This doctrine was applied through denial of license renewals or construction permits, both by the FRC and its successor FCC. After an extended period during which the licensee was obliged not only to cover and to cover fairly the views of others, but also to refrain from expressing his own personal views, *Mayflower Broadcasting Corp.*, 8 FCC 333 (1940), the latter limitation on the licensee was abandoned and the doctrine developed into its present form.

There is a twofold duty laid down by the FCC's decisions and described by the 1949 *Report on Editorializing by Broadcast Licensees*, 13 FCC 1246 (1949). The broadcaster must give adequate coverage to public issues, *United Broadcasting Co.*, 10 FCC 515 (1945), and coverage must be fair in that it accurately reflects the opposing views. *New Broadcasting Co.*, 6 P & F Radio Reg. 258 (1950). This must be done at the broadcaster's own expense if sponsorship is unavailable. *Cullman Broadcasting Co.*, 25 P & F Radio Reg. 895 (1963).

III

The broadcasters challenge the fairness doctrine and its specific manifestations in the personal attack and political editorial rules on conventional First Amendment grounds, alleging that the rules abridge their freedom of speech and press. Their contention is that the First Amendment protects their desire to use their allotted frequencies continuously to broadcast whatever they choose, and to exclude whomever they choose from ever using that frequency. No man may be prevented from saying or publishing what he thinks, or from refusing in his speech or other utterances to give equal weight to the views of his opponents. This right, they say, applies equally to broadcasters.

A

Although broadcasting is clearly a medium affected by a First Amendment interest, differences in the characteristics of new media justify differences in the First Amendment standards applied to them. Just as the Government may limit the use of sound-amplifying equipment potentially so noisy that it drowns out civilized private speech, so may the Government limit the use of broadcast equipment. The right of free speech of a broadcaster, the user of a sound truck, or any other individual does not embrace a right to snuff out the free speech of others.

Only a tiny fraction of those with resources and intelligence can hope to communicate by radio at the same time if intelligible communication is to be had, even if the entire radio spectrum is utilized in the present state of commercially acceptable technology. Where there are substantially more individuals who want to broadcast than there are frequencies to allocate, it is idle to posit an unabridgeable First Amendment right to broadcast comparable to the right of every individual to speak, write, or publish. If 100 persons want broadcast licenses but there are only 10 frequencies to allocate, all of them may have the same "right" to a license; but if there is to be any effective communication by radio, only a few can be licensed and the rest must be barred from the airwaves.

It would be strange if the First Amendment, aimed at protecting and furthering communications, prevented the Government from making radio communication possible by requiring licenses to broadcast and by limiting the number of licenses so as not to overcrowd the spectrum.

By the same token, as far as the First Amendment is concerned, those who are licensed stand no better than those to whom licenses are refused. A license permits broadcasting, but the licensee has no constitutional right to be the one who holds the license or to monopolize a radio frequency to the exclusion of his fellow citizens. There is nothing in the First Amendment which prevents the Government from requiring a licensee to share his frequency with others and to conduct himself as a proxy or fiduciary with obligations to present those views and voices which are representative of his community and which would otherwise, by necessity, be barred from the airwaves.

The people as a whole retain their interest in free speech by radio and their collective right to have the medium function consistently with the ends and purposes of the First Amendment. It is the right of the viewers and listeners, not the right of the broadcasters, which is paramount. It is the purpose of the First Amendment to preserve an uninhibited marketplace of ideas in which truth will ultimately prevail, rather than to countenance monopolization of that market, whether it be by the Government itself or a private licensee. It is the right of the public to receive suitable access to social, political, esthetic, moral, and other ideas and experiences which is crucial here. That right may not constitutionally be abridged either by Congress or by the FCC.

B

Rather than confer frequency monopolies on a relatively small number of licensees, in a Nation of 200,000,000, the Government could surely have decreed that each frequency should be shared among all or some of those who wish to use it, each being assigned a portion of the broadcast day or the broadcast week. The ruling and regulations at issue here do not go quite so far. They assert that under specified circumstances, a licensee must offer to make available a reasonable amount of broadcast time to those who have a view different from that which has already been expressed on his station. The expression of a political endorsement, or of a personal attack while dealing with a controversial public issue, simply triggers this time sharing. As we have said, the First Amendment confers no right on licensees to prevent others from broadcasting on "their" frequencies and no right to an unconditional monopoly of a scarce resource which the Government has denied others the right to use.

Otherwise, station owners and a few networks would have unfettered power to make time available only to the highest bidders, to communicate only their own views on public issues, people and candidates, and to permit on the air only those with whom they agreed. There is no sanctuary in the First Amendment for unlimited private censorship operating in a medium not open to all.

C

It is strenuously argued, however, that if political editorials or personal attacks will trigger an obligation in broadcasters to afford the opportunity for expression to speakers who need not pay for time and whose views are unpalatable to the licensees, then broadcasters will be irresistibly forced to self-censorship and their coverage of controversial public issues will be eliminated or at least rendered wholly ineffective. Should licensees actually eliminate their coverage of controversial issues, the purposes of the doctrine would be stifled.

At this point, however, that possibility is at best speculative. The communications industry, and in particular the networks, have taken pains to present controversial issues in the past, and even now they do not assert that they intend to abandon their efforts in this regard. And if experience with the administration of these doctrines indicates that they have the net effect of reducing rather than enhancing the volume and quality of coverage, there will be time enough to reconsider the constitutional implications. The fairness doctrine in the past has had no such overall effect.

If present licensees should suddenly prove timorous, the Commission is not powerless to insist that they give adequate and fair attention to public issues. It does not violate the First Amendment to treat licensees given the privilege of using scarce radio frequencies as proxies for the entire community, obligated to give suitable time and attention to matters of great public concern. Congress need not stand idly by and permit those with licenses to ignore the problems which beset the people or to exclude from the airways anything but their own views of fundamental questions.

The statute mandates the issuance of licenses if the "public convenience, interest, or necessity will be served thereby." 47 U.S.C. §307 (a). In applying this standard the Commission for 40 years has been choosing licensees based in part on their program proposals. The Court [has previously recognized] that the Commission was more than a traffic policeman concerned with the technical aspects of broadcasting and that it neither exceeded its powers under the statute nor transgressed the First Amendment in interesting itself in general program format and the kinds of programs broadcast by licensees. National Broadcasting Co. v. United States, 319 U.S. 190 (1943).

D

There is no question here of the Commission's refusal to permit the broadcaster to carry a particular program or to publish his own views; of a discriminatory refusal to require the licensee to broadcast certain views which have been denied access to the airwaves; of government censorship of a particular program contrary to §326; or of the official government view dominating public broadcasting. Such questions would raise more serious First Amendment issues.

E

It is argued that even if at one time the lack of available frequencies for all who wished to use them justified the fairness doctrine, this condition no longer prevails so that continuing control is not justified. To this there are several answers.

Scarcity is not entirely a thing of the past. Advances in technology, such as microwave transmission, have led to more efficient utilization of the frequency spectrum, but uses for that spectrum have also grown apace. Among the various uses for radio frequency space, including marine, aviation, amateur, military, and common carrier users, there are easily enough claimants to permit use of the whole with an even smaller allocation to broadcast radio and television uses than now exists.

Comparative hearings between competing applicants for broadcast spectrum space are by no means a thing of the past. Nothing in this record, or in our own researches, convinces us that the resource is no longer one for which there are more immediate and potential uses than can be accommodated, and for which wise planning is essential.

In view of the scarcity of broadcast frequencies, the Government's role in allocating those frequencies, and the legitimate claims of those unable without governmental assistance to gain access to those frequencies for expression of their views, we hold the regulations and ruling at issue here are both authorized by statute and constitutional.

[JUSTICE DOUGLAS did not participate in this decision.]

Notes and Questions

1. A Missing Citation. The Court's decision in *Tornillo* is strong and sweeping, written as if the result flows inexorably from deeply established precedent under the First Amendment. Interestingly, the opinion contains no discussion of—or even citations to—*Red Lion*, which had been decided five years before. Is this because the two cases cannot be reconciled? Because a case about broadcast has no bearing on a case about print media? Was this irresponsible behavior on the part of the Supreme Court, or was the Court simply exercising restraint by, in each instance, deciding only the case before it?

2. Reconciling the Cases. At first blush, at least, all the arguments rejected in *Red Lion* seem to be the very ones accepted in *Tornillo*. More specifically, the *Tornillo* Court overturned the Florida statute for two reasons. First, any government "compulsion...to publish that which 'reason tells newspapers should not be published' is unconstitutional." Second, "under the operation of the Florida statute, political and electoral coverage would be blunted or reduced." These arguments seem to reflect precisely the issues addressed by the *Red Lion* Court. The broadcasters in that case contended "that the First Amendment protects their desire to use their allocated frequencies continuously to broadcast whatever they choose, and to exclude whomever they choose from ever using that frequency" and "that if political editorials or personal attacks will trigger an obligation in broadcasters to afford the opportunity for expression to speakers who need not pay for time and whose views are unpalatable to the licensees, then broadcasters will be irresistibly forced to self-censorship and their coverage of controversial public issues will be eliminated or at least rendered wholly ineffective."

3. Scarcity. *Red Lion* suggests that the basis for special First Amendment treatment of broadcasters is the scarcity of broadcast spectrum. Chapter Two considers the general question of spectrum scarcity in some detail, so that discussion need not be repeated here. But consider the specific reasoning offered by *Red Lion* in the last two paragraphs of the opinion as edited above. Can you think of any resource (including paper and ink) for which there are not "more immediate and potential uses than can be accommodated, and for which wise planning is

[not] essential"? Moreover, similar arguments were raised and rejected in *Tornillo*. Indeed, as the *Tornillo* Court itself reported, there are only a few owners of newspapers; entry into the newspaper market is "almost impossible"; and, just like broadcasts, newspapers are subject to limits on how much information they can transmit. Yet in *Tornillo* none of these considerations softened the First Amendment protection recognized.

4. Print versus Broadcast. Are there other bases for distinguishing broadcast from print that would justify the lesser First Amendment protection afforded to broadcasters? One commonly noted rationale is that the government licenses the spectrum, and for many years distributed licenses without charge, so public interest obligations like a mandated right of reply were perhaps a permissible condition on the use of government resources. But, given our discussion of scarcity and interference in Chapter Two, is that argument convincing? And how does the argument change now that licenses are distributed by auction, not hearing? Are there other bases for distinguishing broadcasting from print? That broadcasting is an unusually powerful medium? That it is ubiquitous? That it greatly influences our culture? But none of these attributes fits only broadcasting, does it? And if broadcasting were unique in one or more of these manners, why would that suggest that broadcasters should receive less rather than more First Amendment protection?

5. Choosing an Approach. It seems, then, that one must choose between the First Amendment jurisprudence of *Tornillo* and that of *Red Lion*. Which makes more sense? Does *Tornillo* overstate the dangers of government regulation and the extent to which editors will be chilled by it? Why did the *Tornillo* Court fail to conclude that "it is the right of the [readers], not the right of the [publishers], which is paramount"? Does *Red Lion* fail to appreciate that the fairness doctrine is enforced by unelected bureaucrats? Does it fail to appreciate the fact that even a minor threat against a very valuable broadcasting license can be weighty? Is *Red Lion* flawed by its failure to submit a content specific speech regulation to strict scrutiny, or is *Tornillo* flawed because it uses such a high standard of review that a beneficial regulation was needlessly found unconstitutional?

6. Multiple First Amendment Constituencies. Consider *Red Lion*'s suggestion that the First Amendment rights of broadcast licensees are counter-balanced by First Amendment rights of viewers and listeners, and particularly its reference to "the right of the public to receive suitable access to social, political, esthetic, moral, and other ideas and experiences." Is such a reading of the First Amendment persuasive? Is it necessary to accept this reading in order to uphold a right-of-reply statute? And what are the implications of the quoted language?

For example, does this language suggest that the fairness doctrine is not merely permissible but is in fact constitutionally required? That is, does it indicate that, by creating a licensing regime but not creating any explicit fairness obligation, the 1934 Act itself violated the First Amendment? Similarly, does the public's right to suitable access mean that television networks are acting unconstitutionally when they imitate each other's most popular programming and, because of that imitation, fail to provide a wide range of programming alternatives? Does the First Amendment thus justify a rule forbidding a radio station to switch from a unique, financially viable format to another format already employed by several stations in the same market? Recall that this issue arose in FCC v. WNCN Listeners Guild, excerpted in Chapter Four. Justice White, who wrote the opinion in both *WNCN Listeners Guild* and *Red Lion*, addressed the point as follows:

> The Listeners Guild contends that the *Policy Statement* conflicts with the First Amendment rights of listeners "to receive suitable access to social, political, esthetic, moral, and other ideas and experiences." Red Lion Broadcasting Co. v. FCC, 395 U.S. 367, 390 (1969). Although observing that the interests of the people as a whole were promoted by debate of public issues on the radio, we did not imply [in *Red Lion*] that the First Amendment grants individual listeners the right to have the Commission review the abandonment of their favorite entertainment programs. The Commission seeks to further the interests of the listening public as a whole by relying on market forces to promote diversity in radio entertainment formats and to satisfy the entertainment preferences of radio listeners. This policy does not conflict with the First Amendment.

450 U.S. 582, 603–04. Are you persuaded?

7. Implications. Would *Red Lion* permit: (a) a prohibition on speech that the government determines to be of little or no "social, political, esthetic, [or] moral" value?; (b) a rule requiring each television broadcaster to provide a minimum amount of programming per day or per week for pre-school age children?; (c) awarding, in comparative hearing cases, a preference for applicants who are women or members of minority races?; (d) application of the fairness doctrine to a cable television system?

8. Subsequent Events. Although the Supreme Court has not abandoned *Red Lion*, the FCC did abandon the fairness doctrine. The path to that abandonment was a complicated one, in the course of which the FCC rejected most of the justifications asserted in the *Red Lion* opinion. In fact, the FCC cast doubt on the standard enunciated in *Red Lion* itself, although more recently it has attempted to revive *Red Lion*. Consider, in reading the FCC materials that follow, whether one of the decisions, or *Red Lion*, or none of the above, provides sound policy analysis.

FAIRNESS DOCTRINE REPORT
102 FCC 2d 145 (1985)

I. INTRODUCTION

3. The fairness doctrine imposes on broadcasters a two-pronged obligation. Broadcast licensees are required to provide coverage of vitally important controversial issues of interest in the community served by the licensees and to provide a reasonable opportunity for the presentation of contrasting viewpoints on such issues.

4. Our past judgment that the fairness doctrine comports with the public interest was predicated upon three factors. First, in light of the limited availability of broadcast frequencies and the resultant need for government licensing, we concluded that the licensee is a public fiduciary, obligated to present diverse viewpoints representative of the community at large. We determined that the need to effectuate the right of the viewing and listening public to suitable access to the marketplace of ideas justifies restrictions on the rights of broadcasters. Sec-

ond, we presumed that a governmentally imposed restriction on the content of programming is a viable mechanism—indeed the best mechanism—by which to vindicate this public interest. Third, we determined, as a factual matter, that the fairness doctrine, in operation, has the effect of enhancing the flow of diverse viewpoints to the public.

5. On the basis of the voluminous factual record compiled in this proceeding, our experience in administering the doctrine, and our general expertise in broadcast regulation, we no longer believe that the fairness doctrine, as a matter of policy, serves the public interest. We believe that the interest of the public in viewpoint diversity is fully served by the multiplicity of voices in the marketplace today and that the intrusion by government into the content of programming occasioned by the enforcement of the doctrine unnecessarily restricts the journalistic freedom of broadcasters. Furthermore, we find that the fairness doctrine, in operation, actually inhibits the presentation of controversial issues of public importance to the detriment of the public and in degradation of the editorial prerogatives of broadcast journalists.

6. We believe that the same factors which demonstrate that the fairness doctrine is no longer appropriate as a matter of policy also suggest that the doctrine may no longer be permissible as a matter of constitutional law.

7. The fairness doctrine has been a longstanding administrative policy and central tenet of broadcast regulation that Congress has chosen not to eliminate. Moreover, there are proposals pending before Congress to repeal the doctrine. As a consequence, we believe that it would be inappropriate at this time for us to either eliminate or significantly restrict the scope of the doctrine. Instead, we will afford Congress an opportunity to review the fairness doctrine in light of the evidence adduced in this proceeding.

II. THE CONSTITUTIONALITY OF THE FAIRNESS DOCTRINE IS SUSPECT

19. As demonstrated *infra*, the compelling evidence in this proceeding demonstrates that the fairness doctrine, in operation, inhibits the presentation of controversial issues of public importance. As a consequence, we believe that the fairness doctrine can no longer be justified on the grounds that it is necessary to promote the First Amendment rights of the viewing and listening public. Indeed, the chilling effect on the presentation of controversial issues of public importance resulting from our regulatory policies affirmatively disserves the interest of the public in obtaining access to diverse viewpoints. In addition, we believe that the fairness doctrine, as a regulation which directly affects the content of speech aired over broadcast frequencies, significantly impairs the journalistic freedom of broadcasters. As set forth in detail below, in light of the substantial increase in the number and types of information sources, we believe that the artificial mechanism of interjecting the government into an affirmative role of overseeing the content of speech is unnecessary to vindicate the interest of the public in obtaining access to the marketplace of ideas.

20. While it is true that the limited availability of the electromagnetic spectrum may constitute a per se justification for certain types of government regulation, such as licensing, it does not follow that all other types of governmental regulation, particularly rules which affect the constitutionally sensitive area of content regulation, are similarly justified.

III. A NUMBER OF FACTORS JUSTIFY A REASSESSMENT OF THE FAIRNESS DOCTRINE

B. The Fairness Doctrine in Operation Lessens the Amount of Diverse Views Available to the Public

1. Broadcasters Perceive That the Fairness Doctrine Involves Significant Burdens

26. A licensee may be inhibited from presenting controversial issues of public importance by operation of the fairness doctrine even though the first prong of that doctrine affirmatively requires the licensee to broadcast such issues. The reason underlying this apparent paradox is that the two parts of the fairness doctrine differ markedly in the scope of the controversial issues that they encompass, the ease by which a licensee can meet the requirements embodied in the two prongs and the degree to which the Commission, in the past, has taken affirmative action to enforce compliance with them.

27. It is well-established that a licensee, in complying with the first prong of the fairness doctrine, has broad discretion in determining the specific controversial issues of public importance that it chooses to present. Indeed, in our 1974 Fairness Report, we stated that "we have no intention of becoming involved in the selection of issues to be discussed, nor do we expect a broadcaster to cover each and every important issue which may arise in his community." Rather, with respect to the affirmative obligation to cover controversial issues of public importance, "a presumption of compliance exists" and only "in rare instances, where a licensee has failed to give coverage to an issue found to be of critical importance to its particular community, would questions be raised as to whether a licensee had fulfilled its fairness obligations."

28. The responsive programming obligation embodied in the second prong of the fairness doctrine arises whenever the licensee airs any controversial issue of public importance, even in situations where the issue broadcast is not "so critical or of such great public importance" to trigger a requirement under the first part of the fairness doctrine. An overwhelming majority of the complaints we receive and virtually all our orders directing licensees to take corrective action to conform to the requirements of the fairness doctrine involve the second prong of that doctrine.

29. As a result of the asymmetry between its two components, the fairness doctrine in its operation encourages broadcasters to air only the minimal amount of controversial issue programming sufficient to comply with the first prong. By restricting the amount and type of controversial programming aired, a broadcaster minimizes the potentially substantial burdens associated with the second prong of the doctrine while remaining in compliance with the strict letter of its regulatory obligations. Therefore, despite the first prong obligation, in net effect the fairness doctrine often discourages the presentation of controversial issue programming.[1]

---

1. We do not believe that more stringent enforcement of the first prong would be an appropriate remedial response to the existence of a "chilling effect." Contrary to the principles of the First Amendment, a stricter regulatory approach would increase the government's intrusion into the editorial decisionmaking process of broadcast journalists. It would enlarge the opportunity for governmental officials to abuse the doctrine for partisan political pur-

30. There are a variety of reasons why a broadcaster might be inhibited from providing comprehensive coverage of controversial issues of public importance by operation of the fairness doctrine. One reason is the fear of government sanction. Indeed, we have characterized the "strict adherence to the fairness doctrine...as the sine qua non for grant of a renewal of license."

31. Therefore, in order to attenuate the possibility that opponents, in a renewal proceeding, will challenge the manner in which a licensee provides balance with respect to the controversial issues it chooses to cover, a broadcaster may be inhibited from presenting controversial issue programming in excess of the minimum required to satisfy the first prong of the fairness doctrine.

32. While denial of a license renewal is the most severe sanction we can impose for failure to abide by the fairness doctrine, it is not the only sanction. Typically, upon a finding that a licensee has violated the fairness doctrine, we order the broadcaster to provide additional programming. In order to avoid these costs, a broadcaster may be inhibited from presenting more than a minimal amount of controversial issue programming.

33. A licensee may also be inhibited from presenting controversial issue programming by the fear of incurring the various expenses and other burdens which may arise in the context of fairness doctrine litigation regardless of whether or not it is ultimately found to be in violation of the doctrine.

34. As one broadcaster noted, licensees are "conscious of the probability that coverage of a highly controversial issue will trigger an avalanche of protests" demanding air time for the presentation of opposing viewpoints. While most requests may be made in good faith, there is evidence that some complainants invoke a licensee's fairness doctrine obligations in an attempt either to pressure a broadcaster to censor specific programming or to harass licensees into presenting a particular spokesman or broadcast.

35. Broadcasters can also be deterred by the financial costs involved in defending a fairness doctrine complaint. Moreover, in addition to the legal costs and other out-of-pocket expenses incurred by a station that is the subject of a fairness doctrine complaint, the licensee will be further burdened by the dislocation of normal operational functions that necessarily result from the significant amount of time expended by high-level management and station employees with respect to this matter.

37. Certain parties take issue with the contention that the fear of fairness doctrine litigation can have an inhibiting effect on the presentation of controversial issues of public importance. These parties argue that the Commission requests broadcasters to respond to only a small number of the complaints it receives annually and, as a consequence, most broadcasters do not in fact incur such costs. The evidence of record in this proceeding, however, reflects that broadcasters are convinced that these costs can in fact be a significant inhibiting factor in the presentation of controversial issues. Moreover, while it may be true that most broadcasters may not be confronted with actual fairness doctrine litigation, virtually all broadcasters do incur administrative and financial costs

poses. Were the chilling effect of the government sanction removed, the result might well be greater coverage of issues and thus more satisfaction of the policy behind the fairness doctrine's first prong.

which result from presenting responsive programming and negotiating with complainants. Furthermore, in light of the fact that the costs involved in fairness doctrine cases which do proceed beyond the complaint stage can be prohibitively expensive, particularly to smaller stations, we believe that there is a substantial danger that many broadcasters are inhibited from providing controversial issues of public importance by operation of the fairness doctrine.

2. The Record Demonstrates that The Fairness Doctrine Causes Broadcasters to Restrict Their Coverage of Controversial Issues.

42. The record reflects that, in operation, the fairness doctrine—in stark contravention of its purpose—operates as a pervasive and significant impediment to the broadcasting of controversial issues of public importance. The requirement that broadcasters provide balance in their overall coverage of controversial public issues in fact makes them more timid than they would otherwise be in airing programming that involves such issues.

44. The record is replete with descriptions from broadcasters who have candidly recounted specific instances in which they decided not to air controversial matters of public importance because such broadcasts might trigger fairness doctrine obligations.

46. Equally or perhaps even more disturbing than the self-censorship of individual broadcasts is the fact that the avoidance of fairness doctrine burdens has precipitated specific "policies" on the part of broadcast stations which have the direct effect of diminishing, on a routine basis, the amount of controversial material presented to the public on broadcast stations. For example, the owner of a broadcast station and two newspapers regularly prints editorials in his newspapers but, inhibited by regulatory restrictions, is reluctant to repeat the same editorials on his radio station. Moreover, the record reflects that even stations which do elect to editorialize are inhibited by fairness doctrine requirements. According to Mr. Donald Gale, News Director of KSL-AM, the regulatory burdens associated with the fairness doctrine were a crucial factor in the decision of his station not to air "guest editorials."

47. As a direct result of fairness doctrine obligations, CBS acknowledges that its owned and operated stations, as a general matter, limit the amount of time they will sell both to persons seeking to place advertisements relating to ballot propositions and to political parties attempting to purchase broadcast time outside of campaign periods. Ms. Karen Maas, Vice President and General Manager of KIUP-AM and KRSJ-FM in Durango, Colorado states that her stations "think twice" about covering state ballot and related political issues.

49. The most compelling evidence of the existence of a "chilling effect" with respect to ballot advertising is presented in the Comments of the Public Media Center ("PMC"), an organization actively involved in prosecuting complaints under the fairness doctrine. In its Comments, PMC vividly illustrates the manner in which a complainant can successfully pressure broadcasters into refusing to sell advertising on ballot issues. For example, PMC recounts the tactics of a pro-bottle bill coalition as follows: "Ads opposing the beverage deposit—sponsored by an industry front group...hit the air in early August. Within ten days, the pro-bottle bill coalition sent a letter to all 500 California stations asking for a 2 to 1 ratio in free spot time. The coalition urged broad-

casters to refuse to sell time and therefore avoid a fairness situation at all." The majority of the California stations followed the coalition's exhortation. Less than one-third of the stations contacted by the coalition sold ballot advertising to the industry group.

51. In addition to political advertisements, the record reflects that the onerous requirements associated with the fairness doctrine have resulted in the widespread practice of many broadcasters to refuse to air any public issue advertisements. For example, one broadcaster employed by a large television station states that his station and six others under common ownership have a "company policy" not to accept issue advertising. A number of trade associations have also documented that broadcast licensees, inhibited by the requirements of the fairness doctrine, have refused to air issue-oriented advertisements.

56. A number of parties characterize the statements made by broadcasters that document the existence of "chilling effect" as mere "self-serving" utterances to which the Commission should accord little probative value.

57. We disagree. Because the existence of a "chilling effect" is a subjective perception, the statements of broadcasters who are personally subject to its requirements on a daily basis are able to present some of the best evidence on whether or not the doctrine, in operation, inhibits the presentation of controversial issues of public importance.

58. In addition, we reject the proposition that the evidentiary value of these statements is undercut by their alleged "self serving" nature. A statement by a broadcaster that he or she is inhibited from presenting controversial issues of public importance is, in a very real sense, an admission against interest.

60. Some parties assert that any inhibiting effect of the fairness doctrine is not attributable to the actual requirements of the doctrine itself but rather to the misperception of broadcasters as to their precise obligations under the doctrine. However, broadcasters are not lawyers. A broadcaster may be uncertain as to the precise boundaries of our detailed and complex regulatory scheme or may be uncertain as to whether he or she will be able to convince us, in the course of fairness doctrine litigation, that the station's overall programming complies with our regulatory requirements. As a consequence, a broadcaster, in order to avoid even the possibility of litigation, may be deterred from airing material even though the Commission, after hearing all the evidence, would have concluded that the program did not trigger fairness doctrine obligations.

68. In sum, we find that the evidence, derived from the record as a whole, leads us to conclude that the fairness doctrine chills speech. Because the fairness doctrine inhibits the presentation of controversial and important issues, in operation, it actually disserves the purpose it was designed to achieve. In our view, an elimination of the doctrine would result in greater discussion of controversial and important public issues on broadcast facilities.

C. The Administration of the Fairness Doctrine Operates to Inhibit the Expression of Unorthodox Opinions

69. While the fairness doctrine has the laudatory purpose of encouraging the presentation of diverse viewpoints, we fear that in operation it may have the paradoxical effect of actually inhibiting the expression of a wide spectrum of

opinion on controversial issues of public importance. In this regard, our concern is that the administration of the fairness doctrine has unintentionally resulted in stifling viewpoints which may be unorthodox, unpopular or unestablished.

70. First, the requirement to present balanced programming under the second prong of the fairness doctrine is in itself a government regulation that inexorably favors orthodox viewpoints. As we stated in our 1974 Fairness Report, it is only "major" or "significant" opinions which are within the scope of the regulatory obligation to provide contrasting viewpoints. As a consequence, the fairness doctrine makes a regulatory distinction between two different categories of opinions: those which are "significant enough to warrant broadcast coverage under the fairness doctrine" and opinions which do not rise to the level of a major viewpoint of sufficient public importance that triggers responsive programming obligations. As a consequence, the fairness doctrine in operation inextricably involves the Commission in the dangerous task of evaluating the merits of particular viewpoints.

71. Second, broadcasters who have been denied or threatened with a denial of the renewal of their licenses due to fairness doctrine violations have generally not been those which have provided only minimal coverage of controversial and important public issues. Indeed, some licensees that we have not renewed or threatened with non-renewal have presented controversial issue programming far in excess of that aired by the typical licensee. In a number of situations it was the licenses of broadcasters who aired opinions which many in society found to be abhorrent or extreme which were placed in jeopardy due to allegations of fairness doctrine violations.[2] We are extremely concerned over the potential of the fairness doctrine, in operation, to interject the government, even unintentionally, into the position of favoring one type of opinion over another.

E. The Fairness Doctrine Creates the Opportunity For Intimidation of Broadcasters by Governmental Officials

74. The broadcast industry is characterized by pervasive regulation. This pervasive regulatory authority, including the intrusive power over program content occasioned by the fairness doctrine, provides governmental officials with the dangerous opportunity to abuse their position of power in an attempt either to stifle opinion with which they disagree or to coerce broadcasters to favor particular viewpoints which further partisan political objectives.

75. For example, a White House official during the Nixon Administration suggested to the President's Chief of Staff that the Administration respond to the

2. *See, e.g.*, Lamar Life Broadcasting Co., 38 FCC 1143 (1965), *rev'd sub nom.* Office of Communication of United Church of Christ v. FCC, 359 F.2d 994 (D.C. Cir. 1966) (FCC refusal to grant a full term license to a station which espoused racially segregationist viewpoints); Brandywine-Main Line Radio, Inc. (FCC refusal to grant a license renewal to an evangelist station; the Hearing Examiner in Brandywine stated that the licensee's "style of presentation over the air — sometimes so racy as to make the gorge rise — was not what men of refined tastes would deem expedient..." Brandywine Main Line Radio, Inc., 24 FCC 2d at 130). *See also* Trinity Methodist Church, South v. Federal Radio Commission, 62 F.2d 850, 851 (D.C. Cir.), *cert. denied*, 284 U.S. 685 (1932) (Federal Radio Commission denied license renewal in a situation in which "the station had been used to attack a religious organization and where the broadcasts aired by the licensee were sensational rather than instructive.")

alleged "unfair coverage" of the broadcast media by showing "favorites within the media," establishing "an official monitoring system through the FCC" and making "official complaints from the FCC." The attempts to coerce broadcast journalists, moreover, have not been restricted to specific partisan viewpoints or politicians of a particular political party. As described in the Notice, a government official in another Administration was reported to state that the "massive strategy of the Administration was to use the fairness doctrine to challenge and harass the right-wing broadcasters and hope that the challenges would be so costly to them that they would be inhibited, and decide that it was too expensive to continue."

G. Need for the Fairness Doctrine In Light of the Increase in the Amount and Type of Information Sources in the Marketplace

1. Nature and Scope of the Information Services Marketplace

85. In a proceeding revising its national multiple ownership rules, the Commission noted:

> The record in this proceeding supports the conclusion that the information market relevant to diversity includes not only TV and radio outlets, but cable, other video media and numerous print media as well. These other media compete with broadcast outlets for the time that citizens devote to acquiring the information they desire. That is, cable, newspapers, magazines and periodicals are substitutes in the provision of such information.

That the various media are in fact information substitutes in the marketplace of ideas is further reflected in our local cable and television, newspaper and broadcast, radio and television cross-ownership rules.

87. Several commenters argued that broadcasting, particularly television, is such a dominant information source that there are no other realistic information alternatives. These commenters frequently point to studies indicating that television is both the primary and most believed source of information in the country. The success of one particular medium in attracting large audiences does not necessarily provide an appropriate justification for imposing governmentally mandated fairness. Moreover, the data do not suggest that other media voices are somehow unavailable. Studies demonstrating the alleged dominance of television broadcasting are based on data in which television was selected as one of several information sources used by the respondents. Such data merely serve to demonstrate the interchangeability of information options.

88. Similarly, we are not persuaded by those who argue that newspapers and broadcast facilities are in different information markets because newspapers must be read as opposed to television or radio which may be casually watched or monitored. That individuals edit and process information from the various media using different senses or while performing different tasks does not suggest that the information sources exist in separate isolated corners within the marketplace of ideas.

90. While programming from traditional advertiser based broadcast facilities has been considered a "zero priced good," there is no evidence in the record suggesting that the alleged price differentials between these facilities and other

"pay" media are significant enough to preclude interchangeability among information systems. Indeed, the monthly cost of a daily newspaper may be comparable to or even less than the monthly cost of basic cable service.

2. Status of the Information Services Marketplace

93. As we observed in the Notice, there has been explosive growth in the communications marketplace since the inception of the fairness doctrine in 1949. Of particular significance is the development of the marketplace since the Supreme Court's decision in *Red Lion Broadcasting* in 1969 and our subsequent analysis of the market in the 1974 Fairness Report.

(a) Broadcasting

94. The growth and development of radio broadcasting since the inception of the fairness doctrine has been dramatic. The total number of radio stations has increased by 280 percent since the 1949 Fairness Report. Moreover, there has been a 48 percent increase in the number of radio stations since the Supreme Court's decision in *Red Lion* and a 30 percent increase since the Commission's 1974 Fairness Report.

98. There has been a 44.3 percent increase in the overall number of over-the-air television broadcasting stations since the Supreme Court's decision in *Red Lion Broadcasting*.

99. The continued growth in television broadcasting has led directly to an increase in signal availability in local markets. As of 1984, 96 percent of the television households received five or more television signals. This figure represents a significant increase in actual signal availability since 1972, where only 83 percent of the television households received five or more signals. The increase is even more dramatic compared to 1964 when only 59 percent of television households were capable of receiving 5 or more stations.

100. Increases in the number of outlets and signal availability does not necessarily provide a complete picture of the fundamental structural changes occurring in the television marketplace. For example, UHF television, once thought to have occupied second class status, is now a significant voice in the marketplace.

101. The impact of the rise of independent television stations can be seen in the steady decline of the networks' audience share. As the Commission previously observed, the overall network audience share declined from 90 percent to 80 percent in 1983. This trend continues as the overall network share dropped from 80 percent in 1983 to 76 percent in 1984.

104. Given the significant development of both radio and television, we believe it is no longer necessary to utilize a mechanism of government imposed "fairness" in order to insure appropriate coverage of controversial issues of public importance. As the above data amply demonstrate, there are a sufficient number of over-the-air television and radio voices to insure the presentation of diverse opinions on issues of public importance. In this regard, we note that even if there had been no increase in alternate electronic information sources, the growth and development of both the radio and television markets by themselves make the fairness doctrine an unnecessary regulatory mechanism.

(b) Substitute Electronic Technologies

105. In addition to traditional over-the-air television and radio broadcasting, we find that there exist numerous alternative electronic technologies making a significant contribution to the marketplace of ideas.

106. U.S. cable households now number 38,673,270 placing national cable penetration at 43.3% of all television households. Growth in subscribership amounts to an astronomical 975 percent since the *Red Lion* decision. Moreover, cable television will continue to expand in the future.

107. The significance of cable television is also demonstrated by its ability to increase the number of viewing options available to the public. The importance of increased channel capacity is enhanced by the ready availability of a wide variety of cable networks which provide a significant array of diverse programming.

108. Cable services are an important media voice in small markets. Cable penetration rates in these markets are far in excess of the national average and significantly higher when compared with larger broadcast markets. The high penetration levels in these small markets suggest that there is a significant degree of substitutability between cable and over-the-air television broadcasting.

115. Sales of video cassette recorders continue to have a major impact on the information marketplace.

116. To the extent VCR's do not utilize spectrum, anyone who desires to communicate by television may do so by means of a VCR. In this regard, we agree with NBC that VCR's have the potential to become the "electronic handbills" or indeed even the electronic newspaper of the future.

(c) Print Media

123. The overall number of broadcast facilities exceeds the total number of daily newspapers in the United States. This does not mean, however, that the print media is not a significant contributor to the information marketplace. As of 1984, there were 1,701 daily newspapers in the country. Their average circulation was 62,544,503.

124. The total number of periodicals has increased from 6,960 in 1950 to 10,688 in 1982. These newspapers are significant sources of information, especially local information, which is available to consumers in each market.

128. On the record before us, we cannot find that there are an insufficient number of voices in local markets to warrant continuation of the fairness doctrine. Increases in signal availability from traditional broadcasting facilities — television and radio — by themselves attenuate the need for a government imposed obligation to provide coverage to controversial issues. The existence of a plethora of alternate electronic voices, as well as numerous locally oriented print voices, augments this argument.

H. The Fairness Doctrine Can Not Be Justified on the Basis that It Protects Either Broadcasters or the Public from Undue Influence

133. Several commenters contend that retention of the fairness doctrine is useful as a "protection against outside pressures" by groups within the commu-

nity which would otherwise exert undue influence on the editorial decisionmaking of broadcasters. Absent the fairness doctrine, these parties contend that broadcasters will simply "cave-in" to the pressures of advertisers, political action committees, or other powerful groups in the community who do not wish to have particular controversial viewpoints expressed.

134. We take issue with the assumption that intrusive governmental regulation is necessary to "protect" broadcasters from groups which allegedly attempt to influence their programming decisions. The First Amendment forbids governmental intervention in order to "protect" print journalists and we believe that broadcast journalists are in no greater need of "protection" than their counterparts in the print media. We think it telling, in this regard, that broadcasters themselves are not seeking this protection.

135. In addition, several commenters, in support of the fairness doctrine, argue that the doctrine serves to safeguard the public against unwarranted influence by what they perceive as biased broadcast reporting. Although the commenting parties differ among themselves in their perception of the bias to which they object, they believe that retention of the fairness doctrine is appropriate to prevent broadcasters from presenting biased or one-sided programming. The argument apparently is predicated upon the presumption that the requirement to provide "balanced" controversial issue programming is not merely a means to assure access to the marketplace of ideas but is itself a valid regulatory objective.

136. Balance may be a laudable editorial goal, but there are grave dangers when the government tries to strike that balance. First, as we have just noted above, determining what constitutes balanced programming is a very subjective endeavor. Second, as we have described, having the government attempt to achieve balance by means of enforcing the fairness doctrine results in a chilling effect to the ultimate detriment of the listening public. Third, there are the inherent dangers of an arm of the federal government influencing the content of programming in an attempt to guarantee balance. Further, the First Amendment does not require and may well not permit a neat apportionment, dictated by the government, in the marketplace of ideas, with equal space assigned to every viewpoint. The fact that a particular viewpoint may have the capability to be extremely influential or offensive does not mean that it is accorded a lesser degree of First Amendment protection than the expression of less influential or more reasonable opinions.

I. Summary

137. We believe the fairness doctrine is an unnecessary and detrimental regulatory mechanism.

138. Three factors form the basis for this determination. First, we believe that the public has access to a multitude of viewpoints without the need or danger of regulatory intervention.

139. Second, the fairness doctrine in operation thwarts the laudatory purpose it is designed to promote. Instead of furthering the discussion of public issues, the fairness doctrine inhibits broadcasters from presenting controversial issues of public importance.

140. Third, the restrictions on the journalistic freedoms of broadcasters resulting from enforcement of the fairness doctrine contravene fundamental consti-

tutional principles, accord a dangerous opportunity for governmental abuse and impose unnecessary economic costs on both the broadcasters and the Commission.

VI. CONCLUSION

176. Notwithstanding these conclusions, we have decided not to eliminate the fairness doctrine at this time. The doctrine has been a long-standing administrative policy and a central tenet of broadcast regulation in which Congress has shown a strong although often ambivalent interest. Because of the intense Congressional interest in the fairness doctrine and the pendency of legislative proposals, we have determined that it would be inappropriate at this time to eliminate the fairness doctrine. We will continue to administer and enforce the fairness doctrine obligations of broadcasters and [expect] that broadcast licensees will continue to satisfy these requirements.

Notes and Questions

1. Regulatory Capture. In ¶¶56–57, the Commission considers allegations that much of the evidence on which it relies—namely, testimony from broadcast licensees—is biased since broadcasters have an obvious interest in convincing the Commission that the fairness doctrine should be eliminated. As the Commission puts it, "A number of parties characterize the statements made by broadcasters...as mere 'self-serving' utterances to which the Commission should accord little probative value." The Commission responds that these subjective perceptions are the best evidence available since the question of chill is itself a question about broadcasters' subjective perceptions of the fairness doctrine. Is this a convincing retort? Or does it suggest that the agency has perhaps grown too sympathetic to broadcasters' perspectives?

The phrase regulatory capture is used to describe situations where a regulatory agency has fallen under the influence of a powerful interest group. The paradigmatic case of capture arises when an agency does the bidding of the very parties it was originally designed to regulate, and therefore stops regulating in the public's interest and starts, instead, regulating for the benefit of the regulated parties. This is not an uncommon allegation, especially because regulators necessarily do work closely with the parties they regulate, for example gathering information from them, and so at least some form of a relationship is bound to form. Moreover, regulators and regulatees in some sense rely on one another for their survival: should the industry disappear or become fully competitive, the regulators might find themselves without work;[3] should the regulators become too strict, the regulatees might find themselves losing considerable profits and freedoms. All this intuitively could cloud a regulator's judgment; but is that what

---

3. Another issue that might lead to some degree of capture: when regulatory officials leave government and return to the private sector, they often choose to stay involved with the very industry they once regulated. While there are limitations on what those former regulators can do—for example, there is a typically a period during which they are not allowed to appear before the agency on behalf of private clients—regulators might nevertheless foresee this shift in their own interests and thus have some tendency to treat the regulatee/possible future employer better than a regulator otherwise would.

happened in the above proceeding? If so, why didn't the Commission fully abandon the doctrine? If not, why didn't the Commission more explicitly discount the testimony referred to in ¶56?

2. A Doctrine in Limbo. An issue edited out of this excerpt of the Commission's *1985 Report* is whether the Communications Act required the FCC to enforce the fairness doctrine. In 1986, the D.C. Circuit held that Congress had not codified the doctrine, finding it to be "an administrative construction, not a binding statutory directive." Telecommunications Research & Action Center v. FCC, 801 F.2d 501, 517, *cert. denied*, 482 U.S. 919 (1987).

That step squarely raised the issue of the fairness doctrine's status in light of the FCC's peculiar decision that the doctrine was inconsistent with the public interest but the Commission would administer and enforce it anyway. In 1987, the D.C. Circuit remanded a case to the FCC for the Commission either to abandon the fairness doctrine as against the public interest, or to defend the doctrine's constitutionality, and thus retain and enforce it. Meredith Corp. v. FCC, 809 F.2d 863 (D.C. Cir. 1987). Backed into a corner by the D.C. Circuit and its own *1985 Report*, the FCC took the next step in the following order and repealed the fairness doctrine.

IN RE COMPLAINT OF SYRACUSE PEACE COUNCIL
Memorandum Opinion and Order, 2 FCC Rcd. 5043 (1987)

III. DISCUSSION

B. Constitutional Considerations Under *Red Lion*

36. As more fully discussed below, the extraordinary technological advances that have been made in the electronic media since the 1969 *Red Lion* decision, together with a consideration of fundamental First Amendment principles, provide an ample basis for the Supreme Court to reconsider the premise or approach of its decision in *Red Lion*. Nevertheless, while we believe that the Court, after reexamining the issue, may well be persuaded that the transformation in the communications marketplace justifies alteration of the *Red Lion* approach to broadcast regulation, we recognize that to date the Court has determined that governmental regulation of broadcast speech is subject to a standard of review under the First Amendment that is more lenient than the standard generally applicable to the print media. Until the Supreme Court reevaluates that determination, therefore, we shall evaluate the constitutionality of the fairness doctrine under the standard enunciated in *Red Lion* and its progeny.

(c) Conclusion

58. Under the standard of review set forth in *Red Lion*, a governmental regulation such as the fairness doctrine is constitutional if it furthers the paramount interest of the public in receiving diverse and antagonistic sources of information. Under *Red Lion*, however, the constitutionality of the fairness doctrine becomes questionable if the chilling effect resulting from the doctrine thwarts its intended purpose. Applying this precedent, we conclude that the doctrine can no longer be sustained.

59. In the 1985 *Fairness Report*, we evaluated whether the fairness doctrine achieved its purpose of promoting access to diverse viewpoints. After compiling a

comprehensive record, we concluded that, in operation, the fairness doctrine actually thwarts the purpose which it is designed to achieve. We found that the doctrine inhibits broadcasters, on balance, from covering controversial issues of public importance. As a result, instead of promoting access to diverse opinions on controversial issues of public importance, the actual effect of the doctrine is to "overall lessen[] the flow of diverse viewpoints to the public." 1985 *Fairness Report*, 102 FCC 2d 145, 171. Because the net effect of the fairness doctrine is to reduce rather than enhance the public's access to viewpoint diversity, it affirmatively disserves the First Amendment interests of the public. This fact alone demonstrates that the fairness doctrine is unconstitutional under the standard of review established in *Red Lion*.

60. Furthermore, almost two decades of Commission experience in enforcing the fairness doctrine since *Red Lion* convince us that the doctrine is also constitutionally infirm because it is not narrowly tailored to achieve a substantial government interest. Because the fairness doctrine imposes substantial burdens upon the editorial discretion of broadcast journalists and, because technological developments have rendered the doctrine unnecessary to ensure the public's access to viewpoint diversity, it is no longer narrowly tailored to meet a substantial government interest. The doctrine requires the government to second-guess broadcasters' judgment on such sensitive and subjective matters as the "controversiality" and "public importance" of a particular issue, whether a particular viewpoint is "major," and the "balance" of a particular presentation. The resultant overbreadth of the government's inquiry into these matters is demonstrated by the chill in speech that we have identified. The doctrine exacts a penalty, both from broadcasters and, ultimately, from the public, for the expression of opinion in the electronic press. As a result, broadcasters are denied the editorial discretion accorded to other journalists, and the public is deprived of a more vigorous marketplace of ideas, unencumbered by governmental regulation.

61. In sum, the fairness doctrine in operation disserves both the public's right to diverse sources of information and the broadcaster's interest in free expression. Its chilling effect thwarts its intended purpose, and it results in excessive and unnecessary government intervention into the editorial processes of broadcast journalists. We hold, therefore, that under the constitutional standard established by *Red Lion* and its progeny, the fairness doctrine contravenes the First Amendment and its enforcement is no longer in the public interest.

C. Preferred Constitutional Approach

62. Our review of the Supreme Court precedent in the application of First Amendment principles to the electronic media leads to an inescapable conclusion: throughout the development of these principles, the Supreme Court has repeatedly emphasized that its constitutional determinations in this area of the law are closely related to the technological changes in the telecommunications marketplace. For example, in the *Red Lion* decision itself, the Court indicated that advances in technology could have an effect on its analysis of the constitutional principles applicable to the electronic media.

63. The Court's most recent statement on this issue came in its decision in FCC v. League of Women Voters of California, 468 U.S. 364 (1984). Acknowledging that certain persons, including former Chairman Mark Fowler, "charge

that with the advent of cable and satellite television technology, communities now have access to such a wide variety of stations that the scarcity doctrine is obsolete," *id.* at 376 n.11, the Court indicated that it may be willing to re-assess its traditional reliance upon spectrum scarcity upon a "signal" from the Congress or this Commission "that technological developments have advanced so far that some revision of the system of broadcast regulation may be re-quired." *Id.*

65. We believe that the 1985 Fairness Report, as reaffirmed and further elab-orated on in today's action, provides the Supreme Court with the signal referred to in *League of Women Voters.* It also provides the basis on which to reconsider its application of constitutional principles that were developed for a telecommu-nications market that is markedly different from today's market. We further be-lieve that the scarcity rationale developed in the *Red Lion* decision and successive cases no longer justifies a different standard of First Amendment review for the electronic press. Therefore, in response to the question raised by the Supreme Court in *League of Women Voters*, we believe that the standard applied in *Red Lion* should be reconsidered and that the constitutional principles applicable to the printed press should be equally applicable to the electronic press.

2. The Scarcity Rationale

73. Some commenters state that the general standards of First Amendment jurisprudence applied by the Court in cases not involving broadcast regulation are irrelevant in determining whether the fairness doctrine and other content based regulations are constitutional. They assert that the increase in the number and types of information sources has nothing to do with the existence of scarcity in the constitutional sense, and emphasize that the appropriate standard of re-view is that applied by the Court in *Red Lion* and its progeny specifically relating to broadcast regulation. These parties describe two different notions of scarcity—numerical scarcity and spectrum (or allocational) scarcity. We do not believe that any scarcity rationale justifies differential First Amendment treat-ment of the print and broadcast media.

3. Divergence of *Red Lion* from Traditional First Amendment Precepts

83. We believe that the articulation of lesser First Amendment rights for broadcasters on the basis of the existence of scarcity, the licensing of broadcast-ers, and the paramount rights of listeners departs from traditional First Amend-ment jurisprudence in a number of respects. Specifically, the Court's decision that the listeners' rights justifies government intrusion appears to conflict with several fundamental principles underlying the constitutional guarantee of free speech.

84. First, this line of decisions diverges from Supreme Court pronouncements that "the First Amendment 'was fashioned to assure *unfettered* interchange of ideas for the bringing about of political and social changes desired by the peo-ple.'" Connick v. Myers, 461 U.S. 138, 145 (1983), quoting Roth v. United States, 354 U.S. 476, 484 (1957) (emphasis added). The framers of that Amend-ment determined that the best means by which to protect the free exchange of ideas is to prohibit any governmental regulation which "abridg[es] the freedom of speech or of the press." They believed that the marketplace of ideas is too del-icate and too fragile to be entrusted to governmental authorities.

85. Consequently, a cardinal tenet of the First Amendment is that governmental intervention in the marketplace of ideas of the sort involved in the enforcement of the fairness doctrine is not acceptable and should not be tolerated.

86. The fairness doctrine is at odds with this fundamental constitutional precept. While the objective underlying the fairness doctrine is that of the First Amendment itself—the promotion of debate on important controversial issues—the means employed to achieve this objective, government coercion, is the very one which the First Amendment is designed to prevent. As the Supreme Court has noted, "By protecting those who wish to enter the marketplace of ideas from governmental attack, the First Amendment protects the public's interest in receiving information." Pacific Gas & Electric Co. v. Public Utility Commission of California, 106 S. Ct. 903, 907 (1986). Yet the fairness doctrine *uses* government intervention in order to foster diversity of viewpoints, while the scheme established by the framers of our Constitution *forbids* government intervention for fear that it will stifle robust debate. In this sense, the underlying rationale of the fairness doctrine turns the First Amendment on its head.

88. The *Red Lion* decision also is at odds with the well-established precept that First Amendment protections are especially elevated for speech relating to matters of public concern, such as political speech and other matters of public importance.

89. The type of speech regulated by the fairness doctrine involves opinions on controversial issues of public importance. This type of expression is "precisely that...which the Framers of the Bill of Rights were most anxious to protect—speech that is 'indispensible to the discovery and spread of political truth'...." *League of Women Voters*, 468 U.S. at 383, quoting Whitney v. California, 274 U.S. 357, 375 (1927) (Brandeis, J., concurring). Yet, instead of safeguarding this type of speech from regulatory intervention, the doctrine anomalously singles it out for governmental scrutiny.

90. Further, the *Red Lion* decision cannot be reconciled with well- established constitutional precedent that governmental regulations directly affecting the content of speech are subjected to particularly strict scrutiny. The Supreme Court has emphasized that "if the marketplace of ideas is to remain free and open, governments must not be allowed to choose 'which issues are worth discussing or debating....'" Consolidated Edison Co. of New York, Inc. v. Public Service Commission of New York, 447 U.S. at 537–38, quoting Police Department of Chicago v. Mosley, 408 U.S. 92, 96 (1982) (ellipsis in original). As noted above, enforcement of the fairness doctrine not only forces the government to decide whether an issue is of "public importance," but also whether the broadcaster has presented "significant" contrasting viewpoints. Unorthodox minority viewpoints do not receive favored treatment as do their "significant" counterparts. As the Court recently asserted, "regulations which permit the Government to discriminate on the basis of the content of the message cannot be tolerated under the First Amendment." Regan v. Time, Inc., 468 U.S. 641, 649 (1984).

94. Finally, we believe that under the First Amendment, the right of viewers and listeners to receive diverse viewpoints is achieved by guaranteeing them the right to receive speech unencumbered by government intervention. The *Red Lion* decision, however, apparently views the notion that broadcasters should come within the free press and free speech protections of the First Amendment as an-

tagonistic to the interest of the public in obtaining access to the marketplace of ideas. As a result, it is squarely at odds with the general philosophy underlying the First Amendment, *i.e.*, that the individual's interest in free expression and the societal interest in access to viewpoint diversity are both furthered by proscribing governmental regulation of speech. The special broadcast standard applied by the Court in *Red Lion*, which sanctions restrictions on speakers in order to promote the interest of the viewers and listeners, contradicts this fundamental constitutional principle.

4. First Amendment Standard Applicable to the Press

97. We believe that the role of the electronic press in our society is the same as that of the printed press. Both are sources of information and viewpoint. Accordingly, the reasons for proscribing government intrusion into the editorial discretion of print journalists provide the same basis for proscribing such interference into the editorial discretion of broadcast journalists. The First Amendment was adopted to protect the people *not from journalists, but from government.* It gives the people the right to receive ideas that are unfettered by government interference. We fail to see how that right changes when individuals choose to receive ideas from the electronic media instead of the print media. There is no doubt that the electronic media is powerful and that broadcasters can abuse their freedom of speech. But the framers of the Constitution believed that the potential for abuse of private freedoms posed far less a threat to democracy than the potential for abuse by a government given the power to control the press. We concur. We therefore believe that full First Amendment protections against content regulation should apply equally to the electronic and the printed press.

Notes and Questions

1. Judicial Review. The D.C. Circuit affirmed the FCC's repeal of the fairness doctrine. The court did so without reaching the constitutional grounds, instead finding the public interest determination to be sufficient. Syracuse Peace Council v. FCC, 867 F.2d 654 (D.C. Cir. 1989), *cert. denied*, 493 U.S. 1019 (1990). In a separate opinion, Chief Judge Wald concurred in the elimination of the second prong of the fairness doctrine, but dissented from the decision to eliminate the first prong. Finding this portion of the decision both unsupported by the record and procedurally deficient (no notice was given prior to the prong's elimination, so there was no opportunity for public comment), Chief Judge Wald categorized the action as "deregulation running riot." *Id.* at 673.

2. Different Rules for Different Markets. The *1985 Report* and the *1987 Order* seem to lump together all broadcasters and all markets. But wouldn't the case for retention be stronger in some markets than in others? For instance, isn't the case for retaining the fairness doctrine stronger for VHF television than for AM or FM radio? What is the significance of the fact that the FCC did not draw such a distinction? Would it have been wiser to retain the fairness doctrine for certain markets? If so, how should such markets be identified and defined?

3. Powerful Media. Is the controversy over the fairness doctrine a debate about broadcasting or about speech? Do proponents of the fairness doctrine believe

THE LICENSEE AS PUBLIC TRUSTEE

that there is something unusual about encoded electromagnetic radiation (would they apply the fairness doctrine to citizens' band radio?) or do they believe that government ought to ensure the fairness of very powerful media (would they have applied the fairness doctrine to book publishing in the 16th century and to weekly newspapers in the 18th)?

4. Principle or Pragmatism? Does the FCC mean to oppose the fairness doctrine as a matter of principle or as a matter of pragmatic regulatory strategy? Suppose that, during the 21st century, an entirely new medium of communication arises (say, communication through ground waves); that initially very few firms are willing to invest the large sums of money required for this strange and untested technology; and that the medium becomes an extraordinary success with the public. If Congress sought to impose a fairness doctrine on the few owners of this new medium of communication, which, if any, of the arguments in the *1985 Report* and the *1987 Order* would be relevant to that issue?

5. Other Public Trustee Obligations. Is it possible to agree with the FCC's conclusions in the *1985 Report* and *1987 Order* and still believe that broadcast licensees should be regulated in some other matters as "public trustees"? If so, on what basis?

6. Chill. The main concern raised in all of these materials is that the fairness doctrine might chill speech, and the main advantage of the fairness doctrine is that it might lead to more balanced presentations of controversial issues. With respect to the chill, could this concern have been mitigated by the adoption of a new, more detailed fairness doctrine that gave licensees clear touchstones as to which broadcasts would (and would not) trigger fairness doctrine obligations? With respect to the desire for balanced coverage, given the increase in broadcast outlets today, is this goal now so well accomplished through competition that the doctrine loses its allure?

7. Empirical Evidence. Recall that in *Red Lion* the Court indicated a willingness to reconsider its approval of the challenged doctrines "if experience with the administration of these doctrines indicates that they have the net effect of reducing rather than enhancing the volume and quality of coverage."[4] In its *1985 Report*, the FCC had anecdotal support for its assertion that the fairness doctrine produced a reduction in coverage of controversial subjects, but it lacked the kind of comparative evidence that would be ideal—for instance, a showing that when broadcasters are not subject to the fairness doctrine they carry more news programming. The absence of such comparative data is not surprising: the fairness doctrine had been in effect for more than forty years, so there was no period free of the fairness doctrine that could be used for purposes of comparison.

The FCC's repeal of the fairness doctrine did afford such an opportunity, however, as researchers could compare pre- and post-1987 broadcasting. Thomas Hazlett and David Sosa undertook just such a study. They examined

---

4. The Supreme Court quoted this language in making the point more forcefully in FCC v. League of Women Voters, 468 U.S. 364 (1984). In that case the Court declined an invitation to reconsider the constitutionality of the fairness doctrine but stated that, "as we recognized in *Red Lion*, were it to be shown by the Commission that the fairness doctrine 'has the net effect of reducing rather than enhancing' speech, we would then be forced to reconsider the constitutional basis of our decision in that case." *Id.* at 379 n.12 (quoting *Red Lion*, 395 U.S. at 393).

THE JOURNAL OF LEGAL STUDIES

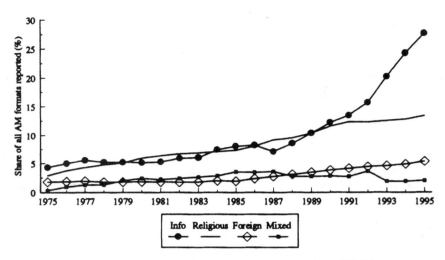

FIGURE 3.—Selected AM format categories (nationwide: 1975–95)

Figure 6.1. EMPIRICAL EVIDENCE. This chart shows the percentage of all AM stations in each of four format categories (information, religious, foreign, mixed) nationwide between 1975 and 1995. This is Figure 3 in the original article. Reprinted with permission.

data on the U.S. radio market from 1975 to 1995 and found that elimination of the fairness doctrine was followed by significant changes in radio station formats—including, notably, an increase in informational programming. They found similar trends for both AM and FM radio. Their chart on AM radio formats is Figure 6.1. It is of course not clear whether the legal change caused the content change; as the authors put it, "correlation is not causality, but the correlation is very strong."[5]

8. Congress and the President. In 1987, just after the FCC repealed the Fairness Doctrine, a statute passed both houses of Congress that would have reinstated the doctrine by Congressional mandate. Then-President Reagan refused to sign the measure, explaining in a statement to the press that, in his view, the fairness doctrine was unconstitutional.[6] Given this pattern of events, should the FCC have reinstated the doctrine of its own accord, following Congress and thus implicitly out-voting Reagan? And what of Reagan's explanation; did he have the authority to deem the doctrine unconstitutional given that the Court had already ruled in *Red Lion* that this sort of regulation of broadcast was constitutional?

---

5. Thomas W. Hazlett & David W. Sosa, Was the Fairness Doctrine a "Chilling Effect"? Evidence from the Postderegulation Radio Market, 26 J. Legal Stud. 279, 299 (1997).

6. *See* Veto of the Fairness in Broadcasting Act of 1987, 23 Weekly Comp. Pres. Doc. 715 (June 19, 1987) (vetoing S. 742-100 (1987), reprinted in 133 Cong. Rec. H4160 (daily ed. June 3, 1987)).

B. The Personal Attack and Political Editorial Rules

The FCC's decision in *Syracuse Peace Council* repealed the fairness doctrine. The focus of *Red Lion*, however, was not the fairness doctrine generally but instead the specific rules mandating that broadcasters provide airtime for responses to any "personal attacks" or "political editorials" that are broadcast. Attempts to repeal those rules have taken their own tortured path, which is significant both in its own right and as an example of the tangled relationships among the Commission, the courts, and private parties.

In response to a 1980 petition by the National Association of Broadcasters (NAB) requesting repeal of the personal attack and political editorial rules, the FCC in 1983 proposed eliminating or substantially modifying those rules, noting its doubts about their consistency with First Amendment objectives. Nothing happened in direct response to that petition, and after the FCC issued *Syracuse Peace Council*, the NAB, the Radio-Television News Directors Association (RTNDA), and other interested groups filed a "petition for expedited rulemaking" to eliminate the personal attack and political editorial rules and clarify *Syracuse Peace Council*'s effect on those rules. After repeated unsuccessful attempts (including another petition in 1990) to prod the FCC to take some sort of action, in 1996 the RTNDA filed a petition in the Court of Appeals for the D.C. Circuit for a writ of mandamus to order the FCC to act on the RTNDA's petition to eliminate the rules. On February 7, 1997, the D.C. Circuit ordered that "the petition be denied without prejudice to its renewal should the Federal Communications Commission fail to make significant progress, within the next six months, toward the possible repeal or modification of the personal attack and political editorial rules." In re Radio-Television News Directors Ass'n, 1997 WL 150084 (D.C.Cir. 1997).

Six months and a day later, on August 8, 1997, the Commission announced that a majority of the Commission could not agree on any resolution, as two commissioners voted to repeal the rules, two voted to keep them and commence a full inquiry into their continued value, and the final Commission seat was vacant. 12 FCC Rcd. 11956 (1997). Shortly thereafter, four new commissioners were confirmed by the Senate, and in May 1998 the Commission voted anew, but again the Commission was deadlocked. This time, there were no open seats, but William Kennard (who had participated in the challenge to the personal attack and political editorial rules when he represented the National Association of Broadcasters) recused himself and the remaining four split two in favor of repeal and two in favor of retention. Two weeks later, the D.C. Circuit ordered the FCC to submit the 2-2 vote as a final agency action, along with a statement of reasons by the Commissioners who wanted to keep the rule.

The D.C. Circuit issued an opinion but did not resolve the underlying debate. In Radio-Television News Directors Ass'n v. FCC, 184 F.3d 872 (D.C. Cir. 1999), the D.C. Circuit declined to review the rules on their merits and instead remanded the matter to the FCC for further consideration. The court rejected the argument (put forward by the RTNDA and NAB, as well as Commissioners Powell and Furchtgott-Roth in a joint dissenting statement) that the repeal of the fairness doctrine necessarily entailed the repeal of the personal attack and political editorial rules. The court stated that it could be theoretically consistent for the agency to repeal the broader fairness doctrine while leaving the more specific rules in place. The court went on to conclude, however, that the joint statement of the Commissioners who favored the rule (Ness and Tristani) failed to present an adequate basis for concluding that these rules were in the public interest and thus was "insufficient to permit judicial review."[7] The reasoning on which Ness and Tristani relied (*e.g.*, that the "'scarcity of broadcast frequencies provides a rationale for imposing public interest obligations on broadcasters'"[8]), after all, was the very same reasoning that the FCC had rejected when it repealed the fairness doctrine. Having found that the FCC (through the joint statement of Commissioners Ness and Tristani) had not provided an adequate justification for keeping the personal attack and political editorial rules, the court ordered the FCC "to provide a more detailed defense—and possibly modifications as well—sufficient to permit meaningful judicial review."[9]

The D.C. Circuit ended its 1999 opinion by stating that "the FCC need act expeditiously,"[10] but months passed with no FCC action. So, in July 2000, the petitioners filed yet another motion for a writ of mandamus. In September 2000, then-Chairman Kennard reversed his prior decision to recuse and thus began to participate in the proceeding. Shortly thereafter, on October 4, 2000, the Commission voted 3-2 (with Kennard joining Ness and Tristani, and Powell and Furchtgott-Roth dissenting) to suspend the personal attack and political editorial rules for sixty days—which, the Commission noted, would correspond with the final month of the 2000 election season. The reason given for this suspension was to see what happened on the airwaves and thus "to enable us to obtain a better record on which to review the rules." *In re Repeal or Modification of the Personal Attack and Political Editorial Rules*, FCC 00-360, 2000 WL 1468707, at ¶1 (2000).

Notably, in this *Order* suspending the personal attack and political editorial rules, the FCC repudiated "the dicta in *Syracuse Peace Council* regarding the appropriate level of First Amendment scrutiny" for broadcast. *Id.* at ¶17. The Commission stated:

> The fundamental error of the Commission's decision in *Syracuse Peace Council* was its confusion of the rationale underlying the fairness doctrine with the basis for public interest regulation of the broadcast spectrum. The fairness doctrine originated at a time when there were only three major television networks, and the proliferation of television stations and the development of cable television reasonably led the Commission to reevaluate the need for the fairness doctrine. The standard of *Red Lion*, however, was not based on the absolute number of media outlets, but on the fact that the spectrum is a public resource and "there are substantially more individuals who want to broadcast than there are frequencies to allocate." 395 U.S. at 388. As both the U.S. Supreme Court and the D.C. Circuit have explained, "a licensed broadcaster is 'granted the free and exclusive use of a valuable part of the public domain; when

---

7. *Id.* at 885.
8. *Id.* at 883 (quoting the joint statement of Commissioners Ness and Tristani).
9. *Id.* at 888.
10. *Id.* at 889.

he accepts that franchise it is burdened by enforceable public obligations.'" CBS v. FCC, 453 U.S. 367, 395 (1981) (quoting Office of Communication of the United Church of Christ v. FCC, 359 F.2d 994, 1003 (D.C. Cir. 1966)). The long-standing basis for the regulation of broadcasting is that "the radio spectrum simply is not large enough to accommodate everybody." NBC v. FCC, 319 U.S. 190, 213 (1943). Under our Nation's system for allocating spectrum, some are granted the "exclusive use" of a portion of this "public domain," even though others would use it if they could. CBS v. FCC, 453 U.S. at 395. That is why "it is idle to posit an unabridgeable First Amendment right to broadcast comparable to the right of every individual to speak, write or publish." *Red Lion*, 395 U.S. at 388.

FCC 00-360, at ¶18.

A few days later, the D.C. Circuit rebuffed the FCC's planned suspension and ordered instead that the rules be repealed. The court did not reach the question of whether the rules were consistent with the First Amendment, and it stated that the FCC could still institute a new rulemaking proceeding "to determine whether, consistent with constitutional constraints, the public interest requires the public attack and political editorial rules." Radio-Television News Directors Ass'n v. FCC, 229 F.3d 269, 272 (D.C. Cir. 2000). The D.C. Circuit instead based its decision on the FCC's response (or lack thereof) to the court's orders. The court emphasized that "the Commission still has not provided adequate justification for the rules, and in its [October 4] *Order* provides no assurance that it will do so. Incredibly, the *Order* reinstates the rules before the Commission will have received any of the updated information that the Commission states it requires in order to evaluate the rules. It is folly to suppose that the 60-day suspension and call to update the record cures anything." On this basis, the court issued a writ of mandamus directing the Commission immediately to repeal the personal attack and political editorial rules. *Id.* at 271–72.

C. Political Broadcasting

Although the FCC disavowed the fairness doctrine, it has never completely dropped its reliance on the general theory of broadcasting and the First Amendment espoused in *Red Lion*—as the above excerpt reminds us. The Commission's insistence that broadcast licensees should be deemed to surrender editorial discretion in return for access to valuable spectrum is nowhere more evident and unrelenting today than in the Commission's control over political broadcasting.[11]

Section 315 of the Communications Act contains the so-called "equal time" rule. The rule provides that, if a broadcaster allows one candidate for an elective office—city, state or federal—to gain air time, the station must allow the candidate's opponent(s) a like opportunity. Thus, if Candidate A is given free broadcast time, A's opponent(s) must be given free broadcast time; and if A bought air

---

11. Scattered paragraphs in this section are based on materials in the "Political Broadcasting" section of Thomas G. Krattenmaker & Lucas A. Powe, Jr., Regulating Broadcast Programming 66–69 (1995).

time, A's opponent(s) must be allowed to buy an equal amount at the same rate.[12]

This rule seems squarely contrary to the theory of free speech on which *Tornillo* rests, but this rule has been part of broadcast regulation from regulation's earliest days, originally appearing as section 18 of the 1927 Radio Act. The legislators who wrote the Radio Act were not about to leave to chance the prospect that the new medium might be turned against them,[13] and the Commission has vigorously enforced the equal time rule to the present day, despite the agency's occasional misgivings about *Red Lion*.

The Commission found enforcement of section 315 rather simple until it encountered a twist in 1959. In February of that year, two Chicago stations included in their evening newscast footage of Mayor Richard Daley greeting the president of Argentina at Midway Airport during a snowstorm. Mayor Daley was at that time running for reelection. One of his opponents, Lar "America First" Daly, demanded equal free air time because of Mayor Daley's "use" of the two stations. The stations refused. They reasoned that Daley's greeting was news, while Lar Daly, a perennial candidate who went about in public in an "Uncle Sam" costume, was a joke. The FCC thought differently. It ordered the stations to grant Daly equal time.[14]

Congress — perhaps acting in its members' self interest — reacted with horror and quickly overruled the agency's interpretation. Within three months, section 315 was amended to exempt both on-the-spot coverage of bona fide news events and bona fide newscasts from the equal time constraints.[15]

That, of course, raised a new question: what is a bona fide news program? Answering that question requires a case-by-case analysis, which the FCC delegates to the chief of its Mass Media Bureau. As the following *Order* reveals, however, the FCC has developed (or thinks it has developed) a set of criteria that provide meaningful guidance as to what constitutes a bona fide news program.

IN RE REQUEST OF ABC, INC. FOR DECLARATORY RULING
15 FCC Rcd. 1355 (1999)

1. The Commission has before it a request for declaratory ruling filed by ABC, Inc. (ABC) on behalf of Buena Vista Television, Inc. ("Buena Vista"), the producer of the program "Politically Incorrect with Bill Maher" ("Politically Incorrect"). ABC seeks a ruling that "Politically Incorrect" is exempt from the "equal opportunities" provision of Section 315(a) of the Communications Act of 1934, as amended (the "Act"). 47 U.S.C. §315(a).

---

12. As discussed more fully below, the rate in both cases is supposed to be the station's "lowest unit charge" for commercials of the same duration and place in the broadcast schedule.

13. Hugh Carter Donahue, The Battle to Control Broadcast News 9–18 (MIT Press 1989); David H. Ostroff, Equal Time: Origins of Section 18 of the Radio Act of 1927, 24 J. Broad. 367 (1980).

14. Reconsideration and Motions for Declaratory Rulings or Orders Relating to the Applicability of §315 of the Communications Act of 1934, as amended, to Newscasts by Broadcast Licensees, Interpretive Opinion, 26 FCC 715 (1959).

15. Donahue, *supra* at 55–66.

I. FACTUAL BACKGROUND

3. ABC explains that "Politically Incorrect" is hosted by "satirist and humorist" Bill Maher, who begins each program with a "monologue" on current news-related issues. He then introduces a panel of four persons from various fields including the media, academia, politics, and popular culture. Mr. Maher poses an issue from his monologue and asks for his guests' opinions. Occasionally, the program will focus on a single issue; more typically it will involve discussion of several current issues of the day. ABC contends that the satirical aspect of Mr. Maher's monologue should not be an impediment to an exemption because satire has long been recognized as an important and serious part of the American political landscape.[16]

4. ABC argues that "Politically Incorrect" fully satisfies the Commission's established criteria for exempt bona fide news interview programs in that: (1) it has been a regularly scheduled half-hour program, broadcast by the ABC television network each weekday evening since January 6, 1997; (2) the producer, Buena Vista, controls all aspects of the program, ensuring that decisions as to format, content, and participants are based on bona fide journalistic judgment and not motivated by partisan purposes; (3) Buena Vista selects the guests from a variety of fields based on the guests' "involvement in newsworthy events," "competence to discuss current issues," and "represent[ation] [of] a cross-section of ideologies to stimulate a lively exchange of views;"[17] (4) prior to the taping of each show, "the producers meet with the guests to review the pre-selected issues and their positions on the issues" and intervene during commercial breaks as they deem necessary to give direction to the participants; and (5) Mr. Maher exercises control over discussions by preventing speechmaking and steering straying comments back to the main topics.

II. DISCUSSION

5. Section 315(a) of the Act provides that if a broadcaster permits a legally qualified candidate for public office to "use" a broadcast station, it must afford equal opportunities to all legally qualified opponents for the same office.[18] In 1959, Congress amended Section 315 so that appearances by legally qualified candidates on the following types of news programs would be exempt from equal opportunities requirements:

1) bona fide newscast,

2) bona fide news interview,

3) bona fide news documentary (if the appearance of the candidate is incidental to the presentation of the subject or subjects covered by the news documentary), or

---

16. ABC notes that the U.S. Supreme Court has recognized satire as constitutionally protected, citing Hustler Magazine v. Falwell, 485 U.S. 46, 51 (1988) ("*Falwell*"), in which a cartoon satirizing the Rev. Jerry Falwell was deemed fully protected by the First Amendment. The Court also stated its view that satirical cartoons had played an important role in political debate throughout our history.

17. ABC states that from the political realm the program often includes elected officials and persons aspiring to be elected.

18. In general, a use is any "positive" identified or identifiable appearance of a legally qualified candidate. This excludes disparaging depictions by opponents or third-party adversaries. *See Report and Order*, 7 FCC Rcd. 678, 684 (1991).

4) on-the-spot coverage of bona fide news events (including but not limited to political conventions and activities incidental thereto).

47 U.S.C. §315(a)(1–4).

6. Congress's fundamental purpose in enacting these exemptions was to encourage increased news coverage of political campaigns and to give broadcasters the discretion to exercise their good faith news judgment in deciding which candidates to cover and in what formats. The legislative history emphasizes the congressional intention:

> To enable what probably has become the most important medium of political information to give the news concerning political races to the greatest number of citizens, and to make it possible to cover the political news to the fullest degree.

105 Cong. Rec. 14451 (1959) (Holland); *see also* Chisholm v. FCC, 538 F.2d 349 (1976). Neither the explicit terms of the statute nor the legislative history of the news exemption amendments, however, reveal the specific format characteristics envisioned by Congress for any of the exemptions. Indeed, the legislative history demonstrates that Congress chose to leave to the Commission the task of interpreting which kinds of programming properly fit the scope of each exemption. In affirming the Commission's 1975 decision that candidate debates should be exempt under Section 315(a)(4) ("on-the-spot coverage of bona fide news events"), the *Chisholm* court observed:

> In creating a broad exemption to the equal time requirements in order to facilitate broadcast coverage of political news, Congress knowingly faced risks of political favoritism by broadcasters, and opted in favor of broader coverage and increased broadcaster discretion. Rather than enumerate specific exempt and non-exempt "uses," Congress opted in favor of legislative generality, preferring to assign that task to the Commission.

Chisholm, 538 F.2d at 366. Although Congress did not specifically detail exempt formats, nor define exactly what it meant by "news,"[19] the legislative history indicates that, in general, the common characteristic envisioned of each exemption is "bona fide news value." Thus, Congress qualified each exemption with the term "bona fide" to emphasize that, to be exempt from the equal opportunities requirement, news programming should be genuinely newsworthy and not designed for the partisan purpose of advancing or harming any particular candidate. The legislative history also shows that Congress expected bona fide news interview programs to be regularly scheduled and under broadcaster control.

7. Thus, in deciding whether a program qualifies as a "bona fide news interview" under Section 315(a)(2), a three-prong test evolved:

(1) whether the program is regularly scheduled;

(2) whether the broadcaster or an independent producer controls the program;[20] and

---

19. While the legislative history lacks any specific discussion of the format of exempt news interviews, there is reference to three programs, "Meet the Press," "Face the Nation" and "Youth Wants To Know" as the kind of interview programming it envisioned.

20. In 1992, the Commission expanded the test to allow exemptions to independently-produced news interview programs. In doing so, the Commission emphasized that a licensee

(3) whether the broadcaster's or independent producer's decisions on format, content and participants are based on newsworthiness rather than on an intention to advance or harm an individual's candidacy.

8. The Commission remained conservative in its analysis of news interview exemption requests under this test for over twenty-five years, essentially limiting the news interview exemption to what it viewed as more traditional question and answer formats like those cited in the legislative history ("Meet the Press," "Face the Nation" and "Youth Wants to Know"). In 1984, however, the Commission reversed an earlier denial of a news interview exemption to the "Donahue" program. Multimedia Entertainment, Inc., 56 RR 2d 143, 146 (1984) ("*Donahue*"). The *Donahue* decision signaled the Commission's willingness to recognize varying less conventional interview formats as being consistent with Congress' overriding intent to increase news coverage of the political campaign process.[21]

9. In *Donahue*, with respect to the second prong of the test, whether sufficient control over the program is present, the Commission concluded that:

> It would be unsound to rule that a program involving a unique or innovative approach to interviewing its guests somehow lacks sufficient licensee control evident in more traditional news interview programs like "Meet the Press" or "Face the Nation" when the licensee has implemented reasonable techniques to ensure control. To do so would discourage programming innovation by sending a signal to broadcasters that to be exempt an interview program should adhere only to the format of certain programs mentioned by Congress over twenty-five years ago.

56 RR2d 146. As to the third prong, good faith news judgment, the Commission reasoned that it should not second-guess broadcasters about the relative newsworthiness of the interviewees or the topics of discussion. The Commission concluded that it should confine its analysis to whether the broadcaster acted reasonably and in good faith. *Donahue* stressed that "reasonable persons may differ" about the newsworthiness of particular topics or guests, and that absent bad faith or unreasonableness, the Commission should follow Congress in its willingness to take risks with the exemptions and thus defer substantially to broadcasters' good faith journalistic judgment.[22]

---

who chooses to carry such programming must still assure itself that the format is nonpartisan and under sufficient producer control to assure against abuse. Request for Declaratory Ruling on Independently Produced News Interviews, In Re Independently Produced News Interview Programs, 7 FCC Rcd. 4681 (1992), *aff'd sub nom*, TRAC v. FCC, 26 F.3d 185 (D.C. Cir. 1994).

21. *Donahue* also discussed the format of "Youth Wants To Know," one of the three programs mentioned in the legislative history and concluded that it too was not a traditional question and answer format. Rather, the Commission stated that it was "an innovative program of its time involving questions posed by students, not professional journalists. To argue that such a format guaranteed adherence to a licensee's journalistic judgment any more than the 'Donahue' format cannot be justified and appears to be inconsistent with the legislative history." 56 RR2d at 146.

22. Since *Donahue*, the Commission has continued to grant exemptions to news interview programs similar to the Donahue program or with other unique and innovative format elements. *See e.g.* Pacifica Radio Town Hall Meetings, 9 FCC Rcd. 2817 (Mass Media Bureau (MMB) 1994); Face to Face, 9 FCC Rcd. 2813 (1994); Larry King, 56 RR2d 956 (MMB 1984). The Commission has also determined that different areas of news coverage are eligible for exemption under 315(a). In 1988, the Mass Media Bureau granted the "En-

10. We believe that ABC has satisfied each prong of the test. First, "Politically Incorrect" has been regularly scheduled for almost two years, clearly meeting this requirement. Second, as to control, ABC has identified various reasonable mechanisms Buena Vista has implemented for exercising control throughout the production of "Politically Incorrect" and those structural safeguards appear reasonably designed to assure that good faith news judgment can be adequately protected. Third, ABC represents that Buena Vista's decisions about format, content and selection of participants are based on newsworthiness and not motivated by any partisan purpose. The presence of satire as an element of "Politically Incorrect" should not prevent the program from being considered bona fide in terms of good faith news judgment absent an indication that the satire is utilized to advance or harm any particular candidate for public office. The Supreme Court in the *Falwell* decision noted the importance of satire in political speech, stating that, "Despite their sometimes caustic nature, from the early cartoon portraying George Washington as an ass down to the present day, graphic depictions and satirical cartoons have played a prominent role in public and political debate." 485 U.S. 46, 54. Satire in the form of a broadcast monologue about news of the day or during discussion of such issues does not appear less important in the realm of political debate than political cartoons.

III. CONCLUSION

11. Congress knowingly gave the Commission substantial discretion to interpret the news exemptions to the equal opportunities requirement and decided that the risk of some broadcasters abusing the exemption for partisan purposes was outweighed by the benefit to the public inherent in increased news coverage of political campaigns. In attempting to fulfill the letter and the spirit of the law, the Commission's decisions in this area have continued to expand the kinds of programming eligible for exemption in recognition of change and innovation in broadcast production. Granting an exemption to "Politically Incorrect" is consistent with these principles.

Notes and Questions

1. Less Conventional Interview Formats. The *Declaratory Ruling* notes that in 1984 the Commission signaled a willingness to expand its definition of bona fide news interview programs to include "less conventional interview formats." ¶8. Was that a wise decision? Was it constitutionally compelled? Note that the *Donahue* decision came one year before the 1985 *Fairness Report*, and the same year that the Commission issued a major report eliminating many broadcast regulations, *In re Deregulation of Commercial Television*, 98 FCC 2d 1076 (1984). Are those actions consistent with the *Donahue* decision? At cross-purposes with it?

---

tertainment Tonight" program an exemption (under 315(a)(1), bona fide newscast), stating that no controlling distinction can be made between various kinds of "news" such as entertainment, business, sports, and religion. The Bureau said that "a determination [of whether a program is bona fide] should not be predicated on the subject matter reported on, but rather should be judged on a basis of whether the program reports news of some area of current events." In re Paramount Communications, Inc., 3 FCC Rcd. 245 (MMB 1988).

2. Defining "Bona Fide" News Programming. Did the decision to expand the definition of bona fide news interview programs increase or decrease the rigor of that definition? As of today, does the definition have meaningful criteria that give it real substance and predictability? If not, does that raise First Amendment concerns? Is such clarity achievable? If not, does *that* raise First Amendment concerns?

3. Televised Political Debates. The amendment to section 315 exempting bona fide news programs has further significance, as it created a new opportunity: televised political debates. Everyone had understood that one effect of section 315 as originally written was that it covered minor party candidates as well as those on the Democratic or Republican tickets. Thus, prior to the 1959 amendment of section 315, no one knew of a way to hold televised debates among candidates for public office without letting all candidates for the position onto the podium. But, in 1975,[23] the FCC ruled that if debates between candidates were scheduled by a third party, then they could be covered as bona fide news events.[24] Under the exception Congress enacted to overrule the *Lar Daly* rule, covering the debates as news events would not trigger an obligation to give equal time to those candidates not represented at the debates. Subsequently, the FCC dropped the window dressing of sponsorship by a third party, ruling that debates are news events within the meaning of section 315 no matter how they come about.[25]

4. Supporters of Candidates. The thrust behind section 315 was to balance different candidates' access to the media. But the language to the provision had a loophole: if supporters of a candidate purchased air time, instead of the candidate himself, the literal text of the provision was not implicated and neither that candidate's opponents, nor supporters of those opponents, were — on the face of the provision — given rights to equal access. The Commission closed this loophole by established the so-called "*Zapple* rule": if a station sells time to supporters of one candidate, it must sell like time to supporters of the candidate's opponents.[26] This rule has become increasingly important in modern campaigns.

5. Candidate Access to the Airwaves. Consistent with section 315, a station may of course refuse to sell air time to any and all candidates. Congress has also enacted, however, section 312(a)(7) of the Act. It grants to candidates for federal office the right to purchase broadcast time for their advertisements at the broadcaster's lowest unit charge.[27] Specifically, the rule states that: (1) candidates must be allowed to purchase broadcast time whether the broadcaster in question wants to sell it or not; and (2) the purchase price must be the station's lowest

---

23. The 1960 debates between candidates Kennedy and Nixon were made possible by Congress suspending section 315 for that one election season. Later, Lyndon Johnson and then Richard Nixon saw to it that section 315 was not suspended for their campaigns, as they did not wish to debate their opponents on national television.

24. Petition of the Aspen Institute Program on Communications and Society and CBS, Inc., for Revision or Clarification of Commission Rulings Under §§315(a)(2) & 315(a)(4), Declaratory Order, Memorandum Opinion and Order, 55 FCC 2d 697 (1975).

25. Petitions to Change Commission Interpretation of Subsections 315(a)(3) and (4) of the Communications Act, Report and Order, BC Dkt. No. 82-564, 54 Rad. Reg. 2d (P & F) 1246 (1983), *aff'd*, League of Women Voters Educ. Fund v. FCC, 731 F.2d 995 (D.C. Cir. 1984).

26. Request by Nicholas Zapple, Communications Counsel, Committee on Commerce for Interpretative Ruling Concerning §315 of the Fairness Doctrine, 23 FCC 2d 707 (1970).

27. 47 U.S.C. §312(a)(7). The statute was held to be constitutional in CBS v. FCC, 453 U.S. 367 (1983) (also known as *Carter/Mondale*).

unit charge for the particular class of advertisement. The FCC determines when a campaign has begun (thus triggering the two-pronged obligation)[28] and the rule applies only to federal candidates.

6. Proposals for Reform. Rules about purchasing air time do little good for candidates who cannot afford the time. Thus, some politicians (including then-President Clinton and then-FCC Chairman Reed Hundt) have embraced the idea of requiring broadcasters to provide candidates with free television time.[29] One variant here would require broadcasters to donate commercial time to a "political time bank" that would be available free of charge to candidates for elective office. Another proposal would mandate that candidates be offered thirty minutes of free television time and discounts fifty percent below the lowest unit charge for additional ads. A third proposal would require that, in the weeks leading up to a federal election, broadcasters set aside five minutes each night for election messages, with the candidates taking turns filling those five-minute periods.

Proponents of this last idea have suggested that the broadcasters be required to provide those five-minute blocks free of charge. But, failing that, they have argued that broadcasters at least be required to sell commercial time in non-standard commercial blocks (like five-minute periods) instead of only selling time in the shorter increments currently used for traditional commercial advertising. The allure of the longer segments from a policy perspective is that they might lead to more substantive messages; the concern is that short messages quickly devolve into sound bites. Broadcasters of course do not relish the prospect of modifying their normal programming schedule in order to allow for five-minute messages, and they have argued that they should not be required to provide special time periods for candidates. The FCC has wavered, ruling in 1994 that there was no such obligation, but reconsidering its own ruling in 1999. Both documents are excerpted below.

IN RE REQUEST FOR DECLARATORY RULING OF NATIONAL ASSOCIATION OF BROADCASTERS REGARDING SECTION 312(A)(7) OF THE COMMUNICATIONS ACT
9 FCC Rcd. 5778 (1994)

1. The Commission has before it a request filed by the National Association of Broadcasters (NAB) seeking a declaratory ruling that broadcast stations need not provide legally qualified candidates for federal office with program time in increments other than those which the station ordinarily sells to commercial advertisers or which it ordinarily programs.

COMMENTS

4. The majority of commenters support NAB's request and recommend that the Commission not promulgate specific rules mandating that broadcast stations

---

28. The specific issues that gave rise to the *Carter/Mondale* case (discussed in the footnote above) were whether the campaign for the 1984 election had begun and whether the FCC could order broadcasters to adopt Jimmy Carter's determination of when it was proper to begin to air political ads. In a straight party line vote, the Commission sided with Carter, a decision that was affirmed by both the D.C. Circuit and the Supreme Court.

29. Heather Fleming, Clinton Calls for Free Airtime, Broadcasting & Cable, March 17, 1997, at 18.

must provide legally qualified candidates for federal office with program time in increments other than those which the station ordinarily sells to commercial advertisers or which it ordinarily programs. These commenters suggest that long-standing Commission precedent prohibits flat bans only in connection with the lengths of time it has made available to commercial advertisers. Many commenters believe that unless a station has made odd program lengths available to commercial advertisers or has chosen to program particular odd lengths such rules would place a substantial burden on broadcasters for two essential reasons: (1) stations could face severe technological burdens because of the difficulty of delaying programming to accommodate political advertisements of nonstandard lengths; and (2) because of contractual obligations with both syndicators and networks, a station may not have five-minute, or other odd length periods of time to offer a client.

5. In contrast, reply comments submitted by the Media Access Project/People for the American Way (MAP/PAW) point to Commission and court decisions which, it contends, hold that a broadcaster cannot arbitrarily refuse to sell an ad of a certain length. They agree, however, that the Commission should not require a broadcaster to sell odd blocks of time to candidates in every circumstance, particularly where the request does not come sufficiently far enough in advance of the requested programming date. MAP/PAW argues that permitting licensees to choose whether or not to sell odd-length program time would conflict with the Commission's longstanding interpretation of Section 312(a)(7), which requires that requests for access by federal candidates must be considered individually on a case-by-case basis thereby prohibiting a blanket policy on sales of any particular length of time.

DISCUSSION

6. Section 312(a)(7) of the Communications Act provides:

> The Commission may revoke any station license or construction permit...for willful or repeated failure to allow reasonable access to or to permit purchase of reasonable amounts of time for the use of a broadcasting station by a legally qualified candidate for Federal elective office on behalf of his candidacy.

47 U.S.C. §312(a)(7). The Commission has not established formal rules outlining specifically how much time would satisfy this requirement. Instead, it has relied on the reasonable good faith judgment of licensees to provide time to federal candidates. In determining whether a particular licensee's judgment in affording access to advertising time is reasonable, the Commission has essentially confined itself to two questions: (1) Did the broadcaster follow the proper standards in deciding whether to grant a candidate's request for access?; and (2) Is the broadcaster's explanation of his decision reasonable in terms of these standards? CBS Inc. v. FCC, 453 U.S. 367, 375–76 (1981) (*Carter/Mondale*).

7. When the Commission formulated its policies for implementing the reasonable access provision in Commission Policy in Enforcing Section 312(a)(7) of the Communications Act ("*1978 Policy Statement*"),[30] it stated:

---

30. 68 FCC 2d 1079 (1978). The guidelines a licensee must follow in evaluating access requests are well-established:

access requests from "legally qualified" candidates for federal elective office... must be considered on an individualized basis, and broadcasters are required to tai-

We believe it to be generally unreasonable for a licensee to follow a policy of flatly banning access by a federal candidate to any of the classes and lengths of program or spot time in the same periods which the station offers to commercial advertisers.

68 FCC 2d at 1090. The Commission elaborated that "we do not believe that this policy will in any way disrupt a station's broadcast schedule. It only requires that the licensee follow its usual commercial practices." *Id.* Finally, in summarizing the various policies it had established, the Commission stated that "licensees may not adopt a policy that flatly bans federal candidates from access to the types, lengths, and classes of time which they sell to commercial advertisers." *Id.* at 1094.

8. In the 1991 political programming *Report and Order*,[31] the Commission emphasized the continued viability of the reasonable access guidelines in the *1978 Policy Statement*. Indeed, in the *Report and Order*'s consideration of whether federal candidates were entitled to gain access to a broadcast facility during the weekend prior to an election to edit existing advertising or to purchase additional time, the Commission decided that such access was required only to the extent weekend access had been made available to commercial advertisers during the preceding year. The Commission stated that:

We confirm that stations are required only to apply the same policies to candidates with respect to weekend access that they apply to commercial advertisers. As noted above, we believe that it is reasonable for federal candidates to expect to be treated in the same manner as commercial advertisers.

7 FCC Rcd. at 4612.

10. Thus, in [this] context the Commission related specific requirements for providing access to candidates to the station's actual practices in its dealings with commercial advertisers. This is fully consistent with the reasoning in the *1978 Policy Statement* that only limitations or flat bans of the kinds and lengths of time offered to commercial advertisers are prohibited. We believe that the same rationale applies to NAB's request and that accordingly broadcasters should be required to make available to federal candidates only the lengths of time offered to commercial advertisers during the year preceding a particular election period. We also believe that stations must make program time available to federal candidates in the same lengths they have programmed the station in the year preceding an election whether or not such lengths of programming time have been sold to commercial advertisers. A station's decision to program odd lengths of time should be treated in the same manner as its decision to sell odd lengths of time. In both cases, it is reasonable to require broadcasters to provide access to quali-

---

lor their responses to accommodate, as much as reasonably possible, a candidate's stated purposes in seeking air time. In responding to access requests, however, broadcasters may also give weight to such factors as the amount of time previously sold to the candidate, the disruptive impact on regular programming, and the likelihood of requests for time by rival candidates under the equal opportunities provision of Section 315(a).
Carter/Mondale at 387. [Footnote relocated.]
    31. Codification of the Commission's Political Programming Policies, 7 FCC Rcd. 678 (1991).

fied federal candidates consistent with their own sales and programming decisions. By establishing the relevant period as one year prior to the election, the Commission is assuring that federal candidates are provided access consistent with a station's current commercial sales or programming practices. It also protects the candidate from the occasional abuse that might occur if a station changed its sales practices or programming just prior to an election period.

12. Finally, with respect to MAP/PAW's argument discussed in ¶5 that the issue of odd lengths of time should be handled on a case-by-case basis, we believe that it is preferable and appropriate to resolve this important issue by declaratory ruling rather than leaving its resolution to case-by-case determinations. The ruling clarifies our reasonable access policies for candidates and broadcasters in a manner which comports with longstanding Commission precedent. Furthermore, taking this action should help to prevent disputes between stations and candidates in the heat of election campaigns, and correspondingly to lessen our case load by providing more specific guidance to interested parties.

IN RE PETITION FOR RECONSIDERATION BY PEOPLE FOR THE AMERICAN WAY AND MEDIA ACCESS PROJECT OF DECLARATORY RULING REGARDING SECTION 312(A)(7) OF THE COMMUNICATIONS ACT

17 Communications Reg. (P&F) 186, FCC 99-231 (1999)

1. The Commission has before it a petition for reconsideration of our October 3, 1994, *Declaratory Ruling*, timely filed by Media Access Project and People for the American Way ("Petitioners"). The *Declaratory Ruling*, 9 FCC Rcd. 5778 (1994), granted a request by the National Association of Broadcasters ("NAB") with respect to a broadcaster's sale of non-standard lengths of time, such as five minutes, to legally qualified candidates for federal elective office. Specifically, the Commission ruled that broadcast stations need not sell or furnish legally qualified candidates for federal office time for political advertising in increments other than those which the station either sold commercial advertisers or programmed during the one-year period preceding an election.

2. For the reasons set forth below, we believe that the petition for reconsideration should be granted and that a broadcast station should not be allowed to refuse a request for political advertising time *solely* on the ground that the station does not sell or program such lengths of time. Our reconsideration finds that the *Declaratory Ruling* did not accord sufficient consideration to the needs of federal candidates.

3. Petitioners argue that the Commission's *Declaratory Ruling* erred both as a matter of policy and law. As to policy, they suggest that allowing broadcasters to refuse in advance the sale of certain lengths of program time based entirely on a station's or network's commercial sales or programming practices wrongly reduces political speech to the level of the commercial marketplace. Petitioners also question the Commission's stated goal of drawing a clear line as to what lengths of time are subject to legitimate access requests in order to avoid potential disputes. According to Petitioners, the record neither demonstrated any need to protect broadcasters from such potential disputes nor evidenced any need to preserve administrative resources. Further, Petitioners contend that only a few cases involving this issue had been brought to the Commission prior to the *Declaratory Ruling*.

4. With regard to the law, Petitioners argue that the *Declaratory Ruling* misconstrued the Commission's longstanding and consistently applied interpretation of Section 312(a)(7), which requires that federal candidates' requests for access must be considered individually, on a case-by-case basis. Petitioners contend that until the *Declaratory Ruling*, Commission decisions had consistently held that a broadcaster cannot arbitrarily refuse, in advance, to sell a program slot of any particular length.[32] Rather, according to Petitioners, the Commission had required broadcasters to consider each request for time on an individualized, *ad hoc* basis. Petitioners maintain that this approach of requiring *ad hoc* responses to access requests properly accorded broadcasters sufficient flexibility without foreclosing the possibility that a candidate may successfully demonstrate the need for a certain non-standard program length. In this way, the candidate has the opportunity to explain individualized campaign needs for a length of program time and the broadcaster retains the ability to counter offer or refuse a request, if warranted by the facts. Petitioners conclude that permitting broadcasters to choose not to sell particular lengths of time based on their own commercial sales and programming practices conflicts with the Commission's and the courts' longstanding interpretation of Section 312(a)(7), which prohibits a broadcaster from establishing blanket bans on sales of any particular length of spot or program time.

5. NAB's Opposition challenges Petitioners' argument that the Commission, by its action, relegated federal candidate speech to that of a commercial advertiser. NAB contends that Petitioners ignored the *Declaratory Ruling* to the extent that it requires a broadcast station to provide access to program lengths either sold *or programmed* in the year preceding an election. Thus, according to NAB, federal candidates are still entitled access to program lengths greater than commercial spot time. NAB argues that the *Declaratory Ruling* struck an appropriate balance between the need of candidates to convey their message and the practical need of broadcasters to minimize the disruption to their schedules. NAB also argues that the *Declaratory Ruling* is entirely consistent with Commission and court precedent, which has avoided forcing broadcasters "to carve up their schedules in order to accommodate a candidate who desires to air an odd-length spot or program."

DISCUSSION

6. Since Congress enacted Section 312(a)(7) of the Communications Act in 1972, the Commission has attempted to interpret it in a manner consistent with Congress's clear intent to promote wider, less fettered dissemination of political speech. Indeed, the legislative history of the access provision emphasizes that the fundamental policy underlying its adoption was "to give candidates for public office greater access to the media so that they may better explain their stand on

---

32. *1978 Policy Statement*, 68 FCC 2d 1079, 1090 (1978). And as noted by Petitioners, the Commission's prohibition against such flat bans was favorably cited by the U.S. Supreme Court in its landmark reasonable access decision. Carter/Mondale Presidential Committee, Inc., 74 FCC 2d 631, *recon. denied*, 74 FCC 2d 657 (1979), *aff'd sub nom.* CBS Inc. v. FCC, 629 F.2d 1 (D.C. Cir. 1980), *aff'd*, 453 U.S. 367, 392 (1981) ("*Carter/Mondale*"). In addition, our *Report and Order* in Codification of the Commission's Political Programming Policies, reaffirmed the ongoing viability of the prohibition against flat bans. 7 FCC Rcd. 678, 681–82 (1991) ("*Political Programming Policies*").

the issues, and thereby more fully and completely inform the voters." 117 Cong. Rec. S12872 (daily ed. Aug. 2, 1971).

8. As articulated by the U.S. Supreme Court in its landmark *Carter/Mondale* decision, the Commission's guidelines a broadcaster must follow in evaluating access requests are well-established:

> [A]ccess requests from "legally qualified" candidates for federal elective office... must be considered on an individualized basis, and broadcasters are required to tailor their responses to accommodate, as much as reasonably possible, a candidate's stated purposes in seeking air time. In responding to access requests, however, broadcasters may also give weight to such factors as the amount of time previously sold to the candidate, the disruptive impact on regular programming, and the likelihood of requests for time by rival candidates under the equal opportunities provision of Section 315(a). These considerations may not be invoked as pretexts for denying access; to justify a negative response, broadcasters must cite a realistic danger of substantial program disruption — perhaps caused by insufficient notice to allow adjustments in the schedule — or of an excessive number of equal time requests.

Carter/Mondale, 453 U.S. at 387. The Commission has consistently followed these guidelines in evaluating complaints under Section 312(a)(7).

9. While determinations regarding access are entitled to deference if the licensee takes into account the appropriate factors and acts reasonably and in good faith, it is well-settled Commission policy that "across-the-board" policies adopted by a broadcaster generally cannot be sustained. This is precisely because "across-the-board" policies do not allow for appropriate consideration of the individualized needs of candidates. The Supreme Court in *Carter/Mondale* considered this issue and stated:

> Whilet he adoption of uniform policies might well prove more convenient for broadcasters, such an approach would allow personal campaign strategies and the exigencies of the political process to be ignored. A broadcaster's "evenhanded" response of granting only time spots of a fixed duration to candidates may be "unreasonable" where a particular candidate desires less time for an advertisement or a longer format to discuss substantive issues.

Id. at 390.

10. On the other hand, in balancing the needs of candidates and broadcasters, the Commission has ruled that candidates do not have a right to a particular placement of their political announcements on a station's schedule, *1978 Policy Statement*, 68 FCC 2d at 1091; nor do candidates have any right to program time "of any particular or minimum duration." *Donald Riegle*, 59 FCC 2d at 1315. These two policies, taken together, require a candidate and a station to negotiate and compromise, in the absence of pre-established ceilings or minimums.

11. The Commission's *Declaratory Ruling* was a departure from the above framework and, on further reflection, we believe it does not afford appropriate consideration to the needs of federal candidates. In effect, the *Declaratory Ruling* permitted what amounts to an "across-the-board" policy, or flat ban, on the sale

of program time in non-standard increments. Thus, upon reconsideration, we now believe that broadcasters should not be allowed to refuse, as the result of such a ban, requests from candidates for non-standard lengths of time. Rather, in considering such requests, broadcasters must take into account the *Carter/Mondale* factors outlined above.

12. We believe that requiring good faith negotiation between an individual federal candidate and a broadcaster concerning access to non-standard lengths of political advertising time better fulfills Congress' intent in enacting Section 312(a)(7). As a practical matter, there may be a variety of circumstances where a federal candidate decides that the best campaign strategy involves the use of non-standard length advertising formats and, applying the *Carter/Mondale* factors, the broadcaster can reasonably make the necessary accommodations. With respect to requests for five-minute increments in particular, we note that, from a candidate's perspective, a five-minute program may be a desirable option because of the expense of purchasing and producing a thirty-minute or longer program, and the brevity of a thirty- or sixty-second spot announcement. As petitioners point out, such non-standard lengths of time may facilitate more substantive political discourse during political campaigns. This, in turn, furthers the purposes of Section 312(a)(7) by giving candidates the opportunity to "better explain their stand on the issues, and thereby more fully and completely inform the voters." 117 Cong. Rec. S12872 (daily ed. Aug. 2, 1971).

14. Our finding herein does not mean that broadcasters will be required to provide five minutes or other non-standard lengths of program time to candidates in every particular instance. Indeed, in several previous decisions involving candidate requests for non-standard length program time, the Commission determined that the broadcaster acted reasonably in denying the request given the circumstances presented in those cases. Thus, the Commission will, as previously, defer to a licensee's discretion, and overturn a decision only if the licensee has acted unreasonably pursuant to the established guidelines.

Notes and Questions

1. Reconciling the Opinions. Which ruling has the more persuasive interpretation of the law? Are both rulings reasonable? If not, what would explain the FCC taking an unreasonable position? If so, is this the sort of policy question that Congress should decide? Relatedly, how do you account for the 1999 reversal of the 1994 ruling? Did something relevant change between 1994 and 1999 that would be an appropriate basis for reversing the existing interpretation?

2. Case-by-Case Resolution. Does a case-by-case approach in this instance make more sense than an across-the-board rule? Whose interests might be served by each approach? What actors are empowered by each approach?

3. Compared to Free Time. How much does the 1999 ruling achieve as compared to the proposal that broadcasters be required to give five-minute blocks of time free of charge? What is the problem to which the 1999 ruling is the solution? What is the problem to which free air time in five-minute blocks is the solution? How tied are all of these questions to broader questions of campaign finance reform?

4. The First Amendment. Is the 1999 ruling subject to First Amendment challenge? Would a requirement of free air time be vulnerable to such a challenge?

Would *Tornillo* be distinguishable because the hypothetical regulation operates without regard to what the broadcaster has (or has not) said? Would *Red Lion* be distinguishable on the grounds that, unlike the fairness doctrine, this hypothetical regulation is not designed to counter misinformation or partial information that the listener or viewer would otherwise receive?

Note that, interestingly, neither *Red Lion* nor *Tornillo* makes any reference to the extensive regulation of political broadcasting, even though it constitutes some of the most intensive political speech in America. Nevertheless, it is no secret that the FCC is charged with enforcing the "equal time," "lowest unit charge," and "guaranteed access" rules, that it enforces these rules with vigor, and that its enforcement has significant impact on political elections across the country in every campaign season. Is there an adequate justification in the *Red Lion* opinion for this kind of administrative oversight of political contests? Can the theory underlying *Tornillo* be reconciled with the fact of FCC regulation of political broadcasting? Does the explosion of new audio and video technologies since the enactments of sections 312(a)(7) and 315 make it easier or harder to defend the FCC's efforts against a First Amendment challenge?

5. Beyond Fairness. The equal time, lowest unit charge, and guaranteed access rules discussed above might seem to suggest that, absent regulation, broadcasters will not treat politicians well. But isn't the real worry here that broadcasters *will* treat particular politicians well—politicians who might then reciprocate with sweetheart regulation or legislation?

In July 1999, broadcasters began airing a series of 30-second public service announcements on topics like literacy, drunk driving, and breast cancer. The ads began in familiar ways, say with a man and women talking in an office or a couple having a conversation over their kitchen table. But then, about 10 seconds before each advertisement ended, the spouse of a local Congressman or Senator would come on camera and says something like, "Hello, I'm Simone-Marie Meeks. My husband, Congressman Gregory Meeks, and I urge you to read with your children. Because literacy is a gift for life." The spouse's face would then fade away and the narrator would announce, "This message brought to you by the National Association of Broadcasters." David Rosenbaum, TV Ads by Congressional Wives are a Sweet Deal for All Involved, N.Y. Times, July 13, 1999, at A-2.

The ads were an obvious boon for all the involved parties. The politicians enjoyed low-risk, favorable public exposure for their names and their families, all without (at least thus far) triggering equal time obligations in favor of their political rivals. The broadcasters meanwhile (arguably) satisfied part of their public trustee obligation by airing public service announcements and, at the same time, surely ingratiated themselves with the featured politicians. But what of the public's interest? Assuming that the spots did, indeed, represent an attempt by the National Association of Broadcasters to ingratiate itself with members of Congress, what changes in the existing regulatory regime would eliminate the NAB's incentive to do so? Would such changes be a good idea, as a policy matter? Is there an argument that these changes are constitutionally compelled? Cf. Matthew L. Spitzer, The Constitutionality of Licensing Broadcasters, 64 N.Y.U. L. Rev. 90 (1989).

6. Gore/Bush 2000. As of October 2000, the Presidential contest between Democratic nominee Al Gore and Republican nominee George W. Bush was a statistical dead heat. The first presidential debate, then, was possibly going to affect the election outcome significantly. That debate took place on Tuesday, October 3, and it was aired live and simultaneously on CBS, ABC, and PBS. Fox and NBC, however—the other two dominant networks—broke with tradition and chose to compete with the debate: Fox aired the series premier of James Cameron's science fiction/adventure program, *Dark Angel*; and NBC took the unusual step of giving its affiliates a choice: either air the debate or air a Major League Baseball playoff game, with the debate available on tape-delay after the game was over.

When it comes time for affiliate renewals, should the FCC punish the affiliates who failed to air the debate live for violating their public trustee obligation? Does it matter that, according to the Neilsen ratings, *Dark Angel* drew an audience of over 17 million viewers, while the debate on ABC and CBS drew a combined audience of roughly 30 million?[33] Which way does that fact cut? Should the FCC distinguish between the NBC affiliates who chose to show the baseball game and the Fox affiliates (who were not given the option of carrying the debate live)? Should the FCC reward the NBC affiliates who did choose to show the debate live? Does it matter whether other affiliates aired the debate later that same evening?

II. INDECENT BROADCASTS

FCC v. PACIFICA FOUNDATION
438 U.S. 726 (1978)

STEVENS, J., delivered the opinion of the Court (Parts I, II, III, and IV-C) and an opinion in which BURGER, C.J., and REHNQUIST, J., joined (Parts IV-A and IV-B). POWELL, J., filed an opinion concurring in part and concurring in the judgment, in which BLACKMUN, J., joined. BRENNAN, J., filed a dissenting opinion, in which MARSHALL, J., joined. STEWART, J., filed a dissenting opinion in which BRENNAN, WHITE, and MARSHALL, JJ., joined.

JUSTICE STEVENS delivered the opinion of the Court (Parts I, II, III and IV-C) and an opinion in which CHIEF JUSTICE BURGER and JUSTICE REHNQUIST joined (Parts IV-A and IV-B).

A satiric humorist named George Carlin recorded a 12-minute monologue entitled "Filthy Words" before a live audience in a California theater. He began by referring to his thoughts about "the words you couldn't say on the public, ah, airwaves, um, the ones you definitely wouldn't say, ever." He proceeded to list those words and repeat them over and over again in a variety of colloquialisms.[34] The transcript of the recording indicates frequent laughter from the audience.

---

33. Shauna Snow, Morning Report, L.A. Times (October 5, 2000), at F-52.
34. [Ed. The words were: shit, piss, fuck, cunt, cocksucker, motherfucker, and tits. At this time, the FCC had seven commissioners. In the aftermath of *Pacifica*, industry rumor had it that, for future enforcement efforts, each commissioner was assigned one word.]

At about 2 o'clock in the afternoon on Tuesday, October 30, 1973, a New York radio station, owned by respondent Pacifica Foundation, broadcast the "Filthy Words" monologue. A few weeks later a man, who stated that he had heard the broadcast while driving with his young son, wrote a letter complaining to the Commission. He stated that, although he could perhaps understand the "record's being sold for private use, I certainly cannot understand the broadcast of same over the air that, supposedly, you control."

The complaint was forwarded to the station for comment. In its response, Pacifica explained that the monologue had been played during a program about contemporary society's attitude toward language and that, immediately before its broadcast, listeners had been advised that it included "sensitive language which might be regarded as offensive to some." Pacifica characterized George Carlin as "a significant social satirist" who "is not mouthing obscenities, but is merely using words to satirize as harmless and essentially silly our attitudes towards those words." Pacifica stated that it was not aware of any other complaints about the broadcast.

On February 21, 1975, the Commission issued a declaratory order granting the complaint and holding that Pacifica had broadcast "indecent language" in violation of federal law. The FCC stated that "the concept of 'indecent' is intimately connected with the exposure of children to language that describes, in terms patently offensive as measured by contemporary community standards for the broadcast medium, sexual or excretory activities and organs, at times of the day when there is a reasonable risk that children may be in the audience." *In re Citizen's Complaint Against Pacifica Foundation*, 56 FCC 2d 94, 98.

II

[Here, the Court concluded that section 326 of the Communications Act, which forbids the Commission to engage in censorship, "does not limit the Commission's authority to impose sanctions on licensees who engage in obscene, indecent, or profane broadcasting." The Court found that the section forbids censorship in advance of broadcast. And, "entirely apart from the fact that the subsequent review of program content is not the sort of censorship at which the statute was directed, its history makes it perfectly clear that it was not intended to limit the Commission's power to regulate the broadcast of obscene, indecent, or profane language."]

III

The only other statutory question presented by this case is whether the afternoon broadcast of the "Filthy Words" monologue was indecent within the meaning of 18 U.S.C. §1464. [The section forbids "any obscene, indecent, or profane language by means of radio communications." The Court held that "obscene" and "indecent," as those words are employed in section 1464, have different meanings. To be obscene, language must appeal to the prurient interest and lack serious value,] but the normal definition of "indecent" merely refers to nonconformance with accepted standards of morality.

IV

Pacifica makes two constitutional attacks on the Commission's order. First, it argues that the Commission's construction of the statutory language broadly encompasses so much constitutionally protected speech that reversal is required even if Pacifica's broadcast of the "Filthy Words" monologue is not itself protected by the First Amendment. Second, Pacifica argues that inasmuch as the recording is not obscene, the Constitution forbids any abridgment of the right to broadcast it on the radio.

A

The first argument fails because our review is limited to the question whether the Commission has the authority to proscribe this particular broadcast.

It is true that the Commission's order may lead some broadcasters to censor themselves. At most, however, the Commission's definition of indecency will deter only the broadcasting of patently offensive references to excretory and sexual organs and activities.[35] While some of these references may be protected, they surely lie at the periphery of First Amendment concern.

B

When the issue is narrowed to the facts of this case, the question is whether the First Amendment denies government any power to restrict the public broadcast of indecent language in any circumstances.[36] For if the government has any such power, this was an appropriate occasion for its exercise.

The fact that society may find speech offensive is not a sufficient reason for suppressing it. If there were any reason to believe that the Commission's characterization of the Carlin monologue as offensive could be traced to its political content—or even to the fact that it satirized contemporary attitudes about four-letter words—First Amendment protection might be required. But that is simply not this case. These words offend for the same reasons that obscenity offends.[37] "Such utterances are no essential part of any exposition of ideas, and are of such slight social value as a step to truth that any benefit that may be derived from them is clearly outweighed by the social interest in order and morality." Chaplinsky v. New Hampshire, 315 U.S. 568, 572 (1942).

In this case it is undisputed that the content of Pacifica's broadcast was "vulgar," "offensive," and "shocking." Because content of that character is not entitled to absolute constitutional protection under all circumstances, we must con-

---

35. A requirement that indecent language be avoided will have its primary effect on the form, rather than the content, of serious communication. There are few, if any, thoughts that cannot be expressed by the use of less offensive language.

36. Pacifica's position would, of course, deprive the Commission of any power to regulate erotic telecasts unless they were obscene under Miller v. California, 413 U.S. 15 (1973). Anything that could be sold at a newsstand for private examination could be publicly displayed on television. We are assured by Pacifica that the free play of market forces will discourage indecent programming. "Smut may," as Judge Leventhal put it, "drive itself from the market and confound Gresham," 556 F.2d at 35; the prosperity of those who traffic in pornographic literature and films would appear to justify skepticism.

37. The Commission stated: "Obnoxious, gutter language describing these matters has the effect of debasing and brutalizing human beings by reducing them to their mere bodily functions." 56 FCC 2d, at 98. Our society has a tradition of performing certain bodily functions in private, and of severely limiting the public exposure or discussion of such matters. Verbal or physical acts exposing those intimacies are offensive irrespective of any message that may accompany the exposure.

sider its context in order to determine whether the Commission's action was constitutionally permissible.

C

We have long recognized that each medium of expression presents special First Amendment problems. And of all forms of communication, it is broadcasting that has received the most limited First Amendment protection.

The reasons for these distinctions are complex, but two have relevance to the present case. First, the broadcast media have established a uniquely pervasive presence in the lives of all Americans. Patently offensive, indecent material presented over the airwaves confronts the citizen, not only in public, but also in the privacy of the home, where the individual's right to be left alone plainly outweighs the First Amendment rights of an intruder. Because the broadcast audience is constantly tuning in and out, prior warnings cannot completely protect the listener or viewer from unexpected program content. To say that one may avoid further offense by turning off the radio when he hears indecent language is like saying that the remedy for an assault is to run away after the first blow. One may hang up on an indecent phone call, but that option does not give the caller a constitutional immunity or avoid a harm that has already taken place.

Second, broadcasting is uniquely accessible to children, even those too young to read. Although Cohen's written message might have been incomprehensible to a first grader, Pacifica's broadcast could have enlarged a child's vocabulary in an instant. Other forms of offensive expression may be withheld from the young without restricting the expression at its source. Bookstores and motion picture theaters, for example, may be prohibited from making indecent material available to children. We held in Ginsberg v. New York, 390 U.S. 629 (1968) that the government's interest in the "well-being of its youth" and in supporting "parents' claim to authority in their own household" justified the regulation of otherwise protected expression.[38] The ease with which children may obtain access to broadcast material, coupled with the concerns recognized in *Ginsberg*, amply justify special treatment of indecent broadcasting.

It is appropriate, in conclusion, to emphasize the narrowness of our holding. This case does not involve a two-way radio conversation between a cab driver and a dispatcher, or a telecast of an Elizabethan comedy. We have not decided that an occasional expletive in either setting would justify any sanction or, indeed, that this broadcast would justify a criminal prosecution. The Commission's decision rested entirely on a nuisance rationale under which context is all-important. The concept requires consideration of a host of variables. The time of day was emphasized by the Commission. The content of the program in which the language is used will also affect the composition of the audience,[39] and differ-

---

38. The Commission's action does not by any means reduce adults to hearing only what is fit for children. *Cf.* Butler v. Michigan, 352 U.S. 380, 383 (1957). Adults who feel the need may purchase tapes and records or go to theaters and nightclubs to hear these words. In fact, the Commission has not unequivocally closed even broadcasting to speech of this sort; whether broadcast audiences in the late evening contain so few children that playing this monologue would be permissible is an issue neither the Commission nor this Court has decided.

39. Even a prime-time recitation of Geoffrey Chaucer's Miller's Tale would not be likely to command the attention of many children who are both old enough to understand

ences between radio, television, and perhaps closed-circuit transmissions, may also be relevant. As Mr. Justice Sutherland wrote, a "nuisance may be merely a right thing in the wrong place—like a pig in the parlor instead of the barnyard." Euclid v. Ambler Realty Co., 272 U.S. 365, 388. We simply hold that when the Commission finds that a pig has entered the parlor, the exercise of its regulatory power does not depend on proof that the pig is obscene.

APPENDIX TO OPINION OF THE COURT

The following is a verbatim transcript of "Filthy Words" prepared by the Federal Communications Commission.

Aruba-du, ruba-tu, ruba-tu. I was thinking about the curse words and the swear words, the cuss words and the words that you can't say, that you're not supposed to say all the time, [']cause words or people into words want to hear your words. Some guys like to record your words and sell them back to you if they can, (laughter) listen in on the telephone, write down what words you say. A guy who used to be in Washington, knew that his phone was tapped, used to answer, Fuck Hoover, yes, go ahead. (laughter) Okay, I was thinking one night about the words you couldn't say on the public, ah, airwaves, um, the ones you definitely wouldn't say, ever, [']cause I heard a lady say bitch one night on television, and it was cool like she was talking about, you know, ah, well, the bitch is the first one to notice that in the litter Johnie right (murmur) Right. And, uh, bastard you can say, and hell and damn so I have to figure out which ones you couldn't and ever and it came down to seven but the list is open to amendment, and in fact, has been changed, uh, by now, ha, a lot of people pointed things out to me, and I noticed some myself. The original seven words were, shit, piss, fuck, cunt, cocksucker, motherfucker, and tits. Those are the ones that will curve your spine, grow hair on your hands and (laughter) maybe, even bring us, God help us, peace without honor (laughter) um, and a bourbon. (laughter) And now the first thing that we noticed was that work fuck was really repeated in there because the word motherfucker is a compound word and it's another form of the word fuck. (laughter) You want to be a purist it doesn't really—it can't be on the list of basic words. Also, cocksucker is a compound word and neither half of that is really dirty. The word—the half sucker that's merely suggestive (laughter) and the word cock is a half-way dirty word, 50% dirty—dirty half the time, depending on what you mean by it. (laughter) Uh, remember when you first heard it, like in 6th grade, you used to giggle. And the cock crowed three times, heh (laughter) the cock—three times. It's in the Bible, cock in the Bible. (laughter) And the first time you heard about a cock-fight, remember—What? Huh? naw. It ain't that, are you stupid? man. (laughter, clapping) It's chickens, you know, (laughter) Then you have the four letter words from the old Angle-Saxon fame. Uh, shit and fuck. The word shit, uh, is an interesting kind of word in that the middle class has never really accepted it and approved it. They use it like, crazy but it's not really okay. It's still a rude, dirty, old kind of gushy word. (laughter) They don't like that, but they say it, like, they say it like, a lady now in a middle-class home, you'll hear most of the time she says it as an expletive, you know, it's

---

and young enough to be adversely affected by passages such as: "And prively he caughte hire by the queynte." The Canterbury Tales, Chaucer's Complete Works (Cambridge ed. 1933), p. 58.

out of her mouth before she knows. She says, Oh shit oh shit, (laughter) oh shit. If she drops something, Oh, the shit hurt the broccoli. Shit. Thank you. (footsteps fading away) (papers ruffling)

Read it! (from audience)

Shit! (laughter) I won the Grammy, man, for the comedy album. Isn't that groovy? (clapping, whistling) (murmur) That's true. Thank you. Thank you man. Yeah. (murmer) (continuous clapping) Thank you man. Thank you. Thank you very much, man. Thank, no, (end of continuous clapping) for that and for the Grammy, man, [']cause (laughter) that's based on people liking it man, yeh, that's ah, that's okay man. (laughter) Let's let that go, man. I got my Grammy. I can let my hair hang down now, shit. (laughter) Ha! So! Now the word shit is okay for the man. At work you can say it like crazy. Mostly figuratively, Get that shit out of here, will ya? I don't want to see that shit anymore. I can't *cut* that shit, buddy. I've had that shit up to here. I think you're full of shit myself. (laughter) He don't know shit from Shinola. (laughter) you know that? (laughter) Always wondered how the Shinola people felt about that (laughter) Hi, I'm the new man from Shinola, (laughter) Hi, how are ya? Nice to see ya. (laughter) How are ya? (laughter) Boy, I don't know whether to shit or wind my watch. (laughter) Guess, I'll shit on my watch. (laughter) Oh, *the* shit is going to hit *de* fan. (laughter). Built like a brick shit-house. (laughter) Up, he's up shit's creek. (laughter) He's had it. (laughter) He hit me, I'm sorry. (laughter) Hot shit, holy shit, tough shit, eat shit. (laughter) shit-eating grin. Uh, whoever thought of that was ill. (murmur laughter) He had a shit-eating grin! He had a what? (laughter) Shit on a stick. (laughter) Shit in a handbag. I always like that. He ain't worth shit in a handbag. (laughter) Shitty. He acted real shitty. (laughter) You know what I mean? (laughter) I got the money back, but a real shitty attitude. Heh, he had a shit-fit. (laughter) Wow! Shit-fit. Whew! Glad I wasn't there. (murmur, laughter) All the animals — Bull shit, horseshit, cow shit, rat shit, bat shit. (laughter) First time I heard bat shit, I really came apart. A guy in Oklahoma, Boggs, said it, man. Aw! Bat shit. (laughter) Vera reminded me of that last night, ah (murmur). Snake shit, slicker than owl shit. (laughter) Get your shit together. Shit or get off the pot. (laughter) I got a shit-load full of them. (laughter) I got a shit-pot full, all right. Shit-head, shit-heel, shit in your heart, shit for brains, (laughter) shit-face, heh (laughter) I always try to think how that could have originated; the first guy that said that. Somebody got drunk and fell in some shit, you know. (laughter) Hey, I'm shit-face. (laughter) Shit-face, *today*. (laughter) Anyway, enough of that shit. (laughter) The big one, the word fuck that's the one that hangs them up the most. [']Cause in a lot of cases that's the very act that hangs them up the most. So, it's natural that the word would, uh, have the same effect. It's a great word, fuck, nice word, easy word, cute word, kind of. Easy word to say. One syllable, short u. (laughter) Fuck. (Murmur) You know, it's easy. Starts with a nice soft sound fuh ends with a *kuh*. Right? (laughter) A little something for everyone. Fuck (laughter) Good word. Kind of a proud word, too. Who are you? I am *FUCK*, (laughter) *FUCK OF THE MOUNTAIN*. (laughter) Tune in again next week to FUCK OF THE MOUNTAIN. (laughter) It's an interesting word too, [']cause it's got a double kind of a life — personality — dual, you know, whatever the right phrase is. It leads a double life, the word fuck. First of all, it means, sometimes, most of the time, fuck. What does it mean? It means to make love. Right? We're going to make love, yeh, we're going to fuck, yeh, we're going to fuck, yeh, we're going to make love. (laughter) we're really going to fuck, yeh, we're going to make love. Right? And it also means the beginning of life, it's the act that begins life, so there's the word hanging around with words like love, and life, and yet on the other hand, it's also a word that we really use to hurt each other with, man. It's a heavy. It's one that you have toward the end of the argument. (laughter) Right? (laughter) You finally can't make out. Oh, fuck you man. I said, fuck you. (laughter, murmur) Stupid fuck. (laughter) Fuck you and everybody that looks like you. (laughter) man. It would be nice to change the movies that we already have and substitute the word fuck for the word kill, wherever we could, and some of those movie cliches would change a little bit. Madfuckers still on the loose. Stop me before I fuck again. Fuck the ump, fuck the ump, fuck the ump, fuck the ump, fuck the ump. Easy on the clutch Bill, you'll fuck that engine again. (laughter) The other shit one was, I don't give a shit. Like it's worth something, you know? (laughter) I don't give a shit. Hey, well, I don't take no shit, (laughter) you know what I mean? You know why I don't take no shit? (laughter) [']Cause I don't give a shit. (laughter) If I give a shit, I would have to pack shit. (laughter) But I don't pack no shit cause I don't give a shit. (laughter) You wouldn't shit me, would you? (laughter) That's a joke when you're a kid with a worm looking out the bird's ass. You wouldn't shit me, would you? (laughter) It's an eight-year-old joke but a good one. (laughter) The additions to the list. I found three more words that had to be put on the list of words you could never say on television, and they were fart, turd and twat, those three. (laughter) Fart, we talked about, it's harmless. It's like tits, it's a cutie word, no problem. Turd, you can't say but who wants to, you know? (laughter) The subject never comes up on the panel so I'm not worried about that one. Now the word twat is an interesting word. Twat! Yeh, right in the twat. (laughter) Twat is an interesting word because it's the only one I know of, the only slang word applying to the, a part of the sexual anatomy that doesn't have another meaning to it. Like, ah, snatch, box and pussy all have other meanings, man. Even in a Walt Disney movie, you can say, We're going to snatch that pussy and put him in a box and bring him on the airplane. (murmer, laughter) Everybody loves it. The twat stands alone, man, as it should. And two-way words. Ah, ass is okay providing you're riding into town on a religious feast day. (laughter) You can't say, up your *ass.* (laughter) You can say, stuff it! (murmur) There are certain things you can say its weird but you can just come so close. Before I cut, I, uh, want to, ah, thank you for listening to my words, man, fellow, uh space travelers. Thank you man for tonight and thank you also. (clapping whistling)

JUSTICE POWELL, with whom JUSTICE BLACKMUN joins, concurring in part and concurring in the judgment.

I join Parts I, II, III, and IV-C of Justice Stevens' opinion.

I do not subscribe to the theory that the Justices of this Court are free generally to decide on the basis of its content which speech protected by the First Amendment is most "valuable" and hence deserving of the most protection, and which is less "valuable" and hence deserving of less protection. In my view, the result in this case does not turn on whether Carlin's monologue, viewed as a whole, or the words that constitute it, have more or less "value" than a candidate's campaign speech. This is a judgment for each person to make, not one for the judges to impose upon him.

The result turns instead on the unique characteristics of the broadcast media, combined with society's right to protect its children from speech generally agreed to be inappropriate for their years, and with the interest of unwilling adults in not being assaulted by such offensive speech in their homes.

JUSTICE BRENNAN, with whom JUSTICE MARSHALL joins, dissenting.

Without question, the privacy interests of an individual in his home are substantial and deserving of significant protection. In finding these interests sufficient to justify the content regulation of protected speech, however, the Court commits two errors. First, it misconceives the nature of the privacy interests involved where an individual voluntarily chooses to admit radio communications into his home. Second, it ignores the constitutionally protected interests of both those who wish to transmit and those who desire to receive broadcasts that many—including the FCC and this Court—might find offensive.

I believe that an individual's actions in switching on and listening to communications transmitted over the public airways and directed to the public at large do not implicate fundamental privacy interests, even when engaged in within the home. Instead, because the radio is undeniably a public medium, these actions are more properly viewed as a decision to take part, if only as a listener, in an ongoing public discourse. Whatever the minimal discomfort suffered by a listener who inadvertently tunes into a program he finds offensive during the brief interval before he can simply extend his arm and switch stations or flick the "off" button, it is surely worth the candle to preserve the broadcaster's right to send, and the right of those interested to receive, a message entitled to full First Amendment protection.

The Court's balance, of necessity, fails to accord proper weight to the interests of listeners who wish to hear broadcasts the FCC deems offensive. It permits majoritarian tastes completely to preclude a protected message from entering the homes of a receptive, unoffended minority.

Parents, not the government, have the right to make certain decisions regarding the upbringing of their children. As surprising as it may be to individual Members of this Court, some parents may actually find Mr. Carlin's unabashed attitude towards the seven "dirty words" healthy, and deem it desirable to expose their children to the manner in which Mr. Carlin defuses the taboo surrounding the words.[40]

I would place the responsibility and the right to weed worthless and offensive communications from the public airways where it belongs and where, until today, it resided: in a public free to choose those communications worthy of its attention from a marketplace unsullied by the censor's hand.

The idea that the content of a message and its potential impact on any who might receive it can be divorced from the words that are the vehicle for its expression is transparently fallacious. A given word may have a unique capacity to capsule an idea, evoke an emotion, or conjure up an image. Indeed, for those of

---

40. The opinions of my Brothers POWELL and STEVENS rightly refrain from relying on the notion of "spectrum scarcity" to support their result. As Chief Judge Bazelon noted below, "although scarcity has justified increasing the diversity of speakers and speech, it has never been held to justify censorship." 556 F.2d, at 29.

us who place an appropriately high value on our cherished First Amendment rights, the word "censor" is such a word.

The opinions of my Brethren display both a sad insensitivity to the fact that such alternatives for adults as purchasing Carlin's records or attending his performances involve the expenditure of money, time, and effort that many of those wishing to hear Mr. Carlin's message may not be able to afford, and a naive innocence of the reality that in many cases, the medium may well be the message.

The airways are capable not only of carrying a message, but also of transforming it. A satirist's monologue may be most potent when delivered to a live audience; yet the choice whether this will in fact be the manner in which the message is delivered and received is one the First Amendment prohibits the government from making.

In our land of cultural pluralism, there are many who think, act, and talk differently from the Members of this Court, and who do not share their fragile sensibilities. It is only an acute ethnocentric myopia that enables the Court to approve the censorship of communications solely because of the words they contain. The words that the Court and the Commission find so unpalatable may be the stuff of everyday conversations in some, if not many, of the innumerable subcultures that compose this Nation. As one researcher concluded, "words generally considered obscene like 'bullshit' and 'fuck' are considered neither obscene nor derogatory in the African American vernacular except in particular contextual situations and when used with certain intonations." C. Bins, "Toward an Ethnography of Contemporary African American Oral Poetry," Language and Linguistics Working Papers No. 5, p. 82 (Georgetown Univ. Press 1972).

Today's decision will thus have its greatest impact on broadcasters desiring to reach, and listening audiences composed of, persons who do not share the Court's view as to which words or expressions are acceptable and who, for a variety of reasons, including a conscious desire to flout majoritarian conventions, express themselves using words that may be regarded as offensive by those from different socio-economic backgrounds. In this context, the Court's decision may be seen for what, in the broader perspective, it really is: another of the dominant culture's inevitable efforts to force those groups who do not share its mores to conform to its way of thinking, acting, and speaking.

JUSTICE STEWART, with whom JUSTICE BRENNAN, JUSTICE WHITE, and JUSTICE MARSHALL join, dissenting.

The statute pursuant to which the Commission acted, 18 U.S.C. §1464, makes it a federal offense to utter "any obscene, indecent, or profane language by means of radio communication." The Commission held, and the Court today agrees, that "indecent" is a broader concept than "obscene" as the latter term was defined in Miller v. California, 413 U.S. 15 (1973), because language can be "indecent" although it has social, political, or artistic value and lacks prurient appeal. But this construction of §1464, while perhaps plausible, is by no means compelled. To the contrary, I think that "indecent" should properly be read as meaning no more than "obscene." Since the Carlin monologue concededly was not "obscene," I believe that the Commission lacked statutory authority to ban it.

Notes and Questions

1. Uniquely Pervasive, Accessible Speech? The Supreme Court's opinion in *Pacifica* was not a surprise, but it did require the Court to juggle precedent somewhat, as a number of precedents outside the broadcasting field seemed to cut against the FCC. The *Pacifica* Court had to distinguish four major cases: (1) Butler v. Michigan, 352 U.S. 380 (1957), which held that the state could not ban the sale to adults of books that were obscene only as to children. (2) Cohen v. California, 403 U.S. 15 (1971), which overturned a conviction for wearing a jacket inscribed with the statement "Fuck the Draft." *Cohen* appeared to leave government equally helpless to regulate the language of speech and its content on the grounds that there was no legitimate distinction between the two. (3) Miller v. California, 413 U.S. 15 (1973), which held that government had wide-ranging powers to regulate "obscene" speech, but defined obscene speech to be speech that (a) described sexual conduct in a patently offensive way; (b) appealed to the prurient interest; and (c) lacked serious literary, artistic, scientific, or political value. (4) And Erznoznik v. City of Jacksonville, 422 U.S. 205 (1975), which held unconstitutional a municipal regulation barring drive-in movies from exhibiting motion pictures visible from public streets in which "the human male or female bare buttocks, human female bare breasts, or human bare pubic areas are shown." When the city sought to justify the regulation as designed to protect children, the Court stated that the law invaded minors' First Amendment rights. "Speech that is neither obscene as to youths nor subject to some other legitimate proscription cannot be suppressed solely to protect the young from ideas or images that a legislative body thinks unsuitable for them." *Id.* at 213–14.

The *Pacifica* Court thus needed to assert that Carlin's speech was of peculiarly low value, notwithstanding these precedents, or to pronounce broadcasting "unique" in order to justify the result. Is the Court convincing in asserting that broadcasting is uniquely pervasive and uniquely accessible to children? That such uniqueness justifies FCC censorship? Of this broadcast? (Are these claims more convincing than the correlative claim in *Red Lion* that broadcasting is unique because it employs scarce resources?)

2. Scarcity. Neither Justice Stevens' opinion nor Justice Powell's concurrence placed any weight on the scarcity rationale, and Justice Brennan's dissent stated flatly that scarcity could not support censorship. The argument for this position is fairly straightforward: the theory of scarcity seeks to justify regulations that expand voices, not those that contract them. But could the scarcity argument apply more broadly? If scarcity justifies requirements that broadcasters provide favored programming, why wouldn't it also justify prohibiting them from wasting that scarce resource on disfavored programming, especially as such a prohibition would them make room for more valuable programming? After all, if the government prohibited all low-value programming, it would not be replaced with silence, but with other programs that would presumably be of greater value.

In this regard, consider the statement in *Red Lion* regarding the "right of the public to receive suitable access to social, political, esthetic, moral, and other ideas and experiences." If, as Justice Stevens' opinion suggests, indecency is "no essential part of any exposition of ideas" and its social value is outweighed by the harms it imposes, then wouldn't the right of the public articulated in *Red*

Lion be vindicated by the replacement of indecency with speech that is more likely to be an essential part of an exposition of ideas?

3. Indecent Speech. Notice that two of the five Justices in the *Pacifica* majority (Powell and Blackmun) relied exclusively on the unique status of broadcasting. For the others (Stevens, Burger, and Rehnquist), it was also important—indeed, perhaps most important—that what was being regulated was "indecent" speech. (*See* Part IV.B. of the Stevens opinion, which Powell and Blackmun declined to join.) What, if any, limits do you suppose the Powell-Blackmun view would place on the ability of the FCC to censor? If AM radio broadcasting is "unique," is it possible that other media are identically unique?

4. Implications. How far does the *Pacifica* rationale reach? The FCC's briefs emphasized that its indecency regulation was aimed at protecting children under the age of 12 from indecent material.[41] Does *Pacifica* suggest that its lenient review applies only to protections of "children...too young to read"? Conversely, would its reasoning apply if the FCC defined "children" as everyone under the age of 18? (On this, see *ACT III*, below.) Does *Pacifica* rest on a special concern for children that could also justify requiring each broadcast licensee to set aside a minimum number of hours per week or per day for broadcasting aimed at children? (On this, see the section on children's television.) Does it rest on a special concern for cleaning up the public airwaves, so that the case might justify restrictions on televised violence? (On this, see the section on televised violence, immediately following.) Does it rest on a special concern for intrusions that most people would find unwarranted, so that the case might justify a ban on harassing telephone calls or on random and gratuitous nudity on a cable channel? (Materials in Chapters Fourteen and Twenty take up the permissibility of prohibiting indecency in cable television programming and telephone transmissions, respectively.)

5. Subsequent Events. Interestingly, the FCC initially was not pleased with its victory in *Pacifica*. The case had been litigated by an FCC appointed by the Nixon and Ford Administrations. By the time the Supreme Court decided the case, Carter appointees had control of the Commission. Through press announcements shortly after *Pacifica*, the Commission stated that it believed the decision applied only to the repeated use, solely for shock value, of the words Carlin employed, when broadcast before 10:00 p.m. (Does this seem to be a correct interpretation of the opinion?) The FCC brought no further indecency cases until 1987.

When the Commission got back into the indecency business it became clear—if it had not already been so—that *Pacifica* left open more questions than it answered. Did the Court mean to authorize a total ban on indecency or simply a limitation on its broadcast, say to certain times of the day? What "children" did the Court mean to protect—preschoolers, elementary school students, high school students? Was speech that was "indecent" but also had serious literary, artistic, political, or scientific value nevertheless subject to proscription? Was the Commission required to come up with evidence of harm to children or of the likelihood that children would be in the listening or viewing audience? As to the

---

41. *See* Action for Children's Television v. FCC, 852 F.2d 1332, 1341–42 (D.C. Cir. 1988) (*ACT I*).

latter, did the Commission need to show a risk that children were watching the specific show broadcast or only that some children were listening to some radio show somewhere? What if the broadcast were preceded by a warning that it contained indecent material? Was the Commission required to adopt a reasonably precise definition of "indecent programming" in order to clarify licensees' responsibilities and confine the FCC's discretion?

The most prominent vehicle that the FCC used both to deal with some of these questions and to announce to the world a policy shift under which it would begin to penalize indecent broadcasts beyond the narrow confines developed in the Carter years, was the *Jerker* case.[42] The presence of *Jerker* on the FCC's docket was in some ways fortunate for an agency inclined to revive and expand indecency regulation, as it contained language that was particularly graphic. Indeed, its language made Carlin's monologue seem remarkably tame by comparison.

IN RE PACIFICA FOUNDATION [*JERKER*]
2 FCC Rcd. 2698 (1987)

I. BACKGROUND

3. The Commission received a complaint alleging that on June 28, 1986, at approximately 7:45 p.m., local time, KPFK-FM aired a program entitled "Shocktime America" ("Shocktime, U.S.A.") which allegedly contained a narration and song lyrics utilizing words and phrases such as "eat shit," "motherfucker," and "fuck the U.S.A." The complaint did not include a transcript or tape recording of the show, and did not indicate whether the use of the expletives described was repetitive.

4. In response Pacifica indicates that "Shocktime, U.S.A." is a live KPFK program that is produced by a Los Angeles-based performance art group. On the program in question, Pacifica indicates that one of the group's members made remarks that were not scripted and which members of the listening audience might well have found offensive. Furthermore, Pacifica asserts that as a result of this incident the other members of the group met and expelled the subject individual. Additionally, the licensee indicates that the program producers, in recognition that "the nature of this spontaneous commentary was so inappropriate," withdrew the program from KPFK. Pacifica expresses regret for the incident and states that it has re-emphasized to all program producers their responsibility to the station and to the listening audience.

5. On September 8, 1986, the Commission received a complaint alleging that on Sunday, August 31, 1986, between 10:00 and 11:00 p.m., local time, KPFK-

---

42. *Jerker* was one of three decisions released on a single day, each of which declared "indecent" material that would not have been so identified under the prior FCC standard. In re Pacifica Foundation, 2 FCC Rcd. 2698 (1987); In re Infinity Broadcasting Corp. of Pa., 2 FCC Rcd. 2705 (1987); In re Regents of the University of California, 2 FCC Rcd. 2703 (1987). To avoid any doubt on this score, the FCC also issued a *Public Notice* summarizing the three orders released that day and "put[ting] all broadcast and amateur radio licensees on notice as to new standards that the Commission will apply in enforcing the prohibition against obscene and indecent transmissions." New Indecency Enforcement Standards to be Applied to All Broadcast and Amateur Radio Licensees, 62 RR2d (P & F) 1218 (1987); *see ACT I*, 852 F.2d at 1336.

FM aired a program "I Am Are You?" ("IMRU") that featured excerpts from a play entitled "Jerker." The complaint alleged that these excerpts involved dramatic readings of sexual fantasies and contained language highly descriptive of sexual and excretory activities.

6. In response, Pacifica states that the program "IMRU" is a regularly aired program directed to the gay population of Los Angeles. Pacifica represents that the play, "Jerker," deals with the issue of Acquired Immune Deficiency Syndrome and that the mood of the play is "the need to affirm life in the face of death." Pacifica contends that the complaint provided no context to the complained-of words and phrases and was, therefore, misleading. A warning was broadcast prior to the commencement of "IMRU" on the night in question: "The following program contains material which some listeners may find objectionable. If you would be disturbed by the use of such sensitive material, please tune out for the next...minutes."

7. Finally, Pacifica asserts that at the time the subject program was broadcast "children would not ordinarily be in the listening audience," and that Arbitron ratings confirm that KPFK's listening audience rarely consists of children. Pacifica also supplied a tape recording of the August 31, 1986, "IMRU" program.

II. DISCUSSION

12. The licensee argues that the holding in *Pacifica* limits a finding of indecency to deliberate, repetitive use of the seven words actually contained in the George Carlin monologue determined to be indecent in *Pacifica*. While Commission action subsequent to the *Pacifica* decision may have indicated this to be our position, we take this opportunity to state that, notwithstanding any prior contrary indications, we will not apply the *Pacifica* standard so narrowly in the future. We find that the definition of indecent broadcast material set forth in *Pacifica* appropriately includes a broader range of material than the seven specific words at issue in *Pacifica*. Those particular words are more correctly treated as examples of, rather than a definitive list of, the kinds of words that, when used in a patently offensive manner as measured by contemporary community standards applicable to the broadcast medium, constitute indecency.

13. While speech that is indecent must involve more than an isolated use of an offensive word, repetitive use of specific words or phrases is not an absolute requirement for a finding of indecency. If a complaint focuses solely on the use of expletives, we believe that under the legal standards set forth in *Pacifica*, deliberate and repetitive use in a patently offensive manner is a requisite to a finding of indecency. When a complaint goes beyond the use of expletives, however, repetition of specific words or phrases is not necessarily an element critical to a determination of indecency. Rather, speech involving the description or depiction of sexual or excretory functions must be examined in context to determine whether it is patently offensive under contemporary community standards applicable to the broadcast medium.

15. The only effective means of restricting the access of minors to indecent programming is to channel such programming to a time during which there is not a reasonable risk that children may be in the audience. Hence, it is the physical attributes of the broadcast medium, not any purported diminished First

Amendment rights of broadcasters based on spectrum scarcity or licensing, that justify channeling of indecent material.[43]

16. In prior determinations related to the broadcast of indecent material, the Commission has indicated that such broadcasts may be legally permissible if they are aired after 10:00 p.m. and are preceded by a warning. Current evidence, however, indicates that there is a reasonable risk that children are still in the audience at 10:00 p.m., at least on weekends (when the program "IMRU" was aired). Significant numbers of children remain in the audience on Sunday evenings as late as midnight. Studies indicate that approximately 112,200 children aged 12–17 are in the Los Angeles metro survey area radio audience per average quarter hour between 7 p.m. and midnight on Sunday night. Thus, we have determined that mechanistically relying on a specific time for broadcasting indecent material no longer satisfies the requirement that indecent material be channeled to a time when there is not a reasonable risk that children may be present in the broadcast audience.

Shocktime, U.S.A.

17. It is uncontested that the June 28, 1986, edition of the "Shocktime, U.S.A." program contained the language at issue. However, we are unable to determine whether the broadcast was indecent. The complainant has merely stated that four specific phrases were used during the course of the broadcast. Without additional information, we cannot determine precisely the context or whether the use of patently offensive speech was isolated.[44]

18. Furthermore, given the circumstances under which the material at issue was aired (i.e., it was live, spontaneous, and unscripted), and the remedial action taken by Pacifica and the group that produced "Shocktime, U.S.A.," even if we could determine that the broadcast was in fact indecent, we would decline to take action in this situation. The Commission has previously indicated that the isolated use of unplanned expletives during live coverage of news or public affairs programming will not necessarily be actionable so long as the licensee exercises reasonable judgment, responsibility and sensitivity to the public's needs and tastes to avoid patently offensive broadcasts.

IMRU

19. We now turn to the "IMRU" broadcast of August 31, 1986. We have reviewed the tape of the program. The program commenced with an interview, by the host of "IMRU," of the director and two actors appearing in the Los Angeles production of the play "Jerker," and was followed by excerpts from the play. The play, which was characterized during the interview with its director, Michael Kearns, as being "blazingly erotic," concerned the telephone relationship of two

---

43. Our regulation of indecent speech is a valid time, place and manner restriction because our objective is not to proscribe the expression of any particular type of protected speech. Rather, our purpose is to promote the content neutral and significant governmental interest in safeguarding the well-being of the nation's youth, while preserving the ability of adults to receive the material during the times of day when there is not a reasonable risk that children may be in the audience.

44. The Commission has been advised that neither a tape recording nor a transcript of the program is available to provide a more detailed review of the words used, the context or the level of repetitiveness.

men who had met accidently over the telephone, but never in person, apparently when one called a wrong number.

20. The conversations broadcast made extensive use of language that describes or depicts sexual or excretory organs or activities in a patently offensive manner. In the first of the three vignettes presented, the words "shit" and "fucking" were used repetitively. In addition, during the first vignette, one character says to the other:

"Yeah, it was loving even if you didn't know whose cock it was in the dark or whose asshole you were sucking."

21. At another point, one of the characters states that he was in Vietnam and that after what he had seen there, no one could tell him that he was immoral if he loved "sucking ass," "taking piss from a guy's cock," or if he had "a quickie blow job in the Union Square men's room."

22. As the presentation moved to the second vignette, the scene shifted to one character's description of an anonymous sexual encounter in which he had participated. He was told by the listening character to "make it hot" and to keep in mind that he would be "playing with" himself while being told the story. That story contained the following language by way of example:

"I'll give you the gentlest fuck west of the Mississippi."

"We cuddled and played around a bit before he started working on my ass."

"I remember he was kneeling between my legs and he worked my asshole with lube for the longest time—just gettin' it to relax so there was no tension, no fear."

"He lowered himself on top of me and slid his dick in all the way, but so gently, so smoothly, there wasn't even a bit of pain."

"His cock felt warm inside me—and full—so nice and full. So he began sliding his cock back and forth inside of my ass—but so gently, so gently."

"I don't think I've ever had such a gentle, sensitive fuck before or after. Well, he must have gone at it for twenty minutes at the very least, just slidin' his cock back and forth inside of my ass."

"And then he whispered to me, 'You're gonna feel me come inside of you.' And I did. Man, I could feel the cum pulse up his shaft inside of my ass. I could count the pulses and it felt warm and good."

And later in the program this exchange:

Actor 1: "You better get yourself ready for some brother-to-brother, sweaty, down and dirty pig sex, you understand?"

Actor 2: "Yeah!"

1: "None of this nicey-nice, lovey-dovey stuff. I want to make you eat ass, suck my balls, and drink my piss like you never have before. You get me?"

2: "Hot throbbing cocks, hard pounding muscles."

1: "You've got it."

23. We believe that the material contained in the aired portion of "Jerker," of which the foregoing is exemplary but by no means exhaustive, supports a finding that the licensee broadcast indecent material within the meaning of 18 U.S.C.

§1464. The material describes sexual and excretory activities and organs in a patently offensive manner as measured by contemporary community standards for the broadcast medium. Notwithstanding the licensee's assertion, we do not believe the context dilutes or ameliorates the patently offensive manner in which the sexual activity was described.

24. We are unpersuaded by Pacifica's argument that "KFPK's listening audience rarely consists of children except where programs are specifically focused on them." First, the test of indecency focuses on the risk of the presence of children in the audience. Second, we note the Supreme Court's observance that radio listeners tune into a station generally without the benefit of a schedule of programs or warning as to potentially offensive content.[45] Finally, we note that listeners often switch indiscriminately from station to station and are thus easily exposed to indecent material not properly channeled to a time during which there is not a reasonable risk that children may be in the broadcast audience.

25. Based upon our review of the material, we conclude that the "IMRU" broadcast falls within the ambit of indecency as prohibited by section 1464 under the standards set forth herein. Thus, we have determined that at a minimum this material warrants restricting children's access. Given our finding that there is a reasonable risk of children remaining in the listening audience at 10:00 p.m. on Sundays, the fact that this program was broadcast at 10:00 p.m. with a warning does not render it permissible. However, because prior Commission actions have indicated that airing programs containing indecent material at 10:00 p.m. might in certain cases be permissible, we hereby limit our action to warning you and all other broadcast licensees that this material would be actionable under the indecency standard as clarified today.

26. We do not decide here whether, based upon the applicable local community standards, the subject material also meets the tests for obscenity set forth in *Miller*. We do believe, however, that there is sufficient possibility of such a finding. We are therefore directing the General Counsel to forward the complaint and tape recording of the subject "IMRU" program to the Department of Justice for its consideration as to whether a criminal prosecution pursuant to 18 U.S.C. §1464 is appropriate.

Notes and Questions

1. The Issues. What view of the indecency prohibition does the FCC espouse in this opinion? Why were the station's responses (¶¶6–7) to the complaint insufficient? Does it matter whether the assertedly indecent broadcast contains matter of redeeming social value? If so, how should the FCC determine whether or not such social value exists? Does it matter if the broadcast is preceded by a warning? Does it matter when the broadcast occurs? Does it matter whether any children in fact heard the program? What does the Commission mean by "child"? Is

---

45. Accordingly, we do not believe a warning preceding a broadcast program is sufficient to restrict the access of children to indecent material at times of day when there is a reasonable risk that children may be in the audience. Nevertheless, we continue to expect advance warnings to be given when broadcasters choose to air indecent programming at a time when there is not a reasonable risk that children may be in the broadcast audience.

the agency legitimately concerned about protecting unwilling or unsuspecting adults (as well as children) from indecent broadcasts?

2. Content Neutral? Think about the content of the broadcasts in this case and in the *Carlin* case. In what sense can it be said that the FCC attacked these broadcasts without regard to their content or viewpoint?

3. Watch Your Language. Suppose you are defending Pacifica's broadcast of "Jerker," and the judge before whom you are appearing suggests that you dispense with a recitation of the language used in "Jerker." Would you refrain from using its language to avoid offending the judge, or would you recite the relevant language, on the theory that failing to do so would implicitly concede its unacceptability?

4. Does Context Matter? Should it matter whether the indecent language is an angry outburst (the statement "suck my dick you fucking cunt" cost a broadcast licensee $5,000[46]) or a Monty Python tune (the song "Sit on My Face and Tell Me That You Love Me" cost another licensee $4,000, less a small reduction for its "long and favorable compliance history"[47])?

5. Howard Stern. As the preceding note suggests, the punishment for the broadcast of indecent material is usually a fine in the thousands of dollars, and broadcasters rarely challenge them in court.[48] Sometimes, though, the stakes are a bit higher. Perhaps the most famous case involved Howard Stern, whose repeated use of language that the FCC deemed indecent led to fines against Stern's employer, Infinity Broadcasting, of more than $1 million. After reflecting on its plans to acquire additional stations and the FCC's indications that a clean record before the FCC would aid the approval of such expansion, Infinity agreed to pay a $1.7 million "voluntary contribution" to the U.S. Treasury. In return, Infinity received assurances that its negative record had been expunged. An Infinity representative explained: "In an era of deregulation, when Infinity is looking forward to acquisitions, our relationship with the FCC has normalized." Infinity Pays the $1.7 million, Broadcasting & Cable, Sept. 4, 1995; In re Infinity Broadcasting, 10 FCC Rcd. 12245 (1995).

6. Reconsidering *Jerker*. Pacifica asked the FCC to reconsider its ruling in *Jerker*, putting in motion a legal process that ultimately involved the Commission, the courts, and Congress. That process culminated in the following en banc decision by the Court of Appeals for the D.C. Circuit.

ACTION FOR CHILDREN'S TELEVISION v. FCC [*ACT III*]
58 F.3d 654 (D.C. Cir. 1995) (en banc), *cert. denied* 516 U.S. 1043 (1996)

Opinion for the court filed by Circuit Judge BUCKLEY, in which Circuit Judges SILBERMAN, WILLIAMS, GINSBURG, SENTELLE, HENDERSON, and RANDOLPH concur. Dissenting opinion filed by Chief Judge EDWARDS. Dis-

---

46. *See* In re LBJS Broadcasting Co., 13 FCC Rcd. 20956 (1998).
47. *See* In re Liability of KGB, Inc., 13 FCC Rcd. 16396 (1998).
48. *See* Action for Children's Television v. FCC, 59 F.3d 1249, 1264 (D.C. Cir. 1995) (Tatel, J., dissenting) (noting that "of the thirty-six FCC indecency forfeiture orders issued since 1987, not one has been reviewed by a court").

senting opinion filed by Circuit Judge WALD, in which Circuit Judges ROGERS and TATEL join.

BUCKLEY, Circuit Judge:

We are asked to determine the constitutionality of section 16(a) of the Public Telecommunications Act of 1992, which seeks to shield minors from indecent radio and television programs by restricting the hours within which they may be broadcast. Section 16(a) provides that, with one exception, indecent materials may only be broadcast between the hours of midnight and 6:00 a.m. The exception permits public radio and television stations that go off the air at or before midnight to broadcast such materials after 10:00 p.m.

I. BACKGROUND

The Radio Act of 1927 provides that "whoever utters any obscene, indecent, or profane language by means of radio communication shall be fined not more than $10,000 or imprisoned not more than two years, or both." 18 U.S.C. §1464 (1988). In enforcing section 1464 of the Radio Act, the Federal Communications Commission defines "broadcast indecency" as "language or material that, in context, depicts or describes, in terms patently offensive as measured by contemporary community standards for the broadcast medium, sexual or excretory activities or organs." In re Enforcement of Prohibitions Against Broadcast Indecency in 18 U.S.C. §1464, 8 FCC Rcd. 704, 705 n.10 (1993) ("*1993 Report and Order*").

While obscene speech is not accorded constitutional protection, "sexual expression which is indecent but not obscene is protected by the First Amendment." Sable Communications of California, Inc. v. FCC, 492 U.S. 115 (1989). "The Government may, however, regulate the content of such constitutionally protected speech in order to promote a compelling interest if it chooses the least restrictive means to further the articulated interest." *Id.* Noting that broadcasting has received the most limited First Amendment protection because of its unique pervasiveness and accessibility to children, the Supreme Court has held that the FCC may, in appropriate circumstances, place restrictions on the broadcast of indecent speech.

In In re Infinity Broadcasting Corp. of Pa., 3 FCC Rcd. 930 (1987) ("Reconsideration Order"), the Commission reviewed its decisions in three cases: In re Pacifica Foundation, 2 FCC Rcd. 2698 (1987) [*Jerker*], In re Infinity Broadcasting Corp. of Pa., 2 FCC Rcd. 2705 (1987), and In re Regents of the University of California, 2 FCC Rcd. 2703 (1987). One of these cases involved a morning broadcast; the other two dealt with programs that were aired after 10:00 p.m. In each of them, the agency found that a radio station had introduced particularly offensive pigs into American parlors in violation of section 1464.

The FCC reaffirmed the Government interest in safeguarding children from exposure to such speech and placed broadcasters on notice that because

> at least with respect to the particular markets involved, available evidence suggested there were still significant numbers of children in the audience at 10:00 p.m.... broadcasters should no longer assume that 10:00 p.m. is automatically the time after which indecent broadcasts may safely be aired. Rather,... indecent material would be actionable (that is, would

be held in violation of 18 U.S.C. §1464) if broadcast when there is a reasonable risk that children may be in the audience.

3 FCC Rcd. at 930–31. The Commission noted, however, that it was its "current thinking" that midnight marked the time after which it is reasonable to expect that it is late enough to ensure that the risk of children in the audience is minimized and to rely on parents to exercise increased supervision over whatever children remain in the viewing and listening audience. *Id.* at 937 n. 47.

In our review of the *Reconsideration Order* in Action for Children's Television v. FCC, 852 F.2d 1332 (D.C. Cir. 1988) ("*ACT I*"), we rejected the argument that the Commission's definition of indecency was unconstitutionally vague and overbroad. 852 F.2d at 1338–40. But although we affirmed the declaratory ruling that found portions of the morning broadcast to be in violation of section 1464, 852 F.2d at 1341, we vacated the Commission's rulings with respect to the two post-10:00 p.m. broadcasts. *Id.* In those instances, we considered the findings on which the Commission rested its decision to be "more ritual than real," *id.*, because the Commission had relied on data as to the number of teenagers in the total radio audience rather than the number of them who listened to the radio stations in question. We were also troubled by the FCC's failure to explain why it identified the relevant age group as children aged 12 to 17 when it had earlier proposed legislation for the protection of only those under 12. 852 F.2d at 1341–42. We further concluded that "the FCC's midnight advice, indeed its entire position on channeling, was not adequately thought through." *Id.* at 1342.

Two months after our decision in *ACT I*, Congress instructed the Commission to promulgate regulations "enforcing the provisions of...section [1464] on a 24 hour per day basis." Pub. L. No. 100-459, §608, 102 Stat. 2186, 2228 (1988). The Commission complied by issuing a regulation banning all broadcasts of indecent material. We reviewed the 24-hour ban in Action for Children's Television v. FCC, 290 U.S. App. D.C. 4, 932 F.2d 1504 (D.C. Cir. 1991) ("*ACT II*"). We again rejected petitioners' vagueness and overbreadth arguments, but we struck down the total ban on indecent broadcasts because "our previous holding in *ACT I* that the Commission must identify some reasonable period of time during which indecent material may be broadcast necessarily means that the Commission may not ban such broadcasts entirely." 932 F.2d at 1509.

Shortly after the Supreme Court denied certiorari in *ACT II*, 112 S. Ct. 1281 (1992), Congress again intervened, passing the Public Telecommunications Act of 1992, Pub. L. No. 102-356, 106 Stat. 949 (1992). Section 16(a) of the Act requires the Commission to

promulgate regulations to prohibit the broadcasting of indecent programming—

(1) between 6 a.m. and 10 p.m. on any day by any public radio station or public television station that goes off the air at or before 12 midnight; and

(2) between 6 a.m. and 12 midnight on any day for any radio or television broadcasting station not described in paragraph (1).

47 U.S.C. §303 note (Supp. IV 1992). Pursuant to this congressional mandate, the Commission issued regulations implementing section 16(a). *1993 Report and Order*, 8 FCC Rcd. at 711; 47 C.F.R. §73.3999 (1994). These are challenged in the petition now before us.

II. DISCUSSION

Petitioners present three challenges to the constitutionality of section 16(a) and its implementing regulations: First, the statute and regulations violate the First Amendment because they impose restrictions on indecent broadcasts that are not narrowly tailored to further the Government's interest, which petitioners define as the promotion of parental authority by shielding unsupervised children from indecent speech in the broadcast media; second, section 16(a) unconstitutionally discriminates among categories of broadcasters by distinguishing the times during which certain public and commercial broadcasters may air indecent material; and third, the Commission's generic definition of indecency is unconstitutionally vague. Petitioners also assert that our decisions in *ACT I* and *ACT II* compel the rejection of the newly enacted restrictions both because there are insufficient data to justify the new statutory ban and because the Commission continues to include children ages 12 to 17 in the protected class.

The Commission argues that the Government's interests extend beyond facilitating parental supervision to include protecting children from exposure to indecent broadcasts and safeguarding the home from unwanted intrusion by such broadcasts. The Commission asserts that restricting indecent broadcasts to the hours between midnight and 6:00 a.m. is narrowly tailored to achieve these compelling governmental interests.

At the outset, we dismiss petitioners' vagueness challenge as meritless. The FCC's definition of indecency in the new regulations is identical to the one at issue in *ACT II*, where we stated that "the Supreme Court's decision in *Pacifica* dispelled any vagueness concerns attending the Commission's definition," as did our holding in *ACT I*. 932 F.2d at 1508. Petitioners fail to provide any convincing reasons why we should ignore this precedent.

We now proceed to petitioners' remaining constitutional arguments.

A. The First Amendment Challenge

The Supreme Court has "long recognized that each medium of expression presents special First Amendment problems. . . . Of all forms of communication, it is broadcasting that has received the most limited First Amendment protection." FCC v. Pacifica Foundation, 438 U.S. 726, 748 (1978) (citation omitted). The Court has identified two reasons for this distinction that are relevant here:

> First, the broadcast media have established a uniquely pervasive presence in the lives of all Americans. Patently offensive, indecent material presented over the airwaves confronts the citizen, not only in public, but also in the privacy of the home, where the individual's right to be left alone plainly outweighs the First Amendment rights of an intruder.

> Second, broadcasting is uniquely accessible to children. . . . Other forms of offensive expression may be withheld from the young without restricting the expression at its source.

Id. at 748–50.

In light of these differences, radio and television broadcasts may properly be subject to different—and often more restrictive—regulation than is permissible for other media under the First Amendment. While we apply strict scrutiny to regulations of this kind regardless of the medium affected by them, our assessment of whether section 16(a) survives that scrutiny must necessarily take into account the unique context of the broadcast medium.

1. The Compelling Government Interests

In examining the Government's interests in protecting children from broadcast indecency, it is important to understand that hard-core pornography may be deemed indecent rather than obscene if it is "not patently offensive" under the relevant contemporary community standards. As Justice Scalia has observed,

> the more narrow the understanding of what is "obscene," and hence the more pornographic what is embraced within the residual category of "indecency," the more reasonable it becomes to insist upon greater assurance of insulation from minors.

Sable, 492 U.S. at 132 (Scalia, J., concurring).

The Commission identifies three compelling Government interests as justifying the regulation of broadcast indecency: support for parental supervision of children, a concern for children's well-being, and the protection of the home against intrusion by offensive broadcasts. Because we find the first two sufficient to support such regulation, we will not address the third.

Petitioners do not contest that the Government has a compelling interest in supporting parental supervision of what children see and hear on the public airwaves. While conceding that the Government has an interest in the well-being of children, petitioners argue that because "no causal nexus has been established between broadcast indecency and any physical or psychological harm to minors," Joint Brief for Petitioners at 32, that interest is "too insubstantial to justify suppressing indecent material at times when parents are available to supervise their children." *Id.* at 33. That statement begs two questions: The first is how effective parental supervision can actually be expected to be even when parent and child are under the same roof; the second, whether the Government's interest in the well-being of our youth is limited to protecting them from clinically measurable injury.

As Action for Children's Television argued in an earlier FCC proceeding, "parents, no matter how attentive, sincere, or knowledgeable, are not in a position to really exercise effective control" over what their children see on television. In re Action for Children's Television, 50 FCC 2dd 17, 26 (1974). This observation finds confirmation from a recent poll conducted by Fairbank, Maslin, Maullin & Associates on behalf of Children Now. The survey found that 54 percent of the 750 children questioned had a television set in their own rooms and that 55 percent of them usually watched television alone or with friends, but not with their families. Sixty-six percent of them lived in a household with three or more television sets. Studies described by the FCC in its 1989 Notice of Inquiry suggest that parents are able to exercise even less effective supervision over the radio programs to which their children listen. According to these studies, each American household had, on average, over five radios, and up to 80 percent of children had radios in their own bedrooms, depending on the locality studied; two-thirds of all children ages 6 to 12 owned their own radios, more than half of whom owned headphone radios. It would appear that Action for Children's Television had a firmer grasp of the limits of parental supervision 20 years ago than it does today.

With respect to the second question begged by petitioners, the Supreme Court has never suggested that a scientific demonstration of psychological harm is required in order to establish the constitutionality of measures protecting minors from exposure to indecent speech. In *Ginsberg,* the Court considered a New York State statute forbidding the sale to minors under the age of 17 of literature displaying nudity even where such literature was "not obscene for adults...." 390 U.S. at 634. The Court observed that while it was "very doubtful" that the legislative finding that such literature impaired "the ethical and moral development of our youth" was based on "accepted scientific fact," a causal link between them "had not been disproved either." *Id.* at 641–42. The Court then stated that it "did not demand of legislatures scientifically certain criteria of legislation. We therefore cannot say that the statute...has no rational relation to the objective of safeguarding such minors from harm." *Id.* at 642–43. In *Ginsberg*, of course, the protection of children did not require simultaneous restraints on the access of adults to indecent speech. The Court, however, has made it abundantly clear that the Government's interest in the "well-being of its youth" justified special treatment of indecent broadcasting.

Finally, we think it significant that the Supreme Court has recognized that the Government's interest in protecting children extends beyond shielding them from physical and psychological harm. The statute that the Court found constitutional in *Ginsberg* sought to protect children from exposure to materials that would "impair[ ] [their] ethical and moral development." 390 U.S. at 641. Furthermore, although the Court doubted that this legislative finding "expressed an accepted scientific fact," *id.*, it concluded that the legislature could properly support the judgment of

> parents and others, teachers for example, who have the primary responsibility for children's well-being by assessing sex-related material harmful to minors according to prevailing standards in the adult community as a whole with respect to what is suitable material for minors.

Id. *at 639.*

Congress does not need the testimony of psychiatrists and social scientists in order to take note of the coarsening of impressionable minds that can result from a persistent exposure to sexually explicit material just this side of legal obscenity. The Supreme Court has reminded us that society has an interest not only in the health of its youth, but also in its quality. *See Prince,* 321 U.S. at 168 ("A democratic society rests, for its continuance, upon the healthy, well-rounded growth of young people into full maturity as citizens, with all that implies."). As Irving Kristol has observed, it follows "from the proposition that democracy is a form of self-government,...that if you want it to be a meritorious polity, you have to care about what kind of people govern it." Irving Kristol, On the Democratic Idea in America 41–42, Harper & Row (1972).

We are not unaware that the vast majority of States impose restrictions on the access of minors to material that is not obscene by adult standards. In light of Supreme Court precedent and the social consensus reflected in state laws, we conclude that the Government has an independent and compelling interest in preventing minors from being exposed to indecent broadcasts.

Petitioners argue, nevertheless, that the Government's interest in supporting parental supervision of children and its independent interest in shielding them from the influence of indecent broadcasts are in irreconcilable conflict. The basic premise of this argument appears to be that the latter interest potentially undermines the objective of facilitating parental supervision for those parents who wish their children to see or hear indecent material. The Supreme Court has not followed this reasoning. Rather, it treats the Government interest in supporting parental authority and its "independent interest in the well-being of its youth," *Ginsberg*, 390 U.S. at 640, as complementary objectives mutually supporting limitations on children's access to material that is not obscene for adults. *Id.* at 639–40.

Today, of course, parents who wish to expose their children to the most graphic depictions of sexual acts will have no difficulty in doing so through the use of subscription and pay-per-view cable channels, delayed-access viewing using VCR equipment, and the rental or purchase of readily available audio and video cassettes. Thus the goal of supporting "parents' claim to authority in their own household to direct the rearing of their children," *id.* at 639, is fully consistent with the Government's own interest in shielding minors from being exposed to indecent speech by persons other than a parent. Society "may prevent the general dissemination of such speech to children, leaving to parents the decision as to what speech of this kind their children shall hear and repeat." *Pacifica*, 438 U.S. at 758 (Powell, J., concurring in part and concurring in the judgment).

The Government's dual interests in assisting parents and protecting minors necessarily extend beyond merely channeling broadcast indecency to those hours when parents can be at home to supervise what their children see and hear. It is fanciful to believe that the vast majority of parents who wish to shield their children from indecent material can effectively do so without meaningful restrictions on the airing of broadcast indecency.

2. Least Restrictive Means

Petitioners argue that section 16(a) is not narrowly drawn to further the Government's interest in protecting children from broadcast indecency for two reasons: First, they assert that the class to be protected should be limited to children under the age of 12; and second, they contend that the "safe harbor" is not narrowly tailored because it fails to take proper account of the First Amendment rights of adults and because of the chilling effect of the 6:00 a.m. to midnight ban on the programs aired during the evening "prime time" hours. We address these arguments in turn.

(a) Definition of "Children"

Although, in *ACT II*, we made no mention of the fact, in its 1990 Report on Broadcast Indecency, the FCC defined "children" to include "children ages 17 and under." 5 FCC Rcd. 5297, 5301 (1990). The agency offered three reasons in support of its definition: Other federal statutes designed to protect children from indecent speech use the same standard (citing 47 U.S.C. §223(b)(3) (Supp. II 1990) (forbidding indecent telephone communications to persons under 18)); most States have laws penalizing persons who disseminate sexually explicit materials to children ages 17 and under; and several Supreme Court decisions have sustained the constitutionality of statutes protecting children ages 17 and under (citing *Sable* and *Ginsberg*). *Id.* We find these reasons persuasive and note, as the

Commission did in the *1993 Report and Order* promulgating regulations pursuant to section 16(a), that the sponsor of that section, Senator Byrd, made specific reference to the FCC's finding that "there is a reasonable risk that significant numbers of children ages 17 and under listen to radio and view television at all times of the day or night." 138 Cong. Rec. S7308 (1992) (statement of Sen. Byrd). In light of Supreme Court precedent and the broad national consensus that children under the age of 18 need to be protected from exposure to sexually explicit materials, the Commission was fully justified in concluding that the Government interest extends to minors of all ages.

(b) The Midnight to 6:00 a.m. "Safe Harbor"

Although, for the reasons set forth in Part II. B. below, we will require the Commission to allow the broadcast of indecent material between 10:00 p.m. and 6:00 a.m., we will address the propriety of section 16(a)'s midnight to 6:00 a.m. safe harbor. We do so for two reasons: First, in addressing the "narrowly tailored" issue, the parties have focused their arguments on the evidence offered by the Commission in support of the section's 6:00 a.m. to midnight ban on indecent programming. Second, the principles we bring to bear in our analysis of the midnight to 6:00 a.m. safe harbor apply with equal force to the more lenient one that the Commission must adopt as a result of today's opinion. Although fewer children will be protected by the expanded safe harbor, that fact will not affect its constitutionality. If the 6:00 a.m. to midnight ban on indecent programming is permissible to protect minors who listen to the radio or view television as late as midnight, the reduction of the ban by two hours will remain narrowly tailored to serve this more modest goal.

The Supreme Court has stated that "a government body seeking to sustain a restriction on...speech must demonstrate that the harms it recites are real and that its restriction will in fact alleviate them to a material degree." Edenfield v. Fane, 113 S. Ct. 1792, 1800 (1993); *see also* Turner Broadcasting System, Inc. v. FCC, 114 S. Ct. 2445, 2470 (1994) (same). The data on broadcasting that the FCC has collected reveal that large numbers of children view television or listen to the radio from the early morning until late in the evening, that those numbers decline rapidly as midnight approaches, and that a substantial portion of the adult audience is tuned into television or radio broadcasts after midnight. We find this information sufficient to support the safe harbor parameters that Congress has drawn.

The data collected by the FCC and republished in the Congressional Record for June 1, 1992, indicate that while 4.3 million, or approximately 21 percent, of "teenagers" (defined as children ages 12 to 17) watch broadcast television between 11:00 and 11:30 p.m., the number drops to 3.1 million (15.2 percent) between 11:30 p.m. and 1:00 a.m. and to less than 1 million (4.8 percent) between 1:45 and 2:00 a.m. Comparable national averages are not available for children under 12, but the figures for particular major cities are instructive. In New York, for example, 6 percent of those aged 2 to 11 watch television between 11:00 and 11:30 p.m. on weekdays while the figures for Washington, D.C., and Los Angeles are 6 percent and 3 percent, respectively.

Concerning the morning portion of the broadcast restriction, the FCC has produced studies which suggest that significant numbers of children aged 2 through 17 watch television in the early morning hours. In the case of Seattle, one of two medium-sized media markets surveyed, an average of 102,200 minors watched television between the hours of 6:00 a.m. and 8:00 a.m., Monday through Friday; in Salt Lake City, the average was 28,000 for the period from 6:00 a.m. to 10:00 a.m.

The statistical data on radio audiences also demonstrate that there is a reasonable risk that significant numbers of children would be exposed to indecent radio programs if they were broadcast in the hours immediately before midnight. According to the FCC, there is an average quarter-hour radio audience of 2.4 million teenagers, or 12 percent, between 6:00 a.m. and midnight. Just over half that number, 1.4 million teenagers, listen to the radio during the quarter hour between midnight and 12:15 a.m. on an average night.

It is apparent, then, that of the approximately 20.2 million teenagers and 36.3 million children under 12 in the United States, a significant percentage watch broadcast television or listen to radio from as early as 6:00 a.m. to as late as 11:30 p.m.; and in the case of teenagers, even later. We conclude that there is a reasonable risk that large numbers of children would be exposed to any indecent material broadcast between 6:00 a.m. and midnight.

Petitioners suggest that Congress should have used station-specific and program-specific data in assessing when children are at risk of being exposed to broadcast indecency. We question whether this would have aided the analysis. Children will not likely record, in a Nielsen diary or other survey, that they listen to or view programs of which their parents disapprove. Furthermore, changes in the program menu make yesterday's findings irrelevant today. Finally, to borrow the Commission's phrase, such station- and program-specific data do not take "children's grazing" into account.

The remaining question, then, is whether Congress, in enacting section 16(a), and the Commission, in promulgating the regulations, have taken into account the First Amendment rights of the very large numbers of adults who wish to view or listen to indecent broadcasts. We believe they have. The data indicate that significant numbers of adults view or listen to programs broadcast after midnight. Based on information provided by Nielsen indicating that television sets in 23 percent of American homes are in use at 1:00 a.m., the Commission calculated that between 21 and 53 million viewers were watching television at that time. Comments submitted to the FCC by petitioners indicate that approximately 11.7 million adults listen to the radio between 10:00 p.m. and 11:00 p.m., while 7.4 million do so between midnight and 1:00 a.m. With an estimated 181 million adult listeners, this would indicate that approximately 6 percent of adults listen to the radio between 10:00 p.m. and 11:00 p.m. while 4 percent of them do so between midnight and 1:00 a.m.

While the numbers of adults watching television and listening to radio after midnight are admittedly small, they are not insignificant. Furthermore, as we have noted above, adults have alternative means of satisfying their interest in indecent material at other hours in ways that pose no risk to minors. We therefore believe that a midnight to 6:00 a.m. safe harbor takes adequate account of adults' First Amendment rights.

Petitioners argue, nevertheless, that delaying the safe harbor until midnight will have a chilling effect on the airing of programs during the evening "prime time" hours that are of special interest to adults. They cite, as examples, news and documentary programs and dramas that deal with such sensitive contemporary problems as sexual harassment and the AIDS epidemic and assert that a broadcaster might choose to refrain from presenting relevant material rather than risk the consequences of being charged with airing broadcast indecency. Whatever chilling effects may be said to inhere in the regulation of indecent speech, these have existed ever since the Supreme Court first upheld the FCC's enforcement of section 1464 of the Radio Act. The enactment of section 16(a) does not add to such anxieties; to the contrary, the purpose of channeling, which we mandated in *ACT I* and reaffirmed in *ACT II*, 852 F.2d at 1343–44; 932 F.2d at 1509, and which Congress has now codified, is to provide a period in which radio and television stations may let down their hair without worrying whether they have stepped over any line other than that which separates protected speech from obscenity. Thus, section 16(a) has ameliorated rather than aggravated whatever chilling effect may be inherent in section 1464.

Petitioners also argue that section 16(a)'s midnight to 6:00 a.m. channeling provision is not narrowly tailored because, for example, Congress has failed to take into consideration the fact that it bans indecent broadcasts during school hours when children are presumably subject to strict adult supervision, thereby depriving adults from listening to such broadcasts during daytime hours when the risk of harm to minors is slight. The Government's concerns, of course, extend to children who are too young to attend school. *See Pacifica*, 438 U.S. at 749 ("broadcasting is uniquely accessible to children, even those too young to read"). But more to the point, even if such fine tuning were feasible, we do not believe that the First Amendment requires that degree of precision.

We believe that deciding where along the bell curves of declining adult and child audiences it is most reasonable to permit indecent broadcasts is the kind of judgment that is better left to Congress, so long as there is evidence to support the legislative judgment. Extending the safe harbor for broadcast indecency to an earlier hour involves "a difference only in degree, not a less restrictive alternative in kind." Burson v. Freeman, 504 U.S. 191 (1992) (reducing campaign-free boundary around entrances to polling places from 100 feet to 25 feet is a difference in degree, not a less restrictive alternative in kind); *see also* Buckley v. Valeo, 424 U.S. 1, 30 (1976) (if some limit on campaign contributions is necessary, court has no scalpel to probe whether $2,000 ceiling might not serve as well as $1,000). It follows, then, that in a case of this kind, which involves restrictions in degree, there may be a range of safe harbors, each of which will satisfy the "narrowly tailored" requirement of the First Amendment. We are dealing with questions of judgment; and here, we defer to Congress's determination of where to draw the line just as the Supreme Court did when it accepted Congress's judgment that $1,000 rather than some other figure was the appropriate limit to place on campaign contributions.

Recognizing the Government's compelling interest in protecting children from indecent broadcasts, Congress channeled indecent broadcasts to the hours between midnight and 6:00 a.m. in the hope of minimizing children's exposure to such material. Given the substantially smaller number of children in the audience after midnight, we find that section 16(a) reduces children's exposure to broadcast indecency to a significant degree. We also find that this restriction does not unnecessarily interfere with the ability of adults to watch or listen to such materials both because substantial numbers of them are active after midnight and because adults have so many alternative ways of satisfying their tastes at other times. Although the restrictions burden the rights of many adults, it seems entirely appropriate that the marginal convenience of some adults be made to yield to the imperative needs of the young. We thus conclude that, standing alone, the midnight to 6:00 a.m. safe harbor is narrowly tailored to serve the Government's compelling interest in the well-being of our youth.

B. The Public Broadcaster Exception

Section 16(a) permits public stations that sign off the air at or before midnight to broadcast indecent material after 10:00 p.m. *See* 47 U.S.C. §303 note. Petitioners argue that section 16(a) is unconstitutional because it allows the stations to present indecent material two hours earlier than all others.

Whatever Congress's reasons for creating it, the preferential safe harbor has the effect of undermining both the argument for prohibiting the broadcasting of indecent speech before that hour and the constitutional viability of the more restrictive safe harbor that appears to have been Congress's principal objective in enacting section 16(a). Congress has failed to explain what, if any, relationship the disparate treatment accorded certain public stations bears to the compelling Government interest—or to any other legislative value—that Congress sought to advance when it enacted section 16(a). Congress and the Commission have backed away from the consequences of their own reasoning, leaving us with no choice but to hold that the section is unconstitutional insofar as it bars the broadcasting of indecent speech between the hours of 10:00 p.m. and midnight.

III. CONCLUSION

"If there is a bedrock principle underlying the First Amendment, it is that the government may not prohibit the expression of an idea simply because society finds the idea itself offensive or disagreeable." Texas v. Johnson, 491 U.S. 397, 414 (1989). The Constitution, however, permits restrictions on speech where necessary in order to serve a compelling public interest, provided that they are narrowly tailored. We hold that section 16(a) serves such an interest. But because Congress imposed different restrictions on each of two categories of broadcasters while failing to explain how this disparate treatment advanced its goal of protecting young minds from the corrupting influences of indecent speech, we must set aside the more restrictive one. Accordingly, we remand this case to the Federal Communications Commission with instructions to limit its ban on the broadcasting of indecent programs to the period from 6:00 a.m. to 10:00 p.m.

EDWARDS, Chief Judge, dissenting:

In this case, the majority upholds as constitutional a total ban of "indecent" speech on broadcast television and radio between the hours of 6 a.m. and midnight. The majority readily acknowledges that indecent speech (as distinguished from obscene speech) is fully protected by the Constitution, and that the Government may not regulate such speech based on its content except when it chooses the least restrictive means to effectively promote an articulated compelling interest. In this case, the Government fails to satisfy the acknowledged constitutional strictures.

The Government advances three goals in support of the statute: first, it claims that the statute facilitates parental supervision of the programming their children watch and hear; second, it claims that the ban promotes the well-being of minors by protecting them from indecent programming assumed to be harmful; and, finally, it contends that the ban preserves the privacy of the home. The majority finds the first two interests compelling, and so finds it unnecessary to address the third. I, too, will focus on the first two interests, which I find to be unsupported.

As an initial matter, I do not comprehend how the two interests can stand together. "Congress may properly pass a law to facilitate parental supervision of their children, *i.e.*, a law that simply segregates and blocks indecent programming and thereby helps parents control whether and to what extent their children are exposed to such programming. However, a law that effectively bans all indecent programming—as does the statute at issue in this case—does not facilitate parental supervision. In my view, my right as a parent has been preempted, not facilitated, if I am told that certain programming will be banned from my... television. Congress cannot take away my right to decide what my children watch, absent some showing that my children are in fact at risk of harm from exposure to indecent programming." Alliance for Community Media v. FCC, 56 F.3d 105, 145 (D.C.Cir.1995) (Edwards, C.J., dissenting).

Furthermore, the two interests—facilitating parental supervision and protecting children from indecent material—fare no better if considered alone. With respect to the alleged interest in protecting children, although the majority strains mightily to rest its finding of harm on intuitive notions of morality and decency (notions with which I have great sympathy), the simple truth is that "there is not one iota of evidence in the record...to support the claim that exposure to indecency is harmful—indeed, the nature of the alleged 'harm' is never explained." *Id*. There is significant evidence suggesting a causal connection between viewing violence on television and antisocial violent behavior; but, as was conceded by Government counsel at oral argument in this case, the FCC has pointed to no such evidence addressing the effects of indecent programming. With respect to the interest in facilitating parental supervision, the statute is not tailored to aid parents' control over what their children watch and hear; it does not, for example, "segregate" indecent programming on special channels, as was the case in *Alliance for Community Media*,[49] nor does it promote a blocking device which individuals control. Rather, section 16(a) involves a total ban of disfavored programming during hours when adult viewers are most likely to be in the audience.

Because the statutory ban imposed by section 16(a) is not the least restrictive means to further compelling state interests, the majority decision must rest primarily on a perceived distinction between the First Amendment rights of broadcast media and cable (and all other non-broadcast) media. The majority appears to recognize that section 16(a) could not withstand constitutional scrutiny if ap-

---

49. *Alliance for Community Media* involved the Cable Television Consumer Protection and Competition Act of 1992, Pub. L. No. 102-385, §10, 106 Stat. 1460, 1468 (1992) and In the Matter of Implementation of section 10 of the Cable Consumer Protection and Competition Act of 1992, 8 FCC Rcd. 2638 (1993), which included a segregate-and-block scheme. [Ed. The Supreme Court granted the petition for certiorari in *Alliance for Community Media*, and affirmed in part and reversed in part in Denver Area Educational Telecommunications Consortium, Inc. v. FCC, 518 U.S. 727 (1996), which is excerpted in Chapter 14.]

plied against cable television operators; nonetheless, the majority finds this irrelevant because it believes that "there can be no doubt that the traditional broadcast media are properly subject to more regulation than is generally permissible under the First Amendment." This is the heart of the case, plain and simple.

Respectfully, I find the majority's position flawed. First, because I believe it is no longer responsible for courts to provide lesser First Amendment protection to broadcasting based on its alleged "unique attributes," I would scrutinize section 16(a) in the same manner that courts scrutinize speech restrictions of cable media. Second, I find it incomprehensible that the majority can so easily reject the "public broadcaster exception" to section 16(a), and yet be blind to the utterly irrational distinction that Congress has created between broadcast and cable operators. No one disputes that cable exhibits more and worse indecency than does broadcast. And cable television is certainly pervasive in our country. Today, a majority of television households have cable, and over the last two decades, the percentage of television households with cable has increased every year. However, the Government does not even attempt to regulate cable with the same heavy regulatory hand it applies to the broadcast media. There is no ban between 6 a.m. and midnight imposed on cable. Rather, the Government relies on viewer subscription and individual discretion instead of regulating commercial cable. Viewers may receive commercial cable, with all of its indecent material, to be seen by adults and children at any time, subject only to the viewing discretion of the cable subscriber.

If exposure to "indecency" really is harmful to children, then one wonders how to explain congressional schemes that impose iron-clad bans of indecency on broadcasters, while simultaneously allowing a virtual free hand for the real culprits—cable operators. And the greatest irony of all is that the majority holds that section 16(a) is constitutional in part because, in allowing parents to subscribe to cable television as they see fit, Congress has facilitated parental supervision of children. In other words, Congress may ban indecency on broadcast television because parents can easily purchase all the smut they please on cable! I find this rationale perplexing.

At bottom, I dissent for three reasons: First, the Government's asserted interests in facilitating parental supervision and protecting children from indecency are irreconcilably in conflict in this case. Second, the Commission offers no evidence that indecent broadcasting harms children. And although it is an easy assumption to make—that indecent broadcasting is harmful to minors—Supreme Court doctrine suggests that the Government must provide some evidence of harm before enacting speech-restrictive regulations. Finally, the Government has made no attempt to search out the least speech-restrictive means to promote the interests that have been asserted. For these reasons, section 16(a) should be struck down as unconstitutional.

I. FIRST AMENDMENT PROTECTIONS FOR THE BROADCAST MEDIA

Over the years, Congress and the Commission have regulated the broadcast media more heavily than they have regulated the non-broadcast media. And courts have upheld speech-restrictive regulations imposed on broadcast which undoubtedly would have been struck down were they imposed on other media. *See, e.g.,* Turner Broadcasting Sys., Inc. v. FCC, 114 S. Ct. 2445, 2456 (1994)

("*TBS*") ("It is true that our cases have permitted more intrusive regulation of broadcast speakers than of speakers in other media."); FCC v. League of Women Voters of California, 468 U.S. 364, 376 (1984) ("Were a similar ban applied to newspapers and magazines, we would not hesitate to strike it down as violative of the First Amendment."). The Supreme Court has explained its tendency to uphold speech-restrictive regulations of broadcast as providing the broadcast media with limited First Amendment protection. *See, e.g.*, FCC v. Pacifica Found., 438 U.S. 726, 748 (1978) (plurality opinion) ("Of all forms of communication, it is broadcasting that has received the most limited First Amendment protection.").

The absurdity of this bifurcated approach—applying a relaxed level of scrutiny to content based regulations of broadcast and a strict level of scrutiny for content based regulations of non-broadcast media—is most apparent in a comparison of the Supreme Court's analysis of broadcast and cable. In *Pacifica*, a plurality of the Court applied a reduced level of scrutiny in determining the First Amendment rights of a broadcasting station. 438 U.S. at 748–50. Last year, however, a majority of the Court held that cable television is entitled to the same First Amendment protection as all other non-broadcast media. *TBS*, 114 S. Ct. at 2456–57. There is no justification for this apparent dichotomy in First Amendment jurisprudence. Whatever the merits of *Pacifica* when it was issued almost 20 years ago, it makes no sense now.

The justification for the Supreme Court's distinct First Amendment approach to broadcast originally centered on the notion of spectrum scarcity. The electromagnetic spectrum was physically limited—there were more would-be broadcasters than frequencies available and broadcasters wishing to broadcast on the same frequency may have interfered with each other—and required regulation to assign frequencies to broadcasters. The Court reasoned that the Government could impose limited content restraints and certain affirmative obligations on broadcasters on account of spectrum scarcity. In 1978, the Court provided two additional rationales—broadcast was uniquely intrusive into the privacy of the home and uniquely accessible to children—which justified relaxed scrutiny and thereby reduced the First Amendment protection accorded to broadcasters. These justifications—spectrum scarcity, intrusiveness, and accessibility to children— neither distinguish broadcast from cable, nor explain the relaxed application of the principles of the First Amendment to broadcast.

A. Spectrum Scarcity

In 1943, the Court determined that the "unique characteristic" of broadcast—that "unlike other modes of expression, radio inherently is not available to all"—explained "why, unlike other modes of expression, it is subject to governmental regulation." National Broadcasting Co., Inc. v. United States, 319 U.S. 190, 226 (1943) ("*NBC*"). Twenty-six years later, the Court spun out the First Amendment implications of this burgeoning scarcity theory. *Red Lion*, 395 U.S. at 388–90. The Court first offered an economic scarcity theory,[50] finding

---

50. Interestingly, in responding to Government's argument that cable and broadcast are alike in that they both are beset by "market dysfunction," the *TBS* Court stated that "the special physical characteristics of broadcast transmission, not the economic characteristics of the broadcast market, are what underlies our broadcast jurisprudence." 114 S. Ct. at 2457 (citations omitted). Apparently, the Court is now prepared to abandon the economic scarcity theory.

that "where there are substantially more individuals who want to broadcast than there are frequencies to allocate, it is idle to posit an unabridgeable First Amendment right to broadcast comparable to the right of every individual to speak, write, or publish." *Id.* at 388. The Court also offered a technological scarcity theory: recognizing the need to prevent "overcrowding of the spectrum,"[51] *id.* at 389, the Court held that, "because of the scarcity of radio frequencies, the Government is permitted to put restraints on licensees in favor of others whose views should be expressed on this unique medium," *id.* at 390.

In my view, it is no longer responsible for courts to apply a reduced level of First Amendment protection for regulations imposed on broadcast based on an indefensible notion of spectrum scarcity. It is time to revisit this rationale. For years, scholars have argued that the scarcity of the broadcast spectrum is neither an accurate technological description of the spectrum, nor a "unique characteristic" that should make any difference in terms of First Amendment protection. First, in response to the problem of broadcast interference when multiple broadcasters attempt to transmit on the same frequency, critics point out that this problem does not distinguish broadcasting from print and is easily remedied with a system of administrative licensing or private property rights. Another problem alluded to by the Court in *Red Lion* is the claim that the spectrum is inherently limited, in contrast to cable stations or newsprint. Today, however, the nation enjoys a proliferation of broadcast stations, and should the country decide to increase the number of channels, it need only devote more resources toward the development of the electromagnetic spectrum.

In response to the economic scarcity argument—that there are more would-be broadcasters than spectrum frequencies available—economists argue that all resources are scarce in the sense that people often would like to use more than exists. Especially when the Government gives away a valuable commodity, such as the right to use certain airwaves free of charge, the demand will likely always exceed the supply. And with the development of cable, spectrum-based communications media now have an abundance of alternatives, essentially rendering the economic scarcity argument superfluous.

In short, neither technological nor economic scarcity distinguish broadcast from other media. And while some may argue that spectrum scarcity may justify a system of administrative regulation as opposed to a free market approach to stations, the theory does not justify reduced First Amendment protection.

B. Accessibility to Children and Pervasiveness

The two additional rationales offered by the plurality opinion in *Pacifica*, attempting to distinguish broadcasting from other media, also fail to justify limited First Amendment protection of broadcast. The plurality found that "broadcasting is uniquely accessible to children, even those too young to read." *Pacifica*, 438 U.S. at 749. This characteristic, however, fails to distinguish broadcast from cable; and, notably, the rationale is absent from the Court's *TBS* opinion.

---

51. The Court recently restated this concern: "if two broadcasters were to attempt to transmit over the same frequency in the same locale, they would interfere with one another's signals, so that neither could be heard at all." *TBS*, 114 S. Ct. at 2456 (citing *NBC*, 319 U.S. at 212).

The plurality in *Pacifica* added another rationale which really has two components. The opinion reasoned that "the broadcast media have established a uniquely pervasive presence in the lives of all Americans.... [The] material presented over the airwaves confronts the citizen, not only in public, but also in the privacy of the home." *Id.* at 748. Again, the pervasiveness of its programming hardly distinguishes broadcast from cable. As noted above, cable is pervasive: a majority of television households have cable today, and this percentage has increased every year over the last two decades. The intrusiveness rationale, that the material confronts the citizen in the privacy of his or her home, likewise, does not distinguish broadcast from cable, nor account for the divergent First Amendment treatment of the two media. Finally, in light of *TBS*, in which the Court omitted any discussion of these rationales, the *Pacifica* rationales no longer can be seen to serve as justifications for reduced First Amendment protection afforded to broadcast.

It seems clear now that *Pacifica* is a flawed decision, at least when one considers it in light of enlightened economic theory, technological advancements, and subsequent case law. The critical underpinnings of the decision are no longer present. Thus, there is no reason to uphold a distinction between broadcast and cable media pursuant to a bifurcated First Amendment analysis.

II. FULL FIRST AMENDMENT PROTECTION OF BROADCAST

Because no reasonable basis can be found to distinguish broadcast from cable in terms of the First Amendment protection the two media should receive, I would review section 16(a) and the Enforcement Order under the stricter level of scrutiny courts apply to content based regulations of cable. This means "the most exacting scrutiny" should be applied "to regulations that suppress, disadvantage, or impose differential burdens upon speech because of its content."

[Judge Edwards then concluded that the "safe harbor" was not narrowly tailored to serve a compelling governmental interest and was therefore an impermissible content based regulation.]

WALD, Circuit Judge, with whom ROGERS and TATEL, Circuit Judges, join, dissenting:

"At the heart of the First Amendment lies the principle that each person should decide for him or herself the ideas and beliefs deserving of expression, consideration, and adherence. Our political system and cultural life rest upon this ideal." Turner Broadcasting System, Inc. v. FCC, 114 S. Ct. 2445, 2458 (1994). Very often this principle is not such an easy one to live up to or to live with. But presumptively, expression that many or even most of us find deeply reprehensible may not be, on that basis alone, proscribed. In R.A.V. v. City of St. Paul, 505 U.S. 377 (1992), for instance, the Court held that racist fighting words could not be penalized on the basis of the hatred they expressed. Thus, whatever our collective interests in a "meritorious polity" and the moral development of the "people [who] govern it," Majority Opinion ("Maj. op.") at 17, governmental enforcement of those interests is radically constrained by the First Amendment's guarantee of freedom of expression.

This principle of free speech admits of limited exceptions, one of which is the permissibility of some government regulation of broadcast indecency. In FCC v.

Pacifica Foundation, 438 U.S. 726, 729, 750–51 (1978), for example, the Supreme Court concluded that the Federal Communications Commission could constitutionally penalize the daytime broadcast of a dialogue containing the repeated use of "filthy words." As Chief Judge Edwards notes, *Pacifica*'s result rested in large part on technological assumptions about the uniqueness of broadcast that have changed significantly in recent years, and the time may be ripe for the Court to recognize those changes by reevaluating its decision in that case. I believe, however, that the "safe harbor" proposed by the government here is unconstitutional even if the Court does not reconsider *Pacifica*.

Because indecent speech is fully within the ambit of First Amendment protection, the permissibility of government regulation of indecency depends crucially on the distinction between banning and channeling speech. Any time-based ban on the airing of indecency intrudes substantially into the rights of adult viewers and listeners and places the government in the extraordinarily sensitive role of censor. By now, at least in the posture of the current case, it is probably too late to revisit our conclusion that the chill brought about by the Commission's open-textured definition of indecency is insufficiently great to invalidate the regulation. *See* Action for Children's Television v. FCC, 271 U.S. App. D.C. 365, 852 F.2d 1332, 1338–40 (D.C. Cir. 1988) ("*ACT I*"). Even a cursory glance at the Commission's enforcement policy to date, however, suggests that that chill is quite substantial, heightening the need for a meaningful safe harbor.

Because the Commission insists that indecency determinations must be made on a case-by-case basis and depend upon a multi-faceted consideration of the context of allegedly indecent material, broadcasters have next-to-no guidance in making complex judgment calls. Thus, conscientious broadcasters and radio and television hosts seeking to steer clear of indecency face the herculean task of predicting on the basis of a series of hazy case-by-case determinations by the Commission which side of the line their program will fall on. When, for instance, radio station hosts read over the air from a Playboy Magazine interview of Jessica Hahn about her alleged rape by the Reverend Jim Bakker, they did not regard the material as indecent because it involved matters of obvious public concern. The Commission, however, issued a notice of apparent liability for a forfeiture of $2,000, explaining that, "while the newsworthy nature of broadcast material and its presentation in a serious, newsworthy manner would be relevant contextual considerations in an indecency determination, they are not, in themselves, dispositive factors." KSD-FM, Notice of Apparent Liability, 6 FCC Rcd. 3689, 3689 (1990). Newsworthiness, the Commission explained, is "simply one of many variables"; no single feature renders a work per se not indecent. *Id.* Although in reading the interview, the hosts had said that the account made them "sick," that it described rape rather than consensual sex, and that they regretted their earlier jokes about the incident, the Commission concluded, without elaboration, that the presentation was "pandering." *Id.* at 3689–90. As this one case exemplifies so well, in enforcing the indecency regulations the Commission takes upon itself a delicate and inevitably subjective role of drawing fine lines between "serious" and "pandering" presentations. And even a "serious" presentation of newsworthy material is emphatically not shielded from liability. This incident and the Commission's discussion of it suggests that enforcement of its indecency regulation involves both government- and self-censorship of much material that presents far harder choices than the glaring examples of smut emphasized to such rhetorical effect by the majority.

Because of this potential for significant incursion into the First Amendment rights of adult viewers and listeners during the hours of the day and evening when the ban is in effect, it is particularly important that the channelling "balance" struck by the government preserve a meaningful place on the spectrum for adult rights to hear and view controversial or graphic nonobscene material— that airing of such material not be restricted to a safe harbor that is in reality a ship's graveyard. Thus, I cannot agree with the majority that determining the perimeter of the safe harbor can be relegated to the category of discretionary line-drawing akin to the distance from polls at which electioneering is allowed and so largely shielded from judicial review. God or the Devil (pick your figure of speech) is in the details. Because the safe harbor constitutes the exclusive repository for the substantial First Amendment rights of adults, its boundaries are of constitutional dimension. For that reason, it cannot be beyond the competence of this court to ensure that the safe harbor ensures *meaningful* as opposed to *pro forma* accommodation of adult rights.

On the basis of the information given us by the Commission and that was before Congress, it is impossible to conclude that the midnight to 6 a.m. safe harbor strikes a constitutionally acceptable balance.[52] Recent Supreme Court cases have made clear that "when the Government defends a regulation on speech as a means to . . . prevent anticipated harms, it must do more than simply posit the existence of the disease sought to be cured. It must demonstrate that the recited harms are real, not merely conjectural, and that the regulation will in fact alleviate these harms in a direct and material way." *Turner*, 114 S. Ct. at 2470. Yet, in the record before Congress, there is as little evidence regarding the magnitude of psychological or moral harm, if any, to children and teenagers who see and hear indecency as there is that such exposure even occurs inside the current safe harbor. In the six years that the safe harbor has been operating from 8 p.m. to 6 a.m., and the prior years in which it covered 10 p.m. to 6 a.m., the government has adduced no concrete evidence of real or even potential harm suffered by the exposure of children to indecent material. We have not a scintilla of evidence as to how many allegedly indecent programs have been either aired or seen or heard by children inside or outside the safe harbor. Thus, even if the government were allowed to presume harm from mere exposure to indecency, surely it cannot progressively constrict the safe harbor in the absence of *any* indication that the presumed harm is even occurring under the existing regime.

Even if the government were acting on a *tabula rasa*, rather than on the basis of years of experience with a less restrictive ban, its delineation of the midnight to 6 a.m. safe harbor would be unjustifiable. In the end, the majority admits the government's own interest in children is limited to "shielding minors from being exposed to indecent speech by persons other than a parent." Maj. op. at 103.

---

52. Although the end result of the majority's decision is to extend the safe harbor from 10 p.m. to 6 a.m., it holds that so long as Congress enacts a uniform rule, the midnight to 6 a.m. safe harbor is constitutionally adequate. Accordingly, I address my discussion to the narrower safe harbor. [Footnote relocated.]

The majority is right: the government's primary if not exclusive interest is in "shielding minors from being exposed to indecent speech by persons other than a parent." Given the significant First Amendment rights of adults at stake, moreover, the government has a constitutional responsibility to key its response to the presumed harm from indecency to facilitating parental control, rather than to government censorship per se. When most parents are presumably able to supervise their children, adult viewers should have access to the speech to which they are entitled.

Because the government can pursue whatever legitimate interests it has in protecting children by facilitating parental control, I do not believe that it can impose a valid ban during any hours it pleases solely because some children are in the audience. Nor do I believe that we can throw up our hands at the assumed impossibility of parental supervision simply because large numbers of children have television sets in their own room. Either or both of these excuses would justify a 24-hour ban as easily as the current 18-hour ban. Reasoning along these lines totally ignores the adult First Amendment interest that the majority purportedly recognizes and, effectively, gives the government unharnessed power to censor.

The government should be put to the task of demonstrating that the banned hours are based on a showing that these are the times of preponderant children viewing and the times when parents are otherwise absorbed in work in or out of the home. As the initial panel opinion explained, "the Commission...appears to assume that, regardless of the time of day or night, parents cannot effectively supervise their children's television or radio habits. Accordingly, the government has not adduced any evidence suggesting that the effectiveness of parental supervision varies by time of day or night, or that the particular safe harbor from midnight to 6 a.m. was crafted to assist parents at specific times when they especially require the government's help to supervise their children." Action for Children's Television v. FCC, 304 U.S. App. D.C. 126, 11 F.3d 170, 178 (D.C. Cir. 1993) ("*ACT III*").

In constructing a safe harbor the government needs to give more careful consideration to those hours in the evening when parental control could reasonably be relied upon in lieu of censorship to protect children. It is only in this manner that the government can genuinely strike the delicate balance between adult freedoms of expression and society's interest in shielding children from indecency and a truly safe harbor can be crafted that "serves the compelling governmental interests without unduly infringing on the adult population's right to see and hear indecent material." Maj. op. at 665

Despite the majority's valiant effort to extract evidence for the government's position from the sparse record before us, the pickings are too slim for constitutional legitimacy. There is no evidence at all of psychological harm from exposure to indecent programs aired inside the current safe harbor. There is no evidence either that parents cannot supervise their children in those safe harbor hours or that "grazing" is leading to any significant viewing of indecency. Finally, the imminence of "V-chip" technology to enable parental control of all violence- and indecency-viewing suggests that a draconian ban from 6 a.m. to midnight is decidedly premature.

In spite of this evidentiary black hole, we have a broadside ban on vaguely defined indecency during all hours when most working people are awake, with a small bow to prior judicial rulings that a complete ban is unconstitutional, but no attempt to fashion an accommodation between the First Amendment and family values. The net effect of the majority's decision is a gratuitous grant of power allowing casual and lightly reviewed administrative decision-making about fundamental liberties. I respectfully dissent.

Notes and Questions

1. The Standard. Under *ACT III*, what is required to show a harm to children that would justify content based regulation of broadcast? What is required to show that the means chosen by Congress are sufficiently tailored? To put the point a bit differently, what would have to happen in order for Congress to fail to satisfy the requirement of a compelling interest or narrow tailoring?

2. Strict Scrutiny? Relatedly, did the court in *ACT III* take seriously the lesson of *Pacifica*? That case seems to hold that broadcast receives the most limited from of First Amendment protection; yet didn't the court here apply strict scrutiny, the highest level of scrutiny used in First Amendment analysis?

3. Empowering Parents, Protecting Children. Note the treatment, in the various opinions, of the goals of empowering parents and of protecting children. Are those goals complementary? In tension with each other? Irrelevant to each other?

III. TELEVISED VIOLENCE

While there is almost no evidence supporting the proposition that exposure to indecent materials harms children,[53] there is considerable evidence linking the viewing of violent images to subsequent antisocial behavior.[54] Correlation is of course not causation (much of the data can be explained by the hypothesis that violent people both watch violent television and commit violent acts); and it is admittedly difficult to define, let alone regulate, exactly what sorts of violent images are most likely to be associated with antisocial behavior. But given that the evidence here is stronger than it is for indecency, it is perhaps surprising that the government has always gone to great lengths to limit broadcast indecency, but there was no legislation related to televised violence until 1996, when Congress took some tentative steps as part of the Telecommunications Act of 1996.

---

53. Indeed, researchers have found that the few studies on the effect of exposure to indecent material have shown no effect or harm to children under the age of eighteen. *See* Edward Donnerstein et al., On the Regulation of Broadcast Indecency to Protect Children, 36 J. Broadcasting & Electronic Media 111, 115 (1992); *see also* Jeremy Harris Lipschultz, Conceptual Problems of Broadcast Indecency Policy and Application, Comm. & L., June 1992. Note that neither the majority in *ACT III* nor the government disputed this point; the court in *ACT III* found that such evidence was not necessary.

54. For an early and extensive review of that literature, *see* Thomas G. Krattenmaker & Lucas A. Powe, Jr., Televised Violence: First Amendment Principles and Social Science Theory, 64 Va. L. Rev. 1123, 1134–1171 (1978). For more recent reviews, *see* Thomas G. Krattenmaker & Lucas A. Powe, Jr., Regulating Broadcast Programming 120–134 (1994); Harry T. Edwards & Mitchell N. Berman, Regulating Violence on Television, 89 Nw. U. L. Rev. 1487, 1536–51 (1995).

Whether any serious attempt to regulate violent images would be upheld by the courts is thus still an open question. Limits on violence would seem to regulate speech based on the effect of the subject matter on viewers and thus be content based.[55] Such a regulation of speech is ordinarily forbidden by the First Amendment unless it is narrowly drawn to effectuate a compelling government interest. If, however, violence were treated as equivalent (for constitutional purposes) to indecency, then the reasoning of *Pacifica* and *ACT III* would suggest that regulation of violent broadcasts would be upheld despite a regulatory emphasis on content. The evidence of harms linked to violent images is stronger, after all, and by hypothesis the legal status of televised violence would be the same as that for indecency. But if regulation of violence is held to the ordinary standard by which courts evaluate content based regulation of speech, any such regulation likely would not survive a First Amendment challenge. The problem is that the social science data do not tell us which programs cause which individuals to commit what acts of violence. So, although the government would seem to have a compelling interest in reducing violence, any conceivable censorship regime would be substantially overbroad in that it would punish speech that cannot be shown to be harmful.

Further, any plausible censorship scheme would have to draw lines that would be hard to defend under strict judicial scrutiny. For example, how could one explain not banning or punishing football telecasts, National Geographic Specials, or news coverage of war scenes even though these constitute some of the most violent fare on broadcast television? And into what category would one place cartoon violence, including not simply "action hero" sequences of the sort featured in cartoons like *Batman* and *G.I. Joe*, but also the playful torture that characterized the interactions of Bugs Bunny and Wile E. Coyote, or the cat-and-mouse team of Tom and Jerry?

The Telecommunications Act of 1996 did not put any of these issues to the test but instead attempted an end-run around the dilemma. Section 551 of the Act[56] is entitled "Parental Choice in Television Programming." It provides that, unless distributors of video programming establish "voluntary rules for rating video programming that contains sexual, violent, or other indecent material" and, further, agree "voluntarily to broadcast signals that contain ratings of such programming," the FCC is to create an advisory committee, develop such a regime, and impose it upon broadcasters through regulation.[57] The provision also requires that television manufacturers include in all new television sets (13" diagonal or greater) a feature—colloquially known as a V-chip—that enables viewers to block the display of programs based on their ratings.[58] Section 551 thus does not directly limit (much less ban) violence on television, but rather creates a mechanism for rating television programming. By broadcasting the ratings, and embedding the ratings in the signals sent to television sets, broadcasters enable television set owners to determine whether violent (or indecent) programming will appear on their televisions.[59]

---

55. *See* United States v. Playboy Entertainment Group, Inc., excerpted in Chapter 14.

56. 110 Stat. 56, 139–42 (1996) (codified as amended in scattered sections of 47 U.S.C.). The text appears in the Statutory Appendix to this book at section 303.

57. §551 (e) (codified as a note to 47 U.S.C. §303).

58. §551 (c) (codified at 47 U.S.C. §303(x)). Details of this requirement, including its phase-in period, were handled by the FCC. *See, e.g.,* In re Implementation of Section 551 of The Telecommunications Act of 1996, 13 FCC Rcd. 8232 (1998).

59. The extent to which the V-chip has this effect depends on A) parents' desire to use it; B) their ability to use it; and C) their children's inability (or lack of desire) to circumvent the V-chip or find another source for the forbidden programming. On this last point, it bears

The following article explains the new Parental Choice in Television Programming provision in more detail. It raises questions about the V-chip method of regulation from both a constitutional and a policy standpoint. Another valuable aspect of this article is its attempt to situate the V-chip legislation in the overall set of actual and potential mechanisms available to give us assistance in, or "filters" for, picking and choosing among information sources.

MEDIA FILTERS, THE V-CHIP, AND THE FOUNDATIONS OF BROADCAST REGULATION

J.M. Balkin, 45 Duke L.J. 1131–75 (1996)

INTRODUCTION—TO V OR NOT TO V

The Telecommunications Act of 1996 requires that all television sets over thirteen inches include a "V-chip," a device that would allow parents to block violent and indecent television programming.[60]

Despite its name, the V-chip is not a single chip at all, but a combination of different technologies. All television programs currently have the capacity to carry extra information—like closed captioning—as well as sound and pictures. An electronic circuit in a television or cable box can be designed to block programs by reading a numerical code broadcast along the same band used for closed captioning. Viewers then use a remote control device to select from a menu of choices as to how much violence, bad language, sex, and nudity they wish to tolerate. A rating system in Canada features a five-number scale, with higher numbers signifying more sex and violence. When the V-chip circuitry reads a rating equal to or higher than the consumer's preselected number, the picture is replaced by a large black box.[61]

The V-chip promises to create a new system for filtering broadcast information. This new technology raises the possibility that in the Information Age, control of filters may be one of the most important forms of power over human thought and human expression. In the Information Age, the informational filter, not information itself, is king.

I. THE DIFFERENCE BROADCASTING MAKES

For many years, broadcast media have been subject to much greater content based regulation than print media. First Amendment scholars are divided as to whether this special treatment is constitutional. They have good reason to be concerned. "Indecency," like violence, is an unclear and wavering category. By

---

noting that several studies have demonstrated that television parental advisory warnings for violent shows have a "forbidden fruit" appeal to children. *See, e.g.*, Brad J. Bushman & Angela D. Stack, Forbidden Fruit Versus Tainted Fruit: Effects of Warnings Labels on Attraction to Television Violence, 2 J. Experimental Psychol.: Applied 207, 208 (1996).

60. §551, 110 Stat. at 139–42. As its name implies, the V-chip technology has been touted primarily as a means of controlling television violence. But its uses are not limited to that category. The Telecommunications Act of 1996 specifically lists its concerns as "sexual, violent, or other indecent material." §551(b)(1), 110 Stat. at 140.

61. The V-chip can also be designed to recall previous settings and block all unrated programs. In order to prevent bad language from being transmitted, it must be able to block sound as well.

definition, it includes sexually explicit speech that could not be regulated as obscene. This is a much larger category than many people imagine. It includes, for example, not only expression expressly designed for sexual stimulation, but also expression that is offensive to some but not obscene because it has genuine literary, artistic, political or scientific value. Thus, indecent expression can include not only the more salacious contents of the Playboy Channel, but also political speeches laced with four-letter words and serious discussions of AIDS and homosexuality.

Similar problems hound the regulation of violence. It is not always clear what kinds of violence do the most harm to children. Is the violence in cartoons worse than the violence in live action programs? Does unrealistic violence do more harm than depictions that bring home the horrors of war and death? Does the violence reported on the local and national news contribute to the problem, and if so, should it also be restricted in the interests of our children?

Traditionally, content based regulations of the broadcast media have been justified on two basic grounds: the scarcity of the airwaves and the pervasiveness of the medium. Other explanations—the fact that broadcasters hold licenses from the government, and the importance of empowering democracy—tend to be parasitic on the scarcity rationale. Unfortunately, each of these justifications becomes problematic when applied to questions of violence and indecency.

The most common argument for special content based regulations of the media is based on the scarcity of the airwaves. The spread of cable television has increasingly made the scarcity argument implausible. In any case, scarcity is a particularly badly suited justification for content based regulation of violence and indecency. At best, scarcity provides a reason to put things on the air, not to keep things off.

The other major justification usually offered for special treatment of the broadcast media is that these media are uniquely "pervasive." Like the term "scarcity," the term "pervasiveness" is also badly chosen. In fact, courts seem to use the term "pervasive" to stand for a conglomeration of five different sorts of justifications about broadcasting, often not fully distinguished.

One interpretation of "pervasive" is, to my mind, the most important, and the only one that really justifies special content based regulation for the broadcast media. It is a concern about parental control of children's viewing habits. Television is pervasive because it is difficult to keep it away from children and children away from it. Once television is in the home, parents must continually supervise what children watch, which is difficult and time-consuming. Many households now own multiple television sets, so that children can watch in the privacy of their own room, away from parental supervision. It is always possible for parents to remove television completely from the home. However, because of television's cultural importance, many parents do not feel able or willing to deny their children the right to watch television at home, especially when the children can watch it at their friends' houses.

Although concerns about children make the most sense doctrinally, it's important to reiterate that they have little to do with scarcity. Even if there were 500 channels, the problem of parental supervision would still exist, and might even be enhanced. Nor does this justification for regulation turn on the fact that broadcast television is an especially powerful medium of communication, or that it is conveyed in the easily assimilable form of pictures. Parents can watch rented movies on a VCR that are every bit as unacceptable for children as anything one might watch on television. But these movies cannot be regulated in the same way that television broadcasting can.

This rationale for broadcast regulation is often described as the protection of children, but the real issue is parental control. The two are not necessarily the same. We generally assume that parents love their children and discipline them in ways that are, on the whole, best for them. But parents do not always do so, and we do not second-guess their decisions except in extreme cases. Parents are currently free to bring home R-rated videos full of violence and nudity and let their children watch them. They can subscribe to premium cable channels showing these movies and leave their cable lock boxes unused. If violence and indecency really are bad for children, and we think protection of children is paramount, we should take steps to criminalize such behavior, whether or not parents misguidedly believe such exposure is harmless. Yet I suspect that such proposals would be severely criticized, and not merely by civil libertarians. Most parents do not want the government deciding what is best for their children when the decisions are contrary to their wishes; they want the government to assist them in controlling their children in ways they think appropriate.

We now live in a time of cultural upheaval, caused by significant economic and technological changes as well as changes in mores. Not surprisingly, many people are especially anxious about these changes; they see the world they once knew slipping away. Like the drunk who searches for his keys near the lamppost because the light is better there, people tend to fix upon the mass media as the likely cause of cultural ills and regulation of the mass media as a likely solution.

The First Amendment prohibits relatively direct control over what adults can be exposed to. Hence the focus naturally turns to control of children, who are under their parents' authority and whom parents see as the natural inheritors and perpetuators of their cultural values. The desire to preserve culture in the face of widespread cultural change (and, in particular, economic and technological change) leads to anxieties over children and the desire to reassert parental control over them.

The problem we face today, however, is that new forms of technology increasingly upset established patterns of parental control. Children can operate VCRs and computers better than their parents. They spend more time in front of the television than at the family dinner table. Technology threatens to render parents' means of cultural reproduction ineffectual. It is no wonder, then, that new forms of communication technology, whether they be movies, records, radio, television, or the Internet, produce new cultural anxieties and new calls for censorship and control.

II. THINKING ABOUT MEDIA IN TERMS OF FILTERS

All media, whether voice, print, or broadcast, share two features in differing degrees. The first is the ability of the recipient to exclude information; the second is the presence or absence of filtering mechanisms. Filtering and excludability are related to each other, because filtering information usually depends on the present or potential ability to exclude it.

Print media lend themselves easily to filtering precisely because print media are easy to exclude. If I want to avoid the information contained in a newspaper, I can simply avoid buying it. If I go into a bookstore, I can buy the book I want without buying other books. I can take the books I want home and then lock them up so that my children cannot see them. Print media are also easy to select and organize. Because my books are discrete units, I can organize them alphabetically. I can read them when I want and in the order I want.

Filtering mechanisms fall into three basic types or functions—they can organize information (for example, by classifying it), they can select information, or they can block information. Within the last category, one can block information for one's self or for others (for example, one's children). All of these functions have important relationships to excludability. Blocking information clearly involves exclusion, but so do selection and organization. To select information, I must be able to take it and not other information. To organize information, I must be able to create categories into which that information (and not other information) falls, and through which that information could (in theory) be selected.

Although I have divided up filters into blocking filters, selecting filters, and organizing filters, these functions substantially overlap. The V-chip is a good example. The V-chip is a blocking filter for children, but it also is a selecting filter for their parents. It lets adults choose whether or not to view violent or indecent material. Equally importantly, the V-chip is an organizing filter, because it creates two types of programming—programming that is blocked by the V-chip and programming that is not. Or, if the V-chip has multiple settings, it creates multiple categories of programming.

If broadcast media are special, they are special in this respect: Broadcast media offer limited practical means of filtering. Parents may want to keep their children from certain kinds of television programs. But their ability to do so is limited. The V-chip and similar technologies promise to change the nature of broadcast media because they offer the possibility of new types of filtering mechanisms. They help the broadcast media become more like the library or the video store, although the former will never be the same as the latter two.

V. PARENTAL CONTROL AND THE V-CHIP

There are two standard objections to blocking filters like the V-chip. The first is that parents will be unable to use the blocking device. The second is that, even if they do, children will be able to break through and watch the programming anyway.

It is important to recognize that some children will be able to "hack through" the blocking devices their parents use. In any population of children, some will be more clever and more computer-literate than others. Some will be very clever, and a few may even be able to break into Defense Department computers. But a filter design need not be foolproof to be acceptable as a constitutionally preferable alternative to a total ban. It need only be able to block most children or make it very difficult for them to break through.

This principle is clear enough from the existing safe harbor provisions in broadcast television. In its *ACT III* opinion, the D.C. Circuit acknowledged that some children would be able to expose themselves to programming not intended for them simply by staying up late, or sneaking a television into their room at night.[62] Indeed, statistics quoted by the court indicate that many, although not most, children watch television after 10 p.m. This did not undermine the value of the ban on indecent programming between 10 p.m. and 6 a.m. Rather, the court reasoned, the safe harbor provisions are a reasonable balance between free expression concerns and the protection of children. If the temporal filters involved in the safe harbor rules need not be perfect in blocking all children, neither do the technological filters involved in the V-chip.

VI. THE KEY ISSUE: AVOIDING ADDITIONAL LAYERS OF REGULATION

Without care and forethought, the V-chip will not liberate broadcast programming from censorial power; rather it will increasingly subjugate it. If the V-chip technology is implemented properly, it will shift the focus of broadcast regulation from regulation of content to regulation of filtering of content. Most importantly, it will turn broadcast regulation towards more appropriate concerns: ensuring access to as many speakers as possible. It will move us away from an improper fixation with what should not be on television and toward a proper concern with what must be.

What I fear is that the V-chip will be used instead to impose an additional layer of content based regulation on top of existing indecency prohibitions and safe harbor provisions. It will be used to ensure not just that children are not exposed to certain programming, but that adults are not exposed either. Proponents of censorship are inevitably tempted to protect adults in the name of protecting children. The V-chip must not be allowed to facilitate this desire.

Courts must be especially vigilant to ensure that a "multi-layered" approach to broadcast regulation does not result. I propose a general principle for assessing the constitutional use of technological filters like the V-chip. Because lack of effective filtering mechanisms is the real justification for content based regulation, creation of new and more effective filtering devices should always create heavy presumptions against any remaining content based restrictions. The more easily and broadly a V-chip or other technological filters can be implemented, the more suspect must be any restrictions on violent and indecent broadcast programming.

The safe harbor provisions offer a good example of how to apply this principle in practice. Even after the V-chip has been perfected, there still may be a limited and temporary need for the safe harbor provisions. By its terms the Telecommunications Act of 1996 applies only to television sets over thirteen inches. Not every television is likely to be replaced as soon as the V-chip is introduced. Most likely there will be a significant period in which many families lack the V-chip. For this reason, it may be necessary to retain the safe harbor provisions for a "sunset" period of, say, seven years.[63] After that point, anyone who uses a non-

---

62. *See ACT III*, 58 F.3d at 665. Moreover, it is at least theoretically possible that children could tape indecent programs during the safe harbor period and view them during the hours they are awake.

63. This figure depends on how one sees the likely future of technological development. If the V-chip is placed in standard cable boxes or in inexpensive add-on devices, it is reasonable to assume that most households that want them will purchase them more quickly, and the sunset period could be reduced accordingly. If, on the other hand, the V-chip is mainly implemented through new television sets, then something like ten years may be necessary for most old sets to wear out and be replaced.

V-chip-compatible television would be on notice that it would not be able to block out programs. If they refused to upgrade their equipment after seven years, they would have only themselves to blame if they were shocked and surprised by what they saw while flipping channels.

The regulatory scheme should not, however, use the lack of V-chip capability as an excuse to pile on additional regulations that put broadcast programming in a worse position than it was in before the Act. The regulatory scheme should not require that the safe harbor rules remain in force indefinitely merely because some televisions do not yet have V-chip equipment.

VII. THE RATINGS SYSTEM

The development of a ratings system poses a second constitutional problem. The Telecommunications Act of 1996 is cleverly drafted to create an almost irresistible set of pressures on private industry to create and implement a voluntary ratings system. It does so because, as the drafters well realized, a government-created ratings system imposed against the will of broadcasters would pose serious constitutional issues. Thus, [§551(b) of] the Act prescribes that "distributors of video programming" have a year to come up with a workable ratings system acceptable to the FCC, "in consultation with appropriate public interest groups and interested individuals from the private sector." If private industry does not come up with rules satisfactory to the FCC, the job will fall to an advisory committee appointed by the FCC. This advisory committee would be comprised of "parents, television broadcasters, television programming producers, cable operators, appropriate public interest groups, and other interested individuals from the private sector."[64] Not surprisingly, this committee sounds like the same groups the FCC would probably consult to determine the acceptability of any industry ratings system.

The Act's "fail-safe" provision deliberately stops short of requiring that broadcasters accept the ratings system devised by the advisory committee. It requires only that, if video programming already is rated by the broadcaster, the rating must also be encoded so that it can be read by a V-chip system. Left unclear is whether the Commission would be empowered to require that broadcasters accept the advisory committee's rating system. Also left unclear is whether the FCC would have the power to insist that all programming be rated before it can be broadcast.

The fail-safe provision is left deliberately toothless to avoid constitutional problems of prior restraint and compelled speech. Instead, the true goal of the legislation is to present broadcasters with a set of unpalatable alternatives. If they do nothing, they risk the appointment of an advisory committee telling them how to rate their programs. Even if the FCC cannot constitutionally require that they accept the ratings system as a condition of broadcasting, there will be enormous public pressure on broadcasters to accept a system that has already been worked out with attendant public fanfare. Faced with this possibility, broadcasters and distributors will instead choose to create their own ratings system.[65]

---

64. §551(b)(2), 110 Stat. at 140. The advisory committee is to be "fairly balanced in terms of political affiliation, the points of view represented, and the functions to be performed by the committee."

65. For similar reasons, if one broadcaster then decides to rate its programming, others will feel enormous pressure to follow suit. Thus, when Rupert Murdoch broke ranks and announced that his Fox network would rate shows regardless of what the other networks

This is precisely what the FCC hopes will happen. If the industry creates its own ratings system, the FCC actually has much greater power and influence than it would have under the fail-safe provisions. The FCC can decide whether to approve the ratings system or not, using basically the same players that would have formed an advisory committee. If the industry does not conform sufficiently to the FCC's wishes, the FCC can declare the industry not to be in compliance and once again hold up the threat of an advisory commission. In this way the FCC can achieve through threats much of what it could not have achieved through direct regulation.

Although the clever drafting of the legislation is designed to avoid constitutional problems, the very idea of an advisory committee, whether as an actual ratings body or as a threat the FCC hopes never to employ, is constitutionally troubling. From one perspective, there is no problem with the government designing a content based information organization system and leaving it up to private parties to decide whether to accept or reject it. For example, there is nothing unconstitutional about the development of the Library of Congress cataloguing system or its near universal acceptance in public and private libraries as a means of organizing information. The problem comes when the government insists that information must be organized according to content in a certain way or it cannot be published at all. And when the government uses threats, whether overt or concealed, to achieve this result, constitutional values are surely implicated.

Although the 1996 Act does not specifically require that all programming be rated before it can be broadcast, this is clearly the eventual goal of the V-chip system. Once a ratings system is in place, the FCC can then issue regulations to discourage or segregate unrated programming. Yet this solution is too facile. It threatens to put enormous numbers of programs in a worse position than they were in before the implementation of the V-chip. It violates the key constitutional principle I have enunciated: that the development of new technological filters should decrease government restrictions on adult viewing, not increase them.

A requirement that all programs be submitted to a private industry council before they can be screened has many of the features of a prior restraint. The problems would be even greater if the ratings (or the guidelines for them) were entrusted to a government-appointed Television Commission. But it should also be constitutionally troublesome for government to insist that speakers gain the imprimatur of a delegated private organization before they can be allowed access to the airwaves.

The constitutional problems posed by unrated programming can easily be solved. V-chip technology should be designed to allow viewers to block out all unrated material. This puts the onus where it belongs, on the parent to avoid watching unrated material, rather than on the networks to rate it.

Sports and news programming will be unrated. However, because much adult-oriented and experimental programming will also be unrated, the industry's solution is likely to cause problems in the future. If news and sports programming remain unrated, the danger is not that people will refuse to watch news and sports programming. The danger is that there will be enormous politi-

---

did, he made it virtually inevitable that NBC, CBS, and ABC would agree to a ratings system.

cal and financial pressures to ensure that all unrated programming is acceptable for all children, so that unrated programming becomes equivalent to a G movie rating. The latter result is the exact opposite of what a V-chip system should accomplish.

I have argued that the constitutional problems of prior restraint can be avoided only if programs can be shown without pre-screening or pre-rating; the burden must be on an external rating organization to provide ratings in time for broadcast. One might object that my solution allows broadcasters to do an end run around the V-chip; they can simply refuse to provide or obtain ratings, and put on violent and sexually charged programming without effectively being blocked out. But this result is unlikely to occur as long as parents are empowered to block out all unrated programs. Broadcasters, after all, are not insensitive to advertisers, and advertisers will be unlikely to spend their dollars on unrated programming if they believe that a substantial number of parents will block such programming. Thus, even without the use of a prior restraint, broadcasters will have considerable financial incentives to submit all programming to a private industry ratings board (or rate it themselves) when they can. Thus, for the vast majority of programming that most families want to watch, it will be possible to obtain a rating before broadcast.

This solution is not without costs. Local cable access programming and other programs that do not or cannot submit to ratings can still be shown under my proposed solution. However, they will not be picked up in the homes of parents who have blocked out all unrated programs. Moreover, my solution will still tend to segregate programming that does not submit to pre-screening along with programming that remains unrated for strategic reasons—for example, sexually explicit and violent programming. This will result in a smaller audience for such programming, and less advertising revenues. But it nevertheless ensures that people who want to watch this programming can have access to it, and at any time of day. In this sense it is more consistent with First Amendment values than the alternative.

VIII. THE V-CHIP AND THE DELEGATION OF INFORMATIONAL FILTERING

So far, I have spoken only about the constitutional issues raised by the V-chip. Yet the deeper problems that the V-chip raises lie elsewhere, and it is likely that these problems are not constitutionally cognizable ones. They concern the power over individual thought and national culture that arises with increasingly powerful forms of delegation of informational access. This problem is by no means new. Delegation of informational access has always existed in one form or another. But my concern is that, in the Information Age, the shape of culture will increasingly be determined by those persons and organizations who organize, filter, and present information for others and to others.

The regulatory apparatus surrounding the V-chip will work an enormous new delegation of informational filtering to a centralized bureaucracy, whether one operated by the federal government or one operated by private industry. This new bureaucracy will be entrusted with the task of devising and implementing filters for virtually all of the television programs available in the United States. It will have to determine the salient characteristics of all programming and evaluate which programs fit within the boundaries defined by these characteristics. These characteristics and these evaluations will in turn be employed by viewers and, more importantly, by advertisers, cable providers, video rental stores, public libraries, television production companies, writers, composers, and directors. As these evaluations become commonly employed, further choices and social arrangements will then be organized around them. In this way, the divisions of the cultural and informational world created by the custodians of the V-chip, however innocent, will be amplified throughout our culture, shaping and skewing the social world in unforeseen ways. It is possible that we shall have nothing to fear from these effects. But it is equally likely that there is much to fear.

Filtering mechanisms are not neutral means of organization, blocking and selection. They have important effects on what kinds of materials are subsequently produced and how social arrangements are subsequently organized.

The first problem of any ratings system is what characteristics count in making programming unsuitable for children. The most likely ratings system will focus on the categories of sexual content, nudity, violence, and profane language. These factors basically track the considerations currently employed by the Motion Picture Association of America (MPAA) ratings system. It is much less likely that racist, sexist, or homophobic language and depictions will be included as salient categories. Yet if parents are concerned with what their children pick up from television, they might be particularly concerned whether their children are picking up habits of intolerance. The harm to our children from these influences, one might think, would be equally as great as the harm from exposure to sex, violence, and bad language. And both sets of criteria involve content based distinctions.

Nevertheless, it is very unlikely that either an industry ratings board or an FCC-appointed television advisory committee will code for racist, sexist, or homophobic expression. The Telecommunications Act of 1996 expressly states that ratings systems are to avoid political and ideological categorizations.[66] These bodies will probably argue that coding or blocking programming as racist, sexist, or homophobic would give the unmistakable appearance of political favoritism.

Yet this objection reveals the problems that already exist with the most likely system of ratings—one organized around depictions of sexual conduct, violence, and profanity. The choice to protect our children from these things rather than others cannot be said to be truly apolitical, even if it can be assured to be mainstream. While overt expressions of homophobia are likely to remain uncoded, overt homosexual expressions of affection will probably be among the first to be coded as inappropriate for children. The social equality of homosexuals is currently a political hot potato, and one is quite sure in which direction this particular potato will get dropped.

The very assumption that exposure to racist messages is less harmful to our children and our community than exposure to violence already carries considerable political freight. Although coding for violence but not for racism seems to exclude political and ideological controversy, it does not avoid politics or ideol-

---

66. The Act insists that "nothing in (the requirement of ratings provisions) shall be construed to authorize any rating of video programming on the basis of its political or religious content." §551(b)(2).

ogy. Rather it installs them in the very process of coding. The actual practice of political and religious "neutrality" will be achieved by the selective avoidance of topics; it will produce the appearance but hardly the reality of apolitical judgment.

Another set of problems with any ratings system concerns equivalency. Even after the basic categories are determined, any ratings system will have to decide what gets coded within each category. More important for present purposes, it will have to decide what gets coded as possessing equal levels of inappropriateness. Like decisions about the categories themselves, these decisions cannot avoid political controversy; they are likely to have wide-ranging effects.

Take, for example, discussions of homosexuality or of safe sex as a means of preventing AIDS. How should these be coded in a ratings system? And what should they be coded as equivalent to? Some parents would see a big difference between such discussions and a sexually titillating love scene, while other parents would find both categories equally unsuitable for people under the age of eighteen.

Questions of equivalency severely test any facade of political neutrality. Does the ratings system regard two men kissing as equivalent to a woman being raped or another being slashed with a knife? Does the system regard a discussion of contraception as more or less inappropriate than a discussion of drug use? Whether or not we regard these events as really being different in kind is irrelevant. What is important is whether the ratings system makes them equivalent, by coding them as equally appropriate or inappropriate for children. Once materials are coded as equivalent, they become equivalent for all purposes for which the ratings system is used. And, make no mistake, the ratings system will be used for purposes other than its designers intended.

Nevertheless, it is possible that events will play out quite differently. If cable bandwidth is expanded—for example, through digital delivery systems—there may be room for several different ratings systems. Groups like the Christian Coalition may offer their own ratings system using V-chip technology, employing their own conception of what is family-friendly and what is not. Consumers can then subscribe to the ratings system of their choice, much as they now subscribe to magazines like TV Guide. Moreover, an explosion of space on cable systems promises the possibility of filtering systems based on any number of programming criteria. The only limitation upon would-be filterers is their ability to catalogue and categorize the millions of hours of materials that will eventually exist for television, and their ability to gain sufficient market share to underwrite the costs of rating this material.

This possible future presents a different set of problems. Consumers will be able to insulate themselves in increasingly specialized programming universes. By delegating their choices to specialized media filtering companies, they can filter out the great mass of programming to focus narrowly on their own special interests. Some, I suspect, will see this as the ultimate vindication of autonomy. Others will mourn the loss of a common televisual culture. In any case, this scenario produces effects completely opposite of the first. Instead of a single filtering system uncannily structuring and skewing thought and culture, the alternative scenario imagines an increasingly fractured community of individuals fixated on their personal programming universe and increasingly oblivious to everything else.

The inevitable emergence of filtering organizations, whether public or private, underscores the importance of distinguishing between delegation and choice—the distance between the informational future that awaits us and the attractive homilies of autonomy and personal empowerment now used to describe it. We are on the verge of installing a series of new filtering mechanisms that will transform the most important systems of mass communication available to us. We do this to satisfy the concerns of parents and the ambitions of politicians. But as we do this, we might be well advised to stop for a moment, and try to imagine what is as yet unimaginable—the profound though unintended effects of this potent combination of bureaucracy and technology on the health of our democracy and the evolution of our culture.

Notes and Questions

1. **"Voluntary" Self-Regulation.** Once section 551 was enacted, the broadcast industry, of course, was not about to permit a group picked by the FCC to rate its programs, so the industry "voluntarily" took it upon itself to come up with a ratings system. In December 1996 industry groups proposed and implemented a system that rates programs by viewer age but not by content. There was no problem with this system technologically, but it failed politically: a number of groups complained that the age-based ratings provided too little information about why the program might be inappropriate. Members of Congress and the White House pressured the broadcast industry to "voluntarily" add information on content to its ratings system, and in the summer of 1997 the industry did just that. In March of 1998, the FCC adopted an order finding these modified ratings (the "TV Parental Guidelines") acceptable and mandating that television receivers include a blocking system that incorporates them. *In re Implementation of Section 551 of The Telecommunications Act of 1996*, 13 FCC Rcd. 8232 (1998). These TV Parental Guidelines apply to all television programming except for news, sports, and unedited MPAA (Motion Picture Association of America) rated movies on premium cable channels. The age-based categories are: TV-Y (appropriate for all children); TV-Y7 (designed for children age 7 and older); TV-G (suitable for general audiences); TV-PG (may be unsuitable for younger children); TV-14 ("contains some material that many parents would find unsuitable for children under 14 years of age," *id.* at ¶7); and TV-MA (designed for mature viewers). The following content labels are appended to the age-based ratings as appropriate: FV (for fantasy violence); S (for sexual situations); V (for violence); L (for coarse language); and D (for suggestive dialogue).[67]

Some broadcasters complained that a principal effect of the ratings would be to give impetus to consumer boycotts of advertisers who buy spots on programs with disfavored ratings. Other broadcasters feared that the ratings system was just a first step toward banning programs that do not receive "acceptable" ratings. Notably, one broadcast network (NBC) agreed to provide the age-based

---

67. Some have already found the ratings categories too constricted. For example, two writers have proposed several additions, including "VP—Features lowlife confessions of interpersonal indiscretions that would make a vulture puke" and "M—Program features painfully strained metaphors, such as baseball representing the indomitable soul of a young and restless nation, or music as religion." Gene Weingarten & Richard Leiby, TV Ratings That The Industry Forgot, The Washington Post, July 15, 1997, at D6.

ratings but not the content ratings, and one cable network (BET) refused to provide any ratings at all. NBC's action proved particularly unpopular in Congress, with a number of Congressmen threatening to retaliate.[68] (Why would NBC run that risk?)

2. Market Response. The initial consumer response to the V-chip was less than overwhelming.[69] If that trend continues, would it suggest that the V-chip is not an effective alternative to regulatory limits on inappropriate television? That it has not been sufficiently publicized? (Whose fault would that be?) That in reality parents are far less interested in limiting the programs that their children watch than politicians imagine them to be? (Note that similar questions arose in United States v. Playboy Entertainment Group, Inc., 529 U.S. 803 (2000), excerpted in Chapter Fourteen.) What, as a legal matter, turns on the answer to these questions?

3. Alternate Rating Systems. The FCC required that television receivers be equipped with a blocking system that responds to the TV Parental Guidelines. Balkin suggests that some organizations might be unsatisfied with those ratings and want alternative ratings systems—for example, ratings that correspond to a particular religious or political perspective. Indeed, some commenters proposed to the FCC that it require television receivers to be accessible to alternative rating systems. The FCC rejected that proposal, based on its reading of the V-chip provision and its concern about the costs and complications (for manufacturers and consumers) of mandating such a system in every television. The FCC added that, "although we are not mandating that TV receiver manufacturers provide for alternative rating systems, we encourage manufacturers to design TV receivers to provide for additional rating systems to the extent practical." *In re Technical Requirements to Enable Blocking of Video Programming Based on Program Ratings*, 13 FCC Rcd. 11248 (1998), at ¶11. What is the point of adding that sentence? Who is the intended audience for it?

4. Market Deference. One of the arguments frequently made against additional ratings systems is that the marketplace can determine whether there is a need or demand for TV receivers to accommodate supplemental rating systems, and manufacturers will respond accordingly. *See, e.g., id.* at ¶9. Indeed, the Commission explicitly stated that, in its view, "manufacturers will be driven by the marketplace to meet any consumer demands to accommodate additional rating systems." *Id.* at ¶11. If that argument is persuasive, why doesn't it also apply to (and therefore undercut) the rationale behind mandating a rating system and the V-chip in the first place?

5. Mandatory Rating and the First Amendment. Is Balkin correct in arguing that the Act, properly construed, does not permit the government to require that any

---

68. *See* Joshua Micah Marshall, Free Speech Gets Tangled in Web, Sacramento Bee, Dec. 28, 1997, at F1 (discussing threat made by Senator John McCain, then-chairman of the Senate committee overseeing broadcasters, to revoke broadcasting licenses of NBC affiliates if it did not adopt the ratings system); Matt Pottinger, Ratings Don't Satisfy Senators, Hollywood Rep., July 11, 1997 (noting Senators' threats to impose content based ratings on broadcasters if NBC did not adopt them on its own).

69. *See, e.g.*, Paul Farhi, Parents Not Tuned To V-Chip; New TV Device Arrives Unnoticed, The Washington Post, June 29, 1999, at A1; Tara Weiss, At Long Last, V-Chip (Yawn) Arrives, Hartford Courant, June 30, 1999, at F1.

program be rated as a condition of being telecast? If not, does the First Amendment nevertheless require that the rating scheme be structured so that producers or broadcasters can avoid ratings altogether if they so desire?

6. Safe Harbors. Balkin suggests that the ratings system may lead to segregation of disfavored programs. In other words, Balkin worries that the Commission (perhaps prodded by Congress) will ultimately require that programs with certain ratings be shown only at certain hours. Would such a "safe harbor only" system be permissible under the rationale of the en banc D.C. Circuit in *ACT III*, excerpted above?

7. Bans. If segregation is upheld, would the next step be an attempt to ban programs with socially unacceptable ratings? Would this pass constitutional muster by analogy to *Pacifica*, or have subsequent cases clarified that *Pacifica* authorizes only segregation (or "zoning") of low-level broadcast speech and not its banishment?

8. Filters. What about Balkin's larger argument that in the information age it is informational filters that will dominate? Is that suggestion insightful or self-evident? For example, we have lived for decades in a world where the commodities marketplace is crammed with millions of goods. In that marketplace, informational filters—advertisers, labels, product reviewers, and so on—play a major role. Do Balkin's informational filters play a role in the information services marketplace that is any different from, or more unusual than, the role these more familiar entities play in the marketplace for commodities? If so, who would stand to gain and who to lose from the fragmentation of viewing practices that filters will likely produce? (Is fragmentation the likely result?) How might the government prevent it? Would such policies be wise? Constitutional?

IV. CHILDREN'S TELEVISION

The Commission has long struggled to identify the best way to encourage broadcast licensees to air educational children's television; and, as the documents that follow will reveal, the agency has over the last twenty years wavered considerably in its approach. Should licensees be given explicit requirements—told, for example, exactly what constitutes an "educational program" and how many hours of such programming are required per week? Should educational television instead be handled more subtly, with licensees simply warned that they have an obligation to serve the educational needs of children and told that performance on this score will be evaluated come renewal time? Are educational goals best served by requiring every broadcast licensee to provide suitable content? Might they be better served by a regulatory regime where only a small number of licensees develop expertise in this area and then provide all the content needed? On these and related issues, the Commission's answer has been both "yes" and "no"—and, at that, all in a relatively short time period.

As you work through these documents, then, see if you can understand why the Commission's position has changed so much over time. Are these adjustments the result of pressure from Congress and interest groups? Are we witnessing an agency that is learning from its early attempts and making adjustments in response? Did the agency in the beginning overestimate how cooperative licensees would be when it came to furthering this public interest goal and then, in the later proceedings, adopt regulations that better reflect a more cynical view? Overall, are the conflicting policy pronouncements that follow evidence that children's television is so far outside the Commission's areas of core competence that the Commission is bound to have trouble defining the problem, let alone crafting a sensible solution; or does the evidence more charitably suggest that the administrative process here has been a success, providing a forum for continued examination of (and flexible responses to) what is an inherently complex and contentious public policy issue?

IN RE CHILDREN'S TELEVISION PROGRAMMING AND ADVERTISING PRACTICES
96 FCC 2d 634 (1983)

2. In 1970, Action for Children's Television (ACT) submitted a petition proposing a rule requiring commercial television broadcasters to provide, on a weekly basis, minimum amounts of age-specific programming for children. In 1971, we adopted our First Notice of Inquiry to explore and define the fundamental issues in children's television. A Children's Television Task Force ("Task Force") was set up at that time to help achieve these goals. We concluded the inquiry in 1974 with the issuance of a Report and Policy Statement ("Policy Statement"). The Policy Statement specifically asked commercial television licensees to: (1) make a "meaningful effort" to increase the amount of programming for children; (2) air a "reasonable amount" of programming for children designed to educate and inform and not simply to entertain; (3) air informational programming separately targeted for both preschool and school-age children; and (4) air programming for children scheduled during weekdays as well as on weekends. Commercial television broadcasters also were expected to: (1) limit the amount of advertising in children's programming; (2) insure an adequate separation between program content and commercial messages; and (3) eliminate host-selling and tie-in practices.[70]

3. On appeal, the U.S. Court of Appeals affirmed the *Report and Policy Statement*. The Court held that the Commission's decision to provide policy guidelines and not to adopt specific regulations governing advertising and programming practices for children's television was a reasoned exercise of its broad discretion.

4. In 1978, the Commission re-established the Children's Television Task Force to inquire into the effectiveness of broadcast industry self-regulation under the Report and Policy Statement. The Task Force presented its report to the Commission on October 30, 1979. It concluded that broadcasters had not complied with the programming guidelines of the Policy Statement but, in general, had complied with the advertising guidelines.

6. In the opinion of the Task Force, the economic incentives of the advertiser-supported broadcasting system do not encourage the provision of specialized

---

70. The Task Force believed that the advertising guidelines in the Policy Statement had been complied with and therefore recommended no changes in this area. Accordingly, we regard requests for changes in these policies to be beyond the scope of this proceeding. [Footnote relocated].

programming for children. Advertisers desire the largest possible audience of potential buyers for their advertised products, but young children have an influence on decisions to buy only a relatively few advertised products. Thus, the amount of money spent on children's advertising appears to be small relative to the amount spent advertising to adults. The Task Force believed that the small numbers of children and the limited appeal of the children's market to advertisers, combined with the small number of outlets in most markets, create incentives for the commercial television system to neglect the specific needs of the child audience.

10. On March 28, 1983, the Commission reopened the children's television proceeding. We sought to update the record to enable us better to resolve the important questions raised by the Notice.

23. The Children's Television Task Force, believing that greater attention to the needs of the child audience was desirable, focused on three broad options to improve the situation: 1) mandatory programming requirements, 2) increased governmental funding (or other incentives) for the production and distribution of such programming, and 3) increasing the number of video outlets so as to improve the commercial incentives for serving subgroups in the audience and to increase the available distribution paths for children's programming. The recommended mandatory programming requirement could be enforced either through a specific rule or through processing guidelines applied to the renewal of station licenses.[71]

24. Our weighing of what we think are the relevant considerations in this proceeding leads us to believe that the recommended mandatory programming obligations are undesirable and should not be adopted. The other recommendations of the Task Force, relating to public funding for the production and distribution of informational and instructional children's programming and for the creation of additional video outlets and commercial funding mechanisms, we agree with fully. While issues relating to public funding are beyond our jurisdiction, we have moved aggressively to create new video outlets.

Availability of Children's Programming

26. In several important respects we disagree with the predicate upon which the Task Force based its recommendations and on which many parties base arguments supporting mandatory programming requirements. The first of these disagreements relates to the issue of the actual availability of programming for the child audience. In particular, we find the Task Force conclusion erroneous for its failure to properly consider: (1) the growth in number of commercial stations and their increased receivability; (2) programming on noncommercial stations;

---

71. [Ed. The use of "processing guidelines" is discussed more fully in the Commission's 1996 report, *infra*. The basic idea is that the Commission might establish guidelines, in this case a minimum amount of children's programming. Broadcasters who did not meet these guidelines would not break any FCC rule, but would face different procedures at license renewal time. For licensees whose past performance and proposed future programming met or exceeded the guidelines, the Commission's staff would be delegated authority to renew their licenses. Stations not meeting these guidelines would have their applications referred to the Commission for full review.]

(3) cable program services; and (4) child viewing of "family" oriented television. These failures undermine the conclusions drawn by the Report. The second disagreement concerns practical, legal, and policy problems with our ability to adopt and enforce programming obligations.

27. With respect to the first of these concerns, the Task Force focused its attention on the amount and scheduling of children's programming by the average commercial station. We must, of course, exercise our regulatory authority with respect to individual licensees. The objective of the Commission's involvement, however, is to assure that the telecommunications system as a whole is responsive to the needs of the public. It is therefore appropriate to look to that system as a whole in reviewing developments relating to the accessibility of programming for the child audience.

28. The data developed by the Task Force reveal a 7.2 percent increase, during the years studied (1973–74 and 1977–78), in the amount of time commercial broadcast stations, on average, devoted to children's programming. Not focused on, however, was the fact that since this docket was commenced, the total number of licensed commercial stations increased from 668 (1971) to 844 (1983), an increase of approximately 25 percent. Moreover, the reach of these stations was being constantly increased through more efficient operations (increased power and antenna height), through reductions in the UHF handicap, and through increased cable television carriage. Summary data show the average television household now receives 9.8 signals, an increase of 3 (44 percent) since 1970. Thus, not only was the average output of children's programming per station increasing but the average number of stations accessible to the child viewer was increasing as well.

29. Even this broader focus, which includes the totality of programming from all commercial stations however, is unduly narrow since it excludes from the product available to the child audience that which by almost any measure must be the most significant programming—that produced and distributed by the public broadcasting system. This system was created precisely for the purpose of supplementing the commercial broadcasting system and in specific recognition of the desirability of providing public support to increasing the availability of programming that might not be fully supported by commercial incentives. The public broadcasting system has recognized this mandate with respect to the broadcasting of children's programming and its successes in this field have been broadly recognized. The Corporation for Public Broadcasting has recently recognized children's programming as the number one priority in its Program Fund guidelines. We do not expect the public broadcasting system to bear the sole responsibility for meeting the needs of the child television audience or its existence to provide an excuse for the failings of the commercial broadcasting system. But we do not believe it appropriate to exclude its output from consideration as a significant factor in measuring the extent to which the needs of this audience are being served. The Commission has reserved channels in its television broadcast table of allotments for the specific use of noncommercial broadcasting stations so that the public would have access to the kinds of informational, instructional, and cultural programming that these stations deliver. Today, almost 300 stations—more than a quarter of all the licensed television stations—are of the noncommercial variety. The Public Broadcasting System, during the 1982–83 season, provided stations in the public broadcasting system, reaching over 90

percent of all television households, with some 2,050 hours of children's programming.

30. An additional important component of the national children's television programming market consists of the programming available to the child audience from nonbroadcast sources, including in particular that programming available over the facilities of cable television systems. Cable television now passes some 54 percent of all homes and cannot be avoided in any assessment of the accessibility of programming to the child audience. The most popular of the cable television delivered children's programming services, "Kidstime," reaches some 18 million subscribers or about 20 percent of all television households. Millions of households have access to other children's program services by cable as well, including "Nickelodeon," (14 million subscribers) and the recently inaugurated Disney Channel.

31. The Task Force's concern was principally with that programming defined in the Commission's rules as children's programming. This definition covers only programs "originally produced and broadcast primarily for a child audience twelve years old and under." Explicitly excluded from coverage are programs that might be appealing to children and significantly viewed by them but which were, when produced, intended for a broader audience as well. This exclusion of what has been broadly referred to as "family" programming, clearly resulted in an unduly narrowed definition of the programming of interest and value to the child audience. By using limitations that excluded programs such as "The Wonderful World of Disney," relevant programming of value could not be fully comprehended by the study. Such a definitional limitation serves to encourage the broadcasting of programming that is likely, given the dynamics of program selection within the household, to have not only a smaller total audience but a smaller child audience. Moreover, it suggests that positive values should be associated with programs, directed to the child audience, whatever the social utility of those programs, while programs specifically designed to bridge age levels and be shared by parents and children are of lesser value on the regulatory scale.

32. In sum, the adequacy of the programming to which children have access must be based on a consideration of the whole of the video distribution system. Viewing that system broadly, there is no national failure of access to children's programming that requires an across-the-board, national quota for each and every licensee to meet.

Issues of Law and Policy

33. Much of the discussion has addressed the overall quantity and scheduling of programming created for children. Yet, in fact, much of the actual concern has only to do with the availability of "quality" children's programming, programming that through its educational, intellectual, or cultural content is mentally or developmentally uplifting to the child audience.

34. Any analysis of the service received by the child audience that is entirely content neutral—which equates hours of television viewing with needs satisfaction—must conclude that this audience is well served. Children watch enough television, and no regulatory initiative need be introduced to get them to watch more. Thus, we are not persuaded that efforts to adopt specific mandatory pro-

gram hours obligations can achieve their intended objective in the absence of some control over or attention to the issue of quality.

36. Because of concerns with problems of this type, we have believed, with only the rarest of exceptions, that selection of programming is a matter that should be decided by station licensees and by the audience through its viewing pattern voting. Program quota systems have been viewed historically as fundamentally in conflict with the statutory scheme of broadcast regulation.

41. The Court of Appeals for the D.C. Circuit stated that it failed to see the logic in policies that imply that a regular schedule of cartoons would satisfy the public interest when a more limited schedule of educational specials would not. This raises again the issue of program quality. If it is assumed that station licensees will provide children's programming only involuntarily, then there is no logical way to disassociate quantity and quality. At a given cost, a specific regulatory requirement to respond to the needs and interests of children could be responded to either by the broadcasting of a limited number of more costly programs (more costly either in terms of production cost or lost audience) or a larger number of less costly programs. Although from the point of view of the station enterprise both approaches are equal in cost, rules that require or reward quantity create a strong bias to follow the "more programs lower cost" approach. Proponents of mandatory requirements urge, however, that with mandatory time requirements at least some programming would be available and, having to provide that programming, stations would then have an incentive to make their best efforts to produce attractive programming. While we agree that stations would attempt to maximize their returns within the constraints imposed, the hypothetical example posed by the Court of Appeals—regularly scheduled cartoons receiving more credit than less frequently scheduled better quality programs—would still seem to be the likely result.

42. As the Children's Television Task Force has suggested, such specialization as is made possible by the development of more programming outlets provides the surest long run chance of providing better service to all segments of society, including children. No sophisticated survey is required to observe that such specialization is occurring. During weekday mornings, independent (as well as public) stations in many markets compete for the child audience. Network affiliated stations concentrate on news and public affairs. On weekends, when network stations target the child audience, the independent (and the public) stations do not. As predicted, market segmentation leads to station specialization better serving the needs of the entire viewing public.

43. Recognizing that a balance must be reached, we believe this balance is best struck through a continued stress on the general licensee obligations emphasized by the Commission in its 1974 Children's Television Policy Statement and through the general requirement that stations provide programming responsive to the needs and interests of the communities they serve. We continue to believe "that the broadcasters' public service obligation includes a responsibility to provide diversified programming designed to meet the varied needs and interests of the child audience."

Notes and Questions

1. The Commission's Rationale. The Commission majority's rationale seems to incorporate two key arguments. First, the majority argues that the extent to which the public interest is being served should be measured by the performance of the entire market—including all video services, not simply free broadcast services. This is, of course, the usual method of evaluating the performance of an industry. For example, no one would say the shoe industry is performing badly if some stores do not carry all makes of all brands of shoes for men, women, and children. Rather, the question would be whether the shoe market, as a whole, provided quality shoes at reasonable prices that were responsive to people's various needs and tastes. But, as applied to television (or radio), isn't this approach completely inconsistent with the concept of the licensee as public trustee? What can remain of a public trustee obligation, in any programming area, under the FCC's rationale in this proceeding? Is this rationale also unduly insensitive to the needs of low income people?

Second, the majority makes clear that, in their view, the real issue here is quality, not quantity. Is this assertion inconsistent with the previous one? If video markets function well, shouldn't a requirement to program for children lead to competition to capture a large children's audience with quality programming? Is the FCC's discussion of this issue in ¶41 convincing?

2. The Next Round. The 1983 *Report and Order* was not the final word on children's television. Congress changed the legal landscape by passing the Children's Television Act of 1990, Pub. L. No. 104-437, 104 Stat. 996. That legislation prompted a return to the issue of children's television in the following *Order.*

POLICIES AND RULES CONCERNING
CHILDREN'S TELEVISION PROGRAMMING
6 FCC Rcd. 2111 (1991)

III. PROGRAMMING RENEWAL REVIEW REQUIREMENTS

14. The Children's Television Act of 1990 requires that, in reviewing television license renewal applications, we consider whether the licensee has served "the educational and informational needs of children through the licensee's overall programming, including programming specifically designed to serve such needs."[72] We may "in addition" consider (1) "any special nonbroadcast efforts... which enhance the educational and informational value of such programming" and (2) any "special effort" to produce or support programming broadcast by another station in the licensee's market that is "specifically designed to serve the educational and informational needs of children." We will implement this programming provision by reviewing a licensee's renewal application to determine whether, over the course of its license term, it has served the educational and information needs of children in its overall programming, including programming specifically designed to serve such needs.

A. Age Range of "Children"

15. The Act does not define "children" for purposes of the educational and informational programming renewal review requirement. Older as well as

---

72. [Ed. The Act also required the FCC to adopt rules limiting the commercials that broadcast stations and cable operators may air during children's programming. Discussion of that topic has been edited out of these materials.]

younger children have unique needs and can benefit from programming directed to them. Teenagers are undergoing a transition to adulthood. They are still very influenced by adult role models and peers, including those portrayed on television. They are generally inexperienced and yet face many crucial decisions concerning sex, drugs, and their own identities. We believe that we must interpret the programming renewal review requirement to apply to programs originally produced and broadcast for an audience of children 16 years of age and under.

18. Requiring each broadcaster to serve all age groups in order to pass our renewal review would probably result in less expensive and lower quality programming, possibly engendering what the Association of Independent Television Stations describes as "sameness and mediocrity." We thus decline to adopt suggestions that broadcasters program to all ages or to each subset of children within the under 16 range. Stations may select the age groups they can most effectively serve.

B. Standard

1. Programming

21. [The Commission seeks a definition of "educational and informational" programming for children] close to the spirit of the Act and to our desire to stimulate, and not dictate, programming responsive to children's needs. Thus, programming that furthers the positive development of the child in any respect, including the child's cognitive/intellectual or emotional/social needs, can contribute to satisfying the licensee's obligation to serve the educational and informational needs of children.

22. The Notice proposed to require each licensee to assess the needs of children given (1) the circumstances within the community, (2) other programming on the station, (3) programming aired on other broadcast stations within the community, and (4) other programs for children available in the broadcaster's community of license. Licensees would then air programs intended to meet "the educational and informational needs of children" responding to this assessment. In order to avoid unnecessary burdens, we are not requiring use of the proposed assessment criteria. We do, however, adopt them as permissive guidelines for exercise of licensee discretion in applying this definition. These factors can serve to make licensees' decisionmaking process more objective and may make it easier for licensees to justify programming decisions that are questioned. We therefore encourage their use.

24. The Act imposes no quantitative standards and the legislative history suggests that Congress meant that no minimum amount criterion be imposed. Given this strong legislative direction, and the latitude afforded broadcasters in fulfilling the programming requirement, we believe that the amount of "specifically designed" programming necessary to comply with the Act's requirement is likely to vary according to other circumstances, including but not limited to, the type of programming aired and other nonbroadcast efforts made by the station. We thus decline to establish any minimum programming requirement for licensees for renewal review independent of that established in the Act.

26. The legislative history provides a wealth of examples of children's programming that is educational and informational. These include "Fat Albert and

the Cosby Kids" (dealing with issues important to kids, with interruptions by host reinforcing purpose of show), "CBS Schoolbreak Specials" (original contemporary drama educating children about the conflicts and dilemmas they confront), "Winnie the Pooh and Friends" (show based on books designed to encourage reading), "ABC Afterschool Specials" (everyday problems of youth), "Saved by the Bell" (topical problems and conflicts faced by teens), "Life Goes On" (problems of a retarded child, emphasizing pro-social values), "The Smurfs" (prosocial behavior), "Great Intergalactic Scientific Game Show" (basic scientific concepts), and "Action News for Kids" (weekly news program for and by kids).

2. Nonbroadcast efforts

27. Section 103(b) of the Act permits the Commission, in evaluating compliance with the broadcaster's obligation to demonstrate at renewal time that it served the educational and informational needs of children, to consider "in addition" to its programming (1) "any special nonbroadcast efforts...which enhance the educational and informational value" of programming meeting such needs and (2) any "special effort" to produce or support programming broadcast by another station in the licensee's market that is specifically designed to meet such needs.

29. If a station produces or buys children's programs broadcast on another station, so as to qualify under section 103(b)(2) of the Act, we hold that both stations may rely on such programming in their renewal applications. The extent of support, measured in both time and money, given to another station's programming will determine the weight afforded it. Nonprogramming efforts, however, will not entirely eliminate the obligation to air some "specifically designed" educational and informational programming.

D. Record-keeping and Reporting

36. We do not adopt proposed processing guidelines based on percentages of children's programming, as these would conflict with Congress' rejection of quantitative standards.

IV. PENALTIES

39. We will assess forfeitures for violations of rules implementing the Act if violations are "willful or repeated" within the meaning of 47 U.S.C. §503. Given that the Act's programming requirement is to be measured over the course of the license term, however, forfeitures for violation of that requirement would be appropriately considered only at renewal. Similarly, violations of the Act should be considered along with a licensee's overall performance in determining whether it is entitled to a renewal.

Notes and Questions

1. **The Commission's Interpretation.** Did the Commission's implementation of the Act substantially reduce its force? Just what did the 1991 rules require of licensees with respect to children's programming? A public interest law group reported that, in the year after the FCC's *Report and Order*, licensees seeking renewals filed such descriptions of their children's programming as: (a) Program: "Bucky O'Hare" (animation), Description: "Good-doer Bucky fights off the evil

toads from aboard his ship. Issues of social consciousness and responsibility are central themes of the program." (b) Program: "Leave It to Beaver," Description: "Eddie misunderstands Wally's help to girlfriend, Cindy, and confronts Wally with his fist. Communication and trust are shown in this episode." Harry F. Waters, On Kid TV Ploys R Us, Newsweek, Nov. 30, 1992, at 88.

2. Another Round. In March 1993, shortly after the Clinton Administration took office, the FCC issued a Notice of Inquiry on Children's Television. A Notice of Proposal Rulemaking followed in 1995. These formed the basis for the Commission's dramatic reversal of course in 1996.

POLICIES AND RULES CONCERNING CHILDREN'S TELEVISION PROGRAMMING
11 FCC Rcd. 10660 (1996)

I. INTRODUCTION

1. In this Order, we take action to strengthen our enforcement of the Children's Television Act of 1990 (CTA).[73] The rules we adopt today are intended to counteract market disincentives and to ensure that broadcasters fulfill the promise of the Children's Television Act to our nation's children.

2. Our initial regulations implementing the CTA have not been fully effective in prompting broadcasters "to increase the amount of educational and informational broadcast television programming available to children." Senate Report at 1. Our review of the record in this proceeding reveals several problems. First, because of their imprecision in defining the scope of a broadcaster's obligation under the Children's Television Act, our rules have led to a variation in the level and nature of broadcasters' compliance efforts that is incompatible with the intent of the CTA. In so doing, our rules fail to adequately counterbalance the marketplace disincentives as Congress intended when it enacted the CTA. Indeed, some broadcasters are carrying very little regularly scheduled standard length programming specifically designed to educate and inform children. Second, some broadcasters are claiming to have satisfied their statutory obligations with shows that, by any reasonable benchmark, cannot be said to be "specifically designed" to educate and inform children within the meaning of the CTA. Third, parents and others frequently lack timely access to information about the availability of programming in their communities specifically designed to educate and inform children, exacerbating market disincentives. Therefore, we refine our policies and rules implementing the CTA to remedy these problems.[74]

3. First, we adopt a number of proposals designed to provide better information to the public about the shows broadcasters air to fulfill their obligation to

---

73. Children's Television Act of 1990, Pub. L. No. 101-437, 104 Stat. 996–1000, *codified at* 47 U.S.C. §§303(a), 303(b) & 394.

74. The actions we take today are consistent with a proposal submitted by President Clinton on behalf of "a group including educators, child advocates, and broadcast industry representatives" on how to revise our rules "to provide educational programming for America's children in fulfillment of the purpose of the 1990 Children's Television Act." Letter from President Clinton to Chairman Reed Hundt (July 31, 1996). The National Association of Broadcasters ("NAB") participated in this group and submitted the identical proposal in supplemental comments. *See* NAB Supplemental Comments (filed July 29, 1996).

air educational and informational programming under the CTA. Such information will assist parents who wish to guide their children's television viewing and, if large numbers of parents use that information to choose educational programming for their children, increase the likelihood that the market will respond with more educational programming. In addition, better information should help parents and others have an effective dialogue with broadcasters in their community about children's programming and, where appropriate, to urge programming improvements without resorting to government intervention.

4. Second, we adopt a definition of programming "specifically designed" to educate and inform children (or "core" programming) that provides better guidance to broadcasters concerning programming that fulfills their statutory obligation to air such programming. In order to qualify as core programming, a show must have serving the educational and informational needs of children as a significant purpose. The Commission will ordinarily rely on the good faith judgments of broadcasters as to whether programming satisfies this test and will evaluate compliance of individual programs with this definition only as a last resort. Our new definition of core programming includes other objective elements. A core program must be a regularly scheduled, weekly program of at least 30 minutes, and aired between 7:00 a.m. and 10:00 p.m. The program must also be identified as educational and informational for children when it is aired and must be listed in the children's programming report placed in the broadcaster's public inspection file.

5. Third, we adopt a processing guideline that will provide certainty for broadcasters about how to comply with the CTA and facilitate our processing efforts. As described more fully below, under this guideline, broadcasters will receive staff-level approval of the CTA portion of their renewal applications if they air three hours per week of core programming or if, while providing somewhat less than three hours per week of core programming, they air a package of programming that demonstrates a level of commitment to educating and informing children that is at least equivalent to airing three hours per week of core programming. Broadcasters that do not meet this guideline will be referred to the full Commission for consideration, where they will have a full opportunity to demonstrate compliance with the CTA, including through efforts other than "core" programming and through nonbroadcast efforts.[75]

6. A processing guideline will help ensure that broadcasters who wish to provide an ample amount of children's educational programming will not find themselves at an unfair disadvantage in the market relative to competing broadcasters who do not, and will not find themselves facing competitive pressure to forgo airing educational programs. A processing guideline will also facilitate speedy and consistent application processing by Commission staff. In short, a processing guideline is a clear, fair and efficient way to implement the Children's Television Act.

---

75. *See* 47 U.S.C. §303b(b) (providing that, in addition to considering educational and informational programming aired on the licensee's station, the Commission may consider "any special nonbroadcast efforts" by the licensee to enhance the value of such programming, and "any special efforts" by the licensee to sponsor programming on another station in its market).

II. BACKGROUND

A. The Importance of Children's Educational Television Programming

9. Congress has recognized that television can benefit society by helping to educate and inform our children. In enacting the CTA, Congress cited research demonstrating that television programs designed to teach children specific skills are effective. For example, children who watch "Mister Rogers' Neighborhood" and "Sesame Street" have been shown to learn task persistence, imaginative play, and letter and number skills.

10. Studies confirm, and many commenters in this proceeding agree, that children can benefit substantially from viewing educational television. In one such study, children who watch "Barney" showed greater counting skills, knowledge of colors and shapes, vocabulary, and social skills, than children who did not watch the program. Although all children can benefit from educational television, it has been found to be particularly beneficial to children from lower income families. Thus, there is substantial information before us showing that television can educate children.

11. That television has the power to teach is important because nearly all American children have access to television and spend considerable time watching it. Recent data show that television reaches 98 percent of all American homes, including well over 90 percent of households with annual incomes below $5,000. Data also show that children from ages 2 to 17 watch on average more than 3 hours of television each day. The significance of over-the-air television for children is reinforced by the fact that fewer children have access to cable television than to over-the-air television. Hence, over-the-air broadcasting is an important source of video programs for children and for all members of low income families, including children.

12. Television reaches children earlier and for more hours per day than any other educational influence except perhaps family. Many children watch television before they are exposed to any formal education. Nearly 70 percent of daycare facilities have a television on for several hours each day. By the time most American children begin the first grade, they will have spent the equivalent of three school years in front of the television set.

13. Some have argued that children will not watch educational programming. But there are studies that show that, where educational programming is available, a large percentage of children watch. The Westat study found that the majority of young children in all demographic groups watch "Sesame Street." Another study submitted by CTW suggests that children do not distinguish between educational and non-educational programming, and that they do not find educational programming less appealing. Fox Broadcasting Company, Fox Children's Network ("FCN"), and Fox Affiliates Association (collectively referred to herein as "Fox") submitted evidence that the educational programs developed by the FCN receive high ratings.

D. The Supply of Children's Educational Television Programming

29. *The Economics of Children's Educational Programming.* In enacting the CTA, Congress found that market forces were not sufficient to ensure that commercial stations would provide children's educational and information programming.

30. A number of factors explain the marketplace constraints on providing such programming. Over-the-air commercial broadcast television stations earn their revenues from the sale of advertising time. Revenues received from the sale of advertising depend on the size and the socio-demographic characteristics of the audience reached by the broadcaster's programming. Broadcasters thus have a reduced economic incentive to promote children's programming because children's television audiences are smaller than general audiences.

31. Broadcasters have even less economic incentive to provide educational programs for children. Educational programming generally must be targeted at segments of the child audience. An educational program for children aged 2–5, however, may well be of little interest to children aged 6–11 or children aged 12–17. By contrast, an entertainment program for children is more likely to appeal to a broader range of children.[76] Thus the market for children's educational television may be segmented by age in ways that do not characterize children's entertainment programming or adult programming. Additionally, the adult audience is much larger than the child audience. There are 59.5 million children in the television audience: 16.0 million children aged 2–5, 22.2 million aged 6–11, and 21.3 million children aged 12–17. Adults aged 18–49 number 122.2 million. Because the adult audience is so much larger than the children's audience, the potential advertising revenues are also much larger and therefore provide broadcasters with an incentive to focus on adult programming rather than children's educational television programming. And within the category of children's programming, broadcasters have an economic incentive to select entertainment programs that appeal to a broader range of children rather than educational programs that appeal to a narrower group.

32. If stations are required to provide some educational programming for children, we believe that the same incentives could cause station owners to prefer to show such programming when relatively few adults would likely be in the audience. For example, it is less costly for broadcasters to show children's educational programs very early in the morning than to show them at later hours because the number of adult viewers lost, and hence the advertising revenues lost, will be relatively low. A significant portion of children's programming is currently aired before 7:00 a.m. and few children's programs are shown in prime time, which draws the largest adult audiences.

33. Furthermore, in the broadcasting marketplace it may be difficult for a small number of parents and others with strong demands for children's educational programming to signal the intensity of their demand for such programming. In other retail markets, consumers can demonstrate the intensity of their preferences by the amount of money they spend, *i.e.*, their dollar "votes." However, broadcasting rating services basically register only one "vote" per viewer. But the signal that matters to the broadcaster is the dollar amount of advertising

76. Nielsen data indicate that children ages 6 to 11 are much more likely to watch general audience or adult-oriented entertainment programs than they are to watch children's programs. Moreover, when asked to name their favorite programs, children ages 10 to 17 were much more likely to include adult-oriented or general audience programs than child-specific shows. The State of Children's Television: An Examination of Quantity, Quality, and Industry Beliefs, conducted by Amy B. Jordan for the Annenberg Public Policy Center of the University of Pennsylvania under the Direction of Kathleen Hall Jamieson, June 17, 1996, *citing* Nielsen Media Research, March, 1996.

revenues. Small audiences with little buying power, such as children's educational television audiences, are unlikely to be able to signal the intensity of their demand for such programming in the broadcasting market. Therefore, broadcasters will have little incentive to provide such programming because the small audiences and small resulting advertising revenues means that there will be a substantial cost to them (the so-called "opportunity cost") of forgoing larger revenues from other types of programs not shown.

34. These and the other factors described above tend to lead to an underprovision of children's educational and informational television programming, as Congress found in the CTA.

36. *The amount of educational programming on broadcast television.* The studies submitted [in this proceeding] are inconclusive in establishing the exact amount of educational programming that currently is being provided by broadcasters. Despite their deficiencies, however, the studies do allow us to conclude that some broadcasters are providing a very limited amount of programming specifically designed to educate and inform children and that broadcasters vary widely in their understanding of the type of programming that the CTA requires. This evidence, viewed together with the rest of the record, leads us to conclude that it is necessary to take the actions adopted here to achieve the goals of the CTA. [A lengthy review of the studies is omitted.]

43. *Availability of educational programming on nonbroadcast media.* A number of broadcasters submitted comments arguing that the Commission should assess not just the educational programming being provided over-the-air by broadcast stations, but rather the overall availability of educational programming in the video marketplace. We believe, however, that the proper focus in this proceeding should be on the provision of children's educational programming by broadcast stations, not by cable systems and other subscription services such as direct broadcast satellite systems that, in contrast to broadcast service, require the payment of a subscription fee. The CTA itself expressly focuses on broadcast licensees. In enacting this statute, Congress found that, as part of their public interest obligations, "*television station operators and licensees* should provide programming that serves the special needs of children," 47 U.S.C. §303a (emphasis added), and the Act applies only to television broadcast stations, *id.* at 303b(a). Thus, the statute focuses on the provision of children's educational programming through broadcasting, a ubiquitous service, which may be the only source of video programming for some families that cannot afford, or do not have access to, cable or other subscription services. While noting an increase in the number of nonbroadcast outlets available for children to receive video programming, the House Report states that "the new marketplace for video programming does not obviate the public interest responsibility of individual broadcast licensees to serve the child audience." House Report at 6.

III. PUBLIC INFORMATION INITIATIVES

47. We conclude that the market inadequacies that led Congress to pass the Children's Television Act can be addressed, in part, by enhancing parents' knowledge of children's educational programming.

48. Commercial television is advertiser supported. Parents can increase the audience of an educational program by encouraging their children to watch the

show, but can only do so if they know in advance when the show will air and that the show is educational. Increasing the audience size for educational programs increases the incentive of broadcasters to air, and producers to supply, more such programs. Access to information can also facilitate viewer campaigns and other community-based efforts to influence stations to air more and better educational programming.

49. In considering the options to improve the information available regarding educational programming, we seek to maximize the access to such information by the public while minimizing the cost to the licensee. We [adopt] three basic methods to improve the public's access to information: commercial broadcasters should identify core programming at the time those programs are aired in a form that is at the sole discretion of the licensee; they should identify such programs to publishers of program guides; and, as detailed below, they should provide improved access to information to the public through standardized reporting and other means. We note that disclosure requirements of the sort we adopt today promote First Amendment interests by increasing the flow of information to the public.[77]

IV. DEFINITION OF PROGRAMMING "SPECIFICALLY DESIGNED" TO SERVE CHILDREN'S EDUCATIONAL AND INFORMATIONAL NEEDS

80. The definition of core programming that we adopt is designed to provide licensees with clear guidance regarding how we will evaluate renewal applications. The elements of our proposed definition are also designed to be as objective as possible so that they are more easily understood by licensees and the Commission staff and to avoid injecting the Commission unnecessarily into sensitive decisions regarding program content. Programming specifically designed to serve children's educational and informational needs is the only category of programming the CTA expressly requires each licensee to provide. Adopting a definition of such programming will promote this statutory objective by more precisely defining the programming that qualifies and, consequently, provide appropriate incentives to increase the amount of such programming. We further believe that the definition we adopt today will continue to provide broadcasters ample discretion in designing and producing such programming. We emphasize that the test of whether programming qualifies as core does not depend in any way on its topic or viewpoint. The test is whether it is "specifically designed" to serve the educational and informational needs of children. We now turn to the specific elements of the new definition of core programming.

Significant Purpose

81. We propose that core programming have serving the educational and informational needs of children as a "significant" instead of "primary" purpose as

---

77. In Meese v. Keene, 481 U.S. 465 (1987), the Supreme Court upheld the Foreign Agents Registration Act, which required the labeling of films distributed by agents of foreign governments to indicate the agent's identity and the identity of the principal for whom the agent acts. The Court agreed with the lower court that "it could not be gainsaid that this kind of disclosure serves rather than deserves the First Amendment," added that such disclosures "better enable the public to evaluate the import of the propaganda," and added that striking down the disclosure requirement under the First Amendment "ironically" would "withhold information from the public." *Id.* at 477, 480 & 481.

suggested in the NOI, in response to the widely-held view that such programming must be entertaining to be successful. We believe that this terminology
makes clear that education need not be the only purpose of programming specifically designed to meet the educational and informational needs of children, but
must be more than an incidental goal.

84. To qualify as core programming, a show must have serving the educational and informational needs of children ages 16 and under as a significant purpose. The "significant purpose" standard appropriately acknowledges the point
advanced by broadcasters and others that to be successful, and thus to serve children's needs as mandated by the CTA, educational and informational programming must also be entertaining and attractive to children. Accordingly, we will
require that core programming be specifically designed to meet the educational
and informational needs of children ages 16 and under and have educating and
informing children as a significant purpose.

87. Several commenters asked us to clarify that our definition of core programming includes educational and informational programs that further children's social and emotional development as well as their cognitive and intellectual development. The CTA speaks of programming specifically designed to serve
"the educational and informational needs of children." 47 U.S.C. §303b(a)(2). It
does not draw a distinction between educational and informational programming that furthers children's cognitive and intellectual development and educational and informational programming that furthers children's social and emotional development. We decline to draw that distinction ourselves and
accordingly conclude that both fall within the scope of our definition.

*Educational and Informational Objective and Target Child Audience Specified in
Writing*

90. With respect to the second element of our core programming definition,
we require licensees to specify in writing in their children's programming report
the educational and informational objective of a core program, as well as its target child audience. We think that such a requirement will help licensees to focus
on children's specific educational and informational needs in compliance with the
CTA. This information will assist parents and other interested parties to understand licensees' programming efforts and afford them the means to participate
with licensees in developing effective educational programming and to play a
more active role in promoting and enforcing the goals of the CTA. Such information must be included in the children's programming report that licensees place in
their public inspection files.

96. We decline to require broadcasters to serve particular segments of the
child audience. We recognize the possibility that licensees may be induced to air
programming for children over 12 because (1) this group has greater spending
power than young children, (2) shows for older children may attract general audiences as well as children, and (3) programming designed for children 12 and
under is subject to commercial limits, while programming for older children is
not. Nonetheless, we conclude that it would be undesirable to require broadcasters to serve particular segments of the child audience, in part because we do not
have adequate data showing that in fact younger age groups are underserved relative to other children.

Times Core Programming May Be Aired

99. To qualify as core, a program must air between the hours of 7:00 a.m. and 10:00 p.m. In specifying this time period, our intention is to encourage broadcasters to air educational programming at times the maximum number of child viewers will be watching. [The Commission then recounted data suggesting that child viewing increases substantially after 7 a.m. and drops considerably after 10 p.m.].

Regularly Scheduled

105. Qualifying core programming should be regularly scheduled, particularly in view of our emphasis on improving the flow of information to parents through published program guides and other means to enable them to select educational and informational programs for their children. Programming that is aired on a regular basis is more easily anticipated and located by viewers, and can build loyalty that will improve its chance for commercial success. We agree with those commenters who argue that programs that air regularly can reinforce lessons from episode to episode. We also believe that regularly scheduled programs can develop a theme which enhances the impact of the educational and informational message. Accordingly, to be considered as core, we will require that educational and informational programs air on a regular basis. Furthermore, to count as regularly scheduled programming, such programs must be scheduled to air at least once a week. Regularly scheduled weekly programming is the dominant form of television programming. Programs that air at less frequent intervals are less likely to attract a regular audience and to be anticipated by parents.

Substantial Length

110. Core programming should be at least 30 minutes in length. The dominant broadcast television format is 30 minutes or longer in length. Programs in these standard formats are more likely than shorter programming to be regularly scheduled and to be listed in program guides, and thus are easier for parents to identify for their child's viewing. In addition, programs that are 30 minutes or longer allow more time for educational and informational material to be presented. There was no evidence presented to support claims by some parties that children have short attention spans and thus will not benefit from substantial length programming.

112. We emphasize that programming with a significant purpose of educating and informing children that is less than 30 minutes in length, although not credited as core programming, can contribute to serving children's needs pursuant to the CTA. Such programming can count toward meeting the three-hour processing guideline when broadcasters air somewhat less than 3 hours per week of core programming, as described below.

Identified as Educational and Informational

113. Stations will be required to identify core programs as educational and informational at the beginning of the program, and to make available the necessary information for listing these programs as educational and informational in program guides. We adopt both of these [rules] in order to improve the information available to parents regarding programming specifically designed for chil-

dren's educational and informational needs, and to assist them in selecting these programs for their children. We also believe this measure will make broadcasters more accountable in classifying programming as specifically designed to educate and inform.

V. PROCESSING GUIDELINE

115. In the NPRM, we sought comment on several proposals for evaluating a licensee's compliance with the Children's Television Act at renewal. Specifically, we proposed to adopt one of three alternative options: (1) Commission monitoring of the amount of educational and informational programming on the air during a period of time following the adoption of measures to improve the flow of programming information to the public and adoption of a definition of "core" programming; (2) adoption of a safe harbor processing guideline specifying an amount of programming specifically designed to serve children's educational and informational needs that would represent one means of satisfying the CTA's programming obligation; and (3) adoption of a programming standard that would require broadcasters to air a specified average number of hours per week of programming specifically designed to serve the educational and informational needs of children. We also sought comment on whether we should adopt "program sponsorship" rules or guidelines, giving licensees the option of satisfying a portion of the prescribed amount by providing financial or other "in kind" support for programming aired on other stations in their market.

118. The National Association of Broadcasters (NAB) filed initial comments also opposing any quantitative guidelines or requirement. In supplemental comments, however, NAB set forth its support for a "processing guideline under which broadcasters could obtain staff approval of the children's television service portion of their renewal applications by showing that they either aired an average of three hours per week of newly defined 'core' educational and informational programming for children or that, while they aired somewhat less than this amount of 'core' programming, they aired a package of other programs that demonstrated the same level of commitment to the needs of children."[78]

120. Based on our review of the record, as well as our experience in enforcing the CTA over the past five years, we have decided to adopt a three-hour processing guideline. Under this guideline, the Mass Media Bureau[79] will be authorized to approve the Children's Television Act portions of a broadcaster's renewal application where the broadcaster has aired three hours per week (averaged over a six month period) of educational and informational programming that has as a significant purpose serving the educational and informational needs of children ages 16 and under. Renewal applications that do not meet this guideline will be referred to the Commission, where the applicant will have a full opportunity to demonstrate compliance with the CTA by, for example, relying in part on sponsorship of core educational and informational programs on other stations in the market that increases the amount of core educational or informational program-

---

78. NAB Supplemental Comments at 1 (filed July 29, 1996). [Ed. The Commission adopted this *Report and Order* on August 8, 1996.]

79. [Ed. The Mass Media Bureau is a subdivision of the FCC that focuses on mass media issues. The FCC has other specialized units, for example the Cable Services Bureau and the Common Carrier Bureau.]

ming on the station airing the sponsored program and/or on special nonbroadcast efforts which enhance the value of children's educational and informational television programming.

124. In the context of the CTA, a processing guideline is clear, fair, and efficient. First, our experience in reviewing the children's programming portions of renewal applications teaches us that a processing guideline is desirable as a matter of administrative efficiency in enforcing the CTA and provides desirable clarity about the extent of a broadcaster's programming responsibilities under the statute. Due to the volume of broadcast television renewal applications received by the Commission—approximately 1500 commercial and noncommercial applications during each renewal cycle—the Commission has for many years delegated to the Mass Media Bureau the authority to act on applications that do not present difficult issues. In the absence of an articulated guideline regarding CTA compliance that the Bureau would use to distinguish applications that are properly processed at the staff level from those that must be sent to the full Commission, a *de facto* processing guideline likely would develop. But this *de facto* guideline, if unpublished, would not provide clear and timely notice of what a licensee can do to guarantee renewal under the CTA. By adopting a safe harbor processing guideline in this order, the Commission is simply giving public notice of the procedures it will use to evaluate a broadcaster's children's educational and informational programming performance.[80] Licensees and the public will consequently know with certainty and in advance what a licensee can do to ensure that it meets its CTA obligations.

129. We recognize that this is contrary to our earlier interpretation of the CTA as precluding quantification of the CTA obligation. We reached this conclusion in 1991 on the grounds that the statute itself "imposed no quantitative standard" and the "legislative history suggested that Congress meant that no minimum amount criterion be imposed." In reaching a contrary conclusion today, we begin with the fact that nothing in the statutory language of the CTA forbids the use of a processing guideline. Furthermore, although there is specific language in the legislative history, cited in our 1991 Report and Order and by parties in this proceeding, stating the "Committee does not intend that the FCC interpret this section as requiring or mandating a quantification standard," this language does not prohibit us from seeking to provide greater clarity and guidance through a processing guideline. Rather, this language simply makes clear that the CTA does not *require* quantitative standards or guidelines. It is not our conclusion today that we *must* adopt a quantitative guideline, but that the processing guideline approach we adopt will clarify the imprecision of our current rules that has led to a variation in the level and nature of broadcasters' compliance efforts that is incompatible with the intent of the CTA. Thus, because of its clarity, fairness, and

---

80. The Commission in the past has adopted processing guidelines to achieve similar purposes. For example, the Commission's non-entertainment programming processing guidelines provided that the applications of licensees that offered less than certain amounts of non-entertainment programming had to be acted upon by the Commission rather than by the Bureau. *See* In re Deregulation of Radio, 84 FCC 2d 968, 975, *recon.*, 87 FCC 2d 797 (1981), *aff'd in part, remanded in part*, Office of Communication of United Christ v. FCC, 707 F.2d 1413, 1432 (D.C. Cir. 1983). It is universally accepted that these guidelines were "purely procedural." *Id.* at 1432.

ease of administration, a processing guideline will remedy the shortcomings of our initial rules and thereby provide the appropriate counterweight to the market forces identified by Congress that tend to discourage broadcasters from airing children's educational and informational programming.

136. If we find that a broadcaster has not complied with the CTA, we will apply the same remedies that we use in enforcing our other rules. These remedies will vary depending on the severity of the deficiency based on objective criteria. For less serious deficiencies, we will consider letters of admonition or reporting requirements. We may also consider using a "promise versus performance" approach. This would be a prospective remedy under which a licensee would detail its plan for coming into full compliance with CTA programming obligations; if this plan meets with Commission approval, the station's license would be renewed on the condition that the licensee adheres to the plan absent special circumstances. For more serious violations, we will consider other sanctions, including forfeitures and short-term renewals. In extreme cases, we will consider designating the license for hearing to determine whether the licensee's violations of the CTA and our implementing rules warrant nonrenewal under the standards set forth in section 309(k) of the Communications Act.

137. *Special Nonbroadcast Efforts.* The CTA states that, "[i]n addition to consideration of the licensee's [educational] programming, the Commission may consider...any special nonbroadcast efforts by the licensee which enhance the educational and informational value of such programming to children." At the Commission level, a licensee may present evidence of such special nonbroadcast efforts. To receive credit under this provision for a "special" nonbroadcast effort, a broadcaster must show that it has engaged in substantial community activity. To receive credit under this provision for a special nonbroadcast effort that "enhance[s]" the educational value of a broadcaster's educational programming, a broadcaster must show a close relationship between its core programming and its nonbroadcast efforts. Finally, we note that the text of this provision plainly does not relieve a broadcaster of the obligation to air core programming. The statute permits the Commission to consider special nonbroadcast efforts only "in addition to consideration of the licensee's [educational] programming."

138. *Special Sponsorship Efforts.* The CTA states that, "in addition to consideration of the licensee's educational programming, the Commission may consider...any special efforts by the licensee to produce or support programming broadcast by another station in the licensee's marketplace which is specifically designed to serve the educational and informational needs of children." Some parties supported giving credit to a sponsoring station in assessing its CTA performance at renewal time, while others opposed the idea. We will allow a licensee to present evidence at the Commission level of such special sponsorship efforts. To receive credit under this provision for a "special" sponsorship effort, a broadcaster must demonstrate that its production or support of core programming aired on another station in its market increased the amount of core programming on the station airing the sponsored core programming. Also, we note again that the text of section 103(b) does not relieve a broadcaster of the obligation to air programming specifically designed to serve the educational and informational needs of children. It permits the Commission to consider sponsorship nonbroadcast efforts only "in addition to consideration of the licensee's [educational] programming."

VII. FIRST AMENDMENT ISSUES

147. The First Amendment arguments raised by opponents of our proposed CTA regulations essentially fall into two categories — arguments that attack the CTA obligation and arguments that attack the quantification of the CTA obligation. To the extent that some commenters argue that the CTA is unconstitutional, Congress itself addressed that issue. It specifically concluded that "it is well within the First Amendment strictures to require the FCC to consider, during the license renewal process, whether a television licensee has provided information specifically designed to serve the educational and informational needs of children in the context of its overall programming." Senate Report at 16. As the Senate Report noted, broadcasters, in exchange for "the free and exclusive use of a valuable part of the public domain," can be expected to serve as a public fiduciary, obliged to serve the needs and interests of their viewers.[81] That obligation includes the obligation to serve the needs of children.[82] Even more specifically, as the FCC, the courts, and Congress have concluded, a broadcaster's public interest obligation properly includes an obligation to serve the educational and informational needs of children.[83] The question in this proceeding is not *whether* the Commission should give effect to the CTA, but *how* it should do so.

149. The course we adopt today — defining what qualifies as programming "specifically designed" to serve the educational needs of children and giving broadcasters clear but nonmandatory guidance on how to guarantee compliance — is a constitutional means of giving effect to the CTA's programming requirement. "It does not violate the First Amendment to treat licensees given the privilege of using scarce radio frequencies as proxies for the entire community, obligated to give suitable time and attention to matters of great public concern." Red Lion Broadcasting Co. v. FCC, 395 U.S. 367, 394 (1969). Congress's authority to order "suitable time and attention to matters of great public concern" includes the authority to require broadcasters to air programming specifically designed to further the educational needs of children. The airwaves belong to the public, not to any individual broadcaster.[84] The fact that Congress elected to retain public ownership of the broadcast spectrum and to lease it for free to private licensees for limited periods carries significant First Amendment consequences.

150. In CBS v. FCC, 453 U.S. 367 (1981), the Supreme Court upheld a challenge to the statute (47 U.S.C. §312(a)(7)) that requires broadcasters to provide reasonable access to individual candidates seeking federal elective office. Similarly, here, the CTA requires broadcasters to serve the educational and informational needs of children through programming specifically designed for those needs. Both provisions require broadcasters to air certain types of programming they might not otherwise choose to provide. However, the obligation imposed by

81. *Id.* (*citing* Red Lion Broadcasting Co. v. FCC, 395 U.S. 367 (1969)).
82. *See id.* (*citing* Prince v. Massachusetts, 321 U.S. 158, 168 (1943)).
83. *Id.* (*citing* ACT v. FCC, 564 F.2d 458 (D.C. Cir. 1977) (affirming our *1974 Policy Statement* specifying that the public interest obligation included an obligation to provide educational and informational programming for children)).
84. *See* 47 U.S.C. §301; FCC v. National Citizens Comm. for Broadcasting, 436 U.S. 755, 806 n.25 (1978).

section 312(a)(7) appears to be significantly more burdensome than the obligation imposed by the CTA. Under section 312(a)(7), broadcasters have no control
over the content of the political advertising. In contrast, under the CTA broadcasters are obligated to provide children's educational programming, yet they retain wide discretion in choosing what programs to provide, a fact little changed
by the clarifying measures we adopt today.

151. In Turner Broadcasting v. FCC, 114 S. Ct. 2445 (1994), the Court made
clear that the Commission has the authority to "inquire of licensees what they
have done to determine the needs of the community they propose to serve," but
not to "impose upon them its private notions of what the public ought to hear."
Id. at 2463. We have chosen to adopt a processing guideline that requires broadcasters to show us how they have served the educational and informational needs
of children, and which provides guidance to them about ways in which they can
meet that obligation. We are not, however, telling licensees what topics to discuss. The *Turner* Court reaffirmed that "broadcast programming, unlike cable
programming, is subject to certain limited content restraints imposed by statute
and FCC regulation." *Id.* at 2462. And, as examples of (presumably) permissible
regulation, the Court cited the Children's Television Act, together with the equal-
time and personal attack rules and the rules channeling indecent programming
away from times when children are most likely to be in the viewing audience. *Id.*
at 2462–63 n.7. If these latter regulations survive constitutional scrutiny, then
so, *a fortiori*, would the Commission's considerably less intrusive proposal for
giving meaningful effect to the Act by defining "core" educational programming
and establishing a procedure that broadcasters can use to assure routine staff
processing of the CTA portion of their renewal applications.

152. Our new regulations, like the CTA itself, impose reasonable, viewpoint-
neutral conditions on a broadcaster's free use of the public airwaves. They do not
censor or foreclose speech of any kind. They do not tell licensees what topics
they must address.

153. The CTA and our regulations directly advance the government's substantial, and indeed compelling, interest in the education of America's children.
As Congress recognized, "it is difficult to think of an interest more substantial
than the promotion of the welfare of children who watch so much television and
rely upon it for so much of the information they receive." Senate Report at 17;
see also House Report at 11.

154. The Children's Television Act is designed to promote programming that
educates and informs children. The framers of the First Amendment understood
that "the greatest menace to freedom is an inert people," as Justice Brandeis
wrote in Whitney v. California, 274 U.S. 357, 372 (1927) (concurring opinion).
It is entirely consistent with the First Amendment to ask trustees of the public
airwaves to pursue reasonable, viewpoint-neutral measures designed to increase
the likelihood that children will grow into adults capable of fully participating in
our deliberative democracy.

155. Such a requirement also is supported by the Supreme Court's decision in FCC v. Pacifica Foundation, 438 U.S. 726 (1978). In that case the
Court recognized that "broadcasting is uniquely accessible to children" and
that "the broadcast media have established a uniquely pervasive presence in
the lives of all Americans." *Id.* at 748, 749–750. Both of those factors sup-

port Congress' decision to require broadcasters to serve the educational needs of children. Television has an influence on children in our society rivalled only by family and school. It would be accurate to blend the two factors noted in *Pacifica* and conclude that television has a pervasive presence in the lives of American children. The Court in *Pacifica* upheld restrictions on the broadcast of indecent material. As stated above, the government's interest in the intellectual development of our nation's children is at least as significant as its interest in protecting them from exposure to indecent material, an interest the Supreme Court "has often found compelling." Denver Area Educational Telecommunications Consortium v. FCC, 116 S. Ct. 2374, 2385, 2387 (1996).

156. *Pacifica* upheld a complete ban on a particular type of programming (indecent programming) during hours when children are likely to be in the audience. The measures we adopt today do not ban programming of any type, they simply notify broadcasters that compliance with the CTA can be achieved with, on average, less than half an hour a day of programming expressing any viewpoint on any topic that broadcasters desire.

Notes and Questions

1. Reversal of Course. With adoption of the 1996 *Report and Order*, the FCC—with some prodding from Congress—had now come full circle. What factor(s) account for the switch in policy? As we asked at the start of this section, can the Commission's changes in policy be explained simply on the grounds that it learned a great deal from its early attempts at regulation and acted later to correct those early errors? Or are these policies more fundamentally inconsistent?

2. Careful Looks. In reviewing the various "kid-vid" proceedings, it is helpful to consider the variety of specific policies that are proposed and debated. What seems to determine whether a policy is considered seriously or brushed aside? Does the Commission overlook any policy angles that might have proven fruitful upon further consideration?

3. Defining Children's Television. What do advocates of regulation mean by "children's programming"? Is it television that children watch? Television that is targeted for children? Television that children should watch? Does the Commission adopt a consistent, complete definition of this term? Does it need to in order to regulate, or is that itself one of the issues being debated in these proceedings?

4. Why Intervene? What is the basic rationale for government intervention? That government should see to it that young children spend more time watching TV? Is the rationale based on the assertion that the television marketplace has failed or that the entire economic and political system has failed? Is the claim that TV uniquely underserves children or that all of society undervalues youngsters' needs and that television is an appropriate or easily available candidate for reform?

5. Children of Different Ages. Recall that, in *ACT III*, the D.C. Circuit did not distinguish teenagers from younger children for purposes of approving the regulations at issue there. Is that consistent with the FCC's emphasis in the 1996 Children's Television rules (see, for example, ¶31) on the different interests and resulting market segmentation of children based on their age? How might you argue that they are consistent?

6. Taxation by Regulation. Why did Congress choose to pursue its educational goals by empowering the FCC to regulate licensees instead of taking a more direct approach, for example taxing broadcasters and using those revenues to pay for the production and distribution of high-quality children's programming? That is, doesn't the current approach in essence operate as a tax on broadcasters, causing them to forfeit the opportunity to engage in their preferred (more profitable) broadcasts and instead air children's television? Why does this make sense? Wouldn't broadcasters be just as happy to buy their way out of this requirement, perhaps airing NBA games and then splitting the revenues with the U.S. Department of Education which could then, in turn, use those monies both to produce quality children's programming and to purchase time on local stations? Indeed, wouldn't such an approach be better for all parties concerned? Surely the U.S. Department of Education can develop better educational content than can some unwilling broadcaster. Further, a tax-and-spend approach would make all the relevant policy choices more explicit, perhaps forcing Congress to consider even better options—like spending all this money on teacher salaries instead of regularly scheduled "educational" cartoons.

As a general matter, the phrase taxation by regulation refers to any situation where the government imposes a financial burden on a regulated party not directly, but instead by requiring a particular unprofitable behavior. The phrase is designed to remind policymakers to consider the explicit alternative—namely, actually taxing the regulated parties in that same amount and then using those monies to further the policy goal at issue. There are myriad examples of taxation by regulation in this book. An important question to consider throughout your study of telecommunications, then, is whether taxation by regulation is a particularly efficient manner of governing in the public interest or, rather, an inefficient option that cases like *Red Lion* unfortunately make easily available to regulators.

7. The 1990 Children's Television Act. The 1990 Children's Television Act is a particularly interesting case study in taxation by regulation since the statute expressly permits stations to buy their way out of certain burdens that they would otherwise bear. Specifically, as implemented in the 1996 *Report and Order*, the Act allows a licensee to receive credit for sponsoring children's programming on another station. Such sponsorship cannot, however, fully "relieve a broadcaster of the obligation to air programming specifically designed to serve the educational and informational needs of children." ¶138. What assumptions about television viewing are reflected in this refusal to allow sponsorship to discharge fully a licensee's kid-vid obligations? If licensees were allowed to discharge all their kid-vid obligations by sponsoring programs on other stations, whose interests would be served? Whose sacrificed?

8. Regulation by Raised Eyebrow. The 1996 *Report and Order* also nicely illustrates the phenomenon of regulation by raised eyebrow, a concept first introduced in Chapter Four. When regulating by raised eyebrow, a regulatory agency announces that it would be pleased if the regulated firm does so-and-so but that the firm is not legally required to do it. The firm, of course, ignores such "advice" at its peril, but at the same time has no apparent basis on which to contest the legality of the agency's announcement since no particular legal penalty attaches to a firm's decision not to comply. Consider, in this regard, ¶22 of the FCC's 1991 *Report and Order*. How would you advise a licensee that was inclined not to follow the "assessment criteria" set out there? Processing guidelines, such as those adopted in the 1996 *Report and Order*, are of course classic "raised eyebrow" approaches. The agency simply announces that licensees who follow the recommended guidelines will breeze through come renewal time, whereas licensees that ignore the guidelines will be subject to full Commission review. Any guesses as to how many licensees opt for full Commission review?

9. The First Amendment. Does the "raised eyebrow" argument dispose of a First Amendment objection to the 1996 rules? Are you persuaded by the Commission's response to the argument that its rules violate the Constitution? Would all of the Commission's arguments apply as well to the imposition of comparable rules on any other medium of expression? Or is the Commission repudiating not only the policy conclusions of its 1983 children's television report, but also the conclusion in its 1985 Fairness Doctrine Report and 1987 *Syracuse Peace Council* Order that television is not a unique medium for constitutional purposes?

Note, too, that the FCC's constitutional argument (in Part VII of the 1996 *Report and Order*) appears wholly divorced from the content of its rules. Part VII appears to describe vague processing guidelines designed to encourage licensees to serve the needs of children. But the rules in fact micromanage the programming process to an unprecedented degree, providing at least six conditions that must be met before a program is a "core" program for purposes of the rules. And this micromanagement takes place in every television market, for every television station, regardless of the number of stations or children's program networks in the market. Suppose the Commission sought to publish a document that justified the constitutionality of the rules which the agency in fact promulgated. This would require, for example, explaining why a highly informative program that is not part of a regularly scheduled series or is twenty-five minutes long is officially disfavored. How might the Commission argue that such rules do not abridge the freedom of speech?

10. The Economics of Children's Educational Programming. Consider the Commission's arguments in its 1996 *Report and Order* concerning the economics of children's educational television programming. *See* ¶¶29–34. If what is said there is accurate, what accounts for the fact that bookstores routinely carry substantial quantities of books geared specifically at "the educational and informational needs of children" and that both PBS and certain cable television networks carry programming of the same sort? Is the Commission's point that none of these other services or media are supported by advertisers? Does the Commission mean to assert that Americans have a right to advertiser-supported television *and* that the exercise of this right also entitles the FCC to enact content regulations that the First Amendment would otherwise forbid? Were a conventional television broadcast station to shift from "free" to "pay" status by scrambling its signal — a shift forbidden by neither law nor technology — would it then be able to argue successfully that the 1996 rules cannot be constitutionally applied to that station?

11. Evaluating Commission Policies. How will members of the Commission judge whether the 1996 rules achieve their purposes? By asking whether children are spending more time watching television? By asking whether children have shifted their viewing patterns from "Sesame Street" to more expensive educational fare produced by commercial networks? By studying whether preschoolers engage in more "imaginative play"? ¶9. Why did Congress assign to the FCC the task of enhancing the imaginative play of three year olds?

V. COMMERCIALIZATION, ASCERTAINMENT, AND OTHER COMMISSION RULES

As we discussed in Chapter Four, the FCC once regulated many aspects of a broadcast licensee's programming performance in addition to the areas covered thus far in the chapter. As we also noted in Chapter Four, the FCC has eliminated almost all of these additional regulations. The *Order* that eliminated many of these detailed performance regulations is excerpted below. The regulations included: guidelines for local, news, and public affairs programs (described in ¶5, below); detailed supervision of the manner in which licensees ascertained the needs and interests of their listening communities (¶45); guidelines limiting the acceptable number of commercials per hour (¶56); and a requirement that stations keep a log of all programs broadcast (¶68). The *Report and Order* thus both describes a previous regime of close regulatory supervision and provides the FCC's rationale for terminating that approach.

IN RE DEREGULATION OF COMMERCIAL TELEVISION
Report and Order, 98 FCC 2d 1076 (1984)

2. We find that market incentives will ensure the presentation of programming that responds to community needs and provide sufficient incentives for licensees to become and remain aware of the needs and problems of their communities. Moreover, we are convinced that these forces will continue to hold levels of commercialization below our existing guidelines. Given these economic and policy conclusions, we no longer believe it appropriate to routinely review the programming, the levels of commercialization, and the formal ascertainment practices of television licensees in the uncontested renewal context.

3. Our action here does not constitute a retreat from our concern with the programming performance of television station licensees. Thus, we are retaining the obligation of licensees to provide programming that responds to issues of concern to the community. A quarterly issues/programs list will provide the public and the Commission with the information needed to monitor licensees' performance under this new regulatory scheme and thus permit us to evaluate the impact of our decision. Existing procedures such as citizen complaints and petitions to deny will continue to function as important tools in this regard.

A. Program Guidelines

5. The guidelines which we are eliminating today originated as informal directions to the staff concerning the routine processing of television renewal applications. The directions indicated which otherwise uncontested applications should be referred to the full Commission for disposition and included both quantitative programming and commercialization standards. The current programming criteria were adopted in 1976 and require Commission action on any commercial television station renewal application reflecting less than five percent local programming, five percent informational programming (news and public affairs) or ten percent total non-entertainment programming.

Need for the Guidelines

10. *Existing Market Performance.* Overall station data indicate that during the six year period from 1973 to 1979, commercial television broadcasters allocated an average of 13.7 percent, 10.3 percent, and 24.3 percent of their broadcast time to informational (news and public affairs), local, and overall non-entertainment programming respectively. These programming levels far exceed our present guidelines in every program category.

11. Moreover, the record indicates that there has been a trend toward increasing amounts of total non-entertainment programming on television. In 1973, commercial television stations devoted 22.6 percent of their time to this program category. By 1979, this amount had risen to 26.1 percent. A similar trend exists for informational programming. In 1973, 13.3 percent of television broadcast time was devoted to informational programming. By 1980, commercial television stations devoted 15.26 percent of their time to informational programming, more than three times the level set by the guidelines.

15. Moreover, in evaluating the above data, it is important to note that the figures cited are percentage averages. They do not, therefore, reflect the significant increase in the absolute supply of programming in the relevant categories resulting from the substantial growth in the number of television stations over time. Since 1973, for example, the number of operating television facilities has increased by approximately 25 percent.

16. Independent UHF stations were subject to the programming guidelines when they were first enacted in 1973. In 1976, however, the Commission exempted UHF independents from the program processing guidelines. An examination of the programming performance for these exempted UHF stations reveals that elimination of the programming guidelines had no material effect on the amount of informational, local and non-entertainment programs broadcast. Prior to the exemption, the average amount of time devoted to informational, local and total non-entertainment programming amounted to 7.9 percent, 14.5 percent, and 22 percent respectively, whereas programming for the three years after the exemption amounted to 8.2 percent, 13.4 percent and 32.9 percent for the same program categories.

18. Finally, our conclusion that television stations' program performance is dictated by market incentives and is essentially independent of our processing guidelines is supported by a third analysis conducted by our own staff concerning programming behavior of commercial television stations during 1980. The study examined the impact of the guidelines on the presentation of informational (news and public affairs) and local programming by comparing the programming performance of exempted UHF independents to all other commercial television stations. Through the use of multivariate regression analysis, the study was able to control for various factors that may influence program performance such as market size, number of competing stations in a local market, number of competing stations, network affiliation, station revenue, and VHF/UHF status. By controlling these variables, the study was able to isolate the impact of the guidelines on the levels of programming. The study found that with respect to local programming, approximately 2 percentage points of the overall non-exempt station average seems attributable to the guidelines. Thus, even in a worst case situation elimination of the guidelines would result in an overall level of station perfor-

mance above the existing standard for local programming. Moreover, the guidelines appear to have no impact on the levels of informational (news and public affairs) programming. Accordingly, it would appear that, absent the current guidelines, overall station performance for informational programming would remain at approximately 15 percent, fully three times the level required by current processing standards.

19. In summary, these three studies provide convincing evidence that existing marketplace forces, not our guidelines, are the primary determinants of the levels of informational, local and overall non-entertainment programming provided on commercial television. It appears, moreover, that these forces have consistently elicited a level of such programming well above the amounts arbitrarily set by our processing criteria.

20. *Future Market Incentives.* We are confident, as well, that the market demand for informational, local, and non-entertainment programming will continue to be met as the video marketplace evolves. Many new video technologies such as Subscription Television (STV), Multipoint Distribution Service (MDS), Satellite Master Antenna Television (SMATV), Low Power Television (LPTV), Direct Broadcast Satellite (DBS), Multi-Channel MDS (MMDS), and Instructional Television Fixed Service Stations (ITFS) have begun, or are just beginning, to assert themselves in the marketplace.

21. The emergence of these new technologies, coupled with the continued growth in the number of television stations, will create an economic environment that is even more competitive than the existing marketplace. Given the market-based demand for these types of programming evidenced by our studies of past broadcast performance, this increased level of competition can, in our view, only further ensure the presentation of sufficient amounts of such programming.

22. We note, however, that there may be individual stations that are not meeting the guidelines with respect to all of the programming categories. We do not believe that such an occurrence is inconsistent with the public interest since the overall data demonstrate that, on average, stations are performing well above the guidelines. It appears, therefore, that the failure of some stations to provide programming in some categories is being offset by the compensatory performance of other stations. In this respect, market demand is determining the appropriate mix of each licensee's programming. For example, a licensee may find it competitively appropriate to emphasize one type of programming within the guidelines rather than presenting programming in all categories. At the same time, other stations in the market may elect to present other types of programming. The net result of this shifting in the programming mix is that overall performance will exceed the guidelines even though individual stations are not presenting required amounts in all program categories.

23. We believe that licensees should be given this flexibility to respond to the realities of the marketplace by allowing them to alter the mix of their programming consistent with market demand. Such an approach not only permits more efficient competition among stations, but poses no real risk to the availability of these types of programming on a market basis. This is particularly true in view of the continuing obligation of all licensees to contribute issue-responsive programming and their responsibility to ensure that the strongly felt needs of all significant segments of their communities are met by market stations collectively.

Disadvantages of the Current Programming Guidelines

25. At the outset, we note that to the extent current levels of programming exceed regulatory standards the guidelines are simply no longer necessary. In this respect, we note that the Court of Appeals has held that regulations, originally adopted to correct a specific problem, may be capricious if the underlying problem no longer exists.

26. Second, we note that the existing guidelines impose administrative costs on licensees. The compliance costs associated with these guidelines with respect to formalized ascertainment and program logging requirements are not market dictated. To the extent that these rules are not necessary to meet our regulatory objectives, we conclude that the costs incident to technical compliance and record keeping are inappropriate.

27. Third, we find that the present regulatory structure raises potential First Amendment concerns. Congress intended private broadcasting to develop with the widest journalistic freedom consistent with its public interest obligation. These concerns with the First Amendment are exacerbated by the lack of a direct nexus between a quantitative approach and licensee performance.

28. To the extent that existing levels of programming are market-dictated, then it may be argued that the overall intrusive nature of the guidelines is not pervasive. This does not mean, however, that there is no current infringement on the editorial discretion of individual broadcasters. For example, each licensee must still monitor its performance in light of this government-imposed standard. Further, the continued existence of the programming guidelines in the context of an evolving video services marketplace could conceivably constitute an unacceptable general level of infringement at some future time.

29. The Commission's traditional policy objectives with respect to programming have never been fulfilled by the presentation of mere quantities of specific programming. Instead, a licensee's programming obligation has always been described in terms of providing programming that responds to the needs of the community. By restating the programming obligation in uncontested renewal proceedings in terms of issue-responsive programming, we are providing broadcasters with a more appropriate description of their programming obligation.

Licensee's Obligations

32. A commercial television broadcaster will remain subject to an obligation to provide programming that is responsive to the issues confronting its community. Moreover, licensees can be expected to demonstrate their compliance with this requirement by using the issues/programs list as discussed below.

33. Moreover, licensees will also have the freedom to decide what amounts of such programming will be offered. Stations should continue to be guided by the needs of the community and their reasonable good faith discretion in selecting issues to be covered and appropriate programming responsive to those issues.[85]

---

85. Of course, broadcasters cannot engage in intentional discrimination in the selection of issues to be addressed in their programming. [Footnote relocated].

34. The significance of our new regulatory scheme lies not only in its impact on the programming behavior of licensees in today's video marketplace, but also in its flexibility in accommodating the natural economic incentives of the developing video marketplace. For example, as the number of video outlets increases, a television licensee may, in response to economic incentives, begin to direct its programming towards a narrower audience. Unlike the existing guidelines, the new regulatory approach fosters this development by allowing the licensee to consider the programming of other television stations in its market in fulfilling its programming responsibilities.[86]

36. *Renewal Standard.* The basic renewal standard will continue to consist of an obligation that a licensee, during its prior license term, addressed community issues with responsive programming and complied with all other legal requirements. A licensee need only have addressed community issues with whatever types of programming, that in its reasonably exercised discretion, it determined was appropriate to those issues. With respect to uncontested applications, our determination With respect to uncontested applications, our determination in this proceeding permits us to make the renewal judgment called for by §309 of the Communications Act of 1934, as amended, on a presumption of compliance with this standard. Accordingly, we will no longer routinely review a licensee's programming in the uncontested renewal context.

37. *Petitions to Deny.* Individual licensees remain obligated to provide programming that is responsive to the community. Therefore, programming will remain a relevant issue in proceedings arising from petitions to deny. While overall programming remains a consideration in petitions to deny, eliminating the guidelines will affect the relevancy of certain types of programming issues. Since we are not concerned with the quantity of specified program categories, arguments based solely on the failure to present amounts of non-entertainment programming will not be appropriate. Petitioners raising programming issues will have to demonstrate that an individual station is failing to address issues facing the community in its programming. Moreover, we believe the obligation of a licensee in this context is to contribute to the overall information flow in its market. Thus, while this obligation is not negated by the existence of other issue-responsive programming in the market, it may be affected by the amounts and types of programming provided by other television broadcasters. The basic responsibility to contribute to the overall discussion of issues confronting the community is a nondelegable duty for which each licensee will be held individually accountable.

38. Similarly, petitioners may make allegations in a petition to deny that an individual station has failed to address issues of particular relevance to a significant segment of the community. Such a petition may be brought even in cases where a licensee has provided some issue-responsive programming. We believe that a station confronted with this type of petition to deny should be able to respond by pointing not only to its own programming that may have addressed such issue, but also to other television stations available in the community that could reasonably have been relied upon to address such issues.[87]

---

86. In this context, the term "television stations" includes both commercial and noncommercial television stations.

87. Under existing regulations licensees cannot look to other stations in determining which issues to address. Allowing licensees to look to other television stations in determin-

B. Ascertainment

45. Currently, applicants for television licenses, and those seeking renewal of existing licenses, are required to follow specific ascertainment procedures set forth in the Primer and Renewal Primer. Specific standards are established for determining the composition of the area to be served, consultation with community leaders and members of the general public, enumerating of community problems and needs, evaluation of the problems and needs, and relating proposed programming to the evaluated problems and needs. In addition, those seeking renewal must maintain an ongoing ascertainment process during their license terms, possess a community leader checklist, maintain information on the composition of the community in the public file, place documentation of ascertainment procedures in the station public inspection file, and annually file a list of not more than ten problems and needs of the station's service area along with a list of programs treating those problems and needs.

47. We believe that the public interest no longer requires adherence to ascertainment procedures.

48. Ascertainment procedures were never intended to be an end in and of themselves. Rather, these procedures were intended as a means of ensuring that licensees actively discovered the problems, needs and issues facing their communities, thereby positively influencing the programming performance of stations by affecting the process of program decision-making. Yet, we have no evidence that these procedures have had such an effect.

49. Commercial necessity dictates that the broadcaster must remain aware of the issues of the community or run the risk of losing its audience.

51. The costs of ascertainment are numerous. The Commission estimates that elimination of ascertainment requirements will result in annual savings of 66,956 work hours to the industry and 761.5 work hours to the Commission.

52. The Commission has previously characterized its experience with ascertainment in the adversarial arena as "litigation over trivia." As we observed in the Notice, the Pike and Fisher Radio Regulation Digest currently contains over sixty pages of ascertainment annotations, most relating to mechanistic aspects of the process. Furthermore, ascertainment hearings unnecessarily delay service to the public. Even without actual litigation, it is clear that substantial resources are expended to make certain that a formalistic challenge is avoided.[88]

54. We do not believe that the benefits of the ascertainment requirements justify the costs of this procedure. Accordingly, in all future proceedings, the focus of our inquiry shall be upon the responsiveness of a licensee's programming, not the methodology utilized to arrive at those programming decisions.

---

ing which issues to address, coupled with the responsibility to contribute issue-responsive programming, may increase the absolute number of issues receiving coverage on television. However, we recognize that significant cross-market diversity benefits may not be fully realized until video markets mature and move towards a narrowcasting model.

88. Counsel must be consulted to assure that formalities have been satisfied. Many of the commenters noted that a major savings from the elimination of formal ascertainment would be a reduction in attorney's fees.

C. Commercial Guidelines

55. The Commission's concern with commercial practices has been shaped by two primary considerations: the desire to prevent the abuse of scarce broadcast resources through excessive commercialization, and a reluctance to adopt rigid quantitative standards.

56. The commercial standard at issue herein is contained in section 0.283(a)(7) of our rules. Under this rule, the authority to review proposed levels of commercialization in new applications, renewals or transfers, is delegated to the Mass Media Bureau, except in the case of "commercial TV applicants for a new station, or assignment or transfer, or renewal of license, proposing to exceed 16 minutes of commercial matter per hour." Those applications which propose to exceed this guideline must be reviewed by the Commission.

58. The record in this proceeding provides convincing evidence that marketplace forces can better determine appropriate commercial levels than our own rules. In addition, such reliance provides a significantly less intrusive and less expensive alternative than our current regulatory scheme. Based on our decision today, the above-noted commercial guideline is herein eliminated. The Commission will no longer consider levels of commercialization in the processing of license applications. Furthermore, we will no longer entertain petitions to deny based on allegations of overcommercialization. Finally, we will rescind our policy banning program length commercials.

Market Incentives

59. The Notice in this proceeding included an analysis of the number of commercial minutes aired on commercial television stations in three states during a recent license renewal period. The data showed that network affiliates averaged 10.87 minutes of commercial matter per hour when the entire broadcast day was considered. The Notice also found that 99.67 percent of all broadcast hours studied were within the guideline. The data convincingly demonstrate that marketplace forces, and not the guideline, are the decisive factor in determining appropriate levels of commercialization for commercial television stations.

Burdens of Existing Regulation

60. Based on the foregoing evidence, we can no longer continue to justify either the direct costs imposed by adherence to the commercial guideline—the paperwork burden of record keeping, reviewing and monitoring—or its more indirect costs such as possible anti-competitive effects or stifling commercial experimentation and intrusion into the realm of commercial speech protected by the First Amendment.

61. The direct burdens imposed by the guideline are straightforward and do not require further illumination herein. However, we believe that closer examination of the indirect costs of our guideline will help to clarify our actions today.

62. *Competitive Effect.* A significant danger posed by our commercial guideline is that it may impede the ability of commercial television stations to present innovative and detailed commercials. Our regulation may also interfere with the natural growth and development of broadcast television as it attempts to compete with future video market entrants.

63. *First Amendment Concerns.* We are concerned about becoming involved in the regulation of program content and of the attendant potential chilling effect on commercial speech which the guideline might exert.

Other Considerations

66. Several commenters objected that market forces will not be adequate to control over-commercialization because of the fractured economic relationship between the licensee and its audience. Suggesting that licensees in fact market their product primarily to advertisers rather than audiences, these parties suggested that elimination of the guideline would increase commercial loading and ultimately result in greater advertiser control over programming. As noted, however, the record does not support the assumption that elimination of the guidelines will lead to increased commercial loading. Moreover, to the extent the concerns raised by these commenters are directed to the fundamental, advertiser supported nature of commercial television, we would readily concede that the advertiser supported nature of the medium has some effect on program content. Again, however, there is no concrete evidence that elimination of the commercial guideline will lead to an increase in the programming power of advertisers to the detriment of the public interest.

67. In sum, it seems clear to us that if stations exceed the tolerance level of viewers by adding "too many" commercials the market will regulate itself, *i.e.*, the viewers will not watch and the advertisers will not buy time.

D. Program Logs

68. Since the beginning of broadcast regulation, some type of program logging requirements have existed. Under present rules, the Commission requires television broadcasters to maintain a contemporaneous listing of all programs broadcast. The program type and source must also be set forth. Program logs must be maintained for a period of two years. Television licensees are required to make these logs available for public inspection if the requester of the information meets certain procedural safeguards.

69. According to a 1978 GAO report, the Commission's logging requirements constituted the largest government burden on business in terms of total burden hours. According to calculations made by Commission staff the burden imposed on commercial television licensees by our program log requirements exceeds 2,468,000 hours per year.

71. We have concluded that the best method of documentation suitable and adequate to our new regulatory scheme for television broadcasting is a quarterly issues/programs list requirement. This list is to be placed in a station's public inspection file and it should contain, in narrative form, a brief description of at least five to ten issues to which the licensee gave particular attention with programming in the past three months with a statement of how each issue was treated. The list also is to include information pertaining to the date and time of broadcast and the duration of listed programming.

77. In the context of a routine license renewal, the existence of the issues/programs list in the station's public file will give the Commission sufficient assurance that the station has met its issue-responsive programming responsibility during the past license term to grant license renewal on that issue. In a con-

tested license renewal the burden of proving that programming relevant to public issues has been provided is on the licensee.

Notes and Questions

1. A Significant Reform. Although each step of this *Report and Order* may seem minor or technical, in its totality the document reflects a deep and fundamental change in the FCC's conception of its responsibility to police the broadcast television program market. Does the evidence recounted by the Commission show that markets are working or only that stations have chosen to stay within the FCC's guidelines and, thus, avoid the expenses and risks associated with not doing so?

2. Guidelines. Note that the guidelines respecting minimum levels of non-entertainment programming and maximum levels of commercialization were just that: guidelines. A television station broke no rule by going under or over the guidelines. Was this "regulation by raised eyebrow" an appropriate response to the concerns that motivated the guidelines? Although a station broke no rule by "violating" the guidelines, it did increase its costs and risks of doing business by doing so. In this way, the processing guidelines functioned like a tax on a licensee who chose to broadcast lots of entertainment programming or commercials. (Is this a good example of taxation by regulation?)

3. The Commission's Rationale. What was the rationale behind the program guidelines? What did the guidelines presume about (a) the way (at least some) people watch television, (b) those viewers' interest in informational, local, and/or non-entertainment programming, and (c) how they will respond when informational, local, and/or non-entertainment programming comes on the station they happen to be watching?

4. Practical Ramifications. Elimination of the guidelines facilitated, among other developments, the rise of television stations largely devoted to displaying and soliciting orders for merchandise. Does the rise of these "home shopping channels" confirm the wisdom of the FCC's actions? Cast doubt upon their wisdom? Neither?

5. Market Deference. If the Commission believes that the market is adequate to protect viewers' interests in receiving non-entertainment programming and avoiding excessive commercialization, why did the FCC choose to retain an obligation for the licensee to provide programming responsive to issues of concern to the community? Is this the one aspect of quality or diverse programming in which regulation performs better than markets?

6. Stations or Markets? Is the Commission's focus on the entire group of stations in a market, and its willingness to allow some individual stations to fail to meet its program guidelines (*see* ¶¶22–23), consistent with the approach that Congress and the Commission have taken toward each broadcaster's obligations with respect to children's television? If a programming regulation is appropriate only when that regulation works better and more cheaply than the market, and if any programming obligations are borne collectively by the stations in the market, then what if anything remains of the notion that each broadcaster individually has a public trustee responsibility?

CHAPTER SEVEN

FOSTERING COMPETITION IN BROADCASTING

The purpose of this chapter is:

- to consider structural regulations that affect the relationship between the major networks (ABC, CBS, NBC, Fox) and their affiliates;

- to likewise consider structural regulations that affect the relationship between networks and independent program suppliers; and

- to consider structural regulations that limit concentration in the broadcast industry and in telecommunications markets more generally.

～

When it comes to regulating broadcast, in recent years the FCC has been increasingly reluctant to get involved—the Commission's logic being that, even given the various imperfections in the broadcast marketplace discussed in Chapter Two, in most cases competitive forces outperform regulatory oversight when it comes to serving listener and viewer tastes. Thus, we saw in Chapter Three, for example, how the FCC has grown increasingly more willing to define the band plan in flexible ways such that market forces can have significant influence over what services use what spectrum; and we saw in Chapter Five how auctions have now displaced regulatory hearings as the preferred mechanism for assigning licenses. Even the public trustee obligations introduced last chapter are, today, a shadow of their former selves, the argument again being that competition disciplines broadcasters sufficiently—or, at least, that competition disciplines broadcasters well enough that it is not worth introducing regulation and its attendant risks, harms, and complexities.

That said, the question remains as to whether the FCC should continue to regulate in ways that might make competition more robust. For example, should the FCC regulate the behavior of the major television networks, the fear being that, in the absence of regulation, the major networks would "dominate" the broadcast industry and be able to dictate terms both to their affiliates and to content providers? Similarly, should the FCC limit the number of broadcast licenses any one entity may own, the worry here being the similar concern that if any one party controls too many media outlets, that party might be able to exert too much influence over the marketplace overall?

In this chapter, we consider questions along these lines, asking whether and how the FCC should address concerns about concentration in the broadcast industry. The first section looks at FCC rules designed to regulate the behavior of the major commercial television networks, namely ABC, NBC, CBS and Fox. The second section examines two types of rules designed to limit concentration more generally: (1) rules that limit how many properties of the same type (say, AM radio stations) a given party can own or control; and (2) rules that limit how many properties of different types (say, FM radio stations and broadcast television stations) a given party can own or control.

One puzzle to keep in mind while reading this material is the question of why the FCC is in the business of structuring the market like this at all. Market structure is traditionally the domain of antitrust law, and antitrust law is typically enforced (at the federal level) by the Department of Justice and the Federal Trade Commission. Is there any reason why there should be a particularized form of antitrust law that applies only to broadcasters and is administered by the FCC? Even though broadcast licensees are fully subject to federal antitrust law[1] and so any collusive or exclusionary practices can be policed under that law of more general applicability?

I. THE TELEVISION NETWORKS

A. Network Dominance

When Americans watch television, they often watch broadcast networks. During the 1950s, '60s, and '70s, television viewership was confined almost exclusively to the three original commercial television networks (ABC, CBS, and NBC) and to a lesser extent the noncommercial television network (PBS). The growth of UHF and cable television in later years increased viewing options, yet, even by the year 2000, over 50% of all television viewing hours were still spent watching ABC, CBS, NBC, or Fox.[2] Consequently, once spectrum allocation and assignment policies are in place, FCC policies toward network structure and behavior become some of the most important determinants of the extent of competition in the television broadcast industry. The following excerpt (importantly, written when there were only three major commercial television networks) explains why networks have been so influential and how FCC policies have shaped the structure of the television network industry.

---

1. *See* United States v. RCA, 358 U.S. 334 (1959); NBC v. United States, 319 U.S. 190, 223 (1943) ("The prohibitions of the Sherman Act apply to broadcasting.").

2. In the Matter of Annual Assessment of the Status of Competition in Markets for the Delivery of Video Programming, Sixth Annual Report, January 14, 2000, at ¶15 ("While audience levels have declined in the last year, the four major television broadcast networks still account for a 52% share of prime time television viewing for all television households."); *see also* Commission Adopts Sixth Annual Report on Competition in Video Markets, 2000 FCC LEXIS 197, at *15 (January 14, 2000) (same quotation).

MISREGULATING TELEVISION

Stanley M. Besen, Thomas G. Krattenmaker,
A. Richard Metzger, & John R. Woodbury[3]
(excerpt from pages 1–2, 4–19 (1984))

1. Introduction: Economic Regulation of Commercial Television Networks

Virtually from its inception in 1934, the FCC has been bedeviled by the issue of network dominance. This issue is frequently expressed as a concern that a few—usually three—corporations dictate the terms on which the business of broadcast home entertainment is conducted and reap the lion's share of profits from the broadcasting industry. During much of the first decade of the FCC's existence, the specific fear was that two firms operating three radio networks had monopolized the business of networking and dominated the programming selections of Commission licensees. In the 1950s, as television became the more popular and profitable medium, the Commission noted with dread the emergence of three dominant television networks: ABC, CBS, and NBC. Consequently, between 1955 and 1970, the FCC conducted an almost uninterrupted series of studies of the phenomenon of television network dominance. At the end of this period, the Code of Federal Regulations contained at least a dozen FCC rules limiting the business dealings between the commercial television networks and their affiliated broadcast stations and program suppliers.

Despite three decades of relentless federal scrutiny, ABC, CBS, and NBC still "dominate" television, notwithstanding the Federal Communications Commission's view, held for over forty years, that such dominance can and should be restrained by limiting or dictating the networks' commercial practices.

2. Network Dominance

Measures of Network Dominance. Although the phrase "network dominance" is sufficiently elastic to encompass a wide variety of specific meanings, by any definition it exists. ABC, CBS, and NBC do indeed "dominate" the television broadcasting industry and form funnels through which most of our television programs flow. For the month of December, 1983, ABC, CBS, and NBC captured 80 percent of the prime-time television viewing audience. In calendar year 1980 these firms, along with network-owned stations and affiliated stations, accounted for about 90 percent of both the revenues and profits of the television broadcasting industry.

Independent commercial television stations (*i.e.*, those not affiliated with ABC, CBS, or NBC) do exist, but these stations are not independent by choice;

---

3. The four authors of this excerpt were all in one way or another involved in formulating the FCC policies that they here analyze. Tom Krattenmaker was the co-director of the FCC's Network Inquiry Special Staff, a unit created by the Commission in 1978 to study the economic structure and commercial practices of the television networks. Stanley M. Besen was the co-director of the Network Inquiry, whose final reports were issued in 1980. A. Richard Metzger, Jr. and John R. Woodbury were, respectively, senior counsel and senior economist on the Network Inquiry staff.

they broadcast exclusively in markets already served by affiliates of each network. Despite diligent searches, we have been unable to locate a single instance in the past twenty-five years when any commercial television station rejected an ABC, CBS, or NBC affiliation offer in order to remain independent or to affiliate with a fourth network. Similarly, firms that produce programs for television regard ABC, CBS, and NBC as a separate market; with few exceptions, they do not at present believe that programs of the sort that the dominant networks acquire can be produced for and sold station-by-station in the syndication market or developed for networks composed of cable television systems or other local outlets employing new technologies, although this is likely to change as cable penetration increases. No firm other than ABC, CBS, or NBC can presently offer an advertiser the opportunity, in one transaction, to gain commercial positions in every part of the broadcast day and on every day in the broadcast week in programs offered to virtually all U.S. television households.

Why Networks are Dominant. Television networks arise because of the interplay between physics and economics. The physical properties of broadcast television signals limit their range; consequently, no single terrestrial television transmitter can reach as much as 10 percent of the U.S. populace today. To provide television service to the entire nation via broadcast stations that utilize the airwaves, then, television signal transmitters (television stations) must be placed throughout the country. That is, the laws of physics dictate that if over-the-air television service is to be earthbound, it must also be provided locally or regionally.

Economic principles, however, pull in the opposite direction. A television program is what economists term a "public good"; its broadcast to one viewer does not reduce its availability or utility to other viewers. A program produced for and transmitted in New York can be broadcast also in Los Angeles at no additional expense aside from the costs of getting the program across the country and operating an additional transmitting tower.

In a nutshell, then, what networks do is to offer physically separated local television stations the economies of scale associated with television program production. By supplying identical programs to many stations, networks both increase the financial base available to fund program production, enabling more expensive programs to be produced, and reduce the per-viewer cost of producing and distributing any given program.

These elementary and unalterable principles explain why nationally distributed television programming will usually have greater viewer appeal than programs produced and aired only locally. The former can cater more lavishly to viewer tastes, yet at a lower cost per viewer than the latter. Nationally distributed programs will not always win out, of course. Viewer tastes may vary from place to place; hence the prevalence of locally produced television news programs. The producer of a program may derive other revenues from producing it, so that large amounts can be spent on production even if exhibition rights are not sold on a national basis. For example, both the existence of gate receipts and variations in tastes among localities probably explain why many professional sports events are telecast regionally or locally rather than nationally.

Economics of Full-Scale Networking. Such exceptions limit, but do not undermine, the principle that nationally disseminated programming will usually be more valuable to viewers, advertisers, and stations than local shows. This principle, however, explains only why national programs are prevalent; it does not explain why every mass distributed program or program series is not distributed by a separate network. ABC, CBS, and NBC are dominant not because they are successful networks, but because they successfully operate full-scale networks, offering programs every day of the week throughout most of the broadcast day.

At least a partial answer to this question is that the economies yielded by networking are not exhausted in the provision of a single program. First, the existence of a full-scale network permits advertisers, in a single transaction, to purchase time on many stations and within diverse programs, and assures them that each ad will appear at the same time in each market. Such a purchasing scheme is obviously less costly than negotiating contracts with each station individually and also makes it easier for the advertiser to predict the audience it will reach. Second, full-scale operation permits the network and a station to negotiate a single contract that covers the processes of offer and acceptance, as well as the amount and manner of compensation, for many programs, thus holding program acquisition and distribution costs below what they would be if networks offered service on a program-by-program and station-by-station basis. Third, a network that provides a schedule of programs can spread the risk of program failure and thus predict more accurately its rate of success than can a network offering only a single program. Because at present the networks finance a substantial portion of the cost of program development, spreading the risk across a large number of programs is a considerable advantage.

Of course, the economies of full-scale networking are not limitless. Indeed, no network offers programs every hour of every day. Variations in local tastes, limits on the amount national advertisers wish to spend on network television, FCC rules on network-affiliate agreements, and bargaining between networks and their affiliated stations over the distribution of profits from broadcasting are some of the factors that work to limit the length of network schedules.

Size vs. Fewness: The Central Issue. Governmental regulation of network organization and behavior would be senseless if such regulation were intended simply to prohibit networking or full-scale networks. At best, regulation of that aspect of network dominance can produce only equivalent programming at higher costs. The question, therefore, that must be addressed in considering the appropriate method of regulating network commercial practices is not why networks are important to the broadcast industry, or why full-scale networks enjoy such competitive success, but rather why the number of effective competing networks is so low.

3. Why So Few Networks Exist

A series of FCC policies effectively blockaded new network entry at least until the mid-1970s, after which many of these policies were abandoned or were circumvented by technological developments. Three types of Commission policies have especially disadvantaged potential networks and are discussed below in ascending order of importance.

Interconnection Costs and FCC Policy. One cost of networking is the expense of interconnecting stations. Prior to the advent of satellites capable of transmitting television signals, the only method for interconnecting stations, short of making multiple copies of films or tapes of programs and distributing them through the mail, was to employ a terrestrial relay system. In the early stages of television industry growth, the FCC permitted AT&T a virtual monopoly over providing this service and, to the present day, AT&T charges substantially different rates for "full-time" and "part-time" service.

In the past decade the FCC has taken steps that reduce the interconnection disadvantage confronting new networks. With respect to terrestrial systems, the Commission has permitted firms to operate private systems that bypass the AT&T monopoly, and allowed intermediaries to purchase blocks of time and to resell that time to part-time users.

More dramatic changes have occurred because of the introduction of communications satellites. The FCC has permitted relatively open entry into the business of owning broadcast satellites, and unrestricted entry into the business of reselling satellite interconnection time. Further, in 1977 the Commission repealed its earlier rules establishing technical design requirements for devices (known as "earth stations") that receive satellite television transmissions and requiring that earth stations be licensed by the Commission.

FCC Restrictions on Program Services. The second manner in which the Commission has impeded new network entry is by limiting the kinds of services non-conventional networks may offer to the public. Until recently, the FCC substantially restricted both distant signal importation by cable television and the programs that could be offered, via broadcast or otherwise, in return for direct viewer payments (*i.e.*, so-called "pay television").

FCC Spectrum Management Policies. The third and most important set of these Commission policies that have acted as a barrier to formation of additional networks has sprung directly or indirectly from the FCC's spectrum management responsibilities. Collectively, these policies made a fourth, full-scale over-the-air network inconceivable until very recently.[4]

The FCC's basic charter, the Communications Act of 1934, gives the Commission two principal responsibilities concerning access to the electromagnetic spectrum that materially affect the number of networks and the extent of competition among them. First, the Commission is empowered to allocate the spectrum among different uses, to determine, for example, which part of the spectrum will be used for FM radio broadcasting. Second, the Commission then assigns spectrum space to specific geographic areas, deciding, for example, whether a transmitter broadcasting on a certain portion of the allocated AM radio spectrum may be based in Newark, N.J. or in New York City.

As noted above, television networks exist because of the economies that accrue from interconnecting geographically dispersed local television stations. Consequently, no action by the FCC could have a greater effect on the conditions of entry confronting television networks than its allocation and assignment decisions since these decisions affect both the number and location of broadcast stations. If, for example, the Commission had exercised its panoply of powers so as

---

4. *See* Thomas L. Schuessler, Structural Barriers to the Entry of Additional Television Networks: The Federal Communications Commission's Spectrum Management Policies, 54 S. Cal. L. Rev. 875 (1981).

to limit every U.S. household to receiving just one television signal, then one full-scale broadcast network, at most, could have emerged.

What the Commission has actually done is somewhat more complicated, although only slightly less draconian. In brief, the FCC initially exercised its spectrum allocation and assignment of powers in a manner that almost guaranteed that no more than three full-scale, advertiser-supported nationwide networks that employed conventional broadcast stations as local outlets would arise. Subsequently, the Commission utilized the same powers, as well as its ancillary jurisdiction over cable, to retard the growth of new technologies or pay TV systems that might have provided alternative bases on which to establish rival networks.

Barriers confronting potential traditional networks. Three distinct FCC spectrum management decisions embodied in a 1952 order have limited the number of conventional networks. (1) First, the Commission chose to assign only limited portions of the VHF and UHF bands to television transmission. If more bandwidth had been given to television, then more stations could have existed and perhaps provided a base for additional networks. (2) Second, to utilize the spectrum assigned to television, the Commission determined to assign, wherever possible, at least one television broadcast station to each U.S. community. In most areas of the United States distinct communities are frequently in close proximity. To avoid interference among signals, the FCC must limit the area television stations serve. But, to authorize transmitters in small communities, the Commission had to limit the number of stations assigned to larger cities. The effect was to limit the number of networks that might arise by restricting the number of available outlets that networks might use to reach large numbers of viewers. (3) Third, in most cases the Commission determined to place both VHF and UHF stations in the same market ("intermixture," in industry parlance). UHF television signals are technically inferior to VHF (poorer signal quality). For this reason, UHF stations compete under a great handicap with their VHF counterparts. Intermixture has affected the number of stations available for network affiliation because UHF stations often cannot survive in intermixed markets. The same policy also affects the nature of competition among those networks that do arise, because a network with a high percentage of UHF affiliates is handicapped in competing vigorously with a network employing primarily VHF outlets.

The interaction of the Commission's choices to limit the TV band, assign stations locally, and intermix VHF and UHF stations produced an overall national assignment plan for commercial television stations, adopted in 1952, that virtually guaranteed that no more than three full-scale, nationwide commercial networks could arise to serve conventional, over-the-air, advertiser-supported stations. The plan does not provide equally valuable outlets in enough markets to enable a fourth network to achieve sufficient economies of scale to enable it to compete on equal, or reasonably close, terms with the other three. This effect can be portrayed most easily by comparing the national coverage the dominant networks obtain with that available to potential new entrants. In 1979, stations owned by or affiliated with ABC, CBS, and NBC reached 98.1, 96.5, and 96.9 percent of U.S. television households respectively. About 13 percent of those households receiving ABC obtained ABC programming via UHF; for CBS and NBC, the figures were 7 percent and 10 percent respectively.

The FCC's table of assignments would impose a dual handicap on any potential additional network. First, such additional networks would face a coverage handicap. If all assigned commercial television frequencies were on the air, a fourth network could reach at most 91.3 percent of U.S. TV households; a fifth could reach 81.1 percent and a sixth 66.8 percent. Second, potential additional networks would face a UHF handicap because, in many markets, the newcomer's UHF affiliate would have to compete with three VHF affiliates of the incumbent networks. Again assuming that all assigned stations were operational, a fourth network could offer only 36 percent of TV households signals technically comparable to those of all three existing networks, and 41 percent of all TV households would receive a fourth network from a UHF affiliate while obtaining ABC, CBS, and NBC programs from a VHF station.

Of course, additional networks are more likely to be erected on the base of operational, rather than assigned, stations. Many stations that have been assigned are not in operation, principally because of the Commission's local assignment and intermixture policies. That is, many stations were authorized in markets too small to support them and other assignments have never been utilized because they authorize UHF stations in markets where many VHF stations also exist. Assuming that a potential new network does not bid away affiliates of the dominant three, the existing base of commercial stations available to such a network would impose severe coverage and UHF handicaps on it. Using existing stations, a fourth network in 1980 could reach at most 63.6 percent of U.S. TV households; a fifth could serve 40.8 percent and a sixth 27.8 percent. Moreover, the fourth network, completely shut out of 36 percent of all households, could also reach another 26 percent with the only UHF affiliate in the market.

Notes and Questions

1. Continued Dominance. Does it surprise you how dominant the major networks are even today? True, many viewers receive the network signals over their cable systems; but, still, these cable subscribers are watching *network* programing instead of programing made specifically for distribution by cable. Why would that be? Doesn't cable television remove most of the barriers mentioned in the excerpt?

2. The Big Four. The Fox Broadcasting Company was launched in 1987. At the start, the network programed only a few hours each week, mainly targeting young audiences and using those weaker UHF stations to carry the network's signal. By 1995, however, the upstart network had outbid CBS for the rights to broadcast football games being played under the auspices of the National Football League's National Football Conference (NFL NFC) and, thanks to a $500 million joint venture with New World Communications, had converted 12 VHF stations formerly associated with the Big Three into Fox affiliates. The conversion significantly hurt CBS (many of the stations were former CBS affiliates), although NBC and ABC also lost VHF outlets in key markets. The station shuffle continued for several years thereafter as ABC, CBS, NBC, and Fox competed to attract VHF affiliates, each trying to maintain a full network of VHF stations in all the major markets despite the increased competition for VHF outlets. Fox survived the game of musical chairs, ending up with a strong network of VHF affiliates. By the 1998/99 television season, Fox enjoyed an average primetime rating of 7.0, meaning that 7% of all television households were tuning in to watch Fox programming; ABC, CBS, and NBC enjoyed ratings during this same time period of 8.1, 9.0, and 8.9, respectively.[5]

3. The Big Seven? More recently, three other networks— Warner Brothers (WB), United Paramount Network (UPN), and Paxson (PAX)—have begun to provide significant broadcast content, although none provide a full schedule of program offerings and none draw audiences comparable to those enjoyed by the Big Four. Does the rise of these alternative networks, however, call the preceding analysis into question, or is this pattern instead consistent with the excerpt's predictions? What about the rise of Fox—consistent or surprising?

B. The Network/Affiliate Relationship

Commercial broadcast television networks and their affiliated stations enjoy a symbiotic relationship, with the networks developing nationally based programming while the affiliates provide local outlets for the distribution of that programming and also supplement those offerings with programs more tailored to local tastes. Jointly, networks and their affiliates exploit the economies of scale that full-time, nationwide networking offers.

The FCC has nevertheless long worried that affiliates need to be protected from network dominance. To that end, the Commission has promulgated several rules that restrict the terms and conditions networks may obtain in their affiliation agreements.[6] Initially, these rules were adopted for radio, a medium "dominated" by three networks in the 1930s. But the rules were extended to television networks in the early days of television and many remain in effect even today. For example, one early FCC regulation forbid stations from officially affiliating with only one network, 47 C.F.R. §73.658(a), while another required that affiliates retain a right to reject any network program, 47 C.F.R. §73.658(e).

The analysis that follows seeks to describe with more rigor and detail the economics of the network/affiliate relationship and to consider the possible effects of the Commission's various rules regulating affiliation agreements. The key conclusions are these: Networks and their affiliates have a symbiotic, not an adversarial, commercial relationship. Networks and their affiliates seek to maximize their joint profits. Occasionally, the tendency toward joint profit maximization will be undercut by one or the other party's strategic use of information, or by the costs of doing business, or by the network's desire to forestall entry by new rivals, but these will be the exceptional cases. Further, where networks and their affiliates clash, the battle will usually be over the distribution of their joint profits, rather than over what are the most efficient methods of networking or the most profitable programs.

If the above conclusions are correct, of course, then one has no choice but to ask what purpose these FCC regulations serve. Do affiliates need to be protected from their partners, the networks? Even if so, can FCC regulation accomplish that goal given the complexity of these relationships and the parties' ability to

---

5. Nielsen Media Research, 2000 Report on Television 18 (2000).
6. These rules are codified at 47 C.F.R. §73.658.

achieve their goals in a variety of practically equivalent but legally distinguishable ways? If the FCC's goal is to promote network competition, isn't the Commission more likely to succeed by concentrating on regulations that create additional local outlets for new networks rather than concentrating on regulations that affect existing affiliation relationships?

MISREGULATING TELEVISION
Stanley M. Besen, Thomas G. Krattenmaker,
A. Richard Metzger, & John R. Woodbury[7]
(excerpt from pages 50–66 (1984))

To appreciate the effects of the various Commission regulations of network affiliation contracts requires an understanding of the economics of the network/affiliate relationship. The specific examples discussed below are drawn from the actual practices of the dominant, conventional networks, but they describe a model that applies to the general phenomenon of linking a variety of scattered, local outlets in order to broadcast television programs widely.

The Organization of the Relationship

Networks exist in a vertical economic relationship to local station outlets. Networks provide programs to broadcasters, cable systems, and other local program distributors who use these programs to provide an overall program schedule to offer to advertisers or viewers or both.

The relationship between the dominant, conventional television networks and their affiliated stations can be characterized in two equivalent ways. On the one hand, the networks can be described as buying access to the time of stations, paying for this time both in cash and by permitting stations to sell spots within and between programs to advertisers. Alternatively, one can think of stations as purchasing programs from the networks, paying for these programs by permitting the networks to sell advertising time within programs and to retain a portion of the resulting revenues.

Each network acquires from independent suppliers, or produces itself, programs that the network offers to its affiliates on terms agreed to in its affiliation contract. For programs of one-half hour or less, the network usually retains control of all advertising time within programs and the stations can sell all commercial time between programs. For longer programs, the stations also have available some time within programs, usually on the hour and the half-hour. The time periods reserved for sale by affiliates are referred to as adjacencies.

In addition to the revenues from advertising time that they sell themselves, stations also receive direct compensation from the network for the carriage (clearance) of network programs. On the average, network compensation

---

    7. The four authors of this excerpt were all in one way or another involved in formulating the FCC policies that they here analyze. Our own Tom Krattenmaker was the co-director of the FCC's Network Inquiry Special Staff, a unit created by the Commission in 1978 to study the economic structure and commercial practices of the television networks. Dr. Stanley M. Besen was the co-director of the Network Inquiry, whose final reports were issued in 1980. A. Richard Metzger, Jr. and John R. Woodbury were, respectively, senior counsel and senior economist on the Network Inquiry staff.

amounts to about 7 percent of the total revenues received by network affiliates. A network can potentially use compensation to distinguish among its affiliates. A network that wishes, for example, to raise compensation for only one of its stations would not do so by increasing the proportion of advertising time made available to affiliates, for in that case all affiliates would benefit. Instead, the network would increase the compensation it pays to that station, so only that station would gain. Station compensation thus provides a vehicle through which networks may treat different stations differently.

The Economics of Program Clearance Decisions

The Affiliate Supply Schedule

In deciding the amount of time and the specific time periods to supply to a network, a station must compare the net revenue it can earn by supplying each time period to the network to what it can earn if it broadcasts nonnetwork material. The affiliate's net revenue from exhibiting a network program, of course, is the sum of network compensation and the receipts the station receives from the sale of adjacencies. The net revenue from a nonnetwork program is equal to the revenue the station generates from selling commercial time minus the costs of acquiring rights to syndicated programs or producing its own shows.

The networks can influence the choices affiliates make by any or all of three methods: (1) adjusting network compensation for a network program; (2) altering the length of time for, and hence the receipts that can be obtained from, the sale of commercial adjacencies in or surrounding network programs; or (3) changing the programs the network offers in order to alter the value of those adjacencies.

From the viewpoint of the network seeking to "buy" clearances from its affiliates, it is possible to construct a "supply schedule of time offered" by each affiliate, showing the relationship between station compensation and the number of hours of network programs that the affiliate will clear. For each available network program, the affiliate calculates the level of network compensation at which it is just willing to clear the program, that is, the affiliate's "reservation price" for that particular program. The reservation price is that amount which, when added to the value of adjacencies, just equates the net revenue from a network program with that of its best nonnetwork program alternative. If network compensation exceeds the reservation price, the station will clear the network program, but if it is below that price the network program will be preempted in favor of nonnetwork material.

The reservation price will most likely differ among programs. For some network programs, the nonnetwork alternatives will be very unattractive because the costs of acquiring or producing these alternatives are high relative to the revenues they can generate. In these cases, the affiliate will prefer the network offering even at low network compensation rates. For other network programs, net revenues for nonnetwork alternatives will be high and network programs will be cleared only at a higher compensation rate. In principle, one can array programs according to the affiliate's reservation price starting with that program for which the reservation price is the lowest, followed by that with the next lowest reservation price, and so on until the array is completed with the program having the highest reservation price.

Joint Clearance Determination

A network, of course, must determine whether it is willing to pay the necessary affiliate reservation prices. In deciding how much it is willing to pay for a clearance, a network must calculate the addition to its revenues provided by the affiliate's clearance.

Once a program has been produced, an affiliation contract has been negotiated, and continuous interconnection arranged, a network can provide the program to an affiliate essentially without cost. The network therefore will seek to have the program carried on a station so long as compensation paid does not exceed the additional advertising revenues from having the program carried by that station. Naturally, however, the network will seek to pay less than this amount. Indeed, a network could not pay all of its advertising revenues as compensation since it would then be unable to cover its other costs such as program acquisition and station interconnection. Thus, for a network to be viable, a substantial number of affiliates must receive compensation lower than the maximum amount a network might be willing to pay to any given affiliate.

The Economics of Profit Distribution: Effects on Program Clearance

Clearly, networks and their affiliates have considerable incentive to maximize joint profits. But program clearance is not the only issue upon which these firms must agree. Some method must be devised to divide the resulting joint profits between a network and its affiliates.

To some extent, the division of profits will depend on differences in bargaining power between a network and its affiliate. For example, suppose two VHF stations are identically situated except that station x exists in a market with three other VHF stations and station y is in a market with only two other VHF stations. We would expect that the network would enjoy more power in bargaining with station x than with station y. In fact, our empirical tests reveal that stations like y do receive significantly higher network compensation rates than do stations like x.

Such differences in bargaining power do not, however, affect the parties' incentive to clear the number and type of programs that maximize joint profits. Nevertheless, other factors may lead the parties to clearance decisions that fail to achieve this goal.

Factors Preventing Clearances That Maximize Joint Profits

The Strategic Use of Information

Maximization of joint profits requires that at least one party have access to all available information regarding the value of each network program and its nonnetwork alternative. Either party (or both), however, may decide not to divulge information unavailable to the other in order to improve its position in bargaining over the division of profits. The affiliate, for example, may overstate its net revenues from nonnetwork programming in order to obtain higher network compensation. Similarly, the network may understate the amount it can pay in order to lower compensation levels.

Transactions Costs

Transactions costs render it uneconomical for the network to negotiate compensation with each affiliate for each network program. Consequently, network/affiliate contracts specify simple formulas by which compensation is determined for a small number of program periods. Since these are negotiated on the basis of the expected profitability of network and nonnetwork programs within each daypart, they do not take account of special situations that occur after the contracts have been signed. Thus, for example, an affiliate may choose not to clear a network program that develops relatively low ratings although the network would be willing and able to pay the higher compensation required to obtain clearance. The problem arises when the high costs of negotiating special compensation for such a program outweigh the advantages of having the program cleared.

The Possibility of New Network Entry

The analysis to this point has proceeded on the assumption that the existing structure of the broadcasting industry (the number of networks and the number of stations) is given. Within this structure, the interests of network and affiliate diverge only with respect to the distribution of joint profits between them. Therefore, if the preemption of a network program produces larger joint profits than does its clearance, both network and station can benefit if the nonnetwork program is carried. In that case, because network compensation would have to exceed the value to the network of the clearance in order for the program to be carried, the network would not attempt to have it cleared.

There is, however, an alternative. The network (and its affiliates) might be willing to forego some profits in the short run if such abstinence could prevent the entry of new program sources (or networks) over the long run. [The intuition here: if a nonnetwork supplier is successful at getting its content picked up by network affiliates, it might develop expertise such that it could be more competitive with the network in later years. Knowing this, the network might not want to allow its affiliates to air the nonnetwork content even if, in the short-run, this would maximize joint profits.]

Conclusions

When one considers the incentives of networks and their affiliates, and the options available to both, the principal conclusion is that both parties have a great incentive to maximize the joint profits that accrue from networking and broadcasting. In most material respects, then, these entities are partners, not adversaries. Networks will not, except in isolated and extreme cases, be able to induce affiliates to clear programs not profitable for affiliates; indeed, except in equally isolated and extreme cases, the network would have no reason to do so if it could. These principles apply whether or not the same firm owns the network and the affiliate.

Volumes of analysis of network economic behavior, by the Commission and by independent researchers, have often seemed filled with fears or assertions that networks plunder affiliates' profits, force them to exhibit unprofitable or unpalatable fare, or prevent them from participating in programming decisions. At first blush, such assertions seem quite incredible; they appear utterly oblivious to the economic system in which the parties in fact cooperate.

Looked at more carefully, such claims probably often stem from a failure to distinguish the parties' shared interests in maximizing their joint profits and their divergent incentives in dividing those profits. Relatively marginal disputes concerning the division of profits are likely to be more visible to the public than the underlying implicit agreement on joint profit maximization, even though this congruence of interests pervades the relationship and, in fact, largely determines the fare offered to viewers.

At the very least, those who advance such fears or assertions would do well to realize that the principal "benefit" of policies, such as a ban on option time, that resolve these disputes externally is likely to be a reallocation of profits from network to affiliate, not any change in the value viewers derive from television.

Notes and Questions

1. What's the Fear? Why wouldn't we expect that a network and its affiliate will negotiate a separate compensation arrangement for each program carried by the affiliate? Given that there is substantial competition between networks, why are we at all concerned that affiliates and networks will fail to clear the most efficient array of television programs?

2. The First Amendment. Is it at all surprising that the above excerpt never brings the First Amendment into the discussion? For example, might we be willing as a society to tolerate less efficient competition in order to promote a First Amendment value, namely diversity in the ownership and control of local stations? Or does efficient competition itself serve First Amendment goals by, for example, increasing quality? Is there a tension between efficiency and diversity in ownership and control, and, if so, does the First Amendment tell us how to resolve it? (We will see the Commission struggle explicitly with these issues in the context of its various ownership limitations, discussed later this chapter.)

3. Deregulation. In 1995, the FCC opened rulemaking proceedings that propose to terminate virtually all of the network affiliate rules for conventional television. (The rules were terminated for radio in 1977.) In March 1995 the FCC repealed the "network station ownership" rule that prohibited ABC, CBS, and NBC from owning TV stations in markets with few stations or stations of unequal desirability. It also repealed the "secondary affiliation" rule that had prevented ABC, CBS, and NBC from establishing a secondary affiliation in markets where two stations had primary affiliations and there was at least one independent unaffiliated station. 10 FCC Rcd. 4538 (1995). Many observers think the FCC will, in the context of this same proceeding, eventually repeal several more, if not all, of its network/affiliate rules. Would you advise the Commission to retain any sort of regulatory influence in this area, or should this relationship be left entirely to market forces?

C. The Network/Program Supplier Relationship

The relationship between networks and their program suppliers is in many ways similar to the network/affiliate relationship in that each party considers its alternatives in determining what prices to bid and ask. Unlike the market for affiliates, however, the program supply industry is unimpeded by entry barriers. Anyone with sufficient time and talent can write a script and then turn to the market to acquire cameras, film, actors, camera operators, and so forth—all of which can be rented and is available in abundant supply at competitive prices. The program supply industry, in short, is much more decentralized and structurally competitive that the broadcasting industry itself. That does not mean that programs will be available at marginal cost; certain programs garner large followings, and the sellers of those particular programs surely enjoy some degree of market power. What this does mean, however, is that there is little the FCC can accomplish by regulating the network/program supplier relationship—at least assuming that the goal in any such regulation would be to increase competition in the program supply market.

Of course, these simple points have not stopped the Commission from getting involved and imposing regulations. Two types of rules were promulgated in the 1970s. First, the prime time access rule (PTAR) limited ABC, CBS, and NBC to supplying their affiliates with only three hours of programing for use during the four-hour "primetime" time block.[8] This meant that, for one primetime hour each night, even network affiliates had to turn to third-party suppliers or in-house talent for program content. Notably, children's programs, half-hour newscasts, and the Rose Bowl were excepted from this prohibition—the first two exemptions having obvious policy allure, while the third seems to be more obviously the result of parochial interests influencing policy. The PTAR was defended largely on the grounds that (1) it carved out a market for independent producers to sell their programs directly to network affiliates and (2) it increased the profits of unaffiliated (especially UHF) stations since, during that one primetime hour, affiliates and independents were on equal footing. The Commission ultimately repealed the PTAR, *see* 11 FCC Rcd. 546 (1995).

Second, and the focus of this section, the Commission adopted the so-called financial interest and syndication rules ("finsyn" for short). 47 C.F.R. §§73.658(i) & (j). These rules, and their subsequent evolution, are described in more detail in the *Schurz Communications* opinion below. For simplicity at this point, however, we can summarize the rules as follows: the finsyn rules prohibited ABC, CBS, and NBC from (1) acquiring profit-sharing positions in network programs produced by independent companies and (2) engaging in the business (called "off-network syndication") of licensing to independent stations the rights to show reruns of program series that have concluded their network runs. The rules respond to two fears. First, the FCC worried that networks would employ their power to overreach program suppliers, extracting from them excessively low fees or excessively generous grants of subsidiary rights. Second, the Commission thought that networks might seek to control the off-network syndication market in order to prevent competition from reruns (especially since these programs are typically telecast, in competition with network affiliates, by independent stations and cable networks).

---

8. 47 C.F.R. §73.658(k).

SCHURZ COMMUNICATIONS v. FCC
982 F.2d 1043 (7th Cir. 1992)

Opinion for the court filed by Circuit Judge POSNER, in which BAUER, Chief Judge, and FAIRCHILD, Senior Circuit Judge, concur.

POSNER, Circuit Judge:

In 1970 the Federal Communications Commission adopted "financial interest and syndication" rules designed to limit the power of the then three television networks—CBS, NBC, and ABC—over television programming. 47 C.F.R. §73.658(j) (1990); *see Network Television Broadcasting*, 23 FCC 2d 382, 387 (1970), aff'd under the name of Mt. Mansfield Television, Inc. v. FCC, 442 F.2d 470 (2d Cir. 1971). Each of the three networks consisted (as they still do) of several television stations, in key markets, owned and operated by the network itself, plus about two hundred independently owned stations electronically connected to the network by cable or satellite. In exchange for a fee paid them by the network, these affiliated stations broadcast programs that the network transmits to them, as well as to its owned and operated stations, over the interconnect system. The networking of programs intended for the early evening hours that are the "prime time" for adult television viewing gives advertisers access to a huge number of American households simultaneously, which in turn enables the networks to charge the high prices for advertising time that are necessary to defray the cost of obtaining the programming most desired by television viewers.

The financial interest and syndication rules adopted in 1970 forbade a network to syndicate (license) programs produced by the network for rebroadcast by independent television stations—that is, stations that were not owned by or affiliated with the network—or to purchase syndication rights to programs that it obtained from outside producers, or otherwise to obtain a financial stake in such programs. If the network itself had produced the program it could sell syndication rights to an independent syndicator but it could not retain an interest in the syndicator's revenues or profits.

Many syndicated programs are reruns, broadcast by independent stations, of successful comedy or dramatic series first shown on network television. Very few series are sufficiently successful in their initial run to be candidates for syndication. Independent stations like to air five episodes each week of a rerun series that originally had aired only once a week or less, so unless a series has a first run of several years—which few series do—it will not generate enough episodes to sustain a rerun of reasonable length. The financial interest and syndication rules thus severely limited the networks' involvement in supplying television programs other than for their own or their affiliated stations.

The concern behind the rules was that the networks, controlling as they did through their owned and operated stations and their affiliates a large part of the system for distributing television programs to American households, would unless restrained use this control to seize a dominating position in the production of television programs. That is, they would lever their distribution "monopoly" into a production "monopoly." They would, for example, refuse to buy programs for network distribution unless the producers agreed to surrender their syndication rights to the network. For once the networks controlled those rights, the access of independent television stations, that is, stations not owned by or affiliated with one of the networks, to reruns would be at the sufferance of the networks, owners of a competing system of distribution.

The Commission hoped the rules would strengthen an alternative source of supply (to the networks) for independent stations—the alternative consisting of television producers not owned by networks. The rules would do this by curtailing the ability of the networks to supply the program market represented by the independent stations, and by protecting the producers for that market against being pressured into giving up potentially valuable syndication rights. And the rules would strengthen the independent stations (and so derivatively the outside producers, for whom the independent stations were an important market along with the networks themselves) by securing them against having to purchase reruns from their competitors the networks.

The basis for this concern was never very clear. If the networks insisted on buying syndication rights along with the right to exhibit a program on the network itself, they would be paying more for their programming. (So one is not surprised that in the decade before the rules were adopted, the networks had acquired syndication rights to no more than 35 percent of their prime-time series, although they had acquired a stake in the syndicator's profits in a considerably higher percentage of cases.) If the networks then turned around and refused to syndicate independent stations, they would be getting nothing in return for the money they had laid out for syndication rights except a long-shot chance—incidentally, illegal under the antitrust laws—to weaken the already weak competitors of network stations. Nor was it clear just how the financial interest and syndication rules would scotch the networks' nefarious schemes. If forbidden to buy syndication rights, networks would pay less for programs, so the outside producers would not come out clear winners—indeed many would be losers. Production for television is a highly risky undertaking, like wildcat drilling for gas and oil. Most television entertainment programs are money losers. The losses are offset by the occasional hit that makes it into syndication after completing a long first run. The sale of syndication rights to a network would enable a producer to shift risk to a larger, more diversified entity presumptively better able to bear it. The resulting reduction in the risks of production would encourage new entry into production and thus give the independent stations a more competitive supply of programs. Evidence introduced in this proceeding showed that, consistent with this speculation, networks in the pre-1970 era were more likely to purchase syndication rights from small producers than from large ones.

Whatever the pros and cons of the original financial interest and syndication rules, in the years since they were promulgated the structure of the television industry has changed profoundly. The three networks have lost ground, primarily as a result of the expansion of cable television, which now reaches 60 percent of American homes, and videocassette recorders, now found in 70 percent of American homes. Today each of the three networks buys only 7 percent of the total video and film programming sold each year, which is roughly a third of the percentage in 1970. (The inclusion of films in the relevant market is appropriate because videocassettes enable home viewers to substitute a film for a television program.) And each commands only about 12 percent of total television advertising revenues. Where in 1970 the networks had 90 percent of the prime-time audience, today they have 62 percent, and competition among as well as with the three networks is fierce. They are, moreover, challenged today by a fourth net-work, the Fox Broadcasting Corporation, which emerged in the late 1980s.

Notwithstanding the fourth network, which might have been expected to re-duce the number of independent stations by converting many of them to Fox net-work stations, the number of independent stations has increased fivefold since 1970. At the same time, contrary to the intention behind the rules yet an expectable result of them because they made television production a riskier business, the production of prime-time programming has become more concentrated. There are 40 percent fewer producers of prime-time programming today than there were two decades ago. And the share of that programming accounted for directly or indirectly by the eight largest producers, primarily Hollywood studios—companies large enough to bear the increased risk resulting from the Commission's prohibition against the sale of syndication rights to networks—has risen from 50 percent to 70 percent.

The evolution of the television industry, sketched above, suggested that the rules, if they were having any effect at all, were working perversely from a com-petitive standpoint. An extensive staff study ordered by the Commission con-cluded that the rules were obsolete and recommended that they be abandoned. Final Report of Network Inquiry Special Staff (1980). In 1983 the Commission issued a tentative decision agreeing with the staff, proposing radical revisions in the rules leading to their eventual repeal, but inviting further public comments on the details of its proposals. *Tentative Decision and Request for Further Com-ments in Docket 82-345*, 94 FCC 2d 1019 (1983). The networks, the Commis-sion found in the tentative decision, had lost any significant monopoly or market power that they may once have had. The financial interest and syndication rules were hampering the entry of new firms into production by blocking an important mechanism (the sale of syndication rights) by which new firms might have shifted the extraordinary risks of their undertaking to the networks.

Mainly as a result of congressional pressure, Hearings before the Subcomm. on Communications of the S. Comm. on Commerce, Science & Transportation on S. 1707, 98th Cong., 1st Sess. 6, 9 (1984), there was no follow-up to the ten-tative decision. The question what to do about the rules remained in limbo until 1990, when the Commission at the request of the Fox network initiated a fresh notice-and-comment rulemaking proceeding. After receiving voluminous submis-sions from the various segments of the television industry, the Commission held a one-day hearing, after which it issued an opinion, over dissents by two of the five commissioners, including the chairman, promulgating a revised set of financial interest and syndication rules. In re Evaluation of the Syndication and Financial Interest Rules, 56 Fed. Reg. 26242 (1991), on reconsideration, 56 Fed. Reg. 64207 (1991). The new rules (published at 47 C.F.R. §§73.658(k), 73.659–73.662, 73.3526(a)(11) (1991)) are different from the old and also more complicated. They define "network" as an entity that supplies at least 15 hours [per week] of prime-time programming to interconnected affiliates. They take off all restrictions on non-entertainment programming (that is, news and sports), and most restrictions on non-prime-time programming and on syndication for the foreign as distinct from the domestic market. But in a provision that has no counterpart in the old rules, the new ones provide that no more than 40 percent of a network's own prime-time entertainment schedule may consist of programs produced by the network itself. The new rules unlike the old permit a network to buy domestic syndication rights from outside producers of prime-time entertainment programming—provided, however, that the network does so pursuant to separate negotiations begun at least 30 days after the network and the producer have agreed on the fee for licensing the network to exhibit the program on the network itself. Even then the network may not arrange for the distribution of the programming to the independent stations; it must hire an independent syndicator for that. And it may acquire syndication rights only in reruns, not in first-run programs, and thus it may not distribute first-run programming other than to its network stations.

Although the Commission conceded that the networks may already have lost so much of their market power as no longer to pose a threat to competition as it is understood in antitrust law, it concluded that some restrictions remain necessary to assure adequate diversity of television programming.

The networks have petitioned this court to invalidate [the new rules] as arbitrary and capricious. 5 U.S.C. §706(2)(A). They argue that the only administrative order supportable by the record compiled by the Commission would be a total repeal of the 1970 rules.

The Communications Act of 1934 gives the Federal Communications Commission authority over the use of the electromagnetic spectrum to propagate communications signals. With the blessing of the Supreme Court the Commission has used this authority, in much the same fashion that it accuses the networks of wanting to use leverage in the distribution market to gain a stranglehold over programming, to regulate activities by networks that are remote from the concerns with signal interference that first summoned federal regulation of the airwaves into being. The handle is the Commission's control over broadcast licenses, including those held by the networks' owned and operated stations. The Commission has been allowed to condition the renewal of those licenses on the networks accepting constraints intended to maximize the Commission's conception of the social benefits of broadcasting. National Broadcasting Co. v. United States, 319 U.S. 190 (1943). The statute provides no guidance for the exercise of this authority other than that the Commission is to act in accordance with the public interest, convenience, or necessity. *Id.* at 215; 47 U.S.C. §303.

If the Commission were enforcing the antitrust laws, it would not be allowed to trade off a reduction in competition against an increase in an intangible known as "diversity." Since it is enforcing the nebulous public interest standard instead, it is permitted, and maybe even required, to make such a tradeoff—at least we do not understand any of the parties to question the Commission's authority to do so. And although as an original matter one might doubt that the First Amendment authorized the government to regulate so important a part of the marketplace in ideas and opinions as television broadcasting, the Supreme Court has consistently taken a different view. FCC v. Pacifica Foundation, 438 U.S. 726 (1978); National Broadcasting Co. v. United States, *supra*, 319 U.S. at 226–27.

The difficult question presented by the petitions to review is not whether the Commission is authorized to restrict the networks' participation in program production and distribution. It is whether the Commission has said enough to justify, in the face of the objections lodged with it, the particular restrictions that it imposed in the order here challenged. It is not enough that a rule might be rational; the statement accompanying its promulgation must show that it is rational—must demonstrate that a reasonable person upon consideration of all the points urged pro and con the rule would conclude that it was a reasonable response to a problem that the agency was charged with solving.

The new rules flunk this test. The Commission's articulation of its grounds is not adequately reasoned. Key concepts are left unexplained, key evidence is overlooked, arguments that formerly persuaded the Commission and that time has only strengthened are ignored, contradictions within and among Commission decisions are passed over in silence. The impression created is of unprincipled compromises of Rube Goldberg complexity among contending interest groups viewed merely as clamoring suppliants who have somehow to be conciliated. The Commission said that it had been "confronted by alternative views of the television programming world so starkly and fundamentally at odds with each other that they virtually defy reconciliation." The possibility of resolving a conflict in favor of the party with the stronger case, as distinct from throwing up one's hands and splitting the difference, was overlooked. The opinion contains much talk but no demonstration of expertise, and a good deal of hand-wringing over the need for prudence and the desirability of avoiding "convulsive" regulatory reform, yet these unquestioned goods are never related to the particulars of the rules—rules that could have a substantial impact on an industry that permeates the daily life of this nation and helps shape, for good or ill, our culture and our politics.

Stripped of verbiage, the Commission's majority opinion, like a Persian cat with its fur shaved, is alarmingly pale and thin. It can be paraphrased as follows. The television industry has changed since 1970. There is more competition—cable television, the new network, etc. No longer is it clear that the networks have market power in an antitrust sense, which they could use to whipsaw the independent producers and strangle the independent stations. So there should be some "deregulation" of programming—some movement away from the 1970 rules. But not too much, because even in their decline the networks may retain some power to extort programs or program rights from producers. The networks offer advertisers access to 98 percent of American households; no competing system for the distribution of television programming can offer as much. Anyway the Commission's concern, acknowledged to be legitimate, is not just with market power in an antitrust sense but with diversity, and diversity is promoted by measures to assure a critical mass of outside producers and independent stations. So the networks must continue to be restricted—but less so than by the 1970 rules. The new rules will give the networks a greater opportunity to participate in programming than the old ones did, while protecting outside producers and independent stations from too much network competition.

All this is, on its face, plausible enough, but it is plausible only because the Commission, ostrich fashion, did not discuss the most substantial objections to its approach, though the objections were argued vigorously to it, by its own chairman among others. To begin with, the networks object that the new rules do not in fact increase their access to the programming market and may decrease it, in the face of the Commission's stated objective. The 40 percent limitation on the amount of prime-time entertainment that a network can supply from its in-house production is a new restriction on the networks, having no counterpart in the original rules. The carving out of nonentertainment programming from the restrictions imposed by the new rules is a throwaway, because there is no syndication market for news and sports programs. Also illusory, the networks argue, is the newly granted right to acquire syndication rights from outside producers, given the restrictions with which the new right is hedged about. A producer cannot wait until 30 days after negotiating the network license fee to sell off syndication rights, because the sale of those rights, the networks contend, is critical to obtaining the financing necessary to produce the program in the first place. These arguments may be right or wrong; our point is only that the Commission did not mention them. We are left in the dark about the grounds for its belief that the new rules will give the networks real, not imaginary, new opportunities in programming.

The new rules, like their predecessors, appear to harm rather than to help outside producers as a whole (a vital qualification) by reducing their bargaining options. It is difficult to see how taking away a part of a seller's market could help the seller. One of the rights in the bundle of rights that constitutes the ownership of a television program is the right to syndicate the program to nonnetwork stations. The new rules restrict—perhaps, as a practical matter, prevent—the sale of that right to networks. How could it help a producer to be forbidden to sell his wares to a class of buyers that may be the high bidders for them? Since syndication is the riskiest component of a producer's property right—for its value depends on the distinctly low-probability event that the program will be a smash hit on network television—restricting its sale bears most heavily on the smallest, the weakest, the newest, the most experimental producers, for they are likely to be the ones least able to bear risk. It becomes understandable why the existing producers support the financial interest and syndication rules: the rules protect these producers against new competition both from the networks (because of the 40 percent cap) and from new producers. The ranks of the outside producers of prime-time programming have been thinned under the regime of financial interest and syndication rules. The survivors are the beneficiaries of the thinning. They consent to have their own right to sell syndication rights curtailed as the price of a like restriction on their potential competitors, on whom it is likely to bear more heavily.

This analysis of risk and its bearing on competition in the program industry is speculative, theoretical, and may for all we know be all wet—though it is corroborated by the increasing concentration of the production industry since the rules restricting the sale of syndication rights were first imposed in 1970. The Commission was not required to buy the analysis. But as the analysis was more than plausible and had been pressed upon it by a number of participants in the rulemaking proceeding, the Commission majority was not entitled to ignore it. Not even to consider the possibility that the unrestricted sale of syndication rights to networks would strengthen the production industry (the industry—not necessarily its present occupants) and thereby increase programming diversity by enabling a sharing between fledgling producers and the networks of the risks of new production was irresponsible. For if the argument about risk sharing is correct, the rules are perverse; by discouraging the entry of new producers into the high-risk prime-time entertainment market, they are likely to reduce the supply of programs to the independent stations and so reduce diversity both of program sources and of program outlets. The Commission's stated desiderata are competition and diversity. The rules adopted by the Commission in order to achieve these desiderata have the remarkable property—if the risk-sharing argument that the Commission did not deign to address is correct—of disserving them both.

If the networks do have market power, the new rules (in this respect like the old) do not seem rationally designed to prevent its exercise. A rule telling a person he may not do business with some firm believed to have market power is unlikely to make the person better off. Suppose that in a competitive market a network would pay $2 million for first-run rights to some program and $1 million for syndication rights, for a total of $3 million, but that because of the lack of perfect substitutes for using this network to distribute his program the producer is willing to sell each of these rights to the network for half their competitive market value (*i.e.,* for $1 million and $500,000 respectively). The producer is made no better off by being forbidden to sell the syndication rights to the network. He gets the same meager first-run license fee ($1 million) and now must cast about for another buyer for the syndication rights. That other buyer is unlikely to pay more than the network would ($500,000); otherwise the producer would have sold the syndication rights to him in the first place. It is no answer that the network would not have given the producer the option of selling it only first-run rights, that it would have insisted on the whole package so that it could control the program supply of the independent stations, which are heavily dependent on reruns and hence on syndication. The producer might indeed be desperate for network distribution, but that desperation would be reflected in the low price at which he was willing to sell the network whatever rights the network wanted. He cannot do better by being forbidden to make such a deal. If he could do better by selling syndication rights to someone else he would not accede to such unfavorable terms as the network offered.

If this is right, the new rules, at least insofar as they restrict network syndication, cannot increase the prices that producers receive. All they can do is increase the costs of production by denying producers the right to share risks with networks.

And we have said nothing as yet of the treatment of the Fox network. That network is built around the production capability and film library of Twentieth Century Fox. At present the network supplies only 12 to 14 hours a week of prime-time programming to its owned and affiliated stations and is therefore exempt from the new rules. Should it reach 15 hours, however, it would be subject to them. Fox argues that, given the importance of program production in its overall corporate activity, the effect of the rules is to limit it to supplying fewer than 15 hours of prime-time programming and therefore to limit its growth as a network. Corroboration of this argument is found in the fact that the Fox network hit 15 hours a week shortly before the rules went into effect, then cut back to the present 12 to 14 hours. By limiting Fox in this way the new financial interest and syndication rules limit competition with the major networks and thus entrench the market power that is the rules' principal rationale. Or so Fox argues; it may be bluffing; maybe the effect of the rules will be to induce Fox to divest its production or network arms, so that the network can grow without constraining Fox's production activities. But once again the Commission failed even to mention the argument that its rules perversely limit competition with the established networks.

More than competition in the economic sense is at stake. Fox's affiliates are for the most part the traditionally weak UHF stations. They do not consider themselves "network" stations in the same sense that a CBS or NBC or ABC affiliate does. Many of them are members of the trade association of independent television stations. Anything that weakens Fox's incentives to furnish prime-time programming weakens them, contrary to the Commission's desire, protectionist though it may be, to strengthen independent stations. This perverse consequence of the rules also went unmentioned.

Finally, while the word diversity appears with incantatory frequency in the Commission's opinion, it is never defined. At argument one of the counsel helpfully distinguished between source diversity and outlet diversity. The former refers to programming sources, that is, producers, and the latter to distribution outlets, that is, television stations. The two forms of diversity are related because the station decides what programs to air and therefore affects producers' decisions about what to produce. A third, and one might suppose the critical, form of diversity is diversity in the programming itself; here "diversity" refers to the variety or heterogeneity of programs. The Commission neither distinguished among the types of diversity nor explained the interrelation among them. As it is very difficult to see how sheer number of producers or outlets could be thought a good thing—and anyway the rules seem calculated, however unwittingly, to decrease, or at least to freeze, but certainly not to increase, the number of producers—we assume that the Commission thinks of source diversity and outlet diversity as means to the end of programming diversity.

Are they? It has long been understood that monopoly in broadcasting could actually promote rather than retard programming diversity. If all the television channels in a particular market were owned by a single firm, its optimal programming strategy would be to put on a sufficiently varied menu of programs in each time slot to appeal to every substantial group of potential television viewers in the market, not just the largest group. For that would be the strategy that maximized the size of the station's audience. Suppose, as a simple example, that there were only two television broadcast frequencies (and no cable television), and that 90 percent of the viewers in the market wanted to watch comedy from 7 to 8 p.m. and 10 percent wanted to watch ballet. The monopolist would broadcast comedy over one frequency and ballet over the other, and thus gain 100 percent of the potential audience. If the frequencies were licensed to two competing firms, each firm would broadcast comedy in the 7 to 8 p.m. time slot, because its expected audience share would be 45 percent (one half of 90 percent), which is greater than 10 percent. Each prime-time slot would be filled with "popular" programming targeted on the median viewer, and minority tastes would go unserved. Some critics of television believe that this is a fair description of prime-time network television. Each network vies to put on the most popular programs and as a result minority tastes are ill served.

Well, so what? Almost everyone in this country either now has or soon will have cable television with 50 or 100 or even 200 different channels to choose among. With that many channels, programming for small audiences with specialized tastes becomes entirely feasible. It would not have been surprising, therefore, if the Commission had taken the position that diversity in prime-time television programming, or indeed in over-the-air broadcasting generally, was no longer a value worth promoting. It did not take that position. Instead it defended its restrictions on network participation in programming on the ground that they promote diversity. But it made no attempt to explain how they do this. It could have said, but did not, that independent television stations depend on reruns, which they would prefer to get from sources other than the networks with which they compete, and—since reruns are the antithesis of diversity—they use their revenue from reruns to support programming that enhances programming diversity. It could have said that programs produced by networks' in-house facilities are somehow more uniform than programs produced by Hollywood studios. It didn't say that either. It never drew the link between the rules, which on their face impede the production of television programs and the interest in diverse programming. The Commission may have thought the link obvious, but it is not. The rules appear to handicap the networks and by handicapping them to retard new entry into production; how all this promotes programming diversity is mysterious, and was left unexplained in the Commission's opinion.

That opinion, despite its length, is unreasoned and unreasonable, and therefore, in the jargon of judicial review of administrative action, arbitrary and capricious. The Commission's order is therefore vacated and the matter is returned to the Commission for further proceedings.

Notes and Questions

1. Subsequent Events. On remand, the Commission essentially repealed the financial interest and syndication rules as well as its newer limitation on networks producing their own programming. *See Evaluation of the Syndication and Financial Interest Rules*, 8 FCC Rcd. 3282 (1993). The agency removed all restrictions on network acquisition of financial interests and syndication rights, and the agency eliminated entirely the cap on in-house production. Retained were the prohibitions on active network domestic syndication, whether in first-run or off-network syndication, but only as to primetime entertainment programming, only for a limited period, and only as to ABC, CBS, and NBC. The Seventh Circuit affirmed, 29 F.3d 309 (1994).

2. Promoting Competition. The 1991 rules were to some extent justified on the grounds that they would promote competition. The court, however, opined that "a rule telling a person he may not do business with some firm believed to have market power is unlikely to make the person better off." Of course, the 1991 rules did not tell program suppliers they could not do business with the networks, only that they could not sell certain rights to them absent certain protections. Didn't the Commission adequately explain why producers might be harmed if, as a consequence of selling syndication rights to the networks, they eventually confronted a syndication market that was dominated by those networks? Precisely what flaw(s) in this argument does the court identify?

3. Regulatory Capture? Note that the court views the program supply industry as including firms that might enter (or be on the verge of entering) the industry, while to the Commission the industry seems to consist only of those firms actively supplying programs to networks and to stations. Is this a manifestation of the industry capturing the regulators? Perhaps the Commission does not understand the argument that restricting the networks' abilities to engage in risk sharing will lead to further concentration in the program supply industry because it cannot see, and therefore cannot imagine, the plight of fledgling entrants?

4. The First Amendment. Can you imagine any conceivable public interest rationale for the 1991 limit on the number of programs networks could produce for themselves? A rationale that would survive First Amendment objections? Might this aspect of the new rules have been a prime source of the court's "impression...of unprincipled compromises...among contending interest groups"?

5. Diversity. The 1991 rules were also to some extent justified on the grounds that they would enhance diversity. Given the court's explanation, near the end of its opinion, for why monopoly in broadcasting may better satisfy viewers' desires than competition would, why does it treat with apparent disdain, earlier in the opinion, the Commission's assertion that it was pursuing diversity, rather than competition, in adopting the 1991 rules? Was the Commission's real failure its omission to define carefully the diversity it meant to stimulate? In what sense might one plausibly assert that the 1991 rules furthered "diversity"?

6. Understanding Monopoly Incentives. On that same point, is it really true that "monopoly in broadcasting [can] actually promote rather than retard programming diversity"? Posner's simple example seems to work; but are there important complexities left out of his discussion that undermine this claim? What assumptions about viewer tastes drive the model? Does the point still have force when we consider viewers who have first, second, and third choices in terms of their viewing preferences? What other refinements help us to evaluate this claim and correctly gauge its implications?

7. Agency Expertise. How confident are you that the FCC can balance all the complicated and competing forces sketched in the above opinion and come to a reasoned conclusion? Can anyone really balance all these countervailing forces? Which way does that cut?

8. More Networks, Less Cash? Consider one more economic wrinkle relevant to understanding the market for program supply. One might suspect that, by increasing the number of networks or supporting the continued development of cable and satellite as distribution technologies, the FCC could increase profits in the program supply industry. The argument would be that the added competition would yield higher bids for any particular program. This is not necessarily true, however, since, as the number of outlets increases, the average audience per outlet likely decreases. Each outlet therefore attracts less advertising revenue and quite possibly each ends up bidding less on content. Does this mean that increasing competition among outlets decreases competition among program suppliers? If so, now what?

9. New Complexities. As we will discuss in Chapter Eleven, many of the networks today provide programming not only to their broadcast affiliates but also to specific cable channels. ABC, for example, has ownership interests in the popular cable sports channel, ESPN. Does this introduce a new reason for Commission regulation, the worry being that the network might not have its affiliates' interests at heart when it determines which programs go to broadcast television and which are carried exclusively on cable? Or is this again a tension that the market can resolve?

II. OWNERSHIP RESTRICTIONS

Another method the FCC employs to foster competition in broadcasting is limiting the number of telecommunications platforms any single entity can own or control. The limitations here come in two forms. First, there are multiple-ownership rules that restrict ownership within the same service or closely connected services. These rules can apply nationally or locally, and they can set caps by stipulating a maximum number of licenses, a maximum percentage of the relevant audience, or both. So, for example, the "local television ownership rules" limit the number of broadcast licenses that a single entity can hold in a given market; and the "national television ownership rules" limit the percentage of the national audience that a single broadcaster can reach through stations it owns or controls. (Note that network affiliates are not necessarily controlled by their associated network since, as was explained earlier in the chapter, an independently owned affiliate has the right to refuse to air particular network programs. This most often happens when an affiliate preempts national programming to focus on an event of local importance, but it also happens when a local owner decides that a program put out by the network is inappropriate given local tastes.)

Second, the Commission also promulgates various cross-ownership rules that restrict ownership across different telecommunications services. For example, in 1999, the Commission announced a radio/television cross-ownership rule that under certain circumstances allows a single party to own as many as one television station and seven radio stations in the same market. *See In the Matter of Review of the Commission's Regulations Governing Television Broadcasting*, 14 FCC Rcd. 12903 (1999) (hereinafter *Local Television Ownership Order*). Cross-ownership rules can include non-broadcast properties as well. For example, the Commission has long restricted cross-ownership of radio stations, television stations, and newspapers all serving the same community; and the Commission similarly has restricted cable, radio, and television cross-ownership, again only with respect to properties that serve the same community.

The FCC frequently revisits these various ownership limitations, and so the key to understanding these provisions is not so much to grasp the specific numerical limitations imposed (since they change so frequently) but instead to understand the underlying policy concerns that animate these rules. Below, then, are excerpts from a recent *Report* filed by the FCC on the topic of both the local radio ownership rules and the national television ownership rules. The *Report* was required by Section 202(h) of the Telecommunications Act of 1996, which orders the Commission to conduct biennial reviews of all its ownership rules to determine whether they continue to be necessary given increased competition in the various telecommunications markets. The Commission does not significantly alter its rules as part of this particular *Review*—mainly because months earlier the Commission had adjusted the local television ownership rules and thus the Commissioners wanted to wait and see the effects of that change before making any further adjustments. The document is nevertheless worth careful attention because it sets out, in comprehensive fashion, the various policy issues at stake.

BIENNIAL REPORT, REVIEW OF THE COMMISSION'S BROADCAST RULES AND OTHER RULES ADOPTED PURSUANT TO SECTION 202 OF THE TELECOMMUNICATIONS ACT OF 1996
15 FCC Rcd. 11058 (2000)

II. BACKGROUND

5. For more than a half century, the Commission's regulation of broadcast service has been guided by the goals of promoting competition and diversity. These goals are separate and distinct, yet also related. Competition is an impor-

tant part of the Commission's public interest mandate because it promotes consumer welfare and the efficient use of resources and is a necessary component of diversity. Diversity of ownership fosters diversity of viewpoints, and thus advances core First Amendment principles. Promoting diversity in the number of separately owned outlets has contributed to our goal of viewpoint diversity by assuring that the programming and views available to the public are disseminated by a wide variety of speakers.

6. We assess current levels of competition in the market for delivered video programming, the advertising market, and the program production market to determine whether such competition has eliminated the need for [any of the rules under consideration in this proceeding]. Our diversity analysis focuses upon the degree to which broadcast and non-broadcast media advance the three types of diversity (viewpoint, outlet and source) that our broadcast ownership rules have attempted to foster. Viewpoint diversity refers to the range of diverse and antagonistic opinions and interpretations presented by the media. Outlet diversity refers to a variety of delivery services (*e.g.*, broadcast stations, cable and DBS) that select and present programming directly to the public. Source diversity refers to the variety of program or information producers and owners.

IV. RULES

A. *National TV Ownership Rule*

1. Regulatory History

14. Section 73.3555(e)(1) sets forth the current national TV ownership rule. That section states:

> No license for a commercial TV broadcast station shall be granted, transferred or assigned to any party (including all parties under common control) if the grant, transfer, or assignment of such license would result in such party or any of its stockholders, partners, members, officers or directors, directly or indirectly, owning, operating or controlling, or having a cognizable interest in TV stations which have an aggregate national audience reach exceeding thirty-five (35) percent.

47 C.F.R. §73.3555(e)(1).

16. The Commission first adopted a national ownership limit for television broadcast stations in the 1940s by imposing numerical caps on the number of stations that could be commonly owned, and originally limited common ownership to no more than three stations nationwide. Several years later this was expanded to allow ownership of no more than five stations. In retaining the five station rule in 1953, the Commission explained:

> The purpose of the multiple ownership rules is to promote diversification of ownership in order to maximize diversification of program and service viewpoint as well as to prevent any undue concentration of economic power contrary to the public interest and thus to carry out the underlying purpose of the Communications Act to effectuate the policy against monopolization of broadcast facilities and the preservation of the broadcasting system on a free competitive basis.

Amendment of Multiple Ownership Rules, 9 RR 1563 (1953).

17. In 1954, the Commission adopted the "Seven Station Rule" by raising the multiple ownership limit from five stations to seven, with no more than five being VHF stations. The Commission believed that the more rapid and effective development of the UHF band warranted permitting the ownership of additional UHF stations. The Commission noted that it was aware of the serious problems confronting the development of the UHF service, especially in markets with VHF-only set saturation, and that it was in these areas particularly where the prestige, capital, and know-how of the networks and other multiple owners would be most effective in aiding UHF.[9]

18. Thirty years later, in 1984, the Commission eliminated the Seven Station Rule and established a six-year transitional period during which common owner-ship of twelve television broadcast stations would be permitted. The Commission determined that repeal of the Seven Station Rule would not adversely affect the Commission's traditional policy objectives of promoting viewpoint diversity and preventing economic concentration. The Commission explained that: 1) changes in the broadcasting and communications markets, 2) new evidence of the positive ef-fects of group ownership on the quality and quantity of public affairs and other pro-gramming responsive to community needs, and 3) the lack of relevance of a national ownership rule to the availability of diverse and independently owned radio and TV voices to individual consumers in their respective local markets led to the conclusion that the rule was unnecessary to ensure diversity of viewpoints. Nevertheless, the Commission recognized the concerns of some commenters that, if the rule were re-pealed immediately and in its entirety, a significant restructuring of the broadcast in-dustry might occur before all ramifications of such a change became apparent. Therefore, the Commission established a transitional limit of twelve television broadcast stations. The transitional limit would automatically sunset in six years unless experience showed that continued Commission involvement was warranted.

19. On reconsideration, the Commission, modified its decision. Specifically, the Commission 1) established an audience reach cap of 25 percent, in addition to the twelve station limit, to better account for the effect that relaxation of the rule would have on population penetration; 2) attributed owners of UHF stations with only 50 percent of their [estimated] audience reach to take cognizance of the limitations inherent in UHF broadcasting; 3) permitted common ownership of an additional two television stations, provided that they were minority con-trolled; and 4) eliminated the automatic sunset provision. The stated objective was to permit reasonable expansion so as to capture the benefits of group owner-ship while avoiding the possibility of potential disruptive restructuring of the na-tional broadcast industry. The Commission explained that a numerical cap would prevent the acquisition of a tremendous number of stations in the smaller markets, thus reducing the possibility of disruptive restructuring in small mar-kets, while an audience reach cap would temper dramatic changes in the owner-ship structure by the largest group owners in the largest markets. The Commis-

---

9. [Ed. Remember, UHF signals are weaker signals and so they can deliver a high-qual-ity television picture only over a small geographic range. Outside that range, UHF channels are significantly less clear than their VHF counterparts. Worse, as the Commission points out, in the 1950s some television sets were incapable of receiving UHF signals, again putting UHF at a competitive disadvantage. None of these limitations matters much in modern times since UHF and VHF are of equal quality when delivered as part of basic cable.]

sion noted that its decision to use both a numerical cap and an audience reach cap was also predicated on concerns regarding the potential impact on industry structure. The Commission further explained that attributing UHF stations with 50 percent of [their expected] audience reach was intended to address the fundamental disadvantage of UHF television in reaching viewers. The Commission found it inadvisable to terminate the multiple ownership rules for television broadcast stations automatically at the end of six years. The Commission explained that 1) it was appropriate to proceed cautiously in relaxing the rules and 2) an automatic sunset of the ownership rules was unnecessary to achieve the Commission's policy objectives.

20. On March 7, 1996, the Commission eliminated the numerical limit on the number of broadcast television stations a person or entity could own nationwide and increased the audience reach cap on such ownership from 25 percent to 35 percent of television households.

2. Comments on National TV Ownership Rule

21. All of the major networks (ABC, CBS, Fox, and NBC) support total repeal of the national television ownership rule. These networks argue that abolition of the rule would have no effect on the level of diversity and competition in local markets, and retention of the rule hinders broadcasters from achieving economic efficiencies. These networks maintain that group owned stations provide more news and public affairs programming than non-group owned stations. They also argue that removal of the audience reach cap would promote the development of new broadcast television networks. Finally, they argue that the only two markets that may be affected by elimination of the rule, the national advertising market and the market for national exhibition rights to video programming, would remain unconcentrated.

24. A number of commenters support retaining the national television ownership rule. [The National Association of Broadcasters (NAB)] argues that the new television ownership limits have not been in effect long enough to warrant any modification at this time. Network Affiliated Stations Alliance (NASA) asserts that an increase in the audience reach cap will increase the bargaining power of networks and, therefore, diminish localism by making it more difficult for affiliates to program their stations in the interests of the communities they are licensed to serve. Center for Media Education (CME) contends that the recent increase in the cap has led to unprecedented concentration and diminished competition that may enable networks to exercise monopsony power in the program production market. According to CME, the public is receiving less news and information from fewer sources. American Federation of Television and Radio Artists (AFTRA) asserts that maintaining the existing 35 percent cap will not harm competition and is essential to protect diversity on the airwaves. AFTRA argues that group owners recycle news and public affairs programming from one reporter or news writer, whereas the public interest is better served by having different reporters and news writers in separate markets provide different angles and perspective on the news.

3. Discussion of National TV Ownership Rule

26. Commenters supporting relaxation or elimination of the cap make credible arguments in favor of their position. These arguments include the contention that elimination of, or increases in, the cap would allow additional economic efficiencies and more news and public affairs, increase minority ownership by re-

moving the cap as an impediment to broadcasters obtaining attributable equity interests in minority-owned television stations, and promote the development of new broadcast television networks. We believe, however, that the competitive concerns of opponents of relaxation or elimination of the cap are more convincing under current circumstances. Until we gain experience under the new local television ownership rules[10] we are disinclined to correspondingly relax them on the national level. While we will reexamine this decision in our future biennial reviews of broadcast ownership rules, we intend to proceed cautiously in this area at the present time.

30. We also intend to proceed cautiously because the Commission has previously recognized that a change in the audience reach cap may well influence the bargaining positions between broadcast television networks and their affiliates. We noted that in some situations, relaxation of the national ownership limits could increase the bargaining power of networks by expanding their option to own rather than affiliate with broadcast television stations. In other situations, however, relaxation of the national ownership limits could increase the bargaining position of group-owned affiliates by creating larger, more powerful groups. In its comments, NASA asserts that the national ownership rule is the essential mechanism for maintaining the balance between networks and their affiliates to ensure that affiliates can program their stations in the interests of the communities they are licensed to serve. NASA argues that an increase in the audience reach cap will increase the bargaining power of networks. We believe that in considering relaxation of the national ownership rule we should act cautiously in light of the potential impact of this rule on the bargaining positions of networks and affiliates, particularly given the restructuring that may be taking place concurrently on the local level. We do not believe that consolidation of ownership of all or most of the television stations in the country in the hands of a few national networks would serve the public interest. The national networks have a strong economic interest in clearing [that is, having affiliates air] all network programming, and we believe that independently owned affiliates play a valuable counterbalancing role because they have the right to decide whether to clear network programming or to air instead programming from other sources that they believe better serves the needs and interests of the local communities to which they are licensed. Independent ownership of stations also increases the diversity of programming by providing an outlet for non-network programming. We do not believe that the role played by independently owned affiliates is any less important today than it was four years ago when [the 35% cap was first established.]

B. Local Radio Ownership Rules

1. Regulatory History

39. Section 73.3555(a)(1) of the Commission's rules sets forth the current local radio ownership rules. [47 C.F.R. §73.3555(a)(1).] These rules currently allow: (1) combinations of up to 8 commercial radio stations, not more than 5 of which are in the same service (AM or FM), in markets with 45 or more commercial radio stations; (2) combinations of up to 7 commercial radio stations, not

---

10. [Ed. The Commission is referring to the local television ownership rules adopted in the 1999 *Local Television Ownership Order* discussed above.]

more than 4 of which are in the same service, in markets with between 30 and 44 commercial radio stations; (3) combinations of up to 6 commercial radio stations, not more than 4 of which are in the same service, in markets with between 15 and 29 commercial radio stations; (4) combinations of up to 5 commercial radio stations, not more than 3 of which are in the same service, if no party controls more than 50 per cent of the stations in the radio market, in radio markets with 14 or fewer commercial radio stations.

40. In 1938, the Commission adopted a strong presumption against granting radio licenses that would create "duopolies" (i.e., common ownership of more than one station in the same service in a particular community) based largely on the principle of diversification of service. In the early 1940s this presumption against duopoly ownership became an absolute prohibition when the Commission 1) adopted rules governing commercial FM service and 2) prohibited the licensing of two AM stations in the same area to a single network. The AM rule barred overlap of AM stations where a "substantial portion of the applicant's existing station's primary service area" would receive service from the station in question, except upon a showing that the public interest would be served through such multiple ownership; and the FM rule prohibited the licensing of a new station which would serve "substantially the same area" as another station owned or operated by the same licensee. 45 FCC 1476, 1476 n.1 (1964). The Commission explained that the radio duopoly rules sought to promote economic competition and diversity of programming viewpoints through station-ownership diversity.

41. In 1964, the Commission [adopted a more objective variant of these rules, specifying with technical precision exactly when two stations would be deemed to be overlapped. In adopting this approach,] the Commission stated: "When two stations in the same broadcast service are close enough together so that a substantial number of people can receive both, it is highly desirable to have the stations owned by different people." *Id.* at 1477. The Commission explained that this objective flowed logically from two basic principles underlying the multiple ownership rules.

> First, in a system of broadcasting based upon free competition, it is more reasonable to assume that stations owned by different people will compete with each other, for the same audience and advertisers, than stations under the control of a single person or group. Second, the greater the diversity of ownership in a particular area, the less chance there is that a single person or group can have an inordinate effect, in a political, editorial, or similar programming sense, on public opinion at the regional level.

Id. The Commission concluded that the rules were based upon the view of the First Amendment that the Amendment "rests on the assumption that the widest possible dissemination of information from diverse and antagonistic sources is essential to the welfare of the public." Associated Press v. U.S., 326 U.S. 1, 10 (1945).

42. In 1988, the Commission replaced the [existing] duopoly standard with a more relaxed standard. [In essence,] the rule prohibited combinations of 2 AM or 2 FM stations in the same "principal city" but permitted AM/FM combinations within the same community. The Commission explained that efficiencies of common ownership might be realized by allowing radio broadcasters to own two or more radio stations in the same geographic area, although not in the same principal city. The Commission also explained that the goals of the duopoly rule

remained the same: to promote economic competition and diversity of programming and viewpoints through local ownership diversity. The Commission noted a changed marketplace, with an increased number of broadcast stations, the introduction of new services and technologies, and the abundance of competition in local markets, as the compelling reasons to relax the local ownership regulation.

43. In 1992, the Commission again cited changed economic conditions in radio markets as a basis for further relaxing the local radio ownership rules. Specifically, the Commission permitted combinations of up to (i) 3 AM and 3 FM in markets with 40 or more stations, (ii) 3 AM and 2 FM in markets with 30 to 39 stations, (iii) 2 AM and 2 FM in markets with 15 to 29 stations and (iv) 3 stations (with no more than 2 in the same service) in markets with 14 or fewer stations. Under cases (i)–(iii), combinations were permitted if the combined audience share did not exceed 25 percent. In case (iv), the combination was permitted if it would not result in a single party controlling 50 percent or more of the stations in the market. The Commission noted growth in the number of radio stations and increased competition from non-radio outlets such as cable and MTV. The Commission noted that stations faced declining growth in radio revenues and concluded that economic circumstances threatened radio's ability to serve the public interest. The Commission explained that consolidation within the industry would allow radio broadcasters to realize economies of scale that would then generate greater programming investment and increase radio stations' competitiveness.

44. In response to petitions for reconsideration, the Commission moderated the relaxation of its rules permitting combinations of up to (i) 2 AM/2 FM in markets with 15 or more stations, if the combined audience share did not exceed 25 percent; and (ii) 3 stations in markets of 14 or fewer stations, with no more than 2 in the same service, if the combination would not control 50 percent or more of the stations in the market. The Commission concluded "that adopting more moderate increases...in the permissible level of station ownership in certain local markets at this time will provide necessary relief while enabling us to monitor marketplace developments as they unfold." 7 FCC Rcd. at 6388.

45. Pursuant to the Telecommunications Act of 1996, the Commission further relaxed its local radio ownership rules in March 1996 [to their current levels.]

2. Comments

47. Commenters were divided on whether the current local radio ownership rules have produced positive or negative results. CME, for example, argues that radio market consolidations have increased the market power of group owners. Some commenters further contend that consolidation has increased radio owners' influence over local advertising rates. Americans for Radio Diversity (ARD) explains that the cost of radio advertising is accelerating at roughly triple the rate of inflation, and that it is common for two or three radio station owners to receive 80% to 90% of the advertising revenues in a local market. ARD further argues that consolidation has negatively impacted small business owners who cannot afford the inflated advertising costs which the current conditions help create.

48. Commenters concerned about ownership consolidation also state that such consolidation has diminished local viewpoint diversity. While group owners may have greater resources to invest in local news and public affairs programming, ARD and CME argue that the scale economies from concentrated radio

ownership arise in part from a homogenization of news reporting . Similarly, Greater Media, Inc., and Press Communications LLC believe that radio consolidation has reduced viewpoint diversity in broadcasting.

49. Other commenters, however, rejoin that consolidation was the intent behind deregulation of local radio ownership restrictions, and that any resulting problems that may arise with market power should be left to antitrust authorities. For example, CBS argues that competitive effects of changes in the local radio ownership limits must be evaluated in the context of the broad advertising markets where radio competes, and cites the fierce inter-media and intra-radio competition that occurs in advertising markets, the willingness of stations to change formats, and the sharp fluctuations in listener preferences as evidence that radio incumbents can easily be challenged. NAB asserts that higher ratings and higher quality service resulting from ownership consolidation account for the higher advertising rates. Commenters supporting further relaxation of the local radio ownership rules also argue that consolidation has produced economic gains that reflect improved economies of scale, in terms of operating cost reductions and the improved quality and quantities of radio services offered. CBS cites transactional efficiencies that occur when a group owner can offer "one stop shopping" for advertisers, with benefits for both buyer and sellers of advertising time. Cumulus cites lower costs and improved radio service, and asserts that the improved economies of scale from group ownership allows radio stations in small and mid-sized markets to compete against local newspaper and television stations, which in many cases have enjoyed near-monopoly status with respect to their service to major local advertisers.

51. Some commenting parties urged the Commission to retain, or even expand, its current radio market definition and station count method. ABC proposes using an all-inclusive measure that includes television, radio, cable, DBS, newspapers, video cassettes, yellow pages, direct mail and the Internet, and would substitute antitrust enforcement for the Commission's current local ownership regulation.

3. Discussion

54. *Competition.* Relaxation of the ownership limits has produced financial benefits for the broadcast radio industry. For the industry as a whole, station profitability has increased and station values have reached new heights. However, it is not clear whether these gains are the result of greater efficiencies, enhanced market power, or both.

55. We are concerned that increasing consolidation may be having adverse effects on competition, especially in the local radio advertising market. Current data show that in 85 out of a total of 270 radio markets, two entities already control more than 80% of advertising revenue; in 143 markets two entities control more than 70 percent of such. We recognize that many advertisers consider alternative media to be good substitutes for radio advertising. However, the Department of Justice (DOJ) has concluded that there are a significant number of advertisers that do not. In distinguishing radio advertising as a distinct market from that of television and newspaper advertising, the DOJ explains that 1) radio advertising is unique in reaching a mobile broadcast audience; 2) radio has a greater ability to target particular audience segments; and 3) radio can be more cost effective and more flexible in responding to changes in local advertising conditions. Thus, for certain advertisers, newspapers, cable, and broadcast television

stations do not constitute an effective substitute for radio stations. For these advertisers, the consolidation of local radio markets may raise significant competitive concerns.

56. *Diversity.* Consolidation of radio stations under group ownership might allow owners to increase investment in news coverage, through the acquisition of more sophisticated news coverage equipment and by maintaining larger, more efficient news staffs.

57. [However] the scale and scope efficiencies discussed above might in part arise from the consolidation of news coverage at commonly-owned stations, leading to a lessening of viewpoint diversity and to a smaller local market for news talent. If this were the case, this would conflict with the longstanding intent of the radio multiple ownership rules to promote viewpoint diversity through independently owned local stations. Viewpoint diversity has traditionally been viewed in terms of the number of independent viewpoints expressed in local markets, in which case ownership consolidation could have a negative impact on both viewpoint and source diversity. A related concern is that even without the loss of news staffs, viewpoint expression might become homogenized within a commonly owned group of radio stations as a result of the sharing of common news facilities and a common corporate culture.

58. Several commenters lend support to these notions. Air Virginia notes a trend by large group-owned stations towards less news and public affairs and more revenue-generating entertainment programming. Americans for Radio Diversity (ARD) believes that group owners tend to ignore public service to demographic groups deemed to be small or unprofitable, which often impacts minorities and those of lower economic status. CME believes that consolidation has led to reduced public-affairs and local-news programming, since group owners increasingly use syndicated programming and out-sourcing to produce news and public affairs programs, often with the same production company as is used by competitors. It reports that, for example, Metro Networks Inc., a Houston-based company, provides all of the news programming to 10 Washington, D.C., radio stations. Similarly, CME reports that Capstar Broadcasting uses ten announcers based in Austin, Texas, to record all between-song breaks and weather and traffic breaks for 37 of its stations in Texas, Arkansas and Louisiana.

59. In view of the large-scale consolidation in the radio industry, we believe that the existing local radio ownership limitations remain necessary to prevent further diminution of competition and diversity in the radio industry. It appears that while there may have been a number of salutary effects flowing from the consolidation that has taken place since 1996, largely in financial strength and enhanced efficiencies, it cannot be said that consolidation has enhanced competition or diversity, and, indeed, may be having the opposite effect. There currently are hundreds of fewer licensees than there were four years ago and, in many communities, far fewer radio licensees compete against each other.

Notes and Questions

1. **Principled Decision-Making?** The court in *Schurz* (excerpted in the previous section) said the FCC's 1991 rules governing television networks' acquisition of programs created the impression "of unprincipled compromises of Rube Gold-

berg complexity among contending interest groups viewed merely as clamoring suppliants who have somehow to be conciliated." Would that be equally accurate as a characterization of the various decisions made in this proceeding? In fact, other than listing all of the various arguments pro and con, what work did the Commission do here before deciding that neither the national television ownership rule nor the local radio ownership rule should be disturbed? In other words, if the concluding paragraph of the local radio ownership section had come out the other way—say, advocating further relaxation of the rule—would the document have been any less convincing? If not, is that troubling?

2. Susceptible to Pressure. Note that the Commission changed the local radio ownership rules twice in 1992, the first change (summarized in ¶43) coming at the end of a full regulatory proceeding, and the second coming, as the Commission puts it, "[i]n response to petitions for reconsideration." ¶44. In fact, the revisions came about because of intense political pressure, including threats of legislative intervention. Are the Commission's multiple- and cross-ownership rules particularly susceptible to this sort of political pressure, on the theory that they do not rest on any objective principle but rather (to some degree at least) seem to involve picking numbers out of the air? Does that mean that the Commission should not be in the business of promulgating these regulations—that this power should be exercised, if at all, by Congress?

3. National Limits. What is the basis for imposing national limits? If listeners choose among local stations, how is competition or diversity affected by whether local stations are affiliated with distant stations or, instead, independently owned? Conversely, if limits are to be imposed, why should they not be very stringent? Does the Commission provide much evidence that national combinations will generate cost savings? And, again, why isn't the choice of any specific numeric cap—say, 35% of the national audience, or 25%, or 10%—a textbook example of an "arbitrary and capricious" decision?

4. Antitrust. With respect to both national and local limits, why not simply leave the regulation of license acquisition to antitrust enforcement? Does the Commission really have any relevant expertise in making decisions about local and national market structure? Can you point to any sentence in the preceding document that evidences Commission expertise? Interestingly, in its comments to the Commission, ABC unabashedly proposed to the FCC substituting antitrust enforcement for the Commission's own rules. (*See* ¶51.)

5. New Technologies. In that same paragraph, ABC is also credited with arguing in favor of an "all-inclusive measure that includes television, radio, cable, DBS, newspapers, video cassettes, yellow pages, direct mail and the Internet" when measuring market power. Why isn't that the right measure? Why does the FCC resist this approach?

6. Newspaper/Broadcast Cross-Ownership. Section 73.3555(d) of the Commission's rules (codified at 47 C.F.R. §73.3555(d)) sets forth a prohibition on newspaper/broadcast cross-ownership. The rule states:

> No license for an AM, FM or TV broadcast station shall be granted to any party (including all parties under common control) if such party directly or indirectly owns, operates or controls a daily newspaper and the grant of such license will result in: (1) The [predicted primary market of an AM station] encompassing the entire community in which such news-

paper is published; or (2) The [predicted primary market of an FM station] encompassing the entire community in which such newspaper is published; or (3) The [primary market of a TV station] encompassing the entire community in which such newspaper is published.

Does this rule implicate any issues not already considered in this chapter? For example, are the First Amendment concerns greater here given that this is a regulation that (indirectly) constrains the individual's right to publish a newspaper? Or is this rule in the end no different from a regulation prohibiting an individual from owning fifteen AM radio stations serving the same community?

Chapter Eight

CASE STUDIES IN LOW POWER FM RADIO AND DIGITAL TELEVISION

The purpose of this chapter is:

- to pull together all the materials on broadcast for one final review of the Commission's regulatory tools by engaging in two case studies:
- a brief case study on the process (both administrative and political) that led to the creation of new licenses for low power FM radio stations; and
- a fuller case study on the creation of new licenses for digital television.

~

I. LOW POWER FM RADIO

In early 2000, the FCC promulgated rules to create a new broadcast radio service called "low power" FM radio (LPFM). *See In re Creation of Low Power Radio Service*, 15 FCC Rcd. 2205 (2000) ("*LPFM Order*"). The idea here was a simple one: in many markets, additional radio stations could go on the air without interfering with existing radio stations, so long as the new stations transmitted their signals at sufficiently low power. Many new, small radio stations could thus be licensed to operate, affording a new opportunity for public, educational, and community (even neighborhood) broadcasting. The FCC accordingly ruled that it would license new classes of licenses for stations to "be operated on a noncommercial educational basis by entities that do not hold an attributable interest in any other broadcast station or other media subject to our ownership rules." *Id.* at ¶1. The maximum power at which such licensees could broadcast under the Commission's ruling was 100 watts, and LPFM stations were prohibited from interfering with the signals of existing broadcasters.

The story of these LPFM licenses reviews, in a microcosm, many of the historical themes and subplots of U.S. broadcasting generally: scarcity, spectrum efficiency, spectrum allocation, the public interest, competition and, last but not least, hardball political economy. The story begins, perhaps, with scarcity and interference. By the end of 2000, there were almost 13,000 radio stations on the air in the United States: 4685 AM stations, 5892 FM stations, and 2140 stations defined as "FM educational." *Id.* at ¶1. This total marked an increase of 102 stations over the total from 1999.[1] Those large numbers notwithstanding, there remained excess demand for broadcast licenses—especially for free ones!—in virtually every U.S. market. As the FCC noted in its *LPFM Order*, it had received "comments and letters from thousands of individuals and groups seeking licenses for new radio stations." 15 FCC Rcd. 2205 at ¶3. But where, in the scarce ether, to put them without interfering with any of the thousands of stations already operating? If the problem was scarcity, a solution might be efficient spectrum management.

Typically, a broadcast licensee is protected not just from interference from signals transmitted on its own channel, but also from signals broadcast on the three adjacent channels. Based on a number of engineering studies, the FCC concluded in the *LPFM Order* that an existing radio broadcaster would be unlikely to suffer interference from low power broadcasts on the third adjacent channel to its own. *Id.* at ¶6. The Commission thus created two classes of low power FM service: a 100 watt service called LP100 which could generally broadcast in a 3.5 mile radius, and a 1 to 10 watt service known as LP10, but also sometimes called "microradio," that could broadcast in a 1 to 2 mile radius. *Id.* at ¶¶13–14. The Commission ruled that, with appropriate technological constraints designed to protect existing broadcasters, these two types of licenses could be issued without raising any significant risk of interference:

> In establishing this new service, we are determined to preserve the integrity and technical excellence of existing FM radio service, and not to impede its transition to a digital future. In this regard, our own technical studies and our review of the record persuade us that 100-watt LPFM stations operating without 3rd-adjacent channel separation requirements will not result in unacceptable new interference to the service of existing FM stations. Moreover, imposing 3rd-adjacent channel separation requirements on LPFM stations would unnecessarily impede the opportunities for stations in this new service, particularly in highly populated areas where there is a great demand for alternative forms of radio service. We will not, therefore, impose 3rd-adjacent channel separation requirements. To avoid any possibility of compromising existing service, given the new nature of the LPFM service, we will impose separation requirements for low power with respect to full power stations operating on co-, 1st- and 2nd-adjacent and intermediate frequency (IF) channels. We believe that the rules we are adopting will maintain the integrity of the FM band and preserve the opportunity for a transition to a digital radio service in the future, while affording significant opportunities for new radio service.

Id. at ¶2.

The next question for the Commission was who these new broadcasters should be. The Commission stated that, in licensing LPFM stations, its goals would be to "encour[age] diverse voices on the nation's airwaves and creat[e] opportunities for new entrants in broadcasting." *Id.* at ¶13. The Commission therefore decided to

> establish LPFM as a noncommercial educational service to allow local groups, including schools, churches and other community-based organi-

---

1. The FCC Mass Media Bureau posts this sort of data on its website. This particular statistic can be found at www.fcc.gov/mmb/obc/fy1999st.txt.

zations, to provide programming responsive to local community needs and interests. We believe that noncommercial licensees, which are not subject to commercial imperatives to maximize audience size, are more likely than commercial licensees to serve small, local groups with particular shared needs and interests, such as linguistic and cultural minorities or groups with shared civic or educational interests that may now be underserved by advertiser-supported commercial radio and higher powered noncommercial radio stations. We note that commenters addressing this issue favored establishing LPFM as a noncommercial service by a substantial margin, though some have argued that a commercial service could provide ownership opportunities for new entrants. While we have considered the entrepreneurial opportunities that low power radio stations might create, we nonetheless conclude that a noncommercial service would best serve the Commission's goals of bringing additional diversity to radio broadcasting and serving local community needs in a focused manner.

Id. at ¶17.

The FCC's stated objectives in licensing LPFM broadcasters have a long historical pedigree. Localism and diversity are two of the main goals the Commission has espoused for programming since the agency's inception in 1934. Indeed, they are at the core of the FCC's public interest regulation of broadcasters and they were two themes we emphasized in this book all the way back in Chapter One. The FCC saw LPFM as affording a new means to advance these familiar goals.

Having decided what kind of licensee would be eligible, the Commission next had to decide how to allocate a limited number of LPFM licenses among a potentially larger pool of eligible applicants. The *LPFM Order* established a filing window after which eligible applicants who did not face competing, mutually exclusive applications would receive licenses. *Id.* at ¶132. But what of competing applications? The Commission considered three familiar alternatives: auctions, comparative hearings, and lotteries. Section 309's requirement of competitive bidding for spectrum licenses does not apply to licenses for noncommercial educational broadcast stations and public broadcast stations, 47 U.S.C. §§309(j)(2)(c) and 397(6), so the FCC was not obliged to distribute the licenses via auctions. The FCC decided instead to adopt a limited comparative review, focusing on very specific criteria:

Based on our consideration of the record, we shall adopt a point system for resolving mutual exclusivity among LPFM applicants. The point system will include three selection criteria: (1) established community presence; (2) proposed operating hours; and (3) local program origination. The system will employ voluntary time-sharing as a tie-breaker, that is, tied applicants will have an opportunity to aggregate points by submitting time-share proposals. As a last resort, where a tie is not resolved through time-sharing or settlement, we shall award successive equal license terms totaling eight years (the normal license term), without renewal expectancy for any of the licensees.

Id. at ¶136.

The above excerpt contains some interesting features, such as allowing applicants to team up through voluntary time sharing and to aggregate their points in the licensing competition. The elimination of the renewal expectancy and the award of successive licenses in the case of unresolved ties is also novel. But in its basic adoption of comparative reviews based on traditional criteria, the *LPFM Order* also seems something of a throwback to an earlier era of spectrum regulation; it thus serves as a reminder of the importance of both that history and the various arguments for and against the different methods of assigning spectrum.

The Commission's decision to license low power radio stations was instantly controversial, both inside and outside the agency. Two Commissioners dissented in part from the *LPFM Order*. Commissioner Furchtgott-Roth found both the costs and the benefits of the policy to be miscalculated. He argued, first, that the Commission had underestimated the risks and costs of interference:

> Even without studying the engineering studies in the record, we can be sure of one thing. As Commissioner Quello once noted, "it is axiomatic that for each new service introduced, interference to existing service is also introduced." Dissenting Statement of Commissioner James H. Quello, Modification of FM Broadcast Station Rules to Increase the Availability of Commercial FM Broadcast Assignments, 48 FR 29486, 29512 (1983). This is true even for 100 watt stations dropped by eliminating "only" third adjacent channel protections. There are real costs — to existing stations, their listeners, and to public perception of the quality of FM radio as a media service — here that the Commission has not even attempted to quantify.

Id. at 2320.

Second, Commissioner Furchtgott-Roth contended that the Commission had overestimated the benefits of new stations. In his analysis, few such stations would be licensed where they might really be needed, and many would be available in places where there would be little demand for them:

> But let's consider what the Commission today has actually achieved in terms of benefits to place on the other side of the ledger. According to the NPRM in this proceeding, elimination of third adjacent channel protections for 100 watt stations will allow for the creation of one such station — in Houston, Texas — in the top five American cities. No such stations will be created in New York, Los Angeles, Chicago, Philadelphia, San Diego, Dallas, San Francisco, Washington, Charlotte, or Miami. So much for the goal of creating low power stations to serve urban communities; there will be precious few new licensees in urban markets.

> To the contrary, the bulk of new licensees will be smaller markets. In many of these areas, full power stations likely could already be dropped in *without* changing third-adjacent channel standards at all. (At least, there is no indication of an effort on the part of the Commission even to consider such an alternative approach.) Given that there is little existing demand for additional full-power stations in these markets, there is no evidence of commercial viability. Indeed, the evidence suggests that such stations are not capable of existence as going concerns.

> Perhaps there *is* a demand for lower power noncommercial stations. Theoretically, however, any such actual demand could be met by the dispensation of licenses within our existing rules — *i.e.*, by giving out 101

watt licenses consistent with the 100 watt minimum requirement. *See* 47 C.F.R. section 73.211(a)(3). Yet again, we receive few if any applications for 101 watt licenses, even in the noncommercial arena. Similarly, if somebody really wanted to operate a 50-watt station, they might file a request for waiver of the 100-watt minimum rule. As far as I can tell, though, no such waiver has ever been filed, again suggesting a lack of any real demand for such licenses. In short, there is no evidence in the behavior of license applicants that suggests any pent-up demand for the stations in question.

Id. at 2320–21.

Commissioner Powell voiced concern that the effect of LPFM on the viability of small, commercial stations had been too quickly dismissed by the Commission, and that some of these commercial stations were serving the very interests the FCC was purporting to further:

> This item's goal is to create a class of radio stations "designed to serve very localized communities or underrepresented groups within communities." *Notice of Proposed Rulemaking*, 14 FCC Rcd. 2471, 2473 (1999). Attempting to give greater voice to narrower interests is generally laudable and I support the objective. But, the question that gives me pause is what the cost is to existing stations that provide equally valuable service to their communities. Because this *Order* fails to give credence to this concern, I respectfully dissent in part.

> I do not quibble with the Commission's objectives. Certainly, the extensive consolidation of radio stations into large commercial groups and the financial challenges of operating full power commercial stations have limited the broadcasting opportunities for highly localized interests. The introduction of a low power FM service may partially address this concern. However, to borrow from the teaching of the medical profession, when trying to treat a problem, we should "first do no harm." There presently exist many small and independent stations across the country that are especially notable for their local focus. This admirable group includes a fair number of stations owned by minorities and women, as well as stations with smaller audiences and limited advertising. These stations have struggled to survive as independent voices against the rising tide of consolidation brought on by the economic stress of small scale production. It would be a perverse result, indeed, if these stations were to fail or the quality of locally originated programming suffer, because new LPFM stations diluted their already tenuous base of support.

> There are two interrelated, yet distinct, threats to these small stations that stem from the new LPFM service: 1) signal interference and 2) erosion of economic viability. The first has garnered all the attention. The Commission has endeavored to minimize the dangers of interference in this item. It wrongly has ignored the second concern. I have met with a number of small market broadcasters that tell me that when they raise concerns about the threat of LPFM to their economic viability they are bluntly rebuked—told that such considerations are of no import, that we are only concerned with spectrum efficiency and that we do not pick winners and losers. I, too, heard this line during our internal delibera-

tions. I find the proposition absurd. We regularly consider the economic impacts of our actions on licensees. Just one example is the degree to which we have attempted to balance the need for consolidation to achieve economic efficiency against our goal to foster myriad diverse voices. Indeed, the Commission itself has recognized that the industry's ability to function in the public interest, convenience and necessity is fundamentally *premised on the industry's economic viability. See* In re Revision of Radio Rules and Policies, 7 FCC Rcd. 6387, 6389 (1992).

Id. at 2323.

Powell's concern was thus that the new LPFM licensees could siphon enough listeners from marginal commercial stations to tip the balance against their viability. The FCC majority viewed this concern in terms of market competition, with then-Chairman Kennard in his own separate statement heralding the virtues of consumer choice and the marketplace: "We should empower consumers to decide what he or she prefers, rather than ruling out some options on our own and depriving the listener of making that choice for him- or herself. That's what faith in the marketplace is all about." *Id.* at 2316.

As for the incumbents? Well, competition and entry have never been on the wish list of any incumbent broadcaster. Recall Thomas Hazlett's arguments (excerpted in Chapter Two) about the origins of spectrum regulation and the role commercial licensees played in fostering the regime of government licensing as a way of protecting themselves from competition. Broadcasters reacted no more happily in 2000 than they did in the 1920s to the prospect of the unwashed masses joining them on the airwaves. Both the National Association of Broadcasters (NAB) (the trade association of the commercial broadcasting industry) and National Public Radio (NPR) vigorously opposed the FCC's *LPFM Order*, seeking reconsideration at the Commission but also taking their battle to Capitol Hill. The incumbents' major argument was interference, and the FCC's allegedly inadequate record for determining that such would not occur. The President of the NAB argued in congressional hearings that the *LPFM Order* should be considered "in light of the history that gave rise to communications regulation in the 1920s—the need to control interference to radio service."[2] He further stated that "NAB believes the FCC has abandoned its mandate and primary function of spectrum manager and has crossed over to social engineering at the expense of the integrity of the spectrum for existing FM broadcast stations and their listeners."[3]

The FCC denied the petitions for reconsideration,[4] but the broadcasters had much better luck with Congress. After holding hearings, Congress substantially cut back the *LPFM Order* by statute. The Radio Broadcasting Preservation Act of 2000[5] not only reduces by an estimated 80 percent the number of LPFM licenses that can be issued, but also takes a further—and unusual—step: it trans-

---

2. Prepared Testimony of Edward O. Fritts, President & CEO, National Association of Broadcasters, Before the House Commerce Committee, Telecommunications & Finance Subcommittee, February 17, 2000.
   3. *Id.*
   4. In re Creation of Low Power Radio Service, Memorandum Opinion and Order on Reconsideration, FCC 00-349, 2000 WL 1434686 (2000).
   5. Pub. L. 106-553.

fers from the FCC to Congress the authority to set technical standards for such licenses. The Act itself exercises that authority by reversing the Commission's decision to eliminate third adjacent channel protection for some incumbent broadcasters and ordering the FCC to review its findings that elimination of such protection would not lead to unacceptable interference. As a result of Congress's action, few LPFM stations are likely to be licensed outside of rural areas or small cities.

Notes and Questions

1. **Basic Justification.** In light of the thousands of commercial and noncommercial broadcasters already on the air, how convincing is the FCC's diversity/localism rationale for LPFM licenses? Should Commissioner Powell's concern for marginal commercial stations dominate? What about Kennard's response?

2. **Support for the Noncommercial Restriction.** In the *LPFM Order*, the FCC notes that most commenters supported restricting LPFM licenses to noncommercial entities. Wouldn't it have been surprising if the balance of sentiment were otherwise? Whose interests would be served or impeded by commercial broadcasting on such bands?

3. **Assignment of LPFM licenses.** What do you think of the FCC's decision to make comparative evaluations of mutually exclusive LPFM applications? Is there a better alternative given the particular goals and distributional objectives of the *LPFM Order*? Given the noncommercial nature of these licenses, were auctions even a possibility? Why not lotteries, especially given that one of the stated goals here was to increase licensee diversity? How better to accomplish that than random assignment?

4. **Interference.** The FCC conducted detailed tests to ensure that LPFM was unlikely to lead to interference with existing broadcasters. In fact, the *LPFM Order* goes out of its way to make clear that preventing interference and preserving the integrity of existing broadcasters was the agency's highest priority in the LPFM proceedings. What, then, are Congress and the incumbent commercial and noncommercial broadcasters worried about? That the FCC's engineering studies were flawed? That the Commission would not be able to enforce its non-interference rules on LPFM licensees? Those are both possible, although the strength of opposition before any LPFM station had even been licensed (let alone caused interference) was remarkably intense if these were the real concerns. And doesn't the FCC have decades of experience enforcing non-interference rules among the thousands of large and small incumbents? Why shouldn't that experience give comfort to the NAB and existing broadcasters? Is it possible that their concerns really are not about interference, but something else? But what would that be? Could small, noncommercial stations really pose an economic threat to the vast bulk of existing broadcasters?

5. **Subsequent Events.** Despite both the legislation cutting back the LPFM program and continued opposition from incumbent broadcasters, the Commission announced in December 2000 that it had found 255 applications in twenty states eligible for LPFM licenses. The Commission stated in its announcement that, in keeping with Congress's mandate, only LPFM stations that fully protected in-

cumbent broadcasters from third adjacent channel interference were being approved.[6]

II. DIGITAL TELEVISION

In 1940, a television broadcasters' group formed to create a common standard for broadcasting that has been used ever since. That standard is known as NTSC, which stands for National Television Systems Committee (the name of the group formed in 1940). In the 1980s, broadcasters, along with consumer electronics manufacturers, began to push the FCC to set aside spectrum for a new broadcasting standard, one that would provide for a clearer picture by offering approximately twice the vertical and horizontal resolution available in NTSC broadcasts.[7] This higher resolution (also termed "higher definition") television format became known as High Definition Television (HDTV).

Advocates sometimes treated the term HDTV as interchangeable with the term Advanced Television (ATV). Technically, this was inaccurate, as ATV referred to all forms of advanced television, of which HDTV was merely the most prominent. (The main alternative in the 1980s was known as Enhanced Definition Television (EDTV), which offered resolution that was superior to NTSC but did not match HDTV.) The conflation of HDTV and ATV was perhaps understandable, as the focus of the early advocates was on a particular form of advanced television—HDTV. Another area of confusion in these early years was the distinction between HDTV and Digital Television (DTV). The former refers to a level of picture quality, and the latter to the type of transmission. HDTV can be analog or digital, and DTV can be high definition or standard definition. As we will see in this chapter, what started out as a proceeding for HDTV ended up providing for DTV.

Neither HDTV nor DTV is limited to any particular means of transmission. Broadcasters can send HDTV and/or DTV signals, but so can cable operators, satellite providers, and so on. In fact, satellite and cable companies often transmit their signals digitally; the signals are then converted to analog for display on consumers' NTSC television sets.[8] Moreover, other countries had developed

---

6. News Release, FCC Announces First 255 Applicants Eligible for Low Power FM Radio Stations (Dec. 21, 2000), www.fcc.gov/bureaus/mass_media/news_releases/2000/nrmm0047.html.

7. According to a history of HDTV in the United States, broadcasters initially pushed for HDTV as a way of avoiding an impending FCC decision to transfer unused UHF spectrum to land mobile radio uses. *See* Joel Brinkley, Defining Vision: The Battle for the Future of Television 3–27 (1997). Consumer electronics manufacturers, meanwhile, were attracted by the prospect of millions of consumers purchasing a new form of television receiver. *See* Michael Dupagne & Peter B. Seel, High-Definition Television: A Global Perspective 135–165 (1998). Politicians saw an opportunity to reclaim the U.S. television receiver market for the U.S. electronics manufacturing industry. *Id.*; *see also* Brinkley at 22–46.

8. Arguably the most frequently used form of digital transmission is information access via the Internet. Notably, increases in bandwidth allow more and more people to download streaming, or real-time, audio and video (via a variety of standards). The computer monitor has thus become a source for programming that is indistinguishable from the television. Should the FCC have taken that into account in its DTV proceeding?

HDTV standards with no intention of using them for broadcast. Both Japan and some European countries had decided to pursue exclusively cable- and satellite-delivered HDTV—a possibility that U.S. broadcasters were particularly anxious to fend off.[9]

In the United States, broadcasters persuaded the FCC to focus its energy on providing for over-the-air terrestrial broadcasting of advanced television (with a strong focus on high definition television). In 1987 the FCC commenced a wide-ranging inquiry to consider the technical and public policy issues surrounding the use of ATV technologies by television broadcast licensees. The broadcasting standard had been updated before, specifically when color television signals gradually replaced black-and-white. That transition was relatively straightforward, because a broadcaster could switch from black-and-white to color broadcasting and still have its signal received by black-and-white television sets. HDTV signals, however, cannot be received by television sets that are designed to receive NTSC signals (absent a converter box, which still would not match full HDTV quality). Implementation of a new standard thus entailed the creation of an entirely new form of broadcasting, which meant that virtually all the issues that had arisen over the decades with respect to conventional broadcasting would have to be hashed out again with respect to the new broadcast standard—and in a much shorter period of time.

Thus the coming of HDTV/DTV—and the FCC's response to this phenomenon—raise most of the problems confronted to this point in the book. How should spectrum be allocated? How should licenses be awarded? When should the Commission substitute regulation by agency oversight for regulation by marketplace discipline? Does the agency have a responsibility to see to it that certain kinds or certain levels of programming are available to all Americans? Should the Commission be more self-conscious in examining and projecting the effects of its station allocation plans on diversity of ownership, or diversity in programming, or competition among networks? In reading the documents excerpted in this section, note not only what the FCC proposes but also what options it has already passed over.

A. Making Room for HDTV

The following *Notice of Proposed Rulemaking* reflects, and makes, several foundational decisions: The FCC focused on HDTV rather than EDTV; an EDTV system might be receivable on current television sets, but HDTV offered a better picture. The FCC proposed to choose among a variety of competing methods for transmitting HDTV signals (just as, in the 1950s, the Commission chose a single system for transmitting color TV signals). Further, the agency proposed to set aside an additional 6 MHz for each television broadcast station that is already authorized and to permit each station to acquire an additional HDTV license for that 6 MHz. The spectrum to be allocated to HDTV would be in the UHF band and would come from (a) unused noncommercial assignments, (b) some spectrum currently assigned to low power television, and (c) reductions in

---

9. *See* Dupagne & Seel at 167–174.

certain spacing requirements that had been designed to protect against interference among stations.

IN RE ADVANCED TELEVISION SYSTEMS

Notice of Proposed Rulemaking, 6 FCC Rcd. 7024 (1991)

I. BACKGROUND

1. This Notice of Proposed Rule Making (*Notice*) proposes policies and rules for implementing advanced television (ATV) service in this country.[10] It is the fourth in a series of Commission actions designed to refine and articulate a regulatory approach for ATV.

2. In the Second Inquiry [in this proceeding], 3 FCC Rcd. 6520 (1988), we tentatively adopted certain principles that continue to guide our policies regarding ATV. These tentative decisions are that: 1) broadcast use of ATV technology would benefit the public; 2) the public can benefit from ATV technology most quickly if current broadcasters are permitted to implement ATV; 3) spectrum needed for ATV broadcasts will be obtained from the spectrum currently allotted to broadcast television; 4) current service to NTSC compatible receivers must continue, at least during a transition period; 5) only systems that utilize 6 MHz or less in broadcasting an ATV signal will be authorized; and 6) it is in the public interest not to retard the independent introduction of ATV in other services or on non-broadcast media. In addition, in our First Order in this proceeding, 5 FCC Rcd. 5627 (1990), we decided that a "simulcast" HDTV system — *i.e.*, a system that employs design principles for ATV service independent of the existing NTSC technology, and that transmits the increased information of an ATV signal in a standard 6 MHz channel as used in the current television plan — will allow for ATV introduction in the most non-disruptive and efficient manner.

4. This *Notice* proposes a tentative plan for ATV terrestrial broadcast implementation. We seek comment on the following fundamental aspects of this plan: (1) who should initially be eligible for ATV frequencies; (2) how we should allot and assign ATV channels to eligible applicants; (3) how we should resolve certain spectrum issues involving the noncommercial reserve, low power, and translator stations, and broadcast auxiliary services; [and] (4) how we should regulate the "conversion" from NTSC to ATV.

---

10. ATV refers to any television technology that provides improved audio and video quality or enhances the current television broadcast system. The existing broadcasting system is referred to as NTSC, after the National Television Systems Committee, an industry group established in 1940 to develop technical standards for television broadcasts.

The term "ATV" embraces both High Definition Television (HDTV) and Enhanced Definition Television (EDTV). HDTV systems aim to offer approximately twice the vertical and horizontal resolution of NTSC receivers and to provide picture quality approaching that of 35 mm film and audio quality equal to that of compact discs. "Simulcast" HDTV systems use design principles independent of existing NTSC technology. They are not receivable on conventional NTSC television sets. EDTV refers to systems that provide limited improvements over NTSC. EDTV signals may be receivable on current NTSC television receivers. We do not envision adopting an EDTV standard, if at all, prior to reaching a decision on an HDTV standard.

II. ELIGIBILITY AND RELATED ISSUES

A. Initial Eligibility

5. Our objective in this proceeding is to effect a major technological improvement in television transmission by allowing broadcasters to implement ATV. Our goal is not to launch a new and separate video service.

6. We continue to believe that the public interest would best be served by limiting the pool of initial ATV applicants to existing broadcasters. First, existing broadcasters have invested considerable resources and expertise in the present system and represent a large pool of experienced talent. As we have previously stated, given the risks inherent in ATV, existing broadcasters' continued involvement appears to be the most practical and expedient way to bring improved ATV television service to the American public. Second, conversion to ATV represents a major change in broadcast technology nationwide. We believe that it would increase the potential for disruption to the viewing public if a technological change of this magnitude were accompanied by a change in the ownership structure of the entire television broadcasting industry. Initially restricting eligibility for ATV frequencies to existing broadcasters thus would appear to serve the public interest by hastening and smoothing the transition to ATV transmission.

7. It is still our tentative view that restricting eligibility to existing broadcasters is legally permissible and consistent with the Supreme Court's decision in Ashbacker Radio Corp. v. FCC, 326 U.S. 327 (1945). In that case, the Supreme Court held that the Commission is required under section 309 of the Communications Act to give comparative consideration to all bona fide mutually exclusive applications. In so holding, however, the Court did not preclude the Commission from establishing threshold qualification standards that must be met before applicants are entitled to comparative consideration.

9. In order to ensure a smooth transition to ATV technology, we also propose to suspend application of the television multiple ownership rules, 47 C.F.R. §73.3555, for ATV spectrum on a limited basis. We propose to permit existing licensees that are awarded an additional ATV channel to hold both their NTSC and ATV licenses, even though their signals overlap, and to permit group owners to hold both NTSC and paired ATV channels, even though nationwide ceilings are exceeded, until such time as existing licensees are required to convert to ATV service exclusively.

IV. SPECTRUM ISSUES

A. Noncommercial Allotments

27. Our technical studies thus far indicate that, for the most part, we will be able to offer an additional 6 MHz of spectrum to existing stations for ATV without using vacant spectrum now reserved in specific communities for noncommercial stations.

28. Our tentative conclusions assume, of course, that the transmission system ultimately selected can function within the spacings ultimately adopted and will not require spacings equal to those in effect for NTSC today.[11]

---

11. Staff studies have assumed 100 mile co-channel spacings, and no UHF taboo spacings for ATV. These spacings are less than those in effect for NTSC today. The current co-

29. However, in the exceptional case where it may be necessary to use a vacant noncommercial allotment to allow present delivery of ATV service, we propose to do so.

B. LPTV and Translator Services

30. It is likely that LPTV and translator stations will be displaced to some degree in the major markets.[12]

31. From the time we first authorized low power service, we stressed that we would permit low power service only as a secondary service, despite the public benefits flowing from the diverse, locally responsive programming it could produce. Although low power interests have argued that displacement of LPTV stations by ATV would contravene the Communications Act by reducing diversity, diversity is not the only criterion that we are bound to consider, or indeed, did consider when we authorized the low power service. One of the other factors leading us to accord secondary status to the low power service was the spectrum demands of competing services, precisely the decisional factor motivating us today.

V. CONVERSION TO ATV

A. The Future Role of NTSC

34. We envision ATV as an improved form of television that, if successful, will eventually replace existing NTSC. In order to make a smooth transition to this technology, we earlier decided to permit delivery of ATV on a separate 6 MHz channel. As we explained in the First Order, a "simulcast" system will transmit the increased information of an HDTV signal in a channel of a size—6 MHz—equivalent to that used in the current television channel plan.

35. In order to continue to promote spectrum efficiency, we intend to require broadcasters to "convert" entirely to ATV—i.e., to surrender one 6 MHz frequency and broadcast only in ATV once ATV becomes the prevalent medium.

B. Surrendering a Frequency

37. It is our tentative view that the public interest requires that we set a firm deadline or other triggering event for broadcasters to surrender their NTSC frequencies and convert entirely to ATV. Establishing a definite point by which conversion must take place will provide clear notice of this transition to the broadcast industry, the viewing public, and other potential users of the spectrum to be relinquished. We seek comment on this tentative conclusion, as well as on the un-

---

channel separation varies from 155 miles to 205 miles for UHF channels and from 170 miles to 220 miles for VHF channels, depending on which part of the country the stations are located in; the current UHF taboo spacings are 20 to 75 miles.

12. A low power station is a broadcast television facility with secondary service status that is authorized at maximum power levels lower than those of full-service television stations. Low power stations may retransmit the programs of a full-service station and may originate programming. Translators are low-power stations that do not originate programming and act only to retransmit the signals of a full-service station.

derlying assumption that there may be other, superior uses for the spectrum to be surrendered.

38. In fixing an appropriate ATV conversion date, we are most concerned that sufficient numbers of consumers purchase ATV receivers by that point so as to justify discontinuance of NTSC broadcasts.[13]

39. There are several ways in which a conversion date for ATV could be selected. One option would use achievement of a specific nationwide penetration rate (defined as a percentage of households with ATV receivers) as the triggering event for ATV conversion, with all broadcast stations being required to convert to ATV transmission within a certain period of time (for example, three years) after a particular penetration rate was achieved.

40. We recognize, however, that use of a nationwide penetration rate as a conversion point for ATV conceivably may pose a hardship to stations in smaller or less affluent markets. In such cases, there might be fewer financial resources to permit either consumers to purchase receivers or stations to construct and equip an ATV facility.[14] We thus seek comment on whether we should modify the first option to require conversion for ATV only after a specific penetration rate is achieved on a market-by-market basis. Such an option would appear to better calibrate consumers' readiness to convert to ATV, and would probably result in stations in larger markets converting more quickly than those in smaller markets. On the other hand, such piecemeal conversion might adversely affect the availability of network or other nationwide ATV programming.

41. A final option would be to establish a firm date by which one frequency would have to be surrendered and the conversion to ATV completed. Such a date in itself would allow sufficient time for consumers to purchase new ATV receivers and adjust to this new transmission form. We believe that this option has the advantage of providing clear notice to licensees and to the public of the date by which conversion must take place. It would also be more efficient to administer than the other options discussed above because the Commission would not

---

13. *See, e.g.,* Fourth Interim Report of the Working Party 5 on Economic Factors and Market Penetration of the Planning Subcommittee of the Advisory Committee on Advanced Television Service (March 4, 1991), at 8 (PS WP5 Market Penetration Report). The report states that the Chairman of Working Party 5 believes that an "optimistic" view of ATV penetration—*i.e.,* 40% penetration 10 years after 1% penetration is reached—is merited. In this view, "it remains likely that ATV home video players and ATV cable service will in fact precede the introduction of ATV terrestrial broadcasting, and even seed the market to the one percent penetration point before the ATV terrestrial service is inaugurated." PS WP5 Market Penetration Report at 7–8. [Footnote relocated.]

14. The PS WP5 Market Penetration Report cites both a PBS study (projecting a cost for an ATV facility ranging from a low $1.7 million for pass-through of network programming on a low-band VHF station, to $12.3 million for full program origination capability on a UHF station) and a CBS Study projecting a $1.5 million cost for network pass-through and $11.6 million for total transmission/studio facility for the first stations that construct, and $741,000 for network pass through and $6.9 million for total plant construction for the last group of stations that move to ATV. CBS projects that the $11.6 million investment for the first 30 stations in the largest markets serving 31% of television households will occur over a period of five years. The CBS Study projects that the cost for stations in smaller markets starting construction of ATV facilities four years later, would fall to less than $8 million. [Footnote relocated.]

have to make determinations of nationwide or market penetration rates in scheduling alternative conversion dates.

B. Compatibility with Other Media

47. Until this point, we have considered implementation issues that bear on
the use of ATV technology in the television transmission medium. However, this
technology may have an impact on, or applications to, other media. ATV compatibility with other forms of transmission and applications would appear to be
a desirable policy objective, provided that it does not unduly compromise other
goals in this proceeding. To what extent can or should we encourage compatibility of a terrestrial broadcast ATV system with other media, including other video
delivery media such as satellite transmission or video cassette recorders, and with
computer applications and other forms of data transmission?

Notes and Questions

1. **Spectrum Allocation.** The Commission seems to be making two distinct major
spectrum allocation decisions. First, it proposes to allocate for advanced television a very large chunk of spectrum (almost as much as is currently occupied by
conventional television broadcasters) and award that chunk to those same broadcasters. (Parts I and II.) Does this seem wise? How does the Commission know
that this is a valuable use of these frequencies? Might there be preferable alternative uses? How might the Commission figure out the answer to that question?
And how could the Commission determine that the reduction in diversity caused
by the loss of low power stations was outweighed by the benefit (in terms of increased picture quality) enjoyed by those willing to purchase HDTV sets? (*See*
¶31). Why not simply tell broadcasters that they may broadcast NTSC or HDTV
or both (if they can invent a signal compression technique that will allow both
signals to be transmitted within 6 MHz)? Note that no federal commission dictated when would be the appropriate time to start manufacturing compact disc
players. Is that a regrettable fact? An inappropriate analogy? Is this just another
instance of "industry capture," in which the agency turns out to be regulated by
the firms rather than vice versa?

Second, the Commission proposes to set a date by which broadcasters must
surrender their NTSC frequencies and convert to HDTV. (Part V.) How does the
agency know that there are more valuable uses for the old NTSC frequencies
than continuing to broadcast NTSC signals?

2. **HDTV/DTV on Other Platforms.** Note the Commission's comment (in a footnote in ¶38) that "it remains likely that ATV home video players and ATV cable
service will in fact precede the introduction of ATV terrestrial broadcasting."
This prediction has been borne out: satellite and cable operators have chosen to
transmit their programs digitally, and most of them paid for their spectrum and
wires. Does this cast doubt on the decision to give away an extra 6 megahertz to
broadcasters? What might be the rationale for giving away that spectrum but
charging satellite companies for spectrum and cable companies for wire? In addition, these cable and satellite digital services probably would have spurred the
creation of a market for higher definition digital receivers absent either an FCC
push or digital terrestrial broadcasting: some consumers would be willing to buy

a new (and more expensive) television to receive the much clearer digital picture from the cable or satellite company, rather than having it converted to the inferior NTSC system. If that assertion is incorrect, what, if anything, does that tell us about the underlying assumption in the FCC's proceeding that consumers will buy a new and much more expensive television to receive digital over-the-air broadcasts? Does the possibility of a digital receiver market arising from cable and satellite transmissions cast doubt on the wisdom of the entire enterprise of a policy aimed at fostering digital and/or high-definition television via terrestrial broadcast? Why did the FCC not simply wait to see whether video technologies that do not create interference — such as cable TV or video cassettes — would evolve toward HDTV/DTV as a norm and permit broadcasters to shift as well if they wished to do so?

3. Reclaiming NTSC Spectrum. As part of the Balanced Budget Act of 1997,[15] Congress provided that broadcasters must give up one of their two sets of frequencies by the end of 2006 (the broadcasters get to choose which one); this extra spectrum will ultimately be auctioned.[16] Thus, it is now established that the extra spectrum granted to conventional broadcasters for HDTV/DTV purposes will be returned at a date certain. Or will it? The 1997 Act also provides that the FCC can extend a broadcaster's use of both sets of spectrum beyond 2006 if 15% of the households in a given market do not either subscribe to a multichannel service that carries the available digital transmissions or have a television receiver capable of receiving digital signals. Does a requirement of 85% market penetration represent a too-generous safety net for broadcasters? Does requiring *only* 85% represent an abandonment of the commitment to free television for all Americans?

4. Allotments. Giving every broadcaster an HDTV license perpetuates the results of the 1952 *Report and Order* establishing that most Americans would receive fewer television signals in return for having television transmitters more widely scattered and operated at lower power. Is this sensible? Would it have been preferable to adopt an allotment plan for HDTV that focused more on providing increased viewing options to households and less on promoting "localism"? Basing HDTV allotments on such novel principles would greatly increase the potential for more broadcast TV networks, and those new networks might compete with existing commercial television networks. Such an approach would, of course, require abandoning the decision to give every existing broadcaster an HDTV license. Would that abandonment cause any harm? To whom?

5. Licensing. By making it a precondition of seeking an HDTV license that the applicant have an NTSC license, and by proposing to offer every NTSC licensee an HDTV license, the Commission avoided the need for comparative hearings.[17] Does the desire to avoid comparative hearings explain why the agency wants to give every NTSC licensee an HDTV license? Why wouldn't a lottery work just as

---

15. This is the same statute that broadened auctions of spectrum to include broadcast applicants; *see* Chapter Five.

16. 47 U.S.C. §309(j)(14).

17. Unless its legal conclusion in ¶7 is wrong. This aspect of the NPRM also calls into question just how seriously the FCC takes its stated goal of promoting diversity of ownership. What has become of the arguments advanced by the FCC, in support of its minority preference policies, in *Metro Broadcasting*?

well? Note that the Telecommunications Act of 1996 ratified the FCC's decision to limit eligibility for digital television spectrum assignments to existing broadcasters.[18] Relatedly, now that Congress has provided that broadcast licenses will be assigned via auction, and that the spectrum allocated for digital television (or its equivalent) will be reclaimed at the end of 2006, is the argument for giving existing broadcasters an additional license strengthened or weakened?

B. Choosing a Standard

From the outset, it was clear that one of the big issues in the ATV proceeding was going to be the choice of a broadcasting standard. One obvious possibility was the existing HDTV system that had been developed in Japan, whose government had helped to fund development of an HDTV system since the early 1970s. That system was available as of the beginning of the FCC proceeding in 1987. The availability of the Japanese system produced not acceptance but instead a gnashing of Congressional teeth at the thought that, with respect to this technology, the United States had fallen behind the more organized and directed Japan. The irritated members of Congress publicly opposed the adoption of the Japanese standard, pushing instead for a new broadcasting standard to be developed in the U.S. The FCC responded to these sentiments by declining to adopt the Japanese system and setting up a process for choosing a new (presumably U.S.-centric) HDTV standard.[19]

The resulting process for choosing a standard proved to be a lengthy one. Various groups developed competing standards, and only after long negotiations did they agree to a "Grand Alliance" that would put forward a single proposal. The Grand Alliance's proposal was heralded by the FCC (among others) as a "single, best-of-the-best system," and in May 1996 the FCC issued a formal notice proposing its adoption.[20] A sense of real achievement was perhaps understandable. The government had let the industry take the lead in developing different kinds of HDTV. The result was a combined system that was far superior to that developed in Japan, thus presenting an apparent instance of private creativity showing its superiority to government-directed innovation. But just when everyone in the broadcasting industry was feeling triumphant, a spoiler came on the scene—the computer industry. It proposed that the FCC refrain from setting any standard at all. This was not something that the FCC had seriously considered. The message from the computer companies was that, in contrast to the FCC's long history of setting standards for broadcasting, standards for computing had been winnowed through market competition to see which ones gained the greatest acceptance; and, the computer companies added none too subtly, which of these two industries had shown greater dynamism, growth, and improvements in services offered? As the following *Order* reveals, the computer industry eventually agreed to a compromise with the proponents of the Grand Alliance; the compromise provided for a standard, but a much more skeletal one

---

18. 47 U.S.C. §336(a).
19. This episode is described in greater detail in Brinkley, *supra* note 7.
20. In re Advanced Television Systems, Fifth Further Notice of Proposed Rule Making, 11 FCC Rcd. 6235 (1996).

than had originally been proposed. The video format constraints—the number of lines of resolution, the number of pixels (picture elements) per line, the aspect ratio, and the scanning parameters—would be left to market forces. Along the way, the *Order* deals with some fundamental questions about not only whether it is wise to have a standard ex ante, but also what specific sort of standard might be appropriate and what role the government should take in the standard-setting process.

IN RE ADVANCED TELEVISION SYSTEMS
Fourth Report and Order, 11 FCC Rcd. 17771(1996)

I. INTRODUCTION

1. In this, the *Fourth Report and Order* in our digital television (DTV) proceeding, we adopt a standard for the transmission of digital television.[21] This standard is a modification of the ATSC DTV Standard proposed in the *Fifth Further Notice of Proposed Rule Making* [in this proceeding], 11 FCC Rcd. 6235 (1996), and is consistent with a consensus agreement voluntarily developed by a broad cross-section of parties, including the broadcasting, consumer equipment manufacturing and computer industries. The Standard we adopt does not include requirements with respect to scanning formats, aspect ratios, and lines of resolution. For clarity, we will refer to this modified standard as the "DTV Standard."

2. This proceeding demonstrates how competing industries, working together, can develop de facto industry selected standards that satisfy the interests of contending parties. We commend these industries for their efforts. We also commend the many dedicated individuals and entities who voluntarily contributed their talents and resources to the development of a world leading digital broadcast television technology.

II. BACKGROUND

4. This proceeding began in 1987, when we issued our first inquiry into the potential for advanced television (ATV) services. Subsequently, over the course of the past decade, we have issued a series of Notices concerning ATV and, based upon the comments received, have made a number of decisions. In the fall of 1987, a few months after initiating this rulemaking proceeding, we established the Advisory Committee on Advanced Television Service ("Advisory Committee" or "ACATS") to provide recommendations concerning technical, economic and public policy issues associated with the introduction of ATV service. Early in the process we decided that no additional spectrum would be allocated for television broadcasting, but that existing broadcasters should be permitted to upgrade their transmission technology so long as the public remains served throughout any transition period. We later decided "that an ATV system that transmits the increased information of an ATV signal in a separate 6 MHz channel independent from an existing NTSC channel will allow for ATV introduction in the most non-disruptive and efficient manner." As the proceeding progressed, all-digital

---

21. This standard will apply only to terrestrial digital television broadcasting and not to other video delivery services.

advanced television systems were developed and we began to refer to advanced television as digital television (DTV) in recognition that, with the development of the technology, it was decided any ATV system was certain to be digital. In February of 1993, the Advisory Committee reported that a digital HDTV system was achievable, but that all four competing digital systems then under consideration would benefit significantly from further development and none would be recommended over the others at that time. In May of 1993, seven companies and institutions that had been proponents of the four tested digital ATV systems, joined together in a "Grand Alliance" to develop a final digital ATV system for the standard. Over the next two-and-a-half years, that system was developed, extensively tested, and is documented in the ATSC DTV Standard. On November 28, 1995, the Advisory Committee voted to recommend the Commission's adoption of the ATSC DTV Standard.

5. The system described by the ATSC DTV Standard is generally recognized to represent a significant technological breakthrough. In addition to being able to broadcast one, and under some circumstances two, high definition television (HDTV) programs, the Standard allows for multiple streams, or "multicasting," of Standard Definition Television (SDTV) programming at a visual quality better than the current analog signal. Utilizing this Standard, broadcasters can transmit three, four, five, or more such program streams simultaneously.[22] The Standard allows for the broadcast of literally dozens of CD-quality audio signals. It permits the rapid delivery of large amounts of data; an entire edition of the local daily newspaper could be sent, for example, in less than two seconds. Other material, whether it be telephone directories, sports information, stock market updates, information requested concerning certain products featured in commercials, computer software distribution, interactive education materials, or virtually any other type of information access can also be provided. It allows broadcasters to send, video, voice and data simultaneously and to provide a range of services dynamically, switching easily and quickly from one type of service to another.

6. On May 9, 1996, we adopted the *Fifth Further Notice*, recommending adoption of the ATSC DTV Standard, and seeking comment on additional issues.

7. Several commenters to the May 9 *Fifth Further Notice*, including representatives of the computer industry and filmmakers, objected to adoption of the ATSC DTV Standard. After several efforts to reach consensus among the industry groups failed, the groups came together again. On November 25, 1996, representatives of a broad cross section of the broadcast, computer and receiver manufacturing industries reached an agreement ("the Agreement") and, the following day, submitted it to the Commission.[23]

---

22. This is made possible through the use of digital compression technology and a packetized transport structure using packet headers and descriptors, which have been described as "a kind of translator to tell all digital devices what type of data is being transmitted." Advisory Committee Final Report and Recommendation, Advisory Committee on Advanced Television Service, November 28, 1995, at p. 15.

23. Filmmaker representatives, although party to the negotiations leading to the agreement, oppose the agreement because it does not require the transmission of motion pictures in their original aspect ratios.

III. COMMENTS[24]

8. Technical Standards for DTV. We received a broad range of comments regarding the *Fifth Further Notice* about whether and how to adopt technical standards for digital broadcast and the proper role of government in the standard setting process. There is widespread agreement among commenters that selection of a DTV standard should be analyzed in terms of network effects, that is the indirect benefits that accrue to other DTV users when any particular user adopts DTV. Broadcasters, computer interests and cable interests agree that broadcasting is a network product; that issues surrounding selection of a DTV standard are influenced by network effects; and that in order to evaluate the various alternatives, it is important to understand how network effects will operate. While commenters agreed on a common analytical framework, they disagreed on the relative severity of the startup, coordination and potential splintering problems facing digital broadcast television. Startup refers to the situation where everyone would be better off adopting DTV technology but no one has the incentive to move first. Coordination is the collaborative effort by broadcasters, consumer equipment manufacturers, and program producers that is necessary to introduce DTV. Splintering refers to the breakdown of the consensus or agreement to use the DTV Standard.

9. Commenters also disagreed on the availability and effectiveness of market-based mechanisms to solve these problems and to facilitate the goals and objectives established in this proceeding. Broadcasters, equipment manufacturers and some consumer groups contend that DTV has startup, coordination and splintering problems that are more severe than those of other network industries and that a DTV standard adopted by the Commission is needed to overcome these problems. In contrast, cable and computer interests contend that all sectors of the broadcast industry have significant incentives to reach a consensus on transmission and reception standards without a government mandate.

10. Broadcasters warn that a market-driven selection of a standard would result in barriers to the introduction of DTV if different incompatible systems develop. Under a market-based approach, for example, broadcasters in the same community could select different and incompatible transmission systems so that consumers would only be able to obtain service from those television stations using the system that is compatible with the receiver they have purchased and be denied access to those using another transmission system. Broadcasters maintain that a government-mandated standard is essential to ensure a universally available, advertiser-supported over-the-air digital broadcast service in the future. In contrast, cable interests do not agree that there are unique characteristics or public policy goals attendant to broadcast DTV, or that there would be a market failure unless a mandatory transmission standard is adopted. They argue that the rationale for not adopting transmission standards for DBS, PCS, MMDS [Multichannel Multipoint Distribution Service, or "wireless cable"], and DARS [Digital Audio Radio Service] applies to DTV.

11. There is likewise a range of opinion on the merits of the ATSC DTV Standard. Broadcasters, equipment manufacturers, the Grand Alliance, and

---

24. This Section will first summarize the initial positions of parties. The extent to which their positions have changed since their initial filings is summarized in the subsection concerning the Agreement.

ATSC urge the Commission to adopt the complete ATSC DTV Standard. They contend that only a Commission-adopted standard will supply the certainty needed by all parties to undertake the transition to DTV and that the ATSC DTV Standard is the best DTV standard in the world. The Grand Alliance contends that "the system's all-digital layered architecture, its packetized data transport structure, its use of headers and descriptors, its support of multiple picture formats and frame rates with a heavy emphasis on progressive scan[25] and square pixels,[26] and its compliance with MPEG-2 international compression and transport standards, give it unprecedented and unmatched interoperability with computers and telecommunications."

12. Computer interests, lead by the Computer Industry Coalition on Advanced Television Service (CICATS), urge us not to adopt a DTV standard but state that if we decide to the contrary we should only mandate a minimum baseline standard based exclusively on progressive scanning technology. The National Telecommunications and Information Administration (NTIA) stresses the need for a single mandatory DTV standard but recommends limiting a standard to only those elements necessary to provide certainty, encourage adoption, ensure the opportunity for technological developments, and promote evolution to an all-progressive scan system. NTIA concludes that the best solution would be for interested parties to reach a consensus on disputed issues.

13. As noted above, the cable industry opposes adoption of mandatory standards. The National Cable Television Association (NCTA) is not critical of the specific ATSC DTV Standard, but questions whether any standard should be dictated by government.

14. Public interest groups generally favor adoption of a single mandatory standard although they differ on what that standard should be. For example, Consumer Federation of America and Media Access Project (CFA/MAP) believes that the public interest will be served if the Commission adopts a digital television standard that 1) reduces the cost of digital receivers and converters and 2) permits the convergence of video and computer technologies. In contrast, National Consumers League urges adoption because "in the absence of a standard, consumers will be confused. The marketplace will send a number of conflicting messages as new products will diverge in purpose and application. Demand for HDTV and related products will not materialize, and we will not experience the dramatic price reductions normally associated with consumer electronics products. The market will simply not be able to function efficiently, and consumers will literally pay the price." Citizens for HDTV contends that the Commission should adopt the Standard for several reasons, which include "the unique 'open' and 'universal' nature of the Nation's broadcasting system, as distinguished from

---

25. In interlaced scanning, which is currently used in NTSC television, odd and even numbered lines of the picture are sent consecutively, as two separate fields. Alternate scans through the picture scan all even numbered, then all odd numbered lines. These two fields are superimposed to create one frame, or complete picture, at the receiver. In progressive scanning, instead of skipping rows as in interlaced scanning, each line is scanned in succession from the top of the picture to the bottom, with a complete image sent in each frame. This type of scanning is commonly found in computer displays today.

26. A pixel is an abbreviation for "picture element," the smallest distinguishable portion of a picture. "Square pixels" means that picture elements are equally spaced in the vertical and horizontal direction. This simplifies computer processing of images.

other media; the appropriate role of government in adopting and mandating this Standard; the certainty and confidence [it] affords for investments by consumers; and the importance of the Standard to DTV compatibility with today's NTSC broadcast system and the Commission's planned recapture of part of the TV bands after the transition is completed."

15. Alternatives to Standards. Little comment was received concerning the two alternative approaches to standards specifically mentioned in the *Fifth Further Notice*: that we authorize use of and prohibit interference to users of the ATSC DTV Standard, or adopt the ATSC DTV Standard for allocation and assignment purposes only. The many parties that support adoption of the complete standard generally believe that these less inclusive options would not provide the certainty necessary for the successful launch of DTV and would not provide an adequate basis for either the design or the purchase of DTV receivers.

16. The ATSC DTV Standard. Substantial comment was received concerning the merits of, and objections to, the ATSC DTV Standard. Broadcasters, equipment manufacturers, the Grand Alliance, ATSC, and the ATTC praise the Standard as representing the best digital television system in the world and one that is unmatched in terms of flexibility, extendibility, interoperability and headroom for growth. They note it uses primarily progressive scan and square pixels, the latter being used in all HDTV formats. These features, they contend, make it the most computer-compatible digital television system in the world because computer monitors use these features. They argue that the Standard's inclusion of four interlaced formats will benefit broadcasters by allowing for the use of interlaced scan where broadcasters determine it desirable to do so, such as when broadcasting archived material that was filmed in interlaced scan or where interlaced scan may be superior, such as in low- light conditions often accompanying electronic news gathering.

17. Commenters representing computer interests and some public interest groups generally oppose the standard. Computer interests object to discrete features of the Standard, including the presence of interlaced scanning and the use of non-square pixels in some of the formats, as well as the maximum frame (or "refresh") rate of 60 Hz[27]. These features, when taken together, assertedly hinder the compatibility of the system with computer applications, drive up the cost of receiving equipment, and delay the convergence of computer and television technologies. CICATS recommends that the Commission adopt a standard consisting of a single video format with 480 lines of progressive scanning, a broadcaster determined picture aspect ratio, and the utilization of only square pixel spacing. Such a standard would allow for an enhancement layer that would permit, but not require, the transmission of high definition television by stations equipped to do so. This approach, it contends, would enable all consumers to receive, at a minimum, an SDTV picture on their digital equipment, at equal or better quality and significantly lower costs than under the ATSC DTV Standard. Public interest groups such as CFA and MAP believe that the ATSC DTV Standard uses too many formats and that the baseline CICATS system will be cheaper, promoting both a more rapid and orderly transition to DTV (and the return of spectrum) and convergence of computer and television technologies.

---

27. This is the number of frames transmitted per second.

18. Supporters of the Standard respond that it is far more computer friendly than any other digital television system in use anywhere in the world, relying as it does primarily on progressive scan and square pixels. While these commenters assert that current technology prohibits the use of progressive scanning for images of more than 1000 lines in the 6 MHz channel, they concede that an all progressive system would be preferred once possible. In the interim, convergence will not be hampered because the Standard enables consumers to choose the display formats they prefer, as interlaced programs may be displayed on progressive receivers (and vice versa). In any case, supporters of the Standard assert that interlaced source material will continue to be widely used for many years and progressive scan receivers such as those advocated by computer interests will have to include a de-interlacer even if only to display NTSC transmissions during the simulcast period. Moreover, they contend that there are already PC/TV products on the market using analog NTSC technology, which relies on interlace scanning, thus proving that interlaced scanning is not incompatible with computers. Therefore, they do not believe it credible that the introduction of the primarily progressive scan ATSC DTV Standard would somehow stymie further convergence, especially given its flexible design which permits future innovations to be accommodated.

20. *Review or Sunset of Standard.* Most commenters addressing the issue advocate either proceeding under our current processes for regulatory change or reviewing the Standard at some definite future time. Broadcasters and equipment manufacturers, for instance, believe that we should consider modifications but should not establish a specific review date or a sunset. They argue that doing so would inject an element of uncertainty into the transition process, discourage consumers, broadcasters and manufacturers from making investments, and be arbitrary because the transition timetable, the timing of production of DTV sets, and the timing of consumer acceptance of DTV sets is unknown at the present time. These parties emphasize the inherent flexibility of the Standard and argue that this mitigates the need for a fixed review or sunset.

21. NTIA urges us to ensure that the industries involved develop a clearly defined plan to promote speedy migration to an all-progressive scan system that moves expeditiously and includes a target date for full transition. NTIA suggests that we periodically review the migration to an all progressive system.

26. *November 26, 1996, Agreement.* As noted above, some of the commenters have altered their positions since the initial round of comments. After further discussions and negotiations, the parties to the November 26, 1996, Agreement urge us to adopt the modified standard we are calling the DTV Standard. The Grand Alliance and ATSC view it as a way to resolve the controversy that has delayed adoption of a DTV standard. They believe that reliance on voluntary industry standards for the formats to be used for digital television is preferable to the cost of the further delay that would result if we fail to act while the parties remain at an impasse. Full service broadcasters endorse the Agreement for similar reasons. The Association for Maximum Service Television, Inc. (MSTV), believes the Agreement is a "workable compromise" that will permit the compatible development of progressive technologies. One low power television broadcaster, International Broadcasting Network, objects to the process that resulted in the Agreement and contends that low power television broadcasters were excluded.

27. Equipment manufacturers endorse the Agreement as "an important step toward reducing reliance on Government-mandated standards," that makes it likely that "the industry standard becomes the vehicle around which the marketplace organizes." They believe that the Agreement will provide sufficient certainty and that the video formats, although not mandated by the Commission, will remain viable nevertheless because there is a voluntary industry standard in place.

IV. THE DIGITAL TELEVISION STANDARD

30. Adoption of the Digital Standard. In the *Fifth Further Notice*, we listed four objectives regarding the authorization and implementation of a DTV standard: 1) to ensure that all affected parties have sufficient confidence and certainty in order to promote the smooth introduction of a free and universally available digital broadcast television service; 2) to increase the availability of new products and services to consumers through the introduction of digital broadcasting; 3) to ensure that our rules encourage technological innovation and competition; and 4) to minimize regulation and assure that any regulations we do adopt remain in effect no longer than necessary. In addition to these objectives, we stated our intentions to consider how adoption of the DTV Standard would affect other goals enumerated in this proceeding including facilitating the provision of digital video services, spurring a rapid conversion from NTSC to DTV, and recovering the analog broadcast spectrum after conversion.

31. In the *Fifth Further Notice*, we proposed to adopt the ATSC DTV Standard. We sought comment on requiring use of some layers of the ATSC DTV Standard but making others optional. In this *Report and Order*, we decide to adopt this last alternative and to require the use of all layers of the ATSC DTV Standard, except the video format layer, which will remain optional.

32. Our decision today to adopt the ATSC DTV Standard, as modified, is based on a careful weighing and balancing of the various goals and objectives outlined in this proceeding. We conclude that adopting the DTV Standard will fulfill the four objectives set out in the *Fifth Further Notice*.

33. First, we conclude that the DTV Standard will serve our goal of ensuring that all affected parties have sufficient confidence and certainty in order to promote the smooth introduction of a free and universally available digital broadcast television service. As we have recognized before, broadcast television is unique. It is free, available to nearly every American, and many Americans rely on broadcast television programming as a primary source of information and entertainment. Because of these characteristics, we stated that the goals of certainty and reliability take on special significance and strengthen the case for our adoption of a DTV standard. The DTV Standard we adopt today will help ensure that broadcast television remains available to all Americans in the digital era.

34. Many commenters argued that startup, coordination and potential splintering problems are so severe in digital broadcast television that they cannot be adequately solved without the Commission adopting a single DTV standard. We recognize that these problems may be more troublesome for digital broadcast television than cable, DBS, MMDS and other subscription video services which have a greater degree of control over the equipment used by their customers. While we are not convinced that these problems are so severe that they would

absolutely preclude us from allowing the market to operate without a set standard, we are concerned that market solutions may result in more than one sustainable transmission standard. Such an outcome might result in compatibility problems and increase the risk that consumer DTV equipment purchased in one city would not work well in another city; that a receiver would not display all the broadcast channels in a city; or that a digital television set purchased one year might not work several years later. Such results would hurt consumers and make it more difficult to preserve a universally available broadcast television service.

35. More than one transmission standard could also cause some consumers and licensees to postpone purchasing DTV equipment, because they do not wish to take the risk of investing in what may soon become obsolete technology, or because they believe better technologies will soon become available. This could slow investment during the early stages of the transition to DTV and, thereby, slow the transition to DTV.

36. In addition, more than one transmission standard would make it more difficult to facilitate an efficient allotment of broadcast channels and protect against interference. Determining interference performance becomes more complicated as the number of transmission systems increases, because each system's interference characteristics must be tested against every other system. This could complicate moving some licensees to new channels following the conversion to DTV and decrease the amount of spectrum recovered.

37. For all of these reasons, we believe that adopting the DTV Standard provides additional certainty that the public policy goals unique to broadcast DTV are realized. Simply protecting a standard, or using a standard for allocation purposes, would not address our concerns with "wait-and-see" behavior and preserving a universally available broadcast television service. We also reject the argument that the Agreement is too restrictive and still includes too many mandatory aspects of the DTV Standard. As more fully explained below, we believe that the entire DTV Standard is needed to achieve our goals.

38. Second, we conclude that adopting the DTV Standard will increase the availability of new products and services for consumers. The DTV Standard is flexible and extensible and permits data broadcasting as well as new services. With respect to data broadcasting, the DTV Standard provides for multiple 19 Mega (Million) bits per second (Mbps) digital pipelines directly into the home of every American. While we would anticipate that licensees would, at the very least, continue to provide tomorrow what consumers have come to expect today—that is, at least one free program per 6 MHz channel—we also expect to authorize its use to transmit, for example, newspapers, stock market or sports data and, perhaps of greatest significance, software applications directly to computing devices.

39. Third, we conclude that incorporating the DTV Standard into our Rules will encourage technological innovation and competition. In particular, we conclude that our decision not to specify video formats will result in greater choice and diversity of equipment, allow computer equipment and software firms more opportunity to compete by promoting interoperability, and result in greater consumer benefits by allowing an increase in the availability of new products and services. By not adopting video formats, we are allowing consumers to choose which formats are most important to them. Thus, we avoid the possibility that

we could inhibit development of services which might, in fact, draw consumers more readily to embrace digital broadcasting and thus, hasten its adoption. By not specifying video formats in this respect we foster competition among those aspects of the technology where we are least able to predict the outcome, choosing instead to rely upon the market and consumer demand.

40. Moreover, the DTV Standard itself is highly extensible. The DTV Standard remains fully digital and incorporates packet identifiers (PIDs) which provide a large amount of "headroom" for further development without requiring changes to the DTV Standard. We note that ATSC is already at work on technical standards to facilitate data broadcasting with DTV systems. It has formed a new ATSC Specialist Group on Data Broadcasting to develop data broadcasting standards that "will provide the mechanism for distribution of computer files including programs (executable code) and data."

41. Furthermore, there is little risk in such extensibility making obsolete consumer investment in digital receivers or decoders. While not all receivers would be capable of interpreting new PIDs, we are satisfied that, "backward compatibility is assured when new bit streams are introduced into the transport system as existing decoders will automatically ignore new PIDs" and continue to decode and display the intended material. The resultant conditions would be reminiscent of the introduction of color or stereo sound to the NTSC system. Earlier equipment continued to work unimpaired even as newer equipment provided additional or improved features.

42. Finally, we conclude that adopting this Standard provides for the minimum of regulation needed to provide for a smooth transition. At the same time, we provide the certainty needed for the transition. The DTV Standard eliminates an unnecessary government requirement by not specifying video formats. A key point of contention throughout this proceeding has been the migration to progressive scan transmission formats. While almost all parties agree that, ultimately, progressive scanning is superior to interlaced across a variety of dimensions, the record has been marked by dissent and contradiction about the desirability of allowing both interlaced and progressive scanning, given the over-the-air bandwidth limitation of 6 MHz. Adoption of the DTV Standard, which will allow video formats to be tested and decided by the market, avoids the risk of a mistaken government intervention in the market and is consistent with the deregulatory direction of the Telecommunications Act of 1996.

43. The consensus among the broadcast, set manufacturing and computer industries gives us confidence that the DTV Standard we are adopting does not reflect overreaching or overregulation by government. The Agreement itself recognizes that the ATSC DTV Standard is a "voluntary" one, selected by private parties under the auspices of the ATSC, an American National Standards Institute-accredited organization. That parties representing major segments of such widely divergent industries have forged a consensus over the appropriate standard at once furthers our confidence in the DTV Standard itself and ameliorates concerns that adoption of a standard might retard competition and innovation.

46. We are not persuaded by those who contend that not specifying video formats in the DTV Standard will inject uncertainty into the transition process and delay implementation of digital television. As explained above, we believe that by adopting a transmission standard, we are providing the appropriate level

of certainty that the digital television market will need to move forward. Our belief in this regard is supported by the fact that the major industries affected by this decision have reached an agreement that video formats need not be part of the DTV Standard. The confidence expressed by these parties gives us reasonable assurance it is not necessary to require video formats. We recognize that some parties contend that the Commission should not rely on the Agreement in considering an appropriate digital standard. As the analysis above shows, we are not relying solely on the fact that these parties reached agreement. Nevertheless, we believe the consensus flows from a sufficiently broad segment of the affected industries to warrant our recognition of the end result and factor it into our analysis.

49. We believe that in view of the DTV Standard that we are adopting, a sunset is not necessary. Nonetheless, unforeseeable innovations eventually may require modification of this standard. We want to be sure that we do not inadvertently deter experimentation and innovation by adopting the DTV Standard. Our concern is lessened substantially by the broad range of parties who have agreed that deleting the video format constraints will permit experimentation and innovation and eliminate the need for either a sunset or a scheduled review. Moreover, the ATSC has committed to continue to review the ATSC DTV Standard and to implement compatible extensions of, and deviations from, the ATSC DTV Standard that evolve in the future. We also have adopted a schedule of periodic reviews to monitor the progress of DTV implementation and have requested comment on updating that schedule. We intend to keep abreast of developments and will review our rules as appropriate based upon technological developments and marketplace conditions.

Notes and Questions

1. The Compromise. Is this the triumph of private initiative that the Commission suggests it is? (*See, e.g.*, ¶2) Why did the parties compromise?

2. Regulatory Parity. As the *Fourth Report and Order* notes, the FCC chose not to impose a particular standard on DBS or wireless cable, but to impose nonetheless a skeletal standard on broadcast. What is different about free, over-the-air broadcasting that makes a government-imposed standard necessary? If a standard is necessary for broadcasting, why such a skeletal standard that does not even specify video formats?

3. Serving Which Public's Interest? Note the FCC's emphasis on the flexibility of the standard as allowing for new products and services. Does that reflect a concern for the well-being of broadcasters or consumers (or both or neither)? Are the interests of broadcasters and consumers compatible? Are they separable?

4. Compatibility. This *Order* applies to terrestrial digital television broadcasting and not to other video delivery services such as cable and DBS. Most Americans, of course, receive their television signals via such other services. Cable companies have their own digital services (and conversion devices for them), but even after the adoption of the above *Order* they moved slowly to adopt cable converters compatible with the new DTV broadcast standard, citing (among other concerns) the lack of a significant demand for DTV-compatible cable boxes. Does this absence of demand undercut the entire rationale for having a DTV broadcast standard? Does it show the necessity of such a standard, and in fact justify FCC action to compel cable operators to introduce compatible products? Note that your answer to this second question implicates a more fundamental question that will arise again in Chapter Eleven as part of a discussion of cable must-carry—namely, is it in cable companies' interests to have broadcasters fail?

The FCC chose to answer these questions by initiating a proceeding to impose compatibility standards on cable companies. *In re Compatibility Between Cable Systems and Consumer Electronics Equipment*, FCC 00-137, 2000 WL 377467 (2000). The FCC noted another concern about DTV-cable compatibility, namely that without it "the reclamation and reallocation of a portion of the spectrum now allocated for analog television service will be delayed." Is that a peripheral issue, or a central one?

C. Services Required and Permissible on Spectrum Given to Broadcasers for DTV

One important aspect of the standard approved in the *Order* excerpted above is that it is digital. Because of the compression that digital transmission allows, the standard may not in the end require the use of all 6 megahertz. Furthermore, in light of this new standard, it might be possible for licensees to transmit a lower-definition signal (*i.e.*, not HDTV) and use the rest of the spectrum for other purposes. The FCC tackled the considerations raised by these developments in the following *Order*, which it billed as its final major order in its lengthy advanced television proceeding.

IN RE ADVANCED TELEVISION SYSTEMS
Fifth Report and Order, 12 FCC Rcd. 12809 (1997)

II. ISSUE ANALYSIS

A. Goals

3. Digital technology holds great promise. It allows delivery of brilliant, high-definition, multiple digital-quality programs, and ancillary and supplementary services such as data transfer. But, while the opportunities afforded by digital technology are great, so are the risks. In recent years, competition in the video programming market has dramatically intensified. Cable, Direct Broadcast Satellite (DBS), Local Multipoint Distribution System (LMDS), wireless cable, Open Video Systems (OVS) providers, and others vie, or will soon vie, with broadcast television for audience. Many operators in those services are poised to use digital. Some, like DBS, actually transmit digitally today but must convert the signals to analog NTSC service for display on home receivers, while others have plans to implement digital technology in the future. Broadcasters have long recognized that they must make the switch to digital technology. The viability of digital broadcast television will require millions of Americans to purchase digital television equipment. Because of the advantages to the American public of digital technology—both in terms of services and in terms of efficient spectrum manage-

ment—our rules must strengthen, not hamper, the possibilities for broadcast DTV's success.

4. [There are] two essential objectives that underlie the decisions we make today.

5. First, we wish to promote and preserve free, universally available, local broadcast television in a digital world. Only if DTV achieves broad acceptance can we be assured of the preservation of broadcast television's unique benefit: free, widely accessible programming that serves the public interest. DTV will also help ensure robust competition in the video market that will bring more choices at less cost to American consumers. Particularly given the intense competition in video programming, and the move by other video programming providers to adopt digital technology, it is desirable to encourage broadcasters to offer digital television as soon as possible. We make decisions today designed to promote the viability of digital television services. Digital broadcasters must be permitted the freedom to succeed in a competitive market, and by doing so, attract consumers to digital. In addition, broadcasters' ability to adapt their services to meet consumer demand will be critical to a successful initiation of DTV.

6. Second, we wish to promote spectrum efficiency and rapid recovery of spectrum. Decisions that promote the success of digital television—our first goal—promote this goal as well. The more quickly that broadcasters and consumers move to digital, the more rapidly spectrum can be recovered and then be reallocated or reassigned, or both. The faster broadcasters roll out digital television, the earlier we can recover spectrum.

B. Channel Bandwidth

8. Background. In the Fourth Further Notice/Third Inquiry [in this proceeding], 10 FCC Rcd. 10541 (1995), we noted that we had previously decided that DTV would be introduced by assigning existing broadcasters a temporary channel on which to operate a DTV station during the transition period. We also noted that the DTV transmission system was designed for a 6 MHz channel and added that "we continue to believe that providing 6 MHz channels for ATV purposes represents the optimum balance of broadcast needs and spectrum efficiency." Nonetheless, we invited comment on any means of achieving greater spectrum efficiency, and, in this section, we will discuss whether 6 MHz channels should be allotted.

9. Comments. All broadcasters filing comments support affording a second 6 MHz channel per broadcaster for DTV.

10. However, Media Access Project, et al. (MAP) argues that the Commission should provide broadcasters only enough spectrum to provide one "free" digital program service, either by allocating less than 6 MHz channels to broadcasters, by allocating the spectrum to others and only affording broadcasters "must carry" rights; or by allocating the spectrum to broadcasters but requiring them to lease out excess capacity to unaffiliated programmers. Further, Home Box Office (HBO) asserts that if the Commission determines that the public interest demands Standard Definition Television (SDTV) or other auxiliary applications, it must take another look at whether an entire 6 MHz slice of new spectrum should go to incumbent broadcasters.

12. Contrary to those comments that disagreed with allotting 6 MHz channels for DTV, we believe that the use of 6 MHz channels is necessary to provide viewers and consumers the full benefits of digital television made possible by the DTV Standard, including high definition television (HDTV), standard definition television, and other digital services. The DTV Standard was premised on the use of 6 MHz channels. To specify a different channel size at this late date would not promote our goals in adopting the DTV Standard and would prolong the conversion to DTV. Specifically, we believe that failing to specify a 6 MHz channel would undermine our goals of fostering an expeditious and orderly transition to digital technology and managing the spectrum to permit the recovery of contiguous blocks of spectrum and promote spectrum efficiency. The conversion to DTV would undoubtedly be significantly delayed if we set aside the longstanding expectations of the parties, on which they have based the technology and established their plans, and specified a different channel bandwidth. Accordingly, we reaffirm our earlier judgment and will allot 6 MHz channels for DTV.

D. Definition of Service

1. Spectrum Use

20. The DTV Standard, adopted by the Commission in the *Fourth Report and Order*, 11 FCC Rcd. 17771(1996), permits broadcasters to offer a variety of services. It allows broadcasters to offer free television of higher resolution than analog technology. It allows the broadcast of at least one, and under some circumstances two, high definition television programs; and it allows "multicasting," the simultaneous transmission of three, four, five, or more digital programs. The Standard also allows for the broadcast of CD-quality audio signals. And it permits the rapid delivery of large amounts of data: an entire edition of the local newspaper in less than two seconds, sports information, computer software, telephone directories, stock market updates, interactive educational materials and, indeed, any information that can be translated into digital bits. In addition to allowing broadcasters to transmit video, voice, and data simultaneously, the DTV Standard allows broadcasters to do so dynamically, meaning that they can switch back and forth quickly and easily. For example, a broadcaster could transmit a news program consisting of four separate SDTV programs for local news, national news, weather and sports; while interrupting that programming with a single high definition television commercial with embedded data about the product; or transmit a motion picture in a high definition format, while simultaneously using the excess capacity for transmission of data unrelated to the movie.

21. In light of the flexibility and new capabilities of digital television, we asked to what extent we should permit broadcasters to use their DTV spectrum for uses other than free, over-the-air television. Recognizing that broadcasters are currently allowed to use a portion of their broadcast spectrum for ancillary or supplementary uses that do not interfere with the primary broadcast signal, we asked whether we should permit such uses of the DTV spectrum, and, if so, how such uses should be defined and what portion of the DTV system's capacity should be allowed for such ancillary and supplementary services. Assuming we permitted ancillary and supplementary services, we also asked to what extent we should allow broadcasters to use DTV spectrum for services that go beyond traditional broadcast television or ancillary and supplementary uses analogous to

those allowed under the current regulatory structure. We also asked whether broadcasters should be permitted to provide nonbroadcast and/or subscription services, and, if permitted, how such services should be defined, how much of the DTV capacity should be allowed for such uses, and what, if any, regulation would be appropriate for such services.[28]

22. Comments. Most commenters support affording flexibility to broadcasters to provide ancillary and supplementary services. Joint Broadcasters favor the provision of any ancillary and supplementary services other than those limited by the Telecommunications legislation then pending. AAPTS/PBS favors ancillary broadcast and nonbroadcast use of the DTV channel, noting that flexible use will serve the public interest by helping to spur development of new technologies and to provide greater opportunities for noncommercial stations to enhance their public service to their respective communities. Further, noncommercial stations could use ancillary and supplementary services, without regard to the educational content, as a revenue source to support nonprofit services and operations and the transition to DTV.

23. Microsoft argues that licensees should be given maximum flexibility to provide a wide variety of services and any definition of free over-the-air broadcasting should be narrowly defined in the DTV environment. Indeed, Microsoft argues that the Commission's goal of preserving free over-the-air broadcasting would seem to be an outmoded policy goal.[29] Texas Instruments, Inc. ("Texas Instruments") argues that it is premature for the Commission to regulate the mix of DTV services by requiring a certain amount of capacity to be used for video programming; freedom from regulatory restraints will enhance television's functionality and appeal beyond entertainment to encompass new and unforeseen services.

24. Equipment manufacturers such as General Instrument, Motorola, Thomson, and Zenith, and EIA urge that the Commission should permit flexible use of the DTV channel consistent with the preservation of free over-the-air television and as long as there is a substantial commitment to HDTV. Motorola, however, supports a more restrictive definition of ancillary services.[30] The Digital Grand Alliance states that, while the predominant use should be for free over-the-air television and a minimum number of HDTV hours should be broadcast, the Commission should permit flexible uses of the DTV channel.

25. NYNEX and Personal Communications Industry Association (PCIA) urge that the primary use of the DTV channel should be free over-the-air broadcasting. NYNEX urges that allowing broadcasters to provide nonbroadcast and subscription services would threaten free, universal broadcasting and should be

28. In the *Third Report/Further Notice* [in this proceeding], 7 FCC Rcd. 6924, 6981 (1992), we noted that we did not want ancillary uses to predominate over the primary use of the channel for "ATV" programming. In the *Fourth Further Notice/Third Inquiry*, however, we noted that this presumption had been overtaken by technological developments, specifically the development of the Grand Alliance digital transmission system.

29. [Ed. In the original document, this sentence appears in a footnote.]

30. Motorola believes that ancillary services should be confined to traditional broadcast ancillary services, and ancillary information or interactive services should be substantially related to the video carried by the license holder. According to Motorola; it would be unfair to permit broadcasters to obtain spectrum free of charge and offer non-broadcast subscription services.

permitted only as a residual use of spectrum capacity. PCIA urges that a DTV licensee should be permitted to offer broadcast-related services, such as closed captioning, pay programming, broadcast or narrowcast audio service, and home shopping, but should not be allowed to offer mobile radio services like paging without open competition for DTV licenses by all qualified applicants. HBO argues that the second channel should be used for HDTV and opposes affording broadcasters flexible use of the channel, but adds that if the Commission permits flexibility in the use of the channel, it should nonetheless require that a substantial portion of the day be devoted to HDTV programming. The Benton Foundation opposes spectrum flexibility as affording broadcasters an unfair competitive advantage over competitors and argues that the principal use of the second channel, defined as a minimum of 75% of capacity, should be for broadcast.

27. Decision. As we have noted before, an overarching goal of this proceeding is to promote the success of a free, local television service using digital technology. Broadcast television's universal availability, appeal, and the programs it provides—for example, entertainment, sports, local and national news, election results, weather advisories, access for candidates and public interest programming such as education television for children—have made broadcast television a vital service. It is a service available free of charge to anyone who owns a television set, currently 98% of the population.

28. We expect that the fundamental use of the 6 MHz DTV license will be for the provision of free over-the-air television service. In order to ease the transition from our current analog broadcasting system to a digital system, we will require broadcasters to provide on their digital channel the free over- the-air television service on which the public has come to rely. Specifically, broadcasters must provide a free digital video programming service the resolution of which is comparable to or better than that of today's service and aired during the same time periods that their analog channel is broadcasting.

29. We wish to preserve for viewers the public good of free television that is widely available today. At the same time, we recognize the benefit of permitting broadcasters the opportunity to develop additional revenue streams from innovative digital services. This will help broadcast television to remain a strong presence in the video programming market that will, in turn, help support a free programming service. Thus, we will allow broadcasters flexibility to respond to the demands of their audience by providing ancillary and supplementary services that do not derogate the mandated free, over-the-air program service. Ancillary and supplementary services could include, but are not limited to, subscription television programming, computer software distribution, data transmissions, teletext, interactive services, audio signals, and any other services that do not interfere with the required free service.

30. In addition, we will not impose a requirement that the ancillary and supplementary services provided by the broadcaster must be broadcast-related.

31. The approach we take here, of allowing broadcasters flexibility to provide ancillary and supplementary services is supported both generally and specifically by the 1996 Act. Section 336(a)(2) of the Communications Act, contained in Section 201 of the 1996 Act, provides that if the Commission issues additional licenses for advanced television services, it "shall adopt regulations that allow the holders of such licenses to offer such ancillary or supplementary services on des-

ignated frequencies as may be consistent with the public interest, convenience, and necessity."

32. Under Section 336(b)(2), the Commission is required to limit ancillary and supplementary services to avoid derogation of any advanced television services that the Commission may require. We herein require that any ancillary and supplementary services broadcasters provide will not derogate that required service.

33. Moreover, we believe that the approach we take here will serve the public interest by fostering the growth of innovative services to the public and by permitting the full possibilities of the DTV system to be realized. One of our goals is to promote spectrum efficiency. Encouraging an expeditious transition from analog to digital television and a quick recovery of spectrum will promote that goal. By permitting broadcasters to assemble packages of services that consumers desire, we will promote the swift acceptance of DTV and the penetration of DTV receivers and converters. That, in turn, will help promote the success of the free television service. As discussed above, digital television promises a wealth of possibilities in terms of the kinds and numbers of enhanced services that could be provided to the public. Indeed, we believe that giving broadcasters flexibility to offer whatever ancillary and supplementary services they choose may help them attract consumers to the service, which will, in turn, hasten the transition. In addition, the flexibility we authorize should encourage entrepreneurship and innovation. For example, it may encourage the development of compression technologies that could allow even more digital capacity on a 6 MHz channel, paving the way for multiple high definition programs and more free programming than would otherwise be offered.

2. High Definition

37. *Background.* The Commission requested comment as to whether it should require broadcasters to provide a minimum amount of high definition television and, if so, what minimum amount should be required.

38. *Comments.* Many commenters are opposed to a minimum HDTV requirement. The National Association of Broadcasters (NAB) notes that mandating a certain amount of HDTV could impair broadcasters' ability rapidly to fuel development of the DTV market with complementary program offerings and could prolong the transition to digital television. NAB states: "By providing maximum latitude, the Commission will encourage development of diverse new programming services that will facilitate the most rapid acceptance of ATV and lead to the most rapid return of NTSC spectrum." According to ALTV, independent stations rely on syndicated and local programming, which is less likely to be produced in an HDTV format, so a minimum HDTV requirement would have a disproportionately burdensome impact on independents. Telemundo Group, Inc. ("Telemundo") notes that a minimum HDTV requirement would negatively impact foreign language stations and networks, many of which feature programming produced outside the United States, where HDTV production is likely to lag domestic HDTV production. AAPTS and PBS, in joint comments, oppose a minimum HDTV requirement, noting that the Commission can rely on broadcasters and public television's commitment to HDTV, and argue that if the Commission adopts an HDTV requirement, it should be "liberally waived" for noncommercial stations (particularly those analog stations that may share a DTV channel in the transition). The Benton Foundation argues that mandating an

HDTV minimum serves no public interest because it does not increase the number of voices in the marketplace or contribute to the civic discourse of democracy.

39. Support for a minimum HDTV requirement is expressed by three networks [CBS, ABC, and NBC], HBO, NYNEX Corporation, receiver manufacturers, Viacom, Golden Orange Broadcasting Co., Inc. ("Golden Orange"), and the National Consumers League. Supporters of a minimum requirement generally argue that a requirement will help promote the early availability of HDTV programming, create demand for HDTV receivers, stimulate the market, and speed the transition. Golden Orange, for example, notes that without HDTV, the public will not be motivated to buy receivers. HBO argues that the legal and policy principles that justify awarding incumbent broadcasters a second channel for DTV do not permit broadcasters to use this second channel for anything other than HDTV programming, and, if the FCC allows other than HDTV programming, it should require that a substantial portion of the broadcast day, especially during dayparts and prime time, be devoted exclusively to HDTV. These commenters vary on the amount of HDTV programming that should be required and on how the minimum should be implemented.

41. Decision. Our decisions today, and our previous adoption of the DTV Standard, give broadcasters the opportunity to provide high definition television programming, but we decline to impose a requirement that broadcasters provide a minimum amount of such programming and, instead, leave this decision to the discretion of licensees. The DTV Standard will allow broadcasters to offer the public high definition television, as well as a broad variety of other innovative services. We believe that we should allow broadcasters the freedom to innovate and respond to the marketplace in developing the mix of services they will offer the public. In this regard, we endeavor to carry out the premises of the 1996 Act which, as noted above, seeks "to promote competition and reduce regulation in order to secure lower prices and higher quality services for American telecommunications consumers and encourage the rapid deployment of new telecommunications technologies." There is no reason to involve the government in a decision that should properly be based on marketplace demand. The 1996 Act specifically affords the Commission discretion whether or not to require minimum high resolution television programming.

42. Our decisions to adopt the DTV Standard and to use 6 MHz channels permit broadcasters to provide high definition television in response to viewer demand. If we do not mandate a minimum amount of high resolution television, we anticipate that stations may take a variety of paths: some may transmit all or mostly high resolution television programming, others a smaller amount of high resolution television, and yet others may present no HDTV, only SDTV, or SDTV and other services. We do not know what consumers may demand and support. Since broadcasters have incentives to discover the preferences of consumers and adapt their service offerings accordingly, we believe it is prudent to leave the choice up to broadcasters so that they may respond to the demands of the marketplace. A requirement now could stifle innovation as it would rest on a priori assumptions as to what services viewers would prefer. Broadcasters can best stimulate consumers' interest in digital services if able to offer the most attractive programs, whatever form those may take, and it is by attracting consumers to digital, away from analog, that the spectrum can be freed for additional uses. Further, allowing broadcasters flexibility as to the services they provide will

allow them to offer a mix of services that can promote increased consumer acceptance of digital television, which, in turn, will increase broadcasters' profits, which, in turn, will increase incentives to proceed faster with the transition.

43. We have also been persuaded by the arguments that a minimum high definition television requirement would be burdensome on some broadcasters. We note the arguments of ALTV and Telemundo as to the difficulties a minimum high resolution television requirement might impose on independent stations and foreign language stations, respectively. We acknowledge the contributions of such stations and the programming they provide to the diversity of our broadcast television service and hesitate to impose a requirement that might make it more difficult for such stations to convert to digital television, perhaps even undermining their ability to do so. We are not convinced that high definition television programming should be mandated where to mandate it might impose significant burdens on stations, particularly where, as will be discussed below, it appears that the marketplace will provide high definition television programming even absent a governmental requirement to that effect.

44. We note that some commenters argued that a high definition television mandate is necessary to give program producers and equipment manufacturers the necessary incentives to support high resolution television, and to provide viewers and consumers enough high resolution television programming to foster demand for such programming and to drive DTV receiver purchases. To the contrary, however, we believe that a minimum high definition television requirement is unnecessary to achieve these goals. We note in this regard that broadcasters and networks have emphasized their commitment to high definition television. We find nothing in the record that identifies a market failure or other reason to impose a governmental requirement for high definition television. High definition television will afford broadcasters an important tool in the increasingly competitive video programming market. There is no reason to believe that a government mandate is necessary to ensure that high definition television gets a fair chance in the marketplace.

F. Transition

1. Simulcast

51. Background. In our 1992 Second Report/Further Notice [in this proceeding], 7 FCC Rcd. 3340 (1992), we determined that DTV licensees should simulcast on their NTSC channel the programming offered on their DTV channel. Specifically, we adopted, as a preliminary matter, a 50 percent simulcasting requirement, beginning one year after the six-year application and construction period, increasing to 100 percent two years later. Our early simulcast decisions were based on the expectation that DTV would primarily consist of the broadcast of a single HDTV program service. However, as DTV technology developed, we learned that DTV would be able to do much more than we initially expected and that it would be possible to transmit multiple simultaneous SDTV program services on a single 6 MHz channel. Recognizing that a licensee would be unable to simulcast multiple program services on its NTSC channel, we stated in the *Fourth Further Notice* that our simulcast requirement must be revisited and we must consider alternatives. In addition, we stated that we still perceived a need for a simulcast requirement, albeit different from that first envisioned, and proposed to require the simulcast of all material being broadcast on the licensee's

NTSC channel on a program service of the DTV channel. We requested comment on this proposal.

55. We do not adopt a simulcast requirement during the early years of the transition in order to give broadcasters the ability to experiment with program and service offerings. We are convinced by commenters who argue that many consumers' decisions to invest in DTV receivers will depend on the programs, enhanced features, and services that are not available on the NTSC service, and a simulcast requirement might limit broadcasters' ability to experiment with the full range of digital capabilities. Because the DTV channels represent valuable resources with large opportunity costs, we believe licensees will have economic incentives to provide programming and services that will attract consumers to DTV. In any event, a simulcast requirement during this initial transition phase appears to be unnecessary because the record suggests that marketplace forces will ensure that the best NTSC programming will be simulcast on the digital channel and broadcasters have indicated that they will simulcast NTSC programs on the DTV channel even in the absence of a requirement.

56. While we believe that a simulcast requirement is not warranted during the early years of the transition, there are benefits to a simulcast requirement near the end of the transition period. Such a requirement will help ensure that consumers will enjoy continuity of free over-the-air program service when we reclaim the analog spectrum at the conclusion of the transition period. It may be difficult to terminate analog broadcast service if broadcasters show programs on their analog channels but not on their digital channels. We believe that it will be easier to terminate analog services and reclaim the spectrum at the end of the transition if most broadcast households are capable of receiving DTV signals and these households do not suffer the loss of a current program service only offered on analog channels. Thus, we will require a phased-in simulcasting requirement as follows: By the sixth year from the date of adoption of this *Report and Order*, we adopt a 50% simulcasting requirement; by the seventh year, we adopt a 75% simulcasting requirement; by the eighth year, we adopt a 100% simulcasting requirement which will continue until the analog channel is terminated and the analog spectrum returned. We recognize that we will need to define clearly "simulcasting" in the context of DTV and will do so as part of our two-year reviews or other appropriate proceeding.

Notes and Questions

1. Outmoded Goals? Suppose that, tomorrow, the FCC becomes persuaded that preserving free over-the-air broadcasting is, as Microsoft argued, an "outmoded policy goal." Under those circumstances, what actions should the FCC take with respect to the DTV issues addressed in this chapter?

2. Simulcasting. The Commission does not require simulcasting for the early years of DTV. Does the FCC provide an adequate rationale for such forbearance? If so, then why require simulcasting beginning in the sixth year? Is this an unwarranted intrusion into program content or an unjustifiable limitation on the potential for increased diversity of programming?

3. Evolution from HDTV to DTV. Overall, a system that once started out as 6 megahertz for HDTV (either digital or analog) has become 6 megahertz for a number of services, one of which will be DTV—but perhaps not "high definition" television at all. In fact, licensees now need only provide television service "comparable" to the existing NTSC signal. ¶28. Was this a sensible transformation? Was it inevitable? Is there a point in the process at which a different decision should have been made?

4. Fees for Ancillary or Supplementary Services. As the *Fifth Report and Order* indicates, digital compression allows broadcasters to use some of their 6 megahertz for non-broadcast services, and the abandonment of a requirement of high definition television gives broadcasters still more opportunities for such services (known as "ancillary or supplementary" services). Section 201 of the Telecommunications Act of 1996, 47 U.S.C. §336, authorized the FCC to permit (and regulate) such ancillary services, so long as those services do not interfere with advanced television services. The preceding *Order* deals with those matters. Section 336 also directed the FCC to establish a licensing fee that broadcasters would have to pay to the government for the privilege of using this spectrum to provide ancillary or supplementary services. Specifically, the provision mandates the creation of a licensing fee applicable to any ancillary or supplementary services for which the broadcaster itself receives compensation from a third party. Commercial advertisements used to support non-subscription broadcasting are excepted from this requirement. In a separate proceeding, the Commission asked for proposals for such a fee. It found that

> Commenters advocated percentages for the fee that ranged from less than one percent to more than ten percent. Those commenters who proposed a low fee—two percent or less of gross revenues—based their proposal on the declining auction values of the non-broadcast spectrum and on the possibility that a higher fee would discourage broadcasters from offering innovative services. Commenters proposing a high fee— ten percent or more—argued that such a fee would be consistent with other government licensing fees and would be necessary to prevent unjust enrichment.[31]

The FCC set the fee at five percent of gross revenues from the ancillary or supplementary services.

D. Public Interest Obligations

The transition to digital television, and in particular the grant of an additional 6 megahertz of spectrum to broadcasters for a period of at least nine years, has given rise to serious questions about the public interest obligations that should be attached to digital television. What sort of obligations can and should the government seek from broadcasters in exchange for this new grant of spectrum? The Clinton Administration, under the aegis of then-Vice President Al Gore, empaneled a commission to produce recommendations on this issue. The commission included representatives from a wide variety of interested groups (notably including commercial broadcasters, public broadcasters, and various public interest groups). In light of this diversity, it is perhaps unsurprising that there was a wide range of opinion; in addition to the formal report of the com-

---

31. In re Fees for Ancillary or Supplementary Use of Digital Television Spectrum, 14 FCC Rcd. 3259 (1998), at ¶20.

mission, there were eleven separate statements issued by some combination of the commission's twenty-two members. Below is an excerpt from the Gore Commission's main report, as well as an excerpt from one of these separate statements.

FINAL REPORT OF THE ADVISORY COMMITTEE ON PUBLIC INTEREST OBLIGATIONS OF DIGITAL TELEVISION BROADCASTERS
http://www.ntia.doc.gov/pubintadvcom/piacreport.pdf (1998)

Executive Summary

Section I. *The Origins and Future Prospects of Digital Television*

One of the primary rationales for the Nation's transition to digital television is high-definition television, or HDTV. This transmission mode contains up to six times more data than conventional television signals and at least twice the picture resolution. But digital television (DTV) also enables a broadcast station to send as many as five digital "standard-definition television" (SDTV) signals, which are not as sharp as HDTV but still superior to existing television images. This new capacity, known as "multicasting" or "multiplexing," is expected to allow broadcasters to compete with other multichannel media such as cable and direct broadcast satellite systems.

Another DTV capability is the ability to provide new kinds of video and data services, such as subscription television programming, computer software distribution, data transmissions, teletext, interactive services, and audio signals, among others. Referred to as "ancillary and supplementary services" under the Telecommunications Act of 1996, these services include such potentially revenue-producing innovations as providing stock prices and sports scores, classified advertising, paging services, "zoned" news reports, advertising targeted to specific television sets, "time-shifted" video programming, and closed-circuit television services.

These choices—HDTV, SDTV, and innovative video/information services— are not mutually exclusive. Within a single programming day, a broadcaster will have the flexibility to shift back and forth among different DTV modes in different day parts. Although many existing programming genres and styles will surely continue, innovations in video programming and information services will arise, fueled in no small part by the anticipated convergence of personal computer and television technologies.

Section II. *The Public Interest Standard in Television Broadcasting*

Federal oversight of all broadcasting has had two general goals: to foster the commercial development of the industry and to ensure that broadcasting serves the educational and informational needs of the American people. In many respects, the two goals have been quite complementary, as seen in the development of network news operations and in the variety of cultural, educational, and public affairs programming aired over the years.

In other respects, however, Congress and the Federal Communications Commission have sometimes concluded that the broadcast marketplace by itself is not adequately serving public needs. Specific policies have sought to foster diversity of programming, ensure candidate access to the airwaves, provide diverse views on public issues, encourage news and public affairs programming, promote localism, generate more educational programming for children, and sustain a separate realm of noncommercial television programming services.

The fundamental legal framework that still governs the broadcast industry, based on the notion of "spectrum scarcity," sets it apart from other media. Congress has mandated that licensees serve as "public trustees" of the airwaves. Broadcasters have affirmative statutory and regulatory obligations to serve the public in specific ways. The U.S. Supreme Court has upheld the public trustee basis of broadcast regulation as constitutional.

Section III. *Recommendations of the Advisory Committee*

The vast new range of choices inherent in digital television technology makes it impossible to transfer summarily existing public interest obligations to digital television broadcasting. A key mandate for the Committee, therefore, has been to suggest how traditional principles of public-interest performance should be applied in the digital era. A second mandate has been to consider what additional public interest obligations may be appropriate, given the enhanced opportunities and advantages that broadcasters may receive through digital broadcasting.

Mindful of the uncertainties in how digital television will evolve, the Advisory Committee has operated under several basic principles in formulating its recommendations. The first is that the public, as well as broadcasters, should benefit from the transition to digital television. Second, flexibility is critical to accommodate unforeseen economic and technological developments. Third, the Advisory Committee has favored, whenever possible, policy approaches that rely on information disclosures, voluntary self-regulation, and economic incentives, as opposed to regulation.

The Advisory Committee recommends:

- *Disclosure of Public Interest Activities by Broadcasters.* Digital broadcasters should be required to make enhanced disclosures of their public interest programming and activities on a quarterly basis, using standardized checkoff forms that reduce administrative burdens and can be easily understood by the public.

- *Voluntary Standards of Conduct.* The National Association of Broadcasters, acting as the representative of the broadcasting industry, should draft an updated voluntary Code of Conduct to highlight and reinforce the public interest commitments of broadcasters.

- *Minimum Public Interest Requirements.* The FCC should adopt a set of minimum public interest requirements for digital television broadcasters in the areas of community outreach, accountability, public service announcements, public affairs programming, and closed captioning.

- *Improving Education Through Digital Broadcasting.* Congress should create a trust fund to ensure enhanced and permanent funding for public broadcasting to help it fulfill its potential in the digital television environment and remove it from the vicissitudes of the political process. When spectrum now used for analog broadcasting is returned to the government, Congress should reserve the equivalent of 6 MHz of spectrum for each viewing community in order to establish channels devoted specifically to noncommercial educational programming. Congress should establish an orderly process for allocating the new channels as well as provide adequate funding from appropriate revenue sources. Broadcasters that choose to implement datacasting should transmit information on behalf of local schools, libraries, community-based nonprofit organizations, governmental bodies, and public safety institutions. This activity should count toward fulfillment of a digital broadcaster's public interest obligations.

- *Multiplexing and the Public Interest.* Digital television broadcasters who choose to multiplex, and in doing so reap enhanced economic benefits, should have the flexibility to choose between paying a fee, providing a multicasted channel for public interest purposes, or making an in-kind contribution. Given the uncertainties of this still-hypothetical market, broadcasters should have a 2-year moratorium on any fees or contributions to allow for experimentation and innovation. Small-market broadcasters should be given an opportunity to appeal to the FCC for additional time. The moratorium should begin after the market penetration for digital television reaches a stipulated threshold.

- *Improving the Quality of Political Discourse.* If Congress undertakes comprehensive campaign finance reform, broadcasters should commit firmly to do their part to reform the role of television in campaigns. This could include repeal of the "lowest unit rate" requirement in exchange for free airtime, a broadcast bank to distribute money or vouchers for airtime, and shorter time periods of selling political airtime, among other changes. In addition, the television broadcasting industry should voluntarily provide 5 minutes each night for candidate-centered discourse in the 30 days before an election. Finally, blanket bans on the sale of airtime to all State and local political candidates should be prohibited.

- *Disability Access to Digital Programming.* Broadcasters should take full advantage of new digital closed captioning technologies to provide maximum choice and quality for Americans with disabilities, where doing so would not impose an undue burden on the broadcasters. These steps should include the gradual expansion of captioning on public service announcements, public affairs programming, and political programming; the allocation of sufficient audio bandwidth for the transmission and delivery of video description; disability access to ancillary and supplementary services; and collaboration between regulatory authorities and set manufacturers to ensure the most efficient, inexpensive, and innovative capabilities for disability access.

- *Diversity in Broadcasting.* Diversity is an important value in broadcasting, whether it is in programming, political discourse, hiring, promotion, or business opportunities within the industry. The Advisory Committee recommends that broadcasters seize the opportunities inherent in digital television technology to substantially enhance the diversity available in the television marketplace. Serving diverse interests within a community is both good business and good public policy.

- *New Approaches to Public Interest Obligations in the New Television Environment.* Although the Advisory Committee makes no consensus recommendation about entirely new models for fulfilling public interest obligations, it believes that the Administration, the Congress, and the FCC should explore alternative approaches that allow for greater flexibility and efficiency while affirmatively serving public needs and interests.

MEMBERS BENTON, BLYTHE, CHARREN, CRUZ, MASUR, MINOW, RUIS, SCOTT, SOHN, STRAUSS, and YEE file this separate statement, which SUNSTEIN and GLASER join only in Part I.

I. *Political Discourse*

The FCC should require broadcasters to provide a reasonable amount of "free time," to national and local political candidates, under conditions that promote in-depth discussion of issues and ideas.

The Advisory Committee's recommendations on political discourse are well-intentioned, but insufficient. We recommend that, unless Congress enacts comprehensive campaign finance reform legislation:

> (1) The FCC should require broadcasters to provide "free time" to national and local candidates for candidate-centered discourse;
>
> (2) The FCC should consider whether a portion of this "free time" should be administered by political parties;
>
> (3) In implementing this obligation, the FCC should consider whether it should specify an administrative scheme such as the "time bank" or "voucher" models presented to the Advisory Committee by the Alliance for Better Campaigns and the Center for Governmental Studies; and
>
> (4) The FCC should give broadcasters broad discretion over the format of candidate appearances, except that qualifying "free time" segments must be of no less than 1 minute in duration, and the candidate should appear for no less than one-half of the duration of the segment.

The Advisory Committee recommendations on political discourse include, among other things: (1) a challenge to broadcasters to support "free time" proposals that are part of comprehensive campaign finance reform legislation and (2) broadcasters' voluntarily providing 5 minutes per night of free candidate centered discourse. For the reasons discussed below, we believe that these recommendations will likely fall short of achieving the very worthy goals of ensuring that citizens have broad access to candidate speech that results in informed decisions at the ballot box and reducing the influence of money on the political process.

First, despite what appears to be majority support in both Houses, Congress failed to pass comprehensive campaign finance reform last year, and is unlikely to do so in the future. If Congress does not pass comprehensive campaign finance reform, including a "free time" component, the FCC should require broadcasters to provide a modest amount of free candidate-centered discourse. This approach allows Congress to have the first opportunity to act to broaden political speech. If Congress does not act, we believe that it is necessary for the FCC to step in.

Second, we believe that exclusive reliance on voluntary standards in this area will be ineffective. Many broadcasters provide candidate-centered discourse today and the new mandate will not affect them. Rather, this obligation is directed at the substantial number of broadcasters that have chosen not to do so. There is no reason to believe that voluntary standards will impel those broadcasters that choose not to carry any such programming to do so now. It is this reasoning that led the Advisory Committee to recommend mandatory minimum requirements for local public affairs programming and public service announcements. In light of the expanded capacity and increased opportunities that digital transmission will provide for broadcasters, the burden on broadcasters of providing a minimal amount of free candidate-centered discourse would be small.

Although we recommend that the FCC should require broadcasters to provide "free time," the obligation should not be unlimited. The Advisory Committee has been presented with several "time bank" and "voucher" models that would result in broadcasters providing very modest amounts of "free time" for political candidates 60 days before a general election. It has also considered other models that would require broadcasters to provide some specific amount of time (for example, 5 minutes a night for the 60 days before an election). None of these models will unreasonably burden broadcasters, and all provide them with flexibility in the choice of the format.

The goal of ensuring an informed electorate will not be achieved, however, if the benefits of "free time" are used only for 30 second attack ads and 7-second sound bites that are segregated onto one of multiple channels. If the FCC provides a benefit of "free time," it may, and should, also require that this time be of a specified minimum length, and that candidates actually appear for a specified amount of time. It should also prohibit broadcasters from segregating the candidate-centered programming onto one of multiple program channels. Such segregation would violate Federal candidates' rights to "reasonable access" to the broadcast airwaves, *see* 47 U.S.C. §312(a)(7), and might also violate candidates' rights to equal opportunities, 47 U.S.C. §315(a).

II. *Mandatory Minimum Standards*

The FCC should adopt processing guidelines based upon 3 hours per week of local news and 3 hours per week of locally originated or locally oriented educational and/or public affairs programming outside of local news.

We agree with the principle underlying the Advisory Committee's recommendation on mandatory minimum public interest requirements—broadcasters should be required to provide some minimum amount of public interest programming in return for the free use of the public airwaves. We write separately to address the absence of specific minima in the Report. At the very least, we believe it is critical to specify how many hours per week of each type of public interest programming should be carried, and to specify the time period in which it should be carried (to ensure that such programming is not relegated to hours when few viewers are watching).

In addition, to ensure that all broadcasters serve the public interest, the FCC should adopt minimum public interest requirements that are stronger and more specifically targeted to address the absence of local news and locally originated and locally oriented educational and public affairs programming over many broadcast stations.

We recommend, therefore, that the FCC adopt a processing guideline calling for 3 hours per week of local news and 3 hours per week of locally originated or locally oriented educational and public affairs programming outside of local news. A broadcaster that airs this minimum amount would receive automatic approval of that portion of its license renewal application that addresses local programming. Local programming, outside of local news, should be dedicated to programming that addresses issues of local importance and/or is specifically tailored to meet a need in the community that is otherwise underserved, including minority communities. To ensure that such programming is not buried in "graveyard" time periods, the Commission should specify that a significant amount of this programming should be aired between 6 p.m. and 11 p.m. and that no programming to fulfill this mandate should be aired before 7 a.m. or after 11 p.m. Public service announcements would not fulfill this requirement.

The proposed recommendation has its roots both in the Communications Act of 1934 and the Telecommunications Act of 1996. Under the 1934 Act, television broadcasters are licensed to serve localities to which they are licensed. 47 U.S.C. §307(b). It has long been understood both by the FCC and by broadcasters that at the core of this local licensing requirement is an obligation that broadcasters provide locally originated and locally oriented programming. Most broadcasters take this obligation to serve as public trustees for their communities seriously, and consequently provide programming that meets local needs. However, evidence presented to the Advisory Committee demonstrates that a significant number of broadcasters provide neither local news nor local public affairs programming, and avoid controversial topics, no matter how important.

As discussed above, broadcasters receive a license to use public spectrum free of charge in exchange for providing in-kind payment through programming services that are not market-driven. Under the same rationale, the FCC, pursuant to Congress's mandate in the Telecommunications Act of 1996, gave incumbent broadcasters free additional spectrum (for a period of no less than 9 years) to convert to digital TV. In the 1996 Act, Congress emphasized three times the need for digital broadcasters to provide programming and services that serve the public. 47 U.S.C. §§336(a)(2), 336(a)(5) & 336(d). The processing guidelines discussed above will ensure that broadcasters that provide little or no local programming do not benefit from the free grant of spectrum in the digital world. We believe that these guidelines would not burden those broadcasters who already provide adequate amounts of local news and programming.

Notes and Questions

1. Is Digital Television Special? Do the recommendations in the formal report go far enough? Do the recommendations in the separate statement go too far? Is there anything in either the report or the separate statement that would not apply as well to conventional (NTSC) broadcasting? Are there reasons why there should be a different public interest standard for digital broadcasting than for conventional broadcasting?

2. The "Free Time" Proposal. Regarding the separate statement's "free time" proposal, is it appropriate for the FCC to promulgate by regulation what Congress fails to pass as legislation? Not only would there be no specific authorization for the FCC's action, but Congress would have specifically declined to pass that authorization. Under such circumstances, would action by the FCC be a violation of our principles of government, or an exemplar of them? Would it follow from the FCC's statutory mission to regulate according to the "public interest, convenience, and necessity"?

3. Requirements per Stream vs. Overall. Should a licensee's public interest obligations attach to the DTV channel as a whole, such that a licensee that chooses to multicast would have discretion to fulfill them on one of its program streams? Should, instead, the obligations attach to each program stream offered by the licensee? Is there a good analogy here to the debate, with respect to children's television obligations (for old-fashioned NTSC signals), over whether a licensee should be allowed to discharge its obligations by sponsoring children's programming to be presented by another broadcaster? Is this the same issue that is presented by multicasting of DTV signals, or does the possibility of DTV multicasting raise different considerations? Remember, too, the debates (with respect to format and equal employment obligations) about intrastation versus interstation diversity. How do they apply to multicasting? 47 U.S.C. §336(d) provides that a "television licensee shall establish that all of its program services on the existing or advanced spectrum are in the public interest." What do you make of that language? Is it a routine authorization of FCC authority or does it indicate that Congress wants public interest obligations applied to each program stream?

4. Ancillary and Supplementary Services. Should a licensee's public interest obligations apply to its ancillary and supplementary services? Does the licensee's obligation to pay a 5% fee on its revenues from these services affect the fairness or wisdom of such obligations?

5. Relationship to Free Television. Is it important that broadcasters did not pay the government for their extra spectrum for digital television? Is it relevant that digital television has been presented as the means by which free over-the-air broadcasting will remain vibrant? If digital television really is essential to broadcasting's continued success, which way does that fact cut in terms of public interest obligations?

PART TWO

CABLE TELEVISION

Cable television began in the 1940s as a relatively modest technology. Cable providers back then were simple antenna owners. They would use large antennas to capture broadcast signals from the air, and they would then pipe those captured transmissions through coaxial cable to communities where over-the-air reception was poor. Cable at this time thus typically served two types of communities: those located far away from broadcast transmission facilities, and those where trees, mountains, and other terrain features interfered with over-the-air reception. Importantly, in this early incarnation, cable was not a *competitor* to broadcast. Cable and broadcast were complements, with broadcast supplying content to cable, and cable helping broadcast reach an audience that it would otherwise inadequately serve.

Times, of course, have changed, and today cable no longer plays only a supporting role. Cable providers do still echo broadcast transmissions, but they also offer a broad range of original dramatic, comedic, educational, sports, and informational programming. Cable competes with broadcast to obtain exclusive rights to air particular programs and events. And cable no longer limits itself to serving only those households where over-the-air reception is poor. Indeed, by the end of 1999, approximately 96% of all television-equipped households were passed by coaxial cable or fiber optics from at least one cable provider,[1] and over 76% of all television-equipped households actually subscribed to cable service.[2] Broadcasters still do better—over 98% of all households receive at least one broadcast station over the air, with most households receiving at least ten broadcast channels[3]—but cable is no longer in any way a second-class media platform.

The story of cable regulation, then, is the story of this changing relationship between broadcast and cable television. Chapter Nine begins with a discussion of cable's history and basic issues like the problem of natural monopoly and the question of whether cable should be regulated, if at all, by federal or state authorities. Next, Chapters Ten and Eleven look at cable regulation today. Chapter Ten covers rate regulation and the franchising authority; Chapter Eleven considers the various regulations that mediate rights as between cable operators, broadcasters, and content producers—namely, the copyright, syndicated exclusivity, network nonduplication, retransmission consent, and must-carry rules. Chapter

---

1. Paul Kagan Associates, Inc., The Cable TV Financial Databook (1999) (reporting that there are 100,000,000 television households in the United States, of which 96,600,000 are passed by cable infrastructure).

2. Nielsen Media Research, 2000 Report on Television 13.

3. *See* In the Matter of Review of the Commission's Regulations Governing Television Broadcasting, 7 FCC Rcd 4111, at ¶3 (1992).

Twelve looks at structural rules that define the cable marketplace, for example the horizontal and vertical ownership limits; while Chapter Thirteen contrasts these rules with the regulations that apply to direct broadcast satellite (DBS) television, a service that has grown up in the shadow of cable just as cable once grew up in the shadow of broadcast. Finally, this Part of the book concludes in Chapter Fourteen with a discussion of the regulation of indecent content on cable.

CHAPTER NINE

CABLE BASICS AND
THE EARLY HISTORY

The purpose of this chapter is

- to provide an introduction to some of the basic issues implicated by cable television service, by:

- introducing the concept of a natural monopoly and showing why markets that exhibit this characteristic might benefit from government regulations that limit entry, constrain price, and enforce minimum quality standards;

- surveying some of the early problems identified with respect to cable and the regulatory responses thereto; and

- examining the question of whether, if cable is to be regulated, that regulation is more appropriately accomplished at the federal or state level.

$\sim$

I. INTRODUCTION

Americans watch a great deal of television. Indeed, Nielsen Media Research reports that over 98% of all U.S. households are equipped with at least one television set and, even more interestingly, the average household has at least one of those sets on and in use over seven hours per day.[4] That's over fifty hours of television every week, with the exact number of course varying with household size and other demographic variables.

What are Americans watching? Figure 9.1 lists the ten most watched programs on broadcast television between March 6 through March 12, 2000.[5] Figure 9.2 shows corresponding information for programs that originated on cable during this same time period. The top programs on broadcast are a somewhat predictable mix of game shows, situational comedies, dramas, and the occasional sporting event or news program. But the top ten cable shows are overwhelmingly children's fare and professional wrestling, two categories that rarely make the

---

4. Nielsen Media Research, 2000 Report on Television 13–14.
5. Nielsen ratings are reported online at www.zap2it.com. The website offers current ratings and also archives historical data. Earlier data can be acquired from Nielsen Media Research itself, which publishes a variety of reports and periodicals.

broadcast list. The total audience numbers here are perhaps a bit surprising as well. While the top broadcast programs attract fifteen to twenty million viewers, the top cable offerings are watched by only three to six million people—a substantial difference even when you account for the fact that only three-fourths of all households subscribe to basic cable.

Figure 9.1
Most Watched Programs on Broadcast Television, 3/6/00—3/12/00
Nielsen Media Research (as reported on www.zap2it.com)

Rank	Program Name	Millions of Viewers
1	Who Wants to be a Millionaire (Tuesday)	19.6
2	Who Wants to be a Millionaire (Sunday)	17.7
3	Who Wants to be a Millionaire (Thursday)	17.3
4	60 Minutes	14.8
5	Friends	14.0
6	The Practice	13.4
7	ABC News Special Report	13.2
8	Touched by an Angel	13.0
9	ABC News Special Report	12.1
10	Everybody Loves Raymond	11.1

Figure 9.2
Most Watched Programs on Cable Television, 3/6/00—3/12/00
Nielsen Media Research (as reported on www.zap2it.com)

Rank	Program Name	Millions of Viewers
1	Raising the Mammoth (DISC Special)	6.0
2	WWF Entertainment (Monday)	5.3
3	WWF Entertainment (Monday)	4.5
4	Prime Movie (LIFETIME)	3.2
5	Sunday Movie 1 (LIFETIME)	2.9
6	Rugrats (Saturday)	2.8
7	Rugrats (Monday)	2.8
8	Sunday Movie II (LIFETIME)	2.7
9	Rugrats (Sunday)	2.7
10	Snick House 3 (NICK)	2.6

One might suspect that these differences can be explained by the fact that cable is pay television whereas broadcast is advertiser-supported. According to this argument, advertisers prefer bland fare that attracts large audiences, whereas pay television serves niche markets where smaller groups of subscribers pay the costs of producing and transmitting programs that are more specifically tailored to their interests. Such an argument, however, just pushes the question one level deeper, in that it fails to explain why cable is pay television but broadcast is available at no charge. True, this has been the case historically, but is there anything in either delivery mechanism that necessitates this result?

Broadcast television could be a subscriber service. Broadcast signals could be scrambled and broadcasters could easily charge for decoder boxes that would then allow paying subscribers to view particular programs or channels but exclude non-paying customers from viewing that content. In fact, some of the earliest pay television systems did deliver their content in exactly this way—in Hartford, Los Angeles, Chicago, and San Francisco, for example, during the 1950s and 1960s.[6] Similarly, cable television could be funded entirely by advertisers. Advertising today accounts for less than one-fourth of cable revenues nationwide,[7] but there is no reason why, in principle, increased advertising could not cover the costs of the cable infrastructure and fund free cable television hookups.

In short, despite very real differences in viewer habits and pricing structures, at the end of the day cable and broadcast are remarkably similar: these are two platforms for delivering streams of audio and video content to the home. This, as Stanley Besen and Robert Crandall point out in the excerpt that follows,[8] makes the cable industry a particularly interesting case study in regulation.

> First, like trucking or intrastate natural gas, the cable television industry developed as a substitute for a regulated service. Television broadcasting had been regulated by the FCC for some time when cable television operators began to offer retransmissions of distant broadcast signals. It is not surprising that this new industry was soon viewed as a threat to the established, regulated television industry. Extension of regulation to the new challenger was a natural response for the regulators.
>
> Second, cable television offers a classic example of how markets operate to thwart regulators' attempts to cross subsidize "meritorious" services. The FCC limits the number of television outlets in each major market and requires that part of the profits generated as a result be devoted to "public service" programming. But cable television was capable of adding immensely to the number of signals available in a market, increasing the competition broadcasters face and reducing local broadcasters' ability to offer these merit programs. Perceiving a threat to its policy of cross-subsidization, the Commission naturally (at first) attempted to limit cable's ability to compete.
>
> Third, cable television provides an excellent example of how difficult it is to restrict entry when technology is changing rapidly. Just as the Interstate Commerce Commission [saw] its ability to regulate railroads compromised by the invention of the truck and then the airplane, the FCC has found it difficult to continue to protect its television broadcast licensees from the onslaught of technology. The lesson here is simple: If technological change is sufficiently rapid, deregulation may be unavoidable in almost any sector.

---

6. Roger Noll et al., Economic Aspects of Television Regulation 129–50 (1973).

7. Cable revenue for fiscal year 1999, for example, broke down as follows: the cable industry earned $11.2 billion in advertising revenue ($2.9 billion from local/spot revenue and $8.3 billion from national advertisements) but received $36.9 billion in direct payments from cable subscribers. Paul Kagan Associates, Inc., The Cable TV Financial Databook 2 (1999).

8. Stanley M. Besen & Robert W. Crandall, The Deregulation of Cable Television, 44 Law & Contemp. Probs. 77, 78 (1981).

Notes and Questions

1. Was Deregulation Inevitable? What exactly are Besen and Crandall claiming? Is their claim that, with the advent of cable television, deregulation was inevitable? If so, what should we make of the fact that, as of this writing—six decades after the introduction of cable technology and two decades since the authors wrote the paragraphs quoted above—both broadcast and cable are still subject to heavy regulation?

2. Competition or Regulatory Parity. Is their claim instead that competition and deregulation are desirable? But how do they know? Does the excerpt above convincingly argue for deregulation, or does it instead simply point out that, if regulation is to be successful, similar regulations must apply to all similar services?

II. THE PROBLEM OF NATURAL MONOPOLY

While much of this Part will focus on the relationship between cable and broadcast, we must not forget to think about cable television in isolation as well. After all, there are plausible reasons to intervene in the market for cable television independent of any goals the FCC might have for broadcast television. Consider in this light the following excerpt from Judge Richard Posner, taken from a case in which a would-be cable franchisee accused the City of Indianapolis of violating antitrust law by discouraging competition in the local cable market.[9]

> The cost of the cable grid appears to be the biggest cost of a cable television system and to be largely invariant to the number of subscribers the system has. Once the grid is in place—once every major street has a cable running above or below it that can be hooked up to the individual residences along the street—the cost of adding another subscriber probably is small. If so, the average cost of cable television would be minimized by having a single company in any given geographical area, for if there is more than one company and therefore more than one grid, the cost of each grid will be spread over a smaller number of subscribers, and the average cost per subscriber, and hence price, will be higher.

> If the foregoing accurately describes conditions in Indianapolis it describes what economists call a "natural monopoly," wherein the benefits, and indeed the very possibility, of competition are limited. You can start with a competitive free-for-all—different cable television systems frantically building out their grids and signing up subscribers in an effort to bring down their average costs faster than their rivals—but eventually there will be only a single company, because until a company serves the whole market it will have an incentive to keep expanding in order to lower its average costs. In the interim, there may be wasteful duplication of facilities. This duplication may lead not only to higher prices to cable television subscribers, at least in the short run, but also to higher costs to other users of the public ways, who must compete with the cable televi-

---

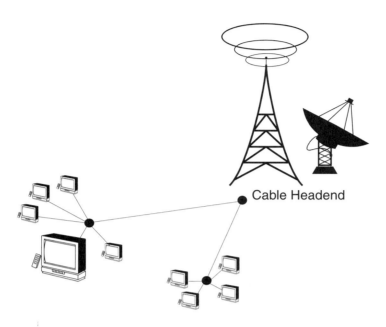

Figure 9.3. THE CABLE NETWORK. As Judge Posner explains, cable television is provided over a grid of coaxial (or fiber optic) cable that runs along city streets and ultimately connects individual subscriber residences into the cable network. In this simple illustration, we also show the *headend*, which is where the cable network receives incoming signals, typically by satellite but sometimes off the airwaves and sometimes by wire directly from the relevant source.

sion companies for access to them. An alternative procedure is to pick the most efficient competitor at the outset, give him a monopoly, and extract from him in exchange a commitment to provide reasonable service at reasonable rates. In essence the antitrust allegations in this case accuse the City of Indianapolis of having taken this alternative route to the monopoly that may be the inevitable destination to which all routes converge.

Notes and Questions

1. Virtues of Competition. To evaluate Judge Posner's discussion, it is important first to articulate the reasons why, in general, good social policy favors competition. Is competition merely about keeping prices low? If it is, do you believe that local government can accomplish this goal through regulation just as well as the market could through competition? More precisely, do you think that the benefits from eliminating the wasteful duplication Posner identifies outweigh the harms caused by inevitable errors in price-setting by the local government? Is competition about something more than mere price-setting? Can local government accomplish that through regulation, too?

2. Periodic Competition. Suppose that the City of Indianapolis were to announce that it was going to authorize only one firm to lay cable lines under city streets, but that every five years it would auction off the right to be that firm. Would this structured, periodic competition produce the same benefits as more open competition? Can you come up with a variant that would?

* * *

In the United States, the preferred method of regulating markets for goods and services is usually to rely on competition, with many firms offering identical or substitutable goods and services and thus trying to sell to the same customers. This competition among firms for consumers' patronage tends to force firms to set prices at or near the marginal cost of producing the relevant good or service. A firm that prices above its marginal cost will find its customers flocking to competitors that charge lower prices. For the same reason, competition tends to reward firms that produce goods and services efficiently; because their costs are lower, these firms can underprice less efficient rivals. Ideally, then, competition forces firms both to be efficient—that is, to use resources in their most productive uses—and to allocate their products efficiently—that is, to sell their wares to anyone willing to pay the marginal costs of producing them.

As Judge Posner points out, however, natural monopoly, where it occurs, confounds this ideal. A natural monopoly is said to exist in any market where the costs of production are such that it is less expensive for demand to be met by one firm than it would be for that same demand to be met by more than one firm. This typically occurs when, over a sufficiently large range of output, the addition of each new customer lowers the average cost of serving every other customer. *Total costs* in such a case increase as demand increases; the important feature is that the firm's average cost *per unit* of output declines with increasing demand.

Declining per-unit average cost can arise for three principal reasons. One possibility is that the good or service at issue requires a very large "fixed" expense that must be incurred no matter how many units are sold. As the firm increases production, those fixed costs can be spread over an ever larger number of units of output, reducing the per-unit average cost. The telephone system was long considered to fit this pattern. A telephone company must build its network of wires, purchase switching machinery, create databases, and hire personnel before it can transmit its first call. The company recovers that investment by factoring a share of these fixed costs into the retail price of telephone service. With each new subscriber, the phone company can further spread its fixed costs and thereby allocate a lower proportion of those costs to each customer. The cost of each individual's phone service thus declines as the number of callers on the network increases.

A second reason that a firm might have declining per-unit costs—and might thereby possibly be a natural monopoly—does not depend at all on fixed costs. A firm that has already recovered its fixed costs, or that has few fixed costs to begin with, might still have *incremental* costs of production that decline as output increases. In this case the firm is not gaining a cost advantage by spreading its fixed costs ever more thinly, but instead is gaining a cost advantage by experiencing reduced variable costs for each successive unit of output. This kind of "increasing returns to scale" could arise for a number of reasons. Machinery might become more fuel and labor efficient when operated at higher capacities. Or marginal costs may decline as a workforce becomes more experienced. Such increas-

ing returns will not often occur over very broad ranges of output, and will therefore rarely be sufficient to lead to natural monopoly, but it bears considering the
theoretical possibility that a natural monopoly could arise even if fixed costs are
not substantial.

The third common reason for declining per-unit costs is demand variability.
In order to provide adequate electric service, your local electric company must
be ready to supply you with a great deal of power at any instant. Having all
that idle capacity is expensive, however, since outside of peak times your electricity needs are likely modest. The same is true for your neighbor, and her
neighbor too, of course, so if each of you were being served by separate firms,
those firms would have significant resources invested in idle equipment. By having a single firm serve all of you, however, the costs of providing electricity can
be lowered dramatically. You three can share a given amount of excess capacity,
putting the equipment to better use since the variance in each of your demands
will to some degree tend to cancel out, and thus you three can share some of
that excess capacity without any of you experiencing a noticeable degradation
in service.

Important to all of the above arguments is not only that per-unit costs are
declining, but also that they are declining over *most of the range of output that
the market will demand*. To see why, think about the automobile industry. The
fixed costs of automobile production are very high. An automobile maker
must build a manufacturing plant, purchase machinery, and install a management system before it can produce its first car. The firm recovers those fixed
costs by including a share of them in the price of each car it makes. So the average cost per car decreases as the number of cars produced at the plant increases. Should automobile manufacturing be considered a natural monopoly,
then? Probably not. First, if a single plant cannot meet the market's entire demand for cars, then the decline in per-unit costs will stop before all consumers
are served. At that point the firm would have to build a new plant and incur a
new set of fixed costs. In such a case, there is no efficiency gain from having
just one firm serve the market, and preventing entry would needlessly sacrifice
all the familiar benefits of competition like lower prices, higher output, better
quality, and product innovation. Second, even if a single plant could produce
enough cars to satisfy consumer demand, it might still not be the case that per-
unit costs are declining over a large enough range of output to make the producer a natural monopoly. Fixed costs might be spread so thinly as to be almost zero on a per-unit basis well before the market's demand has been
satisfied. In that case, it might be possible for multiple firms to be in the market without affecting each other's ability to reach the most efficient scale of
production.

What about conventional television broadcasting? On one hand, once a program is transmitted, the marginal cost to the broadcaster of serving an additional
viewer is zero. So if the market at issue were that for distribution of a particular
program, then there might be a case for calling broadcast a natural monopoly.
Having additional broadcasters distribute the same program would only raise
costs. But that is much too narrow a market definition. Consumers don't watch
some generic product called "broadcast;" they watch particular programs that in
many cases are not substitutes for each other. So, at issue in broadcasting is not
just the production and distribution of a single program at any point in time, but

of multiple, simultaneous programs. Given that fact, the question becomes whether a single broadcaster can make and/or distribute programming more cheaply than can multiple, competing broadcasters. On the program production side, there is little case to be made for the existence of a natural monopoly. Putting aside the important point that it is probably not beneficial to confine a creative enterprise to one or a few producers, the incremental costs of producing programming (actors, writers, and so on) are very large in comparison to the small fixed costs (*e.g.* studios and equipment) and there seems little reason that the incremental costs should decline as a studio produces more shows. On the distribution side, a single broadcaster does not have the capacity to deliver all programs that air at a given time. And once a new set of transmission facilities is needed to broadcast the programming the market demands, the benefits of spreading fixed costs are truncated and the conditions for natural monopoly probably disappear. The arguments for natural monopoly in conventional broadcasting are thus weak. (Although note that there are some economies of scale in the broadcast industry, and that networks group individual broadcasters together into larger units in order to take advantage of those efficiencies. Chapter Seven considers networks from this perspective.)

This brings us back to cable television, long regulated as a natural monopoly. Does it qualify? There seems little question that the fixed costs of building a cable system are very high. Moreover, building a high-capacity system that can carry all the program channels needed to meet market demand probably doesn't cost much more than building a low-capacity system. Finally, the cost per customer of providing cable distribution declines as more households subscribe to the service. The incremental costs of connecting additional homes to the cable system are very modest and probably constant. So, spreading the fixed costs of cable distribution over an increasing number of households reduces the cost per subscriber. And, once a complete cable network is in place, there is good reason to think that the per-unit distribution costs decline over the entire range of consumer demand. Entry by a second cable system would therefore raise the average per-household costs of providing service. At least as far as program distribution (as distinguished from program production, packaging and marketing) is concerned, then, there is at least a plausible argument that cable systems exhibit natural monopoly properties.

The policy implications associated with natural monopolies are complicated. The existence of natural monopoly conditions would seem to argue in favor of legal rules restricting entry. That is, the existence of a natural monopoly seems to tell us that, as a policy matter, law should ensure that the good or service in question is provided by a single firm. However, monopoly supply is a problem in and of itself; for example, monopolists tend to charge prices far above marginal cost and/or provide goods and services of inferior quality. Government could in theory solve those problems by regulating price and quality, but regulation, too, is no straightforward task. The question thus ultimately devolves into a choice between various evils: allow competition to regulate the market knowing full well that either (a) there will be competitive supply and thus higher costs or (b) a monopolist will emerge, with the attendant harms in terms of high prices and possibly inferior quality; or use law to restrict entry and regulate behavior, knowing that due to politics, imperfect information, rent-seeking, and the like, those regulations will introduce inefficiencies of their own.

Notes and Questions

1. Naturally a Monopoly? Commentators, including Judge Posner in the excerpt above, often suggest that markets that exhibit natural monopoly properties tend to become monopolistic markets. In essence they interpret the phrase "natural monopoly" to mean "naturally, this market will become a monopoly." Does that follow from the definition of a natural monopoly? If it does, why is it that often the legal response to natural monopoly is to restrict entry?

Phrased another way, does the entrance of a competitor into a market mean that the market is not properly characterized as a natural monopoly? Can you think of any reasons why a firm might enter a natural monopoly market even though another firm is already present? Would that threat of entry cause the firm already in the market to price at or near the competitive level? If so, do we still need government regulation? And what if "natural monopoly" does mean "naturally, this market will become a monopoly"? Is the implication here that we have no choice but to regulate these markets?

2. Test Your Understanding. Evaluate the following statement: "Natural monopoly is only problematic where the good has no ready substitute. It does not matter whether 'purple rubber bands' are a natural monopoly because, even if this were true, rubber bands of other colors would supply competition."

3. Setting Prices. If you were regulating a natural monopoly market, what price would you choose as the "right" price for firms to charge? Suppose, for example, that average price decreases as the number of customers increases; does that mean that there should be a range of prices based on whether a customer happens to purchase the 200th unit as opposed to the 300th? Should all customers be charged the same price? What price should that be? Consider a simple example. Suppose that it costs $16 to build a bridge and $2 in wear and tear every time a truck crosses the bridge. Further, imagine that five truck drivers are willing to pay $15, $10, $10, $5, and $2, respectively, for the privilege of crossing the bridge. Can you show that bridge service in this example exhibits the properties of a natural monopoly? What price would the unregulated bridge owner charge if his were the only bridge available? What is the better, "efficient" price? How can the government encourage the bridge owner to charge it?

4. Natural Monopoly When Average Cost Increases. The discussion above emphasizes the various ways that decreasing average costs can lead to natural monopoly. Note, however, that natural monopoly conditions can arise even in instances where average costs are increasing. Such examples are somewhat less intuitive and hence are not discussed in this introductory text; but the broad point is simply this: a market exhibits natural monopoly properties in any case where total costs are minimized by having a single firm serve the market. This happens when average cost is constantly declining over the relevant range of output, but it can be true in other instances as well. (Readers interested in pursuing this topic should consult the economic literature on the topic of "subadditivity.")

* * *

Many people believe that the provision of cable television service is a natural monopoly. Many people (often the same ones) believe that provision of local telephone service is a natural monopoly. Be careful not to accept these natural monopoly claims uncritically, however. For example, it may be that providing the wires for cable television is a natural monopoly, but that selecting or providing the programs that go over them is not. It may be that even if telephone and cable television services are natural monopolies, there is no need for price (or quality) regulation because consumers find other services — such as cellular telephony or direct broadcast satellite television — to be substitutes for the natural monopoly services and, thus, these other services keep the natural monopolists from either charging prices that are too high or offering services of inferior quality. Lastly, many parties benefit from the regulated structure of the cable and telephone markets and therefore have a strategic interest in arguing that cable and/or telephone service are natural monopoly services. So be wary as you evaluate natural monopoly claims, and always ask yourself whether the proposed regulatory response is well suited to the alleged market imperfection.

III. EARLY REGULATORY RESPONSES TO CABLE

Cable television began in the 1940s as "community antenna television" (CATV), with cable operators using towers and well-placed antennas to pick up broadcast signals that could then be transmitted through coaxial cable to nearby residents. This retransmission of local signals alarmed neither broadcasters nor the FCC. At worst it was redundant, with cable bringing signals to consumers who could already receive them over the air. And at best it benefitted both consumers and broadcasters, with cable in these cases bringing broadcast signals to consumers who otherwise would have gone unserved.

As cable began to take on an expanded role, however, both broadcasters and the FCC became concerned. Should cable operators be allowed to "import" broadcast signals from distant communities, in essence bringing new broadcasters into the local marketplace? If so, should they have to compensate the foreign broadcasters who, perhaps unwittingly, supplied the content? Should they have to compensate instead (or in addition?) the copyright owners who licensed those foreign broadcasters to air the content in the first place? The local broadcasters who would now face new competition in the local market? And should cable providers themselves be allowed to originate content, either charging subscribers a flat fee or offering programs on a pay-as-you-go basis? These were some of the issues that needed to be addressed early in cable's history.

The text that follows is a continuation of the Besen & Crandall article excerpted above. It is an overview of early FCC policy with respect to cable television, and it provides a good snapshot of the FCC's original understanding of cable as both friend and foe to the broadcast-dominated media marketplace.

THE DEREGULATION OF CABLE TELEVISION
Stanley M. Besen & Robert W. Crandall
44 Law & Contemporary Problems 77 (1981)

The first cable television (CATV) system began operation in Astoria, Oregon in 1949; the first commercial system was initiated one year later in Lansford,

Pennsylvania. By the end of the 1950s, there were approximately 640 systems serving about 650,000 subscribers, and the nascent industry had begun to receive the attention of the FCC. It is fair to say, however, that during this period the attitude of the Commission was essentially one of "benign neglect," of permitting cable to develop without government intervention absent a definitive showing that such growth was not in the public interest.

A. The "Auxiliary Service" Inquiry

The Commission's early views on cable television are provided extensively in its 1959 *Report and Order* on its inquiry into the effect of cable and other "auxiliary services" on the development of television broadcasting. The Commission's basic concern, one that continued over the two decades of cable regulation, was stated at the outset of its *Report*:

> There is presented a problem of conflicting interests and objectives. On the one hand are the interests of the general public of the areas involved in the preservation of a local television outlet, with the attendant advantages which a community gains from having a local means of self-expression, and (in some cases but not in all) the preservation of the only television service to some of the public, such as rural residents who cannot be served by CATV. On the other hand is the interest of another group, such as city residents who want and can afford to pay for CATV service, in obtaining multiple television service.

The conflict the Commission described was the basis of the claims of some broadcasters who argued that, where cable systems carry signals which viewers in their markets cannot receive over-the-air, local stations lose audiences and advertising revenues. This, in turn, leads to a reduction in local service and, in the extreme, to the local station being forced off the air. Thus, the broadcasters held, if cable were permitted to import distant signals, some viewers might lose their only television service. This claim influenced the next two decades of government regulatory policy toward cable.

In examining the "evidence" presented on the relation of station viability to the existence of cable and the other auxiliary services, the Commission in 1959 first concluded that it believed the public would benefit substantially from essentially unfettered growth of auxiliary services, including cable: "We do not now envision where we could find that the public interest would be disserved by affording an opportunity for choice of service and the benefits of competition and diversity of expression." The only possible exception might be where it was the one and only local broadcast service whose existence was threatened: "There is some merit in the broadcasters' position that the 'only service' must be maintained...especially...where the number losing their only service is considerably greater than the number who would receive the multiple service."

The Commission did feel that regulation might be required in two areas. First, the Commission had been asked to rule that Section 325(a) of the Communications Act, which forbids the rebroadcast of the signal of a broadcast station without its permission, applied also to the retransmission by cable systems of broadcast signals. The Commission indicated that it did "not believe that section 325(a) in its present form includes the requirement that CATVs get the consent of the stations whose signals they carry." But, the Commission went on, "we intend to recommend to Congress that an appropriate amendment to section 325(a) be enacted, so as to extend the 'consent' requirement to CATVs." This marks the first public-policy pronouncement in favor of "retransmission consent," an issue which has remained before the Commission for over two decades in one form or another.

The Commission also found favor with the suggestion that cable systems be required to carry the signals of local or nearby stations (if they so request) and indicated that it would recommend such an amendment to the Communications Act. This pronouncement initiated the on-going debate over "must carry" rules. However, the agency rejected a proposal that cable systems be forbidden to duplicate programs carried by local stations, even when those stations protest the duplication.

B. A Change in Policy: *Carter Mountain*

The first policy change occurred in connection with what appeared to be a routine authorization of microwave facilities to carry broadcast signals to cable systems. Carter Mountain Transmission Corporation had applied for FCC authorization and, nine days after the Commission's report on the impact of "auxiliary services" on television broadcasting, its application was granted without a hearing. Shortly thereafter, a protest was filed by a local broadcast station and the effective date of the authorization was suspended. In 1961, the Commission's Hearing Examiner, echoing the Commission's views in the auxiliary services inquiry, denied the protest:

> Whatever impact the operations of the CATV systems may have on protestant's operation of station KWRB-TV, these are matters of no legal significance to the ultimate determination made that a grant of the subject application of Carter, a bona fide communications common carrier, will serve the public interest. Further, even if considered, the record precludes any reliable approach to an accurate estimate of that impact.

A year later, on appeal to the Commission, the authorization was denied. In what can only be regarded as a startling reversal of its earlier views, the Commission argued:

> A grant of common carrier radio facilities requires a finding that the public interest will be served thereby; certainly the well-being of existing television facilities is an aspect of this public interest. Thus it is not only appropriate, it is necessary that we determine whether the use of the facility applied for would directly or indirectly bring about the elimination of the only television transmission or reception service to the public.

Moreover, the Commission apparently no longer harbored doubts about its ability to determine whether cable would harm broadcasters: "If the CATV pattern is permitted to be altered, the local station would find it more difficult to sell its advertising in the face of a split audience, and this situation results in our judgment that the demise of this local operation would result."

Finally, where previously it could find no reason why it should not afford "an opportunity for choice of service and the benefits of competition and diversity of expression" it now found:

> A grant of the instant application would permit the rendition of better service by the CATV, but at the expense of destroying the local station

and its rural coverage. It must be concluded that the need for the local outlet and the service which it would provide to outlying areas outweighs the need for the improved service which Carter would furnish.

The Commission invited Carter to refile its application if it could show that the cable system would carry the signal of the local station and not carry the signals of other stations which duplicated its programming.[10]

C. Rules Concerning Microwave-Served CATV

Three years later, in 1965, the Commission moved to codify its policies respecting the authorization of microwave facilities which served cable systems. There were to be two kinds of regulations, both in the form of conditions imposed on the authorization of microwave facilities to serve cable systems. One requirement was that the cable system carry the signals of all local stations. The second rule was that a cable system not carry the programs of a distant station when they duplicated the programs of local stations during a period of fifteen days before or after the local broadcast.

Both requirements derived from the Commission's view that the competition provided by cable television systems to local broadcasters is different from the competition provided by additional broadcast stations. When a cable system did not carry the local signals, a viewer subscribing to the service could only receive a local station by disconnecting the cable and attaching an antenna. To the extent that this proved cumbersome, access to cable subscribers was denied to local broadcasters. The requirement that local signals be carried was designed to remedy this difficulty.

The nonduplication requirement was designed to deal with the fact that cable systems carried broadcast signals without obtaining the consent of either the originating station or the producers of its programs. The Commission held: "The CATV system that provides its subscribers with the signals of distant stations presently stands outside of the program distribution process." Also: "In the absence of a market in which the question of competitive access to programming by stations and CATVs can be resolved, our aim is to preserve for stations the competitive exclusivity they have been able to obtain as against other stations, but nothing more." The asserted rationale for the nonduplication rule was preservation of this exclusivity.

Although the Commission's stated purpose in adopting these rules was to make competition between broadcasting and cable "fair and reasonable," the Commission clearly was concerned as much with the outcome as with the fairness of the process: "The question at the heart of these proceedings is whether and to what extent rulemaking action is necessary or appropriate to integrate CATV service into our existing television system—to ensure that CATV performs its valuable supplementary role without unduly damaging or impeding the growth of television broadcast service."

The Commission continued to be concerned with the impact of cable in the smallest markets, but its list of concerns had grown since 1959:

We think it clear that the most serious effects will be felt by (1) stations in smaller one- and two-station markets, where the public does not receive

---

10. The D.C. Circuit affirmed the Commission's decision. *See* Carter Mountain Transmission Corp., 321 F.2d 359 (D.C. Cir. 1963), *cert. denied*, 375 U.S. 951 (1963).

the full services of all three national networks off-the-air, (2) by marginal stations in larger markets, and (3) by new stations coming on the air.

Since, by definition, there will always be marginal stations in larger markets so long as not all channel assignments are filled, the Commission was no longer limiting its purview to situations in which the only local broadcast service was threatened. Indeed, it was likely that every market would contain at least one station in one of the Commission's three areas of concern.

D. The *Second Report and Order*

The following year, 1966, was a watershed in the regulation of cable. Never before or since has the Commission's regulation of cable been more wide-ranging or restrictive. In adopting its *Second Report and Order*, the Commission stated that its actions were designed to prevent "unfair" competition by cable systems and to foreclose any "adverse impact" on broadcasting that CATV growth might produce. The role of cable was to be that of a "supplement" to the over-the-air broadcast system.

The *Second Report and Order* marked three notable shifts in FCC policy. First, the Commission had progressed from 1959, when it claimed that it was unable to measure the harm caused by cable, to a point where, seven years later, it stated confidently that "the materials before us would appear to indicate substantial growth and substantial impact by CATV in the large markets."

Second, the Commission's locus of concern had shifted from markets where the only local broadcast service is threatened by cable to the major markets which have many stations:

> We have selected the top 100 markets for special attention because it is in these markets that UHF stations or wire pay-TV based upon CATV operations are most likely to develop and therefore the problems raised are most acute. The top 100 markets include roughly 90 percent of the television homes in this country. Our policy therefore focuses on the critically important areas.

Third, for the first time in its deliberations respecting cable, the Commission expressed concern for the impact that cable growth might have on the emergence of UHF television stations, especially in the major markets. The Commission's policy of placing many television allocations in the UHF band and intermixing VHF and UHF stations in the same markets, established in its *Sixth Report and Order on Television Allocations*, had encountered serious problems. Many of the UHF stations which had gone on the air in 1954 had failed. More than 40 percent of UHF stations reported operating at a loss compared to less than 15 percent of VHF stations.

With the passage of the All-Channel Receiver Act in 1962 and the subsequent enactment of Commission rules to implement its provisions, the Commission assumed responsibility for the healthy growth of UHF. In its *Second Report and Order*, the Commission determined that the expansion of cable would harm the prospects for UHF. Thus, the Commission concluded, cable development would have to be tightly circumscribed in those markets where it believed that UHF prospects were brightest, the top 100.

The Commission's new cable policy had two facets. First, it extended to all cable systems, not just those employing microwave, the requirement that all local stations be carried and that imported signals not duplicate local programming. Second, and more importantly, the Commission announced that it would not permit the carriage of a distant broadcast signal into one of the top 100 markets without a showing in an evidentiary hearing that such carriage "would be consistent with the public interest, and particularly the establishment and healthy maintenance of UHF television broadcast service." Thus, even cable systems which adhered to the local carriage and nonduplication rules would still be required to demonstrate that their carriage of distant signals would not threaten even marginal UHF stations.

In the only evidentiary hearing completed for a major market, the Commission reversed the decision of its Hearing Examiner and imposed restrictions on the ability of one of the San Diego cable systems to carry the signals of Los Angeles independent stations. This decision, combined with the administrative burden of the evidentiary hearing process, made it clear that the development of cable in the major markets would be stopped completely unless the rules were regularly evaded by staff action or were abandoned completely.

E. Affirmation of Jurisdiction

The Commission's authority to adopt the rules contained in its *Second Report and Order* was upheld by the Supreme Court in *Southwestern Cable*. Relying on the Communications Act, which obligates the Commission to provide "a fair, efficient, and equitable distribution" of television service, and on the Commission's findings that achievement of this goal requires the use of the UHF band and that cable threatens UHF television, the Supreme Court upheld the Commission's authority to regulate cable. Without determining the limits of the Commission's regulatory authority, the Court found that the rules adopted in 1966 were "reasonably ancillary" to the fulfillment of the Commission's responsibilities in regulating broadcasting.[11]

F. The Copyright Question

As the Commission made clear in its *Second Report and Order*, the fact that when cable television imported distant signals it "stands outside of the program distribution process" was a matter of some concern. Henry Geller, General Counsel to the Commission at the time, has argued that the *Second Report* can best be understood as a holding action until this issue was definitely resolved in the courts. He argued, further, that the Commission was prepared to relax or eliminate its distant signal rules, when, as was generally anticipated, federal courts held that cable systems were liable when they carried distant signals without obtaining permission.

The matter received the attention of the courts when a program supplier, relying on the Copyright Act of 1909, sued a cable system for carrying the supplier's programs on an imported signal. Both the District Court and the Court of Appeals ruled that the cable system was engaged in a "performance" within the meaning of the Act and was liable for copyright infringement. However, in 1968, the Supreme Court, reversing the decisions of the lower courts, held that the carriage of the signals in question was not a violation on the grounds that the activities of cable systems are closer to those of viewers than of broadcasters.[12]

---

11. United States v. Southwestern Cable Co., 392 U.S. 157 (1968).
12. Fortnightly Corp. v. United Artists Television, Inc., 392 U.S. 390 (1968).

G. Cablecasting: Prescriptive Rather than Proscriptive Regulation

In 1969, the Commission addressed the issue of origination by requiring all cable systems with 3,500 or more subscribers to originate programming. The Commission described the benefits which could be expected from origination and why it had refused to accede to broadcaster requests that origination be banned entirely because it would divert audience from "free" television:

> We do not think that the public should be deprived of an opportunity for greater diversity merely because a broadening of selections may spread the audience and reduce the size of the audience for any particular selection. Such competition is not unfair, since broadcasters and CATV originators stand on the same footing in acquiring the program material with which they compete.

In addition, the Commission saw benefits from the potential for cable networking of originated programming. But despite the Commission's words, some doubts remained about its sincerity. First, the Commission imposed a rule limiting advertising on originated programming to "natural breaks" which reduced the attractiveness of providing such programs on an advertiser-supported basis. Second, by leaving the question whether to permit advertising on cable network operation "open," it discouraged such networking. Finally, while it stated that it saw no need to place limits on originated programs supported by direct subscriber payments, in the following year it did just that.

In extending the rules which had been applied to over-the-air pay television to pay-cable operations, the Commission stated that:

> where cablecasting is accompanied by a per-program or per-channel fee, it is akin to subscription television and presents the same threat of siphoning programs away from free television in favor of a service limited to those to whom the cable is geographically available. Remedial action in this area should not wait upon the threat becoming actuality.

The rules prevented cablecasting for which a per-program or per-channel charge was made of: (i) movies which had been in theatrical release more than 2 years prior to the cablecast, (ii) sporting events which had been telecast in the community on a non-subscription basis during the previous two years, and (iii) series programming of any type.

These regulations also limited feature films and sporting events to 90 percent or less of total programming hours and banned advertising on pay channels entirely.

H. After the Freeze — Cable Television in the Seventies

Cable entered the 1970s as a small business relegated principally to rural areas and small communities and held hostage by television broadcasters to the Commission's hope for the development of UHF. The opportunity for cable to break these shackles occurred in 1970 when Dean Burch replaced Rosel Hyde as Chairman of the FCC, several other Commissioners' terms expired, and the Office of Telecommunications Policy was established under Clay T. Whitehead.

Is it not very difficult to characterize the political obstacles to cable development which faced Burch and Whitehead. They were: (i) The continuing fear that distant signal importation would imperil the development of UHF broadcasting and reduce the rents flowing from VHF broadcasting in major markets. (ii) The failure of the courts and Congress to resolve the cable copyright problem which caused copyright owners (producers, artists, motion picture companies) to ally themselves with broadcasters. (iii) The concern that cable systems would not serve "the public interest" by extending an array of new services to the communities they served. Some feared that they would simply augment the entertainment choices for subscribers while threatening to diminish the choices available on advertiser supported commercial stations for households unable to afford subscriptions to cable services.

The joint efforts of Burch and Whitehead produced the 1972 cable rules, also known as the "Consensus Agreement." These rules can only be described as baroque. They limited the importation of distant signals in a manner which varied with market size; they provided that "significantly viewed" signals from adjacent markets could be carried in addition to the distant-signal quota and provided an intricate test for determining whether a signal was "significantly viewed;" they continued the mandatory carriage requirement for local signals; they provided for two different forms of exclusivity protection for non-network (syndicated) programs; and they placed a rather heavy burden of local origination, franchising, and technical standards upon all cable operators. As we shall see, thorough enforcement of these many rules proved to be beyond the wherewithal of the Commission.

Despite the numerous restrictions on cable services that they contained, the new rules were clearly a liberalization of policy. Where distant signal importation into major markets had previously been virtually prohibited, now at least a modicum of such importation could take place. But why did the Commission move from its rigid anti-cable stance? Why did broadcasters allow such a liberalization? There are a number of possible answers.

First, the personalities had changed. For whatever reason, Burch and Whitehead clearly were interested in promoting a policy which would permit some cable growth in the major markets. Second, the agreement on the part of cable interests to accept some form of copyright liability when they retransmitted distant signals served to reduce the opposition of program producers to cable growth.

Third, a number of economic studies published between 1966 and 1972 may have allayed some of the Commission's fears. Several of these studies—particularly those undertaken at the Rand Corporation—demonstrated that UHF stations might actually benefit from the presence of a local cable system. For many UHF stations, the gain from being able to compete on an equal basis with local VHF stations in homes served by cable was greater than any loss they might experience from audience diversion to distant stations. Moreover, these studies demonstrated that the gain in viewer welfare from the increase in viewing choices afforded by cable could be substantial.

Finally, while the extent of the influence of these studies upon policymakers remains an open question, they clearly provided support for the positions taken by an increasingly powerful cable industry. That industry continued to grow between 1966 and 1970, nearly trebling in size as it continued to wire the smaller markets. Simultaneously, large multiple system owners and equipment suppliers acquired wider representation in Washington and some broadcasters acquired substantial positions in cable, making it difficult for that industry to take a monolithic position with respect to cable.

As the cable industry passed the 5 million subscriber level in 1971, with no demonstrable harm to broadcasters, it became increasingly difficult to ignore the accumulating evidence that the Commission's fear of injury to broadcasters was overdrawn and the growing political power of groups that would benefit from cable growth. Some liberalization of the cable rules became an obvious course.

J. "Reregulation" Effort

It was clear that full enforcement of the rules by the new Cable Bureau would be very difficult, if not impossible. They were extremely detailed, requiring approval of franchise agreements, supervision of the number and identity of all signal importations, enforcement of technical requirements, and enforcement of program exclusivity on every imported commercial signal in the largest 100 markets. With more than 3,000 systems in operation, it would be naive to expect thorough, consistent enforcement of all of these rules.

Equally important, the numerous provisions could hardly be justified as necessary to protect UHF broadcasting. If, for instance, very small systems were granted exemptions from the rules, it would be unlikely that UHF stations would be imperiled. Similarly, if signal-carriage requirements were waived during periods of limited viewing, it could not be argued that broadcast stations would suffer.

In 1977, the Commission announced a detailed inquiry into the relationship between cable television and television broadcasting. Coming only five years after the adoption of 1972 Cable Rules, this Inquiry could only be a signal that the Commission had reached a point in reregulation where deregulation might be considered. It resulted in the issuance of *Notices of Proposed Rulemaking* to drop all distant-signal carriage rules and to eliminate the syndicated exclusivity rules. The Commission had thus arrived at a position where it was willing to undo the Consensus Agreement altogether only eight years after Burch and Whitehead had fashioned it.

K. Court Interpretations of the Commission's Rules

Two actions taken by the courts were especially important for the development of cable during this period. The first, and more significant, came when, in Home Box Office v. FCC, the Court of Appeals for the District of Columbia vacated the Commission's pay cable rules.[13] These rules had sharply limited the ability of cable systems to offer feature films and sports events on subscription channels in order to prevent the "siphoning" of programming from broadcasting to cable. In effect, the Commission was regulating a nonbroadcasting activity, pay cable, in order to provide protection to broadcasters. Although the court ruled that "we think that the strategy the Commission has employed in implementing its interest in preventing siphoning creates a restriction 'greater than is

---

13. Home Box Office v. FCC, 567 F.2d 9 (1977), *cert. denied*, 434 U.S. 829 (1978).

essential to the furtherance of that interest,'" it also appeared to say that, in any event, it would not have affirmed any pay-cable rules because of doubts that the Commission had jurisdiction to impose them. In light of this chastisement by the court of appeals, the Commission has not tried to reimpose pay-cable rules.

A second significant ruling occurred in FCC v. Midwest Video Corp.[14] In United States v. Midwest Video Corp.,[15] the Supreme Court had ruled, in a five-to-four decision, that the FCC had the authority to require cable systems to originate programming. A plurality of four found that there was no rational distinction between regulations designed to avoid adverse impact, such as those upheld in *Southwestern Cable*, and those whose purpose was to enhance the quality of television service, such as the Commission's origination rules.

In *Midwest Video II*, however, the Commission's rules requiring that channels be made available by cable operators for access by third parties on a non-discriminatory basis and that cable systems be required to have a minimum capacity of 20 channels were overturned by the Supreme Court. The majority reasoned that, while the origination rules required cable operators only to fulfill a role comparable to that played by broadcasters, the access rules required them to operate as common carriers. The Communications Act prohibits the imposition of common carrier regulation of broadcasters and the majority held that this stricture applied to cable systems as well.

L. The Copyright Problem Again

During the year in which the consensus agreement was being negotiated, a second cable copyright case, CBS v. Teleprompter,[16] began wending its way through the courts. The Columbia Broadcasting System attempted to distinguish this case from *Fortnightly* by arguing that Teleprompter had employed microwave relays to carry signals over hundreds of miles to its cable systems while Fortnightly had used nothing more than a strategically placed antenna. Thus, CBS argued, its copyrights had been infringed by Teleprompter even if Fortnightly was not liable on the facts of its case. In 1974, on essentially the same grounds that it had employed in *Fortnightly*, the Supreme Court ruled that Teleprompter was not liable for an infringement of copyright.

This set the stage for the enactment of the General Revision of the Copyright Act in 1976.[17] The Revision contained a compulsory license provision in which cable systems were allowed to carry distant signals without authorization from the imported station — hence, the phrase "compulsory license" — but were required to pay statutorily set fees for importation. In addition, while the consensus agreement had called for a compulsory license only for those signals authorized by the 1972 cable rules, the General Revision provided for a compulsory license for all signals authorized by the FCC. The General Revision created a Copyright Royalty Tribunal which would be required to consider adjustments to the fee schedule whenever the carriage rules were changed.

---

14. FCC v. Midwest Video Corp., 440 U.S. 689 (1979) [hereinafter *Midwest Video II*].
15. United States v. Midwest Video Corp., 406 U.S. 649 (1972).
16. CBS v. Teleprompter, 415 U.S. 394 (1974).
17. Copyright Revision Act of 1976, 17 U.S.C. §§101-810 (1976) (effective Jan. 1, 1978).

M. The Economic Inquiry and Its Aftermath

By 1978, the Commission had dropped many of the limitations upon cable which it had imposed in 1972, and the courts had forced abandonment of others. The major remaining rules related to distant signal carriage and syndicated exclusivity, but, a year earlier, the Commission had initiated an *Economic Inquiry* directed at examining whether to retain even these rules. The FCC's Cable Bureau, aided by a group of academic economists specializing in communications policy research, reported its findings to the Commission in 1979. This report, which was adopted by the Commission, concluded that cable provided only a minor threat to broadcasters' profits and even less to their ability to perform in the public interest. As a result, the Commission adopted a *Notice of Proposed Rulemaking* looking toward complete elimination of the broadcast signal carriage and syndicated exclusivity rules and in 1980 it deleted the rules entirely.

The Commission's decision to accept the *Economic Inquiry* report and to issue the *Notice of Proposed Rulemaking* marked the first time since 1959 that it had voted to accept the proposition that television broadcasters did not require protection from cable to survive, prosper, and serve the public interest. How could it have reached such a conclusion so much at odds with the policies it had adopted in 1972 or 1966? One possible answer is that broadcasters did not argue very strongly in favor of continuing the restrictive distant signal rules during the *Economic Inquiry*. These rules had been designed to protect large market broadcasters, and cable's threat to the development of UHF stations had been the asserted rationale for such a policy. But as the evidence accumulated that cable did not provide much of a threat to large-market stations, it became increasingly difficult to defend this rationale.

With the battle over pay-cable having been lost in the *Home Box Office* case, with new developments such as expanded subscription television, videocassettes, and direct satellite-to-home broadcasting on the horizon posing potentially greater threats than cable, and with substantial broadcaster ownership interests in cable, it is hardly surprising that broadcaster participation in the *Economic Inquiry* seemed perfunctory. Indeed, the "new" economic evidence provided by broadcasters varied little from the "old" evidence available to the Commission in the early 1970s.

Notes and Questions

1. Why Protect Broadcast? From 1959 until 1980, the FCC generally seemed to regulate cable television with an eye toward protecting the preexisting broadcast industry. But is it clear to you why the FCC favored broadcast? Was this just politics, with the well-funded broadcast lobby championing its own interests over those of the public? Was it a simple reluctance to disturb the status quo? It should be noted that the FCC never seemed to consider the possibility of the opposite regulatory approach, namely regulating broadcast so as to promote the development of cable. This is not so ridiculous as it might at first sound; if the FCC's real concern was providing free or inexpensive television to families who could not afford pay television, that goal could in theory have been accomplished by a thriving, advertiser-supported cable system.

2. The Cable/Broadcast Relationship. An important case discussed briefly in the preceding excerpt is Home Box Office v. FCC, excerpted below. As you consider that case, think through the complicated relationship between cable and broad-

cast television. Are you confident that the FCC understood this relationship sufficiently, such that the regulations at issue were likely to further the Commission's
intended goals?

HOME BOX OFFICE (HBO) v. FCC

567 F.2d 9 (D.C. Cir. 1977), *cert. denied*,
434 U.S. 829 (1978)

Before WRIGHT and MacKINNON, Circuit Judges, and WEIGEL, District
Judge (sitting by designation). Opinion for the court filed PER CURIAM. Concurring opinions filed by Circuit Judge MacKINNON and District Judge WEIGEL

PER CURIAM:

These 15 consolidated cases challenge four orders of the Federal Communications Commission which, taken together, regulate and limit the program fare cablecasters and subscription broadcast television stations may offer to the public for a
fee set on a per-program or per-channel basis. The Commission in 1975 issued rules
which prohibited pay exhibition of: (1) feature films more than three, but less than
10, years old; (2) specific sports events (*e.g.*, the World Series) shown on broadcast
television within the previous five years; and (3) more than the minimum number
of non-specific (*i.e.*, regular season) sports events which had not been broadcast in
any of the five preceding years, and in some cases only half that number. In addition, the Commission prohibited commercial advertising in conjunction with pay
exhibition of programming and limited the overall number of hours of pay operation which could be devoted to sports and feature films to 90% of total pay operations.

The stated purpose of these rules was to prevent competitive bidding away of
popular program material from the free television service to a service in which
the audience would have to pay a fee to see the same material. Such competitive
bidding, or "siphoning," is said to be possible because the money received from
pay viewers is significantly more for some programs than money received from
advertisers to attach their messages to the same material. For this reason, even a
relatively small number of pay viewers could cause a program to be siphoned regardless of the wishes of a majority of its free viewers.

I. THE FACTUAL BACKGROUND

To understand the postulated "siphoning" phenomenon and its potential
harm, it is useful to consider the structure of the television industry today. In
1975 there were 70.1 million American homes with television sets, of which 9.8
million had access to some cable system. Although the number of cable subscribers is large, individual cable systems are quite small, with the largest having
only 101,000 customers and with only 224 of approximately 3,405 systems having more than 10,000 subscribers. The number of homes that presently have access to pay cable facilities is about a half million and is growing rapidly. Most of
these homes are located outside major television markets, with the exception of
the New York City area and parts of California. Extension of service to other
urban areas might be accomplished at a capital cost of some $8 billion, but lay-

ing cable to reach that half of the American population which lives in rural areas would by any estimate be extremely expensive, perhaps requiring an additional $240 billion. Because of these capital requirements, extension of cable service with cablecasting capability to the country as a whole does not seem possible in the immediate future.

Similarly, access of all Americans to cable seems foreclosed by the cost of cable service. Technical capability exists today to distribute and bill for cablecast programs on a program-by-program basis, but this is not currently done. Instead a single fee of $5–$7 monthly, in addition to the $5–$6 monthly basic fee, is charged for access to the cablecasting channels. Nonetheless, as the name of one petitioner suggests, it is quite literally possible to turn the home receiver into a "Home Box Office," thereby marketing television features in much the same way that movies are marketed in theaters today. As with other box offices, however, only those with enough money to buy a ticket can get in to see the show.

Siphoning is said to occur when an event or program currently shown on conventional free television is purchased by a cable operator for showing on a subscription cable channel. If such a transfer occurs, the Commission believes, the program or event will become unavailable for showing on the free television system or its showing on free television will be delayed. In either case a segment of the American people—those in areas not served by cable or those too poor to afford subscription cable service—could receive delayed access to the program or could be denied access altogether. The ability of the half-million cable subscribers thus to preempt the other 70 million television homes is said to arise from the fact that subscribers are willing to pay more to see certain types of features than are advertisers to spread their messages by attaching them to those same features. For example, according to Commissioner Robinson, subscribers may be willing to pay 15 to 30 cents per viewing hour for the privilege of viewing a recent feature film, while advertisers are willing to pay only three cents per viewer. As a result a pay audience of one million could routinely buy a film away from a nonpaying audience of five to ten million.

Whether such a siphoning scenario is in fact likely to occur and, if so, whether the result of siphoning would be to lower the quality of free television programming available to certain areas of the country or to certain economic strata of the population are matters of great dispute among the Commission and the various petitioners and intervenors seeking review of the Commission's regulations in this case. Some petitioners argue that the rules which ostensibly place cable in a subordinate role in order to increase program diversity—a goal which has been basic to a number of Commission regulations—in fact diminish diversity by prohibiting subscription cable operators from showing the programs that are most likely to be the financial backbone of a successful cable operation. As a result, it is claimed, cultural and minority programming that could otherwise "piggyback" on a cable system supported by more broadly popular fare is precluded. Finally, other petitioners take the position that the threat of siphoning is very real and that the Commission's rules do not adequately cope with this threat to conventional television service.

II. PAY CABLE RULES

A. Statutory Authority

[Editor's note: When the opinion was written, the FCC had no express, direct jurisdiction over cable television operators. The Supreme Court had held, however, that the Commission might regulate cable where such regulation was "reasonably ancillary" to achieving "long established" goals of broadcast regulation.]

2. Applying the Jurisdictional Standard

Although there is dispute over the effectiveness of the rules, it is clear that their thrust is to prevent any competition by pay cable entrepreneurs for film or sports material that either has been shown on conventional television or is likely to be shown there. How such an effect furthers any legitimate goal of the Communications Act is not clear. The Commission states only that its "mandate to act in the public interest requires that it strive to maintain the public's ability to receive the informational and entertainment programming now provided by conventional television at no direct cost," *First Report and Order*, *supra*, 52 FCC 2d at 43, and that its action "is designed to enhance the integrity of broadcast signals and is a proper execution of our responsibility under the Communications Act." *id.* at 45.

Insofar as the Commission places reliance on such conclusory phrases as "enhance the integrity of broadcast signals," we think it has crossed "the line from the tolerably terse to the intolerably mute." Greater Boston Television Corp. v. FCC, 143 U.S.App.D.C. at 394. Beneath such generalities, however, the Commission seems to be making two more specific arguments which relate the public interest to retention of the conventional television structure. First, the Commission appears to take the position that it has both the obligation and the authority to regulate program format content to maintain present levels of public enjoyment. For this reason, and because the Commission also seems to assert that the overall level of public enjoyment of television entertainment would be reduced if films or sports events were shown only on pay cable or shown on conventional television only after some delay, it concludes that anti-siphoning rules are both needed and authorized. Second, and closely related, is the argument that the Communications Act mandates the Commission to promulgate anti-siphoning rules since cable television cannot now and will not in the near future provide a nationwide communications service. Before considering each of these arguments in turn, we note that we do not understand the Commission to be asserting that subscription cable television will divide audiences and revenues available to broadcast stations in such a manner as to put the very existence of these stations in doubt.

The question of the Commission's obligation or authority to regulate television to maintain public enjoyment is one whose analysis takes us into a thicket of disagreement between this court and the Commission. Although this controversy has taken place in the context of the Commission's obligation to regulate changes in radio broadcast formats,[18] much of what has been said is directly relevant here.

The position of this Circuit, as expressed in the cases concerning FCC regulation of radio station formats, is unmistakable: The Communications Act not only allows, but in some instances requires, the Commission to consider the preferences of the public, and the Commission in discharging this authority must regu-

---

18. [Ed. This issue is explored in Chapter Four in the section on transfer hearings.]

late the entertainment programming which station owners can present whenever a significant segment of the public is threatened with the loss of a preferred broadcast format. Were *WEFM* (the court's latest format opinion) the last word, it is at least possible that the Commission could promulgate the anti-siphoning rules under the theory of jurisdiction recognized by the plurality in *Midwest Video Corp.*, since the end to be achieved—protection of preferred television service for those not served by cable television—would also justify regulation of the broadcast media.

The Commission has not, however, acquiesced in *WEFM*. Instead, it recently launched and concluded a proceeding on "Changes in the Entertainment Formats of Broadcast Stations." *See Notice of Inquiry*, 57 FCC 2d 580 (1976); *Memorandum Opinion and Order*, 60 FCC 2d 858 (1976). Its conclusions there bear repeating in some detail. First, the Commission has reiterated its conclusion that it has no statutory authority to dictate entertainment formats. Format regulation, it is argued, is analogous to imposing common carrier responsibilities on broadcasters. Since Section 3(h) of the Communications Act, 47 U.S.C. §153(h) (1970), specifically excludes broadcasters from the category of "common carriers," "Congress intentionally refrained from extending the full range of regulatory tools deemed appropriate for common carrier regulation to the field of broadcast regulation." A second point relevant here is the Commission's professed inability to determine the boundaries of a "particular entertainment format." *Id.* at 862. "The Commission does not know, as a matter of indwelling administrative expertise, whether a particular format is 'unique' or, indeed, assuming that it is, whether it has been deviated from by a licensee." *Id.* In any case, concludes the Commission, "it is impossible to determine whether consumers would be better off with or without any particular format without reference to the actual preferences of real people." *Id.* at 864.

If the Commission's own recently announced standards are applied to the rules challenged here, it seems clear that the rules cannot stand. The very essence of the feature film and sports rules is to require the permission of the Commission "to commence programming, including program format services, offered to the public." However, it has been the consistent position of the Commission itself that cablecasters, like broadcasters, are not to be regulated as common carriers, a view sustained by a number of courts. Thus, even if the siphoning rules might in some sense increase the public good, this consideration alone cannot justify the Commission's regulations.

In addition, the record before us is devoid of any "reference to the actual preferences of real people." While we would be willing to concede that certain formats, such as the World Series, are sufficiently unique and popular that a factual inquiry into actual preferences might not be required, this would not seem to be the case with either feature films or "non-specific" sports events. Moreover, there is not even speculation in the record about what material would replace that which might be "siphoned" to cable television. Without such a comparative inquiry, we do not understand how the Commission could define the current level of programming as a baseline for adequate service. Finally, with regard to feature films we question how the Commission, which has stated that it has no criteria by which to distinguish among formats, could have determined that feature films are a sufficiently unique format to warrant protection.

The Commission has, in this proceeding, seemingly backed into an area of regulation in which it would not assert jurisdiction were it to face the issues directly. Indeed, in this very proceeding, and despite the Commission's definition of current quantity and quality levels of films and sporting events as the minimum level consistent with adequate television service, there is no indication that the Commission is prepared to require broadcasters to continue to present material presently on conventional television. Because we are hesitant to approve rules which seem inconsistent with the Commission's best thinking in a closely analogous area, we think we should not affirm the feature film and sports regulations on the basis of *WEFM*.

Before reaching a conclusion on whether remand is necessary, however, we must consider the Commission's second theory of jurisdiction. Counsel for the Commission at oral argument, stressing that Section 1 of the 1934 Act mentions that the Commission is to foster "nation-wide" service, argued that cable could not be a nationwide service in the reasonably foreseeable future and that "siphoning" would, therefore (the logic behind this "therefore" is by no means clear), destroy nationwide service in contravention of the policy of Section 1. The Commission has nowhere spelled out even a theory of the dynamic which could result in loss of broadcast television service to regions not served by cable. Nor is such a dynamic readily apparent. For example, cablecasters are unlikely to withhold feature film and sports material from markets they do not serve since broadcast of this material in such markets could not reduce the potential cable audience and because exhibition rights to this material would undoubtedly have substantial value. In these circumstances, the postulated loss of regional service is too speculative to support jurisdiction.

B. The Evidence

2. Applying the Standard of Review

(a) The Need for Regulation

Here the Commission has framed the problem it is addressing as "how cablecasting can best be regulated to provide a beneficial supplement to over-the-air broadcasting without at the same time undermining the continued operation of that 'free' television service."

To state the problem this way, however, is to gloss over the fact that the Commission has in no way justified its position that cable television must be a supplement to, rather than an equal of, broadcast television. Such an artificial narrowing of the scope of the regulatory problem is itself arbitrary and capricious and is ground for reversal. Moreover, by narrowing its discussion in this way the Commission has failed to crystallize what is in fact harmful about "siphoning." Sometimes the harm is characterized as selective bidding away of programming from conventional television, sometimes delay, and sometimes (perhaps) the financial collapse of conventional broadcasting. As a result, informed criticism has been precluded and formulation of alternatives stymied.

Setting aside the question whether siphoning is harmful to the public interest, we must next ask whether the record shows that siphoning will occur. The Commission assures us that siphoning is "real, not imagined." Our own review of the record in these cases suggests that, if there is any evidentiary support at all for this assurance, it is indeed scanty. As to the potential financial power of cable television, we are left to draw the inference from two facts—that championship boxing matches often appear only on closed-circuit television in theaters and that Evel Knievel chose to televise his jet-cycled dive into the Snake River in the same fashion—and a series of mathematical demonstrations. While the former may be directly relevant to siphoning of what the Commission has characterized as "specific" sports events, it is not at all clear what light they shed on the question of who is going to pay how much to see feature films and non-specific sports events on pay cable.

The meaning of the various mathematical demonstrations is even less certain. [Here, the court reviewed a study by ABC that predicted that pay cable might grow sufficiently by 1980 so that HBO might pay more for the rights to exhibit a hit movie than ABC would pay. The court rejected this study because (a) it compared prices ABC paid in 1972 with prices HBO was assumed to pay in 1980 and (b) it did not account for the possibility that, when faced with competition, the TV networks might reduce their profits and pay more for programs and movies.]

We have similar difficulties with the second cardinal assumption of the Commission, *i.e.*, that "siphoning" would lead to loss of film and sports programming for audiences not served by cable systems. To reach such a conclusion the Commission must assume that cable firms, having purchased exhibition rights to a program, will not respond to market demand to sell the rights for viewing in those areas that cable firms do not reach. We find no discussion in the record supporting such an assumption. Indeed, a contrary assumption would be more consistent with economic theory since it would prima facie be to the advantage of cable operators to sell broadcast rights to conventional television stations in regions of the country where no cable service existed.

We find the Commission's argument that "siphoning" could lead to loss of programming for those too poor to purchase cable television more plausible. Cable operators, to be able to sell a show, would require exclusive exhibition rights in the markets they served, with the result that events purchased by cable operators for subscription presentation would be unavailable to broadcasters, or would be available only after a delay. What follows from this scenario, even assuming that cable operators would have the financial strength to outbid broadcasters, is by no means clear. There is uncontradicted evidence in the record, for example, that the popularity of film material does not decline with an increase in the interval between first theater exhibition and first television broadcast. At least as to movies, therefore, "siphoning" may not harm the poor very much.

Equally important, the pay cable rules taken as a whole scarcely demonstrate a consistent solicitude for the poor. Thus, although "free" home viewing relies upon advertiser-supported programming, the Commission has in this proceeding barred cable firms from offering advertising in connection with subscription operations. As a result, the Commission forecloses the possibility that some combination of user fees and advertising might make subscription cable television available to the poor, giving them access to the diverse programming cable may potentially bring. We are thus left with the conclusion that, if the Commission is serious about helping the poor, its regulations are arbitrary; but if it is serious about its rules, it cannot really be relying on harm to the poor.

III. FIRST AMENDMENT

The First Amendment theory espoused in *Red Lion Broadcasting Co.* cannot be directly applied to cable television since the essential preconditions of that theory—physical interference and scarcity—are absent. And even though there is some evidence that local distribution of cable signals is a natural economic monopoly, which may raise the specter of private censorship by the system owner, there is no readily apparent barrier of physical or electrical interference to operation of a number of cable systems in a given locality. In any case, scarcity which is the result solely of economic conditions is apparently insufficient to justify even limited government intrusion into the First Amendment rights of the conventional press, *see* Miami Herald Publishing Co. v. Tornillo, 418 U.S. 241, 247–256 (1974), and there is nothing in the record before us to suggest a constitutional distinction between cable television and newspapers on this point.

The absence in cable television of the physical restraints of the electromagnetic spectrum does not, however, automatically lead to the conclusion that no regulation of cable television is valid. Regulations which transform cacophony into ordered presentation can often be consistent with the First Amendment. Regulations evincing a "governmental interest unrelated to the suppression of free expression," United States v. O'Brien, 391 U.S. 367, 377 (1968), are valid (1) if such regulations "further an important or substantial governmental interest" and (2) "if the incidental restriction on alleged First Amendment freedoms is no greater than is essential to the furtherance of that interest."

Applying *O'Brien* here, we cannot say that the pay cable rules were intended to suppress free expression. The narrow purpose espoused by the Commission—protecting the viewing rights of those not served by cable or too poor to pay for cable—is neutral. The Commission seeks only to channel movie and sports material to its intended recipients over broadcast television, rather than pay cable, whenever the economics of advertiser-supported programming permit.

We nonetheless hold that the rules cannot be squared with *O'Brien*'s other requirements and, consequently, they violate the First Amendment. The no-advertising and 90-percent rules clearly violate *O'Brien*'s first criterion. Not only do they serve no "important or substantial interest," 391 U.S. at 377, they serve no purpose which will withstand scrutiny on this record. The sports and features films rules fare no better. We have already concluded that the Commission has not put itself in a position to know whether the alleged siphoning phenomenon is a real or merely a fanciful threat to those not served by cable. Instead, the Commission has indulged in speculation and innuendo. Moreover, we doubt that the Commission's interest in preventing delay of motion picture broadcasts could be shown to be important or substantial on any record.

The rules are grossly overbroad. Examples of this are legion. It is undisputed, for example, that many films will never be suitable for broadcast television because of their limited appeal, their sophisticated subject matter, or their repeated releases to theaters. Yet, after a film is three years old its exhibition on cable television is restricted regardless of whether it was ever suitable for broadcast. Similarly, in some circumstances the sports rules reduce the number of non-specific games that can be shown on cable television at the same time that broadcasters are reducing the number of games they will show.

WEIGEL, District Judge, concurring:

In joining the court's opinion, I wish to emphasize the view that the Federal Communications Commission lacks the power to control the content of programs originating in the studios of cablecasters. Such programs involve neither retransmission of signals received over the air from conventional television broadcasting nor transmission over television broadcasting frequencies. They are offered to users of television sets on terms the users are free to accept or reject.

It seems to me that if there could be any governmental interest justifying this species of censorship, it is an interest which Congress has not empowered the Commission to assert. In relation to cablecasting, the power is so fraught with the potential for impingement upon First Amendment rights that it should not be sanctioned by implication.

[Concurring opinion of Judge MacKINNON is omitted.]

Notes and Questions

1. Ramifications. The D.C. Circuit's opinion in *HBO* is important both for what it did and for what it said. First, what it did: as a result of the *HBO* decision, the FCC removed all rules concerning programs that cable systems could offer for a fee. This move greatly expanded cable's ability to attract subscribers; cable operators now could offer programs other than those fully funded by advertising. Cable penetration and subscription rates moved steadily upward after *HBO*.

2. Implications. Now, what it said: the *HBO* opinion seems to suggest that cable operators enjoy First Amendment rights identical to those afforded newspaper publishers and, further, that this constitutional protection requires that courts subject content neutral regulation of cable programming to searching scrutiny. In part because the Supreme Court declined to review the *HBO* decision and in part because so many FCC decisions are appealable to the D.C. Circuit, this view of cable's constitutional status became very influential. Accordingly, as subsequent materials reveal, many other cable regulations—such as those requiring cable operators to provide access channels, and those forbidding the cablecast of "indecent" programs—became vulnerable to First Amendment challenge.

3. The First Amendment. If the *HBO* court is correct in its First Amendment approach to cable regulations, would it still be permissible to require cable systems: (a) to provide "access channels," in which citizens are allowed, without charge, to offer their own programming over the cable system on a first-come, first-served basis; (b) to carry, without compensation, the signals of broadcast stations licensed to the community which the cable system serves; or (c) to agree, in order to obtain permission (*i.e.*, a franchise) to build a cable system, that the system will offer (1) program service to every resident or (2) burglar alarm services along with its program packages? These and other constitutional issues are raised in the materials that follow.

4. Fears of Siphoning. Note that the policy said to underlie the pay cable rules was designed not to protect broadcasters, but to protect television viewers. Does the *HBO* court believe that there is something intrinsically erroneous or impermissible about the Commission's "siphoning" fears, or is the court's objection only that these fears were inadequately documented? Based on our experience without pay cable programming restrictions in the years since *HBO*, does it appear that a modified "anti-siphoning" rule might be a good idea, especially to protect low income viewers?

5. Siphoning by Other Broadcasters? The *HBO* decision makes much of the threat of siphoning, this idea that a new cable provider might divert both viewers and content away from broadcast. But are these phenomena unique to the cable/broadcast relationship? Suppose a new broadcast licensee seeks to set up shop in SmallTown. Should the existing licensees be allowed to oppose the new licensee on grounds that the new licensee will divert viewers away from the existing channels? That the new licensee might compete with existing channels for the exclusive rights to air popular programs? (The FCC did allow this sort of objection at one time but no longer does.)

6. The Truth is Out There. Is siphoning an argument without end? For example, don't movie theaters siphon both viewers and content? And what about video cassette rentals? Fans of the broadcast television program *The X-Files* know this all too well. In 1998, the story arcs that were on-going all season as part of the advertiser-supported broadcast program were concluded (or, in typical *X-Files* fashion, further confused) in a pay-at-the-box-office theatrical release. Producers of the program figured that they could earn greater profits selling this content to a smaller audience at $10 a head than they could by reaching the full *X-Files* audience but earning only pennies per viewer through advertising. Is this siphoning any different from cable siphoning?

IV. THE JURISDICTION PUZZLE: WHO SHOULD REGULATE?

Siphoning is an important argument in the context of cable television for another reason: until 1984, siphoning was the argument the FCC used to establish jurisdiction over cable. Under the 1934 Act, the FCC had no explicit authority to regulate cable. So, until Congress amended the Act in 1984, the FCC asserted jurisdiction by arguing that, because of siphoning, the Commission could not achieve long-established broadcast goals without having at least some power over cable television. The Supreme Court accepted this argument in its 1968 decision in United States v. Southwestern Cable, concluding that the FCC did have jurisdiction over cable to the extent necessary to promulgate rules "reasonably ancillary to the effective performance of the Commission's various responsibilities for the regulation of television broadcasting." 392 U.S. 157, 178 (1968).

In some ways, this is just a note of historical interest. Section 2 of the Act now clearly states that the "provisions of this [Act] shall apply with respect to cable service, to all persons engaged within the United States in providing such service, and to the facilities of cable operators which relate to such service." 47 U.S.C. §152. However, this sort of argument can easily arise again. For example, many companies today produce computer software that enables a computer with Internet access to be used for long distance telephone communication. As we will learn in Part Three, telephone carriers are subject to significant FCC regulation. Should the FCC therefore regulate the provision of this computer software, or indeed this use of the Internet? Does it matter whether Internet long distance service offers the same voice quality and features (like call waiting) as does the regulated service? Do the same arguments mean that the FCC should have been allowed to regulate email, another new technology that significantly affected telephone utilization? The answers to these questions reveal a problem with regulation more generally: once government starts to regulate an area, it becomes difficult to stop those regulations from expanding.

While the FCC's jurisdictional arguments were largely based on the effects cable might have on broadcast, local government attempted to regulate cable for reasons much more closely tied to cable. Most states, in fact, today require that would-be cable providers obtain a franchise from either state or, more often, local government officials before constructing a cable system. This franchising power is typically justified as a method of controlling those who would disrupt the local community by burying wires in the ground or hanging them off poles. A more cynical explanation would be that local authorities want control over the makeup and quality of the cable system—perhaps for noble but also for self-interested reasons.

All of these rationales for local government involvement are reflected in the opinion that follows. It bears emphasis at the outset that the *Group W* opinion is included in these materials not because it is necessarily correct or convincing, but because of the number of issues it describes and the vigor with which one clear position is asserted.

GROUP W CABLE, INC. v. CITY OF SANTA CRUZ
669 F. Supp. 954 (N.D. Cal. 1987)

SCHWARZER, District Judge:

Plaintiff, Group W Cable, Inc. ("Group W"), brings this action to enjoin defendants, the City and the County of Santa Cruz ("Santa Cruz"), from terminating its cable television franchise in the Santa Cruz area. Group W moves for summary judgment on grounds that Santa Cruz's policy of granting only one franchise to operate a cable television system violates the First Amendment and that the criteria Santa Cruz employed in evaluating proposals for cable franchises abridge Group W's rights under the First Amendment.

I. BACKGROUND

Group W is the sole operator of a cable television system in Santa Cruz under a so-called "non-exclusive" franchise granted by Santa Cruz in May 1966 to Group W's predecessor. The franchise agreement with Santa Cruz expired by its terms in May 1986. Despite negotiations stretching over the period 1982–84, Group W and Santa Cruz could not reach accord on terms for renewal.

In June 1984, Santa Cruz published a Request for Proposals to Provide Cable Television Service ("RFP") which solicited offers from cable television companies to provide service to the Santa Cruz community. The RFP established minimum criteria for granting a franchise proposal, including that the franchisee provide free access channels for public, governmental, and educational or institutional users; provide two-way institutional service capacity; promise basic service to every home in the Santa Cruz service area requesting such service; pay an annual franchise fee of 5% of gross revenue; provide video facilities for free use by local public, educational, and governmental programmers; meet certain technical requirements; and provide extensive information relating to financial capability. Group W and three other cable companies submitted proposals in response to the RFP.

On September 23, 1986 Santa Cruz denied Group W renewal of its franchise and also denied Group W a new franchise under the RFP procedure. Santa Cruz determined that Group W's RFP application was nonresponsive to the RFP criteria and, in any event, placed last among the four contenders for the franchise. It granted a franchise to Greater Santa Cruz Cable TV Associates, Inc. The parties then stipulated that Santa Cruz would not disrupt or discontinue Group W's cable services until final determination of the merits of this action.

On October 10, 1986 Group W moved for summary judgment on its claim that Santa Cruz's policy of granting a monopoly franchise violated the First Amendment. The Court concludes, for the reasons discussed in this opinion, that the policy of granting only a monopoly franchise violates the First Amendment, and that conditioning the award of a franchise on the provision of concessions violates the First Amendment, except that Santa Cruz is entitled (a) to require appropriate evidence of financial responsibility and (b) to charge a reasonable administrative fee and a reasonable fee for Group W's use of public streets and rights of way.

II. DISCUSSION

C. First Amendment protection of cable television

Cable operators, like newspapers, exercise considerable editorial discretion in selecting the mix and content of cable programming. These speech aspects of cable television clearly warrant a degree of First Amendment protection. Santa Cruz contends that the standards governing the broadcast media apply as well to cable, while Group W claims the broader range of protections afforded the print media.

Although differences in the characteristics of the media justify differences in the First Amendment protections afforded them, *Red Lion*, 395 U.S. at 386, "the basic principles of freedom of speech and the press, like the First Amendment's command, do not vary. Those principles...make freedom of expression the rule." Joseph Burstyn, Inc. v. Wilson, 343 U.S. 495, 503 (1952). Therefore, the starting point for the Court's analysis is that unless cable television differs in some material respect from the print media, the First Amendment standards that apply to newspapers apply with equal force to cable.

D. Exclusive franchising under the First Amendment

Group W contends that Santa Cruz's de facto policy of granting a single cable franchise to the operator of its choice violates Group W's First Amendment rights to freedom of speech and of the press. Santa Cruz defends its policy on three grounds: (1) the utility poles and subsurfaces of streets in Santa Cruz can accommodate only one cable system; (2) because cable television is inherently a natural monopoly, Santa Cruz is justified in awarding a franchise to the single cable television operator best able to serve the community; and (3) permitting more than one cable operator to string cables through Santa Cruz would cause undue disruption to the public domain.

Santa Cruz's selection of only one cable operator purports to be a content neutral regulation of the nonspeech aspects of cable television. In United States v. O'Brien, 391 U.S. 367 (1968), the Supreme Court devised the controlling test for weighing the constitutionality of regulations directed at the non-speech elements of First Amendment conduct. This test provides:

> a government regulation is sufficiently justified (1) if it is within the con-
> stitutional power of the government; (2) if it furthers an important or
> substantial governmental interest; (3) if the governmental interest is un-
> related to the suppression of free expression; and (4) if the incidental re-
> striction on alleged First Amendment freedoms is no greater than is es-
> sential to the furtherance of that interest.

O'Brien, 391 U.S. at 377. Moreover, the government bears the burden of satisfying each prong of this test.

1. Authority to award a franchise

California Government Code §53066 expressly authorizes local governing bodies to franchise cable television systems within their jurisdiction, to charge franchise fees, and to prescribe rules and regulations for the protection of sub-scribers. The 1984 Cable Policy Act, 47 U.S.C. §521 et. seq., established a na-tional policy of vesting in local governing bodies authority to franchise and regu-late cable communications, subject only to the Act's specified limitations. The Act clearly envisions a franchising model similar to the Santa Cruz procedure.[19]

2. Substantial or important governmental interest

a. Physical scarcity

Santa Cruz contends that its existing infrastructure of utility poles and un-derground conduits cannot accommodate all the cable operators that initially participated in the RFP process, justifying it in limiting to one the number of op-erators permitted access. This contention is without merit.

[Santa Cruz offered expert testimony that its utility poles would not accom-modate four concurrent systems. But, by 1986, only Group W and one other company were seeking non-exclusive franchises.] Santa Cruz has failed to raise a genuine issue concerning the capacity of its utility poles and conduits to accom-modate two systems.

No doubt the capacity of Santa Cruz's utility infrastructure is finite. But this fact alone cannot justify granting only a single cable franchise. Santa Cruz has

---

19. Section 541(a)(1) of the Cable Policy Act expressly grants local governments the power to award "one or more franchises within its jurisdiction." A franchise authorizes a franchisee to construct a cable system over public rights of way and over easements dedi-cated to compatible uses. §541(a)(2).

therefore failed to demonstrate the existence of a substantial government interest based on physical scarcity justifying an exclusive franchise.

b. Natural monopoly

Santa Cruz next asserts that the market for cable television in its community can support only one cable franchise. According to Santa Cruz, because the cable market will inevitably give rise to a natural monopoly, government regulation must replace competition as the mechanism ensuring cable television's responsiveness to public needs. It therefore has an "important or substantial governmental interest" in selecting the one cable operator best able to serve the public.

Even if Santa Cruz's factual allegations concerning its cable market are taken as true, the natural monopoly rationale cannot as a matter of law justify Santa Cruz's paternalistic regulatory scheme.

In Miami Herald Publishing Co. v. Tornillo, 418 U.S. 241 (1974), the Supreme Court rejected the natural monopoly rationale in the context of newspapers. The Court acknowledged that "the same economic factors which have caused the disappearance of vast numbers of metropolitan newspapers, have made entry into the marketplace of ideas served by the print media almost impossible." *Id.* at 251. Nonetheless, the Court concluded that "press responsibility is not mandated by the Constitution and like many other virtues it cannot be legislated." *Id.* at 256.

This principle applies with equal force to the medium of cable television. Government selection of an exclusive First Amendment speaker, whether a newspaper or a cable operator, "creates a serious risk that government officials will discriminate among speakers on the basis of the content of, or views expressed in, their proposed speech." *Preferred I*, 754 F.2d at 1406. The First Amendment cannot tolerate this risk.

The Seventh, Eighth, and Tenth Circuits have each held that the natural monopoly rationale provides a basis for denying a cable operator access to the market. These courts rely on essentially two theories to reach the conclusion that natural monopoly characteristics of cable justify greater government intrusion into the medium.

First, the courts reason that cable systems, like public utilities, operate most efficiently when they serve the entire market. Until a triumphant cable company competing in a free market drives out its competitors, there will be duplication of facilities and higher prices for consumers. Government regulation of such a natural monopoly avoids these hazards, thereby maximizing economic efficiency and consumer welfare.

While the economic argument standing alone may be persuasive, it ignores the First Amendment values implicated in cable television. So long as physical scarcity does not make some limitation on access to the market unavoidable, the risk of intrusion into editorial judgment is too great to permit the government to select the exclusive cable operator. The notion that economic efficiency warrants such intrusion is to the Court's knowledge unprecedented.

Second, these courts also reason that because government may regulate those physical aspects of the cable industry that affect the public domain, government also has free rein to regulate economic aspects of the industry. For example, in *Community Communications,* the Tenth Circuit distinguished *Miami Herald* from a case involving monopoly franchising of a cable operator on the ground that "Miami Herald involved an effort by state government to compel public access to a medium that is not tied to government in the way cable companies necessarily are. There, the characteristic of economic scarcity was unrelated to the disruptive use of the public domain requiring a government license." *Community Communications,* 660 F.2d at 1379. In other words, the government's interest in regulating cable's impact on the public domain gives it authority to select the operator entitled to exercise the franchise.

This argument, too, ignores First Amendment constraints. Under the *O'Brien* test the government may regulate speakers only as required to further its interests. Whatever monopolistic tendency the cable market may have has nothing to do with the government's interest in licensing potentially disruptive uses of the public domain. Santa Cruz may be correct that only one cable operator will prove economically viable. However, it has not demonstrated that its interest in minimizing physical disruption legitimizes giving it the right to determine who that operator will be.

c. Physical disruption

Santa Cruz also argues that the physical and aesthetic disruption of the public domain that will necessarily result from the construction of multiple cable systems justifies granting a single franchise. According to Santa Cruz, the installation of multiple cable systems will require replacing some utility poles with taller poles, adding anchoring cables to utility poles, and rearranging cables on existing poles. In addition, approximately one-fourth of the new cables will be laid under streets. Underground installations of cables will result in cuts that permanently weaken the road surfaces and may damage the substreet pipes and cables of vital utilities.

Santa Cruz has "legitimate interests in public safety and in maintaining public thoroughfares." *Preferred I,* 754 F.2d at 1406. "This provides a justification for some government regulation." *Id.* The question, however, is whether it provides a sufficient justification for the granting of a monopoly franchise.

Santa Cruz supports its physical disruption argument with the declarations of administrators of the Santa Cruz Department of Public Works. Each declarant states that the non-simultaneous installation of four new cable systems would result in undue disruption to Santa Cruz's thoroughfares. The scenario described by these declarants of four cable operators installing cables without any coordination, however, has no factual basis. In fact, only two cable operators, Group W and another company, would install cable systems.

Indeed, Santa Cruz's own evidence undercuts any claim that the simultaneous installation of two cable systems would result in a significant disruption to the public streets. According to data prepared by Santa Cruz's declarant, two cable systems with shared facilities would call for replacing fewer than two percent of Santa Cruz's utility poles and rearranging one percent of its power lines and ten percent of its telephone lines. Although, according to Santa Cruz, seventy percent of the guy wires and wire anchors supporting the poles would require replacement or rearrangement, this appears unlikely to have any significant effect on traffic or the appearance of the utility poles.

In sum, Santa Cruz has failed to raise a genuine issue as to whether granting a monopoly cable franchise will materially further its interest in minimizing the physical disruption of the public domain.[20]

d. Conclusion

Santa Cruz has failed to come forward with evidence sufficient to raise a genuine issue as to whether its policy of granting only a single cable franchise is supported by any important or substantial government interest. Accordingly, it has failed to sustain its burden under the second prong of the *O'Brien* test, and the policy therefore violates the First Amendment.

e. Conditions imposed on Group W

According to Group W, because the RFP process and criteria empower Santa Cruz to exact a broad range of concessions from a franchise, they are constitutionally invalid. Santa Cruz alleges that imposition of the RFP criteria and rejection of Group W's application for noncompliance with those criteria serve important governmental interests.

Although Santa Cruz is precluded from legislating a cable monopoly, it does not necessarily follow that Santa Cruz must "open its doors to all cable-television comers, regardless of size, shape, quality, qualifications, or threat to the ultimate capacity of the system." Pacific West Cable Company v. City of Sacramento, 798 F.2d 353, 355 (9th Cir. 1986). The question before the Court is whether Santa Cruz can reconcile with the First Amendment the requirements and conditions to which Group W objects. For the purposes of this discussion, these regulations may be divided into four categories: (1) public access requirements; (2) technical requirements; (3) provisions concerning Group W's financial capability; and (4) franchise fees.

1. Public access requirements

The RFP requires the franchisee to devote separate access channels to public, governmental, and institutional users. The franchisee may not charge a fee for use of these channels. In addition, the franchisee must finance, staff, and make available for free public use at least one fully equipped production studio and one to two mobile production units. Santa Cruz plans to create an agency to administer these channels and facilities, which will have primary responsibility for adopting rules governing the use of channel time and facilities and for scheduling and coordinating their use. The franchisee must fund this agency.

Santa Cruz contends that these measures further the First Amendment interests of the community by ensuring that the cable system will carry a diverse range of viewpoints.

If applied to the press, these requirements would surely violate the First Amendment. Santa Cruz attempts to distinguish *Tornillo* on the ground that the

---

20. Santa Cruz also defends its policy on the ground that Group W can continue to transmit its programs over an access channel leased from the franchised cable system. But the First Amendment forbids Santa Cruz from restricting Group W's speech by offering Group W a less adequate alternative to a cable franchise: "one is not to have the exercise of his liberty of expression in an appropriate place abridged on the plea that it may be exercised in some other place." Schneider v. State, 308 U.S. 147, 163 (1939).

access regulations in that case were triggered by the newspapers' content, while the right of access called for in the RFP in not contingent on the content of the cable operator's statements. According to Santa Cruz, "access comes automatically and without extensive governmental intervention."

On closer scrutiny, however, the access requirements cannot be characterized as content neutral. Access does not, as Santa Cruz claims, come "automatically"; rather, under the scheme envisaged in the RFP, access is meted out by a government agency that enjoys unlimited discretion to devise rules governing the use of access time and facilities and to schedule the use of such time and facilities. Santa Cruz has thus reserved to itself broad power to designate the speakers entitled to package their messages using the franchisee's production facilities and to air their views using the franchisee's cable system. Santa Cruz reserved the power to designate when and for how long speakers may produce and transmit their messages. In practice, Santa Cruz can turn the access channels and facilities into forums for attacks on the editorial views expressed by the franchisee. Like the newspaper in *Tornillo*, a cable operator in Santa Cruz may be deterred from airing its views for fear that this will trigger—indeed, force it to produce and fund—the response of an opposing group. Furthermore, this access scheme potentially grants the incumbent government a free platform from which to advance its own view and candidates.

"The First Amendment interest of the public in being informed," *Tornillo*, 418 U.S. at 251, cannot justify the risk that the franchisee's speech will be chilled or that the government will abuse its discretion to serve its own interest, rather than the public's, at the expense of the franchisee.

2. Technical requirements

Group W objects to the array of technical requirements imposed by Santa Cruz. For example, the RFP requires that the franchisee provide a minimum of 54 channels. Basic service to residential subscribers must consist of at least 30 channels. The RFP also dictates the mix of programming the franchisee must offer, including local and distant television broadcast signals; "cable program" packages such as non-pay satellite services; and automated, pay cable, audio, access, handicapped, and regional programming services. All residential subscribers must be offered a basic viewing package of local television broadcast signals, access channels, automated services, and "cable program" services. Separate automated service channels are to be devoted to a program guide and a community bulletin board.

The franchisee is further required to provide a two-way cable for institutional use. The institutional cable must have the capacity for interactive transfer of audio, video, and data information among its users. The franchisee is further required to develop such governmental uses of the cable system as water meter reading, security services, and computer data transfer. All these services are to be provided to governmental users at no charge and to other institutional users at no charge or a reduced fee.

In addition, Santa Cruz requires the franchise to offer basic cable services to every home in the City and County requesting such service. Santa Cruz concedes that line extension to homes in outlying and sparsely populated areas is costlier than extension to other areas, and so permits the franchisee to charge these subscribers a specified surcharge over the basic subscriber rate and, under certain circumstances, a specified capital contribution.

Santa Cruz argues that these requirements maximize the public benefits of cable television while still permitting the cable franchisee to realize a reasonable profit. This justification does not pass the test articulated in *Tornillo* for regulation of the communicative aspects of the press. *Tornillo* made clear that a government regulation that intrudes into the editorial functions of the press cannot survive, even if the newspaper "would face no additional costs to comply and would not be forced to forgo publication of news or opinion." 418 U.S. at 258. Thus the relevant point is not that a franchisee could earn a reasonable profit if it complied with Santa Cruz's technical requirements, but rather that these requirements impermissibly intrude into the editorial functions of cable operators.

Regulations dictating a cable operator's channel capacity, quality of service, mix of programming, institutional service, and extension of service to outlying areas would be akin to legislation requiring a newspaper to print a minimum number of pages, use paper and ink of only a certain quality, cover a specified range of subjects, print information and data of interest to government and institutional readers free of charge, provide free subscriptions to government and institutional readers, and offer home delivery to any subscriber residing anywhere in the community at a price fixed by the government. Such measures, if imposed on a newspaper, would certainly violate the First Amendment. Santa Cruz has not shown why cable operators would be entitled to less protection.

Furthermore, these regulations are not narrowly drawn to advance Santa Cruz's substantial interest in minimizing physical disruption to the public domain. Although Santa Cruz might argue that a one-time installation of a new state-of-the-art cable system will reduce the need for piecemeal repairs and replacement of an obsolete system, it has not demonstrated the inadequacy of more narrowly drawn measures for minimizing the disruptive aspects of cable repairs.

Finally, these regulations cannot be sustained on the ground that they are meant to protect consumers from shoddy cable service provided by inept or unscrupulous cable franchisees. The challenged measures do not attack this evil with sufficient precision. If Santa Cruz wishes to address it, it can do so with consumer protection laws and criminal statutes designed to deter and punish such misconduct.

3. Financial capability

The RFP requires a prospective franchisee to submit extensive information concerning its ownership, finances and experience in the cable field and ten-year projections of operating costs and revenue. Group W objects to these disclosure requirements on the ground that they are expensive and burden the exercise of First Amendment rights.

To the extent the information sought relates only to an applicant's ability to comply with the access and technical regulations invalidated above, Santa Cruz has no legitimate interest in requiring its disclosure. Santa Cruz does, however, have a substantial governmental interest in minimizing the physical disruption that could occur if a cable operator lacks the financial resources to install and maintain a cable system safely and expeditiously. To this end, Santa Cruz may require an applicant to post a reasonable performance bond, obtain adequate insurance, and submit evidence of competence to operate the system, to the extent necessary to prevent harm to the City and the County. It may not, however, demand disclosure of the scope presently required by the RFP. Nor may it reserve to itself discretion to select from among applicants the operator it considers best qualified.

4. Franchise fee

The RFP requires the franchisee to pay a "franchise fee" of 5% of its gross revenue from the franchise. Although a portion of these payments may constitute reimbursement to Santa Cruz for its administrative costs in licensing and administering a cable franchise, Santa Cruz concedes that the franchise fee would exceed its administrative costs and generate revenue.

Group W contends that the First Amendment precludes Santa Cruz from charging a licensing fee greater than necessary to defray its legitimate regulatory costs. The franchise fee is unconstitutional, Group W argues, because it singles out cable operators and conditions the exercise of First Amendment rights on the payment of a tax.[21] Because the franchise fee is directed at the non-communicative aspects of Group W's First Amendment activities, the four-pronged *O'Brien* test determines whether it constitutes a permissible restriction.

a. Authority to charge a fee

Santa Cruz clearly has statutory authority to charge an appropriate franchise fee. Moreover, the 1984 Cable Policy Act authorizes local franchising authorities to charge up to a 5% annual franchise fee over and above the numerous financial exactions permitted under the Act. 47 U.S.C. §542(b).

Group W maintains that Santa Cruz's public thoroughfares are a traditional public forum, access to which may not be conditioned upon the payment of a revenue-raising fee. This argument, however, fails to recognize that cable television's use of public streets differs from that of other First Amendment speakers. Cable television is unique in that it requires the permanent occupation of space on utility poles and through underground conduits to the exclusion of other potential users of the same space.

b. Substantial governmental interest

Like the MTA in *Gannett*, Santa Cruz has a substantial governmental interest in charging a reasonable fee as compensation for the grant of a permanent interest in public property. A cable franchise confers on the franchisee an interest in public property that differs significantly from the public's general right to travel over public streets.

c. Unrelated to the suppression of free speech

Nor can Group W argue that Santa Cruz has singled out cable operators from other similar users of public streets and facilities. For example, Santa

---

21. Group W also objects on the same grounds to such in-kind payments imposed by the RFP as the free access and institutional channels and services discussed above. Because the Court invalidates these requirements on other grounds, it does not reach the question whether they constitute an unconstitutional tax on the exercise of Group W's First Amendment rights.

Cruz charges the Pacific Gas and Electric Company a franchise of 2% of gross revenues attributable to the franchise in return for the right to lay pipes and cables along public streets and highways in which Santa Cruz has a proprietary interest.

d. Burden is no greater than is essential

Finally, Santa Cruz has a substantial interest in being paid the fair market value of what it has conveyed. A charge in excess of fair market value would, however, not be sufficiently tailored to Santa Cruz's proprietary interest in its property and thus would unreasonably burden Group W's ability to exercise its First Amendment freedoms. Although an excessive fee would further Santa Cruz's interest in raising revenue, this interest could be achieved as effectively by a general tax on all businesses. *Minneapolis Star*, 460 U.S. at 586.

Although the RFP nominally requires only a 5% franchise fee, it also calls for a variety of other concessions which, aside from infringing the First Amendment for reasons heretofore discussed, add substantially to the cost imposed on the cable operator.[22] Moreover, neither the 5% fee nor the in-kind charges purport to bear any relationship to the fair market value of the right to use Santa Cruz property pursuant to a franchise.

Determination of what constitutes a reasonable fee must turn principally on an appraisal of the fair market value of the rights of way, easements and other entitlements to use, occupy or traverse Santa Cruz property incidental to the exercise of Group W's cable franchise. Because such appraisals are routinely made in the ordinary course of municipal and private affairs, the Court expects the parties to arrive at an appropriate figure by negotiation.

In addition, Santa Cruz is entitled to charge a reasonable fee to defray the administrative costs of issuing the franchise. For the reasons stated in this opinion, those costs should cover only the relatively minor clerical services required.

Notes and Questions

1. Later Developments. Local government discretion with respect to franchising decisions is today significantly constrained by the Cable Communications Policy Act of 1984 and the Cable Television Consumer Protection and Competition Act of 1992. The next chapter considers these modern rules in detail.

2. The Local Interest. Federal law aside, what are the strongest claims for having local cable regulation? Are the regulations considered in *Group W* consistent with those justifications? For example, if you believe that local government should be allowed to regulate cable so as to minimize the disruption that would otherwise be caused by having multiple companies lay cable lines, does it follow that local government should be allowed devote access channels to public, governmental, and institutional users? What about the argument that space on local

---

22. A study in the early 1980's of a typical cable system in a top 50 television market found that franchise fees, free service to government buildings, and public access facilities and services consume 21% to 24% of subscriber revenues. Cable Television Regulation: Hearings Before the Senate Comm. on Commerce, Science, and Transportation, 97th Cong., 2d Sess. 236–37 (1982).

telephone poles is scarce, and so only a small number of cable providers can be allowed to serve any given community? Isn't this argument just as strong as the scarcity argument that was used in the broadcast context to justify the entire federal regulatory regime?

3. Natural Monopoly. If cable television is a natural monopoly, isn't it sensible to choose who will operate that monopoly at the outset, rather than to endure the potential for duplicated costs, undue disruption, and consumer confusion that can result from permitting several firms to begin to build a system when only one can survive? What is gained and what is lost by permitting the competition for the monopoly position to be conducted (a) in the marketplace or (b) in a franchising process?

4. Franchise Agreements. The conditions Santa Cruz sought to impose on its franchisee are not atypical of the kinds of bargains that characterized the bidding for cable television franchises during cable's early years. Notice especially the "technical requirements" described in Part II. E. 2. Would it be preferable to permit the marketplace to determine precisely what features a city's cable system(s) will offer? Or is the franchise stage—where potential cable operators bargain with city officials—a more appropriate place to determine what the cable system(s) will look like, given the limited marketplace competition a cable operator is likely to face? Does either option promise to give much weight to the interests of low income residents?

5. The First Amendment. The court, in effect, concludes that the First Amendment dictates that the precise nature and scope of the cable system be determined by bargaining between the cable operator(s) and potential subscribers. Why does the court read the First Amendment in this manner? Why does the court conclude that Santa Cruz's "requirements impermissibly intrude into the editorial functions of cable operators"? Might the technical requirements, at least, be viewed alternatively as permissible conditions incident to permitting access to public property and rights of way?

6. Franchise Fees. Note also the court's disposition of the challenge to the franchise fee. Does the Court here give too little deference to Congress's determinations?

7. Open Markets. The opinion, as a whole, seems to suggest that although cities may require cable operators to obtain franchises, officials must award a franchise to anyone willing and able to obey generally applicable laws that are not specific to the cable industry. Thus, for example, the city can require that it be compensated for damage to the streets in the same manner and at the same rate that it charges anyone for the right to dig up the streets, but the city cannot require that the cable system contain a minimum number of channels or be capable of providing burglar alarm services. Is this a sensible way to protect a city's legitimate interests without permitting undue governmental intrusion into cable operators' rights of expression?

8. Level Playing Field Statutes. Many states have adopted so-called "level playing field" statutes that prohibit municipalities from issuing new franchise agreements that are more favorable than the agreements under which incumbent franchisees serve. In Illinois, for example, the relevant statute provides:

(4) If the franchising authority shall determine that it is in the best interest of the municipality to do so, [the municipality] may grant [an] addi-

tional cable television franchise. [However]...no such additional cable television franchise shall be granted under terms or conditions more favorable or less burdensome to the applicant than those required under the existing cable television franchise, including but not limited to terms and conditions pertaining to the territorial extent of the franchise, system design, technical performance standards, construction schedules, performance bonds, standards for construction and installation of cable television facilities, service to subscribers, public educational and governmental access channels and programming, production assistance, liability and indemnification, and franchise fees.

(5) [T]he franchising authority may grant an additional cable television franchise under different terms and conditions than those of the existing franchise, in which event the franchising authority shall enter into good faith negotiations with the existing franchisee and shall, within 120 days after the effective date of the additional cable television franchise, modify the existing cable television franchise in a manner and to the extent necessary to ensure that neither the existing cable television franchise nor the additional cable television franchise, each considered in its entirety, provides a competitive advantage over the other....

65 ILCS 5/11-42-11(e)(4)-(5). The Illinois statute goes on to limit the types of retroactive adjustments allowed, for example disallowing any changes that would require the incumbent to "make any additional payment to the franchising authority" or "engage in any additional construction."

Whose interests are served by these level playing field statutes? Are the statutes a good idea? Needless to say, considerable litigation has arisen out of claims by incumbents that municipalities have not satisfied their states' particular level playing field statutes. *See, e.g.*, New England Cable Television Association, Inc. v. Department of Public Utility Control, 717 A.2d 1276 (Conn. 1998).

9. Overlapping Jurisdiction. On the broader jurisdictional issue, is it sensible to have cable television regulated by both federal and state authorities? Federal regulation of broadcast was intuitively appealing since broadcast does not respect local political boundaries. But doesn't *Group W* make a convincing case that most of cable television's possible harms — at least ones that the First Amendment allows government to rectify — are local in nature, thus justifying only local intervention? Is there a story to be told here about checks and balances, perhaps, with the federal government stopping local government from overreaching? Or is this instead a setting where two levels of government mean double the opportunity for self-dealing, rent-seeking, and bureaucratic waste?

CHAPTER TEN

RATE REGULATION AND LOCAL FRANCHISE AUTHORITY

The purpose of this chapter is

- to begin a two-chapter survey of modern cable regulation, with this chapter focusing on two items: rate regulation, in the form of price caps and rate-of-return regulation; and federal regulation of the local franchise authority.

~

I. RATE REGULATION

Under the Cable Communications Policy Act of 1984, Pub. L. 98-549, 98 Stat. 2779, government involvement with cable rates was minimal. The Act provided that local authorities could not regulate the rates cable systems charged to subscribers in any cases where the FCC determined that those systems faced "effective competition." The Commission determined that a cable system confronted effective competition in any case where its subscribers could receive three or more over-the-air television signals.[1] Since most cable systems operated in environments meeting that criterion, this standard effectively abolished rate regulation for all cable systems.

Cable rates rose significantly in the absence of regulation, and so, a few years later, Congress changed the statutory scheme by passing the Cable Television Consumer Protection and Competition Act of 1992, Pub. L. 102-385, 106 Stat. 1460. This Act requires that cable operators (1) establish a "basic tier" of services consisting largely of whatever retransmitted television stations the system carries (including network affiliates and independent stations); (2) price that basic tier separately; and (3) force subscribers to purchase the basic tier as a precondition to subscribing to other services. The statute then permits local authorities to regulate rates for basic service according to formulas established by the Commission. As it was with the 1984 Act, under the 1992 Act local government

---

1. In the Matter of Amendment of Parts 1, 63, and 76 of the Commission's Rules to Implement the Provisions of the Cable Communications Policy Act of 1984, 1985 FCC LEXIS 3475; 58 Rad. Reg. 2d (P & F) 1 (1985), at ¶100.

authorities are not permitted to regulate prices for cable systems that are subject to "effective competition," but the statutory standard defining effective competition under the 1992 Act assures that rate regulation will be permissible for the vast majority of cable systems.[2]

Rate regulation outside the basic tier is no longer permitted for either the Commission or local authorities. There were times in the past when the FCC regulated upper tier prices. For example, under the 1992 Act, the Commission had authority to entertain complaints regarding cable services that were outside the basic tier. But even then the FCC had no power over cable services sold pay-per-channel or pay-per-program. As of March 31, 1999, however, the Telecommunications Act of 1996 repealed all cable rate regulation except for regulation associated with the basic tier. Thus, rate regulation today mainly consists of local approval for monthly charges related to basic cable service and local approval of any fees related to the use, ownership, or installation of equipment related to basic service. The relevant statutory provision is 47 U.S.C. §543.

The following text is excerpted from the *Executive Summary* of the Commission's *Report and Order* on rate regulation pursuant to the 1992 Cable Act. Read it not so much for the details (which have changed since 1992 and continue to evolve), but instead for the broader issues, such as the question of how government officials should select and enforce price levels in cable markets and when, if ever, specific cable providers should be granted exceptions from those general rules.

RATE REGULATION OF CABLE SERVICES
Executive Summary, Report and Order,
8 FCC Rcd. 5631 (1993)

I. INTRODUCTION

2. The Cable Act of 1992 generally provides that where effective competition is present, cable television rates shall not be subject to regulation by government but shall be regulated by the market. The Act contains a clear and explicit preference for competitive resolution of issues where that is feasible. However, where competition is absent, cable rates are to be regulated to protect the interests of subscribers. This regulation is to be undertaken jointly by the Federal Communications Commission and by state and local governments. Local (or state) governments are primarily responsible for the regulation of rates for programming service and equipment on the basic service tier, and this Commission will entertain complaints against the rates for programming services and equipment for the cable programming services tier or tiers. (Services offered on a per-channel or per-program basis are not subject to rate regulation).

3. The primary results of this proceeding are: 1) development of a process for identifying those situations where effective competition exists (and rate regulation is thus precluded), 2) establishment of the boundaries between local and state, and federal responsibilities, 3) development of procedural and substantive rules to govern the regulation of basic service tier, cable programming service, and leased channel rates, and 4) creation of a process of gathering information to

---

2. In the Matter of Implementation of Sections of the Cable Television Consumer Protection and Competition Act of 1992 Rate Regulation, 8 FCC Rcd 5631 (1993), at ¶¶18-50.

facilitate the regulation that is being undertaken and periodically review its effectiveness.

II. REPORT AND ORDER

A. Rate Regulation of Cable Service

1. Rollback of Cable Service Rates

6. The *Report and Order* finds that Congress was concerned that rates of systems not subject to effective competition reflect undue market power and are unreasonable to the extent they exceed competitive rate levels. This conclusion is based upon the findings and goals of the Cable Act of 1992, the overall scheme of regulation under it, and the fact that the Commission must consider the rates of systems subject to effective competition in establishing rate regulations. Additionally, the Commission conducted a survey of cable system rates as of September 30, 1992, which revealed that, on average, rates of systems not subject to effective competition are approximately 10 percent higher than rates of comparable systems subject to effective competition, as that term is defined in the statute. Thus, the Commission's survey supports the findings of Congress that current rates for cable systems not subject to effective competition reflect pervasive market power.

7. The Commission concludes, therefore, that its initial effort to regulate rates for cable service should provide for reductions from current rates of cable systems exhibiting undue market power. The Commission's initial implementation of rate regulation of cable service will generally lead to significant reductions from current rate levels for most cable systems. Our approach will enable local franchise authorities to require rates for the basic tier, and the Commission to require rates for cable programming services on the basis of individual complaints, to fall approximately 10 percent, unless the operator is already charging rates that are at the "competitive" benchmark level or it can justify a higher rate from September 30, 1992 levels, based on costs. The Commission estimates that this rollback will affect approximately three-quarters of cable systems, with a total consumer benefit of approximately $1 billion. Rates of all regulated systems will then be subject to a price cap that will govern the extent to which rates can be raised in the future without a cost-of-service showing.

2. Standards and Procedures for Identifying Cable Systems Not Subject to Effective Competition

a. Application of Effective Competition Tests

8. Cable service and equipment rates may only be regulated under the Cable Consumer Protection and Competition Act of 1992 ("1992 Act") if the cable system is not subject to effective competition. Under the statute, "effective competition" exists if: (a) fewer than 30 percent of households in the franchise area subscribe to the cable service of a cable system; or (b) (i) the franchise area is served by at least two unaffiliated multichannel video programming distributors ("multichannel distributors"), each of which offers comparable programming to at least 50 percent of households in the franchise area, and (ii) the number of households subscribing to programming services offered by multichannel distributors other than the largest multichannel distributor exceeds 15 percent of

households in the franchise area; or (c) the franchise authority itself is a multi-channel distributor and offers video programming to at least 50 percent of the households in the franchise area.

(2) Availability of Competing Services

10. A multichannel distributor's service is "offered" in a franchise area if the service is both technically and actually available, with no regulatory, technical, or other impediments to households taking service. Service will be deemed to be "technically available" when the multichannel distributor is physically able to deliver the service to a household wishing to subscribe, with only minimal additional investment by the distributor. A service will be considered "actually available" if subscribers in the franchise area are reasonably aware through marketing efforts that the service is available.

(3) Definition of Household

11. We define the term "household" as each separately billed or billable customer, except that we treat individual residences of multiple dwelling units as separate households.

(4) Measurement of Subscribership

12. For purposes of applying the 30 percent threshold in the first effective competition test, the measurement of subscribership will be based on that of the particular system in question, and not an aggregation of all cable systems or competitors in the franchise area. For purposes of applying the 15 percent threshold in the second effective competition test, subscribership of alternative multichannel distributors will be calculated on a cumulative basis; however, only those multichannel distributors that offer programming to at least 50 percent of the households in the franchise area will be included in the 15 percent cumulative measurement.

(5) Program Comparability

13. A multichannel distributor will be deemed to offer "comparable programming" to that provided by a cable system if it offers at least twelve channels of video programming, including at least one non-broadcast channel.

b. Finding of Effective Competition

14. For purposes of implementing rate regulation by local franchising authorities, we presume that cable operators are not subject to effective competition. Franchising authorities may rely on this presumption when filing a certification with the Commission to regulate basic rates. The cable operator will then have the burden of rebutting this presumption with evidence demonstrating that effective competition does in fact exist.

3. Regulation of the Basic Service Tier

a. Assertion of Jurisdiction over Basic Service and Equipment Rates

(1) Jurisdiction Over Basic Rate Regulation

16. The 1992 Cable Act requires local authorities wishing to regulate basic service and equipment rates to certify in writing to the Commission that (1) its

rate regulations will be consistent with the rate regulations we prescribe; (2) it has the legal authority to adopt, and the personnel to administer, rate regulations; and (3) its procedural rules provide an opportunity for consideration of the views of interested parties. Such certification filed with the Commission by a franchising authority will become effective 30 days after filing *unless* the Commission finds, after notice and a reasonable opportunity to comment, that the franchising authority has not met one of the three criteria above. If the Commission disapproves the certification, the franchising authority will be notified of any revisions or modifications necessary to gain approval. If the Commission disapproves or revokes a certification, we will exercise the franchise authority's regulatory jurisdiction until the authority becomes qualified by filing a new certification that meets the requirements set forth above.

(a) Division of Jurisdiction Between FCC and Local Governments

17. Under the statute, local franchising authorities and the Commission have shared jurisdiction over the regulation of basic service and equipment rates. However, the Commission will not exercise jurisdiction unless either (a) a local franchising authority's certification is denied or revoked, or (b) the franchising authority requests us to regulate basic rates because it has insufficient resources to regulate or it lacks the legal authority to do so. Franchising authorities requesting Commission intervention on the basis of insufficient funds must submit a showing explaining why the franchise fees it obtains cannot be used to cover the cost of rate regulation at the local level. The Commission will not regulate basic rates where a local government voluntarily chooses not to seek certification because it is satisfied with the rates charged by the local cable operator.

(2) The Certification Process

(d) Revocation of Certification

27. A cable operator once not subject to effective competition that later becomes subject to effective competition may petition the franchising authority for change in its regulatory status. The operator bears the burden of proving the existence of effective competition.

b. Implementation and Enforcement of Basic Tier Rates

(1) Review by Local Franchising Authorities

(b) Franchising Authority Review of Basic Cable Rates

31. A two-step approach will be used regarding franchise authority review of a cable operator's current rates for the basic service tier and accompanying equipment, or proposed increases in those rates. Under the first step, if a franchising authority is able to determine that a cable operator's current rates are within the Commission's reasonable rate standards, the rates could go into effect 30 days after they were submitted. Also, if the franchising authority found that a proposed rate increase was within the Commission's rate standards, the increase could go into effect 30 days after filing with the franchising authority.

32. Under the second step, if the franchising authority is unable to determine whether the rate in issue is within the Commission's reasonable rate standard, based on the material before it, or if the cable operator has submitted a cost-of-service showing seeking to justify a rate above the Commission's reasonable rate level, the franchising authority may take an additional period of time to make a final determination and toll the effective date of the proposed rates for a commensurate period. A franchising authority may take an additional 90 days if it needs more time to ensure that a rate is within the Commission's rate standard. The authority may take an additional 150 days to evaluate a cost-of-service showing seeking to justify a rate above the reasonable rate level. The authority must issue a brief written decision regarding its invocation of the additional time period. If no action is taken within these time periods, the proposed rates will go into effect, subject to subsequent refund orders if a franchising authority later issues a decision disapproving any portion of the proposed rates.

(c) Due Process Concerns

33. A cable operator is required to notify subscribers in writing of a proposed rate increase at approximately the same time it notifies the franchising authority, *i.e.*, at least 30 days before any proposed increase is effective.

34. A franchising authority is required to issue a written decision to the public whenever it disapproves either an initial basic cable rate or a request for an increase in whole or in part, or approves a proposed rate over the objections of interested parties. However, we will not require an authority to issue a written decision if it is approving a basic cable rate or rate increase in its entirety and there have been no objections.

(2) Remedies and Appeals

(a) Remedies for Unreasonable Basic Cable Rates

36. Franchising authorities may order prospective rate reductions and, where they have determined that existing or proposed rates are unreasonable, prescribe a reasonable rate.

37. Franchising authorities may also invoke the remedy of ordering refunds in three situations: First, if an operator fails to comply with a rate decision and continues to charge unreasonable rates, the authority can order refunds back to the effective date of its rate order. Second, as part of its initial review of existing cable rates, an authority has the discretion to order refunds for unreasonable rates that exceed the Commission's permitted tier charge and are not supported by a persuasive cost-of-service showing by the operator. Third, if an authority has tolled a proposed rate increase for 90 or 150 additional days and has not completed its review by the end of these time periods, the proposed rates can go into effect subject to a refund if portions of the rates are later found to be unreasonable. For situations two and three above, the refund period is limited to a maximum of one year.

(b) Forum for Appeals of Local Authorities' Decisions

38. The Commission will exercise exclusive jurisdiction over appeals of local rate decisions involving whether the franchising authority has acted inconsis-

tently with the rate regulation provisions of the Cable Act or our implementing rules.

(3) Notification of Availability of the Basic Service Tier

39. Cable operators are required to notify subscribers of the availability of basic tier service within 90 days or three billing cycles from the effective date of the rules adopted in this proceeding and are required to notify new subscribers at the time of installation.

c. Regulation of Basic Service Tier Rates and Equipment

(1) Components of the Basic Service Tier Subject to Rate Regulation

(a) Introduction and (b) General Requirements

40. The 1992 Cable Act requires cable operators to offer subscribers a separately available basic service tier to which subscription is required for access to any other tier of service. The basic tier must include, at a minimum, all must-carry signals, all PEG[3] channels, and all domestic television signals other than superstations. The cable operator may add other channels of programming to its basic tier at its discretion. The statutory definition preempts provisions in franchise agreements that require additional services to be carried on the basic tier.

(c) Buying-Through Basic Service to Other Tiers

41. Subscribers must purchase the basic service tier in order to gain access to video programming offered on a per-program or per-channel basis. The *Report and Order* finds that purchase of the basic tier is not required in order to buy non-video programming services such as cable radio.

(d) A Single Basic Tier

42. Cable operators subject to rate regulation may have only one "basic" tier which must be unbundled from all other tiers; multiple basic tiers will not be permitted for rate regulation purposes.

(2) Regulations Governing Rates of the Basic Service Tier

(a) Statutory Standards

43. The Cable Act of 1992 requires the Commission to establish regulations that will assure reasonable rates for the basic service tier, but does not explicitly define "reasonable." Instead, it requires that regulations be designed to achieve statutory goals and take into account the enumerated statutory factors. We have determined that under the statute the Commission can, and should, place primary weight on the rates of systems subject to effective competition. Accordingly, the Commission's regulations governing rates for the basic service tier are aimed

---

3. [Ed. PEG channels are "public, educational, and governmental" channels made available on the cable system by the franchisee for use by the local franchising authority. They are typically required by the franchise agreement. PEG channels are discussed later in this chapter.]

toward achieving rate levels that are closer to rates of systems subject to effective competition.

(b) Benchmarking versus Cost-of-Service Regulation

44. The Commission examines the relative merits of a benchmarking versus a cost-of-service approach as the primary method for regulating rates for the basic service tier.[4] We conclude that we should incorporate a benchmark into our framework for regulation of basic service tier rates because a benchmark can protect consumers from excessive rates and keep the costs of administration and compliance low. The Commission's rules, however, allow cable operators to use cost-of-service principles to justify rates higher than permitted by the system's benchmark.

(c) Local Authority Discretion

45. The *Report and Order* concludes that local authorities may not elect cost-of-service regulation as their primary mode of regulation of the basic service tier because such an approach would establish a regulatory regime for the basic service tier that is less consistent with Congressional intent than benchmark regulation. Rather, local governments must apply the benchmark system of rate regulation adopted by the Commission, unless a cable operator chooses to make a cost-of-service showing.

(d) Basic Rate Level in Comparison to Other Tiers

46. The Commission declines to adopt a regulatory framework for cable service that seeks lower rates for the basic service tier in comparison to higher tiers. We believe that any advantages in producing a low priced basic tier are outweighed by the incentives for cable operators to reduce offerings on the basic service tier. Accordingly, the Commission establishes a tier neutral framework for rate regulation that applies the same standards of reasonableness to the basic service tier and to cable programming services.

(e) Adoption of a Benchmark to Govern Rates for the Basic Service Tier

AA. The Competitive Benchmark

47. The *Report and Order* discusses the various benchmark alternatives proposed in the Notice. We find that the Cable Act of 1992 reflects a Congressional conclusion that current rates for cable service result, in part, from an ability to raise rates to unreasonable levels because of a lack of effective competition, and that rates are unreasonable to the extent they exceed competitive levels. Our industry survey confirms that rates of systems not subject to effective competition exceed competitive levels by approximately 10 percent on an average industry basis. Based on the statute and the results of the Commission's industry survey, we conclude that the reasonableness of rates of the basic service tier shall be determined by reference to the rates of systems subject to effective competition. The Commission, therefore, adopts a table of benchmarks based on the average September 30, 1992 rates of systems subject to effective competition.[5]

---

4. [Ed. "Benchmarking" is defined at ¶¶47–51, and "cost of service" is discussed at ¶¶63–65.]

5. [Ed. The table of benchmarks represents the results of the agency's statistical analyses of the rates of systems subject to effective competition. The table gives the benchmark price per channel for systems defined by (a) the number of subscribers, (b) the number of

BB. System Characteristics

48. The Commission applies different benchmark rates to systems based on the individual system's number of channels, subscribers, and satellite signals, but our industry survey does not provide a sufficient basis for identifying other system characteristics that would warrant application of different rate structures. As the Commission gains more experience with cable rate regulation, it may reevaluate this conclusion.

CC. Application of the Benchmark to Determine Initial Regulated Rate Levels

49. The Commission concludes that it will consider reasonable a per channel rate for the basic service tier that is at, or below, the benchmark level when a system becomes subject to regulation. Where a cable system is not charging rates that are above the competitive benchmark we can assume that its rates do not reflect undue market power, even in the absence of effective competition. Therefore, the initial regulated rate for such a system shall be its rate in effect on the date the system becomes subject to regulation, regardless of the amount that rate is below the benchmark.

50. Rates exceeding the applicable benchmark at the time regulation begins are presumptively unreasonable because they exceed the average rate charged by systems subject to effective competition. Some systems with rates at the onset of regulation that are above the benchmark may have had rates that were below the benchmark on September 30, 1992. Such systems are not subject to a rollback from levels in effect on September 30 because the rates were presumptively reasonable on that date. These systems must reduce rates from existing levels to the benchmark, but they may maintain increases from September 30, 1992 levels up to the benchmark and adjust rates to reflect inflation.

51. For a system with basic tier rates above the benchmark both when it becomes subject to regulation and on September 30, 1992, the maximum permitted rate will be the September 30, 1992, rates reduced 10 percent, but no lower than the benchmark rate for that system.

(f) Adoption of the Price Cap

AA. In General

54. The Commission adopts a price cap mechanism to assure that future rate increases remain within reasonable bounds.[6] We have found that a price

---

satellite signals offered, and (c) the number of channels offered. Thus, a cable system that does not encounter effective competition and therefore is subject to rate regulation and that has 25 basic channels, ten satellite signals and 5,000 subscribers would consult the table for a 25 channel/ten satellite signal/5,000 subscriber system and use those per channel benchmark prices to determine its initial (before adjusting for inflation and other outside factors) regulated price per channel.]

6. [Ed. The use of "price caps" to regulate the prices of telecommunications monopolies is discussed in the Note that follows. In brief, the procedure is that the regulator (here, the FCC) establishes a reasonable price for a service and then "caps" that price. This means that the firm cannot increase the price above the cap, except insofar as the regulator permits periodic systematic increases to account for inflation or other cost increases beyond the firm's control. See ¶56. The asserted value of a price cap system is that it does not require detailed administrative oversight of pricing once the initial prices are set. The principal

cap approach is an effective alternative to cost-of-service regulation in other regulated areas, and that this approach is consistent with our statutory mandate. At the same time, the Commission has provided for adjustments to the price cap, based on inflation and other factors beyond an operator's control, to assure that the cap does not unduly restrict cable operators' ability to recover costs. The possibility of a cost-of-service showing will also assure that cable operators can recover appropriate costs of service. The price cap rate for the basic service tier will be expressed as a rate per channel to facilitate rate calculations and review.

BB. Application of the Cap to Systems with Current Rates Below the Benchmark

55. The price cap applies to all regulated systems, including those systems with rates that are below the benchmark on the date that regulation commences, unless a cable system justifies higher rates based on cost-of-service principles.

(g) External Costs[7]

AA. Retransmission Consent Fees

57. The Commission concludes that retransmission consent costs should be treated as external to the benchmark. However, we are concerned that external treatment during the initial period in which cable operators and broadcasters will establish retransmission consent agreements may unduly skew incentives away from fair bargaining for reasonable retransmission fees. The Commission believes that a delay in onset of external treatment for retransmission consent fees will serve to protect subscribers from any precipitous increase in rates after October 6, 1993. Hence, we will accord retransmission consent costs external treatment only after October 6, 1994 and only for new or additional fees beyond those already in effect on October 6, 1994. The Commission will also monitor initial retransmission consent agreements and their potential impact on subscribers and may reexamine external treatment if it appears that retransmission consent fees have an unwarranted impact on subscribers.

BB. Other External Costs

58. Programming Costs Other Than Retransmission Consent. The Commission will treat programming cost increases, other than retransmission consent, as external to the benchmark. We will monitor the impact of external treatment of

---

drawback is that, because this method does not set prices according to costs, the firm may now have an incentive to offer shoddy goods in order to increase its profit margin or, if it becomes much more efficient, may begin to earn very large monopoly profits.]

7. [Ed. As the phrase is used here, "external costs" refers to costs that, when they increase, may be added to the otherwise capped benchmark price. Under price cap regulation, if the price of executive compensation rises, the permitted price does not increase. These are "internal costs" that the regulated firm must control to survive under a price cap system. But the regulator may conclude that certain costs of doing business (*e.g.*, taxes) are so far removed from the regulated firm's control that an increase in those costs should generate an offsetting increase in the capped price.]

programming cost increases and consider making programming costs subject to the cap if it appears that this treatment is disserving subscribers. The Commission's accounting and cost allocation requirements will determine the share of programming costs to be allocated to the basic service tier.

59. Taxes, Franchise Fees, Cost of Franchise Requirements. The Commission also excludes from the cap taxes, franchise fees, and the costs of satisfying franchise requirements, including the costs of satisfying franchise requirements for local, public, educational, and governmental (PEG) access channels. The Commission's accounting and cost allocation requirements provide that costs associated with PEG channels carried on the basic tier will be directly assigned to the basic tier where possible and remaining costs will be allocated between tiers in proportion to the number of channels on each tier.

DD. Limitation on External Treatment for Increases Less Than Inflation

62. For all categories of external costs, other than franchise fees, the Commission permits external treatment for increases in such costs only to the extent that they exceed inflation as measured by the GNP-PI..

(h) Cost-of-Service Showings

AA. The Opportunity to Justify Rates Above the Cap Based On Costs

63. The Commission has determined that its primary method of regulating cable service rates shall be a price cap mechanism applied to rates determined in relation to the competitive benchmark. However, the starting price cap level is based on industry-wide data and does not necessarily reflect individual systems' costs of providing cable service. Thus, the Commission cannot be certain that the initial capped rate will permit all cable operators to fully recover the costs of providing basic tier service and to continue to attract capital. Accordingly, a cable operator is permitted to make a cost-of-service showing to determine the reasonable rate for its system.[8] The resulting rate determination will supercede our benchmark/rollback provisions. Thus, an operator may exceed the benchmark or capped rate if it can make the necessary cost showings in certain circumstances. Similarly, however, a cost-of-service determination resulting in a rate below that system's September 30, 1992, rate minus 10 percent will prescribe that system's new rate. The Commission rejects the alternative of not permitting cable operators to exceed the cap unless the rate as applied to them is confiscatory.

(3) Regulations Governing Rates for Equipment

66. The Cable Act of 1992 requires the Commission to establish standards for setting, on the basis of actual cost, the rate for installation and lease of equip-

---

8. [Ed. Like price cap regulation, cost of service rate regulation is discussed in the Note that follows this excerpt. In short, this form of price regulation requires the regulator to calculate all the firm's costs, consider the extent to which those costs are reasonable, and then set prices at a level sufficient to cover reasonable costs plus a reasonable profit. In this *Report and Order*, the Commission is, essentially, choosing to follow the price cap rather than the cost of service method of price regulation. Here, however, the Commission is responding to the fear that, by imposing "benchmark" price caps (derived from a study of a few systems) on all cable systems, it may be forcing some of them to price below their costs.]

ment used by subscribers to receive the basic service tier, and the installation and lease of monthly connections for additional television receivers.

67. The Commission concludes that equipment "used to receive the basic service tier" is broadly interpreted and includes converter boxes, remote controls, connections for additional television sets, and cable home wiring. Our expansive reading of the phrase "used to receive the basic service tier" means that equipment and installations used to receive both basic tier service and other services would be regulated according to actual cost guidelines described below. Although the Commission believes that Congress intended the Commission's regulations to encourage a competitive market in the provision of equipment and service installation, the Commission does not have, at this time, the information it would need to establish a separate effective competition test for installation and equipment. The Commission has begun a proceeding to investigate these issues. Therefore, all systems subject to rate regulation must comply with the actual cost standards for equipment and service installations used to receive the basic service tier.

(4) Cost of Franchise Requirements

75. The Commission has determined that costs attributable to satisfying franchise requirements shall include: 1) the sum of per channel costs for the number of channels used to meet franchise requirements for public, educational and governmental channels; 2) any direct costs of providing any other services required under the franchise; and 3) a reasonable allocation of overhead.

4. Regulation of Cable Programming Services

a. Definition of "Cable Programming Service"

80. Under the 1992 Act, regulation of "cable programming service" rates and equipment is to be conducted by the Commission, not local franchising authorities. "Cable programming service" is defined broadly in the statute as all video programming provided over a cable system except that provided on the basic service tier or on a per-channel or per-program basis.

b. Complaints Regarding Cable Programming Service Rates

(1) Procedures for Receiving, Considering, and Resolving Complaints

81. The 1992 Act provides that rate regulation of cable programming services and equipment will occur only in response to specific complaints—*i.e.*, the Commission will not regulate cable programming service rates until it receives a complaint that a particular operator's rates are unreasonable.

82. The 1992 Act permits subscribers, franchising authorities and other relevant government entities to file complaints about the rates for cable programming services and equipment. As required by law, complainants alleging that a cable operator's current cable programming rates are unreasonable will have 180 days from the effective date of the Commission's rules to challenge existing rates. With regard to rate increases, complainants must file complaints about cable programming service and equipment rates within 45 days from the time subscribers receive a bill that reflects the rate increase.

83. In order to avoid dismissal of a complaint, the complainant must supply certain readily available factual information and must allege that the rate is un-

reasonable because it violates the Commission's rate regulations. Complainants must use the complaint form adopted by the Commission and serve a copy on the cable operator and franchising authority.

84. Subscribers need not obtain the franchising authority's concurrence before filing a complaint with the Commission. However, franchising authorities are encouraged to assist subscribers in completing complaint forms and subscribers are free to attach the views of the franchising authority when submitting a complaint to the Commission. Franchising authorities will not be permitted to formally review and adjudicate cable programming service complaints in the first instance.

85. Upon receipt of a cable programming service complaint submitted on the FCC form, the Commission will review the complaint to determine whether it meets the minimum showing needed to permit the complaint to go forward. The operator must respond to a complaint filed on the standard complaint form within 30 days of service of the complaint, unless the Commission notifies the operator that the complaint fails to satisfy the minimum showing requirement.

(2) Remedial and Enforcement Procedures for Rates Found to be
    Unreasonable

86. If cable programming service rates are found to be unreasonable, the Commission will order the operator to reduce rates prospectively and to reflect that reduction in prospective bills to customers. The operator will also be required to refund overages (plus interest) to subscribers, with refunds being calculated from the date the complaint was filed until the date the operator implements the reduced rate prospectively in bills to subscribers.

5. Provisions Applicable to Cable Service Generally

a. Geographically Uniform Rate Structure

95. The Cable Act of 1992 requires cable operators to "have a rate structure, for the provision of cable service, that is uniform throughout the geographic area in which cable service is provided over its cable system." The Commission concludes that a cable system must have a uniform rate structure throughout the franchise area. This requirement, however, does not preclude operators from establishing reasonable categories of customers and services. The Commission concludes that for purposes of the Cable Act of 1992 a geographic area means the franchise area. Thus, a cable operator is generally required by this provision to have a uniform rate structure within each franchise area.

b. Discrimination

96. A cable operator may offer reasonable discounts to senior citizens and other economically disadvantaged individuals. For this purpose, an "economically disadvantaged individual" is defined as a person who receives federal, state or local welfare assistance.

Note on Rate Regulation

The above excerpt in no way represents the Commission's final words on the issue of rate regulation. For one thing, the Commission's authority has since been modified in this area; as was noted above, the Telecommunications Act of 1996 stripped the Commission of its power to regulate cable services outside the basic tier. Moreover, the Commission of its own volition has revisited its cable rate regulations from time to time. In March 1994, for example, the agency decided that the proper benchmark for rate reductions would be a seventeen percent, rather than a ten percent, average reduction in rates, and, further, that cable systems should be permitted to price programs newly added to their systems at cost plus seven and one-half percent.

What is important to take from the *Cable Rate Regulation Executive Summary*, then, is not the particular implementation details related to the 1992 Act, but the broader issues the document raises with respect to the techniques a regulator might use to set prices in a regulated market. As the document suggests, the FCC has used two primary approaches: price cap regulation, and what the FCC refers to as "cost of service" regulation but which we will term "rate-of-return" regulation.

Under price cap regulation, the government regulates by announcing the maximum price that will be allowed for a given service and, usually, by further specifying how that price will change over time given, say, expected efficiency improvements and inflation. Price cap regulation can be accomplished in other ways as well. For instance, instead of specifying a cap for each regulated service, the government might announce a maximum average price for a group of services, in that way leaving the regulated party a little more flexibility in its price-setting decisions.[9] The key intuition to all price cap regulation is simply that the government's maximum price does not vary with the regulated party's costs. If the regulated party can lower its costs, it can maintain its price and keep the extra profits for itself. The main allure of price cap regulation is thus the obvious one: just like competition, price cap regulation creates a strong incentive for regulated firms to minimize their costs.

Rate-of-return regulation implements a different theory. Under this approach, instead of capping prices (at perhaps arbitrary levels), the regulator calculates the fair and reasonable costs of offering a service and permits the cable system to charge that amount plus a reasonable profit. The regulated party is thus no worse off than it would be had it invested its resources in a competitive market; in either case, the party earns back its costs plus a competitive return on its capital investment. This is attractive for consumers since they (in theory) get closer-to-competitive pricing; the idea is that, if these prices earn a competitive level of profit for the regulated party, they must be prices that are somewhat close to the competitive level.

Both price cap and rate-of-return regulation have drawbacks and complications, many of which are apparent on the face of the *Executive Summary* it-

---

9. A helpful analogy here might be to think of the salary cap in professional football. The teams are to a large degree free to set salaries for individual players, but the NFL constrains the maximum amount of money players on a given team can earn in a given season. The league, in other words, sets a price cap on the group of salaries but not on any salary in particular.

self. Let's start with price caps. While price caps do give firms a strong incentive to keep costs down, this is in practice a mixed blessing. The incentive could cause firms to be more efficient since, if they can provide the same service at lower cost, the extra profits are theirs to keep. But the same incentive could also tempt firms to skimp on quality. For example, what prevents regulated cable operators, after price caps are imposed, from slashing costs not by increasing efficiency but, rather, by degrading the quality of their service? Surely not the presence of "effective competition" since, according to the statute, only those operators not faced with effective competition are subject to rate regulation in the first place. Is the adoption of price cap regulation thus antithetical to the professed goal of upgrading the U.S. information transmission infrastructure? Does the imposition of price cap regulation in this context reflect a determination, by Congress or the FCC, that U.S. consumers prefer cheaper, lower quality cable television to more expensive, higher quality systems? Or can regulation solve this problem, perhaps by specifying both maximum price and minimum quality? (Does the FCC say anything about this in the above document?)

Furthermore, price caps are beneficial only if they cap prices at levels below the monopoly level. But how is the regulator to know what prices to set? In the *Executive Summary* you see the FCC struggling to identify benchmark prices by, among other things, looking at markets where cable providers do face "effective competition." But how sure are you that the Commission takes into account enough or the right factors in drawing those comparisons? And what makes the FCC think that its benchmark prices are competitive prices? Simply that they are lower than prevailing prices? Worse, what will the FCC do when it comes time to price new services for which there are no easily-available market analogies, or when a regulated party proposes some more complicated pricing regime—for example, charging low prices early in the life of a new service in order to attract customers but then wanting to charge correspondingly higher prices later in the life of that service to recoup the initial investment?

Lastly, while price caps have the professed benefit of giving firms a strong incentive to be more efficient, even that claim must be questioned. The reason: the government cannot credibly commit not to change the price cap over time. If the regulated firm does a great job at cutting costs, there is some chance that the government will "renege" on the deal and lower the price cap. Similarly, if the regulated firm sees its costs spiral, it is likely that the government will bail the firm out by raising the price cap instead of, say, allowing the lone cable provider to go bankrupt. These possibilities at least partially undermine the aforementioned incentive to cut costs.

All this might seem to argue in favor of rate-of-return regulation, but that approach, too, has several severe limitations. First, under rate-of-return regulation, the regulated party has little incentive to economize on its expenditures. So long as the firm appears to be incurring reasonable costs—and, realistically, how well can the regulator distinguish reasonable from unreasonable expenses?—under rate-of-return regulation the firm will be allowed to increase its prices and in that way recoup those investments. Firms regulated under rate-of-return regulation are thus often accused of "gold-plating"—figuratively, lining their wires with gold when simple copper would do.

Second, and relatedly, firms regulated under rate-of-return principles not only have little incentive to minimize costs, but also have strong incentives to allocate costs from other services to the regulated service. Suppose, for example, that a cable provider has to incur a significant expense in order to upgrade its infrastructure to provide Internet service. If the firm can make the regulator think that this expense was incurred in order to provide a regulated service (say, cable television), the firm will be able to recoup this cost by raising cable prices and thus will have an unfair advantage when it comes to competing in the market for Internet service provision. Note that, unlike the gold-plating example, expenses incurred in this example are not necessarily wasteful or inefficient; the problem here is that the regulation is being used to distort competition in an unregulated market. (This is an important issue in the context of telephone regulation, and we will consider it further in that setting.) Cable prices, though, cannot be increased perpetually; at some point, it will be unprofitable for the cable firm to raise prices even if the relevant regulatory authority would allow further increases.

Again, a well-informed regulator can mitigate these difficulties, but fully eliminating the problems of rate-of-return regulation seems unlikely. For one thing, gathering information from the regulated party is expensive. Moreover, if the regulator really could learn that much and evaluate the information that well, the government could simply provide the service itself. The regulator, then, can only be expected to do so much.

One wrinkle: the fact that there are time delays involved in rate adjustments does to some degree lessen the incentive to gold-plate. For instance, if costs are at a certain level in January and, at that time, the regulator approves particular cable prices effective January through October, the cable provider has some incentive to economize on its expenses since, as it was under price caps, any cost savings accomplished during that time period translate into increased profits. Those profits will be lost once the government resets prices so as to reflect the new (lower) costs; but, during the time lag between changes in costs and changes in the approved schedule of prices, even a firm regulated under rate-of-return regulation has some incentive to spend wisely.

Overall, then, one might say that the choice between price caps on the one hand and rate-of-return regulation on the other should depend on what one fears most. If one fears diminution in product quality more than one fears unjustified price increases, one should choose rate-of-return regulation. Conversely, if price hikes are more of a threat than product deterioration, price caps are perhaps the better alternative. One implication is thus that the balance of these factors might lead to one choice for cable regulation and another for telephone regulation. Perhaps cable services are more of a luxury than phone service, or the cable plant is more in need of incentives to upgrade than is the telephone plant. If so, then rate-of-return regulation might be preferable for cable and price cap for telephone.

Either option, of course, imposes significant costs on regulated firms, and it is unlikely that the total costs of data collection, document filing, and keeping abreast of the rules vary much with firm size. This means that regulatory compliance costs per subscriber are likely to be higher for small cable systems than they are for large cable systems. Rate regulation, then, probably adds an incentive for smaller cable systems to merge with larger ones. The FCC does from time to time attempt to alleviate some of this burden for smaller firms. For example, the

FCC's Cable Bureau has offered to help small system owners complete various computations that are part of the rate regulation process; qualifying firms need only fax the relevant data to the Bureau.

Rate regulation is also costly to taxpayers. To take but one example: Congress authorized the Commission to hire 240 new people to carry out the tasks assigned to the FCC by the 1992 Cable Act. If the average government job costs the fisc $100,000 per year (in salary, benefits, office space, equipment, and other support), then the cost of these new hires—itself just one of many costs associated with rate regulation—was approximately $24 million.

Notes and Questions

1. Temporary or Permanent Solution? Is rate regulation best viewed as a temporary, modest palliative for a transition period during which most cable systems will become subject to effective competition and, thus, not subject to rate regulation? Is that how the FCC views rate regulation in the *Cable Rate Regulation Executive Summary* excerpted above?

2. Test Your Understanding: Gold-Plating. In the Note that follows the *Executive Summary*, we raise the concern that firms might "gold-plate" under rate-of-return regulation. Is it a good response to that worry to say that cable customers will only pay so much for cable service, and as a result cable providers likely cannot gold-plate in practice?

3. Test Your Understanding: Regulatory Lag. In the Note we also point out that, because there is typically some lag in the regulatory process, firms subject to rate-of-return regulation will (during the lag period) have some incentive to economize on their expenses. We explicitly say, in fact, that this lag minimizes the danger of gold-plating; does it also lessen the regulated firm's incentive to (mis)allocate costs as between an unregulated and the regulated service?

4. Setting Prices. In conventional markets, efficiency is maximized by having firms charge marginal cost. As we explained in Chapter Nine, however, in natural monopoly markets, marginal cost pricing does not yield sufficient revenues to cover the relevant firm's fixed costs. How does the FCC implicitly resolve this problem in the *Executive Order*? Is the FCC's solution a good one?

5. Price Caps and the First Amendment. Why doesn't price cap regulation run afoul of the First Amendment? As the D.C. Circuit put it in Time Warner Entertainment Co. v. FCC, 56 F.3d 151 (D.C. Cir. 1995), surely the "government could not, consistently with the First Amendment, cap the price of a newspaper at 25 cents in order to limit monopoly profits and make the paper more affordable." *Id.* at 183. So why is the government allowed to cap the price of basic cable service?

II. LOCAL FRANCHISE AGREEMENTS

Limiting local government's authority to regulate cable rates would be a meaningless gesture if local government were nevertheless free to charge an exorbitant franchise fee, impose unlimited in-kind obligations on cable operators, or otherwise discipline cable operators in subtle ways. So, at the same time that the 1984 and 1992 Acts rewrote the rules on rate regulation, they also imposed new constraints on local government's franchising power by specifically authorizing local government to work with only a handful of policy levers.

Three limitations were of primary importance. First, the 1984 Act limited local government's ability to use the threat of franchise non-renewal as a means by which to discipline cable franchisees. The Act did so by creating a strong presumption that a cable franchisee will have its franchise renewed at the end of its term. Under the Act, local authorities can refuse to renew only by producing evidence of substantial non-compliance with franchise conditions and, at that, the local authority must give the cable operator notice and an opportunity to cure any alleged failures. 47 U.S.C. §546. Renewals cannot be denied on the basis of the mix or quality of the cable services provided by the system, at least if those services comply with franchise terms. Decisions not to renew are subject to judicial review.

Second, the 1984 Act capped the franchise fee that local government can charge, specifically prohibiting local authorities from charging a fee exceeding five percent of the cable system's gross revenues. 47 U.S.C. §542. This was just a maximum; as was noted in the previous chapter, courts might construe the First Amendment to further constrain this number in situations where the franchise fee is out of proportion to the value of the public rights-of-way being used or to the aesthetic and disruptive harms imposed.

Third, the 1992 Act prohibited local government from (1) granting exclusive franchises and (2) unreasonably refusing to award additional competitive franchises. 47 U.S.C. §541. That is, local authorities could neither make a legally binding promise that a particular franchisee would be the exclusive cable provider nor credibly commit to accomplishing the same result de facto by refusing to award later franchises. This seriously constrained local government's clout; after the 1992 Act, local government was no longer in the business of granting lucrative, legally-guaranteed monopolies. Instead, to whatever extent the market would bear, cable franchisees would be subject to competition.

The 1984 and 1992 Cable Acts were not entirely bad news for local authorities, however. Indeed, even though the Acts constrained local government's ability to regulate price and limited the size of any franchise fee, the Acts did at the same time combine to explicitly authorize local government to impose two significant obligations on cable franchisees. First, the Acts added what became section 611 to the Communications Act of 1934. This new section permitted franchising authorities to require that cable operators make available certain channel capacity at no charge for what the statute refers to as "public, educational, or governmental use." 47 U.S.C. §531. As the name implies, "PEG" channels carry governmental and educational information that might be of interest to local subscribers but be under-supplied by market forces. These channels constitute an implicit tax imposed on franchisees; instead of taking a higher fee and then purchasing channel capacity, the local government is allowed to take a fee of no more than five percent of revenues but can then require the franchisee to provide a certain number of PEG channels.

Second, the Acts similarly combined to add section 612 to the Communications Act. This provision requires certain cable systems to lease some of their channel capacity to unaffiliated firms, and to do so at regulated rates. 47 U.S.C. §532. These channels are typically referred to as "leased access" channels. Whether channels must be set aside and, if so, how many, is determined by the statute based on the size of the cable system at issue. The statute further allows cable operators who are required to provide leased access capacity to instead devote up to one third of that capacity to "programming from a qualified minority programming source or from any qualified educational programming source, whether or not such source is affiliated with the cable operator." 47 U.S.C. §612(i).

Cable operators brought suit contending that the PEG and leased access provisions violate their First Amendment rights and therefore are unconstitutional on their face. The highest court to address those claims was the Court of Appeals for the D.C. Circuit, and the portions of its opinion dealing with the PEG and leased access provisions are excerpted below.[10] That excerpt is followed by an excerpt from the *Report and Order* implementing the leased access regime.

TIME WARNER ENTERTAINMENT CO. v. FCC
93 F.3d 957 (D.C. Cir. 1996)

Before BUCKLEY, RANDOLPH, and TATEL, Circuit Judges. Opinion for the Court filed PER CURIAM. Opinion concurring in part and dissenting in part filed by Circuit Judge TATEL.

PER CURIAM:

LEASED ACCESS PROVISIONS

The 1984 Cable Act compelled cable operators of systems with more than thirty-six channels to set aside between 10 and 15 percent of their channels for commercial use by persons unaffiliated with the operator. 47 U.S.C. §532(b)(1). The larger the number of channels in the system, the greater the percentage of channels the operator must set aside. "Leased access" was originally aimed at bringing about "the widest possible diversity of information sources" for cable subscribers. *Id.* §532(a). Congress thought cable operators might deny access to programmers if the operators disapproved the programmer's social or political

---

10. The challenges to the PEG and leased access provisions were part of a larger facial challenge to many different portions of the 1984 and 1992 Cable Acts. All told, the plaintiff cable television system owner/operators and programmers argued that the following provisions infringed upon their First Amendment right to freedom of speech: sections 611 (public, educational, and governmental programming) and 612 (leased access) of the 1984 Act, and sections 3 (rate regulation), 10(d) (obscenity liability), 11(c) (subscriber limitation, channel occupancy, and program creation restrictions), 15 (premium channel preview notice), 19 (vertically integrated programming), 24 (municipal immunity), and 25 (direct broadcast satellite set-aside) of the 1992 Act. *See* Time Warner Entertainment Co. v. FCC, 93 F.3d 957, 962 (D.C. Cir. 1996). In addition, the suit originally included a constitutional challenge to the must-carry provisions (sections 4 and 5) of the 1992 Cable Act. Pursuant to a special jurisdictional provision of the 1992 Cable Act that applied only to challenges to sections 4 and 5, the must-carry challenge was severed, sent to a three-judge panel of the district court, and appealed directly to the Supreme Court, resulting in Turner Broadcasting Sys., Inc. v. FCC, 512 U.S. 622 (1994) (*Turner I*), and, after the *Time Warner* opinion was issued, Turner Broadcasting Sys., Inc. v. FCC, 520 U.S. 180 (1997) (*Turner II*). Both *Turner I* and *Turner II* are excerpted and discussed in Chapter Eleven.

viewpoint, or if the programmers' offerings competed with those the operators were providing. "Diversity," as the 1984 Act used the term, referred not to the substantive content of the program on a leased access channel, but to the entities—the "sources"—responsible for making it available. *See* H.R. Rep. No. 934, 98th Cong., 2d Sess. 48 (1984).

The 1984 Act gave cable operators the authority to establish the price, terms, and conditions of the service on their leased access channels. 1984 Act, §2, 98 Stat. at 2783 (original version of 47 U.S.C. §532(c)(1)). With respect to those channels, then, the operator stood in the position of a common carrier. If an operator refused to provide service, persons aggrieved had the right either to bring an action in district court or to petition the Commission for relief. The operator's rates, terms, and conditions were presumed reasonable, a presumption that could be overcome "by clear and convincing evidence to the contrary." *Id.* §532(f). The operator was free to use any of the channels set aside for leased access until someone signed up.

The 1984 legislation did not accomplish much. Unaffiliated programming on leased access channels rarely appeared. Exactly why is uncertain. Cable operators said the reasons were high production costs and low demand in the face of the already wide array of programming operators were already providing. Others laid the blame at the feet of the operators, claiming they had set unreasonable terms for leased access. The FCC, in a 1990 report, recommended amending the 1984 Act to provide a national framework of leased access rules and to streamline the section's enforcement mechanism. *Competition, Rate Deregulation, and the Comm'ns Policies Relating to the Provision of Cable Television Serv.*, 5 FCC Rcd. 4962, 5048–50 ¶¶177-83 (1990). The House Energy and Commerce Committee thought that cable operators had financial incentives to refuse access to those who would compete with existing programs. The Senate Commerce, Science, and Transportation Committee believed that the Act's permitting operators to establish the rates and terms of leased access service made "little sense." S. Rep. No. 92, 102d Cong., 2d Sess. 30–32 (1991).

Amendments enacted in 1992 authorized the FCC to establish a maximum price for leased access, to regulate terms and conditions, and to establish procedures for the expedited resolution of disputes. At the same time, Congress added a second rationale for leased access: "to promote competition in the delivery of diverse sources of video programming." 47 U.S.C. §532(a), as amended.

Time Warner's initial point regarding the leased access provisions is that they should be subject to the most stringent of the standards used to evaluate restrictions on speech. As the company sees it, the provisions are content based; the government therefore must demonstrate a compelling interest to overcome their presumptive invalidity. There is nothing to this. The provisions are not content based. They do not favor or disfavor speech on the basis of the ideas contained in the speech or the views expressed. Whether, and how many, channels a cable operator must designate for public leasing depends entirely on the operator's channel capacity. What programs appear on the operator's other channels—that is, what speech the operator is promoting—matters not in the least. So too with respect to the speech of those who use the leased access channels. Their qualification to lease time on those channels depends not on the content of their speech, but on their lack of affiliation with the operator, a distinguishing characteristic stemming from considerations relating to the structure of cable television. The statutory objective, as well as the provisions carrying it forth, are framed in terms of the sources of information rather than the substance of the information. This is consistent with the First Amendment's "assumption that the widest possible dissemination of information from diverse and antagonistic sources" promotes a free society. Associated Press v. United States, 326 U.S. 1, 20 (1945). The Supreme Court has determined that regulations along these lines are content neutral. Turner Broadcasting Sys., Inc. v. FCC, 114 S.Ct. 2445, 2469–70 (1994).

Hence the standard must be intermediate scrutiny: it is enough if the government's interest is important or substantial and the means chosen to promote that interest do not burden substantially more speech than necessary to achieve the aim. Time Warner thinks the leased access provisions fail even this test. The company's attack is not on the sufficiency of the governmental interest. After *Turner*, "promoting the widespread dissemination of information from a multiplicity of sources" and "promoting fair competition in the market for television programming" must be treated as important governmental objectives unrelated to the suppression of speech. 114 S.Ct. at 2469–70. The problems Time Warner sees are elsewhere: there is first the lack of any demonstration that the leased access provisions address a real, non-conjectural harm; and there is second the loose fit between the remedy of setting aside a percentage of channel capacity and the supposed harm.

As to the alleged lack of any real harm, the Commission recently said: "Cable operators and leased access programmers agree that relatively little leased access capacity is being used by unaffiliated programmers." *Implementation of Sections of the Cable Television Consumer Protection and Competition Act of 1992: Rate Regulation, Leased Access*, MM Docket No. 92-26, slip op. at 5 ¶6 (1996). Four years earlier, the Committee reports accompanying the 1992 Amendments reached the same conclusion. When we get to reasons why there have been so few takers, the finger-pointing begins. The unaffiliated programmers blame the operators, claiming that their high rates made leased access unaffordable. The "operators claim that the demand for leased access is weak regardless of the leased access rate, because, at least in part, programming production costs are high." *Id.* If we treated this as a factual dispute and tried to resolve it in light of the evidence, we could not do so on the current record. The Committee reports, which side with the unaffiliated programmers, carry weight; but they are basically conclusory, as one would expect. In their brief in this court, the United States and the Commission point to the increasing vertical integration of the cable industry: "Many of the most popular cable programming services are owned in whole or in part by cable operators," which gives operators an incentive to favor programmers affiliated with them. Opening Brief for the FCC and the United States at 46–47. A finding in the 1992 Act is more circumspect: vertical integration "could make it more difficult for non-cable-affiliated programmers to secure carriage on cable systems." 1992 Act, §2(a)(5), 106 Stat. at 1460–61. Still, we do not have before us any specific evidence showing either the extent to which operators have refused to carry unaffiliated programmers or the effect of the leased access provisions on the speech of the operators. No section of the statute directly addresses these evidentiary points.

If this were purely an economic regulation subject to rational basis review, we would say that the legislative decision embodied in the leased access provisions "is not subject to courtroom fact-finding and may be based on rational speculation unsupported by evidence or empirical data." FCC v. Beach Communications, Inc., 508 U.S. 307, 315 (1993). But the *Turner* plurality, applying a higher standard of review, believed that fact-finding was needed. Suppose we too followed that course and remanded. A series of questions would then present themselves. This is a facial challenge to the constitutionality of the leased access provisions. Should the facts be determined as of the time Congress enacted the provisions? At the time the complaint was filed? At the time of the hearing on remand? Or should the district court consider the state of affairs expected to develop sometime in the future, taking into account rapidly changing technology and new legislation opening up cable operators to greater competition?

The parties do not provide answers. Time Warner thinks it sufficient to allege in its brief that there is not now, nor will there be under new FCC regulations, any appreciable demand by unaffiliated programmers for access to cable systems because cable systems are already carrying a wide variety of programs from diverse sources and because leased access does not make economic sense in light of the costs of production. For the sake of argument, we shall accept this assertion as true. We will assume, in other words, that on remand Time Warner could prove the factual propositions contained in its brief. Would that render the leased access provisions unconstitutional? We think not. If unaffiliated programmers have not and will not lease time on the channels set aside for them—if, in other words, Time Warner made its best case—we fail to see how the company could establish that the provisions violate its First Amendment right to free speech. In *Turner*, there was no doubt that local broadcasting would occupy channels in cable systems; the open evidentiary questions, according to the plurality, were whether this was necessary to preserve local broadcasting and whether the effect would be to force cable operators to drop programs they would otherwise carry. Our case is very different. Under section 532(b)(4), a "cable operator may use any unused channel capacity" set aside for leased access "until the use of such channel capacity is obtained, pursuant to a written agreement, by a person unaffiliated with the operator." That is, if unaffiliated programmers have not and, as Time Warner predicts, will not exploit the leased access provisions, then the provisions will have no effect on the speech of the cable operators. *See Turner*, 114 S.Ct. at 2456. None of their programming would have to be dropped. The channels set aside for leasing will either be vacant or they will be occupied according to the wishes of the cable operators. The operators' editorial control will remain unimpaired and so will their First Amendment right to determine what will appear on their cable systems.

The same analysis applies to Time Warner's argument that the leased access provisions are not narrowly tailored to achieve their ends. One of the alleged defects stems from the statutory requirement that the larger the number of channels in the system, the greater the number of channels the operator must set aside. 47 U.S.C. §532(b)(1). The company states that "because a cable system has more channels does not mean there are any more unaffiliated programmers" being excluded, and that "the more channels a cable operator has, the fewer unaffiliated programmers would be excluded from carriage." Brief for Appellants at 68–69. Yet if this is accurate, operators of large cable systems would scarcely have any customers asking to lease the access channels; and the operators would thus be free to fill the unused capacity as they saw fit.[11]

We therefore see no reason to remand this portion of the case to the district court for factual findings. Time Warner has mounted a facial challenge to the leased access provisions. If it succeeded in establishing that few unaffiliated programmers will take advantage of the provisions, section 532(b)(4) would insulate it and other operators from suffering any infringement of their First Amendment rights.

PEG PROVISION

Section 611 of the 1984 Cable Act provides that local franchising authorities "may...require as part of a [cable] franchise...[or] franchise renewal...that channel capacity be designated for public, educational, or governmental use." 47 U.S.C. §531(b). The District Court upheld the "PEG" provision, as it is commonly known, finding: that it was content neutral and thus subject to intermediate scrutiny, that it served a significant regulatory interest by giving speakers with lesser market appeal access to cable, and that it was narrowly tailored to accomplish that purpose.

To prevail in its facial challenge, Time Warner must "establish that no set of circumstances exists under which the Act would be valid." United States v. Salerno, 481 U.S. 739, 745 (1987). Except in the case of an overbreadth challenge, which Time Warner does not make here, "a holding of facial invalidity expresses the conclusion that the statute could never be applied in a valid manner." Members of the City Council v. Taxpayers for Vincent, 466 U.S. 789, 797–98 (1984). Consideration of this standard is somewhat tricky here since rather than requiring PEG channel capacity, the statute merely permits local franchise authorities to require PEG programming as a franchise condition. In fact, prior to the passage of the 1984 Cable Act, and thus, in the absence of federal permission, many franchise agreements provided for PEG channels. In passing the PEG provision, Congress thus merely recognized and endorsed the preexisting practice of local franchise authorities conditioning their cable franchises on the granting of PEG channel access. *See* H.R. Rep. No. 934, *supra*, at 30. All the statute does, then, is preempt states from prohibiting local PEG requirements (if any states were to choose to do so) and preclude federal preemption challenges to such requirements, challenges that cable operators might have brought in the absence of the provision. Preemption issues aside, a statute that simply permits franchise authorities to regulate where they had previously done so raises no First Amendment problems unless the localities themselves infringe on cable operators' speech. For this reason, although the concept of an "application" of a federal statute that permits non-federal franchise authorities to act is somewhat unusual, we consider each individual franchise authority's

---

11. Time Warner asks us to consider "a cable operator that voluntarily has carried each and every programmer that asked for carriage up until the point where it had no excess capacity and yet still must set aside channels under the leased access system scheme to carry other programming." *Brief for Appellants* at 70. This seems to assume the opposite of the company's argument that there is no demand for leased access. In any event, Time Warner has mounted a facial constitutional challenge to the leased access provisions. If an individual operator finds itself in the position Time Warner describes, that operator may mount its own as-applied First Amendment challenge. Our decision today deals only with the facial validity of the provisions.

PEG requirements to be an "application" of the statute for purposes of this facial challenge.

Time Warner must therefore show that no franchise authority could ever exercise the statute's grant of authority in a constitutional manner. We can, of course, imagine PEG franchise conditions that would raise serious constitutional issues. For example, were a local authority to require as a franchise condition that a cable operator designate three-quarters of its channels for "educational" programming, defined in detail by the city council, such a requirement would certainly implicate First Amendment concerns. At the same time, we can just as easily imagine a franchise authority exercising its power without violating the First Amendment. For example, a local franchise authority might seek to ensure public "access to a multiplicity of information sources," *Turner*, 114 S.Ct. at 2470, by conditioning its grant of a franchise on the cable operator's willingness to provide access to a single channel for "public" use, defining "public" broadly enough to permit access to everyone on a nondiscriminatory, first-come, first-serve basis. Under *Turner*, such a scheme would be content neutral, would serve an "important purpose unrelated to the suppression of free expression," *id.*, and would be narrowly tailored to its goal. Time Warner's facial challenge therefore fails.

[Separate opinion of Judge TATEL (concurring in this portion of the opinion and dissenting from a different portion) is omitted.]

Notes and Questions

1. PEG / Leased Access. Note the differing rationales behind PEG and leased access channels. The idea behind PEG channels is to expand the information provided to the public on crucial issues. In this way, the goal of increasing valuable programming via PEG channels is similar to the theory of *Red Lion*. Commercial leased access regulations, by contrast, are usually defended on the grounds that they promote competition among program suppliers. The theory is that a cable network might seek to enter into a contract with a cable operator that effectively excludes other networks, but the leased access capacity will enable those other networks to get on the system nevertheless. Thus the rationale behind leased access is to make sure that cable companies do not freeze out potentially popular channels with which the cable companies are not affiliated.

2. Interpreting the Statute. What, according to *Time Warner*, do the PEG and leased access provisions actually mandate? What does this case tell us about the constitutionality of a federal statute that mandates the surrender of a specified percentage of channels for leased access channels or for PEG channels? What does it tell us about the likelihood of success of an as-applied challenge?

3. Heads I Win, Tails You Lose? With regard to leased access, was Time Warner in a no-win position? If Time Warner argued (as it did) that it already carried a wide variety of programs from different sources so there was no demand (and thus no need) for leased access, the D.C. Circuit could respond (as it did) that the leased access regime did not harm Time Warner. If Time Warner argued instead that many unaffiliated programmers were clamoring for leased access channels and filling up the leased access channels, then the court might well respond that this demonstrated the need for leased access, and thus showed that leased access was responding to a real, non-conjectural harm. Could Time Warner have made an argument that would have avoided both of these responses? If not, what does that tell us?

4. Compelled Access. The general problem of compelled access to media platforms is one that we have seen and will continue to see throughout this casebook. The question is always the same: should we impose on broadcasters, cable operators, newspaper publishers, and other owners of communication infrastructure "common carrier" obligations, in essence separating legal authority over the conduit from legal authority over the content? Despite the prevalence of the issue, courts have not settled on a single approach to the question of whether mandated access can be squared with the First Amendment principle of freedom of speech and the press. Meanwhile, we never question the imposition of common carrier duties on telephone companies, but—following the apparent lead of *Tornillo*—seem to assume that it is flatly unconstitutional to impose common carrier obligations on the print media. Is a single, coherent principle available for resolving questions about compelled access to the mass media?

5. Market Alternatives. Printing presses, recording studios, sound stages, and so on, are today regularly available for rent in the marketplace. Does this cut against the rationale for requiring leased access channels, implying that the market already allows speakers to make use of communications technology that they cannot afford to purchase themselves?

6. The Basic Tier. Notice that the rate regulation provisions of the 1992 Cable Act intersect with the PEG and leased access regulations discussed here to create what is arguably a common carrier platform within the cable system. The rate regulations require that cable systems not subject to effective competition offer a separate "basic" tier of video programming, a tier that essentially consists of PEG channels and retransmitted broadcast signals. By law, subscribers must purchase the basic tier before they may buy any another video programming from that cable system. And the price of the basic tier is regulated by local authorities. In short, then, within each cable system not subject to effective competition, the 1992 Act creates a tier of service for which firms other than the cable operator control the content and the FCC and local authorities control the price. Is this in any way different from a pure "common carrier" approach to regulating the basic tier?

What explains this rather substantial recasting of the concept of cable television services? Does Congress now perceive cable operators as somewhat akin to owners of bridges or local telephone loops—*i.e.*, as providers of essential transport services whose rates should be held down and who should be forced to relinquish control of the traffic they carry? Is this wise? Does it adequately account for the free speech rights of cable operators? Should this model be extended to all tiers of the cable system?

7. In Cash or In Kind. Is it surprising that local authorities are significantly constrained in their ability to extract cash from cable franchisees (in the form of franchise fees) but are given broad discretion to extract in-kind compensation in the form of PEG and leased access channels? Is there a logic here? Aren't we more likely to see an efficient use of resources if, instead, local authorities were allowed to take cash but then had to purchase channel space?

8. The Federal/Local Relationship. Looking back at your answers to all of the above questions, does the very fact that the federal government imposes so many limitations on local discretion raise concern? Has the federal government left local officials with sufficient discretion to allow them to vindicate genuine local interests? And why is the federal government the better arbiter of what are and are not beneficial policies with respect to cable television? Any reason to trust the judgment of federal officials more than local ones?

9. Rate Regulation. The following is another excerpt from the *Cable Rate Regulation Executive Summary* that was included earlier in this chapter. The bulk of that document deals with the regulation of rates charged by operators to subscribers, but this section considers rates charged by operators to those who lease commercial access capacity.

RATE REGULATION OF CABLE SERVICE
Executive Summary, Report and Order,
8 FCC Rcd. 5631 (1993)

B. Leased Commercial Access

1. Leased Access: Background

103. The Communications Act requires that cable systems with 36 or more channels make available a portion of their channel capacity for lease by outside unaffiliated parties. Under section 9 of the Cable Act of 1992, the Commission is provided with expanded authority to regulate the commercial leasing of cable channels for those cable systems required to make such channel capacity available.

2. Leased Access: Terms and Conditions of Use

104. The cable operator and commercial leased access user may negotiate channel placement and tier access for leased programming. Parties must take into account the nature of the service; the relationship between the charge imposed and the desirability of the channel; and the need to provide competition in delivery service and diversity of programming. Cable operators may not apply programming production standards to leased access users that are any higher than those applied to PEG channels. Operators must also provide the minimal amount of technical support necessary for users to air their material. Operators are also entitled to be reimbursed for such services. Reasonable security deposits to lease channels may be requested from users by cable operators. Cable operators may not set terms and conditions for users based on content except to the extent necessary to establish a reasonable price for use of channel capacity and to comply with the Commission's indecency standards. Cable operators are also required to provide billing and collection services for leased access users, unless the operator demonstrates the existence of third party billing and collection services which, in terms of cost and accessibility, offer leased access users an alternative substantially equivalent to that offered comparable non-leased programmers.

3. Leased Access: Maximum Reasonable Rates

a. Leased Access

105. The maximum commercial leased access rates that a cable operator may charge is [the "average implicit fee" charged to non-affiliated programmers on

the same programming services tier. To calculate the average implicit fee, the operator must first take the total amount it receives in subscriber revenues per month for all programming on the tier and then subtract the total amount it pays in programming costs per month for the tier. The remaining figure represents what the cable operator effectively charges (its implicit fee) for use of those channels in that tier. For example, suppose a cable operator offers a cable programming services tier for $5 per subscriber per month. The tier includes five programmers: ESPN, CNN, BET, MTV, and TLC. The operator pays each of those five programmers a total of fifty cents per month. The operator's average implicit fee is fifty cents per subscriber per channel per month. The calculation is: $5 from subscribers minus $2.50 (50 cents to each of 5 programmers) in program costs equals $2.50, which may be viewed as the total amount per subscriber per month that the five programmers "pay" the operator in order to "rent" its channels. Since five channels are "rented" the average implicit fee per channel is fifty cents per subscriber per month.][12]

5. Leased Access: Procedures for Resolution of Disputes

108. Review of leased access rates or terms and conditions will be triggered by the filing of a complaint at the Commission. A streamlined process has been developed to handle these complaints so that they can be handled expeditiously.

6. Leased Access: Minority and Educational Programmers Alternative

109. In accordance with the statutory provisions, up to 33 percent of a system's designated leased channel capacity may be used for qualified minority or educational programming purchased by the system operator rather than by leased channel programming.

Notes and Questions

1. **Rationale for Regulation.** What programs will be shown on cable under the present leased access regime that would not have obtained carriage without leased access? Won't cable operators, seeking to satisfy a wide range of viewers' desires, carry any available programming that is expected to be profitable? If a hypothetical XYZ pay cable network offering movies and sports can make more money for the cable system than, say, HBO, won't the cable system carry XYZ? If not, how is XYZ helped by offering it leased access at the "net implicit fee" the system charges HBO? Besides, what specific governmental interest does leased access promote that is sufficient to overcome constitutional objections?

2. **The Exception for Qualified Minority or Educational Programming.** Is the 33 percent set-aside described in ¶109 vulnerable to separate constitutional attack? Does it violate equal protection principles? Is it a content based departure from an otherwise content neutral rule? Or is it just a determination to forbear from regulation as to these programs, so that the government is not implicated in the

---

12. [Ed. The material in brackets is paraphrased from the Commission's 1997 revision of the method by which the leased access fee is to be computed. *See* In re Implementation of Sections of The Cable Television Consumer Protection And Competition Act of 1992, 12 FCC Rcd. 5267 (1997).]

operator's choice to substitute "qualified minority or educational programming" for leased access? If owners of such programming had to pay the "net implicit fee" for access, how would that fee be determined? Would requiring such a fee effectively deny minority and educational programming the benefits of leased access?

CHAPTER ELEVEN

THE BROADCAST/CABLE RELATIONSHIP

The purpose of this chapter is:

- to study how copyright law, the 1992 Cable Act, and FCC regulations implementing the 1992 Cable Act combine to mediate rights among cable operators, broadcasters, and content producers.

∼

One of the most significant tasks to be accomplished in the regulation of cable television is to define the relative rights and obligations of broadcasters, the content producers who supply content to broadcasters, and cable providers who under certain conditions capture and retransmit broadcast signals. Two basic questions arise in this context. First, under what conditions should cable operators be obligated to compensate broadcasters and/or program producers for echoed content? Second, is it the cable operator's decision, the broadcaster's decision, the content producer's decision, or some combination thereof that determines whether a given program will be echoed on cable? The law with respect to both of these issues comes from a combination of three primary sources: federal copyright law, the 1992 Cable Act, and FCC regulations implementing the 1992 Act.

Before turning to the details, however, it is helpful to consider the various interests at stake by playing out a simple hypothetical. So, suppose that you are a broadcast television licensee in Cleveland, Ohio, in 1960. You hear that a cable television system will soon be built in your area. How do you react?

From our knowledge of cable's early years, we know that you are likely to be of two minds about cable. On the one hand, cable television might make you better off by enhancing the quality of your signal and extending its reach. And whether your viewers receive your signal over the air or over cable, they are your viewers; they are watching your programs and they are thus people whose attention you can sell to your advertisers. On the other hand, cable is also a threat. Cable might compete with you for viewers, offering original programming of its own or importing broadcast television signals from other markets. These imported stations might even carry programming—for example, reruns of network-produced situational comedy—that you carry and for which you have paid substantial sums.

The details of your relationship with the cable system might also have you concerned. You might believe that the cable system will unjustly enrich itself by carrying your signal (thus increasing the appeal of basic cable) and thus think that you should be compensated if the cable operator does indeed echo your content. At the same time, you might worry that the cable operator will decide not to carry your station, putting you at a significant disadvantage as compared to your broadcast competitors. You might further worry about intermediate issues, for example whether the cable provider will be allowed to cherry-pick the good content from your station, airing your better programs but replacing your less popular ones with programs of its own choosing. You might also worry about whether your content will be shown on cable on the same numeric channel you use over the air; after all, if you've spent a fortune promoting the slogan "Channel Five Cares," you are going to be upset if your signal is not shown on the cable operator's channel five—and even more upset if a rival is given that channel position.

The statutory provisions and FCC regulations that are our focus this chapter address all of these concerns. Must cable operators compensate content producers for echoed programming? May content producers refuse to permit retransmission if they so desire? Both of these questions have been considered by the Supreme Court and are today answered by specific provisions of the Copyright Act of 1976. In the first section of this chapter we will consider those provisions and their evolution. The next section then looks at the syndicated exclusivity and network nonduplication rules, two FCC regulations that allow a broadcaster to purchase the exclusive right to air a particular program in a given market and, by contract, stipulate that no other broadcaster will be allowed to authorize the local cable company to retransmit that same program. The final section considers the controversial must-carry and retransmission consent provisions of the 1992 Act. Under the must-carry provision, qualifying broadcasters can force their local cable provider to retransmit their signals (indeed, at the correct dial positions) even if the cable provider would rather not echo the signals at all. Retransmission consent, meanwhile, establishes the converse right, empowering broadcasters to deny cable operators the right to retransmit. As is likely apparent, retransmission consent is important not because broadcasters typically refuse retransmission, but instead because broadcasters can threaten to deny retransmission consent and in that way extract payments from cable providers who as a practical matter need to retransmit at least some broadcast stations in order to attract subscribers.

I. COPYRIGHT AND COMPULSORY LICENSES

When cable television first began to retransmit broadcast stations, issues of copyright liability were unclear. True, many of the programs aired on broadcast television were protected by copyright and so clearly *broadcasters* had to pay the relevant copyright owners before airing copyrighted content. But cable operators were simply retransmitting content that had already been made public. Once the copyright holders were paid by broadcasters and once they had agreed to put their programs out for all to see, did they really have any claim to additional royalties when a cable operator wanted to echo that same program?[1]

---

1. Interestingly, copyright owners did have an indirect ability to claim additional payments from any other broadcaster who might have wanted to retransmit content that was

In the 1968 case of Fortnightly Corp. v. United Artists, 392 U.S. 157 (1968), the Supreme Court confronted exactly this question. The facts were simple. A West Virginia cable operator had begun to retransmit five broadcast signals that were already available over the air in his local market. United Artists, which represented copyright holders who held rights in many of the programs being aired on those broadcast channels, sued the cable operator for infringement, arguing that the cable operator could not air copyrighted content without first obtaining a license from the relevant copyright holders. The Supreme Court ruled that there was no infringement. Just as a viewer was free to receive the broadcasts by antenna and then display the content on his home television, cable operators too, in the Court's view, were free to capture these signals by antenna and display them on the multiple television sets attached to the cable network.

The Supreme Court reaffirmed and expanded this logic a few years later in the 1974 case of CBS v. Teleprompter, 415 U.S. 394 (1974). In this instance, the cable provider was capturing broadcast signals in one community and then using microwave relays to transport those signals to its cable system hundreds of miles away. The issue, then, was not the local retransmission of broadcast signals (*Fortnightly*), but instead the importation of broadcast signals from distant communities. Again, the Supreme Court held that the cable company was acting more like a viewer than like a broadcaster; it was receiving a publicly available signal and then displaying that signal on television sets connected to its system. There was no copyright liability for the cable provider, just as there was no copyright liability for normal viewers.

None of this would remain good law for very long. The Copyright Act of 1976 changed a good many details of copyright law,[2] and one of those changes effectively reversed *Fortnightly* and *Teleprompter*. Under the new Act, the retransmission of copyrighted broadcast content by a cable operator was defined to be copyright infringement.[3] Home viewers were still implicitly licensed to capture broadcast signals off the air and display them privately, but cable operators could no longer borrow broadcast content with impunity.

Had the Copyright Act of 1976 stopped there—defining cable retransmission to be infringement but doing no more—then every time a cable operator wanted to retransmit a local signal, it would have had to acquire a license from every relevant content owner. If the local NBC affiliate was airing thirty copyrighted programs a day, that would mean that the cable operator would need thirty licenses to air the full day's content. This might have meant tracking down and negotiating with each and every copyright owner, or there might have developed some sort of clearinghouse organization (like BMI and ASCAP are for the music industry) to handle these permissions en masse.

Congress apparently thought that either result would be unwise, so, in addition to defining cable retransmission as infringement, Congress added to the Copyright Act what is today 17 U.S.C. §111. That provision establishes a system

---

first transmitted by a rival. This power came from 47 U.S.C. §325(a), a provision which forbid one broadcaster from retransmitting another's signal without that broadcaster's explicit permission.

2. Copyright Act of 1976, Pub. L. 94-533, codified as amended at 17 U.S.C. §101 et seq.

3. 17 U.S.C. §501(c).

of compulsory licenses in favor of cable operators who want to retransmit copyrighted broadcast content. These are *compulsory* licenses: copyright owners are deemed to authorize retransmission so long as the cable operators satisfy the terms of the licenses as set out by Congress.

Section 111(c)(1) establishes the basic rule that "secondary transmissions to the public by a cable system of a performance or display of a work embodied in a primary transmission made by a broadcast station licensed by the Federal Communications Commission...shall be subject to statutory licensing" upon compliance with various conditions. Particularly important among those conditions is §111(c)(3)'s stipulation that neither the content of the particular program at issue, nor any commercial advertising or station announcements transmitted by the primary transmitter immediately before or after the program's transmission, be "willfully altered by the cable system through changes, deletions, or additions."

Section111(d) sets out the royalty structure for these compulsory licenses. The details of that provision are not important for our purposes, but it is important to note that cable operators pay royalties only to the extent they retransmit "nonnetwork programming of a primary transmitter in whole or in part beyond the local service area" of that primary transmitter. That is, cable operators enjoy a compulsory license for all retransmitted broadcast content, and they pay royalties only for the subset of content that is nonnetwork and from a broadcaster outside the cable operator's local service area. There is no royalty for network programming and also no royalty for local nonnetwork programming.

The House Report on the Copyright Act of 1976, H.R. Rep. No. 1476, explains all of the above as follows:

> In general, the Committee believes that cable systems are commercial enterprises whose basic retransmission operations are based on the carriage of copyrighted program material and that copyright royalties should be paid by cable operators to the creators of such programs. The Committee recognizes, however, that it would be impractical and unduly burdensome to require every cable system to negotiate with every copyright owner whose work was retransmitted by a cable system. Accordingly, the Committee has decided to establish a compulsory copyright license for the retransmission of over-the-air broadcast signals.
>
> The Committee determined however that there was no evidence that the retransmission of local broadcast signals by a cable operator threatens the existing market for copyright program owners. Similarly, the retransmission of network programming, including network programming which is broadcast in distant markets, does not injure the copyright owner. The copyright owner contracts with the network on the basis of his programming reaching all markets served by the network and is compensated accordingly.
>
> By contrast, retransmission of distant non-network programming by cable systems causes damage to the copyright owner by distributing the program in an area beyond which it has been privately licensed. Such retransmission adversely affects the ability of the copyright owner to exploit the work in the distant market. It is also of direct benefit to the cable system by enhancing its ability to attract subscribers and increase

revenues. For these reasons, the Committee has concluded that the copy-right liability of cable television systems under the compulsory license should be limited to the retransmission of distant non-network programming.

Notes and Questions

1. The *Fortnightly* Approach. Who was being hurt under the Supreme Court's interpretation of copyright law under *Fortnightly*? Local broadcasters? The copyright holders? Was the real problem just that the legal rule was unclear? That is, had copyright owners known that cable operators could retransmit their programs with impunity, could they have been fully compensated by raising the prices they charged broadcasters in the first place?

2. Drawing Distinctions. Was the Supreme Court's interpretation of copyright law defensible? Was it really that difficult to distinguish television viewers from cable operators for copyright purposes? Doesn't copyright law draw those sorts of distinctions all the time?

3. Compulsory Licenses. Why did Congress choose a compulsory licensing scheme as opposed to defining secondary transmission to be copyright infringement and then allowing the market to establish the terms and royalties for retransmission? Is the House Report's claim that this would have been "impractical" and "unduly burdensome" convincing given that BMI and ASCAP have long successfully acted as copyright clearinghouses for the music industry, collecting royalties from radio stations, restaurants, and other entities that broadcast and otherwise perform musical compositions and then distributing those moneys to the appropriate copyright holders?

4. The Logic of the House Report. Are there any situations where the logic of the House Report with respect to network programming, local programming, and nonnetwork distant programming fails, or did Congress get things right when it established royalties only for a small subset of copyrighted programs?

5. Thinking Ahead. Do the copyright provisions considered here apply to retransmissions of broadcast content by any third party? For example, suppose that a firm launches a satellite and begins to provide "direct broadcast satellite" service by capturing broadcast signals in Los Angeles and then echoing them into Portland. Will this firm benefit from the compulsory license? If not, should Congress have drafted the provision more broadly? (We will consider direct broadcast satellite more fully in Chapter Thirteen.)

II. SYNDICATED EXCLUSIVITY AND NETWORK NONDUPLICATION

Overall, the Copyright Act of 1976 represented a compromise: cable operators had to pay for some of the content they retransmitted, but neither broadcasters nor copyright holders were able to deny cable operators the right to carry once-broadcasted programming. Section 111, however, had an important exception: secondary transmissions were subject to compulsory licenses only "where the carriage of the signals comprising the secondary transmission [was also] permissible under the rules, regulations, or authorizations" of the FCC. Prior to the 1976 Act, there existed many FCC rules designed to balance cable operators', broadcasters', and copyright holders' respective rights. Most of those rules were repealed after the 1976 Act took effect so as to not interfere with the compulsory licensing scheme devised by Congress. In 1988, however, two of those rules— syndicated exclusivity[4] and network nonduplication[5]—were reinstated.

Syndicated exclusivity ("syndex") and network nonduplication ("network nondupe") are companion rules, the former applicable to the syndicated programs that are distributed to and aired by broadcast stations and the latter applicable to programs that are distributed within and aired by the networks. Syndex rules enable a local broadcaster to prevent a cable system from exhibiting that part of an imported distant broadcaster's signal that contains programs (or episodes from a television series) for which the local broadcaster has obtained exclusive broadcast rights, in that local area, from the copyright holder. Network nonduplication rules give local broadcasters similar rights with respect to network programming for which they have obtained local exclusivity.

The syndex rules were challenged as, among other things, inconsistent with Congress' compulsory license regime. The D.C. Circuit upheld the rules in the 1989 case reprinted below.

UNITED VIDEO v. FCC
890 F.2d 1173 (D.C. Cir. 1989)

Opinion for the court filed by Chief Judge WALD, in which Circuit Judges EDWARDS and SILBERMAN concur.

WALD, Chief Judge:

A syndicated television program is a program marketed from its supplier to local television stations by means other than a television network. In 1988, the Federal Communications Commission reinstated its "syndicated exclusivity" rules. These rules allow the supplier of a syndicated program to agree with a broadcast television station that the station shall be the exclusive presenter of the program in its local broadcast area. A broadcast station with exclusive rights to a syndicated program can forbid any cable television station from importing the program into its local broadcast area from a distant station.

Petitioners, mostly cable television companies whose distant signal offerings will be restricted under the new rules, challenge the rules as arbitrary and capricious, and as violative of the Copyright Act of 1976, the Cable Act of 1984, and the First Amendment. We find that the Commission's action is within its authority and is not arbitrary or capricious.

---

4. 47 CFR §76.101.
5. 47 CFR §76.92.

I. BACKGROUND

The volatile relationship between cable and broadcast television has traditionally hinged on the ability of cable television stations to receive the signal that a broadcast station sends over the air, and to retransmit that signal to subscribers via a cable. The Communications Act forbids a broadcast station from rebroadcasting another broadcast station's signal without permission, 47 U.S.C. §325(a), but does not forbid cable retransmission.

Prior to the 1976 revision of the copyright laws, cable companies were free, as far as copyright law was concerned, to pick up signals aired by broadcasters and retransmit them throughout the country.

The distress felt by originating broadcasters whose signals were retransmitted in this way was matched only by the anger of local broadcasters in the receiving end communities, who watched the cable companies importing into their markets the very programs that they were themselves showing, and to which they had purchased exclusive broadcast rights. The FCC decided that this was an unfair form of competition. Beginning in 1965, the Commission promulgated exclusivity rules that protected local broadcasters from the importation into their markets of distant signals that duplicated signals to which they had purchased exclusive rights.

In 1976, Congress finally got around to addressing the question of the copyright liability of cable companies that carried distant signals. Congress provided, in the Copyright Revision Act of 1976, a compulsory licensing scheme whereby cable companies paid an administratively-set fee for such carriage. Subsequently, in 1980, the FCC decided that, given the new copyright regime, syndex protection was no longer in the public interest, although network exclusivity was retained. CATV Syndicated Program Exclusivity Rules, 79 F.C.C.2d 663 (1980). The Commission stated that the elimination of syndex would cause no significant harm to broadcast stations. *Id.* at 814.

Broadcast stations petitioned the Commission for a reconsideration of its negative position on syndex in 1984, but the Commission refused to budge, saying that there had been no change in circumstances that would justify a change in its position. In 1987, however, the Commission began another review of its 1980 decision to eliminate syndex, and in 1988 it promulgated the rules challenged in this case. The Commission decided that its 1980 decision reflected an imperfect understanding of the role cable was to assume in the ensuing decade as a full competitor to broadcast television. The Commission found that with the enormous growth in cable's audience and advertising revenues, the lack of syndex was harming broadcast stations, and might have been significantly affecting the supply of syndicated programs. The Commission decided to reinstate syndex in view of the changes in the cable television industry that occurred between 1980 and 1988.

II. ARBITRARINESS AND CAPRICE

A. The Commission's Factual Findings

The Commission's decision to reinstate syndex rests on its finding that syndex rules will promote diversity in syndicated programming. In the report accompanying the rules, the Commission found that unrestricted importation of distant signals (*i.e.*, no syndex protection) leads to duplication of programming in local broadcasting areas; this duplication lessens the value of syndicated programs to broadcast stations; that loss of value in turn lowers the price syndicated program suppliers will receive for their programs; and all of this ultimately reduces the incentive for syndicated program suppliers to produce programs, which translates into a reduction in the diversity of programming available to the public. On the basis of this scenario, the Commission concluded that syndex rules should be reinstated in order to promote diversity of programming.

The petitioners challenge the FCC's rule as arbitrary and capricious, for want of support in the rulemaking record.

1. Duplication

The petitioners do not challenge the Commission's finding that unrestricted importation of distant signals leads to duplication of programming between broadcast and cable channels.

2. Lessening of the Value of Syndicated Programs to Local Broadcast Stations

The petitioners hotly contest the Commission's finding that program duplication lessens the value of syndicated programs purchased by local broadcast stations. However, the Commission's report cites substantial evidence from which it could reasonably draw this conclusion. The Commission discusses two related ways in which duplication lessens the value of syndicated programs: audience diversion and the loss of exclusivity as a competitive tool.

The Commission found that duplication of programming diverts a substantial portion of the broadcast audience to cable. The evidence was strongest regarding diversion caused by a cable station's simultaneous transmission of a program being aired by a broadcast channel, for such diversion can be gauged by ratings information. Numerous stations reported a substantial number of viewers that chose to watch a duplicated program on the cable rather than the broadcast channel. Although the Commission correctly observed that not every viewer who watched the program on cable would watch it on the broadcast channel if that were the only way to watch it, and that these numbers therefore did not provide a mathematically precise measure of audience diversion, the Commission was surely justified in concluding that significant diversion was occurring.

The Commission reasonably inferred that diversion lessened the value of the programming by lowering advertising revenues.

The Commission's report does not specify quite so clearly how it reached the conclusion that nonsimultaneous transmission of duplicative programming (including transmission of different episodes of the same program) also causes audience diversion. The one sentence explicitly devoted to this question in the report says that "the quantity of non-simultaneous duplication documented in the record in this proceeding, taken as a whole, presents compelling evidence that substantial diversion is taking place." *Id.* at 5306. This sentence suggests that the Commission has simply assumed diversion from the conceded fact of non-simultaneous duplication. The Commission points to no specific empirical support for this statement in the record.

While it is intuitively reasonable to assume that simultaneous duplication causes diversion, the question of nonsimultaneous duplication seems more varied and complex. A cable company's transmission of a feature film, for example, might reduce the audience for a broadcast of that film for weeks afterwards. But if a broadcast channel airs an old episode of M*A*S*H at 6:00 p.m., will a substantial number of viewers be diverted because a cable channel is offering a different old episode at 11:00 p.m.? The Commission's report offers no way to tell, and it is possible that the 6:00 p.m. and 11:00 p.m. time slots attract quite diverse audiences. If the Commission had relied solely on its assumption of audience diversion as evidence that nonsimultaneous duplication lessens the value of programs to broadcast stations, we might well have felt obliged to require some supplementation or further explanation of its reasoning.

However, the Commission relies on more solid evidence that duplication makes programming less valuable. The evidence is that all stations, broadcast and cable, want exclusivity. Many broadcasters, in their comments supporting the syndex rules, identify exclusivity as the key to programming success. Even more telling, cable companies themselves regularly take advantage of their ability to obtain exclusive rights in programming. The reason, as the FCC notes in its report, is that exclusivity gives stations the opportunity to promote themselves as the only presenter of a certain program. If a broadcaster spends money promoting a duplicated program, some of the value of the expenditure will be captured by the cable company that is importing the same program. Syndex will give the local broadcaster a competitive tool that it can use both to call attention to the particular program and to "alert viewers to the general attractiveness of the broadcaster's whole range of programming." The strong desire of all stations for complete exclusivity is evidence that even non-simultaneous duplication lessens the value of programming, whether because of audience diversion or for other reasons.

While the Commission's report may leave something to be desired in its detail on the dangers of nonsimultaneous duplication, we do not think its conclusion that even this type of duplication lessens the value of programming for broadcast stations can be called arbitrary or capricious. The record as a whole shows that both broadcast and cable companies want complete exclusivity; the Commission did not act without reason in concluding that exclusivity must be a valuable commodity, and conversely that lack of exclusivity diminishes the value of a program.

3. Effects on Program Supply

We think the Commission's conclusion about the link between lack of program diversity and lowered broadcast revenues due to lack of exclusivity is sufficiently in accord with accepted economic theory that it can stand without empirical support, particularly since we agree with the Commission that it would be very difficult for it to show the degree to which programs are currently not being produced because of the lack of syndex protection. The FCC has assumed only that increasing the value of programs to broadcast companies will increase the amount paid for them, and that these higher prices will improve product supply.

The petitioners argue in response that despite the lack of syndex protection, syndicated programming and broadcast television are thriving. Absent any actual evidence that syndex would increase program supply, they claim that the current robust health of the market shows that syndicators and broadcast stations are suffering no harm that requires FCC correction. However, the Commission properly rejected this argument as irrelevant. Syndicators may be doing well, but that does not show that they would not do better if they could capture the full value of their programs. The FCC is not empowered to regulate the market only in cases where regulation is necessary to save broadcast stations or syndicators from economic peril. Increasing program diversity is a valid FCC regulatory goal and increasing revenues for program originators a likely means of achieving it.[6]

Having tested each link in the Commission's causal chain, we find that it used valid reasoning to conclude that syndex rules will increase the diversity of programming options available to the public. Its imposition of syndex was adequately supported by the rulemaking record.

B. Change in Agency Course

The Commission's report notes several ways in which the Commission now feels the 1980 decision to have been inadequate. First, the report discusses how circumstances have changed since 1980. The principal change has been the unforeseen emergence of cable television as a full competitor to broadcast television. In 1980, cable served 19% of television households, but in 1988 it served 51%, a percentage the FCC projected would rise to 60% by 1996. In 1980, the Commission had predicted that cable penetration would never go beyond 48%. Cable advertising revenues were $45.5 million in 1980, but they grew to over $1 billion in 1988; cable's share of total television advertising revenue climbed from less than 0.5% to more than 6%. *Id.* This unexpected growth, the Commission notes, substantially undermines its 1980 findings that repeal of syndex would not cause significant audience diversion or otherwise harm broadcast stations.

The Commission also faults its earlier studies for focusing on the effects repeal of syndex would have on individual stations, rather than its effects on the competitive process and the incentive for production of new programs. Lack of syndex protection, as discussed above, distorts the broadcaster's promotional incentives and makes it impossible for syndicators to capture the full value of their programs. A competitive process in which exclusivity contracts are enforceable will, the Commission now believes, produce the best programming for the public.

The Commission's report also examines the negative aspects of syndex rules. It acknowledges the costs in reimposing syndex: cable companies will need to purchase new equipment to comply, and the necessity of deleting protected programs will cause some disruption in cable service. However, the report concludes

---

6. Furthermore, the Commission notes that syndex can improve the programming mix in the local television markets even if it does not lead to a change in program supply. Without syndex protection, local broadcasters may find it uneconomical to purchase certain programs that they would purchase if they could get exclusivity. As a result, television viewers in that area who do not subscribe to cable will not be able to see those programs at all. Of course, with syndex rules in place, the program could become unavailable on cable if a local broadcaster buys exclusive rights to it, but that result is still preferable to the market distortion caused by lack of syndex rules, because with syndex, the broadcasters and the cable companies can engage in competition that results in the program being carried by the station whose viewers value it most.

that the equipment cable companies will need is currently available and reasonably priced, and disruption will be lessened by the one-year delay between the announcement and effective date of the rules.

The Commission in its report also acknowledges that the absence of syndex provides consumers with the benefit of "time and episode diversity." A cable station, free of syndex restraints, may import a different episode of a program than the one aired by a broadcast station, or the same episode at a different time of day. The Commission suggests, however, that this diversity must be balanced against the lack of diversity engendered by duplication, and by the reduced incentive for the production of new programs. The Commission also suggests that market forces will allow duplication where viewers value it sufficiently, since stations with exclusive rights to a program can always sell the right to duplicate it. Finally, the Commission notes that the value of cable in providing time diversity has been lessened by the significant increase in the penetration of video cassette recorders (up from 1.5% of television households in 1979 to 58.1% today), since VCRs allow viewers to provide time diversity for themselves.

III. THE COMMISSION'S AUTHORITY

Syndex rules are rules that the Commission has found necessary to carry out its mandate under the Communications Act; they clearly fall within the Act's general authority, the regulation of interstate and foreign communication by wire or radio, 47 U.S.C. §152(a); and, as we concluded above, the rules were reasonably adopted in furtherance of a valid communications policy goal. Hence, they fall under the Commission's §303(r) powers unless they are "inconsistent with law." We therefore turn to the provisions of law with which the petitioners claim syndex is inconsistent.

A. The Copyright Act

The 1976 Copyright Act, now Title 17 of the United States Code, struck a balance between the rights of copyright owners and the needs of cable television stations. Congress decided that when a cable station carries a broadcast station's signal into a distant market, it ought to pay a fee for the carriage. But Congress also believed that it would be impracticable for cable companies to negotiate individually with every copyright owner whose work they wished to carry. Congress therefore created a compulsory licensing scheme, embodied in §111 of the Act, that provides for payment to copyright owners without the need for individual negotiations. Under the Act, cable stations may carry copyrighted signals into distant markets upon payment of a fee set by the Copyright Royalty Tribunal. The Tribunal distributes these fees to copyright owners.

Syndex therefore represents, according to the petitioners, an impermissible attempt by the FCC to impose on cable television stations the very copyright liability that Congress decided should not exist.

The fundamental problem with the petitioners' argument is that syndex rules were in place when Congress passed the Copyright Act in 1976. Congress was fully aware of syndex and chose to let it remain in place until the Commission decided to change it. The 1976 Act says: "secondary transmissions to the public by a cable system of a primary transmission made by a broadcast station licensed by the [FCC]...shall be subject to compulsory licensing...where the carriage of the signals comprising the secondary transmission is permissible under the rules, regulations, or authorizations of the [FCC]." 17 U.S.C. §111(c)(1). The Act thus explicitly withholds a compulsory license from cable companies in cases where the FCC forbids the cable companies' transmissions.

The petitioners compare syndex to a "retransmission consent requirement"—a requirement that a cable station obtain the consent of each broadcaster whose signal it wishes to carry—which the Commission concedes would be an impermissible interference with compulsory licensing. It is true that if enough broadcasters take advantage of their ability to obtain exclusive rights in programming, the practical difference between syndex and a retransmission consent requirement may be small. We confess that we find it somewhat surprising that Congress, on the one hand, created a compulsory licensing scheme and, on the other hand, let stand a regulation that could greatly limit the set of signals for which that scheme would be effective. However, we think it clear that that is precisely what Congress did, with full knowledge of what it was about. It is not for us to tell Congress how to create a compulsory licensing scheme.

B. The Cable Act

The Cable Communications Policy Act of 1984 amended the Communications Act to explicitly grant the FCC a power it had previously only inferred from its general authority to regulate television: the power to regulate cable television. *See* Pub.L. No. 98-549, §3(a), 98 Stat. 3801 (1984) (codified at 47 U.S.C. §152(a)). However, the Act also set some limits on that power, and in particular it provided: "(1) Any Federal agency, State, or franchising authority may not impose requirements regarding the provision or content of cable services, except as expressly provided in this subchapter." The petitioners claim that this section forbids syndex rules.

The key to understanding what Congress meant by the term "requirements" in §544(f) is whether a regulation is content based or content neutral. The House report suggests that Congress thought a cable company's owners, not government officials, should decide what sorts of programming the company would provide. But it does not suggest a concern with regulations of cable that are not based on the content of cable programming, and do not require that particular programs or types of programs be provided. Such regulations are not requirements "regarding the provision or content" of cable services.

Syndex is clearly different from a requirement or prohibition of the carriage of a particular program or channel. Although it will certainly affect the content of cable programming, it is content neutral. The basis on which syndex forbids carriage of certain programs is not their content, but ownership of the right to present them. Syndex itself does not require carriage of any particular program or type of program, nor does it prevent a cable company from acquiring the right to present, and presenting, any program.

C. The First Amendment

The petitioners repeatedly claim that syndex restrains the expression of fully protected speech which has been paid for and authorized under the compulsory licensing scheme of §111 of the Copyright Act. The fact is, however, that because of the provisions of §111, cable companies will not be able to obtain a compulsory license to transmit a program if transmission would violate the syndex rules. The petitioners are therefore in the position of claiming that they have a First Amendment right to express themselves using the copyrighted materials of others.

IV. CONCLUSION

The Commission has considered anew the question of how to balance the rights of broadcast and cable television companies so as best to serve the public interest in receiving diverse programming. Congress decided that this question should be resolved by the agency, and on the record before us we uphold its resolution.

Notes and Questions

1. The Logic of Syndex. What interests are the syndex rules designed to protect? Suppose a major market independent station (say, a non-network station in Washington, D.C.) is imported into a small market (Quincy, Illinois) by the small market cable system. Suppose further that both the imported D.C. station and a Quincy station hold rights to exhibit episodes of *Seinfeld*. Is the D.C. station harmed by the importation of its signal? How about the Quincy station? Although the Quincy station may suffer the "audience diversion" discussed in *United Video*, won't it also be able, as a consequence, to obtain *Seinfeld* rights for a smaller fee? How about the producer of *Seinfeld*? Won't that firm now be able to charge higher prices to the D.C. station due to its expanded audience in Quincy?

2. Increasing Diversity. What explains the somewhat puzzling claim in the *United Video* opinion that "increasing program diversity is a valid FCC regulatory goal *and increasing revenues for program originators a likely means of achieving it*" (emphasis added)? If you were a program producer and were given a million dollars would you be more likely to (a) increase the diversity of your programs or (b) spend the money with wanton and profligate abandon on your own luxurious desires?

3. Any More Rights to Allocate? If the Copyright Act of 1976 was not adequate to regulate the relationship between cable and broadcast television—presumably for something like the reasons raised by the first question above—then are the syndex and network nonduplication rules sufficient? With these rules in place, what is the point of (a) retransmission consent regulations or (b) any other regulation of cable?

4. Contract Law. Are the syndex and network nonduplication rules redundant to simple contract law? Is there anything more here than the FCC saying that parties can contract for exclusive rights, which arguably they could do without the FCC's permission?

III. MUST-CARRY AND
RETRANSMISSION CONSENT

While both copyright law and the network nonduplication/syndex regulations focus primarily on program content, two important types of statutory provisions focus instead on the broadcast signal itself: 47 U.S.C. §325(b) states that a cable operator cannot retransmit a broadcaster's signal without that broadcaster's explicit permission; and 47 U.S.C. §§534–535 give certain broadcasters the right to insist that their signals be carried without charge on the local cable system. These provisions are typically referred to as the "retransmission consent" and "must-carry" obligations, respectively; both were added to federal law by the Cable Television Consumer Protection and Competition Act of 1992.

Consider, first, retransmission consent. Again, retransmission consent refers to the permission a cable operator must today receive in order to retransmit the signal of almost any broadcast station. The only stations for which consent is not needed are the so-called "super-stations" (such as WTBS, WGN, and WWOR) that, as of 1991, had established themselves as national broadcast stations. Retransmission consent is required in addition to any permissions needed under copyright law. That is, retransmission consent recognizes an intellectual property right in the signal that is independent of, and in addition to, the intellectual property rights already recognized in the copyrighted content being transmitted by the signal. The provision gives broadcasters the power to negotiate with cable operators for a share of the revenues generated by the retransmission of broadcast signals.

So, whose interests does retransmission consent protect? That, unfortunately, is not entirely clear. The copyright, syndicated exclusivity and network nonduplication rules seem to already protect program suppliers. And, if retransmission consent was designed to protect the additional value in a station's signal that is contributed by the station—for example, the value created when a station assembles a package of programs that provide a continuous sequence of entertainment—one still must explain why broadcasters could not be adequately compensated for this value in other ways. For example, would not copyright owners charge these broadcasters lower prices, the copyright owners wanting their content mixed in with the otherwise desirable signal and thus willing to take a lower fee? Phrased another way, it is not intuitively clear why retransmission consent is important given that copyright law, the syndicated exclusivity rules, and the network nonduplication rules already combine to force both broadcasters and cable operators to negotiate with copyright holders and, hence, each other.

Relatedly, think about the relationship between retransmission consent and the 1992 Cable Act's establishment of rate regulation for cable systems. The rate regulation provisions suggest that Congress believes cable systems, when unregulated, can engage in monopoly pricing, but that rate regulation will be effective at lowering prices to competitive levels. However, why won't broadcast stations, through exercising retransmission consent, bargain for prices for their consent that capture the monopoly profits the cable systems used to receive? Note that the FCC allows cable systems to treat retransmission consent fees as costs that can be added to their prices. Insofar as rate regulation prevents cable systems from gaining monopoly profits by forcing them to reduce their prices from x (the monopoly price) to y (something closer to the competitive price), will retransmission consent enable powerful local broadcasters to gain x-y for themselves? If so, the net effect here would be that consumers would receive no price reduction while monopoly profits would be shifted from cable operators to broadcast station owners. Must the FCC now engage in retransmission consent price regulation in order to preserve cable service price regulation?

Retransmission consent took effect in 1993, and thus in that year the major networks had their first experience negotiating with cable providers. CBS took a hard line and attempted to hold out for huge fees. Cable operators refused to pay, and ultimately CBS caved in and authorized retransmission at no charge.[7] Meanwhile, NBC and ABC granted retransmission consent, but not for money. Instead, these networks gave their consent in exchange for space on the various cable systems. NBC used that space for an ultimately unsuccessful cable channel called "America's Talking." ABC more profitably used its space for the sports channel ESPN2. (Fox also traded retransmission consent for system capacity, using its cable capacity to launch a cable channel called "FX".) These deals over-all meant that cable operators did not have to pay out cash for retransmission privileges, and the networks—except, of course, CBS—were able to introduce new cable channels that immediately at launch reached upwards of 18 million subscribers.[8]

Bargaining over retransmission consent continued to be contentious in subsequent rounds of these triennial negotiations. For example, in 1999, ABC took an aggressive stance with respect to retransmission consent, trying both to increase subscribership for its affiliated "Lifetime" network and to introduce a new movie channel. Negotiations went well past the expiration date of the then-existing retransmission consent agreement, and so for several weeks ABC's status on a number of major cable systems was precariously maintained through *ad hoc* extensions of the old deal.[9] All this, of course, raises the question of whether the logic of retransmission consent has played out in practice. A cynical summary might suggest not—arguing that retransmission consent serves only to threaten the reach of some broadcast channels (*e.g.*, ABC) while on a broader scale diverting broadcaster attention away from broadcast and toward, instead, the development of (often second-rate) cable properties like America's Talking, ESPN2, and FX. If the purpose of retransmission consent was to bolster the broadcast market by ensuring broadcasters their share of cable revenues, is it fair to say that retransmission consent has backfired?

The must-carry provisions are in some ways the converse of the retransmission consent provision. Under must-carry, certain broadcasters can relinquish their rights to demand retransmission consent and instead insist that the local cable provider retransmit their broadcast signals at no charge. This is an option only for broadcasters in the local area covered by the cable system, the logic being that these broadcasters could be significantly harmed were the cable operator to decide not to retransmit their signals and instead to devote that channel capacity to other programming. Must-carry in these cases works to force that cable provider's hand; even if the cable provider does not want to retransmit these signals, under the must-carry provisions the signals must be carried.

To be more specific, the must-carry provisions apply to two types of broadcast channels: local commercial television stations including both network affili-

7. Joe Flint, "CBS Extends Retrans Deal," Daily Variety (August 10, 1994) at 5.
8. "Cable on the March," Variety (May 2, 1994) at 35; *see also* "ABC Avoided Cable Fight," Television Digest (Jan. 17, 1994) at 8.
9. *See, e.g.*, "Keeping Tabs on Retrans," Cable World (January 12, 2000) at 2; Linda Moss, "Charter, Hearst-Argyle Agree to Retrans Deal," Multichannel News (Jan. 31, 2000) at 6.

ates and independents, 47 U.S.C. §534(a), and noncommercial educational television stations, 47 U.S.C. §535(a). Cable operators are not required to carry all local commercial stations nor are they required to carry all noncommercial educational stations. Instead, sections 534(b) and 535(b) establish specific numeric requirements for commercial and educational channels, respectively, that are tied to the number of subscribers the cable system has and the maximum number of channels it is capable of delivering. Cable operators are of course free to carry more stations than this on a voluntary basis and, by FCC rule, stations carried under retransmission consent count toward the numeric requirements.[10] Section 534(b)(6) stipulates that any station carried in fulfillment of the must-carry provision for local commercial stations must be carried on the cable system at the same channel number on which the local commercial station is broadcast over the air unless the parties otherwise agree. Section 535(b)(5) establishes the same right for educational channels. Once every three years broadcasters must elect to either invoke the must-carry obligation or pursue fees under retransmission consent. 47 CFR §76.64(f).

The must-carry provisions have twice been considered by the Supreme Court. Opinions from both cases are excerpted below.

TURNER BROADCASTING SYSTEM, INC. v. FCC [*TURNER I*]
512 U.S. 622 (1994)

KENNEDY, J., announced the judgment of the Court and delivered the opinion for a unanimous Court with respect to Part I, the opinion of the Court with respect to Parts II-A and II-B, in which REHNQUIST, C.J., and BLACKMUN, O'CONNOR, SCALIA, SOUTER, THOMAS, and GINSBURG, JJ., joined, the opinion of the Court with respect to Parts II-C, II-D, and III-A, in which REHNQUIST, C.J., and BLACKMUN, STEVENS, and SOUTER, JJ., joined, and an opinion with respect to Part III-B, in which REHNQUIST, C.J., and BLACKMUN and SOUTER, JJ., joined. BLACKMUN, J., filed a concurring opinion. STEVENS, J., filed an opinion concurring in part and concurring in the judgment. O'CONNOR, J., filed an opinion concurring in part and dissenting in part, in which SCALIA and GINSBURG, JJ., joined, and in Parts I and III of which THOMAS, J., joined. GINSBURG, J., filed an opinion concurring in part and dissenting in part.

JUSTICE KENNEDY announced the judgment of the Court and delivered the opinion of the Court, except as to Part III-B.

Sections 4 and 5 of the Cable Television Consumer Protection and Competition Act of 1992 require cable television systems to devote a portion of their channels to the transmission of local broadcast television stations. This case presents the question whether these provisions abridge the freedom of speech or of the press, in violation of the First Amendment.

---

10. *See* Rules Implementing Must-Carry and Retransmission Consent Provisions of 1992 Cable Act Adopted, Report No. DC-2364, 1993 FCC LEXIS 1229, at *11 (March 11, 1993).

The United States District Court for the District of Columbia granted summary judgment for the United States, holding that the challenged provisions are consistent with the First Amendment. Because issues of material fact remain unresolved in the record as developed thus far, we vacate the District Court's judgment and remand the case for further proceedings.

I

B

Section 4 requires carriage of "local commercial television stations," defined to include all full power television broadcasters, other than those qualifying as "noncommercial educational" stations under §5, that operate within the same television market as the cable system. §4, 47 U.S.C. §§534(b)(1)(B), (h)(1)(A) (1988 ed., Supp. IV). Cable systems with more than 12 active channels, and more than 300 subscribers, are required to set aside up to one-third of their channels for commercial broadcast stations that request carriage. Cable systems with more than 300 subscribers, but only 12 or fewer active channels, must carry the signals of three commercial broadcast stations.[11]

If there are fewer broadcasters requesting carriage than slots made available under the Act, the cable operator is obligated to carry only those broadcasters who make the request. If, however, there are more requesting broadcast stations than slots available, the cable operator is permitted to choose which of these stations it will carry.[12] The broadcast signals carried under this provision must be transmitted on a continuous, uninterrupted basis and must be placed in the same numerical channel position as when broadcast over the air. Further, subject to a few exceptions, a cable operator may not charge a fee for carrying broadcast signals in fulfillment of its must-carry obligations.

Section 5 of the Act imposes similar requirements regarding the carriage of local public broadcast television stations, referred to in the Act as local "noncommercial educational television stations." 47 U.S.C. §535(a) (1988 ed., Supp. IV). A cable system with 12 or fewer channels must carry one of these stations; a system of between 13 and 36 channels must carry between one and three; and a system with more than 36 channels must carry each local public broadcast station requesting carriage. As with commercial broadcast stations, §5 requires

---

11. If there are not enough local full power commercial broadcast stations to fill the one-third allotment, a cable system with up to 35 active channels must carry one qualified low power station and an operator with more than 35 channels must carry two of them. *See* §534(c)(1); *see also* §534(h)(2) (defining "qualified low power station"). Low power television stations are small broadcast entities that transmit over a limited geographic range. They are licensed on a secondary basis and are permitted to operate only if they do not interfere with the signals of full power broadcast stations.

12. Cable systems are not required to carry the signal of any local commercial television station that "substantially duplicates" the signal of any other broadcast station carried on the system. §534(b)(5); *see also* In re Implementation of the Cable Television Consumer Protection and Competition Act of 1992 (Broadcast Signal Carriage Issues), No. 92-259, March 29, 1993, ¶19 (defining "substantial duplication" as a 50% overlap in programming). Nor are they required to carry the signals of more than one station affiliated with each national broadcast network. If the cable operator does choose to carry broadcast stations with duplicative programming, however, the system is credited with those stations for purposes of its must-carry obligations. §534(b)(5).

cable system operators to carry the program schedule of the public broadcast station in its entirety and at its same over-the-air channel position.

Taken together, therefore, §§4 and 5 subject all but the smallest cable systems nationwide to must-carry obligations, and confer must-carry privileges on all full power broadcasters operating within the same television market as a qualified cable system.

C

Congress enacted the 1992 Cable Act after conducting three years of hearings on the structure and operation of the cable television industry. The conclusions Congress drew from its fact-finding process are recited in the text of the Act itself. *See* §§2(a)(1)-(21). In brief, Congress found that the physical characteristics of cable transmission, compounded by the increasing concentration of economic power in the cable industry, are endangering the ability of over-the-air broadcast television stations to compete for a viewing audience and thus for necessary operating revenues. Congress determined that regulation of the market for video programming was necessary to correct this competitive imbalance.

In particular, Congress found that over 60 percent of the households with television sets subscribe to cable, §2(a)(3), and for these households cable has replaced over-the-air broadcast television as the primary provider of video programming. §2(a)(17). This is so, Congress found, because "most subscribers to cable television systems do not or cannot maintain antennas to receive broadcast television services, do not have input selector switches to convert from a cable to antenna reception system, or cannot otherwise receive broadcast television services." *Ibid.* In addition, Congress concluded that due to "local franchising requirements and the extraordinary expense of constructing more than one cable television system to serve a particular geographic area," the overwhelming majority of cable operators exercise a monopoly over cable service. §2(a)(2). "The result," Congress determined, "is undue market power for the cable operator as compared to that of consumers and video programmers." *Ibid.*

According to Congress, this market position gives cable operators the power and the incentive to harm broadcast competitors. The power derives from the cable operator's ability, as owner of the transmission facility, to "terminate the retransmission of the broadcast signal, refuse to carry new signals, or reposition a broadcast signal to a disadvantageous channel position." §2(a)(15). The incentive derives from the economic reality that "cable television systems and broadcast television stations increasingly compete for television advertising revenues." §2(a)(14). By refusing carriage of broadcasters' signals, cable operators, as a practical matter, can reduce the number of households that have access to the broadcasters' programming, and thereby capture advertising dollars that would otherwise go to broadcast stations. §2(a)(15).

Congress found, in addition, that increased vertical integration in the cable industry is making it even harder for broadcasters to secure carriage on cable systems, because cable operators have a financial incentive to favor their affiliated programmers. §2(a)(5). Congress also determined that the cable industry is characterized by horizontal concentration, with many cable operators sharing common ownership. This has resulted in greater "barriers to entry for new program-

mers and a reduction in the number of media voices available to consumers."
§2(a)(4).

In light of these technological and economic conditions, Congress concluded
that unless cable operators are required to carry local broadcast stations, "there
is a substantial likelihood that... additional local broadcast signals will be
deleted, repositioned, or not carried," §2(a)(15); the "marked shift in market
share" from broadcast to cable will continue to erode the advertising revenue
base which sustains free local broadcast television, §§2(a)(13)–(14); and that, as
a consequence, "the economic viability of free local broadcast television and its
ability to originate quality local programming will be seriously jeopardized."
§2(a)(16).

D

Appellants, plaintiffs below, are numerous cable programmers and cable op-
erators. Although the Government had not asked for summary judgment, the
District Court, in a divided opinion, granted summary judgment in favor of the
Government, ruling that the must-carry provisions are consistent with the First
Amendment. 819 F. Supp. 32 (D.D.C. 1993). This direct appeal followed.

II

There can be no disagreement on an initial premise: Cable programmers and
cable operators engage in and transmit speech, and they are entitled to the protection of the speech and press provisions of the First Amendment. Leathers v.
Medlock, 499 U.S. 439, 444 (1991). Through "original programming or by exercising editorial discretion over which stations or programs to include in its reper-
toire," cable programmers and operators "seek to communicate messages on a
wide variety of topics and in a wide variety of formats." Los Angeles v. Preferred
Communications, Inc., 476 U.S. 488, 494 (1986). By requiring cable systems to
set aside a portion of their channels for local broadcasters, the must-carry rules
regulate cable speech in two respects: The rules reduce the number of channels
over which cable operators exercise unfettered control, and they render it more
difficult for cable programmers to compete for carriage on the limited channels
remaining. Nevertheless, because not every interference with speech triggers the
same degree of scrutiny under the First Amendment, we must decide at the outset
the level of scrutiny applicable to the must-carry provisions.

A

We address first the Government's contention that regulation of cable television should be analyzed under the same First Amendment standard that applies
to regulation of broadcast television. It is true that our cases have permitted
more intrusive regulation of broadcast speakers than of speakers in other media.
Compare Red Lion Broadcasting Co. v. FCC, 395 U.S. 367 (1969) (television),
and National Broadcasting Co. v. United States, 319 U.S. 190 (1943) (radio),
with Miami Herald Publishing Co. v. Tornillo, 418 U.S. 241 (1974) (print), and
Riley v. National Federation of Blind of N.C., Inc., 487 U.S. 781 (1988) (personal solicitation). But the rationale for applying a less rigorous standard of First
Amendment scrutiny to broadcast regulation, whatever its validity in the cases
elaborating it, does not apply in the context of cable regulation.

The justification for our distinct approach to broadcast regulation rests upon the unique physical limitations of the broadcast medium. *See* FCC v. League of Women Voters of Cal., 468 U.S. 364, 377 (1984); *Red Lion, supra,* at 388–389, 396–399; *National Broadcasting Co.,* 319 U.S., at 226. As a general matter, there are more would-be broadcasters than frequencies available in the electromagnetic spectrum. And if two broadcasters were to attempt to transmit over the same frequency in the same locale, they would interfere with one another's signals, so that neither could be heard at all. *Id.,* at 212. The scarcity of broadcast frequencies thus required the establishment of some regulatory mechanism to divide the electromagnetic spectrum and assign specific frequencies to particular broadcasters. In addition, the inherent physical limitation on the number of speakers who may use the broadcast medium has been thought to require some adjustment in traditional First Amendment analysis to permit the Government to place limited content restraints, and impose certain affirmative obligations, on broadcast licensees. *Red Lion,* 395 U.S., at 390. As we said in *Red Lion,* "where there are substantially more individuals who want to broadcast than there are frequencies to allocate, it is idle to posit an unabridgeable First Amendment right to broadcast comparable to the right of every individual to speak, write, or publish." *Id.,* at 388.

Although courts and commentators have criticized the scarcity rationale since its inception, we have declined to question its continuing validity as support for our broadcast jurisprudence, *see* FCC v. League of Women Voters, *supra,* at 376, n. 11, and see no reason to do so here. The broadcast cases are inapposite in the present context because cable television does not suffer from the inherent limitations that characterize the broadcast medium. Indeed, given the rapid advances in fiber optics and digital compression technology, soon there may be no practical limitation on the number of speakers who may use the cable medium. Nor is there any danger of physical interference between two cable speakers attempting to share the same channel. In light of these fundamental technological differences between broadcast and cable transmission, application of the more relaxed standard of scrutiny adopted in *Red Lion* and the other broadcast cases is inapt when determining the First Amendment validity of cable regulation.

The Government and some appellees maintain that the must-carry provisions are nothing more than industry-specific antitrust legislation, and thus warrant rational basis scrutiny under this Court's "precedents governing legislative efforts to correct market failure in a market whose commodity is speech," such as Associated Press v. United States, 326 U.S. 1 (1945), and Lorain Journal Co. v. United States, 342 U.S. 143 (1951). *See* Brief for Federal Appellees 17. This contention is unavailing. *Associated Press* and *Lorain Journal* both involved actions against members of the press brought under the Sherman Antitrust Act, a law of general application. But while the enforcement of a generally applicable law may or may not be subject to heightened scrutiny under the First Amendment, *compare* Cohen v. Cowles Media Co., 501 U.S. 663, 670 (1991), *with* Barnes v. Glen Theatre, Inc., 501 U.S. 560, 566–567 (1991), laws that single out the press, or certain elements thereof, for special treatment "pose a particular danger of abuse by the State," Arkansas Writers' Project, Inc. v. Ragland, 481 U.S. 221, 228 (1987), and so are always subject to at least some degree of heightened First Amendment scrutiny. Because the must-carry provisions impose special obligations upon cable operators and special burdens upon cable programmers, some measure of heightened First Amendment scrutiny is demanded.

B

At the heart of the First Amendment lies the principle that each person should decide for him or herself the ideas and beliefs deserving of expression, consideration, and adherence. Our political system and cultural life rest upon this ideal. Government action that stifles speech on account of its message, or that requires the utterance of a particular message favored by the Government, contravenes this essential right. Laws of this sort pose the inherent risk that the Government seeks not to advance a legitimate regulatory goal, but to suppress unpopular ideas or information or manipulate the public debate through coercion rather than persuasion.

For these reasons, the First Amendment, subject only to narrow and well-understood exceptions, does not countenance governmental control over the content of messages expressed by private individuals. Our precedents thus apply the most exacting scrutiny to regulations that suppress, disadvantage, or impose differential burdens upon speech because of its content. Laws that compel speakers to utter or distribute speech bearing a particular message are subject to the same rigorous scrutiny. In contrast, regulations that are unrelated to the content of speech are subject to an intermediate level of scrutiny, because in most cases they pose a less substantial risk of excising certain ideas or viewpoints from the public dialogue.

Deciding whether a particular regulation is content based or content neutral is not always a simple task. We have said that the "principal inquiry in determining content neutrality . . . is whether the government has adopted a regulation of speech because of [agreement or] disagreement with the message it conveys." Ward v. Rock Against Racism, 491 U.S. 781, 791 (1989).

As a general rule, laws that by their terms distinguish favored speech from disfavored speech on the basis of the ideas or views expressed are content based. By contrast, laws that confer benefits or impose burdens on speech without reference to the ideas or views expressed are in most instances content neutral.

C

Insofar as they pertain to the carriage of full power broadcasters, the must-carry rules, on their face, impose burdens and confer benefits without reference to the content of speech.[13] Although the provisions interfere with cable opera-

---

13. The must-carry rules also require carriage, under certain limited circumstances, of low power broadcast stations. 47 U.S.C. §534(c). Under the Act, a low power station may become eligible for carriage only if, among other things, the FCC determines that the station's programming "would address local news and informational needs which are not being adequately served by full power television broadcast stations because of the geographic distance of such full power stations from the low power station's community of license." §534(h)(2)(B). We recognize that this aspect of §4 appears to single out certain low-power broadcasters for special benefits on the basis of content. Because the District Court did not address whether these particular provisions are content based, and because the parties make only the most glancing reference to the operation of, and justifications for, the low-power broadcast provisions, we think it prudent to allow the District Court to consider the content neutral or content based character of this provision in the first instance on remand.

In a similar vein, although a broadcast station's eligibility for must-carry is based upon its geographic proximity to a qualifying cable system, §534(h)(1)(C)(i), the Act permits the FCC to grant must-carry privileges upon request to otherwise ineligible broadcast stations.

462 TELECOMMUNICATIONS LAW AND POLICY

tors' editorial discretion by compelling them to offer carriage to a certain minimum number of broadcast stations, the extent of the interference does not depend upon the content of the cable operators' programming. The rules impose obligations upon all operators, save those with fewer than 300 subscribers, regardless of the programs or stations they now offer or have offered in the past. Nothing in the Act imposes a restriction, penalty, or burden by reason of the views, programs, or stations the cable operator has selected or will select. The number of channels a cable operator must set aside depends only on the operator's channel capacity; hence, an operator cannot avoid or mitigate its obligations under the Act by altering the programming it offers to subscribers. *Cf.* Miami Herald Publishing Co. v. Tornillo, 418 U.S., at 256–257 (newspaper may avoid access obligations by refraining from speech critical of political candidates).

The must-carry provisions also burden cable programmers by reducing the number of channels for which they can compete. But, again, this burden is unrelated to content, for it extends to all cable programmers irrespective of the programming they choose to offer viewers. And finally, the privileges conferred by the must-carry provisions are also unrelated to content. The rules benefit all full power broadcasters who request carriage — be they commercial or noncommercial, independent or network-affiliated, English or Spanish language, religious or secular. The aggregate effect of the rules is thus to make every full power commercial and noncommercial broadcaster eligible for must-carry, provided only that the broadcaster operates within the same television market as a cable system.

It is true that the must-carry provisions distinguish between speakers in the television programming market. But they do so based only upon the manner in which speakers transmit their messages to viewers, and not upon the messages they carry: Broadcasters, which transmit over the airwaves, are favored, while cable programmers, which do not, are disfavored. Cable operators, too, are burdened by the carriage obligations, but only because they control access to the cable conduit. So long as they are not a subtle means of exercising a content preference, speaker distinctions of this nature are not presumed invalid under the First Amendment.

That the must-carry provisions, on their face, do not burden or benefit speech of a particular content does not end the inquiry. Our cases have recognized that even a regulation neutral on its face may be content based if its manifest purpose is to regulate speech because of the message it conveys.

Our review of the Act and its various findings persuades us that Congress' overriding objective in enacting must-carry was not to favor programming of a particular subject matter, viewpoint, or format, but rather to preserve access to free television programming for the 40 percent of Americans without cable.

In acting upon these requests, the FCC is directed to give "attention to the value of localism" and, in particular, to whether the requesting station "provides news coverage of issues of concern to such community ... or coverage of sporting and other events of interest to the community." §534(h)(1)(C)(ii). Again, the District Court did not address this provision, but may do so on remand.

In unusually detailed statutory findings, *supra*, Congress explained that because cable systems and broadcast stations compete for local advertising revenue, §§2(a)(14)–(15), and because cable operators have a vested financial interest in favoring their affiliated programmers over broadcast stations, §2(a)(5), cable operators have a built-in "economic incentive...to delete, reposition, or not carry local broadcast signals." §2(a)(16). Congress concluded that absent a requirement that cable systems carry the signals of local broadcast stations, the continued availability of free local broadcast television would be threatened. *Ibid.* Congress sought to avoid the elimination of broadcast television because, in its words, "such programming is...free to those who own television sets and do not require cable transmission to receive broadcast television signals," §2(a)(12), and because "there is a substantial governmental interest in promoting the continued availability of such free television programming, especially for viewers who are unable to afford other means of receiving programming." *Ibid.*

By preventing cable operators from refusing carriage to broadcast television stations, the must-carry rules ensure that broadcast television stations will retain a large enough potential audience to earn necessary advertising revenue—or, in the case of noncommercial broadcasters, sufficient viewer contributions—to maintain their continued operation. In so doing, the provisions are designed to guarantee the survival of a medium that has become a vital part of the Nation's communication system, and to ensure that every individual with a television set can obtain access to free television programming.

The design and operation of the challenged provisions confirm that the purposes underlying the enactment of the must-carry scheme are unrelated to the content of speech. The rules, as mentioned, confer must-carry rights on all full power broadcasters, irrespective of the content of their programming. They do not require or prohibit the carriage of particular ideas or points of view. They do not penalize cable operators or programmers because of the content of their programming. They do not compel cable operators to affirm points of view with which they disagree. They do not produce any net decrease in the amount of available speech. And they leave cable operators free to carry whatever programming they wish on all channels not subject to must-carry requirements.

Appellants and Justice O'Connor make much of the fact that, in the course of describing the purposes behind the Act, Congress referred to the value of broadcast programming. In particular, Congress noted that broadcast television is "an important source of local news, public affairs programming, and other local broadcast services critical to an informed electorate," §2(a)(11), and that noncommercial television "provides educational and informational programming to the Nation's citizens." §2(a)(8). We do not think, however, that such references cast any material doubt on the content neutral character of must-carry. That Congress acknowledged the local orientation of broadcast programming and the role that noncommercial stations have played in educating the public does not indicate that Congress regarded broadcast programming as more valuable than cable programming. Rather, it reflects nothing more than the recognition that the services provided by broadcast television have some intrinsic value and, thus, are worth preserving against the threats posed by cable.

We likewise reject the suggestion, advanced by appellants and by Judge Williams in dissent, that the must-carry rules are content based because the preference for broadcast stations "automatically entails content requirements." 819 F. Supp., at 58. It is true that broadcast programming, unlike cable programming, is subject to certain limited content restraints imposed by statute and FCC regulation.[14] But it does not follow that Congress mandated cable carriage of broadcast television stations as a means of ensuring that particular programs will be shown, or not shown, on cable systems.

As an initial matter, the argument exaggerates the extent to which the FCC is permitted to intrude into matters affecting the content of broadcast programming. The FCC is forbidden by statute from engaging in "censorship" or from promulgating any regulation "which shall interfere with the broadcasters' right of free speech." 47 U.S.C. §326. In particular, the FCC's oversight responsibilities do not grant it the power to ordain any particular type of programming that must be offered by broadcast stations; for although "the Commission may inquire of licensees what they have done to determine the needs of the community they propose to serve, the Commission may not impose upon them its private notions of what the public ought to hear." Network Programming Inquiry, Report and Statement of Policy, 25 Fed. Reg. 7293 (1960).

Indeed, our cases have recognized that Government regulation over the content of broadcast programming must be narrow, and that broadcast licensees must retain abundant discretion over programming choices. See FCC v. League of Women Voters of Cal., 468 U.S., at 378–380, 386–392 (invalidating under the First Amendment statute forbidding any noncommercial educational station that receives a grant from the CPB to "engage in editorializing"); Columbia Broadcasting System, Inc. v. Democratic National Committee, 412 U.S. 94, 126 (1973) (describing "the risk of an enlargement of Government control over the content of broadcast discussion of public issues" as being of "critical importance" to the First Amendment). Thus, given the minimal extent to which the FCC and Congress actually influence the programming offered by broadcast stations, it would be difficult to conclude that Congress enacted must-carry in an effort to exercise content control over what subscribers view on cable television. In a regime where Congress or the FCC exercised more intrusive control over the content of broadcast programming, an argument similar to appellants' might carry greater weight. But in the present regulatory system, those concerns are without foundation.

D

Appellants advance three additional arguments to support their view that the must-carry provisions warrant strict scrutiny. In brief, appellants contend that

---

14. See, e.g., 47 U.S.C. §303b (1988 ed., Supp. IV) (directing FCC to consider extent to which license renewal applicant has "served the educational and informational needs of children"); Pub. L. 102-356, §16(a), 106 Stat. 954, note following 47 U.S.C. §303 (1988 ed., Supp. IV) (restrictions on indecent programming); 47 U.S.C. §312(a)(7) (allowing FCC to revoke broadcast license for willful or repeated failure to allow reasonable access to broadcast airtime for candidates seeking federal elective office); 47 CFR §73.1920 (1993) (requiring broadcaster to notify victims of on-air personal attacks and to provide victims with opportunity to respond over the air); En Banc Programming Inquiry, 44 FCC 2d 2303, 2312 (1960) (requiring broadcasters to air programming that serves "the public interest, convenience or necessity").

the provisions (1) compel speech by cable operators, (2) favor broadcast programmers over cable programmers, and (3) single out certain members of the press for disfavored treatment. None of these arguments suffices to require strict scrutiny in the present case.

1

Appellants maintain that the must-carry provisions trigger strict scrutiny because they compel cable operators to transmit speech not of their choosing. Relying principally on Miami Herald Publishing Co. v. Tornillo, 418 U.S. 241 (1974), appellants say this intrusion on the editorial control of cable operators amounts to forced speech which, if not per se invalid, can be justified only if narrowly tailored to a compelling government interest.

The same principles invoked in *Tornillo* led us to invalidate a similar content based access regulation in Pacific Gas & Elec. Co. v. Public Util. Comm'n of Cal., 475 U.S. 1 (1986). At issue was a rule requiring a privately owned utility, on a quarterly basis, to include with its monthly bills an editorial newsletter published by a consumer group critical of the utility's ratemaking practices. Although the access requirement applicable to the utility, unlike the statutory mechanism in *Tornillo*, was not triggered by speech of any particular content, the plurality held that the same strict First Amendment scrutiny applied. Like the statute in *Tornillo*, the regulation conferred benefits to speakers based on viewpoint, giving access only to a consumer group opposing the utility's practices. The plurality observed that in order to avoid the appearance that it agreed with the group's views, the utility would "feel compelled to respond to arguments and allegations made by the group in its messages to the utility's customers." *Id.*, at 16. This "kind of forced response," the plurality explained, "is antithetical to the free discussion that the First Amendment seeks to foster." *Ibid*.

Tornillo and *Pacific Gas & Electric* do not control this case for the following reasons. First, unlike the access rules struck down in those cases, the must-carry rules are content neutral in application. They are not activated by any particular message spoken by cable operators and thus exact no content based penalty. Likewise, they do not grant access to broadcasters on the ground that the content of broadcast programming will counterbalance the messages of cable operators.

Second, appellants do not suggest, nor do we think it the case, that must-carry will force cable operators to alter their own messages to respond to the broadcast programming they are required to carry. Given cable's long history of serving as a conduit for broadcast signals, there appears little risk that cable viewers would assume that the broadcast stations carried on a cable system convey ideas or messages endorsed by the cable operator.

Finally, the asserted analogy to *Tornillo* ignores an important technological difference between newspapers and cable television. Although a daily newspaper and a cable operator both may enjoy monopoly status in a given locale, the cable operator exercises far greater control over access to the relevant medium. A daily newspaper, no matter how secure its local monopoly, does not possess the power to obstruct readers' access to other competing publications—whether they be weekly local newspapers, or daily newspapers published in other cities. Thus, when a newspaper asserts exclusive control over its own news copy, it does not thereby prevent other newspapers from being distributed to willing recipients in the same locale.

The same is not true of cable. When an individual subscribes to cable, the physical connection between the television set and the cable network gives the cable operator bottleneck, or gatekeeper, control over most (if not all) of the television programming that is channeled into the subscriber's home. Hence, simply by virtue of its ownership of the essential pathway for cable speech, a cable operator can prevent its subscribers from obtaining access to programming it chooses to exclude. A cable operator, unlike speakers in other media, can thus silence the voice of competing speakers with a mere flick of the switch.[15]

The potential for abuse of this private power over a central avenue of communication cannot be overlooked. The First Amendment's command that government not impede the freedom of speech does not disable the government from taking steps to ensure that private interests not restrict, through physical control of a critical pathway of communication, the free flow of information and ideas.

2

Second, appellants urge us to apply strict scrutiny because the must-carry provisions favor one set of speakers (broadcast programmers) over another (cable programmers). Appellants maintain that as a consequence of this speaker preference, some cable programmers who would have secured carriage in the absence of must-carry may now be dropped. Relying on language in Buckley v. Valeo, 424 U.S. 1 (1976), appellants contend that such a regulation is presumed invalid under the First Amendment because the government may not "restrict the speech of some elements of our society in order to enhance the relative voice of others." Id., at 48–49.

At issue in *Buckley* was a federal law prohibiting individuals from spending more than $1,000 per year to support or oppose a particular political candidate. The Government justified the law as a means of "equalizing the relative ability of individuals and groups to influence the outcome of elections." *Buckley*, 424 U.S., at 48. We rejected that argument with the observation that Congress may not "abridge the rights of some persons to engage in political expression in order to enhance the relative voice of other segments of our society." *Id.*, at 49, n. 55.

Our holding in *Buckley* does not support appellants' broad assertion that all speaker-partial laws are presumed invalid. Rather, it stands for the proposition that speaker-based laws demand strict scrutiny when they reflect the Government's preference for the substance of what the favored speakers have to say (or aversion to what the disfavored speakers have to say). *Buckley* thus stands for the proposition that laws favoring some speakers over others demand strict scrutiny when the legislature's speaker preference reflects a content preference.

The question here is whether Congress preferred broadcasters over cable programmers based on the content of programming each group offers. The answer, as we explained above, is no.

---

15. As one commentator has observed: "The central dilemma of cable is that it has unlimited capacity to accommodate as much diversity and as many publishers as print, yet all of the producers and publishers use the same physical plant.... If the cable system is itself a publisher, it may restrict the circumstances under which it allows others also to use its system." I. de Sola Pool, TECHNOLOGIES OF FREEDOM 168 (1983).

3

Finally, appellants maintain that strict scrutiny applies because the must-carry provisions single out certain members of the press—here, cable operators—for disfavored treatment. In support, appellants point out that Congress has required cable operators to provide carriage to broadcast stations, but has not imposed like burdens on analogous video delivery systems, such as multi-channel multipoint distribution (MMDS) systems and satellite master antenna television (SMATV) systems. Relying upon our precedents invalidating discriminatory taxation of the press, *see, e.g.,* Arkansas Writers' Project, Inc. v. Ragland, 481 U.S. 221 (1987); Minneapolis Star & Tribune Co. v. Minnesota Comm'r of Revenue, 460 U.S. 575 (1983), appellants contend that this sort of differential treatment poses a particular danger of abuse by the government and should be presumed invalid. But such heightened scrutiny is unwarranted when the differential treatment is justified by some special characteristic of the particular medium being regulated. *Ibid.*

The must-carry provisions, as we have explained above, are justified by special characteristics of the cable medium: the bottleneck monopoly power exercised by cable operators and the dangers this power poses to the viability of broadcast television. Appellants do not argue, nor does it appear, that other media—in particular, media that transmit video programming such as MMDS and SMATV—are subject to bottleneck monopoly control, or pose a demonstrable threat to the survival of broadcast television. It should come as no surprise, then, that Congress decided to impose the must-carry obligations upon cable operators only.

In addition, the must-carry provisions are not structured in a manner that carries the inherent risk of undermining First Amendment interests. The regulations are broad-based, applying to almost all cable systems in the country, rather than just a select few. *See* 47 U.S.C. §534(b)(1) (1988 ed., Supp. IV) (only cable systems with fewer than 300 subscribers exempted from must-carry). As a result, the provisions do not pose the same dangers of suppression and manipulation that were posed by the more narrowly targeted regulations in *Minneapolis Star* and *Arkansas Writers' Project*.

III

A

In sum, the must-carry provisions do not pose such inherent dangers to free expression, or present such potential for censorship or manipulation, as to justify application of the most exacting level of First Amendment scrutiny. We agree with the District Court that the appropriate standard by which to evaluate the constitutionality of must-carry is the intermediate level of scrutiny applicable to content neutral restrictions that impose an incidental burden on speech. *See* Ward v. Rock Against Racism, 491 U.S. 781 (1989); United States v. O'Brien, 391 U.S. 367 (1968).

B

That the Government's asserted interests are important in the abstract does not mean that the must-carry rules will in fact advance those interests. When the

Government defends a regulation on speech as a means to redress past harms or prevent anticipated harms, it must do more than simply "posit the existence of the disease sought to be cured." Quincy Cable TV, Inc. v. FCC, 768 F.2d 1434, 1455 (CADC 1985). It must demonstrate that the recited harms are real, not merely conjectural, and that the regulation will in fact alleviate these harms in a direct and material way.

Thus, in applying *O'Brien* scrutiny we must ask first whether the Government has adequately shown that the economic health of local broadcasting is in genuine jeopardy and in need of the protections afforded by must-carry. Assuming an affirmative answer to the foregoing question, the Government still bears the burden of showing that the remedy it has adopted does not "burden substantially more speech than is necessary to further the government's legitimate interests." *Ward*, 491 U.S., at 799. On the state of the record developed thus far, and in the absence of findings of fact from the District Court, we are unable to conclude that the Government has satisfied either inquiry.

Because of the unresolved factual questions, the importance of the issues to the broadcast and cable industries, and the conflicting conclusions that the parties contend are to be drawn from the statistics and other evidence presented, we think it necessary to permit the parties to develop a more thorough factual record, and to allow the District Court to resolve any factual disputes remaining, before passing upon the constitutional validity of the challenged provisions.

[Concurring opinion of JUSTICE BLACKMUN is omitted.]

JUSTICE STEVENS, concurring in part and concurring in the judgment.

While I agree with most of Justice Kennedy's reasoning, and join Parts I, II(C), II(D), and III(A) of his opinion, I part ways with him on the appropriate disposition of this case. In my view the District Court's judgment sustaining the must-carry provisions should be affirmed.

An industry need not be in its death throes before Congress may act to protect it from economic harm threatened by a monopoly. The mandatory access mechanism that Congress fashioned in §§4 and 5 of the 1992 Act is a simple and direct means of dealing with the dangers posed by cable operators' exclusive control of what is fast becoming the preeminent means of transferring video signals to homes. The must-carry mechanism is analogous to the relief that might be appropriate for a threatened violation of the antitrust laws; one need only refer to undisputed facts concerning the structure of the cable and broadcast industries to agree that that threat is at least plausible. Moreover, Congress did not have to find that all broadcasters were at risk before acting to protect vulnerable ones, for the interest in preserving access to free television is valid throughout the Nation. Indeed, the Act is well tailored to assist those broadcasters who are most in jeopardy. Because thriving commercial broadcasters will likely avail themselves of the remunerative "retransmission consent" procedure of §6, those broadcasters who gain access via the §4 must-carry route are apt to be the most economically vulnerable ones. Precisely how often broadcasters will secure carriage through §6 rather than §4 will depend upon future developments; the very unpredictability of this and other effects of the new regulatory scheme militates in favor of allowing the scheme to proceed rather than requiring a perfectly documented or entirely complete *ex ante* justification.

It is thus my view that we should affirm the judgment of the District Court. Were I to vote to affirm, however, no disposition of this appeal would command the support of a majority of the Court. An accommodation is therefore necessary. Accordingly, because I am in substantial agreement with Justice Kennedy's analysis of the case, I concur in the judgment vacating and remanding for further proceedings.

JUSTICE O'CONNOR, with whom JUSTICE SCALIA and JUSTICE GINS-BURG join, and with whom JUSTICE THOMAS joins as to Parts I and III, concurring in part and dissenting in part.

I

A

The 1992 Cable Act implicates the First Amendment rights of two classes of speakers. First, it tells cable operators which programmers they must carry, and keeps cable operators from carrying others that they might prefer. Though cable operators do not actually originate most of the programming they show, the Court correctly holds that they are, for First Amendment purposes, speakers. Selecting which speech to retransmit is, as we know from the example of publishing houses, movie theaters, bookstores, and Reader's Digest, no less communication than is creating the speech in the first place.

Second, the Act deprives a certain class of video programmers—those who operate cable channels rather than broadcast stations—of access to over one-third of an entire medium. Cable programmers may compete only for those channels that are not set aside by the must-carry provisions. A cable programmer that might otherwise have been carried may well be denied access in favor of a broadcaster that is less appealing to the viewers but is favored by the must-carry rules. It is as if the government ordered all movie theaters to reserve at least one-third of their screening for films made by American production companies, or required all bookstores to devote one-third of their shelf space to nonprofit publishers. As the Court explains in Parts I, II-A, and II-B of its opinion, which I join, cable programmers and operators stand in the same position under the First Amendment as do the more traditional media.

Under the First Amendment, it is normally not within the government's power to decide who may speak and who may not, at least on private property or in traditional public fora. I agree with the Court that some speaker-based restrictions—those genuinely justified without reference to content—need not be subject to strict scrutiny. But looking at the statute at issue, I cannot avoid the conclusion that its preference for broadcasters over cable programmers is justified with reference to content. The findings, enacted by Congress as §2 of the Act, and which I must assume state the justifications for the law, make this clear. "There is a substantial governmental and First Amendment interest in promoting a diversity of views provided through multiple technology media." §2(a)(6). "Public television provides educational and informational programming to the Nation's citizens, thereby advancing the Government's compelling interest in educating its citizens." §2(a)(8)(A). "A primary objective and benefit of our Nation's system of regulation of television broadcasting is the local origination of programming. There is a substantial governmental interest in ensuring its continuation." §2(a)(10). "Broadcast television stations continue to be an important source of local news and public affairs programming and other local broadcast services critical to an informed electorate." §2(a)(11).

Similar justifications are reflected in the operative provisions of the Act. In determining whether a broadcast station should be eligible for must-carry in a particular market, the FCC must "afford particular attention to the value of localism by taking into account such factors as...whether any other eligible station provides news coverage of issues of concern to such community or provides carriage or coverage of sporting and other events of interest to the community." §4. In determining whether a low-power station is eligible for must-carry, the FCC must ask whether the station "would address local news and informational needs which are not being adequately served by full power television broadcast stations." §4. Moreover, the Act distinguishes between commercial television stations and noncommercial educational television stations, giving special benefits to the latter. *Compare* §4 *with* §5.

Preferences for diversity of viewpoints, for localism, for educational programming, and for news and public affairs all make reference to content. They may not reflect hostility to particular points of view, or a desire to suppress certain subjects because they are controversial or offensive. They may be quite benignly motivated. But benign motivation, we have consistently held, is not enough to avoid the need for strict scrutiny of content based justifications. The First Amendment does more than just bar government from intentionally suppressing speech of which it disapproves. It also generally prohibits the government from excepting certain kinds of speech from regulation because it thinks the speech is especially valuable.

This is why the Court is mistaken in concluding that the interest in diversity—in "access to a multiplicity" of "diverse and antagonistic sources,"—is content neutral. Indeed, the interest is not "related to the suppression of free expression," but that is not enough for content neutrality. The interest in giving a tax break to religious, sports, or professional magazines, *see Arkansas Writers' Project, supra*, is not related to the suppression of speech; the interest in giving labor picketers an exemption from a general picketing ban, *see* Carey v. Brown, 447 U.S. 455 (1980), is not related to the suppression of speech. But they are both related to the content of speech—to its communicative impact. The interest in ensuring access to a multiplicity of diverse and antagonistic sources of information, no matter how praiseworthy, is directly tied to the content of what the speakers will likely say.

B

The Court dismisses the findings quoted above by speculating that they do not reveal a preference for certain kinds of content; rather, the Court suggests, the findings show "nothing more than the recognition that the services provided by broadcast television have some intrinsic value and, thus, are worth preserving against the threats posed by cable." The controversial judgment at the heart of the statute is not that broadcast television has some value—obviously it does—

but that broadcasters should be preferred over cable programmers. The best explanation for the findings, it seems to me, is that they represent Congress' reasons for adopting this preference; and, according to the findings, these reasons rest in part on the content of broadcasters' speech.

It may well be that Congress also had other, content neutral, purposes in mind when enacting the statute. But we have never held that the presence of a permissible justification lessens the impropriety of relying in part on an impermissible justification. In fact, we have often struck down statutes as being impermissibly content based even though their primary purpose was indubitably content neutral. When a content based justification appears on the statute's face, we cannot ignore it because another, content neutral justification is present.

C

Content based speech restrictions are generally unconstitutional unless they are narrowly tailored to a compelling state interest. This is an exacting test. It is not enough that the goals of the law be legitimate, or reasonable, or even praiseworthy. There must be some pressing public necessity, some essential value that has to be preserved; and even then the law must restrict as little speech as possible to serve the goal.

The interest in localism, either in the dissemination of opinions held by the listeners' neighbors or in the reporting of events that have to do with the local community, cannot be described as "compelling" for the purposes of the compelling state interest test. It is a legitimate interest, perhaps even an important one—certainly the government can foster it by, for instance, providing subsidies from the public fisc—but it does not rise to the level necessary to justify content based speech restrictions. It is for private speakers and listeners, not for the government, to decide what fraction of their news and entertainment ought to be of a local character and what fraction ought to be of a national (or international) one. And the same is true of the interest in diversity of viewpoints: While the government may subsidize speakers that it thinks provide novel points of view, it may not restrict other speakers on the theory that what they say is more conventional.

The interests in public affairs programming and educational programming seem somewhat weightier, though it is a difficult question whether they are compelling enough to justify restricting other sorts of speech. We have never held that the Government could impose educational content requirements on, say, newsstands, bookstores, or movie theaters; and it is not clear that such requirements would in any event appreciably further the goals of public education.

But even assuming arguendo that the Government could set some channels aside for educational or news programming, the Act is insufficiently tailored to this goal. To benefit the educational broadcasters, the Act burdens more than just the cable entertainment programmers. It equally burdens CNN, C-SPAN, the Discovery Channel, the New Inspirational Network, and other channels with as much claim as PBS to being educational or related to public affairs. Even if the Government can restrict entertainment in order to benefit supposedly more valuable speech, I do not think the restriction can extend to other speech that is as valuable as the speech being benefited.

Finally, my conclusion that the must-carry rules are content based leads me to conclude that they are an impermissible restraint on the cable operators' editorial discretion as well as on the cable programmers' speech. For reasons related to the content of speech, the rules restrict the ability of cable operators to put on the programming they prefer, and require them to include programming they would rather avoid. This, it seems to me, puts this case squarely within the rule of *Pacific Gas & Electric Co.*, 475 U.S., at 14–15 (plurality); *id.*, at 23–24 (Marshall, J., concurring in judgment); *see also* Miami Herald Publishing Co. v. Tornillo, 418 U.S. 241, 257–258 (1974).

II

Even if I am mistaken about the must-carry provisions being content based, however, in my view they fail content neutral scrutiny as well. Assuming arguendo that the provisions are justified with reference to the content neutral interests in fair competition and preservation of free television, they nonetheless restrict too much speech that does not implicate these interests.

Sometimes, a cable system's choice to carry a cable programmer rather than a broadcaster may be motivated by anticompetitive impulses, or might lead to the broadcaster going out of business. That some speech within a broad category causes harm, however, does not justify restricting the whole category. If Congress wants to protect those stations that are in danger of going out of business, or bar cable operators from preferring programmers in which the operators have an ownership stake, it may do that. But it may not, in the course of advancing these interests, restrict cable operators and programmers in circumstances where neither of these interests is threatened.

The must-carry provisions are fatally overbroad, even under a content neutral analysis: They disadvantage cable programmers even if the operator has no anticompetitive motives, and even if the broadcaster that would have to be dropped to make room for the cable programmer would survive without cable access. None of the factfinding that the District Court is asked to do on remand will change this.

III

Having said all this, it is important to acknowledge one basic fact: The question is not whether there will be control over who gets to speak over cable — the question is who will have this control. Under the FCC's view, the answer is Congress, acting within relatively broad limits. Under my view, the answer is the cable operator. Most of the time, the cable operator's decision will be largely dictated by the preferences of the viewers; but because many cable operators are indeed monopolists, the viewers' preferences will not always prevail. Our recognition that cable operators are speakers is bottomed in large part on the very fact that the cable operator has editorial discretion.

I have no doubt that there is danger in having a single cable operator decide what millions of subscribers can or cannot watch. And I have no doubt that Congress can act to relieve this danger. In other provisions of the Act, Congress has already taken steps to foster competition among cable systems. Congress can encourage the creation of new media, such as inexpensive satellite broadcasting, or fiber-optic networks with virtually unlimited channels, or even simple devices that would let people easily switch from cable to over-the-air broadcasting. And of course Congress can subsidize broadcasters that it thinks provide especially valuable programming.

Congress may also be able to act in more mandatory ways. If Congress finds that cable operators are leaving some channels empty—perhaps for ease of future expansion—it can compel the operators to make the free channels available to programmers who otherwise would not get carriage. *See* PruneYard Shopping Center v. Robins, 447 U.S. 74, 88 (1980) (upholding a compelled access scheme because it did not burden others' speech). Congress might also conceivably obligate cable operators to act as common carriers for some of their channels, with those channels being open to all through some sort of lottery system or timesharing arrangement. Setting aside any possible Takings Clause issues, it stands to reason that if Congress may demand that telephone companies operate as common carriers, it can ask the same of cable companies; such an approach would not suffer from the defect of preferring one speaker to another.

But the First Amendment as we understand it today rests on the premise that it is government power, rather than private power, that is the main threat to free expression; and as a consequence, the Amendment imposes substantial limitations on the Government even when it is trying to serve concededly praiseworthy goals.

[Concurring and dissenting opinion of JUSTICE GINSBURG is omitted.]

Notes and Questions

1. Overlooked Elements? What explains the failure of the Court to acknowledge that (1) broadcast stations and cable systems compete in a wide variety of different local markets; (2) broadcast stations differ greatly in their ability to reach large numbers of viewers without the aid of cable transmission (especially in size of market and quality of over-the-air signal reception); and (3) cable operators may compete with commercial stations, but not with noncommercial stations, for advertising revenues?

2. Content Neutral? Precisely why do the majority and dissenting opinions differ on the key question of whether the must-carry provisions are content neutral? Are you convinced by the majority's argument that the content neutral criterion Congress used was "the manner in which speakers transmit their messages to viewers?" *Opinion of the Court*, Part II. C. The Act does not direct cable systems to carry all broadcasters or even a number of randomly selected broadcasters; only local broadcasters were selected for must-carry status. On the other hand, are the dissenting justices straining in finding a content based explanation for must-carry provisions that appear more plainly to rest on an economic premise: that cable operators control a facility to which their rival broadcast stations need access in order to compete?

3. Valuable Speech. The dissent argues that the "First Amendment does more than just bar government from intentionally suppressing speech of which it disapproves. It also generally prohibits the government from excepting certain kinds of speech from regulation because it thinks the speech is especially valuable." *Dissent*, Part I. A. Does the majority agree with this proposition? Does it explain why it is not applicable in this case?

4. Taxation by Regulation. In Part I. C, the dissent draws a distinction between forcing cable operators to carry stations under a must-carry regime and, instead, using tax revenues to pay cable operators to carry particular stations. Specifically, while strenuously objecting to the must-carry provisions, Justice O'Connor writes that the government could "certainly" foster its interest in the case by "providing subsidies from the public fisc." Is O'Connor's distinction a good one? Defensible? Do you see how this relates to our earlier discussion (in Chapter Six) of "taxation by regulation"? What would O'Connor say is the best way to encourage the development of children's television?

5. Why Must-Carry in Addition to Retransmission Consent? What is the policy rationale for giving local commercial television broadcast stations both a right to insist on retransmission consent and a right to must-carry status?[16] Is Justice Stevens correct that, once local TV stations are afforded retransmission consent rights, the sole or principal function of must-carry will be to protect those stations that are most "economically vulnerable"? If so, what is the public policy justification for mandating carriage of these not-so-successful stations instead of using that channel capacity for other programming? Does your answer to this question change if you assume that, in the absent of a must-carry obligation, the cable capacity at issue would be used for (a) C-SPAN versus (b) The Cartoon Network?

6. The Constitutional Status of Broadcast. The opinion of the Court may also be important for what it says about the constitutional status of content regulation of broadcasting. Part II. A seems to reaffirm the notion that broadcasters enjoy diminished protection under the First Amendment. (If this is the Court's intention, is it noteworthy that the defense of this notion seems rather sketchy and flimsy?) On the other hand, at the conclusion of Part II. C, the Court seems to portray television broadcasters as being legally protected against most forms of censorship. Might *Turner I*, as a whole, be read as a tentative first step toward re-ordering the First Amendment jurisprudence that applies to broadcast regulation?[17]

7. Round Two. Justice Blackmun retired the day after *Turner I* was handed down. Although *Turner II* technically raised questions not resolved in *Turner I*, it turned out that the only vote that mattered was that of Justice Breyer, Blackmun's replacement. With Breyer's decisive fifth vote, a majority upheld the law.

TURNER BROADCASTING SYSTEM, INC. v. FCC [*TURNER II*]
520 U.S. 180 (1997)

KENNEDY, J., announced the judgment of the Court and delivered the opinion of the Court, except as to a portion of Part II-A-1. REHNQUIST, C.J., and

---

16. Is there an answer to this question that accounts for the fact that Congress gave retransmission consent, but not must-carry, rights to radio stations?

17. Two examples: The Court's statement in Part II. C. that "the FCC's oversight responsibilities do not grant it the power to ordain any particular type of programming that must be offered by broadcast stations" is hard to square with the result in Red Lion Broadcasting Co. v. FCC, 395 U.S. 367 (1969), enforcing an FCC order that a radio station air a particular program—in that case a response to a "personal attack." Further, that same statement is at least in some tension with the premises underlying the present regulation of children's television (discussed in Chapter Six of this book).

STEVENS and SOUTER, JJ., joined that opinion in full, and BREYER, J., joined except insofar as Part II-A-1 relied on an anticompetitive rationale. STEVENS, J., filed a concurring opinion. BREYER, J., filed an opinion concurring in part. O'-CONNOR, J., filed a dissenting opinion, in which SCALIA, THOMAS, and GINSBURG, JJ., joined.

JUSTICE KENNEDY delivered the opinion of the Court, except as to a portion of Part II-A-1.

Sections 4 and 5 of the Cable Television Consumer Protection and Competition Act of 1992 require cable television systems to dedicate some of their channels to local broadcast television stations. Earlier in this case, we held the so-called "must-carry" provisions to be content neutral restrictions on speech, subject to intermediate First Amendment scrutiny under United States v. O'Brien, 391 U.S. 367, 377 (1968). A plurality of the Court considered the record as then developed insufficient to determine whether the provisions were narrowly tailored to further important governmental interests, and we remanded the case to the District Court for the District of Columbia for additional factfinding.[18]

On appeal from the District Court's grant of summary judgment for appellees, the case now presents the two questions left open during the first appeal: First, whether the record as it now stands supports Congress' predictive judgment that the must-carry provisions further important governmental interests; and second, whether the provisions do not burden substantially more speech than necessary to further those interests. We answer both questions in the affirmative, and conclude the must-carry provisions are consistent with the First Amendment.

II

We begin where the plurality ended in *Turner*, applying the standards for intermediate scrutiny enunciated in *O'Brien*. A content neutral regulation will be sustained under the First Amendment if it advances important governmental interests unrelated to the suppression of free speech and does not burden substantially more speech than necessary to further those interests. *O'Brien*, 391 U.S., at 377. As noted in *Turner*, must-carry was designed to serve "three interrelated interests: (1) preserving the benefits of free, over-the-air local broadcast television, (2) promoting the widespread dissemination of information from a multiplicity of sources, and (3) promoting fair competition in the market for television programming." 512 U.S., at 662. We decided then, and now reaffirm, that each of those is an important governmental interest. We have been most explicit in holding that "'protecting noncable households from loss of regular television broadcasting service due to competition from cable systems' is an important federal in-

---

18. [Ed. The following is taken from a subsequent passage in the text of the Court's opinion:] The District Court oversaw another 18 months of factual development on remand "yielding a record of tens of thousands of pages" of evidence, Turner Broadcasting v. FCC, 910 F. Supp. 734, 755 (DC 1995), comprised of materials acquired during Congress' three years of pre-enactment hearings, *see Turner, supra,* at 632–634, as well as additional expert submissions, sworn declarations and testimony, and industry documents obtained on remand. Upon consideration of the expanded record, a divided panel of the District Court again granted summary judgment to appellees. 910 F. Supp., at 751.

terest." *Id.*, at 663 (quoting Capital Cities Cable, Inc. v. Crisp, 467 U.S. 691, 714 (1984)). Forty percent of American households continue to rely on over-the-air signals for television programming. Despite the growing importance of cable television and alternative technologies, "'broadcasting is demonstrably a principal source of information and entertainment for a great part of the Nation's population.'" *Turner, supra*, at 663 (quoting United States v. Southwestern Cable Co., 392 U.S. 157, 177 (1968)). We have identified a corresponding "governmental purpose of the highest order" in ensuring public access to "a multiplicity of information sources," 512 U.S., at 663. And it is undisputed the Government has an interest in "eliminating restraints on fair competition, even when the individuals or entities subject to particular regulations are engaged in expressive activity protected by the First Amendment." *Ibid.*

The Congressional findings do not reflect concern that, absent must-carry, "a few voices," Tr. of Oral Arg. 23, would be lost from the television marketplace. In explicit factual findings, Congress expressed clear concern that the "marked shift in market share from broadcast television to cable television services," Cable Act §2(a)(13), resulting from increasing market penetration by cable services, as well as the expanding horizontal concentration and vertical integration of cable operators, combined to give cable systems the incentive and ability to delete, reposition, or decline carriage to local broadcasters in an attempt to favor affiliated cable programmers. §§2a(2)–(5), (15). Congress predicted that "absent the reimposition of [must-carry], additional local broadcast signals will be deleted, repositioned, or not carried," §2(a)(15); *see also*§2(a)(8)(D), with the end result that "the economic viability of free local broadcast television and its ability to originate quality local programming will be seriously jeopardized." §2(a)(16).

At the same time, Congress was under no illusion that there would be a complete disappearance of broadcast television nationwide in the absence of must-carry. Congress was concerned not that broadcast television would disappear in its entirety without must-carry, but that without it, "significant numbers of broadcast stations will be refused carriage on cable systems," and those "broadcast stations denied carriage will either deteriorate to a substantial degree or fail altogether." 512 U.S., at 666.

We have noted that "'it has long been a basic tenet of national communications policy that "the widest possible dissemination of information from diverse and antagonistic sources is essential to the welfare of the public."'" *Turner*, 512 U.S., at 663–664. "'Increasing the number of outlets for community self-expression'" represents a "'long-established regulatory goal in the field of television broadcasting.'" United States v. Midwest Video Corp., 406 U.S. 649, 667–668 (1972) (plurality opinion). Consistent with this objective, the Cable Act's findings reflect a concern that Congressional action was necessary to prevent "a reduction in the number of media voices available to consumers." §2(a)(4). Congress identified a specific interest in "ensuring the continuation" of "the local origination of broadcast programming," §2(a)(10), an interest consistent with its larger purpose of promoting multiple types of media, §2(a)(6), and found must-carry necessary "to serve the goals" of the original Communications Act of 1934 of "providing a fair, efficient, and equitable distribution of broadcast services," §2(a)(9). In short, Congress enacted must-carry to "preserve the existing structure of the Nation's broadcast television medium while permitting the concomitant expansion and development of cable television." 512 U.S., at 652.

Although Congress set no definite number of broadcast stations sufficient for these purposes, the Cable Act's requirement that all cable operators with more than 12 channels set aside one-third of their channel capacity for local broadcasters, §4, 47 U.S.C. §534(b)(1)(B), refutes the notion that Congress contemplated preserving only a bare minimum of stations. Congress' evident interest in "preserving the existing structure," 512 U.S., at 652, of the broadcast industry discloses a purpose to prevent any significant reduction in the multiplicity of broadcast programming sources available to noncable households. To the extent the appellants question the substantiality of the Government's interest in preserving something more than a minimum number of stations in each community, their position is meritless. It is for Congress to decide how much local broadcast television should be preserved for noncable households, and the validity of its determination "'does not turn on a judge's agreement with the responsible decisionmaker concerning' the degree to which the Government's interests should be promoted." *Ward*, 491 U.S., at 800.

The dissent proceeds on the assumption that must-carry is designed solely to be (and can only be justified as) a measure to protect broadcasters from cable operators' anticompetitive behavior. Federal policy, however, has long favored preserving a multiplicity of broadcast outlets regardless of whether the conduct that threatens it is motivated by anticompetitive animus or rises to the level of an antitrust violation. Broadcast television is an important source of information to many Americans. Though it is but one of many means for communication, by tradition and use for decades now it has been an essential part of the national discourse on subjects across the whole broad spectrum of speech, thought, and expression. Congress has an independent interest in preserving a multiplicity of broadcasters to ensure that all households have access to information and entertainment on an equal footing with those who subscribe to cable.

A

The expanded record permits us to consider whether the must-carry provisions were designed to address a real harm, and whether those provisions will alleviate it in a material way. We turn first to the harm or risk which prompted Congress to act. The Government's assertion that "the economic health of local broadcasting is in genuine jeopardy and in need of the protections afforded by must-carry," *id.*, at 664–665, rests on two component propositions: First, "significant numbers of broadcast stations will be refused carriage on cable systems" absent must-carry, *id.*, at 666. Second, "the broadcast stations denied carriage will either deteriorate to a substantial degree or fail altogether." *Ibid.*

1

We have no difficulty in finding a substantial basis to support Congress' conclusion that a real threat justified enactment of the must-carry provisions.

As to the evidence before Congress, there was specific support for its conclusion that cable operators had considerable and growing market power over local video programming markets. Cable served at least 60 percent of American households in 1992, and evidence indicated cable market penetration was projected to grow beyond 70 percent. As Congress noted, §2(a)(2), cable operators possess a local monopoly over cable households. Only one percent of communities are served by more than one cable system. Cable operators thus exercise "control over most (if not all) of the television programming that is channeled into the subscriber's home" and "can thus silence the voice of competing speakers with a mere flick of the switch." *Turner*, 512 U.S., at 656.

Evidence indicated the structure of the cable industry would give cable operators increasing ability and incentive to drop local broadcast stations from their systems, or reposition them to a less-viewed channel. Horizontal concentration was increasing as a small number of multiple system operators (MSO's) acquired large numbers of cable systems nationwide. The trend was accelerating, giving the MSO's increasing market power. In 1985, the 10 largest MSO's controlled cable systems serving slightly less than 42 percent of all cable subscribers; by 1989, the figure was nearly 54 percent.

Vertical integration in the industry also was increasing. As Congress was aware, many MSO's owned or had affiliation agreements with cable programmers. Evidence indicated that before 1984 cable operators had equity interests in 38 percent of cable programming networks. In the late 1980's, 64 percent of new cable programmers were held in vertical ownership. Extensive testimony indicated that cable operators would have an incentive to drop local broadcasters and to favor affiliated programmers.

After hearing years of testimony, and reviewing volumes of documentary evidence and studies offered by both sides, Congress concluded that the cable industry posed a threat to broadcast television. The Constitution gives to Congress the role of weighing conflicting evidence in the legislative process. Even when the resulting regulation touches on First Amendment concerns, we must give considerable deference, in examining the evidence, to Congress' findings and conclusions, including its findings and conclusions with respect to conflicting economic predictions. Furthermore, much of the testimony, though offered by interested parties, was supported by verifiable information and citation to independent sources.

In addition, evidence before Congress, supplemented on remand, indicated that cable systems would have incentives to drop local broadcasters in favor of other programmers less likely to compete with them for audience and advertisers. Independent local broadcasters tend to be the closest substitutes for cable programs, because their programming tends to be similar and because both primarily target the same type of advertiser: those interested in cheaper (and more frequent) ad spots than are typically available on network affiliates. The ability of broadcast stations to compete for advertising is greatly increased by cable carriage, which increases viewership substantially. With expanded viewership, broadcast presents a more competitive medium for television advertising. Empirical studies indicate that cable-carried broadcasters so enhance competition for advertising that even modest increases in the numbers of broadcast stations carried on cable are correlated with significant decreases in advertising revenue to cable systems. Empirical evidence also indicates that demand for premium cable services (such as pay-per-view) is reduced when a cable system carries more independent broadcasters. Thus, operators stand to benefit by dropping broadcast stations.

Cable systems also have more systemic reasons for seeking to disadvantage broadcast stations: Simply stated, cable has little interest in assisting, through carriage, a competing medium of communication. Evidence adduced on remand indicated cable systems have little incentive to carry, and a significant incentive to drop, broadcast stations that will only be strengthened by access to the 60% of the television market that cable typically controls. Congress could therefore reasonably conclude that cable systems would drop broadcasters in favor of programmers—even unaffiliated ones—less likely to compete with them for audience and advertisers. The cap on carriage of affiliates included in the Cable Act, 47 U.S.C. §533(f)(1)(B); 47 CFR §76.504) (1995), and relied on by the dissent, *post*, at 11, 25, is of limited utility in protecting broadcasters.

The dissent contends Congress could not reasonably conclude cable systems would engage in such predation because cable operators, whose primary source of revenue is subscriptions, would not risk dropping a widely viewed broadcast station in order to capture advertising revenues. *Post*, at 12. However, if viewers are faced with the choice of sacrificing a handful of broadcast stations to gain access to dozens of cable channels (plus network affiliates), it is likely they would still subscribe to cable even if they would prefer the dropped television stations to the cable programming that replaced them. Substantial evidence introduced on remand bears this out: With the exception of a handful of very popular broadcast stations (typically network affiliates), a cable system's choice between carrying a cable programmer or broadcast station has little or no effect on cable subscriptions, and subscribership thus typically does not bear on carriage decisions.

It was more than a theoretical possibility in 1992 that cable operators would take actions adverse to local broadcasters; indeed, significant numbers of broadcasters had already been dropped. The record before Congress contained extensive anecdotal evidence about scores of adverse carriage decisions against broadcast stations. Congress considered an FCC-sponsored study detailing cable system carriage practices. It indicated that in 1988, 280 out of 912 responding broadcast stations had been dropped or denied carriage in 1,533 instances. Even assuming that every station dropped or denied coverage responded to the survey, it would indicate that nearly a quarter (21 percent) of the approximately 1,356 broadcast stations then in existence had been denied carriage. The same study reported 869 of 4,303 reporting cable systems had denied carriage to 704 broadcast stations in 1,820 instances, and 279 of those stations had qualified for carriage under the prior must-carry rules. A contemporaneous study of public television stations indicated that in the vast majority of cases, dropped stations were not restored to the cable service.

Substantial evidence demonstrated that absent must-carry the already "serious," Senate Report, at 43, problem of noncarriage would grow worse because "additional local broadcast signals will be deleted, repositioned, or not carried," §2(a)(15). The record included anecdotal evidence showing the cable industry was acting with restraint in dropping broadcast stations in an effort to discourage reregulation. There was also substantial evidence that advertising revenue would be of increasing importance to cable operators as subscribership growth began to flatten, providing a steady, increasing incentive to deny carriage to local broadcasters in an effort to capture their advertising revenue. A contemporaneous FCC report noted that "cable operators' incentive to deny carriage...appears to be particularly great as against local broadcasters." Defendants' Joint Statement of Evidence Before Congress ¶155 (JSCR).

Additional evidence developed on remand supports the reasonableness of Congress' predictive judgment. Approximately 11 percent of local broadcasters were not carried on the typical cable system in 1989. The figure had grown to even more significant proportions by 1992. According to one of appellants' own experts, between 19 and 31 percent of all local broadcast stations, including network affiliates, were not carried by the typical cable system. Based on the same data, another expert concluded that 47 percent of local independent commercial stations, and 36 percent of noncommercial stations, were not carried by the typical cable system. The rate of noncarriage was even higher for new stations.

The dissent cites evidence indicating that many dropped broadcasters were stations few viewers watch, and it suggests that must-carry thwarts noncable viewers' preferences. Undoubtedly, viewers without cable—the immediate, though not sole, beneficiaries of efforts to preserve broadcast television—would have a strong preference for carriage of any broadcast program over any cable program, for the simple reason that it helps to preserve a medium to which they have access. The methodological flaws in the cited evidence are of concern. Even aside from that, the evidence overlooks that the broadcasters added by must-carry had ratings greater than or equal to the cable programs they replaced. (Indeed, in the vast majority of cases, cable systems were able to fulfill their must-carry obligations using spare channels, and did not displace cable programmers.) On average, even the lowest-rated station added pursuant to must-carry had ratings better than or equal to at least nine basic cable program services carried on the system. If cable systems refused to carry certain local broadcast stations because of their subscribers' preferences for the cable services carried in their place, one would expect that all cable programming services would have ratings exceeding those of broadcasters not carried. That is simply not the case.

The evidence on remand also indicated that the growth of cable systems' market power proceeded apace. By 1994, the 10 largest MSO's controlled 63 percent of cable systems, a figure projected to have risen to 85 percent by the end of 1996. MSO's began to gain control of as many cable systems in a given market as they could, in a trend known as "clustering." Cable systems looked increasingly to advertising (and especially local advertising) for revenue growth, and cable systems had increasing incentives to drop local broadcasters in favor of cable programmers (whether affiliated or not). The vertical integration of the cable industry also continued, so by 1994, MSO's serving about 70 percent of the Nation's cable subscribers held equity interests in cable programmers. The FTC study the dissent cites takes a skeptical view of the potential for cable systems to engage in anticompetitive behavior, but concedes the risk of anticompetitive carriage denials is "most plausible" when "the cable system's franchise area is large relative to the local area served by the affected broadcast station," Reply Comment of FTC, at 20, and when "a system's penetration rate is both high and relatively unresponsive to the system's carriage decisions," *id.*, at 18. That describes "precisely what is happening" as large cable operators expand their control over individual markets through clustering. Second Declaration of Tom Meek ¶35 (App.1867). As they do so, they are better able to sell their own reach to potential advertisers, and to limit the access of broadcast competitors by denying them access to all or substantially all the cable homes in the market area.

The issue before us is whether, given conflicting views of the probable development of the television industry, Congress had substantial evidence for making the judgment that it did. We need not put our imprimatur on Congress' economic theory in order to validate the reasonableness of its judgment.

2

The harm Congress feared was that stations dropped or denied carriage would be at a "serious risk of financial difficulty," 512 U.S., at 667, and would "deteriorate to a substantial degree or fail altogether." *Id.*, at 666. Congress had before it substantial evidence to support its conclusion. Congress was advised the viability of a broadcast station depends to a material extent on its ability to secure cable carriage. One broadcast industry executive explained it this way:

> "Simply put, a television station's audience size directly translates into revenue—large audiences attract larger revenues, through the sale of advertising time. If a station is not carried on cable, and thereby loses a substantial portion of its audience, it will lose revenue. With less revenue, the station can not serve its community as well. The station will have less money to invest in equipment and programming. The attractiveness of its programming will lessen, as will its audience. Revenues will continue to decline, and the cycle will repeat." Hearing on Competitive Issues, at 526–527 (statement of Gary Chapman) (App. 1600).

Considerable evidence, consisting of statements compiled from dozens of broadcasters who testified before Congress and the FCC, confirmed that broadcast stations had fallen into bankruptcy, curtailed their broadcast operations, and suffered serious reductions in operating revenues as a result of adverse carriage decisions by cable systems. The record also reflected substantial evidence that stations without cable carriage encountered severe difficulties obtaining financing for operations, reflecting the financial markets' judgment that the prospects are poor for broadcasters unable to secure carriage. Evidence before Congress suggested the potential adverse impact of losing carriage was increasing as the growth of clustering gave MSO's centralized control over more local markets. Congress thus had ample basis to conclude that attaining cable carriage would be of increasing importance to ensuring a station's viability. We hold Congress could conclude from the substantial body of evidence before it that "absent legislative action, the free local off-air broadcast system is endangered." Senate Report, at 42.

To be sure, the record also contains evidence to support a contrary conclusion. Appellants (and the dissent in the District Court) make much of the fact that the number of broadcast stations and their advertising revenue continued to grow during the period without must-carry, albeit at a diminished rate. Evidence introduced on remand indicated that only 31 broadcast stations actually went dark during the period without must-carry (one of which failed after a tornado destroyed its transmitter), and during the same period some 263 new stations signed on the air. New evidence appellants produced on remand indicates the average cable system voluntarily carried local broadcast stations accounting for about 97 percent of television ratings in noncable households. Appellants, as well as the dissent in the District Court, contend that in light of such evidence, it is clear "the must-carry law is not necessary to assure the economic viability of the broadcast system as a whole." NCTA Brief 18.

This assertion misapprehends the relevant inquiry. The question is not whether Congress, as an objective matter, was correct to determine must-carry is necessary to prevent a substantial number of broadcast stations from losing cable carriage and suffering significant financial hardship. Rather, the question is whether the legislative conclusion was reasonable and supported by substantial evidence in the record before Congress.

Although evidence of continuing growth in broadcast could have supported the opposite conclusion, a reasonable interpretation is that expansion in the cable industry was causing harm to broadcasting. Growth continued, but the rate of growth fell to a considerable extent during the period without must-carry (from 4.5 percent in 1986 to 1.7 percent by 1992), and appeared to be tapering off further. At the same time, "in an almost unprecedented development," 5 FCC Rcd, at 5041, ¶¶153–154, stations began to fail in increasing numbers. Broadcast advertising revenues declined in real terms by 11 percent between 1986 and 1991, during a period in which cable's real advertising revenues nearly doubled. While these phenomena could be thought to stem from factors quite separate from the increasing market power of cable (for example, a recession in 1990–1992), it was for Congress to determine the better explanation.

Despite the considerable evidence before Congress and adduced on remand indicating that the significant numbers of broadcast stations are at risk, the dissent believes yet more is required before Congress could act. It demands more information about which of the dropped broadcast stations still qualify for mandatory carriage, *post,* at 13; about the broadcast markets in which adverse decisions take place, *post,* at 14; and about the features of the markets in which bankrupt broadcast stations were located prior to their demise. *Post,* at 19. The level of detail in factfinding required by the dissent would be an improper burden for courts to impose on the Legislative Branch.

We think it apparent must-carry serves the Government's interests "in a direct and effective way." *Ward,* 491 U.S., at 800. Must-carry ensures that a number of local broadcasters retain cable carriage, with the concomitant audience access and advertising revenues needed to support a multiplicity of stations. Appellants contend that even were this so, must-carry is broader than necessary to accomplish its goals. We turn to this question.

B

The second portion of the *O'Brien* inquiry concerns the fit between the asserted interests and the means chosen to advance them. Content neutral regulations do not pose the same "inherent dangers to free expression," *Turner, supra,* at 661, that content based regulations do, and thus are subject to a less rigorous analysis, which affords the Government latitude in designing a regulatory solution. Under intermediate scrutiny, the Government may employ the means of its choosing "'so long as the...regulation promotes a substantial governmental interest that would be achieved less effectively absent the regulation,'" and does not "'burden substantially more speech than is necessary to further'" that interest. *Turner, supra,* at 662 (quoting *Ward, supra,* at 799).

The must-carry provisions have the potential to interfere with protected speech in two ways. First, the provisions restrain cable operators' editorial discretion in creating programming packages by "reducing the number of channels over which they exercise unfettered control." *Turner,* 512 U.S., at 637. Second, the rules "render it more difficult for cable programmers to compete for carriage on the limited channels remaining." *Ibid.*

Appellants say the burden of must-carry is great, but the evidence adduced on remand indicates the actual effects are modest. Significant evidence indicates the vast majority of cable operators have not been affected in a significant manner by must-carry. Cable operators have been able to satisfy their must-carry obligations 87 percent of the time using previously unused channel capacity; 94.5 percent of the 11,628 cable systems nationwide have not had to drop any programming in order to fulfill their must-carry obligations; the remaining 5.5 percent have had to drop an average of only 1.22 services from their programming; and cable operators nationwide carry 99.8 percent of the programming they carried before enactment of must-carry. Appellees note that only 1.18 percent of the approximately 500,000 cable channels nationwide is devoted to channels added because of must-carry; weighted for subscribership, the figure is 2.4 percent. Appellees contend the burdens of must-carry will soon diminish as cable channel capacity increases, as is occurring nationwide.

We do not understand appellants to dispute in any fundamental way the accuracy of those figures, only their significance. They note national averages fail to account for greater crowding on certain (especially urban) cable systems and contend that half of all cable systems, serving two-thirds of all cable subscribers, have no available capacity. Appellants argue that the rate of growth in cable programming outstrips cable operators' creation of new channel space, that the rate of cable growth is lower than claimed, and that must-carry infringes First Amendment rights now irrespective of future growth. Finally, they say that regardless of the percentage of channels occupied, must-carry still represents "thousands of real and individual infringements of speech." Time Warner Brief 44.

While the parties' evidence is susceptible of varying interpretations, a few definite conclusions can be drawn about the burdens of must-carry. It is undisputed that broadcast stations gained carriage on 5,880 channels as a result of must-carry. While broadcast stations occupy another 30,006 cable channels nationwide, this carriage does not represent a significant First Amendment harm to either system operators or cable programmers because those stations were carried voluntarily before 1992, and even appellants represent that the vast majority of those channels would continue to be carried in the absence of any legal obligation to do so. The 5,880 channels occupied by added broadcasters represent the actual burden of the regulatory scheme. Appellants concede most of those stations would be dropped in the absence of must-carry so the figure approximates the benefits of must-carry as well.

Because the burden imposed by must-carry is congruent to the benefits it affords, we conclude must-carry is narrowly tailored to preserve a multiplicity of broadcast stations for the 40 percent of American households without cable. Congress took steps to confine the breadth and burden of the regulatory scheme. For example, the more popular stations (which appellants concede would be carried anyway) will likely opt to be paid for cable carriage under the "retransmission consent" provision of the Cable Act; those stations will nonetheless be counted towards systems' must-carry obligations. Congress exempted systems of 12 or fewer channels, and limited the must-carry obligation of larger systems to one-third of capacity; allowed cable operators discretion in choosing which competing and qualified signals would be carried; and permitted operators to carry public stations on unused public, educational, and governmental channels in some circumstances.

Appellants say the must-carry provisions are overbroad because they require carriage in some instances when the Government's interests are not implicated: the must-carry rules prohibit a cable system operator from dropping a broadcaster "even if the operator has no anticompetitive motives, and even if the broadcaster that would have to be dropped would survive without cable access." 512 U.S., at 683 (O'Connor, J., dissenting). We are not persuaded that either possibility is so prevalent that must-carry is substantially overbroad. As discussed *supra,* cable systems serving 70 percent of subscribers are vertically integrated with cable programmers, so anticompetitive motives may be implicated in a majority of systems' decisions not to carry broadcasters. It appears that no more than a few hundred of the 500,000 cable channels nationwide are occupied by network affiliates opting for must-carry, a number insufficient to render must-carry "substantially broader than necessary to achieve the government's interest." *Ward,* 491 U.S., at 800.

Our precedents establish that when evaluating a content neutral regulation which incidentally burdens speech, we will not invalidate the preferred remedial scheme because some alternative solution is marginally less intrusive on a speaker's First Amendment interests. "So long as the means chosen are not substantially broader than necessary to achieve the government's interest, the regulation will not be invalid simply because a court concludes that the government's interest could be adequately served by some less-speech-restrictive alternative." *Ward, supra,* at 800.

In any event, after careful examination of each of the alternatives suggested by appellants, we cannot conclude that any of them is an adequate alternative to must-carry for promoting the Government's legitimate interests. First among appellants' suggested alternatives is a proposal to revive a more limited set of must-carry rules, known as the "Century rules" after the 1987 court decision striking them down, *see* Century Communications Corp. v. FCC, 835 F.2d 292. Those rules included a minimum viewership standard for eligibility and limited the must-carry obligation to 25 percent of channel capacity. The parties agree only 14 percent of broadcasters added to cable systems under the Cable Act would be eligible for carriage under the Century rules. The Century rules, for the most part, would require carriage of the same stations a system would carry without statutory compulsion. While we acknowledge appellants' criticism of any rationale that more is better, the scheme in question does not place limitless must-carry obligations on cable system operators. In the final analysis this alternative represents nothing more than appellants' disagreement with the responsible decisionmaker concerning' the degree to which the Government's interests should be promoted. *Cf. Ward, supra,* at 800.

The second alternative appellants urge is the use of input selector or "A/B" switches, which, in combination with antennas, would permit viewers to switch between cable and broadcast input, allowing cable subscribers to watch broadcast programs not carried on cable. Congress examined the use of A/B switches as an alternative to must-carry and concluded it was "not an enduring or feasible method of distribution and...not in the public interest." §2(a)(18). The data showed that: many households lacked adequate antennas to receive broadcast signals; A/B switches suffered from technical flaws; viewers might be required to reset channel settings repeatedly in order to view both UHF and cable channels; and installation and use of the switch with other common video equipment (such as videocassette recorders) could be "cumbersome or impossible." Senate Report, at 45, and nn. 115–116; House Report, at 54, and nn. 60–61. Even the cable industry trade association (one of appellants here) determined that "the A/B switch is not a workable solution to the carriage problem." Senate Report, at 45, House Report, at 54. Congress also had before it "considerable evidence," including two empirical studies, that "it is rare" for cable subscribers ever to switch to receive an over-the-air signal, Senate Report, at 45; House Report, at 54, and n. 62.

Appellants also suggest a leased-access regime, under which both broadcasters and cable programmers would have equal access to cable channels at regulated rates. Because this alternative is aimed solely at addressing the bottleneck control of cable operators, it would not be as effective in achieving Congress' further goal of ensuring that significant programming remains available for the 40 percent of American households without cable. Indeed, unless the number of channels set aside for local broadcast stations were to decrease (sacrificing Congress' interest in preserving a multiplicity of broadcasters), additional channels would have to be set aside for cable programmers, further reducing the channels under the systems' control. Furthermore, Congress was specific in noting that requiring payment for cable carriage was inimical to the interests it was pursuing, because of the burden it would impose on small broadcasters.

Appellants next suggest a system of subsidies for financially weak stations. A system of subsidies would serve a very different purpose than must-carry. Must-carry is intended not to guarantee the financial health of all broadcasters, but to ensure a base number of broadcasters survive to provide service to noncable households. Must-carry is simpler to administer and less likely to involve the Government in making content based determinations about programming. The must-carry rules distinguish between categories of speakers based solely on the technology used to communicate. The rules acknowledge cable systems' expertise by according them discretion to determine which broadcasters to carry on reserved channels, and (within the Cable Act's strictures) allow them to choose broadcasters with a view to offering program choices appealing to local subscribers. Appellants' proposal would require the Government to develop other criteria for giving subsidies and to establish a potentially elaborate administrative structure to make subsidy determinations.

Appellants also suggest a system of antitrust enforcement or an administrative complaint procedure to protect broadcasters from cable operators' anticompetitive conduct. Congress could conclude, however, that the considerable expense and delay inherent in antitrust litigation, and the great disparities in wealth and sophistication between the average independent broadcast station and average cable system operator, would make these remedies inadequate substitutes for guaranteed carriage. The record suggests independent broadcasters simply are not in a position to engage in complex antitrust litigation, which involves extensive discovery, significant motions practice, appeals, and the payment of high legal fees throughout. An administrative complaint procedure, although less burdensome, would still require stations to incur considerable expense and delay before enforcing their rights.

III

Judgments about how competing economic interests are to be reconciled in the complex and fast-changing field of television are for Congress to make.

Those judgments "cannot be ignored or undervalued simply because appellants cast their claims under the umbrella of the First Amendment." Columbia Broadcasting v. Democratic National Committee, 412 U.S., at 103. The judgment of the District Court is affirmed.

[Concurring opinion of JUSTICE STEVENS is omitted.]

JUSTICE BREYER, concurring in part.

I join the opinion of the Court except insofar as Part II-A-1 relies on an anticompetitive rationale. My conclusion rests not upon the principal opinion's analysis of the statute's efforts to "promote fair competition," *see post*, at 3–4, 9–12, but rather upon its discussion of the statute's other objectives, namely "'(1) preserving the benefits of free, over-the-air local broadcast television,'" and "'(2) promoting the widespread dissemination of information from a multiplicity of sources.'" *Ante*, at 6 (quoting *Turner*, 512 U.S., at 662). Whether or not the statute does or does not sensibly compensate for some significant market defect, it undoubtedly seeks to provide over-the-air viewers who *lack* cable with a rich mix of over-the-air programming by guaranteeing the over-the-air stations that provide such programming with the extra dollars that an additional cable audience will generate. I believe that this purpose—to assure the over-the-air public "access to a multiplicity of information sources," *id.*, at 663—provides sufficient basis for rejecting appellants' First Amendment claim.

I do not deny that the compulsory carriage that creates the "guarantee" extracts a serious First Amendment price. It interferes with the protected interests of the cable operators to choose their own programming; it prevents displaced cable program providers from obtaining an audience; and it will sometimes prevent some cable viewers from watching what, in its absence, would have been their preferred set of programs. This "price" amounts to a "suppression of speech."

But there are important First Amendment interests on the other side as well. The statute's basic noneconomic purpose is to prevent too precipitous a decline in the quality and quantity of programming choice for an ever-shrinking non-cable-subscribing segment of the public. This purpose reflects what "has long been a basic tenet of national communications policy," namely that "the widest possible dissemination of information from diverse and antagonistic sources is essential to the welfare of the public." *Turner*, *supra*, at 663 (internal quotations omitted). That policy, in turn, seeks to facilitate the public discussion and informed deliberation, which, as Justice Brandeis pointed out many years ago, democratic government presupposes and the First Amendment seeks to achieve. Whitney v. California, 274 U.S. 357, 375–376 (1927) (Brandeis, J., concurring). See also New York Times Co. v. Sullivan, 376 U.S. 254, 270 (1964); Red Lion Broadcasting Co. v. FCC, 395 U.S. 367, 390 (1969).

With important First Amendment interests on both sides of the equation, the key question becomes one of proper fit. In particular, I note (and agree) that a cable system, physically dependent upon the availability of space along city streets, at present (perhaps less in the future) typically faces little competition, that it therefore constitutes a kind of bottleneck that controls the range of viewer choice (whether or not it uses any consequent economic power for economically predatory purposes), and that *some* degree — at least a limited degree — of governmental intervention and control through regulation can prove appropriate when justified under *O'Brien* (at least when not "content based"). I also agree that, without the statute, cable systems would likely carry significantly fewer over-the-air stations, that station revenues would therefore decline, and that the quality of over-the-air programming on such stations would almost inevitably suffer. I agree further that the burden the statute imposes upon the cable system, potential cable programmers, and cable viewers, is limited and will diminish as typical cable system capacity grows over time.

Finally, I believe that Congress could reasonably conclude that the statute will help the typical over-the-air viewer (by maintaining an expanded range of choice) more than it will hurt the typical cable subscriber (by restricting cable slots otherwise available for preferred programming). The latter's cable choices are many and varied, and the range of choice is rapidly increasing. The former's over-the-air choice is more restricted; and, as cable becomes more popular, it may well become still more restricted insofar as the over-the-air market shrinks and thereby, by itself, becomes less profitable. In these circumstances, I do not believe the First Amendment dictates a result that favors the cable viewers' interests.

These and other similar factors discussed by the majority lead me to agree that the statute survives "intermediate scrutiny," whether or not the statute is properly tailored to Congress' purely economic objectives.

JUSTICE O'CONNOR, with whom JUSTICE SCALIA, JUSTICE THOMAS, and JUSTICE GINSBURG join, dissenting.

In sustaining the must-carry provisions of the Cable Television Protection and Competition Act of 1992 (Cable Act) against a First Amendment challenge by cable system operators and cable programmers, the Court errs in two crucial respects. First, the Court disregards one of the principal defenses of the statute urged by appellees on remand: that it serves a substantial interest in preserving "diverse," "quality" programming that is "responsive" to the needs of the local community. The course of this litigation on remand and the proffered defense strongly reinforce my view that the Court adopted the wrong analytic framework in the prior phase of this case. Second, the Court misapplies the "intermediate scrutiny" framework it adopts. Although we owe deference to Congress' predictive judgments and its evaluation of complex economic questions, we have an independent duty to identify with care the Government interests supporting the scheme, to inquire into the reasonableness of congressional findings regarding its necessity, and to examine the fit between its goals and its consequences. The Court fails to discharge its duty here.

I

Perhaps because of the difficulty of defending the must-carry provisions as a measured response to anticompetitive behavior, the Court asserts an "independent" interest in preserving a "multiplicity" of broadcast programming sources. *Ante,* at 11; *ante,* at 1–3 (Breyer, J., concurring in part). In doing so, the Court posits existence of "conduct that threatens" the availability of broadcast television outlets, quite apart from anticompetitive conduct. *Ante,* at 11. We are left to wonder what precisely that conduct might be. Moreover, when separated from anticompetitive conduct, this interest in preserving a "multiplicity of broadcast programming sources" becomes poorly defined. Neither the principal opinion nor the partial concurrence offers any guidance on what might constitute a "significant reduction" in the availability of broadcast programming. The proper analysis, in my view, necessarily turns on the present *distribution* of broadcast stations among the local broadcast markets that make up the national broadcast "system." Whether cable poses a "significant" threat to a local broadcast market depends first on how many broadcast stations in that market will, in the absence of must-carry, remain available to viewers in noncable households. It also depends on whether viewers actually watch the stations that are dropped or denied carriage. The Court provides some raw data on adverse carriage decisions, but it never connects that data to markets and viewership. Instead, the Court proceeds from the assumptions that adverse carriage decisions nationwide will affect broadcast markets in proportion to their size; and that all broadcast programming is watched by viewers. Neither assumption is logical or has any factual basis in the record.

Appellees bear the burden of demonstrating that the provisions of the Cable Act restricting expressive activity survive constitutional scrutiny. As discussed below, the must-carry provisions cannot be justified as a narrowly tailored means of addressing anticompetitive behavior. As a result, the Court's inquiry into whether must-carry would prevent a "significant reduction in the multiplicity of broadcast programming sources" collapses into an analysis of an ill-defined and generalized interest in maintaining broadcast stations, wherever they might be threatened and whatever their viewership. Neither the principal opinion nor the partial concurrence ever explains what kind of conduct, apart from anticompetitive conduct, threatens the "multiplicity" of broadcast programming sources. Indeed, the only justification advanced by the parties for furthering this interest is heavily content based. It is undisputed that the broadcast stations protected by must-carry are the "marginal" stations within a given market; the record on remand reveals that any broader threat to the broadcast system was entirely mythical. Pressed to explain the importance of preserving noncable viewers' access to "vulnerable" broadcast stations, appellees emphasize that the must-carry rules are necessary to ensure that broadcast stations maintain "diverse," "quality" programming that is "responsive" to the needs of the local community. Brief for Federal Appellees 13, 30; see also *ante,* at 2 (Breyer, J., concurring in part) (justifying must-carry as a means of preventing a decline in "quality and quantity of programming choice"). Must-carry is thus justified as a way of preserving viewers' access to a Spanish or Chinese language station or of preventing an independent station from adopting a home-shopping format. Undoubtedly, such goals are reasonable and important, and the stations in question may well be worthwhile targets of Government subsidies. But appellees' characterization of must-carry as a means of protecting these stations, like the Court's explicit concern for promoting "'community self-expression'" and the "'local origination of broadcast programming,'" reveals a content based preference for broadcast programming. This justification of the regulatory scheme is, in my view, wholly at odds with the *Turner* Court's premise that must-carry is a means of preserving "access to free television programming—*whatever its content,*" 512 U.S., at 649 (emphasis added).

I do not read Justice Breyer's opinion—which analyzes the must-carry rules in part as a "speech-enhancing" measure designed to ensure a "rich mix" of over-the-air programming—to treat the content of over-the-air programming as irrelevant to whether the Government's interest in promoting it is an important one. The net result appears to be that five Justices of this Court do not view must-carry as a narrowly tailored means of serving a substantial governmental interest in preventing anticompetitive behavior; and that five Justices of this Court do see the significance of the content of over-the-air programming to the Government's and appellees' efforts to defend the law. Under these circumstances, the must-carry provisions should be subject to strict scrutiny, which they surely fail.

II

The principal opinion goes to great lengths to avoid acknowledging that preferences for "quality," "diverse," and "responsive" local programming underlie the must-carry scheme, although the partial concurrence's reliance on such preferences is explicit. I take the principal opinion at its word and evaluate the claim that the threat of anticompetitive behavior by cable operators supplies a content neutral basis for sustaining the statute. It does not.

The *Turner* Court remanded the case for a determination whether the must-carry provisions satisfy intermediate scrutiny under United States v. O'Brien, 391 U.S. 367 (1968). Under that standard, appellees must demonstrate that the must-carry provisions (1) "furthe[r] an important or substantial government interest"; and (2) burden speech no more "than is essential to the furtherance of that interest." *Id.*, at 377; *see also* Ward v. Rock Against Racism, 491 U.S. 781, 799 (1989). The Turner plurality found that genuine issues of material fact remained as to both parts of the *O'Brien* analysis. On whether must-carry furthers a substantial governmental interest, the *Turner* Court remanded the case to test two essential and unproven propositions: "(1) that unless cable operators are compelled to carry broadcast stations, *significant numbers* of broadcast stations will be refused carriage on cable systems; and (2) that the broadcast stations denied carriage will either *deteriorate to a substantial degree or fail altogether*." 512 U.S., at 666 (emphasis added). As for whether must-carry restricts no more speech than essential to further Congress' asserted purpose, the *Turner* plurality found evidence lacking on the extent of the burden that the must-carry provisions would place on cable operators and cable programmers. *Id.*, at 667–668.

A

What was not resolved in *Turner* was whether "reasonable inferences based on substantial evidence," 512 U.S., at 666 (plurality opinion), supported Congress' judgment that the must-carry provisions were necessary "to prevent cable operators from exploiting their economic power to the detriment of broadcasters," *id.*, at 649. Because I remain convinced that the statute is not a measured response to congressional concerns about monopoly power, *see infra*, in my view the principal opinion's discussion on this point is irrelevant. But even if it were relevant, it is incorrect.

1

The *Turner* plurality recognized that Congress' interest in curtailing anticompetitive behavior is substantial "in the abstract." 512 U.S., at 664. The principal opinion now concludes that substantial evidence supports the congressional judgment that cable operators have incentives to engage in significant anticompetitive behavior. It appears to accept two related arguments on this point: first, that vertically integrated cable operators prefer programming produced by their affiliated cable programming networks to broadcast programming, *ante,* at 15–16, 17; and second, that potential advertising revenues supply cable system operators, whether affiliated with programmers or not, with incentives to prefer cable programming to broadcast programming. *Ante,* at 17–19.

To support the first proposition, the principal opinion states that "extensive testimony" before Congress showed that in fact operators do have incentives to favor vertically integrated programmers. *Ante,* at 15. This testimony, noteworthy as it may be, is primarily that of persons appearing before Congress on behalf of the private appellees in this case. Even accepting as reasonable Congress' conclusion that cable operators have incentives to favor affiliated programmers, Congress has already limited the number of channels on a cable system that can be occupied by affiliated programmers. 47 U.S.C. §533(f)(1)(B); 47 CFR §76.504 (1995). Once a cable system operator reaches that cap, it can no longer bump a broadcaster in favor of an affiliated programmer. If Congress were concerned that cable operators favored too many affiliated programmers, it could simply adjust the cap. Must-carry simply cannot be justified as a response to the allegedly "substantial" problem of vertical integration.

The second argument, that the quest for advertising revenue will supply cable operators with incentives to drop local broadcasters, takes two forms. First, some cable programmers offer blank slots within a program into which a cable operator can insert advertisements; appellees argue that "the opportunity to sell such advertising gives cable programmers an additional value to operators above broadcast stations...." Brief for Federal Appellees 24. But that "additional value" arises only because the must-carry provisions *require* cable operators to carry broadcast signals without alteration. 47 U.S.C. §534(b)(3). Judge Williams was correct in noting that the Government cannot have "a 'substantial interest' in remedying a competitive distortion that arises entirely out of a detail in its own purportedly remedial legislation." 910 F. Supp. 734, 777 (DC 1995) (Williams, J., dissenting). Second, appellees claim that since cable operators compete directly with broadcasters for some advertising revenue, operators will profit if they can drive broadcasters out of the market and capture their advertising revenue. There is no dispute that a cable system depends primarily upon its subscriber base for revenue. A cable operator is therefore unlikely to drop a widely viewed station in order to capture advertising revenues—which, according to the figures of appellees' expert, account for between one and five percent of the total revenues of most large cable systems. In doing so, it would risk losing subscribers. Nevertheless, appellees contend that cable operators will drop some broadcast stations in spite of, and not because of, viewer preferences. The principal opinion suggests that viewers are likely to subscribe to cable even though they prefer certain over-the-air programming to cable programming, because they would be willing to trade access to their preferred channel for access to dozens of cable channels. *Ante,* at 19. Even assuming that, at the margin, advertising revenues would drive cable systems to drop some stations—invariably described as "vulnerable" or "smaller" independents, *see* NAB Brief 22; Brief for Federal Appellees 25, and n. 14—the strategy's success would depend upon the additional untested premise that the advertising revenues freed by dropping a broadcast station will flow to cable operators rather than to *other* broadcasters.

2

Under the standard articulated by the *Turner* plurality, the conclusion that must-carry serves a substantial governmental interest depends upon the "essential propositio[n]" that, without must-carry, "significant numbers of broadcast stations will be refused carriage on cable systems." 512 U.S., at 666. In analyzing whether this undefined standard is satisfied, the Court focuses almost exclusively on raw numbers of stations denied carriage or "repositioned" — that is, shifted out of their traditional channel positions.

The Court begins its discussion of evidence of adverse carriage decisions with the 1988 study sponsored by the Federal Communications Commission. But in *Turner*, the plurality criticized this very study, noting that it did not indicate the time frame within which carriage denials occurred or whether the stations were later restored to their positions. 512 U.S., at 667. As for the evidence in the record before Congress, these gaps persist; the Court relies on a study of *public* television stations to support the proposition that "in the vast majority of cases, dropped stations were not restored to the cable service." *Ante,* at 20.

In canvassing the additional evidence offered on remand, the Court focuses on the suggestion of one of appellees' experts that the 1988 FCC survey underestimated the number of drops of broadcast stations in the non-must-carry era. The data do not indicate which of these stations would now qualify for mandatory carriage. Appellees' expert frames the relevant drop statistic as "subscriber instances" — that is, the number of drop instances multiplied by the number of cable subscribers affected. Two-thirds of the "subscriber instances" of drops existing as of mid-1992 remained uncured as of mid-1994, fully 19 months after the present must-carry rules went into effect. The Court discounts the importance of whether dropped stations now qualify for mandatory carriage, on the ground that requiring any such showing places an "improper burden" on the Legislative Branch. It seems obvious, however, that if the must-carry rules will not reverse those adverse carriage decisions on which appellees rely to illustrate the Government "interest" supporting the rules, then a significant question remains as to whether the rules in fact serve the articulated interest. Without some further analysis, I do not see how the Court can, in the course of its independent scrutiny on a question of constitutional law, deem Congress' judgment "reasonable."

In any event, the larger problem with the Court's approach is that neither the FCC study nor the additional evidence on remand canvassed by the Court says anything about the broadcast markets in which adverse carriage decisions take place. The Court accepts Congress' stated concern about preserving the availability of a "multiplicity" of broadcast stations, but apparently thinks it sufficient to evaluate that concern in the abstract, without considering how much local service is already available in a given broadcast market.

Nor can we evaluate whether must-carry is necessary to serve an interest in preserving broadcast stations without examining the value of the stations protected by the must-carry scheme to viewers in noncable households. By disregarding the distribution and viewership of stations not carried on cable, the Court upholds the must-carry provisions without addressing the interests of the over-the-air television viewers that Congress purportedly seeks to protect. The *only* analysis in the record of the relationship between carriage and noncable viewership favors the appellants. A 1991 study by Federal Trade Commission staff concluded that most cable systems voluntarily carried broadcast stations with any reportable ratings in noncable households and that most instances of noncarriage involved "relatively remote (and duplicated) network stations, or local stations that few viewers watch." App. 163.

Appellees—who bear the burden of proof in this case—offer no alternative measure of the viewership in noncable households of stations dropped or denied carriage. Instead, appellees and their experts repeatedly emphasize the importance of preserving "vulnerable" or "marginal" independent stations serving "relatively small" audiences. When appellees are pressed to explain the Government's "substantial interest" in preserving noncable viewers' access to "vulnerable" or "marginal" stations with "relatively small" audiences, it becomes evident that the interest has nothing to do with anticompetitive behavior, but has everything to do with content—preserving "quality" local programming that is "responsive" to community needs. Brief for Federal Appellees 13, 30. Indeed, Justice Breyer expressly declines to accept the anticompetitive rationale for the must-carry rules embraced by the principal opinion, and instead explicitly relies on a need to preserve a "rich mix" of "quality" programming. *Ante*, at 1, 2 (Breyer, J., concurring in part).

3

I turn now to the evidence of harm to broadcasters denied carriage or repositioned. The record on remand does not permit the conclusion, at the summary judgment stage, that Congress could reasonably have predicted serious harm to a significant number of stations in the absence of must-carry.

The purported link between an adverse carriage decision and severe harm to a station depends on yet another untested premise. Even accepting the conclusion that a cable system operator has a monopoly over *cable* services to the home, it does not necessarily follow that the operator also has a monopoly over all *video* services to cabled households. Cable subscribers using an input selector switch and an antenna can receive broadcast signals. Widespread use of such switches would completely eliminate any cable system "monopoly" over sources of video input. Growing use of direct-broadcast satellite television also tends to undercut the notion that cable operators have an inevitable monopoly over video services entering cable households.

In the Cable Act, Congress rejected the wisdom of any "substantial societal investment" in developing input selector switch technology. §2(a)(18). In defending this choice, the Court purports to identify "substantial evidence of technological shortcomings" that prevent widespread, efficient use of such devices. But nearly all of the "data" in question are drawn from sources pre-dating the enactment of must-carry by roughly six years. The Court notes the importance of deferring to congressional judgments about the "interaction of industries undergoing rapid economic and technological change." *Ante*, at 13. But this principle does not require wholesale deference to judgments about rapidly changing technologies that are based on unquestionably outdated information.

The Court concludes that the evidence on remand meets the threshold of harm established in *Turner*. The Court begins with the "considerable evidence" that broadcast stations denied carriage have fallen into bankruptcy. The analysis, however, does not focus on features of the market in which these stations were located or on the size of the audience they commanded. The "considerable evidence" relied on by the Court consists of repeated references to the bankruptcies of the same 23 commercial independent stations—apparently, new stations. Because the must-carry provisions have never been justified as a means of *enhancing* broadcast television, I do not understand the relevance of this evidence, or of the evidence concerning the difficulties encountered by *new* stations seeking financing.

The Court also claims that the record on remand reflects "considerable evidence" of stations curtailing their broadcast operations or suffering reductions in operating revenues. Most of the anecdotal accounts of harm on which the Court relies are sharply disputed. *Compare* JSCR ¶¶618, 619, 622, 623, 692 (App. 1553–1555, 1591) *with* Time Warner Entertainment Company, L. P.'s Broadcast Station Rebuttal ¶8 (TWE Rebuttal) (App. 2299) (ABC affiliate claiming harm from denial of carriage experienced $3.8 million net revenue increase between 1986 and 1992); TWE Rebuttal ¶83 (App. 2372–2373) (station alleged to have lost half of its cable carriage in fact obtained carriage on systems serving 80 percent of total cable subscribers within area of dominant influence); TWE Rebuttal ¶30 (App. 2318) (some systems on which station claimed anticompetitive carriage denials were precluded from carrying station due to signal strength and quality problems).

Unlike other aspects of the record on remand, the station-specific accounts cited by the Court do permit an evaluation of trends in the various broadcast markets, or "areas of dominant influence," in which carriage denials allegedly caused harm. The Court does not conduct this sort of analysis. Were it to do so, the Court would have to recognize that all but *one* of the commercial broadcast stations cited as claiming a curtailment in operations or a decline in revenue was broadcasting within an area of dominant influence that experienced net growth, or at least no net reduction, in the number of commercial broadcast stations operating during the non-must-carry era. Indeed, in 499 of 504 areas of dominant influence nationwide, the number of commercial broadcast stations operating in 1992 equaled or exceeded the number operating in 1987. Only two areas of dominant influence experienced a reduction in the number of noncommercial broadcast stations operating between 1987 and 1992.

The Court acknowledges that the record contains much evidence of the health of the broadcast industry. But the Court dismisses such evidence, emphasizing that the question is not whether Congress correctly determined that must-carry is necessary to prevent significant financial hardship to a substantial number of stations, but whether "the legislative conclusion was reasonable and supported by substantial evidence in the record before Congress." *Ante,* at 29. Even accepting the Court's articulation of the relevant standard, it is not properly applied here. The principal opinion disavows a need to closely scrutinize the logic of the regulatory scheme at issue on the ground that it "need not put [its] imprimatur on Congress' economic theory in order to validate the reasonableness of its judgment." *Ante,* at 25. That approach trivializes the First Amendment issue at stake in this case. A highly dubious economic theory has been advanced as the "substantial interest" supporting a First Amendment burden on cable operators and cable programmers. In finding that must-carry serves a substantial interest, the principal opinion necessarily accepts that theory. The partial concurrence does not, but neither does it articulate what threat to the availability of a "multiplicity" of broadcast stations would exist in a perfectly competitive market.

B

I turn now to the second portion of the *O'Brien* inquiry, which concerns the fit between the Government's asserted interests and the means chosen to advance them. The Court observes that "broadcast stations gained carriage on 5,880 channels as a result of must-carry," and recognizes that this forced carriage imposes a burden on cable system operators and cable programmers. *Ante,* at 33. But the Court also concludes that the other 30,006 cable channels occupied by broadcast stations are irrelevant to measuring the burden of the must-carry scheme. The must-carry rules prevent operators from dropping these broadcast stations should other more desirable cable programming become available, even though operators have carried these stations voluntarily in the past. The must-carry requirements thus burden an operator's First Amendment freedom to exercise unfettered control over a number of channels in its system, whether or not the operator's present choice is aligned with that of the Government.

Even assuming that the Court is correct that the 5,880 channels occupied by added broadcasters "represent the actual burden of the regulatory scheme," *ante,* at 33, the Court's leap to the conclusion that must-carry "is narrowly tailored to preserve a multiplicity of broadcast stations," *ante,* at 33–34, is nothing short of astounding. The Court's logic is circular. Surmising that most of the 5,880 channels added by the regulatory scheme would be dropped in its absence, the Court concludes that the figure also approximates the "benefit" of must-carry. Finding the scheme's burden "congruent" to the benefit it affords, the Court declares the statute narrowly tailored. The Court achieves this result, however, only by equating the *effect* of the statute—requiring cable operators to add 5,880 stations— with the governmental *interest* sought to be served. The Court's citation of *Ward* reveals the true nature of the interest at stake. The "evi[l] the Government seeks to eliminate," 491 U.S., at 799, n. 7, is not the failure of cable operators to carry *these 5,880 stations.* Rather, to read the first half of the principal opinion, the "evil" is *anticompetitive behavior* by cable operators. As a factual matter, we do not know whether these stations were not carried because of anticompetitive impulses. Positing the effect of a statute as the governmental interest "can sidestep judicial review of almost any statute, because it makes all statutes look narrowly tailored." Simon & Schuster, Inc. v. Members of N. Y. State Crime Victims Bd., 502 U.S. 105, 120 (1991). Without a sense whether *most* adverse carriage decisions are anticompetitively motivated, it is improper to conclude that the statute is narrowly tailored simply because it prevents *some* adverse carriage decisions.

In my view, the statute is not narrowly tailored to serve a substantial interest in preventing anticompetitive conduct. I do not understand Justice Breyer to disagree with this conclusion. *Ante,* at 1, 3 (examining fit between "speech-restricting and speech-enhancing consequences" of must-carry). Congress has commandeered up to one third of each cable system's channel capacity for the benefit of local broadcasters, without any regard for whether doing so advances the statute's alleged goals. To the extent that Congress was concerned that anticompetitive impulses would lead vertically integrated operators to prefer those programmers in which the operators have an ownership stake, the Cable Act is overbroad, since it does not impose its requirements solely on such operators. Moreover, Congress has placed limits upon the number of channels that can be used for affiliated programming. 47 U.S.C. §533(f)(1)(B). The principal opinion does not suggest why these limits are inadequate or explain why, once a system reaches the limit, its remaining carriage decisions would also be anticompetitively motivated. Even if the channel limits are insufficient, the principal opinion does not explain why requiring carriage of *broadcast* stations on *one third* of the system's channels is a measured response to the problem.

Finally, I note my disagreement with the Court's suggestion that the availability of less-speech-restrictive alternatives is never relevant to *O'Brien's* narrow tailoring inquiry. *Ante*, at 35–36. The *Turner* Court remanded this case in part because a plurality concluded that "judicial findings concerning the availability and efficacy of constitutionally acceptable less restrictive means of achieving the Government's asserted interests" were lacking in the original record. 512 U.S., at 668 (internal quotation marks omitted). The Court's present position on this issue is puzzling.

Our cases suggest only that we have refrained from imposing a *least*-restrictive-means requirement in cases involving intermediate First Amendment scrutiny. It is one thing to say that a regulation need not be the *least*-speech-restrictive means of serving an important governmental objective. It is quite another to suggest, as I read the majority to do here, that the availability of less-speech-restrictive alternatives cannot establish or confirm that a regulation is substantially broader than necessary to achieve the Government's goals. The availability of less intrusive approaches to a problem serves as a benchmark for assessing the reasonableness of the fit between Congress' articulated goals and the means chosen to pursue them.

As shown above, in this case it is plain without reference to any alternatives that the must-carry scheme is "substantially broader than necessary," *Ward*, 491 U.S., at 800, to serve the only governmental interest that the principal opinion fully explains—preventing unfair competition. If Congress truly sought to address anticompetitive behavior by cable system operators, it passed the wrong law. Nevertheless, the availability of less restrictive alternatives—a leased-access regime and subsidies—reinforces my conclusion that the must-carry provisions are overbroad.

Consider first appellants' proposed leased-access scheme, under which a cable system operator would be required to make a specified proportion of the system's channels available to broadcasters and independent cable programmers alike at regulated rates. Leased access would directly address both vertical integration and predatory behavior, by placing broadcasters and cable programmers on a level playing field for access to cable. Must-carry quite clearly does not respond to the problem of vertical integration. In addition, the must-carry scheme burdens the rights of cable programmers *and* cable operators; there is no suggestion here that leased access would burden cable *programmers* in the same way as must-carry does. In both of these respects, leased access is a more narrowly tailored guard against anticompetitive behavior. Finally, if, as the Court suggests, Congress were concerned that a leased access scheme would impose a burden on "small broadcasters" forced to pay for access, subsidies would eliminate the problem.

Subsidies would not, of course, eliminate anticompetitive behavior by cable system operators—a problem that Congress could address directly or through a leased-access scheme. Appellees defend the must-carry provisions, however, not only as a means of preventing anticompetitive behavior, but also as a means of protecting "marginal" or "vulnerable" stations, even if they are *not* threatened by anticompetitive behavior. The principal opinion chooses not to acknowledge this interest explicitly, although Justice Breyer does. Even if this interest were content neutral—which it is not—subsidies would address it directly. The Court adopts appellees' position that subsidies would serve a "very different purpose than must-carry. Must-carry is intended not to guarantee the financial health of all broadcasters, but to ensure a base number of broadcasters survive to provide service to noncable households." *Ante*, at 40. I take appellees' concern to be that subsidies, unlike must-carry, would save some broadcasters that would not survive even *with* cable carriage. There is a straightforward solution to this problem. If the Government is indeed worried that imprecision in allocation of subsidies would prop up stations that would not survive even with cable carriage, then it could tie subsidies to a percentage of stations' advertising revenues (or, for public stations, member contributions), determined by stations' access to viewers. For example, in a broadcast market where 50 percent of television-viewing households subscribe to cable, a broadcaster has access to all households without cable as well as to those households served by cable systems on which the broadcaster has secured carriage. If a broadcaster is carried on cable systems serving only 20 percent of cable households (*i.e.,* 10 percent of all television-viewing households in the broadcast market), the broadcaster has access to 60 percent of the television-viewing households. If the Government provided a subsidy to compensate for the loss in advertising revenue or member contributions that a station would sustain by virtue of its failure to reach 40 percent of its potential audience, it could ensure that its allocation would do no more than protect those broadcasters that would survive with full access to television-viewing households. In sum, the alleged barrier to a precise allocation of subsidies is not insurmountable. The Court also suggests that a subsidy scheme would involve the Government in making "content based determinations about programming." Even if that is so, it does not distinguish subsidies from the must-carry provisions. In light of the principal opinion's steadfast adherence to the position that a preference for "diverse" or local-content broadcasting is not a content based preference, the argument is ironic indeed.

IV

In sustaining the must-carry provisions of the Cable Act, the Court ignores the main justification of the statute urged by appellees and subjects restrictions on expressive activity to an inappropriately lenient level of scrutiny. The principal opinion then misapplies the analytic framework it chooses, exhibiting an extraordinary and unwarranted deference for congressional judgments, a profound fear of delving into complex economic matters, and a willingness to substitute untested assumptions for evidence. In light of gaps in logic and evidence, it is improper to conclude, at the summary judgment stage, that the must-carry scheme serves a significant governmental interest "in a direct and effective way." *Ward*, 491 U.S., at 800. Moreover, because the undisputed facts demonstrate that the must-carry scheme is plainly not narrowly tailored to serving the only governmental interest the principal opinion fully explains and embraces—preventing anticompetitive behavior—appellants are entitled to summary judgment in their favor.

Justice Breyer disavows the principal opinion's position on anticompetitive behavior, and instead treats the must-carry rules as a "speech-enhancing" measure designed to ensure access to "quality" programming for noncable households. Neither the principal opinion nor the partial concurrence explains the nature of the alleged threat to the availability of a "multiplicity of broadcast programming sources," if that threat does not arise from cable operators' anticompetitive conduct. Such an approach makes it impossible to discern whether Congress was addressing a problem that is "real, not merely conjectural," and whether must-carry addresses the problem in a "direct and material way." *Turner, supra,* at 664 (plurality opinion).

I therefore respectfully dissent, and would reverse the judgment below.

Notes and Questions

1. **Deference to Congress.** Is there any fact, or set of facts, that opponents of the law might have submitted to the Court that would have persuaded the majority to change its mind? Or is the majority's point that the factual disputes underlying must-carry policies are for Congress to resolve? If so, what task, if any, remained for the Court?

2. **The Importance of Technology.** Suppose that, at an appropriate moment in the litigation, researchers at MIT had come forward to show the Court a relatively inexpensive remote control unit that would allow television viewers to switch from cable to broadcast and back again without climbing out of their chairs. Suppose further that economists had testified that, if the Court were to strike down the must-carry provisions, demand for this technology would be significant and would lead, among other things, to even better variations of the technology and even cheaper prices. Would that have changed the Court's ultimate decision in the case? If so, how does the Court deal with its implicit reliance on the state of existing technology? Is this a normal problem faced by courts, or an aberrational one peculiar to this controversy?

3. **Predictive Harms.** In both *Turner I* and *Turner II*, the Court suggested that the asserted harms to broadcast television had not yet occurred and that the legislative assertions of such harms were therefore predictions. Should the predictive nature of these harms affect the constitutional analysis, and if so, how? In this regard, note that *Turner I* emphasized that the harms on which the must-carry legislation rested must be "real, not merely conjectural," but in *Turner II* the "not merely conjectural" language fell out of the equation (the Court simply referred to "a real harm" and "a real threat"). What is the difference between these formulations? Which one makes more sense?

4. **Understanding the Standard.** Is it the position of the *Turner II* dissenters that every remedy for—or protection against—anticompetitive behavior by a cable operator must be closely tailored to achieve no more competition or protection than is necessary?

5. **Test Your Understanding.** Suppose the FCC adopted the following rule with respect to MMDS (a subscription video service often called "wireless cable"):

> Whereas MMDS operators receive free use of the public airwaves and because we believe that MMDS operators may soon acquire significant shares of viewers in local markets now that digital compression technology allows transmission of over 100 signals by most MMDS operators, the Commission has determined that each MMDS operator must carry, without charge, the three television stations in its viewing area

that are the least often viewed by local television viewers and the three radio stations in its listening area that are the least often listened to by local radio listeners, so long as the stations in question consent to such carriage.

Would this hypothetical rule survive a First Amendment challenge in light of *Turner I* and *Turner II*?

6. Digital Television. As described in Chapter Eight, the FCC has allocated an additional channel to each television broadcaster in order to promote advanced television service. By employing digital technologies, broadcasters will be able to deliver several signals over that one channel. The advent of these new signals from broadcasters has raised the question of what, if any, must-carry obligations should be imposed upon cable operators in addition to their obligation to carry the broadcasters' analog signal during the period (scheduled to extend until 2006) when broadcasters are utilizing both their original analog spectrum and their new spectrum for digital television. The FCC issued a *Notice of Proposed Rulemaking* in July of 1998 requesting comment on the extent to which cable operators should be required to carry the digital signal(s) that broadcasters will deliver, and more proceedings will surely follow.

Broadcasters argue that digital must-carry is perhaps even more important than analog must-carry, on the theory that, without cable carriage, digital television will never gain the market penetration it needs to succeed. They also argue that Congress and the FCC should share their desire to increase cable carriage, because the recovery of the spectrum planned for 2006 depends upon high digital market penetration, without which consumers will rebel at the prospect of losing their traditional analog (NTSC) signals. Broadcasters contend, in other words, that it would be both good policy and good politics for the government to require carriage and thereby avoid infuriating consumers in the future.

Cable operators, meanwhile, argue that the burdens imposed by digital must-carry are much greater than for the regime approved in *Turner II*. Carrying the digital signals in addition to the analog NTSC signals represents a doubling (or more) of the channels occupied by broadcasters, thereby multiplying the number of channels not being devoted to cable networks. Cable operators contend, in other words, that being required to carry a single station from each broadcaster, most of which they would want to carry anyway, is quite different from being required to carry one or more digital signals in addition to the analog signal (especially as the audience for the digital signals might be so small that the cable operator would want to carry few if any of the new signals).

Do these considerations affect the applicability of *Turner II* to digital must-carry, and, if so, how? What reading of *Turner II* would effectively doom challenges to digital must-carry? What reading of *Turner II* would call digital must-carry into question? Which reading is the more persuasive? Finally, note that the proceeding on digital must-carry has arisen at the same time that the FCC and Congress are considering what, if any, public interest obligations to impose on digital broadcasters. Are these two matters related? Should they be?

CHAPTER TWELVE

STRUCTURAL LIMITATIONS

The purpose of this chapter is:
- to survey several types of structural rules that limit concentration in the cable marketplace.

$\sim$

So far in our study of cable regulation we have considered a series of rules and statutory provisions designed to resolve conflicts between cable operators, broadcasters, and content owners with respect to particular programs and particular signals. In this chapter, we turn our attention to a different set of legal rules, namely rules that shape the cable television market by limiting the market power enjoyed both by particular cable operators and by the cable industry overall. These rules protect two groups: firms that supply program content and firms that distribute program content by technologies other than transmission via cable.

Consider first the restrictions designed to benefit firms that supply programs. Many firms create and produce informational, educational, and entertainment programming that they then supply to cable operators—as well as to broadcasters, operators of direct broadcast satellite television, and so on. Among these firms are the major Hollywood production studios, companies that operate specialized cable networks such as USA and MTV, and the major professional sports leagues. These firms worry about two threats. First, they worry that a given cable operator might grow so large that it will have monopolistic purchasing power and be able to demand content at particularly low prices or particularly favorable terms. Second, they worry that cable providers will start to produce and favor their own content, effectively blocking independent program suppliers from their wires.

The first concern is addressed by the FCC's rules on horizontal ownership. Section 11(c)(2) of the 1992 Cable Act requires the Commission to promulgate rules "establishing reasonable limits on the number of cable subscribers" a given cable operator can reach through commonly owned or controlled cable systems. The current rule forbids a single cable provider from serving, through owned or controlled cable systems, more than 30% of all multiple video programming distribution (MVPD) subscribers nationwide. Note that the latter number includes not just cable subscribers (which would have constrained cable operators more) but all subscribers to services comparable to cable, for example DBS and video services delivered over the telephone network.

The second concern is addressed by the FCC's rules limiting vertical ownership, again promulgated under the authority of section 11(c)(2) of the 1992

Cable Act. The worry here is that cable providers will favor content produced either in-house or by affiliated firms. The vertical ownership restrictions limit vertical integration between cable providers and content producers, thus limiting the number of programs for which this concern is relevant. (The leased access provisions, discussed in Chapter Eleven, address this same issue from another angle by giving unaffiliated program suppliers the opportunity to purchase cable access at regulated rates.)

Other provisions of the 1992 Act focus not so much on possible harms to program suppliers, but instead on possible harms to competing program distribution technologies. The must-carry provisions fit into this category, protecting as they do conventional broadcasters. So, too, does 47 U.S.C. §548, an umbrella provision designed to increase "competition and diversity in the multichannel video programming market." §548(a). In fact, section 548 requires the FCC to issue regulations that, among other things, prohibit cable operators from causing affiliated content providers to discriminate against other players in the multichannel video programming market. §548(c)(2)(B).

The materials that follow consider in greater detail these and other structural regulations. Specifically, the chapter takes up, in turn: first, the controls on vertical integration and horizontal concentration, each of which protects program suppliers; and second, regulations promulgated under the authority of §548 and thus designed to protect competing multichannel video programmers from anti-competitive behavior by cable operators. In studying these materials, be sure to ask yourself what specific fears each regulation addresses, whether those fears are well-founded, and to what extent each regulation is likely to be effective in mitigating the identified problem. Also consider the regulations as a package. Are some more likely to be effective than others? Does the presence of one of these rules—or one of the rules considered earlier in this Part—make another redundant? Does the 1992 Act represent a measured and coherent response to cable's present role in the telecommunications marketplace or does it reflect a grab-bag approach in which every conceivable "solution" was thrown at every imaginable "problem"? Would Congress have been better advised to leave the issues to resolution by application of existing (and continually maturing) antitrust law, or was Congress wise to try to devise more detailed and specific provisions to deal with the cable industry in particular?

I. PROTECTING PROGRAM SUPPLIERS

Section 11(c)(2) of the 1992 Cable Act (amending section 613 of the Communications Act and codified at 47 U.S.C. §533(f)(1)), required the Commission to conduct a proceeding:

> (A) to prescribe rules and regulations establishing reasonable limits on the number of cable subscribers a person is authorized to reach through cable systems owned by such person, or in which such person has an attributable interest;

> (B) to prescribe rules and regulations establishing reasonable limits on the number of channels on a cable system that can be occupied by a

video programmer in which a cable operator has an attributable interest; and

(C) to consider the necessity and appropriateness of imposing limitations on the degree to which multichannel video programming distributors may engage in the creation or production of video programming.

The Commission implemented these statutory provisions by prescribing both national subscriber limits (in response to subsection (A)) and channel occupancy limits (in response to subsection (B)). The Commission declined, however, to impose any limitations on cable operators' creation or production of video programming. The materials that follow consider each of these decisions in turn, starting with the 1993 *Report and Order* that restricted cable operators' freedom to fill their channels with content provided by affiliated firms.

A. Controls on Vertical Integration

IMPLEMENTATION OF SECTION 11 OF THE CABLE TELEVISION CONSUMER PROTECTION AND COMPETITION ACT OF 1992

Second Report and Order, 8 FCC Rcd. 8565 (1993)

IV. CHANNEL OCCUPANCY LIMITS

A. Background

41. Section 11 of the 1992 Cable Act, 47 U.S.C. §533 (f)(1)(B), requires the Commission to establish reasonable limits on the number of cable channels that can be occupied by a video programmer in which a cable operator has an attributable interest. Congress adopted this provision to address its concerns that the cable industry has become increasingly vertically integrated and that as a result cable operators have the ability and the incentive to favor their affiliated programmers over unaffiliated or competing distributors. Vertical integration in this context refers to common ownership of both programming and distribution systems. Such integration, Congress determined, could make it difficult for non-cable affiliated or competing programmers to secure carriage on vertically integrated cable systems. Congress similarly found that vertically integrated program suppliers have the incentive and the ability to favor their affiliated cable operators over unaffiliated operators and program distributors using other technologies.

42. According to the House Report [on the 1992 Cable Act], some vertically integrated cable multiple system operators (MSOs) favor video programming services in which they have an ownership interest, denying system access to unaffiliated programmers and programmers affiliated with rival MSOs. The House Report also found that such vertically integrated MSOs may discriminate against rival video programming services with regard to price, channel positioning, and promotion. In addition, Congress was concerned that vertical integration limits diversity of cable programming and reduces the number of voices available to the public. In this respect, the Senate Report likens the channel occupancy limits to

the Commission's broadcast one-to-a-market rule, which is similarly designed to increase the diversity of voices available to the public.

43. On the other hand, the House Report cites a study by the National Telecommunications and Information Administration (NTIA), which concluded that common ownership of cable systems and cable programming services did not appear to affect adversely the supply of cable programming or diversity of viewing choices for cable subscribers. NTIA found that none of the top five MSOs showed a pattern of favoring basic services with which they were affiliated. Congress also acknowledged that significant benefits have resulted from vertical relationships in the cable industry. In particular, the House Report cited C-Span, CNN, Black Entertainment Television, Nickelodeon, and the Discovery Channel as examples of innovative programming that would not have been feasible without the financial support of cable system operators.

44. In the *1990 Cable Report*, the Commission also found that the cable industry had become vertically integrated. In this regard, the Commission observed that MSOs had equity interests in 13 of the top 20 national basic cable networks and in 6 of the top 8 pay cable networks. We concluded that vertical integration had accelerated in the cable industry, but that such vertical relationships had increased both the quality and quantity of cable programming services. We found that MSO investment was responsible for the development and survival of several of the most popular video programming services. We also determined that vertical integration among the largest MSOs had contributed to program diversity by providing new video programming services with an extensive subscriber base and information regarding viewer tastes and desires for new programming.

45. We seek to establish channel occupancy limits which strike the proper balance between competing statutory objectives: to ensure that vertically integrated cable operators do not favor affiliated video programmers, or unfairly impede the flow of video programming to cable subscribers, on the one hand and, on the other, to encourage MSOs to continue to invest in the development of diverse and high quality video programming services.

B. Application of Channel Occupancy Limits.

51. Section 11(c)(2)(B) requires the Commission to "establish reasonable limits on the number of channels on a cable system that can be occupied by a video programmer in which a cable operator has an attributable interest." The language contained in section 11(c)(2)(B) of the 1992 Cable Act is not entirely clear because it can also be read as applying to carriage of video programmers affiliated with the particular cable operator or to carriage of any vertically integrated cable programmer on any cable system.

52. The most logical interpretation of the statutory language is to apply such limits only to video programmers that are vertically integrated with the particular cable operator in question.

53. Cable operators have very little incentive to favor video programming services that are affiliated solely with a rival MSO. Moreover, a vertically integrated cable operator appears to have significantly less power to control the content or distribution of a programming service in which it has no ownership interest. Further, we believe that application of the channel occupancy limits to all

vertically integrated programmers, regardless of whether they are affiliated with the particular cable operator, would severely inhibit MSO investment in video programming services, since the mere fact of such MSO investment may restrict carriage of the video programming service on all cable systems.

54. With respect to calculating channel capacity, we conclude that all activated channels should be taken into account. We note that cable operators are obligated by the 1992 Cable Act to carry local broadcast and noncommercial educational channels, and are required to reserve channel capacity for lease to unaffiliated programmers. Consequently, we conclude that it would be unreasonable to use such channels to reduce the base of channels available for carriage of vertically integrated programming. We believe that such an approach would penalize cable operators who carry the broadest array of broadcast channels by decreasing the number of channels available for carriage of vertically integrated programming. Moreover, carriage of broadcast, PEG, and leased access channels promotes diversity and provides alternative sources of unaffiliated programming to cable subscribers in furtherance of the statutory objectives.

C. Vertical Ownership Attribution Standard.

61. Section 11(c)(2)(B) of the 1992 Cable Act does not indicate the appropriate criteria for determining vertical ownership attribution. We conclude that the broadcast attribution criteria are appropriate for this purpose.

62. In the context of establishing limits on vertical integration in the cable industry we are concerned with identifying interests in cable programming services that are sufficient to afford influence or control over programming decisions. We also seek to identify interests that might potentially provide cable operators with an incentive to favor an affiliated video programming service over an unaffiliated or competing video programming service. However, we must balance these concerns with the objective of preserving the benefits and efficiencies of vertical integration and encouraging continued MSO investment in new video programming services. The broadcast attribution criteria are appropriate to address these competing concerns. The [broadcast] attribution criteria were designed to identify all interests that could potentially afford influence or control over management or programming decisions, while providing exceptions for interests above 5% if there is no realistic possibility of such interests imparting control.[1] Thus, we conclude that the broadcast attribution criteria are strict enough to identify all interests that afford the potential to exert influence or control over management or programming decisions, yet flexible enough to permit continued MSO investment in new video programming services. Moreover, we believe that interests of 5% or greater may be substantial enough to motivate cable systems to favor an affiliated programmer over a programmer in which the cable system has no attributable interest.

---

1. [Ed. In 1999, the FCC slightly modified the broadcast attribution criteria to which it refers in the previous sentence, and a few months later the Commission similarly modified the cable attribution rules. The current rules for both cable and broadcast, like the ones to which this 1993 order refers, provide that all active voting stock interests of 5% or more are attributable; but passive (institutional) investor voting stock interests are attributable only if they are 20% or more (rather than an original 10%) of the outstanding voting stock of a corporation. *See* 14 FCC Rcd. 19014 (1999).]

D. Percentage Limitation.

68. We conclude that a 40% limit on the number of channels[2] that can be occupied by affiliated video programming services is reasonable to serve Congress' competing objectives in requiring such restrictions. We believe that a 40% limit is appropriate to balance the goals of increasing diversity and reducing the incentive and ability of vertically integrated cable operators to favor their affiliated programming, with the benefits and efficiencies associated with vertical integration.[3] Congress and the Commission have both recognized that there are benefits which result from vertical integration. First, MSO investment has produced a wealth of high quality cable programming services. Many of the most popular cable programming services were initiated or sustained with the help of MSO investment. Second, vertical integration between cable operators and video programming services appears to produce efficiencies in the distribution, marketing, and purchase of programming. Third, vertical integration can reduce programming costs, which in turn may reduce subscriber fees and cable rates. Fourth, vertical integration may in certain circumstances foster investment in more innovative and riskier video programming services.

69. Moreover, cable operators are already required to reserve a substantial percentage of their channel capacity for carriage of local broadcast and PEG stations.[4] In addition, cable operators are subject to leased access requirements, pursuant to which they may be required to designate an additional 15% of their activated channel capacity for commercial use by programmers unaffiliated with the cable operator. See 47 U.S.C. §532. Significantly, the leased access obligations are parallel in purpose to the channel occupancy requirements, since they also obligate cable operators to provide system access to unaffiliated video programmers. Thus, cable operators' ability to carry affiliated programming is already significantly curtailed by statutorily mandated carriage obligations.

70. We also note that channel occupancy limits are not the only means by which Congress intended to prevent anticompetitive conduct by vertically integrated MSOs. Sections 12 and 19 of the 1992 Cable Act establish specific behavioral restrictions prohibiting discrimination by vertically integrated cable operators and video programming services. These provisions impose more narrowly tailored behavioral restraints, specifically prohibiting anticompetitive

---

2. We will measure the vertical ownership limits on a per channel basis, using the traditional 6MHz per channel definition. However, given the dynamic state of cable technology, we recognize that it may soon be common for cable operators to provide several channels using a single 6MHz bandwidth segment. Accordingly, we intend to review periodically this definition.

3. We disagree with MPAA's assertion that a 40% limit could result in many instances in no channels being made available to unaffiliated video programmers. First, MPAA's calculation does not take into account the availability of leased access channels to unaffiliated video programmers. Second, MPAA appears to assume that TCI owned systems will drop popular unaffiliated programming services such as ESPN, USA Network, and A&E in favor of other less popular affiliated programming services. The record evidence suggests that such conduct is fairly unlikely. Finally, MPAA fails to acknowledge that cable systems carrying the maximum number of broadcast must carry and PEG stations are devoting substantial capacity to the carriage of unaffiliated programming.

4. Cable operators with more than 12 channels may be required to reserve 33% of their activated channel capacity for local broadcast and PEG channels. See 47 U.S.C. §§531, 534, 535.

conduct by vertically integrated cable operators and programmers, while channel occupancy limits impose broader structural constraints, which affect the ability of all cable operators to carry programming in which they have an attributable interest.

71. In addition, in order to promote the presentation of a diversity of viewpoints on cable, we will allow carriage of vertically integrated video programming services on two additional channels or up to 45% of a cable system's channel capacity, which ever is greater, provided such additional video programming services are minority-controlled. The Commission has long recognized that the public interest is enhanced when cable programming reflects a diversity of viewpoints. We believe that allowing such expanded carriage of minority-controlled video programming services will encourage additional MSO investment in minority-owned programming services, which will in turn promote minority ownership of video programming services and increase the diversity of viewpoints presented to cable subscribers. In this regard, we believe that the diversity benefits of such increased minority ownership outweigh the access concerns associated with such an increase in integration. We decline, however, to adopt a similar policy for minority oriented-programming. Although we seek to encourage the presentation of a diversity of viewpoints on cable television including those of minorities, we believe that increasing minority ownership of cable systems and video programming services is the most effective and legally sound means of promoting such diversity.[5]

E. Treatment of Pay Channels, Multiplexed Channels and Local and Regional Networks.

76. We conclude that vertically integrated pay channels and multiplexed channels should not be exempted from the 40% channel occupancy limits. While we recognize that such channels provide subscribers with a valuable service and increase the diversity of programming available on cable, we see no compelling public interest objective to be served by such an exemption.

77. We also disagree with commenters who argue that multiplexed channels should not be counted toward the channel occupancy limits because they provide subscribers with time diversity and counter programming. We recognize that such diversity is beneficial to consumers, but we believe that Congress was specifically concerned with ensuring that a diversity of non-vertically integrated programming sources is available to cable subscribers.

78. We have determined, however, to apply channel occupancy limits only to video programming services distributed to cable systems on a nationwide basis. We consider an exemption for local and regional programming services to be an important means of encouraging continued MSO investment in the development of local cable programming, which is responsive to the needs and tastes of local audiences and serves Congress' objectives of promoting localism.[6] Moreover, we

5. *See* Metro Broadcasting v. FCC, 110 S. Ct. 2997, 3019 & n.36 (1990) (noting substantial practical and constitutional difficulties that would be presented by FCC promotion of broadcast program diversity through direct program regulation rather than through structural means such as ownership).

6. The 1992 Cable Act states that "A primary objective and benefit of our nation's system of regulation of broadcast television is the local origination of programming." 1992 Cable Act, §2(a)(10).

recognize that because local and regional programming services are usually costly to produce and appeal only to a limited population of subscribers, such an exception may be necessary to encourage MSOs to continue investing in such local programming. Without such an exception commenters argue that MSOs will favor national programming services which can be marketed to larger audiences across the country producing greater subscriber and advertising revenues.

F. Effect of Fiber Optic Cable and Digital Signal Compression.

83. We believe the expanded channel capacity that will result from fiber optic cable and digital compression technology will help obviate the need for channel occupancy limits as a means of encouraging cable operators to carry unaffiliated or competing video programming services. Although information on how multichannel video distributors will respond to greatly increased channel capacity is necessarily somewhat speculative, the record indicates that vastly larger cable systems will likely be inclined to deliver targeted "niche" video programming services aimed at correspondingly smaller audience sizes. In addition, pay-per-view and pay-per-channel offerings — also with more limited audiences — will increase as channel capacity increases. Also, as channel capacity becomes more abundant and relatively less costly, "multiplexing" is likely to increase and more capacity will be used to increase the convenience of program starting times rather than to distribute separate channels of original programming. Thus, for example, a feature film service ("near-video-on-demand") intended to be competitive with video tape rentals might involve the distribution of films on numerous channels simultaneously with starting times staggered by only a few minutes.

84. Occupancy limits in these circumstances do not parallel occupancy limits for more restricted capacity systems where most services are distributed on discrete channels to a significant portion of a system's subscribership. Accordingly, we believe that occupancy limits can be relaxed once the number of cable channels on a system increases beyond the number distributed using traditional technology. Conventional cable distribution, in the absence of dual cable distribution plant, signal compression, or "fiber to the block," enables the distribution of approximately 75 video channels. At the present time, this threshold appears to be a reasonable cut-off for application of the channel occupancy limit. Thus, we will apply the channel occupancy limits only up to 75 channels on a cable system owned by a vertically integrated MSO. Any additional channel capacity made possible through the use of advanced cable technologies will not be subject to the channel occupancy limits at this time.

H. Grandfathering Carriage of Vertically Integrated Programmers.

93. We believe that the public interest would be disserved by requiring cable operators to delete vertically integrated video programming services in order to comply with the channel occupancy caps. Accordingly, we will grandfather all vertically integrated video programming services carried as of December 4, 1992 (the effective date of the 1992 Cable Act), which exceed the channel occupancy limits we adopt herein. We believe that this proposal will minimize the disruption to existing programming relationships and will prevent subscriber confusion, which could result from divestiture or program deletion. We note, however, that once additional capacity becomes available on a grandfathered system, the cable operator shall be

prohibited from expanding its carriage of vertically integrated video programming services until such system is in full compliance with the channel occupancy limits.

94. We recognize that grandfathering existing vertical programming relationships to some extent may protect established services and favor the largest and most vertically integrated cable operators. However, we believe that such considerations are outweighed by the need to prevent subscriber confusion and minimize the disruption to existing carriage agreements. Moreover, given the trend toward increased channel capacity as a result of improved cable technologies, it appears that no useful purpose would be served by requiring cable operators to drop existing services.

Notes and Questions

1. **Necessary Given Horizontal Restrictions?** The next part of the chapter considers limitations on horizontal concentration in the cable industry—in essence, restrictions on the number of subscribers a given cable operator can serve. But suppose for the moment that horizontal restrictions exist and are effective. If so, what public purpose is achieved by the rules limiting vertical integration? How, for example, could an MSO that accounted for, say, seven percent of cable subscribers nationwide hope to benefit by favoring programming in which it has an "attributable interest" over programming that the market prefers?

Of course, horizontal restrictions might not be very effective. In the same *Report and Order* excerpted above, the Commission established rules on horizontal concentration that permitted single MSOs to serve up to 30 percent of all U.S. cable subscribers. At such levels of concentration, might MSOs find it in their interest to favor programs they owned, thus denying substantial channel capacity to rival programmers? If so, were the vertical integration restrictions adopted in this *Order* sufficient to protect unaffiliated programmers? Or was the Commission relying on other provisions—such as the provisions establishing and regulating leased access channels—to provide this protection?

2. **Necessary Given Leased Access Channels?** And what of those leased access channels, or the provisions of the 1992 Act that required the FCC to adopt rules that would preserve for all multichannel video program distributors "equal access" to program content? Even putting the horizontal limitations to one side, aren't these other provisions sufficient to protect unaffiliated programmers? Was there any reason *also* to impose the limitations on vertical integration discussed in the *Report*? What distinct goals might the channel occupancy rules achieve? And is the case for this additional regulation strong enough to withstand First Amendment challenge? If the answer to this question is affirmative (as the D.C. Circuit indicated in Time Warner Entertainment Co. v. United States, discussed below), then what does that tell us about the need for, and constitutionality of, leased access?

3. **The Commission's Perspective.** Does the Commission's implementation of the vertical integration section of the statute reflect skepticism about the need for this sort of regulation? What else explains the decisions (a) to express the limit as a percentage of all activated channels, including those subject to must-carry, leased access, and PEG obligations [¶54], but (b) only up to 75 channels [¶84], while (c) grandfathering all vertical integration as of 1992 that exceeds the new limits [¶93]?

4. *Metro Broadcasting* Revisited. The Commission suggests in ¶71 that legitimate concern for assuring the diversity of viewpoints on cable justifies the agency's decision to provide a small increase in the vertical integration limits for programming that is minority controlled (but not for programming that is minority oriented). Are these conclusions consistent with the rationale of *Metro Broadcasting*? Does this program stand on different constitutional footing from the one struck down in *Missouri Synod*?

B. Controls on Horizontal Concentration

IMPLEMENTATION OF SECTION 11(C) OF THE CABLE TELEVISION CONSUMER PROTECTION AND COMPETITION ACT OF 1992
Third Report and Order, 14 FCC Rcd. 19098 (1999)

II. BACKGROUND

7. Section 613(f) of the Communications Act, 47 U.S.C. §533(f)(1)(A), requires the Commission to "prescribe rules and regulations establishing reasonable limits on the number of cable subscribers a person is authorized to reach through cable systems owned by such person, or in which such person has an attributable interest."

8. Congress did not direct the Commission to use a mathematical formula in determining the horizontal limits. Rather, Congress directed in Section 613(f)(2) that the Commission must consider and balance, among other public interest objectives, seven specific public interest guidelines in determining the appropriate horizontal limits. These public interest guidelines are:

(A) ensure that no cable operator or group of cable operators can unfairly impede, either because of the size of any individual operator or because of joint actions by a group of operators of sufficient size, the flow of video programming from the programmer to the consumer;

(B) ensure that cable operators affiliated with video programmers do not favor such programmers in determining carriage on their cable systems or do not unreasonably restrict the flow of video programming of affiliated video programmers to other video distributors;

(C) take particular account of the market structure, ownership patterns, and other relationships of the cable industry, including the nature and market power of the local franchise, the joint ownership of cable systems and video programmers, and the various types of non-equity controlling interests;

(D) account for any efficiencies and other benefits that might be gained through increased ownership or control;

(E) make such rules and regulations reflect the dynamic nature of the communications marketplace;

(F) not impose limitations which would bar cable operators from serving previously unserved rural areas; and

(G) not impose limitations which would impair the development of diverse and high quality programming.[7]

9. The 1992 Cable Act and its legislative history indicate heightened Congressional concern over horizontal concentration among cable operators. Witnesses at the congressional hearings, including representatives of the MSOs themselves, testified to the need for cable horizontal ownership limits to preserve competition and protect the public interest. Congress was concerned that the concentration of cable systems in the hands of a few "media gatekeepers" could potentially bar entry to new programmers and reduce the number of media voices available to consumers.

10. However, Congress also recognized that multiple system ownership could provide benefits to consumers. The House Report stated that cable industry consolidation had benefited consumers by allowing efficiencies in the administration, distribution and procurement of programming, and also noted that concentration of cable operators could promote the introduction of new programming services by providing capital and a ready subscriber base for new services. The House Report also observed that large cable MSOs can take competitive and programming risks that smaller operators cannot. Similarly, the Senate Report acknowledged that horizontal concentration could create efficiencies from lower transaction costs in carriage negotiations between programmers and cable operators.

III. BASIS FOR THE RULES

12. Congress directed the Commission to establish horizontal rules; yet in response to the *Notice* in this proceeding and in the course of the judicial proceedings relating to Section 613, a number of commenters make arguments that, while sometimes couched as pleas for a higher limit, appear to challenge the legitimacy and rational basis of any regulations of the type Section 613(f) requires the Commission to adopt. They argue:

> that increases in channel capacity, through system upgrades and the introduction of digital channels, reduce the practical need as well as the ability of operators to select among alternative content sources;

> that other rules, including mandatory broadcast signal carriage, channel occupancy, leased access, and public access rules, eliminate the need for ownership limits that are also designed to promote programming competition and content diversity;

> that cable system operators as purchasers of programming content for their subscribers are bound by marketplace forces so that they acquire only that product which their subscribers demand and there is no evidence that cable operators have ever used their editorial discretion to deny an outlet for unorthodox or unpopular speech;

> that, if any problems exist in this area, they can be addressed through ordinary antitrust enforcement processes.

We are not persuaded that these arguments are responsive to Congress' concerns in adopting Section 613(f).

---

7. 47 U.S.C. §533(f)(2)(A)–(G).

13. With respect to the channel capacity argument, system operators are implicitly suggesting that increased capacity translates into an increased demand for programming. This change in the supply and demand relationship between purchasers and sellers of programming would, it appears they are arguing, tend to mitigate concerns that are based on the buying (monopsony) power of system operators.

14. In most markets, a single incumbent cable operator is likely to have more than 80% of the multichannel video distribution market. Although calculations of market power are almost always complex, a frequently cited compendium of monopoly cases concludes that "market share in excess of 70% is almost always deemed sufficient to support an inference of monopoly power, although that inference may be overcome by other evidence." I Antitrust Law Developments (Third) 213–214 (1992) (citations omitted). The cable television industry has become, in the words of the 1992 Cable Television Consumer Protection and Competition Act, "A dominant nationwide video medium." Public Law 102-385, §2(a)(3). On the other hand, the programming supply market is extremely competitive with increases in cable channel capacity, with the growth rate of new programmers rapidly outpacing the growth of new channels. The Commission's 1998 Competition Report found that there were 245 national cable networks and that 65 new cable networks were planned to launch in the near future. The decreasing marginal value of additional channels, the more limited exposure these channels receive by virtue of their placement on digital or other tiers to which subscribership is restricted and the associated difficulties of attracting an audience base to support advertising sales all tend to suggest that capacity increases have not had the consequence suggested and that channel expansion has not negated the Congressional concerns. Cable operators still have the power to decide which cable networks will "make it" even as channel capacity grows.

15. The suggestion that other statutory provisions and Commission rules effectively address the same concerns we find equally unpersuasive. We believe Congress passed Section 613 to address specific concerns regarding the development of the video-programming market. Since Congress was aware of the interplay between the horizontal rule and the other rules addressing programming, it is clear that Congress intended for all the rules to work together in a complementary fashion. In any event, we do not believe that the goals of Section 613 are addressed by other statutory provisions. The channel occupancy rules adopted pursuant to Section 613 of the Communications Act are intended to address only that programming that is controlled through direct ownership rather than through purchase and apply only to channel capacity up to 75 channels. The leased access rules, while intended to address some of the same kinds of concerns, require the programmer to pay for carriage, a model which thus far has not resulted in any significant amount of nationally distributed programming content being made available to the public. The must-carry requirement applies only to broadcasters, not to other unaffiliated programmers. Moreover, the content of the broadcast stations that are carried, even when carried pursuant to mandatory obligations, is not totally divorced in terms of ownership and editorial voice from the cable systems involved. There are significant common ownership ties between a number of the broadcast networks involved and cable television system operators, including for example, significant AT&T (Liberty) ownership interests in News Corp. (the Fox networks), Time Warner and MediaOne ownership in The WB network, AT&T (Liberty) ownership in Telemu-

ndo, and Comcast and AT&T interests in QVC and HSN. These statutory based requirements thus share common objectives with the horizontal rules and function in a mutually supportive fashion with them but the contention that they are less restrictive methods of accomplishing the same substantive result is not correct. None of these rules fully address the core concern of national programming content diversity to which the horizontal limits are directed.

16. The Commission specifically considered how the behavioral rules interact with the horizontal ownership rules when it adopted the rules in this proceeding. The limit is a structural complement to the other access provisions. Thus, for example, it was explained that the horizontal ownership rules limit the potential for anticompetitive abuses of purchasing power in areas outside of the core areas covered by the program access rules, such as programming contracts between cable operators and non-vertically integrated programmers or contracts involving programming that is not delivered to cable operators via satellite. In addition, structural regulations generally are more easily enforced and their violation more easily detected than conduct regulations. We recognize that a large market share does not in and of itself indicate that a firm or a collection of firms has the ability to exercise market power or engage in anticompetitive behavior. The cable operators have presented no new arguments in response to the *Further Notice* [in this proceeding] that would alter these findings.

17. The suggestion that cable system operators are somehow involved in content decisions only as somewhat mechanical purchasing agents for their subscribers, without independent discretion over the nature of that product, is equally unavailing as a response to the concerns reflected in Section 613. Because there are more programming services available for distribution than there are cable channels to be used for distribution, systems operator inevitably must make judgments as to which services will be carried. Marketing and other economic considerations that involve both the desire to satisfy consumer demands and independent profit calculations certainly play a major role in programming distribution decisions. But there would also seem to be little doubt, especially when the value of programming content may be difficult to determine in advance of its distribution, that issues of judgment, showmanship, social conscience, and personal taste are also involved. The cable television industry has programming expenditures of almost eight billion dollars annually. If these expenditures were allocated evenly across the industry, a firm with 30% of the market would pay $2.5 billion annually for programming, making it one of the largest purchasers of entertainment programming in the world.

18. With respect to the argument that ordinary antitrust policies and enforcement are sufficient to address any legitimate issues raised, we fail to understand why the statutory provisions and policies incorporated into antitrust law should be favored over the more targeted legislative mandate incorporated in Section 613. We agree with Ameritech that, if Congress had intended for us to rely on an antitrust analysis by itself, it would have directed us to do so or would not have adopted Section 613. Instead, Congress directed that the Commission, in setting the horizontal limit, consider "among other public interest objectives" seven specific factors [listed in ¶8], none of which involves an antitrust analysis. Indeed, in enacting Section 613, Congress was aware that the cable industry at that time was far from being concentrated under a traditional antitrust analysis assuming a national market for cable competition, but nevertheless empowered

the Commission to enact horizontal limits using a public interest analysis.[8] The House Report stated that a traditional antitrust analysis should not be the "sole measure of concentration in media industries:"

> Both Congress and the Commission have historically recognized that diversity of information sources can only be assured by imposing limits on the ownership of media outlets that are substantially below those that a traditional antitrust analysis would allow. The Committee believes that concentration of media presents unique problems that must be considered by the Commission.[9]

19. In sum, we do not find persuasive arguments that the concerns leading to the adoption of Section 613 are adequately addressed by market forces or technical changes, are not significant enough to warrant remedial action, or are properly addressed through other regulatory mechanisms.

V. USING TOTAL MVPD SUBSCRIBERSHIP TO CALCULATE THE HORIZONTAL LIMIT

A. Background

26. In the *Further Notice*, we proposed that the horizontal ownership rules reflect the presence of all MVPDs rather than cable MVPDs alone in order to reflect changes in the MVPD market and their impact on programming power. We noted that the emergence of non-cable MVPDs diminishes an operator's market power over programming while conversely an operator's interest in non-cable MVPDs increases its market power. We requested comment on whether such a revision would be consistent with the Commission's statutory authority under Section 613. In calculating a cable operator's market share, we proposed that the numerator would contain the operator's cable subscribers plus that operator's non-cable MVPD subscribers, and the denominator would contain the total number of cable subscribers plus non-cable MVPD subscribers nationwide.

---

8. There are two prevailing measures of market concentration—the four firm concentration ratio ("Four Firm Ratio") and the Hirfindahl-Hirschman Index (HHI). The Four Firm Ratio measures the percentage of the market captured by the four largest companies in the market. The HHI reflects the distribution of market share among all firms in a given market, giving proportionately greater weight to the market shares of the larger firms. A market is generally considered concentrated when one firm, or a small group of firms, has a sufficient share of the market to exercise power over it. The Justice Department considers an industry concentrated when the HHI exceeds 1800 (although an HHI that exceeds 1000 prompts further evaluation) or when the four firm ratio exceeds 50%. According to the 1992 House Report, the HHI for the top 20 MSOs was 491 and the Four Firm ratio for the largest MSOs was 36%, well below the Justice Department's threshold. *See* House Report at 42.

9. House Report at 42. To the extent commenters are simply urging that the rules we adopt should be informed by an antitrust type of analysis, we note that no party has provided a specific analytical framework whereby this might be accomplished unless it is to suggest that the aggregation of interests within the cable industry does not pose an antitrust concern. Because cable operators are frequently monopolists in their local area, traditional horizontal analysis may not find harm in mergers. To the extent that is the case it reinforces, rather than undermines, the need for a separate analysis based on the standards set forth in Section 613.

B. Discussion

27. We conclude that it is appropriate under Section 613 to include all MVPD subscribers in the horizontal limits calculation in order to reflect changes in the marketplace since 1993. In order to encourage competition through over-building, however, we will not include cable subscribers that an MSO serves through non-incumbent cable systems, as that phrase is defined below. In the Commission's determination of the appropriate measurements under the horizontal ownership rules, Section 613(f)(2)(A) requires the Commission to ensure that a cable operator cannot, by virtue of its size or by acting in concert with other cable operators, unfairly impede the distribution of video programming. Moreover, Section 613(f)(2)(E), 47 U.S.C. §533(f)(2)(E), requires the Commission to consider "the dynamic nature of the communications marketplace."

28. The MVPD marketplace has changed since 1993. In our *Competition Reports*, we have stated that the effect of horizontal concentration on programming should take into account the presence of all MVPDs [including providers of cable, digital broadcast satellite (DBS) service, and so on, because the market significance of all these services is increasing over time.][10]

29. Although cable continues to be the primary source of multichannel programming, its share of the MVPD market fell to approximately 81.77% in June 1998 from 93.37% in December 1994. Currently, DBS has a 12.47% market share, home satellite delivery (HSD) has a 2.21% market share, [and so on for other delivery platforms.] Between June 1997 and June 1998, DBS grew from approximately 5 million subscribers to 7.2 million subscribers, an increase of almost 43%. By June 1999, DBS had grown to 10.078 million subscribers.

30. Given the past and expected future growth of non-cable MVPDs, we believe that it is consistent with Section 613's mandate to include all MVPD subscribers in both the denominator and the numerator when calculating an MSO's market share under the cable horizontal limits. We reject the argument that non-cable MVPDs should not be placed in the denominator because cable has certain types of competitive advantages over non-cable MVPDs. Although we agree that cable is still dominant in the MVPD marketplace, non-cable MVPDs have a growing impact on that marketplace. Inclusion of both cable and non-cable MVPD subscribers in the denominator will reflect the dynamic nature of the marketplace and the diminishing market power of cable operators as non-cable MVPDs increase their subscribership.

31. Likewise, when calculating an MSO's horizontal ownership, inclusion of both its cable and non-cable MVPDs subscribers in the numerator will reflect the market power held by that MSO through its total number of MVPD subscribers, whether reached through cable or other MVPD systems. This rule recognizes the increased market power gained by an MSO through its non-cable MVPD subscribers. This rule thus serves the objectives of Section 613 by reflecting both the dynamic nature of the marketplace and the ability of an MSO to impede the flow of programming by virtue of its total number of subscribers.

---

10. Fourth Annual Report, In the Matter of Annual Assessment of the Status of Competition in the Market for the Delivery of Video Programming, FCC 97-423, CS Docket No. 97-141 at §150 (Jan. 13, 1997).

32. This rule is also consistent with Section 613's directive that the Commission establish limits on the number of cable subscribers a person may serve. The rule will not limit the number of subscribers a cable operator may reach through alternative MVPD systems. It also will not apply to persons who have no attributable ownership interests in cable systems. This rule will create a sliding or adjustable cable horizontal ownership limit, under which the number of subscribers a cable operator is authorized to reach through cable systems would decrease in proportion with any increase in the number of subscribers that that entity reaches through other MVPD systems. Conversely, the cable horizontal ownership limit would be higher for a cable operator that reaches fewer subscribers through other MVPD systems. This sliding scale calculation will more accurately reflect a cable operator's potential monopsony power and the extent of its control in the MVPD marketplace as a whole.

33. In order to promote competition in the marketplace, we find it appropriate at this time to include in an MSO's horizontal limit only those cable subscribers that it serves through incumbent cable franchises. For purposes of the horizontal ownership rule, "incumbent cable franchise" shall mean all cable franchises in existence on the date this order is released, October 20, 1999, and all successors in interest to those franchises. An MSO's cable subscribers shall include all subscribers served by those incumbent cable franchises, regardless of when the subscribers were added to the incumbent cable franchise system.

34. This rule will continue to limit an MSO's growth through acquiring incumbent cable franchises where cable-programming power is dominant. On the other hand, the rule sets no limits on an MSO overbuilding "incumbent cable franchises," thereby encouraging competition, more outlets for programming networks and more choices for consumers. Thus, we find that the benefits of not counting customers served via overbuilding outweigh any potential anticompetitive impact on the programming marketplace.

VI. THE LEVEL OF THE HORIZONTAL OWNERSHIP LIMIT

A. Background

36. In the *Second Report and Order* issued in this proceeding, 8 FCC Rcd. 8565 (1993) [the document excerpted earlier this chapter], we found that a limit of 30 percent of households passed by all cable operators represented a careful balance between: (1) limiting the possible exertion by a cable operator of excessive market power in the purchase of video programming; and (2) ensuring that cable operators are able to expand and benefit from the economies of size necessary to encourage investment in new video programming technology and the deployment of other advanced technologies. In the *Further Notice*, we requested comment on whether 30% remains the appropriate horizontal limit in light of any changes in market conditions since 1993, when the initial rules in this proceeding were issued.

37. Because we agree with the cable operators that emerging non-cable MVPDs have an impact on the programming marketplace, we will, as discussed above, amend the horizontal limits rule to include all cable and non-cable MVPD subscribers in the calculation of the appropriate horizontal market. In addition, as discussed below, to the extent that cable operators have concerns regarding ef-

ficiencies of scale and competition with incumbent telephone service providers, we will permit cable operators to grow in size through overbuilding without counting subscribers reached in that manner towards an operator's horizontal limit. With these exceptions, which we will take into account in the calculation of the horizontal limit, the commenters have not presented any new or credible facts that would alter our conclusion regarding the need for and the considerations applicable to the adoption of an appropriate horizontal limit. Although the theoretical underpinnings for the rule remain unchanged and we continue to believe a 30% rule is appropriate, the effect of changing to a calculation based on the total size of the MVPD market results in a significant relaxation of the rule. The rule we adopt, a cable subscriber limit of no more than 30% of MVPD subscribers, is equivalent to a 36.7% limit based on cable subscribership alone. We find this change justified by the record and a consideration of the criteria specified in Section 613. Otherwise, however, we find nothing in the record that would justify upsetting the balance established in the initial rules. We discuss below the commenters' arguments regarding the cable operator's role as a media gatekeeper, competition, and the efficiencies of consolidation.

38. Guidelines A, B, C and G of Section 613(f) [quoted in ¶8] require the Commission to ensure that cable operators, unilaterally or in coordination, do not unreasonably restrict the flow of video programming to consumers and do not hinder the development of new programming from diverse voices. When Congress enacted Section 613(f)(1)(A), it concluded that cable industry concentration may enable MSOs to exercise excessive market power, or monopsony power, to bar the entry of new programmers and to reduce the number of media voices available to consumers:

> The cable industry has become highly concentrated. The potential effects of such concentration are barriers to entry for new programmers and a reduction in the number of media voices available to consumers.[11]

In particular, Congress was concerned with the possibility that "media gatekeepers will (1) slant information according to their own biases, or (2) provide no outlet for unorthodox or unpopular speech because it does not sell well, or both."[12] At the time of the 1992 Cable Act, cable served over 56 million households representing over 60% of all television households. As of June 1999 cable served more than 66 million homes, representing approximately 82% of all MVPD households. Thus, cable television remains the primary source of information and programming for many households in the United States. The horizontal rule limits the extent to which one or a few operators could reduce the number of diverse programming voices in the United States.

39. In the search for appropriate decisional criteria on which to base the Congressionally mandated ownership limit, one important element of the equation is the issue of what limit will sufficiently assure that no single cable operator "or group of cable operators" can "unfairly impede the flow of video programming from the video programmer to the consumer." 47 U.S.C. §533(f)(2)(A). If the rule can help to assure that no single operator or group of operators can unilaterally determine the success or failure of a new programming service, then the rule can achieve one important congressional purpose.

---

11. 1992 Cable Act, at §2(a)(4); 47 U.S.C. §521 note.
12. Senate Report at 32–33.

40. In our *1996 Competition Report*, based on information supplied by program providers in proceedings before the Commission, we suggested that, to have a long term prospect for success, the initial subscriber requirement for a new channel would be at least 10 to 20 million households. In our 1998 Competition Report, we noted the conventional understanding that in the typical mass market, an advertiser supported programming network needs between 15 and 20 million subscribers in order to ensure its long-term viability.

41. Staff analysis further supports 15 million as a minimum subscriber number for viability. In analyzing data consisting of 1988–98 subscription figures for 68 cable networks along with the launch date for each, staff found that networks that survive for a long period of time almost always obtain more than 15 million subscribers. Of the 39 networks started in or before 1988, 38 had more than 15 million subscribers in 1998. Thus, we find no basic disagreement as to the general requirement for a cable programmer to succeed and have a reasonable prospect for survival.

42. We will assume that a new programmer needs 15 million subscribers in order to have a reasonable chance to achieve economic viability. We use the lower number 15 over 20 million as a baseline in order to counterbalance the competing objectives of Section 613 to recognize the dynamics of the marketplace and the efficiencies of size. Fifteen million subscribers are not an absolute minimum for viability. It is instead a number of subscribers that provides a reasonable probability of long-term success for a cable network. Fifteen million subscribers represent approximately 18.56% of the MVPD market.

43. Using the 15 million-subscriber number, a programmer could still theoretically obtain the minimum necessary circulation even if one system operator held 35, 40, or even 80% of the market. We do not agree, however, with the position of the cable operators that this is the end of the analysis. We disagree with the cable operators' assumption that the horizontal limit should be designed with only a single large operator in mind. Congress was concerned not only by the behavior of a single operator, but also with the possibility that a group of operators might decline to carry the programmer. Section 613(f)(2)(A) specifically directs the Commission to

> ensure that no cable operator or *group of cable operators* can unfairly impede, either because of the size of any individual operator or because of joint actions by a *group of operators* of sufficient size, the flow of video programming from the video programmer to the consumer.[13]

Thus, the horizontal limit must account for the possibility that a group of operators will collectively deny carriage to a new programmer, either by unilateral, independent decisions or by tacit collusion. The limit should be set at a level such that, if each member of the group reaches the horizontal limit, the operators' "collective market share" will still leave enough of the market available to the programmer so that the programmer has a reasonable chance of obtaining the subscribers it needs in order to become financially viable. The legislative assumption is not unreasonable given an environment in which all the larger operators in the industry are vertically integrated so that all are both buyers and sellers of programming and have mutual incentives to reach carriage decisions beneficial to each other. Operators have incentives to agree to buy their programming from one another. Moreover,

---

13. Section 613(f)(2)(A) (emphasis added).

they have incentives to encourage one another to carry the same non-vertically integrated programming in order to share the costs of such programming.

44. The limit should also take into account that both cable operators and cable networks benefit from having a certain number of large MSOs. The MSOs benefit from the efficiencies of economies of scale. The cable networks benefit in that, if a new cable network obtains carriage on one large MSO, it will incur significantly lower transaction costs.

45. Examining the horizontal limit from the cable network's perspective, given that 20% of the market is the share that a cable network must reach to ensure viability, and assuming that there is a public value in minimizing transaction costs, one could argue that 20% is a lower bound on the appropriate MSO limit. A 20% limit would preserve the possibility that a cable network could acquire its minimum subscriber level in a single negotiation. In addition, if 5 MSOs were to divide the market, the cable network would have five chances of obtaining carriage. This would also serve the public interest by maximizing the potential that there would be at least 5 voices.

46. However, it is unlikely that a network could, in fact, achieve 20% penetration via a single MSO that reaches 20% of total subscribers. First, some of the MSO's cable systems may lack channel capacity and will be unable to carry the cable network at all. Second, those systems of the MSO that have channel capacity may place the cable network on an upper or digital tier or on a premium channel that not all subscribers receive. A 20% limit might therefore be unreasonably small in terms of efficiency from the cable network's point of view.

47. In addition, we find no reason to believe that the remaining four MSOs, comprising 80% of the market, would collectively decline to carry the new cable network, thereby leaving the programmer with only one MSO. Balancing the efficiencies of size against the possibility of group action, we believe that assuming coordinated action by two operators rather than by three or more operators is appropriate at this time. Under this scenario, if two MSOs, comprising 40% of the market, declined to carry a new cable network, this would leave 60% of the market available to the network. However, giving the cable operators the benefit of the doubt, we do not believe that a cable network requires an open field of 60% of the market in order to secure the 15 million subscribers the new cable network needs on average to succeed.

48. In this regard, we will examine and weigh various market factors to approximate a typical cable network's probable rate of success of reaching subscribers through cable operators that do not flatly deny the cable network carriage. [One recent census of cable network subscribers found cable networks had an average carriage rate of 53%, while another found an average carriage rate of 36%.]

49. A programming network's ability to obtain carriage on cable systems may be limited by market conditions such as the lack of channel capacity on certain cable systems, the high cost of competitive entry, the competitive advantages of networks carried by the largest MSOs, the demographics of audiences in certain viewing areas, and other non-quantifiable factors, such as the programming tastes of particular cable operators. In addition, given the process of selling cable service by tiers, even where a programming network is added to a particular system it is unlikely that all subscribers to the system will purchase the network.

Given these inherent roadblocks to carriage, we find that it is reasonable to assume that a programming network will have at the most a 50% success rate of overcoming these roadblocks with respect to each subscriber available to it.

50. Like the 15 million-subscriber figure, the 50% success rate figure is a rough attempt to quantify a multitude of business conditions that may vary widely from programmer to programmer. Some new cable networks may have a higher success rate if they are affiliated with existing networks or cable operators, while other new cable networks produced by parties new to the cable market may have a lower success rate. We believe that the 50% figure takes into account the varying factors for market entrance. Because we believe that a cable network has a 50% chance of successfully obtaining carriage, only 40% of the market need be available to a new cable network for it to reach the 15 million subscribers (or 20% of the market) it needs. Accordingly, it is not necessary to maximize the number of MSOs controlling 20% of the market or to protect 60% of the market for a new cable network. Moreover, given the limited benefit to the cable networks, a 20% cable horizontal ownership limit threatens to limit unduly an MSO's ability to achieve economies of scale.

52. A [limit as high as 40%] would pose problems. Although a cable network would have a reasonable chance of success if it gained access to an MSO at the 40% limit, two MSOs at the 40% limit, representing a total of 80% of the market, might decline to carry the new network. Even assuming that the remaining 20% of the market was in the hands of one MSO and that MSO agreed to carry the programmer, it is highly unlikely that the programmer would reach 100% of that MSO's subscribers for the reasons stated above. In addition, if the remaining 20% of the market is fragmented among several cable operators, the cable network again would be highly unlikely to succeed given a 50% success rate at carriage.

53. Approaching a horizontal limit from these two ends, a 20% limit favoring cable networks and a 40% limit favoring cable operators, we select a 30% limit as a reasonable balance between the interests of the cable networks and the cable operators. We believe that adopting a limit between 20% and 40% is reasonable given that the tradeoffs for the cable networks and the operators are roughly even. Based on this analysis, a new programmer would have a reasonable chance of success if 40% of the 80,000,000 subscriber MVPD market is available to it after two operators have denied it access to the other 60% of the market. In other words, a 30% limit on a single operator's size will thereby prevent two large operators from obtaining control over 60% of the market. Thus, even if two operators, covering 60% of the market, individually or collusively deny carriage to a programming network, the network will still have access to 40% of the market, thereby giving it a reasonable chance of financial viability.

54. While permitting cable operators to obtain economies of scale, the 30% limit serves the salutary purpose of ensuring that there will be at least 4 MSOs in the marketplace. The rule thus maximizes the potential number of MSOs that will purchase programming. With more MSOs making purchasing decisions, this increases the likelihood that the MSOs will make different programming choices and a greater variety of media voices will therefore be available to the public.

55. We conclude that a 30% limit would fulfill Section 613(f)(2)'s mandate to strike a proper balance between the dangers to new programmers and the bene-

fits to cable operators of economies of scale. Under current market conditions, we find that a 30% horizontal limit provides a new programmer with a reasonable chance of success, even if the largest operators decline to carry it. We acknowledge that the new cable programmer who is denied carriage by the largest operators may be at a severe competitive and financial disadvantage in the marketplace given the declining marginal cost basis of the programming distribution business.

56. The market power of large cable operators has the potential to prevent nascent cable networks from even launching and to cause current networks to fail. While the exercise of market power could result in lower negotiated programming costs for cable operators in the short run, it could also adversely affect the development of diverse and innovative programming in the long run. Studies have shown that increased horizontal concentration has both efficiency and negative market consequences. New networks might not be able to operate successfully subject to the lower prices that large operators are able to demand by virtue of their size. Launch costs for a new cable network are estimated to be between $100 to $125 million. New networks often must initially pay for carriage. In addition, although advertising revenue is critical for a cable network's long-term success, some industry analysts believe that new networks cannot attract significant advertising until they surpass at least 30 million subscribers. In particular, niche networks targeting small audiences with specific interests have difficulty attracting advertising. Given the significant amount of debt a new network must therefore carry before it begins earning affiliation and advertising revenues, nascent networks may not launch and new networks may fail because of an inability to carry this debt. The 30% limit recognizes this dynamic of the communications marketplace and the dynamic's ability to foreclose new programming. TCI's argument that consumers benefit from lower rates (as a result of lower programming costs enjoyed by large MSOs due to their bargaining power) takes into account only the efficiency effect of horizontal concentration.

61. If the sole guideline in adopting rules were to encourage the largest number of sources of editorial control possible, the horizontal limit would be quite low. Guidelines E and F of Section 613(f)(2), however, require the Commission to include in the rulemaking balance the efficiencies and benefits of consolidation and the dynamic nature of the communications marketplace. In the *Second Report and Order* and in the *Second Order on Reconsideration*, we recognized and weighed the benefits of clustering and economies of scale and determined that 30% was the appropriate number to encourage growth without unduly raising competitive concerns. We find no basis in this record to alter this balance. Cable operators argue that the limit should be raised so that they may compete with common carriers for the provision of Internet and telephony services. However, under the current rules, a cable operator may obtain as much as 30% of the cable nationwide market. A 30% limit allows a cable operator to gain access to a substantial portion of the market to provide Internet access and telephony. The cable operators have presented no credible evidence that a larger size is necessary for the deployment of advanced technologies or telephony. Moreover, we note the possibility of cooperative arrangements among operators to offer coordinated telephony services through their cable systems, so that a cable operator does not necessarily need to grow in absolute

size beyond the limit in order to participate in the offering of a national telephony service.

62. In addition, we disagree with the cable operators' arguments that the horizontal ownership rules prevent an MSO from clustering its systems in order to enjoy an economy of scale and to compete with incumbent local phone companies. As we stated earlier in this proceeding, "the 30% limit permits cable MSOs to cluster systems in order to gain efficiencies related to economies of scale and scope in administration, deployment of new technologies and services, extension into previously unserved territories, etc. Accordingly, the 30% limit simultaneously guards against the potential anticompetitive effects of horizontal concentration and allows cable MSOs to realize the benefits of clustering."[14] The horizontal limit permits an MSO to consolidate its systems in one area in order to compete with a local telephone company rival, if it wishes to do so. If an MSO must divest a system in order to comply with the horizontal ownership rules, the MSO has the discretion to decide what cluster of systems to retain in order to serve its business plans and customers.

63. Ameritech and Consumers Union raise the negative aspects of clustering, observing that clustering may enable cable operators to deny their competitors access to affiliated video programming and may deter overbuilders. RCN Telecom Services, Inc. requests that we limit the size of cable clusters in order to promote competition. In the *Second Report and Order*, we considered whether to adopt regional subscriber limits, but declined to do so. We stated that other provisions of the Cable Television Consumer Protection and Competition Act of 1992 that were specifically designed to introduce local competition would better address issues regarding regional concentration. In addition, there was no evidence in the record that indicated that any anticompetitive effects outweighed the potential benefits of cable clustering, such as regional programming, upgraded cable infrastructure and improved customer services. Likewise, the record in this proceeding shows that the benefits of clustering—including market efficiencies and the deployment of telephony and Internet access services—outweigh any alleged anticompetitive effects on local programming.

Notes and Questions

1. **Regional and National Limits.** Why would Congress want the Commission to prescribe any rule that deals with horizontal concentration of cable systems on a national basis? Don't cable systems compete for viewers within local, not national, markets? It seems highly unlikely that many people move from one region of the country to another in order to get better cable service. So why does the FCC focus on national subscribership limits?

The reason, of course, is that this section of the 1992 Cable Act responds to fears that cable systems might affect competition in the national program supply

---

14. In re Implementation of Section 11(c) of the Cable Television Consumer Protection and Competition Act of 1992: Horizontal Limits, MM Docket No. 92-264 (June 26, 1998), at ¶41.

market through their power as purchasers of programming ("monopsony" power). A firm that owned cable systems in many different regions of the country might have more power to affect competition in the program supply market than a firm that owned a cable system in only one of these towns. Given this, however, does it make sense to allow cable operators to cluster their service? And what about local or regional limits in addition to national ones—would such regulations serve any purpose?

2. Picking the Number. If the goal, then, is to stop large MSOs from exercising monopsony power in the supply market, why did the Commission choose 30 percent rather than some lower figure as the limit? Does the Commission have reason to believe that monopsony power would be curtailed in an industry in which three firms each accounted for 30 percent of all video subscribers? Did the agency choose to permit such a high degree of ownership concentration because it wanted to protect, as far as possible, substantial efficiencies that MSOs gain by integrating on a national scale? (If so, what are those efficiencies?) Was the FCC motivated, in part, by a belief that the markets in which cable operators compete are local and regional rather than national?[15]

3. Arbitrary Lines? Regardless of your response to the previous question, can you defend the various calculations the Commission used to reach the 30 percent limit against the charge that they are arbitrary? Consider, for example, the Commission's statement that "assuming coordinated action by two operators rather than by three or more operators is appropriate at this time." ¶47. Is this decision based on empirical evidence? Economic theory? Policy considerations? Magic? What of the two boundaries created in this proceeding—the 20% limit favoring cable networks and the 40% limit favoring cable operators? ¶53. The Commission states that a "20% limit would preserve the possibility that a cable network could acquire its minimum subscriber level in a single negotiation." ¶45. Isn't the same thing true of a 40% limit? What balance does the FCC purport to be striking?

4. Redundancy. How do the horizontal concentration regulations integrate into the panoply of restraints established by the 1992 Cable Act? Why wasn't this the only necessary regulation respecting competition in the national program supply market? Once horizontal concentration is confined within reasonable bounds, what need could remain for rules limiting vertical integration, or rules mandating leased access? As we asked in the questions following the materials on vertical integration: how could a cable firm with a small share of the national purchasing market profit from seeking to exclude other cable firms or unaffiliated program suppliers from its segment of the market?

The Commission responds to this sort of concern by stating that "Congress intended all the rules to work together in a complementary fashion." ¶15. But do

---

15. To the extent that cable companies compete locally for customers, "horizontal concentration" is a different issue. If cable is a natural monopoly, we expect each cable system to control a large percentage of its local market. At the local level, then, the 1992 Cable Act focuses on regulating the rates of cable systems, providing competing multichannel video program distributors equal access to cable programming, and favoring local broadcasters' carriage on cable systems.

they? If not, why doesn't the Commission more carefully relate the horizontal concentration and vertical integration rules to each other? Have the questions above convinced you that they are, in fact, integrally related?

5. The Commission's Perspective, Part II. Section 11(c)(2) of the 1992 Cable Act not only required the Commission to promulgate rules regarding vertical integration and horizontal concentration, but also required the Commission to "consider the necessity and appropriateness of imposing limitations on the degree to which multichannel video programming distributors may engage in the creation or production of video programming." §11(c)(2)(C). The Commission did just that— in the very same *Report and Order* excerpted in the section on vertical integration. Interestingly, in just a few small paragraphs, the Commission determined that no restrictions were necessary. "In view of the structural and behavioral restrictions already required under the 1992 Act, we do not believe that additional restrictions on the ability of multichannel distributors to engage in the creation or production of video programming are warranted at the present time. We conclude that at the present time the objectives of such a restriction are fully addressed by the other provisions...of the 1992 Cable Act." 8 FCC Rcd. 8562, at ¶106. This category was the only category for which the Commission had the discretion to decide not to regulate. Given its decision, do you think the Commission would also have chosen not to promulgate vertical or horizontal restraints, were that option available? If so, what, if anything, should that tell Congress? What should it tell a court reviewing a constitutional challenge to §§533(f)(1)(A) and (B)?

6. Cross-Ownership Limitations. Lastly, remember that, in addition to the horizontal and vertical restrictions discussed here, cable operators are also subject to cross-ownership restrictions of the sort introduced in Chapter Seven. In particular, section 76.501(a) of the Commission's rules (codified at 47 C.F.R. §76.501(a)) provides:

> No cable television system (including all parties under common control) shall carry the signal of any television broadcast station if such system directly or indirectly owns, operates, controls, or has an interest in a TV broadcast station whose [primary market] overlaps in whole or in part the service area of such system (i.e., the area within which the system is serving subscribers).

Given the discussions above, is this rule necessary? Is it surprising that the rule does not actually forbid cross-ownership but instead only prohibits the relevant cable operators from "carry[ing] the signal of any television broadcast station"? Or is that just semantics given that most cable operators *must* carry local broadcast channels under the federal must-carry provisions?

Judicial Review

In the course of a long and tortuous review process, the D.C. Circuit upheld the statutory provisions requiring vertical and horizontal limits but rejected the FCC orders (excerpted above) imposing those limits. One part of the broad facial challenge that resulted in the two *Turner* Supreme Court opinions (excerpted in Chapter Eleven) and the 1996 D.C. Circuit opinion in *Time Warner* (excerpted in Chapter Ten) was a constitutional challenge to 47 U.S.C. §§533(f)(1)(A) and (B), the provisions requiring vertical and horizontal restraints. The district court that heard these challenges held that subscriber limits were unconstitutional, but that the channel occupancy provision was constitutional. Daniels Cablevision, Inc. v. United States, 835 F. Supp. 1 (D.D.C. 1993). One week later, the FCC adopted the *Second Report and Order* excerpted above (which included both subscriber and channel occupancy limits), and Time Warner then petitioned the D.C. Circuit for review of those regulations. The D.C. Circuit's 1996 *Time Warner* decision, in a portion edited out of the excerpt in Chapter Ten, consolidated the facial constitutional challenge to §§533(f)(1)(A) and (B) with the challenges to the *Second Report and Order*, and thus declined in 1996 to consider the challenge to the statute separately from the challenge to the FCC's rules. *See* Time Warner Entertainment Co. v. FCC, 93 F.3d 957, 979-80 (D.C. Cir. 1996).

The judicial economies that the D.C. Circuit apparently envisioned in consolidating these challenges did not materialize. In October 1999 (after the consolidated cases had been scheduled for oral argument), the FCC issued the *Third Report and Order* excerpted above. The D.C. Circuit then severed the challenges to the statutory provisions from the challenges to the regulations, held the latter in abeyance, and considered only the facial challenge to §§533(f)(1)(A) and (B) — the same challenge that it had deferred in 1996. In Time Warner Entertainment Co. v. United States, 211 F.3d 1313 (D.C. Cir. 2000), the D.C. Circuit found that neither the subscriber limits provision nor the channel occupancy provision, on their face, violated the First Amendment.

Time Warner argued that both provisions were content based and thus subject to strict scrutiny. The D.C. Circuit, relying heavily on *Turner I*, concluded that §§533(f)(1)(A) and (B) were premised on cable operators' bottleneck power over the programming that enters the subscriber's home; according to the D.C. Circuit, "the legislative concern was not with the speech of a particular source but solely with promoting diversity and competition in the cable industry." *Id.* at 1321.[16] The court thus declined to apply strict scrutiny and applied intermediate scrutiny instead. On the application of this standard, Time Warner argued that the requirement of an important government interest was not met because the harms to which §§533(f)(1)(A) and (B) responded were speculative, and thus failed the requirement that they be "real, not merely conjectural." *Turner I*, 512 U.S. at 664. The D.C. Circuit, this time following the lead of *Turner II*, required only that Congress's inferences be reasonable; and it found that Congress met that deferential standard in positing that, first, increases in the concentration of cable operators threatened diversity and competition in the cable industry, and, second, that a cable company has an incentive to favor its affiliated programmers. *See* 211 F.3d at 1320, 1322. Lastly, in response to Time Warner's final argument that these provisions were unnecessary in light of other provisions, the D.C. Circuit stated: "Nor is it a fatal flaw that the subscriber limits provision focuses upon behavior already arguably proscribed by other laws. As a structural limitation, the subscriber limits provision adds a prophylaxis to the law and

---

16. *See also id.* at 1318 ("The subscriber limits preserve competition between the cable operator and its affiliated programmers on the one hand and unaffiliated providers of cable programming on the other. By placing a value upon diversity and competition in cable programming the Congress did not necessarily also value one speaker, or one type of speech, over another; it merely expressed its intention that there continue to be multiple speakers.").

avoids the burden of individual proceedings to remedy particular instances of anticompetitive behavior." *Id.* at 1320.[17]

Time Warner thus did not succeed in overcoming the high hurdle confronting a facial challenge to a statute.[18] Time Warner's challenge to the regulations excerpted above, however, still remained—and that challenge was successful. In Time Warner Entertainment Co. v. FCC, 2001 WL 201978, No. 94-1035 (D.C. Cir. March 2, 2001), the D.C. Circuit vacated both the channel occupancy limits and the subscriber limits. The court did not question the Commission's objective of ensuring program diversity on cable systems, nor did it think the FCC wrong in trying to ensure that no programmer could have its fate in the marketplace decided by the decision of a single cable operator. But the court did find the actual levels of the limitations to have been arbitrarily set and insufficiently justified by evidence on the administrative record.

As with the facial challenge to the statute, the D.C. Circuit applied the intermediate scrutiny of *Turner I* and *Turner II.* It found that the interests supporting the regulations were the same as the interests supporting §§533(f)(1)(A) and (B)—promoting diversity in ideas and speech and preserving competition—and it reiterated its conclusion in the 2000 opinion that Congress had drawn reasonable inferences that increases in the concentration of cable operators threatened diversity and competition. But, the court added: "the FCC must still justify the limits that it has chosen as not burdening substantially more speech than necessary. In addition, in 'demonstrat[ing] that the recited harms are real, not merely conjectural,' *Turner I,* 512 U.S. at 664, the FCC must show a record that validates the regulations, not just the abstract statutory authority." 2001 WL 201978, at *3.

As to the channel occupancy rules that limit a cable system's carriage of affiliated programming to forty percent of the system's channels, the court stated that "the FCC seems to have plucked the 40% limit out of thin air." *Id.* at *11. The court reversed the FCC's adoption of this limit:

> We recognize that in drawing a numerical line an agency will ultimately indulge in some inescapable residue of arbitrariness; even if 40% is a highly justifiable pick, no one could expect the Commission to show why it was materially better than 39% or 41%. But to pass even the arbitrary and capricious standard, the agency must at least reveal a rational connection between the facts found and the choice made. Here the FCC must also meet First Amendment intermediate scrutiny. Yet it appears to provide nothing but the conclusion that "we believe that a 40% limit is appropriate to balance the goals." See *Second Report and Order,* 8 FCC Rcd. 8565, at ¶68 (1993). What are the conditions that make 50% too high and 30% too low? How great is the risk presented by current market conditions? These questions are left unanswered by the Commission's discussion.

---

17. *See also id.* at 1322-23 (rejecting this argument against the channel occupancy provision, stating that "a prophylactic, structural limitation is not rendered unnecessary merely because preexisting statutes impose behavioral norms and *ex post* remedies").

18. In the 2000 opinion, the D.C. Circuit emphasized the nature of the broad, facial challenge to the statute: "Time Warner argues that both provisions facially—that is, no matter how sensitively or sensibly they might be implemented—violate the First Amendment to the Constitution of the United States." *Id.* at 1315.

Id.

With regard to the horizontal ownership limit, the court noted the FCC's assumption that there was a serious risk that two competitors would engage in collusion, but the court found that Congress made no judgment regarding collusion and that the FCC's assumption of collusion was "mere conjecture." *Id.* at *4. The court also discussed the FCC's suggestion, in ¶54 of the *Third Report and Order*, that the thirty percent limit could be justified as enhancing diversity. The court found, however, that "Congress has not given the Commission authority to impose, solely on the basis of the 'diversity' precept, a limit that does more than guarantee a programmer two possible outlets (each of them a market adequate for viability)." *Id.* at *9. Thus, as to the FCC's subscriber limits, the court concluded that

> the 30% horizontal limit is in excess of statutory authority. While a 60% limit might be appropriate as necessary to ensure that programmers had an adequate "open field" even in the face of rejection by the largest company, the present record supports no more. In addition, the statute allows the Commission to act prophylactically against the risk of "unfair" conduct by cable operators that might unduly impede the flow of programming, either by the "joint" actions of two or more companies or the independent action of a single company of sufficient size. But the Commission has pointed to nothing in the record supporting a non-conjectural risk of anticompetitive behavior, either by collusion or other means.

Id. at *11.

II. REGULATION OF PROGRAM SUPPLY CONTRACTS

A principal purpose of the 1992 Cable Act was to encourage the continued deployment of multichannel technologies (like direct broadcast satellite) that might ultimately compete with cable television. One barrier facing those rival technologies was the possibility that cable operators might make it difficult for them to obtain high-quality programming. Congress thus drafted a provision that empowered the FCC to intervene on behalf of rival MVPDs and ensure "equal access" to program content. The following *Report and Order* summarizes that statutory provision and explains the agency's implementing regulations.

DEVELOPMENT OF COMPETITION AND DIVERSITY IN VIDEO PROGRAMMING DISTRIBUTION AND CARRIAGE
First Report and Order, 8 FCC Rcd. 3359 (1993)

I. INTRODUCTION

1. This *Report and Order* adopts rules to implement section 19 of the Cable Television Consumer Protection and Competition Act of 1992 ("1992 Cable Act"), which adds a new section 628 prohibiting unfair or discriminatory prac-

tices in the sale of satellite cable and satellite broadcast programming to the Communications Act of 1934. Section 628 [codified at 47 U.S.C. §548] is intended to increase competition and diversity in the multichannel video programming market, as well as to foster the development of competition to traditional cable systems, by prescribing regulations that govern the access by competing multichannel systems to cable programming services.

2. Section 628(a) states that the purpose of this provision "is to promote the public interest, convenience, and necessity by increasing competition and diversity in the multichannel video programming market, to increase the availability of satellite cable programming and satellite broadcast programming to persons in rural and other areas not currently able to receive such programming, and to spur the development of communications technologies." Section 628(b) states that "it shall be unlawful for a cable operator, a satellite cable programming vendor in which a cable operator has an attributable interest, or a satellite broadcast programming vendor to engage in unfair methods of competition or unfair or deceptive acts or practices, the purpose or effect of which is to hinder significantly or to prevent any multichannel video programming distributor from providing satellite cable programming or satellite broadcast programming to subscribers or consumers."

3. Section 628(c) instructs the Commission to adopt regulations to specify particular conduct that is prohibited by subsection (b). Specifically, the regulations are to:

(1) establish safeguards to prevent undue influence by cable operators upon actions by affiliated program vendors related to the sale of programming to unaffiliated distributors;

(2) prohibit price discrimination by vertically integrated satellite cable programming vendors and satellite broadcast programming vendors; and

(3) prohibit exclusive contracts between a cable operator and a vertically integrated programming vendor in areas that are not served by a cable operator and any such exclusive arrangements in areas served by cable that are not found in the public interest by the Commission.

The statute provides parties aggrieved by conduct alleged to violate the program access provisions the right to commence an adjudicatory proceeding before the Commission.

6. The *Notice of Proposed Rulemaking* [in this proceeding] observed that the statute permits programming vendors to impose certain requirements to account for different characteristics among multichannel video programming distributors (MVPDs),[19] including cost and volume-related factors, and inquired whether other legitimate economic factors may exist to explain price differences that are consistent with the statute.

---

19. For the purposes of the regulations to implement section 628, we will define a "multichannel video programming distributor" as an entity engaged in the business of making available for purchase, by subscribers or customers, multiple channels of video programming. Such entities include, but are not limited to, a cable operator, a multichannel multipoint distribution service, a direct broadcast satellite service, a television receive-only satellite program distributor, and a satellite master antenna television system operator, as well as buying groups or agents of all such entities.

II. SUMMARY OF DECISION

9. In enacting the program access provisions of the 1992 Cable Act, Congress expressed its concern that potential competitors to incumbent cable operators often face unfair hurdles when attempting to gain access to the programming they need in order to provide a viable and competitive multichannel alternative to the American public. Various distributors have described numerous situations in which their ability to secure programming has been impaired, either by refusals to sell cable programming by certain vendors or by discriminatory terms and conditions imposed upon the acquisition of various programming services.

10. With respect to the entities covered by section 628, we will follow the plain language of the statute by applying the general prohibition in section 628(b) against "unfair methods of competition" and "unfair or deceptive acts or practices" to all cable operators, all satellite broadcast programming vendors and vertically integrated satellite cable programmers. Thus, a cable operator or satellite broadcast programmer may become subject to this provision of the 1992 Cable Act even if it is not vertically integrated.[20] By contrast, for the more specific proscriptions in section 628(c), vertical integration is more often an essential element of a complaint.

11. As a general matter, in order to file a complaint regarding discrimination, exclusive contracts, or undue influence under section 628(c), vertical integration need not exist in the specific market at issue. Rather, the complainant need show only that the relevant programmer or cable operator is vertically integrated in any market. We believe that this approach best addresses Congress' apparent concern with industry-wide influences that can occur even in the absence of a vertical relationship in the complainant's specific market.

17. In order to fulfill Congress' directive that section 628 complaints be resolved expeditiously, we have developed a streamlined complaint process that will enable us to settle uncomplicated complaints quickly while still resolving complex cases in a timely manner. Our rules will encourage program vendors to provide relevant information to distributors before a complaint is filed with the Commission. In the event that a vendor declines to provide such information, it will be sufficient for a distributor to submit a sworn complaint alleging, upon information and belief, that an impermissible price differential or exclusive arrangement exists, or that other prohibited conduct—such as undue influence or an unreasonable refusal to sell—has occurred. The programmer will have the opportunity to refute the charge. Complainants may then submit a reply, after which the Commission will review the pleadings and assess whether the complaint can be resolved on the written record or whether further investigation is required. If further action is necessary, the staff will have the discretion either to require the submission of further information or, where appropriate, allow discovery and/or designate the proceeding for a hearing before an Administrative Law Judge.

21. The program access requirements of section 628 have at their heart the objective of releasing programming to the existing or potential competitors of

---

20. [Ed. By "vertical integration" the Commission means that the MVPD has a five percent or greater ownership interest in the programmer or vice versa.]

traditional cable systems so that the public may benefit from the development of competitive distributors. The 1992 Cable Act and its legislative history reflect congressional findings that horizontal concentration in the cable television industry,[21] combined with extensive vertical integration (*i.e.*, combined ownership of cable systems and suppliers of cable programming),[22] has created an imbalance of power, both between cable operators and program vendors and between incumbent cable operators and their multichannel competitors (*i.e.*, other cable systems, home satellite dish (HSD) distributors, direct broadcast satellite (DBS) providers, satellite master antenna television (SMATV) systems, wireless cable operators, etc.). This imbalance has limited the development of competition and restricted consumer choice. Congress further concluded that vertically integrated program suppliers have the incentive and ability to favor their affiliated cable operators over other multichannel programming distributors.[23] To address this problem, Congress chose program access provisions targeted toward cable satellite programming vendors in which cable operators have an "attributable" interest and toward satellite broadcast programming vendors regardless of vertical relationships.

IV. UNFAIR METHODS OF COMPETITION AND DECEPTIVE PRACTICES

36. Section 628(b) provides that:

> It shall be unlawful for a cable operator, a satellite cable programming vendor in which a cable operator has an attributable interest, or a satellite broadcast programming vendor to engage in unfair methods of competition or unfair or deceptive acts or practices, the purpose or effect of which is to hinder significantly or to prevent any multichannel video programming distributor from providing satellite cable programming or satellite broadcast programming to subscribers or consumers.

37. The provisions of section 628(c) that follow this general prohibition make it clear that certain types of exclusive contracting, undue influence among affiliates, and discriminatory sales practices are to be treated as unfair methods of competition or unfair or deceptive acts. In the *Notice*, we sought comment on whether Congress intended for the Commission to regulate any additional "unfair methods of competition or unfair or deceptive acts or practices" beyond

---

21. For example, the House Report observes that the largest multiple system operator (MSO), TCI, controls access to almost 25 percent of the nation's cable subscribers.

22. The legislative history lists 15 of the most popular cable programming services as being owned by cable operators. The House Report notes that, according to the National Cable Television Association, 39 of the 68 nationally delivered cable networks have some ownership affiliation with cable operators.

23. In Report in MM Docket No. 89-600, 5 FCC Rcd. 4962 (1990) (*1990 Cable Report*), the Commission similarly concluded that the cable television industry has become increasingly concentrated and vertically integrated, thus providing multiple system operators and vertically integrated cable operators the potential to pursue anticompetitive actions against programming services or competing multichannel providers. The 1990 Cable Report also found evidence that some cable operators have indeed used this potential anticompetitively. For example, alternative distributors presented evidence that some programming vendors refused to sell cable programming, and wireless cable and SMATV operators, HSD distributors, and second competitive cable systems described the discriminatory terms and conditions imposed on their acquisitions of various programming services. *See 1990 Cable Report*, 5 FCC Rcd. 5006, 5008, and 5021.

those specifically referenced in subsection (c). In particular, we asked whether other practices that are precluded by the various antitrust laws—such as refusals to deal or "tying" arrangements—are encompassed within the terms of section 628 and warrant Commission regulation. We also noted that the language of section 628(b) itself addresses only practices that are (i) "unfair," "deceptive," or "discriminatory," and (ii) could significantly hinder multichannel video programming distributors from providing satellite programming to consumers. Moreover, because practices that a particular competitor might consider "unfair" or "discriminatory" may not significantly harm competition generally in distributing multichannel video programming, we questioned whether our analysis should consider harm to (i) consumers, measured by the amount or availability of programming to consumers in the market; (ii) other distributors in the market; or (iii) both consumers and distributors.

41. Although the types of conduct more specifically referenced in the statute, *i.e.*, exclusive contracting, undue influence among affiliates, and discriminatory sales practices, appear to be the primary areas of congressional concern, section 628(b) is a clear repository of Commission jurisdiction to adopt additional rules or to take additional actions to accomplish the statutory objectives should additional types of conduct emerge as barriers to competition and obstacles to the broader distribution of satellite cable and broadcast video programming. In this regard, it is worth emphasizing that the language of section 628(b) applies on its face to all cable operators. Elements of an offense under this provision would, however, include a demonstration that "the purpose or effect" of the conduct was to "hinder significantly or to prevent any multichannel video programming distributor from providing satellite cable programming or satellite broadcast programming to subscribers or consumers." In particular, the complainant must show that its ability to distribute programming to customers has been hampered in some fashion.

V. COMPETITIVE HARM OR HINDRANCE TO ACCESS AS AN ELEMENT OF RULES

42. We have concluded that parties bringing complaints under section 628(b) must demonstrate how the allegedly unfair practice has hampered or prevented the distribution of programming. A related question asked in the *Notice* was whether a similar showing of "harm" must be made by complainants seeking relief under the more specific provisions of section 628(c).

46. One interpretation of the words of section 628 is that subsection (b) generally proscribes anticompetitive behavior that causes harm to MVPDs, and that subsection (c) defines specific conduct which the Commission's rules must prohibit and which Congress has already determined causes anticompetitive harm. Alternatively, because subsection (c) requires the Commission to "prescribe regulations to specify particular conduct that is prohibited by subsection (b)," it is possible to read subsection (b)'s limitations as equally applicable to the behavior specified in subsection (c), such that the conduct specified in subsection (c) is only prohibited if it is shown to "hinder significantly or prevent" any MVPD from providing programming.

47. The legislative history indicates that Congress did not intend to place a threshold burden on aggrieved MVPDs to show either specific or generalized harm to competition in those circumstances specifically prescribed in subsection

(c). We conclude, therefore, that the language in subsection (b) was not intended to impose an additional burden or threshold showing on complainants with respect to the activities specified in subsection (c). Rather, we believe that if behavior meets the definitions of the activities proscribed in subsection (c), such practices are implicitly harmful.[24]

VI. LIMITATIONS ON EXCLUSIVE CONTRACTING

50. As indicated above, the Commission is directed to prescribe program access regulations to specify particular conduct that is prohibited in three specific areas. The record in this proceeding reveals that there are two key areas of concern for cable competitors. First, a number of MVPDs assert that they have been unable to secure certain programming at all because programming vendors have exclusive contracts with cable operators, even in areas not currently served by cable. The first area we address thus relates to limitations of exclusive contracting. Second, even where MVPDs have been able to gain access to programming, they contend that they must pay unreasonably high prices for it. We accordingly will next turn to a discussion of the price discrimination prohibitions of section 628(c)(2)(B). Finally, we address the prohibition against "undue influence" in section 628(c)(2)(A), which received much less attention in the record.

A. Exclusive Contracts in Areas Not Served by Cable

59. Section 628(c)(2)(C) is specific in mandating implementing regulations that prohibit "practices, understandings, arrangements, and activities, including exclusive contracts" between cable operators and vertically integrated satellite cable programming vendors or satellite broadcast programming vendors that prevent MVPDs from obtaining such programming for distribution "in areas not served by a cable operator as of the date of enactment of this section." The statute is unequivocal in this regard and thus the rules adopted will provide that such practices constitute a per se violation. As indicated in the Conference Report, an area "served" by a cable system is defined as "an area actually passed by a cable system and which can be connected for a standard connection fee."

61. As for "other practices, understandings, arrangements, and activities" that should come within the scope of our rules, we will prohibit vertically integrated programmers from engaging in activities that result in de facto exclusivity, or from imposing requirements on MVPDs that prevent or restrict them from delivering their programming to any unserved area.

B. Exclusive Contracts in Areas Served by Cable

62. Section 628(c)(2)(D) treats exclusive contracts between vertically integrated programming vendors and cable operators in areas served by cable in a somewhat less restrictive manner. Contracts of this type are to be prohibited unless the Commission determines that "such contract is in the public interest." In

---

24. In other words, if a price differential, or the magnitude of a particular price differential, between competing MVPDs cannot be justified under the statutory allowances, then discrimination has occurred, and a finding of harm is implicit. Similarly, if a vertically integrated programming vendor enters into an exclusive contract with a cable operator that governs an unserved area, or an exclusive contract governing a served area that does not meet the statutory public interest standard, a finding of harm is implicit.

making this judgment, the Commission is to consider each of the following factors with respect to the effect of such contract on the distribution of video programming in that area:

(A) the effect of such exclusive contract on the development of competition in local and national multichannel video programming distribution markets;

(B) the effect of such exclusive contract on competition from multichannel video programming distribution technologies other than cable;

(C) the effect of such exclusive contract on the attraction of capital investment in the production and distribution of new satellite cable programming;

(D) the effect of such exclusive contract on diversity of programming in the multichannel video programming distribution market; and

(E) the duration of the exclusive contract.

63. We note that exclusivity under this provision is not prohibited. As a general matter, the public interest in exclusivity in the sale of entertainment programming is widely recognized. Indeed, elsewhere in the 1992 Cable Act, in the context of the broadcast station-cable system relationship, specific steps have been taken to protect exclusive rights. In the unique situation presented here, however, it is clear that exclusivity is not favored. Congress has clearly placed a higher value on new competitive entry than on the continuation of exclusive distribution practices that impede this entry. In its 1990 Cable Report, the Commission itself articulated this balance as follows: "While we agree with the cable commenters that the Commission should and does generally support exclusivity rights, we believe that the public interest in developing competition to the local cable operator justifies temporary, limited and targeted intervention to ensure that alternative multichannel program providers have fair and equitable access to programming."[25] Moreover, as stated by one of the authors of section 628, "exclusive programming that is not designed to kill the competition is still permitted."[26] Cable systems have generally developed without effective competition and it is recognized that if "facilities-based"[27] competition is to develop, access to programming is an essential prerequisite. We thus believe and find it entirely consistent with the objectives of the Act that, while exclusivity may be shown to be in the public interest in certain circumstances, the burden must be on the party seeking exclusivity to demonstrate persuasively that it is justified.

64. *Public Interest Standard.* As for the appropriate standard to be applied when making this public interest determination, we do not believe that it is necessary or consistent with the statutory language to articulate a single standard in this proceeding that can govern the public interest assessment generally. We believe, at least at the outset, that it is more consistent with the statute to require individual, case-by-case determinations using the five statutory criteria specified.

---

25. *1990 Cable Report*, 5 FCC Rcd. at 5031.

26. Congressional Record, July 23, 1992 at 6534 (Statement of Representative Tauzin).

27. "Facilities-based competition" is a term used in the legislative history of the Act to emphasize that program competition can only become possible if alternative facilities to deliver programming to subscribers are first created. The focus in the 1992 Cable Act is on assuring that facilities-based competition develops.

This flexible approach will permit us to evaluate and weigh each factor within a specific fact situation. We emphasize, moreover, that we believe that the statute requires that the burden be placed on the proponent of exclusivity to demonstrate that exclusivity is in the public interest.

65. Many commenters urged us to particularize in advance, by rule if possible, specific situations in which it could be established that an exclusive contract would be in the public interest. For example, many commenters argue that exclusivity is essential for the development, promotion and launch of new programming services. One commenter suggests that exclusivity should be prohibited only if it deprives an MVPD of a vital program service necessary to its competitive survival; another suggests that exclusivity should be permitted if "substitute" programming is available; another suggests that a party seeking to enforce cable-only exclusivity must make a positive showing that such exclusivity will not preclude effective competition. Particularly with respect to new programming, we recognize that there may well be circumstances in which exclusivity could be shown to meet the public interest test, especially when the launch of local origination programming is involved that may rely heavily on exclusivity to generate financial support due to its more limited appeal to a specific regional market.[28] The record is insufficient, however, on this point, or with respect to the other suggestions received, to support a general finding or to identify appropriate general limitations on, for example, such factors as the permissible duration of exclusivity.[29] Thus, we will handle such exclusivity proposals on a case-by-case basis.

66. *Approval of Contracts.* Section 628(c)(2)(D) states on its face that exclusive contracts in served areas are prohibited unless the Commission finds that exclusivity is in the public interest. Thus, as many commenters observed, the statute itself requires that the Commission make an affirmative finding that a specific exclusive contract meets the statutory public interest standard before the contract can be enforced.

67. Thus, we will require any vertically integrated programmer or any cable operator seeking to execute an exclusive contract to seek and obtain our public interest judgment before doing so. This may be accomplished through the submission of a petition containing those portions of the programming contract relevant to exclusivity to the Commission for approval, along with a statement setting forth the petitioner's reasons that support a finding that the contract meets the public interest test that addresses each of the five criteria outlined in section 628(c)(4). The petition will be placed on public notice for 30 days, and any MVPD that actually or potentially competes with the cable operator may file an opposition,[30] arguing that, under the statutory criteria, exclusivity in this case is

28. For example, it is possible that local or regional news channels could be economically infeasible absent an exclusivity agreement.

29. For example, the record reflects wide disagreement on the appropriate duration of such exclusivity, with proposals ranging from two to seven years, ten years, and even longer. None of the commenters expressing a view, however, supports its proposal with any empirical evidence or concrete support to justify its conclusion. While we sought comment on whether any additional considerations were relevant to the public interest determination, the commenters did not suggest anything that is not already well within the scope of the statutory factors.

30. In view of the underlying purpose of section 628—to promote a competitive multichannel video marketplace—we believe parties with sufficient standing to challenge an ex-

not in the public interest. If the Commission determines that the petitioner has made a persuasive public interest showing, it will issue an order granting the petition and approving the contract.

VII. PROHIBITIONS AGAINST DISCRIMINATION

82. Section 628(c)(2)(B) requires the Commission to:

prohibit discrimination by a satellite cable programming vendor in which a cable operator has an attributable interest or by a satellite broadcast programming vendor in the prices, terms, and conditions of sale or delivery of satellite cable programming or satellite broadcast programming among or between cable systems, cable operators, or other multichannel video programming distributors, or their agents or buying groups; except that such a satellite cable programming vendor in which a cable operator has an attributable interest or such a satellite broadcast programming vendor shall not be prohibited from—

(i) imposing reasonable requirements for creditworthiness, offering of service, and financial stability and standards regarding character and technical quality;

(ii) establishing different prices, terms, and conditions to take into account actual and reasonable differences in the cost of creation, sale, delivery, or transmission of satellite cable programming or satellite broadcast programming;

(iii) establishing different prices, terms, and conditions which take into account economies of scale, cost savings, or other direct and legitimate economic benefits reasonably attributable to the number of subscribers served by the distributor; or

(iv) entering into an exclusive contract that is permitted under subparagraph (D).

A. Definitions of "Competing" and "Similarly-Situated" Distributors

96. *"Competing" Distributors.* Because section 628 is intended to prevent and remedy anticompetitive conduct in the multichannel video marketplace, complaints of discriminatory conduct should logically involve competing distributors. Thus, we will require that a complainant demonstrate that it has been offered or is paying a higher price, or has received less favorable terms, than a competing distributor. In establishing that another distributor is a competitor for these purposes, we will require that there be some overlap in actual or proposed service area. Moreover, the geographic market for assessing whether distributors compete with each other (either actually or potentially) can be local, regional or national, depending on how the distributor buys and distributes programming. For example, certain locally-oriented distributors, such as cable, MMDS, and SMATV operators, compete directly within a particular local market. Such distributors therefore will generally file discrimination complaints if another local

---

clusive arrangement will be those alternative distributors that provide actual or potential competition in any area covered by the program contract. A similar analysis will be applied when evaluating discrimination complaints.

distributor received a more favorable programming contract. With respect to nationally-oriented competitors that buy programming and serve subscribers beyond a local or regional market — such as DBS and HSD distributors — parties may make complaints based on comparisons between contracts of national competitors, provided that the complaint includes a justification for that comparison.

99. In evaluating a discrimination complaint, we believe that it will often be useful to conduct a two-step analysis. First, we will compare the difference in programming prices (or terms or conditions) paid by (or offered to) the complainant and the competing distributor. Second, we will allow the programmer to justify the difference under the statutory factors by either (i) submitting a showing that one or more of the factors is involved and the price differential reflecting those factors is reasonable, or (ii) submitting an alternative contract for a more reasonably comparable, or more "similarly situated", distributor. Although such a contract will not necessarily provide definitive evidence that the price difference can be explained under the statutory factors, we believe that it will often be useful in assessing whether the programmer has adequately explained the difference. For purposes of evaluating alternative contracts offered by programmers, we will define a distributor as "similarly situated" with respect to the complainant if it operates within a proximate geographic region, has roughly the same number of subscribers, and purchases a similar service, while also using the same distribution technology as the "competing" distributor with whom the complainant seeks to compare itself. We emphasize that an analysis of "similarly situated" distributors may be useful in demonstrating that the vendor has offered comparable terms to distributors with similar attributes. However, additional evidence may be needed to establish that the magnitude of a price difference for a consistently applied term (such as a standard volume discount) is reasonably justified under the statute's permissible factors.

100. We believe that these regulations will effectively prohibit discriminatory practices by programming vendors, while still following the statute's objectives to "rely on the marketplace, to the maximum extent feasible, to achieve greater availability" of the relevant programming. In this regard, we believe that certain practices involving price differentials benefit the public by increasing the availability of programming — as well as reducing the price of service — to consumers. For instance, we conclude that our rules must allow for fundamental differences in pricing of satellite cable programming as opposed to satellite broadcast programming, because satellite broadcast programming vendors face a unique, artificial ceiling on program prices as well as comparative ease of entry barriers for potential competitors seeking to offer the same signal.[31] In addition, we also recognize that certain regional programming services use a form of graduated prices to promote broad distribution of the service into more distant communities. We also believe that our regulations regarding discriminatory practices will satisfy the stated policy of Congress to "ensure that cable operators continue to expand, where economically justified, their capacity and the programs offered over their

---

31. Given the virtual lack of entry barriers for potential competitors to satellite broadcast programming, vendors of such programming are constrained to set their prices below a potential competitor's cost of obtaining the signal directly from the satellite. If the vendor's price exceeds this cost, the potential competitor has an incentive to obtain the signal directly rather than purchase it from the vendor.

cable systems."[32] Furthermore, we believe that faithful implementation of the statute requires us to allow for differences based on the permissible factors enumerated in section 628(c)(2)(B)(i)–(iv), as defined below, and that we must deny claims of discrimination resulting from factors that the 1992 Cable Act has established as entirely justified and reasonable.

C. Justifiable Price Differences

105. We will generally permit vendors to employ legitimate discounts associated with the factors specified in section 628(c)(2)(B), provided that similar terms are standardly available to various distributors. Therefore, we adopt the following definitions and guidelines for the factors involving, in general terms: (i) cost differences at the wholesale level among distributors, (ii) volume differences, (iii) creditworthiness and financial stability, and (iv) differences in "offering of service."[33]

106. *Cost Justifications.* Section 628(c)(2)(B)(ii) allows a vendor to establish different prices, terms, and conditions to take into account actual and reasonable differences in the cost of creation, sale, delivery, or transmission of satellite cable programming or satellite broadcast programming. We agree with those commenters suggesting that the record in this proceeding supports the preliminary conclusion in the *Notice* that service to HSD distributors may be more costly than service to others using different delivery systems such as cable operators, as additional costs are often incurred for advertising expenses, copyright fees, customer service, DBS Authorization Center charges, and signal security. The record indicates that these cost differences are particularly evident when providing program services to HSD distributors who do not provide a complete distribution path to individual subscribers. We also recognize that cost differences may occur within a given technology as well as between technologies. Therefore, the adopted regulations will allow vendors to base programming prices on legitimate cost factors. Vendors will not have to use a uniform rate card, although they will incur the risk and burden of showing that the cost factors they claim cause a price differential are legitimate and are not designed to conceal prohibited discrimination.

107. The record also raises the issue of whether a vendor may take into account those cost differences incurred by distributors in providing service to subscribers—cost differences at the retail level—when justifying price differences for programming as charged to distributors. Although we recognize that costs incurred by some distributors when delivering their services to consumers may be lower than for others (*e.g.*, HSD vs. cable), we believe that it would be contrary to the purposes of the Act and disserve the public to allow vendors to charge higher prices based on this factor. In particular, we believe that such a result could artificially raise the retail price of programming and discourage the development of low-cost technologies contrary to the statute's goals. Moreover, contrary to the claims of some commenters that HSD distributors will simply retain

---

32. *See* 1992 Cable Act, §2(b)(3).

33. We note that §628(c)(2)(B) also permits a programming vendor to make allowances for differences in "character" and "technical quality" in establishing prices for various distributors. Due to the nature of these considerations, we believe that these aspects are most appropriately considered on a case-by-case basis.

any savings rather than pass them on to HSD users, we believe the HSD market is sufficiently competitive to ensure that savings will inure to the benefit of the public. Accordingly, we will generally reject a vendor's consideration of a distributor's costs in delivering service to subscribers. A vendor who can show that the lower price offered to the distributor will not result in lower prices to consumers because the distributor is simply retaining the potential cost savings in the form of higher profits, can justify a price differential based on retail costs.

108. *Volume Justifications.* As a second consideration, section 628(c)(2)(B)(iii) permits a vendor to establish different prices, terms, and conditions that take into account economies of scale, cost savings, or other direct and legitimate benefits reasonably attributable to the number of subscribers served by the distributor. The record in this proceeding indicates that volume-related information is often available on some rate cards through "volume discounts" based upon a distributor's number of subscribers. We observe, however, that the statute speaks of "economies of scale, cost savings, or other direct and legitimate economic benefits reasonably attributable to the number of subscribers" rather than simple volume discounts. As possible standards related to volume, we could establish rules to require that rate cards reflect economies due to volume differences between distributors or adopt the recommendations of certain alternative distributors to permit only cost-based volume discounts. Alternatively, other parties have argued that in addition to cost economies, a larger number of subscribers confers direct non-cost "economic benefits" by delivering more viewers, thus increasing revenue from advertising more than proportionally, and providing a larger base for amortizing the costs of the programming service. We believe that this interpretation most closely follows the language of section 628 regarding "direct and legitimate economic benefits," which distinguishes "volume differences" from the "cost differences" considered in the first permissible factor. Therefore, we will permit vendors to establish pricing schedules based on volume-related factors reflecting direct economic benefits to the extent that such pricing schedules are standardly available to similarly situated distributors.

109. *Justifications based on creditworthiness, offering of service, and financial stability and standards regarding character and technical standard.* As provided in the statute, our adopted regulations also will allow programming vendors to take into account a distributor or customer's creditworthiness or financial stability when it negotiates a price for a programming service. However, any distinctions based on considerations of creditworthiness must be applied on a technology neutral basis. Although we note Viacom's statement that certain types of distribution systems have created greater "bad debt" problems, we also seek to avoid situations where individual distributors are forced to pay higher programming prices, without regard to their own creditworthiness, solely due to the perceived creditworthiness of cable systems as opposed to wireless cable systems or other distribution means.

110. *Differences in offering of service.* Neither the statute nor its legislative history provides much guidance on the proper definition of this term, although we believe that it refers to differences related to the actual service exchanged between the vendor and the distributor. For example, such considerations could be manifested in standard contract terms based on a distributor's willingness to provide secondary services that are reflected as a discount or surcharge in the programming service's price.

111. Consequently, we adopt regulations that will allow programming vendors to establish price differentials based on factors related to offering of service. Such factors could include, for example, penetration of programming to subscribers or to particular systems;[34] retail price of programming to the consumer for pay services;[35] amount and type of promotional or advertising services provided by a distributor; a distributor's purchase of programming in a package or a la carte; channel position; importance of location for non-volume reasons;[36] prepayment discounts; contract duration; date of purchase, especially purchase of service at launch;[37] and other legitimate factors as standardly applied in a technology neutral fashion.[38] We emphasize that this list of considerations is intended to provide examples of frequently used contractual terms, and is not exclusive.

D. Non-price Discrimination

116. We believe that non-price "discrimination" by a programming vendor between competing distributors is also covered within section 628(c). While specific practices within this prohibition are not well identified or discussed by commenters, we believe that one form of non-price discrimination could occur through a vendor's "unreasonable refusal to sell," including refusing to sell programming to a class of distributors, or refusing to initiate discussions with a particular distributor when the vendor has sold its programming to that distributor's competitor. We believe that the Commission should distinguish "unreasonable" refusals to sell from certain legitimate reasons that could prevent a contract between a vendor and a particular distributor, including (i) the possibility of parties reaching an impasse on particular terms, (ii) the distributor's history of defaulting on other programming contracts, or (iii) the vendor's preference not to sell a program package in a particular area for reasons unrelated to an existing exclusive arrangement or a specific distributor. In addition, we believe that section 628(c)'s prohibition against non-price discrimination would also encompass situations in which a vendor refuses to offer particular

---

34. For instance, a vendor may justify a price differential for an MSO that purchases a programming service for all its cable systems, rather than only selected markets. Likewise, for pay or premium services, a vendor may offer incentive discounts to encourage distributors to offer the programming service to a larger percentage of the distributor's total subscribers.

35. As an example, a vendor may offer discounts to distributors as an incentive for lower retail prices for subscribers, especially in the case of premium services that are sold a la carte.

36. We note that a vendor may offer discounts to secure contracts for a programming service in key markets, such as Manhattan or Los Angeles, for purposes of enhancing advertising or program production. Such discounts could appropriately apply, then, for all competitors in those markets.

37. For example, a vendor could conceivably justify rate differences, or a separate rate structure, to distinguish those distributors that were "charter members" or longstanding customers of a service, provided that such discounts are or were available to distributors of any technology. Any such potential rates, however, must result from specific provisions of a contract that predates the complainant's attempt to purchase the same programming.

38. Certain commenters have argued in favor of the merits of price differentials based upon a vendor's attempt to "meet competition" at the price level for another vendor's service. We recognize that such practices may benefit the public in certain instances by increasing the availability of programming and reducing the price of programming to consumers, and we will determine whether these benefits are likely to occur on a case-by-case basis.

terms to an individual distributor, or class of distributors, that are offered to competing distributors. This would prohibit such practices, for example, as selling programming to one distributor on an a la carte basis, but refusing to permit that distributor's competitors to purchase the same programming on the same terms or conditions.

E. Application of Rules to Existing Contracts

120. Consistent with federal court cases that proscribe retroactive application of regulations absent clear Congressional intent, the anti-discrimination rules adopted herein will not affect prices paid for past video programming services or penalize vendors for practices preceding passage of the Act. The Commission will, however, apply the rules adopted under section 628 prospectively to all existing contracts, whether they were executed before or after the effective date of the rules.

VIII. PROHIBITIONS AGAINST UNDUE OR IMPROPER INFLUENCE

142. As indicated above, the Commission is directed to prescribe regulations to specify particular conduct that is prohibited by section 628(b) in three specific areas. The first of these relates to the exercise of certain types of "undue influence." Specifically, the Commission must: "establish effective safeguards to prevent a cable operator which has an attributable interest in a satellite cable programming vendor or a satellite broadcast programming vendor from unduly or improperly influencing the decision of such vendor to sell, or the prices, terms, and conditions of sale of, satellite cable programming or satellite broadcast programming to any unaffiliated multichannel video programming distributor."

145. Based on information presented in the record, we conclude that the concept of undue influence between affiliated firms is closely linked with discriminatory practices and exclusive contracting, the direct regulation of which is to be undertaken pursuant to sections 628(c)(2)(B), (C), and (D) based on externally ascertainable pricing and contracting information. Section 628(c)(2)(A) can play a supporting role where information is available (such as might come from an internal "whistleblower") that evidences "undue influence" between affiliated firms to initiate or maintain anticompetitive discriminatory pricing, contracting, or product withholding.

Notes and Questions

1. The Rationale for Section 19. The intended beneficiaries of section 19 are the multichannel video program distributors that compete with entrenched cable systems. Why was Congress anxious to provide these emerging technologies—such as wireless cable (MMDS) and direct broadcast satellite (DBS)—access to programming identical to that already available on cable? Does the Act, in effect, declare that such networks as HBO, MTV, and TNT are "essential facilities" that rivals need in order to compete with cable?

2. Vertical Integration and Horizontal Concentration. Note further that the FCC believes that section 19's regulation of exclusive and discriminatory program supply contracts is necessary only because of existing horizontal concentration and vertical integration in the cable industry. Does that mean that the agency views its own horizontal and vertical restrictions as inadequate? Why not issue new regulations on horizontal concentration and vertical integration, then, instead of attempting an entirely new family of regulatory constraints?

3. Implications. The key practical effect of the Commission's implementation of section 19 has been to render invalid most exclusive programming contracts for well-established programs. Not all exclusivity is outlawed, however. According to the *Report and Order*, how will the Commission distinguish between permissible and impermissible exclusive contracts? What factors seem likely to play a central role in the FCC's analysis? Similarly, how will the Commission distinguish between tolerable and intolerable differences in the terms of program supply contracts?

4. What Kind of Harm? Do the rules require a showing of harm to competition? Or is it enough to prove harm to a cable system's competitor? (Given the paucity of competition that cable systems currently face, is there much difference between harm to competition and harm to competitors?)

5. Antitrust. Overall, are any of the rules articulated in this chapter really necessary given the existence of antitrust law? Perhaps so. After all, maybe the rules surveyed here are more generous to new entrants than antitrust would be—the purpose being to give emerging multichannel technologies the same kind of boost cable received in its infancy when cable operators had free access to the signals of broadcast stations. Then again, it might be argued that, just as cable developed its own sources of programs (HBO, CNN, MTV, ESPN), so should its competitors. We are, after all, seeking more than just increased competition among various pathways for distributing the same programming.

CHAPTER THIRTEEN

DIRECT BROADCAST SATELLITE

The purpose of this chapter is:

- to consider the regulation of direct broadcast satellite service and contrast it with the regulatory regime used for cable.

~

We started this Part by pointing out that cable in many ways grew up in the shadow of broadcast. The FCC from very early on assumed that cable should be regulated such that it would be a supplement to, but not a competitor with, conventional broadcast television. The story of cable regulation was thus the story of the changing relationship between cable and broadcast, a story that brings us today to a point where cable is a major media platform that delivers content to a substantial majority of American homes.

The story of direct broadcast satellite (DBS) service is in many ways the same story, this time with cable playing the role of the established and politically powerful incumbent and DBS playing the part of the struggling new technology at first regulated into a secondary role. We consider DBS here, then, because thus far in this Part we have focused almost exclusively on regulations that explicitly affect cable competition. But equally important to the competitive stance of the cable industry are regulations that indirectly affect it; and recently the most important of those have been regulations that govern cable's rising competitor, DBS.

Although this chapter discusses DBS in relation to cable, note that direct broadcast service was originally viewed, like cable, as a service that could extend and improve upon traditional broadcast television. DBS did not begin successful commercial entry until the early 1990s — by which time its prime importance, as this chapter will reveal, was its role as a competitor to cable. Direct broadcast satellite television received regulatory approval long before its actual commercial rollout, however, and back then DBS was a technology that made broadcasters (as well as cable franchisees) nervous.

Broadcasters' fears were easy to understand. Like cable, DBS was a threat to local advertising revenues since DBS could import distant signals and in that way diminish the audience for local stations. Broadcasters accordingly opposed the allocation of spectrum for DBS and asked the Commission at least to subject DBS operators to the public interest and other obligations already at that time imposed on broadcast under the authority of the 1934 Act. The FCC considered all of these arguments and, in 1982, approved its first DBS licenses.[1] In related proceedings the Commission declined to apply its public interest obligations—or indeed almost any existing regulations—to the new service. DBS transmissions could therefore contain the operator's own programming, programs for which an independent entity purchased carriage from the DBS operator, or any mix of the two.[2] DBS providers were also left free to choose whether to send signals to viewers at no charge (like a broadcaster) or to transmit signals addressed only to paying subscribers. The Commission foresaw five principal benefits flowing from the introduction of DBS service: (1) services for remote viewers of the same quality and variety as for urban viewers; (2) additional program channels throughout the country; (3) programming better suited to particular viewers' tastes because of programming incentives created by greater availability of channels; (4) innovative services like dual-language sound tracks and teletext; and (5) non-entertainment services like data transmission.[3]

In making the above determinations, the Commission soundly rejected broadcasters' contention that DBS would not be in the public interest.[4] The Commission also rejected the argument that DBS would harm conventional broadcasters, finding a lack of evidence that DBS would have more than a "negligible" effect on local broadcasting.[5] That conclusion was perhaps in some tension with the Commission's finding that one of the benefits of DBS would be an increase in competition among programmers for advertising revenues and a decrease in the sale price of broadcast stations. Nonetheless, the Commission in the end focused heavily on the potential benefits of the then-nonexistent DBS service and decided not to regulate satellite broadcasts.

Broadcasters challenged these FCC decisions in court, claiming that space-based stations with national footprints (1) violated the 1934 Act's requirement of local licensing, (2) robbed free local television service of advertising revenues, and (3) undercut programming directed at local interests.[6] The United States Court of Appeals for the D.C. Circuit rejected those arguments and generally upheld the FCC's decision not to impose its Title III public interest obligations on DBS operators.[7] The court agreed that DBS promised many advances and expressly commended the Commission for "assuring that regulation...not impede new technologies that offer substantial public benefits."[8] The court rejected the petitioners' localism arguments as "luddite"[9] and rejected their competitive con-

---

1. *See* Application of Satellite Television Corp. for Authorization to Construct an Experimental Direct Broadcast Satellite System, 91 FCC 2d 953 (1982).
2. 90 FCC 2d at 706–09.
3. Inquiry into the Development of Regulatory Policy in Regard to Direct Broadcast Satellites, 90 FCC 2d 676, 680–82 (1982), *aff'd in part sub nom.* National Ass'n of Broadcasters v. FCC, 740 F.2d 1190, 1199–1206 (D.C. Cir. 1984).
4. *Id.* at 680–82.
5. *Id.* at 685.
6. National Ass'n of Broadcasters v. FCC, 740 F.2d 1190 (D.C. Cir. 1984).
7. *Id.* at 1195. In a partial remand, the court asked the Commission to explain its departure from its previously broad definition of "broadcaster." The FCC was eventually upheld entirely. *See* National Ass'n for Better Broadcasting v. FCC, 849 F.2d 665 (D.C. Cir. 1988).
8. *Id.*
9. The Luddites were 19th century British handcraftsmen who destroyed labor-saving textile machinery because they believed it would hurt employment. The term is more broadly used to describe those who are opposed to technological development.

Figure 13.1. DIRECT BROADCAST SATELLITE. Direct broadcast satellite systems use satellites to transmit content to subscribers. Content is sent to the satellite from an uplink station and received by small antenna receptors situated near subscriber homes. Note that any given satellite has a specific geographic footprint, which is the geographic area the satellite is capable of serving. In this diagram, the satellite arbitrarily has been shown to have a footprint covering Ohio and Indiana.

cerns with the finding that "existing systems, like existing licensees, have no entitlement that permits them to deflect competitive pressure from innovative and effective technology."[10] This ruling opened the way for the Commission's eventual decisions to exempt from conventional broadcast regulations all signals that were "addressed" rather than freely available to the public at large and to reclassify all "subscription" services—everything not wholly advertiser-supported—as "nonbroadcast services."[11] The path was thus set for DBS to enter the video market as a direct competitor to cable.

That takes us to modern times. As most readers surely know, DBS today is a multichannel service that uses a network of satellites to transmit programing directly to subscribers' homes. Like cable, DBS provides both original program content and retransmissions of content already available through other platforms. The big difference between cable and DBS is the technology; whereas cable uses physical connections to deliver its content to the home, DBS sends content over the airwaves. Subscribers use small and increasingly inexpensive home satellite dishes to receive their DBS signal. Equipment at the home then descrambles the signal (if necessary) and builds the appropriate television image. Leading firms providing DBS today include EchoStar and DirecTV.

---

10. *Id.* at 1197–98.
11. In re Subscription Video, 2 FCC Rcd. 1001 (1987).

The major contemporary issue in DBS regulation is the scope of the statutory license granted to satellite providers that, in certain cases, allows them to retransmit local and/or distant broadcast signals without permission from the relevant copyright holders. This statutory license has strong parallels to the compulsory licenses ultimately created in response to the cable cases of *Fortnightly* and *Teleprompter*. The issue is a contentious one because, as a practical matter, the ability to retransmit local broadcast stations is critical if DBS is ultimately to compete with cable. Since the statutory license affects this ability to retransmit local signals, the scope of the license was bound to be a hotly contested issue.

The materials in this chapter begin with an excerpt from a district court opinion which laid out the status of the statutory license as of 1998. The materials then continue with a discussion of the Satellite Home Viewer Improvement Act of 1999 (SHVIA), a statute that altered the rules at issue in the case and arguably brought DBS regulation more in line with cable regulation. The chapter concludes with discussion of a statute imposing public interest obligations on DBS providers and a case addressing the constitutionality of that mandate.

I. THE PRIMETIME LITIGATION

CBS BROADCASTING v. PRIMETIME 24
48 F.Supp.2d 1342 (1998)

I. INTRODUCTION

This is a copyright infringement action in which the Plaintiffs (CBS, Fox, and various affiliates) seek injunctive relief pursuant to Section 502 of the Copyright Act, 17 U.S.C. §502.

Plaintiffs own exclusive rights in copyrighted network television programs that PrimeTime 24 Joint Venture ("PrimeTime") is retransmitting via satellite to its subscribers nationwide. Plaintiffs claim that PrimeTime's retransmissions violate Plaintiffs' copyright in its network television broadcasts. The principal issue is whether PrimeTime's actions are permitted by the Satellite Home Viewer Act (SHVA), 17 U.S.C. §119, which provides a limited statutory license to satellite carriers. The license in the SHVA permits PrimeTime to transmit network programming only to "unserved households."

An "unserved household" is defined in 17 U.S.C. §119(d)(10) as a household that—

> (a) cannot receive, through the use of a conventional outdoor rooftop receiving antenna, *an over-the-air signal of grade B intensity (as defined by the Federal Communications Commission)* of a primary network station affiliated with that network, and

> (b) has not, within 90 days before the date on which that household subscribes, either initially or on renewal, to receive secondary transmissions by a satellite carrier of a network station affiliated with that network, subscribed to a cable system that provides the signal of a primary network station affiliated with that network.

Id. (emphasis added).

The principal dispute between the parties is over the meaning of the phrase "over-the-air signal of grade B intensity (as defined by the [FCC])" in Section 119(d)(10)(A) and what remedy the Court should impose to ensure compliance with the statute.

III. THE PARTIES

A. Plaintiffs

Plaintiffs CBS Broadcasting Inc. ("CBS") and Fox Broadcasting Co. ("Fox") are two separate national television broadcast networks. The remaining Plaintiffs consist of several individual CBS network stations and a trade association of CBS affiliate stations. CBS and Fox own exclusive rights in copyrighted network television programs such as "60 Minutes" and "The Simpsons." CBS and Fox broadcast their network programs nationwide through local television stations that, in turn, transmit the network's programming to viewers in their local markets. Some of the local CBS and Fox stations are owned by the CBS or Fox networks or by sister companies, but most local CBS and Fox stations are owned by third parties. These local television stations — affiliates — are licensed to broadcast CBS or Fox programs to their local markets.

The partnership between national broadcast networks and their affiliates enables local network stations to offer the viewing public a mix of (1) national programming provided centrally by the networks (*i.e.,* "60 Minutes"), (2) local programming, such as news, weather, and public affairs, produced in-house by many local stations, and (3) syndicated programming acquired by local stations from third parties. This programming is typically available to the public for free, as long as they can receive the local broadcast signal.

As well as relying upon each other to provide programming to households nationwide, networks and affiliates rely upon each other financially. Both network stations and local affiliates derive a majority of their revenue from the sale of advertising time. The advertising dollars are split such that the network receives the advertising dollars for network commercials, and the local affiliate receives the advertising dollars for local commercials. Network stations sell advertising during all three of the categories of programming they offer: network programs (such as NFL Football and "60 Minutes"), local programs (such as the "6 O'Clock News"), and syndicated programs (such as "Rosie O'Donnell"). While local stations sell commercial time for their local programming, the sale of advertising during network programs accounts for as much as half of total station revenues. The price of such advertising is dependent on the type and size of a program's audience.

Networks and affiliates both promote the programming of the other so as to increase a program's audience. Both networks and individual stations design their programming schedules and the promotional spots that appear during their programs to encourage maximum "audience flow" — where viewers stay tuned to the same channel from one program to the next. For example, CBS provides local stations with time for a "local news tease" at 10:59 p.m. to promote the station's upcoming 11 p.m. news program. Given that advertising dollars increase when viewership increases, maximizing viewership for both network and local stations is of great importance to maintaining the network/affiliate relationship.

B. PrimeTime

PrimeTime is a satellite carrier engaged in the business of uplinking the signals of network television stations—including CBS and Fox television networks—via satellite and retransmitting those signals for a fee to subscribers of its services. PrimeTime does not retransmit the signals of each local affiliate to its subscribers in that area; rather, it offers the same network signals to all of its subscribers. [This differs from retranmission via cable, since cable operators must, under the must-carry provision, retransmit local stations.]

Specifically, pursuant to contractual arrangements with two CBS affiliates (WRAL from Raleigh, North Carolina, and WPIX from San Francisco, California) and also FoxNet, Inc., PrimeTime broadcasts programming from these three affiliates to all PrimeTime subscribers. In PrimeTime's retransmissions of network programming, local commercials are replaced with national advertisements and the revenues from this advertising is split between PrimeTime and the affiliates (*i.e.*, FoxNet, WPIX, and WRAL).

PrimeTime sells its service through distributors, such as DirecTV and Echostar, or directly to owners of certain satellite dishes. As of June, 1998, PrimeTime had approximately three million subscribers, and most of Prime-Time's growth is through customer sales to owners of small dishes who purchase programming from packagers such as DirecTV or Echostar.

PrimeTime does not have a license from CBS or Fox to retransmit its programming. PrimeTime has contracted with a Fox subsidiary, FoxNet, and the two CBS affiliates, WRAL and WPIX, to transmit network broadcasts; however, the agreement limits these broadcasts to "unserved households" as defined by the SHVA.

IV. FINDINGS OF FACT

A. PrimeTime's Efforts to Comply with the SHVA

PrimeTime has made some attempts to comply with the "unserved household" limitation contained in the SHVA. PrimeTime or its distributors, ask potential subscribers three questions: 1) whether they intend to use the programming for residential use; 2) whether they have subscribed to cable in the last 90 days; and 3) whether the household receives an acceptable picture through the use of a conventional rooftop antenna.[12] PrimeTime has always made its initial eligibility determinations exclusively on what the subscriber tells the customer service representative in response to these three questions.

Congress imposed an objective test to determine whether a subscriber was eligible for network programming from PrimeTime. PrimeTime was fully aware that the SHVA's grade B standard did not take into account a viewer's perception of picture quality. PrimeTime simply ignored the grade B test even though it

---

12. Before asking the third question, PrimeTime suggests that its distributors tell potential subscribers that, if they say that they receive an acceptable quality picture, they will not be eligible to receive network service.

"tried and failed to persuade Congress to adopt a test of eligibility based on subscriber statements about over-the-air reception." In a December 18, 1996, mailing to subscribers regarding the SHVA, PrimeTime stated that the Act imposes "a technical standard used by the FCC as an indicator of adequate service. Unfortunately, this technical standard often does not reflect the quality of the picture that you are actually getting on your television set." Similarly, in efforts to persuade subscribers to write their legislative representative, PrimeTime stated that "under the current law, your ability to view satellite network TV is based upon the intensity of the signal you receive from your local station, not based upon the quality of the picture on your TV set."

PrimeTime's efforts to comply with the SHVA [through] its use of questionnaires is insufficient to meet Congress' objective test. Asking potential subscribers about picture quality simply fails to provide evidence that such subscribers fit within Congress' definition of an "unserved household."

B. PrimeTime Has Not Met Its Burden of Proof under the SHVA

The SHVA places the burden upon PrimeTime to prove that it is not transmitting network programming to ineligible households. PrimeTime's evidence consists of: 1) its questionnaire regarding whether a household receives an "acceptable picture;" 2) signal intensity tests conducted at or near the homes of 13 PrimeTime subscribers in or near Missoula, Montana; and 3) affiliate stations' consent that certain locations in their local markets do not receive grade B intensity signals from the stations. After carefully considering the evidence and the applicable law as discussed in the Conclusions of Law section, the Court finds that PrimeTime has failed to meet its burden.

1. PrimeTime's Questionnaires

PrimeTime's questionnaires fail to consider that the SHVA imposed an objective standard to determine whether a household is "unserved." The emphasis in the SHVA was whether a household can receive a grade B signal from a local station. Although there is evidence that there is a strong correlation between signal intensity and picture quality when multiple, neutral observers evaluate picture quality using properly functioning rooftop antennas, PrimeTime has presented no credible evidence that there is a strong correlation between signal intensity and answers about picture quality supplied by prospective PrimeTime customers.

As noted in the Magistrate Judge's Report, "there are a variety of reasons, unrelated to being an 'unserved household' why a customer might sign up for Prime-Time 24." For example, "viewers with access to additional network stations can watch network programs several hours later (or earlier) by watching a station from a distant time zone and can see sports programs (such as NFL football) that are not available locally." Additionally, PrimeTime subscribers receive digital programming, and do not need to install or maintain a conventional rooftop antenna.

As PrimeTime's own expert witness testified, if a potential subscriber stated that he could not receive a good quality picture over the air, such an answer would provide him with "no scientifically or engineering valid data on which to have an opinion about the signal intensity at that location." In addition, PrimeTime's experts have admitted that subjective assessments of picture quality by biased observers are not reliable.

Even if PrimeTime's subscribers were unbiased observers, PrimeTime has presented no evidence that its subscribers have properly functioning and correctly oriented rooftop antennas. In fact, PrimeTime's subscriber questionnaires reflect that many of their subscribers do not have rooftop antennas at all. And for those customers who do have rooftop antennas, PrimeTime presented no evidence that the antennas and transmission lines are properly oriented and in good working order.

For these reasons, the Court finds that PrimeTime cannot rely on statements by subscribers about picture quality as a substitute for actual signal intensity measurements.

2. PrimeTime's Signal Intensity Tests

PrimeTime submitted the results of signal tests taken by one of PrimeTime's experts at 13 subscriber homes in Missoula, Montana. For many reasons, PrimeTime cannot rely on these 13 tests in Montana to meet its burden of proof. Most fundamentally, these households were not selected on a random basis; rather, they were selected by PrimeTime itself. As such, these tests cannot be used to generalize as to PrimeTime's subscribers as a whole. In addition, the majority of these tests did not measure the household's signal intensity because the expert used each homeowners' own antenna and transmission line. Because the expert was using unknown equipment, it is impossible to measure signal intensity with precision.

3. Local Network Affiliates' Consent to Satellite Broadcasts in Certain Areas

PrimeTime has presented, through deposition testimony and documents, evidence that some local stations have conceded that there may be certain locations in their markets that do not receive a grade B intensity signal. This evidence does not establish that PrimeTime's subscribers fall within the definition of "unserved households." First, such admissions do not mean that PrimeTime subscribers are only located in those areas. Second PrimeTime does not restrict its sale of network programming to locations that local stations have stated are unserved. In fact, PrimeTime places no geographical limits on its sale of CBS and Fox programming.

As none of PrimeTime's evidence establishes that its subscribers do not receive a signal of grade B intensity, PrimeTime has failed to meet its burden of proving that it is providing network services only to "unserved households."

D. The Result of PrimeTime's Conduct

PrimeTime's actions have affected the network/affiliate relationship because individuals who subscribe to its service do not watch local network programs provided by the affiliates. This is due to the fact that PrimeTime does not transmit local affiliate programming or advertising. Instead, as mentioned previously, PrimeTime transmits the network programs broadcast by the handful of affiliates with which it has a contractual agreement, and substitutes local advertising with national advertising. Accordingly, PrimeTime's violation of the SHVA is reducing the number of viewers for local affiliate programming and advertising, which in turn reduces an affiliate's revenue stream.

PrimeTime maintains that its subscribers would not be watching affiliate programming because they cannot adequately receive the affiliate's programming.

However, PrimeTime assumes that its subscribers cannot receive an adequate picture from their local affiliates. PrimeTime's own evidence at trial belies this position. During trial, PrimeTime presented evidence of picture quality received at 13 homes in Missoula, Montana. PrimeTime's own expert found that not only did several of the homes receive a signal of grade B intensity, but the picture quality at several of these homes was adequate for viewing purposes. Thus, the Court disagrees with PrimeTime that affiliates are not affected by PrimeTime's retransmissions of network programming to subscribers who can receive a signal of grade B intensity or better.

V. CONCLUSIONS OF LAW

A. The Satellite Home Viewer Act (SHVA)

In 1988, Congress crafted the satellite carrier "compulsory license" which contains a narrow exception to a network's exclusive copyright over its programming. This exception, codified at 17 U.S.C. §119, allows satellite carriers to deliver network programming to certain satellite dish owners without the copyright owner's permission. By enacting this provision, Congress sought to achieve two goals: (1) to make network programming available to the small number of households that otherwise lack access to it, while (2) preserving the existing national network/affiliate television distribution system by preventing satellite delivery of network programming to other households.

To address these twin goals, Congress limited the satellite compulsory license to "unserved households" for private home viewing. 17 U.S.C. §119(a)(2)(B). As discussed above, the definition of "unserved household" has two parts. First, an "unserved household" is one that "cannot receive, through the use of a conventional outdoor rooftop receiving antenna, an over-the-air signal of grade B intensity (as defined by the [FCC])" from a local network station of the same network. 17 U.S.C. §119(d)(10)(A). Second, to be "unserved," a household must not have recently received network stations via cable. 17 U.S.C. §119(d)(10)(B). Unless a customer meets these criteria, PrimeTime has no statutory license to transmit CBS or Fox programming to that customer.

The first requirement—inability to receive a signal of grade B intensity—is a strictly objective standard. Congress rejected a bill proposed by PrimeTime and other satellite carriers that would have permitted viewers to receive network services by satellite if they submitted affidavits indicating that they did not receive adequate service over the air. Although Congress rejected this bill, PrimeTime continues to argue to this Court that Congress meant to adopt such a standard. However, when Congress has expressly considered and rejected a proposal to include particular provisions in a statute, there could hardly be a clearer indication that a law does not have the meaning it would have had if the proposal had been accepted.

The Court finds that PrimeTime's actions constitute a pattern or practice of violating the SHVA. PrimeTime has failed to establish that any of its three million subscribers meet SHVA's criteria for eligibility. Furthermore, the evidence shows that PrimeTime made a conscious decision to flout the law when it was well aware of what the law required. PrimeTime's attempt to comply with the

SHVA was largely ineffectual and has led to systematic violation of SHVA's white area restriction. Accordingly, the Court finds that PrimeTime has engaged in a nationwide willful or repeated pattern or practice of infringements.

Notes and Questions

1. Aftermath. The Court went on to grant a permanent injunction against Prime-Time's unauthorized use of the copyrighted material, an injunction that could have affected as many as 2.5 million subscribers had its importance not been mitigated first by a negotiated settlement (that allowed PrimeTime to continue to retransmit certain signals for an agreed-upon period of time) and then by Congressional action, discussed below.

2. Regulatory Parity? How do you explain the SHVA? Did it treat DBS providers the same way the Supreme Court treated cable providers in *Fortnightly* and *Teleprompter*? Did it treat DBS the way Congress treated cable providers under the Copyright Act of 1976? Can any differences in treatment be explained on policy grounds, or were those differences instead simply the result of interest group politics that favored established broadcasters and cable providers over fledgling DBS providers and their subscribers?

3. Protecting Cable. The definition of "unserved households" includes an intuitive prong about the quality of the signal the household receives but also a more surprising prong about the household's consumption of cable services during the previous ninety days. What policy goal was being served by that second prong? Now do you see the analogy between DBS and cable on the one hand, and cable and broadcast on the other?

II. THE SATELLITE HOME VIEWER IMPROVEMENT ACT OF 1999

As was mentioned above, *PrimeTime* turned out to be just a prelude to the storm. The satellite, cable, and broadcast industries took their arguments to Congress and, in November 1999, Congress responded with the Satellite Home Viewer Improvement Act of 1999, Pub. L. No. 106–113, 113 Stat. 1501 (codified at scattered sections of 17 U.S.C. and 47 U.S.C.).[13] The new Act amends both federal copyright law (those are the changes codified at 17 U.S.C.) and the Communications Act of 1934 (codified at 47 U.S.C.), substantially changing the legal rules at issue in *PrimeTime*.

According to Congressional documents, the general purpose of the new Act is to make DBS regulation more consistent with cable regulation and, in that way, to promote competition between the two media platforms. A Senate Report in support of an early version of the SHVIA explains the bill as follows:

---

13. Be careful with your acronyms: the SHVIA is an entirely different statute from the Satellite Home Viewer Act of 1988, Pub. L. No. 100–667, 102 Stat. 3949 (codified as amended at 17 U.S.C. §§ 111 & 119 (1994)), which uses the similar acronym "SHVA."

THE SATELLITE TELEVISION ACT OF 1999
Senate Report 106–51 (May 20, 1999)

Purpose of the Bill. The purpose of the bill is to amend the Communications Act of 1934 to promote competition in the provision of multichannel video service while protecting the availability of free, local over-the-air television.

Background and Needs. Cable rates have increased more than 20 percent since the enactment of the 1996 Telecommunications Act, far exceeding other consumer price increases. Even the Federal Communications Commission has recognized that cable rates have risen excessively in recent years notwithstanding the agency's implementation of cable rate regulation rules.

Regulation of most tiers of cable television service ceased on April 1, 1999. This regulatory "sunset" date was enacted into law based on the belief that, by that date, cable television operators would face competition from a number of other multichannel video services, including direct-to-home satellite television, wireless cable, and telephone company-provided video dialtone systems.

This anticipated competition failed to develop as expected. Technical and operational problems resulted in financial difficulties for wireless cable systems; telephone companies concentrated their efforts on voice and data delivery rather than on video; and direct-to-home satellite service struggled due to a series of statutorily-imposed limitations on the nature and terms of the service it could offer.

Despite these adverse occurrences, the cable rate regulation sunset took place as required by statute on April 1. Therefore, under current circumstances, most cable television systems have become virtually unregulated providers of a monopoly service, with unconstrained power to raise consumer rates due to the lack of an effectively competitive alternative provider of multichannel video service.

Recognizing this fact, the cable industry has volunteered to hold future subscriber rate increases to around 5 percent annually. This, however, would still be more than twice the projected inflation rate, and no voluntary commitment, however sincerely intentioned, can actually be enforced.

Return to a prescriptive rate regulation regime would not be a satisfactory alternative. Experience shows that cable rate regulation is ineffective in holding cable rates down without also hurting investment in cable service. In 1992 the FCC reduced cable rates 17 percent and imposed limits on subsequent rate increases. Investment in programming and in cable plant improvements was immediately and sharply curtailed. Total capital investment plunged from $8.17 billion in 1989 to $1.9 billion in 1993. In contrast, with rate deregulation slated to take effect on April 1, capital flow from debt, equity, and other sources has increased 25 percent each year since 1996. And because many cable systems are making the substantial investment needed to provide high-speed cable modem service, reimposition of rate regulation now would impede cable's capital flow at precisely the time it is most needed.

Conversely, experience shows that competition is effective in constraining cable rates without harming cable service. In fact, competition has been shown to produce improved service at lower rates. Testimony before the Committee last year showed that head-to-head competition between cable systems typically caused the incumbent cable operator to increase the number of channels offered while cutting monthly rates dramatically, in one case almost in half. Effective competition from other providers of multichannel video service remains the only workable antidote to cable rate increases.

Direct-to-home satellite service, commonly referred to as Direct Broadcast Service (DBS), is currently the best potential competitor to cable television. DBS systems are the fastest-growing consumer electronics product in history: the number of DBS subscribers jumped an astonishing 97 percent in 1996 and another 30 percent the following year. However, despite this growth, some current statutes and regulations impede DBS's ability to compete with cable.

Satellite television companies are prohibited under the terms of the Satellite Home Viewer Act (SHVA) and the Copyright Act from providing their subscribers with signals from local network stations as a component of their satellite television service. Cable television providers, however, face no such prohibitions. They can, and do, provide local television stations to their customers.

Direct-to-home satellite service providers' inability to offer local television stations as part of an integrated service package puts it at a significant competitive disadvantage to cable television service. When the FCC surveyed people who "investigated" DBS systems but did not buy them, 55 percent of these people reported that they did not buy a DBS system because of a lack of local television networks. Therefore, to compete effectively with cable television systems, DBS must be allowed to provide local television stations to subscribers.

Under current law, satellite television providers are also prohibited from providing distant network signals to a subscriber unless that subscriber resides in an area considered to be "unserved" by the local television station. "Unserved" areas are in turn defined as being those beyond the local television station's predicted Grade B contour. The area closest to the television station is referred to as the station's "Grade A" contour. This area is where the television station's over-the-air signal strength is likely to be strongest and is the core of the local television station's market.

As a result, many consumers who subscribed to direct-to-home satellite service believed that, because they got poor reception of their local stations off-air, they lived in an "unserved" area and were entitled to receive distant network signals from their satellite television provider. It has been estimated that over 2,000,000 satellite television subscribers received distant network signals although they resided in the local television station's predicted Grade A and Grade B contours, and therefore were ineligible to receive them under the terms of SHVA.

In 1997 and 1998, a number of lawsuits were brought under SHVA by broadcasters against satellite carriers, alleging that the satellite carriers were distributing the signals of distant network-affiliated television broadcast stations to subscribers that were not unserved households within the meaning of SHVA. Perhaps the most far-reaching of these was brought before the United States District Court for the Southern District of Florida in Miami by CBS, Fox, and several affiliates against PrimeTime 24. [This is the case excerpted earlier in the chapter.]

Finding that PrimeTime had willfully provided distant network programming to served households in violation of SHVA, the Miami court issued a preliminary and, later, a permanent injunction ordering PrimeTime not to deliver CBS or Fox television network programming to any customer living in a "served" household. The court further enjoined PrimeTime from providing distant network signals to any house predicted by a computer model to be served without first either: (1)

obtaining the written consent of the affected stations; or (2) providing the affected station with copies of a signal intensity test showing that the household in question is actually unserved.

The preliminary injunction took effect on February 28, 1999, and the permanent injunction was to have taken effect on April 30, 1999. The preliminary injunction resulted in the termination of network signals to the estimated 700,000 to one million subscribers nationwide who subscribed to PrimeTime after the networks filed their lawsuit on March 11, 1997. The permanent injunction, which applies to the PrimeTime customers who subscribed before March 11, 1997, could affect an additional 1.5 million subscribers nationwide. The total number of PrimeTime subscribers affected by the Miami injunctions could therefore reach 2.2–2.5 million. Several other lawsuits have been filed by broadcasters and satellite carriers in the federal courts, and so the number of affected subscribers will likely continue to grow.

Some of these cases have settled, of course. For example, DirecTV and the networks recently announced an agreement that settles some of the litigation before the Miami federal court. Under the agreement, DirecTV will temporarily restore distant CBS and Fox network signals to its estimated 700,000 customers who lost network service on February 28. However, subscribers predicted (by an FCC model) to receive a Grade A signal over the air will be disconnected from distant network service on June 30, 1999. Those predicted to receive a Grade B signal will have distant network service cut off on December 31, 1999. These cut-off households can have their service restored if actual signal measurements show them to be unable to receive at least a Grade B signal. The settlement also requires DirecTV to provide its cut-off subscribers a substantial discount on outdoor over-the-air antennas.

While they may serve as a partial stop-gap measure, agreements like this do not lessen the need for congressional action to avoid the disenfranchising of millions of consumers. The Miami agreement, for instance, does not change the fact that, as a result of the litigation, millions of satellite television subscribers stand to lose the distant network stations that they have enjoyed receiving for some time. Many will be required to go to the trouble and expense of installing off-air antennas to improve their reception of local television signals. For those satellite television subscribers living at the fringes of the predicted Grade B contour, these measures may still not allow for reception of television signals that these viewers consider acceptable.

The direct-to-home satellite service providers argue that consumers should not be arbitrarily deprived of channels that enable them to enjoy decent network television signals and more program options, and whose carriage has not appeared to injure local television stations. Many consumers agree. However, broadcasters argue that satellite television companies should not be rewarded for breaking the law, that the Grade B contour does in fact predict adequate television service, that satellite carriage of distant network stations is, in fact, harming local network television stations, and that local stations give television subscribers sufficient access to network programming.

Note on the SHVIA

The Senate Report excerpted above accompanied Senate bill S. 303, which was ultimately combined with a similar bill and enacted as the SHVIA in November 1999. The new Act made several important changes. First, in section 1002(a), the SHVIA amends federal copyright law by adding a new section, 17 U.S.C. §122, which states that "a secondary transmission of a performance or display of a work embodied in a primary transmission of a television broadcast station in the station's local market shall be subject to statutory licensing." In other words, DBS providers enjoy a compulsory license to retransmit even copyrighted local broadcast content back into the local market. Subsection 1002(c) further provides that DBS providers do not have to pay any royalty in exchange for this compulsory license. Other provisions in this section establish rules comparable to those in effect with respect to cable, for example prohibiting DBS providers from willfully altering the retransmitted signal.

Note that the compulsory license created by section 1002(a) does not perfectly mirror the compulsory license created by the Copyright Act of 1976 for the benefit of cable providers. Most importantly, the SHVIA license applies only to the retransmission of local content back into the local market; it is explicitly not a license to retransmit distant signals. The provisions relating to cable's compulsory license, by contrast, do apply to distant programing—both distant network programing (for which there is no royalty) and distant non-network programing (for which there is a royalty). The license granted to DBS operators, then, is considerably narrower than the one granted to cable providers back in 1976.

Second, in section 1005, the SHVIA addresses the issue of distant signal importation for the benefit of unserved households. The provision has prospective and retrospective components. Looking prospectively, the Act amends 17 U.S.C. §119 (part of the Copyright Act) so as to establish a new standard for what it means to be an "unserved" household. According to the new standard:

> The term "unserved household," with respect to a particular television network, means a household that…cannot receive, through the use of a conventional, stationary, outdoor rooftop receiving antenna, an over-the-air signal of a primary network station affiliated with that network of Grade B intensity as defined by the Federal Communications Commission.

17 U.S.C. §119(d)(10)(A). Grade B intensity is an objective measure of signal intensity. Just as before, section 1005 recognizes in DBS providers a compulsory license to retransmit copyrighted program content to unserved households, subject to the payment of a statutory fee. Note that, unlike the old standard, the new one does not include any reference to a ninety-day waiting period for households once served by cable.

Looking retrospectively, section 1005 further amends 17 U.S.C. §119 to grandfather many of the subscribers caught up in litigation like the *PrimeTime* case excerpted above. That amendment in essence creates a moratorium on the enforcement of copyright law with respect to these illegal retransmissions. The moratorium lasts until December 31, 2004, at which time DBS providers can face liability for copyright infringement with respect to any retransmission that does not either qualify for a compulsory license under the new Act or occur subject to a valid negotiated license. (In documents on the FCC website, the FCC advises customers slated to lose retransmission service to purchase and install outdoor antennas such that they can pick up local signals off the air.)

Third, section 1009 of the Act amends 47 U.S.C. §325(b) to create a retransmission consent requirement for DBS. That requirement went into effect in May of 2000 (six months after the SHVIA was enacted). The DBS requirement is similar to that already in effect for cable and, in fact, it was simply added to the existing statutory provision regarding cable retransmission consent. The new provision reads, in relevant part: "No cable system or other multichannel video programming distributor shall retransmit the signal of a broadcasting station, or any part thereof, except with the express authority of the originating station."

Fourth, section 1008 of the Act amends the Communications Act of 1934 by adding a new provision, codified at 47 U.S.C. §338, that creates a must-carry regime for DBS. The provision states that, if a DBS provider chooses to retransmit the signal of a local television station pursuant to the statutory copyright license made available under §1002, the provider will have the obligation to carry the signals of all television broadcast stations located within that same local market. This requirement differs from the cable must-carry regime in a number of notable respects. For one thing, its effective date was set at January 1, 2002, which means that Congress gave DBS providers a period of a little more than two years after passage of the SHVIA during which there would be no must-carry obligations. Moreover, even after 2002, the must-carry obligation is triggered only if a DBS provider retransmits a station through reliance on the compulsory license created by §1002.[14] As the FCC noted in a *Notice of Proposed Rulemaking* on the SHVIA, "if satellite carriers provide local television signals pursuant to private copyright arrangements, the [must-carry] obligations do not apply."[15] What this means is simply that, if in a given local market a DBS provider makes its own arrangements without relying on the compulsory license, or chooses not to retransmit local signals at all, then that carrier will have no must-carry obligations in that local market. Lastly, note that (unlike the 1992 Cable Act) the SHVIA neither creates a "basic tier" of service that must include all broadcast stations that opt for must-carry, nor authorizes local government to regulate the rates charged by DBS providers for access to these stations. The Act only requires that the DBS provider set a "nondiscriminatory price" and offer the channels in a "nondiscriminatory manner."

In all these ways, the DBS requirements might be seen as less onerous than the must-carry regime for cable. Other differences, however, may pose a greater burden on DBS providers. Most significantly, in contrast to the provision in the 1992 Cable Act that tied the number of local stations that had to be carried to

---

14. The relevant language states that "each satellite carrier providing, under section 122 of title 17, United States Code, secondary transmissions to subscribers located within the local market of a television broadcast station of a primary transmission made by that station shall carry upon request the signals of all television broadcast stations located within that local market." 47 U.S.C. §338.

15. *See* Notice of Proposed Rule Making, Implementation of the Satellite Home Viewer Improvement Act of 1999, 15 FCC Rcd. 12147, at ¶10 (2000).

the total number of channels a cable provider offered,[16] section 1008 of the SHVIA does not by its own terms limit the number of local stations that DBS providers must carry. Section 1008 does allow a DBS provider to refuse to carry more than one network affiliate in any given market, and also to refuse to carry a signal that "substantially duplicates" the signal of a local station it is already re-transmitting; but unless the FCC decides to limit the DBS must-carry obligation to a specified percentage of local stations, the requirement, when it applies at all, will apply to all local stations.

Notes and Questions

1. Syndicated Exclusivity and Other FCC Rules. A section of the SHVIA not discussed above requires the FCC to establish regulations applying network nonduplication, syndicated exclusivity, and sports blackout rules to DBS. Interestingly, Congress ordered the FCC to apply the network nonduplication and syndicated exclusivity rules only with respect to superstations; in the cable context, by contrast, these apply to any imported signal, be it superstation or no. The SHVIA does seem to leave the FCC with discretion to expand the DBS rules to stations other than superstations, but, in the *Report and Order* implementing these regulations, the Commission chose not to do so. *See In re Implementation of the Satellite Home Viewer Improvement Act of 1999, Applications of Network Nonduplication, Syndicated Exclusivity, and Sports Blackout Rules to Satellite Retransmission of Broadcast Signals,* FCC 00–388, 2000 WL 1639016 (2000). Said the Commission, "In implementing the SHVIA, the Commission attempts to be faithful to the clear Congressional intent to place satellite carriers on an equal footing with cable operators, while taking into consideration that the operational structures of these two Multichannel Video Programming Distributors (MVPDs) are very different." *Id.* at ¶5.

2. Test Your Understanding. In its explanation for why a new law was required, the Senate Report asserts that, before the SHVIA, satellite television companies were "prohibited under the terms of the Satellite Home Viewer Act and the Copyright Act from providing their subscribers with signals from local network stations as a component of their satellite television service." Is that a correct statement of the law as it stood before the SHVIA? Why not? Does this seemingly minor error suggest that Congress overlooked an important alternative to the compulsory licensing scheme it ultimately adopted?

3. Regulatory Parity, Part II. The SHVIA imposes on satellite television a must-carry scheme somewhat analogous to the one imposed on cable; but, as the summary above points out, the schemes do differ in several respects. Can you justify the various differences? If you cannot, does that indicate that either the cable or the DBS provisions should be modified? Or would regulatory consistency be a false consistency in this case since the same regulation might have very different implications for DBS as opposed to cable? The Senate Report, at least, claims that the reason must-carry obligations will not take effect until January 1, 2002 is because requiring immediate compliance would have imposed an impossible burden on DBS providers due to the sheer number of satellite transponders re-

---

16. *See* 47 U.S.C. §534 (section 4 of the Cable Act of 1992, discussed in Chapter Eleven).

quired to capture and retransmit that many broadcast signals. Does that sound plausible to you?

4. Must-Carry and Retransmission Linked. The SHVIA couples the compulsory license to retransmit local broadcast stations into local markets with must-carry obligations. Is it logical to link these two issues, or should Congress have dealt with them separately—say, requiring carriage of local broadcasters only if DBS becomes a dominant media platform?

5. Why Retransmission Consent? In our study of cable regulation, we puzzled over the need for retransmission consent. Why add retransmission consent, we asked, to a legal regime that already recognized copyright in every program? Was retransmission consent redundant to copyright law or (even worse) was it in direct tension with the compulsory licensing scheme established for cable? Note that the SHVIA seems to again raise these questions in that it again creates a legal regime with copyright protection for program content, compulsory licenses for the retransmission of certain copyrighted programs, and retransmission consent for broadcast signals as a whole. Do these interwoven provisions make more sense in the DBS context than they did in the cable context?

III. REQUIRING EDUCATIONAL PROGRAMMING ON DBS

Broadcasters are subject to public interest obligations; that was the subject of Chapter Six. And, as we know from Chapter Ten, most cable providers are required to provide PEG channels. May and should the government impose public interest obligations on DBS providers?

This question is of more than academic interest. Section 25 of the 1992 Cable Act, codified at 47 U.S.C. §335(b)(1), provides:

> The Commission shall require, as a condition of any provision, initial authorization, or authorization renewal for a provider of direct broadcast satellite service providing video programming, that the provider of such service reserve a portion of its channel capacity, equal to not less than 4 percent nor more than 7 percent, exclusively for noncommercial programming of an educational or informational nature.

In addition, DBS providers can have no editorial control over the educational or informational programming they are required to carry under this provision. *Id.* §335(b)(3).

As part of the massive litigation challenging various provisions of the 1992 Cable Act (part of which was split off and became Turner Broadcasting v. FCC), cable companies challenged section 25 as violating the First Amendment. The District Court for the District of Columbia agreed, stating that it was "clearly unconstitutional":

> There is absolutely no evidence in the record upon which the Court could conclude that regulation of DBS service providers is necessary to serve any significant regulatory or market-balancing interest. There is

nothing in the record purporting to demonstrate that educational television is presently in short supply in the homes of DBS subscribers, nor is there a reason to conclude that section 25 was designed (or deemed necessary) by Congress to quell anti-competitive DBS provider practices. In the absence of a record identifying a valid regulatory purpose or some other legitimate government interest to be advanced by conscripting DBS channel space, there is no justification for any First Amendment burdens occasioned by section 25.[17]

On appeal, in the same opinion that was excerpted back in Chapter Ten for its holdings with respect to leased access and PEG channels on cable, a panel of the Court of Appeals for the District of Columbia Circuit saw matters differently.

TIME WARNER ENTERTAINMENT CO. v. FCC
93 F.3d 957 (D.C. Cir. 1996)

Before BUCKLEY, RANDOLPH, and TATEL, Circuit Judges. Opinion for the Court filed PER CURIAM. Opinion concurring in part and dissenting in part filed by Circuit Judge TATEL.

PER CURIAM:

Time Warner insists, for a variety of reasons, that the DBS set-aside provisions must be subjected to strict scrutiny; it also maintains that we may not consider the government's argument that DBS systems are analogous to broadcast television and therefore subject to no more than heightened scrutiny, because that argument had not been raised before the district court. While it is true that we will not ordinarily entertain an argument that the trial court had no opportunity to consider, the instant case is concerned with the validity of a federal statute governing the application of a new technology of enormous significance. Our resolution of the legal issue presented here does not require the consideration of facts not already in the record, and for us to ignore the obvious similarity between DBS and broadcasting would do nothing to preserve the integrity of the judicial process.

The Supreme Court recognized, in 1969, that because of the limited availability of the radio spectrum for broadcast purposes, "only a tiny fraction of those with resources and intelligence can hope to communicate by radio at the same time." Red Lion Broadcasting Co., Inc. v. FCC, 395 U.S. 367, 388 (1969). The same is true for DBS today. Because the United States has only a finite number of satellite positions available for DBS use, the opportunity to provide such services will necessarily be limited. Even before the first DBS communications satellite was launched in 1994, the FCC found that "the demand for channel/orbit allocations far exceeds the available supply." Recently, the last DBS license was auctioned off for $682.5 million, the largest sum ever received by the FCC for any single license to use the airwaves. As the Supreme Court observed,

---

17. Daniels Cablevision, Inc., v. United States, 835 F. Supp. 1 (D.D.C. 1993), *aff'd in part, rev'd in part*, Time Warner Entertainment Co. v. FCC, 93 F.3d 957 (D.C. Cir. 1996).

where there are substantially more individuals who want to broadcast than there are frequencies to allocate, it is idle to posit an unabridgeable First Amendment right to broadcast comparable to the right of every individual to speak, write, or publish.

Red Lion, 395 U.S. at 388.

In such cases, the Court applies a "less rigorous standard of First Amendment scrutiny," based on a recognition that

the inherent physical limitation on the number of speakers who may use the…medium has been thought to require some adjustment in traditional First Amendment analysis to permit the Government to place limited content restraints, and impose certain affirmative obligations, on broadcast licensees.

Turner Broadcasting Sys., Inc. v. FCC, 114 S.Ct. 2445, 2456, 2457 (1994). Because the new DBS technology is subject to similar limitations, we conclude that section 25 should be analyzed under the same relaxed standard of scrutiny that the court has applied to the traditional broadcast media.

Both broadcasters and the public have First Amendment rights that must be balanced when the government seeks to regulate access to the radio spectrum. Nonetheless, the Supreme Court has held that "it is the right of the viewers and listeners, not the right of the broadcasters, which is paramount. It is the right of the public to receive suitable access to social, political, esthetic, moral and other ideas and experiences which is crucial here." *Red Lion*, 395 U.S. at 390. An essential goal of the First Amendment is to achieve "the widest possible dissemination of information from diverse and antagonistic sources." FCC v. National Citizens Comm. for Broadcasting, 436 U.S. 775, 799 (1978) (*NCCB*). Broadcasting regulations that affect speech have been upheld when they further this First Amendment goal. For example, in *NCCB*, the Supreme Court recognized that "efforts to enhance the volume and quality of coverage of public issues through regulation of broadcasting may be permissible where similar efforts to regulate the print media would not be." *Id*. at 800.

The government asserts an interest in assuring public access to diverse sources of information by requiring DBS operators to reserve four to seven percent of their channel capacity for noncommercial educational and informational programming. Indeed, a stated policy of the 1992 Act is to "promote the availability to the public of a diversity of views and information through cable television and other video distribution media." 1992 Act, §2(b)(1), 106 Stat. at 1463. This interest lies at the core of the First Amendment: "Assuring that the public has access to a multiplicity of informational sources is a governmental purpose of the highest order, for it promotes values central to the First Amendment." *Turner*, 114 S.Ct. at 2470.

While Time Warner does not dispute the validity of these interests, it asserts that the government made no findings regarding the need for channel set-asides on DBS. We have recognized that "when trenching on first amendment interests, even incidentally, the government must be able to adduce either empirical support or at least sound reasoning on behalf of its measures." Century Communications Corp. v. FCC, 835 F.2d 292, 304 (D.C.Cir.1987), *clarified*, 837 F.2d 517 (D.C.Cir. 1988). Nevertheless, while it is true that Congress made no specific findings in support of section 25, "Congress is not obligated, when enacting its statutes, to make a record of the type that an administrative agency or court does to accommodate judicial review." *Turner*, 114 S.Ct. at 2471 (plurality opinion). Indeed,

> sound policymaking often requires legislators to forecast future events and to anticipate the likely impact of these events based on deductions and inferences for which complete empirical support may be unavailable.

Turner, 114 S.Ct. at 2471 (plurality opinion).

In this instance, Congress could not have made DBS-specific findings for the simple reason that no DBS system was in operation at the time the 1992 Act was enacted. Congress had to base its decision to require set-asides on its long experience with the broadcast media. In 1967, when it enacted the Public Broadcasting Act, Congress recognized that "the economic realities of commercial broadcasting do not permit widespread commercial production and distribution of educational and cultural programs which do not have a mass audience appeal." H.R. REP. NO. 572, 90th Cong., 1st Sess. 10–11 (1967). Congress noted the same problem in 1989, when it established the National Endowment for Children's Educational Television. As the Supreme Court has observed, since 1939, the government has "recogniz[ed] the potential effect of...commercial pressures on educational stations" by reserving radio frequencies and television channels for educational use. FCC v. League of Women Voters, 468 U.S. 364, 367 (1984).

Section 25, then, represents nothing more than a new application of a well-settled government policy of ensuring public access to noncommercial programming. The section achieves this purpose by requiring DBS providers to reserve a small portion of their channel capacity for such programs as a condition of their being allowed to use a scarce public commodity. The set-aside requirement of from four to seven percent of a provider's channel capacity is hardly onerous, especially in light of the instruction, in the Senate Report, that the FCC "consider the total channel capacity of DBS systems operators" so that it may "subject DBS systems with relatively large total channel capacity to a greater reservation requirement than systems with relatively less total capacity." S. Rep. No. 92, *supra*, at 92. Furthermore, a DBS provider "may utilize for any purpose any unused channel capacity required to be reserved under this subsection pending the actual use of such channel capacity for noncommercial programming of an educational or informational nature." 47 U.S.C. §335(b)(2).

We note, further, that the government does not dictate the specific content of the programming that DBS operators are required to carry. What the Court in *Turner* found to be true with regard to the must-carry rules is just as true for DBS:

> The design and operation of the challenged provisions confirm that the purposes underlying their enactment are unrelated to the content of speech. The rules do not require or prohibit the carriage of particular ideas or points of view. They do not penalize DBS operators or programmers because of the content of their programming. They do not compel DBS operators to affirm points of view with which they disagree. They do not produce any net decrease in the amount of available speech. And they leave DBS operators free to carry whatever programming they wish on all channels not subject to the set-aside requirements.

114 S.Ct. at 2461–62.

The Supreme Court found that Congress's "overriding objective in enacting must-carry was not to favor programming of a particular subject matter, viewpoint, or format, but rather to preserve access to free television programming for Americans without cable." 114 S.Ct. at 2461. Section 25 serves a similar objective; its purpose and effect is to promote speech, not to restrict it. Because section 25 is "a reasonable means of promoting the public interest in diversified mass communications," it does not violate the First Amendment rights of DBS providers. *See NCCB*, 436 U.S. at 802.

[Separate opinion of Judge TATEL (concurring in this portion of the opinion and dissenting from a different portion) is omitted.]

* * *

Time Warner sought a rehearing in banc (by the full court of appeals) but that request was denied. Although there were many different issues in the case — including the PEG and leased access issues discussed previously — only the DBS provision drew a written dissent from the decision to deny the in banc rehearing.

TIME WARNER ENTERTAINMENT CO. v. FCC
On Suggestions for Rehearing In Banc
105 F.3d 723 (D.C. Cir. 1997)

Before EDWARDS, Chief Judge, WALD, SILBERMAN, WILLIAMS, GINSBURG, SENTELLE, HENDERSON, RANDOLPH, ROGERS and TATEL, Circuit Judges.

PER CURIAM:

The Suggestions for Rehearing In Banc and the response thereto have been circulated to the full court. The taking of a vote was requested. Thereafter, a majority of the judges of the court in regular active service did not vote in favor of the suggestions. Upon consideration of the foregoing, it is ordered that the suggestions be denied.

Circuit Judges WALD and HENDERSON did not participate in this matter.

WILLIAMS, Circuit Judge, with whom Chief Judge EDWARDS, Judge SILBERMAN, Judge GINSBURG and Judge SENTELLE concur, dissenting from the denial of rehearing in banc:

Although I dissent from the denial of the suggestion for rehearing in banc, I do so with genuine uncertainty about the correct outcome. But I believe there were fatal defects in the panel's legal theory for upholding the 1992 Cable Act's requirement that direct broadcast satellite (DBS) providers set aside several channels for noncommercial programming of an educational or informational nature. DBS is not subject to anything remotely approaching the "scarcity" that the Court found in conventional broadcast in 1969 and used to justify a peculiarly relaxed First Amendment regime for such broadcast. Accordingly *Red Lion* should not be extended to this medium.

If the 1992 Act's content rules for DBS can be sustained at all, in my view it would only be on the theory that the government is entitled to more leeway in setting the terms on which it supplies "property" to private parties for speech purposes (or for purposes that include speech).

1. *Red Lion*

The panel concluded that DBS is more like broadcasting than like cable, and that therefore *Red Lion* applied. As the *Red Lion* doctrine relies on an idea of extreme physical scarcity, I disagree. The new DBS technology already offers more channel capacity than the cable industry, and far more than traditional broadcasting.[18]

DBS is more than an order of magnitude less scarce than traditional broadcasting. Over 50% of the conventional broadcast markets receive fewer than five commercial broadcast channels (including UHF channels), and only 20% receive seven or more. While this number of channels is greater than those available in 1969 when *Red Lion* was decided, it pales in comparison to cable or DBS. Cable operators currently offer about fifty channels, but compression techniques and new technology may eventually lead to 500 channels or more.

DBS has even greater channel capacity. The three orbital slots that permit broadcast throughout the continental United States can accommodate at least 120 video channels each, using existing compression technology, for a total of 360 channels. This does not include the other five orbital slots (4 usable for west coast broadcasting and 1 for east coast broadcasting), which raise the number of channels available to 480 (4 X 120) for the east coast, and 840 (7 X 120) for the west coast. DBS compression is expected to increase the number of channels fivefold by the year 2000. Currently, there are four DBS providers, each providing between 45 and 75 video channels and up to 30 music channels. Thus, even in its nascent state, DBS provides a given market with four times as many channels as cable, which (even without predicted increases in compression) offers about 10 times as many channels as broadcast.

Accordingly, *Red Lion*'s factual predicate—scarcity of channels—is absent here. And the *Red Lion* Court implied that its result would have been different in the absence of such a predicate. Similarly, to the extent that *Turner* distinguishes *Red Lion* on grounds of lack of scarcity in cable, *see* Turner Broadcasting System, Inc. v. FCC, 512 U.S. 622, 637 (1994) (observing that "distinct approach to broadcast regulation rests upon the unique physical limitations of the broadcast medium"), DBS falls on the cable rather than the broadcast side of the line.

---

18. Even in its heartland application, *Red Lion* has been the subject of intense criticism. Partly this rests on the perception that the "scarcity" rationale never made sense—in either its generic form (the idea that an excess of demand over supply at a price of zero justifies a unique First Amendment regime) or its special form (that broadcast channels are peculiarly rare). And partly the criticism rests on the growing number of available broadcast channels. While *Red Lion* is not in such poor shape that an intermediate court of appeals could properly announce its death, we can think twice before extending it to another medium.

Turner, to be sure, appears in part to ground its distinction between cable and broadcast on technological characteristics independent of sheer numbers. "If two broadcasters were to attempt to transmit over the same frequency in the same locale, they would interfere with one another's signals, so that neither could be heard at all." *Id.* But this can hardly be controlling. Alleviation of interference does not necessitate government content management; it requires, as do most problems of efficient use of resources, a system for allocation and protection of exclusive property rights. A cable operator enjoys property rights in the cables in which he transmits his signal (as well, of course, as in the structures he uses to make the transmission). That is the reason would-be cable operators do not interfere with each other's "signals." If I were to burst into Time Warner's studio full of zest to run my program or attempt to transmit signals through wires owned by a cable operator, I would be guilty of trespass and Time Warner could have me ejected. There is no technological obstacle to applying this regime to the broadcast spectrum; indeed, under the current regime a licensee is subject to legal sanctions if he broadcasts outside the wavelengths covered by his license.

Accordingly, it seems to me more reasonable to understand *Red Lion* as limited to cases where the number of channels is genuinely low.

2. Validity of the DBS regulations as "content neutral"?

The panel also justified its decision by analogizing the DBS provision to the must-carry rules, which the Supreme Court in *Turner* classified as content neutral. But whereas the must-carry provisions reviewed in *Turner* mandate access for particular stations regardless of their programming content, the DBS provision speaks directly to content, creating an obligation framed in terms of "noncommercial programming of an educational or informational nature." 47 U.S.C. §335(b)(1). As a subject-matter specification, then, the DBS requirement would normally be "content based" and subject to strict scrutiny if viewed as garden-variety government regulation of speech.

Turner hardly provides support for categorical programming requirements of this type, as the Court there took pains to distinguish the must-carry rules from such requirements. 512 U.S. at 648 ("the operation of the Act further undermines the challenging parties' suggestion that Congress' purpose in enacting must-carry was to force programming of a 'local' or 'educational' content"); *id.* at 651 ("noncommercial licensees are not required by statute or regulation to carry any specific quantity of 'educational' programming").

The panel opinion states that Congress's purpose is not to favor particular programming, but to promote "diversified mass communications," 93 F.3d at 977, which would be a content neutral purpose under *Turner*. I don't see that one can accurately characterize Congress's concern in §25 as relating merely to variety of programming. Rather, §25 explicitly seeks to advance one particular type of programming—"noncommercial programming of an educational or informational nature." 47 U.S.C. §335(b)(1).

Thus, it would appear to me that as a simple government regulation of content, the DBS requirement would have to fall. Or, to put it another way, if this regulation is acceptable, it is hard to see what content regulation (short of viewpoint based ones) would be impermissible. Perhaps, however, the DBS regulation could be saved as a condition legitimately attached to a government grant. I turn briefly to that subject.

3. Rust v. Sullivan, et al.

The government may subsidize some activities and not others. In Rust v. Sullivan, the Court held that Congress could prohibit grantees of federal funds for certain family planning services from using those funds for the "counseling, referral, and the provision of information regarding abortion." 500 U.S. 173, 193 (1991). Rejecting arguments that the requirement was unconstitutionally viewpoint-based, the Court stated that the government was "simply insisting that public funds be spent for the purposes for which they are authorized." *Id.* at 196. In its response to the petition for rehearing, the government makes an oblique allusion to this analysis, suggesting that it was within the government's power to retain control over the "public domain" to have reserved 4-to-7% of channel capacity for itself.

Echoes of this idea can be found in the various opinions in the recent case of Denver Area Educational Telecommunications Consortium v. FCC, 116 S.Ct. 2374 (1996). Speaking of the rule allowing cable operators to veto indecency on "leased" channels, Justice Breyer (joined in this aspect by Justices Stevens, O'-Connor & Souter) stressed that the section merely gave operators permission to "regulate programming that, but for a previous Act of Congress, would have had no path of access to cable channels free of an operator's control." 116 S.Ct. at 2386. Part of Justice Breyer's reasoning seems to be that Congress may, in its redistribution away from the cable operators, attach content based strings to its grant to the lessees. The opinion of Justice Thomas, for himself as well as Chief Justice Rehnquist and Justice Scalia, takes a similar tack, observing that the rights of the petitioners to access to cable have been "governmentally created at the expense of cable operators' editorial discretion." 116 S.Ct. at 2424. Compare *id.* at 2407–16 (Kennedy, J., concurring in part and dissenting in part, with whom Ginsburg, J., joined) (analyzing the provision under the public forum doctrine).[19] And in *Red Lion* itself, the Court used the language of conditioned grants:

> To condition the granting or renewal of licenses on a willingness to present representative community views on controversial issues is consistent with the ends and purposes of those constitutional provisions forbidding the abridgment of freedom of speech and freedom of the press.

395 U.S. at 394.

On the other hand, the Court has not clearly committed itself to treating spectrum licenses as conditioned grants. For example, when in FCC v. League of Women Voters, 468 U.S. 364 (1984), it struck down Congress's ban on editorializing by stations receiving monetary grants from the Corporation for Public

---

19. If spectrum regulation is to be analyzed as conditioned grants of government property, of course the analysis should mesh with the public forum doctrine. That doctrine is merely a specialized set of rules limiting the conditions that government may impose on use of its resources, either traditional public fora such as streets, sidewalks or parks, or "designated" public fora, *i.e.*, "property that the State has opened for expressive activity for part or all of the public." International Soc. for Krishna Consciousness, Inc. v. Lee, 505 U.S. 672, 678 (1992).

Broadcasting, it considered only those grants and found them inadequate to justify the restriction. It did not consider the stations' positions as holders of broadcast licenses.

There is, perhaps, good reason for the Court to have hesitated to give great weight to the government's property interest in the spectrum. First, unallocated spectrum is government property only in the special sense that it simply has not been allocated to any real "owner" in any way. Thus it is more like unappropriated water in the western states, which belongs, effectively, to no one. Indeed, the common law courts had treated spectrum in this manner before the advent of full federal regulation. *See* Chicago Tribune Co. v. Oak Leaves Broadcasting Station, Ill. Circuit Ct., Cook County, Nov. 17, 1926, reprinted in 68 Cong. Rec. 215–19 (1926) (recognizing rights in spectrum acquired by reason of investment of time and money in application of the resource to productive use, and drawing on analogy to western water rights law).

Further, the way in which the government came to assert a property interest in spectrum has obscured the problems raised by government monopoly ownership of an entire medium of communication. We would see rather serious First Amendment problems if the government used its power of eminent domain to become the only lawful supplier of newsprint and then sold the newsprint only to licensed persons, issuing the licenses only to persons that promised to use the newsprint for papers satisfying government-defined rules of content. The government asserted its monopoly over broadcast spectrum long before the medium attained dominance, making the assertion of power seem modest and, by the time dominance was manifest, normal. While this sequence veiled the size and character of the asserted monopoly, it is not clear why it should justify an analysis any different from what would govern the newsprint hypo.

If the subsidy model is suitable for spectrum, the DBS licenses are properly viewed as subsidies, even though there is no cash transfer to the DBS providers for the support of educational programming. The character varies depending on whether the license was granted free, or in an auction occurring after the enactment of the 1992 Act. (There appear to be no licenses auctioned before the 1992 Act.) As for DBS providers that received their licenses gratis, the subsidy is clear, although it is troubling that all the DBS providers that did so received them before the condition was attached.

There is also a subsidy in the auction setting. Those bidding for the DBS channels necessarily discounted their bids in light of the known prospect that a portion of the channels would be allocated for educational programming (and that the DBS provider would bear at least some of the operating costs and overhead). This differential — money that the government could have received had it not imposed the programming requirement — constitutes a subsidy exactly matching the pecuniary burden imposed by the provision. Thus the government may be said to have given the educational channels to the DBS providers.

Analogizing from Rust v. Sullivan, then, the government may argue that it has not required the licensee to give up non-educational speech, but simply to use those channels granted by the government for educational and informational programming for that "specific and limited purpose." 500 U.S. at 196.

Because I can see no principled basis for upholding the requirements imposed on DBS operators without resolving these questions, I dissent from the denial of the petition for rehearing in banc.

Notes and Questions

1. Contrasting Bases. The panel opinion extends *Red Lion* to DBS. The dissent from the denial of rehearing in banc rejects the application of *Red Lion* to DBS, but suggests that a governmental subsidy model might justify regulation of DBS. What are the implications of extending *Red Lion* versus finding regulation justified because of a subsidy? Which line of reasoning would trouble you more if you were the lawyer for: (a) a cable television provider; (b) a wireless paging service (would it matter whether your service used satellites to transmit messages?); (c) a rural incumbent local exchange carrier; (d) a company hoping to gain FCC approval for the use of previously unusable spectrum to transmit information to home receiving appliances (would you need more knowledge about what kind of information and/or what kind of appliances?); or (e) a newspaper?

2. Content Neutral. The panel opinion suggests that §25 is content neutral because it "does not dictate the specific content of the programming." Does that follow from *Turner I*? Is it consistent with *Turner I*? What does the panel opinion mean by "specific content"? If a statute required DBS providers to show "programming aimed at 2- and 3-year-old children that uses music and games to teach them how to speak and read," would that not constitute "specific content" just because several different shows meet those criteria? If that would be content neutral under the panel's reasoning, is the dissent correct that "it is hard to see what content regulation (short of viewpoint-based ones) would be impermissible"? If, on the other hand, the hypothetical language would constitute "specific content," what is the relevant distinction between that language and the actual language of §25? Are your answers the same for a statute requiring "programming designed to show children how beneficial an education can be"? How is that different from simply requiring "programming of an educational...nature"? After all, isn't the point in both cases simply to encourage an interest in education?

3. Subsequent Events. By the slimmest of margins, the full D.C. Circuit voted not to reconsider the panel opinion. Afterwards, the FCC implemented section 335 by requiring that DBS providers set aside four percent of their channel capacity exclusively for noncommercial programming of an educational or informational nature. Reserving channels for these purposes would, the FCC said, "expand programming choices for consumers."[20]

---

20. In re Implementation of Section 25 of the Cable Television Consumer Protection and Competition Act of 1992, 13 FCC Rcd. 23254, 13 FCC Rcd. 24279 (1998).

Chapter Fourteen

INDECENCY REVISITED

The purpose of this chapter is:

- to liven up an otherwise dull book by including some cases that contain inappropriate language that might be offensive to some. (Just kidding.)

⁓

Earlier in the casebook we considered various indecency regulations that applied to broadcast. The topic of course comes up in the context of cable television as well. The purpose of this chapter, then, is to revisit the issue of indecency, asking two primary questions: first, is there anything about cable that might change our analysis here as compared to our analysis with respect to broadcast?; and, second, does adding cable to the mix in any way change our earlier analysis, which, to some degree at least, assumed that broadcast was the only mass media platform available?

We begin with Cruz v. Ferre, a case that is representative of judicial opinions reviewing local efforts to suppress cable indecency. To date, these opinions uniformly have struck down such regulations.

CRUZ v. FERRE
755 F.2d 1415 (11th Cir. 1985)

Opinion for the court filed by District Judge STAFFORD (sitting by designation), in which Circuit Judges HATCHETT and CLARK concur.

STAFFORD, District Judge:

This case involves a challenge to the constitutionality of a Miami ordinance regulating the distribution of obscene and indecent material through cable television. The district court found the provisions of the ordinance regulating the distribution of "indecent material" constitutionally overbroad.

On January 13, 1983, the City of Miami enacted Ordinance No. 9538. This ordinance is intended to regulate "indecent" and "obscene" material on cable television. The relevant portions of this ordinance provide:

Section 1. No person shall by means of a cable television system knowingly distribute by wire or cable any obscene or indecent material.

Section 2. The following words have the following meanings:

. . . .

(g) "Indecent material" means material which is a representation or description of a human sexual or excretory organ or function which the average person, applying contemporary community standards, would find to be patently offensive.

[Plaintiff-appellee Cruz is a cable television subscriber. After holding two hearings, the district court granted Cruz' motions for summary judgment and enjoined Miami from enforcing the sections of the ordinance that regulate "indecent material" on cable television.]

The United States Supreme Court has recognized only limited categories of speech that fall outside of the First Amendment's protection. The Court has declined to extend protection to obscenity, Roth v. United States, 354 U.S. 476 (1957). In Miller v. California, 413 U.S. 15 (1973) the Court reaffirmed that obscene material is unprotected by the First Amendment and set forth the current permissible limits of regulation. However, the *Miller* court "acknowledge[d]... the inherent dangers of undertaking to regulate any form of expression. State statutes designed to regulate obscene materials must be carefully limited." *Id.* at 23–24.

Appellees did not challenge the Miami ordinance's definition of "obscene" material or the city's constitutional authority to regulate obscenity on cable television. Rather, appellees challenged the provisions of the ordinance which attempt to regulate "indecent" materials. The ordinance's definition of indecent materials goes beyond the *Miller* definition of obscenity in two significant respects. First, the ordinance does not require that the challenged materials, "taken as a whole, appeal to the prurient interest in sex." *Miller*, 413 U.S. at 24. Second, the ordinance does not inquire whether the materials, "taken as a whole, do not have serious literary, artistic, political, or scientific value." *Id.* Therefore, if materials falling within the ordinance's definition of "indecent" are to be regulated, the city's authority to do so must be found somewhere other than in the Supreme Court's obscenity cases.

Appellants' primary argument on appeal is that authority for the city's regulation is found in the Supreme Court decision FCC v. Pacifica Foundation, 438 U.S. 726 (1978). The district court, after "a careful consideration of *Pacifica*," found *Pacifica* to be "inapplicable to the facts herein." The district court contrasted the cable medium with broadcast television. A Cablevision subscriber must make the affirmative decision to bring Cablevision into his home. By using monthly program guides, the Cablevision subscriber may avoid the unpleasant surprises that sometimes occur in broadcast programming. Additionally, the district court noted, the ability to protect children is provided through the use of a free "lockbox" or "parental key" available from Cablevision.

Pacifica, it must be remembered, focused upon broadcasting's "pervasive presence," and the fact that broadcasting "is uniquely accessible to children, even those too young to read." The Court's concern with the pervasiveness of the broadcast media can best be seen in its description of broadcasted material as an "intruder" into the privacy of the home. Cablevision, however, does not "intrude" into the home. The Cablevision subscriber must affirmatively elect to have cable service come into his home. Additionally, the subscriber must make the additional affirmative decision whether to purchase any "extra" programming services, such as HBO. The subscriber must make a monthly decision whether to continue to subscribe to cable, and if dissatisfied with the cable service, he may cancel his subscription. The Supreme Court's reference to "a nuisance rationale" is not applicable to the Cablevision system, where there is no possibility that a non-cable subscriber will be confronted with materials carried only on cable. One of the keys to the very existence of cable television is the fact that cable programming is available only to those who have the cable attached to their television sets.[1]

Probably the more important justification recognized in *Pacifica* for the FCC's authority to regulate the broadcasting of indecent materials was the accessibility of broadcasting to children. This interest, however, is significantly weaker in the context of cable television because parental manageability of cable television greatly exceeds the ability to manage the broadcast media. Again, parents must decide whether to allow Cablevision into the home. Parents decide whether to select supplementary programming services such as HBO. These services publish programming guides which identify programs containing "vulgarity," "nudity," and "violence." Additionally, parents may obtain a "lockbox" or "parental key" device enabling parents to prevent children from gaining access to "objectionable" channels of programming. Cablevision provides these without charge to subscribers.

Pacifica represents a careful balancing of the First Amendment rights of broadcasters and willing adult listeners against the FCC's interests in protecting children and unwilling adults. The Court held that, under the particular facts of *Pacifica*, the balance weighed in favor of the FCC. Because we determine that under the facts of the instant case the interests of the City of Miami are substantially less strong than those of the FCC in *Pacifica*, we believe that we must hold *Pacifica* to be inapplicable to this case.

Even if we were to find the rationale of *Pacifica* applicable to this case, we would still be compelled to strike the ordinance as facially overbroad. As the district judge noted, the ordinance "prohibits far too broadly the transmission of indecent materials through cable television. The ordinance's prohibition is wholesale, without regard to the time of day or other variables indispensable to the decision in *Pacifica*." The ordinance totally fails to account for the variables identified in *Pacifica*: the time of day; the context of the program in which the material appears; the composition of the viewing audience. In ignoring these variables, the ordinance goes far beyond the realm of permissible regulation envisioned by the *Pacifica* Court.

Notes and Questions

1. Bans on Indecent Content. Although the issue has not been frequently litigated, no federal court decision permits states or municipalities to bar indecent programs from cable television. Is this because (as the *Cruz* court suggests in its concluding paragraph) *Pacifica* itself, properly read, does not permit a total ban

---

1. Appellants seem to want to extend Justice Stevens' "pig in the parlor" analogy. *See* Brief of Appellants at 16 ("it makes no difference whether the pig enters the parlor through the door of broadcast, cable, or amplified speech: government is entitled to keep the pig out of the parlor"). It seems to us, however, that if an individual voluntarily opens his door and allows a pig into his parlor, he is in less of a position to squeal.

on indecent radio or television broadcast programs? If so, could regulators "channel" indecent programs to certain times of the day, or to certain channels on the cable system, in order to reduce children's opportunities to see indecent programs?

2. Broadcast vs. Cable. Or is the point that cable differs from broadcasting? Did the court identify any material difference between cable and conventional broadcasting other than the availability of lockboxes for cable subscribers? Given that the government could require that radio and television sets be engineered so that parents can lock out broadcast channels, did the *Pacifica* Court err in failing to insist on this less intrusive alternative?

* * *

As *Pacifica* and *ACT III* reminded us back in Chapter Six, the federal government has long sought to reduce the amount of indecent programming available on broadcast television. The federal government's efforts at regulating cable indecency, by contrast, are both of more recent vintage and of somewhat narrower scope. It wasn't until the 1992 Cable Act that Congress made any serious effort to regulate cable indecency. And, even then, the regulation of choice was not a complete ban, but instead a statutory provision that allowed cable operators to decide whether or not to prohibit indecent programs on the only channels (apart from those subject to must-carry) that they do not themselves program: the commercial leased access and PEG channels. The Supreme Court's splintered response follows.

DENVER AREA EDUCATIONAL TELECOMMUNICATIONS CONSORTIUM, INC. v. FCC
518 U.S. 727 (1996)

BREYER, J., announced the judgment of the Court and delivered the opinion of the Court with respect to Part III, in which STEVENS, O'CONNOR, KENNEDY, SOUTER, and GINSBURG, JJ., joined, an opinion with respect to Parts I, II, and V, in which STEVENS, O'CONNOR and SOUTER, JJ., joined, and an opinion with respect to Parts IV and VI, in which STEVENS and SOUTER, JJ., joined. STEVENS, J., and SOUTER, J., filed concurring opinions. O'CONNOR, J., filed an opinion concurring in part and dissenting in part. KENNEDY, J., filed an opinion concurring in part, concurring in the judgment in part, and dissenting in part, in which GINSBURG, J., joined. THOMAS, J., filed an opinion concurring in the judgment in part and dissenting in part, in which REHNQUIST, C.J., and SCALIA, J., joined.

JUSTICE BREYER announced the judgment of the Court and delivered the opinion of the Court with respect to Part III, an opinion with respect to Parts I, II, and V, in which JUSTICE STEVENS, JUSTICE O'CONNOR, and JUSTICE SOUTER join, and an opinion with respect to Parts IV and VI, in which JUSTICE STEVENS and JUSTICE SOUTER join.

These cases present First Amendment challenges to three statutory provisions that seek to regulate the broadcasting of "patently offensive" sex-related material on cable television. Cable Television Consumer Protection and Competition Act of 1992 (1992 Act or Act), §§10(a), 10(b), and 10(c), 47 U.S.C. §§532(h), 532(j), and note following §531. The provisions apply to programs broadcast over cable on what are known as "leased access channels" and "public, educational, or governmental channels." Two of the provisions essentially permit a cable system operator to prohibit the broadcasting of "programming" that the "operator reasonably believes describes or depicts sexual or excretory activities or organs in a patently offensive manner." 1992 Act, §10(a); see §10(c). The remaining provision requires cable system operators to segregate certain "patently offensive" programming, to place it on a single channel, and to block that channel from viewer access unless the viewer requests access in advance and in writing. 1992 Act, §10(b).

We conclude that the first provision—that *permits* the operator to decide whether or not to broadcast such programs on *leased* access channels—is consistent with the First Amendment. The second provision, that *requires* leased channel operators to segregate and to block that programming, and the third provision, applicable to public, educational, and governmental channels, violate the First Amendment, for they are not appropriately tailored to achieve the basic, legitimate objective of protecting children from exposure to "patently offensive" material.

I

A "leased channel" is a channel that federal law requires a cable system operator to reserve for commercial lease by unaffiliated third parties. About 10 to 15 percent of a cable system's channels would typically fall into this category. See 47 U.S.C. §532(b). "Public, educational, or governmental channels" (which we shall call "public access" channels) are channels that, over the years, local governments have required cable system operators to set aside for public, educational, or governmental purposes as part of the consideration an operator gives in return for permission to install cables under city streets and to use public rights-of-way. See §531; see also H.R.Rep. No. 98–934, p. 30 (1984) (authorizing local authorities to require creation of public access channels). Between 1984 and 1992 federal law (as had much pre-1984 state law, in respect to public access channels) prohibited cable system operators from exercising *any* editorial control over the content of any program broadcast over either leased or public access channels. See 47 U.S.C. §§531(e) (public access), 532(c)(2) (leased access).

In 1992, in an effort to control sexually explicit programming conveyed over access channels, Congress enacted the three provisions before us. The first two provisions relate to leased channels. The first says:

"This subsection shall permit a cable operator to enforce prospectively a written and published policy of prohibiting programming that the cable operator reasonably believes describes or depicts sexual or excretory activities or organs in a patently offensive manner as measured by contemporary community standards." 1992 Act, §10(a)(2), 106 Stat. 1486.

The second provision applicable only to leased channels requires cable operators to segregate and to block similar programming if they decide to permit, rather than to prohibit, its broadcast. The provision tells the Federal Communications Commission (FCC or Commission) to promulgate regulations that will (a) require "programmers to inform cable operators if the program[ming] would be indecent as defined by Commission regulations"; (b) require "cable operators to place" such material "on a single channel"; and (c) require "cable operators to block such single channel unless the subscriber requests access to such channel in writing." 1992 Act, §10(b)(1).

The third provision is similar to the first provision, but applies only to public access channels. The relevant statutory section instructs the FCC to promulgate regulations that will

> "enable a cable operator of a cable system to prohibit the use, on such system, of any channel capacity of any public, educational, or governmental access facility for any programming which contains obscene material, sexually explicit conduct, or material soliciting or promoting unlawful conduct." 1992 Act, §10(c).

The FCC, carrying out this statutory instruction, promulgated regulations defining "sexually explicit" in language almost identical to that in the statute's leased channel provision, namely as descriptions or depictions of "sexual or excretory activities or organs in a patently offensive manner" as measured by the cable viewing community.

The upshot is, as we said at the beginning, that the federal law before us (the statute as implemented through regulations) now *permits* cable operators either to allow or to forbid the transmission of "patently offensive" sex-related materials over both leased and public access channels, and *requires* those operators, at a minimum, to segregate and to block transmission of that same material on leased channels.

II

We turn initially to the provision that *permits* cable system operators to prohibit "patently offensive" (or "indecent") programming transmitted over leased access channels. 1992 Act, §10(a). [The Court of Appeals] viewed this statute's "permissive" provisions as not themselves restricting speech, but, rather, as simply reaffirming the authority to pick and choose programming that a private entity, say, a private broadcaster, would have had in the absence of intervention by any federal, or local, governmental entity.

Nonetheless, petitioners point to circumstances that, in their view, make the analogy with private broadcasters inapposite and make this case a special one, warranting a different constitutional result. As a practical matter, they say, cable system operators have considerably more power to "censor" program viewing than do broadcasters, for individual communities typically have only one cable system, linking broadcasters and other program providers with each community's many subscribers. Moreover, concern about system operators' exercise of this considerable power originally led government—local and federal—to insist that operators provide leased and public access channels free of operator editorial control. To permit system operators to supervise programming on leased access channels will create the very private-censorship risk that this anticensorship effort sought to avoid.

Under these circumstances, petitioners conclude, Congress' "permissive" law, *in actuality*, will "abridge" their free speech. And this Court should treat that law as a congressionally imposed, content based, restriction unredeemed as a properly tailored effort to serve a "compelling interest."

Like petitioners, Justices Kennedy and Thomas would have us decide these cases simply by transferring and applying literally categorical standards this Court has developed in other contexts. For Justice Kennedy, leased access channels are like a common carrier, cablecast is a protected medium, strict scrutiny applies, §10(a) fails this test, and, therefore, §10(a) is invalid. For Justice Thomas, the case is simple because the cable operator who owns the system over which access channels are broadcast, like a bookstore owner with respect to what it displays on the shelves, has a predominant First Amendment interest. Both categorical approaches suffer from the same flaws: They import law developed in very different contexts into a new and changing environment, and they lack the flexibility necessary to allow government to respond to very serious practical problems without sacrificing the free exchange of ideas the First Amendment is designed to protect.

The history of this Court's First Amendment jurisprudence, however, is one of continual development, as the Constitution's general command that "Congress shall make no law... abridging the freedom of speech, or of the press," has been applied to new circumstances requiring different adaptations of prior principles and precedents.

This tradition teaches that the First Amendment embodies an overarching commitment to protect speech from government regulation through close judicial scrutiny, thereby enforcing the Constitution's constraints, but without imposing judicial formulas so rigid that they become a straitjacket that disables government from responding to serious problems. This Court, in different contexts, has consistently held that government may directly regulate speech to address extraordinary problems, where its regulations are appropriately tailored to resolve those problems without imposing an unnecessarily great restriction on speech. Justices Kennedy and Thomas would have us further declare which, among the many applications of the general approach that this Court has developed over the years, we are applying here. But no definitive choice among competing analogies (broadcast, common carrier, bookstore) allows us to declare a rigid single standard, good for now and for all future media and purposes. That is not to say that we reject all the more specific formulations of the standard—they appropriately cover the vast majority of cases involving government regulation of speech. Rather, aware as we are of the changes taking place in the law, the technology, and the industrial structure related to telecommunications, we believe it unwise and unnecessary definitively to pick one analogy or one specific set of words now. We therefore think it premature to answer the broad questions that Justices Kennedy and Thomas raise in their efforts to find a definitive analogy, deciding, for example, the extent to which private property can be designated a public forum; whether public access channels are a public forum; whether the Government's viewpoint neutral decision to limit a public forum is subject to the same scrutiny as a selective exclusion from a pre-existing public forum; whether exclusion from common carriage must for all purposes be treated like exclusion from a public forum; and whether the interests of the owners of communications media always subordinate the interests of all other users of a medium.

Rather than decide these issues, we can decide these cases more narrowly, by closely scrutinizing §10(a) to assure that it properly addresses an extremely important problem, without imposing, in light of the relevant interests, an unnecessarily great restriction on speech. The importance of the interest at stake here—

protecting children from exposure to patently offensive depictions of sex; the accommodation of the interests of programmers in maintaining access channels and of cable operators in editing the contents of their channels; the similarity of the problem and its solution to those at issue in *Pacifica*; and the flexibility inherent in an approach that *permits* private cable operators to make editorial decisions, lead us to conclude that §10(a) is a sufficiently tailored response to an extraordinarily important problem.

First, the provision before us comes accompanied with an extremely important justification, one that this Court has often found compelling—the need to protect children from exposure to patently offensive sex-related material. *Sable Communications*, 492 U.S., at 126; Ginsberg v. New York, 390 U.S. 629, 639–640 (1968).

Second, the provision arises in a very particular context—congressional *permission* for cable operators to regulate programming that, but for a previous Act of Congress, would have had no path of access to cable channels free of an operator's control. The First Amendment interests involved are therefore complex, and involve a balance between those interests served by the access requirements themselves (increasing the availability of avenues of expression to programmers who otherwise would not have them) and the disadvantage to the First Amendment interests of cable operators and other programmers (those to whom the cable operator would have assigned the channels devoted to access).

Third, the problem Congress addressed here is remarkably similar to the problem addressed by the FCC in *Pacifica*, and the balance Congress struck is commensurate with the balance we approved there. In *Pacifica* this Court considered a governmental ban of a radio broadcast of "indecent" materials, defined in part, like the provisions before us, to include

> "'language that describes, in terms patently offensive as measured by contemporary community standards for the broadcast medium, sexual or excretory activities and organs, at times of the day when there is a reasonable risk that children may be in the audience.'" 438 U.S. at 732 (quoting 56 F.C.C.2d 94, 98 (1975)).

The Court found this ban constitutionally permissible primarily because "broadcasting is uniquely accessible to children" and children were likely listeners to the program there at issue—an afternoon radio broadcast. *Id.*, at 749–750. In addition, the Court wrote, "the broadcast media have established a uniquely pervasive presence in the lives of all Americans," *id.*, at 748, "patently offensive, indecent material...confronts the citizen, not only in public, but also in the privacy of the home," generally without sufficient prior warning to allow the recipient to avert his or her eyes or ears, *id.*; and "adults who feel the need may purchase tapes and records or go to theaters and nightclubs" to hear similar performances. *Id.*, at 750, n. 28.

All these factors are present here. Cable television broadcasting, including access channel broadcasting, is as "accessible to children" as over-the-air broadcasting, if not more so. Cable television systems, including access channels, "have established a uniquely pervasive presence in the lives of all Americans." *Pacifica, supra,* at 748. "Patently offensive" material from these stations can "confron[t] the citizen" in the "privacy of the home," *Pacifica, supra,* at 748, with little or no prior warning. There is nothing to stop "adults who feel the need" from finding similar programming elsewhere, say, on tape or in theaters.

Fourth, the permissive nature of §10(a) means that it likely restricts speech less than, not more than, the ban at issue in *Pacifica*. Although the provision does create a risk that a program will not appear, that risk is not the same as the certainty that accompanies a governmental ban. Finally, the provision's permissive nature brings with it a flexibility that allows cable operators, for example, not to ban broadcasts, but, say, to rearrange broadcast times, better to fit the desires of adult audiences while lessening the risks of harm to children. In all these respects, the permissive nature of the approach taken by Congress renders this measure appropriate as a means of achieving the underlying purpose of protecting children.

The existence of this complex balance of interests persuades us that the permissive nature of the provision, coupled with its viewpoint-neutral application, is a constitutionally permissible way to protect children from the type of sexual material that concerned Congress, while accommodating both the First Amendment interests served by the access requirements and those served in restoring to cable operators a degree of the editorial control that Congress removed in 1984.

III

The statute's second provision significantly differs from the first, for it does not simply permit, but rather requires, cable system operators to restrict speech—by segregating and blocking "patently offensive" sex-related material appearing on leased channels (but not on other channels). 1992 Act, §10(b). In particular, this provision and its implementing regulations require cable system operators to place "patently offensive" leased channel programming on a separate channel; to block that channel; to unblock the channel within 30 days of a subscriber's written request for access; and to reblock the channel within 30 days of a subscriber's request for reblocking. Also, leased channel programmers must notify cable operators of an intended "patently offensive" broadcast up to 30 days before its scheduled broadcast date.

These requirements have obvious restrictive effects. The Government argues that, despite these adverse consequences, the "segregate and block" requirements are lawful because they are "the least restrictive means of realizing" a "compelling interest," namely "protecting the physical and psychological well-being of minors." *See* Brief for Federal Respondents 11 (quoting *Sable,* 492 U.S. at 126).

We agree with the Government that protection of children is a "compelling interest." But we do not agree that the "segregate and block" requirements properly accommodate the speech restrictions they impose and the legitimate objective they seek to attain. Nor need we here determine whether, or the extent to which, *Pacifica* does, or does not, impose some lesser standard of review where indecent speech is at issue, *compare* 438 U.S., at 745–748 (opinion of Stevens, J.) (indecent materials enjoy lesser First Amendment protection), with *id.,* at 761–762 (Powell, J., concurring in part and concurring in judgment) (refusing to accept a lesser standard for nonobscene, indecent material). That is because once one examines this governmental restriction, it becomes apparent that, not only is it not a "least restrictive alternative" and is not "narrowly tailored" to meet its legitimate objective, it also seems considerably "more extensive than necessary." That is to say, it fails to satisfy this Court's formulations of the First Amendment's "strictest," as well as its somewhat less "strict," requirements.

Several circumstances lead us to this conclusion. For one thing, the law, as recently amended, uses other means to protect children from similar "patently offensive" material broadcast on *un*leased cable channels, *i.e.*, broadcast over any of a system's numerous ordinary, or public access, channels. The law, as recently amended, requires cable operators to "scramble or...block" such programming on any (unleased) channel *"primarily dedicated* to sexually-oriented programming." Telecommunications Act of 1996, §505, 110 Stat. 136 (emphasis added). In addition, cable operators must honor a subscriber's request to block any, or all, programs on any channel to which he or she does not wish to subscribe. §504. And manufacturers, in the future, will have to make television sets with a so-called "V-chip"—a device that will be able automatically to identify and block sexually explicit or violent programs. §551, *id., at* 139–142.

Although we cannot, and do not, decide whether the new provisions are themselves lawful (a matter not before us), we note that they are significantly less restrictive than the provision here at issue. They do not force the viewer to receive (for days or weeks at a time) all "patently offensive" programming or none; they will not lead the viewer automatically to judge the few by the reputation of the many; and they will not automatically place the occasional viewer's name on a special list. They therefore inevitably lead us to ask why, if they adequately protect children from "patently offensive" material broadcast on ordinary channels, they would not offer adequate protection from similar leased channel broadcasts as well? Alternatively, if these provisions do not adequately protect children from "patently offensive" material broadcast on ordinary channels, how could one justify more severe leased channel restrictions when (given ordinary channel programming) they would yield so little additional protection for children?

The record does not answer these questions. It does not explain why, under the new Act, blocking alone—without written access-requests—adequately protects children from exposure to regular sex-dedicated channels, but cannot adequately protect those children from programming on similarly sex-dedicated channels that are leased. It does not explain why a simple subscriber blocking request system, perhaps a phone-call based system, would adequately protect children from "patently offensive" material broadcast on ordinary non-sex-dedicated channels (*i.e.*, almost all channels) but a far more restrictive segregate/block/written-access system is needed to protect children from similar broadcasts on what (in the absence of the segregation requirement) would be non-sex-dedicated channels that are leased. Nor is there any indication Congress thought the new ordinary channel protections less than adequate.

Consequently, we cannot find that the "segregate and block" restrictions on speech are a narrowly, or reasonably, tailored effort to protect children. Rather, they are overly restrictive, "sacrific[ing]" important First Amendment interests for too "speculative a gain." Columbia Broadcasting System, Inc. v. Democratic National Committee, 412 U.S. 94, 127 (1973). For that reason they are not consistent with the First Amendment.

IV

The statute's third provision, as implemented by FCC regulation, is similar to its first provision, in that it too *permits* a cable operator to prevent transmission of "patently offensive" programming, in this case on public access channels. 1992 Act, §10(c); 47 CFR §76.702 (1995). But there are four important differences.

The first is the historical background. Cable operators have traditionally agreed to reserve channel capacity for public, governmental, and educational channels as part of the consideration they give municipalities that award them cable franchises. Significantly, these are channels over which cable operators have not historically exercised editorial control. Unlike §10(a) therefore, §10(c) does not restore to cable operators editorial rights that they once had.

The second difference is the institutional background that has developed as a result of the historical difference. When a "leased channel" is made available by the operator to a private lessee, the lessee has total control of programming during the leased time slot. Public access channels, on the other hand, are normally subject to complex supervisory systems of various sorts, often with both public and private elements. *See* §531(b) (franchising authorities "may require rules and procedures for the use of the [public access] channel capacity"). Municipalities generally provide in their cable franchising agreements for an access channel manager, who is most commonly a nonprofit organization, but may also be the municipality, or, in some instances, the cable system owner. Access channel activity and management are partly financed with public funds—through franchise fees or other payments pursuant to the franchise agreement, or from general municipal funds and are commonly subject to supervision by a local supervisory board.

This system of public, private, and mixed nonprofit elements, through its supervising boards and nonprofit or governmental access managers, can set programming policy and approve or disapprove particular programming services. And this system can police that policy by, for example, requiring indemnification by programmers, certification of compliance with local standards, time segregation, adult content advisories, or even by prescreening individual programs. Whether these locally accountable bodies prescreen programming, promulgate rules for the use of public access channels, or are merely available to respond when problems arise, the upshot is the same: there is a locally accountable body capable of addressing the problem, should it arise, of patently offensive programming broadcast to children, making it unlikely that many children will in fact be exposed to programming considered patently offensive in that community.

Third, the existence of a system aimed at encouraging and securing programming that the community considers valuable strongly suggests that a "cable operator's veto" is less likely necessary to achieve the statute's basic objective, protecting children, than a similar veto in the context of leased channels.

Finally, our examination of the legislative history and the record before us is consistent with what common sense suggests, namely that the public/nonprofit programming control systems now in place would normally avoid, minimize, or eliminate any child-related problems concerning "patently offensive" programming. The Commission itself did not report *any* examples of "indecent" programs on public access channels. Moreover, comments submitted to the FCC undermine any suggestion that prior to 1992 there were significant problems of indecent programming on public access channels.

The upshot, in respect to the public access channels, is a law that could radically change present programming-related relationships among local community and nonprofit supervising boards and access managers, which relationships are established through municipal law, regulation, and contract. In doing so, it would not significantly restore editorial rights of cable operators, but would greatly increase the risk that certain categories of programming (say, borderline offensive programs) will not appear. At the same time, given present supervisory mechanisms, the need for this particular provision, aimed directly at public access channels, is not obvious. We conclude that the Government cannot sustain its burden of showing that §10(c) is necessary to protect children or that it is appropriately tailored to secure that end. Consequently, we find that this third provision violates the First Amendment.

VI

For these reasons, the judgment of the Court of Appeals is affirmed insofar as it upheld §10(a); the judgment of the Court of Appeals is reversed insofar as it upheld §10(b) and §10(c).

[Concurring opinions of JUSTICES STEVENS and SOUTER are omitted.]

JUSTICE O'CONNOR, concurring in part and dissenting in part.

I agree that §10(a) is constitutional and that §10(b) is unconstitutional, and I join Parts I, II, III, and V, and the judgment in part. I am not persuaded, however, that the asserted "important differences" between §§10(a) and 10(c), are sufficient to justify striking down §10(c). I find the features shared by §10(a), which covers leased access channels, and §10(c), which covers public access channels, to be more significant than the differences. For that reason, I would find that §10(c) too withstands constitutional scrutiny.

Both §§10(a) and 10(c) serve an important governmental interest: the well-established compelling interest of protecting children from exposure to indecent material. Furthermore, both provisions are permissive. Neither presents an outright ban on a category of speech, such as we struck down in Sable Communications of Cal. Inc. v. FCC, *supra*.

It is also significant that neither §10(a) nor §10(c) is more restrictive than the governmental speech restriction we upheld in FCC v. Pacifica Foundation, 438 U.S. 726 (1978). I agree with Justice Breyer that we should not yet undertake fully to adapt our First Amendment doctrine to the new context we confront here. Because we refrain from doing so, the precedent established by *Pacifica* offers an important guide. Section 10(c), no less than §10(a), is within the range of acceptability set by *Pacifica*.

I am not persuaded that the difference in the origin of the access channels is sufficient to justify upholding §10(a) and striking down §10(c). The interest in protecting children remains the same, whether on a leased access channel or a public access channel, and allowing the cable operator the option of prohibiting the transmission of indecent speech seems a constitutionally permissible means of addressing that interest. Nor is the fact that public access programming may be subject to supervisory systems in addition to the cable operator, sufficient in my mind to render §10(c) so ill-tailored to its goal as to be unconstitutional. Given the compelling interest served by §10(c), its permissive nature, and fit within our precedent, I would hold §10(c), like §10(a), constitutional.

JUSTICE KENNEDY, with whom JUSTICE GINSBURG joins, concurring in part, concurring in the judgment in part, and dissenting in part.

Though I join Part III of the opinion (there for the Court) striking down §10(b) of the Act, and concur in the judgment that §10(c) is unconstitutional, with respect I dissent from the remainder.

I

Two provisions of the 1992 Act, §§10(a) and (c), authorize the operator of a cable system to exclude certain programming from two different kinds of channels. Section 10(a) concerns leased access channels. Section 10(c) involves public, educational, and governmental access channels (or PEG access channels, as they are known).

Though the two provisions differ in significant respects, they have common flaws. In both instances, Congress singles out one sort of speech for vulnerability to private censorship in a context where content based discrimination is not otherwise permitted. Sections 10(a) and (c) disadvantage nonobscene, indecent programming, a protected category of expression, Sable Communications of Cal., Inc. v. FCC, 492 U.S. 115, 126 (1989), on the basis of its content. The Constitution in general does not tolerate content based restriction of or discrimination against speech. R. A. V. v. St. Paul, 505 U.S. 377, 382 (1992) ("Content based regulations are presumptively invalid"). In the realm of speech and expression, the First Amendment envisions the citizen shaping the government, not the reverse; it removes "governmental restraints from the arena of public discussion, putting the decision as to what views shall be voiced largely into the hands of each of us, in the hope that use of such freedom will ultimately produce a more capable citizenry and more perfect polity." Cohen v. California, 403 U.S. 15, 24 (1971).

Sections 10(a) and (c) are unusual. They do not require direct action against speech, but do authorize a cable operator to deny the use of its property to certain forms of speech. As a general matter, a private person may exclude certain speakers from his or her property without violating the First Amendment, and if §§10(a) and (c) were no more than affirmations of this principle they might be unremarkable. Access channels, however, are property of the cable operator dedicated or otherwise reserved for programming of other speakers or the government. A public access channel is a public forum, and laws requiring leased access channels create common carrier obligations. When the government identifies certain speech on the basis of its content as vulnerable to exclusion from a common carrier or public forum, strict scrutiny applies. These laws cannot survive this exacting review. However compelling Congress' interest in shielding children from indecent programming, the provisions in this case are not drawn with enough care to withstand scrutiny under our precedents.

II

Before engaging the complexities of cable access channels and explaining my reasons for thinking all of §10 unconstitutional, I start with the most disturbing aspect of the plurality opinion: its evasion of any clear legal standard in deciding these cases.

The creation of standards and adherence to them, even when it means affording protection to speech unpopular or distasteful, is the central achievement of our First Amendment jurisprudence. Standards are the means by which we state in advance how to test a law's validity, rather than letting the height of the bar be determined by the apparent exigencies of the day. They also provide notice and fair warning to those who must predict how the courts will respond to attempts to suppress their speech. Yet formulations like strict scrutiny, used in a number of constitutional settings to ensure that the inequities of the moment are subordinated to commitments made for the long run, mean little if they can be watered down whenever they seem too strong. They mean still less if they can be ignored altogether when considering a case not on all fours with what we have seen before.

The plurality cannot bring itself to apply strict scrutiny, yet realizes it cannot decide these cases without uttering some sort of standard; so it has settled for synonyms. "Close judicial scrutiny," is substituted for strict scrutiny, and "extremely important problem," or "extraordinary proble[m]," is substituted for "compelling interest." The admonition that the restriction not be unnecessarily great in light of the interest it serves, is substituted for the usual narrow tailoring requirements. All we know about the substitutes is that they are inferior to their antecedents. We are told the Act must be "appropriately tailored," "sufficiently tailored," or "carefully and appropriately addressed," to the problems at hand — anything, evidently, except narrowly tailored.

These restatements have unfortunate consequences. The first is to make principles intended to protect speech easy to manipulate. The words end up being a legalistic cover for an ad hoc balancing of interests; in this respect the plurality succeeds after all in avoiding the use of a standard. Second, the plurality's exercise in pushing around synonyms for the words of our usual standards will sow confusion in the courts bound by our precedents.

Another troubling aspect of the plurality's approach is its suggestion that Congress has more leeway than usual to enact restrictions on speech where emerging technologies are concerned, because we are unsure what standard should be used to assess them.

III

B

In providing public access channels under their franchise agreements, cable operators are not exercising their own First Amendment rights. They serve as conduits for the speech of others. Cf. PruneYard Shopping Center v. Robins, 447 U.S. 74, 87 (1980). Section 10(c) thus restores no power of editorial discretion over public access channels that the cable operator once had; the discretion never existed. It vests the cable operator with a power under federal law, defined by reference to the content of speech, to override the franchise agreement and undercut the public forum the agreement creates. By enacting a law in 1992 excluding indecent programming from protection but retaining the prohibition on cable operators' editorial control over all other protected speech, the

Federal Government at the same time ratified the public-forum character of public access channels but discriminated against certain speech based on its content.

It seems to me clear that when a local government contracts to use private property for public expressive activity, it creates a public forum. Regulations of speech content in a designated public forum, whether of limited or unlimited character, are "subject to the highest scrutiny" and "survive only if they are narrowly drawn to achieve a compelling state interest." International Soc. for Krishna Consciousness, Inc. v. Lee, 505 U.S. 672, 678 (1992).

C

The constitutionality under *Turner Broadcasting,* 512 U.S. at 665–668, of requiring a cable operator to set aside leased access channels is not before us. For purposes of this case, we should treat the cable operator's rights in these channels as extinguished, and address the issue these petitioners present: namely, whether the Government can discriminate on the basis of content in affording protection to certain programmers.

Laws removing common-carriage protection from a single form of speech based on its content should be reviewed under the same standard as content based restrictions on speech in a public forum. Making a cable operator a common carrier does not create a public forum in the sense of taking property from private control and dedicating it to public use; rather, regulations of a common carrier dictate the manner in which private control is exercised. A common-carriage mandate, nonetheless, serves the same function as a public forum. It ensures open, nondiscriminatory access to the means of communication. This purpose is evident in the statute itself and in the committee findings supporting it.

Giving government free rein to exclude speech it dislikes by delimiting public forums (or common carriage provisions) would have pernicious effects in the modern age. Minds are not changed in streets and parks as they once were. To an increasing degree, the more significant interchanges of ideas and shaping of public consciousness occur in mass and electronic media. The extent of public entitlement to participate in those means of communication may be changed as technologies change; and in expanding those entitlements the Government has no greater right to discriminate on suspect grounds than it does when it effects a ban on speech against the backdrop of the entitlements to which we have been more accustomed. It contravenes the First Amendment to give Government a general license to single out some categories of speech for lesser protection so long as it stops short of viewpoint discrimination.

D

Pacifica teaches that access channels, even if analogous to ordinary public forums from the standpoint of the programmer, must also be considered from the standpoint of the viewer. An access channel is not a forum confined to a discrete public space; it can bring indecent expression into the home of every cable subscriber, where children spend astounding amounts of time watching television. Though in *Cohen* we explained that people in public areas may have to avert their eyes from messages that offend them, 403 U.S. at 21, we further acknowledged that "government may properly act in many situations to prohibit intrusion into the privacy of the home of unwelcome views and ideas which cannot be totally banned from the public dialogue," *id.*

These concerns are weighty and will be relevant to whether the law passes strict scrutiny. They do not justify, however, a blanket rule of lesser protection for indecent speech. Other than the few categories of expression which can be proscribed, *see R. A. V.,* 505 U.S. at 382–390, we have been reluctant to mark off new categories of speech for diminished constitutional protection. Our hesitancy reflects skepticism about the possibility of courts' drawing principled distinctions to use in judging governmental restrictions on speech and ideas, *Cohen, supra,* at 25, a concern heightened here by the inextricability of indecency from expression. "We cannot indulge the facile assumption that one can forbid particular words without also running a substantial risk of suppressing ideas in the process." 403 U.S. at 26. The same is true of forbidding programs indecent in some respect. In artistic or political settings, indecency may have strong communicative content, protesting conventional norms or giving an edge to a work by conveying "otherwise inexpressible emotions," *id.* In scientific programs, the more graphic the depiction (even if to the point of offensiveness), the more accurate and comprehensive the portrayal of the truth may be. Indecency often is inseparable from the ideas and viewpoints conveyed, or separable only with loss of truth or expressive power. Under our traditional First Amendment jurisprudence, factors perhaps justifying some restriction on indecent cable programming may all be taken into account without derogating this category of protected speech as marginal.

IV

At a minimum, the proper standard for reviewing §§10(a) and (c) is strict scrutiny. The plurality gives no reason why it should be otherwise. I would hold these enactments unconstitutional because they are not narrowly tailored to serve a compelling interest.

The Government has no compelling interest in restoring a cable operator's First Amendment right of editorial discretion. As to §10(c), Congress has no interest at all, since under most franchises operators had no rights of editorial discretion over PEG access channels in the first place. As to §10(a), any governmental interest in restoring operator discretion over indecent programming on leased access channels is too minimal to justify the law. First, the transmission of indecent programming over leased access channels is not forced speech of the operator. *Turner Broadcasting, supra,* at 655–656. Second, the discretion conferred by the law is slight. The operator is not authorized to place programs of its own liking on the leased access channels, nor to remove other speech (racist or violent, for example) that might be offensive to it or to viewers. The operator is just given a veto over the one kind of lawful speech Congress disdains.

Congress does have, however, a compelling interest in protecting children from indecent speech. Sections 10(a) and (c) nonetheless are not narrowly tailored to protect children from indecent programs on access channels. First, to the extent some operators may allow indecent programming, children in localities those operators serve will be left unprotected. The interest in protecting children from indecency only at the caprice of the cable operator is not compelling.

Second, to the extent cable operators prohibit indecent programming on access channels, not only children but adults will be deprived of it. The Government may not "reduce the adult population...to [viewing] only what is fit for children." Butler v. Michigan, 352 U.S. 380, 383 (1957). A block-and-segregate requirement similar to §10(b), but without its constitutional infirmity of requiring persons to place themselves on a list to receive programming, protects children with far less intrusion on the liberties of programmers and adult viewers than allowing cable operators to ban indecent programming from access channels altogether.

Sections 10(a) and (c) present a classic case of discrimination against speech based on its content. There are legitimate reasons why the Government might wish to regulate or even restrict the speech at issue here, but §§10(a) and 10(c) are not drawn to address those reasons with the precision the First Amendment requires.

VI

In agreement with the plurality's analysis of §10(b) of the Act, insofar as it applies strict scrutiny, I join Part III of its opinion. Its position there, however, cannot be reconciled with upholding §10(a). In the plurality's view, §10(b), which standing alone would guarantee an indecent programmer some access to a cable audience, violates the First Amendment, but §10(a), which authorizes exclusion of indecent programming from access channels altogether, does not. There is little to commend this logic or result. I dissent from the judgment of the Court insofar as it upholds the constitutionality of §10(a).

JUSTICE THOMAS, joined by CHIEF JUSTICE REHNQUIST and JUSTICE SCALIA, concurring in the judgment in part and dissenting in part.

I agree with the plurality's conclusion that §10(a) is constitutionally permissible, but I disagree with its conclusion that §§10(b) and (c) violate the First Amendment. For many years, we have failed to articulate how and to what extent the First Amendment protects cable operators, programmers, and viewers from state and federal regulation. I think it is time we did so, and I cannot go along with Justice Breyer's assiduous attempts to avoid addressing that issue openly.

I

The Court in Turner Broadcasting System, Inc. v. FCC, 512 U.S. 622 (1994), found that the FCC's must-carry rules implicated the First Amendment rights of both cable operators and cable programmers. The rules interfered with the operators' editorial discretion by forcing them to carry broadcast programming that they might not otherwise carry, and they interfered with the programmers' ability to compete for space on the operators' channels. We implicitly recognized in *Turner* that the programmer's right to compete for channel space is derivative of, and subordinate to, the operator's editorial discretion. Like a free-lance writer seeking a paper in which to publish newspaper editorials, a programmer is protected in searching for an outlet for cable programming, but has no free-standing First Amendment right to have that programming transmitted. *Cf.* Miami Herald Publishing Co. v. Tornillo, 418 U.S. at 256–258. Likewise, the rights of would-be viewers are derivative of the speech rights of operators and programmers. Viewers have a general right to see what a willing operator transmits, but, under

Tornillo and *Pacific Gas*, they certainly have no right to force an unwilling operator to speak.

By recognizing the general primacy of the cable operator's editorial rights over the rights of programmers and viewers, *Turner* raises serious questions about the merits of petitioners' claims. None of the petitioners in these cases are cable operators; they are all cable viewers or access programmers or their representative organizations. It is not intuitively obvious that the First Amendment protects the interests petitioners assert, and neither petitioners nor the plurality have adequately explained the source or justification of those asserted rights.

In the process of deciding not to decide on a governing standard, Justice Breyer purports to discover in our cases an expansive, general principle permitting government to "directly regulate speech to address extraordinary problems, where its regulations are appropriately tailored to resolve those problems without imposing an unnecessarily great restriction on speech." *Ante*, at 2385. This heretofore unknown standard is facially subjective and openly invites balancing of asserted speech interests to a degree not ordinarily permitted. It is true that the standard I endorse lacks the "flexibility" inherent in the plurality's balancing approach, but that relative rigidity is required by our precedents and is not of my own making.

In any event, even if the plurality's balancing test were an appropriate standard, it could only be applied to protect speech interests that, under the circumstances, are themselves protected by the First Amendment. But, by shifting the focus to the balancing of "complex" interests, *ante*, at 2386, Justice Breyer never explains whether (and if so, how) a programmer's ordinarily unprotected interest in affirmative transmission of its programming acquires constitutional significance on leased and public access channels. It is that question, left unanswered by the plurality, to which I now turn.

II

A

As I read [the provisions on leased access and PEG channels], they provide leased and public access programmers with an expansive and federally enforced statutory right to transmit virtually any programming over access channels, limited only by the bounds of decency.

Petitioners must concede that cable access is not a constitutionally required entitlement and that the right they claim to leased and public access has, by definition, been governmentally created at the expense of cable operators' editorial discretion. Just because the Court has apparently accepted, for now, the proposition that the Constitution permits some degree of forced speech in the cable context does not mean that the beneficiaries of a government-imposed forced speech program enjoy additional First Amendment protections beyond those normally afforded to purely private speakers.

The question petitioners pose is whether §§10(a) and (c) are improper restrictions on their free speech rights, but *Turner* strongly suggests that the proper question is whether the leased and public access requirements (with §§10(a) and (c)) are improper restrictions on the *operators'* free speech rights. In my view, the constitutional presumption properly runs in favor of the operators' editorial discretion, and that discretion may not be burdened without a compelling reason for doing so.

It is one thing to compel an operator to carry leased and public access speech, in apparent violation of *Tornillo*, but it is another thing altogether to say that the First Amendment forbids Congress to give back part of the operators' editorial discretion, which all recognize as fundamentally protected, in favor of a broader access right. It is no answer to say that leased and public access are content neutral and that §§10(a) and (c) are not, for that does not change the fundamental fact, which petitioners never address, that it is the operators' journalistic freedom that is infringed, whether the challenged restrictions be content neutral or content based.

§§10(a) and (c) do not burden a programmer's right to seek access for its indecent programming on an operator's system. Rather, they merely restore part of the editorial discretion an operator would have absent government regulation without burdening the programmer's underlying speech rights.

B

That the leased access provisions may be described in common-carrier terms does not demonstrate that access programmers have obtained a First Amendment right to transmit programming over leased access channels. Labeling leased access a common carrier scheme has no real First Amendment consequences. It simply does not follow from common carrier status that cable operators may not, with Congress' blessing, decline to carry indecent speech on their leased access channels. Common carriers are private entities and may, consistent with the First Amendment, exercise editorial discretion in the absence of a specific statutory prohibition.

C

Petitioners argue that public access channels are public fora in which they have First Amendment rights to speak and that §10(c) is invalid because it imposes content based burdens on those rights.

Cable systems are not public property. Cable systems are privately owned and privately managed, and petitioners point to no case in which we have held that government may designate private property as a public forum. The public forum doctrine is a rule governing claims of "a right of access to public property," Perry Ed. Assn. v. Perry Local Educators' Assn., 460 U.S. 37, 44 (1983), and has never been thought to extend beyond property generally understood to belong to the government.

Government control over its own property or private property in which it has taken a cognizable property interest is consistent with designation of a public forum. But we have never even hinted that regulatory control, and particularly direct regulatory control over a private entity's First Amendment speech rights, could justify creation of a public forum.

Even were I inclined to view public access channels as public property, which I am not, the numerous additional obligations imposed on the cable operator in managing and operating the public access channels convince me that these channels share few, if any, of the basic characteristics of a public forum. For this reason, and the other reasons articulated earlier, I would sustain both §10(a) and §10(c).

III

Most sexually oriented programming appears on premium or pay-per-view channels that are naturally blocked from nonpaying customers by market forces, and it is only governmental intervention in the first instance that requires access channels, on which indecent programming may appear, to be made part of the basic cable package. Section 10(b) does nothing more than adjust the nature of government-imposed leased access requirements in order to emulate the market forces that keep indecent programming primarily on premium channels (without permitting the operator to charge subscribers for that programming).

Unlike §§10(a) and (c), §10(b) clearly implicates petitioners' free speech rights. Though §10(b) by no means bans indecent speech, it clearly places content based restrictions on the transmission of private speech by requiring cable operators to block and segregate indecent programming that the operator has agreed to carry. Consequently, §10(b) must be subjected to strict scrutiny and can be upheld only if it furthers a compelling governmental interest by the least restrictive means available. *See Sable*, 492 U.S. at 126. The parties agree that Congress has a "compelling interest in protecting the physical and psychological well-being of minors" and that its interest "extends to shielding minors from the influence of [indecent speech] that is not obscene by adult standards." *Id.* Because §10(b) is narrowly tailored to achieve that well-established compelling interest, I would uphold it.

The Court strikes down §10(b) by pointing to alternatives, such as reverse-blocking and lockboxes, that it says are less restrictive than segregation and blocking. Though these methods attempt to place in parents' hands the ability to permit their children to watch as little, or as much, indecent programming as the parents think proper, they do not effectively support parents' authority to direct the moral upbringing of their children.[2] The FCC recognized that leased-access programming comes "from a wide variety of independent sources, with no single editor controlling [its] selection and presentation." In re Implementation of Section 10 of the Consumer Protection and Competition Act of 1992: Indecent Programming and Other Types of Materials on Cable Access Channels, First Report and Order, 8 FCC Rcd. 998, 1000 (1993). Thus, indecent programming on leased access channels is "especially likely to be shown randomly or intermittently between non-indecent programs." *Id.* Rather than being able to simply block out certain channels at certain times, a subscriber armed with only a lockbox must carefully monitor all leased-access programming and constantly reprogram the lockbox to keep out undesired programming. Thus, even assuming that cable subscribers generally have the technical proficiency to properly operate a lockbox, by no means a given, this distinguishing characteristic of leased access channels makes lockboxes and reverse-blocking largely ineffective.

---

2. In the context of dial-a-porn, courts upholding the FCC's mandatory blocking scheme have expressly found that voluntary blocking schemes are not effective. *See Dial Information Servs., supra*, at 1542; *Information Providers' Coalition, supra*, at 873–874. [Footnote relocated.]

Petitioners argue that forcing customers to submit a written request for access will chill dissemination of speech. However, petitioners' allegations of an official list "of those who wish to watch the 'patently offensive' channel," as the majority puts it, are pure hyperbole. The FCC regulation implementing §10(b)'s written request requirement, 47 CFR §76.701(b) (1995), says nothing about the creation of a list, much less an official government list. It requires only that the cable operator receive written consent. Other statutory provisions make clear that the cable operator may not share that, or any other, information with any other person, including the Government. Section 551 mandates that all personally identifiable information regarding a subscriber be kept strictly confidential and further requires cable operators to destroy any information that is no longer necessary for the purpose for which it was collected. 47 U.S.C. §§551.

Any request for access to blocked programming—by whatever method—ultimately will make the subscriber's identity knowable. But this is hardly the kind of chilling effect that implicates the First Amendment.

The United States has carried its burden of demonstrating that §10(b) and its implementing regulations are narrowly tailored to satisfy a compelling governmental interest. Accordingly, I would affirm the judgment of the Court of Appeals in its entirety. I therefore concur in the judgment upholding §10(a) and respectfully dissent from that portion of the judgment striking down §§10(b) and (c).

Notes and Questions

1. Do No Harm. Justice Souter's concurring opinion in *Denver Area* expresses agreement with Justice Breyer's unwillingness to choose a doctrinal category in analyzing the First Amendment issues, and Souter closes by invoking a "rule familiar to every doctor of medicine: 'First, do no harm.'" 518 U.S. at 778. Justice Kennedy, in his partial concurrence and partial dissent, quotes this statement but adds: "The question, though, is whether the harm is in sustaining the law or striking it down." *Id.* at 787. What is the "do no harm" position in this case? Is there an answer to that question that does not subsume the entire controversy?

2. Zoning Indecency. *Denver Area*, at least to some extent, translates to cable television *Pacifica*'s toleration of "zoning" broadcast indecency. Does this mean that the current Court no longer believes that over-the-air broadcasting is a "*uniquely* pervasive" medium that is also "*uniquely* accessible to children" (emphases added)? If so, then just what is the surviving rationale of *Pacifica*? Note that several members of the Court voted to uphold some provisions of the Act on the grounds that those provisions are no more intrusive than the policies upheld in *Pacifica*.

3. Rules or Standards. Justice Breyer explicitly refuses to pick a rigid standard of scrutiny, and Justices Kennedy and Thomas criticize him for so refusing. This clash invokes the longstanding dispute over whether we should prefer clear rules or fluid standards. One added element in this instance is that everyone expects continued technological change. Both sides, though, suggest that the uncertainty produced by such change supports their position. Who is right? Does the likelihood of continued technological development indicate that courts should lay down clear rules so that people can rely on them in choosing a course of action, or that courts should allow themselves the flexibility to craft new approaches when they seem appropriate?

4. Satisfying the Standard. In Part II of his opinion—joined by three other justices—Justice Breyer describes §10(a) as "a sufficiently tailored response to an extraordinarily important problem." In what respects is §10(a) "tailored"? What is the "extraordinarily important problem" the provision cures? Perhaps it is the risk that a sixteen year old child will hear an "offensive sex-related" word? If this constitutes an "extraordinarily important problem" confronting the federal government, how do you suppose Justice Breyer might describe, for example, the threat of nuclear war?

5. The 1996 Act. The Telecommunications Act of 1996 added three provisions affecting "indecency" on cable. Section 506, codified at 47 U.S.C. §531(e) and §532(c)(2), informs cable operators that they can refuse to transmit any PEG or leased access program or portion thereof "which contains obscenity, indecency, or nudity." Is the portion of section 506 applicable to PEG channels constitutional after *Denver Area*? The portion applicable to leased access? What does section 506 add to the powers that cable operators already had under pre-1996 law?

The other two provisions are sections 504 and 505 of the Telecommunications Act. Both provisions are discussed in the following case, which invalidated §505, in part because of the less restrictive alternative presented by §504.

UNITED STATES v. PLAYBOY ENTERTAINMENT GROUP, INC.
529 U.S. 803 (2000)

KENNEDY, J., delivered the opinion of the Court, in which STEVENS, SOUTER, THOMAS, and GINSBURG, JJ., joined. STEVENS, J., and THOMAS, J., filed concurring opinions. SCALIA, J., filed a dissenting opinion. BREYER, J., filed a dissenting opinion, in which REHNQUIST, C. J., and O'-CONNOR and SCALIA, JJ., joined.

JUSTICE KENNEDY delivered the opinion of the Court.

This case presents a challenge to §505 of the Telecommunications Act of 1996 (Act), 47 U.S.C. §561. Section 505 requires cable television operators who provide channels "primarily dedicated to sexually-oriented programming" either to "fully scramble or otherwise fully block" those channels or to limit their transmission to hours when children are unlikely to be viewing, set by administrative regulation as the time between 10 p.m. and 6 a.m. 47 U.S.C. §561(a); 47 CFR §76.227 (1999). Even before enactment of the statute, signal scrambling was already in use. Cable operators used scrambling in the regular course of business, so that only paying customers had access to certain programs. Scrambling could be imprecise, however; and either or both audio and visual portions of the scrambled programs might be heard or seen, a phenomenon known as "signal bleed." The purpose of §505 is to shield children from hearing or seeing images resulting from signal bleed.

To comply with the statute, the majority of cable operators adopted the second, or "time channeling," approach. The effect of the widespread adoption of time channeling was to eliminate altogether the transmission of the targeted programming outside the safe harbor period in affected cable service areas.

Appellee Playboy Entertainment Group, Inc., challenged the statute as unnecessarily restrictive content based legislation violative of the First Amendment. After a trial, a three-judge District Court concluded that a regime in which viewers could order signal blocking on a household-by-household basis presented an effective, less restrictive alternative to §505. 30 F.Supp.2d 702, 719 (D. Del.1998).

II

Two essential points should be understood concerning the speech at issue here. First, we shall assume that many adults themselves would find the material highly offensive; and when we consider the further circumstance that the material comes unwanted into homes where children might see or hear it against parental wishes or consent, there are legitimate reasons for regulating it. Second, all parties bring the case to us on the premise that Playboy's programming has First Amendment protection. As this case has been litigated, it is not alleged to be obscene; adults have a constitutional right to view it; the Government disclaims any interest in preventing children from seeing or hearing it with the consent of their parents; and Playboy has concomitant rights under the First Amendment to transmit it. These points are undisputed.

The speech in question is defined by its content; and the statute which seeks to restrict it is content based. Section 505 applies only to channels primarily dedicated to "sexually explicit adult programming or other programming that is indecent." The statute is unconcerned with signal bleed from any other channels. The overriding justification for the regulation is concern for the effect of the subject matter on young viewers.

Not only does §505 single out particular programming content for regulation, it also singles out particular programmers. The statutory disability applies only to channels "primarily dedicated to sexually-oriented programming." 47 U.S.C. §561(a). Laws designed or intended to suppress or restrict the expression of specific speakers contradict basic First Amendment principles. Section 505 limited Playboy's market as a penalty for its programming choice, though other channels capable of transmitting like material are altogether exempt.

The effect of the federal statute on the protected speech is now apparent. It is evident that the only reasonable way for a substantial number of cable operators to comply with the letter of §505 is to time channel, which silences the protected speech for two-thirds of the day in every home in a cable service area, regardless of the presence or likely presence of children or of the wishes of the viewers. According to the District Court, "30 to 50% of all adult programming is viewed by households prior to 10 p.m.," when the safe-harbor period begins. 30 F.Supp.2d, at 711. To prohibit this much speech is a significant restriction of communication between speakers and willing adult listeners, communication which enjoys First Amendment protection. It is of no moment that the statute does not impose a complete prohibition. The distinction between laws burdening and laws banning speech is but a matter of degree. The Government's content based burdens must satisfy the same rigorous scrutiny as its content based bans.

Since §505 is a content based speech restriction, it can stand only if it satisfies strict scrutiny. If a statute regulates speech based on its content, it must be narrowly tailored to promote a compelling Government interest. If a less restrictive alternative would serve the Government's purpose, the legislature must use that alternative. To do otherwise would be to restrict speech without an adequate justification, a course the First Amendment does not permit.

Our precedents teach these principles. Where the designed benefit of a content based speech restriction is to shield the sensibilities of listeners, the general rule is that the right of expression prevails, even where no less restrictive alternative exists. We are expected to protect our own sensibilities "simply by averting [our] eyes." Cohen v. California, 403 U.S. 15, 21 (1971). Here, of course, we consider images transmitted to some homes where they are not wanted and where parents often are not present to give immediate guidance. Cable television, like broadcast media, presents unique problems, which inform our assessment of the interests at stake, and which may justify restrictions that would be unacceptable in other contexts. *See* Denver Area Educational Telecommunications Consortium, Inc. v. FCC, 518 U.S. 727, 744 (1996) (plurality opinion); *id.*, at 804–805 (Kennedy, J., concurring in part, concurring in judgment in part, and dissenting in part); FCC v. Pacifica Foundation, 438 U.S. 726 (1978). No one suggests the Government must be indifferent to unwanted, indecent speech that comes into the home without parental consent. The speech here, all agree, is protected speech; and the question is what standard the Government must meet in order to restrict it. As we consider a content based regulation, the answer should be clear: The standard is strict scrutiny. This case involves speech alone; and even where speech is indecent and enters the home, the objective of shielding children does not suffice to support a blanket ban if the protection can be accomplished by a less restrictive alternative.

There is, moreover, a key difference between cable television and the broadcasting media, which is the point on which this case turns: Cable systems have the capacity to block unwanted channels on a household-by-household basis. The option to block reduces the likelihood, so concerning to the Court in *Pacifica*, that traditional First Amendment scrutiny would deprive the Government of all authority to address this sort of problem. The corollary, of course, is that targeted blocking enables the Government to support parental authority without affecting the First Amendment interests of speakers and willing listeners — listeners for whom, if the speech is unpopular or indecent, the privacy of their own homes may be the optimal place of receipt. Simply put, targeted blocking is less restrictive than banning, and the Government cannot ban speech if targeted blocking is a feasible and effective means of furthering its compelling interests. This is not to say that the absence of an effective blocking mechanism will in all cases suffice to support a law restricting the speech in question; but if a less restrictive means is available for the Government to achieve its goals, the Government must use it.

III

The District Court concluded that a less restrictive alternative is available: §504 [of the Act], with adequate publicity. [§504 provides that "[u]pon request by a cable service subscriber, a cable operator shall, without charge, fully scramble or otherwise fully block" any channel the subscriber does not wish to receive. 47 U.S.C. §560.] No one disputes that §504, which requires cable operators to block undesired channels at individual households upon request, is narrowly tailored to the Government's goal of supporting parents who want those channels blocked. The question is whether §504 can be effective.

When a plausible, less restrictive alternative is offered to a content based speech restriction, it is the Government's obligation to prove that the alternative will be ineffective to achieve its goals. The Government has not met that burden here. In support of its position, the Government cites empirical evidence showing that §504, as promulgated and implemented before trial, generated few requests for household-by-household blocking. Between March 1996 and May 1997, while the Government was enjoined from enforcing §505, §504 remained in operation. A survey of cable operators determined that fewer than 0.5% of cable subscribers requested full blocking during that time. The uncomfortable fact is that §504 was the sole blocking regulation in effect for over a year; and the public greeted it with a collective yawn.

The District Court was correct to direct its attention to the import of this tepid response. Placing the burden of proof upon the Government, the District Court examined whether §504 was capable of serving as an effective, less restrictive means of reaching the Government's goals. It concluded that §504, if publicized in an adequate manner, could be.

The District Court employed the proper approach. When the Government restricts speech, the Government bears the burden of proving the constitutionality of its actions. When the Government seeks to restrict speech based on its content, the usual presumption of constitutionality afforded congressional enactments is reversed.

This is for good reason. "The line between speech unconditionally guaranteed and speech which may legitimately be regulated, suppressed, or punished is finely drawn." Speiser v. Randall, 357 U.S. 513, 525 (1958). Error in marking that line exacts an extraordinary cost. It is through speech that our convictions and beliefs are influenced, expressed, and tested. It is through speech that we bring those beliefs to bear on Government and on society. It is through speech that our personalities are formed and expressed. The citizen is entitled to seek out or reject certain ideas or influences without Government interference or control.

When a student first encounters our free speech jurisprudence, he or she might think it is influenced by the philosophy that one idea is as good as any other, and that in art and literature objective standards of style, taste, decorum, beauty, and esthetics are deemed by the Constitution to be inappropriate, indeed unattainable. Quite the opposite is true. The Constitution no more enforces a relativistic philosophy or moral nihilism than it does any other point of view. The Constitution exists precisely so that opinions and judgments, including esthetic and moral judgments about art and literature, can be formed, tested, and expressed. What the Constitution says is that these judgments are for the individual to make, not for the Government to decree, even with the mandate or approval of a majority. Technology expands the capacity to choose; and it denies the potential of this revolution if we assume the Government is best positioned to make these choices for us.

It is rare that a regulation restricting speech because of its content will ever be permissible. Indeed, were we to give the Government the benefit of the doubt when it attempted to restrict speech, we would risk leaving regulations in place that sought to shape our unique personalities or to silence dissenting ideas. When First Amendment compliance is the point to be proved, the risk of non-persuasion—operative in all trials—must rest with the Government, not with the citizen.

With this burden in mind, the District Court explored three explanations for the lack of individual blocking requests. First, individual blocking might not be an effective alternative, due to technological or other limitations. Second, although an adequately advertised blocking provision might have been effective, §504 as written did not require sufficient notice to make it so. Third, the actual signal bleed problem might be far less of a concern than the Government at first had supposed.

To sustain its statute, the Government was required to show that the first was the right answer. According to the District Court, however, the first and third possibilities were "equally consistent" with the record before it. As for the second, the record was "not clear" as to whether enough notice had been issued to give §504 a fighting chance. The case, then, was at best a draw. Unless the District Court's findings are clearly erroneous, the tie goes to free expression.

The District Court began with the problem of signal bleed itself, concluding "the Government has not convinced us that [signal bleed] is a pervasive problem." 30 F.Supp.2d, at 708–709, 718. The District Court's thorough discussion exposes a central weakness in the Government's proof: There is little hard evidence of how widespread or how serious the problem of signal bleed is. Indeed, there is no proof as to how likely any child is to view a discernible explicit image, and no proof of the duration of the bleed or the quality of the pictures or sound. To say that millions of children are subject to a risk of viewing signal bleed is one thing; to avoid articulating the true nature and extent of the risk is quite another. Under §505, sanctionable signal bleed can include instances as fleeting as an image appearing on a screen for just a few seconds. The First Amendment requires a more careful assessment and characterization of an evil in order to justify a regulation as sweeping as this.

The Government relied at trial on anecdotal evidence to support its regulation, which the District Court summarized as follows:

> "The Government has presented evidence of only a handful of isolated incidents over the 16 years since 1982 when Playboy started broadcasting. The Government has not presented any survey-type evidence on the magnitude of the 'problem.'" 30 F .Supp. 2d, at 709.

Spurred by the District Court's express request for more specific evidence of the problem, the Government also presented an expert's spreadsheet estimate that 39 million homes with 29.5 million children had the potential to be exposed to signal bleed. The Government made no attempt to confirm the accuracy of its estimate through surveys or other field tests, however. Accordingly, the District Court discounted the figures and made this finding: "The Government presented no evidence on the number of households actually exposed to signal bleed and thus has not quantified the actual extent of the problem of signal bleed." *Id.*, at 709. The finding is not clearly erroneous; indeed it is all but required.

Once §505 went into effect, of course, a significant percentage of cable operators felt it necessary to time channel their sexually explicit programmers. This is an indication that scrambling technology is not yet perfected. That is not to say, however, that scrambling is completely ineffective. Different cable systems use different scrambling systems, which vary in their dependability. "The severity of the problem varies from time to time and place to place, depending on the weather, the quality of the equipment, its installation, and maintenance." *Id.*, at 708. At even the good end of the spectrum a system might bleed to an extent sufficient to trigger the time-channeling requirement for a cautious cable operator. (The statute requires the signal to be "*fully* block[ed]." 47 U.S.C. §561(a) (emphasis added).) A rational cable operator, faced with the possibility of sanctions for intermittent bleeding, could well choose to time channel even if the bleeding is too momentary to pose any concern to most households. To affirm that the Government failed to prove the existence of a problem, while at the same time observing that the statute imposes a severe burden on speech, is consistent with the analysis our cases require. Here, there is no probative evidence in the record which differentiates among the extent of bleed at individual households and no evidence which otherwise quantifies the signal bleed problem.

In addition, market-based solutions such as programmable televisions, VCR's, and mapping systems (which display a blue screen when tuned to a scrambled signal) may eliminate signal bleed at the consumer end of the cable. Playboy made the point at trial that the Government's estimate failed to account for these factors. Without some sort of field survey, it is impossible to know how widespread the problem in fact is, and the only indicator in the record is a handful of complaints. Cf. Turner Broadcasting System, Inc. v. FCC, 520 U.S. 180, 187 (1997) (reviewing "'a record of tens of thousands of pages' of evidence" developed through "three years of pre-enactment hearings, ... as well as additional expert submissions, sworn declarations and testimony, and industry documents" in support of complex must-carry provisions).

No support for the restriction can be found in the near barren legislative record relevant to this provision. Section 505 was added to the Act by floor amendment, accompanied by only brief statements, and without committee hearing or debate. One of the measure's sponsors did indicate she considered time channeling to be superior to voluntary blocking, which "put[s] the burden of action on the subscriber, not the cable company." 141 Cong. Rec. 15587 (1995) (statement of Sen. Feinstein). This sole conclusory statement, however, tells little about the relative efficacy of voluntary blocking versus time channeling, other than offering the unhelpful, self-evident generality that voluntary measures require voluntary action. The Court has declined to rely on similar evidence before. *See* Sable Communications of Cal., Inc. v. FCC, 492 U.S. 115, 129–130 (1989) ("Aside from conclusory statements during the debates by proponents of the bill, the congressional record presented to us contains no evidence as to *how* effective or ineffective the regulations were or might prove to be"); Reno v. American Civil Liberties Union, 521 U.S. 844, 858, and n. 24, 875–876, n. 41 (1997) (same). This is not to suggest that a 10,000 page record must be compiled in every case or that the Government must delay in acting to address a real problem; but the Government must present more than anecdote and supposition. The question is whether an actual problem has been proven in this case. We agree that the Government has failed to establish a pervasive, nationwide problem justifying its nationwide daytime speech ban.

Nor did the District Court err in its second conclusion. The Government also failed to prove §504 with adequate notice would be an ineffective alternative to

§505. Once again, the District Court invited the Government to produce its proof. Once again, the Government fell short. There is no evidence that a well-promoted voluntary blocking provision would not be capable at least of informing parents about signal bleed (if they are not yet aware of it) and about their rights to have the bleed blocked (if they consider it a problem and have not yet controlled it themselves).

The Government finds at least two problems with the conclusion of the three-judge District Court. First, the Government takes issue with the District Court's reliance, without proof, on a "hypothetical, enhanced version of Section 504." Brief for United States et al. 32. It was not the District Court's obligation, however, to predict the extent to which an improved notice scheme would improve §504. It was for the Government, presented with a plausible, less restrictive alternative, to prove the alternative to be ineffective, and §505 to be the least restrictive available means.

The Government also contends a publicized §504 will be just as restrictive as §505, on the theory that the cost of installing blocking devices will outstrip the revenues from distributing Playboy's programming and lead to its cancellation. This conclusion rests on the assumption that a sufficient percentage of households, informed of the potential for signal bleed, would consider it enough of a problem to order blocking devices—an assumption for which there is no support in the record. It should be noted, furthermore, that Playboy is willing to incur the costs of an effective §504. One might infer that Playboy believes an advertised §504 will be ineffective for its object, or one might infer the company believes the signal bleed problem is not widespread. In the absence of proof, it is not for the Court to assume the former.

It is no response that voluntary blocking requires a consumer to take action, or may be inconvenient, or may not go perfectly every time. A court should not assume a plausible, less restrictive alternative would be ineffective; and a court should not presume parents, given full information, will fail to act. If unresponsive operators are a concern, moreover, a notice statute could give cable operators ample incentive, through fines or other penalties for noncompliance, to respond to blocking requests in prompt and efficient fashion.

Having adduced no evidence in the District Court showing that an adequately advertised §504 would not be effective to aid desirous parents in keeping signal bleed out of their own households, the Government can now cite nothing in the record to support the point. The Government instead takes quite a different approach. After only an offhand suggestion that the success of a well-communicated §504 is "highly unlikely," the Government sets the point aside, arguing instead that society's independent interests will be unserved if parents fail to act on that information. Brief for United States et al. 33 ("Even an enhanced version of Section 504 would succeed in blocking signal bleed only if, and after, parents affirmatively decided to avail themselves of the means offered them to do so. There would certainly be parents—perhaps a large number of parents—who out of inertia, indifference, or distraction, simply would take no action to block signal bleed, even if fully informed of the problem and even if offered a relatively easy solution").

Even upon the assumption that the Government has an interest in substituting itself for informed and empowered parents, its interest is not sufficiently compelling to justify this widespread restriction on speech. The Government's argument stems from the idea that parents do not know their children are viewing the material on a scale or frequency to cause concern, or if so, that parents do not want to take affirmative steps to block it and their decisions are to be superseded. The assumptions have not been established; and in any event the assumptions apply only in a regime where the option of blocking has not been explained. The whole point of a publicized §504 would be to advise parents that indecent material may be shown and to afford them an opportunity to block it at all times, even when they are not at home and even after 10 p.m. Time channeling does not offer this assistance. The regulatory alternative of a publicized §504, which has the real possibility of promoting more open disclosure and the choice of an effective blocking system, would provide parents the information needed to engage in active supervision. The Government has not shown that this alternative, a regime of added communication and support, would be insufficient to secure its objective, or that any overriding harm justifies its intervention.

There can be little doubt, of course, that under a voluntary blocking regime, even with adequate notice, some children will be exposed to signal bleed; and we need not discount the possibility that a graphic image could have a negative impact on a young child. It must be remembered, however, that children will be exposed to signal bleed under time channeling as well. Time channeling, unlike blocking, does not eliminate signal bleed around the clock. Just as adolescents may be unsupervised outside of their own households, it is hardly unknown for them to be unsupervised in front of the television set after 10 p.m. The record is silent as to the comparative effectiveness of the two alternatives.

Basic speech principles are at stake in this case. When the purpose and design of a statute is to regulate speech by reason of its content, special consideration or latitude is not accorded to the Government merely because the law can somehow be described as a burden rather than outright suppression. We cannot be influenced, moreover, by the perception that the regulation in question is not a major one because the speech is not very important. The history of the law of free expression is one of vindication in cases involving speech that many citizens may find shabby, offensive, or even ugly. It follows that all content based restrictions on speech must give us more than a moment's pause. If television broadcasts can expose children to the real risk of harmful exposure to indecent materials, even in their own home and without parental consent, there is a problem the Government can address. It must do so, however, in a way consistent with First Amendment principles. Here the Government has not met the burden the First Amendment imposes.

[Concurring opinions of JUSTICES STEVENS and THOMAS, and dissenting opinion of JUSTICE SCALIA, are omitted.]

JUSTICE BREYER, with whom CHIEF JUSTICE REHNQUIST, JUSTICE O'-CONNOR, and JUSTICE SCALIA join, dissenting.

I

At the outset, I would describe the statutory scheme somewhat differently than does the majority. I would emphasize three background points. First, the statutory scheme reflects more than a congressional effort to control incomplete scrambling. Previously, federal law had left cable operators free to decide whether, when, and how to transmit adult channels. Most channel operators on their own had decided not to send adult channels into a subscriber's home except on request. But the operators then implemented that decision with inexpensive technology. Through signal "bleeding," the scrambling technology (either inadvertently or by way of enticement) allowed non subscribers to see and hear what was going on. That is why Congress decided to act.

The statute is carefully tailored to respect viewer preferences. It regulates transmissions by creating two "default rules" applicable unless the subscriber decides otherwise. Taken together, [§§504 and 505] create a scheme that permits subscribers to choose to see what they want. But each law creates a different "default" assumption about silent subscribers. Section 504 assumes a silent subscriber wants to see the ordinary (non adult) channels that the cable operator includes in the paid-for bundle sent into the home. Section 505 assumes that a silent subscriber does not want to receive adult channels. Consequently, a subscriber wishing to view an adult channel must "opt in," and specifically request that channel. See §505. A subscriber wishing not to view any other channel (sent into the home) must "opt out." See §504.

The scheme addresses signal bleed but only indirectly. From the statute's perspective signal "bleeding"—i.e., a failure to fully "rearrange the content of the signal...so that the programming cannot be viewed or heard in an understandable manner," §505(c),—amounts to transmission into a home. Hence "bleeding" violates the statute whenever a clear transmission of an unrequested adult channel would violate the statute.

Second, the majority's characterization of this statutory scheme as "prohibit[ing]...speech" is an exaggeration. Ante, at 7. Rather, the statute places a burden on adult channel speech by requiring the relevant cable operator either to use better scrambling technology, or, if that technology is too expensive, to broadcast only between 10 p.m. and 6 a.m. Laws that burden speech, say, by making speech less profitable, may create serious First Amendment issues, but they are not the equivalent of an absolute ban on speech itself. The difference— between imposing a burden and enacting a ban—can matter even when strict First Amendment rules are at issue.

Third, this case concerns only the regulation of commercial actors who broadcast "virtually 100% sexually explicit" material. 30 F.Supp.2d 702, 707 (Del. 1998). The channels do not broadcast more than trivial amounts of more serious material such as birth control information, artistic images, or the visual equivalents of classical or serious literature. This case therefore does not present the kind of narrow tailoring concerns seen in other cases.

With this background in mind, the reader will better understand my basic disagreement with each of the Court's two conclusions.

II

The majority first concludes that the Government failed to prove the seriousness of the problem—receipt of adult channels by children whose parents did not request their broadcast. This claim is flat-out wrong. For one thing, the parties concede that basic RF scrambling does not scramble the audio portion of the program. For another, Playboy itself conducted a survey of cable operators who were asked: "Is your system in full compliance with Section 505 (no discernible audio or video bleed)?" To this question, 75% of cable operators answered "no." Further, the Government's expert took the number of homes subscribing to

Playboy or Spice, multiplied by the fraction of cable households with children and the average number of children per household, and found 29 million children are potentially exposed to audio and video bleed from adult programming. Even discounting by 25% for systems that might be considered in full compliance, this left 22 million children in homes with faulty scrambling systems. And, of course, the record contains additional anecdotal evidence and the concerns expressed by elected officials, probative of a larger problem.

If signal bleed is not a significant empirical problem, then why, in light of the cost of its cure, must so many cable operators switch to night time hours? There is no realistic answer to this question. I do not think it realistic to imagine that signal bleed occurs just enough to make cable operators skittish, without also significantly exposing children to these images.

If, as the majority suggests, the signal bleed problem is not significant, then there is also no significant burden on speech created by §505. The majority cannot have this evidence both ways. And if, given this logical difficulty and the quantity of empirical evidence, the majority still believes that the Government has not proved its case, then it imposes a burden upon the Government beyond that suggested in any other First Amendment case of which I am aware.

III

The majority's second claim—that the Government failed to demonstrate the absence of a "less restrictive alternative"—presents a closer question. The specific question is whether §504's "opt-out" amounts to a "less restrictive," but *similarly* practical and *effective*, way to accomplish §505's child-protecting objective. As *Reno* tells us, a "less restrictive alternative" must be "at least as effective in achieving the legitimate purpose that the statute was enacted to serve." 521 U.S., at 874.

The words I have just emphasized, "similarly" and "effective," are critical. In an appropriate case they ask a judge not to apply First Amendment rules mechanically, but to decide whether, in light of the benefits and potential alternatives, the statute works speech-related harm (here to adult speech) out of proportion to the benefits that the statute seeks to provide (here, child protection).

These words imply a degree of leeway, however small, for the legislature when it chooses among possible alternatives in light of predicted comparative effects. Without some such empirical leeway, the undoubted ability of lawyers and judges to imagine *some* kind of slightly less drastic or restrictive an approach would make it impossible to write laws that deal with the harm that called the statute into being. As Justice Blackmun pointed out, a "judge would be unimaginative indeed if he could not come up with something a little less 'drastic' or a little less 'restrictive' in almost any situation, and thereby enable himself to vote to strike legislation down." Illinois Bd. of Elections v. Socialist Workers Party, 440 U.S. 173, 188–189 (1979) (concurring opinion). Used without a sense of the practical choices that face legislatures, "the test merely announces an inevitable [negative] result, and the test is no test at all." *Id.*, at 188.

Unlike the majority, I believe the record makes clear that §504's opt-out is not a similarly effective alternative. Section 504 (opt-out) and §505 (opt-in) work differently in order to achieve very different legislative objectives. Section 504 gives parents the power to tell cable operators to keep any channel out of their home. Section 505 does more. Unless parents explicitly consent, it inhibits the transmission of adult cable channels to children whose parents may be unaware of what they are watching, whose parents cannot easily supervise television viewing habits, whose parents do not know of their §504 "opt-out" rights, or whose parents are simply unavailable at critical times. In this respect, §505 serves the same interests as the laws that deny children access to adult cabarets or X-rated movies. These laws, and §505, all act in the absence of direct parental supervision.

This legislative objective is perfectly legitimate. Where over 28 million school age children have both parents or their only parent in the work force, where at least 5 million children are left alone at home without supervision each week, and where children may spend afternoons and evenings watching television outside of the home with friends, §505 offers independent protection for a large number of families. I could not disagree more when the majority implies that the Government's independent interest in offering such protection—preventing, say, an 8-year-old child from watching virulent pornography without parental consent—might not be "compelling." *Ante*, at 19. No previous case in which the protection of children was at issue has suggested any such thing. Indeed, they all say precisely the opposite. *See Reno*, 521 U.S., at 865 (State has an "independent interest in the well-being of its youth"); *Denver Area*, 518 U.S., at 743. They make clear that Government has a compelling interest in helping parents by preventing minors from accessing sexually explicit materials in the absence of parental supervision.

By definition, §504 does *nothing at all* to further the compelling interest I have just described. How then is it a similarly effective §505 alternative?

The record, moreover, sets forth empirical evidence showing that the two laws are not equivalent with respect to the Government's objectives. As the majority observes, during the 14 months the Government was enjoined from enforcing §505, "fewer than 0.5% of cable subscribers requested full blocking" under §504. *Ante*, at 11. The majority describes this public reaction as "a collective yawn," *id.*, adding that the Government failed to prove that the "yawn" reflected anything other than the lack of a serious signal bleed problem or a lack of notice which better information about §504 might cure. The record excludes the first possibility—at least in respect to exposure, as discussed above. And I doubt that the public, though it may well consider the viewing habits of *adults* a matter of personal choice, would "yawn" when the exposure in question concerns young children, the absence of parental consent, and the sexually explicit material here at issue.

Neither is the record neutral in respect to the curative power of better notice. Section 504's opt-out right works only when parents (1) become aware of their §504 rights, (2) discover that their children are watching sexually-explicit signal "bleed," (3) reach their cable operator and ask that it block the sending of its signal to their home, (4) await installation of an individual blocking device, and, perhaps (5) (where the block fails or the channel number changes) make a new request. Better notice of §504 rights does little to help parents discover their children's viewing habits (step two). And it does nothing at all in respect to steps three through five. Yet the record contains considerable evidence that those problems matter, *i.e.*, evidence of endlessly delayed phone call responses, faulty installations, blocking failures, and other mishaps, leaving those steps as significant §504 obstacles.

Further, the District Court's actual plan for "better notice"—the only plan that makes concrete the majority's "better notice" requirement—is fraught with difficulties. The District Court ordered Playboy to insist that cable operators place notice of §504 "inserts in monthly billing statements, barker channels... and on-air advertising." 30 F.Supp.2d, at 719. But how can one say that placing one more insert in a monthly billing statement stuffed with others, or calling additional attention to adult channels through a "notice" on "barker" channels, will make more than a small difference? More importantly, why would doing so not interfere to some extent with the cable operators' own freedom to decide what to broadcast?

Even if better notice did adequately inform viewers of their §504 rights, exercise of those rights by more than 6% of the subscriber base would itself raise Playboy's costs to the point that Playboy would be forced off the air entirely—a consequence that would not seem to further anyone's interest in free speech. Section 504 is not a similarly effective alternative to §505 (in respect to the Government's interest in protecting children), unless more than a minimal number of viewers actually use it; yet the economic evidence shows that if more than 6% do so, Playboy's programming would be totally eliminated.

Of course, it is logically *possible* that "better notice" will bring about near perfect parental knowledge (of what children watch and §504 opt-out rights), that cable operators will respond rapidly to blocking requests, and that still 94% of all informed parents will decided not to have adult channels blocked for free. But the *probability* that this remote *possibility* will occur is neither a "draw" nor a "tie." *Ante*, at 14. And that fact is sufficient for the Government to have met its burden of proof.

IV

Section 505 raises the cost of adult channel broadcasting. In doing so, it restricts, but does not ban adult speech. Adults may continue to watch adult channels, though less conveniently, by watching at night, recording programs with a VCR, or by subscribing to digital cable with better blocking systems. The Government's justification for imposing this restriction—limiting the access of children to channels that broadcast virtually 100% "sexually explicit" material—is "compelling." The record shows no similarly effective, less restrictive alternative. Consequently §505's restriction, viewed in light of the proposed alternative, is proportionate to need. That is to say, it restricts speech no more than necessary to further that compelling need. Taken together, these considerations lead to the conclusion that §505 is lawful.

I repeat that my disagreement with the majority lies in the fact that, in my view, the Government has satisfied its burden of proof. In particular, it has proved both the existence of a serious problem and the comparative ineffectiveness of §504 in resolving that problem. This disagreement is not about allocation of First Amendment burdens of proof, basic First Amendment principle nor the importance of that Amendment to our scheme of Government. First Amendment standards are rigorous. They safeguard speech. But they also permit Congress to enact a law that increases the costs associated with certain speech, where doing so serves a compelling interest that cannot be served through the adoption of a less restrictive, similarly effective alternative. Those standards at their strictest make it difficult for the Government to prevail. But they do not make it impossible for the Government to prevail.

The majority here, however, has applied those standards without making a realistic assessment of the alternatives. It thereby threatens to leave Congress without power to help the millions of parents who do not want to expose their children to commercial pornography—but will remain ill served by the Court's chosen remedy. Worse still, the logic of the majority's "505/504" comparison (but not its holding that the problem has not been established) would seem to apply whether "bleeding" or totally unscrambled transmission is at issue. If so, the public would have to depend solely upon the voluntary conduct of cable channel operators to avert considerably greater harm.

Case law does not mandate the Court's result. To the contrary, as I have pointed out, our prior cases recognize that, where the protection of children is at issue, the First Amendment poses a barrier that properly is high, but not insurmountable. It is difficult to reconcile today's decision with our foundational cases that have upheld similar laws, such as *Pacifica*. It is not difficult to distinguish our cases striking down such laws—either because they applied far more broadly than the narrow regulation of adult channels here, *see, e.g., Reno*, imposed a total ban on a form of adult speech, *see, e.g., Sable*, or because a less restrictive, similarly effective alternative was otherwise available, *see, e.g., Denver Area*, 518 U.S., at 753–760.

Congress has taken seriously the importance of maintaining adult access to the sexually explicit channels here at issue. It has tailored the restrictions to minimize their impact upon adults while offering parents help in keeping unwanted transmissions from their children. By finding "adequate alternatives" where there are none, the Court reduces Congress' protective power to the vanishing point. That is not what the First Amendment demands.

Notes and Questions

1. *Pacifica*. Is Justice Breyer correct that the majority opinion is in tension with *Pacifica*? If so, what does that mean for *Pacifica*?

2. **What's the Disagreement?** What, precisely, is the disagreement between the majority and the dissent? Justice Breyer contends that "this disagreement is not about allocation of First Amendment burdens of proof, basic First Amendment principle nor the importance of that Amendment to our scheme of Government." What does he believe is the basis of the disagreement, then?

3. **A Severe Burden on Speech?** Does it make sense "to affirm" (as the majority did) "that the Government failed to prove the existence of a problem, while at the same time observing that the statute imposes a severe burden on speech"? What are the implications of a negative answer to that question?

4. **Protecting Children.** In this case the government relied not only on its interest in empowering parents, but also on its interest in protecting children. Section 504 gives concerned parents the opportunity to block the signal from any channel they do not want to receive. But, as the government pointed out, that may not protect the children of parents who "out of inertia, indifference, or distraction" fail to avail themselves of this option. If the Court accepted such an interest as sufficient, could the Court have later deemed any limitations on indecency impermissible? That is, can you imagine any indecency restriction not responsive to the goal of protecting children from inattentive parents? Relatedly, does the

Court's rejection of the government's argument regarding inattentive parents mean that, if a filter is available, no regulation limiting indecency will be constitutional?

5. *ACT III* and Parental Control. The issue of empowering parents versus protecting children also arose in *ACT III*. Are there any differences between the way *Playboy* and *ACT III* handle the interest in protecting children? Does *Playboy* suggest that the court in *ACT III* erred, and, if so, how?

6. Revising the Law. If Congress wanted to enact a new §505 that would pass muster under *Playboy*, what sort of factual support would it need to amass? Is satisfying that standard a realistic possibility? Is the *Playboy* standard consistent with the standard imposed on Congress by *ACT III*? With *Turner II*? How might these cases be harmonized?

PART THREE

TELEPHONE REGULATION

Throughout the textbook, a central theme has been the choice between competition and regulation as two possible means by which to discipline firm behavior. Alfred Kahn explained the choice this way back in 1970:

> The essence of regulation is the explicit replacement of competition with government orders as the principal institutional device for assuring good performance. The regulatory agency determines specifically who shall be permitted to serve; and when it licenses more than one supplier, it typically imposes rigid limitations on their freedom to compete. So the two prime prerequisites of competition as the governing market institution— freedom of entry and independence of action—are deliberately replaced. Instead, the government determines the conditions of service, and imposes an obligation to serve.[1]

We turn to telephone regulation not only to understand how the choice between competition and regulation played out in yet another context, but also to examine the emergence of an important third option: the attempt to use regulation not as an alternative to competition, but rather as a means to facilitate competition. The story of the telephone system is thus the story of how policymakers have, over time, reconceptualized telecommunications regulation, shifting from the early view that regulation should displace competition as the mechanism for determining price and quality to the later (and current) view that regulation should strive to counterbalance any factors that might limit competition but, beyond that, defer to market forces.

At the same time, the story of telephone regulation is also a story about how legal rules sometimes outlast the economic realities that first motivated them. The market for telephone service changed dramatically over the last hundred years, as new technologies changed the economics of existing services and made possible entirely new alternatives as well. Yet, for most of this time and until 1996, telephone regulation was based on the same (increasingly suspect) premise—that local telephone service was a natural monopoly. Economics and technology changed at a pace much faster than the pace of legal reform, it turns out. Some questions we will consider as we move through this history, then, are why legal rules lag, and how legal rules might be constructed so as to avoid this difficulty in the future.

We begin in Chapter Fifteen with a brief history of telephone regulation as well as an introduction to the basic vocabulary, concepts, and economics of telephone communication. Chapter Sixteen focuses on a critical event: the breakup

---

1. Alfred E. Kahn, 1 The Economics of Regulation: Principles and Institutions 20 (1970).

of the Bell Telephone Company, the firm that dominated both interstate and intrastate telephone communication from almost the moment the telephone was invented until the early 1980s. Chapter Seventeen looks at the aftermath of the Bell antitrust litigation, in particular considering the difficulties that faced the FCC in establishing fair telephone rates, keeping regulated firms from unfairly gaining advantage in competitive markets, and maintaining a system of financial subsidies for low income and other favored telephone subscribers. Chapter Eighteen considers the Telecommunications Act of 1996, legislation that radically restructured the telephone industry and established the current pro-competitive regulatory scheme. Finally, Chapter Nineteen examines what today might be seen as the biggest threat to robust telecommunications competition: mergers and acquisitions that are increasingly bringing former competitors under common control.

CHAPTER FIFTEEN

AN INTRODUCTION TO TELEPHONE REGULATION

The purpose of this chapter is:

- to survey the early history of telephone regulation as a way of helping readers to better contextualize the modern regulatory framework;

- to introduce basic telephone concepts and vocabulary, including the universal service cross-subsidies and the economics of natural monopoly; and

- to set the stage for the breakup of the Bell system by examining several precursors to divestiture, including: the introduction of competition into the markets for telephone equipment and interstate telephone communication; the convergence of markets for computer and telecommunications equipment; and the development of increasingly intricate but ultimately unsuccessful forms of cost-based rate regulation.

∼

I. TELEPHONE SYSTEM BASICS

A. The Early History[2]

On March 10, 1876, Alexander Graham Bell declared "Mr. Watson, come here, I want you" and with those words began what would be a technological revolution of extraordinary import. Bell knew it from early on, confidently predicting what must have sounded unthinkable at the time—that "a telephone in every house [would someday] be considered indispensable."[3]

Of course, even Bell didn't get all the details quite right. For example, an 1878 version of Bell's telephone required two devices, one for listening and the other for speaking. Handsets that contained both transmitter and receiver—so-called "French" handsets—would not arrive in the United States until 1927. An

---

2. Many excellent sources survey the early history of the telephone industry. Interested readers might consult, among others, Huber et al., Federal Telecommunications Law (2d ed. 1999); R. Garnet, The Telephone Enterprise: The Evolution of the Bell System's Horizontal Structure 1876–1909 (1985).

3. Garnet, *supra* note 2, at 12.

even more important oversight in Bell's original concept was his assumption that phones would be linked one-to-one instead of being linked together into web-like networks. From a legal standpoint, this is much more than a technical detail, as Peter Huber, Michael Kellogg, and John Thorne explain:

> Initially, telephones were linked one to one. It took until 1878, two years after the invention of the telephone itself, for the budding new telephone companies to grasp the necessity of a telephone "exchange." The telephone exchange — a simple switchboard at first — radically increased a telephone's utility by enabling each phone to reach any other phone connected to the same exchange. Demand for service increased dramatically. By the mid-1880s, multiple unit switching systems allowed operators to work in banks, each serving the same array of telephones. The first automatic switching system was patented in 1889; a series of pulses was used to raise and then rotate a shaft to make the appropriate connection. A patent for dialing devices was granted in 1898. Newark, New Jersey, boasted the first semi-automatic switching system in 1914. Omaha, in 1921, housed the first fully automated system.
>
> The advent of the telephone exchange gave rise to the first rumblings about the need for — or inevitability of — monopoly provision of telephone service. A central switchboard and the wires leading to it represented a large, fixed capital investment; the costs of an exchange seemed to decline rapidly as more subscribers were added. By fragmenting the market, competition appeared to drive up costs and nullify the key advantage of a central exchange, which was to connect everyone to everyone else.[4]

Bell the inventor had overlooked the network concept; but Bell's company — the Bell Telephone Company ("Bell") — would not make that same mistake. Bell had originally been built on the telephone patents awarded to its namesake. But by the time telephone service was achieving significant market penetration, those early patents were expiring. New patents on long distance technology would ultimately help to reaffirm the Bell Telephone Company's dominant intellectual property position, but denying interconnection to competitors would also be an important strategic tool. Roger Noll and Bruce Owen put the point this way:

> The value of telephone service to a subscriber is directly related to the number of other subscribers to the system; the more subscribers a system has, the greater the number that any given customer can call. As calls are the source of consumer demand for service, the number of people with whom one can talk determines the value of the service. The Bell System was the largest and hence could offer the greatest number of people with whom a prospective subscriber could talk. By denying its competitors interconnection — that is, a link between two telephone exchanges that would allow each exchange's customers to talk to subscribers of the other system — Bell could use its absolute size to gain a competitive edge.

---

4. Huber et al., *supra* note 2, at 8.

Denial of interconnection, however, was by itself insufficient to give the Bell System a clear victory in the telephone wars of the early twentieth century. The companies that composed the other half of the industry had an effective response: they formed an alliance by interconnecting with each other. Hence, the industry was growing in the direction of two competing systems of roughly equal size, each unable to communicate with the other.[5]

The Bell Telephone Company thus adopted a two-pronged strategy. First, as Noll and Owen explain, Bell denied interconnection to rival telephone service providers and in that way made sure that the size of the Bell network would work to Bell's advantage. Second — because smaller rivals could have solved the interconnection problem by forming an alliance of their own — Bell aggressively pursued patent protection for critical telephone system components and used those patents to ensure that Bell phone service would be of higher quality than that offered by any rival. Huber, Kellogg, and Thorne pick up the story here:

FEDERAL TELECOMMUNICATIONS LAW
Peter W. Huber, Michael K. Kellogg & John Thorne
(excerpts from 1st. ed., 1992, pp. 11–17,
and 2d. ed., 1999, pp. 11–17)[6]

When commercial telephone service began in the United States in 1877, Bell held all the essential patents. The company thus enjoyed a complete and legal monopoly. By 1894, however, the essential patents had either expired or been narrowly construed by the courts. Thousands of independent telephone companies took advantage of this opportunity. By 1902, 451 out of the 1002 cities with phone service had two or more companies providing it. By 1907, when a phone census was taken, the "independents" owned nearly as many phone stations as Bell. Average rates were cut in half, and Bell's average return on investment had fallen over 80 percent.

At about this time, Theodore Vail, a brilliant administrator, took charge of the declining Bell empire. The Bell System had lost its original patents on the telephone, but it had acquired new ones through which it now enjoyed a critical edge at providing quality long distance connections. Vail believed passionately that all telephone service should be supplied by one company — his own. Bell therefore offered its superior long distance service to its own local affiliates but not to others. The company likewise refused to sell equipment or to provide interconnection even to those independents that did not directly compete with it. As a result, phone companies not affiliated with the Bell System either folded or were acquired. In 1876 Western Union — then the largest corporation in the world — had declined to purchase Alexander Graham Bell's basic telephone patents. In 1910 it was Vail's turn to buy Western Union — for the then astronomical sum of $30 million.

---

5. *See* Noll & Owen, *supra* note 1, at 291–92.

6. This excerpt includes text from both editions of the Huber treatise. This is a somewhat unusual editorial decision, we know, but the earlier edition had some useful language that the later edition omits, presumably to conserve space in the treatise. The later version obviously was in other respects an improvement over the old, so merging the two seemed to maximize the educational value of the excerpt.

By 1915, when Bell had established transcontinental service, Vail could describe the Bell System as "an ever-living organism" that possessed "one of the largest laboratories of the application of science to industrial development in the world." Vail's slogan, announced in 1908, had an almost Orwellian ring to it: One Policy, One System, Universal Service.

Common Carriage

It is at this point in the history of telecommunications that regulation could have forcefully intervened to prevent the rise of monopoly service by forbidding boycotts and requiring carriers to interconnect with one another. Multiple carriers might well have coexisted and competed under such a regime without a balkanized network in which telephone owners could only talk with other customers of the same carrier. The fundamental question arose early on: must carriers carry other carriers? At first, the answer was no; the direct result was the creation of the largest, most powerful telecommunications monopoly the world had ever known.[7]

The earliest common carriers were created when the Crown awarded an exclusive monopoly to a company operating such things as a ferryboat, a wharf, or, for a time, a printing press. The English common law gradually developed rules that both constrained monopolists' excesses and defended their monopolies. Crown monopolies were required to charge only "reasonable and nondiscriminatory" rates, provide adequate service, and accept all customers on the same terms, without discrimination. In time, these principles came to extend to any firm "affected with a public interest" that held itself open to the general public and purported to serve all comers. In return, common carriers enjoyed important legal privileges, most particularly limits on their liabilities — limits appropriate to a business that could not legally discriminate among those it chose to serve. America inherited these core principles from England.

Telegraph and telephone companies are quite clearly "common carriers." They have long been expected to serve all comers and charge similar rates for similar services. They could not generally be sued for the content transmitted over their systems, or for the damage caused by garbled or lost transmissions. They soon came to be viewed as paradigm "common carriers," so common, so ubiquitous, so routinized that one could scarcely imagine them operating any other way — except, as it turned out, when a would-be "customer" happened to be another carrier.

The problem had been faced — and resolved correctly — half a century before the birth of telephony, in legislation for telegraphy. The Post Roads Act of 1866 required telegraph companies to interconnect and accept each other's traffic. If similar obligations had been imposed on telephone companies, local exchanges might have remained competitive as companies could have differentiated their prices and services. They all might have offered interconnection with other companies, including long distance connections. But legislators, regulators, and the courts missed the opportunity and adopted instead a narrow understanding of a common carrier's obligations to carry its competitors' traffic.

---

7. [Ed. As the authors point out in a part not included in the above excerpt, that answer would ultimately change to a tentative yes between 1960 and 1996, and later to a forceful yes with the passage of the Telecommunications Act of 1996. We will consider these changes in due course, later in these materials.]

[Consider, for example, the case of Pacific Telephone & Telegraph Co. v. Anderson, 196 F. 699 (E.D. Wash. 1912).] In 1903, a company that would soon be acquired by the Interstate Telephone Company won permission to install a telephone system in Newport, Washington. The owner of the system agreed not to compete against Pacific Telephone and to connect all long distance calls to Pacific's network. When Interstate bought the system in 1911, it ceased both practices. Pacific demanded to be reconnected; Interstate responded that the original agreement illegally excluded other carriers. A federal judge disagreed, ruling that "each telephone company is independent of all other telephone companies," and, hence, common carrier law did not require telecommunications companies "to accord to any such outside organization or its patrons connection with its switchboard on an equality with its own patrons." Other cases around this time reached the same result, despite the existence of state statutes requiring universal carriage. For example, the Supreme Court of Tennessee conceded that although "telephone and telegraph companies are common carriers, this does not mean that a telephone company is bound to permit another telephone company to make a physical connection with its lines." (Home Tel. Co. v. People's Tel. & Tel. Co., 141 S.W. 845, 848 (1911)).

In 1910, Congress had its first major chance to correct this imbalance when it passed the Mann-Elkins Act of 1910 (36 Stat. 539 (1910)). The Act brought interstate telecommunications within the regulatory jurisdiction of the Interstate Commerce Commission (ICC) and included telecommunications companies within the definition of "common carrier," thereby obligating them "to provide service on request at just and reasonable rates, without unjust discrimination or undue preference." But the Act did not require a common carrier to carry other carriers. The ICC might have taken steps to remedy this, but the agency was fixated at the time on railroads and was insecure with respect to exercising its powers. As a result, the Bell System continued its march toward monopoly unchecked.

Antitrust

In 1912, fresh on the heels of its victory against Rockefeller, the U.S. Justice Department threatened to take on Vail. There followed a great deal of sound and fury, no doubt reflecting America's traditional populist mistrust of monopoly. In the end, however, government officials would conclude that monopoly in communications was much more tolerable than monopoly in oil.

In a 1913 agreement between the U.S. Attorney General and a Bell vice president, N. C. Kingsbury, the company agreed to stop acquiring independent phone companies and to connect the remaining independents to Bell's long distance network. Bell also agreed to divest itself of Western Union. It appeared to be at least a partial victory for the trustbusters at the Justice Department—an honorable armistice signed by vigilant public servants to contain all-too-acquisitive private interests. But the Kingsbury Commitment was really nothing of the sort.

It did indeed stop the growth of Bell's financial empire—for a few short years, in any event—but it did nothing to promote competition in either telephony or telegraphy. Local exchange monopolies were left intact, utterly free to continue to refuse interconnection to other local exchange companies. Bell's monopoly long distance service was reinforced: Bell would be required to interconnect with all local exchanges, but there was no provision for any competition—or interconnection—among long distance carriers. Western Union was indeed spun off, but only to provide telegraphy, not telephony.

The government solution, in short, was not the steamy, unsettling cohabitation that marks competition, but rather a sort of competitive apartheid, characterized by segregation and quarantine. Markets were carefully carved up: one for the monopoly telegraph company, one for each of the established monopoly local telephone exchanges, one for Bell's monopoly long distance operations. Bell might not own everything, but some monopolist or another would dominate each discrete market. The Kingsbury Commitment could be viewed as a solution only by a government bookkeeper who counted several separate monopolies as an advance over a single monopoly, even absent any trace of competition among them.

Notes and Questions

1. Events after Kingsbury. Bell continued to grow and prosper after 1913, considerably extending the reach of both its local and long distance services. That had its benefits; the American phone system was, by most accounts, the best in the world, and Bell did extend phone service to rural and low income communities that a more competitive phone system might have chosen to ignore. But Bell's dominance continued to raise concern. A second major antitrust prosecution was undertaken in 1949; and a third was commenced in 1974. That last one would ultimately lead to "divestiture"—the breakup of the Bell Telephone Company—an event we consider at great length in Chapter Sixteen.[8]

2. Non-Overlapping Monopolists. Are Huber and his coauthors too harsh in their evaluation of the Kingsbury Commitment, or are they correct that there are few gains to breaking one monopolist into several non-overlapping monopolists? For instance, are smaller monopolists easier for local government to control? (Which way does that cut?) Do non-overlapping monopolists provide regulators with useful comparative information about costs, prices and performance?

B. Federal Versus State Regulation

From its creation in 1934, the FCC has always shared jurisdiction over telephony with state regulators. The 1934 Act's limitation of federal authority is clearly stated, if not always so easily implemented in practice: the Act is not to be construed "to give the Commission jurisdiction with respect to... practices, services, facilities, or regulations for or in connection with *intra*state communication service by wire or radio of any carrier." 47 U.S.C. §152(b) (emphasis added). Indeed, the 1934 Act on its face restricts FCC jurisdiction to "*inter*state and foreign communication by wire or radio." 47 U.S.C. §152(a) (emphasis added). The Act

---

8. The word "divestiture" comes from the verb "divest" which means to separate or take away. The breakup separated Bell's various business units into legally independent entities; hence the breakup is often referred to as the "divestiture" of the Bell System.

thus appears to keep the Commission out of the business of regulating what, in 1934, accounted for the vast bulk of telephone usage: local telephony.

The 1934 Act in this way marked an important departure from earlier telephone regulation. Before the Act, telephone service had been regulated by the Interstate Commerce Commission (ICC), an agency charged with the task by the Mann-Elkins Act of 1910.[9] The ICC had enjoyed broad power to preempt any state regulation with which it disagreed. In fact, in *The Shreveport Rate Case*, the Supreme Court in 1914 affirmed that the ICC had preemption authority whenever an intrastate rate would frustrate the achievement of a federal statutory goal.[10] Although that case involved railroad rates, not telephony, the Court was interpreting the ICC's authority under a statute that applied equally to both.

The scope of federal authority in telephony had received a further, though less direct, boost from the Supreme Court in 1930 as well. In Smith v. Illinois Bell Telephone Company, 282 U.S. 133 (1930), the Court ruled that state regulations must be strictly limited to intrastate facilities and services. Rates for local service could not incorporate the full costs of local network facilities so long as even a tiny fraction of the traffic on those facilities was interstate. The costs imposed on the local network by interstate calls had to be "separated" from the intrastate costs for the purposes of setting local rates. While this case did not directly broaden federal authority, it did narrow state authority.

The Communications Act of 1934 thus effectively nullified *The Shreveport Rate Case*'s applicability to telecommunications. The rule of construction contained in §152(b) of the 1934 Act is sweeping: "*nothing* in this chapter shall be construed" to preempt state jurisdiction over intrastate services or facilities. The implication is that, even if state regulation of intrastate service might make implementation of some telephony provision of the 1934 Act more difficult, federal regulators cannot, as they could under *Shreveport*, preempt the inconvenient state law. Section 152(b) thus appears to give clear primacy to state regulators where intrastate telephony is involved. One limitation on that primary state role: §410(c) of the Act gives the FCC ultimate authority, after consultation with a joint board of state and federal regulators, to decide the respective degrees to which network facilities are used for interstate and intrastate service. Section 410 thus gives the Commission some discretion to decide where to draw the line between interstate and intrastate telecommunications and, within reason, to adjust its jurisdiction accordingly.

The practical complications of §410 aside, the 1934 Act quite consciously tried to reserve substantial authority to the States. But the actual operation and judicial interpretation of §152(b) turned out, for a time at least, to be somewhat different from what might have been expected given the text of the provision. After several decades during which there was little conflict between state and federal goals — and correspondingly few jurisdictional squabbles — some disagreement began to arise, notably as the FCC began to promote competition in certain areas of telecommunications.[11] One particular set of conflicts (the substance of which we will consider later this chapter) resulted in a

---

9. Mann-Elkins Act of 1910, ch. 309, 36 Stat. 539 (1910).
10. Houston & Texas Railway v. U.S., 234 U.S. 342 (1914) (known as *The Shreveport Rate Case*).
11. Huber et al., *supra* note 2, at 232–233.

series of court decisions that greatly expanded federal regulatory power at the expense of the states. The first such decision was the decision in North Carolina Utilities Commission v. FCC, 537 F.2d 787 (4th Cir. 1976) (*NCUC I*). There, the United States Court of Appeals for the Fourth Circuit ruled that the FCC could preempt a state law regulating certain types of basic telephone equipment so long as the equipment affected by the regulation would be used for interstate, as well as intrastate, telephone communication. The FCC had been trying to promote competition in the market for telephone equipment and found the state law at issue to be antithetical to that policy. Notable about the Fourth Circuit's decision is that it allowed preemption even though the telephone equipment at issue was at that time still used almost exclusively for local calling.

A second case arising one year later out of the same regulatory proceeding even more radically expanded federal jurisdiction. In North Carolina Utilities Commission v. FCC, 552 F.2d 1036 (4th Cir. 1977) (*NCUC II*), the Fourth Circuit decided that it was a practical impossibility to separate the interstate and intrastate uses of most telephone equipment and thus granted the FCC even broader authority to preempt state law. In short, while under *NCUC I* the FCC could preempt a state law only if it could be shown to affect interstate telephone service, under *NCUC II* the FCC could preempt a state law in any case where the effects on interstate and intrastate service were inseparable.[12] This in some ways turned §152(b) on its head by shifting the presumption in favor of federal rather than state regulation. Moreover, it seemed to reinstate the pro-preemption doctrine of *The Shreveport Rate Case*, a doctrine that was well known when Congress decided to adopt a contrary rule of construction in the 1934 Act.

The *NCUC* cases would not remain good law for long. A number of other federal courts had adopted the *NCUC* tests[13] when, in 1986, the question of federal authority in telecommunications finally reached the Supreme Court. The case was Louisiana Public Service Commission v. FCC, 476 U.S. 355 (1986) ("*Louisiana PSC*"). At issue was the FCC's decision that its depreciation rules for the installation of wires on a customer's premises would preempt any state regulations prescribing different depreciation rates. The Supreme Court reversed the Commission's ruling, holding that, although 47 U.S.C. §220 gave the Commission broad authority to prescribe depreciation rates, it did not unambiguously provide for preemption of contrary state depreciation rules. The Court further found that the rates at issue did not involve either costs that were incapable of separation between interstate and intrastate components or a conflict that would completely negate the federal rule. The Court therefore held that, where separation is not impossible and where application of a federal rule will not be nullified by contrary state provisions, preemption of state regulation of intrastate telecommunications can occur only where expressly and unambiguously provided for by statute. *Id.* at 375–76.

The principle for allocation of jurisdiction between state authorities and the FCC has not changed much since *Louisiana PSC*. As we will see in Chapter Eigh-

---

12. Huber et al., *supra* note 2, at 236.
13. *See, e.g.*, California v. FCC, 567 F.2d 84 (D.C. Cir. 1977), *cert. denied* 434 U.S. 1010 (1978); New York Telephone Co. v. FCC, 631 F.2d 1059 (2nd Cir. 1980).

teen, however, there have been some underlying statutory changes that in some instances give the Commission the kind of express authority that, under *Louisiana PSC*, is necessary for preemption of state regulations governing intrastate communications. But let us hold off on those issues and consider them later, in the context of the events that made them important.

C. Telephone System Vocabulary

As the above discussions make clear, one hurdle to studying telephone regulation is simply mastering the vocabulary of telephone service provision. To assist in that process, let us pause here a moment and survey the key terminology.

Consumers have in their homes standard equipment (like telephones) capable of encoding and receiving voice communications. Businesses have similar basic equipment. This equipment is what insiders call customer premises equipment, which is abbreviated "CPE." The Telecommunications Act of 1996 defines CPE as "equipment employed on the premises of a person (other than a carrier) to originate, route, or terminate telecommunications." 47 U.S.C. §153(14). This category, as implemented by the FCC, includes not only basic telephones but also answering machines, fax machines, modems, and even private branch exchange (PBX) equipment (in which a large entity maintains, in effect, its own switchboard to various internal extensions).

CPE is used in the provision of basic telephone service. Basic telephone service, in turn, is termed "POTS," which stands for plain old telephone service. This is in contrast to both newer services (for example, Internet access) and less conventional services (for example, home burglary protection systems) that are not considered as fundamental as the basic ability to originate and terminate telephone communications. Some arguably witty insiders today refer to new, high-technology services under the acronym "PANS," which stands for "pretty amazing new services."

CPE is connected by wire to a central hub, often located in the telephone company's central office. In olden days, the key piece of equipment kept in this hub was a switchboard where an operator would connect one party to another by plugging the caller's and recipient's wires into a common jack. This was all done by voice; so a caller would first identify to the operator the person he wanted to ring, and the operator would then make the connection manually. Privacy issues were significant under this system and affected how telephones were used at this time.

Today, automatic equivalents to the switchboard—called routers, switches, and exchanges—serve this same basic purpose. There are minor distinctions that can be drawn here, but the basic idea is the same for each of these devices: these are computers that direct telephone traffic from one part of the network to another. They are in a very real sense just substitutes for wire. The modern telephone network could in theory be accomplished by having every telephone connected to every other telephone via billions of one-to-one wires. Given the expense associated with laying wires, we use fewer wires and allow switches, routers, exchanges and sometimes human operators to connect phones in a web-like pattern instead.

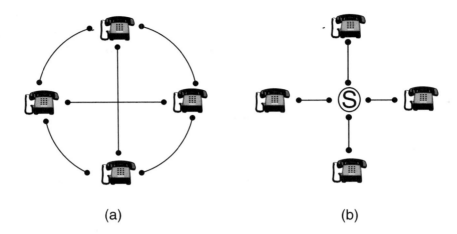

(a)   (b)

Figure 15.1. SWITCHES. We are not kidding when we say that switches substitute for wire. The panel to the left shows how four telephones might be connected one-to-one by wire. The panel to the right replaces those wires with a switch. As is clear in even this four-telephone example, switches significantly decrease the complexity of the telephone network.

Building on the word "exchange," insiders typically refer to the local phone company as the local exchange carrier (LEC) since there is typically one major switch that serves each large geographic area and the local phone company is the business entity that owns and operates that switch. Long distance phone companies, by contrast, are referred to as interexchange carriers (IXCs) since their job is to carry phone traffic from one local exchange to another.

Two other phrases often associated with the local phone company are the phrases the local loop and the last mile. The local loop is the part of the network that connects individual subscribers to the main local switch. This is in a very literal sense the "last mile" of the phone system. This part of the phone network has always been the subject of considerable attention and concern since many people believe this part to be a natural monopoly. The belief is that the costs of operating two or more local switches—and then either connecting them to each other or connecting each telephone to each local switch—would greatly exceed the costs of simply operating one switch to which all local telephones were connected. Understanding this claim is of central importance to understanding the entire regulatory regime related to telephone service; and so it is to this claim, and its logical extensions, that we now turn our attention.

II. TELEPHONY AS A MONOPOLY SERVICE

Throughout his career, Theodore Vail argued that one firm—namely, his firm—should provide all telephone service nationwide. His argument was of course in part self-serving; yet it is important to ask at the outset whether there

Figure 15.2. INTEREXCHANGE CARRIERS. IXCs carry telephone traffic from one local exchange to another. In the diagram, for example, an IXC connects the two local exchange carriers in Nevada. Note that an IXC can operate within a single political jurisdiction (here, Nevada), and an IXC can also operate across jurisdictions (for example connecting the Nevada LEC with the California LEC).

might have been some merit to Vail's view. That is, despite our normal affinity for markets and competition, is it possible that Vail's monopoly was not only in his own interest but also in society's as well?

For a long time, one common answer here was to say that a nationwide telephone monopoly was desirable because the telephone system exhibits what some people call "network externalities" and others term "network effects."[14] For our purposes, both terms refer to the benefits that accrue as the size of a network grows. In the context of telephony, for example, a lone telephone is of no practi-

---

14. The seminal papers on network economics are Michael Katz & Carl Shapiro, Network Externalities, Competition, and Compatibility, 75 Am. Econ. Rev. 424 (1985), and Joseph Farrell & Garth Saloner, Standardization, Compatibility, and Innovation, 16 Rand J. Econ. 70 (1985). A helpful survey of this literature and analysis of possible legal implications is Mark Lemley & David McGowan, Legal Implications of Network Economic Effects, 86 Cal. L. Rev. 479 (1998). Note that some authors draw distinctions between the terms "network externalities" and "network effects" (*see* Lemley & McGowan, *supra*, at 482 n.5) but that is by no means a common practice. We use the terms interchangeably in this text.

cal value to its user because there is no one to call. But the usefulness of that first phone, and of all other phones, increases with each additional customer on the network; there are simply more people to call, and more people from whom to receive calls as well. Phrased another way, then, the telephone system exhibits the properties of a network externality: the value a given subscriber places on telephone service increases as the number of other subscribers increases.

How does this relate to Vail's monopoly claims? Well, suppose that there were a bunch of competing local telephone companies, each denying interconnection to the others, and you had to choose which network to join. All else held equal, wouldn't you have a strong incentive to select the phone company that had the largest number of customers with whom you might want to converse? Once you join, can you see how this same phenomenon would increase the pressure on, say, your friends and family — which in turn would put pressure on their friends and family — to join this same phone network, thus increasing any monopoly tendency already at play in this market? Further, can you see why it might be in society's interest to stop this strategic fragmentation of the market, perhaps by establishing a single dominant telephone network to which everyone would subscribe?

That the telephone system exhibits network properties is relatively uncontroversial; significantly more controversial are the implications. After all, while it might be true that, if left with the discretion to do so, a company like Bell will refuse to interconnect with competitors as a way of taking strategic advantage of any network externalities, it is also true (as hinted at above) that interconnection can be imposed even on unwilling firms. For one thing, subscribers can create de facto interconnection simply by purchasing access to multiple networks. If every family had both a Bell telephone with which to contact Bell customers and also, say, a Sprint telephone with which to contact all Sprint customers, there would be no need for interconnection between the Bell and Sprint networks. A more efficient and direct option might be to use legal rules to force Bell and Sprint to interconnect. The real question in both cases is whether the costs associated with interconnection are so great that competition/interconnection makes society worse off than would monopoly/no interconnection.

Society is getting more information on this question right now because, under current law, there is a statutory obligation imposed on telephone carriers to interconnect with their rivals. We'll consider the details in Chapter Eighteen; but what is important to note here is that the costs of mandatory interconnection are turning out to be non-trivial. It is expensive for federal and state authorities to monitor compliance with interconnection obligations, for example by holding hearings and overseeing negotiations and arbitrations between rivals. Aside from that, there are also costs associated with good faith attempts at interconnection. For instance, every time the technology changes, rivals must exchange protocol information and otherwise ensure that each is encoding and interpreting telephone signals in compatible ways. Admittedly, it is possible that over time many of these costs will be mitigated by thoughtful regulatory policy. But they cannot be entirely eliminated, and so, again, there is at least some truth to the claim that having just one firm provide all telephone service nationwide might be less expensive than having multiple firms each operate their own (even interconnected) networks.

A stronger argument in favor of Vail's monopoly vision is that, like the provision of cable television, the provision of telephone service might be a natural monopoly. As we explained in Chapter Nine, this means that—due to the structure of costs in this market—the cheapest way to provide nationwide telephone service might be to have a single firm provide service to all interested customers. The logic here is basically the same logic that was put forward for cable: to provide telephone service, a firm must incur a significant fixed investment (this time to build the initial network of wires, switches, and so on); but, once that investment has been made, the marginal cost of adding an additional phone customer is almost zero. There is an economy of scale, then, in having a single firm build the local loop instead of having multiple firms each build their own possibly overlapping infrastructures.

Demand variability bolsters this claim. An individual's demand for phone service varies significantly from moment to moment and day to day; yet, in order to provide adequate phone service, the phone company has to be ready to serve a given user whenever that user happens to pick up the telephone. If a different firm were to serve each user, there would be significant waste since almost all of each phone system's capacity would sit idle for most of the day. By having a single firm serve a large number of users, by contrast, the costs of providing phone service can be lowered dramatically. Several users can share a given amount of capacity, putting the equipment to better use since the variance in each consumer's demand would to some degree cancel out, leaving less of the phone system's capacity to sit idle at a given time. Sometimes—say, Mother's Day—everyone will want to use the phone at the same moment, and, at that time, some customers will be denied service; but, for most of the year, users can share capacity without any degradation in service, and thus it is cheaper to have a single firm serve many customers as opposed to having multiple firms serve that same number of customers.[15]

Vail's vision of a single telephone company was supported not just by network externality arguments and not just by conventional natural monopoly arguments, but also by the concept of economies of scope. An economy of scope is said to exist in settings where a single firm can produce a given quantity of each of two or more goods more cheaply than can multiple firms produce those same total quantities. Shoe production is an intuitive example; once a given firm is producing left shoes of a certain style, it is likely true that this same firm can produce the corresponding right shoes more cheaply than could any rival. The economy of scope argument is not a straightforward natural monopoly argument. We know, for example, that a great many shoe companies today compete in the shoe market, and we have no reason to believe that costs would be reduced were all shoes made by a single firm. The economy of scope argument suggests only that,

---

15. A telephone system natural monopoly is also sometimes said to result from an "economy of density." This is just a variety of an economy of scale. Economies of density are the efficiencies that result from more intense use of existing facilities. A density efficiency can be thought of as a scale economy at the facility, as opposed to network, level. For example, a dense network may have more, and shorter, customer lines connected to a switch than does a sparse network. Thus, even if competing networks serve the same overall number of customers, the most dense network may have a cost advantage over rivals. If so, the dense network may be able to extend its service to new customers at lower average cost than its competitors can, perhaps leading to or reinforcing natural monopoly conditions.

if a company is in the business of selling one of two interrelated products, it likely makes sense for that same company to sell both.

In the telephone setting, this argument combined with the various natural monopoly arguments to make a strong case in favor of a large, integrated phone company. First, because the provision of local telephone service to some degree exhibited the properties of a natural monopoly, Vail could argue that there should be a single telephone company in each community. Second, because of economies of scope, it was likely that having the same firm provide telephone service in both local and long distance markets would minimize overall costs as telephone traffic moved from one part of the network to another. The economy of scope argument thus completed Vail's intuitive claim: to realize the full efficiencies possible in this setting, not only should there be a single network in every community, but those networks should all be jointly operated by a single national firm. Naturally, in Vail's view, that company was Bell.[16]

Efficiency arguments were not the only arguments supporting Vail's view that a single firm should provide all telephone service. There were equity arguments on his side as well. In particular, state regulators realized that a unified telephone system might accord them greater freedom to keep telephone service affordable for favored categories of consumers. The key intuition is this: so long as there was an integrated phone service provider, the prices charged for any one service did not necessarily have to reflect the costs of providing that service. True, the integrated provider needed to make an overall profit; but that provider did not need to make a profit on every service. An integrated provider could therefore price its services such that some were priced artificially low as compared to their actual costs whereas others were priced artificially high. The latter would in essence "cross-subsidize" the former. Three such cross-subsidies had strong political appeal in the early days of telephone regulation:

First, business service could subsidize the costs of residential service. Bell charged business customers higher rates than it charged residential customers for the same services, and those extra profits in the business sector were used to keep prices low for residential customers. That is, in a neighborhood in which two identical structures sat side by side, each containing one telephone and one telephone line, if the only difference between them was that one was a barbershop and the other was a residence, the barbershop would still have paid a higher

---

16. For readers with a more mathematical bent, it might be helpful to capture the concepts of economies of scale and economies of scope in symbolic form. As you might recall from Chapter Nine, an economy of scale is said to exist whenever the average cost of producing one unit of a good is constantly declining over the normal range of consumer demand. If we define $f(x)$ to be the total cost of making x units of a good, then an economy of scale exists whenever: $f(x_1+x_2)<f(x_1)+f(x_2)$.

Similarly, an economy of scope is said to exist whenever a single firm can produce a given quantity of each of two or more goods more cheaply than could multiple firms. If we define $f(x,y)$ to be the total cost of making x units of one good and y of another, an economy of scale exists whenever: $f(x, y)<f(x, 0) + f(0, y)$. Comparable notation can be used to represent cases with more goods or more firms.

monthly fee. Note that this cross-subsidy takes the form of charging different prices for services with identical costs.

Second, urban service could subsidize the costs of rural service. In general, the per-customer cost of providing telephone service decreases as population density increases. More people can be served by one switch, and the phone lines from the residences to the switch need not be so long. Nevertheless, policymakers thought it good policy to set monthly subscriber fees such that they were generally equal regardless of whether the area was densely or sparsely populated. This served to overcharge urban customers and undercharge rural ones. Note that, unlike the cross-subsidy for residential over business services, this cross-subsidy involves charging identical prices for services that have different costs.

Third and finally, long distance rates could be used to subsidize the costs of local telephone service. The Communications Act of 1934 vested jurisdiction over interstate rates in the FCC but left intrastate telephone rates to state regulation. This required federal and state regulators to decide jointly which parts of the telephone system to allocate to interstate and which parts to intrastate service. This process of "separations and settlements" gave government officials a great deal of discretion because many costs (for example, the basic connection of a home to the network) were not obviously allocable to either service exclusively. In order to keep residential rates low—presumably so that more low income consumers would join the network[17]—in the early days there was strong policy support for erring on the side of allocating costs to the interstate system.[18] This artificially raised long distance rates but correspondingly lowered the rates charged for basic telephone service.

These three cross-subsidies would ultimately come to be known under the political banner "universal service," and, again, they are important to our current conversation because together they represented yet another argument in favor of allowing Bell to dominate the telephone industry. Implicit cross-subsidies like these would not have survived in a competitive market since competitive markets force prices to line up with costs. So long as Bell served the vast majority of consumers, however, these implicit cross-subsidies were an option.

In summary, then, from the late 1800s until the breakup in 1982, the natural monopoly and universal service arguments put Vail and his successors in an envi-

---

17. This policy of "universal access" was likely attractive for two reasons. First, there was the intuitive allure of helping to ensure that low income individuals were included in the technology revolution. This continues to be a policy goal even today, as we will see later in this Part. Second, because of the network externality discussed earlier in this chapter, the telephone system was more valuable as more people, regardless of their income, subscribed. To some extent, then, having (typically wealthy) long distance users subsidize lower income subscribers might have been desirable on grounds that it increased the overall efficiency of this market.

18. One study concludes that, in 1983, the average monthly price charged for local residential service was about $11, while the average monthly cost of providing this service was about $26. The difference was made up by interstate charges. *See* Paul Dempsey, Adam Smith Assaults Ma Bell with his Invisible Hands: Divestiture, Deregulation, and the Need for a New Telecommunications Policy, 11 Hastings Comm. & Ent. L. J. 527, 535 (1989).

able position. They were able to establish and maintain Bell's domination of the telephone industry, all the while arguing that Bell domination was actually in the public interest.

Notes and Questions

1. Other Cross-Subsidies. While the cross-subsidies outlined in the text were the ones with the strongest political appeal, a variety of other implicit cross-subsidies have long been built into telephone rates. For example, long distance calls tend to be more costly the longer they travel and the longer they last because, in both cases, more system capacity is occupied by the call. Rates were and are set on both of these bases. But, time and distance being equal, frequency of use also affects the cost of a call. If the line from, say, St. Louis to Chicago is used more frequently than another line of about the same length (say, Quincy, Illinois, to South Bend, Indiana) then the cost per call on the heavily used route is lower. Due to a policy of "nationwide rate averaging" in effect throughout the early history of telephone regulation, these cost differences were not reflected in long distance prices and, hence, St. Louis/Chicago callers subsidized their Quincy/South Bend peers. (Prices much more closely reflect actual costs today, although certain cross-subsidies are still implemented through FCC pricing regulations, and phone companies do from time to time adopt pricing strategies that similarly cause prices and costs to diverge.)

2. An Explicit Tax Alternative. Was the desire to subsidize certain services by raising the rates on other services really a good reason to favor an integrated telephone service provider? Couldn't these same policies have been achieved in a world with multiple carriers simply by implementing a targeted system of telecommunications taxes? Suppose, for example, that it is good policy to have business users subsidize residential ones. Why not just impose a tax on all business telephone service (no matter which firm provides it) and then use that money to subsidize the purchase of residential service?

Phrased another way, are there reasons why an implicit subsidy scheme (the cross-subsidies) would be more desirable than an explicit equivalent (taxation)? Is it because implicit subsidies are somehow easier for politicians to slip into legislation? Does that mean that the subsidies serve special interests? But what do you make of the fact that the implicit subsidy scheme hurt powerful constituencies like business and urban users but benefitted relatively weak constituencies like residential and rural users? Can cross-subsidies really be understood as a means by which elected officials pandered to powerful special interests?

3. Common Carrier Regulation. In our study of cable, one question we considered was whether cable natural monopolies could to some extent be "quarantined" such that one firm would build the cable infrastructure but then many firms would be allowed to use that infrastructure to provide competing content options. Is this sort of solution possible with respect to the telephone system? Is that, in fact, what common carrier regulation is all about?

4. Economies of Scope. While economies of scale give rise to natural monopoly conditions, economies of scope do not have the same implication. As the text points out, there are many companies that produce and sell shoes, yet there has never been any significant support for the creation of a Federal Shoe Commission

(FSC). Can you explain why it is that economies of scope do not lead to natural monopoly conditions but economies of scale do? Why, then, is the economy of scope a concept relevant to understanding the telephone system?

Note on Ramsey Pricing

Universal service policies manipulate prices: they keep some prices artificially high in order to keep other prices artificially low. This raises the concern that universal service policies cause firms and individuals to make inefficient decisions—consuming too much of the goods priced below cost while consuming too little of the goods priced above cost. For example, if long distance rates overstate the actual costs of providing long distance service, consumers will see those higher rates and react by making fewer long distance calls. Conversely, if residential rates are subsidized by business rates, residential users will underestimate the burden their calls impose on the telephone network and thus residential users will make an inefficiently large number of calls. Equity and efficiency are thus in tension when it comes to setting prices in the telephone system; policies that manipulate rates on pure policy grounds often inadvertently lead to inefficient use of the telephone network.

The tension between equity and efficiency is actually a much broader problem in the telephone network, however. Even if there were no cross-subsidies built into telephone prices, the economic structure of the telephone industry would still pit efficiency against equity when it came to setting prices for various telephone services. To see why, consider the following simple example.

Suppose that, in order to offer two services—say, local service and long distance service—a telephone company must incur a significant fixed cost of $20,000. This figure represents the costs of laying the necessary telephone lines, purchasing and deploying routers, and so on. Suppose, further, that having made that initial infrastructure investment, the firm can offer local service to its customers at a cost of $20 per month and long distance service at a cost of $25 per month. What price should the firm set for these two services in a purely efficiency-driven world?

Our initial inclination might be to suggest marginal cost, in this case $20 for local service and $25 for long distance service. Were that feasible, that would of course be the right answer. By charging marginal cost, the firm would ensure that every consumer who values either service above its cost would buy that service, and, conversely, the firm would also ensure that service would be denied to any consumer for whom the benefits did not exceed the costs. This would be efficient, but, again, this is not practical. Marginal cost pricing would not allow the firm to in any way recoup its up-front fixed cost investment of $20,000.

It is clear, then, that the prices of one or both of these services must be set above the level of marginal cost. But by how much? One possibility would be to price local service at its marginal cost ($20) but raise the price of long distance until the revenues there covered both long distance costs and the fixed cost investment. Another possibility would be to price long distance at its marginal cost ($25) but raise the price of local service until those revenues covered both the costs of local service and the fixed cost investment. But there are an infinite number of other possibilities between these two extremes, and the puzzle here is to identify the most efficient choice.

British economist and mathematician Frank Ramsey considered this sort of problem in 1927.[19] Ramsey found that the best approach is to raise the prices of both products such that each experiences the same percentage reduction in demand. In other words, if marginal cost pricing would have led 4,000 consumers to purchase local service and 5,000 consumers to purchase long distance service, then the most efficient prices that nevertheless allow the firm to recoup its fixed cost investment will result in the same 4:5 ratio in the consumption of the two goods. So, if the firm found that it could recover its fixed costs by raising prices such that, in the end, 3,600 people purchased local service and 4,500 purchased long distance, we would know that it had raised prices in the most efficient way possible because the ratio of the quantities demanded is the same before and after the price increase.

The intuition here is as follows. Marginal cost pricing would be the most efficient option were it plausible but, because of the fixed cost expenditure, it is not. We thus have to raise prices and, in turn, reduce consumption. Ramsey pricing suggests that, in raising prices, we should at least maintain the desirable relative output level as between the two services. That is, if a 4:5 ratio was the ratio of local service demanded versus long distance service demanded under marginal cost pricing, the 4:5 ratio is still the best outcome in a world where prices must exceed marginal cost. The absolute levels of demand unavoidably must change; given that, the best option is to at a minimum avoid skewing the relative consumption levels.

Ramsey's insight has an important policy implication, one that significantly sharpens the tension between equity and efficiency in this setting: under Ramsey pricing, price is raised more for the product that has the less "elastic" demand. Elasticity measures how sensitive consumers are to price. It is defined to be the percentage change in quantity demanded that results from a one percent change in price. The more elastic the demand, the more output changes for a given price change. What this means is that, because Ramsey pricing requires that both services experience the same percentage decrease in quantity demanded, the most efficient price pair will raise the price more on the good for which consumers are less sensitive to price. If consumers have a strong desire for local telephone service no matter what its price, but are more sensitive to price when it comes to long distance calling, Ramsey pricing would suggest that the fixed costs of the telephone system be recovered mainly by increasing the price of local phone service. Long distance prices should stay near marginal cost—at least according to Ramsey's theory.

On policy grounds, of course, this outcome is distinctly unappealing. Indeed, it runs in the exact opposite direction of the relevant universal service subsidy. Remember, universal service keeps local service inexpensive by raising the price of long distance service. Hence, efficiency and equity really are in sharp tension in the telephone setting. Not only do universal service cross-subsidies cause inefficient over-use and under-use of particular telephone services, but, more broadly, universal service policies tend to push prices in one direction whereas efficiency concerns would move them in the exact opposite direction.

---

19. Frank Ramsey, A Contribution to the Theory of Taxation, 37 Economic Journal 47 (1927). An accessible and helpful explanation of Ramsey pricing can be found in Kenneth Train, Optimal Regulation 117–40 (1991).

This sort of tension between efficiency and public policy is not unique to telephone pricing: Ramsey pricing is often unattractive on policy grounds. For example, demand for clean drinking water is not very sensitive to price, yet it is unlikely that policymakers would be willing to raise the costs of drinking water as a way to fund the sewage and water treatment infrastructure. Similarly, people without cars likely have relatively inelastic demand for public transportation, yet few policymakers would be willing to pay for highway maintenance by raising the prices charged for public transportation. The question here is whether local phone service is so like drinking water (and public transportation) that equity concerns should trump Ramsey's efficiency-based logic.

Notes and Questions

1. **How Broad a Principle?** We consider, above, increasing the prices of various telephone services as a way of paying for the telephone infrastructure. But would anything change if, instead of trying to pay for the telephone infrastructure, we were trying to pay for something completely unrelated to telephone service? Suppose, for instance, that a local politician wants to subsidize school lunches and has decided to do so by taxing telephone usage. Does Ramsey pricing tell us anything about how that tax should be collected, or is Ramsey irrelevant because school lunches are not logically related to telephone service?

2. **Cross-Subsidies and Ramsey.** How would Ramsey suggest that policymakers resolve the tension between universal service policies on the one hand, and economic efficiency on the other? Can equity and efficiency goals both be satisfied simultaneously? Can the tension at least be mitigated?

3. **Test Your Understanding.** In order to raise money for new computers at Yale Law School, the law school dean has decided to increase the prices charged for law textbooks at the bookstore, food at the law school cafeteria, and candy at a vending machine located in the law school basement. What do the economics behind Ramsey pricing suggest about which of these prices should be increased most significantly? Should the dean instead just charge for computer access?

4. **Paying the Fixed Costs.** It would seem that we could avoid the difficult trade-offs inherent in Ramsey pricing by having the government pay the fixed costs of telephone service. Would this be a better approach? If the fixed costs were paid in this manner, would there still be an argument in favor of cross-subsidies in telephone pricing? Would those cross-subsidies still raise efficiency concerns?

III. PRECURSORS TO DIVESTITURE

The third antitrust prosecution of the Bell Telephone Company began in 1974. The suit would culminate eight years later in the breakup of the Bell System. But the events that set the stage for the eventual breakup began well before 1974. Divestiture, in other words, was hardly a surprise. As former FCC Commissioner Glen Robinson puts it, the antitrust decree that finally accomplished the Bell breakup was "almost anticlimactic."[20] By the time the decree was accepted by Judge Greene in 1982, "most of the events that would transform the shape of the industry" were already "well under way."[21]

In this section, we consider four important precursors to divestiture. In the first two sections, we look at the process by which competition was introduced in the markets for consumer premises equipment (CPE) and interstate toll service, respectively. The third section considers the convergence of telecommunications and computer technology and the resulting pressures that were imposed on the regulatory scheme. Finally, the fourth section surveys the Commission's early experiences with rate-of-return regulation, noting how difficult it was for the agency to regulate Bell given that Bell had more information about the costs of telephone service that did its regulator.

A. Competition in Customer Premises Equipment

FEDERAL TELECOMMUNICATIONS LAW
Peter W. Huber, Michael K. Kellogg & John Thorne
(excerpts from 1st. ed., 1992, pp. 499–505,
and 2d. ed., 1999, pp. 663–670)

The Bell System had never cared to recognize the equipment market as a separate market. Bell did not sell equipment; it sold service. Its customers in turn bought service, and service alone. Thus, Bell supplied not only the wires and switches of the network, but also all CPE and inside wiring.[22] To freeze out alien CPE, Bell [prohibited subscribers from interconnecting any non-Bell product] with Bell's network. Such prohibitions appeared in private contracts with telephone subscribers as early as 1899, and they were incorporated in Bell company tariff schedules [public documents that described the services Bell offered and stipulated price and other conditions of service] by 1913. The ostensible purpose of these provisions was to protect the physical integrity of the network from dangers such as erratic voltage generation caused by defective equipment. Their practical effect was to eliminate all competitive suppliers of CPE.

It took some time before the FCC seriously questioned the equipment monopoly; the first suggestion that the link [between provision of equipment and provision of service] might not be inextricable did not come until 1948. That year, the Commission struck down "foreign attachment" provisions that prohibited the use of recording devices in connection with interstate service. Bell had not had the temerity to insist that any device used to record a phone call had to be supplied by Bell, perhaps because Bell did not sell any such devices. But Bell

---

20. Glen O. Robinson, The Titanic Remembered: AT&T and the Changing World of Telecommunications, 5 Yale J. Reg. 517, 520 (1988) (book review).
21. Id.
22. [Ed. Note that, at this time, most phone system subscribers rented their CPE from Bell instead of owning their CPE outright. This made the CPE more analogous to other Bell components — wires, switches, and so on — than it might seem to modern audiences.]

did contend that any device connecting a recorder to the network was "of primary importance to the telephone service and a part of the telephone facilities"; it was therefore "essential" that any such device be "furnished, installed, and maintained by the telephone companies."[23] The Commission disagreed. Recording devices could in fact be used without causing "any perceptible effect on the functioning of the telephone apparatus or the quality of the telephone service";[24] all federal tariffs purporting to bar the use of recording devices were therefore rejected. It was a bold beginning, but one the Commission was unable to vindicate fully until three decades later.

Indeed, by 1954, only six years later, the Commission was in full retreat. That year it upheld Bell's refusal to permit the Jordaphone, a prototype of today's answering machine, to be connected to the network.[25] Unlike ordinary "recording devices," the Jordaphone "opens and closes the telephone circuit"; this was enough to justify different treatment.[26] Bell had made no showing whatsoever that the network would suffer any substantial harm from Jordaphones. Nevertheless, the Commission decided that this kind of recording device would be used primarily with intrastate calls and should thus be left to the jurisdiction of individual state public utility commissions.

The following year the Commission issued perhaps its most comical order, revealing how a regulatory mind-set can sometimes overwhelm common sense. At issue was the "Hush-A-Phone," a metal device (packed with sound-muffling asbestos) that snapped onto the mouthpiece of the phone to provide some privacy and quiet in crowded office environments. Bell complained to the Commission that the Hush-A-Phone might muffle voices and lower the overall quality of telephone service; moreover, there was "no appreciable public demand" for the product.[27] The FCC agreed: "the unrestricted use of foreign attachments...may result in impairment to the quality and efficiency of telephone service, damage to telephone plant and facilities, or injury to telephone company personnel."[28] Foreign attachments would have to be analyzed one case at a time. And, after lengthy analysis, the Commission concluded that this particular snap-on cup would "be deleterious to the telephone system and injure the service rendered by it."[29] As a general principle, "telephone equipment should be supplied by and under control of the carrier itself."[30]

The D.C. Circuit sensibly reversed in a brief per curiam. The court found no support for the Commission's suggestion "that the use of a Hush-A-Phone affects more than the conversation of the user—that its influence pervades, in some fashion, the whole telephone system."[31] But the court went on to establish a principle of much wider significance: it affirmed "the telephone subscriber's right reasonably to use his telephone in ways which are privately beneficial without being

---

23. Use of Recording Devices in Connection with Telephone Services, 11 FCC 1033, 1048 (1947).

24. *Id.* at 1036.

25. Jordaphone, 18 F.C.C. 644 (1954).

26. *Id.* at 699.

27. Hush-A-Phone Corp. v. American Tel. & Tel. Co., 20 FCC 391, 397 (1955).

28. *Id.* at 419.

29. *Id.* at 420.

30. *Id.*

31. Hush-A-Phone Corp. v. U.S., 238 F.2d 266, 268 (D.C. Cir. 1956).

publicly detrimental."[32] Moreover, the court explained, "the mere fact that the telephone companies can provide a rival device would seem to be a poor reason for disregarding Hush-A-Phone's value in assuring a quiet line."[33]

On remand, the FCC recognized the potential significance of the court's opinion. It accordingly directed Bell to permit its customers to use the Hush-A-Phone device and any other similar device that "does not injure defendants' employees or facilities, the public in its use of defendants' services, or impair the operation of the telephone system."[34] Future tariffs, the Commission warned, must distinguish "between the harmful and harmless" and avoid encroaching "upon the right of the user to make reasonable use of the facilities furnished by the defendants."[35]

The full implications of *Hush-A-Phone* were not realized for over a decade, when the Commission handed down its 1968 *Carterfone* decision.[36] At issue was a device permitting direct communication between a mobile radio and the landline network.[37] True to form, Bell objected to the device, but failed to demonstrate that it would harm the network. The Commission rejected Bell's argument. Instead, the Commission ruled that the basic principle of *Hush-A-Phone* applied: any form of CPE could be attached to the network "so long as the interconnection does not adversely affect the telephone company's operations or the telephone system's utility for others."[38] Unvarnished claims of threatened harm to the network would no longer suffice. [As the Commission put it: "The vice of the present tariff, here as in *Hush-A-Phone*, is that it prohibits the use of harmless as well as harmful devices."[39]]

Technical problems aside, Bell had also argued that interconnection would have adverse economic effects and undercut universal service. But it had made no substantial effort to document the likelihood of such harms. "Economic effects upon the carriers' rate structure might well be a public interest question," the Commission acknowledged, but "it is an issue, if a carrier seeks to raise it, to be decided upon the facts."[40] Thus the Commission put Bell on notice that, if it wanted to rely on such claims, it would have to document them thoroughly.

Even after *Carterfone*, competitive providers of CPE did not have unfettered access to the network. Bell responded to *Carterfone* by filing new tariffs, tariffs

---

32. *Id.* at 269.
33. *Id.*
34. Hush-A-Phone Corp. v. American Tel. & Tel. Co., 22 FCC 112, 114 (1957).
35. *Id.* at 113.
36. In re Use of the Carterfone Device in Message Toll Telephone Service, 13 FCC 2d 420 (1968) [hereinafter *Carterfone*].
37. [Ed. The Commission described the Carterfone device as follows: "The Carterfone is designed to be connected to a two-way radio at the base station serving a mobile radio system. When callers on the radio and on the telephone are both in contact with the base station operator, the handset of the operator's telephone is placed on a cradle in the Carterfone device. A voice control circuit in the Carterfone automatically switches on the radio transmitter when the telephone caller is speaking; when he stops speaking, the radio returns to a receiving condition. A separate speaker is attached to the Carterfone to allow the base station operator to monitor the conversation, adjust the voice volume, and hang up when the conversation has ended." *Id.* at 420–21.]
38. *Id.* at 424.
39. *Id.*
40. Use of the Carterfone Device in Message Toll Service, 14 FCC 2d 571, 573 (1968).

that permitted customers to connect to the telephone network, but only through interconnecting devices called "protective connecting arrangements" (PCAs) [that Bell itself would sell to interested parties.] Further, any "network control signalling" devices—devices, like the ordinary dial telephone, that actually put electronic signals onto the phone network—still had to be furnished, installed, and maintained by Bell. The Commission turned aside the immediate challenges to these tariffs on the ground that although *Carterfone* permitted the interconnection of competitive CPE with the "telephone system," that "system" already included "(1) the telephone set, usually located on the customer's premises; (2) the pair of wires, and its supporting structures, which connect the telephone set to the central office; (3) the switching equipment in the central office; and (4) the trunk facilities that connect central offices to each other."[41] *Carterfone*, the Commission reasoned, permitted interconnections with—but not substitutions or replacements for—the "system," expansively defined. This substantially eviscerated *Carterfone*.

Notes and Questions

1. Subsequent Events. The FCC would ultimately reverse course. In 1972, the Commission began an inquiry into the issue of competitive CPE; that inquiry culminated in 1976 in a program of "technical registrations" for all CPE. Under this program, CPE suppliers had a choice: they could purchase a "protective connecting arrangement" (PCA) interface from Bell, or they could register their CPE with the Commission and show that the equipment would not harm the telephone network. Bell's stranglehold on the CPE market was thereby broken.

2. Other Bell Arguments. Bell raised two additional arguments in the context of the *Carterfone* decision, neither of which is summarized in the Huber excerpt. First, Bell argued that allowing the installation of unauthorized equipment would "divide the responsibility for assuring that each part of the system is able to function effectively," the implication apparently being that divided responsibility would not only introduce consumer confusion but also increase the coordination costs involved in keeping the telephone network operational. *Carterfone*, at 424. Second, Bell argued that unauthorized equipment would "retard development of the system since independent equipment suppliers would tend to resist changes which would render their equipment obsolete." *Id.* The FCC responded to these objections as follows:

> No one entity need provide all interconnection equipment for our telephone system any more than a single source is needed to supply the parts for a space probe. We are not holding that the telephone companies may not prevent the use of devices which actually cause harm, or that they may not set up reasonable standards to be met by interconnection devices. These remedies are appropriate; we believe they are also adequate to fully protect the system.

> Nor can we assume that the telephone companies would be hindered in improving telephone service by any tendency of the manufacturers and

---

41. American Tel. & Tel. Co. "Foreign Attachment" Tariff Revisions in AT&T Tariff FCC Nos. 263, 260, and 259, Memorandum Opinion and Order, 15 FCC 2d 605, 606 (1968).

users of interconnection devices to resist change. The telephone companies would remain free to make improvements to the telephone system and could reflect any such improvements in reasonable revised standards for interconnection. An owner of a device which failed to meet reasonable revised standards for such devices would either have to have the device rebuilt to comply with the revised standards or discontinue its use. Such is the risk inherent in the private ownership of any equipment to be used in connection with the telephone system.

Id.

3. Ulterior Motives. The FCC rejected Bell's various justifications for its CPE tariff, apparently disbelieving Bell and suspecting ulterior motives. The Huber excerpt suggests that perhaps Bell's ulterior motive was the desire to eliminate competition in the CPE market. But why would that be in Bell's interest? After all, Bell already controlled the phone network; why would it need two "stacked" monopolies—first, the phone network, then the attached CPE? In fact, wouldn't Bell be better off having competitive supply of CPE, since competitive supply would likely mean decreased costs and higher quality? Wouldn't those changes increase the profits Bell could make through its service monopoly? If so, why was the FCC so sure that Bell's objections to competitive CPE were disingenuous?

4. Bell/Microsoft. How similar is the Bell CPE issue to the modern claims that Microsoft has intentionally made it difficult for unaffiliated firms to develop software for the Windows operating system? That is, as we ask immediately above, wouldn't Microsoft be better off allowing competition in the software market, the argument being that high quality and low prices in the software market would drive demand for the operating system, and so it would actually be in Microsoft's interest to allow competition in the software market so long as Microsoft could maintain its monopoly on the operating system?

5. Test Your Understanding. Suppose that Western Electric—the Bell subsidiary that manufactured most of Bell's CPE—was in fact not affiliated with Bell. That is, imagine that Bell was purchasing almost all of its CPE from a single supplier, but that Bell did not have any ownership interest in that supplier. Would Bell still have had an incentive to thwart competition in the market for CPE?

B. Competition in the Long Distance Market

At the same time that competition was emerging in the market for CPE, competition in the provision of interstate telephone service was also on the rise. This incipient competition resulted in part from the development of a new technology that eroded major barriers to entry in the long distance market: microwave transmission.

For our purposes, microwave transmission is a technology through which large amounts of information can be transmitted efficiently over the airwaves. Why was the introduction of this technology so important? To be sure, AT&T's monopoly over long distance telephony was supported by its control over local exchange service in most markets. But it was also supported by the high costs to an entrant of, first, digging the trenches and, second, obtaining the rights of way needed to lay the transmission cable essential for providing telephone service. Microwave technology helped to reduce the entry barriers created by these two costs by greatly reducing the need to lay cable. A firm could transmit information by microwave, incurring only the more modest costs of constructing transmission and relay towers at sufficient intervals.

At first resistant to new entry in the market for interstate communications, the FCC in its 1959 *Above 890* decision[42] authorized the use of this new technology only as part of a tailored form of interstate service called "private line service." Private line service allowed large corporations to customize transmission capacity to meet their specialized needs. Instead of using the traditional telephone system, these firms could use their own "private" service to, for example, transmit traffic from one branch office to another. Importantly, private line service was not generic long distance service. Private lines did not compete head-on with Bell long distance because private lines served only particularly demanding users with peculiar transmission requirements—or so it was at first.

THE TITANIC REMEMBERED: AT&T AND THE CHANGING WORLD OF TELECOMMUNICATIONS

Glen Robinson, 5 Yale Journal on Regulation 517, 523–527 (1988)

In 1959, the FCC's decision in *Allocation of Frequencies in the Bands Above 890 MHz* first opened up the possibility of privately supplied microwave transmission facilities. As in *Carterfone*, the logic of allowing users to do for themselves what previously only Bell could do for them would lead to competitive supply of telephone services. In this instance the competitive effects trailed the decision by a decade; the effects were first manifest in 1969 by an authorization to MCI to provide private line services between Chicago and St. Louis. The MCI decision in turn prompted a general rulemaking, the *Specialized Common Carrier Services* proceeding, which in 1971 authorized competition in private line services more generally.

The FCC's "original intent" in the *Specialized Common Carrier Services* decision was the subject of much controversy in the mid-1970s and early 1980s. The debate recalls Robert Browning's response to an inquiry into the meaning of one of his early poems: "When I wrote that only God and Robert Browning knew what it meant; now only God knows." If God knew what the FCC meant in 1971, He didn't say; neither did the FCC. It seems that what the FCC originally had in mind was specialized services tailored to distinctive service needs of particular customers, as opposed to the homogenized common carrier services provided by Bell. But this was never precisely stated in the FCC's decision.

The issue of intent arose specifically in connection with whether the specialized carriers would have access, on nondiscriminatory terms, to Bell's foreign exchange (FX) and common control switching arrangement (CCSA) services, in essence the infrastructure that allowed interstate phone traffic to interconnect with the local exchange. In 1974 the FCC ordered access, over Bell's vigorous opposition. Bell's resistance to providing access to its FX and CCSA services was to

---

42. Allocation of Frequencies in the Bands Above 890 MHz, 27 FCC 359 (1959) ("*Above 890*").

be a key element in the Justice Department's ultimate antitrust case, as well as in private antitrust actions. However, neither Bell nor the FCC then appreciated that a little adroit packaging of these interconnections would allow MCI to provide [traditional] long distance service in direct competition with Bell's long distance service. This was what MCI accomplished with its "Execunet" offering. When the FCC learned (from Bell) that this is what access to FX and CCSA produced, it rejected MCI's Execunet tariff: direct competition with AT&T's basic [long distance] service was not part of the "original intent" of *Specialized Common Carrier*.

The court of appeals rejected the FCC's rejection, remanding for a clearer rationale of why long distance competition was not in the public interest.[43] This was the beginning of the end. *Execunet* would be as devastating to the Bell monopoly as the iceberg was to the Titanic. On remand the Commission instituted a rulemaking proceeding to consider the scope of competition in Bell's service markets, concluding in 1980 that there should be open competition [in the long distance market.]

A series of decisions constraining Bell's rate-cutting responses to the new competition was perhaps as important as the decisions authorizing competition in the first place. The Commission's *Specialized Common Carrier* decision had acknowledged that it would lead to adjustment of Bell rates in different markets to bring them more in line with costs—a departure from the pattern of uniform nationwide pricing that the FCC had historically approved. It could hardly be otherwise. Competition was being induced in high-density/low-cost markets where rates had been kept artificially high in order to subsidize low-density/high-cost markets. It would have been indefensible to deny Bell the right to defend its market position by reducing rates in competitive markets and raising them in subsidized, noncompetitive markets. This would, of course, undo some of the cross-subsidies that had long been built into telephone system pricing.

While the FCC clearly accepted this principle of rate de-averaging to bring rates into line with the actual costs of service, practical details here were complex. The heart of the problem was the difficulty of determining on which costs rates should be based. In unregulated competitive markets, such questions are occasionally raised in the context of alleged "predatory pricing" behavior. Predation in unregulated markets is rare because it can succeed only under very special conditions; in regulated competitive markets, on the other hand, the availability of monopoly rents from protected segments of the market makes predation a more viable and likely strategy for the regulated firm.[44]

---

43. MCI Telecommunications Corp. v. FCC, 561 F.2d 365 (D.C. Cir. 1977) (*Execunet I*); *see also* MCI Telecommunications Corp. v. FCC, 580 F.2d 590 (D.C. Cir.) (*Execunet II*), *cert. denied*, 439 U.S. 980 (1978).

44. [Ed. To elaborate on Robinson's implicit concern: Bell might have had an incentive to understate its costs in competitive markets, its purpose being to justify low prices that would in turn drive competitors out of that market. This is a form of predatory pricing—which more generally is a strategy of charging prices below cost in order to drive competitors out, but then raising prices once all competitors have left. Note that many economists question whether predatory pricing of this sort is workable. After all, so long as competitors can re-enter, the original firm will never be in a position to raise its prices sufficiently to recoup the losses incurred by underpricing. We discuss predatory pricing—and question whether this was Bell's actual strategy—in Chapter Sixteen.]

Unsurprisingly, insistent claims of predation were heard from Bell's competitors throughout the 1970s and ultimately appeared in the Justice Department's 1974 antitrust suit. The FCC's response to these charges was not a model of clear thinking. It got off to a bad start by adopting a highly dubious cost allocation standard: in 1976 the Commission ruled that Bell's competitive rates must cover fully distributed costs (FDC pricing) to ensure that Bell service in competitive markets was not subsidized by its monopoly services. Few economists applauded this standard. There was much criticism that the FCC was becoming a great handicapper of competition.

The problem is both theoretical and practical. In theory, FDC pricing violates a venerated axiom of economic efficiency, the principle of marginal cost pricing. In practice, there are also measurement problems. How do you allocate joint costs among different products? Not only is there no generally accepted principle for choosing FDC over marginal cost, there is no accepted formula for defining either one. In the early 1960s the Commission devised seven different methods covering a range of particular cost assignments that blurred the classic simple dichotomy between marginal and average costs. In 1976 it chose the most extreme fully distributed cost standard, though it later relaxed that standard.

Defining general standards was only half the task. Applying them was the other. The Commission did the first poorly and the second questionably. The Commission rejected major Bell tariffs on the ground that the particular cost assignments were not adequately justified, but refused to provide any real guidance as to what they should be.

The FCC's conduct over this period is not easy to interpret, but I suspect there was more to it than was officially reported. After the *Execunet* remand, the Commission became committed to a policy of open competition, apparently envisioning that after a "decent interval" all would be left to compete with little or no regulatory constraint. Yet well into the 1980s the Commission also feared that without a helping regulatory hand the infant competition could not survive open competition with Bell.

Notes and Questions

1. Skimming the Cream: Negligible? Bell's main argument against allowing rival firms to provide interstate service was that these new entrants would upset the established rate structure by "cream-skimming"—that is, siphoning off the high-profit business but leaving Bell to continue to supply phone service in less profitable areas. Such siphoning, Bell rightly pointed out, was in direct conflict with the FCC's cross-subsidy policies; those policies helped to create the "cream" by encouraging Bell to set prices without regard to costs, at least in certain circumstances.

Just to be clear about the link between FCC policy and the possibility of cream-skimming: because the FCC required Bell to charge artificially high prices to business users and artificially low prices to residential ones, rival firms could "skim cream" by offering service only to business users. In other words, the rival firms could undercut Bell's rates simply by setting prices more in line with actual costs. Similarly, because Bell was required to keep long distance rates high in order to subsidize local service, rivals could "skim cream" by entering the long distance market. In neither case would the rivals need to be more efficient than

Bell; they could win business simply because they were not obligated to engage in the cross-subsidy.

The D.C. Circuit and the Commission both responded to this objection by arguing that specialized carriers would not compete to such a degree that Bell would be seriously threatened. In *Execunet*, for example, the D.C. Circuit framed the issue as a question of whether rivals should be allowed to compete "on the fringes" of Bell's interstate service. 561 F.2d at 378. In the context of that same case, the Commission's position was that only a very small percentage of Bell's market was vulnerable to private carrier competition in the first place. Events would later reveal these predictions to be incorrect.

2. Skimming the Cream: Pro-Competitive? Even if MCI were cream-skimming to a substantial degree, why would that be an argument in support of Bell's position? Isn't cream-skimming a good thing in that it tends to bring prices more in line with costs? Besides—and as we asked earlier in this chapter—why couldn't the federal government remove the incentive to cream-skim simply by imposing a tax on all interstate service providers and using that tax to subsidize rural and residential service?

3. Predatory Pricing. A second argument against the introduction of competition in interstate service was the claim that it was just too difficult to determine whether Bell was engaging in predatory pricing. The upshot here was that the FCC would have trouble protecting any new entrants from being driven out of the market by Bell. Predatory pricing arguments are made in many markets; Wal-Mart, for example, is often accused of pricing below cost to drive out rival stores. But Robinson says that predatory pricing is different in the telephone industry because "in regulated competitive markets, the availability of monopoly rents from protected segments of the market makes predation a more viable and likely strategy for the regulated firm." Can you defend this statement? Why would the regulated firm use its monopoly profits in this way instead of just taking those profits to the bank? Does Robinson's argument prove too much? Wouldn't the logic of the argument suggest that McDonald's, Dell Computer, and IBM—all very profitable companies—also have the necessary profits to engage in predatory pricing and so these firms, too, must be regulated? Is there something special about Bell?

4. Benefits of Competition. Even if competition were workable (that is, even if the predatory pricing worry could be addressed through regulation), what benefits could competition bring? Could competition help the FCC establish more efficient rates, or do the above complexities suggest that rates would still be determined more by regulation than by market forces? If not that, what?

5. Quarantine. How much of the problem here is caused by the FCC's attempt to allow one firm, Bell, to compete in both regulated and unregulated markets? Why not ban Bell from competitive markets entirely? Wouldn't that have solved the predatory pricing worries? The cream-skimming worries?

C. Communications/Computer Convergence

A third precursor to the Bell breakup involved the technological convergence of computer and communications technology. In 1949, the government filed its second antitrust action against Bell, this time arguing that Bell had impermissibly used its patents on telecommunications equipment to monopolize "almost the entire telephone operating and manufacturing fields."[45] That case settled in 1956, in large part because the Eisenhower administration was unsympathetic to the suit; and the settlement at the time appeared to be a total victory for Bell. Under the settlement terms, Bell agreed that its Western Electric subsidiary (by that time a manufacturing arm) would manufacture only equipment used in the provision of telecommunications services, and, further, that Bell itself would limit its business to the "provision of common carrier communications services."[46] These were seemingly token sacrifices; at the time, they represented Bell's approximate policies anyway.

As the market for computer services matured, however, the restrictions began to seem more binding. Bell scientists had invented the transistor—a key computer component—and yet the 1956 decree seemed to bar Bell from participating in the industry that the transistor made possible. As Roger Noll and Bruce Owen put it, "with its leadership in semiconductor technology, Bell was positioned to be a very effective early competitor in computers; indeed, one can speculate that AT&T might well have been better off giving up the telephone but retaining its rights in transistors and computers."[47] Bell sought to offer services in new areas, and on several occasions, most notably 1980, the question arose whether that 1956 agreement really did prohibit Bell from providing so-called "advanced" services.

For example, in the early 1980s, large mainframe computers were very expensive both to build and to operate. Because of this, many firms wanted to be able to pool their resources, building a single large computer and then sharing access to that computer. Then (as now) the easiest way to accomplish that sharing was to access the commonly owned computer over the telephone system, with each firm having a remote connection (a "dummy terminal") that linked to the shared computer resource. But did the consent decree bar Bell from providing this sort of distributed computing service? Or was this a permissible "common carrier communications service"? As the excerpt below explains, questions like these did not admit to easy answers.

THE TITANIC REMEMBERED: AT&T AND THE CHANGING WORLD OF TELECOMMUNICATIONS

Glen Robinson, 5 Yale Journal on Regulation 517, 527–529 (1988)

Not long after *Carterfone*, the Commission initiated an inquiry into data processing uses of communications facilities. The inquiry was prompted by the growth of computer technology leading to a logical integration of computers and communications. The major questions were whether Bell should be permitted to

---

45. Huber et al., *supra* note 1, at 355 n.115 (quoting the government's complaint in United States v. Western Elec. Co., No. 17–49 (D.N.J. Jan 14, 1949)).

46. Huber et al., *supra* note 2, at 355–57 (discussing the settlement agreement).

47. Roger Noll & Bruce Owen, The Anticompetitive Uses of Regulation: United States v. AT&T, in The Antitrust Revolution 294 (J. Kwoka & L. White, eds., 1989).

market data processing services, and whether data processing services should be regulated when they are integrated with communications services.

The FCC answered the first question in the affirmative in 1971 but conditioned its permission on the formation of separate subsidiaries. It answered the second question in the negative. Both of these regulatory issues presented the definitional problem of distinguishing between data processing and communications. The Commission attempted sharply to distinguish "data processing" from "communications" in this decision, but its attempt was overtaken by technological advances that made the two virtually indistinguishable. The same device that could act as a telecommunications terminal (a network signaling device and modem) could be designed to handle general data processing functions.

In 1976 the FCC instituted a second inquiry to review the rules. While that inquiry was pending, the problem came to a head with a Bell tariff for a "smart" terminal device known as Dataspeed 40 which Bell defined as a "communications" (not "data processing") device and sought to offer as part of a tariffed communications service. The distinction was critical for Bell, which was precluded under a 1956 antitrust consent decree from offering non-communications services or products except as an incidental aspect of providing a tariffed (regulated) communications service. Thus, if Dataspeed 40 were declared a data processing device (rather than a communications device), Bell could not provide it at all. Meanwhile, computer firms were afraid that if Bell succeeded in getting the FCC to characterize it as a communications terminal, this could lead to an FCC extension of regulation to general purpose computer terminals whenever they incorporated functions usable for communications purposes.

The FCC decided that Dataspeed 40 was a communications device, and its decision was affirmed despite challenges by IBM and others. But the Commission had misgivings over its resolution of the dilemma. While sympathetic to Bell's argument that it ought not to be foreclosed from a market in which it had as much to offer as IBM, the FCC had no desire to regulate the computer industry.

The FCC's second computer inquiry (commonly called *Computer Inquiry II* or simply *Computer II*) was of greater scope. The Commission could now effect a dramatic measure which would avoid the need to distinguish between data processing and communications services: the deregulation of all CPE and those services that were most subject to competition—so-called "enhanced" services (any service other than "basic" transmission and switching). *Computer II* (1980), in short, was a momentous decision, comparable to *Carterfone* (1968) and *Specialized Common Carrier* (1971) in its effect on the character of telecommunications markets. *Computer II* differed from the other two, however, in that its primary interest was not so much to open particular telecommunications markets to outsiders as it was to open new markets—specifically, the various data processing markets—to Bell. For Bell's competitors, then, *Computer II* was a mixed blessing. On the one hand, by this decision the FCC declined to extend regulation to include computers with telecommunications uses. On the other hand, the decision unleashed into a host of computer-related markets a powerful new competitor: Bell.

Anxiety over the prospect of competing with Bell was compounded by the fact that Bell had a unique advantage: it controlled long distance switched services via its "AT&T Long Lines" subsidiary, and it controlled local exchange service via the so-called "Bell Operating Companies." Competitors feared that Bell would use its basic service monopoly to cross-subsidize its competitive CPE and enhanced services. Perhaps more important, competitors also feared that Bell's control of access to the basic services network (on which all competitors depended) gave Bell the means to handicap the competition, for example by manipulating network design or access arrangements. Fears of predatory conduct thus had not disappeared.

To meet these concerns the Commission required that Bell provide CPE and enhanced services only through corporate subsidiaries fully separated from both AT&T Long Lines and the Bell Operating Companies (BOCs). The FCC's theory was that this structural separation would make it more difficult for Bell to handicap competitors and to subsidize its own services and equipment. No doubt it did. However, it was also very costly to Bell, and it prevented efficient integration of services. (These concerns would lead to its ultimate undoing.)

Notes and Questions

1. Structural Separation. Did the Commission adequately balance the benefits and harms when it chose to abandon its attempt at line-drawing and instead to rely on structural remedies? The benefit, of course, was that structural remedies allowed the FCC to defer to market forces in the markets for both CPE and "enhanced" services. But the harm was a possibly significant loss of the efficiencies that would have been possible had Bell been allowed to integrate its telecommunications and computer arms.

2. Microsoft. Have the courts handled these arguments better in the context of the Microsoft litigation, where again a large firm has argued that there are significant efficiency benefits from integrated product development, this time integrating computer operating systems with applications software?

D. Rate-of-Return Regulation

The Commission's experience with rate-of-return regulation was the fourth experience that in many ways foreshadowed the coming breakup of Bell. Vail's argument that the Bell monopoly was good for society on both equity and efficiency grounds turned on an important assumption—namely that, when it came time to define appropriate rates for telephone service, government regulation would be an adequate substitute for competitive forces. But, as the FCC gradually came to realize, rate regulation in the context of monopoly is a tricky business, for the most part because the regulated party is also the party that has all the information the regulator needs.

We introduced rate-of-return and price cap regulation in Chapter Ten. (If you have not yet read that material, you might want to turn specifically to the "Note on Price Regulation" before reading any further.) The excerpt that follows is taken from a 1989 *Report and Order* adopting a new system of rate regulation in the post-divestiture world. It is included here because, in these paragraphs, the FCC describes its historical (and largely unsuccessful) efforts to regulate Bell. Also mixed into the Commission's discussion of rate regulation are summaries of the three other topics considered in this section: the introduction of competition in the market for CPE, the introduction of competitive interstate service, and the convergence of computer and telecommunications technology. The document thus serves as a nice overview of all the precursors to divestiture.

IN THE MATTER OF POLICY AND RULES CONCERNING RATES FOR DOMINANT CARRIERS
4 FCC Rcd. 2873 (1989)

1. Our current approach to regulating rates for interstate basic service is based on the following theory: that limiting a dominant carrier's profit on invested capital to "normal" levels is the most effective means of restraining its market power, enhancing consumer welfare, and furthering the public interest in just, reasonable, and non-discriminatory rates. For more than twenty years we have been administering an increasingly elaborate regulatory system based on this theory.

16. The Communications Act of 1934 (Act) charges this Commission with regulating "so as to make available...to all the people of the United States a rapid, efficient, Nation-wide, and world-wide...communication service with adequate facilities at reasonable charges...." We attempt to carry out this mandate within the regulatory structure established under the Act, which provides for dual regulation of telephone companies by this Commission and the individual states. Pursuant to this regulatory structure, telephone company costs are apportioned between the state and the interstate (federal) jurisdictions in accordance with rules adopted by this Commission after consultation with the states. Such costs are thereafter recovered by the telephone companies according to applicable federal and state regulatory policies.

17. The Act provides this Commission with various powers and tools to use in regulating the recovery of costs apportioned to the interstate jurisdiction.[48] With regard to the ratemaking process, the courts have determined that there is no single method or formula that agencies must use to satisfy the requirements in Title II of the Act and other similar statutes that rates be just and reasonable, and not unreasonably discriminatory. Instead, courts evaluate the end result of particular regulatory methodologies to determine whether they produce rates that fall within a "zone of reasonableness," an area bounded at the lower end by investor

---

48. Title II of the Act contains provisions granting this Commission the powers commonly associated with public utility regulation. These powers include the authority to require a carrier to interconnect with other carriers and to establish through routes and to determine whether carriers' rates and conditions of service are just and reasonable and without unreasonable preferences or discriminations. Section 203 authorizes this Commission to determine the information that must accompany carriers' tariff filings, while section 204 of the Act empowers this Commission to suspend and investigate proposed rates on our own initiative or in response to a petitioner's request. Should investigation establish the unlawfulness of rates, this Commission may prescribe just and reasonable terms to replace the offending conditions. Section 214 enables this Commission to control entry into and exit from the interstate market and to control to some extent a carrier's expansion of its rate base. Title II also permits this Commission, *inter alia*: to determine the value of the property a carrier includes in its rate base; to prescribe depreciation rates as well as accounting systems to be used by carriers subject to the Act; and to require such carriers to file any additional information this Commission may need to fulfill its statutory mandate.

interests in maintaining financial integrity and access to capital markets and at the upper end by consumer interests against non-exploitative rates.

18. At the present time, we employ a regulatory system known as rate-of-return, or cost of service, regulation. This approach requires not only that we establish a carrier's allowable rate-of-return, but also that we establish whether: (1) its investment and cash expenses are properly calculated and efficiently incurred; (2) the level of non-cash expenses such as depreciation and other accruals is properly reflected in rate calculations; and (3) the rates proposed or in effect cover these costs and produce a fair rate-of-return.

19. This elaborate approach is often thought of as "traditional" regulation. In fact, we did not begin to develop this system until the mid-1960s. Prior to that time, there were no explicit criteria for determining whether Bell System rates were just and reasonable. Instead, we followed a policy of "continuing surveillance" of Bell System earnings levels to ensure that rates remained within the zone of reasonableness. This process operated without regular formal proceedings of any kind, and rate adjustments occurred only if this Commission or Bell System representatives initiated "discussions looking toward appropriate rate changes" whenever the level of total interstate earnings "appeared to warrant such action."

20. During the period when the "continuing surveillance" policy was in effect, a voice occasionally was raised in complaint that the Bell System's costs and rates might be too high, but only once during this period did this Commission initiate a comprehensive investigation of such matters. This inquiry in the late 1930s cost millions of dollars and occupied approximately 300 researchers for several years. The staff's efforts culminated in the preparation of a voluminous report on Bell System costs and operations, but allegations of inflated costs and rates—and substantial cost shifting between unregulated Western Electric (at this time a Bell subsidiary) and regulated telephone company operations—were never documented to the Commission's satisfaction. Ultimately, no action was taken on the report's major recommendations, and the investigation produced no significant changes in Commission or Bell System procedures.

21. The use of "continuing surveillance" to assure just and reasonable rates occurred during a period when the Bell System faced little or no competition in the domestic interstate telecommunications market.

22. In the 1950s and 1960s, technological developments began to lower economic barriers to entry into the telephone business and to put pressure on the boundary between telephone companies and other firms. The development of microwave technology rendered scale economies insignificant at the "high" end of the telephone market. As a result, entities using large amounts of telephone service, which generally had been telephone company customers, could operate their own telephone systems and, potentially, compete against their former suppliers. The development of satellite technology as a cost-effective method of transmitting messages transformed firms with satellite expertise into potential entrants into the telephone field. Previously unrelated firms, such as aerospace companies and the Bell System, thus came into competitive interaction. Rapid development of digital electronics and transistor technology blurred the line between computers and communications. Computer systems took on the characteristics of telephone systems—i.e., switches linked by transmission lines—while, at the

same time, telephone companies were adopting computer technology for use in communications systems and expanding their operations into the domain of computer firms.

23. In the face of such developments, and often following the lead of the courts (*e.g., Execunet*), we embarked on two paths of regulatory change.

24. The first path consisted of a series of proceedings in which we addressed the impact of technological advances that made it possible for companies outside the Bell System to provide telecommunications equipment and services. The second path consisted of a series of proceedings in which we abandoned the "continuing surveillance" policy and began to construct the regulatory system currently relied upon to regulate dominant carriers. In retrospect, it is easy to see how the two paths of regulatory change were related, with the second coming as a response to the first. Permitting entry into certain segments of telecommunications allowed competition to develop in part, but not all, of that market. New competitors called upon this Commission to police the boundary between the competitive and less competitive portions of the market, and to arbitrate disputes among all competitors. Issues that had been left largely to telephone companies during the period of "continuing surveillance," such as rate structure, became crucial competitive variables. The allocation of telephone company costs among competitive and less competitive services became a subject of intense controversy.

25. With regard to both paths, this Commission's efforts were devoted to structuring regulatory policies that affirmatively promote competition, that rely on competitive forces as an effective means of assisting us in achieving our statutory goals, or that attempt to emulate the operations of a competitive market. The public interest rationale for applying this competition-based regulatory model is readily understandable. Companies subject to competition are forced to operate in ways that generally result in just, reasonable, and non-discriminatory rates. Although firms operating in a competitive environment simply are attempting to maximize their profits, the various means each uses to achieve this result—innovating, enhancing efficiency, providing quality services—benefit consumers individually and society as a whole.[49]

26. Commission proceedings directed toward affirmatively promoting competition in telecommunications markets yielded clear and substantial public interest benefits. For example, decisions to deregulate the provision of customer premises equipment (CPE) resulted in greatly increased consumer choice among a wide range of such products, and a sharp decrease in prices. Likewise, after we opened entry into the market for interstate long distance services, and determined that the lack of market power among most new entrants made it unnecessary to regulate their operations comprehensively, the prices for such services fell and the number of service providers grew exponentially.

---

49. The competitive model may not be sufficient by itself to achieve all the objectives established in the Act. For example, we have construed our mandate under the Act to include the promotion of universal service. Achieving this goal requires us on occasion to exercise our powers in ways that do not conform to a competitive paradigm. We also have acted on many occasions to preserve the policy of geographic rate averaging, again a policy that to some degree conflicts with the competitive model.

27. This Commission did not achieve similarly clear-cut and uniform benefits in connection with proceedings devoted to applying detailed rate-of-return regulation to the Bell System and its progeny after divestiture.

28. Throughout most of the 1970s, we conducted extensive and complex investigations of the Bell System's rate base and cost allocation systems, and of its tariffed rates. In a repeat of our rate base investigation in the 1930s, no significant disallowances of carrier investment resulted from these inquiries.

Notes and Questions

1. Justifying Rate Regulation. Why does the FCC conclude that permitting competition in telephone equipment and long distance services logically compels a shift to rate-of-return regulation? Isn't the whole purpose of competition to obviate the need for any form of rate regulation?

2. Changing Policy at the FCC. The history as recounted by the FCC suggests that, over time, the Commission reduced the extent of internal cross-subsidization in Bell's rates and began to rely heavily on competition to regulate and discipline Bell. Why did the agency believe that these regulatory shifts would benefit consumers? What had changed since the early years when it was considered to be an advantage of monopoly that prices did not have to accurately reflect costs?

3. Inevitable Progress? Does the gradual march toward competition seem inevitable in retrospect? Given the changing technologies—especially the developing convergence between computers and telephones, and the introduction of satellite and microwave for long distance hookups—could the regulatory regime in place in 1960 plausibly have survived into the 1990s?

CHAPTER SIXTEEN

BREAKUP OF THE BELL MONOPOLY

The purpose of this chapter is:

- to examine in careful detail an event of extraordinary import in the regulation of telecommunications, the breakup of the Bell Telephone System.

~

I. INTRODUCTION

Two main themes would undergird the government's 1974 antitrust case against Bell, themes that are likely apparent from last chapter's discussion of the four precursors to the Bell breakup. First, the government would argue that Bell was gaining an unfair advantage in the CPE, computer, and long distance markets because it could discriminate against rivals who needed access to Bell's local telephone exchanges in order to compete effectively. Second, the government would claim that Bell was engaged in predatory pricing against its rivals, a scheme made more plausible in the government's view by the fact that Bell was simultaneously operating in both regulated/monopolistic and unregulated/competitive markets. Anticompetitive discrimination in interconnection and predatory cross-subsidization were thus the cornerstones of what would become the lawsuit that brought down Bell.

The case was filed on November 20, 1974, but the judge originally assigned to oversee the matter got little done during the first four years of the litigation.[1] When that judge fell ill in 1978, the case was transferred to U.S. District Court Judge Harold Greene. It was his first day on the federal bench. The case would stay on his docket in one form or another for eighteen years.

Greene pushed the parties to move quickly through early hearings and stipulations, and by January of 1981 the trial was underway. There was one six-week break during which the parties attempted (and failed) to negotiate a settlement; but, beyond that, the trial moved forward with haste. The court heard more than one hundred witnesses between March and September 1981. In September, at the end of the government's case but before Bell had put forward its

---

1. For a fuller telling of the history of the 1974 antitrust case, *see* Huber et al., Federal Telecommunications Law 351–71 (2d ed. 1999), as well as the many sources cited therein.

defense, Bell filed a motion to dismiss. Judge Greene rejected the motion. Shortly thereafter, Bell and the government submitted to Judge Greene a proposed settlement decree.[2]

Judge Greene thus never had an opportunity to rule on the merits of the government's antitrust claim. Under the Tunney Act (codified at 15 U.S.C. §16), Greene could review the proposed consent decree only to determine whether its acceptance would be "in the public interest." Greene conducted that review, imposed several changes, and then accepted the decree as changed. That decree is known today as the Modification of Final Judgment, Modified Final Judgment, or MFJ. It stripped Bell of its local exchange carriers but then freed Bell—now a long distance and equipment company—to compete in virtually any market. Meanwhile, the agreement imposed upon the now-separate LECs strict limitations in terms of their business ventures outside the provision of basic local telephone service. All of these results stemmed from a desire to keep the computer, telephone equipment, long distance, and enhanced services markets free of both discriminatory interconnection and predatory cross-subsidization.

The principal reading that follows is an excerpt from Judge Greene's opinion modifying, and then accepting as modified, the agreement reached by the Department of Justice and the American Telephone & Telegraph Company. Note that we have thus far in these materials referred to the latter entity as "Bell" in order to avoid confusion between the pre-divestiture entity (Bell) and the company that emerged from divestiture to provide long distance service (AT&T). Judge Greene's opinion uses the more common, and potentially confusing, naming convention; readers should thus be careful to distinguish between the opinion's references to AT&T (meaning the entire Bell System), his references to the Bell Operating Companies (BOCs) (meaning the subdivisions of Bell that provided local exchange service), and his references to AT&T Long Lines (meaning the subdivision of Bell that, prior to divestiture, provided interstate long distance service).

After that excerpt, we include portions of an article by economists Roger Noll and Bruce Owen. Their article, in very accessible terms, explains and critiques the theory behind the government's case.

---

2. Interestingly, the decree was negotiated not only in the shadow of the antitrust litigation, but also in the shadow of direct intervention by Congress. The decree language, in fact, closely tracks a Senate bill then under consideration. *See* Senate Bill S. 898, 97th Cong. 1st Sess. (Oct. 20, 1981). Some commentators claim that the Justice Department intentionally modeled the proposed consent decree after the Senate bill. *See, e.g.,* Steve Coll, The Deal of the Century 304–05 (1986).

II. THE MODIFICATION OF
FINAL JUDGMENT (MFJ)

UNITED STATES v. AMERICAN
TELEPHONE & TELEGRAPH CO.
552 F. Supp. 131 (D.D.C. 1982),
aff'd, 460 U.S. 1001 (1983)

HAROLD GREENE, District Judge:

These actions are before the Court for a determination whether a consent decree proposed by the parties is in the "public interest" and should therefore be entered as the Court's judgment.

I. Preliminary Considerations

A. History of the Litigation

On January 14, 1949, the government filed an action in the District Court for the District of New Jersey against the Western Electric Company, Inc.[3] and the American Telephone and Telegraph Company, Inc. The complaint alleged that the defendants had monopolized and conspired to restrain trade in the manufacture, distribution, sale, and installation of telephones, telephone apparatus, equipment, materials, and supplies, in violation of the Sherman Act. The relief sought included the divestiture by AT&T of its stock ownership in Western Electric; termination of exclusive relationships between AT&T and Western Electric; divestiture by Western Electric of its fifty percent interest in the Bell Telephone Laboratories research facility; separation of telephone manufacturing from the provision of telephone service; and the compulsory licensing of patents owned by AT&T on a non-discriminatory basis.

The court record reveals little activity in the case between the date of the filing of the complaint in 1949 and the entry of a consent decree in 1956.

The gaps in the court record are partly filled by a report of a committee of the United States House of Representatives which conducted an intensive investigation of the circumstances surrounding the entry of the consent decree. *Report of the Antitrust Subcommittee of the House Committee on the Judiciary on the Consent Decree Program of the Department of Justice*, 86th Cong., 1st Sess., January 30, 1959 (Committee Print) (hereinafter *Subcommittee Report*).

As early as February 28, 1952, the president of Bell Laboratories, Dr. M. J. Kelly, met with Secretary of Defense Robert A. Lovett and other members of the Department of Defense to enlist their help in persuading the Justice Department

---

3. Western Electric is the wholly owned subsidiary of AT&T that manufactures telecommunications equipment for AT&T's Long Lines Department and the Operating Companies. In addition, Western Electric provides telecommunications equipment and services to government agencies and, to a limited extent, the independent telephone companies.

to suspend prosecution of the action until the end of the Korean War, a suspension the Attorney General refused to grant.

> Indefinite postponement was requested by the Defense Department despite the fact that neither Mr. Lovett...nor anyone else in the Department had made an independent investigation to determine whether trial of the suit would actually impede the mobilization effort or whether Bell System personnel working on defense matters would actually be needed for preparation of trial of the case. *Subcommittee Report* at 47.

AT&T continued its attempts to end the litigation as soon as the Eisenhower Administration took office. These efforts culminated in a meeting on June 27, 1953, between T.B. Price, AT&T's general counsel, and Attorney General Herbert Brownell. According to a memorandum prepared by Price following this meeting, Attorney General Brownell said that he believed that "a way ought to be found to get rid of the case," and that AT&T "could readily find practices that they might agree to have enjoined with no real injury to their business." *Subcommittee Report* at 53—54.

Shortly after this meeting, AT&T again urged the Defense Department "to intercede with the Justice Department to have the case settled on a basis that would not require divorcement of Western." *Subcommittee Report* at 55. To that end, Secretary of Defense Charles E. Wilson had a letter hand-carried to Attorney General Brownell urging him to end the litigation without divesting Western Electric. The rationale stated for this position was that the severance of Western Electric would "effectively disintegrate the coordinated organization which is fundamental to the successful carrying forward of these critical defense projects," and would "be contrary to the vital interests of the Nation." *Subcommittee Report* at 56. The Wilson letter was actually prepared by AT&T.

The consent decree which was the product of this process included neither the divestiture of Western Electric nor any of the other structural relief originally requested by the government. Instead, an injunction was issued which precluded AT&T from engaging in any business other than the provision of common carrier communications services; precluded Western Electric from manufacturing equipment other than that used by the Bell System; and required the defendants to license their patents to all applicants upon the payment of appropriate royalties.

This was the status of the Western Electric suit when the government filed a separate antitrust action on November 20, 1974, in this Court against AT&T, Western Electric, and Bell Telephone Laboratories, Inc. The complaint in the new action alleged monopolization by the defendants with respect to a broad variety of telecommunications services and equipment in violation of §2 of the Sherman Act. The government initially sought the divestiture from AT&T of the Bell Operating Companies (hereinafter generally referred to as Operating Companies or BOCs)[4] as well as the divestiture and dissolution of Western Electric.

---

4. The twenty-two Bell Operating Companies, most of which are wholly owned by AT&T, provide the means by which local telephone service is furnished. Bell customers presently also gain access to the network for both local and long distance telecommunications services through the Operating Companies. These Operating Companies are regulated by the various state public utility commissions. They may encompass several states, a single state, or only a single metropolitan area.

B. The Proposed Decree

Section I of the proposed decree would provide for significant structural changes in AT&T. In essence, it would remove from the Bell System the function of supplying local telephone service by requiring AT&T to divest itself of the portions of its twenty-two Operating Companies which perform that function.

The geographic area for which these Operating Companies would provide local telephone service is defined in the proposed decree by a new unit, the "exchange area." According to the Justice Department, an exchange area "will be large enough to comprehend contiguous areas having common social and economic characteristics but not so large as to defeat the intent of the decree to separate the provision of intercity services from the provision of local exchange service."

The Operating Companies would provide telephone service from one point in an exchange area to other points in the same exchange area — "exchange telecommunications"[5] — and they would originate and terminate calls from one exchange area to another exchange area — "exchange access." The interexchange portion of calls from one exchange area to another exchange area[6] would, however, be carried by AT&T and the other interexchange carriers, such as MCI and Southern Pacific Co.

Section II of the proposed decree would complement these structural changes by various restrictions which are said to be designed (1) to prevent the divested Operating Companies from discriminating against AT&T's competitors, and (2) to avoid a recurrence of the type of discrimination and cross-subsidization that were the basis of the AT&T lawsuit.

The first group of these provisions would require the divested Operating Companies to provide services to interexchange carriers equal in type, quality, and price to the services provided to AT&T and its affiliates. In addition, they would be prohibited from discriminating between AT&T and other companies in their procurement activities, the establishment of technical standards, the dissemination of technical information, their use of Operating Company facilities and charges for such use, and their network planning.

The second type of restriction imposed upon the Operating Companies is said to be intended to prevent them from engaging in any non-monopoly business so as to eliminate the possibility that they might use their control over exchange services to gain an improper advantage over competitors in such businesses. Thus, the Operating Companies would not be permitted (1) to manufacture or market telecommunications products and customer premises equipment; (2) to provide interexchange services; (3) to provide directory advertising such as the Yellow Pages; (4) to provide information services; and (5) to provide any other product or service that is not a "natural monopoly service actually regulated by tariff."

Finally, the proposed decree would vacate the final judgment entered on January 24, 1956, in the Western Electric case, eliminating the restrictions imposed upon AT&T by that decree.

---

5. Also referred to herein as intra-exchange service. This may roughly be equated with local telephone service.

6. In general, this is the service commonly known as long distance service.

IV. The Divestiture

A. Conditions Necessitating Antitrust Relief

1. Evidence of Anticompetitive Actions by AT&T

The government asserted that AT&T monopolized the intercity telecommunications market and the telecommunications product market in a variety of ways in violation of the Sherman Act. The evidence that was produced during the AT&T trial indicates that, at least with respect to several of the government's claims, this charge may be well taken.

In its intercity case, the government alleged that AT&T used its control over its local monopoly to preclude competition in the intercity market. The government proved *inter alia* that after 1968 AT&T included a "customer premises" provision in its interconnection tariff which deterred potential competitors from entering that market;[7] that it refused to provide FX and CCSA services to specialized common carriers and domestic satellite carriers until 1974 when the FCC specifically ordered it to do so;[8] and that it attempted to prevent competitors from offering metered long distance service that would compete with AT&T's own regular long distance service.

AT&T's basic rationale for these policies was that it was attempting to prevent competitors from "cream-skimming." As viewed by AT&T, it would have been able successfully to combat cream-skimming if it had priced each of its routes on the basis of the costs for operating that route. However, it concluded that the FCC had rejected this approach when it endorsed national rate averaging in the interest of promoting the goal of universal service. Accordingly, AT&T argued that, since rate averaging is inconsistent with competition, and since the basic rate averaging policy had been required by the FCC as being in the public interest, it was acting reasonably under the Communications Act in preventing competition as best and as long as it could.

What this line of reasoning fails to consider is that, at least by the mid-1970s, the FCC had clearly begun to promote competition in telecommunications. The government contended during the trial—correctly, in the Court's

---

7. Under this provision, a competitor could interconnect with the AT&T network only if the interconnection occurred in switching equipment located on the customer's premises where the telecommunication originated or terminated. The effect of this restriction was to prevent competitors from entering the intercity market gradually, and thus effectively from entering the market at all. For example, because of this restriction, a customer whose sole office was in St. Louis could not choose to use the services of an AT&T competitor for part of a route (*e.g.*, from St. Louis to Chicago), and then AT&T's services for the remainder of the route (*e.g.*, from Chicago to Bethesda, Maryland) because the St. Louis customer did not have the "premises" in Chicago that AT&T required for interconnection. Thus, to receive service for Bethesda as well as for Chicago, the customer was required to purchase both services from AT&T.

8. FX (foreign exchange) service permits a customer to make or receive local calls through a distant switching center by effectively providing a long extension cord in the form of a dedicated line between the customer's location and a telephone company switching system in the distant location (the foreign exchange). CCSA (common control switching arrangement) is essentially a miniature AT&T long distance network, except for the fact that it is used by only one customer, albeit a customer, such as the federal government, with large telecommunications needs.

view—that AT&T had an obligation to follow the more recent FCC policy rather than previous policies which may have suited AT&T better, particularly since there was never a direct FCC rule against de-averaging.

What is significant about these events is that AT&T was able to adopt the policies described above in large part because of its control over the local exchange facilities. For example, it was because of its ownership and control of the local Operating Companies—whose facilities were and are needed for interconnection purposes by AT&T's competitors—that AT&T was able to prevent these competitors from offering FX and CCSA services. Similarly, AT&T was able to deter competition by manipulating prices for access to the Operating Company networks.

AT&T's control over the local Operating Companies was central also to the anticompetitive behavior alleged with respect to the second facet of the government's case, that involving customer-provided terminal equipment.

The government proved that AT&T prohibited the attachment of competitors' equipment to the network except through a protective connecting arrangement (PCA). There was evidence that some experts (including a panel of the National Academy of Sciences) believed that such a PCA was necessary if the nationwide telephone network was to be protected from a variety of harms. On the other hand, the government's evidence indicated that AT&T required PCAs for equipment that in all probability could not harm the network; that there were delays in providing PCAs; that the PCAs were over-designed and over-engineered, and, thus, over-priced; that PCAs were required for competitive equipment while identical equipment sold by AT&T did not require their use; and that PCAs could not guard against all of the harms to the network that AT&T professed to fear.

Additionally, the alternative option of certification[9] was available but never seriously pursued by AT&T. Moreover, when ultimately certification was directly mandated by the FCC as a substitute for the protective connecting arrangement, the telephone network did not cease to function in its customary fashion. Indeed, AT&T was unable during the trial to prove any actual harm to the network from the elimination of the PCAs.

In its procurement part of the case, the government alleged, and there was proof, that AT&T used its control over the local Operating Companies to force them to buy products from Western Electric even though other equipment manufacturers produced better products or products of identical quality at lower prices. Here, too, AT&T's control of the Operating Companies was central to the allegedly anticompetitive behavior.[10]

2. Concentration of Power in the Telecommunications Industry

There is an additional reason, largely independent of the factors discussed above, which supports some type of antitrust relief in this case: AT&T's substantial domination of the telecommunications industry in general.

---

9. Under a certification program, non-Bell equipment may be connected directly to the AT&T network—without the use of a PCA—provided that the equipment has been certified as meeting certain technical standards.

10. It should be noted, however, that the government's procurement case was not extremely strong.

Many commentators have asserted that we are entering an age in which information will be the keystone of the economy. The only pervasive two-way communications system is the telephone network. It is crucial in business affairs, in providing information to the citizenry, and in the simple conduct of daily life. In its present form, AT&T has a commanding position in the industry. The men and women who have guided the Bell System appear by and large to have been careful not to take advantage of its central position in America's economic life. There is no guarantee, however, that future managers will be equally careful.[11] In any event, it is antithetical to our political and economic system for this key industry to be within the control of one company.

B. Effect of the Divestiture

As indicated in Part IV(A), *supra*, the ability of AT&T to engage in anticompetitive conduct stems largely from its control of the local Operating Companies. Absent such control, AT&T will not have the ability to disadvantage competitors in the interexchange and equipment markets.

For example, with the divestiture of the Operating Companies, AT&T will not be able to discriminate against intercity competitors, either by subsidizing its own intercity services with revenues from the monopoly local exchange services, or by obstructing its competitors' access to the local exchange network. The local Operating Companies will not be providing interexchange services, and they will therefore have no incentive to discriminate. Moreover, AT&T's competitors will be guaranteed access that is equal to that provided to AT&T, and intercity carriers therefore will no longer be presented with the problems that confronted them in that area. *See* Part VIII, *infra*.

Abuses will also be unlikely in the equipment interconnection area, because the Operating Companies will not manufacture equipment and will therefore lack AT&T's incentive to favor the connection of one manufacturer's equipment over another's. Any pro-Western Electric bias on the part of these companies will be eliminated once the intra-enterprise relationship between the Operating Companies and Western Electric is broken.[12]

C. Alternative Remedies

1. Divestiture of Western Electric and Bell Laboratories

The inadequacy of the divestiture from the Bell System of its research and manufacturing arms as an antitrust remedy is obvious: it would not eliminate AT&T's ability and incentive to take anticompetitive actions against its competitors in the intercity market. The remedy would thus be ineffective in the very area in which the government's proof in the AT&T action was strongest. In addition, this remedy would not eliminate AT&T's de facto control of the national

---

11. One may speculate, for example, on the effect on the political life of this nation if a company or group with strong political or ideological opinions were to gain effective control of the present Bell System (particularly if the company, additionally, were not precluded from entry into information and electronic publishing services). *See* Part VI(B).

12. Any cross subsidization of AT&T's intercity services and equipment manufacturing operations with revenue from its monopoly local exchange services will likewise be eliminated.

telecommunications system. Although the company would no longer dominate the manufacturing and research markets, it would still control the essentials of American telecommunications—virtually all intercity and local services. The divestiture would thus not fulfill the goal of deconcentrating AT&T's vast economic power.

2. Injunction

It is unlikely that, realistically, an injunction could be drafted that would be both sufficiently detailed to bar specific anticompetitive conduct yet sufficiently broad to prevent the various conceivable kinds of behavior that AT&T might employ in the future.

An even more formidable obstacle is presented by the question of enforcement. Two former chiefs of the FCC's Common Carrier Bureau, the section of the Commission charged with regulating AT&T, testified that the Commission is not and never has been capable of effective enforcement of the laws governing AT&T's behavior. The problems of supervision by a relatively poorly-financed, poorly-staffed government agency over a gigantic corporation with almost unlimited resources in funds and gifted personnel are no more likely to be overcome in the future than they were in the past.

D. Effect of the Divestiture Upon Other Interests

The divestiture of the Operating Companies will not necessarily have an adverse effect upon the cost of local telephone service. The decree would leave state and federal regulators with a mechanism—access charges—by which to require a subsidy from intercity service to local service.

There is simply no evidence or reason to believe that, funding aside, the quality of service will decline as a result of divestiture. The divested Operating Companies will not be technical backwaters: they will have substantial incentives to upgrade their networks and to provide high-quality interconnections for other carriers in order to maximize revenues from access charges and from local rates.

The evidence adduced during the AT&T trial indicates that the Bell System has been neither effectively regulated nor fully subjected to true competition. The FCC officials themselves acknowledge that their regulation has been woefully inadequate to cope with a company of AT&T's scope, wealth, and power. The efforts of various arms of government to introduce true competition into the telecommunications industry have been similarly feeble. The antitrust suit brought by the Department of Justice in 1949 ended in 1956 with a consent decree which imposed injunctive relief that was patently inadequate. It took from 1968 when the *Carterfone* decision was handed down by the FCC to 1978 when the United States Court of Appeals decided *Execunet II* to establish even the very principle of competition so that it was beyond dispute. In short, the choice is between a Bell System restrained by neither regulation nor true competition and a Bell System reorganized in such a way as to diminish greatly the possibility of future anticompetitive behavior.

V. Absence of Restrictions on AT&T

Under the terms of the proposed decree, the line of business restrictions and the licensing requirements imposed by the 1956 consent decree in the *Western*

Electric case would be removed and AT&T would be free to compete in all facets of the marketplace. The Court finds that, with one exception concerning electronic publishing services (*see* Part VI(B), *infra*), the imposition of restrictions on AT&T would not be in the public interest.

Past restrictions on AT&T were justified because of its control over the local Operating Companies. With the divestiture of these local exchange monopolies, continued restrictions are not required unless justified by some other rationale.

A. AT&T Power in the Interexchange Market

Virtually all those who suggest that restrictions beyond those in the proposed decree be imposed on AT&T make the same general arguments. Their basic claim is that AT&T still possesses monopoly power in the interexchange market and that it will leverage this power by cross-subsidizing its competitive services with monopoly revenues. These interexchange monopoly revenues, it is said, will subsidize a variety of business activities, ranging from competitive interexchange routes to equipment manufacturing to alternative local distribution facilities.

The validity of these arguments depends, of course, upon the soundness of the claim that after the divestiture AT&T will still possess monopoly power in the interexchange market.

There can be no doubt that AT&T's market share in the interexchange market is high. Even AT&T concedes that as late at 1981 its share of interexchange revenue was around 77 percent. But the inquiry of whether AT&T possesses monopoly power in the interexchange areas does not end with a description of AT&T's size or its market share.

As defined by the Supreme Court, monopoly power is "the power to control prices or exclude competition." United States v. Grinnell Corp., 384 U.S. at 571 (1966); United States v. duPont & Co., 351 U.S. 377, 391 (1956). Size alone is not synonymous with market power, particularly where entry barriers are not substantial.

Both the Department of Justice and AT&T contend that competition in the interexchange market is growing and that this increase in competition demonstrates an absence of monopoly power. The interexchange market is now being served not only by relatively young businesses but also by subsidiaries of such well established firms as ITT, Southern Pacific, and IBM.

That is not to say, however, that competition has flourished without impediment or that it would soar if the Bell System were not broken up. But the overriding fact is that the principal means by which AT&T has maintained monopoly power in telecommunications has been its control of the Operating Companies with their strategic bottleneck position. The divestiture required by the proposed decree will thus remove the two main barriers that previously deterred firms from entering or competing effectively in the interexchange market.

First. AT&T will no longer have the opportunity to provide discriminatory interconnection to competitors. The Operating Companies will own the local exchange facilities. Since these companies will not be providing interexchange services, they will lack AT&T's incentive to discriminate. Moreover, they will be required to provide all interexchange carriers with exchange access that is "equal in type, quality, and price to that provided to AT&T and its affiliates." *See* Part VIII, *infra*.

Second. Once AT&T is divested of the local Operating Companies, it will be unable either to subsidize the prices of its interexchange service with revenues from local exchange services or to shift costs from competitive interexchange services.

With the removal by the decree of all these burdens on competition, the number of firms entering the interexchange market is thus likely to increase. This development should be further assisted by the reduction of other barriers to entry. For example, although the cost of entering the telecommunications business is still substantial, the size of the required capital investment is not as great as it once was. In addition, as more competitors begin to offer more services that are comparable to those offered by AT&T, entrenched customer preferences in favor of AT&T will decrease.

Thus, unless proposed restrictions on AT&T are premised on more than the claim that AT&T has monopoly power in the interexchange area, they will have to be rejected.

B. Interexchange Restrictions

Some of those who have commented on the proposed decree urge that the Court require a modification guaranteeing access to AT&T's interexchange network for its competitors.

However, as the proponents of a clause which would guarantee access to AT&T's interexchange competitors concede, such access is already required by existing FCC decisions and regulations. These regulations make it possible for competing carriers to interconnect freely and to expand their facilities by "piecing out" AT&T's network, that is, by using AT&T's facilities to complete portions of routes that must traverse low density, sparsely populated, and hence presumably not very profitable territory.

C. Equipment Restrictions

After divestiture, AT&T's position in the equipment market will be diminished, and that market is certain to become more competitive. To the extent that prior to divestiture AT&T was able to engage in anticompetitive conduct in the equipment market, that ability stemmed basically from its control of the Operating Companies. Once these local companies are divested, Western Electric will lose its captive customers.

There is likewise no merit to the argument that Western Electric will have an anticompetitive edge in the production of new equipment because its affiliation with Bell Laboratories and Long Lines will give it early access to technical information and network standards. This claim ignores the fact that after divestiture, the Operating Companies, not AT&T, will control the information necessary for local exchange and exchange access services. Thus, if equipment manufacturers need information about interconnecting their equipment to the local exchange network, it will be provided by companies that are not engaged in the manufacturing of equipment.[13]

---

13. To the extent that manufacturers need information from Long Lines, market forces will help to ensure their access: since Long Lines will increasingly be forced to compete with

D. Bypass

A considerable number of persons have suggested that the Court prohibit AT&T from using new local distribution technologies that would allow it to "bypass" the networks of the Operating Companies to reach its local subscribers directly. The fear is that, early on, use of this technology will tend to exert pressure on Operating Companies' rates and their ability to levy access charges on interexchange carriers, and that, in time, the new technology will render the Operating Companies and their plants obsolete.

AT&T is not the only carrier to possess the technical know-how necessary for bypassing the Operating Companies' local networks. Imposition of this restriction on AT&T is thus unlikely to be effective. Furthermore, because other interexchange carriers possess this technology, to prohibit only AT&T from developing and using it would artificially and unfairly restrict competition.

Bypass would provide telecommunications service directly to the subscriber by means of satellites, microwave towers, or other advanced technological innovations at a lower cost than such service is available now.

Neither the Court nor those who object to the decree can halt the electronic revolution any more than the Luddites could stop the industrial revolution at the beginning of the last century. If and when bypass technology becomes technically and economically feasible for widespread use, it should have the effect of reducing telephone costs and charges across the board, to the benefit of consumers, the economy, and the nation. Should it turn out instead that, as some fear, this technology will be used to reduce charges unevenly so as to threaten the goal of universal service, then those with legislative authority may at that time wish to take steps, through a program of subsidies, special charges, or other regulatory means, to make the benefits of the new technology available to all, including those who are relatively low-volume users of telephone service.

E. Patent Licensing Requirements

Under the terms of the 1956 consent decree, AT&T was required to grant to all applicants non-exclusive licenses for all existing and future Bell System patents. Until now, AT&T's research and development have been financed primarily through the licensing contracts with the local Operating Companies. As long as ratepayer financed local exchange revenues were supporting this research and development, it made sense to require AT&T to share the fruits of its monopoly financing with others. But under the proposed decree, the licensing contracts will be terminated, and this rationale for exclusive licensing thus fails.

VI. The 1956 Decree and Line of Business Restrictions

The basic agreement embodied in the 1956 consent decree in the Western Electric case was that AT&T would not be required to divest itself of Western

---

other interexchange competitors, it will have the incentive to purchase the best equipment at the lowest prices without regard to corporate affiliation. It will therefore be in Long Lines' own interest to disseminate its own technical information and standards as broadly as possible to enable it to choose from among the widest range of products. Finally, as technology in interexchange services advances and carriers turn increasingly to the use of microwave towers and satellites, reliance on the AT&T network will decline and the need for obtaining information about the AT&T network will increasingly be reduced.

Electric, provided that AT&T would restrict its operations to the provision of common carrier communications services and that Western Electric would manufacture only the types of equipment used by the Bell System.

The decree which has now been submitted by the parties would eliminate all of the restrictions of the 1956 consent judgment. If that decree is entered by the Court, AT&T would be free to enter the computer market as well as to provide the full range of so-called information services.

There has been no serious opposition to the entry of AT&T into manufacturing and marketing of computers and other electronic equipment. By contrast, others who have submitted comments object to AT&T's entry into the information services market.

"Information services" are defined in the proposed decree as:

the offering of a capability for generating, acquiring, storing, transforming, processing, retrieving, utilizing or making available information which may be conveyed via telecommunications.

Two distinctly different types of information services fall within this general category: services which would involve no control by AT&T over the content of the information other than for transmission purposes (such as the traditional data processing services), and services in which AT&T would control both the transmission of the information and its content (such as news or entertainment). Because these two types of services raise different concerns, they will be addressed separately.

A. Data Processing and Other Computer-Related Services

As technology has advanced, the line between communications and data processing has become blurred. Advances in communications technology, for example, now allow otherwise incompatible computers to converse with each other. New sophisticated telephone equipment located on a customer's premises not only performs switching and call routing functions but it also retrieves information much as does a traditional computer. Even ordinary telephones may be capable of performing functions that formerly required the support of a separate computer.

As explained in Part V, *supra*, there is little possibility that AT&T will be able to use its revenues from the interexchange market to subsidize its prices for computer services. That being true, AT&T would not possess any anticompetitive advantages over competitors on this basis.

Since AT&T will be offering its own computer-related services, it may well have an incentive to discriminate in transmitting competitors' services. But what defeats the objections is that AT&T's actual ability to discriminate is quite remote. This segment of the information services industry is already well established, comprised of some of the nation's leading corporate giants, as well as many smaller concerns. The FCC has found that "there are literally thousands of unregulated computer service vendors offering competing services connected to the interstate telecommunications network." These strongly competitive conditions will limit AT&T's ability to practice discrimination in two ways. First, AT&T's competitors will have the economic resources necessary to combat any attempt at discrimination. Second, the growing demand for information services will necessarily increase the demand for transmission facilities for these services. Such an increase in demand is likely to stimulate AT&T's interexchange competitors to offer satisfactory alternatives to the AT&T network, and any attempt by AT&T to discriminate would only further enhance this eventuality.

This fairly limited possibility of discrimination clearly does not outweigh the substantial advantages to the public that would be gained by allowing AT&T to develop this new technology.

B. Electronic Publishing Services

The second type of information service which AT&T would be permitted to provide under the proposed decree are those services in which it would control, or have a financial interest in, the content of the information being transmitted. Those services are generally referred to as electronic publishing or information publishing services. After drawing on various sources, the Court has concluded that, for purposes of this opinion, electronic publishing will be regarded as:

> the provision of any information which a provider or publisher has, or has caused to be originated, authored, compiled, collected, or edited, or in which he has a direct or indirect financial or proprietary interest, and which is disseminated to an unaffiliated person through some electronic means.

While the possibility of cross-subsidization is as remote here as it is with respect to other subjects considered herein, there is a real danger that AT&T will use its control of the interexchange network to undermine competing publishing ventures.

AT&T could discriminate against competing electronic publishers in a variety of ways. It could, for example, use its control over the network to give priority to traffic from its own publishing operations over that of competitors. A second concern is that, inasmuch as AT&T has access to signalling and traffic data, it might gain proprietary information about its competitors' publishing services. Furthermore, it appears that AT&T would have both the incentive and the opportunity to develop technology, facilities, and services that favor its own publishing operations and the areas served by these operations rather than the operations of the publishing industry at large. Similarly, AT&T could discriminate in interconnecting competitors to the network and in providing needed maintenance on competitors' lines. Finally, AT&T might submit tariffs that would have the effect of favoring AT&T's publishing operations to the disadvantage of competing concerns.

AT&T and the Department of Justice provide the same response to these arguments that they make in other contexts: that market forces will curtail AT&T's ability effectively to engage in these practices. However, in the view of the Court, a different conclusion is appropriate here, for the peculiar characteristics of the electronic publishing market would both render anticompetitive acts more damaging to AT&T's competitors in that market and insulate such acts from correction by market forces.

The electronic publishing industry is still in its infancy. Although this business may some day be a very significant part of the American communications system, at present, and most likely for the next several years, a small number of relatively small firms will be experimenting with new technology to provide services to an American public that is, for the most part, still almost totally unfamiliar with them. There can be no doubt that, if AT&T entered this market, the combination of its financial, technological, manufacturing, and marketing resources would dwarf any efforts of its competitors.

It is also readily apparent that competitors in the electronic publishing industry—far more so than competitors in any other industry—could easily be crushed were AT&T to engage in the types of anticompetitive behavior described above. Unlike most products and services, information in general and news in particular are by definition especially sensitive to even small impediments or delays. Information is only valuable if it is timely; by and large it is virtually worthless if its dissemination is delayed. This quality is especially important in electronic publishing because up-to-date information and constant availability are the features likely to be sought by subscribers.

The trial record in the AT&T case reveals many instances when AT&T was slow to respond to the needs of competitors, both in providing essential products or parts and in servicing these products and parts. Any delays of that kind, were they to occur in the context of the transmission of electronic publishing information, would quickly cause subscribers to desert their unreliable publishers and thus cripple AT&T's competitors in that business.

Finally, electronic publishers remain more dependent upon the AT&T network than others in the telecommunications business. In some areas, AT&T is the sole provider of intercity services. Elsewhere, where competition does exist, the other common carriers—although capable of handling voice transmissions—frequently lack the sophisticated facilities necessary to meet the needs of the electronic publishers.

Thus, should AT&T engage in anticompetitive activity, publishers would have no realistic alternative transmission system by which to reach their subscribers. The low level of demand for these services that exists at present makes it unlikely that competing interexchange carriers would construct transmission systems to be used solely for the delivery of electronic publishing services, and publishers would therefore be forced to accept the inferior services provided by AT&T.

Based on competitive considerations alone, therefore, the Court might well be justified in barring AT&T from the electronic publishing industry. Beyond that, AT&T's entry into the electronic publishing market also poses a substantial danger to First Amendment values.

During the last thirty years, there has been an unremitting trend toward concentration in the ownership and control of the media. Diversity has disappeared in many areas; newspapers have gone out of business; others have merged; and much of the flow of news and editorial opinion appears more and more to be controlled and shaped by the three television networks and a handful of news magazines and metropolitan newspapers. Unless care is taken, both the concentration and the attendant dangers will be significantly increased by the new technologies. Indeed, it is not at all inconceivable that electronic publishing, with its speed and convenience, will eventually overshadow the more traditional news media, and that a single electronic publisher would acquire substantial control over the provision of news in large parts of the United States.

It is the intention of the Court to remove the prohibition on electronic publishing at the end of seven years from the entry of the decree should application for such removal be made.[14] That seven-year period should be sufficient for the development of electronic publishing as a viable industry, for the acquisition of sufficient strength by individual publishers adequate to permit them to compete, and for the development of means other than the AT&T network for the transmission of the messages of electronic publishers.

VII. Restrictions on the Divested Operating Companies

The proposed decree limits the Operating Companies, upon their divestiture, to the business of supplying local telephone service. In addition to a general prohibition against the provision of "any product or service that is not a natural monopoly service actually regulated by tariff," there are more specific restrictions that deny the Operating Companies the opportunity to engage in the following activities: (1) the provision of interexchange services; (2) the provision of information services; (3) the manufacture of telecommunications products and customer premises equipment; (4) the marketing of such equipment; and (5) directory advertising, including the production of the "Yellow Pages" directories.

These restrictions are justified, according to the Justice Department, because the Operating Companies will have "both the ability and the incentive" to thwart competition in these markets by leveraging their monopoly power in the intra-exchange telecommunications market. In the absence of the restrictions, it is reasoned, the Operating Companies will be able (1) to subsidize their prices in competitive markets with supra-competitive profits earned in the monopoly market, and (2) to hinder competitors by restricting their access to the intra-exchange network. In short, it is the Department's view that the divested Operating Companies may appropriately be equated with the present Bell System complex in that, if permitted to enter competitive markets, they may be expected to engage in the same type of anticompetitive behavior that was the crux of the AT&T lawsuit.

The government's approach, while not without conceptual neatness, fails to take account of circumstances far more complex than these undifferentiated rules acknowledge. The Bell System is a vast, vertically integrated company which dominates local telecommunications, intercity telecommunications, telecommunications research, and the production and marketing of equipment. Each of the divested Operating Companies will have a monopoly in only one geographic portion of one of these markets—local telecommunications. In addition, the Bell System as presently constituted has few powerful competitors in any of the activities in which it is engaged. The Operating Companies, by contrast, will, if permitted to enter competitive markets, be faced with the most potent conceivable competitor: AT&T itself. Thus, the only similarity between the divested Operating Companies and the present Bell System is that both possess a monopoly in local telecommunications.

A. Interexchange Services

To permit the Operating Companies to compete in this market would be to undermine the very purpose of the proposed decree—to create a truly competi-

---

14. [Ed. Seven years later, the application was made and granted.]

tive environment in the telecommunications industry. The key to interexchange competition is the full implementation of the decree's equal exchange access provisions. *See* Part VIII, *infra*. If the Operating Companies were free to provide interexchange service in competition with the other carriers, they would have substantial incentives to subvert these equal access requirements.

B. Information Services

The proposed decree prohibits the Operating Companies from providing information services, an umbrella description of a variety of services including electronic publishing and other enhanced uses of telecommunications.

All information services are provided directly via the telecommunications network. Here, too, the Operating Companies could discriminate by providing more favorable access to the local network for their own information services than to the information services provided by competitors, and here, too, they would be able to subsidize the prices of their services with revenues from the local exchange monopoly.[15]

There is also the effect on the configuration of the local networks to consider. Many of the competitive problems in the interexchange market resulted from the fact that competition was introduced after AT&T had designed the local networks to service only its own Long Lines department. If the Operating Companies are excluded from the information services market, they will have an incentive, as time goes on, to design their local networks to accommodate the maximum number of information service providers, since the greater the number of carriers the greater will be the Operating Companies' earnings from access fees. Thus, competition will be encouraged from the outset. If, however, the Operating Companies were permitted to provide their own information services, their incentive would be the precise opposite: it would be to design their local networks to discourage competitors, and thus to thwart the development of a healthy, competitive market.

C. Manufacture of Equipment

There is a substantial likelihood that, should the Operating Companies be permitted to manufacture telecommunications equipment, nonaffiliated manufacturers would be disadvantaged in the sale of such equipment and the development of a competitive market would be frustrated. The Operating Companies would have an incentive to subsidize the prices of their equipment with the revenues from their monopoly services as well as to purchase their own equipment, even though it was more expensive and not of the highest quality. In that respect, the Operating Companies lack the competitive restraints that ordinarily prevent the typical vertically integrated company from engaging in such practices: the absence of competition in the end product market—exchange telecommunications—im-

---

15. For similar reasons, the Court rejects the argument that the Operating Companies can most efficiently provide information services by taking advantage of various economies (such as using the same equipment for exchange telecommunications and for information services). It would be impossible to determine at any time whether the Operating Companies' advantages were due to inherent efficiencies, or to efficiencies created by structuring the network so as to hinder competition.

munizes these purchasing decisions from competitive pressures. The Operating Companies therefore would be able to pay inflated prices for poor quality equipment and to reflect these costs in their rates without suffering a diminution in revenues.[16]

Moreover, if they were permitted to manufacture CPE, the Operating Companies would have substantial incentives to favor their own manufacturing arms by providing to them information regarding changes in network standards, thus permitting them to gain an advantage over non-affiliated manufacturers.[17] In addition, they could subsidize the price of this equipment with revenues from the exchange monopoly.

D. Marketing of Customer Premises Equipment

The proposed decree would also prohibit the Operating Companies from selling or leasing customer premises equipment. Given the ban on BOC manufacturing of CPE, this issue arises only if an Operating Company desires to sell equipment made by another firm. Based upon a realistic assessment, marketing of CPE presents little potential for anticompetitive behavior by the Operating Companies.

Anticompetitive activities undertaken by two separate corporations rather than by two components of the same corporation are likely to be far more difficult to accomplish because of increased problems of coordination and the greater possibility of detection. For example, it would be quite difficult for an Operating Company to conspire successfully with a manufacturer to provide advance information about revised network standards or to impose interconnection restrictions which favored that manufacturer's products and no one else's.

Under the proposed decree, AT&T will retain both the embedded customer premises equipment and the existing network of retail outlets. These factors, combined with Western Electric's large market share, will, at a minimum, ensure its continuation as a formidable provider of CPE for a considerable period of time. The Operating Companies, with their existing relationship to telephone users, are more likely than any other competitive entity to provide an effective counterbalance to AT&T's market strength and thereby to promote a genuinely competitive market.

---

16. This rationale does not require the divestiture of Western Electric from the Bell System because AT&T's end products—interexchange services and information services—will be subject to competitive pressures. If AT&T paid a higher price for its equipment and that cost was reflected in higher rates, consumers would switch to a carrier with prices which reflected purchasing decisions based upon the principles of best quality and least cost.

17. The Department of Justice acknowledges that the registration program established by the FCC, see 47 C.F.R. §§68.1, et seq. (1981), would somewhat limit the Operating Companies' opportunities to obstruct the attachment to their networks of equipment manufactured by others. However, it seems possible that, where the Operating Company is the manufacturer of a type of equipment, it would still be able to impose interconnection requirements designed to favor that equipment. In addition, the Operating Companies retain the ability to discriminate against equipment manufactured by others with respect to types of interconnections, testing, maintenance and similar matters.

E. Directory Advertising

The proposed decree would bar the divested Operating Companies from all activities related to directory advertising, including the production of the so-called Yellow Pages.[18] This restriction lacks an appropriate basis and is not in the public interest.

All parties concede that the Yellow Pages currently earn supra-competitive profits. There is no warrant therefore for proceeding on the premise that the advertising prices charged by the Operating Companies are artificially low as the result of a subsidy from local exchange service. Similarly, there is no possibility of improper discrimination by the Operating Companies against competing directory manufacturers since access to the local exchange network is not required for production of a printed directory.

All those who have commented on or have studied the issue agree that the Yellow Pages provide a significant subsidy to local telephone rates. This subsidy would most likely continue if the Operating Companies were permitted to continue to publish the Yellow Pages.

The loss of this large subsidy would have important consequences for the rates for local telephone service. For example, the State of California claims that a two dollar increase in the rates for monthly telephone service would be necessary to offset the loss of revenues from directory advertising. Other states assert that increases of a similar magnitude would be required. This result is clearly contrary to the goal of providing affordable telephone service for all Americans.

F. Removal of the Restrictions

It is probable that, over time, the Operating Companies will lose the ability to leverage their monopoly power into the competitive markets from which they must now be barred. This change could occur as a result of technological developments which eliminate the Operating Companies' local exchange monopoly or from changes in the structures of the competitive markets. Thus, a restriction will be removed upon a showing that there is no substantial possibility that an Operating Company could use its monopoly power to impede competition in the relevant market.

VIII. Equal Exchange Access

One of the government's principal contentions in the AT&T case was that the Operating Companies provided interconnections to AT&T's intercity competitors which were inferior in many respects to those granted to AT&T's own Long Lines Department.

Although after divestiture the Operating Companies will no longer have the same incentive to favor AT&T, a substantial AT&T bias has been designed into the integrated telecommunications network, and the network, of course, remains

---

18. The Operating Companies are appropriately prohibited from producing electronic versions of the Yellow Pages, for the reasons stated in Subpart B.

in that condition. It is imperative that any disparities in interconnection be eliminated so that all interexchange and information service providers will be able to compete on an equal basis.

The governing principle established by the proposed decree is that by September 1, 1986, the Operating Companies must provide access services to interexchange carriers and information service providers which are "equal in type, quality, and price" to the access services provided to AT&T and its affiliates.

XII. Conclusion

The American telecommunications industry is presently dominated by one company: AT&T. It provides local and long distance telephone service; it manufactures and markets the equipment used by telephone subscribers as well as that used in the telecommunications network; and it controls one of the leading communications research and development facilities in the world. According to credible evidence, this integrated structure has enabled AT&T for many years to undermine the efforts of competitors seeking to enter the telecommunications market.

The key to the Bell System's power to impede competition has been its control of local telephone service. The local telephone network functions as the gateway to individual telephone subscribers. It must be used by long distance carriers seeking to connect one caller to another. Customers will only purchase equipment which can readily be connected to the local network through the telephone outlets in their homes and offices. The enormous cost of the wires, cables, switches, and other transmission facilities which comprise that network has completely insulated it from competition. Thus, access to AT&T's local network is crucial if long distance carriers and equipment manufacturers are to be viable competitors.

AT&T has allegedly used its control of this local monopoly to disadvantage these competitors in two principal ways. First, it has attempted to prevent competing long distance carriers and competing equipment manufacturers from gaining access to the local network, or to delay that access, thus placing them in an inferior position vis-a-vis AT&T's own services. Second, it has supposedly used profits earned from the monopoly local telephone operations to subsidize its long distance and equipment businesses in which it was competing with others.

The divestiture of the local Operating Companies from the Bell System will sever the relationship between this local monopoly and the other, competitive segments of AT&T, and it will thus ensure—certainly better than could any other type of relief—that the practices which allegedly have lain heavy on the telecommunications industry will not recur.

With the loss of control over the local network, AT&T will be unable to disadvantage its competitors, and the restrictions imposed on AT&T after the government's earlier antitrust suit—which limited AT&T to the provision of telecommunications services—will no longer be necessary.

The decree will thus allow AT&T to become a vigorous competitor in the growing computer, computer-related, and information markets. Other large and experienced firms are presently operating in these markets, and there is therefore no reason to believe that AT&T will be able to achieve monopoly dominance in these industries as it did in telecommunications. At the same time, by use of its formidable scientific, engineering, and management resources, including particularly the capabilities of Bell Laboratories, AT&T should be able to make significant contributions to these fields, which are at the forefront of innovation and technology, to the benefit of American consumers, national defense, and the position of American industry vis-a-vis foreign competition.[19]

After the divestiture, however, the Operating Companies will possess a monopoly over local telephone service. Therefore, the Operating Companies should be prohibited from providing long distance services and information services, and from manufacturing equipment used in the telecommunications industry. Participation in these fields carries with it a substantial risk that the Operating Companies would use the same anticompetitive techniques used by AT&T in order to thwart the growth of their own competitors. Moreover, contrary to the assumptions made by some, Operating Company involvement in these areas could not legitimately generate subsidies for local rates. Such involvement could produce substantial profits only if the local companies used their monopoly position to dislodge competitors or to provide subsidies for their competitive services or products—the very behavior the decree seeks to prevent.

Different considerations apply, however, to the marketing of customer premises equipment—the telephone and other devices used in subscribers' homes and offices—and the production of the Yellow Pages advertising directories. For a variety of reasons, there is little likelihood that these companies will be able to use their monopoly position to disadvantage competitors in these areas. In addition, their marketing of equipment will provide needed competition for AT&T, and the elimination of the restriction on their production of the Yellow Pages will generate a substantial subsidy for local telephone rates.[20]

Note on the Government's Theory

The two main charges leveled against Bell were predatory cross-subsidization and discriminatory interconnection. The Noll & Owen excerpt *infra* describes these claims in detail, but it is good to review the basics first. To do so, consider two possible competitors to Bell: a firm that manufactures and sells interactive data processing telephones (let's call them "computer phones"), and an ordinary hot dog stand.

(1) *Predatory cross-subsidization.* In both Judge Greene's opinion and the Robinson excerpt from last chapter, the cross-subsidization claim is framed as follows: because Bell was not effectively controlled by price regulation, Bell was able to earn monopoly profits from its ownership of local exchange carriers; Bell could use, or threaten to use, those monopoly profits to subsidize below-cost pricing in other markets. In the context of our simple example, the argument

---

19. [Ed. The court reiterated, however, its view that competitive and First Amendment concerns justified a seven year ban on AT&T's entry into electronic publishing.]

20. The decree also provides for another method of subsidizing these rates. It permits the Operating Companies, under the supervision of state and federal regulators, to levy access charges upon long distance carriers and those companies that provide information services. These charges may, if the regulators desire, be set at levels which continue the present level of subsidy for local telephone rates.

would be that Bell could sell its computer phones below cost due to its monopoly profits from local exchange service, driving out any would-be competitor not on the merits of its computer phone but, instead, simply because Bell had such large cash reserves that it could subsidize this form of anticompetitive behavior.

That characterization of the cross-subsidization argument is problematic, however, in that it implies that Bell could use the same tactic in *any* market. That is, with the kind of cross-subsidization described above, why couldn't Bell use its monopoly profits to subsidize the costs not only of long distance telephony, but also of hot dog production, selling Bell hot dogs at prices below cost and driving Oscar Mayer out of the hot dog business? That, in fact, was not the government's theory; and so it is important to understand how the government's actual argument distinguished computer phones from hot dogs.

The key insight for understanding the government's theory of the case is this: the government's claim is not that Bell could monopolize computer phones because it had a lot of money. It does not ordinarily make sense for a company to sell its products below cost. Even cash-rich firms do not like to waste money. Moreover, if the government feared that Bell would cross-subsidize computer phones because Bell had large revenues, then it should have been suing other firms with lots of money, too—for example, General Motors. The government sued Bell, however, because it had significantly more reason to believe that Bell would spend profits from its local phone service to subsidize computer phones than it did to believe that GM would use its profits from selling pick-up trucks to subsidize GM computer phones.

Why? Well, the government's claim was that Bell could sell computer phones below cost but nevertheless not lose money. Instead, Bell could, as an accounting matter, shift costs from the competitive computer phone market to its regulated local exchange business. If additional costs in the regulated business would simply be factored into the rate base and thereby produce additional revenue in the regulated market (as ordinarily would be the case with rate-of-return regulation), then Bell could both recover its costs incurred in the competitive market and enjoy a competitive advantage in that market.

Here's how the scheme would work. If some of the costs of manufacturing computer phones could show up on Bell's books as costs of running the local exchange service, then the firm could underprice computer phones but recoup the difference by raising local telephone rates. Bell's captive local telephone customers would in essence subsidize prices for Bell's not-at-all-captive computer phone customers. Bell could get away with this cost shifting because the phony costs would be so similar to costs legitimately incurred in the provision of local telephone service that, to some extent at least, Bell's regulators would not notice. Charges related to the production of hot dog buns would be obvious to even the least competent regulator; but costs related to computer phones might be hard to distinguish from costs legitimately incurred in developing and maintaining the local telephone system. That is the subterfuge that makes "cross-subsidization" possible. Bell was in a special situation because it could use a regulated market to subsidize costs from a competitive one—something General Motors, McDonald's, and Oscar Mayer cannot do.

This wrinkle in the cross-subsidy theory is also the theory's Achilles heel: if cross-subsidy is a realistic fear only in cases where it may be difficult to sort out improper from proper cost accounting, then there is always a risk that legitimate cost accounting might be condemned (inadvertently) as predatory. To return to computer phones, suppose that there are economies of scope in making computer phones such that it is cheaper for a firm to make computer phones if the firm also runs a local exchange service. Perhaps, for example, expenditures to design and configure the local telephone network also help a firm to design and configure computer phones. If Bell were to allocate some of these joint costs to local service, is that a predatory act against competing computer phone makers? If not, how will regulators or antitrust authorities know which acts are predatory and which are not? Has the regulated firm engaged in illegal predation every time it allocates costs in a manner that regulators subsequently deem inappropriate?

In any event, note that there are several preconditions that must be satisfied before a firm like Bell has an incentive to engage in predatory cross-subsidization. First, the firm has to have a dominant position in a market where demand is relatively inelastic. That is, the theory requires that the firm raise prices in its regulated market, something the firm would not want to do if those higher prices would cause its customers to leave in droves. Second, rate regulation has to be such that the regulator allows the regulated firm to increase its price only if the firm can show increased costs. Without that link between its asserted costs and the regulated price, the regulated firm would have had no reason to misallocate its costs since claiming higher costs in the regulated market would not accomplish anything for the firm. Third, there has to exist a competitive market with sufficiently overlapping costs such that the firm can incur costs in that competitive market but persuade regulators that those costs should be attributed to the regulated market instead. In Bell's case, for example, the market for hot dogs would not have sufficed. Arguably, however, the markets for computer equipment, CPE, and long distance service did.

(2) *Discriminatory interconnection.* The second major charge leveled against Bell was that Bell used its monopoly over local exchange services to deny competitors in other markets (for example, computer phones) necessary access to the local exchange. The claim, in short, is that Bell raised its rivals' costs; or, in other words, that Bell was able to sell computer phones more cheaply because its costs of interconnection were lower. While subsidization claims focus on cost allocation as an accounting matter, then, discrimination claims focus on engineering and technology issues related to local exchange service itself.

Discriminatory interconnection is relevant only in instances where access to the monopolized telecommunications service (here, the local loop) is crucial to success in some otherwise-competitive market. Thus, if Bell said that only Bell computer phones could be connected to Bell-owned local exchanges, Bell might well gain a monopoly over computer phone sales. People would not want to buy computer phones that could not be connected to the phone system. But Bell could not plausibly threaten to obtain a monopoly in selling hot dogs by refusing to provide phone service to non-Bell hot dog stands. One can operate a hot dog stand without connecting it to the phone system.

An important question to ask when considering the discrimination theory is the question we considered last chapter (that time, in the context of the market for CPE), namely: why would Bell try to expand its monopoly in local phone service provision into some related competitive market? Think, for example, about computer phones. Wouldn't Bell be better off allowing for competitive provision of computer phones, since more competition would lead to better computer phones and hence more demand for local service? Wouldn't Bell have been able to extract the value of any efficiency gains by raising the prices it charged for local phone service? Why not? (Aha!)

Thus, again, it is the fact that Bell was regulated in one market that made anticompetitive behavior attractive in another. If Bell could have exercised its monopoly power unchecked in the local exchange market, it is very possible that Bell would not have engaged in discriminatory interconnection. Competition in computer phones would have led to increased demand for telephone service; and Bell would have adjusted its price and reaped rewards accordingly. Because Bell was constrained in the local exchange market, however, Bell had good reason to try to shift its market power from the regulated market to a competitive one where that power could be exercised more freely.

We consider the MFJ in further detail at the end of this chapter. For now, however, we continue with an excerpt from an article by Roger Noll and Bruce Owen. In it, the authors — both of whom worked with the government on the Bell litigation — explore in more detail the theory behind the government's antitrust case.

III. ANTITRUST THEORIES UNDERLYING THE MFJ

THE ANTICOMPETITIVE USES OF REGULATION: UNITED STATES v. AT&T
Roger Noll & Bruce Owen, *in* THE ANTITRUST REVOLUTION
290, 295–326 (J. Kwoka & L. White, eds., 1989)

The Government's Case

The essence of the government's case against the Bell System was that it had used its status as a regulated monopoly in most of its markets to erect anticompetitive barriers to entry in potentially competitive markets. The novel feature of this line of argument was that much of the Bell System's anticompetitive behavior was economically rewarding to the company only because it was regulated and, consequently, that one arena of public policy, economic regulation, was a cause of illegal acts in another area, antitrust.

The essence of the government's conception of regulation was that regulators did constrain the behavior of the Bell System, but not perfectly. As a result, the Bell companies had an important degree of flexibility in setting prices and deciding which services to provide, and they succeeded in earning profits that, while substantially below the monopoly returns that might be earned in an unregulated market, were nonetheless greater than a firm in a competitive industry could expect.

The importance of the government's perception of how regulation works is very great. If regulation is perfect, in that a firm can never earn more than the competitive rate-of-return and can never incur unnecessary expenditures that benefit managers, or if regulation is completely ineffective so that a firm can evade its constraints without limit, then it is doubtful that the regulated firm would have any financial incentive to engage in the anticompetitive practices that

Bell was alleged to employ. But partially effective regulation creates an entering wedge for attempted evasion of regulatory constraints and for financially lucrative anticompetitive actions. Moreover, as we shall discuss, the methods used by regulators to control profits, costs, and prices actually increase the financial return to some anticompetitive practices.

The Role of Regulation

Although each regulatory agency proceeds to regulate a utility in its own way, all take essentially the same fundamental steps. First, the regulators determine the "rate base"—that is, the stock of capital facilities that the company uses to provide regulated services. The key test is whether a given piece of equipment is "used and useful." This means not only that the equipment is in service, but that it makes sense for the company to be using that equipment, rather than something else. The idea is to force the company to use the right technology for providing services. Once the capital facilities satisfying this test are identified, they enter the rate base at their current book value. Usually, this is their original cost to the utility, less depreciation.

The second step in the process is to determine the firm's cost of capital. The question addressed here is what interest rate on debt and returns on equity investment must the company pay in order to attract the funds necessary to make its investments, and in what ratio of debt to equity? The point of this phase is to guarantee a firm sufficiently high returns to attract investors, but no more.

The third step of the process is to add depreciation and operating costs to the product of the rate base and the allowed rate-of-return. This sum is the "revenue requirement" of the firm, which it is permitted to recover from its customers.

The last step of the process is to set prices. The pricing policy followed by regulators in the telephone industry for several decades has been "residual pricing." Regulators closely scrutinize what they regard as the socially significant (or politically expedient) prices: installation charges and basic monthly service charges for residential customers, and pay-telephone prices. These have been permitted to grow only very slowly, substantially less rapidly than the overall rate of inflation. The regulated firm is then free to set prices for other services (*e.g.*, business local service, toll calls, CPE other than ordinary telephones), subject to the limitation that it must not exceed its overall revenue requirement. Although regulators can control these prices as well, in practice they generally did not. Regulatory agencies rarely even bothered to articulate a policy regarding the price structure for other than the three services regarded as most important.

A key point in the government's arguments was that this process of price regulation did not preclude anticompetitive price increases for customers of telephone companies. Hence, the captive nature of customers to local telephone companies also held the danger that they would face anticompetitive prices. The government argued that this could occur in two important ways. First, state regulators had no way of knowing whether the prices paid for equipment (both CPE and telephone company equipment) were too high. For almost all large local telephone companies and for the Bell System's long distance carrier, equipment was not acquired through competitive bidding, but from a corporate affiliate at posted prices. In the absence of a benchmark of competitive procurement outside of a vertical relationship, regulators had no basis for assessing the reasonableness of equipment prices. If manufacturing affiliates earned excess profits or simply were inefficient, telephone companies would pay too much for equipment. This would translate into a bloated rate base and bloated profits on that rate base. This in turn would raise the firm's revenue requirements and hence prices charged to at least some customers for some services.

The second way in which customers of a regulated monopoly could face prices above the competitive level is through cross-subsidization, which occurs when one group of customers pays part of the cost of providing service to another group. Once again, regulation causes the problem by creating an incentive to use price increases for some monopoly customers to offset losses elsewhere. Suppose that at all feasible prices one market has elastic demand (demand very sensitive to price), while another has inelastic demand (not sensitive to price). If a regulated firm lowers the price in the former, it will increase sales by a relatively large amount, requiring that it commit substantially more capital to that market. But if it increases prices in the latter market, it will suffer a relatively small reduction in sales, and hence a small reduction in capital requirements. Thus, changing both prices simultaneously in this way increases the total required capital that is "used and useful" by the firm. This, in turn, increases the firm's allowed profits. Because regulators do not exercise very close control over most prices, such behavior, within bounds at least, is seldom effectively controlled by regulation.

It is important to emphasize that these strategies become financially rewarding only if regulation is effectively holding down prices in a market in which the firm could otherwise profitably increase its prices. The best possible strategy for a firm is always to raise prices without paying higher costs or lowering prices elsewhere; however, regulation presumably prevents such a straightforward monopolistic practice. If so, inflated equipment prices and cross-subsidization are profitable, if imperfect, substitutes.

Monopolistic Abuses

The government argued that the Bell System retained its virtual monopoly not by superior efficiency, for there was no assurance that the Bell System had settled on the most efficient technology or the least costly means of providing service, but through a series of anticompetitive practices against firms that were willing and able to compete in virtually all of the Bell System's lines of business except local service. The specific charges were: (1) refusals to deal—denial of interconnection to competing services and CPE; (2) discriminatory practices that raised the costs of competitors; (3) abuse of the regulatory process—failures to provide complete information to regulators that sought to promote competition, and the use of regulatory process as a means of retarding entry and raising competitors' costs; and (4) setting prices in a manner designed to exclude competitors and that did not preclude predatory pricing.

Refusals to deal. A major component of the government's equipment case at trial was a set of "horror stories" from competitors to the Bell System about the company's persistent refusal either to buy their products or to permit the Bell System's customers to buy them. In addition, the Bell System refused to permit its customers to own nearly all types of CPE, instead insisting that CPE be leased from the telephone company. Similarly, in the case of competing long distance services, there was evidence that Bell systematically refused to provide rivals with interconnection, or comparable interconnection, with its local facilities.

Prior to divestiture, the Bell System owned either all of or a controlling interest in twenty-three local telephone companies. In all but a few cases, the Bell Operating Companies purchased essentially all of their equipment from Western Electric, the Bell System's manufacturing arm. Hence, the government contended that the Bell System's vertical relationships prevented other manufacturers that produced good equipment at lower prices from taking away the business of Western Electric. The effect was greater sales and higher profits at both ends of the Bell System's business—unregulated equipment manufacture, and regulated telephone service (because higher costs and inelastic demand meant higher allowed profits).

In CPE, the government's case turned on the practices of the Bell System prior to the FCC's decisions in the early 1970s that forced the Bell System to permit its customers to buy equipment from competitors. The Bell System had insisted that CPE posed a serious threat to the integrity of the telephone system and the safety of its employees. Bad CPE, it argued, could emit electrical charges into the network, disrupting the quality of service. Moreover, these charges might be sufficiently powerful that they could electrocute workers attempting to repair the system. Thus, in order to maintain the integrity of the system, the Bell System first insisted that it be permitted to own all CPE, thereby taking responsibility for its quality. This placed the decision about the source of such equipment in the hands of the local Bell Operating Company, which in turn purchased exclusively Western Electric devices.

The Bell System's motives for undertaking such a policy, according to the government's argument, were another by-product of regulation. If local telephone companies owned CPE, the Bell System could earn profits twice for every CPE sale: once at the manufacturing level, and then again as part of the rate base of the local telephone company. In the absence of regulation, the Bell System could have charged monopoly prices for basic telephone service. It would have had no incentive to insist on owning and leasing CPE unless to do so would reduce the customer's cost of service or improve the quality of service (and thereby cause customers to be willing to pay prices that yielded a higher profit). Nor would an unregulated monopoly want to stay in the business of manufacturing CPE if others could do so more cheaply, for expensive CPE would simply reduce the profits it could extract from its telephone monopoly. But once regulation is imposed on telephone services, profits become dependent on costs, and as long as demand is inelastic, higher costs mean greater revenues and greater allowed profits.

Eventually, the FCC required that the Bell System allow its customers to own CPE and to buy it from whomever they pleased. Initially, at the urging of the Bell System and other telephone companies, the local telephone company insisted that it be permitted to require that customers who owned their CPE purchase a "protective" interface device that would prevent dangerous electrical feedback to the network. Eventually, the FCC adopted its own testing procedures whereby CPE could be licensed for interconnection to the nation's telecommunications system without the protective device, and the Commission simultaneously insisted that the Bell System separate its CPE leasing business from other activities. By the time the case came to trial, these policies had opened the doors to a competitive CPE market, and by the time divestiture actually took place, most lines of CPE were highly competitive. Nevertheless, the government used CPE as an illustration of the Bell System's generally anticompetitive corporate policy.

The final example of refusals to deal was the Bell System's actions regarding private telecommunications systems and competitive long distance companies. Again, once the FCC had permitted corporations to own their internal telecommunications systems and to interconnect corporate offices with private, long distance links, the Bell System effectively thwarted this policy for several years by refusing to permit these systems to be connected to its national network. Without interconnection, the large fixed costs of private networks were useful only for intercity intracorporate communications, and not for communications between the same two cities that were directed at people outside the company. Only companies with large corporate facilities in several cities would find a noninterconnected system worthwhile.

The Bell System had lost numerous battles in court and regulatory agencies over its interconnection policies, and by the late 1970s it could no longer deny interconnection without facing the possibility of stiff fines. Nonetheless, it persisted in denying interconnection that had the best technical properties. At the time of trial, the issue of access quality was being litigated at the FCC, and undoubtedly some "equal access" requirement would have emerged from the agency.

Raising costs of competitors. The Bell System's practices in both CPE and long distance interconnection were also cited as discriminatory practices designed to preserve the company's monopoly in these areas. For example, the protective device that the Bell System required for all "foreign attachments"—that is, CPE manufactured by someone other than the Bell System—was expensive, yet, as the FCC's tests proved, totally unnecessary. Some of the government's most devastating evidence was testimony from AT&T employees that, indeed, during the periods in which the Bell System forbade foreign attachments altogether, and then insisted on the protective interface device, the company's own technicians were reporting that the policy was unnecessary. Hence, the requirement to use an expensive interface device amounted to nothing more than a means to make more expensive the use of competitive CPE relative to the Bell System's products. By imposing costs on users of competitive CPE, the Bell System guaranteed that it could retain most of the market even if its prices were higher (but by less than the cost of the interface device), thereby earning supra-competitive profits for products it produced efficiently and lower but positive profits on products that it produced less efficiently than its rivals.

Abuse of process. In presenting its case, the government had to deal with a pervasive problem. Politically legitimate regulatory agencies could in principle have put an end to the Bell System's anticompetitive activities by making appropriate decisions and enforcing them through legal action and franchising decisions. That the agencies had either not done so, or had done so only slowly and cautiously, was attributed in part to the behavior of the Bell System. The essential points were that the Bell System had strategically withheld information that was harmful to its self-interested claims, had purposely entangled its competitors in numerous regulatory and judicial proceedings to inhibit their ability to compete, and had refused to comply with procompetitive regulatory policies that were clearly enunciated by the agencies.

Two examples of refusals to supply relevant information were with regard to the alleged dangers of foreign attachments and the costs of providing competitive services. Throughout the 1950s and 1960s, the Bell System claimed that it had to have control of CPE to protect the network and its employees, yet it also knew these claims to be false for a wide variety of competitive manufacturers. Moreover, the Bell System also claimed that to build an effective interface device to protect the network was technically infeasible. Yet, the Bell System's Bell Laboratories had in fact invented such a device, and when the FCC finally ordered that competitive CPE be permitted with an effective interface, the Bell System was ready to provide it.

The Bell System was also charged with failing to supply regulators with proper cost information for the purpose of determining whether prices proposed in competitive markets were reasonable. The issue first became important when the FCC decided to permit companies to build their own private telecommunications networks. The Bell System responded in 1960 by substantially lowering the price of service for very large customers, essentially offering huge quantity discounts. These prices were controversial, and some charged that they were below cost. The FCC then embarked on an investigation to determine the actual costs of service, but the proceeding dragged on for nearly two decades and was never resolved. The FCC repeatedly found that the Bell System had provided insufficient information to permit the government to determine whether the prices were justified.

The conclusion that this represented a strategic decision to withhold information was clearly incorrect at a superficial level. The Bell System could not have withheld this information, because, as the government learned in the discovery phase of the case, the Bell System did not possess decent cost information itself. Estimates of the costs of components of the Bell System were calculated using computational algorithms developed within the Bell System. The estimates were based on hypothetical configurations of components of the long distance network, with average prices of inputs, rather than with the actual design of real components of the network and the prices actually paid. The estimates were also "bottom up" engineering cost estimates, rather than estimates derived from actual experience in constructing and operating the network. The result was cost estimates that were only loosely related to actual costs of providing service, or even to the actual book costs of the Bell System's local and long distance companies. As a result Bell companies never could answer questions such as "What is the cost of providing local telephone service to households in Cambridge, Massachusetts?" or "What is the cost of a peak-period long distance telephone call from Cambridge, Massachusetts, to Palo Alto, California?" Instead, Bell could only provide hypothetical answers from engineering cost analysis, or average book costs for broad categories of services over large geographic areas.

To claim that this constitutes abuse of process requires arguing not that the Bell System willfully withheld information that its own managers possessed, but that it designed an accounting system that obscured the actual sources of costs within the company. Here the government offered no evidence that Bell consciously adopted a policy of not gathering such information for anticompetitive reasons, but relied instead on arguments that such a policy could serve no other purpose than the anticompetitive benefit it provided. The benefit was that it made the regulator's job of preventing anticompetitive pricing next to impossible. Specifically, if regulators were to impose a price structure on the Bell System that was based on principles of cost causation (*e.g.*, that prices for each service ought to be related to the cost of providing it), they would have to sustain a burden of proof in subsequent court appeals. Without reliable cost data, the best that regulators could do was to require that the company abandon its proposed price structure until it could be supported by data. The company, in turn, could then submit a new proposed set of prices, which under the regulatory statute would go into effect until an evidentiary hearing in support of them was completed. Thus, by failing to collect relevant information, the Bell System prevented regulators from regulating the price structure effectively.

Regulatory agencies were helpless to prevent anticompetitive pricing. Their procedures had been designed with the problem of overcharges in mind. If an FCC investigation of overcharges was underway, the company could be forced by an "accounting order" to keep track of the money received, so that it might later be refunded. But in an investigation of possible below-cost or predatory pricing, these procedures were useless. Nothing could deter the Bell System from continuing to charge the questionable prices until the investigation finally ended, and if the Bell System continually failed to supply necessary information, the investigation could never end.

The final allegation regarding abuse of process was that the Bell System purposely entangled its competitors in needless regulatory and judicial processes before the latter could compete effectively. A principal example was the company's stonewalling tactics regarding interconnection with long distance companies. After the FCC required interconnection, the Bell System continued to deny it on the grounds that state regulatory policy precluded it. This required the competitors to fight the battle in other forums. First, they had to deal with state agencies to attempt to induce them to order interconnection as well, but regardless of the outcome, the issue eventually then ended up in the courts.

The government had to deal with a highly significant problem in this part of the case. The United States Constitution protects the right of citizens (and hence corporations) to plead their cases to government officials and before the courts. A key question, then, is when simple exercise of constitutional rights becomes abuse of process. The government did not argue that the Bell System had no right to appeal FCC decisions, nor to try to get state regulators to undo what the FCC had done. The argument was that the Bell System persisted in using this tactic long after the outcomes were completely predictable. By litigating the issue in a large number of states, the Bell System's use of process was argued to have become abusive after the first few court decisions had ruled (in favor of the competitors) that, indeed, the FCC had the jurisdictional authority to require interconnection and that its ruling had to be obeyed.

Pricing without regard to cost. Because the Bell System did not itself possess reasonably accurate information about the costs of its individual services, one could not prove that it had engaged in predatory pricing, which requires a demonstration that prices are set below some measure of costs. Thus, closely in step with the allegations regarding abuse of process, the government proposed a new variant of an exclusionary pricing claim: "pricing without regard to cost." The central argument was that, as implied by the absence of reasonable cost data, the Bell System set prices for competitive services purely on the basis of competitive market conditions, or more specifically on the basis of an objective to exclude competitors, paying no attention at all to whether prices bore any relation to costs. Thus, Bell's sole pricing goal in competitive markets was to retain a monopoly, regardless of the costs of doing so.

The pricing allegations were made in the context of private line services during the period when the Bell System faced competition on a very limited range of its services. Such pricing behavior clearly would be irrational for an ordinary, unregulated firm. But the Bell System could readily have assumed that losses in these services, even from prices that were a small fraction of cost, would be negligible compared to the Bell System's total revenues and so could readily be made up by increasing regulated monopoly prices by a very small amount. Thus, pricing competitive services without regard to cost was not irrational for the Bell System as long as regulators held its prices and overall return below the level that it would achieve as an unconstrained monopolist. In addition, there was documentary and other evidence that the prices in question were established by Bell System officials who did not consult, or even possess, cost information.

The Bell System price response to competitive entry in long distance was simply to lower prices to whatever level was necessary to keep the market. Not asking whether these prices recovered even marginal costs was consistent with the incentives facing the company. As long as the revenue requirement remained the same, and some services could have their prices profitably raised, it did not matter whether the competitive services were profitable in their own right, and it was reasonable for the Bell System not to worry even about meeting these conditions as long as the competitive sector was a small part of the business.

The implication of this allegation for regulated monopolies is profound. It implicitly confers on regulated firms a positive antitrust obligation to know their costs and to be sure that their prices are not anticompetitive, even if the regulators approve their price structure and do not care whether prices are anticompetitive. The Bell System was not charged with actually setting competitive prices below any cost standard; it was charged with not knowing or caring whether such a cost standard was satisfied and hence introducing the possibility that its prices would fail the cost test for predation.

The reason that the government's argument makes sense as antitrust policy is that if pricing without regard to cost is permitted, it retards all entry, whether warranted or not. A potential competitor with lower costs than the Bell System would be unlikely to enter because of the certainty that no matter how low its costs might be as compared to the Bell System, the Bell System's prices would be set to preserve its monopoly.

Relief

Although the government did not present a detailed relief proposal until the settlement agreement, the principles of the case dictated divestiture. The cornerstone of all aspects of the case was the perniciousness of combining economic regulation with competition. Hence, the regulated parts of the business had to be separated from the unregulated or competitive parts. In theory, this could have meant even more divestiture than that which took place. Because local telephone service was likely to remain a regulated monopoly for the foreseeable future, it had to be quarantined from competitive markets. In addition, at the time of divestiture, long distance service, although subject to some competition, was still dominated by AT&T and regulated by both the FCC (interstate) and the states (for long distance calls within individual states). Hence, an argument could be made for separating AT&T Long Lines, the regulated long distance carrier, from Western Electric, the unregulated equipment manufacturer.

Nevertheless, the government decided not to pursue total dissolution. For one thing, it could not establish that vertical integration between manufacturing and service did not provide some efficiency benefits. Second, with several competitors busily constructing national networks at the time of divestiture, the durability of AT&T's ability to use its remaining vertical connections to damage competition was dubious. The FCC had removed entry restrictions for services subject to its jurisdiction, leaving few, if any, long distance services free of potential competitive discipline. Moreover, a practice of inefficient production and an irrational price structure in a regime of open entry would simply hasten the entry and growth of competitors. Thus, the government was willing to rely on the FCC's decision not to let AT&T have any remaining protected regulated monopolies as sufficient to prevent regulation-induced anticompetitive behavior.

The second aspect of the relief proposal was to decide how many local operating companies to create. Permitting the Bell Operating Companies to remain as a single entity was potentially damaging to the equipment market, for the companies would have considerable monopsony power. In addition, creating multiple operating companies could also assist state regulators. Over the years, differences in the performances of the companies could form the base of more realistic and accurate tests of the efficiency of operations, including the "used and useful" tests for capital investments. Finally, if the quarantine on competitive activities by local service companies were relaxed, one could expect local telephone companies to have some incentive to begin competing with each other in services that had no geographic tie to their franchise areas. Examples are Yellow Pages directories and radio telephone systems, where in fact, after divestiture, the local operating companies have invaded each other's territories to offer competition.

Given that multiple operating companies made sense, the next step was to determine how many there should be. One possibility was to make all the twenty-three Bell Operating Companies separate. Another approach was simply to allow combination up to the point at which the market shares would begin to raise competitive questions. The government opted for the latter, ultimately settling on seven Regional Holding Companies (RHCs)—namely, US West, Pacific Telesis, Southwestern Bell, Ameritech, Nynex, Bell Atlantic, and BellSouth—each of which would operate in several states. This line of argument does not support seven companies, rather than eight or six, and so the final configuration of the divestiture must be regarded as somewhat arbitrary, at least from the perspective of antitrust analysis.

The next issue was to decide where to draw the boundary between the local companies and long distance. The government case at trial implied that the place to divest the local companies was at the local service switch. All calling from one local service area to another would be regarded as long distance and open to competition. During settlement negotiations, however, AT&T convinced government officials that this was impractical. Within metropolitan areas, adjacent local switches often had dedicated trunks connecting them. To allocate these trunks to AT&T rather than the local companies would give it a large number of stand-alone trunks that really were a part of a somewhat expanded local network.

Once the dedicated trunks were assigned to local companies, it was difficult to determine precisely where to draw the line between local and long distance. Whether a pair of switches was connected by a dedicated trunk became a question of the level of demand and hence could be expected to change over time with changes in population, commuting patterns, and the structure of local

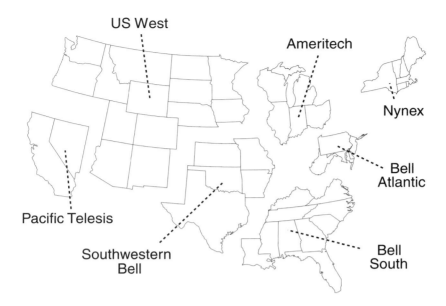

US West

Ameritech

Nynex

Bell
Atlantic

Pacific Telesis

Southwestern
Bell

Bell
South

Figure 16.1. REGIONAL HOLDING COMPANIES. Under the MFJ, seven Regional Holding Companies were established and the local Bell Operating Companies were divided among them.

economies. From this discussion emerged what amounts to a new political jurisdiction: "Local Access and Transport Areas" (LATA), of which there are 160. In each state, the Bell Operating Company was subdivided into one or more LATAs. The center of a LATA is normally a Consolidated Metropolitan Statistical Area. Smaller towns do not have their own LATAs, but instead are adjoined to a larger city somewhere else in the state — not necessarily on the basis of economic integration or even propinquity. Within the LATAs, BOCs can provide long distance service. Between the LATAs, they cannot provide service, whether interstate or intrastate.

The Bell System's Defense

"Defendants contend that modern Bell management accurately perceived the fact that the elimination of competition was an essential element of the creation of an efficient industry structure and necessary for the provision of efficient telephone service."

AT&T proposed stipulation 127, Episode 5/57A.

In broadbrush terms, the Bell System's defenses were as follows:

(1) The Bell System lacked market power because its businesses were subject to regulation by state and federal commissions. These regulators controlled both prices and entry in the telephone business. Hence the Bell System did not meet the legal standard for possession of market power, which courts had held to be "the power to control prices and exclude competitors."

(2) The Bell System had not earned monopoly profits and hence had not exercised monopoly power.

(3) The court had no legal jurisdiction over the issues in the case because only regulators could exercise such jurisdiction.

(4) The specific acts that the government alleged were denied. For example, the Bell System denied that it had abused the regulatory process and denied that it had priced its intercity services below or without regard to cost.

(5) To the extent the Bell System engaged in any anticompetitive behavior, it was inadvertent and excusable in light of the massive and sudden changes taking place in the industry. The telephone industry had been run as a monopoly for many years with the active encouragement of state and federal regulators; the change in policy designed to encourage competition was very recent; and signals from the regulators to the Bell System were ambiguous or contradictory, leaving Bell System employees in great doubt not only as to the permissible nature and extent of competition, but also as to the proper course of behavior for the Bell System in response to entry.

(6) To the extent the Bell System had acted to eliminate competition, its behavior was justified by the natural monopoly characteristics of the telephone industry. The telephone business had economies of scale, scope, and vertical integration that only a monopolist could exploit fully. Dismemberment of the Bell System was an inappropriate and unnecessary remedy, on account of the economies that would be lost.

Several of these defenses are concerned with legal rather than economic issues, and we will not discuss them further except to say that Judge Greene generally rejected these arguments in the course of denying the Bell System's motion to dismiss at the close of the government's case.

The bulk of the economic evidence offered by the Bell System focused on two areas: the pricing of intercity services and the natural monopoly characteristics and historical economic performance of the Bell System. The pricing evidence was designed to show that the Bell System's difficulties in satisfying the FCC's criticisms of its pricing practices did not amount to an antitrust violation because the FCC had adopted the wrong pricing standard. Other evidence was introduced to show that if the correct pricing standard were considered, the Bell System had priced its competitive services above cost. Experts testified that AT&T personnel had carefully and accurately measured costs, so that the company had not priced without regard to cost. The natural monopoly evidence was designed to show that the Bell System's actions in excluding competitors were economically justified and that the Bell System's dissolution would be harmful to consumers.

Research and Development

The Bell System has long operated industrial research facilities of the highest quality, organized as Bell Telephone Laboratories. Bell Labs has been a national leader in all phases of communications R&D, from basic research in physical sciences and mathematics to developmental work in equipment and network architecture. A key element of Bell's defense was that divestiture threatened the continuing excellence of Bell Labs research.

Bell's basic contentions regarding R&D were as follows. First, the ultimate uses of much of Bell's R&D could not easily be predicted in advance. One could not predict whether local service, long distance, or manufacturing would be the principal beneficiary of a given line of research. Divested portions of the company, then, would no longer be able to benefit from some of the products of its research. Hence, facing lower expected benefits, the divested company would undertake less R&D, thereby slowing productivity advances in the industry. This appropriability problem is used to explain the general empirical finding in the economics literature that the private sector tends to invest too little in R&D. Economic theory predicts that a profit-seeking enterprise will invest in R&D up to the point where the marginal cost of further research effort equals the marginal benefit *to the firm* of the results of that effort. If the benefits to the firm are only a fraction of the larger social benefits of R&D, the firm will spend too little on R&D. Applied to a divested AT&T, Bell's argument was that after divestiture Bell Labs would produce some research output that was valuable primarily to its divested operating companies. AT&T would not benefit from these applications and so would have no incentive to invest in producing them.

Second, Bell argued that intra-organizational methods of communication are better suited to designing research projects than inter-organizational relationships. Hence, dissolving the Bell System would reduce the ability of Bell Labs to identify the most promising lines of research from the perspective of the national telecommunications network. The basis of this argument is that, after divestiture, conflicts of interest were likely to emerge between AT&T and its divested operating companies. As a result, each was likely to withhold some potentially important information from the other. Consequently, even if AT&T ignored the appropriability problem arising from research that benefitted the operating companies, it would still be less favorably positioned to undertake the most desirable research projects.

Bell's arguments amount to a defense of the proposition that a monopoly will do more and better R&D than a competitive firm. While both arguments have merit, they are incomplete as an analysis of the economics of R&D in a regulated industry. Empirical economics research provides no factual support for the proposition that monopolists do more or better R&D. As a theoretical matter, the appropriability argument must be augmented by two additional considerations. One is that the optimal R&D by a firm depends on its expectations regarding R&D by its rivals. In an industry with rapidly evolving technology, incomplete appropriability must be balanced against the likely consequences of doing significantly less R&D than a rival, and thereby facing the loss of the entire business. The other is the effect of regulation, which by setting prices on the basis of costs tends to pass the gains from R&D on to customers, though with a lag. Even if the technology, costs, and demand conditions of an industry suggest that a monopoly has a greater incentive to pursue R&D than a competitive firm, it may still be the case that a *regulated* monopolist has less incentive to invest in R&D than an *unregulated* competitor. Because the government's case foresaw competition as a means to relax if not eliminate regulation of long distance services, the latter comparison was the appropriate one.

Moreover, the regulated status of the Bell System could have provided an incentive to invest too much in R&D as a means of preserving monopoly. Like investment in excess capacity, expenditures on R&D constitute a commitment to lower costs and higher quality in the future. Investing too much in R&D—that is, expenditures beyond the point at which a dollar of R&D can be justified on the basis of its expected long term effects on cost and quality of service—can retard warranted entry. If regulators do not, or for informational reasons cannot, force the regulated firm to be efficient in its R&D intensity, the costs of excessive

R&D are simply passed on in regulated prices, thereby imposing little cost on the firm. The benefit, however, is to deter entry, even by firms that are more efficient. Entrants will expect that the incumbent's excessive R&D will eventually erode the entrant's ability to compete.

Which of these arguments is most applicable to the telecommunications industry is a matter of considerable uncertainty. Indeed, probably the least predictable ultimate effect of divestiture is what it will do to R&D in the industry.

Notes and Questions

1. The Importance of Being Regulated. Why was it important to the government's antitrust theory that regulation of Bell was partially, but only partially, successful? What if Bell were completely unregulated? Regulated more effectively?

2. Universal Service or Cross-Subsidization? Was it unfair to hold Bell accountable for cross-subsidization given that "pricing without regard to cost" was in fact what the government's universal service policies themselves required? Did Judge Greene himself endorse cross-subsidization in Part VII(E) of his opinion, at least to the extent that revenues from the sale of advertisements in the Yellow Pages might subsidize local phone service?

3. Other Solutions. Focus on the government's claim that Bell might be using its local phone service monopoly to subsidize its activities in the possibly competitive market for CPE. Instead of solving this problem by divestiture, could the government have solved it by switching to price cap regulation (a concept introduced in Chapter Ten) in the market for local exchange service? Alternatively, could the danger have been eliminated by somehow introducing competition into the market for local exchange service? What about by allowing new entry into the market for CPE?

4. Local Service. Under the terms of the MFJ, was post-divestiture AT&T allowed to offer local telephone service to its customers, or was AT&T instead limited to providing only interexchange service? Is your answer here consistent with the government's theory of the case?

5. Restrictions Post-Divestiture. In Part V(A) of his opinion, Judge Greene considers the possibility of imposing restrictions on AT&T even after divestiture of the BOCs. He summarizes the argument in favor as follows:

> Virtually all those who suggest that restrictions beyond those in the proposed decree be imposed on AT&T make the same general arguments. Their basic claim is that AT&T still possesses monopoly power in the interexchange market and that it will leverage this power by cross-subsidizing its competitive services with monopoly revenues. These interexchange revenues, it is said, will subsidize a variety of business activities, ranging from competitive interexchange routes to equipment manufacturing to alternative local distribution facilities.

First, does the above language convince you that Judge Greene understood the cross-subsidy argument, or does this passage instead suggest that Greene wasn't clear on the difference between the government's theory and standard arguments about predatory pricing? Second, either way, was Judge Greene's decision here correct? As you will recall, he ultimately did not impose any additional restrictions (except with respect to electronic publishing), his logic being that AT&T would not possess market power in the interexchange market after divestiture. Is he right that the absence of market power obviates any worries about cross-subsidization?

6. Bell's Domination. Relatedly, note that in Part IV(A) of his opinion, Judge Greene states that an additional reason for antitrust action against Bell is its "substantial domination of the telecommunications industry in general." What does this add to the arguments based on cross-subsidization and discriminatory interconnection? If a firm had a large market share but no ability to engage in cross-subsidization or discriminatory interconnection, would antitrust relief against that firm nonetheless be appropriate? If so, then why did Judge Greene leave AT&T a unified interexchange company with its massive market share in interexchange service, and why did he leave the BOCs with monopolies in the local exchanges? What further steps might he have taken to reduce the "vast economic power" of these companies, if such power alone was an independent concern?

7. "The Most Potent Conceivable Competitor." Elsewhere in the opinion (specifically, Part VII), the judge considers whether the divested Bell Operating Companies should be restricted to providing only local exchange service. According to the judge, the government thought so, its fear being that these firms would, if left unchecked, themselves adopt anticompetitive cross-subsidization and predatory interconnection policies. Did Judge Greene find this argument compelling? Should he have? In calculating the desirability of such restrictions, does the judge place too little emphasis on the fact that, whereas before divestiture there was only one AT&T, after divestiture there would be seven RHCs made up of a total of twenty-three BOCs? Is this what the judge means when he criticizes the government for failing to take into account "circumstances" that distinguish the Bell situation from the situation facing the divested BOCs? And what is he getting at when he points out that the BOCs "will, if permitted to enter competitive markets, be faced with the most potent conceivable competitor: AT&T itself"? Does the existence of this extra competition really decrease the opportunity for cross-subsidization or discriminatory interconnection?

8. The First Amendment. In Part VI(B), Judge Greene invokes "a substantial danger to First Amendment values" as an independent, and apparently significant, reason to prevent AT&T from entering the electronic publishing market for a period of seven years. Is his invocation of and reliance on these First Amendment values persuasive? Is his articulation of First Amendment values consistent with *Tornillo*? With *Red Lion*? (Both cases were discussed at length in Chapter Six.)

9. Equal Access. Part VIII of the MFJ is labeled "equal exchange access" and, in this section, Judge Greene considers the obligations to be imposed upon the Bell Operating Companies with respect to their treatment of IXCs. Judge Greene points out that, prior to divestiture, significant "bias [had] been designed into the integrated telecommunications network" and thus, in Judge Greene's view, it was "imperative that any disparities in interconnection be eliminated so that all interexchange and information service providers will be able to compete on an equal basis." Equal access rules were the decree's means for accomplishing just that, ensuring that AT&T would not enjoy an artificial advantage in the long distance market after divestiture. As the Commission later explained the rule:

> Equal access not only ensured that IXCs would receive equal transmission quality, but also that callers would have the opportunity to pre-sub-

scribe their telephones to an IXC other than AT&T. Before the advent of equal access, all interstate...calls dialed on a 1+ basis were routed to AT&T. A caller could reach an [alternative carrier] only by dialing a seven-digit phone number, as well as an often-lengthy identification code, prior to dialing the called number. Equal access enabled callers to select a carrier other than AT&T to provide them long-distance phone service on a simple "1+" dialing basis. Moreover, the balloting process through which equal access was implemented educated customers as to the availability of alternative suppliers of telecommunications services and encouraged them to make a choice among IXCs.

In re Competition in the Interstate Interexchange Marketplace, 5 FCC Rcd. 2627, at ¶41 (1990).

The BOCs were not the only local exchange carriers required to grant equal access to long distance companies. In 1985, the FCC extended that obligation to all independent local exchange carriers,[21] basing its decision in part on a 1983 consent decree between the government and a large independent LEC in which that LEC had, like the BOCs in the MFJ, agreed to provide equal access.[22] The Commission's 1985 decision thus evened the playing field, applying the same equal access requirement to all LECs whether they were subject to a particular consent decree or no.

10. Alternatives to the MFJ. Overall, were preferable alternatives to the breakup of the Bell System overlooked? How about:

(a) Confining the relief to divestiture of Western Electric and Bell Laboratories (to rid Bell of its incentive to monopolize CPE) and adoption of the equal access rules in the decree (to level the playing field in the long distance market).

(b) Going through with divestiture, but refusing to shackle the new BOCs.

(c) Leaving all of these issues to the FCC. The Commission could continue its technical registration program for CPE; develop and implement equal access rules for long distance service providers; monitor Bell's prices and costs; and so on.

(d) Spending these energies on attacking the problem at its source—the absence of competition in the local exchange service. (Does the recent growth of cellular telephone and cable television services suggest that this might have been a fruitful strategy?)

(e) Treating the phone system as we treat highways: have the government (or a private/public corporation) build and operate the network of wires and switches, and leave the provision of equipment and services to others.

11. LATAs. As Noll and Owen explain in the excerpt, under the MFJ, telephone service was broken into small geographic regions called "Local Access and Transport Areas" (LATAs). Calls that originated and terminated within a single LATA were called "intraLATA" and they were to be carried by the relevant local phone company—either a divested Bell Operating Company or an unaffiliated

---

21. In re MTS and WATS Market Structure Phase III, 100 FCC 2d 860 (1985).
22. *Id.* at ¶9 (discussing GTE decree).

competitor. IntraLATA calls could show up on customer bills as local calls, but they could also show up as "in-state long distance"; the precise rates and categories were determined by the local phone company subject to approval by the applicable state public utility commission. InterLATA calls, by contrast, were calls that crossed LATA boundaries. BOCs, and the Regional Holding Companies (RHCs) that owned the BOCs, were forbidden to carry interLATA traffic, and so these calls had to be handed off to interexchange carriers (IXC) like MCI, Sprint, and the post-divestiture AT&T. One way to think about LATAs is to remember that the MFJ in essence quarantined the local telephone market, and LATAs were the boundary lines of that quarantine.[23]

12. Vocabulary. The MFJ created seven regional holding companies (RHCs). Some people refer to these firms as the "Baby Bells" since they are small versions of the original Bell Company. Other people refer to these firms as the "Regional Bell Operating Companies" or RBOCs, this phrase emphasizing the fact that RHCs own and operate several, usually contiguous, BOCs. Thus, the acronym RBOCs and the phrase "Baby Bells" both refer to the same entities, the RHCs.

---

23. Under the MFJ, LATAs were established according to the following criteria: (1) LATAs were to "encompass one or more contiguous local exchange areas serving common social, economic, and other purposes, even where such configuration transcends municipal or other local governmental boundaries"; (2) "every point served by a BOC within a State" had to be included in one and only one LATA; (3) no LATA "which includes part or all of one standard metropolitan statistical area (or a consolidated statistical area, in the case of densely populated States) shall include a substantial part of any other standard metropolitan statistical area (or a consolidated statistical area, in the case of densely populated States), unless the Court shall otherwise allow"; and (4) except with approval of the Court, no LATA located in one State was to include "any point located within another State." 552 F. Supp. at 229.

CHAPTER SEVENTEEN

ISSUES POST-DIVESTITURE

The purpose of this chapter is:

- to introduce three key issues that were on the regulatory agenda between divestiture and the passage of the Telecommunications Act of 1996, namely: rate regulation reform, implementation of the MFJ's line of business restrictions, and a restructuring of universal service.

∼

The Modification of Final Judgment might sound as if it was a document designed to end the Bell antitrust litigation; but, in reality, all parties to the case knew that the MFJ would need to be adjusted over time. Experience would teach which restrictions were too broad or too onerous, and changes in market conditions would make some once-reasonable restrictions unnecessary in later years. To handle all this, Judge Greene maintained significant flexibility both to eliminate decree provisions and to grant specific waivers, either in response to a request by one of the parties or completely of his own accord. The Bell System divestiture thus remained on Judge Greene's docket from 1982, the year he first approved the consent decree, until 1996, when the Telecommunications Act of 1996 explicitly took Judge Greene out of the telecommunications business.[1] It is not an overstatement, then, to say that the MFJ not only introduced a new structure to the telecommunications industry but also introduced a new regulator. Judge Greene was, for fourteen years, a one-man Federal Telephony Commission—advised by the FCC and the Department of Justice, but personally exercising enormous power over the industry.

In this chapter, we consider three big issues that were on the regulatory agenda during those fourteen years. First, we look at rate regulation. Even after divestiture, consumers were still vulnerable to market power. Although the decree opened the long distance market to competition, AT&T would still for some time dominate that market. And the local Bell Operating Companies, while no longer part of the large Bell monopoly, nonetheless were still monopoly providers in their respective service territories. So consumers in both the local and long distance markets faced the danger of monopoly pricing even after Bell was broken up. Traditionally, the FCC and the state regulatory commissions sought to avoid

---

1. For a discussion of the standards by which Judge Greene was to evaluate any proposed waivers or modifications, *see* Huber et al., Federal Communications Law 386–391 (2d ed. 1999).

monopoly pricing by regulating phone companies' rates of return. The materials in the first section of this chapter survey the FCC's struggle with rate-of-return regulation during the post-divestiture period, a struggle that ultimately led to the adoption of price cap regulation, at least with respect to core services provided by dominant carriers.

Another post-divestiture issue, foreshadowed by Judge Greene's ruling, was how to prevent the spun-off Bell Operating Companies from repeating Bell's alleged policies of discriminatory interconnection and predatory cross-subsidization. One method to limit the BOCs' potential for anticompetitive behavior would have been to reduce their market power by introducing local competition. But the consent decree assumed that local monopolies in phone service were inevitable, and so the "solution" to BOC market power embodied in the MFJ was instead to limit substantially the lines of business, other than the provision of traditional telephone service, that the BOCs would be permitted to pursue. The second set of materials in this chapter traces the subsequent history of those restrictions. The FCC adopted different responses to the question of reining in the BOCs; its principal conclusions are treated in the Ninth Circuit's review of the Commission's *Computer III* decision.

Finally, universal service was an issue of extraordinary import in the post-divestiture world. When the Bell System was intact, universal service could be handled implicitly by keeping some rates below cost and others above cost. Long distance rates, for example, could be inflated as a way of subsidizing the costs of local service. This was all relatively easy to do since, before divestiture, the same firm offered both long distance and local service, and thus universal service was mainly about moving money from one of Bell's pockets to another. Divestiture changed all that, of course, and so the Commission had to find new ways of moving revenues from long distance carriers (like the post-divestiture AT&T) to local exchange carriers (for example, the newly independent BOCs). The third subsection below thus considers two new approaches to universal service that came into existence at this time: the subscriber line charge (SLC) and access charges.

I. RATE REGULATION IN A POST-DIVESTITURE WORLD

As explained above, constraining the market power of both AT&T and the newly independent Bell Operating Companies remained a major regulatory concern in the wake of the Bell divestiture. The worry was that, if left unregulated, both the BOCs and AT&T would exercise some degree of monopoly power in their respective markets.[2] The then-traditional way of restraining monopoly power was "rate-of-return" regulation, but even before divestiture the FCC had

---

2. This concern was probably more significant for the BOCs, since they were still monopolist providers of local telephone service. AT&T, by contrast, did enjoy certain competitive advantages thanks to its long association with the Bell System, but its market power was surely less than that of the BOCs due to incipient competition in the long distance market from both Sprint and MCI.

begun to realize that this approach was both costly and ineffective. The materials that follow show how the Commission mitigated these concerns in the years after divestiture by switching from rate-of-return regulation to the incentive-based method known as "price cap" regulation. Price caps, introduced in Chapter Ten, avoid many of the pitfalls inherent in rate-of-return regulation in that price caps are not as directly tied to the regulated party's costs. Price caps therefore dampen the incentive to cross-subsidize and also (in theory at least) empower the regulator to regulate effectively even in cases where the regulated party is uncooperative when it comes to sharing information about the regulated activity.

IN RE POLICY & RULES CONCERNING RATES FOR DOMINANT CARRIERS

4 FCC Rcd. 2873 (1989)

I. INTRODUCTION

1. We have been evaluating our current approach to regulating dominant carriers' rates for interstate basic service offerings to determine if our policies continue to further the objectives they originally were designed to achieve.[3] Our current approach is based on the following theory: that limiting a dominant carrier's profit on invested capital to "normal" levels is the most effective means of restraining its market power, enhancing consumer welfare, and furthering the public interest in just, reasonable, and non-discriminatory rates. For more than twenty years we have been administering an increasingly elaborate regulatory system based on this theory. During that time circumstances in telecommunications markets have changed dramatically. Our examination of these changes and our experience administering this system lead us to conclude that our approach actually impedes, rather than facilitates, the achievement of our statutory goals with regard to the regulation of the American Telephone and Telegraph Company (AT&T) and local exchange carriers (LECs).

2. We also have been considering whether our statutory goals are more likely to be achieved by implementing an alternative regulatory approach, commonly referred to as incentive regulation. In comparison with existing regulation, this approach is more likely to help strengthen the competitiveness of American industry in domestic and international telecommunications markets, and, most importantly, help ensure that consumers share in the benefits of the information age through lower rates and a wide array of high quality services.

3. In this *Order*, we find that incentive regulation represents an improvement over our existing regulation of AT&T and the LECs. We adopt rules implement-

---

3. [Ed. When the Commission refers to "dominant carriers" in this report, it means AT&T and the local exchange carriers. These are the firms that the Commission regards as having sufficient market power to require some form of rate regulation. "Non-dominant carriers," such as MCI or Sprint, are not subject to such regulation because the Commission determined that it would "forbear" from exercising its authority to regulate these non-dominant carriers. That decision to forbear was ultimately challenged in the Supreme Court. *See* MCI v. AT&T, 512 U.S. 218 (1994).]

ing incentive regulation for AT&T on a mandatory basis and take the first tentative steps toward adopting price cap regulation for dominant LECs as well.

A. Procedural History

7. In the *Notice of Proposed Rulemaking* that initiated this proceeding, we tentatively concluded that the existing approach to rate regulation is flawed for several reasons. Foremost among them: that current regulation does not encourage the kinds of economically efficient behavior by dominant carriers that result in cost savings, product innovations, and, ultimately, lower rates for consumers. We also determined that rate-of-return regulation is particularly counterproductive when applied in markets characterized by emerging competition.

8. In the *Notice*, we considered a different approach to regulating dominant carriers, one that presents such carriers with a more consumer-oriented set of incentives than exist under rate-of-return. We referred to this approach as "price caps" because its implementation entails placing limits on the rates carriers may charge for their services. In the face of such restraints, a carrier's profit level would be tied directly to its management of underlying costs and its responsiveness to consumer demand. Carriers that improved efficiency and responded to consumer demand effectively would see their profits rise. Carriers that failed to achieve these results would see their profits fall. We proposed to adjust price caps each year according to a predetermined formula that is designed to ensure a continuing nexus between tariffed [that is, public and approved] rates and the underlying cost of providing service. We also demonstrated that the formula would provide carriers with an incentive to reduce their total costs and rates each year to levels lower than existing regulation could be expected to produce — thus assuring that consumers would benefit from price cap regulation.

12. In a *Further Notice of Proposed Rulemaking* we tentatively found that our current practices are expensive and difficult to enforce, and create incentives for carriers to pad their costs, forego efficient innovation, and cross-subsidize services in ways that harm ratepayers and the competitive process. We considered arguments that incentive regulation is unsuitable for LECs due to the lack of competitive alternatives for the services they offer, and we tentatively found such arguments unsupported in theory and at odds with record evidence of successful administration of incentive-based regulation of LECs at the state level and in the United Kingdom.

14. The record compiled in response to the *Further Notice* supports our tentative conclusion that price caps represent a regulatory approach that is superior to rate-of-return because price caps are better suited to encouraging efficiency and innovation in the provision of services and, thus, are better able to satisfy the goals of regulation as set forth in the Communications Act.

B. Background and Summary of Order

1. Synopsis of Historical Dominant Carrier Regulation

[This portion of the *Report and Order*, covering paragraphs 16–28 and summarizing the FCC's experience under rate-of-return regulation, is reprinted in Chapter Fifteen and thus is omitted here.]

2. The Rate-of-Return System

29. In theory, rate-of-return regulation is intended to replicate competitive market results. However, there are many differences in the manner in which rate-of-return regulation and competitive forces operate. Competition holds each firm to "normal" profit levels as a result of a dynamic process that operates over time — a firm strives to maximize profits and secure advantage over other firms by responding to consumer demand effectively. Under rate-of-return, however, "normal" profit levels are established in advance by regulatory fiat. The dynamic process that produces socially beneficial results in a competitive environment is strongly suppressed. In fact, rather than encourage socially beneficial behavior by the regulated firm, rate-of-return actually discourages it.

30. The distorted incentives created by rate-of-return regulation are easily illustrated. In a competitive environment, where prices are dictated by the market, a company's unit costs and profits generally are related inversely. If one goes up, the other goes down. Rate-of-return regulation stands this relationship on its head. Although carriers subject to such regulation are limited to earning a particular percentage return on investment during a fixed period, a carrier seeking to increase its dollar earnings often can do so merely by increasing its aggregate investment. In other words, under a rate-of-return regime, profits (*i.e.*, dollar earnings) can go up when investment goes up. This creates a powerful incentive for carriers to "pad" their costs, regardless of whether additional investment is necessary or efficient. And, because a carrier's operating expenses generally are recovered from ratepayers on a dollar-for-dollar basis, and do not affect shareholder profits, management has little incentive to conserve on such expenses. This creates an additional incentive to operate inefficiently. Moreover, in situations in which carriers providing more than one service face competition for one or more of such services, rate-of-return regulation enables carriers to distort the competitive process by manipulating their reported cost allocations.

31. A system that establishes such incentives is unlikely to encourage efficiency. Moreover, administering rate-of-return regulation in order to counteract these incentives is a difficult and complex process, even when done correctly and well. This is so primarily for two reasons. First, such regulation is built on the premise that a regulator can determine accurately what costs are necessary to deliver service. In practice, however, a regulator may have difficulty obtaining accurate cost information as the carrier itself is the source of nearly all information about its costs. Furthermore, no regulator has the resources to review in detail the thousands of individual business judgments a carrier makes before it decides, for example, to install a new switching system.

32. The second inherent difficulty associated with administering rate-of-return regulation relates to its requirement that determinations be made about how to allocate a carrier's costs among services that often are provided jointly or in common. Such determinations tend to become more economically problematic as they become more detailed. A cost allocation system can present a strong deterrent to anticompetitive activity and, at the same time, be so detailed and rigid that it imposes on a carrier a complex and inflexible rate structure, one that may have little relation to consumer demand. If such a rate structure is deployed in a competitive environment, it may result in distorted consumption decisions, distorted production decisions, and distortions of the competitive process.

34. We have every reason to expect, moreover, that the telecommunications industry will continue to be marked in the future by the same steady technological advancement it has demonstrated in the past. This will lead to greater competition than at present and a continuing shift in the boundaries between the competitive and less competitive segments of the telecommunications marketplace. Notwithstanding this technological change and growing competition, we could continue our current practice of implementing cost allocation systems that present strong deterrents to anticompetitive activity associated with those boundaries, but it will become increasingly difficult to obtain these benefits while concomitantly holding to a minimum the costs such deterrents impose on society. We conclude, therefore, that it is prudent to implement regulatory systems that are better able than rate-of-return to operate effectively in an environment marked by competition and technological change.[4]

3. The Incentive System

36. The attractiveness of incentive regulation lies in its ability to replicate more accurately than rate-of-return the dynamic, consumer-oriented process that characterizes a competitive market. In general, such regulation operates by placing limits on the rates carriers may charge for services. In the face of such constraints, a carrier's primary means of increasing earnings are to enhance its efficiency and to innovate in the provision of service. Because cost padding and cross-subsidization do not justify higher prices under this system—but instead lower profits—the incentives to engage in such activity are limited. The system also is less complex than rate-of-return regulation and easier to administer in the long run, which should reduce the cost of regulation.

37. Because cost allocation requirements do not play as central a role under incentive regulation as they do under rate-of-return, incentive regulation represents a more effective method of policing shifting industry boundaries than rate-of-return. The restraints on price increases become less significant when competition develops because competitive forces hold prices down while the pricing limitations offer consumers strong protection against attempted exercises of market power.

---

4. The difficulties of policing the shifting boundaries of the telecommunications industry are not eliminated even by very strong attempts to establish regulatory boundaries, such as by establishing structural conditions on market entry or restricting market entry altogether. For example, divestiture was an attempt to draw a very distinct boundary between more and less competitive telecommunications services. The basic theory of the antitrust case which resulted in the divestiture was that the local exchange constituted a bottleneck that provided a base from which monopoly power could be extended to the adjacent long distance market. By separating local exchange from interstate toll operations, it was thought that competition could flourish in the potentially competitive latter segment of the market, and all competitors could draw on the services of carriers operating in the former segment of the market. United States v. Western Electric, 569 F. Supp. 990 (1983). The boundary drawn between what was thought to be the "bottleneck" and the more competitive portions of the Bell System, however, has proven to be far less precise than originally supposed. Competition is beginning to take root in a few segments of the local exchange market, particularly regarding the provision of services to the high end of that market (e.g., provision of high-capacity lines to large users of telecommunications services). AT&T, moreover, retains significant market power in portions of the long distance market.

38. The incentive regulatory approach adopted for tariff review purposes in this *Order* for AT&T and proposed for the LECs operates according to the following model. A carrier's services are grouped together in accordance with common characteristics, and the weighted prices in each group are adjusted annually pursuant to formulas designed to ensure that rates are based on the cost of providing service. The formulas provide for adjustments similar to those carriers make to their rates under the current system. For example, all carriers currently adjust their rates in accordance with changes in their input costs. Our formulas accomplish the same result, measuring such changes with reference to the Gross National Product Price Index (GNP-PI), a government-administered index that reflects broad-based input cost changes experienced by dominant carriers more accurately than the Consumer Price Index. We also will continue under price caps the current policy of adjusting rates for known cost changes, such as those caused by regulatory decisions, that are beyond a carrier's direct control. For example, AT&T's rates will be adjusted to reflect regulatory changes, such as changes in the level of access charges.

39. Although the GNP-PI already reflects productivity gains for the economy as a whole, it does not reflect the degree of productivity gains experienced by the telecommunications industry historically. The telecommunications sector has been more productive than the economy as a whole. A number of long term historical studies of pre-divestiture Bell System productivity persuade us that, on a long term basis, productivity has been approximately 2.1 percent per year higher than the general economy. Our analysis of AT&T's price changes during the post-divestiture period indicates that AT&T's productivity differential since 1984 has been approximately 2.3 percent per year. Because we are sufficiently impressed with evidence of the more recent trend in telecommunication productivity indicating a productivity level slightly above the long term view, and because we wish to err, if we must, on the side of consumers, we have decided that AT&T's productivity factor under our plan should be 2.5 percent per year.

40. For the LECs, we similarly found that the available data suggest a long term historical productivity differential of slightly over 2 percent per year above the general economy, with a slightly higher differential in the more recent period. Unlike for AT&T, however, we are unable to corroborate to the same degree the LECs' productivity experience since divestiture. Because of this and possible variations in individual LEC productivity around the industry average, we tentatively have decided to proceed with a 2.5 percent productivity factor, while proposing other adjustments to LEC aggregate prices in order to ensure just and reasonable rate levels.

41. The downward pressure on rates exerted by the 2.5 percent productivity offset assures that consumers will be as well off under caps as they likely would have been under rate-of-return. Because our goal is to make consumers better off under price caps than they likely would be if we continued rate-of-return regulation, however, our plan requires carriers to meet goals that exceed the historic productivity of the telephone industry. In addition to the 2.5 percent adjustment noted above, carriers would be required to lower rates by another 0.5 percent—an amount we refer to as the Consumer Productivity Dividend—in order to ensure that consumers receive a guaranteed, up-front share of the additional efficiencies flowing from the improved incentives created by price cap regulation.

42. In effect, the price cap rate adjustment formula establishes a rule of thumb to use in evaluating a carrier's performance for tariff review purposes: a benchmark. The rates filed by carriers are self-initiated, but the relationship of those filed rates to the price cap formula will trigger various types and levels of Commission scrutiny. If a carrier achieves results superior to this benchmark as a result of its own initiative, it is permitted to keep the resulting profits, at least for a while. If a carrier claims that it cannot achieve the benchmark, we will suspend its tariff revisions and examine its proffered justification. Suspension and investigation is a reasonable response to such an event because the benchmark is based in part on a measurement of carriers' past performance, calculated on a long run basis, and failure to achieve that level of performance is legitimate grounds for inquiry. After the fourth year of the plan, the mark is subject to adjustment as a result of our comprehensive review of the price cap system, which will be conducted in light of the information the carrier reveals about itself in the course of operating pursuant to the plan. This ensures that consumers will be the beneficiaries of all achieved efficiencies.

43. In addition to lower rates, consumers will receive other benefits as a result of incentive regulation implemented through price caps. First, for example, they will receive assurances of rate stability that do not exist under existing regulation. These assurances result from banding limitations that mark the boundaries of potential annual price changes that would be permitted without triggering detailed investigation through the tariff process. Second, price cap regulation should spur innovations that result in consumers enjoying a wider range of high quality services at cost-effective prices. This spur to innovation should occur because, quite simply, carriers operating under price caps can make more money in the short term than under existing regulation if they respond to consumer demand for more and better services. And these are just the direct consumer benefits. The incentives for greater efficiency and innovation established by price caps should provide indirect benefits for society as a whole. Increased productivity will make the telecommunications industry more competitive both at home and abroad. In addition, a system that promotes efficiency and innovation has the indirect effect of lowering the cost of non-telecommunications goods and services because telecommunications services are a significant and growing input of the economy generally.

47. Many forces constrain a carrier's ability to degrade its quality of service. First, cutting back on quality does not necessarily increase profits because permitting the network to deteriorate would ultimately reduce the number of completed calls and, therefore, a carrier's revenues. A second practical restraint is that quality declines manifest themselves readily. No customer needs special training to detect an increase in busy signals, wrong numbers, or static on the line. And as this Commission demonstrated in the post-divestiture period when such complaints were made, we can respond swiftly and effectively to customer complaints about quality. A third restraint is that competition in the long distance market has turned quality into an important selling point, indicating that AT&T could permit quality to decline only at peril to its market position.

50. As adopted in this *Order*, AT&T services used primarily by residential customers are placed in their own basket. Separating such services in this manner ensures that residential customers will receive a larger proportion of expected

AT&T future productivity achievements than would be guaranteed under the proposal in the *Further Notice* or under existing regulation.

51. We also have grouped AT&T's remaining services into two baskets, according to an evaluation of the degree of competition AT&T faces in the provision of such services. All of these services are targeted primarily toward business customers. The record reflects a persuasive consensus that AT&T faces varying degrees of competition for such services, and that they should be separated accordingly. Consequently, we have created a separate basket for 800 services, in which AT&T retains substantial market power. All other AT&T business services—those provided in what the majority of commenters agree is the most competitive segment of the telecommunication market—are grouped together in what constitutes the third "service basket" contained in our plan. Grouping services in this fashion provides greater assurances than exist under existing regulation that AT&T will not raise prices for services for which it retains substantial market power and use revenues generated thereby to fund price decreases for other, more competitive services.

52. Because these changes in the structure of the baskets in our price cap plan significantly reduce AT&T's ability to shift costs among its various services, they also enable us to place upper and lower banding limitations on service categories. The upper band constitutes a service category price ceiling which AT&T must establish substantial cause to pierce. The lower band constitutes a price "floor." AT&T may propose service category rate decreases lower than 5 percent, but such a proposal must be accompanied by cost materials demonstrating that the proposed reduction is not predatory.

Notes and Questions

1. The Basics. Chapter Ten includes a lengthy and thorough discussion of the advantages and disadvantages of both rate-of-return and price cap regulation, there specifically in the context of cable rate regulation. Readers might want to review that discussion before proceeding here.

2. Telephone vs. Cable. As compared to its application in other industries, is rate-of-return regulation particularly difficult or undesirable in the telephone setting? For example, one problem with rate-of-return regulation is that the regulator has to be able to police all of the firm's operating and capital expenditures in order to ascertain that all are efficient rather than inefficient attempts to pad costs at consumers' expense. In the cable context, we saw the Commission attempt to mitigate this problem by examining the costs incurred in communities where cable faced what the Commission deemed to be "effective" competition. Would a similar approach work here? In cable, we also pointed out that such comparisons would not work with respect to new services. What does the FCC say about that problem in the telephone context?

3. Costs Shared by Multiple Products. The general theory behind rate-of-return regulation does not tell us very much about how common costs should be allocated among various intertwined products. For example, how should a regulator assign the capital costs of installing, and the operating costs of maintaining, a local switch that will be used to provide local, long distance, and 800 number services? This is a particularly important question in instances where one of those services is subject to competition (here, long distance) but the others are not. In such a case, after all, the regulated firm has an incentive to allocate the bulk of the common cost to the monopolized service, thereby enhancing its ability to underprice rivals in the competitive market while simultaneously tricking the regulator into thinking that higher prices in the regulated market would be appropriate. This is a variant of the now familiar predatory cross-subsidization argument.

The allure of price cap regulation in this setting, then, is in part the standard attraction (that price caps give firms an incentive to economize on costs) but in part a more tailored advantage: under price caps, a firm has less of an incentive to cross-subsidize by unfairly allocating common costs to monopolized markets. This is true because, in theory, price cap regulation is not tied to costs. That is not strictly true in practice, however, insofar as price caps do respond over time to changes in cost. Suppose, for example, that the FCC or Congress were to discover that, while staying under its price cap, AT&T had cut costs so much that it was earning a 25% return on its capital investments. Would those institutions forbear from either reimposing rate-of-return regulation or lowering the price cap? If AT&T today thinks that there is some probability that the government will react in that manner, won't AT&T again have an incentive to allocate a disproportionate share of its common costs to the regulated market, in essence continuing to behave as if rate-of-return regulation were still in place? In short, unless the FCC and Congress can credibly commit not to react to unexpected profits, this strategic interaction will be in play and price cap regulation will not completely eliminate the incentive to engage in predatory cross-subsidization.

4. Regulating AT&T. In light of the above discussion, should the FCC have adopted price cap regulation for AT&T? Assuming it had legal authority to do so (see below), should the FCC instead have removed rate regulation altogether for AT&T? What arguments can be made for and against forbearance in the years just after the decree? Would forbearance have eliminated the incentives to cross-subsidize and/or gold-plate?

5. Forbearance. The Commission's policy is to regulate the rates of only those carriers that the agency regards as having sufficient market power to require some form of rate regulation. The FCC calls these firms "dominant carriers." "Non-dominant" carriers, such as MCI or Sprint, were not subjected to rate regulation, because the Commission determined that it would "forbear" from exercising its authority to regulate in those instances. A Supreme Court case cast some doubt on the FCC's authority to forbear from regulating non-dominant carriers. MCI v. AT&T, 512 U.S. 218 (1994). Section 401 of the Telecommunications Act of 1996, however, added a new section 10 to the 1934 Act that grants extensive forbearance authority to the FCC. Oversimplifying a bit, if the agency decides that the public interest will be furthered by FCC forbearance, the FCC may refuse to enforce a regulation or even a statutory provision.

In 1995, the Commission determined that AT&T was no longer a dominant carrier in any of the domestic telecommunications markets in which it operated. The Commission cited both the number of firms then providing long distance phone service and the apparent lack of entry barriers to long distance markets. *AT&T Reclassification Order*, 11 FCC Rcd. 3271 (1995). It therefore removed price caps on these services. In 1996, the Commission concluded that AT&T was also non-dominant in the markets for international telephone service offerings and removed price caps on those services, too. *Motion of AT&T to Be Declared Non-Dominant for International Service*, 11 FCC Rcd. 17963 (1996).

II. THE BOC "LINE OF BUSINESS" RESTRICTIONS

The exercise of monopoly power in pricing was just one of the regulatory issues that needed to be addressed after the MFJ was entered. A concern more central to the decree itself was the danger that certain competitive markets could be harmed if the BOCs were to enter those markets and adopt either discriminatory interconnection or predatory cross-subsidization policies. In particular, the government was concerned that a BOC could use its control over the local telephone "bottleneck" to discriminate in its own favor in the markets for long distance telephone service, telephone equipment, and information services. For that reason the decree banned the BOCs from these lines of business. The materials that follow further explain the rationale for the line of business restrictions and then examine how those restrictions, including some related FCC rules that were not part of the MFJ itself, were treated over time by reviewing courts.

We begin with another excerpt from Glen Robinson's article on the Bell divestiture. Note that the article was written in 1988, so the MFJ was still in effect, and Judge Greene's tenure as the country's de facto telecommunications czar was by that time well under way. Robinson's references to particular technologies will seem a bit dated to modern eyes; however, his discussion is still worth careful consideration since these were the very technologies and policy debates motivating continued telecommunications reform in the post-divestiture period.

A. An Overview of the Restrictions

THE TITANIC REMEMBERED: AT&T AND THE CHANGING WORLD OF TELECOMMUNICATIONS

Glen Robinson, 5 Yale Journal on Regulation 517, 534–44 (1988)

A. Judging Regulation

The MFJ restrictions on BOC entry into interexchange service markets, like the restrictions on BOC equipment manufacturing and provision of information service, are designed to implement the central premise of Justice's antitrust case, which was that a monopolist with control over a vital bottleneck facility should not be allowed to compete with those who depend on access to that facility. Whether that premise is still correct is now the dominant controversy in telecommunications.

On the one hand, anyone who thinks competition should be the business of businessmen and not their lawyers will experience revulsion at the avidity with which favored telecommunications interests defend the existing restrictions on additional competition. It is all the more unsettling to see who the protected are: AT&T and IBM, leading electronic equipment manufacturers, newspaper publishers, and the cable television industry. These are not infants of American industry needful of a helping hand while they grow up.

On the other hand, anyone who accepts the legal and economic theory that prompted the antitrust case must concede that the MFJ restrictions follow the logic of that theory. One may think it unseemly that businesses like AT&T and IBM are the beneficiaries of these legal shackles on competition. But, unseemliness aside, the case for these restraints is just as persuasive as the case for the original divestiture order. If it is true that BOC entry into competitive lines of business is not a significant threat to competition, why wasn't AT&T allowed to continue to own and operate the BOCs?

This question is not answered simply by saying that conditions were different in the early 1980s. Of course they were. But most of the changes that have occurred have not been the consequence of divestiture but the product of evolving competition set in motion by the FCC and by technological innovation wholly independent of and even prior to the MFJ.

B. Regulating Judges

Given the complexity of the MFJ, it is not objectionable for the court to retain jurisdiction to interpret the decree for some initial period. As Greene has defined his role, however, it is not merely that of interpretation and enforcement, but one of policymaker, evaluating and acting on requests for waivers of MFJ restrictions as deemed fit in the circumstances.

Virtually all parties continue to acknowledge that the RHC/BOCs "bottleneck" monopoly over local exchange service puts the RHC/BOCs in a strategic position to handicap or gain an advantage over competitive service or equipment suppliers. The controversy boils down to how effectively this strategic position could be controlled by regulations short of a total ban on RHC/BOC participation in competitive markets. Judge Greene's skepticism about the efficacy of limited regulation (and consequent refusal to lift the absolute restrictions on RHC/BOC participation) is understandable in light of his interpretation of what the antitrust case was all about—the FCC's apparent inability to police AT&T. Nevertheless, one must balance the possible costs of ineffective regulation of strategic behavior against the plain costs of the alternative currently in effect: preventing the potential strategists—the RHC/BOCs—from competing.

How important would BOC competition really be, given that there appears to be fairly vigorous competition in all of the markets where they are now excluded?

The answer differs for the various markets. The case for additional competition is undoubtedly weakest in equipment manufacturing; there is scarcely any sector of the economy where competition is more robust and durable. The case for allowing RHC/BOCs to manufacture telecommunications equipment (recall that they are permitted to sell it) has to rest entirely on the desirability of increasing their entrepreneurial options, and on the absence of any significant risk of harm to competition from allowing them to compete. While these reasons may be sufficient to justify lifting the restrictions, they should not be confused with an argument that such entry will produce any direct contribution to the consuming public in terms of cost savings or innovation.

With interexchange transmission service (that is, long distance telephone service), the case for RHC/BOC entry is probably stronger. AT&T still retains eighty to eighty-five percent of the interLATA market compared to five to eight percent for MCI and four for US Sprint (the remainder is divided among other carriers), which suggests that competition may be less than optimally robust. Of course, one should not make too much turn on market shares alone; so long as MCI and US Sprint are large enough to be viable, their ability to enter AT&T's markets cheaply should operate as an effective competitive constraint on AT&T. The important question that supporters of RHC/BOC competition raise is whether these carriers (which currently compete with AT&T) will remain viable over the long term. In contrast, there is little doubt that the RHC/BOCs could provide strong and durable competition for AT&T.

The strongest case for RHC/BOC entry is in the provision of information services.[5] Whatever the arguments for additional competition in both CPE and interexchange service, no one argues that in those areas consumers are presently denied important services at competitive prices. In contrast, prohibiting RHC/BOCs from providing information services has meant that some electronic information services cannot be provided because they are not economically viable as separate services. A prime example is videotex, an all-purpose electronic information service. Despite popularity in Great Britain and France, videotex has failed to develop significantly in the United States. It is not clear that the requisite demand now exists to support videotex service on a major scale in the United States; however, the integration of videotex with basic telecommunications services might offer economies that would make such service less costly and more attractive. The present MFJ restrictions have made it difficult to find out.

I suspect that the MFJ's restrictions on RHC/BOC entry into CPE manufacturing, interexchange transmission, and information services markets will not survive much longer in the current environment of deregulation and competition, despite Judge Greene's present disposition to retain them. But I would not expect their sudden abandonment. We are more likely to see increasing erosion of the restraints—for example, partial entry or conditioned entry subject to open network architecture, comparably efficient integration, and other requirements of the kind the FCC has recently substituted for its former structural separation rules.

B. Judicial Review of the Restrictions

i. The Consent Decree

UNITED STATES v. WESTERN ELECTRIC CO.
900 F.2d 283 (D.C. Cir. 1990)

Before MIKVA, EDWARDS and SILBERMAN, Circuit Judges.

PER CURIAM:

As part of the 1982 consent decree that severed the seven Regional Bell Operating Companies ("RBOCs") from AT&T, the parties agreed that the RBOCs,

---

5. These cover a broad array of distinctive services such as access-retrieval services (*e.g.*, LEXIS and videotex), message storage and retrieval, transactional services (*e.g.*, shop-by-phone), and home monitoring (*e.g.*, alarm monitoring).

which inherited AT&T's local exchange monopoly, would be prohibited from providing interexchange (long distance) or information services, manufacturing telephone equipment, and participating in any non-telecommunications industry. The district judge retained jurisdiction over the case, and the Department of Justice ("DOJ") pledged to report to the court every three years as to the continuing need for these "line of business" restrictions. In the first such "Triennial Review," after considering the DOJ's report, as well as the comments of the other parties and dozens of other individuals and organizations, the district judge issued two opinions lifting the restriction against BOC participation in non-telecommunications businesses, modifying the restriction against their entering the information services market, and leaving intact the interexchange and manufacturing restrictions. With the exception of the district judge's ruling dealing with information services — which we reverse and remand — we affirm.

I.

A. The 1982 Consent Decree

Under the consent decree, AT&T retained its long distance and equipment manufacturing operations but agreed to divest itself of its local exchange monopoly, transferring those operations to the BOCs which were to become totally separate from AT&T. In turn, the BOCs were to be limited to the provision of local exchange services and precluded from participating in the markets for interexchange (long distance) services, equipment manufacturing, information services, and all other non-telecommunications businesses. The BOCs were, however, permitted to provide — but not manufacture — customer premises equipment and also to produce, publish, and distribute "Yellow Pages" directories. These line of business restrictions were premised on the notion that, because the BOCs still controlled the local exchange bottlenecks, there was a risk that they would engage in the same sort of anticompetitive abuses that AT&T had.

Before approving the restrictions, the district judge scrutinized them carefully to ensure "that they will not actually limit competition by unnecessarily barring a competitor from a market." He rejected as overly simplistic the DOJ's equation of the post-divestiture BOCs with the pre-divestiture Bell System based simply on the proposition that they both possessed a monopoly in local telecommunications. The separated BOCs, the district judge recognized, would be far more manageable monopolists for regulators to oversee than AT&T had been because they would be regional rather than national in scope, they would not be vertically integrated, and, if permitted to enter competitive markets, they would face "the most potent conceivable competitor: AT&T itself." He therefore ruled that the public interest standard would permit banning the BOCs from a market only if there was a substantial possibility that the BOCs would use monopoly power to impede competition in that market. The district judge ultimately determined that the proposed restrictions were indeed warranted.

The line of business restrictions were not meant necessarily to be permanent, however. The district judge retained jurisdiction and insisted that a mechanism be inserted into the decree for removing them at a later date.

B. The Triennial Review

When the decree was entered, the DOJ pledged to report to the court on the third anniversary of divestiture and every three years thereafter on the continuing need for the line of business restrictions. Since divestiture was not actually accomplished until 1984, the first such Triennial Review was held in 1987. The DOJ hired an independent consultant, Peter Huber, to conduct in-depth research on the telecommunications industry as a whole as well as on each of the relevant sub-markets. The Huber Report provided the factual basis for the DOJ's preliminary submission, filed with the district court in February 1987, in which it recommended the complete removal of the manufacturing, non-telecommunications, and information restrictions as well as the modification of the interexchange restriction. Quite clearly, the DOJ's position—which conceded the continued existence of the BOCs' local exchange monopoly—represented a significant change from its position when the decree was entered that mere monopoly power in local exchange services necessitated the restrictions.

After discussing the standard for removal of restrictions, the district judge determined that the BOCs still possessed a bottleneck monopoly over local exchange service. The court then analyzed each line of business restriction to decide whether the BOCs had nevertheless met their burden to justify removal. In reviewing the restriction concerning non-telecommunications businesses, the court noted that it had routinely reviewed and granted requests to waive this restriction since the decree became operational in 1984. Despite losing the safeguards that the waiver process afforded by virtue of the conditions imposed whenever a waiver was granted, the district court removed the restriction entirely because potential competitors did not actively oppose the removal and because cross-subsidization is more difficult in enterprises unrelated to telecommunications. In addition, the court asserted that lifting the restriction would eliminate a significant burden on BOCs' business planning and free the court from unnecessary and detailed oversight of BOC decisions.

The district judge left largely intact the decree's so-called "core" restrictions—those regarding interexchange services, manufacturing, and information services. The manufacturing and interexchange restrictions remained completely unchanged since the district court rejected arguments that circumstances had changed since the issuance of the decree so as to justify the BOCs' entrance into those markets. The district judge did grant partial relief to the BOCs on the information services provision but rejected the request of the DOJ and the BOCs to remove the restriction entirely for much the same reasons as he left the manufacturing and interexchange restrictions in place. The court asserted that information services are vulnerable even to slight manipulation and discrimination in access or transmission quality, thereby making it especially easy for the BOCs to use their bottleneck monopolies anticompetitively if they entered the market. Nevertheless, the information restriction was lifted insofar as it prevented the BOCs from providing transmission of information services generated by others. The district judge described the economic and social advantages of making information services more widely available and noted that the telephone system was perhaps the only means of accomplishing that goal, because it uniquely offers providers a means "to reach large, dispersed audiences over reasonably priced, interactive facilities." So long as the BOCs do not compete with the companies that generate the information services, the district judge reasoned, they would have an incentive to afford the widest, fastest, and highest quality access and transmission to all information providers, thereby maximizing their own revenues. All of these rulings have been appealed.

III

A. Interexchange Services

The BOCs, supported by the FCC but not the DOJ, argue that the interexchange restriction should be removed in spite of the conceded persistence of their local exchange monopoly—upon which interexchange carriers rely for access to ultimate consumers—because changed circumstances since the decree would prevent them from impeding competition if they were permitted to enter the market. The DOJ opposes the BOCs' petition.

The district court noted that the interexchange market is currently competitive. Even though AT&T still retains a lion's share of the market, there are hundreds of long distance carriers in the United States, eight of them serving twenty-five or more states. This apparently undisputed fact leads the district court to the curious observation that "the entry of the BOCs into that market is not necessary to give it vitality." The consent decree does not put the BOCs in the "Catch-22" that the district judge seems to imply by that statement—that the restriction will not be lifted if the market to be entered is not competitive because the BOC will grab and wield market power, nor will it be lifted if the market to be entered is highly competitive because the BOCs' presence is not "necessary."

Nevertheless, we agree with the district court's conclusion regarding the changes in the interexchange market. The crux of the BOCs' argument is that equal access for all interexchange carriers has been achieved and cross-subsidization eliminated, thus closing off the primary way for the BOCs to acquire market power anticompetitively. This has allegedly come about primarily through FCC regulation that was made more effective by the fragmentation of the Bell System's local exchange monopoly into seven BOCs. According to the DOJ, those FCC regulations, combined with the BOCs' own equal access plans, have "eliminated most of the anticompetitive advantages AT&T formerly enjoyed." At the time this case was before the district court, however, the DOJ asserted that "the FCC's equal access rules are based on the assumption that the BOCs will not provide interexchange services. Thus the FCC has not yet developed rules that would apply the nondiscrimination and cost separation principles developed in recent FCC proceedings to BOC provision of interexchange services." And until those regulations are adjusted to take account of BOC entry into the interexchange market—entry which would, of course, provide an incentive to deny equal access and to cross-subsidize if possible—the DOJ represents that equal access and proper cost allocation cannot be assured.

The DOJ also points out that violations of the equal access policy are extremely difficult to detect and remedy, thereby underscoring the danger of allowing entry before the FCC's regulations are designed to deal with the problem. Finally, the DOJ warns that the BOCs will have an easier time acquiring market power in the interexchange market than in other markets because many of the firms that began providing interexchange services after the decree have not yet become stable in the highly capital-intensive field. We affirm the district judge's conclusion that the BOCs failed to show that there was no substantial possibility that they could use their monopoly power to impede competition in the interexchange market.

B. Manufacturing

The "manufacturing restriction" is really more properly conceived of as two restrictions. First, it forbids the BOCs from manufacturing (but permits them to provide) customer premises equipment ("CPE"), which "includes equipment employed on the premises of anyone other than a carrier that is utilized to originate, route, or terminate telecommunications." Second, it prohibits the BOCs from manufacturing or providing telecommunications equipment, that is, equipment other than CPE used by a carrier to provide telecommunications services. The BOCs petitioned, with DOJ support, for the complete removal of the manufacturing restriction, and the district court left the restriction intact.

1. Telecommunications Equipment

The BOCs and the DOJ argue that market changes since the decree and regulatory adaptations to the post-divestiture market warrant removal of the telecommunications equipment restriction. The Justice Department further divides the telecommunications equipment market into separate markets for central office switches and for transmission equipment (primarily metal cable). The DOJ makes the significant concession that any BOC that chooses to manufacture central office switches, either unilaterally or through a joint venture, will buy all (or nearly all) of its requirements from the affiliated producer—thereby foreclosing a certain portion of the market, whether or not there are economies to be gained from such integration. Nevertheless, the BOCs will not impede competition (although competitors will surely be hurt) in the switch market, it is argued, because large economies of scale would prevent any BOC from remaining in the market solely to sell to itself. Even the largest BOC buyer of switches in 1985 purchased only 1.4 million lines of new switching capacity, about 17 percent of the U.S. market. Only two other BOCs purchased over one million switches and two BOCs bought less than 500,000. The Huber Report estimates that switch producers must sell upwards of 1.5 million switches per year to survive and many more to be profitable. Of the three major U.S. switch producers, two (AT&T and Northern Telecom) sold over 4.5 million switches in the U.S. in 1985, and perhaps twice that many worldwide. The third (GTE) sold only about 1.5 million switches in 1985 and is losing money in its equipment businesses. Assuming that there are no joint ventures among BOCs (which the DOJ admits would alter its assessment), the DOJ argues that only a few BOCs would enter the switch market and those that did could not afford to produce idiosyncratic (or overpriced) switches since they would have to attract at least some significant number of non-affiliated buyers who, of course, can choose among many producers.

The DOJ further concedes, however, that the image they convey of the efficient BOC producer of switches is somewhat clouded by the danger of anticompetitive interconnection discrimination and of cross-subsidization. The risk of interconnection discrimination, by which a BOC would design its switches in a way that would favor the BOC's self-produced equipment over rival manufacturers, has allegedly been "substantially decreased" by more effective regulatory control—especially the availability of benchmark comparisons among the BOCs. Cross-subsidization is a "plausible concern" in the switch market, the DOJ tells us, because of the need to attract a large market share, the extensive shared costs with local exchange services (especially research and development), and traditional difficulty encountered by regulators in discovering cost misallocations. Indeed, according to the DOJ, a BOC "might not have to produce efficiently to attract its own operating companies as buyers if regulators did not prevent recovery of excessive switch costs." And while the risk of cross-subsidization cannot be eliminated completely, FCC regulation—especially the availability of benchmarks to enforce effective accounting rules—would "significantly mitigate" it. Finally, the DOJ maintains that a small amount of cross-subsidization would not impede competition in the entered market; rather its primary effect would be to raise the price of local exchange service, a problem that the DOJ suggests is to be handled by regulators and is irrelevant to this proceeding.

The DOJ's assessment of the transmission equipment market is substantially similar to that for central office switches. In the transmission equipment market, as was true of central office switches, any BOC would purchase all or most of its own equipment from its own manufacturing affiliate; not all BOCs would manufacture every type of transmission equipment. There is some danger of discrimination and of cross-subsidization, but, due in large part to the availability of benchmark comparisons, that risk is substantially less than it was prior to divestiture. Among the salient differences is that the market has supported competition even though the BOCs have already been allowed to provide transmission equipment in the form of CPE, and therefore already possess an incentive to discriminate in interconnection. In addition, cross-subsidization is allegedly less probable than in the switch market because research and development costs, normally the prime source of cross-subsidization, are so low.

Even if we did accept the DOJ's market forecasts and regulatory assessments wholesale, they would not suffice to compel removal of the telecommunications equipment restriction. The possibility of self-dealing bias in the telecommunications equipment market poses dangers to competition that do not exist in the other markets the BOCs seek to enter. The DOJ's submissions provide little solace against those dangers. As we noted above, the DOJ "assumes that any BOC that manufactures equipment would purchase substantially all of its requirement from its affiliate," presumably regardless of price or quality. While the BOCs and the DOJ contend that not all BOCs will produce each type of equipment and therefore dispute the district judge's conclusion that the BOCs would foreclose 70% of the telecommunications equipment market, there seems to be no dispute that some substantial portion (5–15%) of the equipment market will be foreclosed.

Such foreclosure, if combined with cross-subsidization, would appear to allow the BOCs, in effect, to raise prices (and therefore exercise a form of market power) in the foreclosed sectors of the equipment market by disguising inflated equipment prices as costs in the local exchange market. At least in this first Triennial Review, it is not enough for the BOCs (independently or through the DOJ) to show that a significant number of stable competitors will be able to survive BOC entry.

2. Customer Premises Equipment

The DOJ subdivides the CPE market into the private branch exchange ("PBX") market and the terminal equipment market.[6] While it analyzed those submarkets separately, the DOJ believes—for reasons similar to those offered for the telecommunications equipment market—that BOC entry into both would not threaten competition. The PBX market is described as "moderately concentrated"—with three major and many minor producers—but nevertheless competitive. The DOJ points out that the BOCs have been permitted to provide PBXs (as well as all other forms of CPE) since the decree, and that they therefore have always had the incentive to provide discriminatory interconnection. If allowed to produce PBXs, that discrimination could manifest itself through BOC manipulation of its local network or through discriminatory dissemination of network information. We are assured, however, that the BOCs' ability to discriminate will be blocked, as it has been until now, by numerous obstacles, especially FCC regulation. Similarly, any danger of cross-subsidization in the PBX market is dismissed by the DOJ as negligible.

The DOJ's argument with respect to the terminal equipment market is based again on the premise that no BOC could successfully discriminate against its rivals, either by way of interconnection or by failing to provide critical network information. Their ability to discriminate is asserted to be undercut somewhat by the advent of PBX use, as well as cellular and paging systems for which the BOCs do not even provide the interconnection with the terminal equipment and which all contribute to the prevalent use of standards in interconnection. Residual risk of discrimination, as well as the risk of cross-subsidization, are adequately prevented by FCC regulation.

While we certainly have some reservations concerning the DOJ's assessment of the CPE market, we are inclined to think that the question is much closer than it was for telecommunications equipment. Since the BOCs purchase only a minute percentage of the nation's CPE output, there is no risk of the combined cross-subsidization and foreclosure that is so crucial to our decision on telecommunications equipment. Indeed, on appeal, the BOCs and the DOJ complain primarily that when the district judge discussed foreclosure, he did not differentiate between CPE and the various types of telecommunications equipment that the BOCs do purchase themselves in great quantity. However, the BOCs petitioned for complete removal of the manufacturing restriction, and the DOJ explicitly urged the district judge not to distinguish between the two types of equipment in making his decision, because line-drawing between them is so difficult. Given the risks to competition we identified in the telecommunications equipment market, the district court understandably did not allow the entire manufacturing restriction to be removed in this first Triennial Review, and the motions were properly denied.

C. Information Services

The BOCs and the DOJ also appeal from the district court's decision not to lift the restriction on "information services" under section II(D)(1), as that restriction is applied to the generation of information. The district court found that there had "been no significant, relevant change in" market conditions justifying

---

6. [Ed. A private branch exchange (PBX) is in essence a privately owned local exchange, typically one that operates inside a particular company or office building.]

removal of this restraint. [The court remanded this issue to the district court for reconsideration. The opinion that follows finally disposed of the issue.]

Notes and Questions

1. Triennial Reviews. Because of continuing appellate litigation surrounding the 1987 Triennial Review, the Reviews scheduled for 1990 and 1993 were called off. The Telecommunications Act of 1996 obviated the need for any further Triennial Reviews.

2. Logic of the Appellate Court. Why does the appellate court treat as relatively noncontroversial (a) ending the ban on BOC entry into non-telecommunications services and (b) retaining the prohibition on offering interexchange services?

3. First Amendment Concerns. Does the ban on BOCs' offering of information services run afoul of the First Amendment, properly construed? In the opinion that follows, the D.C. Circuit finally disposed of the information services restriction. Does its opinion adequately address Judge Greene's reservations? What does the circuit court believe will be gained by removing the ban?

UNITED STATES v. WESTERN ELECTRIC CO.
993 F.2d 1572 (D.C. Cir. 1993)

Opinion for the Court filed by Circuit Judge WILLIAMS, in which Circuit Judges BUCKLEY and SENTELLE concur.

WILLIAMS, Circuit Judge:

When the government and AT&T settled the government's antitrust suit against AT&T, the Department of Justice pledged to report to the district court every three years as to whether there was a continuing need for the "line of business" restrictions that the settlement decree, the "Modified Final Judgment," imposed on the Bell operating companies (or BOCs). In 1987, the Department proposed that many of the restrictions be removed, including those on entry into the information services market. The district court rejected the information services proposal and several others. On review, this court largely affirmed, but reversed and remanded as to information services, finding that the district court had employed the wrong standard in reviewing the Department's proposal.

On remand, the district court modified the decree, in an opinion that is something of a pushmi-pullyu. While on the one hand asserting that "none of the Department of Justice's intermediate contentions is supported by credible evidence," the court also concluded that under the standard established by this court in the Triennial Review Opinion, it was bound to defer to those conclusions. The district court thus removed the ban on entry into information services.

Although the district court in certain places mischaracterized the standard under which it was to review the Department's proposal, the evidence was such that, under the standard laid down in the Triennial Review Opinion, rejection of the Department's proposal would have been error. We therefore affirm.

The district court may reject an uncontested modification only if it has exceptional confidence that adverse antitrust consequences will result—perhaps akin to the confidence that would justify a court in overturning the predictive judgments of an administrative agency.

In advocating removal of the information services ban, the Department made the following contentions: (1) that there was no substantial risk that removal of the ban would lessen competition either through the BOCs' use of their "bottleneck" power over local loop connections (*i.e.*, intra-exchange services) to discriminate against competing information service providers, or through cross-subsidization of their own information services; (2) that under current conditions regulation would play a substantial role in minimizing any anticompetitive risks; and (3) that removal of the ban would benefit consumers by enhancing competition in information services. Participants on all sides of the dispute submitted affidavits on these issues, many by very distinguished economists.

(1) It is undisputed that the BOCs have monopolies over local telephone exchange service in their respective service areas. The district court was convinced that the BOCs could use that monopoly power to raise the transmission costs of any rival information service provider, thereby raising the costs and reducing the output of information services. Raising the costs could take the form either of raising prices explicitly or degrading service (as by delayed installation of equipment, low priority restoration of service after an outage, or poor maintenance).

In assessing the ability of BOCs to raise rivals' costs in this way, we assume for the sake of argument that devices for avoiding the local loop altogether, such as satellite dishes, are inadequate. But the record provides strong support—which the district court did not address at all—for the view that, quite apart from such end-runs, BOCs will be unable to discriminate against competing providers. Such discrimination could theoretically occur at either end of the information service transaction—the provider's or the customers'. Take the provider's end first. Professor Fisher notes that providers may prevent such discrimination by exploiting competition between BOCs, and between BOCs and non-BOC telephone companies, by moving or threatening to move their distribution facilities (the point where their information is fed into the telephone system) to a different region or to an independent company within the BOC's region. Further, as Professors Stigler and Carlton say, large information service providers not only can but already do bypass the BOCs by constructing private networks.

This takes us to the customer end. Despite the local monopoly, the record indicates that even here there is much to undercut the threat of discrimination. First, it is evidently difficult, if not impossible, for BOCs to distinguish between information service provider messages and others, as both may come over regular voice lines. Moreover, as Professor Fisher notes, a BOC would not only have to distinguish between voice and data messages, but also between those data messages coming from a competitor and those from a noncompetitor (*e.g.*, interoffice transmissions by corporations). The necessary scale of BOC detections would be enormous; Fisher observes that on one information system alone (DunsNet) customers gain access 60,000 times a day.

The discrimination hypothesis appears to assume, moreover, that local interconnections are a major element of the total costs of providing information services. This seems untrue. One major information service provider well known to lawyers, Commerce Clearing House, reports that only 15–20% of its costs are due to telecommunications, of which 30% are local exchange costs.

Thus only about 4.5% to 6% of CCH's costs are susceptible to BOC discrimination. Even a 50% increase in local exchange costs would raise CCH's costs by only 3%.

The BOCs also offered evidence that non-BOC local exchange companies such as GTE have entered the information services market without using their bottleneck control anticompetitively. The affidavits in the record offer persuasive evidence that, despite their local monopoly power, the BOCs will be unable to discriminate against competing information service providers.

(2) The BOCs and the Department of Justice pointed to regulatory safeguards that could limit anticompetitive effects even if the BOCs otherwise had the incentive and ability to discriminate or cross-subsidize. The district court dismissed these contentions. It believed instead that regulators had never been successful at stopping the Bell system from engaging in anticompetitive activities, and that there were no changes tending to enhance their ability to do so. It disposed of references to current FCC rules that require the BOCs to charge themselves the same access rates as they charge others, for instance, with the observation that a comparable rule did not work before the Bell system breakup. Indeed, the court believed that the increasing complexity and diversity of the industry, including BOC entry into other fields, might make it harder than ever to detect or stamp out discrimination and cross-subsidization.

There is a lot of evidence that the breakup and other recent developments have enhanced regulatory capability. The seven independent BOCs are not the old AT&T. As this court noted in the Triennial Review Opinion, the existence of seven BOCs increases the number of benchmarks that can be used by regulators to detect discriminatory pricing. Indeed, federal and state regulators have in fact used such benchmarks in evaluating compliance with equal access requirements (*i.e.*, the requirements disparaged by the district court) and in comparing installation and maintenance practices for customer premises equipment. Moreover, information service giants operating throughout the country, such as IBM, AT&T and GE, will notice any discrepancies in treatment by the various BOCs and will have the capacity and incentive to bring anticompetitive conduct to the attention of regulatory agencies. The BOCs themselves will be each other's customers in the transmission of information services, with a unique capacity to spot misbehavior and notify regulators. Finally, any effort to establish a reputation for predatory responses to new entry will require that potential new entrants be aware of such predation; a BOC may have great difficulty establishing such a reputation among potential entrants while keeping it a secret from regulators.

Changes independent of the AT&T breakup also support the likelihood of more effective regulation. For example, Professor Kahn pointed to the FCC move in the direction of price cap regulation, which the FCC has in fact extended to the BOCs since his affidavit. This reduces any BOC's ability to shift costs from unregulated to regulated activities, because the increase in costs for the regulated activity does not automatically cause an increase in the legal rate ceiling. In addition, the FCC has acted since the breakup to tighten its accounting rules, especially its treatment of joint costs, all tending to increase the chances of catching any attempts at cost-shifting.

Similarly, Kahn argued that it was by no means valid to assume the prevalence of regulatory "capture." Noting state agencies' overwhelming concern for keeping the rates for local residential service low, he reasoned that this would inhibit any effort by the BOCs to shift costs into those (monopoly) services.

(3) Parties favoring removal of the ban pointed to substantial benefits that they believed were likely to follow. For example, they pointed to several segments of the information services market that are highly concentrated (*e.g.*, alarm services, financial transactions, and airline reservations), arguing that BOC entry would make the market more competitive. Further, there is reason to believe that BOCs entering the information services market will have some economies of scope (the capacity to produce related goods or services at an aggregate cost lower than the total for each produced separately), with resulting consumer benefits.

The district court brushed these contentions aside as "preposterous," partly on the theory that BOC competition could contribute no consumer benefit because the BOCs had no prior experience in the content or substance of information services. This is a curious idea, as businesses are capable of acquiring expertise and experienced talent. Under the court's view, new entry could rarely create competitive benefits; even a development so close to home as recent entries into long distance telephone service could not be expected to generate consumer benefits.

Instead of consumer benefit, the court envisioned a nightmare in which the BOCs would drive out the current competitors and perhaps "extinguish" competition altogether. The latter scenario is of course internally contradictory; because there are seven BOCs, competition would exist even if they drove out all the incumbents. More generally, the district court's scenario necessarily depends upon successful use of some combination of discrimination and cross-subsidization; we have already reviewed the obstacles that such efforts would confront. It is worth noting here the character of some of the firms that the BOCs would have to drive out. They include GE (with annual revenues about five times those of a BOC), AT&T itself (revenues three times those of a BOC), IBM and Sears with their Prodigy service, Merrill-Lynch, ITT, Mead Corporation, American Express, Citicorp, Chase Manhattan Bank, and a variety of foreign and independent telephone companies. These firms are not pushovers. Also, we have already noted evidence that local exchange costs represent only a tiny share of information service providers' total costs, so that the BOCs' bottlenecks do not, in perspective, seem like invincible weapons.

If appellants are right, BOC entry will raise prices and reduce output in the information services industry; if the Department is right, BOC entry will lower prices and expand output. Firms that sell goods and services that are inputs to the production and use of information services stand to gain an expanding market if the Department's prediction is right, and have the incentive to make a completely unbiased judgment on the matter. It is something of a vindication of the Department's view that representatives of those firms, the Computer and Communications Industry Association and the United States Telephone Association (which includes about 1000 independent local telephone companies), filed briefs with the district court supporting removal of the ban.

We therefore affirm the judgment removing the information services line of business restriction from the Modified Final Judgment.

Notes and Questions

1. What Remains. After this decision, the consent decree contained no line of business restrictions on AT&T and only two on the BOCs—bans that prevented the BOCs from (a) providing interexchange service and (b) manufacturing telecommunications equipment. These two restrictions were significantly modified by the 1996 Act, a change that is described more fully next chapter.

2. Independent LECs. Independent local exchange carriers—local phone companies that were unaffiliated with Bell—were of course not subject to the MFJ's restrictions. As a policy matter, should the FCC have imposed line of business restrictions on those firms comparable to those imposed on the BOCs? Or were the BOCs somehow different from other local exchange carriers?

ii. FCC Rules Independent of the Decree

Even before the MFJ, the FCC had to consider the implications of Bell's entry into competitive, unregulated lines of business. The issue was particularly salient in the area of remote computing and data processing because consumers often connected to shared computing facilities through telephone lines. The Commission had two principal (and by now familiar) concerns. The first was that Bell might use its monopoly over access to local exchange customers to discriminate in its own favor in lines of business that depended on such access. Second, the Commission was concerned that the Bell companies might use their regulated monopoly on local telephone service to cross-subsidize (and thereby gain a competitive advantage in) other lines of business.

In a series of rulings known as *Computer I*, *Computer II*, and *Computer III*, the FCC first imposed but later relaxed restrictions under which Bell (and other telephone companies) could provide "enhanced" services that were outside the core telephone business. We considered *Computer I* and *Computer II* back in Chapter Fifteen's discussion of the four precursors to divestiture. The excerpt below continues that story by providing an overview of how the Commission dealt with these same issues in the post-divestiture period.

CALIFORNIA v. FCC [*COMPUTER III*]
905 F.2d 1217 (9th Cir. 1990)

Opinion for the court filed by Circuit Judge NORRIS, in which Circuit Judge FARRIS concurs and in which Circuit Judge BOOCHEVER concurs except fo Part II. Circuit Judge BOOCHEVER filed an opinion concurring in part and dissenting in part.

NORRIS, Circuit Judge:

Petitioners seek review of orders of the Federal Communications Commission issued in a rulemaking proceeding known in the telecommunications industry as the *Third Computer Inquiry* or *Computer III*. Petitioners dispute two discrete rulings by the Commission. First, petitioners challenge the ruling that the divested Bell Operating Companies (BOCs) no longer be required to maintain corporate separation between their common carrier communications services, which are regulated under tariff pursuant to Title II of the Federal Communications Act, and the unregulated provision of enhanced or data processing services over the telecommunications network.[7]

Second, petitioners challenge the Commission's decision to preempt state regulation of communications common carriers' provision of enhanced services on the ground that the FCC's decision violates section 2(b)(1) of the Communications Act, which denies the Commission jurisdiction over "charges, classifications, practices, services, facilities, or regulations for or in connection with intrastate communication service by wire or radio of any carrier...." 47 U.S.C. §152(b)(1).

I

By the 1960s, the growing interdependence of the telephone and the computer created regulatory problems for the Federal Communications Commission. Increasingly, providers of data processing services, such as IBM, were using the transmission facilities of communications common carriers to deliver computer-based information to customers' terminals. An entire new industry based upon the rapidly advancing technology of both the telephone and the computer took root and flourished. Because the provision of enhanced services—as the FCC has labeled telecommunications services combining both data processing and communications components—involves the use of the transmission facilities of communications common carriers, some argued that the Commission was statutorily required to regulate the new industry. The Commission rejected that argument in favor of a regulatory policy of promoting competition in the enhanced services industry notwithstanding the fact that enhanced services contained regulated communications as well as an unregulated data processing component.

The decision to foster a competitive enhanced services industry did not fully resolve the Commission's regulatory problems. The Commission remained concerned that communications carriers would use their telephone exchange monopolies to obtain leverage in the competitive enhanced services market. First, because non-carrier providers of enhanced services were required to obtain access to the telecommunications network through local exchange "bottlenecks," the Commission was concerned that carriers would gain an unfair competitive edge by discriminating in favor of their own enhanced service offerings in providing access. Second, the Commission was concerned that carriers would exploit their

---

7. Throughout this opinion we use the FCC's terms "basic" and "enhanced" to distinguish between regulated common carrier communications services, which consist largely of plain old telephone service (POTS), and unregulated data processing services which use the telephone network to convey information from remote computers to customers' terminals. In the FCC's formal terms, basic service is the offering of a "pure transmission capability over a communications path that is virtually transparent in terms of its interaction with customer supplied information." An enhanced service combines basic service with "computer processing applications that act on the format, content, code, protocol or similar aspects of the subscriber's transmitted information, or provide the subscriber additional, different or restructured information, or involve subscriber interaction with stored information." Database services, in which a customer dials a number to obtain access to stored information, such as Dow Jones News, Lexis, and "Dial It" sports scores, are examples of enhanced services.

exchange monopolies by passing on to telephone ratepayers costs properly attributable to their unregulated enhanced services business. Such improper cost-shifting effectively subsidizes a carrier's unregulated activities with monopoly profits from its regulated activities, to the detriment of both its monopoly ratepayers and its competitors in the enhanced services market.

A. The First and Second Computer Inquiries

In the *First Computer Inquiry* (*Computer I*, 1970), the FCC required that any telephone carrier offering such enhanced services do so by means of a separate corporate subsidiary. Structural separation was not initially regarded as applying to the American Telephone & Telegraph Company (AT&T) and its local exchange affiliates (the Bell System), because those companies were thought to be barred from offering data processing services by a 1956 antitrust consent decree.

In its 1980 *Second Computer Inquiry* (*Computer II*) decision, the FCC continued to rely on structural separation as the principal means of preventing cross-subsidization and discriminatory access. But the Commission restricted the requirement to members of the Bell System and removed it from all other carriers. The FCC attempted to predicate the need for regulation on a carrier's national market power, which only AT&T had. However, the Commission neither defined the "national market" at issue nor explained why it drew its regulatory line between national market power and substantial regional market power.

B. The Breakup of AT&T

Under the AT&T divestiture, AT&T was free to enter virtually all other facets of the marketplace, including data processing. The divested BOCs could not provide interexchange telephone service, or offer "information services," a category that substantially overlaps, but may not be identical to, the FCC's "enhanced services."

C. The BOC Separation Order

In preparation for the January 1984 restructuring of the Bell System, the FCC opened a proceeding to determine whether and how the *Computer II* rules should be applied to the divested BOCs. In the BOC Separation Order rulemaking proceeding, the BOCs argued that divestiture had eliminated the need for *Computer II's* structural separation requirements. The FCC rejected this argument because the BOCs had inherited AT&T's monopoly power and control over access to the telecommunications network. In the Commission's view, the critical fact was that each BOC would retain ownership of the local exchange monopolies in the region in which it operated. Such bottleneck control, in the Commission's view, created the same danger of anticompetitive activity that existed before divestiture.

The FCC also determined in its order that non-structural regulations on BOC cost-accounting and network-access practices would be ineffective safeguards against anticompetitive behavior by the BOCs. Absent a structural separation rule, the FCC found, the BOCs could install their own enhanced services equipment within the local networks, and would be free to market enhanced services through the same organizations used for basic telephone service. For example, the FCC found that if joint marketing were permitted, the personnel who contact customers to market regulated services could be selling enhanced services at the same time. Difficult, sometimes impossible, problems of fairly allocating the costs of marketing between regulated and unregulated accounts would again occur. This integrated operation of regulated and unregulated activities would, in the FCC's words, be "impossible" to monitor for cross-subsidization. Because the services were so closely related, the Commission reasoned, the BOCs could easily reclassify enhanced services costs or joint costs as basic telephone service costs without being detected by the FCC.

Analogous enforcement problems, in the FCC's view, would beset efforts to use network-access rules to assure that the BOCs would not provide inferior access to competitors. Because of the BOCs' exclusive control over the connection and switching equipment of the local exchanges, it would be difficult for the Commission to know whether the BOCs were providing competitors with transmission services of comparable quality at comparable prices. By integrating their enhanced services equipment into the telephone network, the BOCs could favor their own enhanced services with superior signals and switching capacities without being detected.

In contrast, the FCC found that structural separation continued to be an effective means of preventing cost-shifting and discrimination. It viewed structural separation as essentially a prophylactic measure. The separate subsidiary requirement forces the BOCs to produce and market enhanced services independent of basic telephone services, and maintain different books, different staffs, and different equipment premises for each service. This separation eliminates the problem of determining the proper allocation of joint costs, and makes it difficult for the BOCs to masquerade enhanced services costs as basic telephone service costs. It also reduces the chance of discrimination by putting a BOC's enhanced services subsidiary on substantially the same footing as the subsidiary's competitors. Like its competitors, the subsidiary must deal with the BOC at arm's length in purchasing transmission services, and must maintain its enhanced services equipment at a location separate from the BOC's local exchange facilities. The subsidiary thus receives its transmission services along the same telephone lines, and through the same switching systems, as its competitors.

In part, the separation requirements were designed to benefit participants in the enhanced services market by creating an even playing field for the BOCs' competitors. Structural separation also protected the basic telephone service market by preventing the BOCs from extracting, through cost-shifting, monopoly rents from captive telephone consumers. The "ratepayers"—that is, ordinary telephone customers—would not be forced to subsidize the BOCs' expansion into the data processing business.

D. The Third Computer Inquiry

In August 1985, just fourteen months after concluding the *BOC Separation Proceeding* in which the FCC rejected the argument that divestiture had reduced the need for structural separation, the Commission reversed course and announced its intention to relieve the BOCs of the separation requirements. The FCC adopted new regulations permitting the BOCs to integrate their basic and enhanced services upon implementation of a plan of nonstructural safeguards approved by the FCC.

The FCC decided that its structural separation regulations had imposed costs in terms of the unavailability of certain services, lost economies and efficiencies, and the inability of customers to obtain complete telecommunications and data processing solutions from a single vendor. The FCC also determined that the BOCs' ability to cross-subsidize had been restricted because of divestiture, the growth of competitive alternatives to the BOCs' ordinary telephone service, and political and regulatory pressures at the state level to keep local phone rates down. The BOCs' ability to discriminate by providing inferior network access had also diminished, according to the FCC, because of industry-wide coordination of network standards and the threat that enhanced services competitors could bypass the BOCs' local exchanges.

The FCC concluded that the regulatory goals served by structural separation could be achieved by two nonstructural safeguards. First, the FCC would develop cost allocation methods to minimize the BOCs' ability to shift costs from their unregulated to regulated activities. Second, the FCC adopted regulations specifically designed to prevent the BOCs from using their "substantial market power in providing network access" to discriminate against competing providers of enhanced services. These anti-discrimination regulations contained three prongs. First, the FCC endorsed an open-network policy of requiring the BOCs to make the telephone networks as accessible to competitors as they are to the BOCs themselves.[8] Second, each BOC must notify its competitors in the enhanced services industry of changes in the network that may affect the provision of enhanced services so as to permit competitors to take advantage of the changes. Third, each BOC must provide its competitors with information about customer use of the telephone network so that the competitors may design their services to suit customer needs.

II

Petitioners claim that it was irrational for the FCC to abandon structural safeguards so soon after imposing them on AT&T in *Computer II* and reimposing them on the divested BOCs in the *BOC Separation Order*. The FCC explains its lifting of the structural separation requirements by arguing that certain developments in telecommunications markets and technologies have materially changed circumstances in the industry.

A. The Costs of Structural Separation

In appraising the social costs of structural separation, the FCC makes a fair case that the integration of regulated and unregulated telecommunications services by the BOCs would yield some economies of scale. On the technological side, the BOCs could integrate enhanced services equipment more closely into the telephone network. On the marketing side, the BOCs could offer customers — particularly business customers — packages of basic and enhanced services. These packages would minimize transaction costs, and reduce delays and coordination problems in satisfying consumer demands. Moreover, the BOCs would not have to maintain, and customers would not have to pay for, separate organizations

---

8. There are two components to this open-network policy: CEI (for "Comparably Efficient Interconnection"), which means each BOC must, pending more permanent changes, provide competitors with connections to the local exchange network that are equal to the connections available to the BOCs' own enhanced services; and ONA (for "Open Network Architecture"), which means each BOC must ultimately incorporate CEI concepts into the overall design of its basic service network.

and facilities for operating and repairing basic and enhanced services. While the Commission concludes that these costs are "potentially very significant," it makes no attempt to quantify them.

The FCC makes a plausible case that its separation requirements have impeded the marketing and even development of some new forms of enhanced services. The Commission invokes the example of the Custom Calling II VMS (voice message system), which AT&T developed in the early 1980s. AT&T unsuccessfully sought a waiver from the *Computer II* structural separation rules so it could market the system through its local exchange operating companies. The result, according to the Commission, is that neither this system nor any substantial equivalent has been available to the public. The *Computer III* record is replete with BOC assertions that because their ownership of the local exchanges gives them control of access to the telecommunications network, they are best situated to develop and market products that take full advantage of the network's capabilities. Yet the only concrete example in the record is the voice message system cited by AT&T. We recognize that because the BOCs have never had an opportunity to offer enhanced services in a deregulated environment, the real benefits, if any, of integrated operations may not be quantifiable at this time.

B. The Benefits of Structural Separation

The FCC has consistently identified the social benefits of structural separation as safeguarding both captive ratepayers and enhanced services competitors against the twin evils of discriminatory access and cross-subsidization. In *Computer III*, the Commission found that changed technological and market circumstances had reduced the need for structural separation as a safeguard against access discrimination and cross-subsidization of the BOCs' own enhanced services with monopoly revenues derived from ratepayers.

(1) Prevention of Discriminatory Access

The FCC could reasonably conclude that the emergence of powerful competitors such as IBM, which have the resources and expertise to monitor the quality of access to the network, reduces the BOCs' ability to discriminate in providing access to their competitors. The record also supports the proposition that these large corporate competitors—unlike the average telephone user—have a growing capability of bypassing local exchanges by using microwave systems or cable networks for linking their computers with their customers' terminals.

Moreover, the network-access policies that the FCC proposes to substitute for structural separation involve new technologies for detecting inferior access that have not previously been available. The FCC's policy of Comparably Efficient Interconnection (CEI) is designed to ensure that each BOC will provide competitors with connections to the local exchange that equal the connections available to the BOCs' own enhanced services offerings. Moreover, the Open Network Architecture (ONA) policy requires each BOC to incorporate CEI concepts into the overall design of its basic service network.

(2) Prevention of Cross-Subsidization

We cannot agree, however, that there is adequate record support for the Commission's conclusion that changed circumstances have reduced the danger that the BOCs will effectively subsidize their competitive activities with monopoly revenues improperly derived from captive ratepayers. The FCC points to four changes in the telecommunications market that allegedly have reduced this danger following *Computer II* and the *BOC Separation Order*: (1) the enhanced services market has become "extremely competitive"; (2) the growth of "bypass" and other alternatives to local exchange facilities has eroded the BOCs' monopoly power; (3) political and regulatory forces at the state level exert pressure on the BOCs to keep the price of basic telephone service down; and (4) divestiture has dissipated the monolithic power of the Bell System. Given these changes, the FCC asserts that nonstructural safeguards such as accounting controls may be substituted for structural separation requirements without increasing the risk of cross-subsidization.

The Commission does not explain how the fact that the enhanced services market is "extremely competitive" reduces the BOCs' ability to cross-subsidize their unregulated enhanced services businesses by misallocating costs to their regulated activities. The BOCs' ability to shift costs derives from the fact that they are monopoly providers of basic telephone service. If anything, increased competition in the enhanced services market simply increases the BOCs' incentive to shift costs so they can engage in predatory price-cutting as a means of maintaining or increasing their share of the market for enhanced services.

The Commission also asserts that the BOCs' monopoly power over the local networks has been "eroded" by new technologies permitting some telephone users to bypass the BOCs' local exchange facilities. These new bypass technologies include "Teleport" fiber networks, cable networks, and microwave systems, all of which enable some circumvention of the local exchanges. The record indicates that such services are available in some metropolitan areas to large business subscribers.

Although the record contains an impressive array of evidence demonstrating the technical feasibility of bypass, the record contains no evidence that bypass has become a realistic option for any appreciable number of ordinary telephone users. More importantly, the record is devoid of evidence that the potential for bypass is significant enough to reduce the BOCs' ability, as a practical matter, to exact monopoly rents from basic service customers by burdening them with costs from unregulated activities. On the basis of the record before us, therefore, the FCC's contention that the availability of bypass will hamper BOC attempts at cost-shifting must be characterized as speculative at best.

We are also unpersuaded by the Commission's new-found faith in *Computer III* that political and regulatory forces in the states will exert pressure on the BOCs to "minimize rural, residential, and small business local exchange rates, even to levels below cost," thereby limiting "the BOCs' ability to shift costs to regulated basic services." The Commission refers to nothing in the record; it simply relies upon the bald assertion that state regulators have become more effective in protecting ratepayers against improper cost-shifting.

We do not dispute that the FCC has the authority to rethink its post-divestiture policies in light of changed circumstances. It must, however, provide reasoned explanations for its policy changes.

In sum, the four purported "changes" in the telecommunications market identified by the FCC lend no support to its conclusion that the risk of cross-subsidization by the BOCs has decreased. We are left with the Commission's assurance that cost-accounting regulations will be sufficient to "minimize" the BOCs' ability to misallocate costs. But the Commission's consistent position before *Computer III* has always been that monitoring and enforcement problems make cost-accounting regulations an ineffective tool in detecting cost-shifting.

C. The Reasonableness of the FCC's Decision

The *Computer III* nonstructural regulations are designed to protect both ordinary telephone customers and the competitive enhanced services market. We agree that the Commission has made a plausible case that lifting the structural separation requirements will benefit consumers of enhanced services by permitting the BOCs to operate more efficiently in the enhanced services market. We also agree that the Commission has made a plausible case that ONA, CEI, and the growth of bypass technology will be effective in reducing the risk of BOC access discrimination. Thus, the record supports the FCC's determination that *Computer III*'s substitution of nonstructural for structural safeguards will benefit the enhanced service industry. On the other hand, the record yields no support for the Commission's position that market and technological changes since *Computer II* and the *BOC Separation Order* have reduced the danger of cross-subsidization by the BOCs. We therefore hold that it was arbitrary and capricious within the meaning of section 10(e) of the Administrative Procedure Act for the Commission to abandon structural separation and rely on cost accounting regulations to provide regulatory protection for ratepayers.

[Concurring and dissenting opinion of Judge BOOCHEVER is omitted.]

Notes and Questions

1. On Remand. The Ninth Circuit thus remanded the issue to the FCC for further consideration. The agency, in turn, reaffirmed its *Computer III* rules, albeit with further explanation specifically tailored to respond to the court's criticisms. *See Computer III Remand Proceedings*, 57 Fed. Reg. 4373 (1992). That decision would itself go up on appeal to the Ninth Circuit in California v. FCC, 39 F.3d 919 (9th Cir. 1994), and the back-and-forth would continue until 1996 when the Telecommunications Act of 1996 established an entirely new set of restrictions and thus mooted these debates.

2. What Was the FCC's Error? The FCC in essence determined in *Computer III* that (a) the loss in efficiency generated by forcing the BOCs to utilize separate subsidiaries when supplying enhanced services was greater than (b) the risk of anticompetitive behavior by the BOCs if they were allowed to offer enhanced services in-house subject to (1) closer supervision by accountants and (2) a regulatory requirement that they engage in a particular form of open access called "open network architecture" (ONA). According to the Ninth Circuit, which parts of this calculus did the FCC get wrong? Precisely whom is the court seeking to protect? The state regulatory agencies that filed the suit? IBM? Residential telephone service customers? From what is it trying to protect them?

3. Alternatives. If you were an FCC commissioner, what steps would you take to respond to this decision? For example, would you seek to quantify the costs of structural regulation to see whether a more compelling case could be made for the agency's *Computer III* decision? Or would you simply reimpose the structural separation rules? In choosing what steps to take, which facts would influence your choices most heavily?

4. The Buck Stops Where? Overall, what does all this teach you about who does, and who should, bear ultimate responsibility for these types of judgments? The judges administering the consent decree? The Federal Communications Commission? The state regulatory agencies? Does the advent of the 1996 Act suggest that maybe Congress is the right answer? Do the above documents tell you that one or another of these institutions does a better job when it comes to analyzing inherently complex telecommunications concepts?

III. UNIVERSAL SERVICE AFTER DIVESTITURE

It was only in the decade before the MFJ that universal service policies received explicit and systematic attention from federal regulators. Before then, universal service was something of a catchall, referring to a wide array of cross-subsidies that each seemed to further one or another policy goal. For example, universal service meant that all citizens should enjoy telephone service at reasonable costs, and thus rates in urban areas should be used to subsidize rates in rural ones. Universal service also meant that residential users should receive POTS at low prices and, thus, business rates should be set so as to subsidize residential rates. Universal service also encompassed the idea that low income families should be charged low rates, a goal achieved by pricing long distance service above cost and local service below cost, as well as by using revenues collected from long distance providers to fund direct subsidies to low income subscribers. Universal service was therefore something of a jumble, and it was mostly implemented implicitly through the rate approval process.

In 1970, however — just before the antitrust prosecution began — the Commission made universal service more explicit by implementing the so-called "Ozark Plan" for federal universal service support.[9] Under that plan, regulators subsidized telephone penetration by manipulating the "separations and settlement" process that was used to apportion the costs of the local telephone network between federally regulated interstate traffic and state-regulated intrastate traffic.

The Ozark plan worked by disproportionately allocating the fixed costs of the local telephone network to long distance traffic. This would drive long distance prices up, but keep basic POTS prices down. In particular, for every 1 percent of traffic consisting of long distance calls, the plan required that 3.3 percent of local network costs be covered through long distance prices. So, if there were 1000 total calls on a network, 900 of which were local and 100 of which were long distance, the costs of the network would be recovered 33 percent through long distance rates and only 67 percent through local rates. It was in this way

---

9. Prescriptions of Procedures for Separating and Allocating Plant Investment, Operating Expenses, Taxes and Reserve Between the Intrastate and Interstate Operations of Telephone Companies, 26 FCC 2d 247 (1970) ("the Ozark Plan").

that the Ozark plan expressly subsidized local rates; the plan was implemented in 1971 and, by 1980, long distance calls paid for approximately 25 percent of the common local line infrastructure even though those calls made up only 8 percent of traffic on the local networks.[10]

One might have thought that this highly disproportionate rate structure would have led to court challenge, but it did not. Bell, after all, was providing both local and long distance service at this time, and so (as we have pointed out before) it did not much matter whether money was coming into its left pocket or its right pocket. Further, Bell might have thought that these sorts of cross-subsidies would, as a political matter, protect it from antitrust challenge. After all, just as having a single integrated telephone service provider made it easy for AT&T to engage in the sorts of cross-subsidization challenged in the antitrust litigation, having a single integrated telephone service provider made these sorts of policy-motivated cross-subsidies easy to accomplish as well.

The 1984 breakup required the Commission to revisit its universal service policies, however, because long distance and local rates would no longer be paid to the same firm. In the post-divestiture world, raising the price on long distance service to subsidize local service would not work without a mechanism by which AT&T and the other long distance carriers could be forced to transfer funds to the Bell Operating Companies and other local exchange carriers. At the same time, and in obvious tension with the Ozark Plan, the Commission during this period was ready to reduce long distance rates and allocate costs more accurately, the policy motivation being that the exaggerated long distance rates were causing inefficient underutilization of long distance service. (In other words, cross-subsidization had pushed rates far away from the efficient prices suggested by Ramsey pricing and explained in Chapter Fifteen.)

The Commission's post-divestiture universal service plan thus had two parts. The first was to create "access charges" paid by long distance companies to local carriers for originating and terminating long distance calls.[11] The second was to allocate more of the fixed costs of the local network to local rates through a "subscriber line charge" (SLC) that would be paid by local phone service customers. The original plan was to peg the SLC at a fixed $6 per month, which would be offset by an immediate decrease in long distance rates of 5 to 10 cents a minute. However, in the face of virulent opposition from Congress, consumer advocates and state regulators—all of whom liked the idea of keeping local rates low and who either did not factor long distance spending into their assessment of consumer welfare or did not believe long distance prices would actually fall—the FCC backed off. In the end, the Commission left the $6 SLC in place only for business users and capped the residential SLC at $3.50 per month. The FCC did not alter those charges until 2000, when it raised the residential SLC to $4.35 with conditional provision for increases up to $6.50 over the following three years.[12]

The important post-divestiture changes in universal service policies were thus (1) the shifting of a greater proportion of the costs of local service onto the

---

10. Huber et. al, *supra* note 1, at 133.
11. *See* MTS and WATS Market Structure, Phase I, 93 FCC 2d 241 (1983).
12. In re Access Charge Reform, 15 FCC Rcd. 12962 (2000). This *Report and Order* is also discussed in Chapter Eighteen.

charges for those services through the creation of the subscriber line charge; and (2) the creation of interstate access charges through which revenues from interexchange service could be transferred to local exchange carriers. Neither change was received without controversy. Controversy surrounding the former is discussed above; as for the latter, long distance companies claimed that access charges were significantly in excess of the local exchange companies' costs of originating and terminating traffic, thereby improperly inflating the local companies' profits while raising long distance prices for consumers. Access charge reform thus became an important policy issue—one that would ultimately take center stage in the Telecommunications Act of 1996. It is to that momentous legislation that we now turn.

CHAPTER EIGHTEEN

THE TELECOMMUNICATIONS ACT OF 1996

The purpose of this chapter is:

- to examine the central provisions of the Telecommunications Act of 1996, which is the most ambitious piece of telecommunications legislation since the Communications Act of 1934.

∼

A central premise of the Bell divestiture was that the provision of local telephone service was a monopoly enterprise. This view had taken hold back in the 1920s and had led to the system of state-sanctioned local monopolies that both pre-dated and survived the Bell breakup. Indeed, while the MFJ had rejected the notion that long distance service should be provided by a single monopolistic firm, even the MFJ took local exchange monopolies as a given. The consent decree did nothing to promote competition in the local loop. That meant, as we learned last chapter, that state public utilities commissions still had to regulate rates in the local market, and that the FCC (along with appellate courts interpreting the MFJ) still had to design and enforce line of business restrictions so as to protect competitive markets from predatory behavior by the various local phone service monopolists.

By the 1990s, however, both policymakers and entrepreneurs were ready to question the underlying assumption that local service should—or at least as a practical matter would—be provided by state-sanctioned monopolists. New firms had by this time already begun to compete with the incumbent LECs in providing business customers with connections to the long distance networks. And a few firms had even obtained the necessary authorizations to operate switches for the purpose of providing competing residential service, although little such service was actually being offered. The development of wireless (cellular) telephony further suggested that there could be stable competition in the local exchange. True, none of this necessarily meant that there weren't efficiencies to having a single provider of local telephone service; but all of this did suggest that perhaps those efficiencies were not so great as was once thought. The 1990s thus saw increasing political pressure to abandon the complex regulatory framework of the MFJ and instead set free competitive forces. The result was the Telecommunications Act of 1996.[1]

---

1. Telecommunications Act of 1996, Pub. L. No. 104–104, 110 Stat. 56, *codified at* 47 U.S.C. §§151 *et. seq*. The 1996 Act is technically an amendment to the Communications Act of 1934, which remains the umbrella statute for U.S. telecommunications. The 1934 Act, with the 1996 Act and other past amendments, is contained in Title 47 of the United

The 1996 Act has three major themes. First, the Act is designed to facilitate local telephone competition, both by eliminating state-imposed barriers to competition and by forcing existing local exchange carriers to cooperate with potential competitive entrants. This is in many ways the heart of the new Act, in that these provisions implement the new belief that local exchange carriers should not be shielded from competition but should instead be subject to it.

Second, the Act set out to increase competition in telecommunications markets that were already open to competition. Examples of such markets include the long distance services market and certain markets relating to the manufacture and sale of CPE.[2] Under the MFJ, these markets were not as competitive as they might otherwise have been because the RHCs and BOCs were forbidden, by the decree's line of business restrictions, from entering many of them. The Act, however, specifies the conditions under which these restrictions will be removed. The key intuition behind all of these provisions is that, if the Act is successful at introducing competition into the local market, the Bell Operating Companies will no longer enjoy monopoly power and thus will no longer be able to engage in discriminatory interconnection or predatory cross-subsidization. As soon as that happens, there is no reason to keep the BOCs and RHCs from entering competitive markets related to, but distinct from, the local exchange markets.

Third and finally, the Act substantially reforms the funding and definition of universal service. Many of these changes were necessary adjustments motivated by the new competitive structure made possible by the Act. Some, however, reflect a growing policy concern that universal service needs to be redefined so as to promote increased access not just to "plain old telephone service" but also to more advanced telecommunications services like, for example, Internet access.

This chapter is organized around these three themes. The chapter begins with a section on the local competition provisions and then, in the two sections that follow, considers the BOC line of business restrictions and the issue of universal service reform. One question to keep in mind as you work through this material: did the 1996 Act make regulation less determinative of market outcomes, or more so? In other words, does the Act really represent an increased reliance on competitive forces as opposed to regulatory oversight when it comes to setting price and quality, or has the Act instead gone so far in regulating to promote competition that regulation is in fact more outcome determinative today than it was before 1996?

States Code. All statutory sections referred to here, unless otherwise noted, are therefore found in 47 U.S.C.

2. While this was one of Congress's explicit goals for the 1996 Act, there is some debate over whether the Act really will increase competition — or whether all it will accomplish is increasing the number of competitors eligible to enter the above-referenced markets. There is also some debate over whether there is/was even a need for more competition. For example, there is some evidence to suggest that the long distance market was significantly competitive long before the 1996 Act took effect. If true, one might question the wisdom of allowing the BOCs to enter long distance, given all the regulatory complexity that introduces and the danger that regulatory imperfections could again introduce the possibility of predatory cross-subsidization and/or discriminatory interconnection. (The politics here might really have been that the BOCs were allowed to enter these markets under the 1996 Act because the politically powerful BOCs wanted to be able to do so.)

I. THE LOCAL COMPETITION PROVISIONS

The Telecommunications Act of 1996 radically revised prior law by both eliminating state-imposed barriers to competition and forcing existing local exchange carriers to cooperate with potential competitive entrants. The goal of all these provisions is the same: to facilitate, to the extent possible given the economics of the industry, competition in the local loop.

The simplest provisions to understand are the various provisions designed to make it possible for new entrants—so-called "competitive local exchange carriers" or CLECs—to build their own competing local telephone infrastructure and to interconnect that infrastructure with the existing telephone network. Competitors who choose to build their own infrastructure are known as facilities-based competitors since they aim to provide local service either exclusively or predominantly over their own facilities. The provisions most relevant to their efforts are section 253(a), which preempts state and local laws that create barriers to entry into the local exchange markets, and sections 251(a) and 251(c), which require rival local exchange carriers to exchange traffic with entrants such that customers on any one telephone network can communicate with customers on every other network. Note that all of these provisions do important work. The state law preemption provision stops local authorities from protecting favored local exchange carriers. The interconnection provisions, meanwhile, stop incumbent LECs from using the network externalities discussed in Chapter Fifteen to their strategic advantage. After all, refusal by the existing local exchange carrier to interconnect with a rival's system would mean that customers of the new firm would be unable to call, or receive calls from, anyone outside the new network—a result that would effectively eliminate the new firm's business prospects, even if it were to build a state-of-the-art rival telephone network.[3]

A more complicated set of provisions attempts to facilitate entry by firms who might not find it in their interest to build their own entire local telephone networks but who would, if allowed, compete with rival local exchange carriers by providing some services or infrastructure on their own while purchasing other services or infrastructure from rivals. These provisions thus attempt to foster entry by forcing LECs to make their services and infrastructure available to competitors at regulated rates.

Two statutory alternatives are relevant here: the resale provisions and the unbundling provisions. Let's consider the resale provisions first. Under sections 251(b)(1) and 251(c)(4), a CLEC has the right to purchase (at regulated rates) telecommunications services from a rival and then resell those services directly to consumers under the CLEC's own name. Section 251(b)(1) applies to all local exchange carriers and requires that they neither prohibit, nor impose "unreasonable or discriminatory conditions or limitations on," this sort of resale. Section 251(c)(4), meanwhile, applies only to so-called "incumbent local exchange carriers" (ILECs), which the Act defines in section 251(h) to include any LEC that

---

3. If the new entrant were able to gain a majority of subscribers, the network externalities discussed in Chapter Fifteen would start to work in its favor. But getting to that point without interconnection would be difficult (to put it mildly).

provided telephone exchange service as of the date of enactment of the 1996 Act. The provision reaffirms the resale requirement and further stipulates that ILECs must offer to resell relevant telecommunications services "at wholesale rates."

The second option available to a would-be competitor is to use section 251(c)(3) to purchase access, again at regulated rates, to particular components that are part of an incumbent's existing telephone network. These components are referred to in the Act as "network elements"; examples include an incumbent's switches, its transport lines, and its customer loops. This provision is generally referred to as the Act's "unbundling" provision because it requires incumbent firms to separate (or "unbundle") particular elements of their networks and to allow entrants to purchase access to any of those elements. The elements themselves are termed "unbundled network elements" or UNEs. Note that the unbundling provisions allow a CLEC to purchase access to shared building blocks, whereas the resale provisions instead allow a CLEC to purchase complete telecommunications services. And, again in contrast to the resale provisions, the unbundling provision applies only to ILECs.[4]

An example might help to make these provisions concrete. Suppose that the management consulting firm McKinsey & Co. wants to offer to its business clients an integrated telephone/data processing service. If the local incumbent already possesses the ability to provide this service, one approach would be for McKinsey to purchase the service from the ILEC at wholesale rates and then resell it to the firm's customers under the McKinsey brand. McKinsey would add its own marketing and billing infrastructure, but the firm would rely on the ILEC to provide the service. On the opposite extreme, McKinsey could build its own facilities and provide the service entirely by itself. The company might set up some form of cellular telephone system, for example, or install its own switches and wires. McKinsey's more intermediate option is to rent access to some of the ILEC's equipment — say, its switch and particularly expensive transport lines — but to provide the rest of the necessary equipment in-house. Under this approach, McKinsey might use its own computer system to accomplish the data processing, its own CPE placed at each business facility, and so on, cobbling together the full system by connecting those components to components "unbundled" from the ILEC. In short, then, McKinsey has three entry options: entry through resale, entry through pure facilities-based competition, and entry via the purchase of unbundled network elements.

Not surprisingly, the parts of the 1996 Act that impose interconnection and unbundling duties on incumbent local exchange carriers — notably sections 251 and 252 of the Act — have been the source of substantial controversy. We begin our study of that controversy with the first FCC *Report and Order* that explains and implements these provisions. Readers are strongly advised to read sections 251 and 252, as edited in the statutory appendix, before studying the *Report and Order*.

---

4. Standard pronunciations for the various terms here are as follows. The abbreviations LEC, ILEC, and CLEC are pronounced "lek," "aye-lek," and "see-lek," respectively. Meanwhile, the abbreviation UNE is pronounced "yoo-nee."

IN RE IMPLEMENTATION OF THE LOCAL COMPETITION
PROVISIONS OF THE TELECOMMUNICATIONS ACT OF 1996

First Report and Order, 11 FCC Rcd. 15499 (1996)

C. Economic Barriers

10. The removal of statutory and regulatory barriers to entry in the local exchange market, while a necessary precondition to competition, is not sufficient to ensure that competition will supplant monopolies. An incumbent LEC's existing infrastructure enables it to serve new customers at a much lower incremental cost than a facilities-based entrant that must install its own switches, trunking, and loops to serve its customers. Furthermore, absent interconnection between the incumbent LEC and the entrant, the customer of the entrant would be unable to complete calls to subscribers served by the incumbent LEC's network. Because an incumbent LEC currently serves virtually all subscribers in its local serving area, an incumbent LEC has little economic incentive to assist new entrants in their efforts to secure a greater share of that market. An incumbent LEC also has the ability to act on its incentive to discourage entry and robust competition by not interconnecting its network with the new entrant's network or by insisting on supracompetitive prices or other unreasonable conditions for terminating calls from the entrant's customers to the incumbent LEC's subscribers.

11. Congress addressed these problems in the 1996 Act by mandating that the most significant economic impediments to efficient entry into the monopolized local market be removed. The incumbent LECs have economies of density, connectivity, and scale; traditionally, these have been viewed as creating a natural monopoly. The local competition provisions of the Act require that these economies be shared with entrants. We believe they should be shared in a way that permits the incumbent LECs to maintain operating efficiency to further fair competition, and to enable the entrants to share the economic benefits of that efficiency in the form of cost-based prices.

12. The Act contemplates three paths of entry into the local market—the construction of new networks, the use of unbundled elements of the incumbent's network, and resale. The 1996 Act requires us to implement rules that eliminate statutory and regulatory barriers and remove economic impediments to each. We anticipate that some new entrants will follow multiple paths of entry as market conditions and access to capital permit. Some may enter by relying at first entirely on resale of the incumbent's services and then gradually deploying their own facilities. This strategy was employed successfully by MCI and Sprint in the interexchange market during the 1970's and 1980's. Others may use a combination of entry strategies simultaneously—whether in the same geographic market or in different ones. Some competitors may use unbundled network elements in combination with their own facilities to serve densely populated sections of an incumbent LEC's service territory, while using resold services to reach customers in less densely populated areas. Still other new entrants may pursue a single entry strategy that does not vary by geographic region or over time. Our obligation in this proceeding is to establish rules that will ensure that all pro-competitive entry strategies may be explored. As to success or failure, we look to the market, not to regulation, for the answer.

13. We note that an entrant, such as a cable company, that constructs its own network will not necessarily need the services or facilities of an incumbent LEC to enable its own subscribers to communicate with each other. A firm adopting this entry strategy, however, still will need an agreement with the incumbent LEC to enable the entrant's customers to place calls to and receive calls from the incumbent LEC's subscribers. Sections 251(b)(5) and (c)(2) require incumbent LECs to enter into such agreements on just, reasonable, and nondiscriminatory terms and to transport and terminate traffic originating on another carrier's network under reciprocal compensation arrangements. In this item, we adopt rules for states to apply in implementing these mandates of section 251 in their arbitration of interconnection disputes, as well as their review of such arbitrated arrangements, or a BOC's statement of generally available terms. We believe that our rules will assist the states in carrying out their responsibilities under the 1996 Act, thereby furthering the Act's goals of fostering prompt, efficient, competitive entry.

14. We also note that many new entrants will not have fully constructed their local networks when they begin to offer service. Although they may provide some of their own facilities, these new entrants will be unable to reach all of their customers without depending on the incumbent's facilities. Hence, in addition to an arrangement for terminating traffic on the incumbent LEC's network, entrants will likely need agreements that enable them to obtain wholesale prices for services they wish to sell at retail and to use at least some portions of the incumbents' facilities, such as local loops and end office switching facilities.

15. Congress recognized that, because of the incumbent LEC's incentives and superior bargaining power, its negotiations with new entrants over the terms of such agreements would be quite different from typical commercial negotiations. As distinct from bilateral commercial negotiation, the new entrant comes to the table with little or nothing the incumbent LEC needs or wants. The statute addresses this problem by creating an arbitration proceeding in which the new entrant may assert certain rights, including that the incumbent's prices for unbundled network elements must be "just, reasonable and nondiscriminatory." We adopt rules herein to implement these requirements of section 251(c)(3).

D. Operational Barriers

16. The statute also directs us to remove the existing operational barriers to entering the local market. Vigorous competition would be impeded by technical disadvantages and other handicaps that prevent a new entrant from offering services that consumers perceive to be equal in quality to the offerings of incumbent LECs. Our recently-issued number portability *Report and Order* addressed one of the most significant operational barriers to competition by permitting customers to retain their phone numbers when they change local carriers.[5]

---

5. Telephone Number Portability, First Report and Order and Further Notice of Proposed Rulemaking, FCC 96–286 (July 2, 1996). Consistent with the 1996 Act, 47 U.S.C. §251(b)(2), we required LECs to implement interim and long-term measures to ensure that customers can change their local service providers without having to change their phone number. Number portability promotes competition by making it less expensive and less disruptive for a customer to switch providers, thus freeing the customer to choose the local provider that offers the best value.

17. Closely related to number portability is dialing parity. Dialing parity enables a customer of a new entrant to dial others with the convenience an incumbent provides, regardless of which carrier the customer has chosen as the local service provider. The history of competition in the interexchange market illustrates the critical importance of dialing parity to the successful introduction of competition in telecommunications markets. Equal access enabled customers of non-AT&T providers to enjoy the same convenience of dialing "1" plus the called party's number that AT&T customers had. Prior to equal access, subscribers to interexchange carriers (IXCs) other than AT&T often were required to dial more than 20 digits to place an interstate long distance call. Industry data show that, after equal access was deployed throughout the country, the number of customers using MCI and other long distance carriers increased significantly. Thus, we believe that equal access had a substantial pro-competitive impact. Dialing parity should have the same effect.

18. This *Order* addresses other operational barriers to competition, such as access to rights of way, collocation, and the expeditious provisioning of resale and unbundled elements to new entrants. The elimination of these obstacles is essential if there is to be a fair opportunity to compete in the local exchange and exchange access markets. As an example, customers can voluntarily switch from one interexchange carrier to another extremely rapidly, through automated systems. This has been a boon to competition in the interexchange market. We expect that moving customers from one local carrier to another rapidly will be essential to fair local competition.

E. Transition

21. We consider it vitally important to establish a pro-competitive, deregulatory national policy framework for local telephony competition, but we are acutely mindful of existing common carrier arrangements, relationships, and expectations, particularly those that affect incumbent LECs.

22. In this regard, this *Order* sets minimum, uniform, national rules, but also relies heavily on states to apply these rules and to exercise their own discretion in implementing a pro-competitive regime in their local telephone markets. On those issues where the need to create a factual record distinct to a state or to balance unique local considerations is material, we ask the states to develop their own rules that are consistent with general guidance contained herein. The states will do so in rulemakings and in arbitrating interconnection arrangements. On other issues, particularly those related to pricing, we facilitate the ability of states to adopt immediate, temporary decisions by permitting the states to set proxy prices within a defined range or subject to a ceiling. We believe that some states will find these alternatives useful in light of the strict deadlines of the law. For example, section 252(b)(4)(C) requires a state commission to complete the arbitration of issues that have been referred to it, pursuant to section 252(b)(1), within nine months after the incumbent local exchange carrier received the request for negotiation. Selection of the actual prices within the range or subject to the ceiling will be for the state commission to determine. Some states may use proxies temporarily because they lack the resources necessary to review cost studies in rulemakings or arbitrations. Other states may lack adequate resources to complete such tasks before the expiration of the arbitration deadline. However, we encourage all states to complete the necessary work within the statutory deadline.

F.   Executive Summary

1. Scope of Authority of the FCC and State Commissions

24. The Commission concludes that sections 251 and 252 address both inter-state and intrastate aspects of interconnection, resale services, and access to un-bundled elements. The 1996 Act moves beyond the distinction between interstate and intrastate matters that was established in the 1934 Act, and instead expands the applicability of national rules to historically intrastate issues, and state rules to historically interstate issues. In the *Report and Order*, the Commission con-cludes that the states and the FCC can craft a partnership that is built on mutual commitment to local telephone competition throughout the country, and that under this partnership, the FCC establishes uniform national rules for some is-sues, the states, and in some instances the FCC, administer these rules, and the states adopt additional rules that are critical to promoting local telephone com-petition. The rules that the FCC establishes in this *Report and Order* are mini-mum requirements upon which the states may build.

2. Duty to Negotiate in Good Faith

25. In the *Report and Order*, the Commission establishes some national rules regarding the duty to negotiate in good faith, but concludes that it would be fu-tile to try to determine in advance every possible action that might be inconsis-tent with the duty to negotiate in good faith. The Commission also concludes that, in many instances, whether a party has negotiated in good faith will need to be decided on a case-by-case basis, in light of the particular circumstances. The Commission notes that the arbitration process set forth in section 252 provides one remedy for failing to negotiate in good faith.

3. Interconnection

26. Section 251(c)(2) requires incumbent LECs to provide interconnection to any requesting telecommunications carrier at any technically feasible point. The interconnection must be at least equal in quality to that provided by the incum-bent LEC to itself or its affiliates, and must be provided on rates, terms, and con-ditions that are just, reasonable, and nondiscriminatory. The Commission con-cludes that the term "interconnection" under section 251(c)(2) refers only to the physical linking of two networks for the mutual exchange of traffic.

4. Access to Unbundled Elements

27. Section 251(c)(3) requires incumbent LECs to provide requesting telecommunications carriers nondiscriminatory access to network elements on an unbundled basis at any technically feasible point on rates, terms, and conditions that are just, reasonable, and nondiscriminatory. In the *Report and Order*, the Commission identifies a minimum set of network elements that incumbent LECs must provide under this section. States may require incumbent LECs to provide additional network elements on an unbundled basis. The minimum set of net-work elements the Commission identifies are: local loops, local and tandem switches (including all vertical switching features provided by such switches), in-teroffice transmission facilities, network interface devices, signalling and call-re-lated database facilities, operations support systems functions, and operator and

directory assistance facilities. The Commission concludes that access to such operations support systems is critical to affording new entrants a meaningful opportunity to compete with incumbent LECs. The Commission also concludes that incumbent LECs are required to provide access to network elements in a manner that allows requesting carriers to combine such elements as they choose, and that incumbent LECs may not impose restrictions upon the uses to which requesting carriers put such network elements.

5. Methods of Obtaining Interconnection and Access to Unbundled Elements

28. Section 251(c)(6) requires incumbent LECs to provide physical collocation of equipment necessary for interconnection or access to unbundled network elements at the incumbent LEC's premises, except that the incumbent LEC may provide virtual collocation if it demonstrates to the state commission that physical collocation is not practical for technical reasons or because of space limitations. The Commission concludes that incumbent LECs are required to provide for any technically feasible method of interconnection or access requested by a telecommunications carrier, including physical collocation, virtual collocation, and interconnection at meet points.

6. Pricing Methodologies

29. The 1996 Act requires the states to set prices for interconnection and unbundled elements that are cost-based, nondiscriminatory, and may include a reasonable profit. To help the states accomplish this, the Commission concludes that the state commissions should set arbitrated rates for interconnection and access to unbundled elements pursuant to a forward-looking economic cost pricing methodology. The Commission concludes that the prices that new entrants pay for interconnection and unbundled elements should be based on the local telephone companies' Total Service Long-Run Incremental Cost of a particular network element, which the Commission calls "Total Element Long-Run Incremental Cost" (TELRIC), plus a reasonable share of forward-looking joint and common costs. States will determine, among other things, the appropriate risk-adjusted cost of capital and depreciation rates. For states that are unable to conduct a cost study and apply an economic costing methodology within the statutory time frame for arbitrating interconnection disputes, the Commission establishes default ceilings and ranges for the states to apply, on an interim basis, to interconnection arrangements.

8. Resale

32. The 1996 Act requires all incumbent LECs to offer for resale any telecommunications service that the carrier provides at retail to subscribers who are not telecommunications carriers. Resale will be an important entry strategy both in the short term for many new entrants as they build out their own facilities and for small businesses that cannot afford to compete in the local exchange market by purchasing unbundled elements or by building their own networks. State commissions must identify marketing, billing, collection, and other costs that will be avoided or that are avoidable by incumbent LECs when they provide services wholesale, and calculate the portion of the retail rates for those services that is attributable to the avoided and avoidable costs. The Commission identi-

fies certain avoided costs, and the application of this definition is left to the states. If a state elects not to implement the methodology, it may elect, on an interim basis, a discount rate from within a default range of discount rates established by the Commission. The Commission establishes a default discount range of 17–25% off retail prices, leaving the states to set the specific rate within that range, in the exercise of their discretion.

Notes and Questions

1. Judicial Challenge. Many of the rules adopted pursuant to the above *Local Competition First Report and Order* have been challenged in court. Several of the opinions that resulted from those challenges are excerpted in the materials below. Before turning to those details, however, it is helpful to review the basic intuitions that undergird the resale and unbundling provisions.

2. Test Your Understanding. Suppose a firm does not wish to offer full telephone service, but only one or more advanced features. For example, suppose a firm wants to market to businesses a teleconferencing service, whereby one can pick up a phone in the office, dial a predetermined number, and be directly connected to six predetermined recipients. How might the firm take advantage of the new local competition provisions to build such a service without having to build an entire local telephone plant as well?

3. Resale. Now suppose that the firm wants to be a pure reseller, buying local phone service from the incumbent LEC and reselling it to consumers under the firm's own brand. Can the firm do this—resell a service without adding any value other than perhaps its own innovative approach to marketing and billing? If so, what policy goals are advanced by allowing this sort of "competition"? In what way does it challenge an incumbent LEC's monopoly in the local loop, or otherwise benefit consumers?

4. Evaluate the Act. Reviewing your answers to the previous two questions, what are the respective costs and benefits of the local competition rules? How much regulatory oversight is required to make this scheme work? Is the result something more than competition in billing for otherwise identical services? Is this a practical way to facilitate entry by full-service and/or niche-service providers?

5. Finding the Natural Monopoly. How do the resale and interconnection provisions account for claims that the local loop is a natural monopoly? Is the intuition here that these regulations allow competitors to share the natural monopoly portions of the local network but compete in all other respects? If so, who defines which are the natural monopoly portions and which are, instead, the competitive segments? Is it true that these regulations permit competitive forces to answer that question, the idea being that CLECs will exercise the resale and unbundling provisions with respect to portions that exhibit natural monopoly properties but choose to build other portions for themselves? (Think carefully about this; the answer is of critical importance to understanding the political dynamics that follow.)

6. Calling Judge Greene. If, in 1980, someone had conceived of the provisions that are now sections 251 and 252 of the 1996 Act, would Judge Greene have been well advised to reject the consent decree divorcing AT&T from the local exchange operations in favor of mandatory interconnection, unbundling, and the like?

7. *Iowa Utilities Board.* As was noted above, several aspects of the *Local Competition First Report and Order* have been challenged in court, and several of those cases remain unresolved today. Many of the most important issues, however, were raised in a case that has already gone to the Supreme Court, namely the 1999 case of AT&T Corporation v. Iowa Utilities Board. The Court took the case on writ of certiorari to the Court of Appeals for the Eighth Circuit which had ruled, among other things, that the Telecommunications Act of 1996 did not grant the FCC rulemaking jurisdiction over intrastate matters. Accordingly, the Eighth Circuit's decision had invalidated many of the FCC's local competition regulations, including those governing the pricing of unbundled network elements. The Supreme Court's response on the substance of the Commission's regulations is excerpted below; we address the jurisdictional question after the excerpt.

AT&T CORPORATION v. IOWA UTILITIES BOARD
525 U.S. 366 (1999)

SCALIA, J., delivered the opinion of the Court, Parts I, III-A, III-C, III-D, and IV of which were joined by REHNQUIST, C.J., and STEVENS, KENNEDY, SOUTER, THOMAS, GINSBURG, and BREYER, JJ., Part II of which was joined by STEVENS, KENNEDY, SOUTER, and GINSBURG, JJ., and Part III-B of which was joined by REHNQUIST, C. J., and STEVENS, KENNEDY, THOMAS, GINSBURG, and BREYER, JJ. SOUTER, J., filed an opinion concurring in part and dissenting in part. THOMAS, J., filed an opinion concurring in part and dissenting in part, in which REHNQUIST, C. J., and BREYER, J., joined. BREYER, J., filed an opinion concurring in part and dissenting in part. O'CONNOR, J., took no part in the consideration or decision of these cases.

JUSTICE SCALIA delivered the opinion of the Court.

In this case, we address the question of whether the Federal Communications Commission has authority to implement certain pricing and nonpricing provisions of the Telecommunications Act of 1996, as well as whether the Commission's rules governing unbundled access and "pick and choose" negotiation are consistent with the statute.

Until the 1990s, local phone service was thought to be a natural monopoly. States typically granted an exclusive franchise in each local service area to a local exchange carrier (LEC), which owned, among other things, the local loops (wires connecting telephones to switches), the switches (equipment directing calls to their destinations), and the transport trunks (wires carrying calls between switches) that constitute a local exchange network. Technological advances, however, have made competition among multiple providers of local service seem possible, and Congress recently ended the longstanding regime of state-sanctioned monopolies.

The Telecommunications Act of 1996 (1996 Act or Act) fundamentally restructures local telephone markets. States may no longer enforce laws that impede competition, and incumbent LECs are subject to a host of duties intended to facilitate market entry. Foremost among these duties is the LEC's obligation under 47 U.S.C. §251(c) to share its network with competitors. Under this provision, a requesting carrier can obtain access to an incumbent's network in three ways: it can purchase local telephone services at wholesale rates for resale to end users; it can lease elements of the incumbent's network "on an unbundled basis"; and it can interconnect its own facilities with the incumbent's network. When an entrant seeks access through any of these routes, the incumbent can negotiate an agreement without regard to the duties it would otherwise have under §251(b) or (c). *See* §252(a)(1). But if private negotiation fails, either party can petition the state commission that regulates local phone service to arbitrate open issues, which arbitration is subject to §251 and the FCC regulations promulgated thereunder.

Six months after the 1996 Act was passed, the FCC issued its *First Report and Order* implementing the local-competition provisions. In re Implementation of the Local Competition Provisions in the Telecommunications Act of 1996, 11 FCC Rcd. 15499 (1996) (*First Report & Order*). The numerous challenges to this rulemaking, filed across the country by incumbent LECs and state utility commissions, were consolidated in the United States Court of Appeals for the Eighth Circuit.

The basic attack was jurisdictional. The LECs and state commissions insisted that primary authority to implement the local-competition provisions belonged to the States rather than to the FCC. They thus argued that many of the local-competition rules were invalid, most notably the one requiring that prices for interconnection and unbundled access be based on "Total Element Long Run Incremental Cost" (TELRIC)—a forward-looking rather than historic measure.[6] The Court of Appeals agreed and vacated the pricing rules, as well as several other aspects of the *Order*, as reaching beyond the Commission's jurisdiction. Iowa Utilities Board v. FCC, 120 F.3d 753, 800, 804, 805–806 (1997). It held that the general rulemaking authority conferred upon the Commission by the Communications Act of 1934 extended only to interstate matters, and that the Commission therefore needed specific congressional authorization before implementing provisions of the 1996 Act addressing intrastate telecommunications. It found no such authorization for the Commission's rules regarding pricing, dialing parity, exemptions for rural LECs, the proper procedure for resolving local-competition disputes, and state review of pre-1996 interconnection agreements. Indeed, with respect to some of these matters, the Eighth Circuit said that the 1996 Act had affirmatively given exclusive authority to the state commissions.

The Court of Appeals found support for its holdings in 47 U.S.C. §152(b) (§2(b) of the Communications Act of 1934), which, it said, creates a presumption in favor of preserving state authority over intrastate communications. It found nothing in the 1996 Act clear enough to overcome this presumption, which it described as a fence that is "hog tight, horse high, and bull strong, preventing the FCC from intruding on the states' intrastate turf." 120 F.3d at 800.

---

6. TELRIC pricing is based upon the cost of operating a hypothetical network built with the most efficient technology available. Incumbents argued in the lower court that this method was unreasonable because it stranded their historic costs and underestimated the actual costs of providing interconnection and unbundled access. The Eighth Circuit did not reach this issue, and the merits of TELRIC are not before us. [Ed. We consider the merits of TELRIC later in this chapter.]

Incumbent LECs also made several challenges, only some of which are relevant here, to the rules implementing the 1996 Act's requirement of unbundled access. *See* 47 U.S.C. §251(c)(3). Rule 319, the primary unbundling rule, sets forth a minimum number of network elements that incumbents must make available to requesting carriers. The LECs complained that, in compiling this list, the FCC had virtually ignored the 1996 Act's requirement that it consider whether access to proprietary elements was "necessary" and whether lack of access to nonproprietary elements would "impair" an entrant's ability to provide local service. *See* §251(d)(2). In addition, the LECs thought that the list included items (like directory assistance and caller I.D.) that did not meet the statutory definition of "network element." *See* §153(29). The Eighth Circuit rebuffed both arguments, holding that the Commission's interpretations of the "necessary and impair" standard and the definition of "network element" were reasonable and hence lawful thanks to *Chevron* deference. Chevron U.S.A., Inc. v. Natural Resources Defense Council, Inc., 467 U.S. 837 (1984).

When it promulgated its unbundling rules, the Commission explicitly declined to impose a requirement of facility ownership on carriers who sought to lease network elements. Because the list of elements that Rule 319 made available was so extensive, the effect of this omission was to allow competitors to provide local phone service relying solely on the elements in an incumbent's network. The LECs argued that this "all elements" rule undermined the 1996 Act's goal of encouraging entrants to develop their own facilities. The Court of Appeals, however, deferred to the FCC's approach. Nothing in the 1996 Act itself imposed a requirement of facility ownership, and the court was of the view that the language of §251(c)(3) indicated that "a requesting carrier may achieve the capability to provide telecommunications service completely through access to the unbundled elements of an incumbent LEC's network." 120 F.3d at 814.

II

Section 201(b), a 1938 amendment to the Communications Act of 1934, provides that "the Commission may prescribe such rules and regulations as may be necessary in the public interest to carry out the provisions of this Act." 52 Stat. 588, 47 U.S.C. §201(b). Since Congress expressly directed that the 1996 Act, along with its local-competition provisions, be inserted into the Communications Act of 1934, 1996 Act, §1(b), 110 Stat. 56, the Commission's rulemaking authority would seem to extend to implementation of the local-competition provisions.

Respondents argue, however, that §201(b) rulemaking authority is limited to those provisions dealing with purely interstate and foreign matters, because the first sentence of §201(a) makes it "the duty of every common carrier engaged in interstate or foreign communication by wire or radio to furnish such communication service upon reasonable request therefor...." It is impossible to understand how this use of the qualifier "interstate or foreign" in §201(a), which limits the class of common carriers with the duty of providing communication service, reaches forward into the last sentence of §201(b) to limit the class of provisions that the Commission has authority to implement. We think that the grant in §201(b) means what it says: The FCC has rulemaking authority to carry out the "provisions of this Act," which include §§251 and 252, added by the Telecommunications Act of 1996.

[The Court went on here to consider and then reject a large number of nuanced arguments put forward by those who believed that the FCC lacked jurisdiction to promulgate the local competition rules at issue in this case.]

III

A

We turn next to the unbundling rules, and come first to the incumbent LECs' complaint that the FCC included within the features and services that must be provided to competitors under Rule 319 items that do not (as they must) meet the statutory definition of "network element." Among the items included by the FCC but challenged by the incumbent LECs: operator services and directory assistance, operational support systems (OSS), and vertical switching functions such as caller I. D., call forwarding, and call waiting. *See* 47 CFR §§51.319(f)–(g) (1997); *First Report & Order* ¶413. The statute defines a "network element" as

> "a facility or equipment used in the provision of a telecommunications service. Such term also includes features, functions, and capabilities that are provided by means of such facility or equipment, including subscriber numbers, databases, signaling systems, and information sufficient for billing and collection or used in the transmission, routing, or other provision of a telecommunications service." 47 U.S.C. §153(29).

Given the breadth of this definition, it is impossible to credit the incumbents' argument that a "network element" must be part of the physical facilities and equipment used to provide local phone service. Operator services and directory assistance, whether they involve live operators or automation, are "features, functions, and capabilities" provided by means of the network equipment. OSS, the incumbent's background software system, contains essential network information as well as programs to manage billing, repair ordering, and other functions. Section 153(29)'s reference to "databases" and "information sufficient for billing and collection or used in the transmission, routing, or other provision of a telecommunications service" provides ample basis for treating this system as a "network element." And vertical switching features, such as caller I. D., are functions "provided by means of" the switch, and thus fall squarely within the statutory definition. We agree with the Eighth Circuit that the Commission's application of the "network element" definition is eminently reasonable.

B

We are of the view, however, that the FCC did not adequately consider the "necessary and impair" standards when it gave blanket access to these network elements, and others, in Rule 319. That rule requires an incumbent to provide requesting carriers with access to a minimum of seven network elements: the local loop, the network interface device, switching capability, interoffice transmission facilities, signaling networks and call-related databases, operations support systems functions, and operator services and directory assistance. 47 CFR §51.319 (1997). If a requesting carrier wants access to additional elements, it may petition the state commission, which can make other elements available on a case-by-case basis. §51.317.

Section 251(d)(2) of the Act provides:

> In determining what network elements should be made available for purposes of subsection (c)(3) of this section, the Commission shall consider, at a minimum, whether
>
> (A) access to such network elements as are proprietary in nature is necessary; and
>
> (B) the failure to provide access to such network elements would impair the ability of the telecommunications carrier seeking access to provide the services that it seeks to offer.

We agree with the incumbents that the Act requires the FCC to apply some limiting standard, rationally related to the goals of the Act, which it has simply failed to do. In the general statement of its methodology set forth in the *First Report and Order*, the Commission announced that it would regard the "necessary" standard as having been met regardless of whether "requesting carriers can obtain the requested proprietary element from a source other than the incumbent," since "requiring new entrants to duplicate unnecessarily even a part of the incumbent's network could generate delay and higher costs for new entrants, and thereby impede entry by competing local providers and delay competition, contrary to the goals of the 1996 Act." *First Report & Order* ¶283. And it announced that it would regard the "impairment" standard as having been met if "the failure of an incumbent to provide access to a network element would decrease the quality, or increase the financial or administrative cost of the service a requesting carrier seeks to offer, compared with providing that service *over other unbundled elements in the incumbent LEC's network*," ¶285 (emphasis added)—which means that comparison with self-provision, or with purchasing from another provider, is excluded. Since any entrant will request the most efficient network element that the incumbent has to offer, it is hard to imagine when the incumbent's failure to give access to the element would not constitute an "impairment" under this standard.

The Commission asserts that it deliberately limited its inquiry to the incumbent's own network because no rational entrant would seek access to network elements from an incumbent if it could get better service or prices elsewhere. That may be. But that judgment allows entrants, rather than the Commission, to determine whether access to proprietary elements is necessary, and whether the failure to obtain access to nonproprietary elements would impair the ability to provide services. The Commission cannot, consistent with the statute, blind itself to the availability of elements outside the incumbent's network. That failing alone would require the Commission's rule to be set aside. In addition, however, the Commission's assumption that any increase in cost (or decrease in quality) imposed by denial of a network element renders access to that element "necessary," and causes the failure to provide that element to "impair" the entrant's ability to furnish its desired services is simply not in accord with the ordinary and fair meaning of those terms. An entrant whose anticipated annual profits from the proposed service are reduced from 100% of investment to 99% of investment has perhaps been "impaired" in its ability to amass earnings, but has not ipso facto been impaired "in its ability to provide the services it seeks to offer"; and it cannot realistically be said that the network element enabling it to raise its profits to 100% is "necessary."

The Commission began with the premise that an incumbent was obliged to turn over as much of its network as was "technically feasible," and viewed (d)(2) as merely permitting it to soften that obligation by regulatory grace:

> "To give effect to both sections 251(c)(3) and 251(d)(2), we conclude that the proprietary and impairment standards in section 251(d)(2) grant us the authority to refrain from requiring incumbent LECs to provide all network elements for which it is technically feasible to provide access on an unbundled basis." *First Report & Order* ¶279.

The Commission's premise was wrong. Section 251(d)(2) does not authorize the Commission to create isolated exemptions from some underlying duty to make all network elements available. It requires the Commission to determine on a rational basis which network elements must be made available, taking into account the objectives of the Act and giving some substance to the "necessary" and "impair" requirements. The latter is not achieved by disregarding entirely the availability of elements outside the network, and by regarding any "increased cost or decreased service quality" as establishing a "necessity" and an "impairment" of the ability to provide services.

C

The incumbent LECs also renew their challenge to the "all elements" rule, which allows competitors to provide local phone service relying solely on the elements in an incumbent's network. *See First Report & Order* ¶¶328–340. This issue may be largely academic in light of our disposition of Rule 319. If the FCC on remand makes fewer network elements unconditionally available through the unbundling requirement, an entrant will no longer be able to lease every component of the network. But whether a requesting carrier can access the incumbent's network in whole or in part, we think that the Commission reasonably omitted a facilities-ownership requirement. The 1996 Act imposes no such limitation; if anything, it suggests the opposite, by requiring in §251(c)(3) that incumbents provide access to "any" requesting carrier. We agree with the Court of Appeals that the Commission's refusal to impose a facilities-ownership requirement was proper.

It would be gross understatement to say that the Telecommunications Act of 1996 is not a model of clarity. It is in many important respects a model of ambiguity or indeed even self-contradiction. That is most unfortunate for a piece of legislation that profoundly affects a crucial segment of the economy worth tens of billions of dollars. The 1996 Act can be read to grant (borrowing a phrase from incumbent GTE) "most promiscuous rights" to the FCC vis-a-vis the state commissions and to competing carriers vis-a-vis the incumbents—and the Commission has chosen in some instances to read it that way. But Congress is well aware that the ambiguities it chooses to produce in a statute will be resolved by the implementing agency, *see Chevron*. We can only enforce the clear limits that the 1996 Act contains, which in the present case invalidate only Rule 319.

For the reasons stated, the judgment of the Court of Appeals is reversed in part and affirmed in part and is remanded for proceedings consistent with this opinion.

[Concurring and dissenting opinions of JUSTICES SOUTER, THOMAS, and BREYER are omitted.]

Note on Jurisdiction

The jurisdictional battle between the state public utility commissions and the FCC was one of the central points of contention in *Iowa Utilities Board*, but the issues raised turn on a set of materials that are not typically addressed in a basic telecommunications course. In broad strokes, though, the jurisdictional dispute was as follows.

Applying the standard for preemption set forth by the Supreme Court in Louisiana Public Service Commission v. FCC, 476 U.S. 355 (1986), the Eighth Circuit had held that the Commission lacked jurisdiction to promulgate many of the rules that were challenged in *Iowa Utilities Board*. As we discussed in Chapter Fifteen, *Louisiana PSC* stands for the proposition that, under §152(b), the FCC can preempt state regulations governing intrastate telecommunications *only* if the Act expressly and unambiguously provides for such preemption. The Eighth Circuit found that §§251 and 252 of the 1996 Act expressly refer to state commissions as the bodies responsible for setting UNE rates and, further, that neither provision provides the necessary unambiguous authority for preemption by the FCC. Colorfully describing §152(b) as "a *Louisiana*-built fence that is hog tight, horse high, and bull strong, preventing the FCC from intruding on the states' intrastate turf," 120 F.3d at 800, the Eighth Circuit thus found the FCC to be acting outside its authority in promulgating the TELRIC pricing rules.

The Supreme Court reviewed the Eighth Circuit's decision on writ of certiorari and, in parts of the opinion not excerpted above, reversed the Eighth Circuit's holding with respect to jurisdiction. Instead, a majority of the Court found that, by virtue of §201(b) of the 1934 Act, the FCC had jurisdiction to promulgate its pricing rules. That provision provides that the FCC "may prescribe such rules and regulations as may be necessary in the public interest to carry out the provisions of this Act." The Court found that, because Congress expressly incorporated the 1996 Act into the 1934 Act, §201(b) and its attendant rulemaking authority extend to the provisions of the 1996 Act, including the local competition provisions:

> Section 201(b), a 1938 amendment to the Communications Act of 1934, provides that "the Commission may prescribe such rules and regulations as may be necessary in the public interest to carry out the provisions of this Act." Since Congress expressly directed that the 1996 Act, along with its local-competition provisions, be inserted into the Communications Act of 1934, 1996 Act, §1(b), the Commission's rulemaking authority would seem to extend to implementation of the local-competition provisions.

> The incumbent LECs and state commissions (hereinafter respondents) argue, however, that §201(b) rulemaking authority is limited to those provisions dealing with purely *interstate and foreign* matters, because the first sentence of §201(a) makes it "the duty of every common carrier engaged in interstate or foreign communication by wire or radio to furnish such communication service upon reasonable request therefor...." It is

impossible to understand how this use of the qualifier "interstate or foreign" in §201(a), which limits the class of common carriers with the duty of providing communication service, reaches forward into the last sentence of §201(b) to limit the class of provisions that the Commission has authority to implement. We think that the grant in §201(b) means what it says: The FCC has rulemaking authority to carry out the "provisions of this Act," which include §§251 and 252, added by the Telecommunications Act of 1996.

525 U.S. at 377–78 (internal footnotes and some internal citations omitted).

Moreover, the Court found that §152(b) did not constitute a bar to the FCC's UNE pricing rules because the 1996 Act expressly applies to intrastate telecommunications and thus expressly gives the Commission authority to make rules on those intrastate matters covered by the 1996 Act:

Our view is unaffected by 47 U.S.C. §152(b), which reads: "Except as provided in sections 223 through 227..., inclusive, and section 332..., and subject to the provisions of section 301 of this title..., nothing in this chapter shall be construed to apply or to give the Commission jurisdiction with respect to...charges, classifications, practices, services, facilities, or regulations for or in connection with intrastate communication service...."

The local-competition provisions are not identified in §152(b)'s "except" clause. Seizing on this omission, respondents argue that the 1996 Act does nothing to displace the presumption that the States retain their traditional authority over local phone service.

The fallacy in this reasoning is that it ignores the fact that §201(b) *explicitly* gives the FCC jurisdiction to make rules governing matters to which the 1996 Act applies. Respondents argue that avoiding this *pari passu* expansion of Commission jurisdiction with expansion of the substantive scope of the Act was the reason the "nothing shall be construed" provision was framed in the alternative: "Nothing in this Act shall be construed to apply *or to give the Commission jurisdiction*" (emphasis added) with respect to the forbidden subjects. The italicized portion would have no operative effect, they assert, if every "application" of the Act automatically entailed Commission jurisdiction. The argument is an imaginative one, but ultimately fails. For even though "Commission jurisdiction" always follows where the Act "applies," Commission jurisdiction (so-called "ancillary" jurisdiction) *could* exist even where the Act does *not* "apply." The term "apply" limits the substantive reach of the statute (and the concomitant scope of primary FCC jurisdiction), and the phrase "or to give the Commission jurisdiction" limits, in addition, the FCC's *ancillary* jurisdiction.

Id. at 379–380.

In reaching this decision, the Supreme Court seems to have limited the scope of *Louisiana PSC*. The Court interpreted that case to require express and unambiguous preemption authority only in situations where the FCC has not otherwise been given explicit rulemaking authority. *Id.* at 381. In addition to its potential importance for the development of telecommunications markets, then, the Court's decision in *Iowa Utilities* thus marks an important further evolution in the division of regulatory authority between the FCC and state commissions.

The majority opinion on jurisdiction met with vigorous dissent. Justice Thomas's partially dissenting opinion, *id*. at 402, for example, found nothing in §201(b) to trump the overarching rule of construction established in §152(b). Justice Thomas found that, if anything, the local competition provisions of the 1996 Act were deliberately meant to "respect[] the States' historical role as the dominant authority with respect to intrastate communications." *Id*. at 411. In his own partial dissent, *id*. at 412, Justice Breyer further emphasized the role of state commissions in the statutory provisions at issue. He pointed to the express reference in §252(c) to "State commission[s]" as the entities charged to set rates for unbundled network elements. Justice Breyer also argued that *Louisiana PSC* and the legislative history support the dissenters' position:

> Consider the similarities between *Louisiana* and the present cases. The relevant rules of statutory construction—the general and explicit presumptions favoring retention of local authority—are the same. The subject matter is highly similar—both cases involve the way in hich local rates will be set for equipment used for both intrastate and interstate calls. And both cases involve intrastate charges that could affect interstate rates, here because of local competition's interstate impact, in *Louisiana* because more (or less) stringent local depreciation rules would affect the rate of replacement of equipment used for interstate calls.

> Consider, too, the differences. The language of the relevant statute here explicitly refers to "*State commission[s]*," which, it says, will "establish any rates." 47 U.S.C. §252(c)(2) (emphasis added). The language of the relevant statute in *Louisiana*, by contrast, was far more easily read as granting the FCC the authority it sought. That statute said that the FCC would "prescribe" depreciation practices for the relevant local telephone companies, and it prohibited "any depreciation charges...other than those prescribed by the [FCC]," §220(b); it made it "unlawful...to keep any other [depreciation] accounts...than those so prescribed or...approved" by the FCC, §220(g); it ordered the FCC to hear from state commissions before establishing its own rules, §220(i); and it authorized the FCC to exempt state-regulated companies from its depreciation rules, §220(h). These differences, of course, make the argument for local ratemaking in these cases stronger, not weaker, than in *Louisiana*. The majority says its view is "unaffected" by §152(b). But Congress's apparently was not, for when it enacted the 1996 Act, it initially considered amending §152(b) to make it inapplicable to the provisions that we here consider, thereby facilitating an interpretation, like the majority's, that would give the FCC the local rate-setting power it now seeks to exercise. See S. 652, 104th Cong., 1st Sess., §101(c)(2) (1995); H. R. 1555, 104th Cong., 1st Sess., §101(e)(1) (1995). The final legislation, however, rejected that proposed language. It cannot be thought that Congress "intended *sub silentio* to enact statutory language that it had earlier discarded in favor of other language." INS v. Cardoza-Fonseca, 480 U.S. 421, 442–443 (1987).

525 U.S. at 422–23 (most internal citations omitted).

Justice Breyer concluded that no other exigency existed to justify the FCC's decision to promulgate mandatory UNE pricing rules. He rejected both the argument that the Act in some way required the particular method prescribed by the Commission, *id.* at 424, as well as the alternative argument that the states retained sufficient discretion under the Commission rules to have meaningful independent jurisdiction over UNE rates, *id.* at 423.

Notes and Questions

1. Who Should Be in Charge? While the courtroom debate turned on technical detail, the policy issue underlying the Act's jurisdiction provisions is a simple one: are there convincing arguments as to why the Commission should take the lead in implementing the resale and unbundling provisions? Are these issues of primarily local concern? Is the point here that these local regulations can be expected to have a significant effect on the national telecommunications market? Or is it simply that, as an expert agency, the FCC is more likely to set appropriate rules? Does the statute allow the Court to adequately consider these core issues? If so, is that an appropriate task for judges? If not, is that wise (on the theory that this should be Congress's responsibility) or foolish (since it relegates the Justices to arguing over strained readings of ambiguous phrases)?

2. The Statutory Design. Putting jurisdiction to one side and returning to the substance of the excerpt: the majority opinion holds that the FCC erred in interpreting the 1996 Act's provisions on unbundled network elements. What were the Commission's errors and what does the Court's decision require the agency to do on remand? What factors should determine whether an incumbent local exchange carrier must make a particular network element available to competitors? What does the statute say? What should the statute say?

3. Unbundle What? The question of what should constitute an unbundled network element is one that we will further address in the materials that follow; however, even at this early stage, consider what touchstones you might suggest to the FCC as a way of determining which items should be unbundled. Why should the local switch be unbundled but not, say, access to the ILEC's fleet of service trucks? What about historical information regarding customer calling habits? Access to the ILEC's secretarial pool? What policies are motivating your intuitive responses to these suggestions? Can you formulate those into a coherent set of principles for unbundling?

4. Resale vs. Unbundling. One issue along these lines (and also considered in some depth in the opinion) is the question of whether CLECs should have to own some of their own facilities before using the unbundling provision to get access to the ILEC's infrastructure. That is, can a CLEC build its network by buying *all* of the necessary components as UNEs, or are the unbundling provisions open only to CLECs that have built some, but not all, of their own network? What does the FCC say on this issue? The Court? Does the result even matter given that CLECs always have the option to purchase the service in question under the resale provisions?

5. New Infrastructure. Why aren't the unbundling and resale provisions limited to services and infrastructure that were deployed as of the enactment of the 1996

Act? Wouldn't such a limitation level the playing field as of 1996 but also leave ILECs with substantial incentives to innovate? (Do they have incentives to innovate under the Act as interpreted above, given that any new infrastructure must be shared with competitors?) If the FCC had adopted such an interpretation, would the Court have allowed it to stand?

6. Facilities-Based Competition. Overall, what is the logic of having unbundling and resale as entry options? Don't these options discourage facilities-based competition? Isn't that the real goal of the Act? But wait; if facilities-based competition were the real goal of the Act, wouldn't the resale and unbundling provisions sunset after, say, ten years? Looked at another way: if, ten years from now, we still see firms relying on resale and unbundling, should we deem the Act a success, or a failure? Would such a result simply confirm that local exchange service is a natural monopoly? In short, what is the purpose of the local competition provisions of the 1996 Act?

7. The FCC Responds. The FCC's answers to many of the above questions are found in its *Report and Order* issued in response to the remand from the Supreme Court, from which the following excerpt is taken.

IN RE IMPLEMENTATION OF THE LOCAL COMPETITION PROVISIONS OF THE TELECOMMUNICATIONS ACT OF 1996
Third Report and Order, 15 FCC Rcd. 3696 (1999)

I. INTRODUCTION

1. In this proceeding, we respond to the Supreme Court's January 1999 decision in AT&T Corp. v. Iowa Utilities Board that directs us to reevaluate the unbundling obligations of section 251 of the Telecommunications Act of 1996. Specifically, the Court has required us to give some substance to the "necessary" and "impair" standards in section 251(d)(2), and to develop a limiting standard that is "rationally related to the goals of the Act."

8. We believe that the "necessary" and "impair" standards we adopt below address the Supreme Court's mandate and implement the statutory language and goals of the Act. The standards we adopt take into consideration alternatives outside the incumbent LEC's network, and whether those alternatives are actually available to the requesting carrier as a practical, economic, and operational matter. We consider not only the direct costs, but also other costs and impediments associated with using alternative elements that may constitute barriers to entry. We believe the Commission must assess these factors to determine the availability of alternatives, and whether access to the incumbent's network element thereby satisfies the "necessary" and "impair" standards of section 251(d)(2).

9. The unbundling standards we adopt in this *Order* also seek to encourage the rapid introduction of competition in all markets, including residential and small business markets. They seek to create incentives for both incumbents and requesting carriers to invest and innovate in new technologies by establishing a mechanism by which regulatory obligations to provide access to network elements will be reduced as alternatives to the incumbent LECs' network elements become available in the future. In addition, the standards provide reasonable cer-

tainty regarding the availability of unbundled elements, thereby allowing requesting carriers to attract investment capital and move forward with implementing national and regional business plans that will allow them to serve the greatest number of consumers.

10. To date, we have seen the development of facilities-based competition among providers of particular services in certain sectors of the market. For example, as discussed in more detail below, competitors have deployed their own fiber rings and approximately 700 circuit switches to provide local exchange and exchange access services primarily to medium and large business customers in high-density metropolitan areas. In addition, the record in this proceeding suggests that a growing number of carriers are deploying packet switches to provide data services in a number of markets, particularly for end users with substantial telecommunications needs.

11. Other local markets, however, particularly the residential and small business markets, and geographic markets outside of major metropolitan areas, have seen minimal competition. This may be due to the uncertainty surrounding the ability of competitive LECs to use reasonably priced unbundled network elements to serve these areas as a result of litigation concerning the Commission's unbundling rules. Because unbundled network elements have not been made fully available to requesting carriers as the Commission expected in 1996, we do not yet know the extent to which competition will develop once all of the unbundling rules are actually implemented by incumbent LECs.

15. The unbundling standards we adopt in this *Order* also are designed to be administratively practical and respond to changes in the marketplace as alternatives to the incumbent LECs' network elements become available. We are committed to reviewing the unbundling obligations in three years, and as the marketplace changes with the development of new technologies and increased facilities-based competition, we will modify the list of unbundled elements, as warranted.

II. EXECUTIVE SUMMARY

Section 251(d)(2)'s "Necessary" and "Impair" Standards.

Section 251(d)(2)(A)'s "necessary" standard is a stricter standard that applies to proprietary network elements. Section 251(d)(2)(B)'s "impair" standard applies to non-proprietary network elements. [The FCC elsewhere in the *Order* defines a proprietary network element as follows: "if an incumbent LEC can demonstrate that it has invested resources (time, material, or personnel) to develop proprietary information or network elements that are protected by patent, copyright, or trade secret law, the product of such an investment is 'proprietary in nature' within the meaning of section 251(d)(2)(A)."] Applying a stricter standard to proprietary network elements is consistent with Congress' intention to spur innovation and investment by both incumbent and competitive LECs. In applying these standards, we look first to what is occurring in the marketplace today.

> Necessary. A proprietary network element is "necessary" within the meaning of section 251(d)(2)(A) if, taking into consideration the availability of alternative elements outside the incumbent's network, including self-provisioning by a requesting carrier or acquiring an alternative from

a third-party supplier, lack of access to that element would, as a practical, economic, and operational matter, preclude a requesting carrier from providing the services it seeks to offer. There are limited circumstances under which we may unbundle proprietary information or functionalities even if those elements are not strictly "necessary," as long as the "impair" standard is met. These circumstances are: (1) where an incumbent LEC, for the primary purpose of causing a particular network to be evaluated under the stricter "necessary" standard in order to avoid its unbundling obligation, implements only a minor modification to the network element to make the element proprietary; (2) where an incumbent LEC cannot demonstrate that the information or functionality that it claims to be proprietary differentiates its services from its competitors' services, or is otherwise competitively significant; or (3) where lack of access to the proprietary element would jeopardize the goal of the 1996 Act to bring rapid competition to the greatest number of consumers.

Impair. The incumbent LECs' failure to provide access to a non-proprietary network element "impairs" a requesting carrier within the meaning of section 251(d)(2)(B) if, taking into consideration the availability of alternative elements outside the incumbent's network, including self-provisioning by a requesting carrier or acquiring an alternative from a third-party supplier, lack of access to that element materially diminishes a requesting carrier's ability to provide the services it seeks to offer. In order to evaluate whether there are alternatives actually available to the requesting carrier as a practical, economic, and operational matter, we look at the totality of the circumstances associated with using an alternative. In particular, our "impair" analysis considers the cost, timeliness, quality, ubiquity, and operational issues associated with use of the alternative.

Goals of the Act.

We also interpret the obligations imposed in section 251(d)(2) within the larger statutory framework of the 1996 Act. Congress apparently contemplated that we would consider additional factors by directing the Commission, in section 251(d)(2), to "consider at a minimum" the "necessary" and "impair" standards. The Supreme Court decision requires us to apply a limiting standard "rationally related to the goals of the Act." Accordingly, in addition to the factors set forth above, we may consider the following factors:

Rapid Introduction of Competition in All Markets. We may consider whether the availability of an unbundled network element is likely to encourage requesting carriers to enter the local market in order to serve the greatest number of consumers as rapidly as possible.

Promotion of Facilities-Based Competition, Investment, and Innovation. We may consider the extent to which the unbundling obligations we adopt will encourage the development of facilities-based competition by competitive LECs, and innovation and investment by both incumbent LECs and competitive LECs, especially for the provision of advanced services.

Reduced Regulation. We may consider the extent to which we can encourage investment and innovation by reducing regulatory obligations to provide access to network elements, as alternatives to the incumbent LECs' network elements become available in the future.

Certainty in the Market. We may consider how the unbundling obligations we adopt can provide the uniformity and predictability that new entrants and fledgling competitors need to develop national and regional business plans. We also consider whether the rules we adopt provide financial markets with reasonable certainty so that carriers can attract the capital they need to execute their business plans to serve the greatest number of consumers.

Administrative Practicality. We may consider whether the unbundling obligations we adopt are administratively practical to apply.

Modification of the National List of Unbundled Elements.

The *Order* recognizes that rapid changes in technology, competition, and the economic conditions of the telecommunications market will require a reevaluation of the national unbundling rules periodically. In order to encourage a reasonable period of certainty in the market, the Commission expects to reexamine the national list of unbundled network elements in three years.

For now, then, we conclude that the following network elements must be unbundled:

Loops. Incumbent local exchange carriers must offer unbundled access to loops, including high-capacity lines, xDSL-capable loops, dark fiber, and inside wire owned by the incumbent LEC. The unbundling of the high frequency portion of the loop is being considered in another proceeding.

Subloops. Incumbent LECs must offer unbundled access to subloops, or portions of the loop, at any accessible point. Such points include, for example, a pole or pedestal, the network interface device, the minimum point of entry to the customer premises, and the feeder distribution interface located in, for example, a utility room, a remote terminal, or a controlled environment vault. The *Order* establishes a rebuttable presumption that incumbent LECs must offer unbundled access to subloops at any accessible terminal in their outside loop plant.

Network Interface Device (NID). Incumbent LECs must offer unbundled access to NIDs. The NID includes any potential means of interconnection with customer premises inside wiring at the point where the carrier's local loop facilities end, such as at a cross connect device used to connect the loop to customer-controlled inside wiring. This includes all features, functions, and capabilities of the facilities used to connect the loop to premises wiring, regardless of the specific mechanical design.

Circuit Switching. Incumbent LECs must offer unbundled access to local circuit switching, albeit with some technical exceptions explained elsewhere in this *Order*. Local circuit switching includes the basic function of connecting lines and trunks on the line-side and port-side of the switch. The definition of the local switching element encompasses all of the features, functionalities, and capabilities of the switch.

Packet Switching. Incumbent LECs must offer unbundled access to packet switching only in limited circumstances in which the incumbent has placed digital loop carrier systems in the feeder section of the loop or has its Digital Subscriber Line Access Multiplexer (DSLAM) in a remote terminal. The incumbent will be relieved of this obligation, however, if it permits a requesting carrier to collocate its DSLAM in the incumbent's remote terminal on the same terms and conditions that apply to its own DSLAM. Packet switching is defined as the function of routing individual data message units based on address or other routing information contained in the data units, including the necessary electronics (*e.g.*, DSLAMs).

Interoffice Transmission Facilities. Incumbent LECs must offer unbundled access to dedicated interoffice transmission facilities, or transport, including dark fiber. Dedicated interoffice transmission facilities are defined as incumbent LEC transmission facilities dedicated to a particular customer or carrier that provide telecommunications between wire centers owned by the incumbent LECs or requesting telecommunications carriers, or between switches owned by incumbent LECs or requesting telecommunications carriers. State commissions are free to establish reasonable limits governing access to dark fiber if incumbent LECs can show that they need to maintain fiber reserves. Incumbent LECs must also offer unbundled access to shared transport where unbundled local circuit switching is provided. Shared transport is defined as transmission facilities shared by more than one carrier, including the incumbent LEC, between end office switches, between end office switches and tandem switches, and between tandem switches in the incumbent LEC's network.

Signaling and Call-Related Databases. Incumbent LECs must offer unbundled access to signaling links and signaling transfer points (STPs) in conjunction with unbundled switching, and on a stand-alone basis. The signaling network element includes, but is not limited to, signaling links and STPs. Incumbent LECs must also offer unbundled access to call-related databases, including, but not limited to, the Line Information database (LIDB), Toll Free Calling database, Number Portability database, Calling Name (CNAM) database, Operator Services/Directory Assistance databases, Advanced Intelligent Network (AIN) databases, and the AIN platform and architecture. We do not require incumbent LECs to unbundle access to certain AIN software that qualify for proprietary treatment.

Operations Support Systems (OSS). Incumbent LECs must offer unbundled access to their operations support systems. OSS consists of pre-ordering, ordering, provisioning, maintenance and repair, and billing functions supported by an incumbent LEC's databases and information. The OSS element includes access to all loop qualification information contained in any of the incumbent LEC's databases or other records, including information on whether a particular loop is capable of providing advanced services.

The following network elements need not be unbundled:

Operator Services and Directory Assistance (OS/DA). Incumbent LECs are not required to unbundle their OS/DA services pursuant to section 251(c)(3), except in the limited circumstance where an incumbent LEC does not provide customized routing to a requesting carrier to allow it to route traffic to alternative OS/DA providers. Operator services are any automatic or live assistance to a consumer to arrange for billing or completion of a telephone call. Directory assistance is a service that allows subscribers to retrieve telephone numbers of other subscribers. Incumbent LECs, however, remain obligated under the non-discrimination requirements of section 251(b)(3) to comply with the reasonable request of a carrier that purchases the incumbents' OS/DA services to rebrand or unbrand those services, and to provide directory assistance listing updates in daily electronic batch files.

<u>Shared Transport Where Circuit Switching is Not Unbundled</u>. Incumbent LECs are not required to unbundle shared transport where they are not required to offer unbundled local circuit switching, as described above.

Note on the Pricing of Network Elements

In its opinion in *Iowa Utilities Board*, the Supreme Court did not reach the validity of the Commission's pricing rules for unbundled network elements. It instead considered the jurisdictional and definitional issues discussed above and then remanded the challenge to the pricing rules for further consideration by the United States Court of Appeals for the Eighth Circuit. We excerpt the Eighth Circuit's decision on remand below. Before turning to that document, however, it might be helpful to think through a simple example and in that way clarify exactly why this pricing issue has turned out to be such a difficult one. (Unfortunately, and significantly, the Act itself offers little guidance on this issue, with section 252 stipulating only that prices for access to network elements must be based on "cost.")

Suppose that, in 1995, an incumbent local exchange carrier invested $2 million to develop and install an advanced telecommunications device called the HyperSwitch. The HyperSwitch is a fictional component we invented just for this example, but, to be concrete, let us imagine that the HyperSwitch is a switch that is particularly efficient in networks where the amount of data traffic greatly exceeds the amount of voice traffic. Further suppose that, having built the HyperSwitch, the ILEC incurs an additional expense of two cents per call for each call routed through the switch. This marginal cost might represent any number of real-world costs, for example the cost of the electricity required to run the HyperSwitch, or the maintenance costs associated with switch use. The point is that, wholly apart from fixed costs (here, $2 million), there are marginal costs incurred on a per-call basis—which is to say that it costs the ILEC something (two cents) every time anyone uses its switch.

Now, thinking about the HyperSwitch as a possible unbundled network element, our question is a deceptively simple one: what price should the ILEC be allowed to charge a CLEC for use of the HyperSwitch?

Let's state at the outset exactly what is at stake here. First, there is a distributional/fairness issue to keep in mind. The ILEC, at least, will argue that the regulated price must be high enough so as to allow the recovery of not just its marginal costs but also some fair proportion of its fixed costs. Set too low a price and the ILEC will complain that the regulation imposes an unfair burden—perhaps a burden so substantial as to amount to an unconstitutional "taking" of the ILEC's property. Note that this distributional issue affects other parties in addition to the ILEC. For example, if a potential new entrant were to determine that the government is treating the ILEC unfairly, that new entrant might decide to enter instead an unregulated industry, not wanting to take the chance that the government will someday similarly mistreat it. ILEC distributional issues, then, are important to more than just the ILECs.

Second and relatedly, there is the question of the ILEC's future incentives to innovate. If the ILEC knows that its facilities will be offered to rivals at regulated rates and, worse, thinks that those rates will be too low, the ILEC might be reluctant in the future to invest in new technologies like the HyperSwitch. This is particularly troubling if we think that, thanks to their years of experience and considerable resources, incumbents are particularly well-suited to engage in innovation.

Third, there is a short-term efficiency worry to grapple with. Any price above marginal cost threatens to create a state of affairs where the HyperSwitch will be underused. After all, if the regulated price exceeds marginal cost, firms willing to pay more than marginal cost but less than the regulated price will not purchase access. Conversely, prices below marginal cost might lead to overuse.

Fourth and finally, we have to worry about CLECs' incentives to invest in new technologies. If ILEC equipment is available at bargain basement prices, CLECs will be less likely to venture into the business of developing new equipment. This might not matter if we believe that ILECs will handle all necessary innovation; but, to whatever extent we want CLECs to innovate, this is a significant concern. Conversely, if ILEC equipment is priced at too high a level, CLECs might build their own infrastructure even in cases where society would prefer that they share the existing equipment. (Of course, in this situation the ILEC might voluntarily lower its asking price and in that way avoid the inefficient build-around.)

The reason it is so difficult to price unbundled network elements is that it is difficult to write a rule that simultaneously responds to all four of the above concerns. Allow the incumbent to recover some of its up-front investment by charging more than marginal cost, and not only will the network element be underused, but also CLECs might end up building new infrastructure even when, from a societal perspective, that redundant infrastructure is unnecessary. Force the incumbent to charge marginal cost, by contrast, and not only must the incumbent absorb a significant loss, but also in the future incumbent firms will hesitate to invest in new technologies. Pricing our hypothetical HyperSwitch, in short, is a difficult task.

Faced with these competing considerations, the FCC chose what—at first—looks like a rule that sacrifices some degree of efficiency in order to account for the distributional issues discussed above. That rule is a pricing mechanism the FCC calls "TELRIC," which stands for Total Element Long-Run Incremental Cost (see ¶29 of the *Local Competition First Report and Order* excerpted above). Under TELRIC, the price an entrant pays for access to an incumbent's network element reflects the ILEC's marginal costs plus (a) a proportional share of most other, non-marginal costs associated with the relevant network element and (b) a reasonable profit. To be more specific, were an incumbent to install a new switch today, under TELRIC that incumbent would be allowed to charge CLECs a price for access that would include (1) any costs directly attributable to the CLECs' use (marginal costs); (2) a proportional share of the depreciation in the switch's value over time; (3) a proportional share of overhead costs associated with switch use (personnel costs, billing costs, and so on); and (4) a share of the cost of the capital invested in the switch (either interest paid or the foregone returns on alternative investments). TELRIC thus seems to establish prices that allow ILECs to recover nearly all of the costs associated with any particular network element.

A wrinkle, however, undermines this simple logic. The FCC decided that, when calculating rates under TELRIC, it would not consider what insiders call the "embedded costs" of facilities put in place before the Act. These embedded costs include any portion of the fixed costs of building the network that the incumbent has not yet recovered through its service prices. Instead, the Commission decided that, at any point in time, "the total element long-run incremental cost of an element should be measured based on the use of the most efficient telecommunications technology currently available and the lowest cost network configuration, given the existing location of the incumbent LEC's wire centers." 47 C.F.R. §51.505(b)(1). The Commission's rule is therefore the rule explained above, except that the costs are based not on the costs associated with the incumbent LEC's actual network, but on the costs associated with a hypothetically efficient network.

Why did the FCC complicate its rule in this manner? The materials that follow will suggest some possible explanations, but the answer is far from clear. Was the FCC worried that "embedded costs" would include so many inefficient investments (made during the time when ILECs were not disciplined by competition) that a pricing rule based on embedded costs would yield prices so high that CLECs would never want to purchase UNEs? Did the FCC think it would be too hard to calculate these old numbers, especially since any such calculation would have to determine the proportion of the existing infrastructure already paid off during the pre-competitive period? Maybe the FCC thought that pricing as if the most efficient technology were actually in use would increase ILECs' incentive to upgrade their networks—although query whether this claim is true and, further, whether upgrades (artificially) motivated in this manner are desirable in any event.

Unsurprisingly, ILECs challenged the FCC rules. First, the incumbents argued that a rule barring them from recovering the embedded costs of their networks constituted a taking of their property in violation of the Fifth Amendment. Second, the incumbents contended that, even if TELRIC did not represent an unconstitutional taking, the rule violated the plain language and express purpose of the 1996 Act. Section 252 didn't say much, but it did say that prices for access to network elements had to be based on "cost"—and the incumbents argued that "cost" meant real costs and could not reasonably be interpreted to mean costs associated with some hypothetical telephone network that might never even be built. The Eighth Circuit reviewed these claims and struck down the Commission's pricing rules. An excerpt of that opinion follows.

IOWA UTILITIES BOARD v. FCC
219 F.3d 744 (8th Cir., 2000)

Opinion for the Court filed by Circuit Judge HANSEN, in which Chief Judge WOLLMAN and Circuit Judge BOWMAN concur.

HANSEN, Circuit Judge:

These cases are before us on remand from the Supreme Court. Local telephone service providers (known as "incumbent local exchange carriers" or "ILECs") and their industry associations petition for review of the *First Report and Order* issued by the Federal Communications Commission (FCC) which contains the FCC's findings and rules pertaining to the local competition provisions of the Telecommunications Act of 1996 (the Act). On remand we must now review the merits of the FCC's forward-looking pricing methodology.

II. Analysis

In reviewing an agency's interpretation of a statute, we must defer to the agency only if its interpretation is consistent with the plain meaning of the statute or is a reasonable construction of an ambiguous statute. *See* Chevron U.S.A. Inc. v. Natural Resources Defense Council, Inc., 467 U.S. 837, 842–43 (1984). We will overturn an agency interpretation that conflicts with the plain meaning of the statute, is an unreasonable construction of an ambiguous statute, or is arbitrary and capricious. In making our decision regarding reasonableness, the issue "is not whether the Commission made the best choice, or even the choice that this Court would have made, but rather 'whether the FCC made a reasonable selection from among the available alternatives.'" Southwestern Bell Tel. Co. v. FCC., 153 F.3d 523, 559–60 (8th Cir. 1998) (quoting MCI Telecomms. Corp. v. FCC, 675 F.2d 408, 413 (D. C. Cir. 1982)).

A. Pricing Methodology

Congress established pricing standards for the rates that may be charged by ILECs to their new local service competitors for interconnection and for the furnishing of network elements on an unbundled basis. The statute states that the "just and reasonable" rates shall be "based on the cost...of providing the interconnection or network element (whichever is applicable)," and further stipulates that the rates must be nondiscriminatory but "may include a reasonable profit." 47 U.S.C. §252(d)(1).

The FCC promulgated various pricing rules to implement the Act. The FCC's pricing provisions that pertain to the pricing of interconnection and network elements utilize a forward-looking economic cost methodology that is based on the total element long-run incremental cost (TELRIC) of the element. These costs are to be based on an ILEC's existing wire center locations using the most efficient technology available in the industry regardless of the technology actually used by the ILEC and furnished to the competitor. State commissions are to employ TELRIC to determine the price an ILEC may charge its competitors for the right to interconnect with the ILEC and/or to use the ILEC's network elements to compete with the ILEC in providing telephone services.

The petitioners contend the TELRIC method violates the plain language and purpose of the Act and represents arbitrary and capricious decision-making.

1. Hypothetical Network Standard

In its *First Report and Order*, the FCC explained that forward-looking methodologies, like TELRIC, consider the costs that a carrier would incur in the future for providing the interconnection or unbundled access to its network elements. These costs either can be based on the most efficient network configuration and technology currently available, or on the ILEC's existing network infrastructures. The FCC chose an approach which it says combined the two possibilities. Pursuant to section 252(d)(1), the FCC promulgated 47 C.F.R. §51.505 entitled "Forward-looking economic cost." It states in part that "the total element long-run incremental cost of an element should be measured based on the use of the most efficient telecommunications technology currently available and the lowest cost network configuration, given the existing location of the incumbent LEC's wire centers." 47 C.F.R. §51.505(b)(1).

The petitioners contend the language of section 251(d)(1) points inescapably to the actual costs the ILEC incurs for furnishing its existing network to the competitor either through interconnection or on an unbundled network element basis. However, the petitioners explain that the costs under the FCC's pricing methodology are those costs that would be incurred by a hypothetical carrier deploying a hypothetical network that is optimally efficient in technology and configuration. The petitioners argue that the FCC's hypothetical network standard does not reflect what they are statutorily required to furnish to their competitors and is, therefore, flatly contrary to the statute.

The respondents counter the petitioners' assertion that TELRIC costs are based on a hypothetical network. The respondents contend TELRIC does reflect the ILECs' costs but on a predictive forward-looking basis that assumes a reasonable level of efficiency. According to the respondents, setting rates based on the use of the most efficient technology available and on the lowest cost network configuration using existing wire center locations is consistent with the statute, promotes competition, and is a reasonable application of forward-looking costs.

We agree with the petitioners that basing the allowable charges for the use of an ILEC's existing facilities and equipment (either through interconnection or the leasing of unbundled network elements) on what the costs would be if the ILEC provided the most efficient technology and in the most efficient configuration available today utilizing its existing wire center locations violates the plain meaning of the Act. It is clear from the language of the statute that Congress intended the rates to be "based on the cost . . . *of providing the interconnection or network element*," §252(d)(1)(A)(i) (emphasis added), not on the cost some imaginary carrier would incur by providing the newest, most efficient, and least cost substitute for the actual item or element which will be furnished by the existing ILEC pursuant to Congress's mandate for sharing. Congress was dealing with reality, not fantasizing about what might be. The reality is that Congress knew it was requiring the existing ILECs to share their existing facilities and equipment with new competitors as one of its chosen methods to bring competition to local telephone service, and it expressly said that the ILECs' costs of providing *those* facilities and *that* equipment were to be recoverable by just and reasonable rates. Congress did not expect a new competitor to pay rates for a "reconstructed local network," *First Report and Order* ¶685, but for the existing local network it would be using in an attempt to compete.

This does not defeat the purpose of using a forward-looking methodology, despite what the FCC asserts. Costs can be forward-looking in that they can be calculated to reflect what it will cost the ILEC in the future to furnish to the competitor those portions or capacities of the ILEC's facilities and equipment that the competitor will use including any system or component upgrading that the ILEC chooses to put in place for its own more efficient use. In our view it is the cost to the ILEC of carrying the extra burden of the competitor's traffic that Congress entitled the ILEC to recover, and to that extent, the FCC's use of an incremental cost approach does no violence to the statute. At bottom, however, Congress has made it clear that it is the cost of providing the actual facilities and equipment that will be used by the competitor (and not some state of the art presently available technology ideally configured but neither deployed by the ILEC nor to be used by the competitor) which must be ascertained and determined.

Consequently, we vacate and remand to the FCC rule 51.505(b)(1).

2. Use of a Forward-looking Methodology

The petitioners contend that the FCC's use of its forward-looking TELRIC methodology, which denies the ILECs recovery of their historical costs, is contrary to the express terms of the Act and is unreasonable. The petitioners state that the term "cost" plainly refers to historical cost. The respondents argue the term "cost" is an elastic term that can be construed to mean either historical or forward-looking costs and that the FCC's interpretation of cost as forward-looking is reasonable. The respondents also argue the FCC explained in detail its decision to use forward-looking costs and that the decision was reasonable based on the new competitive objectives of the 1996 Act.

We respectfully disagree with the petitioners' contention that cost, as it is used in the statute, means historical cost. The statute simply states that rates "shall be based on the cost...of providing the interconnection or network element." 47 U.S.C. §252(d)(1)(A). We conclude the term "cost," as it is used in statute, is ambiguous, and Congress has not spoken directly on the meaning of the word in this context.

The FCC has the authority to make rules to fill any gap in the Act left by Congress, provided the agency's construction of the statute is reasonable. *See Chevron*, 467 U.S. at 843. Forward-looking costs have been recognized as promoting a competitive environment which is one of the stated purposes of the Act. The Seventh Circuit, for example, explained, "It is current and anticipated cost, rather than historical cost that is relevant to business decisions to enter markets...historical costs associated with the plant already in place are essentially irrelevant to this decision since those costs are 'sunk' and unavoidable and are unaffected by the new production decision." MCI Communications v. American Tel. & Tel. Co., 708 F.2d 1081, 1116–17 (7th Cir.1983). Here, the FCC's use of a forward-looking cost methodology was reasonable.

Notes and Questions

1. Hypothetical Networks. Is the reasoning behind the Eighth Circuit's acceptance of forward-looking pricing consistent with its rejection of the FCC's "hypothetical" network standard? What, in the court's opinion, was the Commission's error? Could the FCC have saved its rule by providing a better explanation of how the "hypothetical" model reflects the forward-looking costs of actual networks? Or is the court saying that no hypothetical network models can be used no matter how well they might predict actual costs? If you were an attorney for the Commission, what would you propose to do in response to this opinion?

2. What is the FCC's Logic? What is the logic of the Commission's position? For example, does the hypothetical network standard encourage the incumbent to upgrade its existing infrastructure to the new technology, perhaps because TELRIC prices are set based on that new technology whether or not the incumbent actually has it? In the alternative, is the Commission just trying to push prices down, subsidizing competitive entry? But what purpose does inefficient competition serve?

3. Too High or Too Low? Should we assume that the Commission's hypothetical network standard systematically sets prices that are below the prices that would result were TELRIC based on the real network actually in place? Might the Commission's hypothetical network yield prices that are higher? As a policy matter, should we be more concerned about one of these possibilities than the other?

4. Takings. One of the claims made before the Eighth Circuit was that TELRIC prices were so low as to constitute an unconstitutional taking under the Takings Clause of the Fifth Amendment to the U.S. Constitution. Gregory Sidak and Daniel Spulber explain the argument this way:

> The Takings Clause of the Fifth Amendment commands: "Nor shall private property be taken for public use, without just compensation." The prototypical takings case involves a physical invasion of land. It arises, for example, when the state needs a piece of private land to build a highway and commences a condemnation proceeding that results in the payment of compensation. The dramatic growth of the regulatory state, however, produced another class of takings case—the regulatory taking—in which the owner of private property is not forced to sell it to the government pursuant to a condemnation action, but rather is allowed to keep his property subject to significant constraints concerning its use. Justice Holmes planted the seed for that legal theory back in 1922 when he observed that a state law making it "commercially impracticable to mine certain coal" on one's property had "very nearly the same effect for constitutional purposes as appropriating or destroying it."

> The "deregulatory taking" derives from a similar logic. The sweeping deregulation of public utilities being proposed and implemented at the state and federal levels promises to bring the benefits of competition to markets for electric power and telecommunications. Those benefits include improvements in operating efficiencies, competitive prices, efficient

investment decisions, technological innovation, and product variety. The benefits of competition, however, do not include forced transfers of income from utility shareholders to their customers and competitors. As regulators dismantle barriers to entry and other regulatory restrictions, they must honor their past commitments and avoid actions that threaten to confiscate or destroy the property of utility investors on an unprecedented scale.[7]

Is this takings argument convincing? Do you agree that TELRIC reneges on some explicit or implicit "past commitment" to the local exchange carriers? Do legislators have the power to make these sorts of commitments, in essence binding future legislators to promises made by their predecessors? Any reason why they should? Does the deregulatory takings argument really suggest a new pricing rule, or does it instead suggest that the federal government should pay a one-time lump sum to the various LECs affected by the new regulation? (Isn't that how we handle physical takings?)

5. Takings: The Eighth Circuit. The Eighth Circuit declined to examine the incumbents' deregulatory takings claim, stating that:

> Because we have vacated 47 C.F.R. §51.505(b)(1), we have some doubt that we need to address the argument that TELRIC also violates the Constitution. Our remand to the FCC of the TELRIC rule should result in a new rule for determining the compensation that the ILECs will receive for the new competitor's use of the ILEC's property—a rule that should accurately determine the actual costs to the ILEC of furnishing its network (either by interconnection or on an unbundled element basis) to its competitors together with a permitted reasonable profit. Whether the new rule will result in rates that do not provide just and reasonable compensation cannot be foretold. We conclude that the present takings claim is not ripe for review.

219 F.3d at 753–54.

6. Takings: The Fifth Circuit. In a case decided several months before the Eighth Circuit released the above decision, however, the United States Court of Appeals for the Fifth Circuit held that TELRIC was not inconsistent with the 1996 Act (in contradiction to the Eighth Circuit's holding on this issue) and also found that it did not violate the Fifth Amendment Takings Clause. That case, Texas Office of Public Utility Counsel v. FCC, 183 F.3d 393 (5th Cir. 1999), is a more complicated vehicle by which to study the issues surrounding TELRIC because it involves not a direct challenge to TELRIC, but a challenge in the context of how TELRIC affects the universal service subsidies incumbent LECs receive. Nonetheless, the underlying issues are identical. On the deregulatory takings issue, the Fifth Circuit had this to say:

> GTE claims that implementing the forward-looking cost methodology will force ILECs to operate at a loss, and this constitutes an unconstitutional taking. Relying on Brooks-Scanlon v. Railroad Comm'n, 251 U.S. 396 (1920), GTE argues that a regulated entity cannot be forced to operate one segment of its business at a loss on the expectation that it can make up the shortfalls from another competitive line of business. At the

7. Sidak & Spulber, Deregulatory Takings and the Regulatory Contract 1–2 (1997).

very least, GTE says, the FCC should adopt a narrow construction of the statutory language to avoid any constitutional infirmities.

The FCC responds that before a narrowing construction should be considered, GTE must show that a taking will "necessarily" result from the regulatory actions. Even if GTE can show that some taking will result, it must demonstrate that its losses are so significant that the "net effect" is confiscatory. *See* Duquesne Light Co. v. Barasch, 488 U.S. 299, 310–16 (1989).

GTE has failed to meet the requirements of *Duquesne*, because it cannot show that it will lose any revenue at all, much less enough to constitute a taking under more recent precedent. *Duquesne* stands for the proposition that "no single ratemaking methodology is mandated by the Constitution, which looks to the consequences a governmental authority produces rather than the techniques it employs." *Duquesne*, 488 U.S. at 299 (Scalia, J., concurring). *Duquesne* does not require courts to engage in a takings analysis whenever an agency opens a previously regulated market to competition. Further, GTE's reliance on *Brooks-Scanlon* is misplaced; [unlike the situation in *Brooks-Scanlon*, the FCC is not requiring the ILECs to remain open or to charge low rates, thereby forcing them to operate at a permanent loss.]

Texas Office of Pub. Util. Counsel v. FCC, 183 F.3d 393, 413 n.14 & 437–38 (5th Cir. 1999), *cert. granted sub nom.* GTE Service Corp. v. FCC, 120 S. Ct. 2214, *cert dismissed* 121 S. Ct. 423 (2000).

7. Practical Difficulties. Our simple examples aside, remember that, in the real world, even once the parties agree on the appropriate pricing rule, implementation of that rule will still be a challenge. TELRIC, for example, theoretically takes into account all costs associated with an element over time. As was noted above, if an incumbent purchases a new switch today, it can under TELRIC charge a price that includes (1) the short-run (marginal) costs of access; (2) a proportional share of the depreciation in the switch's value over time; (3) a proportional share of the joint and common costs (a measure of overhead costs) of operating the switch; and (4) a share of the cost of capital invested to purchase the switch (interest paid or the foregone returns on alternative investments). None of these numbers is easy to determine, and the process of setting each will surely engender significant controversy. Moreover, to whatever extent incumbents are ultimately allowed to recover the sunk costs of the physical plant—those so-called "embedded" or "stranded" costs—there is again likely to be significant dispute, with the parties arguing over how much of the existing physical plant was already paid for under the regulated rates in effect before the 1996 Act.

8. The Resale Provisions. The discussion above focuses on the pricing issue as it applies to unbundled network elements. Remember, however, that the resale provisions require price regulation as well. For example, under section 251(c)(4), incumbents are required to offer their services for resale "at wholesale rates," a phrase which section 252(d)(1) defines to mean "retail rates charged to subscribers for the telecommunications service requested, excluding the portion thereof attributable to any marketing, billing, collection, and other costs that will be avoided by the local exchange carrier." Do the issues raised in the resale context differ at all from those raised in the unbundling context? If not, how do you explain the differences in the statutory language? If so, did Congress do a good job in crafting the pricing rule set out in section 252(d)(1)? Readers familiar with the economic literature might recognize similarities between the statutory provision and the so-called "Efficient Component Pricing Rule" (ECPR). *See* Baumol & Sidak, The Pricing of Inputs Sold to Competitors, 11 Yale J. Reg. 171 (1994)).

9. Excuse me? Did You Say Deregulation? While all of these pricing issues are both complicated and, as yet, unresolved, one thing is abundantly clear: given the above, it would be inaccurate to say that the 1996 Act truly allows the market to replace regulation in determining competitive outcomes. But if the Act does not do that, then what was its purpose?

Note on Interconnection

Although we have surveyed many parts of the 1996 Act by this point, we have focused so far only on the statutory provisions that promote local competition through unbundling and resale. The materials have thus considered what it means when we label something a "network element"; what the difference is between resale and unbundling; and, perhaps ad nauseam, how it is that the government should set prices for both UNEs and resale. As we noted at the start of the chapter, however, the 1996 Act promotes local competition in another, even more fundamental, way as well: it requires that rival LECs interconnect with one another to exchange network traffic. That is, in addition to the requirement that ILECs allow CLECs to "interconnect" for the purpose of using UNEs or even reselling particular services, the 1996 Act—in particular, sections 251 and 252—further requires that all telecommunications carriers accept telephone traffic bound for their customers even if that traffic originates on a rival firm's telephone network.

Why is this important? As we discussed in Chapter Fifteen, back in the early days of the telephone system, Bell strategically refused to connect its telephone network to networks developed and owned by rivals. Denying interconnection was for Bell an effective tool; rivals could not realistically compete with the Bell network if their customers could not call Bell customers. This lesson was not lost on the architects of the 1996 Act, who worried that incumbent LECs would similarly deny interconnection to CLEC entrants and, in that way, undermine local competition. Without interconnection, it would be impossible for those new entrants to match incumbents' established network benefits; thus, without interconnection, it would be impossible for those entrants to seriously challenge the incumbents' dominant positions in the various local exchange markets.

In ¶26 of the *Local Competition First Report and Order* excerpted earlier in this chapter, the FCC defined interconnection as "the physical linking of two networks for the mutual exchange of traffic." Unlike the Act's unbundling provisions, which apply only to ILECs, the basic interconnection provisions of §§251 and 252 apply to all telecommunications carriers, whether established incumbents or new entrants. Section 251(a) sets forth the basic interconnection mandate: carriers must (1) interconnect directly or indirectly with the facilities and equipment of other carriers, and (2) refrain from installing any network facilities or functions that interfere with such interconnection. Section 251(c)(2) imposes some further obligations on the ILECs. In the Commission's words, "section 251(c)(2) requires incumbent LECs to provide interconnection to any requesting telecommunications carrier at any technically feasible point. The interconnection must be at least equal in quality to that provided by the incumbent LEC to itself or its affiliates, and must be provided on rates, terms, and conditions that are just, reasonable, and nondiscriminatory." *Local Competition First Report and Order*, ¶26.

The 1996 Act not only mandated interconnection, but also set out some general guidelines for the terms on which such "mutual exchange of traffic" should proceed. Most generally, §251(b)(5) provides that all telecommunications carriers must "establish reciprocal compensation for the transport and termination of telecommunications." And §252(d)(2) adds that, to qualify as "just and reasonable," reciprocal recovery by each carrier of the costs of transporting and terminating other carriers' traffic must be limited to "a reasonable approximation of the additional costs of terminating such calls." The Huber treatise usefully summarizes the Act's reciprocal compensation scheme as follows:

> When a customer of Carrier A places a local call to a customer of Carrier B, Carrier A must pay Carrier B for terminating the call. Conversely, when a customer of Carrier B places a call to a customer of Carrier A, Carrier B must pay. The Act provides that state commissions shall not consider reciprocal compensation arrangements to be just and reasonable unless they provide for the mutual and reciprocal recovery by each carrier of the costs associated with the transport and termination on each carrier's network of calls that originate on the other's network; such costs are to be determined on the basis of a reasonable approximation of the additional costs of terminating such calls. In other words, the Act looks to the marginal cost of carrying the additional traffic, not the fully distributed costs of the network.[8]

It is important to note that the pricing standard for interconnection is therefore distinct from the pricing standard for access to unbundled network elements (such access is sometimes referred to as "interconnection" to network elements, but that should not be confused with interconnection for the exchange of traffic, which is what we are concerned with here). The price of interconnection for the purpose of exchanging telecommunications traffic should reflect only the additional costs imposed on a network by the calls it receives from other networks—a true marginal cost measure. There is thus, unlike under TELRIC, no recovery through interconnection prices of asset depreciation, overhead, capital costs, or other network costs.

While the Act requires reciprocal agreements for the transport and termination of traffic, note that it does leave open the possibility that carriers would elect not to charge each other for such services. Section 252(d)(2)(B)(i) makes clear that nothing in the Act precludes "arrangements that waive mutual recovery (such as bill-and-keep arrangements)." Bill-and-keep agreements operate differently from the scenario for reciprocal compensation set out in the passage above. Under bill-and-keep, Carriers A and B do not pay each other to terminate calls moving from the network of one to the network of the other. Instead, the carriers assume that these numbers will cancel out in the end and so each agrees to simply charge its own subscribers for local service and then originate and terminate whatever calls happen to pass through the system. Unpacking the phrase, then:

---

8. Huber et al., *supra* note 1 at 476.

under a "bill-and-keep" agreement, our hypothetical Carrier A would *bill* its own subscribers for local service and then *keep* all that revenue itself—neither passing cash on to Carrier B to pay for B's expenses in terminating calls that originate with Carrier A, nor collecting cash from Carrier B to pay for A's own expenses in terminating calls that originate with Carrier B.

Interconnection in general, and reciprocal compensation in particular, raises a number of hard questions in practice. For one, exactly what telecommunications traffic is subject to reciprocal compensation agreements? Does §251(b)(5) apply to any and all traffic, or to local calls only? The question is an important one, for if all traffic is to be interconnected on a reciprocal-compensation basis, the regime of access charges under which long distance carriers pay for origination and termination of their calls would disappear. (As we mentioned last chapter and discuss later in this chapter, much of the modern universal service system relies on these access charges.) The Commission resolved this question in ¶1034 of its *Local Competition First Report and Order*, ruling that reciprocal compensation applies only "to traffic that originates and terminates within a local area." Interestingly, the Commission's restriction of reciprocal compensation to local traffic would raise yet further questions as to what calls are in fact "local." As we will see in Chapter Twenty-Two, that issue has become particularly complex with regard to calls made to Internet service providers.

A second interconnection issue involves the question of which service providers (among local service providers) are eligible for reciprocal compensation. The Act makes clear that the provisions apply to "telecommunications carriers," but the Act leaves it to the Commission to decide what kind of entity qualifies under that designation. For example, must conventional, wireline telephone companies enter into reciprocal compensation agreements with wireless communications providers? The FCC addressed this issue in the same massive interconnection order that we saw earlier in this chapter regarding competition in the local loop. We excerpt here the portion of that order dealing with Commercial Mobile Radio Services (CMRS). CMRS encompasses all mobile telecommunications services that are provided for profit and available for general public use. Increasingly important services in this category include cellular telephony and pager services.

IN RE IMPLEMENTATION OF THE LOCAL COMPETITION PROVISIONS OF THE TELECOMMUNICATIONS ACT OF 1996
First Report and Order, 11 FCC Rcd. 15499 (1996)

X. COMMERCIAL MOBILE RADIO SERVICE INTERCONNECTION

999. In the *Notice of Proposed Rulemaking* in this proceeding, we sought comment on whether interconnection arrangements between incumbent LECs and CMRS providers fall within the scope of sections 251 and 252 of the 1996 Telecommunications Act. Application of sections 251 and 252 to LEC-CMRS interconnection arrangements involves two distinct issues. One is whether the terms and conditions of the physical interconnection between incumbent LECs and CMRS providers are governed under section 251(c)(2), and the corresponding pricing standards set forth in section 252(d)(1). The second, and perhaps more critical issue from the CMRS providers' perspective, is whether CMRS

providers are entitled to reciprocal compensation for transport and termination under section 251(b)(5), and the corresponding pricing standards set forth in section 252(d)(2).

A. CMRS Providers and Obligations of Local Exchange Carriers Under Section 251(b) and Incumbent Local Exchange Carriers Under Section 251(c).

1001. Section 251(b) imposes duties only on LECs, and section 251(c) imposes duties only on incumbent LECs. Section 3(26) of the Act defines "local exchange carrier" to mean "any person that is engaged in the provision of telephone exchange service or exchange access," but "does not include a person insofar as such person is engaged in the provision of a commercial mobile service under section 332(c), except to the extent that the Commission finds that such service should be included in the definition of such term." In the NPRM, we sought comment on whether, and to what extent, CMRS providers should be classified as "local exchange carriers" and therefore subject to the duties and obligations imposed by section 251(b).

1002. Most of the comments on this issue urge that CMRS providers should not be classified as LECs. Some commenters assert that CMRS was expressly excluded from the definition of a LEC in section 3(a)(2)(44) of the 1996 Act and that the legislative history confirms that Congress intended that the Commission reconsider whether CMRS providers should be classified as LECs only if "future circumstances warrant." PCIA maintains that there is no basis for classifying CMRS providers as LECs, because CMRS is not yet a substitute for wireline local exchange service for a substantial number of subscribers, and because CMRS licensees lack the control over essential facilities that underlies the adoption of Section 251. Pronet contends that paging operators do not provide local exchange services, and that Congress did not contemplate treating CMRS providers as LECs. Some CMRS providers propose that the Commission apply the criteria in section 332(c)(3) in considering whether a CMRS provider should be classified as a LEC—that the service is a replacement for a substantial portion of the wireline telephone exchange service within a state. Nextel argues that a CMRS provider should not be classified as a LEC until it has become a substitute for a landline telephone exchange service for a substantial portion of the communications within a state. Omnipoint states that application of the section 332(c)(3) test will permit CMRS providers, which are also small businesses, to be relieved of LEC-type regulatory burdens during their initial entry years, so that they can act as "spirited, if smaller" competitors to the incumbent LEC. The Ohio Commission contends that the Commission should consider market share, diversity of network, and name recognition in classifying CMRS providers as LECs.

1003. COMAV and National Wireless Resellers Association, on the other hand, contend that CMRS entities can provide exchange and exchange access services "and thus are de facto" LECs. COMAV also argues that, if a CMRS provider is a subsidiary of an incumbent LEC, it should be treated as an incumbent LEC, and thus be required to unbundle and allow direct interconnection. NARUC argues that the type of service provided, rather than the technology employed, should determine the appropriate regulatory treatment, and that a CMRS provider should therefore be treated as a LEC if it provides fixed local service. The Illinois Commission similarly indicates that a CMRS provider should be regulated as a LEC when it establishes a wireless local loop for the express purpose of competing against or bypassing the landline loop.

1004. We are not persuaded by those arguing that CMRS providers should be treated as LECs, and decline at this time to treat CMRS providers as LECs. Section 3(26) of the Act, quoted above, makes clear that CMRS providers should not be classified as LECs until the Commission makes a finding that such treatment is warranted. We disagree with COMAV and National Wireless Resellers Association that CMRS providers are de facto LECs (and even incumbent LECs if they are affiliated with a LEC) simply because they provide telephone exchange and exchange access services. Congress recognized that some CMRS providers offer telephone exchange and exchange access services, and concluded that their provision of such services, by itself, did not require CMRS providers to be classified as LECs. We further note that, because the determination as to whether CMRS providers should be defined as LECs is within the Commission's sole discretion, states are preempted from requiring CMRS providers to classify themselves as "local exchange carriers" or be subject to rate and entry regulation as a precondition to participation in interconnection negotiations and arbitrations under sections 251 and 252.

1005. Until such time that we decide otherwise, CMRS providers will not be classified as LECs, and are not subject to the obligations of section 251(b). We further note that, even if we were to classify some CMRS providers as LECs, other types of CMRS providers, such as paging providers, might not be so classified because they do not offer local exchange service or exchange access.

1006. We further note that, because CMRS providers do not fall within the definition of a LEC under section 251(h)(1), they are not subject to the duties and obligations imposed on incumbent LECs under section 251(c).

B. Reciprocal Compensation Arrangements Under Section 251(b)(5)

1007. Some parties contend that LEC-CMRS transport and termination arrangements do not fall within the scope of 251(b)(5), which requires LECs to establish reciprocal compensation arrangements for transport and termination. Other commenters argue that because CMRS providers fall within the definition of "telecommunications carriers," they fall within the scope of section 251(b)(5).

1008. Under section 251(b)(5), LECs have a duty to establish reciprocal compensation arrangements for the transport and termination of "telecommunications." Under section 3(43), the "term 'telecommunications' means the transmission, between or among points specified by the user, of information of the user's choosing, without change in the form or content of the information as sent and received." All CMRS providers offer telecommunications. Accordingly, LECs are obligated, pursuant to section 251(b)(5) (and the corresponding pricing standards of section 252(d)(2)), to enter into reciprocal compensation arrangements with all CMRS providers, including paging providers, for the transport and termination of traffic on each other's networks.

C. Interconnection Under Section 251(c)(2)

1009. Section 251(c)(2)(A) provides that an incumbent LEC must provide interconnection with its local exchange network to "any requesting telecommunications carrier for the transmission and routing of telephone exchange service and exchange access." In the NPRM, we tentatively concluded that CMRS providers may be entitled to request interconnection under section 251(c)(2) for the purposes of providing telephone exchange service and exchange access. We sought comment on this tentative conclusion.

1010. Several commenters argue that many CMRS providers provide telephone exchange service and exchange access as defined by the 1996 Act, and thus section 251(c)(2) should govern their interconnection arrangements with incumbent LECs. NYNEX contends that all CMRS providers, other than providers of one-way paging, provide telephone exchange service. The Ohio Commission contends that all voice grade CMRS providers which provide local exchange service may request interconnection under section 251(c)(2). The Pennsylvania Commission argues that all voice-grade and non-voice grade CMRS providers fit within the definition of telecommunications carriers and fall within the parameters of section 251(c)(2).

1011. Many wireless carriers argue that interconnection arrangements between incumbent LECs and CMRS providers do not fall within the scope of section 251(c)(2). CTIA claims that CMRS was intended to be regulated differently than other services because it entails different traffic flows and different termination costs. Airtouch claims that, if LEC-CMRS interconnection were found to fall within the scope of section 251, the concept of "local exchange areas" could create implementation problems and adverse policy results, thus supporting application of section 332(c)(1)(B).

1012. As discussed in the preceding section, CMRS providers meet the statutory definition of "telecommunications carriers." We also agree with several commenters that many CMRS providers also provide telephone exchange service and exchange access as defined by the 1996 Act. Incumbent LECs must accordingly make interconnection available to these CMRS providers in conformity with the terms of sections 251(c) and 252, including offering rates, terms, and conditions that are just, reasonable and nondiscriminatory.

1013. The 1996 Act defines "telephone exchange service" as "service within a telephone exchange, or within a connected system of telephone exchanges within the same exchange area...and which is covered by the exchange service charge" or "*comparable service* provided through a system of switches, transmission equipment, or other facilities (or combination thereof) by which a subscriber can originate and terminate a telecommunications service." 47 U.S.C. §153(47) (emphasis added). We find that many CMRS services fall within the second part of the definition because they provide "comparable service" to telephone exchange service. These services are comparable because, as a general matter, and as some commenters note, these CMRS carriers provide local, two-way switched voice service as a principal part of their business. Indeed, the Commission has described cellular service as exchange telephone service and cellular carriers as "generally engaged in the provision of local exchange telecommunications in conjunction with local telephone companies." In addition, although CMRS providers are not currently classified as LECs, the fact that most CMRS providers are capable, both technically and pursuant to the terms of their licenses, of providing fixed services, as LECs do, buttresses our conclusion that these CMRS providers offer services that are "comparable" to telephone exchange service and supports the notion that these services may become a true economic substitute for wireline local exchange service in the future.

1015. The arguments that CMRS traffic flows may differ from wireline traffic, that CMRS providers' termination costs may differ from LECs, that CMRS service areas do not coincide with wireline local exchange areas, or that CMRS providers are not LECs, do not alter our conclusion that many CMRS providers do provide telephone exchange service. These considerations are not relevant to the statutory definition of telephone exchange service in section 3(47). Incumbent LECs are required to provide interconnection to CMRS providers who request it for the transmission and routing of telephone exchange service or exchange access, under the plain language of section 251(c)(2).

Notes and Questions

1. Have Your Cake and Eat It Too. How does the Commission reconcile its decision, on one hand, that CMRS providers are not LECs, with its decision, on the other hand, that CMRS providers offer telecommunications services and can request interconnection under §§251 and 252 of the Act?

2. Reciprocal Traffic. Paging providers generally create only one-way traffic: from the originating carrier to the paging provider. The originating LEC might never receive any traffic back from the paging provider for termination on the LEC's network. What does "reciprocal" mean in such a situation? Is the 1996 Act capable of fair application in such an asymmetric case?

3. Bill-and-Keep. In what settings might a local exchange carrier prefer explicit reciprocal compensation over a bill-and-keep arrangement? Would it matter if one LEC had many customers while its interconnected rival had very few? Would it matter if one LEC had a major call center as a customer—say, the call center responsible for answering questions about how to install Microsoft products— while the other LEC served primarily residential subscribers?

4. Judicial Review. In part of its opinion not overruled by the Supreme Court in *Iowa Utilities Board*, the U.S. Court of Appeals for the Eighth Circuit upheld the Commission's authority to regulate interconnection between LECs and CMRS providers:

> Because Congress expressly amended section 2(b) to preclude state regulation of entry of and rates charged by Commercial Mobile Radio Service (CMRS) providers, *see* 47 U.S.C. §§152(b) (exempting the provisions of section 332), 332(c)(3)(A), and because section 332(c)(1)(B) gives the FCC the authority to order LECs to interconnect with CMRS carriers, we believe that the Commission has the authority to issue the rules of special concern to the CMRS providers.

Iowa Utilities Board v. FCC, 120 F.3d 753 n.21 (8th Cir. 1997).

II. BOC LINE OF BUSINESS RESTRICTIONS UNDER THE ACT

The first section of this chapter considered provisions of the 1996 Act that open the local exchange to competition. We just finished thinking, in fact, about the various interconnection obligations that are designed to enable facilities-based entry, and earlier in the chapter we considered the unbundling and resale provisions that together make possible more gradual entry into the local exchange market. In this section, we turn to a related set of provisions: those that attempt to increase competition in telecommunications markets beyond the local loop, including the market for long distance telephone service.

As we pointed out at the start of the chapter, these two sets of provisions are logically related. To whatever extent the local competition provisions are successful, LECs will no longer enjoy monopoly power and thus will no longer be able to engage in discriminatory interconnection or predatory cross-subsidization. Given that, those old "line of business restrictions" lose their principal justification; so long as there is local exchange competition, there is no reason to keep LECs from entering competitive markets and going head-to-head with powerful rivals like (in the long distance market) Sprint, MCI, and AT&T, and (in the market for CPE) IBM and Sun Microsystems.

The relevant provisions of the Act are sections 271–275. These provisions apply only to those LECs that were once part of the Bell System. Any line of business restrictions imposed on other LECs had already been withdrawn by the time of the 1996 Act. The BOCs, by contrast, were still limited by specific provisions of the MFJ.

Under the Act, BOC entry into allied fields is conditioned on detailed regulatory oversight, somewhat reminiscent of the FCC's open network architecture and network disclosure rules (introduced in Chapter Seventeen). In other words, while the new Act does abandon the MFJ's premise that BOCs should be strictly confined to offering only regulated, basic local exchange service, it does not go so far as to permit unrestricted entry into competitive markets. Rather, the 1996 Act attempts to reap the benefits of competition by allowing the BOCs to enter new fields, but at the same time relies on strict regulatory oversight to ensure that entry by these carriers will not lead to predatory behaviors that, perversely, would retard competition.

At this point the reader ought to consult sections 271–275; they are reprinted in the statutory appendix. These sections collectively add to Title II of the 1934 Act a new Part III, called "Special Provisions Concerning Bell Operating Companies." Section 271 removes all restrictions on a Bell Operating Company's ability to offer long distance service originating outside the states where that BOC provides local exchange service under the MFJ; this is known as "out-of-region" service, and §271 lets it begin immediately. By contrast, under §271 a BOC can offer "in-region" service (long distance service originating within a state in which the BOC provides local service under the MFJ) only upon satisfying several specific conditions discussed below. Those same conditions apply, under §273, to another set of activities previously forbidden by the MFJ: the manufacture of telecommunications equipment (that is, the wires, switches, and associated software that make up the local loop) and customer premises equipment (the handsets and switchboards that connect individuals and offices to the local loop). In fact, §273 is explicitly linked to §271: a BOC is allowed to manufacture telecommunications equipment and CPE under §273 only after that BOC has already been authorized by the FCC to provide in-region long distance under §271.

The MFJ also kept the BOCs out of "information services," a vague term that essentially embraced any service for which the phone company itself assembled the data that it purported to also deliver.[9] That restriction was removed in subsequent court proceedings,[10] but a new section 274 imposes restrictions on "electronic publishing" by the BOCs. The Act contains a laundry list definition of electronic publishing, describing several types of data that are included in the term and others that are not. Essentially, electronic publishing is still the transmission by a phone company of information that the company has generated or altered. The definition is, in other words, very close to that employed in the consent decree. The 1996 Act also addresses certain lines of business not expressly covered by the MFJ. For example, section 275 regulates BOC provision of alarm monitoring services.

As noted, the purpose of these provisions is to remove many of the absolute entry barriers that the MFJ's line of business restrictions imposed on the BOCs and to substitute a system of regulated entry to guard against potential predation or discrimination. What types of regulations are substituted? You name it and you'll find it here. For example, section 275 uses a sunset provision; neither BOCs nor their affiliates were allowed to offer alarm monitoring services during the first five years after the Act took effect. Section 274 took a different regulatory approach, allowing BOCs to offer electronic publishing services, but only if done through a separate affiliated entity or joint venture. That requirement had a four year sunset date and so is no longer in effect. Section 272 also imposed a separate affiliate requirement on BOC manufacturing of equipment or provision of in-region long distance services, but that provision employs yet another style of sunset rule. (Interestingly, we saw in Chapter Seventeen that, before the 1996 Act, the FCC had determined that the separate subsidiary requirement was not sound policy because it needlessly sacrificed economies of scale and scope; Congress seems to have determined otherwise in the new Act, at least with respect to competitive activities undertaken in the years just after the Act became law.)

Most importantly, under the Act BOCs may not offer in-region long distance services or manufacture telecommunications equipment until they have first been certified to do so by the FCC. To be certified for these purposes, a BOC must demonstrate to the Commission that it meets the fourteen requirements specified in a "competitive checklist" established by section 271(c)(2)(B). Most of these conditions relate to the local competition provisions discussed earlier in this chapter. For example, before being allowed to offer in-region long distance service, a BOC must show that it is providing or has offered to provide unbundled network elements, number portability, and nondiscriminatory access to its poles. In short, a BOC's ability to offer in-region long distance services and to manufacture equipment is conditioned on its meeting the 1996 Act's new local competition responsibilities, which in turn may make feasible true competition in the market for local exchange services.

There are, of course, other hurdles to clear as well. For example, the agency must ask for an opinion of the Attorney General before approving an in-region long distance application. While the Commission must give "substantial weight"

---

9. United States v. Western Elec. Co., 993 F.2d 1572 (D.C. Cir. 1993). Nynex, for example, could not supply a stock quotation system for which it had assembled the data itself, but it could transmit a ticker service whose content was managed by others.
10. *Id.* at 1582.

to the Attorney General's opinion, 47 U.S.C. §271(d)(2)(A), the Attorney General's opinion is in no way binding on the Commission. A BOC that manufactures and sells equipment must disclose vast quantities of information about its protocols, technical requirements, and network configuration. *See* §273(c). The goal of this latter provision is to prevent the BOC from using inside information gained in its role as a provider of local exchange service to become the sole supplier of equipment to operate that service.

Not surprisingly, entry of the BOCs into in-region long distance services has been the most contentious and visible line of business issue under the 1996 Act. It was not until December 1999—nearly four years after Congress passed the Act—that the FCC approved the first BOC application to provide long distance service in a geographic region where that BOC also provided local service. AT&T Corp. v. FCC, 220 F.3d 607 (D.C. Cir. 2000). And, even then, the filing at issue was opposed by the U.S. Department of Justice. All previous applications had been denied, and the denials had been upheld in court. For example, in 1998 the U.S. Court of Appeals for the D.C. Circuit upheld the Commission's denial of SBC's application to provide long distance service in Oklahoma. SBC Communications Inc. v. FCC, 138 F.3d 410 (D.C. Cir. 1998).

The materials below begin with the D.C. Circuit's decision affirming the FCC's approval of Bell Atlantic's entry into the New York long distance market. The opinion offers a nice overview of the relevant statutory provisions as well as the policy issues at stake. We then turn to the same court's decision affirming the Commission's denial of SBC's Oklahoma application; that opinion presents a more in-depth look at section 271 in particular.

AT&T CORPORATION v. FCC
220 F.3d 607 (D.C. Cir. 2000)

Opinion for the Court filed by Circuit Judge TATEL, in which Circuit Judges RANDOLPH and GARLAND concur.

TATEL, Circuit Judge:

Appellants challenge the Federal Communications Commission's approval of an application by Bell Atlantic to provide long distance service in New York, arguing that the company failed to implement two elements of a fourteen-point competitive checklist prescribed by the Telecommunications Act of 1996. The FCC's approval of Bell Atlantic's application was the first time since the 1982 breakup of AT&T that a Bell operating company received regulatory permission to offer long distance service in a state where it provides local telephone service—so-called "in-region" long distance service. Finding no defect in the Commission's analysis, we affirm in all respects.

Historically, local telephone companies operated as monopolies. "States typically granted an exclusive franchise in each local service area to a local exchange carrier which owned, among other things, the local loops (wires connecting telephones to switches), the switches (equipment directing calls to their destinations), and the transport trunks (wires carrying calls between switches) that constitute a local exchange network." AT&T Corp. v. Iowa Util. Bd., 525 U.S. 366 (1999).

For the better part of the twentieth century, appellant AT&T Corporation provided most local and long distance phone service throughout the country.

In 1974, the United States filed an antitrust action against AT&T alleging monopolization by the defendants with respect to a broad variety of telecommunications services and equipment in violation of section 2 of the Sherman Act. Following several years of discovery and nearly a full year of trial, AT&T and the government settled. Known as the Modification of Final Judgment (MFJ), the resulting consent decree required AT&T to divest itself of the twenty-two Bell operating companies, or "BOCs," that provided local telephone service.

Consolidated into seven regional holding companies (four today as a result of mergers), the BOCs continued to have a monopoly in local phone service in their respective service areas. Because "there are many ways in which the company controlling the local exchange monopoly can discriminate against competitors in the interexchange market," the MFJ prohibited BOCs from offering so-called "interLATA" or long distance service. *AT&T*, 552 F. Supp. at 188. The MFJ left open the possibility that BOCs could someday provide long distance service, but only if they "lost the ability to leverage their monopoly power into the competitive long distance market," either "as a result of technological developments" or as a result of "changes in the structures of the competitive markets." *Id.* at 194. No BOC ever obtained permission to provide long distance telephone service under the MFJ.

Section 601(a)(1) of the 1996 Act frees BOCs from all restrictions and obligations imposed by the MFJ, including the prohibition against providing long distance service. To encourage BOCs to open their markets to competition as quickly as possible, the Act permits them to provide "in-region" long distance service (long distance service originating in a state in which they offered local service under the MFJ) if they demonstrate that they have opened their local markets in that state to competition by fulfilling the requirements of section 271. *See* 47 U.S.C. §271(b)(1). BOCs may immediately begin providing "out-of-region" long distance service (long distance service originating outside the states in which the particular BOC offered local service under the MFJ). *See* §271(b)(2).

Under section 271, a BOC wishing to provide in-region long distance service must apply to the FCC for approval. §271(b)(1). In its application, the BOC must first demonstrate that it has satisfied either section 271(c)(1)(A), known as "Track A," or section 271(c)(1)(B), known as "Track B." To satisfy Track A, the BOC must show that it has entered into an agreement to provide access and interconnection to "one or more unaffiliated competing providers of telephone exchange service...to residential and business subscribers." If no such request for access and interconnection has been made, however, Track B allows the BOC to show that "a statement of the terms and conditions" that the BOC generally offers to provide such access and interconnection "has been approved or permitted to take effect by the State commission."

Once the BOC has shown that it has satisfied either Track A or Track B, it must establish that its offering of services to CLECs meets the fourteen requirements of a "competitive checklist" contained in section 271(c)(2)(B). The checklist incorporates by reference many of the substantive requirements of the Act's local competition provisions, sections 251 and 252. For example, the BOC must demonstrate that it provides "interconnection in accordance with the requirements of sections 251(c)(2) and 252(d)(1)"; "nondiscriminatory access to network elements in accordance with the requirements of sections 251(c)(3) and 252(d)(1)"; and so on. In addition to satisfying the competitive checklist's fourteen requirements, the BOC must demonstrate that it will provide in-region long distance service in accordance with the nondiscrimination and separate affiliate requirements of section 272. See §§271(d)(3)(B) & 272. Finally, the BOC must persuade the FCC that "the requested authorization is consistent with the public interest, convenience, and necessity." §271(d)(3)(C).

The statute gives the FCC ninety days to determine whether an applicant has met section 271's requirements, including whether it has "fully implemented the competitive checklist." The Commission must "consult with the Attorney General," who shall "provide to the Commission an evaluation of the application using any standard the Attorney General considers appropriate." §271(d)(2)(A). Although "the Commission shall give substantial weight to the Attorney General's evaluation," that evaluation "shall not have any preclusive effect on any Commission decision." The FCC must also "consult with the State commission of any State that is the subject of the application in order to verify" the BOC's compliance with that State's requirements for providing in-region long distance service. §271(d)(2)(B).

Prior to the filing of the application at issue in this case, the FCC had received and rejected five section 271 applications. It rejected the first because the applicant, SBC Communications, failed to demonstrate that it satisfied Track A. It rejected the others because the applicants failed to comply with various requirements of the competitive checklist.

Bell Atlantic filed its application to provide in-region long distance service in New York on September 29, 1999. The Bell Atlantic application represented the culmination of more than two years of work by the company and the New York Public Service Commission (NYPSC). After Bell Atlantic submitted a draft application in February 1997, the NYPSC commenced collaborative proceedings involving the company and its competitors to open New York's local exchange market to competition. The NYPSC also issued an order establishing rates for access to certain Bell Atlantic network elements. Spanning over one hundred pages, that order set rates for local loops, local switching, tandem switching, interoffice transport, signal control points, etc. Opinion and Order Setting Rates for First Group of Network Elements, Op. No. 97–2 (NYPSC Apr. 1, 1997).

At about the same time, the NYPSC began developing performance measures and service quality standards to assess whether Bell Atlantic was providing the nondiscriminatory access to its network that the 1996 Act requires. The NYPSC also hired the consulting firm KPMG to test Bell Atlantic's operations support systems for processing orders from Bell Atlantic's competitors. After extensive testing, during which Bell Atlantic corrected many problems, KPMG concluded that the company's operations support systems could adequately accommodate "reasonable, anticipated commercial volumes" of competitors' requests for network access.

On December 21, 1999, the FCC approved Bell Atlantic's application to provide long distance service in New York. The Commission began by observing that "the well established pro-competitive regulatory environment in New York in conjunction with recent measures to achieve section 271 compliance has, in general, created a thriving market for the provision of local exchange and exchange access service. Competitors in New York are able to enter the local market using all three entry paths provided under the Act." The FCC cited Bell Atlantic's estimates that competitors serve over one million phone lines in New York. According to the Department of Justice, moreover, CLECs in New York served approximately 8.9 percent of access lines as of June 1999, an amount "significantly larger than the national average of less than five percent."

Relying on uncontested evidence that Bell Atlantic had entered into interconnection agreements with several competing New York carriers, the Commission determined that the company had satisfied Track A. The Commission next examined Bell Atlantic's compliance with the fourteen components of the competitive checklist, concluding that the company had "fully implemented" each. The Commission also found that Bell Atlantic had demonstrated that it would comply with the separate affiliate and nondiscrimination requirements of section 272. Finding approval of the company's application to be "consistent with promoting competition in the local and long distance telecommunications markets," the Commission concluded that Bell Atlantic's provision of long distance service in New York would be in the public interest.

[The court then discussed, and rejected, each of the arguments presented by those challenging the FCC's approval of Bell Atlantic's provision of long distance service in New York. The opinion concluded as follows:]

Approving a section 271 application requires a delicate judgment about the current state of competition in local markets, as well as how best to foster future competition. The FCC must ensure—as it has in five previous cases—that BOCs failing to comply with the 1996 Act's local competition provisions are not allowed to provide long distance service. The Commission must be equally careful to ensure—as it has in this case—that BOCs that satisfy the statute's requirements are not barred from long distance markets. "Setting the bar for statutory compliance too high would inflict two quite serious harms," as the FCC points out in its brief. "First, it would dampen every BOC's incentive to cooperate closely with state regulators to open local markets to full competition. Second, setting the bar too high would simultaneously deprive the ultimate beneficiaries of the 1996 Act—American consumers—of a valuable source of price-reducing competition in the long distance market."

We believe that the Commission set the bar at a reasonable height. It demanded real evidence that Bell Atlantic had complied with all checklist requirements, but at the same time, it did not allow "'the infeasible perfect to oust the feasible good.'" Given the evidence of growing competition in the New York local telephone market, the NYPSC's careful work on a host of technical and complex issues, and the thorough analysis conducted by the FCC in the limited time permitted by section 271(c), we find no basis for faulting the Commission's conclusion that Bell Atlantic satisfied the statute's requirements for entry into the long distance telephone market.

SBC COMMUNICATIONS, INC. v. FCC
138 F.3d 410(D.C. Cir. 1998)

Opinion for the Court filed by Circuit Judge SILBERMAN, in which Circuit Judges WILLIAMS and SENTELLE concur.

SILBERMAN, Circuit Judge:

Appellant SBC Communications contends that in denying its application to provide long distance telephone service in the State of Oklahoma, the Federal Communications Commission has erroneously interpreted the provisions governing Bell operating company entry into the long distance market in their home region states, specifically 47 U.S.C. §§271(c)(1)(A) & (B). We affirm the Commission's interpretation.

As the first step in meeting the section 271(d)(3) criteria, BOCs must satisfy either §271(c)(1)(A) or §271(c)(1)(B), which the parties refer to as "Track A" and "Track B," respectively. Track A provides:

A [BOC] meets the requirements of this subparagraph if it has entered into one or more [approved] binding agreements...specifying the terms and conditions under which the [BOC] is providing access and interconnection to its network facilities for the network facilities of one or more unaffiliated competing providers of telephone exchange service...to residential and business subscribers. For the purpose of this subparagraph, such telephone exchange service may be offered by such competing providers either exclusively over their own telephone exchange service facilities or predominantly over their own telephone exchange service facilities in combination with the resale of the telecommunications services of another carrier.

Put simply then, Track A visualizes a demonstration of a competitor in the local exchange market. Track B, which first became available 10 months after the date of enactment, is satisfied, on the other hand, if "3 months before...the [BOC] makes its application" to the FCC, "no such provider has requested the access and interconnection described" in Track A, so long as "a statement of the terms and conditions that the [BOC] generally offers to provide such access and interconnection has been approved or permitted to take effect by the State commission." 47 U.S.C. §271(c)(1)(B). As is apparent, Track B is only available to a BOC as a default mechanism if "no such provider" has requested the access and interconnection Track A contemplates. Just what the characteristics of such a provider are and how they are measured—in other words, how useful is Track B to the BOCs—is the key issue in this litigation.

On April 11, 1997, SBC applied to the Commission for authorization to provide interLATA service originating from its in-region State of Oklahoma. Prior to submitting its application, SBC received the Oklahoma Corporation Commission's (OCC) approval of several negotiated access and interconnection agreements, one of which was made with Brooks Fiber Communications. Before the FCC, SBC contended that it satisfied Track A by virtue of its agreement with Brooks. At the time SBC made its application, Brooks owned and operated local telecommunications networks in Tulsa and Oklahoma City, providing service to

20 business customers (13 in Oklahoma City and 7 in Tulsa), and to three Tulsa residents and one other residential customer—each a Brooks employee. This service alone, SBC urged, meant that Brooks qualified as a Track A provider. To bolster its argument, SBC claimed that the tariff Brooks had filed with the OCC obligated Brooks, under Oklahoma law, to provide residential service over its own facilities to any requesting customer in its areas of operation. The OCC had cryptically opined that SBC had satisfied Track A's requirements, and SBC argued that the FCC was obliged to defer to the OCC's decision.

Alternatively, SBC claimed that it satisfied Track B because if the Commission determined that Brooks did not qualify as a Track A provider, neither did any other carrier. (SBC had filed a statement of terms and conditions at which it offered access and interconnection generally, which the OCC allowed to take effect by failing to complete its review within the 60 day requirement imposed by the Act. *See* 47 U.S.C. §252(f)(3)). As it happened, a large number of carriers had "requested" access and interconnection agreements of the sort described in Track A, but none of those requests foreclosed Track B's availability to SBC because, according to SBC at least, the phrase "such provider" means a competing local exchange carrier that was already providing the kind of service described in Track A—local telephone service to residential and business subscribers exclusively or predominantly over its own facilities-based network—at the time it made its request. SBC acknowledged an exception, however, for a requesting carrier who did not have that position at the time of its request but nevertheless achieved it no later than three months before the BOC applied to the FCC for interLATA authorization.[11]

The Commission concluded that appellant had not yet met either Track A or Track B and denied SBC's application. Regarding Track A, the FCC concluded that Brooks—the only provider who could potentially satisfy Track A—was not a competing provider of telephone exchange service to residential subscribers because the four customers to which Brooks provided residential service were its employees and the service was provided on a test basis free of charge. Brooks, in short, did not provide an "actual commercial alternative to the BOC."

The Commission then determined that, whatever legal obligations Brooks had under Oklahoma law, those obligations could not supply evidence of actual competition. Brooks' own executive vice president had averred that Brooks was "'not offering nor had it ever offered residential service in Oklahoma.'" And because it lacked the necessary facilities, Brooks was not "'accepting any request in Oklahoma for residential service." Accordingly, the Commission said Brooks "at present has at most paper commitments to furnish service." In reaching this conclusion, the Commission explicitly relied upon the comments of the United States Department of Justice, whose recommendations the FCC must give "substantial weight." *See* 47 U.S.C. §271(d)(2)(A).

The Commission went on to decide that Track B was not open to SBC. The Commission understood Track B to be foreclosed to a BOC if a provider had

---

11. That exception to SBC's general interpretation helps SBC to claim that Brooks was a Track A provider although it had not been providing all of its relied upon service at the time it made its request. According to SBC, although Brooks did not qualify when it submitted its request in March 1996, it began providing service of the kind described in Track A on January 15, 1997. Since SBC had made its application on April 11 of that year, Brooks became "such provider" a few days too late to foreclose Track B.

made a request that if implemented would satisfy Track A. The phrase "such provider" was not limited, as SBC claimed, to a provider who was already providing the very service contemplated at the time of its request (or one who achieved that status three months before a BOC's application), but rather included one who after implementation of its requested access and interconnection agreement would be a competitor. The Commission recognized, to be sure, that whether such a request satisfied this standard was a potentially difficult question that obliged the Commission to rely on its predictive judgment as an expert agency. On the record before it, the Commission found that SBC had received 45 requests for interconnection; "at the very least, several of which were qualifying requests for access and interconnection that foreclosed Track B."

The FCC rejected SBC's narrow reading of "such provider" in Track B, primarily because under that interpretation, BOCs would have a considerable incentive to delay and prevent interconnection so that they could apply under Track B immediately on December 8, 1996. The Commission thought that "Congress intended Track B to serve as a limited exception to the Track A requirement of operational competition," and believed that its reading "best furthered Congress' goal of introducing competition in the local exchange market by giving BOCs an incentive to cooperate with potential competitors in providing them the facilities they need to fulfill their requests for access and interconnection." The Commission also discarded what it called the "equally unreasonable" position advanced by SBC's potential competitors — that "any request for access and interconnection submitted by a potential new entrant to a BOC is a qualifying request that precludes the BOC from proceeding under Track B" — as that interpretation would allow potential competitors to effectively deny the BOC's entry into the interLATA market by submitting requests that might never satisfy Track A even if implemented.

Track A

We do not think much of appellant's argument that the Commission was obliged to conclude that Brooks was a "competing provider" in the local residential market merely because four Brooks employees were provided free residential service and under Brooks' tariff it is legally bound to offer such service. Track A does not indicate just how much competition a provider must offer in either the business or residential markets before it is deemed a "competing" provider. Nor does the legislative history offer any guidance. Under those circumstances, the Commission's interpretation of the ambiguous phrase "competing provider" is certainly entitled to *Chevron* deference. *See* Chevron U.S.A. Inc. v. Natural Resources Defense Council, Inc., 467 U.S. 837 (1984). It is at least permissible, within the meaning of *Chevron*, for the Commission to interpret "competing provider" as meaning that a satisfactory provider must offer "an actual commercial alternative to the BOC."

Track B

Since appellant's argument is primarily a linguistic one, we think it useful to set forth section 271(c)(1)(B) in its entirety.

(B) FAILURE TO REQUEST ACCESS. A Bell operating company meets the requirements of this subparagraph if, after 10 months after February

8, 1996, no such provider has requested the access and interconnection described in subparagraph (A) before the date which is 3 months before the date the company makes its application under subsection (d)(1) of this section, and a statement of the terms and conditions that the company generally offers to provide such access and interconnection has been approved or permitted to take effect by the State commission under section 252(f) of this title. For purposes of this subparagraph, a Bell operating company shall be considered not to have received any request for access and interconnection if the State commission of such State certifies that the only provider or providers making such a request have (i) failed to negotiate in good faith as required by section 252 of this title, or (ii) violated the terms of an agreement approved under section 252 of this title by the provider's failure to comply, within a reasonable period of time, with the implementation schedule contained in such agreement.

Appellant contends that because the phrase "such provider" in Track B necessarily refers back to the "competing providers" in Track A, Track B must be available to a BOC unless an actual competing provider is on the scene and has requested or entered into binding agreements with a BOC to provide access and interconnection. In SBC's view, it will be recalled, Track B can only be foreclosed if a requesting provider has begun competing in the local telephone market over its own facilities-based network before even asking for an access and interconnection, or, alternatively, if the requesting provider becomes an actual facilities-based competitor at least three months before the BOC makes its application to provide interLATA service (of course, at that point it would not matter if Track B were foreclosed to the BOC because Track A would be available). If the Commission is correct in determining that Brooks is not "such a provider" because it is not sufficiently competitive, then it follows, according to appellant—since no other carrier is claimed to have achieved greater competitive status—that Track B is open to SBC. As we have noted, the Commission read "such provider" differently; it thought that Track B was foreclosed the moment a provider requested interconnection so long as it could predict that the carrier would, after implementing the agreement, provide competitive service to both residential and business customers, at least predominantly over its own facilities.

Appellant argues that the Commission's interpretation makes Track B virtually useless to BOCs because of the flood of interconnection requests. The record showed that SBC received 45 such requests in Oklahoma, and the Commission concluded that four of those would meet the facilities-based competitive standard after being implemented.[12] And SBC asserts that it does not know of any state where no carrier expressing a desire to become a facilities-based competitor requested interconnection. The Commission, on the other hand, contends that ap-

---

12. In making this prediction, the FCC must have at least implicitly determined that the four providers would satisfy Track A's facilities-based requirement. Yet, what it means for a carrier to offer service "exclusively...or predominantly over their own telephone exchange service facilities," 47 U.S.C. §271(c)(1)(A), is nowhere spelled out in the text or by the Commission (it is clear that pure "resale of the BOC's telephone exchange service does not qualify," H.R. CONF. REP. NO. 104–458, at 148). Indeed, the FCC claimed not to have addressed the issue. We are puzzled by the FCC's reasoning, but no party has raised this point, so the FCC's interpretation of what it means to be predominantly facilities-based remains for another case.

pellant's reading would nullify Track A, which it believes Congress intended as the primary path for a BOC seeking to enter the interLATA market.

Carefully parsing the language of the two sections, we come to the conclusion that it is not apparent on their face whether "such provider" in Track B is intended to mean a carrier who has met the requirements of Track A—*i.e.*, is actually providing service, either on its own, or under an access and interconnection agreement with a BOC—or one who has requested such an agreement but has not yet implemented it and begun providing the requisite service. There seems to be an ambiguity as to how close to competitive status a provider must be when the request is made.

Looking further to the structure of the sections to understand their meaning, we see that Track B provides that a BOC will be deemed not to have received an interconnection request if a State commission determines that a requesting provider negotiated in bad faith or violated the terms of an interconnection agreement by delaying its implementation unreasonably. We think that provision supports the Commission's interpretation. As should be apparent, the BOCs have an incentive to protect their local markets from competition, just as the long distance carriers have one to prevent the BOCs from entering the interexchange market. The bad faith and unreasonable delay exceptions explicitly contemplate and seek to deal with the problem that SBC identifies—that a provider might request interconnection only to prevent a BOC from using Track B. If SBC's reading of the statute were correct, a BOC, merely by refusing to enter into an interconnection agreement, could easily prevent a competing facilities-based provider from emerging, thus preserving Track B's availability. To be sure, another provision of the statute obliges the BOCs (as well as requesting carriers) to negotiate access and interconnection agreements in good faith. *See* 47 U.S.C. §251(c)(1). But only the requesting carriers are penalized for negotiating in bad faith in the Track A and B subsections; there is no reciprocal provision that prevents a BOC from using Track B if it in bad faith refused to allow interconnection. Under SBC's reading, the draftsmen would have left an inexplicable loophole in the legislative scheme, one inconsistent with the treatment of requesting providers acting in bad faith.

The Commission's Order is therefore affirmed.

Notes and Questions

1. Summary. The two cases excerpted in this section together provide a thorough discussion of the 1996 Act's provisions related to BOC entry in the interexchange market. To summarize: although BOCs are immediately authorized to provide out-of-region interLATA service (section 271(b)(2)), a BOC is not allowed to provide in-region interLATA service until the Commission concludes that: (1) it has satisfied either section 271(c)(1)(A) or 271(c)(1)(B), the provisions at issue in SBC v. FCC; (2) it has also satisfied the competitive checklist set out in section 271(c)(2)(B); (3) the BOC has established a separate subsidiary as required by section 272; and (4) granting the application would serve the "public interest, convenience, and necessity," as required by section 271(d)(3)(C).

2. In-Region/Out-of-Region. Why does the Act distinguish so sharply between in-region and out-of-region interLATA service? Are the dangers of predatory cross-subsidization and discriminatory interconnection really so different in these two settings?

3. Facilities-Based Competition. Section 271(c)(1)(A) ("Track A") explicitly states that, for purposes of the paragraph, a "telephone exchange service provider" is a provider that offers its services "exclusively" or "predominantly" over that provider's own facilities. This is one of the few provisions of the Act that singles out facilities-based competitors. Why is it so important here that the provider be facilities-based?

4. What is Brooks? The court in SBC v. FCC in essence upheld the Commission's determination that Brooks was *not* a sufficient competitor such that SBC could qualify under Track A but *was* a sufficient competitor such that SBC would be precluded from using, instead, Track B. Is this consistent? Is it a good reading of the statute? The court claims that these interpretations give BOCs "an incentive to cooperate with potential competitors," but, on the facts of the very case at issue, what did SBC fail to do for Brooks that a more cooperative BOC would have done?

5. Why Not Mandates? Overall, the statute seems to set up the removal of the restriction on BOC provision of interLATA service as a quid pro quo: BOCs that cooperate with respect to the local competition provisions are, in exchange, given as a reward the right to enter the long distance service market. Is there a reason why Congress adopted this sort of incentive approach instead of simply mandating particular cooperative behaviors by a date certain?

6. Dealing with the LEC Bottleneck. Reviewing all the materials on telephone regulation to this point in the book—including price cap regulation, the local competition provisions, and the approaches of the MFJ, the FCC, and the 1996 Act to line of business restrictions—we can identify at least seven "responses" to the question of whether to permit local exchange carriers to offer services allied to, but different from, plain old telephone service:

(a) complete ban on entry (original MFJ);

(b) complete ban on entry but only for a few years (*e.g.*, MFJ provision on AT&T entry into electronic publishing);

(c) entry permitted, but only via separate subsidiaries (*e.g.*, FCC decision in *Computer II*);

(d) permit entry while imposing price caps;

(e) permit entry while imposing interconnection duties;

(f) permit entry subject to "open architecture" and disclosure regulations of the sort adopted by the FCC in *Computer III;*

(g) unrestricted entry without specially tailored restraints.

How would you assess the costs and benefits of each approach? What about combining two or three? Does your answer vary with the service at issue? Is there a preferable "solution" not mentioned above?

7. The Buck Stops Where, Part II. These materials also repeatedly raise the question of who (or what institution) is best equipped to answer the questions posed in the preceding note. Are these issues that ought to be resolved by accountable legislators? Left up to the various state agencies? Resolved by politically independent judges? Handled by the FCC because of its expertise and ability to adopt flexible, innovative rules or remedies?

8. Rebuilding Bell. Another noteworthy aspect of the 1996 Act is that it basically freed AT&T of all regulatory constraints. Was this a wise conclusion to the decades of legal wrangling over AT&T's status? For example, should AT&T be allowed to re-enter the local exchange business? The MFJ prevents AT&T from acquiring the stock or assets of any of the former Bell Operating Companies, but it does not by its terms prevent the acquisition of a non-Bell local exchange carrier. When AT&T sought to merge with what was then the country's largest provider of cellular telephone services, McCaw Cellular Communications, Judge Greene initially declared that the acquisition would violate the MFJ because some of the Regional Bell Holding Companies shared cellular licenses with McCaw. Thus, AT&T would technically have acquired some stock or assets of the former Bell companies. 66 Antitrust & Trade Reg. Report 410 (April 14, 1994). Suppose this technical objection did not exist. Should AT&T have been allowed into local cellular telephony, via merger or de novo entry? In fact, AT&T did ultimately merge with McCaw and is thus today involved in the cellular marketplace; does that mean the MFJ ultimately failed, or was perhaps unnecessary?

Does it matter to all of the above that AT&T is, as of this writing, also the nation's largest cable operator? What if it turns out that the cable infrastructure is the most cost-effective way to offer voice service that competes with the voice service available over the wireline telephone network? Do your answers change yet again if it turns out that voice service can be provided over the wires of the electric grid? And lastly, what are we to make of AT&T's decision in 2000 to voluntarily separate itself into several independent operating units?

III. UNIVERSAL SERVICE AND ACCESS CHARGE REFORM

We pointed out in the previous section that the provisions of the Act lifting the BOC line of business restrictions in many ways followed naturally from the provisions designed to facilitate competition in the local loop. The former, we said, were a response to the latter; the new competitive landscape on the local level made competition more workable in allied markets. A similar point can be made with respect to the Act's provisions regarding universal service/access charge reform. The restructuring of the competitive landscape triggered by the local competition provisions necessitated corresponding changes to the system of funding universal service. The old approach—implicit cross-subsidies—could not survive the transition to competitive markets. Monopolists can cross-subsidize. Competitors cannot. As it was with the line of business restrictions, then, many of the 1996 Act's reforms with respect to universal service can be explained as necessary responses to the local competition provisions of the Act.

To explain the 1996 Act's universal service provisions exclusively on this ground, however, would be to sell these reforms short. The 1996 Act went beyond necessary adjustments; it set in motion a process that has already begun to transform not only the way universal service is funded, but also the very scope of the universal service system. Historically, the universal service program had as its principal objective only the relatively modest goal of reducing the costs of basic telephone service and, in that way, increasing national subscribership. The program was phenomenally successful on this score; by 1997, the percentage of homes nationwide with at least basic telephone service was estimated at nearly 95%.[13] But universal service under the 1996 Act is much more. As the materials that follow suggest, the 1996 Act established that a modern program of universal service must include in its goals not only increased penetration for basic telephone service, but also greater access to new telecommunications technologies and services. Under the 1996 Act, in fact, universal service is defined to include an evolving level of support—in short, as technological possibilities expand, so, too, will the nation's universal service commitment.

The key statutory provision is section 254, which sets out various rules and procedures for universal service reform. The section explicitly establishes the basic intuitions sketched above, stating (in §254(c)(1)) that universal service is to be "an evolving level of telecommunications services" that the Commission should adjust over time to account for "advances in telecommunications and information technologies and services." Details beyond that, however, are largely left to a Federal-State Joint Board that was created by the Act (in §254(a)(1)) and charged with the task of recommending to the FCC what should be included within the federal universal service standard. The FCC established this Joint Board in the spring of 1996 and its recommendations were released that November.

The Act directs the Joint Board and the FCC to design policies for preserving and advancing universal service so as to promote several goals: providing services at just, reasonable, and affordable rates; providing access to advanced services in all regions; ensuring that there are comparable rates and quality of services; providing schools, classrooms, libraries, and health care providers with access to advanced telecommunications services; and ensuring that federal and state support mechanisms are predictable, specific, and sufficient. (See §254(b)(1)–(7)). To these goals, the Joint Board added "competitive neutrality," an addition to which the FCC subsequently agreed.

What, then, is universal service? As defined by the Joint Board, universal service includes "voice grade access to the public switched network, with the ability to place and receive calls; touch-tone or dual tone multi-frequency signaling (DTMF) or its functional equivalent; single-party service; access to emergency services; access to operator services; access to interexchange services; and access to directory assistance." Universal service as defined by the Joint Board also includes additional assistance for low income consumers so as to enable them to have access to services such as toll limitation and toll blocking. Note that the Joint Board's definition does not (yet) include the infrastructure necessary for high-speed Internet access.

---

13. In re Federal-State Joint Board on Universal Service, 12 FCC Rcd. 8776, at ¶7 (1997).

How will we pay for universal service? Section 254(d) mandates that "every telecommunications carrier that provides interstate telecommunications services shall contribute, on an equitable and nondiscriminatory basis," to whatever universal service funds the Commission ultimately creates. The Joint Board recommended that the phrase "every telecommunications carrier that provides interstate telecommunications services" be construed broadly to include any company that provides such services to the public for a fee (not necessarily for a profit), or to a substantial part of the public. Interestingly, the Board left Internet service providers off that list, a controversial decision that we will explore in Chapter Twenty-Two. The Board further recommended that "contributions be based on a carrier's gross telecommunications revenues net of payments to other carriers."

Only a telecommunications carrier described under 47 U.S.C. §214(e)(1) will receive federal universal service support. That section states:

> A common carrier designated as an eligible telecommunications carrier under paragraph (2) or (3) shall be eligible to receive universal service support in accordance with section 254 and shall, throughout the service area for which the designation is received—
>
> (A) offer the services that are supported by Federal universal service support mechanisms under section 254(c), either using its own facilities or a combination of its own facilities and resale of another carrier's services (including the services offered by another eligible telecommunications carrier); and
>
> (B) advertise the availability of such services and the charges therefor using media of general distribution.

The Joint Board recommended that the FCC not impose additional criteria and that funds be distributed and collected by a neutral party. The Commission agreed to these funding recommendations.

The Joint Board also recommended that schools and libraries should have access to telecommunications services, specifically the Internet, at a discount. Including the Internet in this recommendation angered many LECs because, as noted above, Internet service providers do not have to contribute to the fund. Health care providers receive similar universal service support. In line with the Act's concept of an evolving definition of universal service, the Joint Board also suggested that the FCC establish another Joint Board "no later than January 1, 2001, to revisit the definition of universal service."

Although the Joint Board sets federal guidelines, states are free to set their own universal service guidelines and collect money for intrastate universal service funds. Indeed, this is to some degree an exception to the requirement in §253(a) that no state or local regulation "prohibit or have the effect of prohibiting" new entry into the local exchange market. The exception, set out in §253(b), recognizes in the states the authority to set their own universal service guidelines for intrastate services so long as any such regulations are competitively neutral and consistent with section 254.

Edited versions of two FCC documents follow. The first is a Commission press release describing the recommendations of the Joint Board. Each of these recommendations was adopted by the Commission in its May 1997 *Universal Service Order*, which is the second document. The first document, then, lists the rules for defining and paying for universal service under the terms of the 1996 Act, while the second document provides, in summary form, the Commission's rationale for these rules.

FCC NEWS RELEASE: JOINT BOARD ADOPTS UNIVERSAL SERVICE RECOMMENDATIONS
Report No. DC 96–100, 1996 WL 648322 (1996)

The Joint Board recommends basing universal service policies on the principles enumerated in the Act, as well as the additional principle of competitive neutrality. By "competitive neutrality," the Joint Board means that all providers of interstate telecommunications services should make an equitable and nondiscriminatory contribution to the preservation and advancement of universal service. The Joint Board believes that the principle of competitive neutrality should be applied to every recipient of and contributor to the universal service support mechanisms, regardless of size, status, or geographic location. The Joint Board's recommendations, in summary, are as follows:

Services Included in Universal Service Support

The Joint Board recommends that support be provided for these services:

1) Voice grade access to the public switched network, including, at a minimum, some usage;

2) Dual-tone multi-frequency (DTMF) signaling or its equivalent;

3) Single-party service;

4) Access to emergency services, including access to 911, where available;

5) Access to operator services;

6) Access to interexchange services; and

7) Access to directory assistance.

Affordability

Whether local telephone service is affordable depends upon several factors apart from local rates. Local calling area size, income levels, cost of living, and other socioeconomic indicators help in assessing affordability. The Joint Board recommends that the states, in their rate-setting roles, make the primary determination as to whether rates are affordable and for taking any necessary actions should they determine the rates are not affordable. The FCC will also assess affordability by continuing to monitor subscribership levels.

Carriers Eligible for Support

The Joint Board recommends that any telecommunications carrier, including, for example, cellular or PCS providers, regardless of the technology that it uses, that meets the criteria for eligibility spelled out in the Act, be eligible to receive universal service support. The statutory criteria for receiving universal service support are as follows:

1) the telecommunications carrier must be a common carrier, and

2) the carrier must offer, throughout a designated service area, all of the services supported by universal service support as described above.

Programs for Low Income Consumers

Over ten years ago, the Commission established two programs that are currently available to assist low income consumers. The Lifeline program reduces qualified low income consumers' monthly phone charges with matching federal and state funds. The Link Up program provides federal support that reduces qualified low income consumers' initial local telephone connection charges by up to one half. Link Up is currently funded by contributions from interexchange carriers. The Joint Board recommends revising the Lifeline and Link Up programs.

Rural, Insular and High Cost Areas

The Joint Board recommends that support for carriers with high costs (except rural carriers) be based on the difference between cost estimates generated by a cost proxy model minus a nationwide benchmark. The Joint Board also states that it is desirable that the benchmark be based on the amount the carrier would expect to recover from other services to cover the cost of providing supported services in rural, insular, and high cost areas, but final determination of the methodology for selecting the benchmark must also consider the revenue base for universal service contributions.

Schools and Libraries

The Joint Board recommends that eligible schools and libraries be able to purchase at a discount any telecommunications services, internal connections among classrooms, and access to the Internet. The Joint Board recommends providing higher discounts for economically disadvantaged schools and libraries and those entities located in high cost areas. Discounts are a minimum of 20% and range from 40–90% for all but the least disadvantaged schools and libraries.

Services for Health Care Providers

The Joint Board estimates that approximately 9,600 health care providers in rural areas in the United States will be eligible to receive telecommunications services supported by the universal service mechanism. Health care providers include teaching hospitals, medical schools, community health centers, migrant health centers, mental health centers, not-for-profit hospitals, local health departments, rural health clinics, and consortia or associations of any of the listed providers. The Joint Board recommends that the Commission seek further information before designating the exact scope of services to be supported for rural health care providers.

Administration of the Universal Service Support Mechanism

The Joint Board recommends that the FCC appoint a universal service advisory board, including state and FCC representatives, to select a neutral, third-party administrator to administer the collection and distribution of the support mechanisms.

The Joint Board recommends that all telecommunications carriers that provide interstate telecommunications services be obligated to contribute to universal service. The Joint Board recommends that contributions be based on carriers' gross revenues from telecommunications services net of payments to other carriers for telecommunications services.

Finally, the Joint Board recommends that universal service support mechanisms for schools, libraries, and rural health care providers be funded by assessing both the intrastate and interstate revenues of providers of interstate telecommunications services.

IN RE FEDERAL-STATE JOINT BOARD ON UNIVERSAL SERVICE
Report and Order, 12 FCC Rcd. 8776 (1997)

I. INTRODUCTION

1. In the Telecommunications Act of 1996, Congress directed the Commission and states to take the steps necessary to establish support mechanisms to ensure the delivery of affordable telecommunications service to all Americans, including low income consumers, eligible schools and libraries, and rural health care providers. Specifically, Congress directed the Commission and the states to devise methods to ensure that "consumers in all regions of the Nation, including low income consumers and those in rural, insular, and high cost areas...have access to telecommunications and information services...at rates that are reasonably comparable to rates charged for similar services in urban areas."[14] Congress further directed the Commission to define additional services for support for eligible schools, libraries, and health care providers, and directed the Commission to "establish competitively neutral rules...to enhance, to the extent technically feasible and economically reasonable, access to advanced telecommunications and information services for all public and non-profit elementary and secondary school classrooms, health care providers, and libraries."[15]

2. Consistent with the explicit statutory principles, our immediate implementation of section 254 is shaped by our commitment to achieve four critical goals. First, we must implement all of the universal service objectives established by the Act, including those for low income individuals, consumers in rural, insular, and high cost areas, schools, libraries, and rural health care providers.[16] Second, we must maintain rates for basic residential service at affordable levels. We believe that the rates for this service are generally at affordable levels today. Third, we must ensure affordable basic service continues to be

---

14. 47 U.S.C. §254(b)(3).

15. 47 U.S.C. §254(h)(2)(A). Telecommunications carriers are required to provide service to rural health care providers "at rates that are reasonably comparable to rates charged for similar services in urban areas." 47 U.S.C. §254(h)(1)(A). Schools and libraries now are entitled under federal law to service "at rates less than the amounts charged for similar services to other parties." 47 U.S.C. §254(h)(1)(B). In addition, Congress directed the Commission to "enhance...access to advanced telecommunications and information services for all public and non-profit elementary and secondary school classrooms, health care providers, and libraries." 47 U.S.C. §254(h)(2).

16. See, e.g., 47 U.S.C. §§254(b), (h), and (i).

available to all users through an explicit universal service funding mechanism. For the present, we believe we can achieve this goal by maintaining our existing high cost mechanism at current funding levels, picking a platform mechanism by December 1997, and implementing a forward-looking economic cost mechanism for universal service for non-rural carriers starting January 1, 1999. Fourth, we must bring the benefits of competition to as many consumers as possible.

3. Today, we adopt rules that reflect virtually all of the Joint Board's recommendations and fulfill the universal service goals established by Congress.[17]

6. In this proceeding, we modify the funding methods for the existing federal universal service support mechanisms so that such support is not generated, as at present, entirely through charges imposed on long distance carriers. Instead, as the statute requires, we will require equitable and non-discriminatory contributions from all providers of interstate telecommunications service.

7. When it enacted section 254 of the Communications Act, Congress emphasized that the preservation and advancement of universal service was to be the result of federal and state action, stating "there should be specific, predictable and sufficient Federal *and State* mechanisms to preserve and advance universal service."[18] Congress also entrusted the states with a role in universal service, including expressly granting states the authority "to adopt regulations not inconsistent with the Commission's rules to preserve and advance universal service," and requiring every telecommunications carrier that provides intrastate telecommunications services to "contribute, on an equitable and nondiscriminatory basis, in a manner determined by the state, to the preservation and advancement of universal service in that state" when such state establishes universal service support mechanisms.[19] States traditionally have promoted universal service by, among other things, assuring affordable residential access by explicitly and implicitly subsidizing and pricing basic telephone service at levels associated with very high telephone subscribership rates, currently 94.2%.

8. Universal service support mechanisms that are designed to increase subscribership by keeping rates affordable will benefit everyone in the country, including those who can afford basic telephone service. At the simplest level, increasing the number of people connected to the telecommunications network makes the network more valuable to all of its users by increasing its usefulness to them. Increasing subscribership also benefits society in ways unrelated to the value of the network per se. For example, all of us benefit from the widespread availability of basic public safety services, such as 911.

9. Congress intended that, to the extent possible, "any support mechanisms continued or created under new section 254 should be explicit, rather than implicit as many support mechanisms are today."[20]

---

17. *See* Federal-State Joint Board on Universal Service, CC Docket No. 96–45, Recommended Decision, 12 FCC Rcd. 87 (1996). [Ed. Subsequent portions of this *Order* adopt those Joint Board recommendations that are listed in the edited press release of November 7, 1996, reprinted above.]

18. 47 U.S.C. §254(b)(5) (emphasis added).

19. 47 U.S.C. §254(f).

20. Joint Explanatory Statement of the Committee of the Conference (H.R. Rep. No. 458, 104th Cong., 2d Sess.) (hereinafter *Joint Explanatory Statement*) at 131.

10. Today, universal service is achieved largely through implicit subsidies.[21] The Commission currently has in place some explicit support mechanisms directed at increasing network subscribership by reducing rates in high cost areas (the high cost fund and Long Term Support) and at making service affordable for low income consumers (the Lifeline and Link Up programs). The current "system," however, consists principally of a number of implicit mechanisms at the state and, to a substantially lesser extent, federal levels designed to shift costs from rural to urban areas, from residential to business customers, and from local to long distance service.

11. The urban-to-rural subsidy has been accomplished through the explicit high cost fund mentioned above, and through geographic rate averaging. The result of state requirements that local telephone rates be averaged across the state is that high-density (urban) areas, where costs are typically lower, subsidize low-density (rural) areas. State pricing rules have also in many cases created a business-to-residential subsidy. Most states have established local rate levels such that businesses pay more on a per-line basis for basic local service than do residential customers, although the costs of providing business and residential lines are generally the same. In addition, rates charged for vertical services such as touch tone, conference calling and speed dialing, subsidize basic local service rates. Finally, interstate and intrastate access charges are set relatively high in order to cover certain loop costs not recovered through local rates. These usage-based charges are then recovered through higher usage charges for interstate long distance service. Thus, interstate long distance customers—and particularly those with higher calling volumes—indirectly subsidize local telephone rates.

12. Of the three implicit subsidy mechanisms—geographic rate averaging, subsidizing residential lines via business lines, and interstate access charges—only the interstate access charge system has been regulated by the Commission, and this contributes the smallest subsidy of the three. Thus, a number of factors operate today to keep basic local telephone rates low, and Congress ordered that we devise a coordinated federal-state scheme to achieve universal service goals.

13. By our *Order* today, we reject the arguments made by some parties that section 254 compels us immediately to remove all universal service costs from interstate access charges. As stated previously, we have met section 254's clear command that we identify the services to be supported by federal universal service support mechanisms, and that we establish a specific timetable for implementation. Under that timetable, we will over the next year identify implicit interstate universal support and make that support explicit, as further provided by section 254(e).

14. We do not, by our *Order* today, attempt to identify existing implicit universal service support presently effected through intrastate rates or other state mechanisms, nor do we attempt to convert such implicit intrastate support into explicit federal universal service support. The Commission, in light of section

---

21. When we refer to "implicit subsidies" in this discussion we generally mean that a single company is expected to obtain revenues from sources at levels above "cost" (*i.e.*, above competitive price levels), and to price other services allegedly below cost. Such intracompany subsidies are typically regulated by states. An example at the federal level, however, is the geographic averaging of interstate long distance rates. In section 254(g) of the Act, Congress expressly directed that this implicit subsidy continue.

2(b) of the Communications Act,[22] does not have control over the local rate-setting process, which generally has aimed at ensuring affordable residential rates. States have maintained low residential basic service rates through, among other things, a combination of: geographic rate averaging, higher rates for business customers, higher intrastate access rates, higher rates for intrastate toll service, and higher rates for vertical features. States, acting pursuant to sections 254(f) and 253 of the Communications Act, must in the first instance be responsible for identifying intrastate implicit universal service support. We further believe that, as competition develops, the marketplace itself will identify intrastate implicit universal service support, and that states will be compelled by those marketplace forces to move that support to explicit, sustainable mechanisms consistent with section 254(f). As states do so, we will be able to assess whether additional federal universal service support is necessary to ensure that quality services remain "available at just, reasonable and affordable rates."[23]

15. Federal universal service support will be distributed based on the interstate portion of the difference between the forward-looking economic cost of providing service[24] and a nationwide revenue benchmark.[25] The amount of support will be explicitly calculable and identifiable by competing carriers, and will be portable among competing carriers, *i.e.*, distributed to the eligible telecommunications carrier chosen by the customer. It will be funded by equitable and nondiscriminatory contributions from all carriers that provide interstate telecommunications services.

16. We wish to avoid action that directly or indirectly raises the price of the basic residential telephone service that guarantees access to the local telephone network. We also believe that raising the existing flat-rate charge on every consumer's line for access to interstate telephone service — the subscriber line charge (SLC) on primary residential lines — is not desirable, because it could adversely affect the affordability of local service. Therefore, we decide that we will not permit any increase in the primary residential line SLC and will not order the creation of any additional end-user charges for local service over these lines. Our primary reason for not mandating the recovery of universal service contributions through basic rates, directly raising charges for basic access through an increase in the primary residence SLC, or adopting any new end-user charge from the local telephone company to the residential consumer for basic access is that we have high subscribership rates today, and therefore believe that current rate levels are "affordable." We see no reason to jeopardize affordability by raising rate levels.

17. At present, the existing system of largely implicit subsidies can continue to serve its purpose, and our current implementation of section 254 relies principally on the continuation of existing mechanisms, with modifications to make

---

22. Section 2(b) of the Act provides that in most cases, "nothing in this Act shall be construed to apply or to give the Commission jurisdiction with respect to…charges, classifications, practices, services, facilities, or regulations for or in connection with intrastate communication service by wire or radio of any carrier." 47 U.S.C. §152(b).

23. 47 U.S.C. §254(b)(1).

24. [Ed. By this phrase the Commission means the costs of providing the service if the carrier employs the most efficient technology currently available. *See* ¶26.]

25. [Ed. By this phrase the Commission means a price that the agency deems just, reasonable, and affordable.]

them more consistent with the statutory requirements and principles. This system is not sustainable in its current form in a competitive environment. Implicit subsidies were sustainable in the monopoly environment because some consumers (such as urban business customers) could be charged rates for local exchange and exchange access service that significantly exceeded the cost of providing service, and the rates paid by those customers would implicitly subsidize service provided by the same carrier to others. By adoption of the 1996 Act, Congress has provided for the development of competition in all telephone markets. In a competitive market, a carrier that attempts to charge rates significantly above cost to a class of customers will lose many of those customers to a competitor. This incentive to entry by competitors in the lowest cost, highest profit market segments means that today's pillars of implicit subsidies—high access charges, high prices for business services, and the averaging of rates over broad geographic areas—will be under attack. New competitors can target service to more profitable customers without having to build into their rates the types of cross-subsidies that have been required of existing carriers who serve all customers.

18. By this *Order*, therefore, we will retain, with some limited modifications, the existing explicit high cost and low income support programs until January 1, 1999, but make collection more equitable and nondiscriminatory and allow carriers other than ILECs to receive support; we will continue to coordinate with the states to determine the appropriate extent of universal service support for high cost areas as competition and related state decisions dictate; and we will fund universal service for eligible schools, libraries, and rural health care providers consistent with the statute. The total amount of federal high cost support (both implicit and explicit) will not decline materially, but will be restructured.

19. Over time, it will be necessary to adjust the universal service support system to respond to competitive pressures and state decisions so that the support mechanisms are sustainable, efficient, explicit, and promote competitive entry. We expect to use both prescriptive (*i.e.*, regulatory) and more permissive (*i.e.*, market-based) approaches to complete this task.

II. EXECUTIVE SUMMARY

D. Carriers Eligible for Universal Service Support

24. Pursuant to section 214(e), eligible carriers must offer and advertise all the services supported by federal universal service support mechanisms throughout their service areas using their own facilities or a combination of their own facilities and resale of another carrier's services. We interpret the term "facilities" in section 214(e)(1) to mean any physical components of the telecommunications network that are used in the transmission or routing of the services designated for support under section 254(c)(1). We also find, as did the Joint Board, that section 214(e) precludes an eligible carrier from offering the supported services solely through resale in light of the statutory requirement that a carrier provide universal service, at least in part, over its own facilities.

E. High Cost Support

26. Consistent with the Joint Board's recommendation, we find that a cost methodology based on forward-looking economic cost should be used to calcu-

late the cost of providing universal service for high cost areas because it best reflects the cost of providing service in a competitive market for local exchange telephone service. We believe that a cost methodology can be designed based upon such consistent assumptions as economic depreciation, forward-looking cost of capital, and forward-looking outside plant cost, including reasonable profits. We agree with the Joint Board that the cost methodologies presented to us thus far are not sufficiently reliable to be used to determine universal service support at this time. As recommended by the Joint Board, we will also continue to explore the use of competitive bidding as a mechanism to provide universal service.

F. Support for Low Income Consumers

27. We adopt the Joint Board's recommendations to make three broad categories of changes to the Lifeline and Link Up programs so that they better comport with our universal service principles and the 1996 Act's renewed concern for low income consumers. First, we agree with the Joint Board's recommendation to expand Lifeline to make it available in all states, territories, and commonwealths of the United States, modify the state matching requirement, and increase the federal Lifeline support amount. We find that these modifications comply with the principles in sections 254(b)(1) and (3), respectively, that rates should be "affordable" and access should be provided to "low-income consumers" in all regions of the nation. Second, we adopt the Joint Board's recommendation to make the contribution and distribution of low income support competitively and technologically neutral by requiring equitable and nondiscriminatory contributions from all providers of interstate telecommunications services, consistent with sections 254(d) and (e), and allowing all eligible telecommunications carriers to receive support for offering Lifeline and Link Up service. Third, we adopt the Joint Board's recommendation to provide low income consumers with access to certain services and policies.

28. Specifically, we agree with the Joint Board that Lifeline consumers should have access to the same services as those supported in rural, insular, and high cost areas: voice grade access to the public switched network, with the ability to place and receive calls; DTMF signaling or its functional equivalent; single-party service; access to emergency services, including in some circumstances, access to 911 and E911; access to operator services; access to interexchange services; and access to directory assistance. In determining the specific services to be provided to low income consumers, we adopt the Joint Board's reasoning that section 254(b)(3) calls for access to services for low income consumers in all regions of the nation, and that universal service principles may not be realized if low income support is provided for service inferior to that supported for other subscribers. In addition, we agree with the Joint Board that Lifeline service should include toll-limitation services, at the customer's request, to the extent that carriers are capable of providing them. We agree with the Joint Board that toll-limitation services will help low income consumers control their toll bills and consequently be better able to maintain access to telecommunications services, as section 254(b)(3) envisions. We concur with the Joint Board's recommendation to prohibit the disconnection of local service for non-payment of charges incurred for toll calls. We are persuaded by the Joint Board's reasoning that such a rule will help improve subscribership among low income consumers, based on

studies indicating that disconnection for non-payment of toll charges is a significant cause of low subscribership among low income consumers. We further find that local and toll services are distinct services, and therefore carriers providing toll service should take action against consumers who do not pay their toll bills. We also adopt the Joint Board's recommendation to prohibit carriers from requiring service deposits from Lifeline customers who elect toll blocking. Service deposits, which primarily serve to guard against uncollectible toll charges, deter subscribership among low income consumers and thus run counter to the principle in section 254(b)(3) that low income consumers should have access to telecommunications services. We therefore find that consumers who receive toll blocking, which bars the placement of toll calls, should be able to benefit from a rule prohibiting service deposits.

G. Support for Schools and Libraries

29. We concur with the Joint Board's recommendation to provide schools and libraries with discounts on all commercially available telecommunications services, Internet access, and internal connections. This program provides schools and libraries with the maximum flexibility to purchase the package of services they believe will meet their communications needs most effectively. We conclude that sections 254(c)(3) and 254(h)(1)(B) authorize us to permit eligible schools and libraries to receive telecommunications services, Internet access, and internal connections at discounted rates from telecommunications carriers.

30. Fiscal responsibility compels us to require schools and libraries to seek competitive bids for all services eligible for section 254(h) discounts. Competitive bidding is the most efficient means for ensuring that schools and libraries are informed about all of the choices available to them. In addition, we agree with the Joint Board that the lowest corresponding price, defined for each telecommunications carrier bidding to serve a school or library as the lowest price that carrier charges to similarly situated non-residential customers in its geographic service area for similar services, shall constitute the ceiling for that carrier's competitively bid pre-discount price for interstate rates.

31. We adopt discounts from 20 percent to 90 percent for all telecommunications services, Internet access, and internal connections, with the level of discounts correlated to indicators of poverty and high cost for schools and libraries. We also establish an annual cap of $2.25 billion on the amount of funds available to schools and libraries.

H. Support for Health Care Providers

35. Sections 254(c) and 254(h) add health care providers to the list of entities that may benefit from universal service support. Recognizing that section 254 requires that universal service support mechanisms be specific, predictable, and sufficient, we establish support for health care providers subject to a $400 million annual cap.

36. Section 254(h)(2)(A) directs the Commission to establish "competitively neutral rules to enhance, to the extent technically feasible and economically reasonable, access to advanced telecommunications and information services for all public and nonprofit health care providers." To meet the goals of this section, and, based on our review of comments filed in response to the Recom-

mended Decision, we adopt mechanisms to provide support for limited toll-free access to an Internet service provider. Each health care provider that lacks toll-free access to an Internet service provider may receive the lesser of the toll charges incurred for 30 hours of access to an Internet service provider or $180 per month in toll charge credits for toll charges imposed for connecting to the Internet.

J. Administration of Support

39. Section 254(d) states that all carriers that provide interstate telecommunications services must contribute to universal service support mechanisms in an equitable and nondiscriminatory manner. To ensure that all providers of similar services make the same contributions to universal service, we adopt the Joint Board's recommendation that all telecommunications carriers that provide interstate telecommunications services must contribute to the support mechanisms and we issue a list of examples of interstate telecommunications services. In addition, we find that the public interest requires providers of interstate telecommunications on a non-common carrier basis and payphone aggregators to contribute to the support mechanisms pursuant to the Commission's permissive authority over "other providers of interstate telecommunications." We adopt the Joint Board's recommendation that contributors whose contribution would be less than the administrator's administrative cost of collecting the contribution will be exempt from contribution and reporting requirements under the *de minimis* exemption contained in section 254(d).

40. Consistent with the Joint Board, we adopt a contribution assessment methodology that is competitively neutral and easy to administer. Contributions will be assessed against end-user telecommunications revenues, revenues derived from end users for telecommunications and telecommunications services,[26] including SLCs [subscriber line charges]. We adopt the Joint Board's recommendation that support for the programs for schools, libraries, and rural health care providers be assessed based on interstate and intrastate telecommunications revenues. Because the Joint Board did not issue a recommendation regarding the revenue base for the balance of the support mechanisms, we will maintain historic jurisdictional lines and will assess contributions for support for the high cost and low income programs on interstate telecommunications revenues.[27]

Notes and Questions

1. Defining Universal Service. What is "universal service"? The specific telecommunications services to be covered (at least initially) are listed in the press release. Is there any rhyme or reason to the types of services that will and will not be eligible for support under the FCC's plan? How about the range of persons and entities who will receive below-cost services under §254?

---

26. [Ed. That is, a sale of services to a reseller will not be taxed. Only sales to actual, ultimate users ("end users") will be taxed.]

27. [Ed. The FCC left for another day the question of how much will be charged for the universal service contribution. It wants to hear first from the states how much revenue they will raise for universal service.]

2. Why Subsidize Phone Service? What is the rationale for subsidizing some telecommunications services for some people and institutions? One claim made in the preceding documents is that people who do not receive direct aid—for example, wealthy subscribers or business subscribers—nevertheless benefit from universal service subsidies because everyone benefits when more people are accessible through the telephone network. But how much does this "network externality" argument explain about the structure of the universal service program? The Act extends universal service benefits to fancy prep schools and wealthy rural landowners. Is this because Congress believes that, absent the subsidy, many such schools and landowners would not buy the services? If not, why include them in the program? That is, why should rich and poor telecommunications service consumers be taxed to provide cheap telecommunications services to rich and poor telecommunications service consumers? Should the programs be limited, then, to low income consumers? To consumers who would not purchase without the subsidy but would purchase with it? (Note that these last two categories will likely have some, but by no means complete, overlap.)

3. Evaluating the Program. Relatedly, how can we evaluate the universal service program? For example, how can we know whether the dominant effect of a universal service subsidy is to increase the number of subscribers as opposed to simply lowering the subscription price for some people who would buy phone service in any event? (And is this a bad thing?)

4. Money is Money. What if people in rural areas, low income consumers, and/or high school principals decide that, rather than subsidized telephone service or Internet access, what they'd really like is subsidies for clothing? Or simply more disposable income? Should we devote funds to telecommunications services because of the network externality even if the beneficiaries of those funds would vastly prefer to use the money for other purposes? Why does Congress know better than rural and low income consumers what are those consumers' most compelling unfulfilled wants?

5. Explicit/Implicit Approaches. Note that the Act appears to promise a shift in universal service support mechanisms from implicit to explicit subsidies. (The Commission, in the above *Universal Service Order*, does precious little to advance this goal, but the agency also notes that most implicit subsidies are creatures of state, not federal, regulation.) The reason for this shift, of course, is that the Act also purports to extend competition to the local exchange service market. Competition and implicit subsidies cannot coexist, as the Commission notes in ¶17 and as was demonstrated by events in the long distance market after that market opened to competition.[28] Interestingly, the Commission also notes that it expects that other implicit subsidies may be revealed as the process of competition unfolds. *See* ¶14.

6. Competitive Neutrality. Section 253 of the Act, which otherwise prevents states from maintaining or erecting barriers to new competition, specifically exempts from this prohibition "requirements necessary to preserve and advance universal service," so long as those requirements are imposed "on a competitively neutral basis and consistent with section 254." What can this mean in practice?

---

28. *See* Chapter Seventeen, especially the discussion of the *Execunet* case.

Consider the problem posed by a firm—a competitive local exchange carrier—that wants to enter a market and compete with the incumbent local exchange carrier. Suppose the state agency puts solely on the ILEC the financial burden of supporting low income consumers' access to the network. This would not be "competitively neutral" as between the ILEC and the CLEC, would it? Alternatively, suppose the state agency makes the incumbent and the entrant share the burden. In almost all cases, the ILEC will operate many more services in many more product markets than the CLEC and will thus have a larger base over which to spread its universal service tax. Could the imposition of such a tax on both firms nevertheless be described as "competitively neutral" as between the two?

Alternatively, suppose the CLEC wishes to enter the local market on a partial basis, solely in order to provide call forwarding and call waiting services. The CLEC believes that it can rapidly obtain a substantial market share in these services because the ILEC is offering both services at prices substantially above the cost of providing them. The ILEC, of course, will complain to state regulators that it is selling those services way above cost in order to recoup the losses the ILEC is required to absorb in selling basic service to low income consumers below cost. Thus, the ILEC argues, to permit the CLEC to enter and sell only call forwarding and call waiting will undermine the universal service goal. Further, the ILEC may argue, granting the CLEC's application will encourage inefficient entry because the ILEC in fact has lower costs—just not lower prices—than the CLEC. In response to these claims, may the state agency then order that the CLEC must, as a condition of doing business in call waiting and call forwarding, also offer basic phone service to low income people? If so, is that an impermissible barrier to entry or a permissible "requirement necessary to preserve and advance universal service"? Alternatively, may the state agency require the CLEC to demonstrate that its call forwarding and call waiting costs will in fact be lower than the ILEC's? On the one hand, what better way could there be to avoid inducing inefficient entry? On the other hand, what could be a clearer case of a state-controlled barrier to entry?

In short, these questions ask in various ways how regulators will reconcile the following two views: (a) under the new Act, firms are permitted and should be encouraged to enter on a partial basis, providing some but not all of the services offered by ILECs; but (b) an important goal of the new Act is to maintain a system of competitively neutral subsidies for some subscribers. The larger point here is that imposing a fee on a service or activity always creates a distortion. As long as there are other services that are not subject to the fee and that can substitute for the taxed service, the untaxed services will become relatively more attractive. Even if the taxed service is more efficient than the untaxed services (as measured by the value of resources expended), many people will choose the latter because of the cost differential created by the tax. Not only can this affect existing services, but it can also have an impact on the development of new technologies. Businesses have an incentive to create methods of data transmission that are not subject to the tax, even if they are not as efficient as existing telecommunications services.

7. Why Not a Broad-Based Tax? The obvious solution to this problem is to collect funds for universal service via a broad-based tax that does not help one service at the expense of another. (After all, assuming that we want to subsidize telecommunications for particular groups, there is no requirement that the funds come from telecommunications services.) Broad-based taxes exist of course — notably, taxes on all income, from whatever source derived. Why not raise the universal service funds through such a tax, thereby ending the regulatory arbitrage opportunities created by a more narrowly focused tax?

Is the answer that money to fund a service should come from users of that service? After all, governments often fund highway construction from highway tolls. But, if that is so, is it consistent with the goal of expanding the network? The answer might be yes, if we assume that the number of net givers who will abandon the network because of higher fees will be smaller than the number of net receivers who will join the network because of the subsidies they will receive. But that takes us back to the question of evaluating the effect of the universal service program, which might be difficult to do. And, in any event, wouldn't we achieve greater expansion of telecommunications service if the fee were not levied on that service?

Is the answer instead that voters would not support an increase in income taxes to fund these programs, but they will not complain as loudly about fees on telecommunications services because they are not as aware of the taxes they effectively pay on such services? On this reasoning, a program that might be politically untenable if funded via a broad-based tax becomes politically viable if funded via a fee on telecommunications services. If that is not the explanation, why not move to a broad-based tax? If it is the explanation, does it cast doubt on the wisdom of the program? To put the point differently, if a program would be unpopular if voters were aware of it and thus is viable only because voters are unaware of it, should that tell members of Congress who support the programs that maybe they have a faulty sense of what is in the public interest? Or would continuation of the program be an example of legislators appropriately acting in the public's best interest, even if the public (or a majority of it, anyway) does not believe that it is in their interest?

8. Why Not Phone Cards? Would it be simpler and fairer to take an approach to universal service based on technology? Why not simply permit local exchange carriers to require that subscribers pay before they call and sell "phone cards" for that purpose? These cards could be inserted into telephones in order to activate the phone, could be issued in various dollar amounts, and could calculate the cost of each call as it is made and deduct that amount from the balance on the card. Governments could then purchase and hand out phone cards to worthy people. What desirable goals of the existing universal service program(s) are not met by such a system?

9. The Access Charge Reform Docket. As the *Order* excerpted above makes clear, universal service reform and access charge reform are intertwined. Again, access charges are the fees local exchange carriers receive from long distance carriers as payment for the origination and termination of interstate calls. These charges overcompensate the LECs, the idea being that the charges not only cover the real expenses associated with origination and termination but also represent a contribution by the IXCs to the universal service infrastructure provided by the LECs. In short, above-cost access charges fund some of the costs of the local exchange and thereby offset the costs of LEC universal service obligations.

On the same day that it adopted the *Universal Service Order* excerpted above, the FCC adopted a companion order that addressed access charge reform directly. The *First Report and Order* in the access charge reform docket explains the problem of above-cost access charges, their relation to universal service, and the difficulty of rapidly adjusting these charges such that they more accurately reflect real costs. An excerpt follows.

IN RE ACCESS CHARGE REFORM
First Report and Order, 12 FCC Rcd. 15982 (1997)

2. Implicit Subsidies in the Existing System

28. Both our price cap and cost-of-service [rate-of-return] rules contain requirements that inevitably result in charges to certain end users that exceed the cost of the service they receive. To the extent these rates do not reflect the underlying cost of providing access service, they could be said to embody an implicit subsidy. Some of these subsidies are due to the rate structures prescribed by our rules, which in some cases prevent incumbent LECs from recovering their access costs in the same way they have been incurred. For example, although the cost of the local loop that connects an end user to the telephone company's switch does not vary with usage, the current rate structure rules require incumbent LECs to recover a large portion of these non-traffic-sensitive costs through traffic-sensitive, per-minute charges. These mandatory recovery rules inflate traffic-sensitive usage charges and reduce charges for connection to the network, in essence creating an implicit support flow from end users that make many interstate long distance calls to end users that make few or no interstate long distance calls.

29. Several Federal-State Joint Boards have observed that additional subsidies and distortions may be due, not only to the rate structure, but to the separations rules that divide costs between the interstate and intrastate jurisdictions. For example, the current separations rules require larger incumbent LECs to allocate the costs of their switching facilities between the interstate and intrastate jurisdictions on the basis of relative use (*i.e.*, if 30 percent of the minutes of use handled by the LEC's switching facilities are interstate long distance calls, 30 percent of the LEC's switching costs are allocated to the interstate jurisdiction and recovered through interstate access charges). Our rules, however, permit smaller incumbent LECs to allocate a greater share of their switching costs to interstate access services than would result from the relative use allocator. These smaller incumbent LECs multiply the interstate use ratio by a factor (as high as 3) specified in the separations rules. In its *Recommended Decision*, the Joint Board on Universal Service observed that these separations rules "shift what would otherwise be intrastate costs to the interstate jurisdiction." 12 FCC Rcd. 87, at ¶189 (1996). The Joint Board found that this allocation structure, known thereby allowing such LECs to charge lower prices for intrastate services. Similarly, another Federal-State Joint Board has observed that the separations rules allocate a share of the incumbent LECs' retail marketing expenses to the interstate jurisdiction that is unreasonably high, given that the interstate access services consist primarily of wholesale service offerings. To the extent these and other separation rules do not apportion costs between the jurisdictions in a manner that reflects the costs incurred to provide service in each jurisdiction, they might be viewed as generating subsidies from the interstate to the intrastate jurisdiction. These subsidies effectively require incumbent LECs to charge higher rates for interstate ser-

vices and lower rates for intrastate services than would otherwise occur if the subsidies were eliminated.

30. This "patchwork quilt of implicit and explicit subsidies"[29] generates inefficient and undesirable economic behavior. For example, a rate structure that requires the use of per-minute access charges where flat-rated fees would be more appropriate increases the per-minute rates paid by IXCs and long distance consumers, thus artificially suppressing demand for interstate long distance services. Similarly, the possible over-allocation of costs to the interstate jurisdiction may, for some consumers, increase long distance rates substantially, suppressing their demand for interstate interexchange services. Implicit subsidies also have a disruptive effect on competition, impeding the efficient development of competition in both the local and long distance markets. For example, where rates are significantly above cost, consumers may choose to bypass the incumbent LEC's switched access network, even if the LEC is the most efficient provider. Conversely, where rates are subsidized (as in the case of consumers in high-cost areas), rates will be set too low and an otherwise efficient provider would have no incentive to enter the market. In either case, the total cost of telecommunications services will not be as low as it would otherwise be in a competitive market. Because of the growing importance of the telecommunications industry to the economy as a whole, this inefficient system of access charges retards job creation and economic growth in the nation.

31. Despite the existence of distortions and inefficiencies, the current system of cross-subsidies has persisted for over a decade. The structure has been justified on policy grounds, principally as a means to serve universal service goals. By providing incumbent LECs with a stream of subsidized revenues from certain customers, the system allows regulators to demand below-cost rates for other customers, such as those in high-cost areas.

3. The Telecommunications Act of 1996

32. The existing system of implicit subsidies and support flows is sustainable only in a monopoly environment in which incumbent LECs are guaranteed an opportunity to earn returns from certain services and customers that are sufficient to support the high cost of providing other services to other customers. The new competitive environment envisioned by the 1996 Act threatens to undermine this structure over the long run. The 1996 Act removes barriers to entry in the local market, generating competitive pressures that make it difficult for incumbent LECs to maintain access charges above economic cost. For example, by giving competitors the right to lease an incumbent LEC's unbundled network elements at cost, Congress provided IXCs an alternative avenue to connect to and share the local network. Thus, where existing rules require an incumbent LEC to set access charges above cost for a high-volume user, a competing provider of exchange access services entering into a market can lease unbundled network elements at cost, or construct new facilities, to circumvent the access charge. In this way, a new entrant might target an incumbent LEC's high-volume access customers, for whom access charges are now set at levels significantly above economic cost. As competition develops, incumbent LECs may be forced to lower

---

29. In re Implementation of the Local Competition Provisions of the Telecommunications Act of 1996, First Report and Order, 11 FCC Rcd. 15499, at ¶5 (1996).

their access charges or lose market share, in either case jeopardizing the source of revenue that, in the past, has permitted the incumbent LEC to offer service to other customers, particularly those in high-cost areas, at below-cost prices. Incumbent LECs have for some time been claiming that this process has already made more than trivial inroads on their high-volume customer base.

33. Recognizing the vulnerability of implicit subsidies to competition, Congress directed the Commission and the states to take the necessary steps to create permanent universal service mechanisms that would be secure in a competitive environment. To achieve this end, Congress directed the Commission to strive to replace the system of implicit subsidies with "explicit and sufficient" support mechanisms. In calling for explicit mechanisms, Congress did not intend simply to require carriers to identify and disclose the implicit subsidies that currently exist in the industry. Rather, as we determine in the *Universal Service Order*, Congress intended to establish subsidies that were both "measurable" and "portable" — "measurable" in a way that allows competitors to assess the profitability of serving subsidized end users; and "portable" in a way that ensures that competitors who succeed in winning a customer also win the corresponding subsidy. A system of portable and measurable subsidies will permit carriers to compete for the subsidies associated with high-cost or low income consumers. In the long run, this approach may even allow us to set subsidy levels through competitive bidding rather than through regulation. By contrast, under the current system of implicit subsidies, the only carriers that will serve high-cost consumers are those that are required to do so by regulation and that are able (because of their protected monopoly positions) to charge above-cost rates to other end users.

34. In the *Universal Service Order*, we establish "explicit and sufficient" support mechanisms to assist users in high-cost areas, low income consumers, schools, and health care providers. By creating explicit support mechanisms, we establish a system to advance the universal service goals of the 1996 Act that is compatible with the development of competition in the local exchange and exchange access markets. By creating a portable and measurable system of subsidies, we utilize the power of the market to serve universal service goals more efficiently. That *Order*, in short, guarantees that Congress's universal service goals are met in a way that conforms with the pro-competitive and deregulatory goals of the 1996 Act.

B. Access Charge Reform

35. In light of Congress's command to create secure and explicit mechanisms to achieve universal service goals, we conclude that implicit subsidies embodied in the existing system of interstate access charges cannot be indefinitely maintained in their current form. In this *Order*, therefore, we take two steps with respect to the rules governing the interstate access charges of price cap incumbent LECs. First, we reform the current rate structure to bring it into line with cost-causation principles, phasing out significant implicit subsidies. Second, we set in place a process to move the baseline rate level toward competitive levels. Together with the *Universal Service Order*, these adjustments will promote the public welfare by encouraging investment and efficient competition, while establishing a secure structure for achieving the universal service goals established by law. Further, the process we set in place to achieve these goals avoids the destabilizing

effects of sudden radical change, facilitating the transformation from a regulated to a competitive marketplace.

1. Rationalizing the Rate Structure

36. In this *Order*, we reshape the existing rate structure in order to eliminate significant implicit subsidies in the access charge system. To achieve that end, we make several modifications to ensure that costs are recovered in the same way that they are incurred. In general, non-traffic-sensitive costs incurred to serve a particular customer should be recovered through flat fees, while traffic-sensitive costs should be recovered through usage-based rates. The present structure violates this basic principle of cost causation by requiring incumbent LECs to recover many fixed costs through variable, per-minute access rates. An important goal of this *Order* is to increase the amount of fixed costs recovered through flat charges and decrease the amount recovered through variable rates.

37. Common Line Costs. Because the costs of using the incumbent LEC's common line (or "local loop") do not increase with usage, these costs should be recovered through flat, non-traffic-sensitive fees. The current rate structure, however, generally allows an incumbent LEC to recover no more than a portion of its interstate common line revenues through a flat-rated Subscriber Line Charge (SLC), which is capped at $3.50 per month for residential and single-line business users, and $6.00 per month for multi-line users. The remaining common line revenues must be recovered through a per-minute Common Carrier Line (CCL) charge assessed on IXCs (which, in turn, may recover these charges through their prices to long distance customers). In order to align the rate structure more closely with the manner in which costs are incurred, we adjust access rates over time until the common line revenues of all price cap LECs are recovered through flat-rated charges.

38. For primary residential and single-line business lines, however, we decline to implement this goal by increasing the SLC ceiling above its existing $3.50 level as urged by many companies, including price cap LECs and IXCs. We do not wish to see increases in the price of basic dial tone charged by local exchange carriers to their end users for fear that such increases might cause some consumers to discontinue service, a result that would be contrary to our mandate to ensure universal service. We agree with the Joint Board's finding that increasing the SLC ceiling may make telecommunications service unaffordable for some consumers. Consequently, to the extent that common line revenues are not recovered through the customer's SLC, we conclude that LECs should recover these revenues through a flat, per-line charge assessed on the IXC to whom the access line is presubscribed—the presubscribed interexchange carrier charge, or PICC. Further, in order to provide IXCs with the opportunity to incorporate these changes into their business plans, we set the PICC for primary residential and single-line business lines at not more than the existing flat-rated line charges for the first year, and we gradually increase the ceiling thereafter until it reaches a level that permits full recovery of the common line revenues from flat charges assessed to both end users and IXCs.

39. For non-primary residential and multi-line business lines, we conclude that affordability concerns do not require us to retain the current ceiling on the monthly SLC. Consequently, we raise the SLC ceiling for these lines to the level

that permits incumbent LECs full recovery for their common line revenues, but never more than $3.00 above the current SLC ceiling for multi-line business lines today, adjusted for inflation. Almost all subscribers will pay SLCs below, and often substantially below, the ceiling. The increase in the SLC ceiling for multi-line businesses will be implemented in the first year. To ameliorate the impact that a dramatic increase in the SLC ceiling might have on residential customers, however, the increase for non-primary residential lines will be phased in over time. The data indicate that raising the SLC ceiling to this level will permit incumbent price cap LECs to recover their average common line revenues from 99 percent of their non-primary residential and multi-line business lines. For the remaining lines, many of which are located in rural areas, the SLC ceiling for non-primary residential and multi-line business lines will ensure that end-user charges are not prohibitive or significantly above the national average, thereby advancing universal service goals of affordability and access.

2. Baseline Rate Level Reductions

42. The rate structure changes that we implement in this *Order* eliminate some of the distortions that have characterized the access charge system for over a decade. These changes, however, are not alone sufficient to create a system that accurately reflects the true cost of service in all respects. To fulfill Congress's pro-competitive mandate, access charges should ultimately reflect rates that would exist in a competitive market. We recognize that competitive markets are far better than regulatory agencies at allocating resources and services efficiently for the maximum benefit of consumers. We conclude, consequently, that competition or, in the event that competition fails to develop, rates that approximate the prices that a competitive market would produce, best serve the public interest.

43. The rate restructuring we implement in this *Order* results in substantial reductions in the charges for usage-rated interstate access services. These reductions move these access charges a long way towards their forward-looking cost levels. Furthermore, in addition to these rate structure adjustments, we also take several steps in this *Order* to address specific cost misallocations that cause access charges to be set above economic costs.

44. We recognize that the prescriptive measures that we implement today represent the first step toward our goal of removing implicit universal service subsidies from interstate access charges and moving such charges toward economically efficient levels. In the NPRM, we identified two separate ways to continue this process in the future—a prescriptive approach in which we actively set rates at economic cost levels, and a market-based approach that relies on competition itself to drive access charges down to forward-looking costs. We conclude in this *Order*, based on our experience in exchange access and other telecommunications markets and the record in this proceeding, that a market-based approach to reducing interstate access charges will, in most cases, better serve the public interest. Although the Commission has considerable expertise in regulating telecommunications providers and services efficiently for the maximum benefit of consumers, we believe that emerging competition will provide a more accurate means of identifying implicit subsidies and moving access prices to economically sustainable levels. Further, as discussed above, we believe that this approach is most consistent with the pro-competitive, deregulatory policy contemplated by the 1996 Act. Accordingly, where competition is developing, it

should be relied upon in the first instance to protect consumers and the public interest.

45. We acknowledge that a market-based approach under this scenario may take several years to drive costs to competitive levels. We also recognize that several commenters have urged us to move immediately to forward-looking rates by prescriptive measures utilizing forward-looking cost models. We decline to follow that suggestion for several reasons. First, as a practical matter, accurate forward-looking cost models are not available at the present time to determine the economic cost of providing access service. Because of the existence of significant joint and common costs, the development of reliable cost models may take a year or more to complete. This situation might be contrasted with that addressed in our *Local Competition Order*, where we endorsed the use of cost models to estimate the cost of providing unbundled network elements. There, we observed that unbundled elements have few joint and common costs, so that devising accurate cost models for unbundled network elements is more straightforward.

46. In addition, even assuming that accurate forward-looking cost models were available, we are concerned that any attempt to move immediately to competitive prices for the remaining services would require dramatic cuts in access charges for some carriers. Such an action could result in a substantial decrease in revenue for incumbent LECs, which could prove highly disruptive to business operations, even when new explicit universal support mechanisms are taken into account. Moreover, lacking the tools for making accurate prescriptions, precipitous action could lead to significant errors in the level of access charge reductions necessary to reach competitive levels. That would further impede the development of competition in the local markets and disrupt existing services. Consequently, we strongly prefer to rely on the competitive pressures unleashed by the 1996 Act to make the necessary reductions.

47. To the extent that some commenters contend that the immediate elimination of all implicit subsidies is mandated by the 1996 Act, we disagree. Neither in the 1996 Act nor its legislative history did Congress state that all forms of implicit universal service support shall be made explicit by May 8, 1997.[30] To the contrary, Congress stated that the conversion of implicit subsidies to explicit support is a goal that "should be" pursued "[t]o the extent possible."[31] Congress most certainly did not state that we must reach that goal by May 8, 1997. Rather, it directed that, by that date, we issue rules that "shall include a definition of the services that are supported by Federal universal service support mechanisms and a specific timetable for implementation." Our companion order satisfies that timetable, and this *Order* establishes a process that will eliminate some implicit subsidies quickly and more gradually eliminate others.

Notes and Questions

1. What Are the Benefits? The *Order* takes two specific steps towards reforming access charges. First, it orders that fewer non-traffic-sensitive costs be recovered

---

30. [Ed. The FCC adopted both this *First Report and Order* and the *Universal Service Order* on May 7, 1997.]

31. Joint Explanatory Statement of the Committee of the Conference, S. CONF. REP. NO. 230, 104th Cong., 2d Sess. 131 (1996) (Joint Explanatory Statement).

through access charges. Second, it allows the LECs to charge an increased SLC on non-primary lines and a new flat charge (the PICC) on long distance service. What benefits are these actions designed to bring? Are those benefits likely to materialize? Is this the type and extent of reform envisioned by Congress when it passed the 1996 Act?

2. Equity or Efficiency? The Commission states that above-cost access charges distort consumers' decisions about how much long distance service to consume. But is the FCC really concerned about that inefficiency? In choosing not to raise the flat-rate subscriber line charge (SLC) on local service—which the Commission seems to recognize would be a more efficient way for LECs to cover costs—is the Commission effectively deciding that it prefers to further equitable objectives rather than to pursue efficiency? Why is there necessarily a tradeoff between the two? If consumers make both local and long distance calls, would they be harmed by lowering the price of the latter (by reducing access charges) while raising the price of the former (by raising the SLC)? What would one need to know to conclude that such a policy would be regressive in its distributional effects?

3. Preserving Telephone Penetration. An important historical goal of universal service policies was to get all Americans connected to the telephone network. In ¶38, the FCC states that raising the SLC would affect the affordability of telephone service and perhaps cause some subscribers to discontinue service. But suppose (as in fact research indicates) that demand for local service is not terribly sensitive to price in the relevant range of rates. Further suppose (as research also indicates) that demand for long distance calling is quite sensitive to price. Given these suppositions, and recalling our discussion of Ramsey pricing back in Chapter Fifteen, is the Commission making exactly the wrong decision here? Or can the Commission's decision be defended?

Note that one worry, at least, with a Ramsey approach to the SLC is that demand for local service might be so inelastic that local rates would end up bearing all the burden of the added tax. That is, the efficient thing to do might be to raise the SLC significantly; consumers might complain, but they will not abandon local telephone service and hence the tax will not be changing behavior in inefficient ways. Of course, this implies that the Commission's real concern here is not a concern about telephone penetration (as the Commission claims) but is instead a broader concern about the distributional effects of telephone prices.

4. Gradual Reductions. Why didn't the Commission simply order access charges to be reduced to cost, much as it has ordered other rates (*e.g.,* TELRIC) to be cost-based? The Commission offers several reasons. On one hand, it seems concerned that no one knows to exactly what extent current access charge levels reflect costs, so any ordered rate might be inaccurate and distort competition. On the other hand, the Commission seems to think that even if costs could be accurately gauged, some LECs' ability to provide service might suffer from a precipitous change, harming universal service objectives. Which concern do you think dominates? Which should dominate under the 1996 Act?

5. Reliance on Competition. What does the FCC mean when it says a market-based approach will be most effective in reducing access charges? What competition is it relying on? If ILECs were to lose twenty-five percent of their monopoly market share to new entrants, would that be enough local competition to induce the ILECs to reduce access charges? Would a competing firm charge a long distance company less for originating and terminating interstate calls than an ILEC would? On the long distance side, the FCC is reducing IXCs' contributions, via access charges, to the cost of operating the local exchange. But what assurance does the Commission have that a long distance carrier will pass savings on to consumers? Isn't it relying on competition among long distance companies to drive long distance rates down as the costs of providing the service decline? Can it so rely?

6. Subsequent Action. In May 2000, the FCC adopted a combined access charge reform and universal service proposal filed by the Coalition for Affordable Local and Long Distance Service (CALLS). *See In re Access Charge Reform*, 15 FCC Rcd. 12962 (2000). The coalition consisted of AT&T, Bell Atlantic, BellSouth, GTE, SBC, and Sprint. The principal goals of the CALLS proposal were (1) to reduce access charges and thereby reduce long distance calling rates; (2) to require local exchange companies to recover more of the universal service subsidy directly from end-users rather than indirectly through charges imposed on long distance calling; and (3) to make the universal service support previously received implicitly through interstate access charges explicit and "portable" to different local carriers. The proposal, which is highly technical and covers many issues, also established various price cap reductions such that target rates would be reached within five years for a variety of services and network elements.

Notably, in adopting CALLS, the FCC agreed to do something it refused to do in the *First Report and Order* on access charge reform: it agreed to gradually raise the SLC on primary lines above the longtime level of $3.50. Why did the FCC change its mind on this? Which, if any, of the following reasons do you find persuasive?

(a) The market competition on which the Commission relied in the *First Report and Order* had not satisfactorily materialized, so the Commission felt compelled to take deliberate action to reduce access charges.

(b) An SLC increase was a quid pro quo for other CALLS reforms. Specifically, given the agreement of the CALLS coalition members to reduce access charges significantly over three years, the LECs needed some other revenue source otherwise they would experience significant revenue losses under the plan.

(c) The CALLs coalition itself made the SLC increase possible. To whatever extent the Commission was reluctant to increase the SLC for political reasons, CALLS—outside of agency processes—brought together a broad coalition of actors with typically divergent interests. Once they had agreed to the increase, the odds of significant political opposition to an SLC increase were low.

Chapter Nineteen

MERGERS AND ACQUISITIONS

The purpose of this chapter is:

- to consider, from a procedural standpoint as well as a substantive one, mergers and acquisitions in the telecommunications industry, focusing in particular on mergers and acquisitions involving one or more of the former Bell Operating Companies; and

- to begin to question the appropriate role for a modern FCC, in this context by asking whether there is reason for the Commission to be involved in merger review, given that other federal agencies (like the Department of Justice) also review mergers and arguably have more expertise on these matters.

~

The last four chapters have shown how the structure of telephone service markets has moved back and forth between monopoly and competition over the last hundred years. Many of these changes were probably not anticipated by the relevant policymakers. For example, the wave of mergers and acquisitions that consolidated the Bell monopoly in the 1920s occurred despite the existence of the Kingsbury Commitment, which in 1913 had, in words at least, endeavored to stop Bell from acquiring rival telephone companies and in that way consolidating the industry. More recently, a wave of high-profile mergers among large incumbent local exchange carriers has caused many observers to wonder why a legal infrastructure so focused on competition has led to private behavior so focused on consolidation.

All this, of course, affects the nature of telecommunications competition. In 1984, right after the Bell divestiture, there were seven RHCs: Ameritech, Bell Atlantic, BellSouth, Nynex, Pacific Telesis, Southwestern Bell, and US West. There were also two large ILECs not associated with the former Bell System: GTE and Southern New England Telephone (SNET). By 2001, only four large local exchange carriers remained. That change in number reflected the merging of SBC, Pacific Telesis, SNET and then Ameritech into SBC Communications, and the merging of Bell Atlantic, NYNEX, and later GTE into Verizon Communications. BellSouth and US West remain the other two large ILECs. This recombination of firms at the local level is certainly not something that Judge Greene would have countenanced under the MFJ, and it seems inconsistent with Congress's apparent expectations under the Telecommunications Act of 1996 as well. In this chapter, we therefore examine these sorts of major telecommunications mergers and ask whether (and on what terms) local telephone competition might survive.

As you read the materials that follow, think about two separate but related issues. First, consider the substance of the various mergers at issue. Should we be worried when two large LECs combine forces, on the theory that the resulting markets will see less vigorous competition? Should we instead celebrate, because mergers likely make possible new efficiencies? Is competition among a smaller number of larger firms better or worse than competition among a larger number of smaller firms? Where do you draw the line? Second, focus on the FCC's merger review procedure itself. On what authority does the FCC get involved in telecommunications mergers? Does the FCC overstep this authority when it imposes conditions on mergers it then approves, or is this an example of the healthy application of administrative expertise? In short, given that other federal agencies (in particular the United States Department of Justice) already engage in merger review, why is the Commission involved, and what exactly is it looking for?

I. BACKGROUND

Mergers, acquisitions, and general concerns about industry concentration have long been on the regulatory agenda in U.S. telecommunications. The Bell breakup in 1984 was neither the beginning nor the end; regulators and antitrust officials had been worried about consolidation in telecommunications markets since long before divestiture, and those worries have continued into modern times.

As we mentioned briefly back in Chapter Fifteen, the Justice Department filed an antitrust suit in 1913 alleging that Bell had improperly used its dominance in the long distance market to pressure competing local carriers to merge into the Bell System. As part of the "Kingsbury Commitment" (the agreement that settled that case) Bell agreed to stop acquiring independent competitors. The Department of Justice nonetheless approved most of Bell's special applications to acquire local companies in the years the consent decree was in force, mostly on the grounds that those acquisitions helped resolve inefficient fragmentation of the phone system by non-interconnecting local carriers. In 1918, Congress and the President gave the Postmaster General emergency wartime powers over the phone system; that led to further consolidations that would remain even after control of the phone system was returned to private parties.

In 1921 Congress suspended the non-acquisition provisions of the Kingsbury Commitment for good and, in addition, gave the Interstate Commerce Commission authority to exempt telephone company mergers from the antitrust laws. The resulting statute, the Willis-Graham Act, was expressly aimed at eliminating the inefficient fragmentation of the phone system caused by the lack of local interconnection.[1] On its face, of course, the Willis-Graham Act did not announce an open season for acquisitions. The Act only withheld antitrust enforcement for consolidations that were "of advantage to the persons to whom service is to be

---

1. Willis-Graham Act of 1921, 42 Stat. 27 (codified as amended at 47 U.S.C. §221(a), *repealed by* Telecommunications Act of 1996, §601(b)(2)).

rendered and in the public interest."[2] In practice, however, the hurdle proved a low one.

When the Communications Act of 1934 passed, the core of the Willis-Graham Act was retained: the relevant agency—now the FCC—had the power to exempt local telephone company mergers from antitrust scrutiny. The FCC could thus trump both the Department of Justice (DOJ) and the Federal Trade Commission (FTC), the agencies normally empowered to review mergers of this sort. Specifically, section 221(a) of the 1934 Act gave the Commission authority to exempt mergers from "any Act or Acts of Congress making the proposed transaction unlawful." That authority remained with the Commission for over 50 years, until §601(b) of the Telecommunications Act of 1996 expressly repealed §221(a). The Act now states that the FCC has no authority "to modify, impair, or supersede the applicability of any of the antitrust laws."

The fact that the FCC can no longer exempt mergers from antitrust review does not mean that the Commission has no role in reviewing these transactions, nor does it mean that the Commission is without power to block them. The Clayton Antitrust Act, for example, grants the FCC concurrent jurisdiction with the Justice Department to act on transactions among "common carriers engaged in wire or radio communications." 14 U.S.C. §18. The FCC has not availed itself of this authority, however, because it has found authority to review transactions under its public interest authority in §§214(a) and 310(d) of Communications Act itself. Section 214(a) requires the Commission to certify that any acquisition of lines by a common carrier will serve the present and future "public convenience and necessity." Similarly, and as we already know from Chapter Four, under §310(d) no transfer of a spectrum license can occur without a finding by the Commission that the transfer will serve the "public interest, convenience, and necessity."

The FCC thus has the authority—indeed the obligation—to review transfers of licenses that are part of a proposed merger or acquisition. As explained by the then-current FCC General Counsel, the Commission has come to apply a four-part test in judging license transfers:

> We ask, first, whether the transfer would violate the statute. For example, section 271 prohibits Bell Operating Companies from providing long distance service until they open their local markets to competition, so interstate lines may not be transferred to a BOC that has not obtained approval under section 271. Second, we ask whether the transfer would violate a regulation. For example, we have spectrum cap rules that prevent wireless companies from having more than 45 MHz in any market, so a wireless license cannot be transferred to a company that would then have more than 45 MHz without a waiver. Third, we ask whether the transfer would frustrate the purposes of the Act or a regulation. The Supreme Court held in 1953 in the *RCA* case [FCC v. RCA Communications, Inc., 346 U.S. 86 (1953)] that competition issues are relevant in applying the public interest standard, and there is no question after 1996 that fostering competition is an important national goal in all communications markets. Accordingly, we ask whether the transfer would frus-

---

2. *Id.*

trate the goal of creating and maintaining competitive communications markets. And fourth, we ask whether the transfer is likely to provide affirmative public benefits. That inquiry is plainly required under the statute, since the applicable statutory provisions direct the Commission to determine whether a transfer would serve the public interest.[3]

The Commission has interpreted the public interest standard it applies to be "a flexible one that encompasses the 'broad aims of the Communications Act.'"[4] In judging common carrier mergers, the Commission has typically focused on competition issues and Commission goals regarding the equitable buildout of new services. Meanwhile, in transactions involving broadcast licenses, the Commission has typically focused on issues related to program diversity. Importantly, however, under the public interest standard as interpreted by the FCC, the Commission need not show that a transaction is likely to reduce competition in order to challenge that transaction. Under the "broad aims" of the Act, the FCC could instead decide that a merger might affect any of the Act's goals (as the FCC interprets them) and, for any of those reasons, block, condition, or approve a transaction regardless of its competitive effects.

The FCC's merger review standards are thus potentially much broader than the standards applied under the antitrust laws by either the Justice Department's Antitrust Division or the Federal Trade Commission. Section 7 of the Clayton Antitrust Act, 15 U.S.C. §18, bars mergers where the effect "may be substantially to lessen competition, or to tend to create a monopoly." Similarly, §1 of the Sherman Act, 15 U.S.C. §1, bars "every contract, combination in the form of trust or otherwise, or conspiracy in restraint of trade or commerce." In interpreting those statutes, the federal antitrust authorities have determined that one factor predominates: whether a transaction will lead to the accumulation of "market power," which the agencies define as the ability of an enterprise "profitably to maintain prices above competitive levels for a significant period of time."[5] On this basis the DOJ and FTC have promulgated guidelines for analyzing when a merger is likely to reduce competition and lead to higher prices for consumers. The sine qua non of merger review under the federal antitrust statutes is thus market power in the sale of a given product or service. In contrast, under the four part test the FCC applies in its public interest analysis, even a merger that would not harm consumers might be challenged because, for example, it would not create "affirmative" benefits for consumers or would make regulatory oversight more difficult.

The Commission's broad interpretation of its authority has created much controversy, but it is a controversy that arises in only an extremely small fraction of the Commission's license transfer proceedings. Indeed, the Commission processes enormous numbers of license transfers that attract no notice whatso-

3. Comments of General Counsel Christopher J. Wright, Introducing the Transactions Team Presentation on Timely Consideration of the Applications Accompanying Mergers (March 1, 2000), www.fcc.gov/Speeches/misc/statements/wright030100.html.

4. In re Application of Teleport Communications Group, Transferor, and AT&T Corp., Transferee, for Consent to Transfer of Control of Corporations Holding Point-to-Point Microwave Licenses and Authorizations to Provide International Facilities Based and Resold Services, 13 FCC Rcd. 15236, 15242–15243 (1998).

5. 1992 Horizontal Merger Guidelines, U.S. Department of Justice and Federal Trade Commission (revised April 8, 1997) at §0.1, www.usdoj.gov/atr/public/guidelines/horiz_book/hmg1.html.

ever. In 1999, for example, the Wireless Telecommunications Bureau of the FCC processed 40,879 license transfers and the Mass Media Bureau processed 4951 audio radio licenses transfers.[6] The fact that a vast number of license transfers have passed smoothly and routinely through the Commission has not, however, insulated the Commission from criticism or controversy. The reason is that in some very large mergers, mostly among common carriers but also among cable operators, license transfer review has been anything but routine. It should not be surprising that the Commission would engage in a much broader and more stringent review of a major merger among carriers than it does to a sale of a given wireless license from one operator to another. What has been controversial is the scope of the Commission's review, the standard it applies on review, and the means it uses to resolve its concerns about a merger. The following excerpts from the Commission's decision allowing RHCs Ameritech and SBC to merge—or, more precisely, allowing Ameritech to transfer its FCC licenses to SBC—exemplifies the Commission's approach to large telecommunications mergers and makes clear why there is such fierce debate over the FCC's role in merger approval.

One final note before turning to the materials. The excerpts that follow in certain passages refer to services that have yet to be formally introduced in this book. For example, the Commission talks about digital subscriber line ("DSL") service (which is a high-speed data service that makes use of slightly upgraded traditional telephone lines) and its variants like ADSL ("asymmetric" DSL) and the generic term xDSL (where the "x" is just a placeholder.) Moreover, the Commission talks about a broad category of high-speed data services called "advanced services" that includes most of the technologies through which consumers will soon access the Internet. All of these topics are considered in Part IV of this textbook. For current purposes, just keep in mind that these are cutting-edge technologies that the Commission is anxious to see developed and implemented on a broad scale.

II. THE SBC/AMERITECH PROCEEDING

IN RE APPLICATIONS OF AMERITECH CORP., TRANSFEROR, AND SBC COMMUNICATIONS, INC., TRANSFEREE, FOR CONSENT TO TRANSFER CONTROL OF LICENSES AND LINES PURSUANT TO SECTIONS 214 AND 310(D) OF THE COMMUNICATIONS ACT

14 FCC Rcd. 14712 (1999)

I. INTRODUCTION

1. In this *Order*, we consider the joint applications filed by SBC Communications Inc. (SBC) and Ameritech Corporation (Ameritech) pursuant to sections 214(a) and 310(d) of the Communications Act of 1934 for approval to

---

6. FCC Public Forum: Merger Transaction Process, March 1, 2000, "Background Information," www.fcc.gov.transactions/background.html.

transfer control of licenses and lines from Ameritech to SBC in connection with their proposed merger. Before we can grant their applications, SBC and Ameritech (collectively, Applicants) must demonstrate that their proposed transaction will serve the public interest, convenience, and necessity. After lengthy discussions with Commission staff and consideration of public comments in this proceeding, SBC and Ameritech supplemented their initial application by attaching to it proposed conditions representing a set of voluntary commitments.

2. We conclude that approval of the applications to transfer control of Commission licenses and lines from Ameritech to SBC is in the public interest because such approval is subject to significant and enforceable conditions designed to mitigate the potential public interest harms of their merger, to open up the local markets of these Regional Bell Operating Companies (RBOCs), and to strengthen the merged firm's incentives to expand competition outside its regions. We believe that the proposed voluntary commitments by SBC and Ameritech substantially mitigate the potential public interest harms while providing public interest benefits that extend beyond those contained in the original applications.

3. Specifically, we conclude in this *Order* that the proposed merger of these RBOCs threatens to harm consumers of telecommunications services by: (a) denying them the benefits of future probable competition between the merging firms; (b) undermining the ability of regulators and competitors to implement the pro-competitive, deregulatory framework for local telecommunications that was adopted by Congress in the Telecommunications Act of 1996; and (c) increasing the merged entity's incentives and ability to raise entry barriers to, and otherwise discriminate against, entrants into the local markets of these RBOCs. Furthermore, the asserted benefits of the proposed merger, absent conditions, do not outweigh these significant harms, as described herein.

4. The proposed conditions, however, change the public interest balance. We expect that with these conditions, competition in the provision of local exchange services, including advanced services, will increase both inside and outside the merged firm's region. Accordingly, assuming the Applicants' ongoing compliance with the conditions described in this *Order*, we find that the Applicants have demonstrated that the proposed transfer of licenses and lines from Ameritech to SBC serves the public interest, convenience, and necessity.

II. EXECUTIVE SUMMARY

5. To implement the dismantling of the Bell System, seven Regional Bell Operating Companies were created in 1984. After the mergers of SBC with Pacific Telesis, and Bell Atlantic with NYNEX, five RBOCs remain. The instant proceeding concerns the proposed transfer of licenses and lines attendant upon a proposed merger of two RBOCs, SBC and Ameritech. We conclude that, with the conditions adopted by this *Order*, the Applicants have demonstrated that the proposed transfer of licenses and lines from Ameritech to SBC will serve the public interest, convenience, and necessity. We also make the following determinations in support of this conclusion:

Harms—The proposed merger of these RBOCs threatens to harm consumers of telecommunications services in three distinct, but interrelated, ways.

1) The merger will remove one of the most significant potential participants in local telecommunications mass markets both within and outside
of each company's region.

2) The merger will substantially reduce the Commission's ability to implement the market-opening requirements of the 1996 Act by comparative
practice oversight methods. Contrary to the deregulatory, competitive
purpose of the 1996 Act, this will, in turn, increase the duration of the
entrenched firms' market power and raise the costs of regulating them.

3) The merger will increase the incentive and ability of the merged entity
to discriminate against its rivals, particularly with respect to the provision of advanced telecommunications services. This is likely to frustrate
the Commission's ability to foster advanced services as it is directed to
do by the 1996 Act.

Benefits — The asserted benefits of the proposed merger do not outweigh the significant harms, detailed above. Specifically:

1) The Applicants have failed to demonstrate that the merger is necessary
in order to obtain the benefits to local competition of the National-Local
Strategy, a plan in which the merged firm will enter 30 out-of-region
markets as a competitive LEC.

2) Only a small portion of the Applicants' claimed cost-saving efficiencies, including procurement savings, consolidation efficiencies, implementation of best practices, faster and broader roll-out of new products
and services, and benefits to employees and communities, are merger-specific, likely and verifiable.

3) The only merger-specific benefits to product markets other than local
wireline telecommunications markets, such as wireless services, Internet
services, long distance and international services, and global seamless
services for large business customers, relate to a somewhat increased
pace of expansion and modest reductions in unit costs. Any benefits in
these regards are both speculative and small.

Conditions — On July 1, 1999, the Applicants supplemented their application by
proffering a set of voluntary commitments that they agreed to undertake as conditions of approval of their proposed transfer of licenses and lines. Following a
period of public comment regarding their proposed conditions, the Applicants
substantially revised their commitments on August 27, 1999, and continued to
refine those commitments in filings with the Commission on September 7, September 17, and September 29, 1999. Assuming satisfactory compliance, implementation of the attached final set of conditions will further the following goals:

1) promoting advanced services deployment;

2) ensuring that in-region local markets are more open;

3) fostering out-of-region competition;

4) improving residential phone service; and

5) enforcing the Merger Order.

These commitments are sufficient to tip the scales, so that, on balance, the application to transfer licenses and lines should be approved.

III. BACKGROUND

1. A Changing Industry

12. In 1982, the United States District Court for the District of Columbia entered a consent decree in an antitrust suit entitled United States v. AT&T Corp. The 1982 Consent Decree, also known as the "Modification of Final Judgment" (MFJ), when fully enforced in 1984, substantially dismantled what had formerly been an integrated end-to-end monopoly of U.S. telecommunications services, the Bell System. Before the MFJ, the Bell System provided local exchange telephone service to over 80 percent of all residential phone subscribers in the United States, and accounted for even higher shares of long distance service, phone plant equipment manufacture and customer premises equipment sales. For most Americans, the Bell System provided virtually all telecommunications needs. By fundamentally altering that environment, the MFJ, together with its underlying rationale, provides the central backdrop against which all telecommunications regulation takes place in this country, and, indeed, the measure against which we evaluate the merger before us.

13. The entry of the 1982 Consent Decree created SBC and Ameritech. The MFJ essentially divorced the Bell System's local exchange operations from its other lines of business by requiring the creation of seven regionally-based operating companies (i.e., the RBOCs). These RBOCs were created as holding companies for the local operating companies that had been owned by AT&T and were forbidden from selling long distance services and information services, and from manufacturing or selling telecommunications equipment. Both SBC and Ameritech therefore are creations of the MFJ, not an outgrowth of natural market forces. Necessarily, then, the rationale behind the 1982 Consent Decree frames most of the issues raised by their proposed merger.

14. To put it simply, the Bell System was broken up because of two firmly held beliefs. One belief was that competition, rather than regulation, could best decide who would sell what telecommunications services at what prices to whom. The other belief was that the principal obstacles to realizing that competitive ideal were the incentive and ability of dominant local exchange carriers, who typically controlled virtually all local services within their regions, to wield exclusionary power against their rivals. The Department of Justice, the federal courts, and this Commission concluded that a firm controlling access to virtually all local phone customers in its region was very likely to exclude those who would directly compete with it and to discriminate against those, such as long distance service providers and equipment manufacturers, who might offer competitive ancillary services that the local exchange carrier also sought to offer. Further, decades of experimentation with various regulatory regimes had taught that regulators could not fully monitor and control such exclusionary and discriminatory behavior. Rather, structural solutions—in this case the divorce of AT&T from its local operating companies—were vitally necessary.

15. The other seminal event in post-World War II telecommunications regulation was the enactment of the 1996 Act. When Congress passed the 1996 Act, it codified the standards and principles established by the Bell System breakup and set forth a framework that governs us today. Two aspects of the 1996 Act in particular drive our analysis of this license transfer application and the companies' subsequent proposed conditions.

16. First, Congress not only firmly ratified the pro-competitive thrust of the MFJ and embraced its rationale, but it extended the goals of the decree. The MFJ principally sought to further competition in ancillary fields, such as long distance, equipment manufacturing, and information services. Based in part on successful state experiments with limited introduction of local competition, the 1996 Act determined that it would also be U.S. telecommunications policy to foster competition nationally in the provision of local exchange and exchange access services to all telephone subscribers, including residential units. From the date of the enactment of the 1996 Act, this Commission, in conjunction with state public utility commissions, has been statutorily charged with opening up local markets to competition, on the specific premise that without regulatory oversight, the incumbent LECs would be able to discriminate against and exclude local rivals.

17. Second, Congress directed this Commission and the state commissions to achieve these competitive ends by deregulatory means. The 1996 Act introduced into our telecommunications law a clearly-stated duty of dominant LECs to interconnect with their competitors—for example, to unbundle their networks and provide advance notice of changes in their network design, to permit rivals to resell incumbent LEC services at a discount, and to allow their competitors to collocate on their premises. Incumbent LECs must accommodate their rivals, not predate against them, and the process of accommodation is to be through commercial negotiation—not regulatory fiat—where possible. Thus, Congress instructed this Commission and state regulators to effectuate the transition from monopoly markets to competitive markets in a deregulatory manner. This means that regulations enforcing interconnection on fair and equitable terms should not impose detailed regulatory oversight on incumbents. Our mandate is to achieve competition, not to devise a complex regulatory regime. We assess this transfer of control application, and its associated conditions, against this mandate.

V. ANALYSIS OF POTENTIAL PUBLIC INTEREST HARMS

A. Overview

55. We conclude that the proposed merger, considered without supplemental conditions, threatens our ability to fulfill our statutory mandate in the following three ways.

56. First, the proposed merger between SBC and Ameritech significantly decreases the potential for competition in local telecommunications markets by large incumbent LECs. The merger eliminates SBC and Ameritech as significant potential participants in the mass market for local exchange and exchange access services in the other's regions. Both firms have the capabilities and incentives to be considered most significant market participants in geographic areas adjacent to their own regions, and in out-of-region markets in which they have a cellular presence. This finding is based partly on our analysis of the plans of Ameritech to expand into St. Louis (in SBC's territory) which would have occurred but for the merger, and SBC's plans to expand into Chicago (in Ameritech's territory). As incumbent LECs, each firm is one of only a few potential entrants with the necessary systems, such as billing and operations support, required to provide local exchange services to residential and small business customers on a large scale. They also bring particular expertise to the process of negotiating and arbitrating interconnection agreements between incumbent and competitive LECs. In adja-

cent markets, each Applicant has an array of nearby switches that can be used to provide local exchange services in the other's traditional operating territories. Moreover, in out-of-region markets in which either Applicant has a cellular affiliate, it also has a base of customers to whom it can offer wireline local exchange services, potentially bundled with cellular and other offerings. Finally, in both adjacent and cellular out-of-region markets, SBC and Ameritech have brand recognition with mass market customers that would provide a strong and often unique advantage in providing competitive wireline services.

57. <u>Second</u>, the proposed merger frustrates the ability of the Commission (and state regulators) to implement the local market-opening provisions of the 1996 Act. The merger of SBC and Ameritech—two of the six remaining major incumbent LECs (the RBOCs and GTE)—would have an adverse impact on the ability of regulators and competitors to implement the competitive goals of the 1996 Act by deregulatory means. Comparing the practices of independent firms can assist federal and state regulators in defining incumbent LEC obligations and in discovering new approaches and solutions to open markets to competition under sections 251 and 271 and state law. Such comparative practice analyses (or "benchmarking") depend upon having a sufficient number of independent sources of observation available for comparison. Indeed, the development of the local competition that exists today can be attributed largely to comparative practice analyses of experiments and developments in various states and among various incumbent LECs.

58. Significant differences between the major incumbent LECs and other carriers preclude the use of other carriers as alternative benchmarks. Large incumbent LECs differ greatly from smaller incumbent LECs, competitive LECs and foreign LECs in regulatory treatment, structure and operation. Furthermore, statistical parity comparisons cannot be used as a substitute for all forms of incumbent LEC benchmarking. The decreased ability to employ comparative practice analysis that would result from the proposed merger ultimately would force regulators and competitors to replace benchmarking with more intrusive and costly methods of regulation, frustrating the goals of the 1996 Act and this Commission of opening markets and easing regulation, to the detriment of the public interest. We and our state colleagues would be forced to adopt more regulations of greater complexity, while competitors would be prevented from gaining valuable information that could help them succeed in breaking down entry barriers.

59. Moreover, the merger's elimination of Ameritech as an independently-owned RBOC is likely to reduce significantly the amount of innovation that regulators and competitors could observe and analyze. Ameritech frequently has taken an approach at the holding-company level that is different from the other RBOCs, examples of which are detailed in the Comparative Practices Analysis section. These differences by Ameritech in one state have allowed regulators and competitors to induce market-opening behavior from other incumbent LECs in other states. Another harm of the merger is that the larger combined entity will have a greater incentive to unify the practices of its separate operating companies to affect the outcome of both best practices and average practices benchmarking by regulators and competitors, resulting in an overall loss of diversity at the operating-company level. The proposed merger of SBC and Ameritech would also directly increase the incentive and ability of remaining incumbent LECs to coordinate their behavior to resist market-opening measures. As the number of rele-

vant independently-owned incumbent LECs shrinks to a small few, the probability of coordination significantly increases.

60. Third, while it would diminish regulatory efficacy, the proposed merger also would increase the incentives and ability of the larger merged entity to discriminate against rivals in retail markets where the new SBC will be the dominant incumbent LEC. The merger will lead the merged entity to raise entry barriers that will adversely affect the ability of rivals to compete in the provision of retail advanced services, interexchange services, local exchange and exchange access services, thereby reducing competition and increasing prices for consumers of those services. The increase in the number of local areas controlled by SBC as a result of the merger will increase its incentive and ability to discriminate against carriers competing in retail markets that depend on access to SBC's inputs in order to provide services. For example, if SBC discriminates against a competitive LEC attempting to enter Houston, it will raise this rival's costs. This competitive LEC will have less capital to spend on common research, product development, and marketing costs, making the competitive LEC a less effective competitor in other areas such as Chicago because of its overall higher costs. Prior to the merger, SBC would not realize the benefits in Chicago from such conduct. After merging with Ameritech, which is the incumbent LEC in Chicago, SBC would realize such benefits. Because SBC after the merger would realize more of the gains from what are presently "external" effects, it would have a greater incentive to engage in discrimination than the combined incentives that the two individual companies would have had in their smaller regions.

61. Any likelihood of increased discrimination and heightened entry barriers causes particular concern in the retail market for advanced services, given the Commission's ongoing efforts to encourage innovation and investment in these emerging markets. Competitors' requests for the type of interconnection and access arrangements necessary to provide new types of advanced services are continually evolving and provide ample scope for incumbents to discriminate in satisfying these requests. The combined entity has an increased incentive to discriminate against a competitor such as Sprint ION that is seeking to enter markets on a national basis, because the merged firm will realize the benefits over the larger combined area in its control. Likewise, once an incumbent LEC has authority to provide interLATA services within its region, it has an incentive to discriminate against the termination of its competitors' calls that originate in that region in order to induce callers at the originating end to choose the incumbent LEC as their interexchange service provider. SBC after the proposed merger will have a much larger "in-region" area, and thus will terminate a greater number of calls from in-region customers. The larger merged firm would therefore have a greater incentive to engage in discrimination, which is likely to be particularly acute with respect to advanced or customized access services where such discrimination would be most difficult to detect.

62. In short, absent stringent conditions, we would be forced to conclude that this merger does not serve the public interest, convenience or necessity because it would inevitably retard progress in opening local telecommunications markets, thereby requiring us to engage in more regulation. Standing alone, without conditions, the initial application proposed a license transfer that would have been inconsistent with the approach to telecommunications regulation and telecommunications markets that the Congress established in the 1996 Act, rati-

fying the fundamental approaches enshrined in the MFJ. For that reason, we conclude that it would be inconsistent with the public interest, convenience and necessity to permit this license transfer in the absence of significant and enforceable conditions. The remainder of Part IV explains these conclusions in detail.

VII. CONDITIONS

349. As noted above, on July 1, 1999, the Applicants supplemented their initial Application to include a package of voluntary commitments that they intended would alter the public interest balance in their favor.

A. Open Process

350. As a threshold matter, we affirm that considering conditions in license and line transfer proceedings is an appropriate and, in circumstances such as this merger, a necessary process in our application review. It is seductively simple, yet short-sighted, to believe that our role is limited to voting an application up or down, measuring an application solely against whether it violates a specific provision of the Act or a specific Commission rule. Such a view rests on the assumption that our market-opening rules will work equally well regardless of the number of major incumbent LECs or RBOCs and of who owns them. As we discussed at some length in Section IV of this Order, however, this would be an incorrect view of our rules, and the current realities of the telecommunications industry.

1. Promoting Equitable and Efficient Advanced Services Deployment

363. Separate Affiliate for Advanced Services. Under this condition, SBC and Ameritech will create, prior to closing the merger, one or more separate affiliates to provide all advanced services in the combined SBC/Ameritech region on a phased-in basis. At present, we note that SBC and Ameritech are only permitted to provide intraLATA advanced services. Establishing an advanced services separate affiliate will provide a structural mechanism to ensure that competing providers of advanced services receive effective, nondiscriminatory access to the facilities and services of the merged firm's incumbent LECs that are necessary to provide advanced services. Because the merged firm's own separate advanced services affiliate will use the same processes as competitors, and pay an equivalent price for facilities and services, the condition should ensure a level playing field between SBC/Ameritech and its advanced services competitors. Given this expectation, we anticipate that this condition will greatly accelerate competition in the advanced services market by lowering the costs and risks of entry and reducing uncertainty, while prodding all carriers, including the Applicants, to hasten deployment.

376. Nondiscriminatory Rollout of xDSL Services. As a means of ensuring that the merged firm's rollout of advanced services reaches some of the least competitive market segments and is more widely available to low income consumers, SBC and Ameritech will target their deployment of xDSL services to include low income groups in rural and urban areas. Specifically, for each SBC/Ameritech in-region state, SBC/Ameritech will ensure that at least 10 percent of the rural wire centers where it, or its separate advanced services affiliate, deploys xDSL service will be low income rural wire centers, meaning those wire centers with the great-

est number of low income households. Similarly, at least 10 percent of the urban wire centers where the merged firm or its separate advanced services affiliate deploys xDSL service in each in-region state will be low income urban wire centers. These requirements will become enforceable for any given state 180 days after the merger closes and after SBC/Ameritech and/or its advanced services affiliate has deployed xDSL service in that state in at least 20 urban wire centers (to activate the urban requirement) or 20 rural wire centers (to activate the rural requirement). After the respective effective date, SBC/Ameritech will provide nondiscriminatory deployment of xDSL services for at least 36 months thereafter. SBC/Ameritech will consult with the appropriate state commission, within 90 days of the merger's closing, to classify all SBC/Ameritech wire centers in that state as urban or rural. Furthermore, to assist in monitoring the merged firm's equitable deployment of xDSL, SBC/Ameritech will publicly file a quarterly report with the Commission describing the status of its xDSL deployment, including the identity and location of each urban and rural wire center where it has deployed xDSL.

2. Ensuring Open Local Markets

377. Carrier-to-Carrier Performance Plan. As a means of ensuring that SBC/Ameritech's service to telecommunications carriers will not deteriorate as a result of the merger and the larger firm's increased incentive and ability to discriminate and to stimulate the merged entity to adopt "best practices" that clearly favor public rather than private interests, SBC/Ameritech will publicly file performance measurement data for each of the 13 SBC/Ameritech in-region states with this Commission and the relevant state commission on a monthly basis. The data will reflect SBC/Ameritech incumbent LECs' performance of their obligations toward telecommunications carriers in 20 different measurement categories. These categories cover key aspects of pre-ordering, ordering, provisioning, maintenance and repair associated with UNEs, interconnection, and resold services. Many of the twenty measurement categories are divided into numerous disaggregated sub-measurements, thereby tracking SBC/Ameritech's performance for different functions and different types of service. Furthermore, the list of measurements reported by SBC/Ameritech under this condition is not static. This list is subject to addition or deletion, and the measurements themselves are subject to modification, by the Chief of the Common Carrier Bureau, through a joint semi-annual review with SBC/Ameritech.

390. Carrier-to-Carrier Promotions. To offset the loss of probable competition between SBC and Ameritech for residential services in their regions and to facilitate market entry, the Applicants propose three promotions designed specifically to encourage rapid development of local competition in residential and less dense areas. SBC/Ameritech will offer these promotions equally to all telecommunications carriers with which it has an existing interconnection and/or resale agreement in an SBC/Ameritech state. Within ten days of the merger closing, SBC/Ameritech will provide each such telecommunications carrier a written offer to amend the carrier's interconnection agreement in that state to incorporate the promotions. [The three promotions involve various pricing discounts that had to be offered to rival firms. These promotions do not have to be offered to all requesting firms; instead, there are caps as to the number of firms that must be allowed to purchase at these lower rates, and there are also specific windows of

opportunity during which interested firms must request to participate in the promotions.]

3. Fostering Out-of-Territory Competition

398. Out-of-Territory Competitive Entry (National-Local Strategy). As a condition of this merger, within 30 months of the merger closing date the combined firm will enter at least 30 major markets outside SBC's and Ameritech's incumbent service area as a facilities-based provider of local telecommunications services to business and residential customers. This will ensure that residential consumers and business customers outside of SBC/Ameritech's territory benefit from facilities-based competitive service by a major incumbent LEC. This condition effectively requires SBC and Ameritech to redeem their promise that their merger will form the basis for a new, powerful, truly nationwide multi-purpose competitive telecommunications carrier. We also anticipate that this condition will stimulate competitive entry into the SBC/Ameritech region by the affected incumbent LECs.

399. Under this condition, SBC and Ameritech will select the 30 out-of-territory markets from the list of 50 major markets that they included in their proposal. As part of the combined firm's entry into each of these new markets, SBC and Ameritech will either meet certain verifiable entry requirements in each market (*i.e.*, installing or obtaining switching capability; providing facilities-based service to each of three business or residential customers; collocating in each of ten wire centers; offering facilities-based service to all business and all residential customers served by each of those ten wire centers; and offering service, whether by resale, unbundled elements or facilities, to all business and all residential customers within the entire service area of the incumbent RBOC or Tier 1 incumbent LEC in the market), or make voluntary incentive payments to a state-designated fund (or as governed by state law) in the amount of $ 110,000 per day for each missed entry requirement, for a total of $ 1.1 million per entry requirement per market. SBC/Ameritech would therefore be obligated to pay $ 39.6 million if it missed all 36 entry requirements in a market, or nearly $ 1.2 billion for missing the entry requirements in all 30 markets.

4. Improving Residential Phone Service

400. Pricing of InterLATA Services. As a direct benefit to consumers, particularly low income consumers and low-volume long distance callers, this condition provides that SBC/Ameritech will not charge residential customers a minimum monthly or minimum flat rate charge for long distance service for a period of not less than three years. This requirement should not only benefit those customers that make few long distance calls, but also should help to ensure that long distance services continue to be available to all consumers at competitive prices. This requirement does not prohibit the merged firm from offering its customers an optional, voluntary pricing plan that may include a minimum monthly charge, minimum flat rate charge, or a prepaid calling card.

5. Ensuring Compliance with and Enforcement of these Conditions

406. The Commission is firmly committed to enforcing the Communications Act and the public interest standard that forms its foundation. Attaching conditions to a merger without an efficient and judicious enforcement program would impair the Commission's ability to protect the public interest. The conditions

therefore establish compliance and enforcement mechanisms that not only will provide SBC/Ameritech with a strong incentive to comply with each of its requirements, but also will facilitate the Commission's oversight of the Applicants' obligations under these conditions. As a general matter, the conditions place the responsibility of taking active steps to ensure compliance on SBC/Ameritech by: (1) establishing a self-executing compliance mechanism; (2) requiring an independent audit of the Applicants' compliance with the conditions; and (3) providing self-executing remedies for failure to perform an obligation.

419. We conclude that, with the conditions that we adopt in this *Order*, the merger of SBC and Ameritech is likely to be beneficial for consumers and spur competition in the local and advanced services markets. Given that the conditions will substantially mitigate the potential public interest harms of the proposed merger and will result in affirmative public benefit, we conclude that the Applicants have demonstrated that the proposed merger, on balance, will serve the public interest, convenience and necessity.

Notes and Questions

1. Preventing Harms or Extracting Benefits? To what extent do you think the above conditions are aimed at mitigating competitive harms from the merger and to what extent are they aimed at achieving affirmative, but perhaps logically unrelated, benefits from the merger? Does the FCC arrogate to itself too much authority here?

2. Overlapping Jurisdiction. Where the conditions are designed to resolve competitive harms, are these harms that the other federal agencies would have overlooked? If we assume that the DOJ and FTC also reviewed this merger with care, does the above document suggest any reasons why the FCC should also analyze the merger? Is the argument that there are distinct benefits that come from the Commission's expertise, just as the DOJ and FTC bring antitrust expertise to the process? Is the argument instead simply that having three agencies review a proposed merger is better than two? What costs do you see from all this overlapping jurisdiction?

3. Limitations to FCC Review. What practical and/or legal concerns are raised by the Commission's use of merger conditions to obtain benefits from, rather than avoid harms from, the transaction? Review §§214(a) and 310(d) of the Act, reproduced in the statutory appendix. What are the possible arguments for and against reading those provisions to support the FCC's broad merger inquiry? What might be the objectives of a narrower inquiry under the language of those provisions?

4. The Debate at the FCC. The next excerpts are from the separate statements of FCC Commissioners Harold Furchtgott-Roth and Michael Powell dissenting in part from the *Order* excerpted above. These separate statements highlight the major issues in the current debate over the FCC's merger review authority.

SEPARATE STATEMENT OF COMMISSIONER HAROLD FURCHTGOTT-ROTH, CONCURRING IN PART, DISSENTING IN PART

14 FCC Rcd. 14712, 15174–189 (1999)

By this *Order*, the Commission imposes legally dubious, overbroad, potentially unenforceable, privately negotiated conditions on a merger that it is statutorily unauthorized to review, and assessment of which was governed by no clear procedural or substantive standards. The item itself is the end-result of an extraordinarily elaborate procedural approach to the review of license transfers that is entirely *sui generis* — that is, never before applied and unlikely ever again to be followed; such a process raises an unfortunate appearance of disparate and unfair treatment of these applicants for license transfers.

Accordingly, I concur only in the narrow decision to grant SBC and Ameritech authorization to transfer lines pursuant to section 214 and licenses pursuant to section 310(d). I cannot support the reasoning of the *Order* and must dissent in full from the adoption of the conditions on these license and authorization transfers.

I. The Conditions Are Inconsistent With The Communications Act

The conditions imposed in this *Order* are, in my opinion, of highly questionable legal validity. In particular, many of the conditions are inconsistent with specific sections of the Communications Act.

To be sure, the Communications Act grants the Commission authority to condition license transfer and section 214 authorizations. This authority is *not* without its limits, however. Rather, section 303(r) provides that "except as otherwise provided in this Act, the Commission...shall...prescribe such...conditions, *not inconsistent with law*, as may be necessary to carry out *the provisions of this Act*." 47 U.S.C. §303(r) (emphasis added). And section 214(c) states that the Commission "may attach to the issuance of [a §214] certificate such terms and conditions as in its judgment the public convenience and necessity may require." Although this provision contains no express language limiting conditions to enforcement of the Act, it is certainly not in the public interest to adopt conditions violative of federal communications law. At a minimum, then, we cannot impose conditions under either section 303(r) or section 214(c) that contradict the Act itself.

The conditions in this *Order* do just that, however. Of especial legal concern are those related to carrier-to-carrier promotions. These conditions limit the number of services and facilities that may be offered to competitive local exchange carriers (CLECs) on a promotional basis. Once the caps are reached, some CLECs will be unable to obtain the same promotional deals as other CLECs. Quite simply, carrier-to-carrier promotions will not be available on an equal basis to all requesting carriers. In this way, then, the conditions violate the "nondiscriminatory access" requirement of section 251(c)(3), as well as the resale nondiscrimination requirement of 251(c)(4)(B).

II. The Conditions Are Disproportionate To The Alleged Potential Harms

A. *The Transaction Does Not Violate The Specific Terms Of Any Extant Communications Statute or Regulation*

Commission regulations take up many bookcases. For a license transfer to run afoul of a specific administrative rule therefore is not an improbable outcome. Given the breadth of our regulation in this area, it is remarkable that the *Order* never asserts that the transfer of licenses between SBC and Ameritech would violate any specific substantive provision of the Communications Act or any Commission regulation. Remedies for such harms, of course, would be easily and clearly prescribed: the transferee would be obliged to bring the license transfers into compliance with existing rules.

How does a regulated entity fall out of compliance, and then revert back into compliance, with a vague idea that has no written rules to define compliance or non-compliance? One must have meetings to discuss and to invent standards that did not previously exist. Indeed, the entire unsavory process of the meetings that ensued from the allegation of statutorily unfounded concerns could have been avoided had the Commission's concerns been directly linked to existing written rules.

B. *The Alleged Harms Are Speculative And Do Not Flow From The Merger*

The Commission foresees three potential harms in the consummation of the license transfers. *First*, that the merger will remove significant potential participants in the local exchange market within, and outside of, each company's current region. *Second*, that the merger will impair this Commission's ability to engage in comparative practice oversight and consequently extend the entrenchment of certain firms and raise the cost of regulating them. *Third*, that the merged entity will have increased incentive and ability to discriminate against competitors, and that this increased incentive and ability will have particular force with respect to the provision of advanced telecommunications services.

The first harm is premised on the Commission's "precluded competitor" doctrine. According to this theory, the license transfers will result in reduced or precluded competition both inside the RBOC territories and outside the SBC/Ameritech regions. The record, however, presents no clear evidence that either SBC or Ameritech had developed plans to provide substantial in-region competition for local exchange services in the other company's territory. Whether plans that might have been developed at some future date are affected by the proposed license transfers is idle speculation. Furthermore, the license transfers themselves do not limit the ability of any other company to offer local exchange services in either SBC or Ameritech territory. Consequently, it is difficult to make a compelling case that competition within either the SBC or Ameritech regions is substantially reduced or precluded by these license transfers.

As to out-of-market competition, the *Order* admits that there is no evidence that SBC intended to enter local exchange markets out of its regions, relying instead on "transitional market analysis." *See Order* at ¶98. This analysis appears to be little more than gussied-up speculation about what markets might look like in the absence of firm evidence. There are many outcomes that are equally plausible as the one reached in the *Order*. The theorizing in the *Order* may be an intriguing intellectual exercise, but it is hardly the basis for an administrative finding about the likely effects on competition out of region and thus for the resultant conditions.

The second harm is similarly conjectural. Can the Commission really defend the proposition that a reduction from six to five local exchange carriers creates a significant, material, and appreciable difference in its ability to make comparative evaluations? Or that the elimination of one company will "severely restrict" the behaviors that regulators can observe in the local exchange market? That is a hard case to make indeed. Currently, the FCC has no duly-promulgated rules that depend on benchmarking performance to industry levels, much less benchmarking performance to industry levels that must be derived from a minimum of six major carriers. Accordingly, this harm is based at most on the possibility that the Commission will, assuming statutory authority to do so, in the future adopt rules benchmarking performance to industry standards.

The second step in this analysis—that the Commission's decreased ability to benchmark will therefore allow entrenched companies to remain that way for an extended period of time—requires a leap in logic. Whatever marginal impairment there may be of the Commission's ability to benchmark, it is a far cry to conclude from that impairment that the Commission will be *so ineffective as a general matter* that entrenched companies will be more able to stay that way. Moreover, there are myriad reasons why—apart from this Commission's regulations—an entrenched company might be pushed into competition: for instance, the marketplace. Even if one assumes that this Commission engaged in no benchmarking at all, it simply does not follow that now-entrenched companies would have longer entrenchment periods than they otherwise would have. Indeed, the Commission cannot even say how much longer, absent its diminished regulatory abilities, that entrenchment would last. If the Commission is truly concerned with the costs of regulation, it ought to reevaluate this *Order*, which creates an entire regulatory and enforcement scheme for a single company.

The third alleged harm is based on an especially large ratio of speculation to actual likelihood. First, the *Order* does not demonstrate why the combined firm has any more incentive and ability to discriminate against competitors than do the separate companies. SBC is a large and powerful company in its territory, as is Ameritech. On this record, there is little compelling evidence that whatever market power either company may exercise in its region would be significantly enhanced by the license transfers. Moreover, incentives to discriminate in a market—as opposed simply to treating all customers either equally well or equally poorly for administrative, financial, legal, and regulatory convenience—depend on many technical factors of market demand and supply. Even for a single service in a narrow geographic market, it would be difficult, even with substantial empirical evidence, to conclude with certainty whether a regulatory action would increase, decrease, or leave unaltered incentives to discriminate. It is a breathtaking to conclude that the proposed license transfers at issue would have a perceptible effect on incentives to discriminate.

Yet even if there were true, I fail to see why those incentives and abilities would be particularly strong in one area of SBC/Ameritech's business, in this case, advanced telecommunication services. What is the rationale as to why that service—as opposed to other services provided by SBC/Ameritech—is uniquely likely to cause the company to engage discriminatory behavior? Although the *Order* focuses on these services, it does not rationally distinguish them from others in terms of the likelihood of discriminatory practices. Indeed, to the extent that SBC/Ameritech has market power generally, it is less likely to be in the market for advanced services, where there are competing alternatives, than in the market for other services where there are fewer alternatives, such as simple dial-tone service. Because the record provides little, if any, basis to even postulate that any existing market power would be enhanced by the proposed license transfers, it is difficult to understand how the subsequent conclusion about the special vulnerability of advanced services to such incentives could be justified.

Moreover, all these alleged harms bear a common characteristic: the merger itself does not increase the likelihood of any of them. That is, they are things that the individual companies would be equally likely to do if the merger never took place. The merger does not in any *appreciable* way make, say, discrimination more likely or benchmarking harder than it is now. Nor are these companies, on a stand-alone basis, distinguishable from other local exchange carriers in terms of their incentives and abilities to engage in these sorts of behaviors. Even if one could quantify it, the differential in the Commission's ability now and post-merger to make such judgments is negligible in comparison to the heavy duties that have been imposed as a remedy for that purported impact.

When it comes to the *benefits* of the merger, the Commission abruptly switches to a more exacting standard of proof and becomes concerned with merger-specificity. It finds that "only a small portion of the Applicants' claim cost-saving efficiencies...are merger-specific, likely and verifiable," and that "the only merger-specific benefits to product markets...are both speculative and small." A scouring of this record will show, however, that applicants' evidence of their asserted benefits is no weaker than the Commission's evidence of its posited harms. It is every bit as, if not more so, founded in empirical and economic reality.

C. The Conditions Do Not Materially Remediate The Alleged Harms

Even if one assumes that the harms have been predicted with adequate certainty, the conditions do not really address those harms. In some instances, there is a complete lack of nexus between the posited harm and the adopted conditions, and in others the conditions will simply not remediate in any direct way the purported harm.

III. The Conditions Impose Undue Administrative Burdens and Costs on The Commission and Participants in the Telecommunications Market

A review of the appendix of conditions attached to this *Order* reveals the great numerosity, length, and intricacy of the conditions. That Appendix lists 30 separate conditions, each with its own subset of interpretive statements, definition, and clarifications, which take up more than 70 pages of text. To really apply and enforce these conditions, the Commission would seem to need to create a separate "SBC/Ameritech" division in the Common Carrier Bureau. Within that division would be teams responsible for overseeing the company's arbitration proceedings; auditing the company; administering the carrier-to-carrier discounts; receiving and processing the company's reports on their advanced services roll-out; reviewing complaints regarding access to cable in multi-unit dwellings; etc.

Moreover, given that this sort of regulation is entirely company-specific, the Commission would have to absorb even more staff resources for each subsequent set of merger-specific conditions it applied to other merged entities. In short, this sort of regulation is very costly to administer, a point that the *Order* fails to consider in its analysis of the efficiency of these conditions with respect to the Commission's future efforts to regulate.

IV. The Conditions Are Either Voluntary And Unenforceable, Or Involuntary And Judicially Reviewable

Throughout this *Order*, the performance of the conditions by SBC/Ameritech is referred to as "voluntary" action. *See, e.g, Order* at ¶1 (describing "proposed conditions" as "representing a set of voluntary commitments"). There are only two possible responses to this assertion. Either the conditions are therefore unenforceable as a matter of law and judicially unreviewable, or the conditions are not voluntary but government-mandated and, thus, their extra-statutory nature in fact injures the applicants and renders the conditions subject to the full panoply of judicial review.

Often, the Commission will term a standard or condition voluntary when, in point of fact, the conditions are the result of intense governmental pressure on regulated entities. The actual voluntariness of action under such conditions is often questioned.

If SBC/Ameritech's adherence to these conditions in the context of agency review of its transfer applications is not really a matter of choice—for instance, if the agency intends to enforce, either directly or indirectly, the conditions—then the conditions take on the force of law. And, as administrative law experts have observed, "even agency statements that purport to be nonbinding can have coercive effects through more subtle, less formal means. To the extent that an agency possesses significant discretionary power over a class of regulatees or beneficiaries, many are likely to "comply" "voluntarily" with an agency's "nonbinding" statement of its preferred policies." Davis & Pierce, I Administrative Law Treatise 232 (3d ed. 1994) As binding obligations, as opposed to voluntary commitments, the conditions would be judicially reviewable and subject to all the provisions of the Communications Act and the Administrative Procedures Act. And if that is true, all the legal deficiencies of the conditions described above are potentially in play.

On the other hand, if the regulations are indeed voluntary, then the company is under no binding legal obligation to perform them. The conditions would therefore be entirely symbolic, doing nothing to effectuate the Commission's purported goals.

At first blush, it might be unclear why the Commission would consciously undermine the enforceability of its own carefully crafted conditions, which it seems to believe in the public good. Characterizing the conditions as "voluntary," however, allows the Commission to achieve other strategic goals: shoring up the item against claims of lack of statutory authority and minimizing the possibility of judicial review of that authority.

As I have previously explained:

The use of voluntary standards allows administrative agencies better to skirt statutory limits on their authority, an offense to the concept of administrative agencies in possession of only those powers delegated to them by Congress....It is no coincidence that the commitments extracted from regulated entities in the guise of voluntary standards tend to be things that the agency lacks statutory authority straightforwardly to require. Voluntary standards, as opposed to duly promulgated rules, can all too easily be used to bootstrap jurisdictional issues: got jurisdiction to approve or disprove the transfer of licenses but no express statutory authority to require unbundling of the licensee's product offerings? Just make it a "optional" condition of the license transfer, add water, mix, and you have fresh jurisdiction to regulate a whole new area. The problem with this approach...is that it renders superfluous Congressional attempts to delineate our areas of responsibility.

There is another reason that agencies might prefer voluntary standards to rules: they are harder to challenge in a court of law. Judicial review of the statutory basis for "voluntary" standards may be difficult to obtain because such guidelines, being technically non-binding, may never formally be announced or enforced against any regulatee.

"Voluntary Standards Are Neither," Speech Before the Media Institute (Nov. 17, 1998).

In this *Order*, the Commission tries to walk a tightrope between the two alternatives as to the legal status of the conditions, referring to the conditions as "voluntary commitments" but hinting elsewhere that it fully expects SBC/Ameritech to carry them out. It is simply not possible to have it both ways, however: either the commitments are *de facto* standards and subject to judicial review, or they are legally unenforceable and thus meaningless as a practical matter.

V. The Commission Lacks "Merger" Review Authority

In addition to the legal problems associated with the nature of the conditions themselves, it is important to step back and recall that, as I have repeated pointed out, this Commission possesses no statutory authority to review "mergers" writ large.

Rather, the Communications Act charge the Commission with a much narrower task: review of the proposed transfer of licenses under Title III from Ameritech to SBC, and consideration of the transfer of common carrier lines between those parties. Nothing in section 310(d) or section 214—the provisions pursuant to which these applications were filed—speaks of jurisdiction to approve or disapprove the merger that has occasioned Ameritech's desire to transfer licenses and section 214 authorizations. [The remainder of this paragraph is relocated from footnote 15 of the original document.] The Commission does possess authority under the Clayton Act, which prohibits combinations in restraint of trade, to review mergers *per se*. *See* 15 U.S.C. §21 (granting FCC authority to enforce Clayton Act where applicable to common carriers engaged in wire or radio communication or radio transmission of energy). If the Commission intends to exercise authority over mergers and acquisitions as such, it ought to do so pursuant to the Clayton Act, with its carefully prescribed procedures and standards of review, not the broad licensing provisions of the Communications Act.

To be sure, the transfer of the licenses and authorizations is an important part of the merger. But it is simply not the same thing. The merger is a much larger and more complicated set of events than the transfer of FCC permits. It includes, to name but a few things, the passage of legal title for many assets other than Title III licenses, corporate restructuring, stock swaps or purchases, and the consolidation of corporate headquarters and personnel. Clearly, then, asking whether the particularized transactions of license transfers and section 214 transfers would serve the public interest, convenience, and necessity entails a significantly more limited focus than contemplating the industry-wide effects of a merger between the transferee and transferor.

For instance, in considering the transfer of licenses, one might ask whether there is any reason to think that the proposed transferee would not put the relevant spectrum to efficient use or comply with applicable Commission regulations; one would not, by contrast, consider how the combination of the two companies might affect other competitors in the industry. One might also consider the benefits of the transfer, but not of the merger generally. And one might consider the transferee's proposed use and disposition of the actual Title III licenses, but one would not venture into an examination of services provided by the transferee that do not even involve the use of those licenses.

By using sections 214 and 310 to assert jurisdiction over the entire merger of two companies that happen to be the transferee and transferor of radio licenses and international resale authorizations, the Commission greatly expands its regulatory authority under the Act. Because the very premise of this *Order* is that it must analyze the competitive effects of the "merger," in contravention of the plain language of sections 214 and 310, I cannot sign on to its reasoning.

STATEMENT OF COMMISSIONER MICHAEL K. POWELL, CONCURRING IN PART, DISSENTING IN PART
14 FCC Rcd. 14712, 15197–99 (1999)

Although I support approval of this merger between SBC and Ameritech, I respectfully disagree with the manner in which the draft weighs the transaction's potential harms and benefits. Specifically, I find fault with the underlying public interest standard, and its application in this proceeding sharpens my concerns with its pitfalls. The approach of rounding up "voluntary" conditions to compensate for largely unrelated potential harms is fraught with public policy problems. Even under this defective standard, however, I believe this *Order*, though carefully written, misses the mark. Although I concur in the conclusion that there are public harms that might well result from this combination that are not entirely offset by the applicants' asserted benefits, I am unsatisfied that any one of these harms bears the weight assigned to it in this *Order*. Thus, I believe fewer conditions, tailored to address the specifically identified harms, would have been the correct result.

I. <u>The Formulation of the Public Interest Standard as an Unconstrained Balancing Test is Both Substantively and Procedurally Flawed</u>

Consistent with my long-standing concerns regarding our license transfer process, I have fundamental difficulties with the public interest standard as developed and applied in this *Order*. Simply put, I am very uncomfortable with a standard that places harms on one side of a scale and then collects and places any hodgepodge of conditions—no matter how ill-suited to remedying the identified infirmities—on the other side of the scale. This balancing approach leads to a number of problems: First, the approach creates a great temptation to load up the benefits side of the scale with a big wish list of conditions that are non-germane to the merger's harmful effects. Second, the approach makes it easier for identified harms, even significant ones, to be visited upon the public in exchange for other benefits. Third, the conditions that are sought are more often surrogates for policies and rules of general, rather than merger-specific, applicability, but without the extensive deliberative process and the check of judicial review normally afforded a rulemaking. And fourth, the process of obtaining "voluntary" conditions inevitably involves bilateral negotiations with the parties that leave the integrity of the Commission's process vulnerable to criticism. I consider each of these in more detail below.

A. *The Problem of the Mountain and the Pebble*

To conceptualize the problems with the public interest standard when reviewing a license transfer (*i.e.*, a merger), consider a simple balancing scale of the "see-saw" variety. On the left side of the scale are public interest harms and, on the right, public interest benefits. The balancing approach used in this *Order* simply requires that the benefits outweigh the harms. If the harms weigh but an ounce more than the proposed benefits, the standard (if faithfully applied as articulated) would require us to block the merger. This approach is troubling on one level, for if the government were neutral with respect to the asserted benefits, it still could be compelled to stop a merger based on essentially negligible harms. This balancing approach becomes even more disconcerting, when the harms we identify require extensive speculation and hypothesis about predicted behavior (as is the case with the "the precluded competitor doctrine") rather than detriments that are more concrete, or at least more time-tested. This is so, for the margin of error in our theories alone may encompass the putative harm, yet we might block the merger nonetheless if unimpressed with the proffered benefits. I believe this describes the case at bar.

The more serious problem arises with the public interest "scale," however, when the Commission, rather than weighing the harms against the *proffered* benefits, attempts to tip the balance by adding weight to the benefits "platter" with conditions—a mountain of goodies designed to leave us, on balance, fat and happy. The public interest standard, as the Commission applies it, does not require that the conditions cure or remedy the identified harms. The conditions need only outweigh the harms. And the standard does not place any limit on how much heavier than the harms the conditions are. Thus, the Commission is free to compensate for a pebble of harm on one side of the public interest scale by throwing a mountain of purportedly beneficial conditions on the other side of the scale, as we have done here. In other words, when conditions are not calibrated to remedy harms, there is no constraint on how voluminous or unrelated they might be. The consequence of this approach is that the slightest harm opens up a quarry of "would-be-nice-to-haves" that can be piled on the scale. Moreover, the coercive effect of having the applicants over a barrel hoping to gain merger approval dramatically improves the chances that the companies will "agree" to abide by the conditions. Thus, the temptation and the enticement to stack the scale with precious gems is irresistible to competing companies and the Commission itself.

B. *"Poor Joshua!"*[7]

The second difficulty I have with the Commission's merger standard is that in theory, it will allow a merger to go forward that it finds will harm the public, as

---

7. This famous refrain is drawn from DeShaney v. Winnebago County Dept. of Social Services, 489 U.S. 189 (1989) (J. Blackmun, dissenting) (holding that state had no constitutional duty to protect Joshua, a child, from his father after receiving reports of possible abuse). In *DeShaney*, Justice Blackmun wrote: "Poor Joshua! Victim of repeated attacks by an irresponsible, bullying, cowardly, and intemperate father, and abandoned by respondents who placed him in a dangerous predicament and who knew or learned what was going on, and yet did essentially nothing except…dutifully record these incidents in [their] files." Id. at 213.

long as the public gets something good in return. In the humorous extreme, one could analogize this to allowing a stranger to beat your dog as long as he commits to giving the dog a bone and some fun squeaky toys.

Jests aside, the point is that when merger conditions are not designed to remedy harms, all the unrelated benefits in the world will not cure the loss to the public. I do not claim that in this *Order* we have allowed unconscionable harm in exchange for some goodies. I happen to believe the harms in general are overstated. Yet if one is convinced of the significance of a proposed merger's harms (as might be the case in future reviews), it is unsettling that the merger would proceed without significantly mitigating those harmful effects with remedial conditions. In this case, for example, nothing in the conditions we impose here reverses the fact that Ameritech will be lost as an independent benchmark for comparative analyses. If this loss is truly significant and harmful, one could argue that we have abdicated our duty to safeguard the public interest by approving the transfer and thereby allowing that harm to befall the public.

Notes and Questions

1. Furchtgott-Roth. Which of Furchtgott-Roth's arguments do you find most compelling? Which least so? Does he find the greater problems to be procedural or substantive?

2. Powell. Powell's statement differs in critical respects from Furchtgott-Roth's statement. What distinctions do you find between them? Do they differ on the fundamental question of whether conditions are ever warranted?

3. Sui Generis Review. Furchtgott-Roth suggests that the Commission's approach to the SBC/Ameritech merger is ad hoc and made up for the purposes of this one transaction ("sui generis," in his words). Is he right? Has the Commission pulled its substantive approach from thin air or is its approach grounded in, and perhaps even required by, established regulatory concerns? Do ¶¶12–17 of the *Order* justify the Commission's actions?

4. Uncertainty. Even if the FCC's merger review process can be used to obtain beneficial results, at the very least the process introduces considerable uncertainty into the regulatory environment. Do any of the above documents address the possible effects this uncertainty might have on firm incentives?

5. Donkeys and Elephants. The authors of the partial dissents above were the two Republican appointees to the Commission. The three Commissioners concurring in full with the *Order* were Democrats. Does this mean that shifts in political administration could also lead to radical shifts in merger review and the kinds of scrutiny firms can expect? Is there some reason this should be more true for FCC merger review than for review by the Department of Justice or the Federal Trade Commission?

6. The DOJ and the FCC. How do procedural differences affect the position of merging parties before the FCC as compared to their position before the DOJ? Both the DOJ and the FCC have the burden of going to court to block a disputed merger. The FCC, though, can prevent a license transfer without going to court, and the burden is then on the merging parties to seek judicial review if they want to go ahead with the disapproved transfer. But that difference may in the end have only limited practical implications. It is very expensive in terms of time and money for parties to fight a suit by the DOJ, so more often than not they either negotiate a settlement that will allow the merger or else abandon the transaction. Similarly, the delays inherent in challenging an FCC license transfer decision could be so costly that often the preferred path from the parties' own perspectives is to bargain with the FCC on "conditions" that will allow the agency to approve the transfer. An important difference, however, is that an FCC decision to approve a license transfer can be challenged in the U.S. Court of Appeals by third parties (*e.g.* competitors of the merging parties), whereas decisions by the DOJ or FTC not to contest a merger cannot be so challenged.

7. Rulemaking vs. Merger Review. One criticism raised by the partial dissents is that the Commission uses its merger review process to impose policies that it could not impose generally through a rulemaking procedure. For example, SBC and Ameritech agreed to provide advanced services through a separate subsidiary that will deal on non-discriminatory terms with the parent companies. But there is no general requirement that ILECs provide advanced services in this manner, and the Commission had indeed backed off from earlier proposals for such a requirement (mainly because of intense political pressure from Congress). Does it raise concern that the Commission now imposes such a requirement as a merger condition? Does this create an opportunity for the FCC to turn a condition on particular parties into a general rule—the Commission's argument being that, once SBC/Ameritech is subject to the condition, it becomes "unfair" to allow SBC/Ameritech's rivals to operate under the normal, less restrictive rules? How might the dynamics of promulgating a particular rule change after the rule's requirements have been imposed, through merger conditions, on particular carriers?

8. Summary. In the end, several important issues of law and policy are raised by the FCC's merger review process. Questions about the FCC's statutory authority, the vagueness of the public interest standard, coercion of merging parties, the lack of judicial review, the social costs of merger conditions, and delay due to duplication of activities among the various federal agencies have all factored into the debate over the Commission's proper role in mergers. The debate has led to calls for reform.

III. MERGER REFORM

In March, 2000, within two weeks of each other, the FCC and Congress each held public proceedings on merger policy in telecommunications. The proximity in timing was not accidental. The Commerce Committee of the U.S. House of Representatives had drafted legislation entitled, "The Telecommunications Merger Review Act of 2000," the purpose of which was to curtail the Commission's authority to impose conditions outside the formal rulemaking process and to accelerate the FCC's review by requiring final action within 60 to 90 days from the filing of a merger application. The Commission, in an effort to preempt some of the concerns raised by the proposed bill, and in anticipation of Congressional hearings on the legislation, held a public forum at which it presented its own proposal for streamlining FCC review of merger-related applications. Below are brief excerpts from testimony presented at the Congressional hearings on the draft legislation, followed by excerpts from the FCC's *Issues Memorandum*[8] presented at its public forum on merger review.

STATEMENT OF CHAIRMAN WILLIAM E. KENNARD
before the House Committee on Commerce; Subcommittee on Telecommunications, Trade and Consumer Products, March 14, 2000

The FCC Has a Legal Duty to Review Mergers

The FCC has the responsibility under Sections 214 and 310 of the Telecommunications Act to review whether the transfers or assignments of licenses or the authorizations sought in connection with a merger are in the public interest. Under the Communications Act, the FCC reviews applications relating to mergers in public proceedings, subject to the Administrative Procedure Act (APA) and judicial review. As a result, the FCC has addressed the often controversial issues surrounding these combinations. We do so in a forum that provides an opportunity to use our substantial expertise to examine the potential consequences of the proposed transactions with full participation by interested members of the public. Applying its expertise and taking the public comments into account, the FCC prepares a written decision addressing the issues. All of the FCC's decisions are subject to judicial review.

Competition remains an important consideration in these proceedings. The FCC must consider the impact of transactions on competition as part of the public interest standard. Also, creating competition where none existed before is a basic goal of the 1996 Act, but it is not the focus of the more general antitrust law provisions administered by the Department of Justice (DOJ) and the Federal Trade Commission (FTC). In addition, preserving competition is of particular concern in an environment where vigorous competition is being relied on to achieve goals formerly served by regulations and where mergers of unprecedented number and size are taking place.

The FCC is Working to Make the Process Better

The dramatic increase in merger activity, the complexity of the issues involved, and the extensive public comment on major mergers have required a substantial commitment of the FCC's resources. The FCC and its staff have worked hard to meet this challenge. I have taken additional steps in the last several months to make the FCC's process for reviewing merger-related applications more efficient, transparent, and predictable.

The Draft Bill Would Deny the FCC Sufficient Flexibility to Resolve Merger Cases

I would like to specifically address some of the proposals in a draft bill circulating on the Hill this past week known as "The Telecommunications Merger Review Act of 2000." I believe that the steps we have taken and are taking address

---

8. Issues Memorandum for March 1, 2000, Transactions Team Public Forum on Streamlining FCC Review of Applications Relating to Mergers, www.fcc.gov/transaction/issuesmemo.html.

the issues of speed, certainty, and inter-agency cooperation in a manner consistent with the FCC's duties and responsibilities under the law.

In contrast, the proposed bill would limit regulation to rulemaking and impose drastically shortened time limits on FCC action. These solutions would create speed and certainty only by sacrificing the meaningful participation of the American people, by eliminating regulatory flexibility in a context where it is most essential, and by casting significantly increased responsibilities (but no additional resources) on the DOJ and FTC while eliminating inter-agency cooperation. The bill is, in short, a recipe for making scrutiny of mergers less public, less flexible, and less likely.

With respect to public participation, the FCC process offers the *only forum* where the merger is considered in a *public proceeding* conducted under the APA. The DOJ and FTC investigations are exercises in prosecutorial discretion, conducted under the cover of confidentiality, with no requirement to explain action or inaction unless a lawsuit is initiated.

The bill requires final agency action within 60 or 90 days from the filing of an application, with no provision that the application be accurate or complete or that the applicant submit information to allow informed consideration by the agency or the public. By statute, the public has at least 30 days from public notice (which can occur only after the application is checked for accuracy and completeness) to file petitions to deny an application, and additional time is needed to allow responses to the petitions. This leaves the FCC very little time to obtain any additional information it needs in order to analyze the transaction and prepare a decision addressing the issues, including those raised by the public, sufficiently to survive judicial review. Speed in the administrative process will do the parties little good if decisions are reversed by the courts.

Requiring regulation by rulemaking, as opposed to case-by-case adjudication, is particularly inappropriate in the context of evaluating mergers in markets where technology is rapidly evolving. Rules work best when the future is fairly predictable and we can anticipate with confidence what factors will be relevant and what standards will reflect sound policy. Rules take a relatively long time to enact and to change and would not adapt to the quickly evolving communications industry. Of course, this oversimplifies the issue, since the question is not whether there will be any rules— there always are—but how much flexibility the standards will allow.

The FCC Role is Not Duplicative of Other Agencies

Finally, with respect to duplication with DOJ and the FTC, let me emphasize that the FCC has a special responsibility and somewhat different standard in cases involving the creation of competition to replace former regulated monopolies. We look at whether the proposed merger is consistent with the pro-competitive and market-opening goals of the 1996 Act, as opposed to the DOJ and FTC, which focus on possible injury to existing competition. As I noted previously, we also provide for public involvement in our review process and engage in procedures that are judicially reviewable.

In sum, I want to emphasize that the FCC plays a crucial role in the review of merger transactions in the communications industry, and we are taking the steps to improve our review process while preserving its integrity and unique contributions. The FCC seeks to preserve a public forum in which proposed mergers can be evaluated and responded to in a flexible way that is most appropriate in a rapidly evolving marketplace, and that makes most efficient use of the combined resources of federal agencies. Thank you again for the opportunity to submit this testimony and for your attention to these important issues.

STATEMENT OF COMMISSIONER HAROLD FURCHTGOTT-ROTH

before the House Committee on Commerce; Subcommittee on
Telecommunications, Trade and Consumer Products, March 14, 2000

The FCC Lacks "Merger" Review Authority

As a threshold matter, I would like to define the scope of the Commission's actual authority when reviewing, under sections 214 and 310 of the Communications, license transactions involving merging parties. Contrary to its frequent assertions, the Commission does not possess statutory authority under those provisions to review, writ large, the mergers or acquisitions of communications companies.

Rather, that Act charges the Commission with a much narrower task: review of the proposed transfer of radio station licenses from one party to another and review of the proposed transfer of interstate operational authorizations for common carriers. Nothing in the Communications Act speaks of jurisdiction to approve or disapprove the mergers that may occasion a transferor's desire to pass licenses on to a transferee. Under that Act, the Commission is required to determine whether the transfer of licenses serves the public interest, convenience and necessity.

By using the license transfer provisions of the Communications Act to bootstrap itself into possession of jurisdiction over the entire merger of two companies that happen to be the transferee and transferor of licenses, the Commission greatly expands its organic authority.

Duplication of Department of Justice & Federal Trade Commission Efforts

The Commission's focus on mergers rather than on license and authorization transfers creates another problem: our work often duplicates that of the Department of Justice's Antitrust Division and the Federal Trade Commission.

Merging companies should not have to jump through excessive federal antitrust hoops, and those hoops should be held out by the institutions with the express statutory authority and expertise to do so. Those agencies are the Department of Justice and the FTC. When the FCC gets into the game as well, it increases the costs of the merging parties and expends taxpayer funds, while adding little value from an antitrust perspective. A report issued last month by the International Competition Policy Advisory Committee reached this very conclusion.

If the Commission limited its review to the actual transfer of radio licenses, as opposed to the proposed merger that triggered the transfer, this problem of duplicated efforts and wasted resources would be avoided.

Potentially Arbitrary Review: Choice of Transfers for Full-Scale Review and Substantive Standards To Be Applied

The Commission annually approves tens of thousands of license transfers without any scrutiny or comment; others receive minimal review, and a select few are subjected to intense regulatory scrutiny. For example, mergers of companies like Mobil and Exxon involve the transfer of a substantial number of radio licenses, many of the same kind of licenses as those at issue in other high-profile proceedings, such as AT&T/TCI, and yet we take no Commission level action on those transfer applications. I do not advocate extensive review of all license transfer applications, but mean only to illustrate that we apply highly disparate levels of review to applications that arise under identical statutory provisions.

Unfortunately, there is no established Commission standard for distinguishing between the license transfers that trigger extensive analysis by the full Commission and those that do not. Nor do any of the Commission's orders in "merger" reviews elucidate the standard. Regulated entities and even their often sophisticated counsel are left to wonder whether or not their applications will receive relatively quick, pro forma review by the relevant Bureau, or whether their applications will take many months to process and engender open meetings, so-called public "fora," and full Commission action.

Moreover, there is clearly a different "public interest" test being applied, *sub silentio*, in different cases under the very same statutory provisions, usually sections 310 and 214. The cases that undergo extensive inquiry exhaustively discuss all kinds of service areas and issues ancillary to the use of the actual radio licenses, and the decisions that are granted at the Bureau level are relatively perfunctory in their public interest analysis. We should, after identifying the threshold test for license transfers that warrant thorough inquiry, articulate clearer substantive criteria to guide the Commission's inquiry.

The long and short of it is this: regulated entities currently have little basis for knowing how their applications will be treated, either procedurally or substantively. The license transfer process at the Commission is lacking in any transparent, fixed and meaningful standards. A person—even a well-trained lawyer— who wished to prepare for this process could find scant guidance in public sources of law. Rather, one would have to be trained in the unwritten ways of this Commission to know what to expect, and those expectations would often have little to do with the text of the Communications Act.

"Conditional" Approval of License Transfer Applications

Finally, I would like to express today, as I have done many times before, great apprehension about the Commission's practice of "conditioning" grants for license transfer applications.

I think it is entirely appropriate, under the Commission's organic statute, for the Commission to condition license transfer on compliance with existing statutory provisions and the FCC regulations that implement them. In fact, the Communications Act specifically contemplates such conditions. Section 303(r) provides that the "Commission shall...prescribe such...conditions, not inconsistent with law, as may be necessary to carry out the provisions of this Act."

All too often, however, this Commission places conditions on license transfers that have no basis in the text of the Communications Act. That is, the Commission requires companies to do certain things—things that it could not for lack of statutory authority require outright in a rulemaking—as a *quo* for the *quid* of receiving a license. Thus, the Commission imposes rules on merging companies that at best have never been considered, and at worst have been considered and rejected, by Congress.

Notes and Questions

1. The Road Ahead. On what points is there room for compromise between the differing positions of Kennard and Furchtgott-Roth? On what points is there fundamental disagreement? Do you think their testimony helped Congress to better understand the issues at stake? Do you think their testimony increased Congress' confidence in the FCC's ability to handle these issues without further legislative guidance?

2. Another Proposal. At about the same time as the above testimony was given, the FCC proposed to "streamline" its merger review process by committing to a timeline that would culminate in a final Commission order within 180 days from the filing of a transfer request. The steps in the proposed timeline are: (1) issuance of a public notice on the day of filing; (2) a public comment period lasting until day 30; (3) a reply comment period lasting until day 45; (3) review by the agency for completeness of the filing lasting until day 75; (4) analysis of the record and discussions with parties until day 110; (5) on day 110, major changes to the transaction at issue could be submitted by the parties, followed on day 130 by a public forum on any such changes; and (6) issuance of a final decision by day 180. *See Issues Memorandum for March 1, 2000, Transactions Team Public Forum on Streamlining FCC Review of Applications Relating to Mergers,* www.fcc.gov/transaction/issuesmemo.html.

In addition to addressing the question of timing, the Commission's *Issues Memorandum* also addressed several other issues that have given rise to concern about the Commission's role in reviewing mergers. Two particularly important issues addressed in the memorandum were: (1) variability in standards from transaction to transaction and (2) coordination with the federal antitrust agencies. With respect to the first point, the Commission wrote:

> The Commission's review process has sometimes been characterized as imposing different levels or even different "standards" of review. For example, in many cases "routine" applications may be granted fairly rapidly; others require more detailed and lengthy consideration; and still others are subject to intensive analysis of competition and other public interest issues on the basis of an extensive record. These differences in procedure do not result from a difference in the applicable standards for Commission review under the Communications Act and the implementing regulations. That Act applies a similar "public interest" test to transfers, assignments, or authorizations relating to mergers. The circumstances of a particular case, however, may present issues that require a more thorough analysis to determine whether the public interest standard is met. For example, (1) the transaction to which the application relates may create a level of horizontal concentration in a market for communications services where the FCC under the 1996 Act is relying on vigorous competition to meet the goals of the Communications Act, (2) granting the application may arguably result in a violation of either the Act or the Commission's rules, (3) the applicant may be seeking a waiver of the Commission's rules, or (4) the transaction may result in a substantial degree of vertical integration that may have a substantial impact on the health of competition with respect to one or more communications services. There may be substantial public comments filed in the review

process addressing these or other issues for which the FCC is given responsibility under the public interest standard in the Communications Act. Cases involving circumstances such as these require more attention than those that can be processed easily under established rules and precedents.

With respect to coordination and potential overlap issues, the *Issues Memorandum* distinguished the Commission's role from that played by the other federal agencies and, indeed, suggested that the inquiries might be complementary:

> The Department of Justice and/or the Federal Trade Commission review the competitive impacts of a number of the transactions that require changes in FCC licenses or authorizations under the antitrust laws. Those reviews differ from the FCC review in substance and procedure. They involve narrower issues than the public interest standard established by the Communications Act. In addition, the process of review by these agencies is an investigation largely hidden from public view that most often results in either no action (with no explanation), a consent decree that is presented to a court after negotiations with the government have been completed, or (rarely) a full trial of a law suit in federal court. The agencies have prosecutorial discretion and no obligation to explain the basis of their decision if they take no enforcement action. In contrast, the FCC review process is a public adjudication, with full opportunity for public participation, which results in a decision that must be agreed to by at least a majority of a five-member Commission (or be made on delegated authority), that must explain its basis and address the arguments made by the parties, and that is subject to judicial review.

Despite the substantive differences, the issues addressed in antitrust review and the FCC's public interest review overlap to some degree. Similarly, despite the procedural differences, the reviews must take place roughly simultaneously. With the increase in these transactions over the last several years, the federal agencies have gained experience in coordinating their efforts to avoid duplication, increase efficient use of the limited government resources, and avoid reaching results that would impose inconsistent requirements on the applicants. Thus, the agencies have found it useful to request waivers from the applicants and other parties to permit FCC review of documents and discussions among the personnel involved in reviewing the transactions in the respective agencies. Discussions and efforts to improve this coordination continue.

PART FOUR

THE INTERNET AND ADVANCED SERVICES

This Part of the book focuses on the area of telecommunications that has seen by far the most explosive growth in recent years—the Internet. As we will discuss, the Internet began simply as a set of protocols and a backbone of physical connections that allowed computers to share data one to another. But, because of the flexibility those protocols allowed, the Internet quickly expanded. It grew in terms of the number of users and host computers involved; and, even more important, it grew in terms of the variety of applications it supported—most notably the graphical interface known as the World Wide Web.

The Internet per se has not been subject to much direct governmental regulation. Indeed, as we will discuss in Chapter Twenty, although the federal government was instrumental in creating the Internet, the government's basic position in recent years has been to favor market deference over substantial government intervention. One significant deviation from this general policy came in the form of the federal government's involvement with the "domain name system," a naming hierarchy that in essence tells connected computers where to find particular websites. The government ultimately transferred management authority to a private nonprofit corporation, however, and so even here a private entity exercises direct control and the government is in the background. Another significant deviation has been Congress's repeated attempts to regulate indecency online. But—despite the significant controversy associated with these various indecency provisions—these attempts have been relatively modest as compared to the government's similar involvement in the broadcast setting.

All this is not to imply that there are no government regulations designed to affect the Internet. Of course there are. What is interesting, however, is that many of them take the indirect form of regulating the services or facilities consumers use to access the Internet rather than regulating the Internet itself. Specifically, many FCC regulations govern the behavior of either firms that themselves provide "broadband" telecommunications capability or firms that operate networks over which this sort of high-speed data transfer can take place. For example, just as there are regulations that foster competition in conventional voice service by requiring incumbent local exchange carriers to allow competitors access to unbundled network elements, there are regulations that foster broadband competition by requiring ILECs to unbundle network elements that are (arguably) critical for broadband deployment. Other regulations are tailored to remove barriers to investment and otherwise promote competition in the cable modem, fixed wireless, and satellite markets. These regulations affect a wide array of applications where fast information transfer is essential, and, taken together, this entire collection of services and technologies has come to be called the market for "advanced services." We discuss these technologies and the relevant regulations in Chapter Twenty-One.

Chapter Twenty-Two moves beyond regulation of infrastructure and turns to the FCC's other significant role in Internet regulation: its regulation of the relationship between Internet service providers (ISPs) and local exchange carriers. As modern readers surely know, one typical way consumers access their ISP is by placing a local telephone call to a computer facility owned by the ISP. The ISP receives the call, manipulates the incoming data, and (in ways we will consider further in the chapter) facilitates end-user access to the Internet. The regulatory puzzle here is to ask how the Commission should characterize that initial call to the ISP. Is the ISP just like any other call recipient, in which case the call is simply a local call between two LEC subscribers? Is the ISP more like an IXC, "receiving" the call but only for the purpose of passing the communication on to computers in other states and countries? If the latter, should ISPs be required to pay access charges and in that way contribute to universal service funding? If the former, should ISP traffic be eligible for reciprocal compensation? Does either answer change insofar as people are using the Internet for real-time voice conversations?

In Chapter Twenty-Three, we conclude this Part—and the book—by taking a step back from the technical and regulatory details to ask some larger questions about the appropriate role for both the FCC specifically and telecommunications law more generally. At the end of the day, have the preceding chapters convinced you that telecommunications markets need an expert agency and highly specialized rules, or are you left with the impression, instead, that telecommunications markets should be subject to the same laws of general applicability that discipline competitors and encourage innovation in other markets, for example the markets for automobiles, food products, and computer equipment?

Chapter Twenty

THE INTERNET AND
ITS REGULATION

The purpose of this chapter is:

- to provide background on what the Internet is, and how it came to be;
- and to consider the main forms of direct regulation imposed on the Internet by briefly discussing regulation of the domain name system and then studying Congress's attempts to regulate indecent content online.

The Internet has risen from obscurity to ubiquity with astonishing speed. Indeed, it has become almost too obvious to say that the Internet has profoundly affected the world of telecommunications—and the world more generally. The Internet's ability to make every person a "broadcaster" or a "publisher," combined with increases in its global reach, the volume of information it can access, and the speeds with which people can interconnect, portend an even bigger impact in the future. But just what is "the Internet"? And what is, and should be, the government's role in it?

To begin to answer these questions, in this chapter we introduce two sets of background materials. In the first section below, we offer an overview of the Internet's history and basic architecture. Our purpose here is to arm the reader with sufficient information to understand the issues raised in the documents that follow later in this Part.[1] In the second section, we survey some of the prominent Internet issues that have been addressed by government entities other than the FCC. We consider the FCC's involvement throughout the remainder of the Part; but we thought it helpful to first consider how other arms of the federal government have thought about the Internet and intervened in its development. In particular, this section considers the Clinton Administration's policy of regulatory forbearance and Congress's recent experience with regulating content online.

---

1. This discussion is far too brief to convey the richness of the Internet's history and structure. For a fuller discussion of the Internet's history (and the source for much of the history that follows), *see* Barry Leiner et al., A Brief History of the Internet, http://www.isoc.org/internet/history/brief.html. For a fuller discussion of Internet architecture, *see, e.g.,* Kevin Werbach, Digital Tornado: The Internet and Telecommunications Policy (1997) (working paper from the FCC's Office of Plans and Policy) http://www.fcc.gov/Bureaus/OPP/working_papers/oppwp29pdf.html; ACLU v. Reno, 929 F. Supp. 824 (E.D. Pa. 1996) (findings of fact), *aff'd*, 521 U.S. 844 (1997).

I. THE HISTORY AND ARCHITECTURE OF THE INTERNET

Early History

A discussion of the birth of the Internet begins to sound as remote today as does the cretaceous period (*e.g.*, "In 1960, when computers were the size of houses, and the mighty behemoth IBM ruled the earth..."). But this history is nevertheless important because, for better or worse, it will for the foreseeable future continue to affect how the U.S. government views the Internet. The idea of a computer "network of networks" was captured by J.C.R. Licklider at MIT in 1962.[2] Licklider was also the first head of the Information Processing Techniques Office at the Defense Advanced Research Projects Agency,[3] an agency of the U.S. Department of Defense. It was at DARPA that Licklider's ideas germinated most fruitfully, and it was under DARPA that the technology we recognize today as the Internet was first developed. At this time—essentially the mid-1960s—the network was known as the ARPANET.

The purpose of the ARPANET was to permit units within the Department of Defense (DOD) and various DOD contractors to share information and hardware with one another easily and quickly, regardless of the distance between them. The ARPANET was first publicly demonstrated in 1972. In this, and many other ways that will be discussed below, the U.S. Government can be said to have paid for and built much of the U.S. portions of the Internet. Contrast this with, for example, the telephone and cable television plant, which have been largely built by private entities using private funds.

New technology, such as the ARPANET, will often flourish when the consumers for that technology are provided with an application that makes the technology too attractive to pass up—sometimes referred to as the "killer app." For television viewers, the killer app may have been the entertainment value of seeing Milton Berle in a dress from their living rooms. For personal computers, perhaps the first killer app to ignite user interest was the VISI-CALC spreadsheet. The first killer app for the ARPANET was email, which was introduced in 1972. Once the utility of ARPANET and email had been demonstrated, it was not long before other constituencies that had ready access to computers began to push for their own networks. By the mid-1970s, networks such as USENET (Unix users), BITNET (research and education users), MFENET (U.S. Department of Energy magnetic fusion energy researchers), and SPAN (NASA space physics researchers) began to spring up, often using government funding, though sometimes using private funds (*e.g.*, BITNET, which was funded by The Corporation for Education and Research Networking).

---

2. He called his idea a "Galactic Network"—an interconnected set of computers throughout the world through which anyone could quickly access data and programs from any site. *See* A Brief History of the Internet, *supra* note 1.

3. Referred to at various times in its history as "DARPA" and "ARPA," but referred to herein under its current acronym of "DARPA."

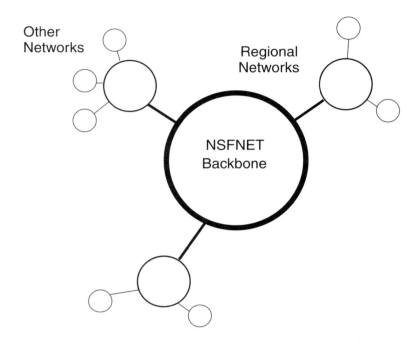

Figure 20.1. THE NSFNET. The NSF helped to build the Internet by providing much of the original backbone infrastructure that connected regional networks into the giant "network of networks" that would mature into today's Internet. This diagram is based on a figure in Kevin Werbach, Digital Tornado: The Internet and Telecommunications Policy (1997).

Networks that sprang up in this era typically relied on disparate networking architectures. That is, each of these networks organized its information differently and so, for the most part, information could not easily move from one of these networks to another. The fundamental principle underlying the Internet, by contrast, is that individual computers and local networks are able to communicate easily regardless of the type of equipment employed. Such a "network of networks" obviously depends on the presence of a single set of communication rules that are followed by every affiliated computer. Two researchers developed such a set of generic rules and made them public in 1973; those rules became what we now know as "TCP/IP"—the Transmission Control Protocol/Internet Protocol.[4] TCP/IP is in many ways the heart of the Internet; the goal of the Internet is connectivity, and the tools used are TCP and IP.[5] In 1974, DARPA contracted with three groups to implement TCP/IP. On January 1, 1983, a milestone event occurred: on that day every host computer on the ARPANET switched to TCP/IP for internetworking.

---

4. *See* V. G. Cerf and R. E. Kahn, A Protocol for Packet Network Interconnection, IEEE Trans. Comm. Tech., Vol. COM-22, V 5, p. 627 (1974). The creators of these protocols were Robert Kahn (then at DARPA) and Vinton Cerf (then at Stanford).

5. *See* Internet Architecture Board, RFC 1958, June 1996; Internet Activities Board, RFC 791, September 1981.

DARPA was not the only government agency to play a central role in the creation of the Internet. In the mid-1980s, the National Science Foundation (NSF) undertook a major new government-funded networking initiative when it began work on the NSFNET, a "network of networks" intended to serve the higher education community. In 1985, a second milestone event occurred—the NSF decided to adopt TCP/IP for the NSFNET and announced that it would from that point onward work with DARPA to ensure interoperability between the two national networks. The agencies would share the costs of common infrastructure, and NSF network traffic would be allowed to travel on DARPA infrastructure. The NSF, in turn, would work with NASA and the Department of Energy to provide an ever-expanding "backbone"—the long-haul segments of the network— and also to fund university network connections and supercomputers. The NSF also contracted with IBM, MCI, and Merit Network, Inc., to manage the NFSNET backbone. Some $200 million was spent on developing the NFSNET between 1986 and 1995. The success of the NFSNET was such that the ARPANET was officially decommissioned in 1990, by which time TCP/IP had largely replaced the disparate networking protocols in earlier use.

A different federal entity (the National Science and Technology Council) formed the Federal Networking Council to coordinate the various government agencies involved and also to coordinate with international organizations supporting the global Internet. The Federal Networking Council passed a resolution providing a definition of the Internet that has become commonly used:

"Internet" refers to the global information system that:

(i) is logically linked together by a globally unique address space based on the Internet Protocol (IP) or its subsequent extensions/follow-ons;

(ii) is able to support communications using the Transmission Control Protocol/Internet Protocol (TCP/IP) suite or its subsequent extensions/follow-ons, and/or other IP-compatible protocols; and

(iii) provides, uses or makes accessible, either publicly or privately, high level services layered on the communications and related infrastructure described herein.[6]

Basic Characteristics

A working paper for the FCC's Office of Plans and Policy[7] lays out the central features of the Internet this way:

The fundamental operational characteristics of the Internet are that it is a distributed, interoperable, packet-switched network.

A distributed network has no one central repository of information or control, but is comprised of an interconnected web of "host" computers, each of which can be accessed from virtually any point on the network. Thus, an Internet user can obtain information from a host computer in another state or another country just as easily as obtaining information from across the street, and there is no hierarchy through which the information must flow or be monitored. Routers throughout the network reg-

---

6. FNC Resolution Defining "Internet" (1995), http://www.fnc.gov/Internet_res.html.
7. Werbach, *supra* note 1.

(a)   (b)

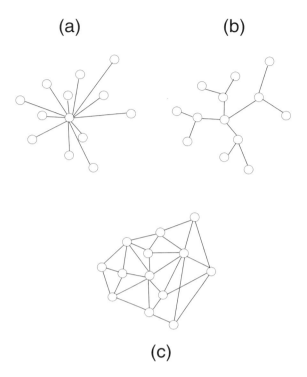

(c)

Figure 20.2. DISTRIBUTED NETWORKS. The Internet is not a centralized network (panel a), nor a decentralized network (panel b), but instead a distributed network (panel c). Among its other virtues, a distributed network can continue to operate even if a given node on the network fails, and a distributed network can easily route traffic around congested areas, thus increasing speed of service.

ulate the flow of data at each connection point. (By contrast, in a centralized network, all users would connect to single location.[8]) The distributed nature of the Internet gives it robust survivability characteristics, because there is no one point of failure for the network, but it makes measurement and governance difficult.

An interoperable network uses open protocols so that many different types of networks and facilities can be transparently linked together, and allows multiple services to be provided to different users over the same network. The Internet can run over virtually any type of facility that can transmit data, including copper and fiber optic circuits of telephone companies, coaxial cable of cable companies, and various types of wireless connections. The Internet also interconnects users of thousands of different local and regional networks, using many different types of computers. The interoperability of the Internet is made possible by the TCP/IP

---

8. In some cases, centralized networks use regional servers to "cache" frequently accessed data or otherwise involve some degree of distributed operation.

protocol, which defines a common structure for Internet data and for the routing of that data through the network.

A packet-switched network means that data transmitted over the network is split up into small chunks, or "packets." Unlike "circuit-switched" networks such as the public switched telephone network (PSTN), a packet-switched network is "connectionless."[9] In other words, a dedicated end-to-end transmission path (or circuit) does not need to be opened for each transmission.[10] Rather, each router calculates the best routing for a packet at a particular moment in time, given current traffic patterns, and sends the packet to the next router. Thus, even two packets from the same message may not travel the same physical path through the network. This mechanism is referred to as "dynamic routing." When packets arrive at the destination point, they must be reassembled, and packets that do not arrive for whatever reason must generally be re-sent. This system allows network resources to be used more efficiently, as many different communications can be routed simultaneously over the same transmission facilities. On the other hand, the inability of the sending computer to ensure that sufficient bandwidth will be available between the two points creates difficulties for services that require constant transmission rates, such as streaming video and voice applications.[11]

Packet Switching and Addressing

As the above excerpt suggests, in terms of structure the Internet is, in many ways, the antithesis of the PSTN. The PSTN is a circuit switched network, which means, in somewhat oversimplified terms, that when you dial a number a pathway is dedicated to that call and remains dedicated to that call until you hang up. Even when no one on the call is speaking, the phone system is still reserving a pathway for the call. The Internet works quite differently. When a request is made by a client computer for a document, the server holding the document responds by sending the requested information across the Internet. No circuit is dedicated to this "call." Instead, the IP protocol breaks the information (whether voice, video, or some other form of data) into "packets," each of which can be thought of as a payload (a small piece of the requested data) and a guidance system (a destination IP address).[12]

---

9. Some newer technologies, such as asynchronous transfer mode (ATM) switching, allow for the creation of "virtual circuits" through the Internet, which allow traffic to follow a defined route through the network. However, information is still transmitted in the form of packets.

10. In actuality, much of the PSTN, especially for long distance traffic, uses digital multiplexing to increase transmission capacity. Thus, beyond the truly dedicated connection along the subscriber loop to the local switch, the "circuit" tied up for a voice call is a set of time slices or frequency assignments in multiplexing systems that send multiple calls over the same wires and fiber optic circuits.

11. "Streaming" voice and video applications are those in which the data available to the receiving user is updated as data packets are received, rather than waiting until an entire image or sound file is downloaded to the recipient's computer.

12. Because no particular route must be used, the Internet is relatively stable to an outage on one part of the network. For example, if Illinois goes off line, remaining network traffic will continue to be routed via whatever route is efficient at the time.

More specifically, each packet includes a header that indicates where the data originates and where it is being sent. In order for the packet to arrive, each computer must be given a unique address, analogous to the unique telephone number used to route phone calls to a given phone. TCP/IP solves this problem by defining locations on the Internet through the use of "IP numbers." IP numbers include four address blocks consisting of numbers between 0 and 256, separated by periods (*e.g.* 216.92.212.164). Fortunately for humans, IP numbers can be represented by alphanumeric domain and host names, which allow Internet addresses to be rendered into more easily recognizable (and memorable) forms such as the ubiquitous "www.EnglishWordHere.com."[13]

The usability of these alphanumeric addresses depends on a system for cross-referencing host names with their associated IP numbers. This translation of host names to the appropriate IP numbers is accomplished via the domain name system. Thus a user's host computer relies on the domain name system to translate a host name into a numeric address that can be understood by the routers that make the Internet work. The domain name system was initially managed by Jon Postel at UCLA (later at the University of Southern California's Information Sciences Institute) under contract with DARPA, and provided to the networking community by SRI International, also under contract with DARPA. When the ARPANET was phased out, the NSF assumed responsibility for the domain name system and, in 1992, entered into a contract with Network Solutions, Inc., to manage the registration of domain names on more or less a first-come, first-served basis. In 1992, NSI registered 200 domain names per month; by 1998, this number had reached 120,000 names per month.

This association of host names with IP numbers highlights a deeper addressing issue: in order for the whole routing scheme to work, and thus for there to be an "Internet" through which all computers can connect, there must be a generally accepted system that tells computers where they can find a given IP number on the network. Without such a system, a computer receiving a message with either a host name or an IP number would not know how to forward the message on toward its destination. Thus at the top of (and in some senses above) the domain name system is a set of "root" servers, each of which lists the IP numbers of the computers containing the authoritative files for each of the top-level domains. At the next level are the computers holding those top-level domain zone files, each of which lists the IP numbers of the servers at the next level of the hierarchy, and so on. This system is central to the smooth operation of the Internet. It, and the domain name system more generally, is considered in greater detail in the next section's discussion of the regulation of the Internet.

Services

The actual services provided to end users through the Internet are not defined through the routing mechanisms of TCP/IP, but depend instead on higher-

---

13. These names can be broken down into the following components: a "host name," *i.e.*, the name of a specific machine; a "domain name," *i.e.*, the name of a specific local network where the host resides; and a "top-level domain name," which identifies which global network is involved. Top-level domains can be further broken down into two categories: generic top-level domains (*e.g.*, .com, .edu, and .gov), and country code top-level domains (*e.g.*, .uk for the United Kingdom, .de for Germany), which are, as the name suggests, designed to host particular countries' networks.

level application protocols that enable particular services. These protocols are not embedded in the Internet itself. This means that a new application-layer protocol, and the new service that it enables, can be added at any time, and it can be operated over the Internet as long as one server computer can transmit data in the proper format and one client computer can receive and interpret the data. Prominent examples of these protocols are the hypertext transport protocol (HTTP), file transfer protocol (FTP), network news transport protocol (NNTP), and simple mail transfer protocol (SMTP).

A number of services were available over the Internet by the late 1980s, including not only email but also other functions like Telnet, which allows a user to log into a proprietary network and retrieve data remotely, and FTP, which allows a user to transfer files between a remote host computer and her own system. These programs were quite useful, but they did not capture the public's attention. Internet use was therefore confined to a relatively small number of people, and even in the early 1990s most Americans were not aware of it (except, perhaps, as a research tool for scientists). Again, explosive growth awaited the next killer app. In 1992, the U.S. Congress turned a corner by granting the NSF the statutory authority to permit commercial traffic on NFS-NET. At about the same time, the killer apps that would lead to the explosive growth of the network appeared in the form of the World Wide Web and the Web browser.

Building on the idea of hypermedia,[14] in 1989 Tim Berners-Lee created the concept of the World Wide Web. The Web contains documents, typically with embedded links to various other documents, written in a standard format such as "hypertext markup language" (HTML). HTML is code that describes the structure of a page, a page that a browser can then render as a screen image in the form of a virtual document. The Web browser provides a "smart" interface that can interpret the page for display without any need for the user to know anything about the underlying data structure.

Berners-Lee also wrote the first Internet browser, but it was the creation of a different browser, Mosaic, by Marc Andreessen and Eric Bina in 1992 while at the National Center for Supercomputer Applications (NCSA) in Illinois, that led to the Web we know today. Browsers rely on standard protocols (FTP, NNTP, or HTTP, for example) layered on top of TCP/IP to retrieve and display documents. This means that browsers can combine text and graphical material—and can incorporate all of the other major Internet services such as FTP, email, and news—into one standard interface, and can even provide for inline images (pictures) within a document. With browsers like Mosaic, however, Web use was limited to relatively sophisticated users running some flavor of the Unix operating system. The Web finally left the computer science world and entered popular culture when several Mosaic developers left the National Center for Supercomputer Applications in Illinois to start Netscape Communications. Netscape developed a browser that was easily installable on personal computers and (relatively) freely available. The availability of a browser that offered easy use, installation, and ac-

---

14. This is a special type of database system in which objects (text, pictures, music, programs, and so on) can be creatively linked to each other. When you select an object, you can see the other objects that are linked to it.

cess to a world of linked documents provided the killer app that drives the growth of the Internet to this day.[15]

II. REGULATION OF THE INTERNET

There are myriad laws that affect the use and development of the Internet. Almost every category of law that applies to offline activity can apply as well to online activity. In many cases, the law is one of general application and questions arise regarding exactly how it will apply to the online world. For instance, a number of lawsuits have involved questions over the online contacts sufficient to establish personal jurisdiction.[16] In other situations, Congress has enacted statutes with the Internet specifically in mind.[17] One of the most prominent examples is the Digital Millennium Copyright Act,[18] which creates protections against the circumvention of technological measures that in turn protect copyrighted works. Such laws will have important effects on both the online and offline worlds.

But what about direct governmental regulation of the Internet? In the context of the other technologies we have addressed in the book, we have seen examples of laws that do not merely peripherally affect a telecommunications technology but instead put the government in the position of squarely regulating some aspect of that technology. Such laws make up the centerpiece of the government's responses to technologies like broadcast, cable, and satellite. To what extent does the government play such a direct role in the regulation of the Internet?

Perhaps the most obvious role for a governing (or at least central) force is in the management of the addressing system. As we discussed above, crucial to the existence of the Internet as a single coherent network is a routing system whereby a message from any point on the network can reach its intended destination elsewhere on the network. This requires not only that each computer have a unique alphanumeric name and an associated IP address, but also that there be agreed-upon repositories of those IP addresses, and a mechanism to resolve the address from the alphanumeric name. When someone sends a message to "fcc.gov," her computer needs to ask a server where to find "fcc.gov," and if servers point in different directions (*i.e.*, to different computers) then some messages will not go to the proper place. The difficulties that would result from such conflicting address systems have been avoided on the Internet because a given server gets its information about where to look for the FCC's IP number from a server above it in the hierarchy, culminating in information at the top from the

---

15. Between 1994 and 2000, for example, the number of people using the Internet increased one-hundredfold, from 3 million to more than 300 million. From 1999 to 2000 alone, the number increased by 80%. U.S. Department of Commerce, Digital Economy 2000 (2000).

16. *See, e.g.*, Cybersell, Inc. v. Cybersell, Inc., 130 F.3d 414 (9th Cir. 1997).

17. States have also passed legislation regulating aspects of online activity, but those statutes face the hurdle posed by the negative implications of the Commerce Clause of the Constitution (often called the "dormant commerce clause"). *See, e.g.*, ACLU v. Johnson, 194 F.3d 1149 (10th Cir. 1999).

18. 17 U.S.C. §§1201–1332.

central root server (known as the "A" root server). Virtually all computers point toward servers that follow this hierarchy, so there is no disagreement about the addresses.

Control of the databases in these servers, and in particular in the "A" root server, is thus in some ways akin to centralized governance. It is not true governance, because users could always direct their computers to servers that look to a different address list; but it would probably take a coordinated defection to topple this hierarchy, and such a defection has never occurred and would be difficult to achieve. Indeed, the U.S. government helps to insure the primacy of the "A" root server by playing a role in the operation of many of the root servers at the next level of the hierarchy.[19] Because all of the servers at this next level get their information from the "A" root server database and dispense it to servers throughout the Internet, any attempt at supplanting the "A" root server would run the risk of "splitting the root" unless the United States government went along.

The government in this way helps to cement the position of the "A" root server database, but, interestingly, it has abjured direct control over that server. For most of the 1990s, the "A" root server database, and the domain name system that rested upon it, were maintained by Network Solutions, a private firm. In 1998 the government issued a statement of policy proposing a privatization of the management of Internet names and addresses. The statement articulated four principles: stability, representation, competition, and—where coordination was necessary—"private, bottom-up coordination" (because "a private coordinating process is likely to be more flexible than government and to move rapidly enough to meet the changing needs.")[20] The document called for the creation of a private nonprofit corporation that would take over responsibility for allocating the IP address space; that entity would also oversee operation of the root server system and determine whether to add new top level domains to the root system.[21] Shortly thereafter, a nonprofit entity called the Internet Corporation for Assigned Names and Numbers (ICANN) was incorporated, and the government (through the Department of Commerce) signed a memorandum of understanding with ICANN transferring these functions to ICANN.[22]

This arrangement with ICANN has generated quite a bit of controversy in the Internet community, with particularly heated concerns raised about its broad powers and its perceived lack of democratic accountability.[23] Space considerations prevent us from doing justice to these issues in this book, but one point bears emphasizing: the U.S. government chose not to control the root server and domain name system itself. It may well be that the government believed that di-

---

19. *See* Statement of Policy, *Management of Internet Names and Addresses*, 63 Fed. Reg. 31741, 31742 (1998).

20. *Management of Internet Names and Addresses*, 63 Fed. Reg. at 31749.

21. *Id.*

22. *See* Memorandum of Understanding Between the U.S. Department of Commerce and Internet Corporation for Assigned Names and Numbers (1998), http://www.icann.org/general/icann-mou-25nov98.htm.

23. *See, e.g.*, A. Michael Froomkin, A Wrong Turn in Cyberspace: Using ICANN To Route Around the APA and the Constitution, 50 Duke L .J. 17 (2000); materials collected by ICANNWatch, www.icannwatch.org. The article by Professor Froomkin also presents comprehensive background on the domain name system and ICANN.

rect governmental control was not a viable option — and that it was correct in so believing — based on, for example, the greater expertise existing outside the government, the increasing internationalization of the Internet, the advantages of decentralized, bottom-up coordination, and so on. The point is simply that, for whatever reason, the government chose not to arrogate this authority to itself. The government helped to create the Internet, and it had an opportunity to attempt to manage it, but it refrained from doing so.

A. The Principles of Internet (Un)Regulation

The government's 1998 decision to privatize the management of Internet names and addresses did not come out of the blue. In fact, it flowed from (and was in many senses preordained by) the Clinton Administration's central statement on Internet policy, the Framework for Global Electronic Commerce.

A FRAMEWORK FOR GLOBAL ELECTRONIC COMMERCE
http://www.ecommerce.gov/framewrk.htm (1997)

PRINCIPLES

1. *The private sector should lead.*

Though government played a role in financing the initial development of the Internet, its expansion has been driven primarily by the private sector. For electronic commerce to flourish, the private sector must continue to lead. Innovation, expanded services, broader participation, and lower prices will arise in a market-driven arena, not in an environment that operates as a regulated industry.

Accordingly, governments should encourage industry self-regulation wherever appropriate and support the efforts of private sector organizations to develop mechanisms to facilitate the successful operation of the Internet. Even where collective agreements or standards are necessary, private entities should, where possible, take the lead in organizing them. Where government action or intergovernmental agreements are necessary, on taxation for example, private sector participation should be a formal part of the policy making process.

2. *Governments should avoid undue restrictions on electronic commerce.*

Parties should be able to enter into legitimate agreements to buy and sell products and services across the Internet with minimal government involvement or intervention. Unnecessary regulation of commercial activities will distort development of the electronic marketplace by decreasing the supply and raising the cost of products and services for consumers the world over. Business models must evolve rapidly to keep pace with the breakneck speed of change in the technology; government attempts to regulate are likely to be outmoded by the time they are finally enacted, especially to the extent such regulations are technology-specific.

Accordingly, governments should refrain from imposing new and unnecessary regulations, bureaucratic procedures, or taxes and tariffs on commercial activities that take place via the Internet.

3. *Where governmental involvement is needed, its aim should be to support and enforce a predictable, minimalist, consistent and simple legal environment for commerce.*

In some areas, government agreements may prove necessary to facilitate electronic commerce and protect consumers. In these cases, governments should establish a predictable and simple legal environment based on a decentralized, contractual model of law rather than one based on top-down regulation. This may involve states as well as national governments. Where government intervention is necessary to facilitate electronic commerce, its goal should be to ensure competition, protect intellectual property and privacy, prevent fraud, foster transparency, support commercial transactions, and facilitate dispute resolution.

4. *Governments should recognize the unique qualities of the Internet.*

The genius and explosive success of the Internet can be attributed in part to its decentralized nature and to its tradition of bottom-up governance. These same characteristics pose significant logistical and technological challenges to existing regulatory models, and governments should tailor their policies accordingly.

Electronic commerce faces significant challenges where it intersects with existing regulatory schemes. We should not assume, for example, that the regulatory frameworks established over the past sixty years for telecommunications, radio and television fit the Internet. Regulation should be imposed only as a necessary means to achieve an important goal on which there is a broad consensus. Existing laws and regulations that may hinder electronic commerce should be reviewed and revised or eliminated to reflect the needs of the new electronic age.

5. *Electronic Commerce over the Internet should be facilitated on a global basis.*

The Internet is emerging as a global marketplace. The legal framework supporting commercial transactions on the Internet should be governed by consistent principles across state, national, and international borders that lead to predictable results regardless of the jurisdiction in which a particular buyer or seller resides.

Notes and Questions

1. **Deference to the Private Sector.** Do these principles give short shrift to problems with private sector leadership? Do they lean too far toward private leadership? Do they not go far enough?

2. **Comparisons to Broadcast, Cable, and Telephone.** Are these principles consistent with the government's regulation of broadcast, cable, and telephony? If not, was the government wrong in those other contexts? Further, note the irony: the government played a crucial role in funding and helping to create the Internet, but it says that it will refrain from regulating the Internet. Meanwhile, the government did not create the broadcast spectrum or pay for cable and telephone wire, and the broadcasting, cable, and telephone industries developed with few

direct financial contributions from government sources,[24] and yet each of those technologies is heavily regulated. Which approach makes more sense? Could both be right?

3. The Domain Name System. Is this statement of principles consistent with the decision made in 1998 to privatize the system of managing Internet names and addresses? What would be a less regulatory position than the one the government adopted in 1998?

4. Electronic Commerce. The above principles, and in fact the entire document of which they are a part, focus on electronic commerce. Is that an appropriate focus? Would it have been better for the Clinton administration to have focused on how to improve the content available on the Internet?

B. Content Regulation

The discussion thus far has focused on direct structural regulation of the Internet but has passed over another regulatory possibility: content regulation. As we have seen with respect to broadcast and cable, content neutral structural regulation is typically only part of the regulatory story. In these other contexts, the government has both sought to increase programming it deems meritorious and decrease programming it deems deleterious. Thus far with respect to the Internet, the government has not attempted to mandate increases in content that it favors, but it has attempted to limit the availability of content it disfavors. Specifically, the government has enacted statutes designed to limit one form of "bad" data—sexual material.

We begin, below, with the regulation of sexual material transmitted via the telephone. Long before the Internet arose, Congress had become concerned about children's ability to call services that offer smut, and Congress addressed that concern with legislation prohibiting indecent or obscene communications over the telephone network. After the Supreme Court invalidated that legislation in *Sable* (which we excerpt below), Congress responded by passing new legislation that sought to respond to the infirmities identified in *Sable*, and that new legislation was upheld by lower courts. When, a few years later, Congress became concerned about the ability of children to gain access to sexual material via the Internet, Congress returned to the provision regulating telephone smut (47 U.S.C. §223) and amended it so that it regulated sexual material delivered not only via telephone but also via the Internet. The Supreme Court then completed the circle by relying in part on *Sable* to strike down this regulation of the Internet.

i. Indecent Communication via Telephone

SABLE COMMUNICATIONS OF CALIFORNIA, INC. v. FCC
492 U.S. 115 (1989)

WHITE, J., delivered the opinion for a unanimous Court with respect to Parts I, II, and IV, and the opinion of the Court with respect to Part III, in which REHN-

---

24. There was a major non-monetary contribution to broadcast, of course, in the granting of spectrum licenses to broadcasters free of explicit fees. *See* Chapter Four.

QUIST, C.J., and BLACKMUN, O'CONNOR, SCALIA, and KENNEDY, JJ., joined. SCALIA, J., filed a concurring opinion. BRENNAN, J., filed an opinion concurring in part and dissenting in part, in which MARSHALL and STEVENS, JJ., joined.

JUSTICE WHITE delivered the opinion of the Court.

The issue before us is the constitutionality of §223(b) of the Communications Act of 1934. 47 U.S.C. §223(b). The statute, as amended in 1988, imposes an outright ban on indecent as well as obscene interstate commercial telephone messages. The District Court upheld the prohibition against obscene interstate telephone communications for commercial purposes, but enjoined the enforcement of the statute insofar as it applied to indecent messages. We affirm the District Court in both respects.

I

In 1983, Sable Communications, Inc., a Los Angeles-based affiliate of Carlin Communications, Inc., began offering sexually oriented prerecorded telephone messages (popularly known as "dial-a-porn") through the Pacific Bell telephone network.[25] Sable arranged with Pacific Bell to use special telephone lines, designed to handle large volumes of calls simultaneously. Those who called the adult message number were charged a special fee. The fee was collected by Pacific Bell and divided between the phone company and the message provider.

In 1988, Sable brought suit in District Court seeking declaratory and injunctive relief against enforcement of the recently amended §223(b). The 1988 amendments to the statute imposed a blanket prohibition on indecent as well as obscene interstate commercial telephone messages. [The FCC appeals the District Court's decision striking down the prohibition on indecent messages, and Sable appeals the decision upholding the ban on obscene messages.]

II

Congress made its first effort explicitly to address "dial-a-porn" when it added subsection 223(b) to the 1934 Communications Act. The relevant provision of the Act made it a crime to use telephone facilities to make "obscene or indecent" interstate telephone communications "for commercial purposes to any person under eighteen years of age or to any other person without that person's consent." The statute required the FCC to promulgate regulations laying out the means by which dial-a-porn sponsors could screen out underaged callers.

The FCC initially promulgated regulations that would have established a defense to message providers operating only between the hours of 9:00 p.m. and 8:00 a.m. Eastern Time ("time channeling") and to providers requiring payment by credit card ("screening") before transmission of the dial-a-porn message. In Carlin Communications, Inc. v. FCC, 749 F.2d 113 (2nd Cir. 1984) (*Carlin I*),

---

25. Dial-a-porn is big business. The dial-a-porn service in New York City alone received six to seven million calls a month for the six-month period ending in April of 1985. Carlin Communications, Inc. v. FCC, 787 F.2d 846, 848 (2nd Cir. 1986). [Footnote relocated.]

the Court of Appeals for the Second Circuit set aside the time channeling regulations and remanded to the FCC to examine other alternatives, concluding that the operating hours requirement was "both overinclusive and underinclusive" because it denied "access to adults between certain hours, but not to youths who can easily pick up a private or public telephone and call dial-a-porn during the remaining hours." The Court of Appeals did not reach the constitutionality of the underlying legislation.

In 1985, the FCC promulgated new regulations which continued to permit credit card payment as a defense to prosecution. Instead of time restrictions, however, the Commission added a defense based on use of access codes (user identification codes). Thus, it would be a defense to prosecution if the defendant, before transmission of the message, restricted customer access by requiring either payment by credit card or authorization by access or identification code. The regulations required each dial-a-porn vendor to develop an identification code database and implementation scheme. Callers would be required to provide an access number for identification (or a credit card) before receiving the message. The access code would be received through the mail after the message provider reviewed the application and concluded through a written age ascertainment procedure that the applicant was at least eighteen years of age. The FCC rejected a proposal for "exchange blocking" which would block or screen telephone numbers at the customer's premises or at the telephone company offices. In Carlin Communications, Inc. v. FCC, 787 F.2d 846 (2nd Cir. 1986) (*Carlin II*), the Court of Appeals set aside the new regulations because of the FCC's failure adequately to consider customer premises blocking. Again, the constitutionality of the underlying legislation was not addressed.

The FCC then promulgated a third set of regulations, which again rejected customer-premises blocking but added to the prior defenses of credit card payment and access-code use a third defense: message scrambling. Under this system, providers would scramble the message, which would then be unintelligible without the use of a descrambler, the sale of which would be limited to adults. On January 15, 1988, in Carlin Communications, Inc. v. FCC, 837 F.2d 546 (2nd Cir.) (*Carlin III*), *cert. denied*, 488 U.S. 924 (1988), the Court of Appeals for the Second Circuit held that the new regulations, which made access codes, along with credit card payments and scrambled messages, defenses to prosecution for dial-a-porn providers, were supported by the evidence, had been properly arrived at, and were a "feasible and effective way to serve" the "compelling state interest" in protecting minors; but the Court directed the FCC to reopen proceedings if a less restrictive technology became available. The Court of Appeals, however, this time reaching the constitutionality of the statute, invalidated §223(b) insofar as it sought to apply to nonobscene speech. *Id.* at 560, 561.

Thereafter, in April 1988, Congress amended §223(b) of the Communications Act to prohibit indecent as well as obscene interstate commercial telephone communications directed to any person regardless of age. The amended statute, which took effect on July 1, 1988, also eliminated the requirement that the FCC promulgate regulations for restricting access to minors since a total ban was imposed on dial-a-porn, making it illegal for adults, as well as children, to have access to the sexually explicit messages, Pub. L. 100–297, 102 Stat. 424. It was this version of the statute that was in effect when Sable commenced this action.

III

The District Court upheld §223(b)'s prohibition of obscene telephone messages as constitutional. We agree with that judgment. We have repeatedly held that the protection of the First Amendment does not extend to obscene speech.

Sable argues that the legislation creates an impermissible national standard of obscenity, and that it places message senders in a "double bind" by compelling them to tailor all their messages to the least tolerant community.

Section 223(b) no more establishes a "national standard" of obscenity than do federal statutes prohibiting the mailing of obscene materials, 18 U.S.C. §1461, *see* Hamling v. United States, 418 U.S. 87 (1974), or the broadcasting of obscene messages, 18 U.S.C. §1464. Furthermore, Sable is free to tailor its messages, on a selective basis, if it so chooses, to the communities it chooses to serve. Whether Sable chooses to hire operators to determine the source of the calls or engages with the telephone company to arrange for the screening and blocking of out-of-area calls or finds another means for providing messages compatible with community standards is a decision for the message provider to make.

IV

The District Court concluded that while the government has a legitimate interest in protecting children from exposure to indecent dial-a-porn messages, §223(b) was not sufficiently narrowly drawn to serve that purpose and thus violated the First Amendment. We agree.

Sexual expression which is indecent but not obscene is protected by the First Amendment; and the federal parties do not submit that the sale of such materials to adults could be criminalized solely because they are indecent. The Government may, however, regulate the content of constitutionally protected speech in order to promote a compelling interest if it chooses the least restrictive means to further the articulated interest. We have recognized that there is a compelling interest in protecting the physical and psychological well-being of minors. This interest extends to shielding minors from the influence of literature that is not obscene by adult standards. Ginsberg v. New York, 390 U.S. 629, 639–640 (1968); New York v. Ferber, 458 U.S. 747, 756–757 (1982). The Government may serve this legitimate interest, but to withstand constitutional scrutiny, "it must do so by narrowly drawn regulations designed to serve those interests without unnecessarily interfering with First Amendment freedoms." Schaumburg v. Citizens for a Better Environment, 444 U.S. 620, 637 (1980). It is not enough to show that the government's ends are compelling; the means must be carefully tailored to achieve those ends.

In Butler v. Michigan, 352 U.S. 380 (1957), a unanimous Court reversed a conviction under a statute which made it an offense to make available to the general public materials found to have a potentially harmful influence on minors. The Court found the law to be insufficiently tailored since it denied adults their free speech rights by allowing them to read only what was acceptable for children. As Justice Frankfurter said in that case, "Surely this is to burn the house to roast the pig." *Id.* at 383. In our judgment, this case, like *Butler*, presents us with "legislation not reasonably restricted to the evil with which it is said to deal." *Id.*

In attempting to justify the complete ban and criminalization of the indecent commercial telephone communications with adults as well as minors, the government relies on FCC v. Pacifica Foundation, 438 U.S. 726 (1978), a case in which the Court considered whether the FCC has the power to regulate a radio broadcast that is indecent but not obscene. In an emphatically narrow holding, the *Pacifica* Court concluded that special treatment of indecent broadcasting was justified.

Pacifica is readily distinguishable from this case, most obviously because it did not involve a total ban on broadcasting indecent material. The FCC rule was not "intended to place an absolute prohibition on the broadcast of this type of language, but rather sought to channel it to times of day when children most likely would not be exposed to it." *Pacifica, supra,* at 733. The issue of a total ban was not before the Court.

The *Pacifica* opinion also relied on the "unique" attributes of broadcasting, noting that broadcasting is "uniquely pervasive," can intrude on the privacy of the home without prior warning as to program content, and is "uniquely accessible to children, even those too young to read." *Id.* at 748–749. The private commercial telephone communications at issue here are substantially different from the public radio broadcast at issue in *Pacifica.* In contrast to public displays, unsolicited mailings and other means of expression which the recipient has no meaningful opportunity to avoid, the dial-it medium requires the listener to take affirmative steps to receive the communication. There is no "captive audience" problem here; callers will generally not be unwilling listeners. The context of dial-in services, where a caller seeks and is willing to pay for the communication, is manifestly different from a situation in which a listener does not want the received message. Placing a telephone call is not the same as turning on a radio and being taken by surprise by an indecent message. Unlike an unexpected outburst on a radio broadcast, the message received by one who places a call to a dial-a-porn service is not so invasive or surprising that it prevents an unwilling listener from avoiding exposure to it.

The federal parties nevertheless argue that the total ban on indecent commercial telephone communications is justified because nothing less could prevent children from gaining access to such messages. We find the argument quite unpersuasive. The FCC, after lengthy proceedings, determined that its credit card, access code, and scrambling rules were a satisfactory solution to the problem of keeping indecent dial-a-porn messages out of the reach of minors. The Court of Appeals, after careful consideration, agreed that these rules represented a "feasible and effective" way to serve the Government's compelling interest in protecting children.

The federal parties now insist that the rules would not be effective enough — that enterprising youngsters could and would evade the rules and gain access to communications from which they should be shielded. But aside from conclusory statements during the debates by proponents of the bill, the congressional record presented to us contains no evidence as to *how* effective or ineffective the FCC's most recent regulations were or might prove to be.

For all we know from this record, the FCC's technological approach to restricting dial-a-porn messages to adults who seek them would be extremely effective, and only a few of the most enterprising and disobedient young people will manage to secure access to such messages. If this is the case, it seems to us that §223(b) is not a narrowly tailored effort to serve the compelling interest of preventing minors from being exposed to indecent telephone messages.

Because the statute's denial of adult access to telephone messages which are indecent but not obscene far exceeds that which is necessary to limit the access of minors to such messages, we hold that the ban does not survive constitutional scrutiny.

JUSTICE SCALIA, concurring.

I join the Court's opinion because I think it correct that a wholesale prohibition upon adult access to indecent speech cannot be adopted merely because the FCC's alternate proposal could be circumvented by as few children as the evidence suggests. But where a reasonable person draws the line in this balancing process — that is, how few children render the risk unacceptable — depends in part upon what mere "indecency" (as opposed to "obscenity") includes. The more narrow the understanding of what is "obscene," and hence the more pornographic what is embraced within the residual category of "indecency," the more reasonable it becomes to insist upon greater assurance of insulation from minors. So while the Court is unanimous on the reasoning of Part IV, I am not sure it is unanimous on the assumptions underlying that reasoning. I do not believe, for example, that any sort of sexual activity portrayed or enacted over the phone lines would fall outside of the obscenity portion of the statute that we uphold, and within the indecency portion that we strike down, so long as it appeals only to "normal, healthy sexual desires" as opposed to "shameful or morbid" ones. Brockett v. Spokane Arcades, Inc., 472 U.S. 491, 498 (1985).

Finally, I note that while we hold the Constitution prevents Congress from banning indecent speech in this fashion, we do not hold that the Constitution requires public utilities to carry it.

JUSTICE BRENNAN, with whom JUSTICE MARSHALL and JUSTICE STEVENS join, concurring in part and dissenting in part.

I agree that a statute imposing criminal penalties for making any indecent telephonic communication for a commercial purpose is patently unconstitutional.

In my view, however, §223(b)(1)(A)'s parallel criminal prohibition with regard to obscene commercial communications likewise violates the First Amendment. The exaction of criminal penalties for the distribution of obscene materials to consenting adults is constitutionally intolerable. The very evidence the Court adduces to show that denying adults access to all indecent commercial messages "far exceeds that which is necessary to limit the access of minors to such messages," also demonstrates that forbidding the transmission of all obscene messages is unduly heavy-handed. Hence, the federal parties cannot plausibly claim that its legitimate interest in protecting children warrants this draconian restriction on the First Amendment rights of adults who seek to hear the messages that Sable and others provide.

* * *

Less than six months after the Supreme Court issued its opinion in *Sable*, Congress passed legislation (labeled "Restoration And Correction of Dial-a-Porn

Sanctions") that amended §223 in order to bring it into conformity with the Court's opinion. *See* Pub. L. 101–166, Title V, §521(1) (1989). The 1989 amendments to §223, and the FCC's response to those amendments, are discussed in the following order.

IN RE REGULATIONS CONCERNING INDECENT COMMUNICATIONS BY TELEPHONE
5 FCC Rcd 4926 (1990)

I. INTRODUCTION

1. Section 223 of the Communications Act of 1934, as amended [in November 1989, in response to the Supreme Court's decision in *Sable*], imposes penalties on those who knowingly make obscene communications by telephone for commercial purposes and on those who knowingly make available indecent communications by telephone for commercial purposes to persons under 18 years of age or to adults without their consent. The section establishes that it is a defense to prosecution for the defendant to restrict access to the prohibited indecent communications to persons eighteen years of age or older by complying with such procedures as the Commission may prescribe by regulation. The statute also requires telephone companies, to the extent technically feasible, to prohibit access to indecent communications from the telephone of a subscriber who has not previously requested access in writing.[26]

2. In this decision we adopt final rules which provide that in order to establish a defense to prosecution under section 223 of the Act, adult information service providers are required to utilize credit card authorization, access codes, or scrambling in order to limit access to consenting adults over the age of eighteen. Finally, we codify that a common carrier shall not provide access to a communication specified in section 223(b) from the telephone of any subscriber who has not previously requested in writing the carrier to provide access to such communication.

III. DISCUSSION

A. Constitutionality

14. We note that the government may regulate indecent speech in order to promote a compelling interest if the means are narrowly tailored to achieve those ends. *Sable*, 109 S.Ct. at 2836. Providers Coalition and Fleishman argue that dial-a-porn providers should also have a defense if they operate in areas served by telephone companies that permit customers to block access to adult messages.[27]

---

26. The statute imposes this obligation to block only if "the carrier collects from subscribers an identifiable charge for [the] communication that the carrier remits, in whole or in part, to the provider of such communication." Section 223(c)(1), 47 U.S.C. §223(c)(1).

27. We use the term "blocking" to include both "voluntary blocking" and "reverse blocking." By "voluntary blocking" we mean the telephone company will, at the central office, prevent calls from going through to specified exchanges or numbers if the customer has requested this blocking service. By "reverse blocking," we mean the telephone company will, at the central office, prevent calls from going through to specified exchanges or numbers unless the customer has requested access. Subsection (c) of the statute requires telephone com-

16. Blocking alone—reverse or voluntary—is insufficient to satisfy Congress' objective of protecting children. Without the additional restrictions on access put in place by dial-a-porn providers (scrambling, access codes, credit cards), children will still be able to gain access to indecent communications. Blocking, as a technical matter, will not prevent children from accessing dial-a-porn messages in another area code. Moreover, even if a child's home telephone is blocked, the child may still be able to receive indecent communications from a payphone, or a telephone in a home or other location where the blocking option has not been exercised.

18. The First Amendment does not preclude Congress from imposing a burden on message providers. *See Sable*. Regulations need not be so weak that they are completely useless. It was reasonable for Congress to conclude that its reverse blocking scheme would be considerably more effective than a voluntary scheme in preventing children from accessing indecent material. A voluntary blocking scheme would be far less effective in protecting children from exposure to indecent material because it is likely that most parents would not realize the need for blocking until their children had already obtained access to indecent messages. Nor would neighbors or relatives where children are only occasional visitors recognize the need to, nor act to, have access blocked. It is reasonable, therefore, to implement a reverse blocking scheme that brings the potential problem to the attention of parents before the damage to children has occurred, rather than waiting until the damage has been done. *See generally* FCC v. Pacifica, 438 U.S. at 748–49.

22. This approach may cause message providers to incur additional costs, and perhaps to raise their prices, but the Supreme Court has said that raising the cost of providing a service is not unconstitutional. *Sable*, 109 S. Ct. at 2836.

B. Defenses to Prosecution.

27. *Credit Cards, Access Codes, and Scrambling.* No single defense is intended as the sole means by which all information providers must operate in order to avoid prosecution. We find that the use of credit card validation, scrambling or access codes before transmission places a minimal burden on the information provider and consenting adult while helping to assure that access by minors is restricted. Nevertheless, we believe Congress could reasonably conclude that each of these is far from foolproof and can be counteracted by less than the "most enterprising and disobedient young [person]," *see Sable*, 109 S. Ct. at 2838. Accordingly, it is necessary to impose reverse blocking, where technically feasible, to achieve Congress's compelling interest in protecting children.

51. Several commenters argue that restrictions on indecent communications will have an adverse impact on the fight against AIDS by restricting open discussion of related issues by telephone. The proposed regulatory scheme does not restrict communications which are clinical discussions of AIDS or any other topic. Legitimate scientific or social endeavors such as community hotlines generally fall outside the definition of obscenity or indecency. In addition, we note that the statute encompasses only those indecent or obscene communications which are produced for commercial purposes.

---

panies to institute reverse blocking where technically feasible if they provide billing and collection services to indecent message providers.

Notes and Questions

1. Comparisons. What are the key features of the reasoning in *Sable*, and how might these materials bear on the government's ability to regulate indecent broadcast programming, cable programming, or material on the Internet?

(a) *Broadcasting.* What is the difference between indecency via broadcast and indecency via telephone? Apparently, broadcast indecency is "uniquely pervasive" and "uniquely accessible." But on what relevant distinctions is the Court relying? What is the factual basis for those distinctions? If *Pacifica* survives *Sable* because the former dealt with the "unique" broadcast medium, does this mean that cellular telephone services, which employ over-the-air transmissions that anyone with the proper tuner can intercept, are subject to *Pacifica*'s rules?

Is the key point that the FCC must use carefully tailored means to regulate indecent broadcasting so that only children are excluded from access to it? If narrowly tailored means are necessary, does this mean that, when regulating broadcast indecency, the Commission must (1) adopt local standards, rather than a single national standard, of indecency (because stations broadcast only to local areas); (2) set aside a "safe harbor" for those times when adults far outnumber children in the audience; or (3) carefully define "child" as someone susceptible to harm from the particular broadcast at issue? Why does the narrow tailoring requirement not mean that government must abandon broadcast program censorship in favor of regulating radio and television set manufacturing so that parents can lock out selected channels?

(b) *Cable.* Does *Sable*, in the manner in which it distinguishes *Pacifica*, undercut or reinforce the view that indecency regulation of cable is unconstitutional? Conversely, if the FCC is persuasive in arguing that voluntary blocking by telephone subscribers is insufficient to protect children from indecent phone messages (¶¶16–22), why does it not follow that government may also protect children from indecent cable programming regardless of subscribers' ability voluntarily to block that programming (by, *inter alia*, not subscribing, or purchasing a lockbox that prevents unauthorized people from gaining access to certain channels)?

(c) *Internet.* Should opponents of Internet indecency regulation be encouraged by the statement that "the message received by one who places a call to a dial-a-porn service is not so invasive or surprising that it prevents an unwilling listener from avoiding exposure to it"? Should the government be encouraged by the lower courts' willingness to uphold the post-*Sable* statute and the Supreme Court's apparent disinterest in disturbing those holdings?

2. Consenting Adults. Precisely what is wrong with Justice Brennan's view in *Sable* that it is unconstitutional to penalize the distribution over telephone wires of obscene materials to consenting adults? Will the *Sable* decision allow government to control other messages that might be sent over telephone lines simply because the government disagrees with the form or content of those messages?

3. Subsequent Litigation. Litigants challenged both the federal dial-a-porn statute (*i.e.*, §223, as amended in 1989) and the 1990 FCC *Report and Order* excerpted above as inconsistent with the First Amendment. The Ninth Circuit Court of Appeals rejected this challenge in Information Providers' Coalition v. FCC, 928 F.2d 866 (9th Cir. 1991), and the Second Circuit upheld the statute against a First

Amendment challenge in Dial Info. Serv. Corp. v. Thornburgh, 938 F.2d 1535 (2d Cir. 1991). There was a petition for certiorari only in the latter case, and the Supreme Court denied it. 502 U.S. 1072 (1992).

ii. Indecent Communication over the Internet

RENO v. ACLU

521 U.S. 844 (1997)

STEVENS, J., delivered the opinion of the Court, in which SCALIA, KENNEDY, SOUTER, THOMAS, GINSBURG, and BREYER, JJ., joined. O'CONNOR, J., filed an opinion concurring in the judgment in part and dissenting in part, in which REHNQUIST, C.J., joined.

JUSTICE STEVENS delivered the opinion of the Court.

At issue is the constitutionality of two statutory provisions enacted to protect minors from "indecent" and "patently offensive" communications on the Internet. Notwithstanding the legitimacy and importance of the congressional goal of protecting children from harmful materials, we agree with the three-judge District Court that the statute abridges "the freedom of speech" protected by the First Amendment.

I[28]

The Internet

The Internet is an international network of interconnected computers. It is the outgrowth of what began in 1969 as a military program called "ARPANET,"[29] which was designed to enable computers operated by the military, defense contractors, and universities conducting defense-related research to communicate with one another by redundant channels even if some portions of the network were damaged in a war. While the ARPANET no longer exists, it provided an example for the development of a number of civilian networks that, eventually linking with each other, now enable tens of millions of people to communicate with one another and to access vast amounts of information from around the world. The Internet is a unique and wholly new medium of worldwide human communication.

The Internet has experienced extraordinary growth. The number of "host" computers — those that store information and relay communications — increased from about 300 in 1981 to approximately 9,400,000 by the time of the trial in 1996. Roughly 60% of these hosts are located in the United States. About 40 million people used the Internet at the time of trial, a number that is expected to mushroom to 200 million by 1999.

---

28. [Ed. This section of the opinion draws heavily on the District Court's extensive findings of fact. ACLU v. Reno, 929 F. Supp. 824 (E.D. Pa. 1996). For the sake of brevity and ease of reading, many citations to that opinion have been removed and many quotation marks identifying phrases located in the lower court's opinion also have been removed.]

29. An acronym for the network developed by the Advanced Research Project Agency.

Individuals can obtain access to the Internet from many different sources, generally hosts themselves or entities with a host affiliation. Most colleges and universities provide access for their students and faculty; many corporations provide their employees with access through an office network; many communities and local libraries provide free access; and an increasing number of storefront "computer coffee shops" provide access for a small hourly fee. Several major national "online services" such as America Online, CompuServe, the Microsoft Network, and Prodigy offer access to their own extensive proprietary networks as well as a link to the much larger resources of the Internet. These commercial online services had almost 12 million individual subscribers at the time of trial.

Anyone with access to the Internet may take advantage of a wide variety of communication and information retrieval methods. These methods are constantly evolving and difficult to categorize precisely. But, as presently constituted, those most relevant to this case are electronic mail ("e-mail"), automatic mailing list services ("mail exploders," sometimes referred to as "listservs"), "newsgroups," "chat rooms," and the "World Wide Web." All of these methods can be used to transmit text; most can transmit sound, pictures, and moving video images. Taken together, these tools constitute a unique medium—known to its users as "cyberspace"—located in no particular geographical location but available to anyone, anywhere in the world, with access to the Internet.

E-mail enables an individual to send an electronic message—generally akin to a note or letter—to another individual or to a group of addressees. The message is generally stored electronically, sometimes waiting for the recipient to check her "mailbox" and sometimes making its receipt known through some type of prompt. A mail exploder is a sort of e-mail group. Subscribers can send messages to a common e-mail address, which then forwards the message to the group's other subscribers. Newsgroups also serve groups of regular participants, but these postings may be read by others as well. There are thousands of such groups, each serving to foster an exchange of information or opinion on a particular topic running the gamut from, say, the music of Wagner to Balkan politics to AIDS prevention to the Chicago Bulls. About 100,000 new messages are posted every day. In most newsgroups, postings are automatically purged at regular intervals. In addition to posting a message that can be read later, two or more individuals wishing to communicate more immediately can enter a chat room to engage in real-time dialogue—in other words, by typing messages to one another that appear almost immediately on the others' computer screens. The District Court found that at any given time tens of thousands of users are engaging in conversations on a huge range of subjects. It is no exaggeration to conclude that the content on the Internet is as diverse as human thought.

The best known category of communication over the Internet is the World Wide Web, which allows users to search for and retrieve information stored in remote computers, as well as, in some cases, to communicate back to designated sites. In concrete terms, the Web consists of a vast number of documents stored in different computers all over the world. Some of these documents are simply files containing information. However, more elaborate documents, commonly known as Web "pages," are also prevalent. Each has its own address—rather like a telephone number. Web pages frequently contain information and sometimes allow the viewer to communicate with the page's (or "site's") author. They generally also contain "links" to other documents created by that site's author or to other (generally) related sites. Typically, the links are either blue or underlined text—sometimes images.

Navigating the Web is relatively straightforward. A user may either type the address of a known page or enter one or more keywords into a commercial "search engine" in an effort to locate sites on a subject of interest. A particular Web page may contain the information sought by the "surfer," or, through its links, it may be an avenue to other documents located anywhere on the Internet. Users generally explore a given Web page, or move to another, by clicking a computer "mouse" on one of the page's icons or links. Access to most Web pages is freely available, but some allow access only to those who have purchased the right from a commercial provider. The Web is thus comparable, from the readers' viewpoint, to both a vast library including millions of readily available and indexed publications and a sprawling mall offering goods and services.

From the publisher's point of view, it constitutes a vast platform from which to address and hear from a world-wide audience of millions of readers, viewers, researchers, and buyers. Any person or organization with a computer connected to the Internet can "publish" information. Publishers include government agencies, educational institutions, commercial entities, advocacy groups, and individuals.[30] Publishers may either make their material available to the entire pool of Internet users, or confine access to a selected group, such as those willing to pay for the privilege. No single organization controls any membership in the Web, nor is there any centralized point from which individual Web sites or services can be blocked from the Web.

Sexually Explicit Material

Sexually explicit material on the Internet includes text, pictures, and chat and extends from the modestly titillating to the hardest-core. These files are created, named, and posted in the same manner as material that is not sexually explicit, and may be accessed either deliberately or unintentionally during the course of an imprecise search. Once a provider posts its content on the Internet, it cannot prevent that content from entering any community. Thus, for example, when the UCR/California Museum of Photography posts to its Web site nudes by Edward Weston and Robert Mapplethorpe to announce that its new exhibit will travel to Baltimore and New York City, those images are available not only in Los Angeles, Baltimore, and New York City, but also in Cincinnati, Mobile, or Beijing—wherever Internet users live. Similarly, the safer sex instructions that Critical Path posts to its Web site, written in street language so that the teenage receiver can understand them, are available not just in Philadelphia, but also in Provo and Prague. Some of the communications over the Internet that originate in foreign countries are also sexually explicit.

Though such material is widely available, users seldom encounter such content accidentally. A document's title or a description of the document will usually appear before the document itself, and in many cases the user will receive detailed information about a site's content before he or she need take the step to ac-

---

30. "Web publishing is simple enough that thousands of individual users and small community organizations are using the Web to publish their own personal 'home pages,' the equivalent of individualized newsletters about the person or organization, which are available to everyone on the Web." 929 F. Supp. at 837 (finding 42).

cess the document. Almost all sexually explicit images are preceded by warnings as to the content. For that reason, the odds are slim that a user would enter a sexually explicit site by accident. Unlike communications received by radio or television, the receipt of information on the Internet requires a series of affirmative steps more deliberate and directed than merely turning a dial. A child requires some sophistication and some ability to read to retrieve material and thereby to use the Internet unattended.

Systems have been developed to help parents control the material that may be available on a home computer with Internet access. A system may either limit a computer's access to an approved list of sources that have been identified as containing no adult material, it may block designated inappropriate sites, or it may attempt to block messages containing identifiable objectionable features. Although parental control software currently can screen for certain suggestive words or for known sexually explicit sites, it cannot now screen for sexually explicit images. Nevertheless, the evidence indicates that a reasonably effective method by which parents can prevent their children from accessing sexually explicit and other material which parents may believe is inappropriate for their children will soon be available.

Age Verification

The problem of age verification differs for different uses of the Internet. The District Court categorically determined that there is no effective way to determine the identity or the age of a user who is accessing material through e-mail, mail exploders, newsgroups or chat rooms. The Government offered no evidence that there was a reliable way to screen recipients and participants in such fora for age. Moreover, even if it were technologically feasible to block minors' access to newsgroups and chat rooms containing discussions of art, politics or other subjects that potentially elicit "indecent" or "patently offensive" contributions, it would not be possible to block their access to that material and still allow them access to the remaining content, even if the overwhelming majority of that content was not indecent.

Technology exists by which an operator of a Web site may condition access on the verification of requested information such as a credit card number or an adult password. Credit card verification is only feasible, however, either in connection with a commercial transaction in which the card is used, or by payment to a verification agency. Using credit card possession as a surrogate for proof of age would impose costs on non-commercial Web sites that would require many of them to shut down. Moreover, the imposition of such a requirement would completely bar adults who do not have a credit card and lack the resources to obtain one from accessing any blocked material.

Commercial pornographic sites that charge their users for access have assigned them passwords as a method of age verification. The record does not contain any evidence concerning the reliability of these technologies. Even if passwords are effective for commercial purveyors of indecent material, the District Court found that an adult password requirement would impose significant burdens on noncommercial sites, both because they would discourage users from accessing their sites and because the cost of creating and maintaining such screening systems would be beyond their reach.

In sum, the District Court found:

"Even if credit card verification or adult password verification were implemented, the Government presented no testimony as to how such systems could ensure that the user of the password or credit card is in fact over 18. The burdens imposed by credit card verification and adult password verification systems make them effectively unavailable to a substantial number of Internet content providers." *Id.* at 847 (finding 107).

II

The Telecommunications Act of 1996, Pub. L. 104–104, 110 Stat. 56, was an unusually important legislative enactment. As stated on the first of its 103 pages, its primary purpose was to reduce regulation and encourage "the rapid deployment of new telecommunications technologies." The major components of the statute have nothing to do with the Internet; they were designed to promote competition in the local telephone service market, the multichannel video market, and the market for over-the-air broadcasting. The Act includes seven Titles, six of which are the product of extensive committee hearings and the subject of discussion in Reports prepared by Committees of the Senate and the House of Representatives. By contrast, Title V—known as the "Communications Decency Act of 1996" (CDA)—contains provisions that were either added in executive committee after the hearings were concluded or as amendments offered during floor debate on the legislation. An amendment offered in the Senate was the source of the two statutory provisions challenged in this case. They are informally described as the "indecent transmission" provision and the "patently offensive display" provision.[31]

The first, 47 U.S.C. §223(a) (Supp. 1997), prohibits the knowing transmission of obscene or indecent messages to any recipient under 18 years of age. It provides in pertinent part:

"(a) Whoever—

"(1) in interstate or foreign communications—

* * *

"(B) by means of a telecommunications device knowingly—

"(i) makes, creates, or solicits, and

"(ii) initiates the transmission of,

"any comment, request, suggestion, proposal, image, or other communication which is obscene or indecent, knowing that the recipient of the communication is under 18 years of age, regardless of whether the maker of such communication placed the call or initiated the communication;

* * *

"(2) knowingly permits any telecommunications facility under his control to be used for any activity prohibited by paragraph (1) with the intent that it be used for such activity,

"shall be fined under Title 18, or imprisoned not more than two years, or both."

---

31. Although the Government and the dissent break §223(d)(1) into two separate "patently offensive" and "display" provisions, we follow the convention of both parties below, as well the District Court's order and opinion, in describing §223(d)(1) as one provision.

The second provision, §223(d), prohibits the knowing sending or displaying of patently offensive messages in a manner that is available to a person under 18 years of age. It provides:

"(d) Whoever—

"(1) in interstate or foreign communications knowingly—

"(A) uses an interactive computer service to send to a specific person or persons under 18 years of age, or

"(B) uses any interactive computer service to display in a manner available to a person under 18 years of age,

"any comment, request, suggestion, proposal, image, or other communication that, in context, depicts or describes, in terms patently offensive as measured by contemporary community standards, sexual or excretory activities or organs, regardless of whether the user of such service placed the call or initiated the communication; or

"(2) knowingly permits any telecommunications facility under such person's control to be used for an activity prohibited by paragraph (1) with the intent that it be used for such activity,

"shall be fined under Title 18, or imprisoned not more than two years, or both."

The breadth of these prohibitions is qualified by two affirmative defenses. One covers those who take "good faith, reasonable, effective, and appropriate actions" to restrict access by minors to the prohibited communications. §223(e)(5)(A). The other covers those who restrict access to covered material by requiring certain designated forms of age proof, such as a verified credit card or an adult identification number or code. §223(e)(5)(B).

III

On February 8, 1996, immediately after the President signed the statute, 20 plaintiffs filed suit against the Attorney General of the United States and the Department of Justice challenging the constitutionality of §§223(a)(1) and 223(d). A second suit was filed by 27 additional plaintiffs. The two cases were consolidated, and a three-judge District Court was convened pursuant to §561 of the Act. After an evidentiary hearing, that Court entered a preliminary injunction against enforcement of both of the challenged provisions.

The judgment of the District Court enjoins the Government from enforcing the prohibitions in §223(a)(1)(B) insofar as they relate to "indecent" communications, but expressly preserves the Government's right to investigate and prosecute the obscenity or child pornography activities prohibited therein. The injunction against enforcement of §§223(d)(1) and (2) is unqualified because those provisions contain no separate reference to obscenity or child pornography.

IV

In arguing for reversal, the Government contends that the CDA is plainly constitutional under three of our prior decisions: (1) Ginsberg v. New York, 390 U.S. 629 (1968); (2) FCC v. Pacifica Foundation, 438 U.S. 726 (1978); and (3) Renton v. Playtime Theatres, Inc., 475 U.S. 41 (1986). A close look at these cases, however, raises—rather than relieves—doubts concerning the constitutionality of the CDA.

In *Ginsberg,* we upheld the constitutionality of a New York statute that prohibited selling to minors under 17 years of age material that was considered obscene as to them even if not obscene as to adults. We rejected the defendant's broad submission that "the scope of the constitutional freedom of expression secured to a citizen to read or see material concerned with sex cannot be made to depend on whether the citizen is an adult or a minor." 390 U.S. at 636. In rejecting that contention, we relied not only on the State's independent interest in the well-being of its youth, but also on our consistent recognition of the principle that "the parents' claim to authority in their own household to direct the rearing of their children is basic in the structure of our society." 390 U.S. at 639.

In four important respects, the statute upheld in *Ginsberg* was narrower than the CDA. First, we noted in *Ginsberg* that "the prohibition against sales to minors does not bar parents who so desire from purchasing the magazines for their children." *Id.* at 639. Under the CDA, by contrast, neither the parents' consent—nor even their participation—in the communication would avoid the application of the statute. Second, the New York statute applied only to commercial transactions, *id.* at 647, whereas the CDA contains no such limitation. Third, the New York statute cabined its definition of material that is harmful to minors with the requirement that it be "utterly without redeeming social importance for minors." *Id.* at 646. The CDA fails to provide us with any definition of the term "indecent" as used in §223(a)(1) and, importantly, omits any requirement that the "patently offensive" material covered by §223(d) lack serious literary, artistic, political, or scientific value. Fourth, the New York statute defined a minor as a person under the age of 17, whereas the CDA, in applying to all those under 18 years, includes an additional year of those nearest majority.

In *Pacifica,* we upheld a declaratory order of the Federal Communications Commission, holding that the broadcast of a recording of a 12-minute monologue entitled "Filthy Words" that had previously been delivered to a live audience "could have been the subject of administrative sanctions." 438 U.S. at 730. The Commission had found that the repetitive use of certain words referring to excretory or sexual activities or organs "in an afternoon broadcast when children are in the audience was patently offensive" and concluded that the monologue was indecent "as broadcast." *Id.* at 735. The respondent did not quarrel with the finding that the afternoon broadcast was patently offensive, but contended that it was not "indecent" within the meaning of the relevant statutes because it contained no prurient appeal. After rejecting respondent's statutory arguments, we confronted its two constitutional arguments: (1) that the Commission's construction of its authority to ban indecent speech was so broad that its order had to be set aside even if the broadcast at issue was unprotected; and (2) that since the recording was not obscene, the First Amendment forbade any abridgement of the right to broadcast it on the radio.

In the portion of the lead opinion not joined by Justices Powell and Blackmun, the plurality stated that the First Amendment does not prohibit all governmental regulation that depends on the content of speech. *Id.* at 742–743. Accordingly, the availability of constitutional protection for a vulgar and offensive monologue that was not obscene depended on the context of the broadcast. *Id.* at 744–748. Relying on the premise that "of all forms of communication" broadcasting had received the most limited First Amendment protection, *id.* at 748–749, the Court concluded that the ease with which children may obtain access to broadcasts, "coupled with the concerns recognized in *Ginsberg*," justified special treatment of indecent broadcasting. *Id.* at 749–750.

As with the New York statute at issue in *Ginsberg*, there are significant differences between the order upheld in *Pacifica* and the CDA. First, the order in *Pacifica*, issued by an agency that had been regulating radio stations for decades, targeted a specific broadcast that represented a rather dramatic departure from traditional program content in order to designate when—rather than whether— it would be permissible to air such a program in that particular medium. The CDA's broad categorical prohibitions are not limited to particular times and are not dependent on any evaluation by an agency familiar with the unique characteristics of the Internet. Second, unlike the CDA, the Commission's declaratory order was not punitive; we expressly refused to decide whether the indecent broadcast "would justify a criminal prosecution." *Id.* at 750. Finally, the Commission's order applied to a medium which as a matter of history had "received the most limited First Amendment protection," *id.* at 748, in large part because warnings could not adequately protect the listener from unexpected program content. The Internet, however, has no comparable history. Moreover, the District Court found that the risk of encountering indecent material by accident is remote because a series of affirmative steps is required to access specific material.

In *Renton*, we upheld a zoning ordinance that kept adult movie theaters out of residential neighborhoods. The ordinance was aimed, not at the content of the films shown in the theaters, but rather at the "secondary effects"—such as crime and deteriorating property values—that these theaters fostered: "'It is th[e] secondary effect which these zoning ordinances attempt to avoid, not the dissemination of "offensive" speech.'" 475 U.S. at 49 (quoting Young v. American Mini Theatres, Inc., 427 U.S. 50, 71, n. 34 (1976)). According to the Government, the CDA is constitutional because it constitutes a sort of "cyberzoning" on the Internet. But the CDA applies broadly to the entire universe of cyberspace. And the purpose of the CDA is to protect children from the primary effects of "indecent" and "patently offensive" speech, rather than any "secondary" effect of such speech. Thus, the CDA is a content based blanket restriction on speech, and, as such, cannot be "properly analyzed as a form of time, place, and manner regulation." 475 U.S. at 46.

These precedents, then, surely do not require us to uphold the CDA and are fully consistent with the application of the most stringent review of its provisions.

<h2 style="text-align:center">V</h2>

In Southeastern Promotions, Ltd. v. Conrad, 420 U.S. 546, 557 (1975), we observed that "each medium of expression…may present its own problems." Thus, some of our cases have recognized special justifications for regulation of the broadcast media that are not applicable to other speakers, *see* Red Lion Broadcasting Co. v. FCC, 395 U.S. 367 (1969); FCC v. Pacifica Foundation, 438 U.S. 726 (1978). In these cases, the Court relied on the history of extensive government regulation of the broadcast medium; the scarcity of available frequencies at its inception; and its "invasive" nature.

Those factors are not present in cyberspace. Neither before nor after the enactment of the CDA have the vast democratic fora of the Internet been subject to the type of government supervision and regulation that has attended the broadcast industry. Moreover, the Internet is not as "invasive" as radio or television. The District Court specifically found that "communications over the Internet do not 'invade' an individual's home or appear on one's computer screen unbidden. Users seldom encounter content 'by accident.'" 929 F.Supp. at 844 (finding 88). It also found that "almost all sexually explicit images are preceded by warnings as to the content," and cited testimony that "'odds are slim' that a user would come across a sexually explicit sight [sic] by accident." *Id.*

We distinguished *Pacifica* in *Sable,* 492 U.S. at 128, on just this basis. In *Sable,* a company engaged in the business of offering sexually oriented prerecorded telephone messages (popularly known as "dial-a-porn") challenged the constitutionality of an amendment to the Communications Act that imposed a blanket prohibition on indecent as well as obscene interstate commercial telephone messages. We held that the statute was constitutional insofar as it applied to obscene messages but invalid as applied to indecent messages. In attempting to justify the complete ban and criminalization of indecent commercial telephone messages, the Government relied on *Pacifica,* arguing that the ban was necessary to prevent children from gaining access to such messages. We agreed that "there is a compelling interest in protecting the physical and psychological well-being of minors" which extended to shielding them from indecent messages that are not obscene by adult standards, 492 U.S. at 126, but distinguished our "emphatically narrow holding" in *Pacifica* because it did not involve a complete ban and because it involved a different medium of communication, *id.* at 127. We explained that "the dial-it medium requires the listener to take affirmative steps to receive the communication." *Id.* at 127–128. "Placing a telephone call," we continued, "is not the same as turning on a radio and being taken by surprise by an indecent message." *Id.* at 128.

Finally, unlike the conditions that prevailed when Congress first authorized regulation of the broadcast spectrum, the Internet can hardly be considered a "scarce" expressive commodity. It provides relatively unlimited, low-cost capacity for communication of all kinds. The Government estimates that as many as 40 million people use the Internet today, and that figure is expected to grow to 200 million by 1999. This dynamic, multifaceted category of communication includes not only traditional print and news services, but also audio, video, and still images, as well as interactive, real-time dialogue. Through the use of chat rooms, any person with a phone line can become a town crier with a voice that resonates farther than it could from any soapbox. Through the use of Web pages, mail exploders, and newsgroups, the same individual can become a pamphleteer. As the District Court found, "the content on the Internet is as diverse as human thought." 929 F. Supp. at 842 (finding 74). We agree with its conclusion that our cases provide no basis for qualifying the level of First Amendment scrutiny that should be applied to this medium.

VI

Regardless of whether the CDA is so vague that it violates the Fifth Amendment, the many ambiguities concerning the scope of its coverage render it problematic for purposes of the First Amendment. For instance, each of the two parts of the CDA uses a different linguistic form. The first uses the word "indecent," 47 U.S.C. §223(a) (Supp. 1997), while the second speaks of material that "in context, depicts or describes, in terms patently offensive as measured by contemporary community standards, sexual or excretory activities or organs," §223(d). Given the absence of a definition of either term, this difference in language will provoke uncertainty among speakers about how the two standards relate to each other and just what they mean.[32] Could a speaker confidently assume that a serious discussion about birth control practices, homosexuality, the First Amendment issues raised by the Appendix to our *Pacifica* opinion, or the consequences of prison rape would not violate the CDA? This uncertainty undermines the likelihood that the CDA has been carefully tailored to the congressional goal of protecting minors from potentially harmful materials.

The vagueness of the CDA is a matter of special concern for two reasons. First, the CDA is a content based regulation of speech. The vagueness of such a regulation raises special First Amendment concerns because of its obvious chilling effect on free speech. *See, e.g.,* Gentile v. State Bar of Nev., 501 U.S. 1030, 1048–1051 (1991). Second, the CDA is a criminal statute. In addition to the opprobrium and stigma of a criminal conviction, the CDA threatens violators with penalties including up to two years in prison for each act of violation. The severity of criminal sanctions may well cause speakers to remain silent rather than communicate even arguably unlawful words, ideas, and images. *See, e.g.,* Dombrowski v. Pfister, 380 U.S. 479, 494 (1965). As a practical matter, this increased deterrent effect, coupled with the "risk of discriminatory enforcement" of vague regulations, poses greater First Amendment concerns than those implicated by the civil regulation reviewed in Denver Area Ed. Telecommunications Consortium, Inc. v. FCC, 518 U.S. 727 (1996).

Given the vague contours of the coverage of the CDA, it unquestionably silences some speakers whose messages would be entitled to constitutional protection. That danger provides further reason for insisting that the statute not be overly broad. The CDA's burden on protected speech cannot be justified if it could be avoided by a more carefully drafted statute.

VII

We are persuaded that the CDA lacks the precision that the First Amendment requires when a statute regulates the content of speech. In order to deny minors access to potentially harmful speech, the CDA effectively suppresses a large amount of speech that adults have a constitutional right to receive and to address to one another. That burden on adult speech is unacceptable if less restrictive alternatives would be at least as effective in achieving the legitimate purpose that the statute was enacted to serve.

In evaluating the free speech rights of adults, we have made it perfectly clear that "sexual expression which is indecent but not obscene is protected by the

---

32. The statute does not indicate whether the "patently offensive" and "indecent" determinations should be made with respect to minors or the population as a whole. The Government asserts that the appropriate standard is "what is suitable material for minors." Reply Brief for Appellants 18, n. 13 (citing Ginsberg v. New York, 390 U.S. 629, 633 (1968)). But the Conferees expressly rejected amendments that would have imposed such a "harmful to minors" standard. *See* S. Conf. Rep. No. 104–230, p. 189 (1996) (S. Conf. Rep.), 142 Cong. Rec. H1145, H1165–1166 (Feb. 1, 1996). The Conferees also rejected amendments that would have limited the proscribed materials to those lacking redeeming value. *See* S. Conf. Rep. at 189, 142 Cong. Rec. H1165–1166 (Feb. 1, 1996).

First Amendment." *Sable*, 492 U.S. at 126. Indeed, *Pacifica* itself admonished that "the fact that society may find speech offensive is not a sufficient reason for suppressing it." 438 U.S. at 745.

It is true that we have repeatedly recognized the governmental interest in protecting children from harmful materials. *See Ginsberg*, 390 U.S. at 639; *Pacifica*, 438 U.S. at 749. But that interest does not justify an unnecessarily broad suppression of speech addressed to adults. As we have explained, the Government may not "reduc[e] the adult population...to...only what is fit for children." *Denver*, 518 U.S. at 759 (internal quotation marks omitted) (quoting *Sable*, 492 U.S. at 128).[33]

The District Court was correct to conclude that the CDA effectively resembles the ban on "dial-a-porn" invalidated in *Sable*. In *Sable*, this Court rejected the argument that we should defer to the congressional judgment that nothing less than a total ban would be effective in preventing enterprising youngsters from gaining access to indecent communications. *Sable* thus made clear that the mere fact that a statutory regulation of speech was enacted for the important purpose of protecting children from exposure to sexually explicit material does not foreclose inquiry into its validity. As we pointed out last Term, that inquiry embodies an "over-arching commitment" to make sure that Congress has designed its statute to accomplish its purpose "without imposing an unnecessarily great restriction on speech." *Denver*, 518 U.S. at 741.

In arguing that the CDA does not so diminish adult communication, the Government relies on the incorrect factual premise that prohibiting a transmission whenever it is known that one of its recipients is a minor would not interfere with adult-to-adult communication. The findings of the District Court make clear that this premise is untenable. Given the size of the potential audience for most messages, in the absence of a viable age verification process, the sender must be charged with knowing that one or more minors will likely view it. Knowledge that, for instance, one or more members of a 100-person chat group will be minor—and therefore that it would be a crime to send the group an indecent message—would surely burden communication among adults.

The District Court found that at the time of trial existing technology did not include any effective method for a sender to prevent minors from obtaining access to its communications on the Internet without also denying access to adults. The Court found no effective way to determine the age of a user who is accessing material through e-mail, mail exploders, newsgroups, or chat rooms. As a practical matter, the Court also found that it would be prohibitively expensive for noncommercial—as well as some commercial—speakers who have Web sites to verify that their users are adults. These limitations must inevitably curtail a significant amount of adult communication on the Internet. By contrast, the District Court found that "despite its limitations, currently available *user-based* software suggests that a reasonably effective method by which *parents* can prevent their children from accessing sexually explicit and other material which *parents*

---

33. *Accord* Butler v. Michigan, 352 U.S. 380, 383 (1957) (ban on sale to adults of books deemed harmful to children unconstitutional); Sable Communications of Cal., Inc. v. FCC, 492 U.S. 115, 128 (1989) (ban on "dial-a-porn" messages unconstitutional); Bolger v. Youngs Drug Products Corp., 463 U.S. 60, 73 (1983) (ban on mailing of unsolicited advertisement for contraceptives unconstitutional).

may believe is inappropriate for their children will soon be widely available." *Id.* at 842 (finding 73) (emphases added).

The breadth of the CDA's coverage is wholly unprecedented. Unlike the regulations upheld in *Ginsberg* and *Pacifica*, the scope of the CDA is not limited to commercial speech or commercial entities. Its open-ended prohibitions embrace all nonprofit entities and individuals posting indecent messages or displaying them on their own computers in the presence of minors. The general, undefined terms "indecent" and "patently offensive" cover large amounts of non-pornographic material with serious educational or other value. Moreover, the "community standards" criterion as applied to the Internet means that any communication available to a nation-wide audience will be judged by the standards of the community most likely to be offended by the message.[34] The regulated subject matter includes any of the seven "dirty words" used in the *Pacifica* monologue, the use of which the Government's expert acknowledged could constitute a felony. It may also extend to discussions about prison rape or safe sexual practices, artistic images that include nude subjects, and arguably the card catalogue of the Carnegie Library.

For the purposes of our decision, we need neither accept nor reject the Government's submission that the First Amendment does not forbid a blanket prohibition on all "indecent" and "patently offensive" messages communicated to a 17-year old—no matter how much value the message may contain and regardless of parental approval. It is at least clear that the strength of the Government's interest in protecting minors is not equally strong throughout the coverage of this broad statute. Under the CDA, a parent allowing her 17-year-old to use the family computer to obtain information on the Internet that she, in her parental judgment, deems appropriate could face a lengthy prison term. *See* 47 U.S.C. §223(a)(2) (Supp. 1997). Similarly, a parent who sent his 17-year-old college freshman information on birth control via e-mail could be incarcerated even though neither he, his child, nor anyone in their home community, found the material "indecent" or "patently offensive," if the college town's community thought otherwise.

The breadth of this content based restriction of speech imposes an especially heavy burden on the Government to explain why a less restrictive provision would not be as effective as the CDA. It has not done so. The arguments in this Court have referred to possible alternatives such as requiring that indecent material be "tagged" in a way that facilitates parental control of material coming into their homes, making exceptions for messages with artistic or educational value, providing some tolerance for parental choice, and regulating some portions of the Internet—such as commercial web sites—differently than others, such as chat rooms. Particularly in the light of the absence of any detailed findings by the Congress, or even hearings addressing the special problems of the CDA, we are persuaded that the CDA is not narrowly tailored if that requirement has any meaning at all.

---

34. Appellees offer an additional reason why, in their view, the CDA fails strict scrutiny. Because so much sexually explicit content originates overseas, they argue, the CDA cannot be "effective." Brief for Appellees American Library Association et al. 33–34. This argument raises difficult issues regarding the intended, as well as the permissible scope of, extraterritorial application of the CDA. We find it unnecessary to address those issues to dispose of this case.

VIII

The Government contends that, even though the CDA effectively censors discourse on many of the Internet's modalities—such as chat groups, newsgroups, and mail exploders—it is nonetheless constitutional because it provides a "reasonable opportunity" for speakers to engage in the restricted speech on the World Wide Web. This argument is unpersuasive because the CDA regulates speech on the basis of its content. A "time, place, and manner" analysis is therefore inapplicable. It is thus immaterial whether such speech would be feasible on the Web (which, as the Government's own expert acknowledged, would cost up to $10,000 if the speaker's interests were not accommodated by an existing Web site, not including costs for data base management and age verification). The Government's position is equivalent to arguing that a statute could ban leaflets on certain subjects as long as individuals are free to publish books.

The Government also asserts that the "knowledge" requirement of both §§223(a) and (d), especially when coupled with the "specific child" element found in §223(d), saves the CDA from overbreadth. Because both sections prohibit the dissemination of indecent messages only to persons known to be under 18, the Government argues, it does not require transmitters to refrain from communicating indecent material to adults; they need only refrain from disseminating such materials to persons they know to be under 18. This argument ignores the fact that most Internet fora—including chat rooms, newsgroups, mail exploders, and the Web—are open to all comers. The Government's assertion that the knowledge requirement somehow protects the communications of adults is therefore untenable. Even the strongest reading of the "specific person" requirement of §223(d) cannot save the statute. It would confer broad powers of censorship, in the form of a "heckler's veto," upon any opponent of indecent speech who might simply log on and inform the would-be discoursers that his 17-year-old child—a "specific person...under 18 years of age," 47 U.S.C. §223(d)(1)(A) (Supp. 1997)—would be present.

IX

The Government's three remaining arguments focus on the defenses provided in §223(e)(5). First, relying on the "good faith, reasonable, effective, and appropriate actions" provision, the Government suggests that "tagging" provides a defense that saves the constitutionality of the Act. The suggestion assumes that transmitters may encode their indecent communications in a way that would indicate their contents, thus permitting recipients to block their reception with appropriate software. It is the requirement that the good faith action must be "effective" that makes this defense illusory. The Government recognizes that its proposed screening software does not currently exist. Even if it did, there is no way to know whether a potential recipient will actually block the encoded material. Without the impossible knowledge that every guardian in America is screening for the "tag," the transmitter could not reasonably rely on its action to be "effective."

For its second and third arguments concerning defenses—which we can consider together—the Government relies on the latter half of §223(e)(5), which applies when the transmitter has restricted access by requiring use of a verified credit card or adult identification. Such verification is not only techno-logically available but actually is used by commercial providers of sexually ex-plicit material. These providers, therefore, would be protected by the defense. Under the findings of the District Court, however, it is not economically feasi-ble for most noncommercial speakers to employ such verification. Accordingly, this defense would not significantly narrow the statute's burden on noncom-mercial speech. Even with respect to the commercial pornographers that would be protected by the defense, the Government failed to adduce any evidence that these verification techniques actually preclude minors from posing as adults.

We agree with the District Court's conclusion that the CDA places an unac-ceptably heavy burden on protected speech, and that the defenses do not consti-tute the sort of "narrow tailoring" that will save an otherwise patently invalid unconstitutional provision. In *Sable,* 492 U.S. at 127, we remarked that the speech restriction at issue there amounted to "burning the house to roast the pig." The CDA, casting a far darker shadow over free speech, threatens to torch a large segment of the Internet community.

X

The "indecency" provision, 47 U.S.C. §223(a) (Supp. 1997), applies to "any comment, request, suggestion, proposal, image, or other communication which is *obscene or indecent.*" (Emphasis added.) Appellees do not challenge the applica-tion of the statute to obscene speech, which, they acknowledge, can be banned totally because it enjoys no First Amendment protection. *See Miller,* 413 U.S. at 18. As set forth by the statute, the restriction of "obscene" material enjoys a tex-tual manifestation separate from that for "indecent" material, which we have held unconstitutional. Therefore, we will sever the term "or indecent" from the statute, leaving the rest of §223(a) standing. In no other respect, however, can §223(a) or §223(d) be saved by such a textual surgery.

XI

In this Court, though not in the District Court, the Government asserts that — in addition to its interest in protecting children — its "equally significant" interest in fostering the growth of the Internet provides an independent basis for upholding the constitutionality of the CDA. Brief for Appellants 19. The Govern-ment apparently assumes that the unregulated availability of "indecent" and "patently offensive" material on the Internet is driving countless citizens away from the medium because of the risk of exposing themselves or their children to harmful material.

We find this argument singularly unpersuasive. The dramatic expansion of this new marketplace of ideas contradicts the factual basis of this contention. The record demonstrates that the growth of the Internet has been and continues to be phenomenal. As a matter of constitutional tradition, in the absence of evi-dence to the contrary, we presume that governmental regulation of the content of speech is more likely to interfere with the free exchange of ideas than to encour-age it. The interest in encouraging freedom of expression in a democratic society outweighs any theoretical but unproven benefit of censorship.

For the foregoing reasons, the judgment of the District Court is affirmed.

JUSTICE O'CONNOR, with whom CHIEF JUSTICE REHNQUIST joins, concurring in the judgment in part and dissenting in part.

I write separately to explain why I view the Communications Decency Act of 1996 (CDA) as little more than an attempt by Congress to create "adult zones" on the Internet. Our precedent indicates that the creation of such zones can be constitutionally sound. Despite the soundness of its purpose, however, portions of the CDA are unconstitutional because they stray from the blueprint our prior cases have developed for constructing a "zoning law" that passes constitutional muster.

Appellees bring a facial challenge to three provisions of the CDA. The first, which the Court describes as the "indecency transmission" provision, makes it a crime to knowingly transmit an obscene or indecent message or image to a person the sender knows is under 18 years old. 47 U.S.C. §223(a)(1)(B) (May 1996 Supp.). What the Court classifies as a single "'patently offensive display'" provision is in reality two separate provisions. The first of these makes it a crime to knowingly send a patently offensive message or image to a specific person under the age of 18 ("specific person" provision). §223(d)(1)(A). The second criminalizes the display of patently offensive messages or images "in a[ny] manner available" to minors ("display" provision). §223(d)(1)(B). None of these provisions purports to keep indecent (or patently offensive) material away from adults, who have a First Amendment right to obtain this speech.

The creation of "adult zones" is by no means a novel concept. States have long denied minors access to certain establishments frequented by adults. States have also denied minors access to speech deemed to be "harmful to minors." The Court has previously sustained such zoning laws, but only if they respect the First Amendment rights of adults and minors. That is to say, a zoning law is valid if (i) it does not unduly restrict adult access to the material; and (ii) minors have no First Amendment right to read or view the banned material. As applied to the Internet as it exists in 1997, the "display" provision and some applications of the "indecency transmission" and "specific person" provisions fail to adhere to the first of these limiting principles by restricting adults' access to protected materials in certain circumstances. Unlike the Court, however, I would invalidate the provisions only in those circumstances.

I

Our cases make clear that a "zoning" law is valid only if adults are still able to obtain the regulated speech. If they cannot, the law does more than simply keep children away from speech they have no right to obtain—it interferes with the rights of adults to obtain constitutionally protected speech and effectively "reduce[s] the adult population...to reading only what is fit for children." Butler v. Michigan, 352 U.S. 380, 383 (1957).

Although the prospects for the eventual zoning of the Internet appear promising, I agree with the Court that we must evaluate the constitutionality of the CDA as it applies to the Internet as it exists today. Given the present state of cyberspace, I agree with the Court that the "display" provision cannot pass muster. Until gateway technology is available throughout cyberspace, and it is not in 1997, a speaker cannot be reasonably assured that the speech he displays will reach only adults because it is impossible to confine speech to an "adult zone." Thus, the only way for a speaker to avoid liability under the CDA is to refrain completely from using indecent speech. But this forced silence impinges on the First Amendment right of adults to make and obtain this speech and, for all intents and purposes, "reduce[s] the adult population [on the Internet] to reading only what is fit for children." As a result, the "display" provision cannot withstand scrutiny. Accord, *Sable*, 492 U.S. at 126–131.

The "indecency transmission" and "specific person" provisions present a closer issue, for they are not unconstitutional in all of their applications. The "indecency transmission" provision makes it a crime to transmit knowingly an indecent message to a person the sender knows is under 18 years of age. 47 U.S.C. §223(a)(1)(B) (May 1996 Supp.). The "specific person" provision proscribes the same conduct, although it does not as explicitly require the sender to know that the intended recipient of his indecent message is a minor. §223(d)(1)(A). Appellant urges the Court to construe the provision to impose such a knowledge requirement, and I would do so.

So construed, both provisions are constitutional as applied to a conversation involving only an adult and one or more minors—*e.g.*, when an adult speaker sends an e-mail knowing the addressee is a minor, or when an adult and minor converse by themselves or with other minors in a chat room. In this context, these provisions are no different from the law we sustained in *Ginsberg*. Restricting what the adult may say to the minors in no way restricts the adult's ability to communicate with other adults.

I would therefore sustain the "indecency transmission" and "specific person" provisions to the extent they apply to the transmission of Internet communications where the party initiating the communication knows that all of the recipients are minors.

II

Whether the CDA substantially interferes with the First Amendment rights of minors, and thereby runs afoul of the second characteristic of valid zoning laws, presents a closer question.

The Court neither "accept[s] nor reject[s]" the argument that the CDA is facially overbroad because it substantially interferes with the First Amendment rights of minors. I would reject it. In my view, the universe of speech constitutionally protected as to minors but banned by the CDA—*i.e.*, the universe of material that is "patently offensive," but which nonetheless has some redeeming value for minors or does not appeal to their prurient interest—is a very small one. Appellees cite no examples of speech falling within this universe and do not attempt to explain why that universe is substantial in relation to the statute's plainly legitimate sweep. That the CDA might deny minors the right to obtain material that has some "value" is largely beside the point. While discussions about prison rape or nude art may have some redeeming education value for *adults*, they do not necessarily have any such value for *minors*, and under *Ginsberg*, minors only have a First Amendment right to obtain patently offensive material that has "redeeming social importance *for minors*," 390 U.S. at 633 (emphasis added). Accordingly, in my view, the CDA does not burden a substantial amount of minors' constitutionally protected speech.

Thus, the constitutionality of the CDA as a zoning law hinges on the extent to which it substantially interferes with the First Amendment rights of adults. Because the rights of adults are infringed only by the "display" provision and by the "indecency transmission" and "specific person" provisions as applied to communications involving more than one adult, I would invalidate the CDA only to that extent. Insofar as the "indecency transmission" and "specific person" provisions prohibit the use of indecent speech in communications between an adult and one or more minors, however, they can and should be sustained. The Court reaches a contrary conclusion, and from that holding that I respectfully dissent.

Notes and Questions

1. Dial-a-Porn. In light of *Reno*, are the FCC's dial-a-porn regulations unconstitutional? Do they impose an excessive burden on adult access to protected speech relative to the harm to minors that is avoided by imposing that burden? Is this the test that emerges from *Reno*?

2. Pacifica. After *Reno*, what is left of the rationale articulated in *Pacifica*? Is the point that *Pacifica* protects children "too young to read" who might be harmed by hearing or learning a dirty word over the radio, but who are unable to access Internet indecency? If this is the case, what are we to make of *ACT III* (from Chapter Six), which affirmed Commission regulations of indecent broadcasting that, among other things, (1) define as a "child" anyone under 18 and (2) do not require that the Commission have evidence that children are in the listening or viewing audience before the agency can conclude that programming on a certain station is indecent?

Is *Pacifica* now explicable only by the *post hoc* justification for it offered in *Reno*—the history of extensive government regulation of broadcast? Does the Court's reliance on the absence of existing Internet regulation mean that Congress's choice was to regulate the Internet at its inception or else? In other words, by waiting for the Internet to develop, did Congress forego its chance to regulate at all? Is that an appropriate message to send to Congress? Does it create the right incentives?

3. Technological Advance. Note Justice O'Connor's emphasis on "the present state of cyberspace." Is a focus on currently existing technology appropriate? Is it necessary, given the Court's task of determining whether the CDA is constitutional? Does this mean that technological change could undermine the finding of unconstitutionality? For instance, suppose someone invents a cheap method for senders to "tag" Internet messages that contain dirty words or graphic descriptions of sex acts, or perhaps a cheap method for cybersurfing recipients to block such messages. Will the Court then enthusiastically embrace "tag and block" rules? Is it unusual for a determination of this magnitude to turn on such a time-sensitive finding of fact? Is there a better way? (Recall that similar concerns came up in *Turner I* and *Turner II*.)

4. The Child Online Protection Act. Is it possible to draft a statute that would pass constitutional muster but nonetheless restrict indecency on the Internet? Congress, in an apparent attempt at doing so, responded to *Reno v. ACLU* by enacting the Child Online Protection Act, Pub. L. No. 105–277, 112 Stat. 2681

(1998) ("COPA"). Like the Communications Decency Act, COPA criminalizes certain disfavored online speech, and like the CDA it has affirmative defenses for those who restrict minors' access to covered material via credit card authorization, adult identification numbers, or other reasonable measures. COPA, however, is narrower than the Communications Decency Act in several ways, including: (a) COPA's restrictions apply only to communications on the World Wide Web; content distributed through other aspects of the Internet (such as e-mail and newsgroups) are not covered; (b) whereas the CDA applied to commercial and non-commercial speakers alike, COPA applies only to communications made "for commercial purposes"; and (c) COPA applies only to "material that is harmful to minors," a term of art that is arguably narrower than "indecent" or "patently offensive" speech.

Shortly after COPA was enacted, the ACLU challenged its constitutionality in federal court. In 1999, a U.S. District Court granted the ACLU's motion for a preliminary injunction and enjoined the United States from enforcing COPA, and in 2000 the United States Court of Appeals for the Third Circuit affirmed. *ACLU v. Reno [II]*, 31 F. Supp.2d 473 (E.D. Pa. 1999), *affirmed*, 217 F.3d 162 (3rd Cir. 2000). The Third Circuit applied the familiar standard for preliminary injunctions and concluded that: (1) the constitutional challenge to COPA was likely to succeed on the merits; (2) Web publishers would be irreparably harmed absent issuance of the preliminary injunction; (3) granting the preliminary injunction would not result in greater harm to the United States than to publishers; and (4) granting the preliminary injunction would be in the public interest. On the crucial first prong, the Third Circuit found that the statute was "more likely than not to be found unconstitutional as overbroad on the merits," 217 F.3d at 181, because of an aspect of COPA that was also present in the CDA: that its definition of "harmful to minors" relied on "contemporary community standards." *See* 47 U.S.C. §231(e)(6). The fatal overbreadth, according to the court, flowed from the fact that

> because material posted on the Web is accessible by all Internet users worldwide, and because current technology does not permit a Web publisher to restrict access to its site based on the geographic locale of each particular Internet user, COPA essentially requires that every Web publisher subject to the statute abide by the most restrictive and conservative state's community standards in order to avoid criminal liability. Thus, because the standard by which COPA gauges whether material is "harmful to minors" is based on identifying "contemporary community standards" the inability of Web publishers to restrict access to their Web sites based on the geographic locale of the site visitor, in and of itself, imposes an impermissible burden on constitutionally protected First Amendment speech.

217 F.3d at 166.

CHAPTER TWENTY-ONE

ADVANCED SERVICES AND INTERNET ARCHITECTURE

The purpose of this chapter is:

- to consider the Commission's approach to the development and deployment of the telecommunications infrastructure necessary to support high-speed Internet access as well as other advanced services.

~

I. AN INTRODUCTION TO ADVANCED SERVICES

Since passage of the Telecommunications Act of 1996, the FCC has devoted substantial attention to promoting the development of "advanced" telecommunications services. Section 706(c)(1) of the 1996 Act (codified as a note to 47 U.S.C. §157) defines "advanced telecommunications capability" as "high-speed, switched, broadband telecommunications capability that enables users to originate and receive high-quality voice, data, graphics, and video telecommunications using any technology." Advanced capability, then, is the power to move beyond low bandwidth communications (like basic voice telephony) to a world in which movies, books, and data can be transmitted quickly and easily among users of telecommunications networks. Section 706 directs the FCC (and state commissions) to "encourage the deployment on a reasonable and timely basis of advanced telecommunications capability to all Americans" and to conduct regular inquiries to ensure such deployment is occurring. §706(a)–(b). Should an FCC inquiry determine that this advanced capability is not being deployed to all Americans in a reasonable and timely fashion, §706 further commands the FCC to "take immediate action to accelerate deployment of such capability by removing barriers to infrastructure investment and by promoting competition in the telecommunications market."§706(b).

Data communications were not, of course, novel at the time Congress passed the 1996 Act. Phone lines had long been used to transmit data to and from computers, between fax machines, and among educational, scientific, corporate and government institutions. Local telephone companies had already begun to implement ISDN technology, a digital standard for higher-speed data and voice transmission. Business users, too, were able long before the Act to purchase dedicated, high-capacity lines for their data traffic. What was new, however, was the growing importance of data communication in the everyday life of average consumers.

Section 706 was therefore designed to promote accessibility and growth in online communications. In 1996, although the Internet had not achieved anything close to the pervasive role it now plays in American life, it had achieved sufficient prominence that members of Congress were aware of its potential. Congress did not refer expressly to the Internet in §706, however, or indeed in other sections addressing advanced telecommunications capability. But there is no question that the Internet is the primary medium across which the majority of telecommunications users "originate and receive high-quality voice, data, graphics, and video"—the activities with which §706 is expressly concerned.

A. The FCC's Implementation of Section 706

Congress's command that the FCC promote the deployment of advanced telecommunications capability empowers the FCC to consider a broad range of regulatory tools, including price cap regulation, regulatory forbearance, promotion of local competition, and "other regulating methods that remove barriers to infrastructure investment." §706(a). Section 706 thus appears to give the FCC discretion to extend existing regulations to advanced services, or alternatively to exempt such services from existing regulations, depending on which will better encourage deployment of advanced network capability and more generally further the public interest.

To undertake this task, the Commission first had to answer, in more specific fashion than Congress did in the Act, several questions about what constitutes "advanced" telecommunications capability. First, what speed represents the dividing line between normal and advanced service? The existing telephone networks, with the proper modem connected, could potentially transmit voice, data, graphics and video at 56 kilobits per second (kbps). Is that "advanced capability" within the meaning of the Act? Or does "high-speed" in the Act mean something faster? Second, what "infrastructure" is at issue in advanced services and what are the advanced networks on or among which Congress charged the FCC to promote competition? Third, what technologies were being used to provide advanced capability and what other regulatory issues did they raise? The Commission addressed each of these questions in the *Second Report* of its ongoing *Inquiry Concerning the Deployment of Advanced Telecommunications Capability*, released in August 2000. This release, excerpted below, provides a useful snapshot of the services, network facilities, and technologies that constitute "advanced telecommunications capability."

INQUIRY CONCERNING THE DEPLOYMENT OF ADVANCED TELECOMMUNICATIONS
Second Report, FCC 00–290, 2000 WL 1199533 (2000)

III. WHAT IS ADVANCED TELECOMMUNICATIONS CAPABILITY?

10. What is advanced telecommunications capability? Section 706 (c) of the 1996 Act defines advanced telecommunications capability as "high-speed,

switched, broadband telecommunications capability that enables users to originate and receive high-quality voice, data, graphics, and video telecommunications using any technology." In the *First Report on Advanced Telecommunications*, we defined "broadband" — and, in effect, advanced telecommunications capability and advanced services — as "having the capability of supporting, in both the provider-to-customer (downstream) and the customer-to-provider (upstream) directions, a speed (in technical terms, 'bandwidth') in excess of 200 kilobits per second (kbps) in the last mile." We stated several reasons for choosing 200 kbps. First, it appeared that Congress intended advanced telecommunications capability to be faster than ISDN service, which operates at a data rate of 128 kbps and was widely available at the time of the 1996 Act. Also, 200 kbps is enough to provide the most popular applications — to change web pages as fast as one can flip through the pages of a book. Finally, we required that both upstream and downstream paths have this capability because Section 706 (c) uses the words "originate *and* receive." (Emphasis added.)

11. In this *Report*, we again examine the availability of 200 kbps, or faster, speeds in both the upstream and downstream paths of the last mile. However, we use the terms "advanced telecommunications capability" and "advanced services" to refer to this capability. Since the *First Report*, the terms "broadband" and "broadband services" have come to include a much broader range of services and facilities. In light of its now common and imprecise usage, we decline to use the term broadband to describe any of the categories of services on facilities that we discuss in this *Report*. Rather, we denominate as "high-speed" those services with over 200 kbps capability in at least one direction. Thus, high-speed is the larger category, consisting of those services and facilities with a transmission speed of 200 kbps in at least one direction. Advanced telecommunications capability and advanced services form a subset of this larger category and denote that portion capable of 200 kbps or greater transmission in *both* directions.

12. In keeping our present definition, we set a standard above the bandwidth that most residential customers use today, but well below the fastest rates possible with today's technologies. We view this definition as a benchmark. If it reflects merely what most residential customers want or are receiving today, then we risk setting our sights unduly low. We think Congress meant us to do more. We are particularly reluctant to lower our standard for the upstream path below 200 kbps. To do so would omit transmissions of home and community events, frustrating important applications of advanced telecommunications capability. It would omit lip-reading and signing, denying a major potential benefit for persons with speech and hearing disabilities and those wanting to converse with them. Narrowband upstream paths would also render difficult, if not impossible, many advanced telecommunications capability applications for telecommuting, consumer-originated broadcasting, distance education, desktop publishing, and health care. We believe that Congress intended advanced telecommunications capability to bring to all Americans a two-way, truly interactive medium, rather than one that is passive and entertainment-oriented.

14. We emphasize that our definition of advanced telecommunications capability will evolve over time. Future reports will reconsider it in light of changing conditions in both supply and demand. We may change the definition, for example, if compression technologies make possible with 100 kbps what now requires more than 200 kbps. We may also increase the speed as higher bandwidths be-

come more affordable, or as demand among millions of residential customers takes firm shape. Periodically reviewing these definitions will ensure flexibility that fits the dynamic, recurrent review process that section 706 contemplates.

IV. IS ADVANCED TELECOMMUNICATIONS CAPABILITY BEING DEPLOYED TO ALL AMERICANS?

A. Overview of the Networks Used to Provide Advanced Services

16. Advanced services are provided using a variety of public and private networks that rely on different network architectures and transmission paths. Some of these networks, like the Internet, are public in the sense that access to the network is open to all users. Other networks, like those built and maintained by corporations for their internal use, are private in the sense that access to the network may be restricted to a particular class of users, often the corporation's employees. Moreover, depending on the network, data may travel from the sender to the recipient over various architectures and transmission paths such as copper wire, cable, terrestrial wireless radio spectrum, satellite radio spectrum, or a combination of these and other media. In addition, data may be transmitted using different communications protocols that manage and direct traffic at different layers of a particular network.

17. Although advanced services are provided over myriad combinations of public and private networks using a variety of transmission paths and protocols, for the purposes of this report we focus on the physical components of the network infrastructure. For simplicity, we have divided network infrastructure into four general categories: backbone, middle mile, last mile, and last 100 feet. In addition, we refer to the points of connection between these components of the network as connection points.

18. In conceptualizing the categories of network infrastructure identified above, we find it helpful to analogize network infrastructure to a system of roads. In our simplified analogy, each of the categories corresponds to a different type of road:

Backbone—Multi-lane Interstate Highway: Backbone provides a long-distance, high-capacity, high-speed transmission path for transporting massive quantities of data, much like the way a large multi-lane interstate highway allows large amounts of traffic quickly to travel long distances. Most backbone consists of fiber optic lines, either buried in the ground or laid under the sea. In addition, backbone can be provided using satellite systems and radio spectrum.

Middle Mile—Divided Highway: As its name suggests, middle mile facilities provide relatively fast, large-capacity connections between backbone and last mile, similar to the way a divided highway may connect local roads to multi-lane interstate highways. Middle mile facilities can range from a few miles to a few hundred miles. They are often constructed of fiber optic lines, but microwave and satellite links can be used as well.

Last Mile—Local Road: The last mile is the link between the middle mile and the last 100 feet to the end-user's terminal. The last mile is analogous to the local road between a larger, divided highway and a traveler's driveway. A last mile with advanced telecommunications capability provides speeds in excess of 200 kbps in each direction. Last miles may consist of cable modem service, digital subscriber line (DSL) service, terrestrial wireless service, or satellite service. Some last-mile segments—for example those on certain cable systems—provide faster downstream speeds than upstream speeds either because their network configurations will not support the higher upstream speed or because they rely on a telephone return path.

Last 100 Feet—Driveway: The last 100 feet is the link between the last mile and the end-user's terminal, which is similar to the way a driveway connects a traveler's home or office to a local road. The last 100 feet includes the in-house wiring found in a consumer's residence, the wiring in an apartment or office building, the more complex wiring in a wireline local area network, or the wireless links in a local wireless network.

Connection Points—Intersections, On-Ramps, and Interchanges: Connection points are the places at which the various components of the network interconnect, often with the aid of an electronic or optical device (*e.g.*, switches and routers between the middle mile and backbone), so that data can move across the network. Connection points are analogous to the intersections, on-ramps, and interchanges between local roads, divided highways, and multi-lane interstate highways.

B. Components of the Network

19. In this section we examine each of the components of the network described above, both in terms of the technology used and the types of entities providing these components. We focus particularly on the last mile because it is a critical link between existing backbone and middle mile infrastructure on the one hand and the last 100 feet to the end-user's terminal on the other hand. In examining each component of the network, we also attempt to identify any major technological barriers to deployment of advanced telecommunications capability.

1. Backbone Facilities

20. At the core of the physical infrastructure supporting advanced telecommunications capabilities are nationwide backbone transport facilities. Much of the terrestrial fiber optic backbone in this country has been constructed along public rights of way created for railroad, telephone, and electric-utility owned companies. Providers have created additional backbone capacity in the form of undersea cables and satellite systems.

21. National backbone transport providers in the United States include large nationwide providers such as AT&T, WorldCom and Sprint and a number of smaller facilities-based transport providers. There are an additional 35 to 50 wireline, terrestrial wireless and satellite-based national Internet backbone providers, with varying amounts of physical facilities. The major Internet backbone providers transport traffic with capacity ranging from approximately 155 Mbps to over 10 Gbps.

22. Although the cost of building and maintaining backbone facilities is high, there do not appear to be significant technological barriers to deployment of these facilities. To date, advances in fiber optic and microwave technologies have allowed backbone capacity to keep pace with demand for backbone facilities.

2. Middle Mile Facilities

23. Middle mile facilities provide transport or routing from last mile aggregation points in order to interconnect and exchange traffic with national backbone providers or directly with other middle mile networks. It appears that most fiber optic, middle-mile facilities, like backbone, exist along public rights of way. Other middle miles include fixed wireless and satellite links.

24. Many middle mile facilities were originally built by telephone and cable companies for ordinary telecommunications or cable television services. For example, the fiber optic connections that transport telephone traffic between telephone company central offices can be considered middle mile facilities. Additional examples of middle mile networks include statewide networks such as the fiber optic network in South Dakota and numerous regional commercial enterprises.

25. Many providers of middle mile transport lease capacity on their networks to non-facilities based Internet service providers (ISPs) and high-speed providers, who find the transport speeds adequate to meet their needs. For example many local exchange carriers (LECs) currently lease the fiber or high-speed lines connecting their central offices. Most cable systems also have fiber or satellite transport facilities to regional and national backbone, which they may lease to other providers. In addition, there are entities known as Global Service Providers providing interLATA transport service.

26. As demand for middle mile facilities has increased, existing providers and new providers have deployed additional facilities. In the past five years, the amount of fiber miles deployed in the United States has doubled. Interexchange carriers, incumbent and competitive local exchange carriers, cable television companies and others, including fixed wireless service providers, have invested enormous amounts of money into construction of fiber facilities.

27. High capacity fiber connects to almost every local exchange carrier central office. Indeed, significant amounts of unused high capacity fiber, typically referred to as dark fiber, exist within the fiber conduit connecting local exchange carrier central offices.

3. Last Mile Facilities

28. Last mile facilities provide the connection between middle mile facilities and the last 100 feet to an end-user's terminal. While all components of the network play important roles in the delivery of advanced services, we focus particular attention on the deployment of last mile facilities because they are often the missing link in communities that do not have access to advanced telecommunications capability. The last mile connection to the end-user can take the form of cable modem service, digital subscriber line service (DSL) or some other LEC-provided service, terrestrial wireless service, or satellite service. Some operators of last mile facilities, like cable providers, transport data entirely over facilities that they own. Others, including many terrestrial wireless providers, lease transport to regional and/or national connection points from local exchange carriers. Last mile facilities called very small aperture terminals (VSATs) may also use satellite links to transport traffic to middle mile facilities or directly to the national backbone networks. In the sections that follow, we examine each of the four major technologies used to provide last mile facilities: cable modem service,

DSL and other LEC-provided services, terrestrial wireless, and satellite service. We discuss the types of entities that provide these last mile facilities, from the technology used to deliver advanced services and subscribership rates, to their investments in infrastructure and analysts' forecasts, as well as the significant technological barriers to deployment of each technology.

a. Overview of Cable Modem Service

29. Cable companies offer advanced services, most notably high-speed Internet access services, using cable modem technologies. Cable modem technologies rely on the same basic network architecture used for many years to provide multichannel video service, but with upgrades and enhancements to support advanced services. The typical upgrade incorporates what is commonly known as a hybrid fiber-coaxial (HFC) distribution plant. HFC networks use a combination of high-capacity optical fiber and traditional coaxial cable. Most HFC systems utilize fiber between the cable operators' offices (the "headend") and the neighborhood "nodes." Between the nodes and the individual end-user homes, signals travel over traditional coaxial cable infrastructure. These networks transport signals over infrastructure that serves numerous users simultaneously, *i.e.*, a shared network, rather than providing a dedicated link between the provider and each home, as does DSL technology. As discussed below, the shared architecture of cable networks poses certain challenges for providers that seek to offer high-speed Internet access or other advanced services over cable infrastructure.

30. Before offering high-speed Internet and other two-way high-speed services, most cable providers upgrade their networks. This process often includes extending optical fiber closer to the end-user and improving system quality to reduce signal leakage. Through this upgrade process, cable operators typically increase the system's transmission capacity to 550 MHz or 750 MHz, which allows the operator greater flexibility in allocating bandwidth for two-way high-speed services without reducing the capacity available for existing video services.

31. Upgrading a system for high-speed Internet service typically requires installation of equipment that enables the transmission of digital data packets: routers, switches, and a cable modem termination system. Further, to allow the high-speed transmission of data over the cable infrastructure in both the upstream and downstream directions, operators install amplifiers and optical lasers in both directions. Without such equipment, providers typically can provide high-speed service only in the downstream direction and must rely on a telephone line return path. Once an HFC network is upgraded, new services are available to all homes passed by the upgraded infrastructure. This contrasts with DSL technologies, where variations in legacy outside plant conditions can limit access to certain end-users even in upgraded areas, and with wireless technologies where line-of-sight requirements may be a factor.

32. Many cable systems providing high-speed data services offer asymmetric service, as the great majority of available bandwidth is allocated for downstream transmissions. The limited remaining bandwidth available for the return path results in lower upstream speeds. Most systems' upstream capacity appears to be sufficient to support current consumer demand for established services such as

web surfing. In some instances, however, this asymmetric service may not offer sufficient upstream speed to qualify under our definition of advanced telecommunications capability. As consumers use applications with higher upstream requirements such as video conferencing, cable operators may need to allocate greater network capacity for upstream transmission.

33. Under optimal conditions, and using the best available technology, an upgraded cable system can provide maximum downstream speeds of 27 Mbps and maximum upstream speeds of 10 Mbps, more than sufficient to qualify as advanced telecommunications capability. In practice, however, cable transmission speeds typically range from several hundred kilobits per second to 1.5 Mbps. The lower speed is attributable to several factors. First, because of the shared architecture of cable networks, the bandwidth—and consequently the speed—available to any single user drops as the number of simultaneously active users increases. Second, a system's transmission speed is affected by the proportion of capacity devoted to advanced services. Third, congestion on the Internet itself often limits the speed of access to well below 10 to 27 Mbps. Given these limitations on system throughput, cable operators typically offer a "maximum speed available" rather than a guaranteed stable speed of service.

34. High-speed Internet access over cable is available primarily to the residential market. Several factors may explain this. First, cable operators historically have deployed facilities for video services to the residential market. This leaves them poorly situated to offer service to many business districts. Second, cable's shared network architecture makes it difficult for providers to guarantee the consistent high speeds and secure transmissions that some business customers require. Third, the relatively narrow bandwidth typically allocated to upstream transmission renders cable unable to provide upstream speeds and symmetric transmission capabilities sufficient to support the requirements of some business customers.

b. Overview of Digital Subscriber Line Service

35. Since 1996, local telephone carriers have offered consumers high-speed data service through their digital subscriber line (DSL) service offerings. With the addition of certain electronics to the telephone line, carriers can transform the copper loop that already provides voice service into a conduit for high-speed data traffic. While there are multiple variations of DSL, some of which we discuss below, most DSL offerings share certain characteristics. With most DSL technologies today, a high-speed signal is sent from the end-user's terminal through the last 100 feet and the last mile (sometimes a few miles) consisting of the copper loop until it reaches a Digital Subscriber Line Access Multiplexer (DSLAM), usually located in the carrier's central office. At the DSLAM, the end-user's signal is combined with the signals of many other customers and forwarded though a switch to middle mile facilities.

36. The most common form of DSL used by residential customers is asymmetric DSL, or ADSL. As its name suggests, ADSL provides speeds in one direction (usually downstream) that are greater than the speeds in the other direction. Many, though not all, residential ADSL offerings provide speeds in excess of 200 kbps in only the downstream path with a slower upstream path and thus do not meet the standard for advanced telecommunications capability. However, ADSL

permits the customer to have both conventional voice and high-speed data carried on the same line simultaneously because it segregates the high frequency data traffic from the voice traffic. This segregation allows customers to have an "always on" connection for the data traffic and an open path for telephone calls over a single line. Thus a single line can be used for both a telephone conversation and for Internet access at the same time.

37. In contrast to ADSL, symmetric DSL (SDSL) provides users with equal speeds in the downstream and upstream path, usually in excess of 200 kbps. Because of the symmetrical nature of SDSL, it is well-suited to applications that require high-speed capacity in the upstream path, such as videoconferencing. Because of its higher capacity needs, SDSL service typically requires a dedicated copper pair for its high-speed data transmissions.

38. DSL service is subject to certain limitations that currently prevent it from being deployed as a last mile facility to all potential end-users. First, it is distance sensitive. Currently, an ADSL customer must be within approximately 18,000 feet of the carrier's central office; SDSL customers must be between 10,000 and 12,000 feet of the central office depending on the speed of the service in question. Eighty percent of the subscriber loop plant falls within these distance limitations, and thus is capable of supporting DSL service, but this factor remains an impediment to DSL deployment in more sparsely populated and remote locations. New technologies may allow DSL deployment at substantially greater distances.

39. The second factor limiting the deployment of DSL to some potential customers is the presence on their loops of load coils and bridged taps, devices that were used to enhance the quality of voice traffic over the copper. While they improve the quality of voice transmission, these devices prevent the deployment of DSL service over a line on which they are installed. Thus, in contrast to an upgraded cable network, which can offer upgraded service to all homes it passes, LECs must "condition" each end-user's line by removing the load coils and bridged taps while increasing the strength of the signal to maintain the quality of the line's voice traffic. Moreover, older loops or loops in need of maintenance, which may occur in poor or inner-city areas, pose additional problems for the deployment of DSL service. Frayed insulation or poorly spliced loops can cause signal leakage, which can result in poor quality transmission.

c. Overview of Other LEC-Provided Wireline Services

41. In addition to DSL offerings, many local exchange carriers offer more traditional high-speed, circuit switched services like T1 lines, which have been available for some time. Additionally, local exchange carriers have used fiber technology for many years for their interoffice plant. It is also used to deliver signals at speeds in excess of 45 Mbps directly to certain large business customers. Most residential and smaller business customers currently do not need the transmission speed of fiber, and the cost of fiber service generally makes it prohibitive for all but the largest users. Several fiber-based residential architectures have been devised; however, the high cost associated with deploying this technology makes it economically viable, if at all, only in the most densely populated of residential settings.

d. Overview of Fixed Wireless Service

43. In a fixed wireless system that provides high-speed services to consumers, a provider generally attaches to a customer's premises a radio transmitter/receiver (transceiver) that communicates with the provider's central antenna site. The central antenna site then acts as the gateway into the public switched telephone network or the Internet for these transceivers. The radio signals that travel over this network architecture serve as a substitute for the copper wire or cable strand that connects customers to the network in traditional, wired technologies.

44. Providers of fixed wireless services typically can deploy their networks much more quickly and with substantially less expense than is required to build a network capable of supporting either cable-modem or DSL service. First, wireless networks are free of the substantial costs associated with installing and maintaining wires that run to a customer's premises. These savings make wireless technology especially well suited to deployment in many rural areas, where substantial distances between customers may be cost-prohibitive for wireline technologies. Wireless technologies may also serve as an economic alternative in urban areas where consumers are not otherwise served by certain forms of wireline technologies. For example, only a small percentage of multi-tenant office buildings are currently served by fiber networks. Thus, fixed wireless services may make high-speed access more affordable for those small and medium-sized businesses for which direct fiber connections remain too expensive.

45. Second, the relative ease of installation of this technology allows wireless providers to deploy their networks much more quickly than is possible for providers that must actually install wires leading to each customer's premises. This permits wireless providers to respond rapidly and dynamically to developing demand for advanced telecommunications capability.

46. Third, the architecture of a wireless network allows providers to roll out their facilities in a manner more closely related to the product demand they encounter. A traditional wired provider often will install the network infrastructure in an entire area before it begins to market its service in that area. Thus, a cable provider will upgrade its cable plant throughout a neighborhood when it begins to offer advanced telecommunications service to the neighborhood's residents even if initial subscription rates are low. Similarly, a DSL provider likely will make certain network investments in an area where it intends to offer service before it signs up its first customer. By contrast, once a wireless provider has installed its antenna in an area, it completes the last-mile connection by installing an on-premises transceiver only for those customers who have actually subscribed to its service. This incremental build-out process allows wireless providers to avoid much of the up-front investment that traditional wired advanced telecommunications capability providers must make.

47. Although wireless services can generally be deployed more rapidly and at lower cost than comparable wireline services, they remain subject to certain technical limitations that may reduce their effectiveness in certain areas and for certain purposes. For example, in addition to requiring access to telecommunications equipment closets and any necessary in-building wiring, wireless providers often must obtain access to rooftops for the placement of antennas. This can become particularly problematic in the case of multi-tenant buildings, in which a building owner may resist permitting access. Also, many, though not all, fixed

wireless technologies are subject to line-of-sight restrictions. Thus, there must be an unobstructed path from a wireless provider's antenna to the customer's antenna on the rooftop of a building. While certain advances in wireless technology may help to overcome this limitation in the future, buildings, topographical features, certain adverse weather conditions, and even vegetation can interfere with the provision of service.

48. While physical infrastructure costs of wireless networks may be significantly less than wireline networks, wireless networks require access to spectrum. Some of the wireless systems providing high-speed services today obtained free spectrum licenses and other providers obtained spectrum through auctions. The explosive growth in recent years of wireless networks has created substantial demand for spectrum. New wireless and satellite services are increasingly constrained by spectrum scarcity and encumbrances, which may result in substantial additional acquisition costs in the future.

49. There are several different bands of spectrum over which wireless providers offer their services. The characteristics of the service, their means of deployment, and the service's potential technical limitations all vary somewhat over the different spectrum bands.

e. Overview of Satellite Service

56. Satellite service provides another option for last mile facilities with its own set of unique characteristics. In most current residential satellite-based last mile facilities, only the downstream path is provided by satellite; the upstream path is often provided by a standard dial-up telephone connection. Thus, many current residential satellite offerings are capable of providing speeds in excess of 200 kbps only in the downstream path, and therefore do not meet the definition of advanced telecommunications capability. Nonetheless, satellite-based last mile facilities may provide consumers and small businesses in geographically remote and sparsely populated areas with access to high-speed services that would not otherwise be available. Moreover, several satellite providers have announced plans to begin offering residential service with the downstream and upstream paths both provided by satellite.

57. High-speed satellite service is currently provided to both residential and business customers. Much of the current business use is for bursty high-speed service and data communications such as credit card verification or inventory control. Most of this traffic apparently is handled under private contractual arrangements similar to private line service. A growing number of business customers are also using satellite service for Internet connections.

59. Satellite-based last mile facilities have some limitations. Consumers must have a clear line of sight to the south in order to access satellite-based services. Areas subject to extreme rain or snow may have difficulty receiving satellite signals in those conditions. Additionally, DirecPC does not provide service using its standard receiving antenna to Alaska and Hawaii, because the satellite currently used to carry DirecPC service does not provide a sufficiently robust signal to operate reliably with small antennas located there. It may be technically feasible, using a larger dish, to receive DirecPC outside the continental United States, however, DirecPC does not support or guarantee its system when installed using a non-standard dish. Furthermore, because DirecPC currently relies on a telephone return path, a subscriber may incur toll charges depending on the distance

to the closest point of presence or may be required also to incur an additional expense to subscribe to a dial-up Internet service provided through a toll-free number.

f. Last 100 Feet Facilities

60. The last 100 feet typically refers to the final infrastructure segment from the end of the local access network to the end-user's terminal. This includes in-building wiring, local area networks and wireless local area networks. There do not appear to be technological barriers for last 100 feet facilities; indeed there are a variety of wireline and wireless options for constructing these facilities. Nevertheless, the cost of some of these facilities may be a significant factor in the deployment of advanced telecommunication capability in the small business or school and library context. Additionally, certain last 100 feet segments may be in poor condition and consequently unable to support advanced services. Unlike a residential setting with a handful of users, small businesses or schools and libraries may have multiple users accessing advanced services simultaneously. This need for simultaneous access may require upgrades to the existing in-building wiring and other last 100 feet facilities, which may have been originally installed only with enough capacity for standard voice telephony services. In addition, access to last 100 feet facilities may be controlled by someone other than the end-user, such as the landlord of a multiple tenant dwelling. This also may create access barriers for these facilities, especially for competitors of the incumbent service provider.

g. Connection points

61. In the preceding discussion, we have examined the various components of the network. In order for advanced services to be delivered to end-users, however, these components must interconnect with each other at the places we loosely describe as connection points—those places at which traffic passes between the various components of networks. High-speed networks exchange traffic at a variety of different places and in a variety of different mechanisms. For example, public telephone networks, including local, long distance and international networks, interconnect at Points of Presence (POPs) or through other interconnection arrangements. Satellite networks exchange traffic with terrestrial networks. Internet backbone service providers exchange traffic at network access points (NAPs), Metropolitan Area Exchanges (MAEs), and through other public and private peering and transit arrangements. National Internet backbone providers report operating commercial exchange points in over 200 cities in the United States and having over 900 POPs where they interconnect with regional networks, private networks and other providers. As usage and demand increase, network operators establish additional arrangements for the exchange of traffic.

B. Regulatory Alternatives

Having defined what "advanced telecommunications capability" is, identified the infrastructure involved, and examined the relevant technologies currently available, the question for the FCC was how, if at all, it should intervene in the advanced services market. Given the dynamic nature of telecommunications—where technology and market shares can change rapidly and continuously—the answer likely needs to be fluid. What might appear to be a monopoly bottleneck one year may well seem subject to adequate competition the next. Conversely, today's promising competitor may be tomorrow's obsolete technology, leaving monopoly where competition once seemed imminent. How should the Commission regulate in such a volatile environment?

The 1996 Act authorizes the Commission to consider a broad range of approaches to promote the development of advanced telecommunications. One approach is simply to let the advanced services market operate without any new or specific regulation so long as "reasonable" progress is being made in deployment. Another option is to be more aggressively deregulatory, exempting advanced services from general regulations (such as rate regulation) in cases where recognizing an exemption might improve investment incentives and/or hurry deployment along. A third approach would be to extend specific preexisting regulations (for example network unbundling) to the services and facilities involved in providing advanced capability. And a fourth possibility would be to implement entirely new regulations specifically designed to enhance competition and investment in advanced services.

Interestingly, the Commission has, in different contexts and at different times, considered all four approaches. For example, the Commission declared its intention to forbear from regulating important aspects of cable modem service in 1998, but opened an inquiry into adopting such regulation in 2000. The Commission's 1996 rule requiring incumbent local exchange companies to provide unbundled loops to new entrants benefitted new DSL providers but was not specifically designed to do so. In 1999, however, the agency did create additional unbundling obligations specific to DSL. (We will look at all of these decisions later in this chapter.)

So, what types of problems might be sufficient to cause the FCC to intervene in telecommunications markets in support of its statutory obligation to "encourage the deployment on a reasonable and timely basis of advanced telecommunications capability?" For one thing, advanced services may be affected by some of the same monopoly bottlenecks that (arguably) justify regulation of conventional telecommunications services. Indeed, the local loop is just as necessary for DSL service as it is for conventional voice telephony. Similarly, just as independent video program producers argued that cable companies should not be allowed to carry only channels and programs in which they have a financial interest, independent ISPs argue that cable companies should not be allowed to close their cable modem service to competing ISPs.

Advanced services might also raise bottleneck issues of a different flavor than those that affect other telecommunications markets. For example, customer loops generally consist of not one, but multiple strands of copper. An incumbent telephone company can provide DSL service over the same copper strand on which it is also offering conventional voice service. This allows economies of scope because the carrier can offer both services while incurring the fixed costs of maintaining and operating only one line. Should a DSL provider that does not also offer voice service be able to "share" the incumbent's voice loop and thereby incur only the cost of one-half of a loop in providing its service? Or is it enough to promote competition to allow the competitor to lease an entire unbundled loop, in which case it must incur the full loop cost to provide its service?

Then again, the potential for different networks and technological platforms to offer similar advanced capabilities might mean there is competition in advanced services even where there is not competition in more conventional telecommunications services. For example, in most areas cable systems do not yet meaningfully compete with telephone networks in the provision of voice communications. But cable modem service does compete with DSL service in the provision of advanced data communications. The prospect of competition most likely weighs against regulatory intervention. In many advanced services settings, then, the first question for the Commission to consider is whether the existence of substitute platforms makes it unnecessary to extend conventional telephone and cable regulations to advanced services. One interesting implication of all this: it may very well be the case that the same platform should be regulated to whatever extent it is used to provide conventional telecommunications services but should not be regulated to whatever extent it is used to provide advanced services.

II. UNBUNDLED ACCESS TO TELEPHONE SYSTEM INFRASTRUCTURE

Regulatory considerations related to the provision of advanced services over the telephone network have largely mirrored those related to the provision of conventional telephone services over that same network. Monopoly power due to bottlenecks, and barriers to entry due to network effects, have been central concerns in the Commission's deliberations about DSL deployment, just as they are central concerns addressed in the various rules that relate to basic voice telephony. Similarly, the primary regulatory tools the Commission has contemplated using to foster DSL deployment are the very same ones it uses to facilitate local exchange competition: unbundling and interconnection.

The materials that follow begin with the Commission's application of its unbundling rules to advanced service capabilities in the telephone network. As a threshold matter, the Commission first had to decide whether the local competition and other telephony provisions of the 1996 Act should apply to advanced services at all. A group of Bell Operating Companies petitioned the FCC for a declaration that DSL services should be entirely unregulated and should not be subject to the unbundling and interconnection requirements of sections 251 and 252. Their basic argument was that, because the DSL market was new and because the incumbents did not possess market power in advanced services the way they did in voice telephony, unbundling for advanced services was unnecessary. Further, according to these incumbent LECs, any such regulatory obligations would deter them from making the investments necessary to develop advanced network capabilities.

The Commission accepted the ILECs' arguments about the undeveloped state of the market and the ILECs' lack of market power, but nonetheless decided that (1) the interconnection requirements of §§251(a)–(c) would apply to packet switched data traffic, and (2) the facilities and equipment the ILECs used for advanced services were network elements under §251(c)(3) and therefore could be unbundled if they met the Act's impairment and technical feasibility criteria. The immediate consequence of the FCC's decision was that

ILECs could not deny unbundled loops to competing DSL providers or refuse to hand off or receive DSL traffic. The two orders that follow show the Commission's further decisions about the unbundling of additional network elements specific to provision of DSL service. The first excerpt is from the Commission's packet switching decision, and the second is from the Commission's line sharing decision.

IN THE MATTER OF IMPLEMENTATION OF THE LOCAL COMPETITION PROVISIONS OF THE TELECOMMUNICATIONS ACT OF 1996

Third Report and Order, 15 FCC Rcd. 3696 (1999)

D. Local Switching

2. Packet Switching

a. Background

300. In an earlier *Notice*, we sought comment on whether packet switches should be unbundled pursuant to section 251(c)(3), and whether there is any basis for treating network elements used in the provisioning of packet-switched advanced services any differently than those used in the provisioning of circuit-switched voice services. Incumbent LECs argue that they generally trail in the deployment of packet switches, and therefore should not be subject to unbundling requirements that might eliminate their incentives to invest in equipment used to provide advanced services. Several competitors argue in favor of unbundling packet switching to encourage the broad-based deployment of advanced services.

b. Discussion

(i) Definition of Packet Switching

302. As a threshold matter, we must define the functionality of the packet switching unbundled network element. In packet-switched networks, messages between network users are divided into units, commonly referred to as packets, frames, or cells. These individual units are then routed between network users. The switches that provide this routing function are "packet switches," and the function of routing individual data units based on address or other routing information contained in the units is "packet switching."

303. We find that a component of the packet switching functionality, and included in our definition of packet switching, is the Digital Subscriber Line Access Multiplexer (DSLAM). The DSLAM splits voice (low band) and data (high band) signals carried over a copper twisted pair. DSLAM equipment sometimes includes a splitter. If not, a separate splitter device separates voice and data traffic. The voice signal is transmitted toward a circuit switch, and the data from multiple lines is combined in packet or cell format and is transmitted to a packet switch, typically ATM or IP. The DSLAM combines: (1) the ability to terminate copper customer loops (which includes both a low-band voice channel and a high-band data channel, or solely a data channel); (2) the ability to forward the voice channels, if present, to a circuit switch or multiple circuit switches; (3) the

ability to extract data units from the data channels on the loops; and (4) the ability to combine data units from multiple loops onto one or more trunks that connect to a packet switch or packet switches.

304. We define packet switching as the function of routing individual data units, or "packets," based on address or other routing information contained in the packets. The packet switching network element includes the necessary electronics (*e.g.*, routers and DSLAMs). We find that packet switching qualifies as a network element because it includes "all features, functions and capabilities... sufficient... for transmission, routing or other provision of a telecommunications service." Because packet switching and DSLAMs are used to provide telecommunications services, packet switching qualifies as a network element. We adopt a definition of packet switching that does not favor or disadvantage one packet switching technology over another. Our intention is to define packet switching in such a way as to capture the functionality of packet networks, without regard to a particular "packetizing" technology that an incumbent LEC has deployed in its network.

(ii) Proprietary Concerns Associated With Packet Switching

305. No party alleged that packet switching was proprietary within the meaning of section 251(d)(2). We find that the record provides no basis for withholding packet switching from competitors based on proprietary considerations or subjecting packet switching to the more demanding "necessary" standard set forth in section 251(d)(2)(A). Instead we examine packet switching under the "impair" standard of section 251(d)(2)(B).

(iii) Unbundling Analysis for Packet Switching

306. We decline at this time to unbundle the packet switching functionality, except in limited circumstances. Among other potential factors, we recognize that the presence of multiple requesting carriers providing service with their own packet switches is probative of whether they are impaired without access to unbundled packet switching. The record demonstrates that competitors are actively deploying facilities used to provide advanced services to serve certain segments of the market—namely, medium and large business—and hence they cannot be said to be impaired in their ability to offer service, at least to these segments without access to the incumbent's facilities. In other segments of the market, namely, residential and small business, we conclude that competitors may be impaired in their ability to offer service without access to incumbent LEC facilities due, in part, to the cost and delay of obtaining collocation in every central office where the requesting carrier provides service using unbundled loops. We conclude, however, that given the nascent nature of the advanced services marketplace, we will not order unbundling of the packet switching functionality as a general matter.

307. Advanced services providers are actively deploying facilities to offer advanced services such as xDSL [a generic term for various DSL services] across the country. Competitive LECs and cable companies appear to be leading the incumbent LECs in their deployment of advanced services. Such marketplace developments suggest that requesting carriers have been able to secure the necessary inputs to provide advanced services to end users in accordance with their

business plans. This evidence indicates that carriers are deploying advanced services to the business market initially as well as the residential and small business markets.

308. Several parties, in addition to the incumbent LECs, argue that the Commission should not unbundle packet switching or DSLAMS generally. We recognize that equipment needed to provide advanced services, such as DSLAMS and packet switches, are available on the open market at comparable prices to incumbents and requesting carriers alike. Incumbent LECs and their competitors are both in the early stages of packet switch deployment, and thus face relatively similar utilization rates of their packet switching capacity. Packet switching utilization rates will differ from circuit switching utilization rates because of the incumbent LEC's monopoly position as carrier of last resort. Incumbent LEC circuit switches, because they serve upwards of 90 percent of the circuit switched market, may achieve higher utilization rates than the circuit switches of requesting carriers. Because the incumbent LEC does not retain a monopoly position in the advanced services market, packet switch utilization rates are likely to be more equal as between requesting carriers and incumbent LECs. It therefore does not appear that incumbent LECs possess significant economies of scale in their packet switches compared to the requesting carriers.

309. Collocating in incumbent LEC central offices imposes material costs and delays on a requesting carrier and materially diminishes a requesting carrier's ability to provide the services it seeks to offer. As discussed above, we identified the costs and delays associated with collocation as factors that impair a requesting carrier's ability to self-provision circuit switches to serve residential and small business market. We see no reason to distinguish a requesting carrier's collocation-related costs and delays to provide circuit-switched service from those collocation costs and delays incurred by requesting carriers to provide packet-switched services. These costs and delays lead us to find that competitors are impaired in their ability to offer advanced services without access to incumbent LEC facilities. That conclusion is not dispositive of whether unbundling is appropriate at this time under section 251(d)(2). In addition to the "impair" standard we consider whether unbundling will open local markets to competition and how access to a given network element will encourage the rapid introduction of local competition to the benefit of the greatest number of customers.

310. NorthPoint argues that an additional impediment it faces when providing advanced services using xDSL technologies is the absence of line sharing. Currently, many incumbent LECs offer advanced services over the high-frequency range of the same loops they use to offer voice services. Although the incumbent LEC may use a single copper pair to provide xDSL services, in the absence of line sharing, requesting carriers providing xDSL services must purchase an additional unbundled loop to serve their customers, thereby incurring additional non-trivial costs. In light of the substantial number of packet switches deployed by competitive LECs, even in comparison to incumbent LEC deployment, we conclude that these non-trivial costs are substantial enough to impair the requesting carrier's ability to provide the services it seeks to offer within the meaning of section 251(d)(2). [The FCC declined, however, to further address the issue of line sharing in this *Order*.]

313. We do find one limited exception to our decision to decline to unbundle packet switching. Access to packetized services to provide xDSL service requires "clean" copper loops without bridge taps or other impediments. Furthermore, xDSL services generally may not be provisioned over fiber facilities. In locations where the incumbent has deployed digital loop carrier (DLC) systems, an uninterrupted copper loop is replaced with a fiber segment or shared copper in the distribution section of the loop [so a customer loop no longer extends all the way to the central office where a competing LEC will typically have its collocated equipment]. In this situation, and where no spare copper facilities [that can bypass the fiber segment] are available, competitors are effectively precluded altogether from offering xDSL service if they do not have access to unbundled packet switching. Moreover, if there are spare copper facilities available, these facilities may not meet the necessary technical requirements for the provision of certain advanced services. For example, if the loop length exceeds 18,000 feet, the provision of ADSL service is technically infeasible. When an incumbent has deployed DLC systems, requesting carriers must install DSLAMs at the remote terminal instead of at the central office in order to provide advanced services. We agree that, if a requesting carrier is unable to install its DSLAM at the remote terminal or obtain spare copper loops necessary to offer the same level of quality for advanced services, the incumbent LEC can effectively deny competitors entry into the packet switching market. We find that in this limited situation, requesting carriers are impaired without access to unbundled packet switching. Accordingly, incumbent LECs must provide requesting carriers with access to unbundled packet switching in situations in which the incumbent has placed its DSLAM in a remote terminal. The incumbent will be relieved of this unbundling obligation only if it permits a requesting carrier to collocate its DSLAM in the incumbent's remote terminal, on the same terms and conditions that apply to its own DSLAM. Incumbents may not unreasonably limit the deployment of alternative technologies when requesting carriers seek to collocate their own DSLAMs in the remote terminal.

314. Policy Goals. Incumbent LECs argue in this proceeding that their incentive to invest and innovate in new technologies capable of providing advanced services will be curtailed if we mandate unbundling. We note that investments in facilities used to provide service to nascent markets are inherently more risky than investments in well established markets. Customer demand for advanced services is also more difficult to predict accurately than is the demand for well established services, such as traditional plain old telephone service (POTS).

315. We acknowledge that the incumbent LEC argument that unbundling may adversely affect innovation is consistent with economic theory, but events in the marketplace suggest that other factors may be driving incumbent LECs to invest in xDSL technologies, notwithstanding the economic theory. For example, in January 1998, U S WEST announced a rollout of ADSL service to 40 in-region metropolitan areas. In October 1998, BellSouth announced its plans to offer ADSL service to 1.7 million customers in 30 markets by the end of 1998, and 23 additional markets in 1999. Combined, Bell Atlantic and GTE have stated that the number of xDSL capable-lines available in region will be 17 million and they will have ADSL capability in 550 central offices, allowing them to serve as many as 6.1 million xDSL customers. Such investments have been planned and undertaken notwithstanding the fact that we sought comment in August 1998 on

whether facilities used to provide advanced services must be unbundled pursuant to section 251.

316. Despite the encouraging signs of investment in facilities used to provide advanced services described above, we are mindful that regulatory action should not alter the successful deployment of advanced services that has occurred to date. Our decision to decline to unbundle packet switching therefore reflects our concern that we not stifle burgeoning competition in the advanced service market. We are mindful that, in such a dynamic and evolving market, regulatory restraint on our part may be the most prudent course of action in order to further the Act's goal of encouraging facilities-based investment and innovation.

317. Our overriding objective, consistent with the congressional directive in section 706, is to ensure that advanced services are deployed on a timely basis to all Americans so that consumers across America have the full benefits of the "Information Age." The advanced services marketplace is a nascent one. Although some investment has occurred to date, much more investment in the future is necessary in order to ensure that all Americans will have access to these services. We remain concerned about the lack of deployment in rural areas. We note that we will carefully monitor the deployment of broadband services to ensure that the objectives of section 706 and the Act are being met. We decline to unbundle packet switching at this time, except for the limited exception described above.

Notes and Questions

1. Why Not Unbundle? Why did the Commission decide not to order unbundling of packet switching given its finding in ¶309 that new competitors are "impaired" without such unbundled access and its finding in ¶315 that the possibility of unbundling did not seem to be harming DSL investment and deployment?

2. Impairment. How, on the other hand, could the FCC conclude that CLECs were impaired in providing DSL service and at the same time find, as it did in ¶307, that the CLECs were in fact leading the ILECs in DSL deployment?

3. Digital Loop Carrier Fiber. As the Commission explains in ¶313, "digital loop carrier" fiber creates a situation where, instead of customer loops going all the way to a central office, they go only to a "remote terminal," which in turn is connected by a fiber feed to the central office. This can be very efficient and can increase the capacity and functionality of the local network. But it has the consequence of making collocation at the central office useless for new entrants because there is no customer loop for them to connect to there. That is why the Commission required either that the ILEC provide collocation at the remote terminal or else unbundle its packet switching with respect to customers whose loops do not go all the way to the central office. Putting in digital loop carrier fiber could therefore have an additional cost for the ILEC in the form of having to either provide unbundled packet switching or else create space for collocation at the usually small remote terminals. If digital loop carrier fiber is efficient, shouldn't the Commission have more carefully considered whether this aspect of its ruling in particular would deter efficient investment?

4. Line Sharing. In ¶310, the Commission raises, but defers, the issue of line sharing, which would have required the Commission to define an entirely new network element specific to DSL. The Commission took on the line sharing issue shortly thereafter, however. That order follows.

IN THE MATTERS OF DEPLOYMENT OF WIRELINE SERVICES OFFERING ADVANCED TELECOMMUNICATIONS CAPABILITY AND IMPLEMENTATION OF THE LOCAL COMPETITION PROVISIONS OF THE TELECOMMUNICATIONS ACT OF 1996

14 FCC Rcd. 20912 (1999)

4. In this *Order* we adopt measures to promote the availability of competitive broadband xDSL-based services, especially to residential and small business customers. We amend our unbundling rules to require incumbent LECs to provide unbundled access to a new network element, the high frequency portion of the local loop. This will enable competitive LECs to compete with incumbent LECs to provide to consumers xDSL-based services through telephone lines that the competitive LECs can share with incumbent LECs. The provision of xDSL-based service by a competitive LEC and voiceband service by an incumbent LEC on the same loop is frequently called "line sharing."

9. In circumstances in which the xDSL-equipped line carries both POTS ("plain old telephone service") and data channels, the carrier must separate those two streams when they reach the telephone company's central office. Generally, this is done by two pieces of transmission equipment, a Digital Subscriber Line Access Multiplexer (DSLAM) and a splitter. The DSLAM sends the customer's voice traffic to the public, circuit-switched telephone network and the customer's data traffic (combined with that of other xDSL users) to a packet-switched data network. Once on the packet-switched network, the data traffic is routed to the location selected by the customer, for example, a corporate local area network or an Internet service provider. That location may itself be a gateway to a new packet-switched network or set of networks, like the Internet.

IV. LINE SHARING

17. Line sharing generally describes the ability of two different service providers to offer two services over the same line, with each provider employing different frequencies to transport voice or data over that line. Section 3(29) of the Act defines a network element as "a facility or equipment used in the provision of telecommunications services" including "features, functions, and capabilities, that are provided by means of such facility or equipment." As discussed in detail below, the frequencies above those used for analog voice services on any loop are a capability of that loop.

    B. Designation of High Frequency Loop Spectrum as an Unbundled
       Network Element

   2. Discussion

25. As discussed below, we conclude that access to the high frequency spectrum of a local loop meets the statutory definition of a network element and satisfies the requirements of sections 251(d)(2) and (c)(3). It is technically feasible

for an incumbent LEC to provide a competitive LEC with access to the high frequency portion of the local loop as an unbundled network element. An incumbent LEC's failure to provide access impairs the ability of a competitive LEC to offer, on a competitive basis, certain forms of xDSL-based service that are capable of line sharing with voice services. The record shows that lack of access to the high frequency portion of the local loop would materially raise competitive LECs' cost of providing xDSL-based service to residential and small business users, delaying broad facilities-based market entry, and materially limiting the scope and quality of competitors' service offerings. Moreover, access to the high frequency portion of the loop encourages the deployment of advanced telecommunications capability to all Americans as mandated by section 706 of the 1996 Act. Because some residential and small business markets may lack the economic characteristics that would support competitive entry in the absence of access to the high frequency spectrum of a local loop, it is clear that spectrum unbundling is crucial for the deployment of broadband services to the mass consumer market.

a) Definition

26. We define the high frequency spectrum network element to be the frequency range above the voiceband on a copper loop facility used to carry analog circuit-switched voiceband transmissions. We affirm our tentative conclusion that any rules we adopt should not mandate a particular technological approach to the use of a line for multiple services. Line sharing relies on rapidly evolving technology and our requirement that incumbent LECs provide the high frequency spectrum of a local loop as an unbundled network element should stimulate technological innovation. We seek to ensure that, in the future, carriers are not denied the opportunity to provision services that rely on different frequency bands within the loop. Consequently, we do not set a specific dividing line between the low frequency channel and a high frequency channel on the loop.

c) Analysis for Unbundled Access to the High Frequency Spectrum of a Local Loop Network Element

29. We conclude that a lack of access to high frequency spectrum of a local loop impairs a competitive carrier's ability to offer certain forms of xDSL-based service. As described below, just as the loop itself remains a facility available only from an incumbent LEC, so too is a competitor seeking to offer certain xDSL-based services impaired if it does not have access to the high frequency spectrum of the local loop available from an incumbent LEC.

30. We recognize that in the *Local Competition Third Report and Order*, the Commission concluded that cable companies and competitive LECs are actively deploying xDSL-based advanced services. We held there that competitors are not impaired in their ability to provide advanced services to medium and large business users without access to the incumbents' packet switching, a component of xDSL-based advanced services. We found that requesting carriers may be impaired in their ability to offer xDSL-based services to residential and small business customers without packet switching capability, but declined to order unbundling of incumbent LEC packet switching capability because of the nascent nature of the advanced services market. However, we also specifically stated that impairment with regard to residential and small business segments may be due "in part, to the cost and delay of obtaining collocation in every central office

where the requesting carrier provides service using unbundled loops." Thus, our impairment analysis for packet switching rests in part on the assumption that the impairment results from the intermediate step of getting to the loop, not from use of the loop. Using the loop to get to the customer is fundamental to competition. The issue before us now, whether competitive LECs are impaired without access to the high frequency portion of the loop when they seek to provide various forms of xDSL-based services, is a different question than whether requesting carriers are impaired without access to unbundled packet switching.

33. There is no question that incumbent LECs are offering xDSL on the same line as their voice service, and competitive LECs are at a significant disadvantage in offering xDSL-based services over the same line that is used to provide voice service. Incumbent LECs generally deploy forms of xDSL-based services that can coexist with voice service on a single line. This enables incumbent LECs to utilize the full capacity of the copper local loop to efficiently provide both voice and data service to a customer. As discussed below, competitive LECs seeking to deploy xDSL-based service to customers subscribing to the incumbent LEC's voice telephone service cannot deploy their xDSL with the same efficiency or at the same cost. Incumbent LECs currently do not permit competitive LECs to access the high frequency portion of the loop to provide xDSL-based services, even though the incumbent LECs utilize the high frequency portion of the loop to deploy their own services. As discussed below, this situation materially diminishes the competitive LEC's ability to provide the particular type of xDSL-based service that it seeks to offer.

39. If competitive LECs were to purchase or self-provision a second unbundled loop to provide voice-compatible xDSL-based services, their provisioning of service would be materially more costly, and coincidentally less efficient, than purchasing the unbundled high frequency portion of the loop. The inability of competing carriers to provide xDSL-based services over the same loop facilities that the incumbents use to provide local exchange service makes the provision of competitive xDSL-based services to customers that want a single line for both voice and data applications—typically small businesses and mass market residential consumers—not just marginally more expensive, but so prohibitively expensive that competitive LECs will not be able to provide such services on a sustained economic basis. Accordingly, a requesting carrier providing voice-compatible xDSL-based services is impaired without access to the unbundled high frequency portion of the loop.

40. Specifically, incumbent LECs refuse to permit competitive LECs to deploy xDSL-based service to their customers on the same customer loops through which incumbents provide voice services, although incumbents regularly deploy both services on the same loop. As a result, a competitive LEC providing xDSL to a customer subscribing to an incumbent LEC's voice service must provide a second customer loop for the customer's xDSL service, effectively doubling the line access charges for that customer's voice and xDSL services, and providing a distinct cost advantage to incumbent LEC-provided xDSL products. The record shows that the combined collocation and unbundled loop costs, exclusive of incremental and fixed network, equipment, and overhead costs, incurred by a competitive LEC seeking to deploy xDSL service can exceed 100% of the retail price for the comparable shared-line xDSL that the incumbent offers to the same customer that the competitor is vying for. The record also shows that incumbents

charge requesting carriers almost as much or more, on a monthly basis, for an unbundled, conditioned loop, as the incumbent charges its retail customers for xDSL service. This price discrepancy between what an incumbent can charge its customer for its own shared-line xDSL and what a competitor must pay to the incumbent just to gain access to that customer materially diminishes the ability of the competitive carrier to offer voice-compatible xDSL-based services in competition with incumbent LEC.

42. A competitive carrier faces a competitive disadvantage in providing xDSL over a second line when competing against the incumbent's single line offering. The incumbent is able to market its own service to customers as a quick and convenient add-on service, while the competitive carrier must persuade the customer to purchase a second line. For example, Bell Atlantic, BellSouth, and US WEST emphasize in their advertising that consumers can subscribe to their xDSL-based products without incurring the installation and additional monthly expense of acquiring an additional telephone line. In comparison, consumers that desire to obtain xDSL service from competitive LECs must encounter complications and expenses, including the need to arrange for a technician to install service, that do not arise if they procure the exact same service from the incumbent LEC. Providing competitive LECs with access to the high frequency portion of the loop would remove that additional burden from consumers that prefer to obtain xDSL service from competitors.

43. Finally, we disagree with commenters who argue that a decision to unbundle the high frequency portion of the loop should be no different than the Commission's analysis of DSLAMs and packet switches, which the Commission decided not to unbundle. These commenters argue that the same reasons which led the Commission to decline to unbundle packet switching should lead to a Commission decision to refrain from creating a high frequency portion of the loop UNE. We disagree. Self-provisioning switches is vastly easier, less expensive, less time consuming, less complicated, and less risky than self-provisioning the outside plant that constitutes the ubiquitous loop network. Moreover, when we considered the impairment issue with regard to packet switches in the *Local Competition Third Report and Order*, we held that the presence of "multiple requesting carriers providing service with their own packet switches is probative of whether they are impaired without access to unbundled packet switching." To follow this line of reasoning in the situation before us, we would be looking at whether competitive LECs have self-provisioned loops, or more precisely, have self-provisioned the high frequency portion of the loop in order to provide xDSL-based services. There can be little dispute that requesting carriers have not duplicated the incumbent LEC's ubiquitous loop plant and generally are not providing service with competitive loop facilities. Thus, we disagree with those commenters who argue that we should treat loops and packet switches as identical for unbundling purposes.

47. Incumbents argue that competitors have the same competitive options as incumbents, that they are free to provide both analog voice and data services in combination, using unbundled network elements, and that as a result, competitors are not impaired without access to the high frequency portion of the loop. We acknowledge that self-provisioning a circuit-switched network is not the sole means of providing voice service. In particular, requesting carriers could obtain combinations of network elements and use those elements to provide circuit-

switched voice service as well data services. This would relieve a competitive carrier from the need to make significant investments in switching technology that may soon become obsolete.

48. We find, however, that despite its ability to purchase transmission facilities from the incumbent to provide voice service, a competitor is still impaired if it must provide analog voice service in order to enter the market for voice-compatible xDSL services. There are additional costs associated with being a provider of voice service than the cost of the circuit switches. In particular, a competitive carrier would need to develop marketing, billing, and customer care infrastructure designed to service the needs of its voice customers. In addition, competitive LECs seeking to enter the traditional voice services market must deploy sales and marketing forces, and invest in creating a recognizable brand. To compete against incumbent LECs that have a long history providing voice services, competitors must overcome the substantial goodwill, experience and market power of the incumbent LECs. These factors make it a considerable challenge for competitive LECs to motivate a consumer to adopt a new local exchange provider that offers much the same service that the consumer already receives from the incumbent LEC.

54. Goals of the Act: Our decision to unbundle the high frequency portion of the loop is consistent with the 1996 Act's goals of rapid introduction of competition and the promotion of facilities-based entry. Moreover, our decision to require spectrum unbundling is consistent with Congress's mandate that the Commission encourage the deployment of advanced telecommunications capability in section 706 of the 1996 Act. We are convinced that line sharing will enable requesting carriers to accelerate the provision of xDSL-based service to residential and small business customers who, to date, have not had the same level access to competitive broadband services as larger businesses.

56. Some commenters argue that unbundling the high frequency portion of the loop will dampen investment by competitive LECs that offer voice services. We do not believe that facilitating competition in xDSL services will necessarily diminish the competitive opportunity in the provision of voice services. Certainly, offering voice service is not a technical prerequisite to the provision of xDSL service on a particular loop. Rather, it is the fact that the incumbent is already providing voice service on a loop that makes the preservation of competitive access to the high frequency portion of that loop so vital. Without line sharing, competitors would face substantial barriers to market entry, such as additional required investment for voiceband equipment and facilities, and the difficulties of competing against an entrenched, market-dominant competitor. Requiring that competitors provide both voice and xDSL services, or none at all, effectively binds together two distinct services that are otherwise technologically and operationally distinct. Such bundling, whether through self-provisioning or through partnerships, will not drive additional investment dollars toward voice, because it does not make voice more lucrative, but will drive investment away from the provision of advanced services, such as xDSL-based services, undermining the Congressional intention articulated in section 706 of the 1996 Act. In addition, without line sharing consumers would need to forego their current voice service provider, virtually always an incumbent LEC, in order to subscribe to a competitive LEC's xDSL service, which robs consumers of market choices.

57. Moreover, the availability of shared-line access will encourage data carriers to continue investing in network facilities such as DSLAMs, interoffice networks, and backbone facilities, and should promote further innovation in xDSL technologies. We conclude that unbundling the high frequency portion of the loop will not deter investment by facilities-based competitive LECs that plan to offer a full range of services to consumers, including both voice and data services. We expect that such carriers will be able to differentiate themselves from competitive LECs offering only data services by offering consumers the benefits of one-stop shopping, or by providing access to superior facilities or technology. In addition, we do not agree that providing competitors with the option to deliver data services will permit incumbent LECs to become entrenched in the provision of voice service. We believe that product integration and technological innovation will, over time, enable competitive LECs to continue to compete with incumbents for the provision of a full range of services.

Notes and Questions

1. Impairment. How does the impairment analysis for the high frequency portion of the local loop differ from the Commission's earlier analysis for packet switching? The answer given by the Commission is that, in the packet switching case, impairment was due to delays in obtaining the loop, and once the loop was obtained there was no further impairment from not having access to the ILEC's DSLAMs. In the line sharing case, an impairment exists even if the unbundled loop can be obtained by the CLEC. Is that a persuasive distinction? Can you think of a better one?

2. A Price Squeeze? The competitive concern that motivates the Commission's decision to order line sharing is that, without it, the ILEC can put competitors in a "price squeeze." A price squeeze occurs when one firm can raise its rival's production costs while at the same time lowering prices in the relevant market. The rival's returns are "squeezed" between its higher costs and its lower revenues and, if the margins turn negative, the rival is pushed out of the market. The problem is raised most often when a vertically integrated firm simultaneously (a) supplies another firm with an essential input and (b) competes with that firm in the final product market. If the vertically integrated firm can charge the competitor more for the input than the firm implicitly charges itself, then it can raise its rival's costs relative to its own costs and create a price squeeze in the final product market. The product market at issue in line sharing was the combined offering of xDSL and regular voice service. Are you persuaded that regulatory action was necessary to prevent a price squeeze in that market? If not, why did the FCC order line sharing? If so, does the FCC's decision alleviate the problem? Should the FCC have done more? Less?

3. Accounting for Cable. The Commission did not consider the competition to DSL service from cable modem service in weighing whether to order line sharing. Should it have? Or is cable modem competition for some reason relevant to the determination of whether to require unbundled packet switching but irrelevant to a determination with regard to line sharing? What might you want to know or predict before deciding whether to consider cable modem competition when regulating DSL?

III. OPEN ACCESS TO CABLE
SYSTEM INFRASTRUCTURE

The telephone infrastructure is not the only infrastructure capable of supporting the kind of high-speed communications necessary for Internet access and other advanced services. The cable plant—and specifically cable modem service—similarly can be used to bring consumers online and/or deliver high bandwidth information products to the home.

In recent years, the main question on the regulatory agenda with respect to high-speed cable service has been the question of whether firms that own cable infrastructure should be forced to open their networks to unaffiliated ISPs in much the same way LECs are forced to open their networks to unaffiliated firms under the 1996 Act's unbundling and resale obligations. The issue arose when specific providers of cable modem service decided to provide Internet access exclusively through a single, affiliated ISP. Unaffiliated ISPs demanded that they, too, be able to reach the affected cable customers and, further, that they be able to do so on non-discriminatory terms. The requested regulation has been labeled "open access."

The FCC early on declined to pursue cable open access policies. In speeches by individual commissioners and decisions not to condition approvals of cable system mergers on open access, the Commission established a de facto policy of non-regulation with regard to cable modem service. The Commission's reasons for not regulating had both legal and economic dimensions. On the legal side, it was and perhaps still is unclear in what statutory category cable modem services fall. Are they cable, telecommunications, or information services? Are they none of the above? The answer to that question has significant consequences for both whether and how cable modem services can be regulated under the 1934 Communications Act. On the economic side, it similarly was and perhaps still is unclear whether open access regulation is desirable as a matter of economic policy. The Commission took the position that the provision of Internet service over cable was in such an embryonic stage, and the investment needed to provide such services was so large, that imposing regulation was more likely to deter growth and deployment than it was to encourage either competition or investment. As then-chair of the FCC William Kennard said in a much-publicized 1999 speech:[1]

> Sometimes people talk about broadband as though it is a mature industry. But, the fact is that we don't have a duopoly in broadband. We don't even have a monopoly in broadband. We have a NO-opoly. Because, the fact is, most Americans don't even have broadband. We have to get these pipes built.
>
> But how do we do it? We let the marketplace do it.

---

1. "The Road Not Taken: Building a Broadband Future for America," Remarks of William E. Kennard, Chairman, Federal Communications Commission, Before the National Cable Television Association, Chicago, Illinois (June 15, 1999).

If we've learned anything about the Internet in government over the last 15 years, it's that it thrived quite nicely without the intervention of government.

If fact, the best decision government ever made with respect to the Internet was the decision that the FCC made 15 years ago not to impose regulation on it. This was not a dodge; it was a decision not to act. It was intentional restraint born of humility. Humility that we can't predict where this market is going.

Who among us could have predicted the incredible advances of the past few years? Who at the beginning of this decade could have predicted the embrace of e-mail by all ages, the birth of the World Wide Web, the advances in communications technology?

In a market developing at these speeds, the FCC must follow a piece of advice as old as Western Civilization itself: first, do no harm. Call it a high-tech Hippocratic Oath.

In the excerpt above, Kennard emphasizes the nascent state of cable modem service as a reason to forbear from regulation. But it is also important to question whether, even if the market for cable modems were well developed, open access regulation would be necessary. What are the incentives for cable operators to monopolize the ISP layer of their Internet service? For example, would allowing consumers their choice of ISP make subscribers more willing to switch from dial-up, narrowband service to cable broadband service, or to choose cable modem service over DSL service? If so, won't cable operators voluntarily adopt open access policies, offering their consumers a choice among several ISPs as a way of attracting or keeping consumers who are free to switch away from cable modem service entirely if they are dissatisfied? And even if consumers view DSL service as inferior to cable modem service, won't cable providers still want to offer ISP choice? After all, to whatever extent consumers value choice, won't they also be willing to pay more for cable modem service? Questions like these lie at the heart of the current debate over cable open access. As you read the material that follows, keep the above questions in mind and critically evaluate the possible incentives cable operators face to be monopolists at the ISP layer on the one hand, and to allow at least some unaffiliated ISPs access to their networks on the other.

While the materials that follow focus exclusively on the open access debate, it should be noted here that open access is not the only major regulatory issue to arise in the context of cable modem service. Another important battle concerns the Commission's horizontal ownership rules. As we noted in Chapter Twelve, any individual cable operator is limited to serving thirty percent of subscription video subscribers nationally. The Commission has a set of rules governing when a subscriber will be attributed to a cable operator for purposes of calculating that operator's market share. In many cases, any subscriber to a system in which an operator has a five percent voting interest will be attributed to that operator for purposes of the subscriber limit. One exception to that attribution rule exists, however, when the operator is only an "insulated limited partner" in the system at issue, in which case that system's subscribers are not attributed to that operator. Before 1999, to qualify as an insulated limited partner a cable operator, among other requirements, had to certify that it was "not materially involved, directly or indirectly, in the management or operation of the media activities of the partnership." 47 C.F.R. §76.501 n.2(g)(1). That rule was subtly but perhaps importantly changed in 1999:

> For the horizontal ownership and channel occupancy limits rules, we will amend the insulation criteria to provide that a limited partnership interest shall be attributed to a limited partner unless the partnership certifies that this limited partner is not materially involved, directly or indirectly, in the management or operation of the video-programming-related activities of the partnership. The horizontal ownership and channel occupancy limits are designed to address the ability of one multiple system operator (MSO) or a group of MSOs, by virtue of their size, to impede the flow of programming from the programmers to consumers. An MSO may extend its ability to affect the programming marketplace when it invests in other cable companies. However, where the MSO is not materially involved in the video-programming activities of a limited partnership, its investment does not extend its national programming power and the concerns of Section 613 are not implicated. In these circumstances where programming is not affected, the current insulation criteria prevent investments between companies whose combination may bring benefits to the public, such as cable broadband and telephony services and competition to the incumbent local exchange carriers or Internet [because such services may qualify as "media activities"]. In order for the limited partnership to benefit from an investor's expertise in these areas, it is necessary to craft insulation criteria that will not prevent the investor from offering its services to the partnership so long as those services are unrelated to the partnership's video-programming activities.[2]

In short, in order to promote the development of cable modem services, the Commission to some degree peeled back its rule against consolidation in the cable industry.

Although the Commission has thus tried to foster the growth of cable as an advanced services platform through actions unrelated to open access, it is open access that has received the most attention and proven the most contentious. Because of the Commission's decision to take a hands-off approach, parties seeking open access had to move the regulatory battle out of the federal arena and instead onto the agenda of state and local cable authorities. That move added further complications. As the materials that follow explain in more detail, once on the state and local level, open access became a two-tiered battle: first, there was the question of whether state and local authorities even had the power to impose open access obligations should they so choose; second, there was the more fundamental question of whether open access obligations were in the public interest no matter who was to impose them. We begin with the jurisdictional issue, our source material being an influential opinion from the Ninth Circuit Court of Appeals.

---

2. In the Matter of Implementation of the Cable Television Consumer Protection and Competition Act of 1992; Implementation of Cable Act Reform Provisions of the Telecommunications Act of 1996; Review of the Commission's Cable Attribution Rules, 14 FCC Rcd. 19014, ¶164 (1999).

AT&T v. CITY OF PORTLAND
216 F.3d 871 (9th Cir. 2000)

Opinion for the court filed by Circuit Judge THOMAS, in which Circuit Judges LEAVY and FERNANDEZ concur.

THOMAS, Circuit Judge:

This appeal presents the question of whether a local cable franchising authority may condition a transfer of a cable franchise upon the cable operator's grant of unrestricted access to its cable broadband transmission facilities for Internet service providers other than the operator's proprietary service. We conclude that the Communications Act prohibits a franchising authority from doing so and reverse the judgment of the district court.

Distilled to its essence, this is a struggle for control over access to cable broadband technology. In broadband data transmission, a single medium carries multiple communications at high transmission speeds. The allure of broadband technology is that it allows users to access the Internet at speeds fifty to several hundred times faster than those available through conventional computer modems connected to what is commonly referenced in the telecommunications industry as "plain old telephone service." Broadband allows transmission, or "streaming," of live video and audio communications, as well as video and audio data files. To satisfy consumer demand for broadband Internet access, cable television operators have replaced coaxial wires with fiber-optic cable, telephone companies have initiated high-frequency digital subscriber line (DSL) services over standard twisted-pair copper wires, fixed wireless providers have upgraded their microwave transmission capacities, satellite providers have launched global two-way digital networks, and researchers have explored the use of quantum communication methods.

The race to acquire broadband transmission systems has, in part, prompted a number of corporate mergers. This appeal concerns the merger between AT&T, at the time the nation's largest long distance telephone provider, and Telecommunications, Inc. (TCI), one of the nation's largest cable television operators. In addition to providing traditional cable television programming, TCI provided cable broadband Internet access to consumers in certain geographic areas. Since acquiring TCI, AT&T has continued to offer cable broadband access as part of its "@Home" service, which bundles its cable conduit with Excite, an Internet service provider (ISP) under an exclusive contract. Like many other ISPs, @Home supplements its Internet access with user e-mail accounts and a Web portal site, a default home page gateway offering Internet search capabilities and proprietary content devoted to chat groups, interactive gaming, shopping, finance, news, and other topics. @Home subscribers also may "click-through" to other free Web portal sites, and may access other Internet service providers if they are willing to pay for an additional ISP; however, subscribers cannot purchase cable broadband access separately from an unaffiliated ISP, and have no choice over terms of Internet service such as content and bandwidth restrictions.

The @Home cable broadband infrastructure differs from that of most ISPs. A typical ISP connects with the Internet via leased telecommunications lines, which its consumers access through "dial-up" connections over ordinary telephone lines. @Home operates a proprietary national "backbone," a high-speed network parallel to the networks carrying most Internet traffic, which connects to those other Internet conduits at multiple network access points. This backbone serves regional data hubs which manage the network and deliver Excite's online content and services, including multimedia content that exploits broadband transmission speeds. Each hub connects to local "headend" facilities, cable system transmission plants that receive and deliver programming, where "proxy" servers cache frequently requested Internet data, such as Web sites, for local delivery. Each headend connects to cable nodes in neighborhoods, each of which in turn connects via coaxial cable to the user's cable modem and computer.

To effect the merger, AT&T and TCI sought three types of regulatory approval. The Department of Justice approved the merger on antitrust grounds, subject to TCI's divestiture of its interest in Sprint PCS wireless services. The Federal Communications Commission approved the transfer of federal licenses from TCI to AT&T, after addressing public interest concerns in four service areas, including residential Internet access. *See Application for Consent to the Transfer of Licenses and Section 214 Authorizations from TCI to AT&T*, 14 FCC Rcd. 3160 (1999).

One of the issues that the FCC considered forms the undercurrent of the present controversy: whether to impose a requirement of open access to cable broadband facilities. A variety of interest groups and competitors argued that allowing AT&T to restrict cable broadband access to the proprietary @Home service would harm competition and reduce consumer choice. In its order approving the license transfer, the FCC rejected any open access condition, citing the emergence of competing methods of high-speed Internet access, and @Home customers' "ability to access the Internet content or portal of his or her choice." It found "that the equal access issues raised by parties to this proceeding do not provide a basis for conditioning, denying, or designating for hearing any of the requested transfers of licenses and authorizations." The FCC concluded that "while the merger is unlikely to yield anticompetitive effects, we believe it may yield public interest benefits to consumers in the form of a quicker roll-out of high-speed Internet access services."

The last regulatory hurdle that AT&T and TCI faced was the approval of local franchising authorities where required by local franchising agreements. *See* 47 U.S.C. §537 (permitting franchising authority approval of cable system sales when the franchise agreement so requires). TCI's franchises with Portland and Multnomah County (collectively, "Portland") permitted the city to "condition any Transfer upon such conditions, related to the technical, legal, and financial qualifications of the prospective party to perform according to the terms of the Franchise, as it deems appropriate." This language parallels the text of 47 U.S.C. §541(a)(4)(C), which describes the conditions a locality may impose on a franchise.

Portland referred the transfer application for recommendation by the Mount Hood Cable Regulatory Commission, an intergovernmental agency overseeing cable affairs in the Portland region. In response to Portland's preliminary questions, AT&T confirmed that TCI was in the process of upgrading its cable system to support @Home over cable broadband, and maintained that @Home was a proprietary product "not subject to common carrier obligations." At public hearings, the incumbent local telephone exchange carrier US WEST and the Oregon Internet Service Providers Association called for open access to TCI's cable broadband network, citing—in addition to consumer welfare—the need for "a level playing field" with US WEST's common carrier obligations and a "very real potential that consumer Internet access businesses could go out of business." The Mount Hood Commission recommended that the city and county approve the transfer of franchise control subject to an open access requirement. On December 17, 1998, Portland and Multnomah County voted to approve the transfer, subject to an open access condition expressed in a written acceptance:

> Non-discriminatory access to cable modem platform. Transferee shall provide, and cause the Franchisees to provide, non-discriminatory access to the Franchisees' cable modem platform for providers of Internet and on-line services, whether or not such providers are affiliated with the Transferee or the Franchisees, unless otherwise required by applicable law. So long as cable modem services are deemed to be "cable services," as provided under Title VI of the communications Act of 1934, as amended, Transferee and the Franchisees shall comply with all requirements regarding such services, including but not limited to, the inclusion of revenues from cable modem services and access within the gross revenues of the Franchisees' cable franchises, and commercial leased access requirements.

AT&T refused the condition, which resulted in a denial of the request to transfer the franchises. AT&T then brought this action, seeking declarations that the open access condition violated the Communications Act of 1934, codified at 47 U.S.C. §151, *et seq.* (collectively, the "Communications Act"), the franchise agreements, and the Constitution's Commerce Clause, Contract Clause, and First Amendment. The district court rejected all of AT&T's claims and granted summary judgment to Portland. *See* AT&T Corp. v. City of Portland, 43 F. Supp. 2d 1146 (D. Or. 1999). We review de novo a grant of summary judgment; there being no disputed factual issues, we face only a question of statutory interpretation.

II

The parties, and numerous amici, forcefully urge us to consider what our national policy should be concerning open access to the Internet. However, that is not our task, and in our quicksilver technological environment it doubtless would be an idle exercise. The history of the Internet is a chronicle of innovation by improvisation, from its genesis as a national defense research network, to a medium of academic exchange, to a hacker cyber-subculture, to the commercial engine for the so-called "New Economy." Like Heraclitus at the river, we address the Internet aware that courts are ill-suited to fix its flow; instead, we draw our bearings from the legal landscape, and chart a course by the law's words. To that end, "we look first to the plain language of the statute, construing the provisions of the entire law, including its object and policy." United States v. Mohrbacher, 182 F.3d 1041, 1048 (9th Cir. 1999). We note at the outset that the FCC has declined, both in its regulatory capacity and as amicus curiae, to address the issue before us. Thus, we are not presented with a case involving potential deference to an administrative agency's statutory construction.

A

Because Portland premised its open access condition on its position that @Home is a "cable service" governed by the franchise, we begin with the question of whether the @Home service truly is a "cable service" as Congress defined it in the Communications Act. We conclude that it is not.

Subject to limited exceptions, the Communications Act provides that "a cable operator may not provide cable service without a franchise." 47 U.S.C. §541 (b)(1). The Act defines "cable service" as "(A) the one-way transmission to subscribers of (i) video programming, or (ii) other programming service, and (B) subscriber interaction, if any, which is required for the selection or use of such video programming or other programming service." 47 U.S.C. §522(6). For the purposes of this definition, "video programming" means "programming provided by, or generally considered comparable to programming provided by, a television broadcast station," 47 U.S.C. §522(20), and "other programming service" means "information that a cable operator makes available to all subscribers generally." 47 U.S.C. §522(14). The essence of cable service, therefore, is one-way transmission of programming to subscribers generally.

This definition does not fit @Home. Internet access is not one-way and general, but interactive and individual beyond the "subscriber interaction" contemplated by the statute. Accessing Web pages, navigating the Web's hypertext links, corresponding via e-mail, and participating in live chat groups involve two-way communication and information exchange unmatched by the act of electing to receive a one-way transmission of cable or pay-per-view television programming. And unlike transmission of a cable television signal, communication with a Web site involves a series of connections involving two-way information exchange and storage, even when a user views seemingly static content. Thus, the communication concepts are distinct in both a practical and a technical sense. Surfing cable channels is one thing; surfing the Internet over a cable broadband connection is quite another.

Further, applying the carefully tailored scheme of cable television regulation to cable broadband Internet access would lead to absurd results, inconsistent with the statutory structure. For example, cable operators like AT&T may be required by a franchising authority to set aside cable channels for public, educational or governmental use, see 47 U.S.C. §531, must designate some of their channels for commercial use by persons unaffiliated with the operator, see 47 U.S.C. §532, and must carry the signals of local commercial and non-commercial educational television stations, see 47 U.S.C. §§534 & 535. We cannot rationally apply these cable television regulations to a non-broadcast interactive medium such as the Internet. As our sister circuit concluded in the context of the abortive "video dialtone" common carrier television technology, regulating @Home as a cable service "simply makes no sense in any respect, and would be infeasible in many respects." National Cable Television Ass'n. v. FCC, 308 U.S. App. D.C. 221, 33 F.3d 66, 75 (D.C. Cir. 1994).

Thus, because the Internet services AT&T provides through @Home cable modem access are not "cable services" under the Communications Act, Portland may not directly regulate them through its franchising authority.

B

Although we conclude that a cable operator may provide cable broadband Internet access without a cable service franchise, we must also determine whether

Portland may condition AT&T's provision of standard cable service upon its opening access to the cable broadband network for competing ISPs. To do so, we must determine how the Communications Act defines @Home.

Under the statute, Internet access for most users consists of two separate services. A conventional dial-up ISP provides its subscribers access to the Internet at a "point of presence" assigned a unique Internet address, to which the subscribers connect through telephone lines. The telephone service linking the user and the ISP is classic "telecommunications," which the Communications Act defines as "the transmission, between or among points specified by the user, of information of the user's choosing, without change in the form or content of the information as sent and received." 47 U.S.C. §153(43). A provider of telecommunications services is a "telecommunications carrier," which the Act treats as a common carrier to the extent that it provides telecommunications to the public, "regardless of the facilities used." 47 U.S.C. §153(44) & (46).

By contrast, the FCC considers an ISP itself as providing "information services" under the Act, defined as "the offering of a capability for generating, acquiring, storing, transforming, processing, retrieving, utilizing, or making available information via telecommunications." 47 U.S.C. §153(20) (1996). As the definition suggests, ISPs are themselves users of telecommunications when they lease lines to transport data on their own networks and beyond on the Internet backbone. However, in relation to their subscribers, who are the "public" in terms of the statutory definition of telecommunications service, they provide "information services," and therefore are not subject to regulation as telecommunications carriers. *See* Federal-State Joint Board on Universal Service, 13 FCC Rcd. 11501; *cf.* Child Online Protection Act, 47 U.S.C. §231(e)(4)), & Internet Tax Freedom Act, Pub. L. No. 105–277, §1101(e), 112 Stat. 2681 (1998) (reproduced at note to 47 U.S.C. §151(e) (1998)) (defining Internet access services as: "a service that enables users to access content, information, electronic mail, or other services offered over the Internet, and may also include access to proprietary content, information, and other services as part of a package of services offered to consumers. Such term does not include telecommunications services.").

Like other ISPs, @Home consists of two elements: a "pipeline" (cable broadband instead of telephone lines), and the Internet service transmitted through that pipeline. However, unlike other ISPs, @Home controls all of the transmission facilities between its subscribers and the Internet. To the extent @Home is a conventional ISP, its activities are one of an information service. However, to the extent that @Home provides its subscribers Internet transmission over its cable broadband facility, it is providing a telecommunications service as defined in the Communications Act.

Under this taxonomy, the Communications Act bars Portland from conditioning the franchise transfer upon AT&T's provision of the @Home transmission element that constitutes telecommunications:

(3)(A) If a cable operator or affiliate thereof is engaged in the provision of telecommunications services —

(i) such cable operator or affiliate shall not be required to obtain a franchise under this title for the provision of telecommunications services; and

(ii) the provisions of this title shall not apply to such cable operator or affiliate for the provision of telecommunications services.

(B) A franchising authority may not impose any requirement under this title that has the purpose or effect of prohibiting, limiting, restricting, or conditioning the provision of a telecommunications service by a cable operator or an affiliate thereof.

(C) A franchising authority may not order a cable operator or affiliate thereof—

(i) to discontinue the provision of a telecommunications service, or

(ii) to discontinue the operation of a cable system, to the extent such cable system is used for the provision of a telecommunications service, by reason of the failure of such cable operator or affiliate thereof to obtain a franchise or franchise renewal under this title with respect to the provision of such telecommunications service.

(D) Except as otherwise permitted by sections 611 and 612, a franchising authority may not require a cable operator to provide any telecommunications service or facilities, other than institutional networks, as a condition of the initial grant of a franchise, a franchise renewal, or a transfer of a franchise.

47 U.S.C. §541(b)(3); *see also* 47 U.S.C. §253(a) ("No State or local statute or regulation, or other State or local legal requirement, may prohibit or have the effect of prohibiting the ability of any entity to provide any interstate or intrastate telecommunications service."). Subsection 541(b)(3) expresses both an awareness that cable operators could provide telecommunications services, and an intention that those telecommunications services be regulated as such, rather than as cable services.

The Communications Act includes cable broadband transmission as one of the "telecommunications services" a cable operator may provide over its cable system. Thus, AT&T need not obtain a franchise to offer cable broadband, *see* 47 U.S.C. §541(b)(3)(A); Portland may not impose any requirement that has "the purpose or effect of prohibiting, limiting, restricting or conditioning" AT&T's provision of cable broadband, *see* 47 U.S.C. §541(b)(3)(B); Portland may not order AT&T to discontinue cable broadband, *see* 47 U.S.C. §541(b)(3)(C); and Portland may not require AT&T to provide cable broadband as a condition of the franchise transfer, *see* 47 U.S.C. §541(b)(3)(D). Therefore, under the several provisions of §541(b)(3), Portland may not regulate AT&T's provision of @Home in its capacity as a franchising authority, and the open access condition contained in the franchise transfer agreement is void.

Notes and Questions

1. **Ninth Circuit Analysis.** The Ninth Circuit's decision proceeds in two steps. First, it examines whether cable modem service is a "cable" service under the Communications Act. Second, upon finding the service not to be "cable," the court examines how it should be characterized under the Act. Why did the court take both steps? Why could it not stop with the determination that cable Internet access can be provided without a franchise under the Act?

2. The Statutory Provisions. Review the statutory provisions (§§541(b)(3)(A)–(D)) on which the court relies to reach its result. Exactly which of those provisions did Portland violate with its ordinance? Did the city do anything to interfere with AT&T's provision of cable modem transmission? Did it improperly require AT&T to provide cable modem service as a condition of license transfer, or did it simply impose obligations on a service AT&T was already providing? Is that a legally meaningful distinction? Consider what textual arguments could be made against the Ninth Circuit's reading of §541(b)(3). Which is the better reading?

3. Implications. In the end, the court does not say that cable operators are immune from open access rules. It says only that, because Internet access constitutes "telecommunications" rather than "cable," a cable license transfer cannot under the Act be conditioned on anything to do with cable modem service. What are the possible outcomes for open access under this decision? Much has been made of the inconsistent patchwork of regulation that might arise if local cable authorities could order open access. But under the Ninth Circuit's reasoning could state telephone regulators decide to enter the fray and themselves impose a patchwork of conflicting local regulations? Or is cable modem service sufficiently interstate that only the FCC can (or should) regulate open access? Does the Ninth Circuit's decision that cable modem service is not "cable" but instead "telecommunications" in any way constrain the FCC's regulatory options?

4. Policy. The Ninth Circuit did not, of course, address the pure policy question of whether open access requirements are in the public interest. The court simply noted that several policy options were open to the Commission, including forbearance, and struck down the City of Portland's ordinance as being outside its powers. Several months after the Ninth Circuit's decision, although not specifically in response to the case, the FCC opened an inquiry into the broader policy question of open access regulation. An excerpt from the Commission's *Notice of Inquiry* follows.

INQUIRY CONCERNING HIGH-SPEED ACCESS TO THE INTERNET OVER CABLE AND OTHER FACILITIES

Notice of Inquiry, FCC 00–355, 2000 WL 1434689 (2000)

I. INTRODUCTION

4. The Commission has heretofore taken a "hands-off" policy with respect to the high-speed services provided by cable operators. This regulatory restraint has been premised, in part, on the belief that "multiple methods of increasing bandwidth are or soon will be made available to a broad range of customers."[3] Nonetheless, this Commission has stated that it would revisit this policy "if competition fails to grow as expected" in the provision of high-speed services.[4] We

---

3. Inquiry Concerning the Deployment of Advanced Telecommunications Capability to All Americans in a Reasonable and Timely Fashion and Possible Steps to Accelerate Such Deployment Pursuant to Section 706 of the Telecommunications Act of 1996, 14 FCC Rcd. 2398, 2448 at ¶101 (1999).

4. Applications for Consent to the Transfer of Control of Licenses and Section 214 Authorizations from MediaOne Group, Inc., Transferor, to AT&T Corp., Transferee, Memorandum Opinion and Order, FCC 00–202, at ¶121 (June 6, 2000).

therefore ask several questions in this proceeding to ascertain whether our hands-off policy for high-speed services provided by cable operators remains the correct approach and how the Commission might introduce a national policy framework for regulating high-speed services. In light of factors such as the differing treatment accorded different providers and services under the Act itself, however, we note that this national framework may or may not impose the same regulatory obligations on all providers.

II. BACKGROUND

A. Evolution of High-Speed Services

8. A number of cable television operators, both incumbents and new entrants, have started offering access to the Internet over their cable plant. These services provide access with much higher transmission speeds than traditional dial-up services and are offered primarily to residential customers over the cable systems' shared media hybrid fiber coaxial networks. The coaxial cable transmits signals to the cable modem, which, in turn, is connected to the computer. For the return path, some cable modem services require the customers' computers to send signals upstream over traditional dial-up telephone connections. With more advanced cable modem networks, both directions of traffic are transmitted via the coaxial cable, which permits the connection to be open at all times and offer higher transmission speeds.

B. The Commission's Approach To High-Speed Services

12. Beginning with our review of the AT&T/TCI merger in 1999, numerous parties have argued that the Commission should require cable operators to provide unaffiliated ISPs with access to cable networks on nondiscriminatory terms and conditions. In the *AT&T/TCI Order*, the Commission declined to condition the transfer on an open access requirement based on the Applicants' representation that subscribers could continue to bypass Excite@Home's proprietary content and reach any content available on the World Wide Web. In its review of the AT&T/MediaOne merger, the Commission again declined to impose an open access condition, based [partly on consideration of] (1) the increasingly rapid deployment of alternative high-speed Internet platforms, especially xDSL and (2) a commitment by AT&T/MediaOne to negotiate non-exclusive contracts with unaffiliated ISPs when the Applicants' exclusive arrangements with affiliated ISPs expire.

13. While the Commission has pursued open access through regulatory restraint, some local governments have sought to achieve open access through regulation. These local efforts have resulted in recent federal court cases that have considered the regulatory status of cable modem service under the Act. In the context of license transfers involving AT&T's cable systems, a number of local franchising authorities (LFAs) enacted ordinances conditioning the license transfer on nondiscriminatory access to the cable modem platform for unaffiliated ISPs. In AT&T Corp. v. City of Portland, the United States Court of Appeals for the Ninth Circuit confirmed this Commission's role in establishing a national broadband policy. The Ninth Circuit also ruled that insofar as Excite@Home provides subscribers with Internet transmission over AT&T's cable network, it was providing a "telecommunications service," and insofar as Excite@Home of-

fers subscribers services traditionally offered by ISPs, the court held that it provides an "information service." The court declined to say whether the Commission should subject the "telecommunications service" provider to the full range of telecommunications common carrier regulations under Title II, observing that the Commission has broad authority to forbear from enforcing those regulations. Reaching a contrary conclusion, the United States District Court for the Eastern District of Virginia has ruled that Excite@Home's cable modem service fits the statutory definition of a "cable service." MediaOne Group v. County of Henrico, 97 F. Supp. 2d 712, 715 (E.D. Va. 2000). Finally, the United States Court of Appeals for the Eleventh Circuit has held that "Internet service does not meet the definition of either a cable service or a telecommunications service." Gulf Power Co. v. FCC, 208 F.3d 1263, 1278 (11th Cir. 2000).

III. DISCUSSION

A. The Classification of Cable Modem Service And/Or The Cable Modem Platform

15. We seek comment on the variety of legal or policy frameworks that might apply to cable modem service and the cable modem platform. Indeed, there may be a number of regulatory approaches possible, from treating cable modem service and/or the cable modem platform as a cable service subject to Title VI; as a telecommunications service under Title II; as an information service subject to Title I; or some entirely different or hybrid service subject to multiple provisions of the Act. We also seek comment on the implications, if any, of adopting a particular framework for classifying cable modem service and/or the cable modem platform as it relates to our regulation of other high-speed service providers, including those that use xDSL, wireless, satellite, broadcast and unlicensed spectrum technologies.

16. More specifically, with respect to applying Title VI, we invite comment on whether cable modem service and/or the cable modem platform is a cable service. "Cable service" is defined under the Act as "(A) the one-way transmission to subscribers of (i) video programming, or (ii) other programming service, and (B) subscriber interaction, if any, which is required for the selection *or use* of such video programming or other programming service." 47 U.S.C. §522(6) (emphasis added). The terms "or use" were added to the definition in the 1996 Act. Does the legislative history indicate that Congress intended by this change to include cable modem service and/or the cable modem platform in the definition of "cable service"? Specifically, we seek comment on whether the addition of the words "or use" expanded the category of services such that cable modem service and/or the cable modem platform fits within the definition. Notwithstanding the 1996 amendment, a service that is not "video programming" cannot be a "cable service" unless it qualifies as "other programming service." Does cable modem service and/or the cable modem platform constitute "other programming service" as defined in the Act?

18. In addition, we seek comment on whether cable modem service and/or the cable modem platform is a telecommunications service subject to Title II. Under the Act, "telecommunications" is a necessary component of a "telecommunications service." Is there a component of cable modem service or the cable modem platform that represents pure transmission capability between a subscriber and a destination which does not alter the form or content of the infor-

mation sent? If so, should we, if only for definitional purposes, sever a telecommunications component from other functions that may be provided? Is it possible for cable subscribers to specify the ultimate points of communication on the Internet? Does it matter, for purposes of determining whether the service is a common carrier offering, that the cable subscriber cannot select ISPs that have not entered into agreements with the cable operator? If cable modem service or the cable modem platform contains a telecommunications component, must the facility used to provide the telecommunications necessarily be classified as a "telecommunications facility"?

20. We note that the Act imposes a wide variety of obligations on telecommunications carriers, including requirements relating to interconnection, universal service contributions, disabilities access, and privacy of subscriber information. How would those statutory provisions, and the Commission's implementing regulations, apply to cable operators? For example, how would the §251(a) interconnection obligation apply to cable operators? How would the Commission determine whether cable modem service was provided at rates that are just, reasonable and not unreasonably discriminatory? How would the Commission determine whether the manner in which cable companies allow unaffiliated ISPs to "interconnect" with the cable modem platform is just, reasonable and not unreasonably discriminatory?

23. We also invite comment on another question, that is whether cable modem service and/or the cable modem platform constitutes an information service. We note that the Commission has classified the end user services commonly provided by dial-up ISPs as information services. Does cable modem service and/or the cable modem platform fit within this definition? We seek comment on the implications, if any, of classifying cable modem service and/or the cable modem platform as an information service under the Act. Information service providers as such are not subject to regulation under Title II as common carriers; the fact that information service is provided "via telecommunications" does not alter that conclusion. With respect to cable modem service, if a cable operator simultaneously offers a telecommunications and information service, should we, if only for definitional purposes, sever the underlying telecommunications, or the telecommunications service, from the information service offering? Is there any reason to treat the cable modem service as if it were solely an information service? Should the Commission's treatment differ depending on whether the provider of cable modem service also owns or controls the underlying transmission platform?

24. Finally, we invite comment on whether cable modem service and/or the cable modem platform is distinct from the regulatory classifications identified above and would require a new legal and policy framework. To the extent the Commission deems it appropriate, under what authority (apart from the authority cited above) could it require cable operators to be subject to the unbundling requirements that stem from the Commission's *Computer Inquiries* or impose similar unbundling requirements?

B. Issues Surrounding Open Access

1. What Is "Open Access"?

27. Currently, there is no universally accepted definition of "open access." Most open access proposals entail two broad requirements, providing unaffili-

ated ISPs with the right to: (i) purchase transmission capability; and (ii) access the customer directly from the incumbent cable operator. Apart from those general requirements, however, there are numerous different technological and economic models for what open access might mean, and technological approaches for how it might be implemented. Should we define open access based on the manner or degree of access we ultimately determine is necessary to achieve particular goals?

28. Industry participants have different conceptions of open access. For example, OpenNet Coalition, a group of ISP and LEC interests, defines open access as "the ability of consumers to choose the Internet service provider of their choice"; "enabling consumers and their chosen Internet service providers to reach each other requires that Internet service providers not chosen by the cable company have the ability to purchase, on a nondiscriminatory basis, the use of 'last mile' communications facilities to reach consumers who are requesting their service."[5] AOL and Time Warner present an alternative conception. Under their conception, open access is achieved through negotiated commercial agreements between cable operators and ISPs operating in a free market. The prices, terms and conditions for such agreements may differ depending on the ISP's needs and the cable operator's resources, but will not vary based on affiliation or lack thereof.

29. In the current environment some cable operators have entered into exclusive arrangements with one particular ISP (*e.g.*, AT&T's arrangement with Excite@Home), and all cable Internet subscribers must pay the cable operator for the Internet service of that particular ISP even if they choose to use an alternative ISP. Although we recognize that these cable operators have recently negotiated access to their networks by certain unaffiliated ISPs, nevertheless, these cable operators currently are not legally prohibited from having an exclusive relationship with one particular ISP. Should the Commission consider the approach of achieving openness through negotiated commercial agreements between cable operators and unaffiliated ISPs an open access model? Does this model provide an appropriate level of openness?

2. Is Open Access A Desirable Policy Goal?

32. We invite comment on the policy considerations that should underlie our analysis of open access issues. Specifically, we invite comment on the desirability of open access as a policy goal. Should the Commission encourage open access to the cable modem platform? If so, what are the appropriate underlying goals that the Commission should seek to achieve through such openness, and what degree of openness is necessary to achieve those goals? Is open access necessary, for example, to benefit consumers or otherwise achieve policy objectives identified by Congress or the Commission, such as promoting competition, deregulation, innovation, and investment in and deployment of high-speed services? What are the best means for the Commission to facilitate the deployment of high-speed services in a manner that benefits consumers? We also ask what costs may be as-

---

5. OpenNet Coalition White Paper, "Frequently Asked Questions about AT&T's Acquisition of MediaOne, Open Access, and the Public Interest," at 23 (Sept. 17, 1999).

sociated with open access and how those costs compare to the benefits of open access.

33. More specifically, commenters should address the services that ISPs currently provide and what new services will likely be offered by ISPs as the Internet enters the high-speed era. Which of these new services, if any, will require ISPs to obtain nondiscriminatory access to the cable modem platform as opposed to other levels or types of access? To the extent nondiscriminatory access is required, why is it required? What are the potential harms of failure to achieve open access? In what specific ways is competition among ISPs important to ensure the widespread availability of high-speed, high-quality services at competitive rates? What benefits does a competitive ISP market bring to other areas of the Internet, such as innovation among content and application providers? How would competition between ISPs affect consumer choice and value, including access by persons with disabilities?

3. If Open Access Is A Desirable Policy Goal, What Are The Most Appropriate Means Of Achieving That Objective?

34. If open access is a desirable policy goal, we invite comment on whether a market-based approach will adequately achieve that objective, or whether the Commission should adopt another approach. Commenters should discuss the implications of our determination of the framework for cable modem services and access to the cable modem platform for providers of similar services using other technologies, such as xDSL, satellite, broadcast, or wireless technologies.

a. Should the Commission Continue a Market-Based Approach?

35. We invite comment on whether market-based approaches are sufficient to achieve the level of access by ISPs to the cable modem platform that the Commission determines is appropriate. Considering the current conditions in the market for cable high-speed services, is there a need for mandated open access or will market forces operate to achieve open access? Specifically, how will mandated open access impact unaffiliated ISPs, unaffiliated content providers, and end users? The decision to provide open access voluntarily may depend on the degree of competition in the provision of local facilities. Are the harms from failure to achieve open access impacted by the presence of competing local facilities? Are any of these harms likely to take place without government intervention? If so, why? To what extent is such regulatory intervention necessary, and what costs would be associated with that intervention? What should be the Commission's role, if any, in promoting and encouraging competition among ISPs?

36. We seek to understand the economic incentives of cable operators, both outside of and under alternative open access models. For example, do cable operators have any incentive to cooperate with multiple ISPs that seek access to their platforms? Do cable operators have an incentive to allow non-exclusive access in order to increase the number of end users purchasing cable modem services? Do cable operators that are vertically integrated with an ISP have less incentive to provide open access in order to decrease competition for the integrated ISP? How do cable operators weigh these competing incentives, and what might induce a vertically integrated cable operator to provide open access? We also seek to determine

how, in a market-based approach, multiple ISPs will be provided access, and how and by whom these ISPs will be chosen. Is the number of ISPs under a market-based approach likely to be sufficient to achieve the goals of open access? Why or why not? Are there significant differences in ISPs? How different, if at all, are the incentives of non-vertically integrated cable operators to offer end users a diverse set of ISPs? What incentives do these operators have not to frustrate end users' access to unaffiliated content? What specific evidence is there that operators have denied their cable modem customers access to unaffiliated content to date? Will the incentives to provide open access change as competition increases in the provision of high-speed access services by DSL providers and providers of other high-speed services? What role, if any, do consumer expectations regarding the availability of multiple, unaffiliated ISPs in the traditional narrowband wireline context have on cable operators' incentives to provide similar availability over cable modem platforms?

37. We also seek comment on the reported development of market-based access initiatives. Initially, cable operators signed exclusive agreements with one ISP (most notably Excite@Home and RoadRunner). Currently, however, there appears to be some movement toward allowing access to additional ISPs. For example, AT&T released a letter, co-signed with Mindspring Enterprises, Inc., promising to allow Mindspring and other ISPs access to its cable platform once its exclusivity agreement with Excite@Home expires in 2002. Similarly, Time Warner, Inc. and AOL released a Memorandum of Understanding promising ISPs open access to Time Warner's cable platform once its exclusivity agreement with RoadRunner expires in 2001. There are further indications that cable operators are moving toward allowing other ISPs access to their platform. Time Warner, for example, recently announced that it had reached an agreement with Juno Online Services, Inc., whereby Juno will become the first unaffiliated ISP to use Time Warner cable systems for the provision of high-speed Internet services.

39. We are further interested in assessments of the current pledges by cable operators for future open access. Are these pledges specific enough to guarantee open access once they are implemented? To what extent is such eventual implementation necessary to promote deployment of high-speed services, competition, deregulation, and other goals contemplated by the Act? If such pledges are lacking in necessary specificity, what additional details or commitments would increase the likelihood that they will eventually be implemented without government intervention? Can such additional details and commitments be fleshed out without favoring certain unaffiliated ISPs or business plans over others?

b. Should The Commission Act To Ensure Open Access?

42. Assuming the Commission has the jurisdiction to require open access, and assuming that open access is desirable as a policy matter, we seek to determine the conditions under which the Commission should mandate open access to the cable modem platform. Specifically, should the Commission intervene if a cable operator is the only facilities-based provider of high-speed services and it owns or controls the ISP providing service to end users? Should the Commission intervene if there is an actual or potential competitor to the cable operator? Commenters should describe any public interest harms that would otherwise result from closed access or requiring open access to the cable modem platform.

Commenters should address whether and the extent to which such harms will be realized if ISPs seeking access to the cable modem platform offer services that are not different from or more attractive to consumers than those provided by the affiliated ISP. Commenters should also describe how requiring open access would alleviate the harms associated with closed access, and discuss any costs that may result from requiring open access. In addition, commenters should address how imposing regulations in this area would comport with the Commission's historical policy of not regulating the Internet. Commenters should compare specifically the advantages and disadvantages associated with regulatory intervention designed to prevent future, potential bottlenecks or impediments to competition and intervention designed to address such impediments that have clearly manifested themselves.

4. Should A Uniform Framework Apply To All Providers Of High-Speed Services?

43. High-speed services are provided using a variety of public and private networks that rely on different network architectures and transmission paths including wireline, wireless, satellite, broadcast, and unlicensed spectrum technologies. Wireline incumbent and competitive LECs currently provide high-speed services in conjunction with affiliated or unaffiliated ISPs and operate pursuant to Title II of the Act. For example, pursuant to the requirements of the Commission's *Computer Inquiries*, certain common carriers must allow ISPs to purchase basic transmission services on a nondiscriminatory basis. As a result, end users are typically given a choice of ISPs, which could be accessed over the telephone network. Cable operators have traditionally provided service pursuant to Title VI of the Act and do not currently operate pursuant to rules requiring end user ISP choice. Wireless and satellite providers, while subject to the Commission's licensing rules and authority to allocate and manage spectrum under Title III, are not currently required to provide network access to multiple ISPs. Likewise, entities providing Internet service pursuant to Part 15 of the Commission's rules are under no obligation to allow multiple ISPs to access their networks.

44. We seek comment on whether uniform requirements for high-speed services provided using different platforms would facilitate the deployment of all such services, and whether we could implement uniform requirements consistent with our statutory mandate. If we determine that a regulatory approach is warranted, could the legal framework we establish apply to incumbent and competitive LECs, as well as cable operators? Could the legal framework apply to other providers of high-speed services including those that employ wireless, satellite, broadcast, and unlicensed spectrum technologies? If so why? If not, why not? In deciding whether the legal framework should apply to a particular high-speed provider, should it matter whether the provider has market power or is vertically integrated? Should it matter that some providers operate under common carrier requirements to serve the public indifferently? Should it matter that some providers must set aside a portion of capacity for purposes other than high-speed services? Should it matter whether the provider is subject to competition from other providers of high-speed services in the geographic area in which it operates?

45. In determining whether to impose the same regulations on different types of providers of high-speed services, what impact, if any, should we give to the

fact that the Act itself imposes different obligations on different service providers and technologies, despite Congress' expectation that providers would begin to compete in new markets (*i.e.*, cable companies entering the local telephone market)? To the extent the Commission attempts to achieve goals such as competitive neutrality, how should the Commission define these goals? For example, should the Commission attempt to achieve competitive neutrality by imposing the same particular requirements on competing providers of a given service, or should the Commission ensure only that the *overall* regulatory burdens imposed on such competitors are roughly equal? Should the notion of competitive neutrality compensate for market or economic advantages that incumbent providers may have over newer entrants, particularly entrants that are beginning to compete in non-traditional markets (*e.g.*, cable companies carrying data processing services)? We also ask for comment on how we should decide which framework should apply when a given service could conceivably be regulated under more than one regulatory framework, as might be the case, for example, [for voice telephony provided over Internet packet switched architecture.] What criteria should guide the Commission's decision on this issue? In particular, if the Commission may legitimately choose between regulatory approaches, we ask commenters to address reasons for adopting one approach over another and how we should consider public interest obligations arising under one approach and not another.

46. In conducting this analysis, should technological differences affect our analysis of which regulatory regime, if any, should apply? Are there any differences or similarities in the inputs used to provide high-speed services over wireline, wireless, satellite, broadcast, and unlicensed spectrum platforms? If so, what are these similarities or differences?

5. What Are The Technical And Operational Issues Associated With Open Access?

47. Various concerns have been raised before the Commission concerning the technical and operational issues surrounding open access to the cable modem platform.

48. To highlight some of the technical and operational issues, we ask what is the meaning of "interconnection" in this context? At what points in the cable network can ISPs interconnect? Are there technically superior locations for ISP interconnection, either from the ISP's perspective or the cable operator's perspective? Does interconnection at other locations yield competitively significant disadvantages for unaffiliated ISPs? If so, what are these disadvantages? Are there multiple methods for implementing open access to cable networks, and to what extent is each method scalable to allow access by the number of ISPs necessary to achieve the goals underlying open access? Will individual subscribers have access to multiple ISPs simultaneously, or will a subscriber have to unsubscribe from one ISP before gaining access to a second? Does use of the same cable plant by multiple ISPs create problems of congestion and network management? What type of bandwidth and quality of service arrangements will cable operators make available? Who will be responsible for network management and customer service? Under an open access regime, what control will the cable operator have over the Internet content available to subscribers? Who will control access to the customer? Will ISPs have the option of marketing and billing their service over

the cable platform directly to the consumer or, alternatively, the option of contracting with the cable company or third parties for this service? What standard(s) should the Commission apply in determining whether access is sufficiently open (nondiscrimination, reasonable opportunity to contract in good faith, etc.)? What steps can be taken to assure that unaffiliated ISPs' access to cable networks satisfies such standards in terms of pricing, service, interconnection, and other relevant factors?

C. The Commission's Options

50. Depending on the classification of cable modem service and the cable modem platform, as well as the desired policy goals, the Commission has various options available to it. In this section, we invite parties to comment on particular courses of action, and to propose other possible outcomes. If market incentives continue to work to foster a competitive environment, the Commission may find regulatory intervention to be unnecessary. Alternatively, the Commission may choose to initiate a rulemaking proceeding or forbear from enforcing statutory and regulatory requirements.

3. Should The Commission Exercise Its Forbearance Authority?

53. If the Commission finds that the marketplace is working and classifies cable modem service and/or the cable modem platform as a telecommunications service, it may choose to forbear from enforcing applicable regulatory requirements. Section 10(a) of the Act, 47 U.S.C. §160(a), grants the Commission authority to forbear from applying any regulation or provision of the Act to "a telecommunications carrier or telecommunications service, or class of telecommunications carriers or telecommunications services, in any or some of its or their geographic markets," if it determines that: (1) enforcement of that regulation or provision is not necessary to ensure just, reasonable and nondiscriminatory charges, practices, classifications or regulations; (2) enforcement of that regulation or provision is not necessary to protect consumers; and (3) forbearance is consistent with the public interest. To the extent the Commission determines that cable modem service and/or the cable modem platform is a telecommunications service, we invite comment on whether the Commission should exercise its forbearance authority, and from what statutory provisions or rules it should forbear. Are there provisions and rules from which forbearance is not appropriate? Parties should address how forbearance from any particular provision or rule would satisfy the necessary statutory criteria. Parties should also discuss for which class of telecommunications carriers or telecommunications services and in which geographic markets the statutory showing would be met.

54. Should the Commission forbear from enforcing section 251(a)'s interconnection requirement in this context? In the event that cable operators are found to be common carriers providing an information service, and therefore subject to the requirements stemming from the *Computer Inquiries*, should the Commission forbear from enforcing the requirement to unbundle basic service from enhanced? What role in its analysis, if any, should the Commission give to the possibility that forbearance will provoke competitors to enter the market? If cable modem service or the cable modem platform is a local exchange service and defined as telephone exchange or exchange access service, are providers of cable modem service or the cable modem platform local exchange carriers subject to

section 251(b) of the Act? Commenters should address whether forbearance would be appropriate if cable modem service and/or the cable modem platform is classified as a local exchange service.

55. We seek to determine the conditions under which the Commission should forbear from imposing or enforcing open access obligations. Specifically, should the Commission forbear if there are potential or actual competing facilities-based providers of high-speed services? Parties should describe how competition in the provision of high-speed services could act to alleviate any harms that may warrant the imposition of open access obligations. Parties should describe the specific conditions that may demonstrate to the Commission that competition is sufficient to forbear from enforcing open access obligations.

Notes and Questions

1. Gathering Information. The NOI raises a broad range of questions that highlight the complexity of regulating cable modem access for independent ISPs. The engineering architecture, economic investment incentives, competitive environment, and legal categorization all come into play, and each raises difficult empirical and theoretical questions, many of which require a prediction of future developments. While such uncertainty counsels humility about regulation, the FCC is also concerned about the long-term effects on advanced services in general and the Internet in particular should monopoly conditions develop and become entrenched. The NOI is thus geared toward gaining the information necessary for the Commission to assess the comparative risks and costs of regulation versus continued non-regulation. For readers of this text, the NOI is also a reminder of how complicated real-world regulatory decision-making actually is. It is one thing to abstract away from the details and ask broad policy questions about open access; quite another to endeavor to write actual regulations on the subject.

2. Kennard's Hippocratic Oath. Is this *Notice of Inquiry* excerpt consistent with the "high-tech Hippocratic Oath" that Kennard invoked in his June 1999 speech? If not, which approach do you prefer? If so, is the difference one of timing? To put the point differently, might it be consistent with such an oath to regulate once the appropriate stage has been reached? How would you define that stage? How will you know when it has been reached? Will there then be a further stage when regulation is once again inappropriate? How would you identify that one?

3. Defining the Term. How should "open access" be defined? The Commission addresses several possible definitions and refers in ¶29 to "an appropriate level of openness." What might that mean and how might "appropriate" be defined? Part of the issue is clearly the number of ISP competitors that might be on a given system. Is there an intermediate option for the Commission between (a) requiring completely open access to all ISPs that want it and (b) leaving the number of competitors up to private negotiations between cable operators and ISPs? What are the potential hazards and benefits of each approach? What incentives might cable operators themselves have to allow multiple ISPs on their systems? Assuming that such incentives exist, is there anything further to be gained from regulation?

4. Solving Which Problems? If the concern is that a cable operator will charge monopoly prices for ISP service to cable modem subscribers on its system, how will open access solve the problem? The cable operator will still control the pipe, so wouldn't it just take the same level of profits by raising the price to subscribers for their basic cable connection or raising the price it charges to ISPs for access to its system? What forces might prevent such behavior by the cable operator?

5. Investment Incentives. The economic considerations for the Commission extend beyond the issue of ISP competition. It clearly remains concerned about preserving investment incentives to deploy advanced cable services and to upgrade cable networks. Would open access deter such investment, or would competitive pressure from DSL push cable operators to invest even if they did not have market power at the ISP level? An additional concern is what effects a cable modem monopoly might have on the development of content and applications for the Internet. If a single ISP gains substantial market power, it has been argued that such an ISP might be able to pressure content and applications providers to enter exclusive deals that harm consumers. How compelling are such arguments? Are you in a position to evaluate them? Is the FCC?

6. Regulatory Parity. The Commission raises the issue of regulatory parity, asking whether two networks that provide the same service should ever be regulated differently because of technological or historical distinctions. The Commission makes clear in ¶50 that the Act might indeed require imposition of different obligations on different providers. At one level the issue is semantic. The Commission devotes numerous questions to the problem of how cable modem service should be labeled—is it "cable," "telecommunications," or "information"? The Act affords distinct tools and mandates for the regulation of each. But on another level the issue is economic and technological. A telephone system connects to each customer through a dedicated line that (usually) runs all the way from a central office. It is thus fairly easy to unbundle one line and pick off one individual customer from the telephone network. But cable is a "shared" medium in which traffic to an individual customer travels from the "headend" on a pipe shared by many, and is routed only at the very end to an individual. How can one define unbundling in such a network? Aren't the traffic management and other engineering questions very different? Finally, the economics of networks may also vary considerably, making apparently similar regulations very different in terms of the actual cost impact across technological platforms. Consider along these lines the following excerpt by William Rogerson, a former Chief Economist at the FCC.

THE REGULATION OF BROADBAND TELECOMMUNICATIONS, THE PRINCIPLE OF REGULATING NARROWLY DEFINED INPUT BOTTLENECKS, AND INCENTIVES FOR INVESTMENT AND INNOVATION

William P. Rogerson, 2000 U. Chi. L. Forum 119, 120–23

Rapid technological change and the enormous potential for innovation create a strong case for the general presumption that the Federal Communications Commission should not attempt at present to regulate extensively the provision of broadband services. Given that multiple competitors are poised to enter most markets, that the vast majority of potential customers have not yet been won by any firm, and that a tremendous need for a diversity of approaches and strong incentives for innovation exist, the advantages to having the FCC simply "get out of the way" are readily apparent.

This Article will argue, however, that in fact a sound economic rationale supports one limited form of regulation that applies to provision of broadband services over copper loops of the local telephone network. More specifically, this Article will argue that regulations requiring local telephone companies (the Incumbent Local Exchange Carriers) to make their copper loops available to other potential broadband suppliers at cost-based rates would be desirable.

My policy prescription can be viewed as an application of a concept that telecommunications regulators are already attempting to use, which I will refer to as the principal of regulating narrowly defined bottleneck inputs instead of outputs. The general idea is that regulators can bring the benefits of competition (increased incentives for innovation and increased diversity) to as many parts of the local telephone network as possible, while still protecting consumers from the exercise of monopoly power, by requiring the incumbent local exchange carrier to sell individual parts of its network to competitors at cost-based prices, instead of regulating final output prices. By this means, competition can infiltrate all parts of the network that are not monopoly bottlenecks and regulators can restrict themselves to regulating only the monopoly bottleneck portions of the network. This principle essentially allows regulators to "have their cake and eat it, too," in situations where the main need for innovation lies in parts of the local telephone network that are not subject to monopoly bottlenecks.

The case of broadband access over the local telephone network is in some ways ideally suited for application of the principle of regulating narrowly defined bottleneck inputs. The existing technology used to provide broadband access over the local telephone network is referred to as direct subscriber line (DSL) technology. In many cases this technology can be used to provide a broadband connection using the existing copper loop of the telephone network between the end user and the ILEC's switch. Electronic equipment is simply added at each end of the loop and, generally speaking, it is possible and economical for multiple DSL providers to install the necessary equipment in the ILEC's switching offices. Almost no additional investment, innovation, or changes are required in the existing copper loops owned by the ILEC. Furthermore, it is possible for different DSL providers to adopt different technological approaches on the same network. That is, requiring the ILEC to make its copper loops available to multiple DSL providers does not constrain the ability of providers to experiment with different DSL technologies on the lines available to them. Therefore, the FCC can create a vibrant and diverse industry of DSL providers over the existing ILEC network of copper loops by requiring the ILEC to sell access to its copper loops at regulated prices and then neither regulating the retail prices of DSL providers (including the retail prices for DSL services charged by the ILEC itself) nor requiring the ILEC to provide any sort of unbundled access at all to any of the equipment on each end of the line that it installs to provide DSL.

While it is true that cable, wireless, and satellite alternatives would provide some competition for the ILEC if the ILEC remained the sole user of its copper loops, allowing multiple providers of DSL access to the ILEC's copper loops would provide a tremendous incentive to diversity and competition without damaging the ILEC's incentives in any important way, because the existing copper network is already largely in place and can be used without significant changes.

One complication raised by this policy is that, in some cases, the traditional all-copper loop is being replaced by connections that use both copper and optical fiber. Employing digital loop carrier (DLC) technology, copper wires run from end users to small remote terminals, at which point the signals are aggregated and carried the remainder of the way to the switching office on high capacity optical fiber. Furthermore, it is possible that the best technological approach to providing broadband connections over the existing ILEC networks may ultimately require that much more copper be replaced by fiber. The problem with a regulation requiring the ILEC to make this new transmission capacity available to CLECs at cost-based prices is that the ILEC will have a reduced incentive to invest and innovate if it is required to sell the fruits of its efforts at cost-based prices. That is, to the extent that the need for innovation is in the loop itself, it is no longer the case that the monopoly bottleneck can be isolated from the parts of the network requiring innovation. Therefore, the issue of whether and how the FCC should require unbundling of mixed copper/fiber loops is a more complex issue that requires further analysis.

With respect to cable firms, there is no analog to the existing set of copper wires that provide the loop connection and that are separable from the new investments required for creating broadband connections. Therefore, the problem identified above would also beset any scheme requiring cable firms to provide unbundled access to their transmission capacity. Specifically, provision of broadband connections requires massive new investments, innovations, and upgrades in the physical plant connecting end users to the network (the analog of the loop). Regulating these facilities (either through regulating retail prices or mandating some type of unbundled access to other providers at regulated prices) would blunt the incentives for investment and innovation. Therefore, I believe that the present asymmetric treatment of ILECs and cable providers may be justified with respect to unbundling obligations, at least insofar as ILECs are required to provide unbundled access to their traditional copper loops.

Notes and Questions

1. More on Investment Incentives. Rogerson argues that, where the relevant infrastructure is already in place, regulation is unlikely to deter innovation and so regulation is less costly than it would otherwise be. But is it possible that access to an unbundled element might deter investment in alternative technologies by new entrants? That is, if copper wires were expensive, wouldn't CLECs have stronger incentives to develop cable modem technology? Similarly, if ISPs are denied access to the cable plant, won't they start pumping more money into DSL deployment? Wouldn't these be desirable outcomes? Don't they cut against Rogerson's thesis? Could Rogerson respond to this argument by making the parallel argument for ILECs—namely that ILECs subject to unbundling obligations face a stronger incentive to invest in new technologies since, to whatever extent they rely on new platforms, they can avoid Rogerson's unbundling requirement?

2. Implementing the Plan. What empirical data would be necessary to implement Rogerson's policy prescription? Is that information likely to be within the reasonable capacity of regulators to determine? For example, how does Rogerson know that copper wire technology is mature and not subject to further innovation?

3. Implications. What does Rogerson's analysis suggest for future regulation of high-speed Internet access? Does it provide a useful way of thinking about such regulation, either as of today or going forward? Does his argument support a more regulatory or a more hands-off approach by the Commission?

IV. NON-REGULATION OF THE INTERNET BACKBONE: PEERING AND TRANSIT ARRANGEMENTS

It would do little good to have high-speed data transmission over the last mile segments of communications networks only to have that same data slow to a crawl somewhere in the many miles that might lie between consumers and the Internet servers they wish to reach. The infrastructure segments that connect computers, linking them into networks, and which then further interconnect to form the network of networks that constitutes the Internet, are called Internet backbones.

Internet backbones are made up of owned or leased national or international high-speed fiber optic networks. These networks are in turn connected by routers, which the backbones use to deliver traffic to and from ISPs, content providers, online service companies and other customers. Each backbone provider essentially creates a network on which customers and content providers can communicate. If Internet users were limited to the content, services, or other customers of a single backbone provider, that would both undercut a central principle of the Internet (*i.e.*, that any computer can connect with any other) and significantly diminish the value of the network. Most users want to be able to communicate with any Internet site or customer regardless of which backbone provider serves it. Different Internet backbones must therefore interconnect with each other to exchange traffic destined for each other's customers.

To date, the FCC has not regulated interconnection among Internet backbones. The fiber optic networks that constitute backbones are major pieces of telecommunications infrastructure; but unlike local exchange networks, cable systems, wireless networks, or long distance telephone facilities, they operate constrained only by market forces and general antitrust law. Is such non-regulation of the critical interconnections among Internet backbones consistent with Congress's mandate to the Commission in §706? Consider the following excerpt from an FCC policy paper.

THE DIGITAL HANDSHAKE:
CONNECTING INTERNET BACKBONES

Michael Kende, FCC Office of Plans and Policy,
OPP Working Paper No. 32 (2000)

II. BACKGROUND

C. Peering and Transit

During the early development of the Internet, there was only one backbone, and therefore interconnection between backbones was not an issue. In 1986, the National Science Foundation (NSF) funded the NSFNET, a 56-kilobit per second (Kbps) network created to enable long distance access to five supercomputer centers across the country. In 1987, a partnership of Merit Network, Inc., IBM, and MCI began to manage the NSFNET, which became a T-1 network connecting thirteen sites in 1988. The issue of interconnection arose only when a number of commercial backbones came into being, and eventually supplanted the NSFNET.

At the time that commercial networks began appearing, general commercial activity on the NSFNET was prohibited by an Acceptable Use Policy, thereby preventing these commercial networks from exchanging traffic with one another using the NSFNET as the backbone. This roadblock was circumvented in 1991, when a number of commercial backbone operators including PSINet, UUNET, and CerfNET established the Commercial Internet Exchange (CIX). CIX consisted of a router, housed in Santa Clara, California, that was set up for the purpose of interconnecting these commercial backbones and enabling them to exchange their end users' traffic. In 1993, the NSF decided to leave the management of the backbone entirely to competing, commercial backbones. In order to facilitate the growth of overlapping competing backbones, the NSF designed a system of geographically dispersed Network Access Points (NAPs) similar to CIX, each consisting of a shared switch or local area network (LAN) used to exchange traffic. The four original NAPs were in San Francisco (operated by PacBell), Chicago (BellCore and Ameritech), New York (SprintLink) and Washington, D.C. (MFS). Backbones could choose to interconnect with one another at any or all of these NAPs. In 1995, this network of commercial backbones and NAPs permanently replaced the NSFNET.

The interconnection of commercial backbones is not subject to any industry-specific regulations. The NSF did not establish any interconnection rules at the NAPs, and interconnection between Internet backbone providers is not currently regulated by the Federal Communications Commission or any other government agency. Instead, interconnection arrangements evolved from the informal interactions that characterized the Internet at the time the NSF was running the backbone. The commercial backbones developed a system of interconnection known as peering. Peering has a number of distinctive characteristics. First, peering partners only exchange traffic that originates with the customer of one backbone and terminates with the customer of the other peered backbone. In Figure [21.1], customers of backbones A and C can trade traffic as a result of a peering relationship between the backbones, as can the customers of backbones B and C, which also have a peering arrangement. As part of a peering arrangement, a backbone would not, however, act as an intermediary and accept the traffic of one peering partner and transit this traffic to another peering partner. Thus, referring back to

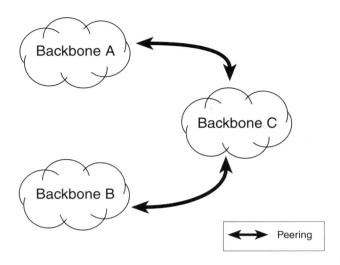

Figure 21.1. PEERING. Backbone C has a peering arrangement with Backbone A and also a peering arrangement with Backbone B. Backbones A and B, however, do not have a peering arrangement. This figure is adapted from Figure 1 in the original article.

Figure [21.1], backbone C will not accept traffic from backbone A destined for backbone B. The second distinctive characteristic of peering is that peering partners exchange traffic on a settlements-free basis. The only costs that backbones incur to peer is that each partner pays for its own equipment and the transmission capacity needed for the two peers to meet at each peering point.

Additional characteristics of peering relate to the routing of information from one backbone to another. Peering partners generally meet in a number of geographically dispersed locations. In order to decide where to pass traffic from one backbone to another in a consistent and fair manner, they have adopted what is known as "hot-potato routing," whereby a backbone will pass traffic to another backbone at the earliest point of exchange. As an example, in Figure [21.2] backbones A and B are interconnected on the West and East coasts. When a customer of ISP X on the East coast requests a web page from a site connected to ISP Y on the West coast, backbone A passes this request to backbone B on the East coast, and backbone B carries this request to the West coast. Likewise, the responding web page is routed from backbone B to backbone A on the West coast, and backbone A is responsible for carrying the response to the customer of ISP X on the East coast. A final characteristic of peering is that recipients of traffic only promise to undertake "best efforts" when terminating traffic, rather than guarantee any level of performance in delivering packets received from peering partners.

The original system of peering has evolved over time. Initially, most exchange of traffic under peering arrangements took place at the NAPs, as it was efficient for each backbone to interconnect with as many backbones as possible at the same location. [Under such an approach, each backbone would only have to] provide a connection to one point, the NAP, rather than providing individual connections to every other backbone. The rapid growth in Internet traffic soon

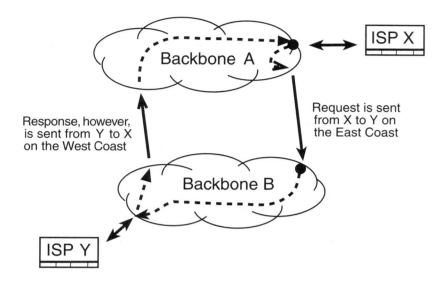

Figure 21.2. "HOT-POTATO" ROUTING. As described in the text, in "hot-potato" routing each backbone attempts to shift traffic to the other backbone as soon as possible. This figure is adapted from Figure 5 in the original article.

caused the NAPs to become congested, however, which led to delayed and dropped packets. For instance, Intermedia Business Solutions asserts that at one point packet loss at the Washington, D.C. NAP reached up to 20 percent. As a result, a number of new NAPs have appeared to reduce the amount of traffic flowing through the original NAPs. For example, MFS, now owned by World-Com, operates a number of NAPs known as Metropolitan Area Exchanges (MAEs), including one of the original NAPs, the Washington, D.C. NAP known as MAE-East, as well as MAE-West in San Jose, and other MAEs in Los Angeles, Dallas, and Chicago.

Another result of the increased congestion at the NAPs has been that many backbones began to interconnect directly with one another. This system has come to be known as private peering, as opposed to the public peering that takes place at the NAPs. This system developed partly in response to congestion at the NAPs, yet it may often be more cost-effective for the backbones. For instance, if backbones were to interconnect only at NAPs, traffic that originated and terminated in the same city but on different backbones would have to travel to a NAP in a different city or even a different country for exchange. With private peering, in contrast, it can be exchanged within the same city. This alleviates the strain on the NAPs. At one point it was estimated that 80 percent of Internet traffic was exchanged via private peering. There are recent indications, however, that as NAPs begin to switch to advanced switch technologies, the NAPs will be able to provide higher quality services and may regain their former attraction as efficient meeting points for peering partners. Unless specified, discussions of peering below refer to both public and private peering.

Because each bilateral peering arrangement only allows backbones to exchange traffic destined for each other's customers, backbones need a significant number of peering arrangements in order to gain access to the full Internet. UUNET, for instance, claims to "peer with 75 other ISPs globally." As discussed below, there are few backbones that rely solely on private or public peering to meet their interconnection needs. The alternative to peering is a transit arrangement between backbones, in which one backbone pays another backbone to deliver traffic between its customers and the customers of other backbones.

Transit and peering are differentiated in two main ways. First, in a transit arrangement, one backbone pays another backbone for interconnection, and therefore becomes a wholesale customer of the other backbone. Second, unlike in a peering relationship, with transit, the backbone selling the transit services will route traffic from the transit customer to its peering partners. [Suppose] backbone A is a transit customer of backbone C; thus, the customers of backbone A have access both to the customers of backbone C as well as to the customers of all peering partners of backbone C, such as backbone B. If backbone A and backbone C were peering partners [by contrast] backbone C would not accept traffic from backbone A that was destined for backbone B.

Many backbones have adopted a hybrid approach to interconnection, peering with a number of backbones and paying for transit from one or more backbones in order to have access to the backbone of the transit supplier as well as the peering partners of the transit supplier. Those few large backbones that interconnect solely by peering, and do not need to purchase transit from any other backbones, will be referred to here as top-tier backbones. Because of the non-disclosure agreements that cover interconnection between backbones, it is difficult to state with accuracy the number of top-tier backbones; according to one industry participant, there are five: Cable & Wireless, WorldCom, Sprint, AT&T, and Genuity (formerly GTE Internetworking).

It is useful to compare Internet interconnection arrangements with more familiar, traditional telephony interconnection arrangements. The practice of peering is similar to the practice of bill-and-keep or sender-keeps-all arrangements in telephony. Transit arrangements between Internet backbones are somewhat similar to resale arrangements between, for instance, long distance carriers; the Internet backbone providing transit service acts as the wholesaler, and the backbone buying transit acts as the reseller of Internet backbone services. There are notable differences in the way Internet and telephony arrangements are regulated, however. The interconnection between Internet backbones is not governed by industry-specific regulations, while the interconnection of traditional telephone carriers is currently regulated both domestically and internationally. Furthermore, unlike telephony, there is no difference between domestic and international Internet interconnection arrangements; backbones treat each other the same regardless of the country of origin or location of customer base.

There is no accepted convention that governs when two backbones will or should decide to peer with one another, nor is it an easy matter to devise one. The term "peer" suggests equality, and one convention could be that backbones of equal size would peer. However, there are many measures of backbone size, such as geographic spread, capacity, traffic volume, or number of customers. It is unlikely that two backbones will be similar along many or all dimensions. One may have fewer, but larger, customers than the other, another may reach into Europe or Asia, and so forth. The question then becomes, how the backbones weigh one variable against another. Given the complexity of such judgments, it may be best to use a definition of equality proposed by one industry participant—that companies will peer when they perceive equal benefit from peering based on their own subjective terms, rather than any objective terms. In sum, peering agreements are the result of commercial negotiations; each backbone bases its decisions on whether, how, and where to peer by weighing the benefits and costs of entering into a particular interconnection agreement with another backbone.

III. INTERCONNECTION ISSUES

This section examines the market outcomes that result from unregulated interconnection agreements between backbone providers. There have been a number of allegations, discussed below, that the entire system of interconnection between backbones is at risk due to the actions of several larger backbones. At least one industry observer argued that the emerging system of private peering enables the larger backbones to act in an anticompetitive manner by excluding smaller backbones from private peering arrangements and then raising prices. While universal connectivity is the norm today, as new real-time services begin to be offered over the Internet, there are fears that in the future backbones may choose to differentiate themselves by not interconnecting for purposes of offering these new services. [This *OPP Report*] examines whether there is any possible market failure in the Internet backbone market that could not be governed adequately by existing antitrust laws.

A. Internet Backbone Market Power Issues

1. Background

Internet backbone providers face conflicting incentives. On one hand, they have an incentive to cooperate with one another in order to provide their customers with access to the full range of Internet users and content. On the other hand, these same backbones have an incentive to compete with one another for both retail and wholesale customers. The need for backbone A to interconnect with backbone B in order to provide its customers access to backbone B's customers creates what might be termed a competitive network externality; this interconnection also enables backbone B to provide its customers access to backbone A's customers. As long as A and B are relatively equally sized, there is a strong incentive for them to cooperate with one another in spite of competitive network externalities; if either unilaterally stops interconnecting, it has no guarantees that it will benefit from such an action. This situation seems to characterize the early days of the commercial Internet, when a number of backbones were relatively similar in size, and readily agreed to peer with one another. Recently, however, there have been allegations that as certain backbones grew they began to engage in uncooperative, if not anticompetitive, practices.

[If these allegations are true and] a market failure is found that leads to anticompetitive actions on the part of one or more Internet backbone providers, then a determination [will then have to be made as to] whether antitrust laws would provide a sufficient remedy, or if industry-specific regulation is required.

The effect of a backbone's refusing to peer with another backbone depends on the degree of competition in the backbone market. In a competitive market, a backbone may refuse to peer with a smaller rival for legitimate, rather than anticompetitive, reasons. In a competitive market, backbones that have been denied peering can nevertheless enter the backbone market, because competition among the larger top-tier backbones gives them an incentive to provide transit arrangements to smaller backbones in place of peering. If, on the other hand, there was a dominant backbone, the dominant backbone might be able to disadvantage actual or potential rivals in an anticompetitive manner by, for instance, not peering or not providing transit to smaller backbones.

2. Analysis

a) Competitive Backbone Market

An important determinant of the competitiveness of any market is whether new firms can enter the market, and smaller firms can expand, thereby constraining any potential exercise of market power by the existing larger firms. In order to enter or expand, Internet backbones need to interconnect with existing backbones in order to enable their customers to exchange traffic with the customers of existing firms, and they need access to fiber capacity to carry their traffic. Fiber capacity is readily available, and thus this section will focus on the ability of smaller Internet backbones to interconnect with larger ones. Much of the current debate focuses on the effects of one backbone refusing to peer with another backbone. [This *OPP Report*] attempts to inform such discussions by showing that, in a competitive backbone market, there may be a number of legitimate reasons for one backbone to refuse to peer with another backbone. Therefore, such a refusal may not constitute a barrier to entering the backbone market. As long as transit arrangements are available on a competitive basis, smaller backbones can enter and ensure that the backbone market remains competitive.

One reason a backbone may refuse to peer is that it believes that peering would enable the other backbone to free ride on its infrastructure investments. [Suppose, for example, that] backbone B, a national backbone, has a presence on both coasts. Backbone A, in contrast, is a regional backbone with a presence only on the East coast. If the two backbones peered on the East coast, when a customer of backbone A requests a web page from a customer of backbone B whose server is on the West coast, then backbone B would carry the request from the East coast to the West coast and also carry the response back to the East coast. The national backbone may thus refuse to peer on the grounds that it would otherwise bear the expense for a national infrastructure from which the regional carrier could then benefit at no cost. As a result of such considerations, a number of backbones require that peering partners be willing and able to interconnect at a number of geographically diverse locations.

The "hot-potato routing" that characterizes peering arrangements may also lead to actual or perceived free-riding, as a result of the decision on the part of some backbones to specialize in providing service mainly to one type of customer, such as content providers. This situation can be illustrated by referring back to Figure [21.2]. Suppose that ISP Y, a customer of backbone B, provides service mainly to content providers, while ISP X, a customer of backbone A, provides service mainly to end users. Given hot-potato routing, when a end user customer of ISP X requests content that is hosted by ISP Y, backbone B will carry the request from the East coast to the West coast, while backbone A would carry the requested content back from the West coast. As a rule, content such as Web pages involve more bits of data than the corresponding requests for the content. Therefore, backbones such as A that carry the Web pages would transport more traffic than would backbones such as B that carry the requests for these Web pages. Backbones may thus refuse to peer with backbones hosting a high proportion of content providers on the grounds that they are bearing the expense for more capacity than the backbone that is actually hosting the content that utilizes this capacity.

The preceding paragraphs show that, in order to prevent free-riding, a large backbone may refuse to peer with a smaller backbone. In a competitive market, these refusals may not have any anticompetitive intent or effect; indeed, such refusals may in fact have a pro-competitive result. A smaller backbone, denied peering on the grounds of free-riding, may then have an incentive to invest in infrastructure and compete for a varied mix of new customers in order to qualify for peering—resulting in an increased number of competing national backbone providers. As discussed below, this is only possible as long as a smaller backbone that has been denied peering is able to enter the market with a transit relationship.

The next example examines the situation of a backbone that is refused peering because it has a small customer base. There are indications that a backbone may refuse to peer with a smaller backbone based on the amount of traffic generated by the smaller backbone. For instance, the published peering policies of UUNET, Sprint, and Genuity all contain a requirement that a peering candidate be able to exchange a certain minimum amount of data at the beginning of the peering relationship. One justification given by the larger backbones is that it is difficult and costly to allocate necessary resources to potential peers with low current volumes that may or may not grow rapidly in the future. Nevertheless, this requirement may place backbones with low volumes in a Catch-22 situation; without a large number of customers generating traffic volume, it is not possible to negotiate peering arrangements with the large backbones, yet without peering, it may be difficult to gain the large number of customers necessary to generate the traffic volume to qualify for peering. In order to determine whether the latter statement is valid, one must examine the implications for smaller backbones of not being able to peer with larger backbones.

It is important to differentiate between larger backbones refusing to *interconnect* with smaller backbones, versus the larger backbones only refusing to *peer* with smaller backbones. Instead of peering with the smaller backbones, the larger backbones may offer them a transit arrangement. For instance, if backbone A is refused peering by backbone B, then backbone A could use a transit arrangement in order for its customers to have access to backbone B's customers. Backbone A could take transit directly from backbone B, or it could become a transit customer of a third backbone C that is interconnected with backbone B. [This *OPP Report*] first argues that in a competitive market, larger backbones that refuse to peer have an incentive to offer smaller backbones transit, and then shows that transit is likely to be offered on a competitive basis.

Having denied peering to smaller backbones, one might question whether the larger top-tier backbones providing transit would either refuse to provide transit to smaller backbones or simply increase the cost of transit in order to squeeze out the smaller rivals. There are two reasons that this would be unlikely in a competitive backbone market. The first reason is unique to the Internet. In negotiating peering, one important bargaining chip is the number of customers to which a backbone provides access; this includes the number of transit customers. Therefore, backbones will compete with each other to win transit customers to use as leverage when negotiating peering relationships with other backbones. The second reason is traditional, that the large backbones will compete for the transit business of smaller backbones in order to increase their revenues, which will keep transit prices down. In a growing market such as the Internet market, in particular, one would not expect it to be profitable for a competitive backbone to raise price, and thereby restrict sales, and growth in sales. Therefore, in a competitive backbone market, no backbone provider is likely to find it profitable to use a price squeeze to disadvantage smaller rivals.

As a transit customer, it may be possible for a smaller backbone provider to grow and later qualify to peer with backbones that initially refused peering, including the transit supplier. Nevertheless, a smaller backbone may prefer peering rather then being a paying transit customer, either for quality or cost reasons. [This *OPP Report*] next examines whether, in a competitive market, a smaller backbone that only interconnects via a transit arrangement is likely to be at a competitive disadvantage.

Because transit does not involve the same service as peering, refusing peering in favor of transit is not simply a means of charging for a service that was otherwise provided free of charge. In a transit relationship, one backbone must pay another for access to the Internet. For instance, at the time that UUNET changed its peering policy in 1997, it announced that wholesale connectivity started at $2,000 per month for a T-1 connection and $6,000 for a fractional T-3 connection. Transit customers receive benefits in return for these payments; when backbones pay for transit they benefit from the infrastructure investments of national or global backbones without themselves having to make or utilize their own investments. In addition, as noted above, transit gives a backbone access to the entire Internet, not just the customers of the peering partner. In order to provide transit customers with access to the entire Internet, the transit provider must either maintain peering arrangements with a number of other backbones or in turn must pay for transit from yet another backbone. In other words, a backbone providing transit services is providing access to a greater array of end users and content than it would as a peer, thereby incurring correspondingly higher costs that are recuperated in the transit payments. In a competitive backbone market, transit prices should reflect costs and should not put entering backbones at a competitive disadvantage.

In conclusion, the presence of a large number of top-tier backbones can prevent any anticompetitive actions. In a competitive backbone market, no large backbone would unilaterally end peering with another, as it has no guarantee that it will benefit from such an action. Furthermore, there would be no insurmountable barrier to entry or growth of smaller backbones. Larger top-tier backbones would continue to compete to provide transit services to smaller backbones. These smaller backbones would be able to resell these services to their own customers, and would not seem to face any barrier to acquiring either the infrastructure or customer base that could enable them eventually to join the ranks of the larger backbones and qualify for peering. Actual, as well as potential, entry by new backbones would act to constrain the actions of larger incumbent backbones, keeping prices at competitive levels.

b) Backbone Market with a Dominant Firm

If, on the other hand, a single backbone were dominant, it would be able to harm the public interest by engaging in a number of anticompetitive actions. As discussed above, it appears unlikely that a firm may organically grow to become dominant. Instead, the route to such dominance would likely be achieved by consolidation between backbone providers, or if a backbone gained market power over a key bottleneck input, such as transmission facilities. The issue of consolidation was at the heart of the debate surrounding WorldCom's acquisition of MCI, and later MCI WorldCom's acquisition of Sprint. This section discusses the potential anticompetitive harms that could be caused by a dominant backbone. Many of these harms were raised by commenters in the MCI/World-Com merger proceeding, and identified in the Commission's *MCI/WorldCom Order*.[6]

A dominant backbone could harm the public interest in a number of ways. First, by definition a dominant firm has the unilateral ability to profitably raise and sustain retail prices above competitive levels. In addition, a dominant backbone would have both the ability and the incentive to stop cooperating with smaller backbones. Failure to cooperate could take a number of forms, including refusing to interconnect at all, executing a price squeeze, or degrading the quality of interconnection by not upgrading the capacity of connections with smaller backbones.

Notes and Questions

1. Different from Telephony? The excerpt above finds current market forces sufficient to ensure adequate backbone interconnection. What distinguishes Internet backbones from rival local exchange carriers? Why is interconnection among the latter regulated under §§251 and 252 of the 1996 Act while backbone interconnection is not? How, if at all, do incentives to interconnect differ between backbone providers on the one hand and local exchange companies on the other?

2. Peering vs. Transit. What is the difference between peering and transit arrangements? The *OPP Report* suggests that refusals to peer are acceptable if transit arrangements are available as an alternative. Why does the *Report* reach this conclusion? Are there conditions under which transit might not adequately substitute for peering?

3. Market Dominance. The excerpt ends with a warning about a breakdown in backbone interconnection if one backbone provider becomes dominant. To date, the excerpt notes, antitrust authorities have been vigilant against mergers that could create market power in backbone services. But what if one backbone becomes dominant simply by dint of being a superior competitor rather than through merger or anticompetitive behavior? If there is no antitrust action to be brought, but dominance nonetheless, should the FCC regulate the rates and relationships between the backbone and customers? Should the backbone be treated like a common carrier?

---

6. Application of WorldCom, Inc. and MCI Communications Corporation for Transfer of Control of MCI Communications Corporation to WorldCom, Inc., 13 FCC Rcd. 18025, at ¶¶149–150 (1998).

4. Going Forward. Are you convinced by the *Report*'s overall argument? Looking forward, do you think the backbone market is likely to remain unregulated or do you see reasons why the FCC might, under §706 or some future Congressional mandate, intervene? What if congestion becomes worse? What if conventional telecommunications services like voice telephony migrate significantly to the Internet? Will the regulatory model for conventional telecommunications migrate to the Internet, or might the current approach to the backbone market form the new model for telecommunications regulation? On what does your answer depend?

Chapter Twenty-Two

CHARACTERIZING INTERNET SERVICE PROVIDERS

The purpose of this chapter is:

- to examine the Commission's attempts at characterizing telephone traffic that is bound for Internet service providers, these attempts all coming in response to pricing disputes that have arisen between local exchange carriers and ISPs.

∼

If local exchange carriers were operating in a completely unregulated, competitive environment, it is unlikely that the FCC would ever have had to deal with questions about the relationship between LECs and Internet service providers (ISPs). In such a world, ISPs would be just like any other LEC customer. True, they would tend to receive more phone calls than the average residential or business customer, and they would tend to make many fewer calls themselves. Moreover, their incoming calls would likely be of longer duration than the average voice communication. But those details would just mean that the local phone company would charge the ISP accordingly, just as the phone company would, under a competitive scenario, likely charge the local pizza place according to its usage pattern and the local barbershop according to its pattern. The relationship between ISPs and LECs would in such a world make for an entirely uninteresting regulatory issue.

In the real world, however, the ISP/LEC interface has been an extraordinarily complicated regulatory issue, and the reason is this: neither ILECs nor CLECs have complete discretion to account for the usage patterns of particular customers in the prices they charge those customers. To some degree — albeit less so for CLECs — state and federal regulations constrain local phone companies in their ability to charge prices that fully reflect each particular customer's usage pattern. So pizza places and barbershops for the most part face similar rate structures for their local service even in cases where the actual burden they put on the telephone network differs in ways the rate structure cannot account for. Similarly, and more important for the current discussion, ISPs are included in that same rough pricing structure even though the phone traffic originating with and terminating at an ISP does not at all comport with the usage pattern regulators had in mind when the various pricing structures were first devised. This little fact opens up a regulatory mess, a mess that ultimately has forced the FCC to take an active role in managing the ISP/LEC relationship.

The Commission defines the term "Internet service provider" as follows:

An ISP is an entity that provides its customers the ability to obtain online information through the Internet. ISPs purchase analog and digital lines from local exchange carriers to connect to their dial-in subscribers. Under one typical arrangement, an ISP customer dials a seven-digit number to reach the ISP server in the same local calling area. The ISP, in turn, combines computer processing, information storage, protocol conversion, and routing with transmission to enable users to access Internet content and services. Under this arrangement, the end user generally pays the LEC a flat monthly fee for use of the local exchange network and generally pays the ISP a flat, monthly fee for Internet access. The ISP typically purchases business lines from a LEC, for which it pays a flat monthly fee that allows unlimited incoming calls.[1]

An ISP is thus a firm that, at a minimum, receives and translates Internet-bound data. The ISP takes data in whatever form it arrives — for traditional ISPs, it comes packaged as a voice communication — and translates it into a form consistent with the TCP/IP protocol of the Internet. Most ISPs also do more than that, of course. For example, in addition to translating data, most ISPs read the outgoing addresses on that data and route the communication appropriately. (ISPs that do not themselves route data pass it on in TCP/IP form to a third-party firm that has computers capable of doing the routing.) Some ISPs provide in addition various services such as email, news, and caching. Some host personal websites. Some provide organized interfaces through which subscribers can access Internet content in convenient forms. Some ISPs even own telecommunications infrastructure (such as high-speed landlines) capable of transporting the data they process and translate.

For our purposes here, what is important is simply this: to the extent that ISP subscribers access their ISPs over the telephone system, ISPs put a significant burden on the local telephone network. Think specifically about a LEC that has as one of its subscribers a successful ISP. This LEC will suddenly find itself receiving (terminating) a huge number of long-duration telephone calls. Again, this wouldn't be a problem if the LEC could charge the ISP for this extra burden. But regulations make it such that, even if the LEC can recoup some of these added costs, it cannot recoup them all. LECs have therefore gone to the FCC and tried to obtain that money in other ways.

The first battle was over access charges. Local exchange carriers argued that ISPs should be characterized as interexchange carriers since ISPs take data from the local exchange and (in some cases at least) carry it to exchanges located far away. This parallels the service provided by long distance carriers and so the LECs contended that ISPs should be treated as IXCs for regulatory purposes. This would have had several implications, the most important being that, as IXCs, ISPs would have been responsible for paying access charges to local ex-

---

1. In re Implementation of the Local Competition Provisions of the Telecommunications Act of 1996, Inter-Carrier Compensation for ISP-Bound Traffic, 14 FCC Rcd. 3689, at ¶4 (1999). This definition is obviously written with the dial-up telephone ISP in mind. ISPs that provide service over the cable plant, for example, do not "purchase analog and digital lines from local exchange carriers." For a definition tailored to the cable setting, see Inquiry Concerning High-Speed Access to the Internet Over Cable and Other Facilities, Notice of Inquiry, FCC 00–355, 2000 WL 1434689, at ¶¶8–10 (2000).

change carriers. (Recall that access charges are the fees that long distance telephone companies pay local exchange carriers to originate and terminate calls. The fees compensate LECs for their legitimate expenses and also help to finance universal service obligations.) In short, if ISPs were deemed to be IXCs, ISPs would be obligated to pay access charges, and LECs would therefore be more fully compensated—maybe even over-compensated—for ISP calls. The FCC considered the issue but declined to characterize ISPs as long distance carriers.

Having lost the battle over access charges, LECs were left to look for another revenue source, and they found it in the form of the reciprocal compensation agreements mandated by the 1996 Act. As we discussed in Chapter Eighteen, when telephone traffic travels from one LEC to another, the two LECs must compensate one another for any added burden. Either the LEC that originates a given call agrees to pay the LEC that terminates it, or the two LECs agree to a "bill-and-keep" scheme where each carries the others' traffic and the payments are assumed to be a draw. Applied to ISPs, did this mean that every time a phone customer from one local provider called an ISP connected to another local provider, the customer's LEC had to pay the ISP's LEC for terminating the call? Given that a good many CLECs had built their entire businesses around ISP service—in that way originating very few calls but terminating a large number—an affirmative answer here had the potential to transfer outlandish sums of money from traditional LECs (that were originating calls from homes and businesses to ISPs) to ISP-focused CLECs (that were terminating all those calls). The FCC thus again had to weigh in on a characterization issue, this time asking not whether ISPs were themselves local or long distance carriers, but instead whether ISP traffic was local telephone traffic for the purposes of reciprocal compensation agreements.

To the extent that both of the above issues were difficult when ISPs were simply providing Internet access, they became all the more so when ISPs began to offer voice communication over the Internet backbone. The packet technology that underlies rapid data transport also can be used for transmitting voice signals. The network was not designed—and is not optimized—for voice traffic; for example, tiny and unpredictable transmission delays that might not be noticed for data pose a problem for voice, where a smooth and uninterrupted flow is desirable. This is in fact one reason why the voice network uses circuits instead of packets, reserving (at the start of any given call) a dedicated path from the point of origination to the point of termination. Nevertheless, because the packet-switched network could be used to provide possibly inferior but also possibly cheaper basic voice service, Internet telephony began to gain market share. That only aggravated the already difficult regulatory challenge sketched above. When ISPs were merely providing Internet access that was one thing. But now that ISPs were competing head-to-head with traditional telephone companies for voice traffic, was it really fair to exempt ISPs from the access charge regime? Wouldn't this skew competition in the long distance voice market, not to mention depriving the universal service fund of necessary funds?

This chapter considers these three issues in turn. The first section below looks at the related battles over access charges and reciprocal compensation payments. The second section shifts gears to focus exclusively on ISP provision of voice communication, what the FCC calls "Internet Protocol telephony" or, more simply, "IP telephony."

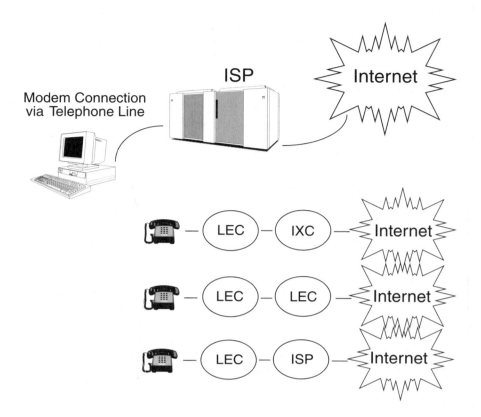

Figure 22.1. CHARACTERIZING ISPs. This diagram offers three possible characteri-zations of a dial-up ISP that customers reach via a LEC (which is represented by the circle on the left). The first imagines the ISP as if it were an IXC. The second treats the ISP as if it were itself a LEC. The third suggests that perhaps a new regulatory category should be created exclusively for ISPs. The question of which mental picture resonates is the subject of this entire chapter. Does any have stronger appeal?

I. ACCESS CHARGES AND RECIPROCAL COMPENSATION

What should be the relationship between the ISPs that connect consumers to the Internet and the local exchange carriers whose networks are necessary to originate and terminate phone connections to the ISPs? Should ISPs be treated like long distance companies and thus asked to pay per-minute access charges to the relevant local carriers? Or are they just regular business subscribers who should be allowed to buy phone service at a flat monthly rate? And what should be the relationship between two local exchange companies, one of whom serves an ISP's customers and the other of whom serves the ISP, given that these two must interconnect in order for the customers and the ISP to interact? Recall that the FCC ruled that advanced services are subject to the interconnection provi-sions of sections 251 and 252 of the 1996 Act. But those provisions apply only to local telecommunications traffic. Should calls to ISPs be considered local for the purposes of these provisions, given that ISP customers often access interstate or foreign content?

The first excerpt below is from the Commission's *Report and Order* on the relationship between ISPs and local exchange carriers. That *Order* is followed by materials addressing in more detail the issue of reciprocal compensation for ISP-bound traffic. Note that in the first of these documents the FCC uses the acronym ISP to refer to "information service providers," a category that includes but is not limited to Internet service providers.[2]

IN THE MATTER OF ACCESS CHARGE REFORM
First Report and Order, 12 FCC Rcd. 15982 (1997)

VI. Other Issues

B. Treatment of Interstate Information Services

1. Background

341. In the 1983 *Access Charge Reconsideration Order*,[3] the Commission decided that, although information service providers (ISPs) may use incumbent LEC facilities to originate and terminate interstate calls, ISPs should not be required to pay interstate access charges. In recent years, usage of interstate information services, and in particular the Internet and other interactive computer networks, has increased significantly. As usage continues to grow, information services may have an increasingly significant effect on the public switched network.

342. As a result of the decisions the Commission made in the *Access Charge Reconsideration Order*, ISPs may purchase services from incumbent LECs under the same intrastate tariffs available to end users. ISPs may pay business line rates and the appropriate subscriber line charge, rather than interstate access rates, even for calls that appear to traverse state boundaries.[4] The business line rates are significantly lower than the equivalent interstate access charges, given the ISPs' high volumes of usage. ISPs typically pay incumbent LECs a flat monthly rate for their connections regardless of the amount of usage they generate, because business line rates typically include usage charges only for outgoing traffic.

---

2. The Telecommunications Act of 1996 defines "information service" in relevant part as "the offering of a capability for generating, acquiring, storing, transforming, processing, retrieving, utilizing, or making available information via telecommunications." 47 U.S.C. §153(20). The basic distinction is between telecommunications service and information service. The FCC has found that these categories are mutually exclusive and, further, that they parallel the same categories used in the Modification of Final Judgment (Chapter Sixteen) as well as the definitions of "basic service" and "enhanced service" that were first developed in the FCC's *Computer II* proceeding (Chapter Fifteen). *See* Inquiry Concerning High-Speed Access to the Internet Over Cable and Other Facilities, Notice of Inquiry, FCC 00–355, 2000 WL 1434689, at n.46 (2000).

3. In the Matter of MTS & WATS Market Structure, 97 FCC 2d 682, 711–22 (1983).

4. To maximize the number of subscribers that can reach them through a local call, most ISPs have deployed points of presence.

343. In the *Notice of Proposed Rulemaking* [in this proceeding], we tentatively concluded that ISPs should not be required to pay interstate access charges. We explained that the existing access charge system includes non-cost-based rates and inefficient rate structures. We stated that there is no reason to extend such a system to an additional class of customers, especially considering the potentially detrimental effects on the growth of the still-evolving information services industry. We explained that ISPs should not be subjected to an interstate regulatory system designed for circuit-switched interexchange voice telephony solely because ISPs use incumbent LEC networks to receive calls from their customers. We solicited comment on the narrow issue of whether to permit incumbent LECs to assess interstate access charges on ISPs. In the companion *Notice of Inquiry*, we sought comment on broader issues concerning the development of information services and Internet access.

2. Discussion

344. We conclude that the existing pricing structure for ISPs should remain in place, and incumbent LECs will not be permitted to assess interstate per-minute access charges on ISPs. We think it possible that had access rates applied to ISPs over the last 14 years, the pace of development of the Internet and other services may not have been so rapid. Maintaining the existing pricing structure for these services avoids disrupting the still-evolving information services industry and advances the goals of the 1996 Act to "preserve the vibrant and competitive free market that presently exists for the Internet and other interactive computer services, unfettered by Federal or State regulation." 47 U.S.C. §230(b)(2).

345. We decide here that ISPs should not be subject to interstate access charges. The access charge system contains non-cost-based rates and inefficient rate structures, and [reforms under the 1996 Act went] only part of the way to remove rate inefficiencies. Moreover, given the evolution in ISP technologies and markets since we first established access charges in the early 1980s, it is not clear that ISPs use the public switched network in a manner analogous to IXCs. Commercial Internet access, for example, did not even exist when access charges were established. As commenters point out, many of the characteristics of ISP traffic (such as large numbers of incoming calls to Internet service providers) may be shared by other classes of business customers.

346. We also are not convinced that the nonassessment of access charges results in ISPs imposing uncompensated costs on incumbent LECs. ISPs do pay for their connections to incumbent LEC networks by purchasing services under state tariffs. Incumbent LECs also receive incremental revenue from Internet usage through higher demand for second lines by consumers, usage of dedicated data lines by ISPs, and subscriptions to incumbent LEC Internet access services. To the extent that some intrastate rate structures fail to compensate incumbent LECs adequately for providing service to customers with high volumes of incoming calls, incumbent LECs may address their concerns to state regulators.

347. Finally, we do not believe that incumbent LEC allegations about network congestion warrant imposition of interstate access charges on ISPs. Even incumbent LEC commenters acknowledge that they can respond to instances of congestion to maintain service quality standards. Internet access does generate

different usage patterns and longer call holding times than average voice usage. However, the extent to which this usage creates congestion depends on the ways in which incumbent LECs provision their networks, and ISPs use those networks. Incumbent LECs and ISPs agree that technologies exist to reduce or eliminate whatever congestion exists; they disagree on what pricing structure would provide incentives for deployment of the most efficient technologies. The public interest would best be served by policies that foster such technological evolution of the network. The access charge system was designed for basic voice telephony provided over a circuit-switched network, and even when stripped of its current inefficiencies it may not be the most appropriate pricing structure for Internet access and other information services.

Notes and Questions

1. Commission Rationales. Why did the Commission decide not to impose access charges on ISPs? In the brief excerpt above, the Commission puts forward three possible rationales for its decision. One is that access charges would retard development of the Internet. The second is that access charges are inefficiently high and should not be perpetuated beyond the context (long distance telephony) where they are already entrenched. And the third is that ISPs use the network differently from long distance telephone carriers and are thus more like other business customers than they are like an interexchange telecommunications service provider. Which of these is the most compelling rationale? Is the FCC here deciding to forbear from imposing access charges that would otherwise apply, or is it deciding that access charges don't apply to begin with?

2. Flat Rates. The Commission dismisses concerns that, because of the high volume of calls they receive and the long duration of those calls, ISPs impose costs on LECs that a regulated, flat monthly rate will not cover. But doesn't this concern have merit? Internet sessions typically last much longer than do regular voice phone calls, and so the traffic put on the telephone network by an ISP will typically require more of a LEC's resources than would traffic put on by a typical business customer. A flat, monthly rate that does not distinguish ISPs from other business customers, then, would seem to under-compensate LECs for their infrastructure costs. Why is the FCC so unsympathetic to this argument? Is the Commission's response just that ISPs might create offsetting benefits for a LEC, for example increased demand for second phone lines? But will those benefits accrue to the same LEC? Is the Commission's response simply that this same sort of harm is caused by other high-volume subscribers, for example pizza shops? Is that a good analogy?

3. Section 706. The FCC frames its policy choice as one between treating ISPs like long distance carriers (and thus imposing per-minute access charges) and treating them like any other business customer that makes or receives a high volume of calls but nonetheless pays a flat monthly line rate. Which option is worse from the perspective of section 706: having ISPs pay too much for access to the conventional voice network through access charges, or having them (arguably) pay too little through flat monthly rates? What happens when we take into account the various parties' incentives to upgrade the telecommunications infrastructure?

4. Reciprocal Compensation. Having determined that ISPs will not be required to pay access charges, the FCC next turned to the question of whether LECs that serve ISPs should be entitled to demand reciprocal compensation from other LECs for calls to the ISPs. We introduced the concepts of reciprocal compensation and bill-and-keep in Chapter Eighteen; but, to fully explore the controversy surrounding ISPs, it is helpful to review in slightly more detail the evolution of reciprocal compensation agreements under the 1996 Act.

When the 1996 Act took effect, ILECs and the relevant state public utilities commissions had a choice: they could craft reciprocal compensation agreements (in essence, detailed contracts) that would govern LEC/LEC relationships, or they could adopt a blanket "bill-and-keep" policy that would obligate every LEC to carry traffic for every other LEC without any money changing hands. At first blush, one might suspect that these options were equally attractive. If a CLEC was going to put x calls on the ILEC's network each month and, in turn, was going to receive x calls back, payments under a reciprocal compensation scheme would cancel out and the parties could seemingly achieve the same result through bill-and-keep. ILECs, however, lobbied vigorously in favor of full-blown reciprocal compensation, probably for a combination of three reasons. First, ILECs likely suspected that, for the foreseeable future, they were going to be net receivers of telephone traffic. For one thing, ILECs already had major call centers as clients, as well as pizza places and other entities that receive many more calls than they originate. Moreover, certain new services—for example, cellular service—tended to be used more for calling into the landline network than for receiving calls from the landline network. If this were true, reciprocal compensation payments would on balance flow to the ILECs, and so of course ILECs favored reciprocal compensation over bill-and-keep. Second, the administrative costs associated with reciprocal compensation are likely more onerous than those associated with bill-and-keep since, under bill-and-keep, there is less of a need for accurate information about the number of calls exchanged, their duration, and so on. ILECs probably hoped that the more costly approach would serve as a barrier to entry, those administrative costs representing a greater proportional burden for CLECs (with their smaller client base) than for ILECs. Third—and admittedly a bit of pure speculation on our part—it is possible that ILECs preferred reciprocal compensation for the simple reason that many ILECs already had a good relationship with their local public utilities commissions. Under bill-and-keep, the terms of the deal were set in stone: no LEC pays any LEC anything. Such a system would have left little room for ILECs to use any inside advantage they might have enjoyed. More complicated reciprocal compensation schemes, by contrast, offered more of an opportunity for subtle favoritism, and hence it is not surprising that ILECs would favor the latter approach.

All this, of course, backfired on the ILECs with the rise of the ISP. With reciprocal compensation agreements in place, CLECs decided that their best strategy was to seek out customers who were net receivers of telephone calls.[5] Naturally, that meant targeting ISPs. This led to the exact opposite payment flow from the one the ILECs had expected; ILECs were paying more to CLECs than they were

---

5. Think about why this statement might be true. It is unquestionably true as a factual matter; but what's the logic here? Is it obvious that this should be so? What assumptions do you need to make in order to explain this statement? (We return to this theme in the "Notes and Questions" that follow the excerpt.)

receiving from CLECs. The ILECs were thus eager to change the terms of their reciprocal compensation agreements — in particular, to have the FCC declare that ISP traffic was not even eligible for reciprocal compensation under the 1996 Act. Whether the ILECs were right in their argument about eligibility hinged on the question of whether the call from the customer to the ISP was a local call. The FCC addressed that question in the *Report and Order* that follows.

IN RE IMPLEMENTATION OF THE LOCAL COMPETITION PROVISIONS IN THE TELECOMMUNICATIONS ACT OF 1996, INTER-CARRIER COMPENSATION FOR ISP-BOUND TRAFFIC
14 FCC Rcd. 3689 (1999)

I. INTRODUCTION

1. The Commission and the Common Carrier Bureau have received a number of requests to clarify whether a local exchange carrier is entitled to receive reciprocal compensation for traffic that it delivers to an information service provider, particularly an Internet service provider (ISP). Generally, competitive LECs (CLECs) contend that this is local traffic subject to the reciprocal compensation provisions of section 251(b)(5) of the Communications Act of 1934 (Act), as amended by the Telecommunications Act of 1996. Incumbent LECs contend that this is interstate traffic beyond the scope of section 251(b)(5).

II. BACKGROUND

B. Incumbent LEC and CLEC Delivery of ISP-Bound Traffic.

7. Section 251(b)(5) of the Act requires all LECs "to establish reciprocal compensation arrangements for the transport and termination of telecommunications." In the *Local Competition Order*,[6] this Commission construed this provision to apply only to the transport and termination of "local telecommunications traffic." In order to determine what compensation is due when two carriers collaborate to deliver a call to an ISP, we must determine as a threshold matter whether this is interstate or intrastate traffic. In general, an originating LEC end-user's call to an ISP served by another LEC is carried (1) by the originating LEC from the end-user to the point of interconnection (POI) with the LEC serving the ISP; (2) by the LEC serving the ISP from the LEC-LEC POI to the ISP's local server; and (3) from the ISP's local server to a computer that the originating LEC end-user desires to reach via the Internet. If these calls terminate at the ISP's local server (where another packet-switched "call" begins), as many CLECs contend, then they are intrastate calls, and LECs serving ISPs are entitled to reciprocal compensation for the "transport and termination" of this traffic. If, however, these calls do not terminate locally, incumbent LECs argue, then LECs serving ISPs are not entitled to reciprocal compensation under section 251(b)(5).

8. CLECs argue that, because section 251(b)(5) of the Act refers to the duty to establish reciprocal compensation arrangements for the "transport and termi-

---

6. In re Implementation of the Local Competition Provisions in the Telecommunications Act of 1996, First Report and Order, 11 FCC Rcd. 15499 (1996).

nation of *telecommunications*," a transmission "terminates" for reciprocal compensation purposes when it ceases to be "telecommunications." "Telecommunications" is defined in the Act as "the transmission, between or among points specified by the user, of information of the user's choosing, without change in the form or content of the information as sent and received." 47 U.S.C. §153(43). CLECs contend that, under this definition, Internet service is not "telecommunications" and that the "telecommunications" component of Internet traffic terminates at the ISP's local server. Incumbent LECs contend, however, that the "telecommunications" terminate not at the ISP's local server, but at the Internet site accessed by the end-user, in which case these are interstate calls for which, they argue, no reciprocal compensation is due.

III. DISCUSSION

9. The Commission has no rule governing inter-carrier compensation for ISP-bound traffic. Generally speaking, when a call is completed by two (or more) interconnecting carriers, the carriers are compensated for carrying that traffic through either reciprocal compensation or access charges. When two carriers jointly provide interstate access (*e.g.*, by delivering a call to an interexchange carrier (IXC)), the carriers will share access revenues received from the interstate service provider. Conversely, when two carriers collaborate to complete a local call, the originating carrier is compensated by its end-user and the terminating carrier is entitled to reciprocal compensation pursuant to section 251(b)(5) of the Act. Until now, however, it has been unclear whether or how the access charge regime or reciprocal compensation applies when two interconnecting carriers deliver traffic to an ISP. As we have already determined, LECs may not impose access charges on ISPs; therefore, there are no access revenues for interconnecting carriers to share. Moreover, the Commission has directed states to treat ISP traffic as if it were local, by permitting ISPs to purchase their PSTN links through local business tariffs. As a result, and because the Commission had not addressed inter-carrier compensation under these circumstances, parties negotiating interconnection agreements and the state commissions charged with interpreting them were left to determine as a matter of first impression how interconnecting carriers should be compensated for delivering traffic to ISPs, leading to the present dispute.

    A. Jurisdictional Nature of Incumbent LEC and CLEC Delivery of
        ISP-Bound Traffic.

10. As many incumbent LECs properly note, the Commission traditionally has determined the jurisdictional nature of communications by the end points of the communication and consistently has rejected attempts to divide communications at any intermediate points of switching or exchanges between carriers.

12. Consistent with our precedents, Petition for Emergency Relief and Declaratory Ruling Filed by BellSouth Corporation, 7 FCC Rcd. 1619 (1992) (*BellSouth MemoryCall*), and Teleconnect Co. v. Bell Telephone Co. of Penn., 10 FCC Rcd. 1626 (1995), *aff'd sub nom.* Southwestern Bell Tel. Co. v. FCC, 116 F.3d 593 (D.C. Cir. 1997),[7] we conclude, as explained further below, that the communications at issue here do not terminate at the ISP's local server, as CLECs and

---

7. Although the cited cases involve interexchange carriers rather than ISPs, and the Commission has observed that "it is not clear that ISPs use the public switched network in a

ISPs contend, but continue to the ultimate destination or destinations, specifically at an Internet website that is often located in another state. The fact that the facilities and apparatus used to deliver traffic to the ISP's local servers may be located within a single state does not affect our jurisdiction. As the Commission stated in *BellSouth MemoryCall*, "this Commission has jurisdiction over, and regulates charges for, the local network when it is used in conjunction with the origination and termination of interstate calls." Indeed, in the vast majority of cases, the facilities that incumbent LECs use to provide interstate access are located entirely within one state. Thus, we reject MCI WorldCom's assertion that the LEC facilities used to deliver traffic to ISPs must cross state boundaries for such traffic to be classified as interstate.

18. Having concluded that the jurisdictional nature of ISP-bound traffic is determined by the nature of the end-to-end transmission between an end-user and the Internet, we now must determine whether that transmission constitutes interstate telecommunications. Section 2(a) of the Act grants the Commission jurisdiction over "all interstate and foreign communication by wire." 47 U.S.C. §152(a). Traffic is deemed interstate "when the communication or transmission originates in any state, territory, possession of the United States, or the District of Columbia and terminates in another state, territory, possession, or the District of Columbia." Federal-State Joint Board on Universal Service Report to Congress, 13 FCC Rcd. 11501, at 11555 (1998). In a conventional circuit-switched network, a call that originates and terminates in a single state is jurisdictionally intrastate, and a call that originates in one state and terminates in a different state (or country) is jurisdictionally interstate. The jurisdictional analysis is less straightforward for the packet-switched network environment of the Internet. An Internet communication does not necessarily have a point of "termination" in the traditional sense. An Internet user typically communicates with more than one destination point during a single Internet call, or "session," and may do so either sequentially or simultaneously. In a single Internet communication, an Internet user may, for example, access websites that reside on servers in various states or foreign countries, communicate directly with another Internet user, or chat on-line with a group of Internet users located in the same local exchange or in another country. Further complicating the matter of identifying the geographical destinations of Internet traffic is that the contents of popular websites increasingly are being stored in multiple servers throughout the Internet, based on "caching" or website "mirroring" techniques. After reviewing the record, we conclude that, although some Internet traffic is intrastate, a substantial portion of Internet traffic involves accessing interstate or foreign websites.

B. Inter-Carrier Compensation for Delivery of ISP-Bound Traffic.

22. Currently, the Commission has no rule governing inter-carrier compensation for ISP-bound traffic. In the absence of such a rule, parties may voluntarily include this traffic within the scope of their interconnection agreements under sections 251 and 252 of the Act, even if these statutory provisions do not apply as a matter of law. Where parties have agreed to include this traffic within their section 251 and 252 interconnection agreements, they are bound by those agreements, as interpreted and enforced by the state commissions.

---

manner analogous to IXCs," *Access Charge Reform Order*, 12 FCC Rcd. 15982, 16133 (1997), the Commission's observation does not affect the jurisdictional analysis.

23. Although we determine, above, that ISP-bound traffic is largely interstate, parties nonetheless may have agreed to treat the traffic as subject to reciprocal compensation. The Commission's treatment of this sort of traffic dates from 1983 when the Commission first adopted a different access regime for ISPs. Since then, the Commission has maintained that exemption, pursuant to which it treats ISPs as end-users under the access charge regime and permits them to purchase their links to the PSTN through intrastate local business tariffs rather than through interstate access tariffs. As such, the Commission discharged its interstate regulatory obligations through the application of local business tariffs. Thus, although recognizing that it was interstate access, the Commission has treated ISP-bound traffic as though it were local.

24. Against this backdrop, and in the absence of any contrary Commission rule, parties entering into interconnection agreements may reasonably have agreed, for the purposes of determining whether reciprocal compensation should apply to ISP-bound traffic, that such traffic should be treated in the same manner as local traffic. When construing the parties' agreements to determine whether the parties so agreed, state commissions have the opportunity to consider all the relevant facts, including the negotiation of the agreements in the context of this Commission's longstanding policy of treating this traffic as local, and the conduct of the parties pursuant to those agreements. Finally, we note that issues regarding whether an entity is properly certified as a LEC if it serves only or predominantly ISPs are matters of state jurisdiction.

25. Even where parties to interconnection agreements do not voluntarily agree on an inter-carrier compensation mechanism for ISP-bound traffic, state commissions nonetheless may determine in their arbitration proceedings at this point that reciprocal compensation should be paid for this traffic. The passage of the 1996 Act raised the novel issue of the applicability of its local competition provisions to the issue of inter-carrier compensation for ISP-bound traffic. Section 252 imposes upon state commissions the statutory duty to approve voluntarily-negotiated interconnection agreements and to arbitrate interconnection disputes. As we observed in the *Local Competition Order*, state commission authority over interconnection agreements pursuant to section 252 "extends to both interstate and intrastate matters." 11 FCC Rcd. at 15544. Thus the mere fact that ISP-bound traffic is largely interstate does not necessarily remove it from the section 251/252 negotiation and arbitration process. However, any such arbitration must be consistent with governing federal law. While to date the Commission has not adopted a specific rule governing the matter, we note that our policy of treating ISP-bound traffic as local for purposes of interstate access charges would, if applied in the separate context of reciprocal compensation, suggest that such compensation is due for that traffic.

26. Some CLECs construe our rules treating ISPs as end-users for purposes of interstate access charges as requiring the payment of reciprocal compensation for this traffic. Incumbent LECs contend, however, that our rules preclude the imposition of reciprocal compensation obligations to interstate traffic and that, pursuant to the ISP access charge exemption, LECs carrying ISP-bound traffic are compensated by their end-user customers—the originating end-user or the ISP. Either of these options might be a reasonable extension of our rules, but the Commission has never applied either the ISP exemption or its rules regarding the joint provision of access to the situation where two carriers collaborate to deliver traffic to an ISP. As we stated previously, the Commission currently has no rule

addressing the specific issue of inter-carrier compensation for ISP-bound traffic. In the absence of a federal rule, state commissions that have had to fulfill their statutory obligation under section 252 to resolve interconnection disputes between incumbent LECs and CLECs have had no choice but to establish an inter-carrier compensation mechanism and to decide whether and under what circumstances to require the payment of reciprocal compensation. Although reciprocal compensation is mandated under section 251(b)(5) only for the transport and termination of local traffic, neither the statute nor our rules prohibit a state commission from concluding in an arbitration that reciprocal compensation is appropriate in certain instances not addressed by section 251(b)(5), so long as there is no conflict with governing federal law. A state commission's decision to impose reciprocal compensation obligations in an arbitration proceeding—or a subsequent state commission decision that those obligations encompass ISP-bound traffic—does not conflict with any Commission rule regarding ISP-bound traffic. By the same token, in the absence of governing federal law, state commissions also are free not to require the payment of reciprocal compensation for this traffic and to adopt another compensation mechanism.

27. State commissions considering what effect, if any, this Declaratory Ruling has on their decisions as to whether reciprocal compensation provisions of interconnection agreements apply to ISP-bound traffic might conclude, depending on the bases of those decisions, that it is not necessary to re-visit those determinations. We recognize that our conclusion that ISP-bound traffic is largely interstate might cause some state commissions to re-examine their conclusion that reciprocal compensation is due to the extent that those conclusions are based on a finding that this traffic terminates at an ISP server, but nothing in this Declaratory Ruling precludes state commissions from determining, pursuant to contractual principles or other legal or equitable considerations, that reciprocal compensation is an appropriate interim inter-carrier compensation rule pending completion of the rulemaking we initiate below.

Notes and Questions

1. Where the Sidewalk Ends. How convincing is the FCC's jurisdictional argument that, because ISP-bound calls eventually may reach foreign or interstate information sources, the calls do not "terminate" locally at the ISP and are thus interstate communications subject to federal regulation? Is this consistent with the FCC's own ruling that ISPs do not have to pay the access charges established for interexchange carriers? That is, if, in the context of the access charge regime, the Commission decided to treat ISPs as regular business customers of a LEC rather than as providers of interstate telecommunications services, doesn't that imply that the local calls ISPs receive terminate with them? If so, why shouldn't reciprocal compensation rules apply?

2. Not So Reciprocal Compensation. The ILECs continue to strongly oppose including ISP-bound traffic in the reciprocal compensation regime of sections 251 and 252. Again, the main reason is that some companies have set themselves up as CLECs that serve only ISPs. Because ISPs do not originate traffic, the CLECs to which they subscribe never pay termination fees to other LECs. On the other hand, because a CLEC serving an ISP terminates a lot of traffic that originated on other LECs, it would, if that traffic is "local," collect a lot of money in termination charges from those other LECs. CLECs serving only ISPs thus receive, but never reciprocate, compensation for interconnection. Intuitively, ILECs in this situation would like to establish a scheme where no money changes hands—for example, bill-and-keep.

3. Equity. While reciprocal compensation has not thus far worked out the way the ILECs' anticipated, it is worth a moment's pause to ask whether there is really anything unfair about treating ISP traffic as eligible for reciprocal compensation. Reciprocal compensation is designed to pay LECs the costs they incur when terminating telephone traffic. ISP-focused CLECs do indeed terminate traffic; so is the argument here that reciprocal compensation payments are bloated and thus overcompensate the CLECs? Does that mean that reciprocal compensation payments are bloated across the board, or could it be that they are set at the correct levels for traditional LECs but only bloated as compared to the costs incurred by ISP-focused LECs? How might state officials go about answering these questions? Are these the sorts of questions state officials should ask?

4. Does Network Size Matter? Suppose that a given ILEC has upwards of two million residential subscribers, whereas an interconnecting rival CLEC has only twenty thousand residential subscribers. For the purposes of this question, assume that neither the ILEC nor the CLEC has any business subscribers. On the basis of the disparity in network size alone, would ILECs have any reason to prefer explicit reciprocal compensation over bill-and-keep? (That is, is this a meaningfully different scenario from the ISP scenario?)

5. Termination. Are the Commission and state regulators too quick to associate the costs of terminating a call with the originating caller's LEC as opposed to the terminating caller's LEC? Throughout the 1990s, users of cellular phones were required to pay fees not only when they chose to originate calls, but also every time they happened to receive a call. Associating termination charges with the phone call recipient would eliminate much of the need for reciprocal compensation agreements; would it be a good idea?

6. The Circle of Life. Consider again the business incentives created if one-way traffic is nonetheless subject to reciprocal compensation. New entrants might have an incentive to sign up customers, like ISPs, pizza parlors, and nursing homes, whose traffic is mostly incoming, rather than customers that generate a lot of outgoing calls or customers who engage in balanced calling patterns. Existing telephone companies would then respond, most likely by petitioning local authorities for higher tariffs—tariffs justified by the significant sums being paid out in reciprocal compensation fees. ISPs would then likely adjust their retail prices downward to compensate, the fear being that the new higher telephone charges would shift consumers away from phone-based ISPs and toward cable, satellite, or other technologies. Does this "circle of life" from consumers to their ISPs, ISPs to local phone companies, local phone companies to other local phone companies, and local phone companies back to consumers suggest that the regulatory decisions here do not matter much? Or does all this distort the development of local exchange competition in ways that should be avoided?

7. Deference to the States. The Commission did not rule that ISP-bound traffic could never be subject to reciprocal compensation. Rather, the FCC left the issue for states or carriers themselves to decide. What considerations might state officials (or carriers negotiating interconnection agreements) take into account in deciding whether to make ISP-bound traffic eligible for reciprocal compensation under particular reciprocal compensation arrangements? Must traffic be symmetric between parties before reciprocal compensation makes sense? Is this in the end a simple question of contract drafting and interpretation? Should it be?

8. Judicial Review. The D.C. Circuit reviewed the Commission's ISP reciprocal compensation decision and found it insufficiently explained to pass judicial review. The court's opinion remanding the issue to the FCC follows.

BELL ATLANTIC TELEPHONE COMPANY v. FCC
206 F.3d 1 (D.C. Cir. 2000)

Opinion for the court filed by Circuit Judge WILLIAMS, in which Circuit Judges SENTELLE and RANDOLPH concur.

WILLIAMS, Circuit Judge:

The Telecommunications Act of 1996 requires local exchange carriers (LECs) to "establish reciprocal compensation arrangements for the transport and termination of telecommunications." *Id.* §251(b)(5). When LECs collaborate to complete a call, this provision ensures compensation both for the originating LEC, which receives payment from the end-user, and for the recipient's LEC. By regulation the Commission has limited the scope of the reciprocal compensation requirement to "local telecommunications traffic." 47 CFR §51.701(a). In the ruling under review, it considered whether calls to internet service providers (ISPs) within the caller's local calling area are themselves "local." In doing so it applied its so-called "end-to-end" analysis, noting that the communication characteristically will ultimately (if indirectly) extend beyond the ISP to websites out-of-state and around the world. Accordingly it found the calls non-local. *See* In the Matter of Implementation of the Local Competition Provisions in the Telecommunications Act of 1996, Intercarrier Compensation for ISP-Bound Traffic, 14 FCC Rcd. 3689, 3690 (¶1) (1999) ("FCC Ruling").

Having thus taken the calls to ISPs out of §251(b)(5)'s provision for "reciprocal compensation" (as it interpreted it), the Commission could nonetheless itself have set rates for such calls, but it elected not to. In [an accompanying] *Notice of Proposed Rulemaking*, the Commission tentatively concluded that "a negotiation process, driven by market forces, is more likely to lead to efficient outcomes than are rates set by regulation," 14 FCC Rcd. at 3707 (¶29), but for the nonce it left open the matter of implementing a system of federal controls. It observed that in the meantime parties may voluntarily include reciprocal compensation provisions in their interconnection agreements, and that state commissions, which have authority to arbitrate disputes over such agreements, can construe the agreements as requiring such compensation; indeed, even when the agreements of interconnecting LECs include no linguistic hook for such a requirement, the commissions can find that reciprocal compensation is appropriate.

This outcome left at least two unhappy groups. One, led by Bell Atlantic, consists of incumbent LECs (the "incumbents"). Quite content with the Commission's finding of §251(b)(5)'s inapplicability, the incumbents objected to its conclusion that in the absence of federal regulation state commissions have the authority to impose reciprocal compensation. Although the Commission's new rulemaking on the subject may eventuate in a rule that preempts the states' authority, the incumbents object to being left at the mercy of state commissions until that (hypothetical) time, arguing that the commissions have mandated exorbitant compensation. In particular, the incumbents, who are paid a flat monthly fee, have generally been forced to provide compensation for internet calls on a per-minute basis. Given the average length of such calls the cost can be substantial, and since ISPs do not make outgoing calls, this compensation is hardly "reciprocal."

Another group, led by MCI WorldCom, consists of firms that are seeking to compete with the incumbent LECs and which provide local exchange telecommunications services to ISPs (the "competitors"). These firms, which stand to receive reciprocal compensation on ISP-bound calls, petitioned for review with the complaint that the Commission erred in finding that the calls weren't covered by §251(b)(5).

The issue at the heart of this case is whether a call to an ISP is local or long distance. Neither category fits clearly. The Commission has described local calls, on the one hand, as those in which LECs collaborate to complete a call and are compensated for their respective roles in completing the call, and long distance calls, on the other, as those in which the LECs collaborate with a long distance carrier, which itself charges the end-user and pays out compensation to the LECs.

Calls to ISPs are not quite local, because there is some communication taking place between the ISP and out-of-state websites. But they are not quite long distance, because the subsequent communication is not really a continuation, in the conventional sense, of the initial call to the ISP. The Commission's ruling rests squarely on its decision to employ an end-to-end analysis for purposes of determining whether ISP-traffic is local. There is no dispute that the Commission has historically been justified in relying on this method when determining whether a particular communication is jurisdictionally interstate. But it has yet to provide an explanation why this inquiry is relevant to discerning whether a call to an ISP should fit within the local call model of two collaborating LECs or the long distance model of a long distance carrier collaborating with two LECs.

In fact, the extension of "end-to-end" analysis from jurisdictional purposes to the present context yields intuitively backwards results. Calls that are jurisdictionally intrastate will be subject to the federal reciprocal compensation requirement, while calls that are interstate are not subject to federal regulation but instead are left to potential state regulation. The inconsistency is not necessarily fatal, since under the 1996 Act the Commission has jurisdiction to implement such provisions as §251, even if they are within the traditional domain of the states. *See* AT&T Corp. v. Iowa Utils. Bd., 525 U.S. 366 (1999). But it reveals that arguments supporting use of the end-to-end analysis in the jurisdictional analysis are not obviously transferable to this context.

In attacking the Commission's classification of ISP-bound calls as non-local for purposes of reciprocal compensation, MCI WorldCom notes that under 47 CFR §51.701(b)(1) "telecommunications traffic" is local if it "originates and terminates within a local service area." But, observes MCI WorldCom, the Commission failed to apply, or even to mention, its definition of "termination," namely "the switching of traffic that is subject to section 251(b)(5) at the terminating carrier's end office switch (or equivalent facility) and delivery of that traffic from that switch to the called party's premises." Local Competition Order, 11 FCC Rcd. at 16015 (¶1040); 47 CFR §51.701(d). Calls to ISPs appear to fit this definition: the traffic is switched by the LEC whose customer is the ISP and then delivered to the ISP, which is clearly the "called party."

In its ruling the Commission avoided this result by analyzing the communication on an end-to-end basis: "The communications at issue here do not terminate at the ISP's local server..., but continue to the ultimate destination or destinations." FCC Ruling, 14 FCC Rcd. at 3697 (¶12). But the cases it relied on for using this analysis are not on point. Both involved a single continuous communication, originated by an end-user, switched by a long distance communications carrier, and eventually delivered to its destination. One, Teleconnect Co. v. Bell Telephone Co., 10 FCC Rcd. 1626 (1995), *aff'd sub nom.* Southwestern Bell Tel. Co. v. FCC, 116 F.3d 593 (D.C. Cir. 1997) (*"Teleconnect"*), involved an 800 call to a long distance carrier, which then routed the call to its intended recipient. The other, In the Matter of Petition for Emergency Relief and Declaratory Ruling Filed by the BellSouth Corporation, 7 FCC Rcd. 1619 (1992), considered a voice mail service. Part of the service, the forwarding of the call from the intended recipient's location to the voice mail apparatus and service, occurred entirely within the subscriber's state, and thus looked local. Looking "end-to-end," however, the Commission refused to focus on this portion of the call but rather considered the service in its entirety (*i.e.,* originating with the out-of-state caller leaving a message, or the subscriber calling from out-of-state to retrieve messages). *Id.* at 1621 (¶12).

ISPs, in contrast, are "information service providers," *In the Matter of Federal-State Joint Board on Universal Service*, 13 FCC Rcd. 11501, 11532–33 (¶66) (1998), which upon receiving a call originate further communications to deliver and retrieve information to and from distant websites. The Commission acknowledged in a footnote that the cases it relied upon were distinguishable, but dismissed the problem out-of-hand: "Although the cited cases involve interexchange carriers rather than ISPs, and the Commission has observed that 'it is not clear that [information service providers] use the public switched network in a manner analogous to IXCs,' Access Charge Reform Order, 12 FCC Rcd. at 16133, the Commission's observation does not affect the jurisdictional analysis." FCC Ruling, 14 FCC Rcd. at 3697 n.36 (¶12). It is not clear how this helps the Commission. Even if the difference between ISPs and traditional long distance carriers is irrelevant for jurisdictional purposes, it appears relevant for purposes of reciprocal compensation. Although ISPs use telecommunications to provide information service, they are not themselves telecommunications providers (as are long distance carriers).

In this regard an ISP appears, as MCI WorldCom argued, no different from many businesses, such as "pizza delivery firms, travel reservation agencies, credit card verification firms, or taxicab companies," which use a variety of communication services to provide their goods or services to their customers. Of course, the ISP's origination of telecommunications as a result of the user's call is instantaneous (although perhaps no more so than a credit card verification system or a bank account information service). But this does not imply that the original communication does not "terminate" at the ISP. The Commission has not satisfactorily explained why an ISP is not, for purposes of reciprocal compensation, simply a communications-intensive business end-user selling a product to other consumer and business end-users.

The Commission nevertheless argues that although the call from the ISP to an out-of-state website is information service for the end-user, it is telecommunications for the ISP, and thus the telecommunications cannot be said to "terminate" at the ISP. As the Commission states: "Even if, from the perspective of the end-user as customer, the telecommunications portion of an Internet call 'terminates' at the ISP's server (and information service begins), the remaining portion of the call would continue to constitute telecommunications from the perspective of the ISP as customer." Commission's Brief at 41. Once again, however, the mere fact that the ISP originates further telecommunications does not imply that the original telecommunication does not "terminate" at the ISP. However sound the end-to-end analysis may be for jurisdictional purposes, the Commission has not explained why viewing these linked telecommunications as continuous works for purposes of reciprocal compensation.

Adding further confusion is a series of Commission rulings dealing with a class, enhanced service providers (ESPs), of which ISPs are a subclass. *See* FCC Ruling, 14 FCC Rcd. at 3689 n.1 (¶1). ESPs, the precursors to the 1996 Act's information service providers, offer data processing services, linking customers and computers via the telephone network. In its establishment of the access charge system for long distance calls, the Commission in 1983 exempted ESPs from the access charge system, thus in effect treating them like end-users rather than long distance carriers. *See* In the Matter of MTS & WATS Market Structure, 97 FCC 2d 682, 711–15 (¶¶77–83) (1983). It reaffirmed this decision in 1991, explaining that it had "refrained from applying full access charges to ESPs out of concern that the industry has continued to be affected by a number of significant, potentially disruptive, and rapidly changing circumstances." In the Matter of Part 69 of the Commission's Rules Relating to the Creation of Access Charge Subelements for Open Network Architecture, 6 FCC Rcd. 4524, 4534 (¶54) (1991). In 1997 it again preserved the status quo. In the Matter of Access Charge Reform, 12 FCC Rcd. 15982 (1997) (*"Access Charge Reform Order"*). It justified the exemption in terms of the goals of the 1996 Act, saying that its purpose was to "'preserve the vibrant and competitive free market that presently exists for the Internet and other interactive computer services.'" *Id.* at 16133 (¶344) (quoting 47 U.S.C. §230(b)(2)).

This classification of ESPs is something of an embarrassment to the Commission's present ruling. As MCI WorldCom notes, the Commission acknowledged in the *Access Charge Reform Order* that "given the evolution in [information service provider] technologies and markets since we first established access charges in the early 1980s, it is not clear that [information service providers] use the public switched network in a manner analogous to IXCs [inter-exchange carriers]." 12 FCC Rcd. at 16133 (¶345). It also referred to calls to information service providers as "local." *Id.* at 16132 (¶342 n.502). And when this aspect of the *Access Charge Reform Order* was challenged in the 8th Circuit, the Commission's brief-writers responded with a sharp differentiation between such calls and ordinary long distance calls covered by the "end-to-end" analysis, and even used the analogy employed by MCI WorldCom here—that a call to an information service provider is really like a call to a local business that then uses the telephone to order wares to meet the need. When accused of inconsistency in the present matter, the Commission flipped the argument on its head, arguing that its exemption of ESPs from access charges actually confirms "its understanding that ESPs in fact use interstate access service; otherwise, the exemption would not be necessary." FCC Ruling, 14 FCC Rcd. at 3700 (¶16). This is not very compelling. Although, to be sure, the Commission used policy arguments to justify the "exemption," it also rested it on an acknowledgment of the real differences between long distance calls and calls to information service providers. It is obscure why those have now dropped out of the picture.

Because the Commission has not supplied a real explanation for its decision to treat end-to-end analysis as controlling, we must vacate the ruling and remand the case.

Notes and Questions

1. The Court's Objections. The Court of Appeals principally objected not to the FCC's result, but rather to what it considered to be gaps in the Commission's reasoning. In particular, the court found that the Commission did not explain why calls don't terminate at an ISP given the Commission's own definition of "termination." Is the court right that the Commission's own definition would cover the ISP case? The court also disagreed with the FCC's end-to-end analysis in this context. What was the court's objection? Was it simply that the precedent the Commission cited to support the analysis was not on point?

2. Remand. What are the FCC's options on remand? Must the FCC choose between rejecting some of its previous decisions or rejecting the 1999 ruling at issue in this case? Consider the regulatory alternatives, including forbearance, open to the Commission. Are there different means the Commission could use, consistent with the 1996 Act, to achieve the same result and yet satisfy the court's concerns?

II. INTERNET PROTOCOL TELEPHONY

Characterizing ISP traffic as local, long distance, or neither was contentious enough when the parties all thought they were arguing about email messages, website graphics, and other standard Internet fare. When it became clear that voice communication would also be in the mix, the frenzy reached new heights. Now the issue wasn't simply one of fair compensation, it was in addition one of fair competition. So long as ISPs were allowed to carry voice traffic but were not required to pay access charges, they would enjoy a seemingly unfair competitive advantage in head-to-head competition with IXCs. Worse, the results of that competition would have implications for universal service. Specifically, if IP telephony were to grow substantially and still remain outside the access charge regime, then fewer and fewer calls would contribute to universal service support and the existing subsidy system would ultimately collapse.

Voice over the Internet thus posed not only an immediate financial and competitive problem for "conventional" local and long distance telephone companies, but also a significant and looming threat to the entire universal service system. The FCC considered both of these issues in the excerpt below.

IN THE MATTER OF THE FEDERAL-STATE JOINT BOARD ON UNIVERSAL SERVICE
Report to Congress, 13 FCC Rcd. 11501,
13 FCC Rcd. 11830 (1998)

3. IP Telephony

83. Having concluded [earlier in this *Report*] that Internet access providers do not offer "telecommunications service" when they furnish Internet access to their customers, we next consider whether certain other Internet-based services might fall within the statutory definition of "telecommunications." We recognize that new Internet-based services are emerging, and that our application of statutory terms must take into account such technological developments. We therefore examine in this section Internet-based services, known as IP telephony, that most closely resemble traditional basic transmission offerings. The Commission to date has not formally considered the legal status of IP telephony. The record currently before us suggests that certain "phone-to-phone IP telephony" services lack the characteristics that would render them "information services" within the meaning of the statute, and instead bear the characteristics of "telecommunications services." We do not believe, however, that it is appropriate to make any definitive pronouncements in the absence of a more complete record focused on individual service offerings.

84. "IP telephony" services enable real-time voice transmission using Internet protocols. The services can be provided in two basic ways: through software and hardware at customer premises, or through "gateways" that enable applications originating and/or terminating on the PSTN. Gateways are computers that transform the circuit-switched voice signal into IP packets, and vice versa, and perform associated signalling, control, and address translation functions. The voice communications can be transmitted along with other data on the "public" Internet, or can be routed through intranets or other private data networks for improved performance. Several companies now offer commercial IP telephony products. For example, VocalTec sells software that end-users can install on their personal computers to make calls to other users with similar equipment, and also makes software used in gateways. Companies such as IDT and Qwest employ gateways to offer users the ability to call from their computer to ordinary telephones connected to the public switched network, or from one telephone to another. To use the latter category of services, a user first picks up an ordinary telephone handset connected to the public switched network, then dials the phone number of a local gateway. Upon receiving a second dialtone, the user dials the phone number of the party he or she wishes to call. The call is routed from the gateway over an IP network, then terminated through another gateway to the ordinary telephone at the receiving end.

85. Commenters that discuss IP telephony are split on the appropriate treatment of these services. Several parties, including Senators Rockefeller, Snowe, Stevens, and Burns, urge that IP telephony providers offer interstate telecommunications services and, consequently, should contribute to universal service sup-

port mechanisms. Other parties, including Senator McCain, Representative White and the National Telecommunications and Information Administration, oppose such regulation. Some commenters argue that IP telephony is a nascent technology that is unlikely to generate significant revenues in the foreseeable future. Regardless of the size of the market, we must still decide as a legal matter whether any IP telephony providers meet the statutory definitions of offering "telecommunications" or "telecommunications service" in section 3 of the 1996 Act [47 U.S.C. §153].

86. As we have observed above in our general discussion of hybrid services, the classification of a service under the 1996 Act depends on the functional nature of the end-user offering. Applying this test to IP telephony, we consider whether any company offers a service that provides users with pure "telecommunications." We first note that "telecommunications" is defined as a form of "transmission." Companies that only provide software and hardware installed at customer premises do not fall within this category, because they do not transmit information. These providers are analogous to PBX vendors, in that they offer customer premises equipment (CPE) that enables end-users to engage in telecommunications by purchasing local exchange and interexchange service from carriers. These CPE providers do not, however, transport any traffic themselves.

87. In the case of "computer-to-computer" IP telephony, individuals use software and hardware at their premises to place calls between two computers connected to the Internet. The IP telephony software is an application that the subscriber runs, using Internet access provided by its Internet service provider. The Internet service providers over whose networks the information passes may not even be aware that particular customers are using IP telephony software, because IP packets carrying voice communications are indistinguishable from other types of packets. As a general matter, our regulations apply only to the provision or offering of telecommunications. Without regard to whether "telecommunications" is taking place in the transmission of computer-to-computer IP telephony, the Internet service provider does not appear to be "providing" telecommunications to its subscribers.

88. "Phone-to-phone" IP telephony services appear to present a different case. In using the term "phone-to-phone" IP telephony, we tentatively intend to refer to services in which the provider meets the following conditions: (1) it holds itself out as providing voice telephony or facsimile transmission service; (2) it does not require the customer to use CPE different from that CPE necessary to place an ordinary touch-tone call (or facsimile transmission) over the public switched telephone network; (3) it allows the customer to call telephone numbers assigned in accordance with the North American Numbering Plan, and associated international agreements; and (4) it transmits customer information without net change in form or content.

89. Specifically, when an IP telephony service provider deploys a gateway within the network to enable phone-to-phone service, it creates a virtual transmission path between points on the public switched telephone network over a packet-switched IP network. These providers typically purchase dial-up or dedicated circuits from carriers and use those circuits to originate or terminate Internet-based calls. From a functional standpoint, users of these services obtain only voice transmission, rather than information services such as access to stored files. The provider does not offer a capability for generating, acquiring, storing, transforming, processing, retrieving, utilizing, or making available information. Thus,

the record currently before us suggests that this type of IP telephony lacks the characteristics that would render them "information services" within the meaning of the statute, and instead bear the characteristics of "telecommunications services."

90. We do not believe, however, that it is appropriate to make any definitive pronouncements in the absence of a more complete record focused on individual service offerings. As stated above, we use in this analysis a tentative definition of "phone-to-phone" IP telephony. Because of the wide range of services that can be provided using packetized voice and innovative CPE, we will need, before making definitive pronouncements, to consider whether our tentative definition of phone-to-phone IP telephony accurately distinguishes between phone-to-phone and other forms of IP telephony, and is not likely to be quickly overcome by changes in technology. We defer a more definitive resolution of these issues pending the development of a more fully-developed record because we recognize the need, when dealing with emerging services and technologies in environments as dynamic as today's Internet and telecommunications markets, to have as complete information and input as possible.

91. In upcoming proceedings with the more focused records, we undoubtedly will be addressing the regulatory status of various specific forms of IP telephony, including the regulatory requirements to which phone-to-phone providers may be subject if we were to conclude that they are "telecommunications carriers." The Act and the Commission's rules impose various requirements on providers of telecommunications, including contributing to universal service mechanisms, paying interstate access charges, and filing interstate tariffs. We note that, to the extent we conclude that certain forms of phone-to-phone IP telephony service are "telecommunications services," and to the extent the providers of those services obtain the same circuit-switched access as obtained by other interexchange carriers, and therefore impose the same burdens on the local exchange as do other interexchange carriers, we may find it reasonable that they pay similar access charges. On the other hand, we likely will face difficult and contested issues relating to the assessment of access charges on these providers. For example, it may be difficult for the LECs to determine whether particular phone-to-phone IP telephony calls are interstate, and thus subject to the federal access charge scheme, or intrastate. We intend to examine these issues more closely based on the more complete records developed in future proceedings.

92. With regard to universal service contributions, to the extent we conclude that certain forms of phone-to-phone IP telephony are interstate "telecommunications," and to the extent that providers of such services are offering those services directly to the public for a fee, those providers would be "telecommunications carriers." Accordingly, those providers would fall within section 254(d)'s mandatory requirement to contribute to universal service mechanisms. Finally, under section 10 of the Act, we have authority to forbear from imposing any rule or requirement of the Act on telecommunications carriers. We will need to consider carefully whether, pursuant to our authority under section 10 of the Act, to forbear from imposing any of the rules that would apply to phone-to-phone IP telephony providers as "telecommunications carriers."

Notes and Questions

1. Universal Service Obligations. What arguments should the FCC consider when deciding whether to extend universal service obligations to ISPs? The above document seems to worry that the Commission does not have the necessary information; but will that information ever be available in the rapidly-changing technology marketplace? Should the FCC withhold judgment until it has good information, perhaps the result being several years during which ISPs are excused from making universal service contributions?

2. Investment Incentives. Should ISPs be exempted from the access charge regime as a way of encouraging the development of IP telephony and related services? Is such an exemption desirable, or might it instead lead firms to invest in packet-switched voice communication not because of the merits of the technology, but, instead, simply because the regulatory regime treats that technology more favorably than other alternatives? Relatedly, if one of the Commission's goals is to encourage investment in IP telephony, does the excerpt above further that mission or simply perpetuate uncertainty about IP telephony's regulatory status?

3. What About Email? Given all of the above, how should the FCC think about email? Should there be access charges associated with long distance emails, the argument being that email is a substitute for long distance telephony and so it, like long distance telephony, should be taxed so as to support the nation's universal service commitment? Don't you think that IXCs view email as a competitive threat to their service? Or is email different from IP telephony in a way that weakens this sort of argument?

4. Hybrid Regulations. Can the FCC treat ISP traffic as long distance traffic if it is a voice communication but as local traffic otherwise? Could such a distinction be justified as a legal matter? Could it be carried out in practice? (What about presumptions—say, assuming that 20% of all ISP traffic is voice traffic? Or would that again invite strategic play?)

5. The Regulatory Perspective. In deciding whether to require firms that offer IP telephony to contribute to universal service, should we look solely at the regulations involved, or should we take a broader perspective? For example, should we account for advantages that flow from the market, or from regulations that helped to entrench a firm in years past but no longer provide such aid? Consider in this regard the following excerpt from Commissioner Michael Powell's separate statement, concurring in the *Report to Congress* excerpted above:

> It is too simple to focus on a single competitive inequity and then declare the game unfair, without examining the totality of advantages and disadvantages among competitors.

> We should recognize that competitive advantages are not limited to whether or not companies must contribute to universal service support. For example, while telecommunications carriers must contribute to universal service, they also enjoy significant benefits under sections 251 and 252 of the Act. Likewise, incumbents often have significant advantages over new entrants, such as capital, business and marketing savvy and technical expertise, such that declining to require new entrants to contribute to universal service may not give the new entrants an appreciable advantage over the incumbent. Leveling the playing field, when the play-

ers do not start from the same place, only institutionalizes the advantage of the stronger, better equipped, experienced players.

Are you persuaded that it is appropriate to focus on these broader considerations? Is it fair to incumbents? On the specific advantages he mentions, do §§251 and 252 confer "significant benefits" on ILECs? Is it appropriate to, in effect, penalize incumbents for their business and marketing savvy?

6. Developments in IP Telephony. Total IP telephony calls in 2000 are estimated at 3 billion minutes, which is trivial compared to the 5.7 trillion minutes of calls carried annually on circuit-switched telephone networks.[8] Neither the FCC nor Congress has thus (as of yet) seen fit to regulate IP telephony or to bring it within the access charge regime.[9] That, however, might soon change. In May 2000, the House passed a bill, H.R. 1291, called the Internet Access Charge Prohibition Act. The bill was aimed at resolving the regulatory issue discussed earlier in this chapter about whether ISPs could be required to pay access charges. The House bill clearly said no but, curiously, included an amendment limiting the bill's reach to data traffic and making clear that nothing in the legislation bars regulating "providers of Internet telephone services regardless of the type of customer premises equipment used in connection with such services." Thus, whether IP voice service operates through computers or the telephone at the customer's end, the FCC could, under the House bill, regulate it.

Such a legislative proposal touches on serious questions about the future relationship between packet- and circuit-switched networks as they increasingly converge. Indeed, it might well not be possible to distinguish voice from data traffic on packet networks since one packet looks much like another. So, if IP telephony develops sufficiently to make a dent in circuit-switched traffic, the FCC's (and Congress's) choice might be either to regulate all Internet traffic to support existing regulatory structures (like universal services) or to regulate none of it and change the underlying structures instead. The ultimate outcome is unclear, but one point bears emphasizing: if this promising service reaches its potential, either current policies towards the Internet, or much of current U.S. telecommunications regulation, will have to change.

---

8. Jason Krause, No Taxes Yet for Net Phone Calls, The Industry Standard (June 26, 2000).
9. In fact, FCC officials have thus far heartily welcomed the growth of IP telephony. *See, e.g.*, Internet Telephony: America Is Waiting, Remarks by FCC Chairman William E. Kennard Before the Voice Over Net Conference, 2000 FCC LEXIS 4787 (2000).

CHAPTER TWENTY-THREE

WHY AN FCC?

The purpose of this chapter is:

- to consider the appropriate future role for the FCC; and
- to raise the question of whether telecommunications markets really need an expert agency and highly specialized rules, or whether, instead, telecommunications markets should be subject to the same laws of general applicability that discipline competitors and encourage innovation in most other markets.

~

In this book we have examined a wide array of telecommunications regulations, and with respect to each we have asked whether the particular regulation makes sense. In this concluding chapter, we want to shift our focus a bit, stepping away from the detail and nuance of particular regulations and asking, instead, some broader questions about both the Federal Communications Commission and this jumble of highly specialized statutes and regulations we call "telecommunications law." Specifically, as you read the excerpts that follow, ask yourself three questions: What should be the role of the FCC in the future? Will there ever come a time when the FCC can be abolished—or, indeed, might that time already be upon us? And (relatedly) will there ever come a time when we can eliminate "telecommunications law" and instead allow statutes and regulations of a more general nature to govern?

The first question—the appropriate role for the FCC—is a question we have seen time and again throughout this book. In virtually every chapter we have tried to weigh the potential capabilities of the FCC on the one hand against the potential capabilities of the market on the other. We've thought hard about the limitations of both approaches, too; after all, it would be foolhardy to define the agency's appropriate role by comparing the strengths of an idealized regulator with the strengths of an idealized market. Perfect regulation, like perfect competition, is difficult to find in the real world. Thus, we have tried to focus on what we can realistically expect from any given level of FCC involvement and, similarly, what we can realistically expect from imperfect market interactions.

We start this chapter with that same balancing question, then, but this time with the entire agency on the line. Drawing on all of the materials we have considered thus far in the book, let us assess regulators and markets in light of their actual capabilities. How do they stack up against each other? Or, perhaps more fairly, in what balance ought the two work together in determining telecommunications outcomes?

A NEW FEDERAL COMMUNICATIONS COMMISSION FOR THE 21ST CENTURY

FCC Report, http://www.fcc.gov/Reports/fcc21.html (1999)

II. The 21st Century: A New Role for the FCC

A. The Transition Period

As history has shown, markets that have been highly monopolistic do not naturally become competitive. Strong incumbents still retain significant power in their traditional markets and have significant financial incentives to delay the arrival of competition. Strong and enforceable rules are needed initially so that new entrants have a chance to compete. At the same time, historical subsidy mechanisms for telecommunications services must be reformed to eliminate arbitrage opportunities by both incumbents and new entrants.

The technologies needed for the telecommunications marketplace of the future are still evolving, and developing them fully requires significant time and investment. Moreover, there is no guarantee that market forces will dictate that these new technologies will be universally deployed. The massive fixed-cost investments required in some industries will mean that new technologies initially will be targeted primarily at businesses and higher-income households. Even as deployment expands, the economics of these new networks may favor heavy users over lighter users, and in some areas of the country deployment may lag behind.

At the same time, consumer preferences will not change overnight. The expansion of communications choices is already leading to greater consumer confusion. Especially in a world of robust competition, consumers will need clear and accurate information about their choices, guarantees of basic privacy, and swift action if any company cheats rather than competes for their business.

In sum, although the long-term future of the telecommunications marketplace looks bright, the length and difficulty of the transition to that future is far from certain. To achieve the goal of fully competitive communications markets in five years, we must continue to work to ensure that all consumers have a choice of local telephone carriers and broadband service providers, and that companies are effectively deterred from unscrupulous behavior. We must also continue to promote competition between different media, promote the transition to digital technology, and continue to ensure that all Americans have a wide and robust variety of entertainment and information sources.

B. The FCC's Role During the Transition to Competition

During the transition to fully competitive communications markets, the FCC, working in conjunction with the states, Congress, other federal agencies, industry, and consumer groups, has six critical goals, all derived from the Communications Act and other applicable statutes:

Promote Competition: Goal number one is to promote competition throughout the communications industry, particularly in the area of local telephony. The benefits of competition are well documented in many communications sectors—

long distance, wireless, customer-premises equipment, and information services. The benefits of local telephone competition are accruing at this time to large and small companies, but not, for the most part, to residential consumers. We must work to ensure that all communications markets are open, so that all consumers can enjoy the benefits of competition.

To meet this goal, we must continue our efforts to clarify the provisions of the Telecom Act relating to interconnection and unbundled network elements, work with the Bell Operating Companies (BOCs), their competitors, states and consumer groups on meeting the requirements of the statute related to BOC entry into the long distance market, reform access charges, and, as required by Sections 214 and 310(d) of the Communications Act and section 7 of the Clayton Act, continue to review mergers of telecommunications companies that raise significant public interest issues related to competition and consumers.

In the mass media area, we must continue the pro-competitive deployment of new technologies, such as digital television and direct broadcast satellites, and the maintenance of robust competition in the marketplace of ideas. To meet these goals, we must continue rapid deployment of new technologies and services and regular oversight of the structure of local markets to ensure multiple voices, all the while updating our rules to keep pace with the ever-changing mass media marketplace.

Deregulate: Our second goal is to deregulate as competition develops. Consumers ultimately pay the cost of unnecessary regulation, and we are committed to aggressively eliminating unnecessarily regulatory burdens or delays. We want to eliminate reporting and accounting requirements that no longer are necessary to serve the public interest. Also, where competition is thriving, we intend to increase flexibility in the pricing of access services. We have already deregulated the domestic, long distance market as a result of increased competition, and we stand ready to do so for other communications markets as competition develops. We have also streamlined our rules and privatized some of the functions involved in the certification of telephones and other equipment. We are currently streamlining and automating our processes to issue licenses faster, resolve complaints quicker, and be more responsive to competitors and consumers in the marketplace.

Protect Consumers: Our third goal is to empower consumers with the information they need to make wise choices in a robust and competitive marketplace, and to protect them from unscrupulous competitors. Consumer bills must be truthful, clear, and understandable. We will have "zero tolerance" for perpetrators of consumer fraud. Further, we will remain vigilant in protecting consumer privacy. We will also continue to carry out our statutory mandates aimed at protecting the welfare of children, such as the laws governing obscene and indecent programming.

Bring Communications Services and Technology to Every American: Our fourth goal is to ensure that all Americans—no matter where they live, what they look like, what their age, or what special needs they have—should have access to new technologies created by the communications revolution. Toward this end, we must complete universal service reform to ensure that communications services in high-cost areas of the nation are both available and affordable. We must also ensure that our support mechanisms and other tools to achieve universal service are compatible and consistent with competition. We must evaluate—and if necessary, improve—our support mechanisms for low income consumers, and in particular Native Americans, whose telephone penetration rates are some of the lowest in the country. We must make certain that the support mechanisms for schools, libraries, and rural health care providers operate efficiently and effectively. We must make sure that the 54 million Americans with disabilities have access to communications networks, new technologies and services, and news and entertainment programming.

Foster Innovation: Our fifth goal is to foster innovation. We will promote the development and deployment of high-speed Internet connections to all Americans. That means clearing regulatory hurdles so that innovation—and new markets—can flourish. We must continue to promote the compatibility of digital video technologies with existing equipment and services. Further, we will continue to encourage the more efficient use of the radio spectrum so that new and expanding uses can be accommodated within this limited resource. More generally, we will continue to promote competitive alternatives in all communications markets.

Advance Competitive Goals Worldwide: Our sixth goal is to advance global competition in communications markets. The pro-competitive regulatory framework Congress set forth in the Telecom Act is being emulated around the world through the World Trade Organization Agreement. We will continue to assist other nations in establishing conditions for deregulation, competition, and increased private investment in their communications infrastructure so that they can share in the promise of the Information Age and become our trading partners. We must continue to intensify competition at home and create growth opportunities for U.S. companies abroad. We will continue to promote fair spectrum use by all countries.

C. The FCC's Core Functions in a Competitive Environment

As we accomplish our transition goals, we set the stage for a competitive environment in which communications markets look and function like other competitive industries. At that point, the FCC must refocus our efforts on those functions that are appropriate for an age of competition and convergence. In particular, we must refocus our efforts from managing monopolies to addressing issues that will not be solved by normal market forces. In a competitive environment, the FCC's core functions would focus on:

Universal Service, Consumer Protection and Information. The FCC will continue to have a critical responsibility, as dictated by our governing statutes, to support and promote universal service and other public interest policies. The shared aspirations and values of the American people are not entirely met by market forces. Equal access to opportunity as well as to the public sphere are quintessential American values upon which the communications sector will have an increasingly large impact. We will be expected to continue to monitor the competitive landscape on behalf of the public interest and implement important policies such as universal service in ways compatible with competition.

In addition, as communications markets become more competitive and take on attributes of other competitive markets, the need for increased information to consumers and strong consumer protection will increase. We must work to ensure that Americans are provided with clear information so that they can make sense of new technologies and services and choose the ones best for them. We must also continue to monitor the marketplace for illegal or questionable market practices.

<u>Enforcement and Promotion of Pro-Competition Communications Goals Domestically and Worldwide</u>. As markets become more competitive, the focus of industry regulation will shift from protecting buyers of monopoly services to resolving disputes among competitors, whether over interconnection terms and conditions, program access, equipment compatibility, or technical interference. In the fast-paced world of competition, we must be able to respond swiftly and effectively to such disputes to ensure that companies do not take advantage of other companies or consumers.

The FCC is a model for other countries of a transparent and independent government body establishing and enforcing fair, pro-competitive rules. This model is critical for continuing to foster fair competition domestically as well as to open markets in other countries, to the benefit of U.S. consumers and firms and consumers and firms worldwide. There always will be government-to-government relations and the need to coordinate among nations as communications systems become increasingly global. As other nations continue to move from government-owned monopolies to competitive, privately-owned communications firms, they will increasingly look to the FCC's experience for guidance.

<u>Spectrum Management</u>. The need for setting ground rules for how people use the radio spectrum will not disappear. We need to make sure adequate spectrum exists to accommodate the rapid growth in existing services as well as new applications of this national and international resource. Even with new technologies such as software-defined radios and ultra-wideband microwave transmission, concerns about interference will continue (and perhaps grow) and the need for defining licensees and other users' rights will continue to be a critical function of the government. We will thus continue to conduct auctions of available spectrum to speed introduction of new services. In order to protect the safety of life and property, we must also continue to consider public safety needs as new spectrum-consuming technologies and techniques are deployed.

Notes and Questions

1. Transitions. The FCC says that we are in a time of transition, and it refers to "the goal of fully competitive communications markets in five years." Recall that this was written in 1999. Does the FCC expect that by 2004 the transition period will be over? Do you? How will we be able to determine if the transition is complete by then? And what exactly will the post-transition, fully competitive period look like? What role does the FCC envision for itself in that post-transition period? Are you persuaded that it will have the role it envisions? That it should?

2. Market Imperfections. The FCC says that "[t]he shared aspirations and values of the American people are not entirely met by market forces." That may be true, but the question is whether FCC involvement improves matters. As to that comparative issue, what does the FCC tell us?

3. And FCC Imperfections, Too. Is the FCC "a model for other countries of a transparent and independent government body establishing and enforcing fair, pro-competitive rules"? Or is that a goal that it rarely meets? If the latter, what does that indicate about the advisability of letting the FCC play the role that it defines for itself in this report? The next excerpt takes up this issue—and takes on the FCC.

ABOLISH THE FCC AND LET
COMMON LAW RULE THE TELECOSM

Peter Huber, Law and Disorder in Cyberspace 3–9 (1997)

Until 1996 the telecosm was governed by laws written half a century ago. The rules for the telephone industry dated back to 1887. They had been written at a time when land, air, water, and energy all seemed abundant, while the telecosm seemed small and crowded, a place of scarcity, cartel, and monopoly, one that required strict rationing and tight, central control.

In the last decade, however, glass and silicon have amplified beyond all prior recognition our power to communicate. Engineers double the capacity of the wires and the radios about every two years, again and again and again. New technology has replaced scarcity with abundance and cartels with competition.

The electronic web of connection that is now being woven amongst us all is a catalyst for change more powerful than Gutenberg's press or Goebbels's radio. Every constraint of the old order is crumbling. The limitless, anarchic possibilities of the telecosm contrast sharply with the limits to growth we now encounter at every turn in the physical world.

In early 1996 Congress passed the most important piece of economic legislation of the twentieth century. The Telecommunications Act of 1996 runs some one hundred pages. The Act's ostensible purpose is to open markets to competition and deregulate them. It may eventually have that effect. The process of deregulating, however, seems to require more regulation than ever. The FCC no longer aspires to immortality through its work. Like Woody Allen, it aspires to immortality through not dying.

It is time for fundamental change. It is time for the Federal Communications Commission to go.

The Future and the Past

The telecosm—the universe of communications and computers— is expanding faster than any other technocosm has ever expanded before. It is the telephone unleashed, the personal computer connected, and the television brought down to human scale at last. Its capacity to carry information has expanded a millionfold in the last decade or two. It will expand another millionfold in our lifetime—or perhaps a billionfold. No one really knows. The only certainty is that the change will be enormous.

This change is characterized by a paradox: It is both fragmentation and convergence.

The old integrated, centralized media are being broken apart. Terminals—dumb endpoints to the network—are giving way to "seminals"—nodes of equal rank that can process, switch, store, and retrieve information with a power that was once lodged exclusively in the massive switches and mainframe computers housed in fortified basements. This is the fragmentation.

At the same time the functions of these nodes are coming together. In digital systems a bit is a bit, whether it represents a hiccup in a voice conversation, a digit in a stock quote, or a pixel of light in a rerun of *I Love Lucy*. This is the convergence.

Then there is the law. Until 1996 most of telephony was viewed as a "natural monopoly." The high cost of fixed plant, the steadily declining average cost of service, and the need for all customers to interconnect with one another made monopoly seem inevitable. The broadcast industry was viewed as a natural oligopoly. It depended on inherently "scarce" airwaves, and was therefore populated by a small, government-appointed elite.

The FCC and comparable state-level commissions were established in the 1920s and 1930s to ration the scarcity and police the monopoly. The administrative structures, their statutory mandates, and the whole logic of commission control reflected the political attitudes of the New Deal. Markets didn't work; government did. Competition was wasteful; central planning was efficient. A fateful choice was made: Marketplace and common law were rejected. Central planning and the commission were embraced.

The common law evolves from the bottom up. Private action comes first. Rules follow, when private conflicts arise and are brought to court. Commission law was to be top-down. A government corps of managers, lawyers, economists, and technicians would settle in at the FCC first. Private action would follow later, when authorized. Common law is created by the accretion of small rulings in discrete, crystallized controversies. Commission law would be published in elaborate statutes and ten-thousand-page rule books; while these were being written, the world would wait. Common law centers on contract and property, legal concepts that are themselves creations of the common law. Commission law would center on public edicts, licenses, and permits. Common law is developed and enforced largely by private litigants. Commission law would come to court only at the end of the process, when public prosecutors filed suits against private miscreants.

Common law would have suited the American ethic of governance far better, particularly in matters so directly related to free speech. But between 1927 and 1934, when the FCC was erected, the winds of history were blowing in the opposite direction. National socialism, right-wing or left, seemed more efficient, the only workable approach to modern industrialism. Around the globe, people in power persuaded themselves that the technical complexities of broadcasting, and the natural-monopoly economics of telephony, had to be managed through centralized control. The night of totalitarian government, always said to be descending on America, came to earth only in Europe. But America was darkened by some of the same shadows. One was the FCC.

Once in place, the FCC grew and grew. Today it has 2,200 full-time employees and a $200 million budget—more offices, more employees, and more money than at any other time in its history. As competition increases, monopolies fade, and the supposed scarcity of spectrum is engineered into vast abundance, the Commission just gets bigger. An institution created to ration scarcity now thrives by brokering plenty. It is an Alice-in-Wonderland sort of world, in which the less reason the Queen has to exist at all, the more corpulent and powerful she becomes.

For the next several years at least, the FCC will have the most important mission in Washington. Wireline and wireless telephony, broadcasting, cable, and significant aspects of network computing together generate some $200 billion in revenues a year. For better or worse, the FCC will profoundly influence how they all develop. And in so doing it will exert a pivotal influence over the entire infrastructure of the information age and thus the economy, culture, and society of the twenty-first century.

The faster that power is dissipated, the better it will be for America.

Deconstructing the Telecosm

The beginning of the end was cable television. Cable demonstrated that spectrum could be bottled, and made abundant. Cable refused to be merely "broadcaster" or merely "carrier." It threatened all the old regulatory paradigms. It was just too capacious and flexible for regulators, even with the relatively primitive technology it used at that time. Now cable is moving into telephony. Meanwhile, by boosting the capacities of their wires, phone companies are poised to move into video. They already carry most of the Internet traffic, which is television in slow motion.

Wireless services are changing even faster. Once dedicated largely to feeding the idiot box, wireless is now the flourishing center of cellular telephony, direct broadcast satellite, wireless cable, and personal communications services. Spectrum is gradually being privatized and dezoned. The new owners are using their wireless bandwidth to provide whatever services they like, to whichever customers they choose.

The fundamentals of deregulation are now clear. The concepts are simple. They can be implemented quickly.

First, throw open the markets. For wireless, this means privatizing the critical asset—spectrum—by giving it away or (better still) selling it. For wires, it means letting anyone deploy new metal and glass alongside the old. Contrary to what Congress assumed for half a century, no commission is needed to protect against "wasteful duplication," "ruinous competition," or "inefficient deployment of resources." Markets take care of that.

Second, dezone the bandwidth. On wire or wireless, a bit is a bit. No government office should zone some bandwidth for pictures, some for voice, some for data. The market can work this out far better than any central planner.

Won't new robber barons then buy up all the wires, corner the spectrum, jack up prices, ruin service, and impoverish consumers? With the entire industry in ferment, with engineers doubling the capacity of every medium every few years, and with the telecosm expanding at big-bang rates, these fears are utterly implausible. But in any event, the traditional antitrust laws will remain in place. For all practical purposes, antitrust law is common law. It addresses specific problems in courts, not commissions. It is decentralized, adaptable, and resilient. Sclerotic commissions just get in the way. Indeed, for decades the FCC has legitimized telecom practices that antitrust courts would never have tolerated in its absence.

Ironically, the Commission can justify much of its current frenetic activity by blaming its predecessors. If the airwaves hadn't been nationalized in 1927, they wouldn't have to be sold off today. If the FCC hadn't spent half a century protecting telephone monopolies, it wouldn't have to dismantle them now. If the Commission hadn't spent so long separating carriage from broadcast, broadcast from cable, and cable from carriage, it wouldn't have to be desegregating those media today. If it hadn't worked so diligently to outlaw competitive entry back then, it wouldn't have to labor so hard to promote it now.

I-broke-it-then-so-I'll-fix-it-now has a certain logic to it, even if the confession of past breaking is always much less emphatic than the promise of future fix. But the fixing somehow always seems to take as long, or longer, than the breaking. And while the Commission plans and plans for perfect competition, competition itself waits uselessly in the wings.

The telecosm would be vastly more competitive today if Congress had just stayed out of session in 1927, in 1934, in 1984, and again in 1992—if Congress had never created the Federal Radio Commission, never folded it into the FCC, never extended the Commission's jurisdiction to cable, and never expanded the Commission's powers over cable further still. The 1996 legislation guarantees that the Commission will grow in size and influence for the rest of this decade while it uproots the anticompetitive vineyard planted and cultivated by its predecessors.

But the uprooting should be done quickly. Five years is time enough; ten would be too long. And then? Then the Commission should shut its doors, once and for all, and never darken American liberty again.

Common Law for the Telecosm

Who, then, will maintain order in all these areas when the Commission is gone? Private actors and private litigants, common-law courts, and the market. It is the Commission that must go, not the rule of law.

We still need laws to defend the property rights of people who lay wires and build transmitters, to enforce contracts and carriage agreements, to defend the freedom to speak and to listen, and to protect copyright and privacy. Anarchy works no better in virtuality than in actuality. The question is not whether there will be rules of law, but where they will come from.

Commissions proclaim the "public interest, convenience, and necessity." They issue general edicts. They publish rules in a massive Code of Federal Regulations. Common law, by contrast, evolves out of rulings handed down by many different judges in many different courtrooms. The good rules gain acceptance by the community at large, as people conform their conduct to rulings that make practical sense. In this kind of jurisprudence, constitutions and codes provide, at most, a broad, general mandate to develop the law by adjudication. They operate like the Bill of Rights or the Sherman Act.

Commission law has been tried. Not just in the telecosm but in command-and-control economies around the globe. Like Communism, commission law has failed. It is rigid, slow, and—despite all the earnest expertise of bureaucrats—ignorant. Market forces, mediated by common law, elicit information faster and more reliably. Markets constantly probe new technology, try out new forms of supply, and assess demand with a determination, precision, and persistence that no commission can ever match. Property-centered, contract-centered, common-law markets allow people to get on with life first and litigate later, if they have to. Most of the time they don't. Rules evolve spontaneously in the marketplace and are mostly accepted by common consent. Common-law courts just keep things tidy at the edges.

The one strength of commission law is that it reduces uncertainty all around. But only because the market must wait for the commission to invent a whole framework of law up front. That often takes years, and the framework is always rigid and inadequate. In a universe where technology transforms itself every few months, where supply and demand grow apace, where new trillion-dollar economies can emerge from thin air in a decade or so—in such a universe, uncertainty is a sign of health and vigor. In a place like that, nothing except common law can keep up. The law must build itself the old-fashioned way, through action in the market first and reaction in the courts thereafter.

If that suggestion seems outlandish, it is only because the FCC has been around so long that people can no longer imagine life without it. Once Henry the Eighth's licensing of printing presses had become routine, it would have seemed equally outlandish to suggest that such an unfamiliar, complicated, and important technology might be left to open markets and common-law courts. When it was created in 1887, the Interstate Commerce Commission seemed essential to proper management of railroads. But when it was abolished in early 1996, hardly anyone even noticed. We never did create a Federal Computer Commission. The computer industry has nonetheless developed interconnection rules and open systems, set reasonable prices, and delivered more hardware and more service to more people faster than any other industry in history.

Now, in the 1990s, with the telecosm growing explosively all around us, with the cacophony of free markets already drowning out the reedy proclamations of a senescent Commission, the only outlandish proposal is that we should keep it.

It is time to finish the job. The Commission must go.

Notes and Questions

1. Huber or the FCC. Relative to the FCC, does Huber have greater faith in markets, less faith in the Commission, or both? Consider the materials we have covered in this book. As between the FCC and Huber, whose faith is more justified?

2. A Difference of Timing? Are Huber's proposals consistent with the FCC's vision for itself once the transition period is over? Put differently, is the difference between the FCC's position and Huber's position that one sees telecommunications as in the middle of a transition and the other sees that transition as complete?

3. The Commission's Record. In evaluating the choice between common-law courts and a federal telecommunications agency, is the Commission's historical record relevant? One could, after all, ignore the history of the FCC and focus instead on the realistic ability of the FCC, or some new replacement agency, to perform in desirable ways. Would that approach make more sense? Does one's choice here change the ultimate answer about the extent to which regulation by a federal telecommunications agency is desirable?

4. Common-Law Courts. Does Huber overestimate the ability of common-law courts to keep order in the telecommunications realm? What about the need to coordinate activities in different states, or among different kinds of technologies? Does Huber reject these as unworthy goals, or does he believe that they are worthy but that common-law courts can handle them? Consider in this regard the following statement from the conclusion of Huber's book: "Nothing grander than common law is even practical anymore. The telecosm is too large, too heterogeneous, too turbulent, too creatively chaotic to be governed wholesale, from the top down." *Id.* at 206. Is he right, or is a "top down" approach necessary in the interconnected world of telecommunications? Are there ways to implement a common-law approach that allow for coordination across state lines and among different technologies and activities? Would that be less bureaucratic than regulation by the FCC? Would it be preferable?

5. Abolish Other Administrative Agencies? Do you think Huber would also be in favor of abolishing other administrative agencies and shifting their duties to common-law courts? Is that because common-law courts have done such a good job in other areas, like tort law, where they dominate?

6. And Abolish Telecommunications Law Too. Huber is not merely suggesting that the FCC should be abolished. He is also challenging the notion that there should be laws specifically aimed at telecommunications. He wants to replace the regime of telecommunications law with generally applicable laws that would be adapted as needed by common-law courts. Many of these would involve traditional common-law causes of action like contract and property claims. Notably, he also wants to rely on antitrust laws (which, he argues, is for all practical purposes common law). This takes us back to the many regulations we have seen that are aimed at telecommunications firms with market power. Huber would do away with all of these regulations and revert to generic antitrust enforcement. To put the question from his perspective: Given that we rely on antitrust to address market power in almost every other industry, why can't we rely on it in the telecommunications context as well? What makes telecommunications so special that ordinary antitrust principles would not suffice?

7. Alternatives. Note that reductions in FCC authority less radical than complete abolition are possible. We could limit the FCC to a few functions that we are confident it will do better than either another regulator (*e.g.*, common-law courts or the Department of Justice) or the market. What would those functions be?

(a) One candidate would be coordinating spectrum assignment and mediating interference claims. Because spectrum does not respect state boundaries and because of the complexities of potential interference problems, we might prefer that a regulator with a national purview, expertise, and continuity be in charge of managing the use of the spectrum. Even if we do not want the government owning or controlling the spectrum, we might want the FCC to play the role of policeman and protect owners' rights to it.

(b) Relatedly, we might want to have a federal entity with the power to negotiate on behalf of the United States with other countries—regarding, for example, which frequencies, and which orbital slots, each country will use.

(c) A third obvious candidate would be a federal entity (or a series of state entities) that would play some role in ensuring that local exchange carriers with entrenched monopoly power provide reasonably priced, technologically sophisticated, and nondiscriminatory access to other providers of allied or competing telecommunications services. These interconnection issues have loomed large in the history of telephony, and many might fear that incumbent LECs would discriminate against other providers unless a regulatory entity watched them carefully.

Option (c) does not suggest that there is anything special about telecommunications, as it is really just an application of traditional antitrust principles to the regulation of telecommunications. Thus, it is not necessarily inconsistent with Huber's approach, and in any event could be accomplished by ordinary antitrust enforcement (which is usually undertaken by the Department of Justice). The first two options, by contrast, do rely on special properties of the spectrum—that it crosses boundaries and that it is subject to fairly subtle and complex forms of interference. But if we stopped at the spectrum management suggested in (a) and (b), that would radically reduce the role for telecommunications law and also for the FCC.

Are there other important functions for which we need laws aimed specifically at telecommunications? Think, for example, about universal service. The Huber excerpt and the three proposals listed above do not provide for a system whereby some users subsidize others. But recall our discussion in Chapter Eighteen about the relative desirability of a program to provide cheap telephone service as compared to a program to provide, say, cheap clothing. The question is whether something about telecommunications justifies subsidizing it specifically, rather than subsidizing other purchases or, more simply, providing the same amount of money in cash to be used for whatever the recipient thought was needed.

The discussion above also leaves out perhaps the most obvious special feature of telecommunications—the "communications" part. Telecommunications systems are an important means of transmitting ideas and values. This raises a host of policy questions about the significance we might attribute to that power. It also raises (as many of the materials in this book demonstrate) complicated First Amendment issues. And, importantly, there may not only be conflicting values but also conflicting visions of the First Amendment, leading different people to draw different conclusions from the communicative power of various media.

The inquiry does not end, of course, with the assertion that telecommunications has certain unique attributes or communicative power. We must still consider what regulatory response is appropriate to those attributes and that power. If, for example, we reject the contention of former FCC Chair Mark Fowler that a television is merely "a toaster with pictures"[1] and instead assert that a televi-

---

1. See Bernard D. Nossiter, Licenses to Coin Money: The FCC's Big Giveaway Show, The Nation, Oct. 26, 1985, at 402 (quoting a radio address given by Fowler).

sion is unlike other appliances in important ways, we still must identify those distinguishing features and then craft the regulatory scheme that most appropriately takes those features into account. The next two excerpts, one from Cass Sunstein, the other from Thomas Krattenmaker and Scot Powe, wrestle with these issues—mainly through the lens of the First Amendment and the power of telecommunications.

THE FIRST AMENDMENT IN CYBERSPACE
Cass R. Sunstein, 104 Yale Law Journal 1757 (1995)

II. THE PRESENT: MARKETS AND MADISON

There are two free speech traditions in the United States, not simply one. There have been two models of the First Amendment, corresponding to the two free speech traditions. The first emphasizes well-functioning speech markets. It can be traced to Justice Holmes' great *Abrams* dissent, where the notion of a "market in ideas" received its preeminent exposition. The market model emerges as well from Miami Herald Publishing Co. v. Tornillo, invalidating a "right of reply" law as applied to candidates for elected office. It finds its most recent defining statement not in judicial decisions, but in an FCC opinion rejecting the fairness doctrine.[2]

The second tradition, and the second model, focuses on public deliberation. The second model can be traced from its origins in the work of James Madison, with his attack on the idea of seditious libel, to Justice Louis Brandeis, with his suggestion that "the greatest menace to freedom is an inert people," through the work of Alexander Meiklejohn, who associated the free speech principle not with laissez-faire economics, but with ideals of democratic deliberation. The Madisonian tradition culminated in the reaffirmation of the fairness doctrine in the *Red Lion* case,[3] with the Supreme Court's suggestion that governmental efforts to encourage diverse views and attention to public issues are compatible with the free speech principle—even if they result in regulatory controls on the owners of speech sources.

Those who endorse the marketplace model do not claim that government may not do anything at all. Of course government may set up the basic rules of property and contract; it is these rules that make markets feasible. Without such rules, markets cannot exist at all. Government is also permitted to protect against market failures, especially by preventing monopolies and monopolistic practices. Structural regulation is acceptable so long as it is a content neutral attempt to ensure competition. It is therefore important to note that advocates of marketplaces and democracy might work together in seeking to curtail monopoly. Of course, the prevention of monopoly is a precondition for well-functioning information markets.

Many people think that there is now nothing distinctive about the electronic media or about modern communications technologies that justifies an additional governmental role.[4] If such a role was ever justified, they would argue, it was be-

---

2. Syracuse Peace Council v. Television Station WTVH, 2 FCC Rcd. 5043, 5054–55 (1987).
3. Red Lion Broadcasting Co. v. FCC, 395 U.S. 367 (1969).
4. *See, e.g., Syracuse Peace Council*; Thomas G. Krattenmaker & Lucas A. Powe, Jr., Regulating Broadcast Programming 277 (1994); Thomas G. Krattenmaker & L.A. Powe, Jr.,

cause of problems of scarcity. When only three television networks exhausted the available options, a market failure may have called for regulation designed to ensure that significant numbers of people were not left without their preferred programming. But this is no longer a problem. With so dramatic a proliferation of stations, most people can obtain the programming they want, or will be able to soon. With cyberspace, people will be able to make or to participate in their own preferred programming in their own preferred "locations" on the Internet. With new technologies, perhaps there are no real problems calling for governmental controls, except for those designed to establish the basic framework.

The second model emphasizes that our constitutional system is one of deliberative democracy. This system prizes both political (not economic) equality and a shared civic culture. It seeks to promote, as a central democratic goal, reflective and deliberative debate about possible courses of action. The Madisonian model sees the right of free expression as a key part of the system of public deliberation.

On this view, even a well-functioning information market is not immune from government controls. Government is certainly not permitted to regulate speech however it wants; it may not restrict speech on the basis of viewpoint. But it may regulate the electronic media or even cyberspace to promote, in a sufficiently neutral way, a well-functioning democratic regime. It may attempt to promote attention to public issues. It may try to ensure diversity of view. It may promote political speech at the expense of other forms of speech. In particular, educational and public-affairs programming, on the Madisonian view, has a special place.

Some people think that the distinction between marketplace and Madisonian models is now an anachronism. Perhaps the two models conflicted at an earlier stage in history; but in one view, Madison has no place in an era of limitless broadcasting options and cyberspace. Perhaps new technologies now mean that Madisonian goals can best be satisfied in a system of free markets. Now that so many channels, e-mail options, and discussion "places" are available, cannot everyone read or see what they wish? If people want to spend their time on public issues, are there not countless available opportunities? Is this not especially true with the emergence of the Internet? Is it not hopelessly paternalistic, or anachronistic, for government to regulate for Madisonian reasons?

I do not believe that these questions are rhetorical. We know enough to know that even in a period of limitless options, our communications system may fail to promote an educated citizenry and political equality. Madisonian goals may be severely compromised even under technologically extraordinary conditions. There is no logical or *a priori* connection between a well-functioning system of free expression and limitless broadcasting or Internet options.

It is foreseeable that free markets in communications will be a mixed blessing. They could create a kind of accelerating "race to the bottom," in which many or most people see low-quality programming involving trumped-up scandals or sensationalistic anecdotes calling for little in terms of quality or quantity of attention. It is easily imaginable that well-functioning markets in communications will bring about a situation in which many of those interested in politics

Converging First Amendment Principles for Converging Communications Media, 104 Yale L.J. 1719 (1995).

merely fortify their own unreflective judgments, and are exposed to little or nothing in the way of competing views. It is easily imaginable that the content of the most widely viewed programming will be affected by the desires of advertisers, in such a way as to produce shows that represent a bland, watered-down version of conventional morality, and that do not engage serious issues in a serious way for fear of offending some group in the audience.

It is easily imaginable that the television—or the personal computer carrying out communications functions—will indeed become what former FCC Chair Mark Fowler described as "just another appliance...a toaster with pictures," and that the educative or aspirational goals of the First Amendment will be lost or even forgotten.

V. SPEECH, EMERGING MEDIA, AND CYBERSPACE

It is possible to describe certain categories of regulation and to set out some general guidelines about how they might be approached. I would suggest that existing law provides principles and analogies on which it makes sense to draw. An exploration of new problems confirms this suggestion. It shows that current categories can be invoked fairly straightforwardly to make sense of likely future dilemmas.

A large lesson may emerge from the discussion. Often participants in legal disputes, and especially in constitutional disputes, disagree sharply with respect to high-level, abstract issues; the debate between Madisonians and marketplace advocates is an obvious illustration. But sometimes such disputants can converge, or narrow their disagreement a great deal, by grappling with highly particular problems. In other words, debate over abstractions may conceal a potential for productive discussion and even agreement over particulars. Perhaps this is a strategy through which we might make much progress in the next generation of free speech law.

1. Requiring Competition

Many actual and imaginable legislative efforts are designed to ensure competition in the new communications markets. There is no constitutional problem with such efforts. The only qualification is that some such efforts might be seen as subterfuge for content regulation, disguised by a claimed need to promote monopoly; but this should be a relatively rare event. If government is genuinely attempting to prevent monopolistic practices, and to offer a structure in which competition can take place, there is no basis for constitutional complaint. Here First Amendment theorists of widely divergent views might be brought into agreement.

2. Subsidizing New Media

It is predictable that government might seek to assist certain technologies that offer great promise for the future. Some such efforts may in fact be a result of interest-group pressure. But in general, there is no constitutional obstacle to government efforts to subsidize preferred communications sources. Perhaps government believes that some technological innovations are especially likely to do well, or that they could receive particularly valuable benefits from national assistance. At least so long as there is no reason to believe that government is favoring speech of a certain content, efforts of this kind are unobjectionable as a matter of law. They may be objectionable as a matter of policy, since government may make bad judgments reflecting confusion or factional influence; but that is a different issue.

3. Subsidizing Particular Programming or Particular Broadcasters

In her dissenting opinion in *Turner* [*I*], Justice O'Connor suggested that the appropriate response to government desire for programming of a certain content is not regulation but instead subsidization. This idea fits well with the idea that the government is unconstrained in its power to subsidize such speech as it prefers. Hence there should be no constitutional objection to government efforts to fund public broadcasting, to pay for high-quality fare for children, or to support programming that deals with public affairs. Perhaps government might do this for certain uses of the Internet.

To be sure, it is doubtful that [this] would be taken to its logical extreme. Could the government fund the Democratic Convention but not the Republican Convention? Could the government announce that it would fund only those public-affairs programs that spoke approvingly of current government policy? If we take the First Amendment to ban viewpoint discrimination, funding of this kind should be held to be improperly motivated. On the other hand, government subsidies of educational and public-affairs programming need not raise serious risks of viewpoint discrimination. It therefore seems unexceptionable for government, short of viewpoint discrimination, to subsidize those broadcasters whose programming it prefers, even if any such preference embodies content discrimination. So too, government might promote "conversations" or fora on e-mail that involve issues of public importance, or that attempt to promote educational goals for children or even adults.

4. Leaving Admittedly "Open" Channels Available to Others Who Would Not Otherwise Get Carriage

Suppose that a particular communications carrier has room for five hundred channels; suppose that four hundred channels are filled, but that one hundred are left open. Would it be legitimate for government to say that the one hundred must be filled by stations that would otherwise be unable be pay for carriage? Let us suppose that the stations would be chosen through a content neutral system, such as a lottery. From the First Amendment point of view, this approach seems acceptable. The government would be attempting to ensure access for speakers who would otherwise be unable to reach the audience. It is possible that as a matter of policy, government should have to provide some payment to the carrier in return for the access requirement. But there does not seem to be a First Amendment problem.

5. Requiring Carriers To Be Common Carriers for a Certain Number of Stations, Filling Vacancies with a Lottery System or Timesharing

In her dissenting opinion in *Turner*, Justice O'Connor suggested the possibility that carriers could be required to set aside certain channels to be filled by a random method. The advantage of this approach is that it would promote access for people who would otherwise be denied carriage, but without involving government in decisions about preferred content. This approach should raise no First Amendment difficulties.

6. Imposing Structural Regulation Designed Not To Prevent a Conventional Market Failure, But To Ensure Universal or Near-Universal Consumer Access to Networks

The protection of broadcasters in *Turner* was specifically designed to ensure continued viewer access to free programming. Notably, the Court permitted government to achieve this goal through regulation rather than through subsidy. Of course subsidy is the simpler and ordinarily more efficient route. If government wants to make sure that all consumers have access to communications networks, why should government not be required to pay to allow such access, on a kind of analogue to the food stamp program? The ordinary response to a problem of access is not to fix prices but instead to subsidize people who would otherwise be without access. The *Turner* Court apparently believed that it is constitutionally acceptable for the government to ensure that industry (and subscribers), rather than taxpayers, provide the funding for those who would otherwise lack access.

The precise implications of this holding remain to be seen. It is impossible to foresee the range of structural regulations that might be proposed in an effort to ensure that all or almost all citizens have access to free programming or to some communications network, including any parts of the "informational superhighway." Some such regulations might in fact be based on other, more invidious motives, such as favoritism toward a particular set of suppliers; this may well be true of the measure in *Turner* itself. The *Turner* decision means that courts should review with some care any governmental claim that regulation is actually based on an effort to promote free access. But the key point here is that if the claim can be made out on the facts, structural regulation should be found acceptable.

7. Protecting Against Obscene, Libelous, Violent, Commercial, or Harassing Broadcasting or Messages

New technologies have greatly expanded the opportunity to communicate obscene, libelous, violent, or harassing messages—perhaps to general groups via stations on (for example) cable television, perhaps to particular people via electronic mail. Invasions of privacy are far more likely. The Internet poses special problems on these counts. As a general rule, any restrictions should be treated like those governing ordinary speech, with ordinary mail providing the best analogy. If restrictions are narrowly tailored, and supported by a sufficiently strong record, they should be upheld.

What of a regulatory regime designed to prevent invasion of privacy, libel, unwanted commercial messages, and obscenity, harassment, or infliction of emotional distress? Some such regulatory regime will ultimately make a great deal of sense. The principal obstacles are that the regulations should be both clear and narrow. It is easy to imagine a broad or vague regulation, one that would seize upon the sexually explicit or violent nature of communication to justify regulation that is far broader than necessary. Moreover, it is possible to imagine a situation in which liability was extended to any owner or operator who could have no knowledge of the particular materials being sent. The underlying question, having to do with efficient risk allocation, involves the extent to which a carrier might be expected to find and to stop unlawful messages; that question depends upon the relevant technology.

Some of the services that provide access to the Internet should not themselves be treated as speakers; they are providers of speech, but their own speech is not at issue. This point is closely related to the debate in *Turner* about the speech status of cable carriers. But whether or not a carrier or provider is a speaker, a harmful effect on speech would raise First Amendment issues. We can see this point with an analogy. Certainly it would not be constitutional to say that truck owners will be criminally liable for carrying newspapers containing articles critical of the President. Such a measure would be unconstitutional in its purposes and in its effects, even if the truck owners are not speakers. From this we can see that a criminal penalty on carriers of material that is independently protected by the First Amendment should be unconstitutional. Thus a criminal penalty could not be imposed for providing "filthy" speech, at least if "filthy" speech is otherwise protected.

But a penalty imposed on otherwise unprotected materials raises a different question. Suppose that the government imposes criminal liability on carriers or providers of admittedly obscene material on the Internet. The adverse effect on unprotected speech should not by itself be found to offend the Constitution, even if there would be a harmful economic effect, and even unfairness, for the provider of the service. Instead the constitutional question should turn on the extent of the adverse effects on the dissemination of materials that are protected by the Constitution. If, for example, the imposition of criminal liability for the distribution of unprotected speech had serious harmful effects for the distribution of protected speech, the First Amendment issue would be quite severe. But that question cannot be answered in the abstract; it depends on what the relevant record shows with respect to any such adverse effects.

To answer that question, we need to know whether carrier liability, for unprotected speech, has a significant adverse effect on protected speech as well. We need to know, in short, whether the proper analogy is to a publisher or instead to a carrier of mail. It is therefore important to know whether a carrier could, at relatively low expense, filter out constitutionally unprotected material, or whether, on the contrary, the imposition of criminal liability for unprotected material would drive legitimate carriers out of business, or force them to try to undertake impossible or unrealistically expensive "searches." The answer to this question will depend in large part on the state of technology.

8. Imposing Content Based Regulation Designed To Ensure Public-Affairs and Educational Programming

It can readily be imagined that Congress might seek to promote education via regulation or subsidy of new media. It might try to ensure attention to public affairs. Suppose, for example, that Congress sets aside a number of channels for public-affairs and educational programming, on the theory that the marketplace provides too much commercial programming. This notion has in fact been under active consideration in Congress. Thus a recent bill would have required all telecommunications carriers to provide access at preferential rates to educational and health care institutions, state and local governments, public broadcast stations, libraries and other public entities, community newspapers, and broadcasters in the smallest markets.

Turner certainly does not stand for the proposition that such efforts are constitutional. By hypothesis, any such regulation would be content based. It would therefore meet with a high level of judicial skepticism. On the other hand, *Turner* does not authoritatively suggest that such efforts are unconstitutional. The Court did not itself say whether it would accept content discrimination designed to promote Madisonian goals. Certainly the opinion suggests that the government's burden would be a significant one. But it does not resolve the question.

It is notable that Justice O'Connor's opinion appears quite sensible on this point, and she leaves the issue open. Her principal argument is that the "must-carry" rules are too crude. Certainly crudely tailored measures give reason to believe that interest-group pressures, rather than a legitimate effort to improve educational and public-affairs programming, are at work. But if the relevant measures actually promote Madisonian goals, they should be upheld. There is of course reason to fear that any such measures have less legitimate purposes and functions, and hence a degree of judicial skepticism is appropriate. But narrow measures, actually promoting those purposes, are constitutionally legitimate.

VI. MADISON IN CYBERSPACE?

Do Madisonian ideals have an enduring role in American thought about freedom of speech? The existence of new technologies makes the question different and far more complex than it once was. It is conceivable that in a world of newly emerging and countless options, the market will prove literally unstoppable, as novel possibilities outstrip even well-motivated government controls.

If so, this result should not be entirely lamented. It would be an understatement to say that a world in which consumers can choose from limitless choices has many advantages, not least from the Madisonian point of view. If choices are limitless, people interested in politics can see and listen to politics; perhaps they can even participate in politics, and in ways that were impossible just a decade ago. But that world would be far from perfect. It may increase social balkanization. It may not promote deliberation, but foster instead a series of referenda in cyberspace that betray constitutional goals.

My central point here has been that the system of free expression is not an aimless abstraction. Far from being an outgrowth of neoclassical economics, the First Amendment has independent and identifiable purposes. Free speech doctrine, with its proliferating tests, distinctions, and subparts, should not lose touch with those purposes. Rooted in a remarkable conception of political sovereignty, the goals of the First Amendment are closely connected with the founding commitment to a particular kind of polity: a deliberative democracy among informed citizens who are political equals. It follows that instead of allowing new technologies to use democratic processes for their own purposes, constitutional law should be concerned with harnessing those technologies for democratic ends—including the founding aspirations to public deliberation, citizenship, political equality, and even a certain kind of virtue. If the new technologies offer risks on these scores, they hold out enormous promise as well. I have argued here that whether that promise will be realized depends in significant part on judgments of law, including judgments about the point of the First Amendment.

CONVERGING FIRST AMENDMENT PRINCIPLES FOR CONVERGING COMMUNICATIONS MEDIA

Thomas G. Krattenmaker and L. A. Powe, Jr.,
104 Yale Law Journal 1719 (1995)

For students of telecommunications law and technology, it has become a trivial ritual to observe that telecommunications technologies and media are converging. Neither producers nor purchasers of audio or video information should find much use, in the near future, for such terms as "television," "computer," "telephone," or "radio." These objects are no longer distinct devices and we believe that any differences among them are ephemeral.

For students of constitutional law and the Supreme Court's jurisprudence of the First Amendment guarantee of freedom of speech, these observations are likely to trigger a different ritual incantation: "Different communications media are treated differently for First Amendment purposes." City of Los Angeles v. Preferred Communications, Inc., 476 U.S. 488, 496 (1986) (Blackmun, J., concurring). How can one reconcile the fact of technological and media convergence with the legal presumption of distinct treatments?

We argue in this Essay that this dilemma should not be resolved by permitting the First Amendment to be used as a sword to prevent communications convergence or as a shield to permit government agencies to force these technologies into distinct, procrustean categories. Rather, the latest advances in telecommunications provide federal courts the opportunity to discard the inherently silly notion that freedom of speech depends on the configuration of the speaker's voicebox or mouthpiece.

If we look behind the facade of broadcast free speech law, we can discern established, durable, fundamental principles that govern regulation of mass communications without regard to the technology employed, that protect freedom of speech while leaving ample room for sober regulation, and that apply equally well to all mass communication media.

III. THE APPROPRIATE SCOPE OF REGULATION

As computers, satellites, and telephone lines become readily available alternatives to VHF, UHF, cable, and microwave transmission of radio and television, it should become simpler even for the Supreme Court Justices to realize that only a unitary First Amendment for all media will do. In the remainder of this Essay, we explain these ground rules of constitutional law and regulatory policy, show how and why they shape government's basic stance toward all nonbroadcast media, and demonstrate how these principles encompass emerging technologies.

A. Basic Principles

Four principles collectively establish the proper responsibilities of government in regulating the structure and performance of the mass media and in supervising access to, and diversity within, those media. They are the principles that, shaped by carefully considered First Amendment values, govern the legal regulation of virtually all other mass media in the United States. These principles provide government with ample authority to regulate the media in ways that can improve their performance, while assuring that government is responsive to, rather than responsible for, American culture, information, and politics. These ground rules of constitutional law and regulatory policy regarding the nonbroadcast media also help to ensure that laws governing the media are targeted at issues government can manage, while avoiding regulations that are simply naive or directed at foisting particular preferences on a pluralist society.

1. First Principle

Editorial control over what is said and how it is said should be lodged in private, not governmental, institutions. Two basic rationales underlie this principle.

They are well stated in Miami Herald Publishing Co. v. Tornillo, and so we only summarize them here.

In the first place, both history and theory clearly teach that the imposition by law of "good journalism" or "fair representation" requirements on speakers operates to chill speech, not to liberate, broaden, or protect it. Telling speakers "if you discuss x, you must do (or discuss) y" has the principal effect of inhibiting discussion of x. Further, such government intervention cannot add more speech; at its very best, that intervention can only substitute speech on one topic for speech on another.

In the second place, editorial control, because it is invariably content based, is an inherently impermissible government function. When government edits, it does so for debatable purposes and with questionable means; that editing necessarily stifles unpopular viewpoints.

The competing principle is drawn from broadcasting: It is regulation in the public interest. As stated by *Red Lion*, government supervision of broadcasters' programming is essential because "[i]t is the right of the viewers and listeners, not the right of the broadcasters, which is paramount." If broadcasters were left to their own discretion (or insufficiently controlled), they would pander to the lowest common denominator, decreasing the quality of important information while simultaneously increasing commercialization. Such programming is not in the public interest and neglects the need to create an intelligent, civically active community where all citizens have access to the full range of information that they need for self-government.

Under the public interest model, government and citizens attentive to civic issues have a role in promoting and improving the community's common values. It is not an adequate response to contend that those who choose to watch, hear, or read information or entertainment that does not further civic values must prefer or enjoy what they choose. "Preferences that have adapted to an objectionable system cannot justify that system. If better options are put more regularly in view, it might well be expected that at least some people would be educated as a result. They might be more favorably disposed toward programming dealing with public issues in a serious way."[5] Accordingly, for adherents to the public interest model, government may, indeed should, regulate access to the media (whether new or old) so as to improve and inform those among its citizens who are not already attuned to the public interest. From this perspective the Supreme Court's observation that "no one has a right to press even 'good' ideas on an unwilling recipient" is simply wrong.[6]

The less attractive results of the public interest model are those regulations that smack of overt censorship. A programmer is forbidden to create, stations are forbidden to air, and adults are forbidden to view and hear programming that would otherwise be available in the market because either Congress or a few commissioners believe that adults are incapable of evaluating what they wish to view. It does not matter whether the banning institution represents a permanent majority of Americans, a transient majority, or a minority that has captured the institution (as appears to have been the case with the 1987 FCC indecency deci-

---

5. Cass R. Sunstein, The Partial Constitution 221 (1993).
6. Rowan v. United States Post Office Dep't, 397 U.S. 728, 738 (1970).

sions). It does not matter whether the purpose of the regulation is to entrench or change the status quo. In each case, government fiat substitutes for the choices that adult Americans would otherwise make.

While censorship is wrong, mandating a more diverse fare often seems right. Thus a newcomer to this area might be tempted to conclude, for example, that a rule requiring television stations to broadcast more children's programming would be a good thing. Ultimately this rests on the view that any "children's program," no matter how bad, is more likely than not to be better than the alternatives (no matter what the audience may think). Unfortunately, however, true quality comes from a program's substance, not its topic, and FCC efforts to create quality programs that broadcasters do not wish to air, while sporadic, have been unsuccessful.

There are basic reasons why regulatory efforts to mandate quality are ineffective. First, even with television there is too much time to fill and too few truly imaginative people to fill it. Second, audiences appear to know what they like and will resist attempts to re-program their tastes.

With newer technologies offering users many more options to watch, hear, or read many more programs and sources of information, these problems will be exacerbated geometrically. Much of the information on the infobahn will be dreck. But users, rather than regulators, will hold the trump cards, because only users can decide how they will spend their time perusing the increased options. Information will have to appeal to users, not government bureaucrats or academic critics, if it is to have a substantial audience. In other words, future users of the infobahn will behave very much like current purchasers of magazines, books, or recordings—and they should be permitted to do so.

2. Second Principle

As a matter of policy, government should foster access by speakers to media. Clearly, government has an important role to play in ensuring that the media are not monopolized and in expanding the opportunities of citizens to speak and to be heard. People who own instrumentalities of communication have incentives to reduce their use in order to charge monopoly prices and equally strong incentives to prevent or retard the development of competing instrumentalities. We cannot assume that those efforts will always fail of their own accord. Further, government funding of basic research is often an efficient way of uncovering new communications technologies or new uses for established vehicles, both of which can widen access by increasing the number of available communication channels.

That government should foster speakers' access to the mass media is not a controversial proposition. What has proved quite contestable, however, although usually only with respect to broadcast regulation, is the meaning of access. In broadcasting, access is often defined as replacing the broadcaster's choice of programming with programming chosen by someone not associated with the station. By contrast, when we examine government's relations to other mass media, it seems reasonably clear that, for purposes of the access principle, access means the ability to reach any willing recipient by any speaker willing to pay the economic costs of doing so (and does not mean that government must or should require others to subsidize the would-be communicator). For example, in book publishing we do not assume that access to book publishers is inadequate if an author is not published because publishers believe her book will not sell enough copies to pay for printing costs.

3. Third Principle

Government policies should foster diversity in the media marketplace. If government adheres to the first and second principles, this third principle will follow automatically because it is the opposite side of the coin. Properly understood, the quest for diversity does not require government to provide people speech that they do not value as much as its costs of production and distribution. And, quite obviously, the quest for diversity does not justify censoring some programming upon a theory that the censorship will necessarily generate some different programming.

Instead, diversity is achieved when people are allowed to bid for any information or entertainment they desire—no censorship—and to receive what they seek, so long as they are willing to pay the economic costs of receiving it. That is, the diversity principle dictates that there be no artificial government-imposed barriers to transmission or reception of speech.

This principle, too, is evident in our settled expectations regarding legal control of the nonbroadcast mass media. For example, the magazine market is regarded as diverse because people are free to subscribe to magazines on any or all topics. We do not regard diversity in the magazine market as incomplete if some topics or formats that might lend themselves to magazine treatment are not published because to do so would cost more than subscribers (or advertisers) are willing to pay.

4. Fourth Principle

Government is not permitted to sacrifice any of the three foregoing principles to further goals associated with either or both of the others. Where such sacrifice is not needed, however, government may extend the goals associated with any of those principles. Put another way, the Constitution does not mandate subsidies for those seeking access to, or diversity from, the mass communications media; neither does the Constitution prohibit such subsidies.

One of the newest technologies traces its rapid growth to the application of this principle. The federal government has borne most of the costs of establishing the infrastructure that is the Internet, thereby increasing the diversity of the fare available and the accessibility of this medium without favoring any speaker or viewpoint. Antecedent similar examples abound. During the era before cable, we were all the richer for the decision to create and subsidize PBS. Perhaps the benefits of PBS did not exceed its economic costs, but government financing of PBS did no damage to the system of freedom of expression. We cannot know how many magazines have been created and continue to exist because of second-class mailing privileges, but, again, we are better for their existence, because more information is better than less.

Indeed, to the extent the marketplace is perceived as impoverished, subsidies may be an effective way of correcting its inadequacies, so long as these are true subsidies rather than extractions from media competitors. Furthermore, the policy issues, while rich and complex, are largely freed from the restraints that the First Amendment otherwise imposes on government actions.

B. Sources of the Basic Principles

For those familiar with basic First Amendment law and general American regulatory policy toward the mass media, reflection will reveal that virtually all First Amendment rules and regulatory policies toward the mass media—other than broadcasting—rest on the four principles set out above. Consider the print media. With little or no controversy, we recognize (or tolerate) the following four propositions. First, a regulation that provides, "If you write about x, you must behave according to specified journalistic norms," puts a chill on writing about x. Second, print media are "accessible" platforms to speakers, even if no one gets published at no cost. Third, the print media provide "diversity," even if we are not assured that every worthwhile view will be offered for sale. Fourth, the First Amendment divested government of power over, or responsibility for, the behavior of editors. Indeed, we might well say that these are the premises underlying *Tornillo*.

We believe American citizens and policymakers embrace those propositions not because they slavishly agree to anything the Supreme Court says, but because of our society's shared belief in the following three empirical assumptions. First, governmental control over editorial policies typically will be exercised in a discriminatory fashion, privileging that which is in vogue, mainstream, and safe while handicapping that which is not. Second, recipients—readers, listeners, viewers—are capable of judging the quality of a speaker's presentation and abandoning those speakers who do not measure up to the recipients' standards. Third, speakers compete within and across media for potential recipients, so that the public is constantly presented with a variety of viewpoints from which to choose. Further, it is only because we believe that markets for ideas and values operate in this fashion that we have chosen to place constitutional constraints on government's authority to regulate speech.

We do not blush to admit that we believe these empirical assumptions are true. Another reason we treat these beliefs about politics, markets, speakers, and listeners as a sound basis for erecting principles to govern legal regulation of the media is "the belief that no other approach would comport with the premise of individual dignity and choice upon which our political system rests." If, for example, we build legal rules on the assumption that recipients can discriminate among speakers and speeches, this should tend to become a self-fulfilling prophecy. Recipients will need to develop the ability to discriminate.

Of course, we cannot prove that those empirical assumptions are generally truthful reflections of reality, and we know that they are not always so. But, for purposes of our argument, it is quite important to note a fact that is not contestable. That fact is that these assumptions about politics, markets, speakers, and listeners underlie virtually every facet of First Amendment law and nonconstitutional regulatory policy toward the (nonbroadcast) mass media. Constitutional and statutory rules aimed at not only the print media, but all mass media other than broadcasting, are premised on the notion that, although government has important duties or opportunities to expand access and diversity through content neutral actions, the goals of an open, stable democracy are best advanced by relying on recipients to choose from among competing speakers unconstrained by government. "To many this is, and always will be, folly; but we have staked upon it our all."

IV. APPLICATION TO CONVERGING TECHNOLOGIES

As we noted at the outset, emerging technologies erase any tenable line delineating that which is broadcasting and exempt from these principles and that which is not. The principles just discussed offer broadcasters and those employing emerging media technologies the full protection of general media law while leaving ample room for progressive and helpful regulation.

What specific forms of regulation should be considered for the era of technological convergence? Three central points emerge: Content control should be forbidden; entry barriers should be reduced and eliminated whenever possible; and common carrier status must be carefully evaluated.

A. No Content Controls

This regulatory strategy flows automatically from our first principle stated earlier. It applies equally to emerging technologies, which must, after all, compete for users' attention, in the same manner that magazines, newspapers, and books seek readers.

B. Reduce Entry Barriers

To help assure that new communications technologies are user friendly rather than centrally controlled—whether by government or by industry— the most important policy government could adopt is a commitment to foster as much competition as possible among would-be speakers for audience attention. This obligation, rooted in free speech concerns, mandates reducing barriers to entry that confront potential speakers. This includes those who wish to employ established technologies, such as television stations broadcasting in the VHF spectrum. For example, long ago the FCC made many decisions that substantially constrict the number of VHF stations that can now be licensed. Those decisions can be reversed. The obligation should extend also to potential speakers desiring to employ new technologies—such as communications networks that link up portable computers. Federal regulation has effectively delayed the entry of, first, portable cellular telephones and, later, portable interactive minicomputers, by failing to establish fluid mechanisms for allocating and reallocating spectrum in response to emerging technologies and consumer demand. That omission can and should be remedied.

Reducing entry barriers and extending the spectrum available for communication of information and entertainment serve the goals of both access and diversity by lowering the costs of communicating and expanding the opportunities for doing so. In this fashion, readers, listeners, and viewers are empowered, without governmental censorship to control what is offered and what is consumed. By simply determining what (if any) materials to access, users of the infobahn can force programmers to serve their interests and desires. To the sober media critic who understands the modest possibilities of achieving real change through regulation, such a program ought to be vastly more appealing than the kinds of clumsy and usually ineffective content controls that were at the center of the fairness doctrine and that underlie present regulation of children's television.

Similarly, government regulation fosters diversity when it helps people make and enforce choices. Thus, no basic principle is violated if government requires that consumers be offered computers or receivers that are engineered so that channels can be permanently or selectively blocked or so that a very wide range of channels can be received. (Where, however, government mandates that only such receivers be offered, it risks reducing access and diversity by increasing the costs of the receivers beyond the willingness of low income viewers to pay for the sets.)

Perhaps the point seems so obvious that to emphasize it is to belabor it. We emphasize it because history teaches a consistent lesson regarding the introduction of new communications technologies: Government should be wary of private barriers to communication and equally wary of public barriers. Indeed, if the past is prologue, entrenched private interests will use public policy to achieve their goals of limiting competition.

Surely, the FCC has known that erecting or maintaining entry barriers is counterproductive. Even Congress has realized this. A key section of the Communications Act of 1934 directs the Commission "to encourage the larger and more effective use of radio in the public interest." 47 U.S.C. §303(g). Yet, although the FCC has always had available the option to reduce barriers to entry and thereby expand the number of broadcast outlets accessible to the public, Commission policy from the agency's inception through at least the next fifty years was to retard the growth of broadcasting.

Proliferating electronic communications technologies make even more compelling a regulatory approach that, resting on the four basic principles, relies on competition rather than direct governmental oversight to discipline firms and to force them to respond to consumer desires. Expanding technologies bring lower access costs and wider opportunities for diversity, thus diminishing the appeal of most proposals to expand government oversight. More recent government actions suggest reason to hope. Broadcast satellites have been launched with comparatively little governmental control. The federal government constructed the infrastructure of the Internet, a communications technology that permits rather easy and nondiscriminatory access.

C. Common Carrier Regulation?

At some point in the evolution of any new communications technology, some important group is sure to argue that the industry should be conducted on a common carrier basis. For example, when cable was in its infancy, a much-debated question was whether cable systems should be required to act as common carriers. The tendency of analysis to gravitate toward the common carrier approach is not surprising. Common carriage is likely to appeal to one who grasps the point of *Tornillo* that editorial control should be left in private hands, but also appreciates the premise of Red Lion that a powerful unregulated medium may exclude valuable information and entertainment.

Reflection reveals that nothing in the basic principles of mass media regulation specifies who must exercise the editorial function. Our traditions, as well as the specific language of the First Amendment, only tell us who must not be the editor. Editing is not government's job. Speakers edit free of governmental control or interference, but they need not own the facilities over which they speak.

Printing presses, sound stages, recording studios, cable systems, and broadcast stations could all be operated as common carriers. They would behave like existing communications common carriers, that is, for example, like local telephone exchange carriers and mobile radio service producers and most long distance microwave services and satellite carriers.

We should make clear that the common carriage discussed here must be consistent with our four principles outlined above. In particular, the regulation must be content neutral, not targeted at particular viewpoints or ideologies. Similarly, randomly choosing one in ten of all AM radio stations for common-carriage status would, at least presumptively, lack the rational basis required by the Fifth Amendment.

In some instances, imposing common carrier obligations can be an effective way to ensure that all speakers receive nondiscriminatory access to platforms. Where this occurs, diversity, as we have defined it, is also enhanced. In simple terms, the appeal of common carrier regulation is that it seems directly responsive to sober claims for content regulation. If, for example, the claim is that we need a fairness doctrine for radio to permit access by speakers whose views are antithetical to advertisers and so would not be carried by advertiser-funded radio stations, one might offer the common carrier alternative. Under such a regime, any speech by a speaker willing to pay the costs of speaking should be carried (access) and can be received by anyone willing to pay any additional costs of receiving it (diversity).

Common-carriage regulation, however, should not be viewed as a panacea. Just because it can be implemented lawfully does not mean it will work well. Indeed, we suspect that, for most media, a thoughtful policy analyst will reject the common carrier model.

First, such regulation is not costless. At a minimum, government resources must be devoted to defining and enforcing the rules. To assure that common carrier prices reflect only the true costs of access may require extensive (and expensive) public-utility-type regulation.

Further, especially as applied to mass communications media, common carrier obligations can prevent the achievement of substantial efficiencies. Magazine publishers and broadcasters do not simply publish articles or air programs. They package groups of articles or programs into a coherent whole. This whole package is often more valuable than the sum of its parts because the package itself communicates. It describes the mix and quality of data or entertainment that the recipient will receive.

Finally, it is not self-evident that common carriers will provide greater access opportunities or diversity of style or viewpoint than will publisher-editors. Where an editor—whether of a newspaper, a broadcast station, or a cable system—has the capacity to add a speaker whom audiences wish to receive, it is usually in that editor's best interests to provide that speech so long as the audiences are willing to pay the (marginal) costs of transmitting it. If a cable system can add a channel at the cost of $5 per month, we expect it will do so for anyone willing to pay that amount.

If the problem is lack of capacity, the preferred government response, as outlined above, is clear: help to increase capacity, to reduce entry barriers. If the cable system cannot or will not add a channel, the better response is to be rid of any rules that constrain cable channel expansion and to provide alternative means—*e.g.*, by microwave or satellite—of transmitting multiple video signals. If the problem is incompatible ideology, the preferred response is the same. By reducing entry barriers and preventing monopolization, government facilitates competition among editors of diverse ideologies, and thus, fosters access to competing viewpoints.

Common carriage, then, should not be viewed as the preferred basis for organizing or regulating the mass media in the United States. In most cases, its costs will exceed its benefits. But, in the unusual case, common carrier regulation can be a cost-effective means of attaining access and diversity goals without engaging in content regulation. For those reasons, a common carrier regime that comports with the four principles described above cannot be said, on *a priori* or philosophical grounds, to impose a threat to civil liberties comparable to that created by empowering government to displace the decisions of private editors.

Common carrier regulation appears to have been a wise choice for common, interactive, wireline audio communication (telephony). With telephones, people largely wish to communicate directly with each other and so little is lost by denying the phone company an editorial voice over these communications. Further, giving telephone companies an editorial discretion would be quite risky. The local telephone loop may well be a natural monopoly; so one would not expect a rival phone company to come into existence to carry messages that the entrenched phone company refused to carry. This suggests, additionally, that a common carrier approach toward the Internet is equally sensible, for the same reasons. People who use the Internet to establish data bases or accessible bulletin boards, however, should not be required to carry all comers, because it is possible to establish many such data bases or bulletin boards along the Internet.

Notes and Questions

1. Missing Pieces. Both of these excerpts attempt to present a fairly comprehensive look at regulation (of mass media, at least). What do they leave out? Which vision seems more consonant with the existing case law? Holding case law aside, which one do you find more appealing as a normative matter?

2. So, What Makes Telecom Unique? According to each article, what, if anything, is special about telecommunications? How much of a role does each envision for government regulation? Which positions would you embrace if you were: (a) an FCC Commissioner; (b) a member of Congress; (c) the head of a fledgling company seeking to bring broadband voice, video, and data to customers' homes; or (d) the head of an ILEC or major cable company seeking to do the same?

3. The Future. Both articles claim to be addressing the appropriate scope of regulation for the future, and in particular for cyberspace. Does either, both, or neither approach make sense for the interconnected future? Are they looking forward, or fighting the last war? What would you advise if you were in charge of reforming (a) the Commission's regulatory authority or (b) telecommunications law more generally? Might you even want to make changes to the First Amendment?

STATUTORY APPENDIX

COMMUNICATIONS ACT OF 1934, AS AMENDED*
47 U.S.C. §§151 *et seq.*

TITLE I—GENERAL PROVISIONS

SEC. 1. [47 U.S.C. 151] PURPOSES OF ACT, CREATION OF FEDERAL COMMUNICATIONS COMMISSION.

For the purpose of regulating interstate and foreign commerce in communication by wire and radio so as to make available, so far as possible, to all the people of the United States, without discrimination on the basis of race, color, religion, national origin, or sex, a rapid, efficient, Nation-wide, and world-wide wire and radio communication service with adequate facilities at reasonable charges, for the purpose of the national defense, for the purpose of promoting safety of life and property through the use of wire and radio communications, and for the purpose of securing a more effective execution of this policy by centralizing authority heretofore granted by law to several agencies and by granting additional authority with respect to interstate and foreign commerce in wire and radio communication, there is created commission to be known as the "Federal Communications Commission", which shall be constituted as hereinafter provided, and which shall execute and enforce the provisions of this chapter.

SEC. 2 [47 U.S.C. 152] APPLICATION OF ACT.

(a) The provisions of this Act shall apply to all interstate and foreign communication by wire or radio and all interstate and foreign transmission of energy by radio, which originates and/or is received within the United States,... and to the licensing and regulating of all radio stations.... The provisions of this Act shall apply with respect to cable service.

(b) Except as provided in sections 223 through 227 of this title, inclusive, and section 332 of this title, and subject to the provisions of section 301 of this title and subchapter V-A of this chapter, nothing in this chapter shall be construed to apply or to give the Commission jurisdiction with respect to (1) charges, classifications, practices, services, facilities, or regulations for or in connection with intrastate communication service by wire or radio of any carrier....

---

* [Ed. These materials have been heavily edited. The complete, unedited text of the Communications Act of 1934, as Amended, is available at the FCC homepage, http://www.fcc.gov.]

SEC. 3 [47 U.S.C. 153] DEFINITIONS.

(14) CUSTOMER PREMISES EQUIPMENT. The term "customer premises equipment" means equipment employed on the premises of a person (other than a carrier) to originate, route, or terminate telecommunications.

(15) DIALING PARITY. The term "dialing parity" means that a person that is not an affiliate of a local exchange carrier is able to provide telecommunications services in such a manner that customers have the ability to route automatically, without the use of any access code, their telecommunications to the telecommunications services provider of the customer's designation from among 2 or more telecommunications services providers (including such local exchange carrier).

(16) EXCHANGE ACCESS. The term "exchange access" means the offering of access to telephone exchange services or facilities for the purpose of the origination or termination of telephone toll services.

(20) INFORMATION SERVICE. The term "information service" means the offering of a capability for generating, acquiring, storing, transforming, processing, retrieving, utilizing, or making available information via telecommunications, and includes electronic publishing, but does not include any use of any such capability for the management, control, or operation of a telecommunications system or the management of a telecommunications service.

(26) LOCAL EXCHANGE CARRIER. The term "local exchange carrier" means any person that is engaged in the provision of telephone exchange service or exchange access. Such term does not include a person insofar as such person is engaged in the provision of a commercial mobile service under section 332(c), except to the extent that the Commission finds that such service should be included in the definition of such term.

(30) NUMBER PORTABILITY. The term "number portability" means the ability of users of telecommunications services to retain, at the same location, existing telecommunications numbers without impairment of quality, reliability, or convenience when switching from one telecommunications carrier to another.

(43) TELECOMMUNICATIONS. The term "telecommunications" means the transmission, between or among points specified by the user, of information of the user's choosing, without change in the form or content of the information as sent and received.

(44) TELECOMMUNICATIONS CARRIER. The term "telecommunications carrier" means any provider of telecommunications services.... A telecommunications carrier shall be treated as a common carrier under this Act only to the extent that it is engaged in providing telecommunications services...

(45) TELECOMMUNICATIONS EQUIPMENT. The term "telecommunications equipment" means equipment, other than customer premises equipment, used by a carrier to provide telecommunications services, and includes software integral to such equipment (including upgrades).

(46) TELECOMMUNICATIONS SERVICE. The term "telecommunications service" means the offering of telecommunications for a fee directly to the public, or to such classes of users as to be effectively available directly to the public, regardless of the facilities used.

SEC. 4. [47 U.S.C. 154] PROVISIONS RELATING TO THE COMMISSION.

(a) The Commission shall be composed of five Commissioners appointed by the President, by and with the advice and consent of the Senate, one of whom the President shall designate as chairman.

* * *

(c) Commissioners shall be appointed for terms of five years...except that any person chosen to fill a vacancy shall be appointed only for the unexpired term of the Commissioner whom he succeeds.

* * *

(i) The Commission may perform any and all acts, make such rules and regulations, and issue such orders, not inconsistent with this Act, as may be necessary in the execution of its functions.

SEC. 7. [47 U.S.C. 157] NEW TECHNOLOGIES AND SERVICES.

(a) It shall be the policy of the United States to encourage the provision of new technologies and services to the public. Any person or party (other than the Commission) who opposes a new technology or service proposed to be permitted under this Act shall have the burden to demonstrate that such proposal is inconsistent with the public interest.

SEC. 10. [47 U.S.C. 160] COMPETITION IN PROVISION OF TELECOMMUNICATIONS SERVICE.

(a) REGULATORY FLEXIBILITY. Notwithstanding section 332(c)(1)(A) of this Act, the Commission shall forbear from applying any regulation or any provision of this Act to a telecommunications carrier or telecommunications service, or class of telecommunications carriers or telecommunications services, in any or some of its or their geographic markets, if the Commission determines that—

    (1)   enforcement of such regulation or provision is not necessary to ensure that the charges, practices, classifications, or regulations by, for, or in connection with that telecommunications carrier or telecommunications service are just and reasonable and are not unjustly or unreasonably discriminatory;

    (2)   enforcement of such regulation or provision is not necessary for the protection of consumers; and

    (3)   forbearance from applying such provision or regulation is consistent with the public interest.

(b) COMPETITIVE EFFECT TO BE WEIGHED. If the Commission determines that forbearance will promote competition among providers of telecommunications services, that determination may be the basis for a Commission finding that forbearance is in the public interest.

* * *

(e) STATE ENFORCEMENT AFTER COMMISSION FORBEARANCE. A State commission may not continue to apply or enforce any provision of this Act that the Commission has determined to forbear from applying under subsection (a).

SEC. 11. [47 U.S.C. 161]. REGULATORY REFORM.

(a) BIENNIAL REVIEW OF REGULATIONS. In every even-numbered year (beginning with 1998), the Commission—

(1) shall review all regulations issued under this Act in effect at the time of the review that apply to the operations or activities of any provider of telecommunications service; and

(2) shall determine whether any such regulation is no longer necessary in the public interest as the result of meaningful economic competition between providers of such service.

(b) EFFECT OF DETERMINATION. The Commission shall repeal or modify any regulation it determines to be no longer necessary in the public interest.

TITLE II—COMMON CARRIERS

PART I—COMMON CARRIER REGULATION

SEC. 201. [47 U.S.C. 201] SERVICE AND CHARGES.

(a) It shall be the duty of every common carrier engaged in interstate or foreign communication by wire or radio to furnish such communication service upon reasonable request therefor; and...to establish physical connections with other carriers....

(b) All charges, practices, classifications, and regulations for and in connection with such communication service, shall be just and reasonable....

SEC. 202. [47 U.S.C. 202] DISCRIMINATION AND PREFERENCES.

(a) It shall be unlawful for any common carrier to make any unjust or unreasonable discrimination in charges, practices, classifications, regulations, facilities, or services for or in connection with like communication service, directly or indirectly, by any means or device, or to make or give any undue or unreasonable preference or advantage to any particular person, class of persons, or locality, or to subject any particular person, class of persons, or locality to any undue or unreasonable prejudice or disadvantage.

SEC. 203. [47 U.S.C. 203] SCHEDULES OF CHARGES.

(a) Every common carrier...shall...file with the Commission and print and keep open for public inspection schedules showing all charges for itself and its connecting carriers for interstate and foreign wire or radio communication... and showing the classifications, practices, and regulations affecting such charges. [E]ach such schedule shall give notice of its effective date...

SEC. 205. [47 U.S.C. 205] COMMISSION AUTHORIZED TO PRESCRIBE JUST AND REASONABLE CHARGES.

(a) Whenever, after full opportunity for hearing,...the Commission shall be of opinion that any charge...or practice of any carrier or carriers is or will be in violation of any of the provisions of this Act, the Commission is authorized and empowered to determine and prescribe what will be the just and reasonable charge...to be thereafter observed, and what...practice is or will be just, fair, and reasonable....

SEC. 214. [47 U.S.C. 214] EXTENSION OF LINES.

(a) No carrier shall undertake the construction of a new line or of an extension of any line, or shall acquire or operate any line, or extension thereof...until there shall first have been obtained from the Commission a certificate that the present or future public convenience and necessity require or will require...such additional or extended line....

(e) PROVISION OF UNIVERSAL SERVICE

(1) ELIGIBLE TELECOMMUNICATIONS CARRIERS

A common carrier designated as an eligible telecommunications carrier under paragraph (2), (3), or (6) shall be eligible to receive universal service support in accordance with section 254 of this title and shall, throughout the service area for which the designation is received:

(A) offer the services that are supported by Federal universal service support mechanisms under section 254(c) of this title, either using its own facilities or a combination of its own facilities and resale of another carrier's services (including the services offered by another eligible telecommunications carrier); and

(B) advertise the availability of such services and the charges therefor using media of general distribution.

(2) DESIGNATION OF ELIGIBLE TELECOMMUNICATIONS CARRIERS

A State commission shall upon its own motion or upon request designate a common carrier that meets the requirements of paragraph (1) as an eligible telecommunications carrier for a service area designated by the State commission. Upon request and consistent with the public interest, convenience, and necessity, the State commission may, in the case of an area served by a rural telephone company, and shall, in the case of all other areas, designate more than one common carrier as an eligible telecommunications carrier for a service area designated by the State commission, so long as each additional requesting carrier meets the requirements of paragraph (1). Before designating an additional eligible telecommunications carrier for an area served by a rural telephone company, the State commission shall find that the designation is in the public interest.

SEC. 220. [47 U.S.C. 220] ACCOUNTS, RECORDS, and MEMORANDA

(a) FORMS

(1) The Commission may, in its discretion, prescribe the forms of any and all accounts, records, and memoranda to be kept by carriers subject to this chapter, including the accounts, records, and memoranda of the movement of traffic, as well as of the receipts and expenditures of moneys.

(2) The Commission shall, by rule, prescribe a uniform system of accounts for use by telephone companies. Such uniform system shall require that each common carrier shall maintain a system of accounting methods, procedures, and techniques (including accounts and supporting records and memoranda) which shall ensure a proper allocation of all costs to and among telecommunications services, facilities, and products (and to and among classes of such services, facilities, and products) which are developed, manufactured, or offered by such common carrier.

(b) DEPRECIATION CHARGES

The Commission may prescribe, for such carriers as it determines to be appropriate, the classes of property for which depreciation charges may be properly included under operating expenses, and the percentages of depreciation which shall be charged with respect to each of such classes of property, classifying the carriers as it may deem proper for this purpose. The Commission may, when it deems necessary, modify the classes and percentages so prescribed. Such carriers shall not, after the Commission has prescribed the classes of property for which depreciation charges may be included, charge to operating expenses any depreciation charges on classes of property other than those prescribed by the Commission, or after the Commission has prescribed percentages of depreciation, charge with respect to any class of property a percentage of depreciation other than that prescribed therefor by the Commission. No such carrier shall in any case include in any form under its operating or other expenses any depreciation or other charge or expenditure included elsewhere as a depreciation charge or otherwise under its operating or other expenses.

(c) ACCESS TO INFORMATION; BURDEN OF PROOF; USE OF INDEPENDENT AUDITORS

The Commission shall at all times have access to and the right of inspection and examination of all accounts, records, and memoranda, including all documents, papers, and correspondence now or hereafter existing, and kept or required to be kept by such carriers, and the provisions of this section respecting the preservation and destruction of books, papers, and documents shall apply thereto. The burden of proof to justify every accounting entry questioned by the Commission shall be on the person making, authorizing, or requiring such entry and the Commission may suspend a charge or credit pending submission of proof by such person. . . .

SEC. 223. [47 U.S.C. 223] OBSCENE OR HARASSING TELEPHONE CALLS . . .

(a) Whoever—

(1) in interstate or foreign communications—

    (A)　by means of a telecommunications device knowingly—

    (i)　makes, creates, or solicits, and

    (ii)　initiates the transmission of, any comment, request, suggestion, proposal, image, or other communication which is obscene, lewd, lascivious, filthy, or indecent, with intent to annoy, abuse, threaten, or harass another person;

    (B)　by means of a telecommunications device knowingly—

    (i)　makes, creates, or solicits, and

    (ii)　initiates the transmission of, any comment, request, suggestion, proposal, image, or other communication which is obscene or indecent, knowing that the recipient of the communication is under 18 years of age, regardless of whether the maker of such communication placed the call or initiated the communication;

(C)   makes a telephone call or utilizes a telecommunications device, whether or not conversation or communication ensues, without disclosing his identity and with intent to annoy, abuse, threaten, or harass any person at the called number or who receives the communications;

(D)   makes or causes the telephone of another repeatedly or continuously to ring, with intent to harass any person at the called number; or

(E)   makes repeated telephone calls or repeatedly initiates communication with a telecommunications device, during which conversation or communication ensues, solely to harass any person at the called number or who receives the communication; or

(2) knowingly permits any telecommunications facility under his control to be used for any activity prohibited by paragraph (1) with the intent that it be used for such activity, shall be fined under title 18, United States Code, or imprisoned not more than two years, or both; and

(b) (1) Whoever knowingly —

(A)   within the United States, by means of telephone, makes (directly or by recording device) any obscene communication for commercial purposes to any person, regardless of whether the maker of such communication placed the call; or

(B)   permits any telephone facility under such person's control to be used for an activity prohibited by subparagraph (A) shall be fined in accordance with title 18, United States Code, or imprisoned not more than two years, or both.

(2) Whoever knowingly —

(A)   within the United States, by means of telephone, makes (directly or by recording device) any indecent communication for commercial purposes which is available to any person under 18 years of age or to any other person without that person's consent, regardless of whether the maker of such communication placed the call; or

(B)   permits any telephone facility under such person's control to be used for an activity prohibited by subparagraph (A), shall be fined not more than $ 50,000 or imprisoned not more than six months, or both.

(3)   It is a defense to prosecution under paragraph (2) of this subsection that the defendant restrict access to the prohibited communication to persons 18 years of age or older in accordance with subsection (c) of this section and with such procedures as the Commission may prescribe by regulation.

(d) Whoever —

(1)   in interstate or foreign communications knowingly —

(A)   uses an interactive computer service to send to a specific person or persons under 18 years of age, or

(B)   uses any interactive computer service to display in a manner available to a person under 18 years of age, any comment, request, suggestion, proposal, image, or other communication that, in context, depicts or describes, in terms patently offensive as measured by contemporary community standards, sexual or excretory activities or organs, regardless of whether the user of such service placed the call or initiated the communication; or

(2)   knowingly permits any telecommunications facility under such person's control to be used for an activity prohibited by paragraph (1) with the intent that it be used for such activity, shall be fined under title 18, United States Code, or imprisoned not more than two years, or both.

(e) In addition to any other defenses available by law:

(1)   No person shall be held to have violated subsection (a) or (d) solely for providing access or connection to or from a facility, system, or network not under that person's control, including transmission, downloading, intermediate storage, access software, or other related capabilities that are incidental to providing such access or connection that does not include the creation of the content of the communication.

(2)   The defenses provided by paragraph (1) of this subsection shall not be applicable to a person who is a conspirator with an entity actively involved in the creation or knowing distribution of communications that violate this section, or who knowingly advertises the availability of such communications.

(3)   The defenses provided in paragraph (1) of this subsection shall not be applicable to a person who provides access or connection to a facility, system, or network engaged in the violation of this section that is owned or controlled by such person.

(4)   No employer shall be held liable under this section for the actions of an employee or agent unless the employee's or agent's conduct is within the scope of his or her employment or agency and the employer (A) having knowledge of such conduct, authorizes or ratifies such conduct, or (B) recklessly disregards such conduct.

(5)   It is a defense to a prosecution under subsection (a)(1)(B) or (d), or under subsection (a)(2) with respect to the use of a facility for an activity under subsection (a)(1)(B) that a person—

(A)   has taken, in good faith, reasonable, effective, and appropriate actions under the circumstances to restrict or prevent access by minors to a communication specified in such subsections, which may involve any appropriate measures to restrict minors from such communications, including any method which is feasible under available technology; or

(B)   has restricted access to such communication by requiring use of a verified credit card, debit account, adult access code, or adult personal identification number.

(6)   The Commission may describe measures which are reasonable, effective, and appropriate to restrict access to prohibited com-

munications under subsection (d). Nothing in this section authorizes the Commission to enforce, or is intended to provide the Commission with the authority to approve, sanction, or permit, the use of such measures. The Commission shall have no enforcement authority over the failure to utilize such measures. The Commission shall not endorse specific products relating to such measures. The use of such measures shall be admitted as evidence of good faith efforts for purposes of paragraph (5) in any action arising under subsection (d). Nothing in this section shall be construed to treat interactive computer services as common carriers or telecommunications carriers.

SEC. 224. (47 U.S.C. 224) REGULATION OF POLE ATTACHMENTS.

(a) (1) The term "utility" means any person who is a local exchange carrier or an electric, gas, water, steam, or other public utility, and who owns or controls poles, ducts, conduits, or rights-of-way used, in whole or in part, for any wire communications.

* * *

(e) (1) The Commission shall, no later than 2 years after the date of enactment of the Telecommunications Act of 1996, prescribe regulations in accordance with this subsection to govern the charges for pole attachments used by telecommunications carriers to provide telecommunications services, when the parties fail to resolve a dispute over such charges. Such regulations shall ensure that a utility charges just, reasonable, and nondiscriminatory rates for pole attachments.

(f) (1) A utility shall provide a cable television system or any telecommunications carrier with nondiscriminatory access to any pole, duct, conduit, or right-of-way owned or controlled by it.

(2) Notwithstanding paragraph (1), a utility providing electric service may deny a cable television system or any telecommunications carrier access to its poles, ducts, conduits, or rights-of-way, on a nondiscriminatory basis where there is insufficient capacity and for reasons of safety, reliability and generally applicable engineering purposes.

SEC. 227. [47 U.S.C. 227] RESTRICTIONS ON THE USE OF TELEPHONE EQUIPMENT.

(b) RESTRICTIONS ON THE USE OF AUTOMATED TELEPHONE EQUIPMENT.

(1) PROHIBITIONS. It shall be unlawful for any person within the United States—

* * *

(B) to initiate any telephone call to any residential telephone line using an artificial or prerecorded voice to deliver a message without the prior express consent of the called party, unless the call is initiated for emergency purposes or is exempted by rule or order by the Commission...

(C) to use any telephone facsimile machine, computer, or other device to send an unsolicited advertisement to a telephone facsimile machine; or

(D)   to use an automatic telephone dialing system in such a way that two or more telephone lines of a multi-line business are engaged simultaneously.

SEC. 230. [47 U.S.C. 230] PROTECTION FOR PRIVATE BLOCKING AND SCREENING OF OFFENSIVE MATERIAL.

(a) FINDINGS. The Congress finds the following:

(1) The rapidly developing array of Internet and other interactive computer services available to individual Americans represent an extraordinary advance in the availability of educational and informational resources to our citizens.

(2) These services offer users a great degree of control over the information that they receive, as well as the potential for even greater control in the future as technology develops.

(3) The Internet and other interactive computer services offer a forum for a true diversity of political discourse, unique opportunities for cultural development, and myriad avenues for intellectual activity.

(4) The Internet and other interactive computer services have flourished, to the benefit of all Americans, with a minimum of government regulation.

(5) Increasingly Americans are relying on interactive media for a variety of political, educational, cultural, and entertainment services.

(b) POLICY. It is the policy of the United States:

(1) to promote the continued development of the Internet and other interactive computer services and other interactive media;

(2) to preserve the vibrant and competitive free market that presently exists for the Internet and other interactive computer services, unfettered by Federal or State regulation;

(3) to encourage the development of technologies which maximize user control over what information is received by individuals, families, and schools who use the Internet and other interactive computer services;

(4) to remove disincentives for the development and utilization of blocking and filtering technologies that empower parents to restrict their children's access to objectionable or inappropriate online material; and

(5) to ensure vigorous enforcement of Federal criminal laws to deter and punish trafficking in obscenity, stalking, and harassment by means of computer.

(c) PROTECTION FOR "GOOD SAMARITAN" BLOCKING AND SCREENING OF OFFENSIVE MATERIAL.

(1)   TREATMENT OF PUBLISHER OR SPEAKER. No provider or user of an interactive computer service shall be treated as the publisher or speaker of any information provided by another information content provider.

(2)   CIVIL LIABILITY. No provider or user of an interactive computer service shall be held liable on account of—

(A)   any action voluntarily taken in good faith to restrict access to or availability of material that the provider or user considers to be obscene, lewd, lascivious, filthy, excessively violent, harassing, or otherwise objectionable, whether or not such material is constitutionally protected; or

(B)   any action taken to enable or make available to information content providers or others the technical means to restrict access to material described in paragraph (1).

PART II—DEVELOPMENT OF COMPETITIVE MARKETS

SEC. 251. [47 U.S.C. 251] INTERCONNECTION.

(a) GENERAL DUTY OF TELECOMMUNICATIONS CARRIERS. Each telecommunications carrier has the duty—

(1)   to interconnect directly or indirectly with the facilities and equipment of other telecommunications carriers; and

(2)   not to install network features, functions, or capabilities that do not comply with the guidelines and standards established pursuant to section 255 or 256.

(b) OBLIGATIONS OF ALL LOCAL EXCHANGE CARRIERS. Each local exchange carrier has the following duties:

(1)   RESALE. The duty not to prohibit, and not to impose unreasonable or discriminatory conditions or limitations on, the resale of its telecommunications services.

(2)   NUMBER PORTABILITY. The duty to provide, to the extent technically feasible, number portability in accordance with requirements prescribed by the Commission.

(3)   DIALING PARITY. The duty to provide dialing parity to competing providers of telephone exchange service and telephone toll service, and the duty to permit all such providers to have nondiscriminatory access to telephone numbers, operator services, directory assistance, and directory listing, with no unreasonable dialing delays.

(4)   ACCESS TO RIGHTS-OF-WAY. The duty to afford access to the poles, ducts, conduits, and rights-of-way of such carrier to competing providers of telecommunications services on rates, terms, and conditions that are consistent with section 224.

(5)   RECIPROCAL COMPENSATION. The duty to establish reciprocal compensation arrangements for the transport and termination of telecommunications.

(c) ADDITIONAL OBLIGATIONS OF INCUMBENT LOCAL EXCHANGE CARRIERS. In addition to the duties contained in subsection (b), each incumbent local exchange carrier has the following duties:

(1)   DUTY TO NEGOTIATE. The duty to negotiate in good faith in accordance with section 252 the particular terms and conditions of agreements to fulfill the duties described paragraphs (1) through (5) of subsection (b) and this subsection. The requesting telecommunications carrier also has the duty to negotiate in good faith the terms and conditions of such agreements.

(2)   INTERCONNECTION. The duty to provide, for the facilities and equipment of any requesting telecommunications carrier, interconnection with the local exchange carrier's network—

(A)   for the transmission and routing of telephone exchange service and exchange access;

(B)   at any technically feasible point within the carrier's network;

(C)   that is at least equal in quality to that provided by the local exchange carrier to itself or to any subsidiary, affiliate, or any other party to which the carrier provides interconnection; and

(D)   on rates, terms, and conditions that are just, reasonable, and nondiscriminatory.

(3)   UNBUNDLED ACCESS. The duty to provide, to any requesting telecommunications carrier for the provision of a telecommunications service, nondiscriminatory access to network elements on an unbundled basis at any technically feasible point on rates, terms, and conditions that are just, reasonable, and nondiscriminatory. An incumbent local exchange carrier shall provide such unbundled network elements in a manner that allows requesting carriers to combine such elements in order to provide such telecommunications service.

(4)   RESALE. The duty—

(A)   to offer for resale at wholesale rates any telecommunications service that the carrier provides at retail to subscribers who are not telecommunications carriers; and

(B)   not to prohibit, and not to impose unreasonable or discriminatory conditions or limitations on, the resale of such telecommunications service, except that a State commission may, consistent with regulations prescribed by the Commission under this section, prohibit a reseller that obtains at wholesale rates a telecommunications service that is available at retail only to a category of subscribers from offering such service to a different category of subscribers.

(5)   NOTICE OF CHANGES. The duty to provide reasonable public notice of changes in the information necessary for the transmission and routing of services using that local exchange carrier's facilities or networks, as well as of any other changes that would affect the interoperability of those facilities and networks.

(6)   COLLOCATION. The duty to provide, on rates, terms, and conditions that are just, reasonable, and nondiscriminatory, for physical collocation of equipment necessary for interconnection or access to unbundled network elements at the premises of the local exchange carrier, except that the carrier may provide for virtual collocation if the local exchange carrier demonstrates to the State commission that physical collocation is not practical for technical reasons or because of space limitations.

(e) NUMBERING ADMINISTRATION-

(1)   COMMISSION AUTHORITY AND JURISDICTION. The Commission shall create or designate one or more impartial entities to administer telecommunications numbering and to make such numbers available on an equitable basis.

* * *

(g) CONTINUED ENFORCEMENT OF EXCHANGE ACCESS AND INTERCONNECTION REQUIREMENTS. On and after the date of enactment of the Telecommunications Act of 1996, each local exchange carrier, to the extent that it provides wireline services, shall provide exchange access, information access, and exchange services for such access to interexchange carriers and information service providers in accordance with the same equal access and nondiscriminatory interconnection restrictions and obligations (including receipt of compensation) that apply to such carrier on the date immediately preceding the date of enactment of the Telecommunications Act of 1996 under any court order, consent decree, or regulation, order, or policy of the Commission, until such restrictions and obligations are explicitly superseded by regulations prescribed by the Commission after such date of enactment.

(h) DEFINITION OF INCUMBENT LOCAL EXCHANGE CARRIER.

(1)   DEFINITION. For purposes of this section, the term "incumbent local exchange carrier" means, with respect to an area, the local exchange carrier that—

(A)   on the date of enactment of the Telecommunications Act of 1996, provided telephone exchange service in such area.

SEC. 252. [47 U.S.C. 252] PROCEDURES FOR NEGOTIATION, ARBITRATION, AND APPROVAL OF AGREEMENTS.

(a) AGREEMENTS ARRIVED AT THROUGH NEGOTIATION.

(1)   VOLUNTARY NEGOTIATIONS. Upon receiving a request for interconnection, services, or network elements pursuant to section 251, an incumbent local exchange carrier may negotiate and enter into a binding agreement with the requesting telecommunications carrier or carriers without regard to the standards set forth in subsections (b) and (c) of section 251. The agreement shall include a detailed schedule of itemized charges for interconnection and each service or network element included in the agreement. The agreement... shall be submitted to the State commission under subsection (e) of this section.

(2)   MEDIATION. Any party negotiating an agreement under this section may, at any point in the negotiation, ask a State commission to participate in the negotiation and to mediate any differences arising in the course of the negotiation.

(b) AGREEMENTS ARRIVED AT THROUGH COMPULSORY ARBITRATION.

(1)   ARBITRATION. During the period from the 135th to the 160th day (inclusive) after the date on which an incumbent local exchange carrier receives a request for negotiation under this section, the

carrier or any other party to the negotiation may petition a State commission to arbitrate any open issues.

* * *

(4)   ACTION BY STATE COMMISSION.

(C)   The State commission shall resolve each issue set forth in the petition and the response, if any, by imposing appropriate conditions as required to implement subsection (c) upon the parties to the agreement, and shall conclude the resolution of any unresolved issues not later than 9 months after the date on which the local exchange carrier received the request under this section.

(c) STANDARDS FOR ARBITRATION. In resolving by arbitration under subsection (b) any open issues and imposing conditions upon the parties to the agreement, a State commission shall—

(1)   ensure that such resolution and conditions meet the requirements of section 251, including the regulations prescribed by the Commission pursuant to section 251;

(2)   establish any rates for interconnection, services, or network elements according to subsection (d); and

(3)   provide a schedule for implementation of the terms and conditions by the parties to the agreement.

(d) PRICING STANDARDS.

(1)   INTERCONNECTION AND NETWORK ELEMENT CHARGES. Determinations by a State commission of the just and reasonable rate for the interconnection of facilities and equipment for purposes of subsection (c)(2) of section 251, and the just and reasonable rate for network elements for purposes of subsection (c)(3) of such section—

(A)   shall be—

(i)   based on the cost (determined without reference to a rate-of-return or other rate-based proceeding) of providing the interconnection or network element (whichever is applicable), and

(ii)   nondiscriminatory, and

(B)   may include a reasonable profit.

(3)   WHOLESALE PRICES FOR TELECOMMUNICATIONS SERVICES. For the purposes of section 251(c)(4), a State commission shall determine wholesale rates on the basis of retail rates charged to subscribers for the telecommunications service requested, excluding the portion thereof attributable to any marketing, billing, collection, and other costs that will be avoided by the local exchange carrier.

(e) APPROVAL BY STATE COMMISSION.

(1)   APPROVAL REQUIRED. Any interconnection agreement adopted by negotiation or arbitration shall be submitted for approval to the State commission. A State commission to which an agreement is submitted shall approve or reject the agreement, with written findings as to any deficiencies.

(2)   GROUNDS FOR REJECTION. The State commission may only reject —

(A)   an agreement (or any portion thereof) adopted by negotiation under subsection (a) if it finds that —

(i)   the agreement (or portion thereof) discriminates against a telecommunications carrier not a party to the agreement; or

(ii)   the implementation of such agreement or portion is not consistent with the public interest, convenience, and necessity; or

(B)   an agreement (or any portion thereof) adopted by arbitration under subsection (b) if it finds that the agreement does not meet the requirements of section 251, including the regulations prescribed by the Commission pursuant to section 251, or the standards set forth in subsection (d) of this section.

* * *

(5)   COMMISSION TO ACT IF STATE WILL NOT ACT. If a State commission fails to act to carry out its responsibility under this section in any proceeding or other matter under this section, then the Commission shall issue an order preempting the State commission's jurisdiction of that proceeding or matter within 90 days after being notified (or taking notice) of such failure, and shall assume the responsibility of the State commission under this section with respect to the proceeding or matter and act for the State commission.

(f) STATEMENTS OF GENERALLY AVAILABLE TERMS.

(1)   IN GENERAL. A Bell operating company may prepare and file with a State commission a statement of the terms and conditions that such company generally offers within that State to comply with the requirements of section 251 and the regulations thereunder and the standards applicable under this section.

(2)   STATE COMMISSION REVIEW. A State commission may not approve such statement unless such statement complies with subsection (d) of this section and section 251 and the regulations thereunder. Except as provided in section 253, nothing in this section shall prohibit a State commission from establishing or enforcing other requirements of State law in its review of such statement, including requiring compliance with intrastate telecommunications service quality standards or requirements.

* * *

(h) FILING REQUIRED. A State commission shall make a copy of each agreement approved under subsection (e) and each statement approved under subsection (f) available for public inspection and copying within 10 days after the agreement or statement is approved.

(i) AVAILABILITY TO OTHER TELECOMMUNICATIONS CARRIERS. A local exchange carrier shall make available any interconnection, service, or network element provided under an agreement approved under this section to which it is a party to any other requesting telecommunications carrier upon the same terms and conditions as those provided in the agreement.

(j) DEFINITION OF INCUMBENT LOCAL EXCHANGE CARRIER. For purposes of this section, the term "incumbent local exchange carrier" has the meaning provided in section 251(h).

SEC. 253. [47 U.S.C. 253] REMOVAL OF BARRIERS TO ENTRY.

(a) IN GENERAL. No State or local statute or regulation, or other State or local legal requirement, may prohibit or have the effect of prohibiting the ability of any entity to provide any interstate or intrastate telecommunications service.

(b) STATE REGULATORY AUTHORITY. Nothing in this section shall affect the ability of a State to impose, on a competitively neutral basis and consistent with section 254, requirements necessary to preserve and advance universal service, protect the public safety and welfare, ensure the continued quality of telecommunications services, and safeguard the rights of consumers.

(c) STATE AND LOCAL GOVERNMENT AUTHORITY. Nothing in this section affects the authority of a State or local government to manage the public rights-of-way or to require fair and reasonable compensation from telecommunications providers, on a competitively neutral and nondiscriminatory basis, for use of public rights-of-way on a nondiscriminatory basis.

(d) PREEMPTION. If, after notice and an opportunity for public comment, the Commission determines that a State or local government has permitted or imposed any statute, regulation, or legal requirement that violates subsection (a) or (b), the Commission shall preempt the enforcement of such statute, regulation, or legal requirement to the extent necessary to correct such violation or inconsistency.

SEC. 254. [47 U.S.C. 254] UNIVERSAL SERVICE.

(a) PROCEDURES TO REVIEW UNIVERSAL SERVICE REQUIRE-MENTS.

(1) FEDERAL-STATE JOINT BOARD ON UNIVERSAL SERVICE. Within one month after the date of enactment of the Telecommunications Act of 1996, the Commission shall institute and refer to a Federal-State Joint Board under section 410(c) a proceeding to recommend changes to any of its regulations in order to implement sections 214(e) and this section, including the definition of the services that are supported by Federal universal service support mechanisms and a specific timetable for completion of such recommendations.

(2) COMMISSION ACTION. The Commission shall initiate a single proceeding to implement the recommendations from the Joint Board required by paragraph (1). The rules established by such proceeding shall include a definition of the services that are supported by Federal universal service support mechanisms and a specific timetable for implementation.

(b) UNIVERSAL SERVICE PRINCIPLES. The Joint Board and the Commission shall base policies for the preservation and advancement of universal service on the following principles:

(1)   QUALITY AND RATES. Quality services should be available at just, reasonable, and affordable rates.

(2)   ACCESS TO ADVANCED SERVICES. Access to advanced telecommunications and information services should be provided in all regions of the Nation.

(3)   ACCESS IN RURAL AND HIGH COST AREAS. Consumers in all regions of the Nation, including low-income consumers and those in rural, insular, and high cost areas, should have access to telecommunications and information services, including interexchange services and advanced telecommunications and information services, that are reasonably comparable to those services provided in urban areas and that are available at rates that are reasonably comparable to rates charged for similar services in urban areas.

(4)   EQUITABLE AND NONDISCRIMINATORY CONTRIBUTIONS. All providers of telecommunications services should make an equitable and nondiscriminatory contribution to the preservation and advancement of universal service.

(5)   SPECIFIC AND PREDICTABLE SUPPORT MECHANISMS. There should be specific, predictable and sufficient Federal and State mechanisms to preserve and advance universal service.

(6)   ACCESS TO ADVANCED TELECOMMUNICATIONS SERVICES FOR SCHOOLS, HEALTH CARE, AND LIBRARIES. Elementary and secondary schools and classrooms, health care providers, and libraries should have access to advanced telecommunications services as described in subsection (h).

(7)   ADDITIONAL PRINCIPLES. Such other principles as the Joint Board and the Commission determine are necessary and appropriate for the protection of the public interest, convenience, and necessity and are consistent with this Act.

(c) DEFINITION.

(1)   IN GENERAL. Universal service is an evolving level of telecommunications services that the Commission shall establish periodically under this section, taking into account advances in telecommunications and information technologies and services. The Joint Board in recommending, and the Commission in establishing, the definition of the services that are supported by Federal universal service support mechanisms shall consider the extent to which such telecommunications services—

(A)   are essential to education, public health, or public safety;

(B)   have, through the operation of market choices by customers, been subscribed to by a substantial majority of residential customers;

(C)   are being deployed in public telecommunications networks by telecommunications carriers; and

(D)   are consistent with the public interest, convenience, and necessity.

* * *

(3)   SPECIAL SERVICES. In addition to the services included in the definition of universal service under paragraph (1), the Commission may designate additional services for such support mechanisms for schools, libraries, and health care providers for the purposes of subsection (h).

(d)   TELECOMMUNICATIONS CARRIER CONTRIBUTION. Every telecommunications carrier that provides interstate telecommunications services shall contribute, on an equitable and nondiscriminatory basis, to the specific, predictable, and sufficient mechanisms established by the Commission to preserve and advance universal service. The Commission may exempt a carrier or class of carriers from this requirement if the carrier's telecommunications activities are limited to such an extent that the level of such carrier's contribution to the preservation and advancement of universal service would be de minimis. Any other provider of interstate telecommunications may be required to contribute to the preservation and advancement of universal service if the public interest so requires.

(e) UNIVERSAL SERVICE SUPPORT. After the date on which Commission regulations implementing this section take effect, only an eligible telecommunications carrier designated under section 214(e) shall be eligible to receive specific Federal universal service support. A carrier that receives such support shall use that support only for the provision, maintenance, and upgrading of facilities and services for which the support is intended.

(f) STATE AUTHORITY. A State may adopt regulations not inconsistent with the Commission's rules to preserve and advance universal service. Every telecommunications carrier that provides intrastate telecommunications services shall contribute, on an equitable and nondiscriminatory basis, in a manner determined by the State to the preservation and advancement of universal service in that State.

(g) INTEREXCHANGE AND INTERSTATE SERVICES. [T]he Commission shall adopt rules to require that the communications services to subscribers in rural and high cost areas shall be no higher than the rates charged by each such provider to its subscribers in urban areas. Such rules shall also require that a provider of interstate interexchange telecommunications services shall provide such services to its subscribers in each State at rates no higher than the rates charged to its subscribers in any other State.

(h) TELECOMMUNICATIONS SERVICES FOR CERTAIN PROVIDERS.

(1)   IN GENERAL.

(B)   EDUCATIONAL PROVIDERS AND LIBRARIES. All telecommunications carriers serving a geographic area shall, upon a bona fide request for any of its services that are within the definition of universal service under subsection (c)(3), provide such services to elementary schools, secondary schools, and libraries for educational purposes at rates less than the amounts charged for similar services to other parties. The discount shall be an amount that the Commission, with respect to interstate services, and the States, with respect to intrastate services, determine is appropriate and necessary to ensure affordable access to and use of such services by such entities.

(2) ADVANCED SERVICES. The Commission shall establish competitively neutral rules - -

(A) to enhance, to the extent technically feasible and economically reasonable, access to advanced telecommunications and information services for all public and nonprofit elementary and secondary school classrooms, health care providers, and libraries; and

(B) to define the circumstances under which a telecommunications carrier may be required to connect its network to such public institutional telecommunications users.

(3) TERMS AND CONDITIONS. Telecommunications services and network capacity provided to a public institutional telecommunications user under this subsection may not be sold, resold, or otherwise transferred by such user in consideration for money or any other thing of value.

(i) CONSUMER PROTECTION. The Commission and the States should ensure that universal service is available at rates that are just, reasonable, and affordable.

SEC. 255. [47 U.S.C. 255] ACCESS BY PERSONS WITH DISABILITIES.

(b) MANUFACTURING. A manufacturer of telecommunications equipment or customer premises equipment shall ensure that the equipment is designed, developed, and fabricated to be accessible to and usable by individuals with disabilities, if readily achievable.

(c) TELECOMMUNICATIONS SERVICES. A provider of telecommunications service shall ensure that the service is accessible to and usable by individuals with disabilities, if readily achievable.

(d) COMPATIBILITY. Whenever the requirements of subsections (b) and (c) are not readily achievable, such a manufacturer or provider shall ensure that the equipment or service is compatible with existing peripheral devices or specialized customer premises equipment commonly used by individuals with disabilities to achieve access, if readily achievable.

SEC. 257. [47 U.S.C. 257] MARKET ENTRY BARRIERS PROCEEDING.

(a) ELIMINATION OF BARRIERS. Within 15 months after the date of enactment of the Telecommunications Act of 1996, the Commission shall complete a proceeding for the purpose of identifying and eliminating, by regulations pursuant to its authority under this Act (other than this section), market entry barriers for entrepreneurs and other small businesses in the provision and ownership of telecommunications services and information services, or in the provision of parts or services to providers of telecommunications services and information services.

(b) NATIONAL POLICY. In carrying out subsection (a), the Commission shall seek to promote the policies and purposes of this Act favoring diversity of media voices, vigorous economic competition, technological advancement, and promotion of the public interest, convenience, and necessity.

(c) PERIODIC REVIEW. Every 3 years following the completion of the proceeding required by subsection (a), the Commission shall review and report to Congress on—

(1)   any regulations prescribed to eliminate barriers within its jurisdiction that are identified under subsection (a) and that can be prescribed consistent with the public interest, convenience, and necessity; and

(2)   the statutory barriers identified under subsection (a) that the Commission recommends be eliminated, consistent with the public interest, convenience, and necessity.

SEC. 259. [47 U.S.C. 259] INFRASTRUCTURE SHARING.

(a) REGULATIONS REQUIRED. The Commission shall prescribe regulations that require incumbent local exchange carriers (as defined in section 251(h)) to make available to any qualifying carrier such public switched network infrastructure, technology, information, and telecommunications facilities and functions as may be requested by such qualifying carrier for the purpose of enabling such qualifying carrier to provide telecommunications services, or to provide access to information services, in the service area in which such qualifying carrier has requested and obtained designation as an eligible telecommunications carrier.

(b) TERMS AND CONDITIONS OF REGULATIONS. The regulations prescribed by the Commission pursuant to this section shall—

(1)   not require a local exchange carrier to which this section applies to take any action that is economically unreasonable or that is contrary to the public interest;

(2)   permit, but shall not require, the joint ownership or operation of public switched network infrastructure and services by or among such local exchange carrier and a qualifying carrier;

(3)   ensure that such local exchange carrier will not be treated by the Commission or any State as a common carrier for hire or as offering common carrier services with respect to any infrastructure, technology, information, facilities, or functions made available to a qualifying carrier in accordance with regulations issued pursuant to this section;

(4)   ensure that such local exchange carrier makes such infrastructure, technology, information, facilities, or functions available to a qualifying carrier on just and reasonable terms and conditions that permit such qualifying carrier to fully benefit from the economies of scale and scope of such local exchange carrier, as determined in accordance with guidelines prescribed by the Commission in regulations issued pursuant to this section;

(5)   establish conditions that promote cooperation between local exchange carriers to which this section applies and qualifying carriers;

(6)   not require a local exchange carrier to which this section applies to engage in any infrastructure sharing agreement for any services or access which are to be provided or offered to consumers by the qualifying carrier in such local exchange carrier's telephone exchange area; and

(7)   require that such local exchange carrier file with the Commission or State for public inspection, any tariffs, contracts, or other arrangements showing the rates, terms, and conditions under which such carrier is making available public switched network infrastructure and functions under this section.

(c) INFORMATION CONCERNING DEPLOYMENT OF NEW SERVICES AND EQUIPMENT. A local exchange carrier to which this section applies that has entered into an infrastructure sharing agreement under this section shall provide to each party to such agreement timely information on the planned deployment of telecommunications services and equipment, including any software or upgrades of software integral to the use or operation of such telecommunications equipment.

(d) DEFINITION. For purposes of this section, the term "qualifying carrier" means a telecommunications carrier that—

(1)   lacks economies of scale or scope, as determined in accordance with regulations prescribed by the Commission pursuant to this section; and

(2)   offers telephone exchange service, exchange access, and any other service that is included in universal service, to all consumers without preference throughout the service area for which such carrier has been designated as an eligible telecommunications carrier.

PART III—SPECIAL PROVISIONS CONCERNING
BELL OPERATING COMPANIES

SEC. 271. [47 U.S.C. 271] BELL OPERATING COMPANY ENTRY INTO INTERLATA SERVICES.

(a) GENERAL LIMITATION. Neither a Bell operating company, nor any affiliate of a Bell operating company, may provide interLATA services except as provided in this section.

(b) INTERLATA SERVICES TO WHICH THIS SECTION APPLIES.

(1)   IN-REGION SERVICES. A Bell operating company, or any affiliate of that Bell operating company, may provide interLATA services originating in any of its in-region States (as defined in subsection (i)) if the Commission approves the application of such company for such State under subsection (d)(3).

(2)   OUT-OF-REGION SERVICES. A Bell operating company, or any affiliate of that Bell operating company, may provide interLATA services originating outside its in-region States after the date of enactment of the Telecommunications Act of 1996, subject to subsection (j).

(4)   TERMINATION. Nothing in this section prohibits a Bell operating company or any of its affiliates from providing termination for interLATA services, subject to subsection (j).

(c) REQUIREMENTS FOR PROVIDING CERTAIN IN-REGION INTERLATA SERVICES.

(1) AGREEMENT OR STATEMENT. A Bell operating company meets the requirements of this paragraph if it meets the requirements of subparagraph (A) or subparagraph (B) of this paragraph for each State for which the authorization is sought.

(A) PRESENCE OF A FACILITIES-BASED COMPETITOR. A Bell operating company meets the requirements of this subparagraph if it has entered into one or more binding agreements that have been approved under section 252 specifying the terms and conditions under which the Bell operating company is providing access and interconnection to its network facilities for the network facilities of one or more unaffiliated competing providers of telephone exchange service to residential and business subscribers.

(B) FAILURE TO REQUEST ACCESS. A Bell operating company meets the requirements of this subparagraph if, after 10 months after the date of enactment of the Telecommunications Act of 1996, no such provider has requested the access and interconnection described in subparagraph (A)...and a statement of the terms and conditions that the company generally offers to provide such access and interconnection has been approved or permitted to take effect by the State commission under section 252(f).

(2) SPECIFIC INTERCONNECTION REQUIREMENTS.

(A) AGREEMENT REQUIRED. A Bell operating company meets the requirements of this paragraph if, within the State for which the authorization is sought—

(i) (I) such company is providing access and interconnection pursuant to one or more agreements described in paragraph (1)(A), or (II) such company is generally offering access and interconnection pursuant to a statement described in paragraph (1)(B), and

(ii) such access and interconnection meets the requirements of subparagraph (B) of this paragraph.

(B) COMPETITIVE CHECKLIST. Access or interconnection provided or generally offered by a Bell operating company to other telecommunications carriers meets the requirements of this subparagraph if such access and interconnection includes each of the following:

(i) Interconnection in accordance with the requirements of sections 251(c)(2) and 252(d)(1).

(ii) Nondiscriminatory access to network elements in accordance with the requirements of sections 251(c)(3) and 252(d)(1).

(iii) Nondiscriminatory access to the poles, ducts, conduits, and rights-of-way owned or controlled by the Bell operating company at just and reasonable rates in accordance with the requirements of section 224.

(iv) Local loop transmission from the central office to the customer's premises, unbundled from local switching or other services.

(v) Local transport from the trunk side of a wireline local exchange carrier switch unbundled from switching or other services.

(vi) Local switching unbundled from transport, local loop transmission, or other services.

(vii) Nondiscriminatory access to—

(I) 911 and E911 services;

(II) directory assistance services to allow the other carrier's customers to obtain telephone numbers; and

(III) operator call completion services.

(viii)White pages directory listings for customers of the other carrier's telephone exchange service.

(ix) Until the date by which telecommunications numbering administration guidelines, plan, or rules are established, nondiscriminatory access to telephone numbers for assignment to the other carrier's telephone exchange service customers. After that date, compliance with such guidelines, plan, or rules.

(x) Nondiscriminatory access to databases and associated signaling necessary for call routing and completion.

(xi) Until the date by which the Commission issues regulations pursuant to section 251 to require number portability, interim telecommunications number portability through remote call forwarding, direct inward dialing trunks, or other comparable arrangements, with as little impairment of functioning, quality, reliability, and convenience as possible. After that date, full compliance with such regulations.

(xii) Nondiscriminatory access to such services or information as are necessary to allow the requesting carrier to implement local dialing parity in accordance with the requirements of section 251(b)(3).

(xiii) Reciprocal compensation arrangements in accordance with the requirements of section 252(d)(2).

(xiv) Telecommunications services are available for resale in accordance with the requirements of sections 251(c)(4) and 252(d)(3).

(d) ADMINISTRATIVE PROVISIONS.

(1)   APPLICATION TO COMMISSION. On and after the date of enactment of the Telecommunications Act of 1996, a Bell operating company or its affiliate may apply to the Commission for authorization to provide interLATA services originating in any in-region State. The application shall identify each State for which the authorization is sought.

(2)   CONSULTATION.

(A)   CONSULTATION WITH THE ATTORNEY GENERAL. Before making any determination under this subsection, the Commission shall consult with the Attorney General. [T]he Attorney General shall provide to the Commission an evaluation of the application using any standard the Attorney General considers appropriate. The Commission shall give substantial weight to the Attorney General's evaluation, but such evaluation shall not have any preclusive effect on any Commission decision under paragraph (3).

(B)   CONSULTATION WITH STATE COMMISSIONS. Before making any determination under this subsection, the Commission shall consult with the State commission of any State that is the subject of the application in order to verify the compliance of the Bell operating company with the requirements of subsection (c).

(3)   DETERMINATION. Not later than 90 days after receiving an application under paragraph (1), the Commission shall issue a written determination approving or denying the authorization requested in the application for each State. The Commission shall not approve the authorization requested in an application submitted under paragraph (1) unless it finds that—

(A)   the petitioning Bell operating company has met the requirements of subsection (c)(1) and—

(i)   with respect to access and interconnection provided pursuant to subsection (c)(1)(A), has fully implemented the competitive checklist in subsection (c)(2)(B); or

(ii)   with respect to access and interconnection generally offered pursuant to a statement under subsection (c)(1)(B), such statement offers all of the items included in the competitive checklist in subsection (c)(2)(B);

(B)   the requested authorization will be carried out in accordance with the requirements of section 272; and

(C)   the requested authorization is consistent with the public interest, convenience, and necessity.

(4)   LIMITATION ON COMMISSION. The Commission may not, by rule or otherwise, limit or extend the terms used in the competitive checklist set forth in subsection (c)(2)(B).

SEC. 272. [47 U.S.C. 272] SEPARATE AFFILIATE; SAFEGUARDS.

(a) SEPARATE AFFILIATE REQUIRED FOR COMPETITIVE ACTIVITIES.

(1)   IN GENERAL. A Bell operating company (including any affiliate) which is a local exchange carrier that is subject to the requirements of section 251(c) may not provide any service described in paragraph (2) unless it provides that service through one or more affiliates that—

(A) are separate from any operating company entity that is subject to the requirements of section 251(c); and

(B) meet the requirements of subsection (b).

(2)   SERVICES FOR WHICH A SEPARATE AFFILIATE IS REQUIRED. The services for which a separate affiliate is required by paragraph (1) are:

(A)   Manufacturing activities (as defined in section 273(h)).

(B)   Origination of interLATA telecommunications services, other than—

(ii)   out-of-region services described in section 271(b)(2); or

(C) InterLATA information services, other than electronic publishing (as defined in section 274(h)) and alarm monitoring services (as defined in section 275(e)).

(b) STRUCTURAL AND TRANSACTIONAL REQUIREMENTS. The separate affiliate required by this section—

(1) shall operate independently from the Bell operating company;

(2) shall maintain books, records, and accounts in the manner prescribed by the Commission which shall be separate from the books, records, and accounts maintained by the Bell operating company of which it is an affiliate;

(3) shall have separate officers, directors, and employees from the Bell operating company of which it is an affiliate;

(4) may not obtain credit under any arrangement that would permit a creditor, upon default, to have recourse to the assets of the Bell operating company; and

(5) shall conduct all transactions with the Bell operating company of which it is an affiliate on an arm's length basis with any such transactions reduced to writing and available for public inspection.

(c) NONDISCRIMINATION SAFEGUARDS. In its dealings with its affiliate described in subsection (a), a Bell operating company—

(1) may not discriminate between that company or affiliate and any other entity in the provision or procurement of goods, services, facilities, and information, or in the establishment of standards; and

(2) shall account for all transactions with an affiliate described in subsection (a) in accordance with accounting principles designated or approved by the Commission.

(d) BIENNIAL AUDIT.

(1) GENERAL REQUIREMENT. A company required to operate a separate affiliate under this section shall obtain and pay for a joint Federal/State audit every 2 years conducted by an independent auditor to determine whether such company has complied with this section and the regulations promulgated under this section.

(e) FULFILLMENT OF CERTAIN REQUESTS. A Bell operating company and an affiliate that is subject to the requirements of section 251(c)—

(1) shall fulfill any requests from an unaffiliated entity for telephone exchange service and exchange access within a period no longer than the period in which it provides such telephone exchange service and exchange access to itself or to its affiliates;

(2) shall not provide any facilities, services, or information concerning its provision of exchange access to the affiliate described in subsection (a) unless such facilities, services, or information are made available to other providers of interLATA services in that market on the same terms and conditions;

(3)   shall charge the affiliate described in subsection (a), or impute to itself (if using the access for its provision of its own services), an amount for access to its telephone exchange service and exchange access that is no less than the amount charged to any unaffiliated interexchange carriers for such service; and

(4)   may provide any interLATA or intraLATA facilities or services to its interLATA affiliate if such services or facilities are made available to all carriers at the same rates and on the same terms and conditions, and so long as the costs are appropriately allocated.

(f) SUNSET.

(1)   MANUFACTURING AND LONG DISTANCE. The provisions of this section (other than subsection (e)) shall cease to apply with respect to the manufacturing activities or the interLATA telecommunications services of a Bell operating company 3 years after the date such Bell operating company or any Bell operating company affiliate is authorized to provide interLATA telecommunications services under section 271(d), unless the Commission extends such 3-year period by rule or order.

(2)   INTERLATA INFORMATION SERVICES. The provisions of this section (other than subsection (e)) shall cease to apply with respect to the interLATA information services of a Bell operating company 4 years after the date of enactment of the Telecommunications Act of 1996, unless the Commission extends such 4-year period by rule or order.

SEC. 273. [47 U.S.C. 273] MANUFACTURING BY BELL OPERATING COMPANIES.

(a) AUTHORIZATION. A Bell operating company may manufacture and provide telecommunications equipment, and manufacture customer premises equipment, if the Commission authorizes that Bell operating company or any Bell operating company affiliate to provide interLATA services under section 271(d), subject to the requirements of this section and the regulations prescribed thereunder.

(c) INFORMATION REQUIREMENTS.

(1)   INFORMATION ON PROTOCOLS AND TECHNICAL REQUIREMENTS. Each Bell operating company shall, in accordance with regulations prescribed by the Commission, maintain and file with the Commission full and complete information with respect to the protocols and technical requirements for connection with and use of its telephone exchange service facilities.

(4)   PLANNING INFORMATION. Each Bell operating company shall provide, to interconnecting carriers providing telephone exchange service, timely information on the planned deployment of telecommunications equipment.

(d) MANUFACTURING LIMITATIONS FOR STANDARD-SETTING ORGANIZATIONS.

(3)   MANUFACTURING SAFEGUARDS.

(A) [A]ny entity which certifies telecommunications equipment or customer premises equipment manufactured by an unaffiliated entity shall only manufacture a particular class of telecommunications equipment or customer premises equipment for which it is undertaking or has undertaken, during the previous 18 months, certification activity for such class of equipment through a separate affiliate.

(C)   Such entity that certifies such equipment shall—

(i)   not discriminate in favor of its manufacturing affiliate in the establishment of standards, generic requirements, or product certification;

(ii)   not disclose to the manufacturing affiliate any proprietary information that has been received at any time from an unaffiliated manufacturer, unless authorized in writing by the owner of the information; and

(iii)   not permit any employee engaged in product certification for telecommunications equipment or customer premises equipment to engage jointly in sales or marketing of any such equipment with the affiliated manufacturer.

(6)   SUNSET. The requirements of paragraphs (3) and (4) shall terminate for the particular relevant activity when the Commission determines that there are alternative sources of industry-wide standards, industry-wide generic requirements, or product certification for a particular class of telecommunications equipment or customer premises equipment available in the United States. Alternative sources shall be deemed to exist when such sources provide commercially viable alternatives that are providing such services to customers.

(8) DEFINITIONS. For purposes of this subsection:

(B)   The term "generic requirement" means a description of acceptable product attributes for use by local exchange carriers in establishing product specifications for the purchase of telecommunications equipment, customer premises equipment, and software integral thereto.

(C)   The term "industry-wide" means activities funded by or performed on behalf of local exchange carriers for use in providing wireline telephone exchange service whose combined total of deployed access lines in the United States constitutes at least 30 percent of all access lines deployed by telecommunications carriers in the United States as of the date of enactment of the Telecommunications Act of 1996.

(D)   The term "certification" means any technical process whereby a party determines whether a product, for use by more than one local exchange carrier, conforms with the specified requirements pertaining to such product.

(E)   The term "accredited standards development organization" means an entity composed of industry members which has been accredited by an institution vested with the responsibility for standards accreditation by the industry.

(e) BELL OPERATING COMPANY EQUIPMENT PROCUREMENT AND SALES.

(1) NONDISCRIMINATION STANDARDS FOR MANU-FACTURING. In the procurement or awarding of supply contracts for telecommunications equipment, a Bell operating company, or any entity acting on its behalf, for the duration of the requirement for a separate subsidiary including manufacturing under this Act—

(A) shall consider such equipment, produced or supplied by unrelated persons; and

(B) may not discriminate in favor of equipment produced or supplied by an affiliate or related person.

(2) PROCUREMENT STANDARDS. Each Bell operating company or any entity acting on its behalf shall make procurement decisions and award all supply contracts for equipment, services, and software on the basis of an objective assessment of price, quality, delivery, and other commercial factors.

(3) NETWORK PLANNING AND DESIGN. A Bell operating company shall, to the extent consistent with the antitrust laws, engage in joint network planning and design with local exchange carriers operating in the same area of interest.

(4) SALES RESTRICTIONS. Neither a Bell operating company engaged in manufacturing nor a manufacturing affiliate of such a company shall restrict sales to any local exchange carrier of telecommunications equipment, including software integral to the operation of such equipment and related upgrades.

SEC. 274 [47 U.S.C. 274] ELECTRONIC PUBLISHING BY BELL OPERATING COMPANIES.

(a) LIMITATIONS. No Bell operating company or any affiliate may engage in the provision of electronic publishing that is disseminated by means of such Bell operating company's or any of its affiliates' basic telephone service, except that nothing in this section shall prohibit a separated affiliate or electronic publishing joint venture operated in accordance with this section from engaging in the provision of electronic publishing.

(b) SEPARATED AFFILIATE OR ELECTRONIC PUBLISHING JOINT VENTURE REQUIREMENTS. A separated affiliate or electronic publishing joint venture shall be operated independently from the Bell operating company. Such separated affiliate or joint venture and the Bell operating company with which it is affiliated shall—

(1) maintain separate books, records, and accounts and prepare separate financial statements;

(3) carry out transactions

(A) in a manner consistent with such independence,

(B) pursuant to written contracts or tariffs that are filed with the Commission and made publicly available, and

(C)   in a manner that is auditable in accordance with generally accepted auditing standards;

(6)   not use for the marketing of any product or service of the separated affiliate or joint venture, the name, trademarks, or service marks of an existing Bell operating company except for names, trademarks, or service marks that are owned by the entity that owns or controls the Bell operating company;

(c) JOINT MARKETING.

(1)   IN GENERAL. Except as provided in paragraph (2)—

(A)   a Bell operating company shall not carry out any promotion, marketing, sales, or advertising for or in conjunction with a separated affiliate; and

(B)   a Bell operating company shall not carry out any promotion, marketing, sales, or advertising for or in conjunction with an affiliate that is related to the provision of electronic publishing.

(2) PERMISSIBLE JOINT ACTIVITIES.

(A)   JOINT TELEMARKETING. A Bell operating company may provide inbound telemarketing or referral services related to the provision of electronic publishing for a separated affiliate, electronic publishing joint venture, affiliate, or unaffiliated electronic publisher: *Provided*, That if such services are provided to a separated affiliate, electronic publishing joint venture, or affiliate, such services shall be made available to all electronic publishers on request, on nondiscriminatory terms.

(B)   TEAMING ARRANGEMENTS. A Bell operating company may engage in nondiscriminatory teaming or business arrangements to engage in electronic publishing with any separated affiliate or with any other electronic publisher if

(i)   the Bell operating company only provides facilities, services, and basic telephone service information as authorized by this section, and

(ii)   the Bell operating company does not own such teaming or business arrangement.

(C)   ELECTRONIC PUBLISHING JOINT VENTURES. A Bell operating company or affiliate may participate on a nonexclusive basis in electronic publishing joint ventures with entities that are not a Bell operating company, affiliate, or separated affiliate to provide electronic publishing services, if the Bell operating company or affiliate has not more than a 50 percent direct or indirect equity interest (or the equivalent thereof) or the right to more than 50 percent of the gross revenues under a revenue sharing or royalty agreement in any electronic publishing joint venture.

(d) BELL OPERATING COMPANY REQUIREMENT. A Bell operating company under common ownership or control with a separated affiliate or electronic publishing joint venture shall provide network access and interconnections for basic telephone service to electronic publishers at just and reasonable rates that are tariffed (so long as rates for such services are subject to regulation) and that are not higher on a per-unit basis than those charged for such services to any other electronic publisher or any separated affiliate engaged in electronic publishing.

* * *

(g) EFFECTIVE DATES.

(1)   TRANSITION. Any electronic publishing service being offered to the public by a Bell operating company or affiliate on the date of enactment of the Telecommunications Act of 1996 shall have one year from such date of enactment to comply with the requirements of this section.

(2)   SUNSET. The provisions of this section shall not apply to conduct occurring after 4 years after the date of enactment of the Telecommunications Act of 1996.

(h) DEFINITION OF ELECTRONIC PUBLISHING.

(1)   IN GENERAL. The term "electronic publishing" means the dissemination, provision, publication, or sale to an unaffiliated entity or person, of any one or more of the following: news (including sports); entertainment (other than interactive games); business, financial, legal, consumer, or credit materials; editorials, columns, or features; advertising; photos or images; archival or research material; legal notices or public records; scientific, educational, instructional, technical, professional, trade, or other literary materials; or other like or similar information.

(2)   EXCEPTIONS. The term "electronic publishing" shall not include the following services:

(A)   Information access, as that term is defined by the AT&T Consent Decree.

(B)   The transmission of information as a common carrier.

(C)   The transmission of information as part of a gateway to an information service that does not involve the generation or alteration of the content of information, including data transmission, address translation, protocol conversion, billing management, introductory information content, and navigational systems that enable users to access electronic publishing services, which do not affect the presentation of such electronic publishing services to users.

(D)   Voice storage and retrieval services, including voice messaging and electronic mail services.

(E)   Data processing or transaction processing services that do not involve the generation or alteration of the content of information.

* * *

(I)   The provision of directory assistance that provides names, addresses, and telephone numbers and does not include advertising.

(J)   Caller identification services.

* * *

(M)   Any other network service of a type that is like or similar to these network services and that does not involve the generation or alteration of the content of information.

(O)   Video programming or full motion video entertainment on demand.

SEC. 275 [47 U.S.C. 275] ALARM MONITORING SERVICES.

(a) DELAYED ENTRY INTO ALARM MONITORING.

(1)   PROHIBITION. No Bell operating company or affiliate thereof shall engage in the provision of alarm monitoring services before the date which is 5 years after the date of enactment of the Telecommunications Act of 1996.

(b) NONDISCRIMINATION. An incumbent local exchange carrier (as defined in section 251(h)) engaged in the provision of alarm monitoring services shall—

(1)   provide nonaffiliated entities, upon reasonable request, with the network services it provides to its own alarm monitoring operations, on nondiscriminatory terms and conditions; and

(2)   not subsidize its alarm monitoring services either directly or indirectly from telephone exchange service operations.

TITLE III—PROVISIONS RELATING TO RADIO

PART I—GENERAL PROVISIONS

SEC. 301. [47 U.S.C. 301] LICENSE FOR RADIO COMMUNICATION OR TRANSMISSION OF ENERGY.

It is the purpose of this Act, among other things, to maintain the control of the United States over all the channels of radio transmission; and to provide for the use of such channels, but not the ownership thereof, by persons for limited periods of time, under licenses granted by Federal authority, and no such license shall be construed to create any right, beyond the terms, conditions, and periods of the license. No person shall use or operate any apparatus for the transmission of energy or communications or signals by radio...except under and in accordance with this Act and with a license in that behalf granted under the provisions of this Act.

SEC. 303 [47 U.S.C. 303] GENERAL POWERS OF COMMISSION.

Except as otherwise provided in this Act, the Commission from time to time, as public convenience, interest, or necessity requires, shall—

(a) Classify radio stations;

(b) Prescribe the nature of the service to be rendered by each class of licensed stations and each station within any class;

(c) Assign bands of frequencies to the various classes of stations, and assign frequencies for each individual station and determine the power which each station shall use and the time during which it may operate;

* * *

(f) Make such regulations not inconsistent with law as it may deem necessary to prevent interference between stations and to carry out the provisions of this Act....

(g) Study new uses for radio, provide for experimental uses of frequencies, and generally encourage the larger and more effective use of radio in the public interest;

* * *

(i) Have authority to make special regulations applicable to radio stations engaged in chain broadcasting;

* * *

(r) Make such rules and regulations and prescribe such restrictions and conditions, not inconsistent with law, as may be necessary to carry out the provisions of this Act, or any international radio or wire communications treaty or convention....

(w) Prescribe—

(1)   on the basis of recommendations from an advisory committee established by the Commission in accordance with section 551(b)(2) of the Telecommunications Act of 1996, guidelines and recommended procedures for the identification and rating of video programming that contains sexual, violent, or other indecent material about which parents should be informed before it is displayed to children: *Provided,* That nothing in this paragraph shall be construed to authorize any rating of video programming on the basis of its political or religious content; and

(2)   with respect to any video programming that has been rated, and in consultation with the television industry, rules requiring distributors of such video programming to transmit such rating to permit parents to block the display of video programming that they have determined is inappropriate for their children.

(x) Require, in the case of an apparatus designed to receive television signals that are shipped in interstate commerce or manufactured in the United States and that have a picture screen 13 inches or greater in size (measured diagonally), that such apparatus be equipped with a feature designed to enable viewers to block display of all programs with a common rating, except as otherwise permitted by regulations pursuant to section 330(c)(4).

SEC. 304. [47 U.S.C. 304] WAIVER BY LICENSEE.

No station license shall be granted by the Commission until the applicant therefor shall have waived any claim to the use of any particular frequency or of the electromagnetic spectrum as against the regulatory power of the United States because of the previous use of the same, whether by license or otherwise.

SEC. 307 [47 U.S.C. 307] ALLOCATION OF FACILITIES; TERM OF LICENSES.

(a) The Commission, if public convenience, interest, or necessity will be served thereby, subject to the limitations of this Act, shall grant to any applicant therefor, a station license provided for by this Act.

(b) [T]he Commission shall make such distribution of licenses, frequencies, hours of operation, and of power among the several States and communities as to provide a fair, efficient, and equitable distribution of radio service to each of the same.

(c) TERMS OF LICENSES.

(1)   INITIAL AND RENEWAL LICENSES. Each license granted for the operation of a broadcasting station shall be for a term of not to exceed 8 years. Upon application therefor, a renewal of such license may be granted from time to time for a term of not to exceed 8 years from the date of expiration of the preceding license, if the Commission finds that public interest, convenience, and necessity would be served thereby.

SEC. 308. [47 U.S.C. 308] REQUIREMENTS FOR LICENSE.

(b) CONDITIONS

All applications for station licenses, or modifications or renewals thereof, shall set forth such facts as the Commission by regulation may prescribe as to the citizenship, character, and financial, technical, and other qualifications of the applicant to operate the station; the ownership and location of the proposed station and of the stations, if any, with which it is proposed to communicate; the frequencies and the power desired to be used; the hours of the day or other periods of time during which it is proposed to operate the station; the purposes for which the station is to be used; and such other information as it may require. The Commission, at any time after the filing of such original application and during the term of any such license, may require from an applicant or licensee further written statements of fact to enable it to determine whether such original application should be granted or denied or such license revoked. Such application and/or such statement of fact shall be signed by the applicant and/or licensee in any manner or form, including by electronic means, as the Commission may prescribe by regulation.

(d) SUMMARY OF COMPLAINTS [ON VIOLENT PROGRAMMING]

Each applicant for the renewal of a commercial or noncommercial television license shall attach as an exhibit to the application a summary of written comments and suggestions received from the public and maintained by the licensee (in accordance with Commission regulations) that comment on the applicant's programming, if any, and that are characterized by the commentor as constituting violent programming.

SEC. 309. [47 U.S.C. 309] APPLICATION FOR LICENSE.

(a) CONSIDERATIONS IN GRANTING APPLICATION

Subject to the provisions of this section, the Commission shall determine, in the case of each application filed with it to which section 308 of this title applies, whether the public interest, convenience, and necessity will be served by the granting of such application, and, if the Commission, upon examination of such application and upon consideration of such other matters as the Commission may officially notice, shall find that public interest, convenience, and necessity would be served by the granting thereof, it shall grant such application.

* * *

(d) (1) Any party in interest may file with the Commission a petition to deny any application....

* * *

(e) If, in the case of any application ... a substantial and material question of fact is presented ... [the Commission] shall formally designate the application for hearing.... Any hearing subsequently held upon such application shall be a full hearing in which the applicant and all other parties in interest shall be permitted to participate....

* * *

(i) (1) (A) [If] there is more than one application for any initial license or construction permit which will involve any use of the electromagnetic spectrum, then the Commission, after determining that each such application is acceptable for filing, shall have authority to grant such license or permit to a qualified applicant through the use of a system of random selection.

* * *

(3) (A) The Commission shall establish rules and procedures to ensure that, in the administration of any system of random selection under this subsection used for granting licenses or construction permits for any media of mass communications, significant preferences will be granted to applicants or groups of applicants, the grant to which of the license or permit would increase the diversification of ownership of the media of mass communications. To further diversify the ownership of the media of mass communications, an additional significant preference shall be granted to any applicant controlled by a member or members of a minority group.

* * *

(C) For purposes of this paragraph:

* * *

(ii) The term "minority group" includes Blacks, Hispanics, American Indians, Alaska Natives, Asians, and Pacific Islanders.

(k) BROADCAST STATION RENEWAL PROCEDURES.

(1) STANDARDS FOR RENEWAL. If the licensee of a broadcast station submits an application to the Commission for renewal of such license, the Commission shall grant the application if it finds, with respect to that station, during the preceding term of its license—

(A) the station has served the public interest, convenience, and necessity;

(B) there have been no serious violations by the licensee of this Act or the rules and regulations of the Commission; and

(C) there have been no other violations by the licensee of this Act or the rules and regulations of the Commission which, taken together, would constitute a pattern of abuse.

(2) CONSEQUENCE OF FAILURE TO MEET STANDARD. If any licensee of a broadcast station fails to meet the requirements of

this subsection, the Commission may deny the application for renewal...or grant such application on terms and conditions as are appropriate, including renewal for a term less than the maximum otherwise permitted.

(4)   COMPETITOR CONSIDERATION PROHIBITED. In making the determinations specified in paragraph (1) or (2), the Commission shall not consider whether the public interest, convenience, and necessity might be served by the grant of a license to a person other than the renewal applicant.

SEC. 310. [47 U.S.C. 310] LIMITATION ON HOLDING AND TRANSFER OF LICENSES.

(b) No broadcast or common carrier...license shall be granted to or held by—

(1) any alien or the representative of any alien;

* * *

(d) No construction permit or station license...shall be transferred...to any person except upon application to the Commission and upon finding by the Commission that the public interest, convenience, and necessity will be served thereby....[B]ut in acting thereon the Commission may not consider whether the public interest, convenience, and necessity might be served by the transfer, assignment, or disposal of the permit or license to a person other than the proposed transferee or assignee.

SEC. 311. [47 U.S.C. 311] SPECIAL REQUIREMENTS WITH RESPECT TO CERTAIN APPLICATIONS IN THE BROADCASTING SERVICE.

(c) (1) If there are pending before the Commission two or more applications for a permit for construction of a broadcasting station, only one of which can be granted, it shall be unlawful, without approval of the Commission, for the applicants or any of them to effectuate an agreement whereby one or more of such applicants withdraws his or their application or applications.

(3)   The Commission shall approve the agreement only if it determines that (A) the agreement is consistent with the public interest, convenience, or necessity; and (B) no party to the agreement filed its application for the purpose of reaching or carrying out such agreement.

(d) (1) If there are pending before the Commission an application for the renewal of a license granted for the operation of a broadcasting station and one or more applications for a construction permit relating to such station, only one of which can be granted, it shall be unlawful, without approval of the Commission, for the applicants or any of them to effectuate an agreement whereby one or more of such applicants withdraws his or their application or applications in exchange for the payment of money, or the transfer of assets or any other thing of value by the remaining applicant or applicants.

(3)   The Commission shall approve the agreement only if it determines that (A) the agreement is consistent with the public interest, convenience, or necessity; and (B) no party to the agreement filed its

application for the purpose of reaching or carrying out such agreement.

SEC. 312. [47 U.S.C. 312] ADMINISTRATIVE SANCTIONS.

(a) The Commission may revoke any station license or construction permit

* * *

(2) because of conditions coming to the attention of the Commission which would warrant it in refusing to grant a license or permit on an original application;

(3) for willful or repeated failure to operate substantially as set forth in the license; [or]

* * *

(7) for willful or repeated failure to allow reasonable access to or to permit purchase of reasonable amounts of time for the use of a broadcasting station by a legally qualified candidate for Federal elective office on behalf of his candidacy.

SEC. 315. [47 U.S.C. 315] FACILITIES FOR CANDIDATES FOR PUBLIC OFFICE.

(a) If any licensee shall permit any person who is a legally qualified candidate for any public office to use a broadcasting station, he shall afford equal opportunities to all other such candidates for that office in the use of such broadcasting station: *Provided*, That such licensee shall have no power of censorship over the material broadcast under the provisions of this section. No obligation is hereby imposed under this subsection upon any licensee to allow the use of its station by any such candidate. Appearance by a legally qualified candidate on any —

(1) bona fide newscast,

(2) bona fide news interview,

(3) bona fide news documentary (if the appearance of the candidate is incidental to the presentation of the subject or subjects covered by the news documentary), or

(4) on-the-spot coverage of bona fide news events (including but not limited to political conventions and activities incidental thereto),

shall not be deemed to be use of a broadcasting station within the meaning of this subsection. Nothing in the foregoing sentence shall be construed as relieving broadcasters, in connection with the presentation of newscasts, news interviews, news documentaries, and on-the-spot coverage of news events, from the obligation imposed upon them under this Act to operate in the public interest and to afford reasonable opportunity for the discussion of conflicting views on issues of public importance.

(b) The charges made for the use of any broadcasting station by any person who is a legally qualified candidate for any public office in connection with his campaign for nomination for election, or election, to such office shall not exceed —

(1)   during the forty-five days preceding the date of a primary or primary runoff election and during the sixty days preceding the date of a general or special election in which such person is a candidate, the lowest unit charge of the station for the same class and amount of time for the same period; and

(2) at any other time, the charges made for comparable use of such station by other users thereof.

SEC. 319. [47 U.S.C. 319] CONSTRUCTION PERMITS.

(a) No license shall be issued under the authority of this Act for the operation of any station unless a permit for its construction has been granted by the Commission.

SEC. 325. [47 U.S.C. 325] FALSE DISTRESS SIGNALS; REBROADCASTING; STUDIOS OF FOREIGN STATIONS.

(a) No person within the jurisdiction of the United States shall knowingly utter or transmit, or cause to be uttered or transmitted, any false or fraudulent signal of distress, or communication relating thereto, nor shall any broadcasting station rebroadcast the program or any part thereof of another broadcasting station without the express authority of the originating station.

(b) (1) [N]o cable system or other multichannel video programming distributor shall retransmit the signal of a broadcasting station, or any part thereof, except—

(A)   with the express authority of the originating station; or

(B)   pursuant to section 614, in the case of a station electing, in accordance with this subsection, to assert the right to carriage under such section.

(2) The provisions of this subsection shall not apply to—

(A)   retransmission of the signal of a noncommercial broadcasting station; [or]

* * *

(D)   retransmission by a cable operator or other multichannel video programming distributor of the signal of a superstation if...the originating station was a superstation on May 1, 1991....

(3)   (A)   [T]he Commission shall...establish regulations to govern the exercise by television broadcast stations of the right to grant retransmission consent under this subsection and of the right to signal carriage under section 614...The Commission shall consider in such proceeding the impact that the grant of retransmission consent by television stations may have on the rates for the basic service tier and shall ensure that the regulations prescribed under this subsection do not conflict with the Commission's obligation under section 623(b)(1) to ensure that the rates for the basic service tier are reasonable....

(B)   The regulations required by subparagraph (A) shall require that television stations...every three years thereafter, make an election between the right to grant retransmission consent under this subsec-

tion and the right to signal carriage under section 614. If there is more than one cable system which services the same geographic area, a station's election shall apply to all such cable systems.

(4)   If an originating television station elects under paragraph (3)(B) to exercise its right to grant retransmission consent under this subsection with respect to a cable system, the provisions of section 614 shall not apply to the carriage of the signal of such station by such cable system.

(5)   The exercise by a television broadcast station of the right to grant retransmission consent under this subsection shall not interfere with or supersede the rights under section 614 or 615 of any station electing to assert the right to signal carriage under that section.

(6)   Nothing in this section shall be construed as modifying the compulsory copyright license established in section 111 of title 17, United States Code, or as affecting existing or future video programming licensing agreements between broadcasting stations and video programmers.

SEC. 326. [47 U.S.C. 326] CENSORSHIP; INDECENT LANGUAGE.

Nothing in this Act shall be understood or construed to give the Commission the power of censorship over . . . any radio station, and no regulation or condition shall be promulgated or fixed by the Commission which shall interfere with the right of free speech by means of radio communication.

SEC. 333. [47 U.S.C. 333] WILLFUL OR MALICIOUS INTERFERENCE.

No person shall willfully or maliciously interfere with or cause interference to any radio communications of any station licensed or authorized by or under this Act or operated by the United States Government.

SEC. 335. [47 U.S.C. 335] DIRECT BROADCAST SATELLITE SERVICE OBLIGATIONS.

(a) PROCEEDING REQUIRED TO REVIEW DBS RESPONSIBILITIES. The Commission shall . . . impose, on providers of direct broadcast satellite service, public interest or other requirements for providing video programming.

(b) CARRIAGE OBLIGATIONS FOR NONCOMMERCIAL, EDUCATIONAL, AND INFORMATIONAL PROGRAMMING.

(1)   CHANNEL CAPACITY REQUIRED. The Commission shall require, as a condition of any . . . authorization . . . for a provider of direct broadcast satellite service providing video programming, that the provider of such service reserve a portion of its channel capacity, equal to not less than 4 percent nor more than 7 percent, exclusively for noncommercial programming of an educational or informational nature.

*   *   *

(3)   PRICES, TERMS, AND CONDITIONS; EDITORIAL CONTROL. A provider of direct broadcast satellite service shall meet

the requirements of this subsection by making channel capacity available to national educational programming suppliers, upon reasonable prices, terms, and conditions, as determined by the Commission. The provider of direct broadcast satellite service shall not exercise any editorial control over any video programming provided pursuant to this subsection.

SEC. 336 [47 U.S.C. 336] BROADCAST SPECTRUM FLEXIBILITY.

(a) COMMISSION ACTION. If the Commission determines to issue additional licenses for advanced television services, the Commission—

(1)   should limit the initial eligibility for such licenses to persons that, as of the date of such issuance, are licensed to operate a television broadcast station or hold a permit to construct such a station (or both); and

(2)   shall adopt regulations that allow the holders of such licenses to offer such ancillary or supplementary services on designated frequencies as may be consistent with the public interest, convenience, and necessity.

(c) RECOVERY OF LICENSE. If the Commission grants a license for advanced television services to a person that, as of the date of such issuance, is licensed to operate a television broadcast station or holds a permit to construct such a station (or both), the Commission shall, as a condition of such license, require that either the additional license or the original license held by the licensee be surrendered to the Commission for reallocation or reassignment (or both) pursuant to Commission regulation.

(d) PUBLIC INTEREST REQUIREMENT. Nothing in this section shall be construed as relieving a television broadcasting station from its obligation to serve the public interest, convenience, and necessity. In the Commission's review of any application for renewal of a broadcast license for a television station that provides ancillary or supplementary services, the television licensee shall establish that all of its program services on the existing or advanced television spectrum are in the public interest.

(e) FEES.

(1)   SERVICES TO WHICH FEES APPLY. If the regulations prescribed pursuant to subsection (a) permit a licensee to offer ancillary or supplementary services on a designated frequency—

(A)   for which the payment of a subscription fee is required in order to receive such services, or

(B)   for which the licensee directly or indirectly receives compensation from a third party in return for transmitting material furnished by such third party (other than commercial advertisements used to support broadcasting for which a subscription fee is not required), the Commission shall establish a program to assess and collect from the licensee for such designated frequency an annual fee or other schedule or method of payment that promotes the objectives described in subparagraphs (A) and (B) of paragraph (2).

(2)   COLLECTION OF FEES. The program required by paragraph (1) shall—

(A)   be designed (i) to recover for the public a portion of the value of the public spectrum resource made available for such commercial use, and (ii) to avoid unjust enrichment through the method employed to permit such uses of that resource; [and]

(B)   recover for the public an amount that, to the extent feasible, equals but does not exceed (over the term of the license) the amount that would have been recovered had such services been licensed pursuant to the provisions of section 309(j) of this Act and the Commission's regulations thereunder.

(f) EVALUATION. Within 10 years after the date the Commission first issues additional licenses for advanced television services, the Commission shall conduct an evaluation of the advanced television services program. Such evaluation shall include—

(1)   an assessment of the willingness of consumers to purchase the television receivers necessary to receive broadcasts of advanced television services;

(2)   an assessment of alternative uses, including public safety use, of the frequencies used for such broadcasts; and

(3)   the extent to which the Commission has been or will be able to reduce the amount of spectrum assigned to licensees.

SEC. 397 [47 U.S.C. 397] DEFINITIONS

(6) The terms "noncommercial educational broadcast station" and "public broadcast station" mean a television or radio broadcast station which:

(A) under the rules and regulations of the Commission in effect on November 2, 1978, is eligible to be licensed by the Commission as a noncommercial educational radio or television broadcast station and which is owned and operated by a public agency or nonprofit private foundation, corporation, or association; or

(B) is owned and operated by a municipality and which transmits only noncommercial programs for education purposes.

TITLE IV—PROCEDURAL AND ADMINISTRATIVE PROVISIONS

SEC. 401. [47 U.S.C. 401] JURISDICTION TO ENFORCE ACT AND ORDERS OF THE COMMISSION.

(a) The district courts of the United States shall have jurisdiction, upon application of the Attorney General of the United States at the request of the Commission, alleging a failure to comply with or a violation of any of the provisions of this Act by any person, to issue a writ or writs of mandamus commanding such person to comply with the provisions of this Act.

SEC. 402. [47 U.S.C. 402] PROCEEDINGS TO ENJOIN, SET ASIDE, ANNUL, OR SUSPEND ORDERS OF THE COMMISSION.

(a) Any proceeding to enjoin, set aside, annul, or suspend any order of the Commission under this Act (except those appealable under subsection (b) of this

section) shall be brought [in the circuit court of appeal where the filing party has its residence or principal office or in the D.C. Circuit].

(b) Appeals may be taken from decisions and orders of the Commission to the United States Court of Appeals for the District of Columbia in [licensing cases or proceedings in which a cease and desist order was issued].

TITLE V—PENAL PROVISIONS—FORFEITURES

SEC. 501. [47 U.S.C. 501] GENERAL PENALTY.

Any person who willfully and knowingly does or causes or suffers to be done any act, matter, or thing, in this Act prohibited or declared to be unlawful, or who willfully and knowingly omits or fails to do any act, matter, or thing in this Act required to be done, or willfully and knowingly causes or suffers such omission or failure, shall upon conviction thereof, be punished for such offense, for which no penalty (other than a forfeiture) is provided in this Act, by a fine of not more than $10,000 or by imprisonment for a term not exceeding one year, or both; except that any person, having been once convicted of an offense punishable under this section, who is subsequently convicted of violating any provision of this Act punishable under this section, shall be punished by a fine of not more than $10,000 or by imprisonment for a term not exceeding two years, or both.

SEC. 502. [47 U.S.C. 502] VIOLATION OF RULES, REGULATIONS, AND SO FORTH.

Any person who willfully and knowingly violates any rule, regulation, restriction, or condition made or imposed by the Commission under authority of this Act...shall, in addition to any other penalties provided by law, be punished, upon conviction thereof, by a fine of not more than $500 for each and every day during which such offense occurs.

SEC. 503. [47 U.S.C. 503] FORFEITURES IN CASES OF REBATES AND OFF-SETS.

(b) (1)   Any person who is determined by the Commission, in accordance with paragraph (3) or (4) of this subsection, to have—

(A)   willfully or repeatedly failed to comply substantially with the terms and conditions of any license, permit, certificate, or other instrument or authorization issued by the Commission;

(B)   willfully or repeatedly failed to comply with any of the provisions of this Act or of any rule, regulation, or order issued by the Commission under this Act...

* * *

shall be liable to the United States for a forfeiture penalty. A forfeiture penalty under this subsection shall be in addition to any other penalty provided for by this Act...

(2)   (A)   If the violator is (i) a broadcast station licensee or permittee, (ii) a cable television operator, or (iii) an applicant for any broadcast or cable television operator license, permit, certificate, or other instrument or authorization issued by the Commission, the

amount of any forfeiture penalty determined under this section shall not exceed $25,000 for each violation or each day of a continuing violation...

(B)   If the violator is a common carrier subject to the provisions of this Act or an applicant for any common carrier license, permit, certificate, or other instrument of authorization issued by the Commission, the amount of any forfeiture penalty determined under this subsection shall not exceed $100,000 for each violation or each day of a continuing violation...

* * *

TITLE VI—CABLE COMMUNICATIONS

PART I—GENERAL PROVISIONS

SEC. 601. [47 U.S.C. 521] PURPOSES.

The purposes of this title are to—

(1)   establish a national policy concerning cable communications;

(2)   establish franchise procedures and standards which encourage the growth and development of cable systems and which assure that cable systems are responsive to the needs and interests of the local community;

(3)   establish guidelines for the exercise of Federal, State, and local authority with respect to the regulation of cable systems;

(4)   assure that cable communications provide and are encouraged to provide the widest possible diversity of information sources and services to the public;

(5)   establish an orderly process for franchise renewal which protects cable operators against unfair denials of renewal where the operator's past performance and proposal for future performance meet the standards established by this title; and

(6)   promote competition in cable communications and minimize unnecessary regulation that would impose an undue economic burden on cable systems.

(a) APPLICABILITY OF AMENDMENTS TO FUTURE CONDUCT.

(1)   AT&T CONSENT DECREE. Any conduct or activity that was, before the date of enactment of this Act, subject to any restriction or obligation imposed by the AT&T Consent Decree shall, on and after such date, be subject to the restrictions and obligations imposed by the Communications Act of 1934 as amended by this Act and shall not be subject to the restrictions and the obligations imposed by such Consent Decree.

SEC. 602. [47 U.S.C. 522] DEFINITIONS.

For purposes of this title—

(1) the term "activated channels" means those channels engineered at the headend of a cable system for the provision of services generally available to residential subscribers of the cable system...

* * *

(3) the term "basic cable service" means any service tier which includes the retransmission of local television broadcast signals;

* * *

(6) the term "cable service" means—

(A) the one-way transmission to subscribers of (i) video programming, or (ii) other programming service,

* * *

(7) the term "cable system" means a facility, consisting of a set of closed transmission paths and associated signal generation, reception, and control equipment that is designed to provide cable service which includes video programming and which is provided to multiple subscribers within a community...

* * *

(11) the term "grade B contour" means the field strength of a television broadcast station computed in accordance with regulations promulgated by the Commission;

(13) the term "multichannel video programming distributor" means a person such as, but not limited to, a cable operator, a multichannel multipoint distribution service, a direct broadcast satellite service, or a television receive-only satellite program distributor, who makes available for purchase, by subscribers or customers, multiple channels of video programming;

(14) the term "other programming service" means information that a cable operator makes available to all subscribers generally;

* * *

(17) the term "service tier" means a category of cable service or other services provided by a cable operator and for which a separate rate is charged by the cable operator;

* * *

(20) the term "video programming" means programming provided by, or generally considered comparable to programming provided by, a television broadcast station.

PART II—USE OF CABLE CHANNELS AND CABLE OWNERSHIP RESTRICTIONS

SEC. 611. [47 U.S.C. 531] CABLE CHANNELS FOR PUBLIC, EDUCATIONAL, OR GOVERNMENTAL USE.

(a) A franchising authority may establish requirements in a franchise with respect to the designation or use of channel capacity for public, educational, or governmental use only to the extent provided in this section.

(b) A franchising authority may in its request for proposals require as part of a franchise, and may require as part of a cable operator's proposal for a franchise renewal, subject to section 626, that channel capacity be designated for public, educational, or governmental use, and channel capacity on institutional networks be designated for educational or governmental use, and may require rules and procedures for the use of the channel capacity designated pursuant to this section.

(c) A franchising authority may enforce any requirement in any franchise regarding the providing or use of such channel capacity. Such enforcement authority includes the authority to enforce any provisions of the franchise for services, facilities, or equipment proposed by the cable operator which relate to public, educational, or governmental use of channel capacity, whether or not required by the franchising authority pursuant to subsection (b).

(d) In the case of any franchise under which channel capacity is designated under subsection (b), the franchising authority shall prescribe—

> (1) rules and procedures under which the cable operator is permitted to use such channel capacity for the provision of other services if such channel capacity is not being used for the purposes designated, and

> (2) rules and procedures under which such permitted use shall cease.

(e) Subject to section 624(d), a cable operator shall not exercise any editorial control over any public, educational, or governmental use of channel capacity provided pursuant to this section, except a cable operator may refuse to transmit any public access program or portion of a public access program which contains obscenity, indecency, or nudity.

(f) For purposes of this section, the term "institutional network" means a communication network which is constructed or operated by the cable operator and which is generally available only to subscribers who are not residential subscribers.

SEC. 612. [47 U.S.C. 532] CABLE CHANNELS FOR COMMERCIAL USE.

(a) The purpose of this section is to promote competition in the delivery of diverse sources of video programming and to assure that the widest possible diversity of information sources are made available to the public from cable systems in a manner consistent with growth and development of cable systems.

(b) (1) A cable operator shall designate channel capacity for commercial use by persons unaffiliated with the operator in accordance with the following requirements:

> (A)   An operator of any cable system with 36 or more (but not more than 54) activated channels shall designate 10 percent of such channels which are not otherwise required for use (or the use of which is not prohibited) by Federal law or regulation.

> (B)   An operator of any cable system with 55 or more (but not more than 100) activated channels shall designate 15 percent of such channels which are not otherwise required for use (or the use of which is not prohibited) by Federal law or regulation.

> (C)   An operator of any cable system with more than 100 activated channels shall designate 15 percent of all such channels.

(D)   An operator of any cable system with fewer than 36 activated channels shall not be required to designate channel capacity for commercial use by persons unaffiliated with the operator.

* * *

(c) (1) If a person unaffiliated with the cable operator seeks to use channel capacity designated pursuant to subsection (b) for commercial use, the cable operator shall establish, consistent with the purpose of this section and with rules prescribed by the Commission...the price, terms, and conditions of such use which are at least sufficient to assure that such use will not adversely affect the operation, financial condition, or market development of the cable system.

(2)   A cable operator shall not exercise any editorial control over any video programming provided pursuant to this section, or in any other way consider the content of such programming, except that a cable operator may refuse to transmit any leased access program or portion of a leased access program which contains obscenity, indecency, or nudity and consider such content to the minimum extent necessary to establish a reasonable price for the commercial use of designated channel capacity by an unaffiliated person.

(4)   (A) The Commission shall have the authority to—

(i)   determine the maximum reasonable rates that a cable operator may establish pursuant to paragraph (1) for commercial use of designated channel capacity, including the rate charged for the billing of rates to subscribers and for the collection of revenue from subscribers by the cable operator for such use;

* * *

(f) In any action brought under this section in any Federal district court or before the Commission, there shall be a presumption that the price, terms, and conditions for use of channel capacity designated pursuant to subsection (b) are reasonable and in good faith unless shown by clear and convincing evidence to the contrary.

* * *

(h) Any cable service offered pursuant to this section shall not be provided, or shall be provided subject to conditions, if such cable service in the judgment of the franchising authority or the cable operator is obscene, or is in conflict with community standards in that it is lewd, lascivious, filthy, or indecent or is otherwise unprotected by the Constitution of the United States. This subsection shall permit a cable operator to enforce prospectively a written and published policy of prohibiting programming that the cable operator reasonably believes describes or depicts sexual or excretory activities or organs in a patently offensive manner as measured by contemporary community standards.

(i) (1) Notwithstanding the provisions of subsections (b) and (c), a cable operator required by this section to designate channel capacity for commercial use may use any such channel capacity for the provision of programming from a qualified minority programming source or from any qualified educational programming source, whether or not such source is affiliated with the cable operator. The channel capacity used to provide programming from a qualified minority

programming source or from any qualified educational programming source pursuant to this subsection may not exceed 33 percent of the channel capacity designated pursuant to this section....

(j) (1) [T]he Commission shall promulgate regulations designed to limit the access of children to indecent programming, as defined by Commission regulations, and which cable operators have not voluntarily prohibited under subsection (h) by—

(A)   requiring cable operators to place on a single channel all indecent programs, as identified by program providers, intended for carriage on channels designated for commercial use under this section;

(B)   requiring cable operators to block such single channel unless the subscriber requests access to such channel in writing; and

(C)   requiring programmers to inform cable operators if the program would be indecent as defined by Commission regulations.

SEC. 613. [47 U.S.C. 533] OWNERSHIP RESTRICTIONS.

(a) (2) It shall be unlawful for a cable operator to hold a license for multichannel multipoint distribution service...in any portion of the franchise area served by that cable operator's cable system....

(c) The Commission may prescribe rules with respect to the ownership or control of cable systems by persons who own or control other media of mass communications which serve the same community served by a cable system.

* * *

(f) (1) In order to enhance effective competition, the Commission shall... conduct a proceeding—

(A)   to prescribe rules and regulations establishing reasonable limits on the number of cable subscribers a person is authorized to reach through cable systems owned by such person...

(B)   to prescribe rules and regulations establishing reasonable limits on the number of channels on a cable system that can be occupied by a video programmer in which a cable operator has an attributable interest; and

(C)   to consider the necessity and appropriateness of imposing limitations on the degree to which multichannel video programming distributors may engage in the creation or production of video programming.

(2)   In prescribing rules and regulations under paragraph (1), the Commission shall, among other public interest objectives—

(A)   ensure that no cable operator or group of cable operators can unfairly impede, either because of the size of any individual operator or because of joint actions by a group of operators of sufficient size, the flow of video programming from the video programmer to the consumer;

(B)   ensure that cable operators affiliated with video programmers do not favor such programmers in determining carriage on their

cable systems or do not unreasonably restrict the flow of the video programming of such programmers to other video distributors;

* * *

(D)   account for any efficiencies and other benefits that might be gained through increased ownership or control; [and]

* * *

(G)   not impose limitations which would impair the development of diverse and high quality video programming.

SEC. 614 [47 U.S.C. 534] CARRIAGE OF LOCAL COMMERCIAL TELEVISION SIGNALS

(a) CARRIAGE OBLIGATIONS

Each cable operator shall carry, on the cable system of that operator, the signals of local commercial television stations and qualified low power stations as provided by this section. Carriage of additional broadcast television signals on such system shall be at the discretion of such operator, subject to section 325(b) of this title.

(b) SIGNALS REQUIRED

(1) IN GENERAL

(A) A cable operator of a cable system with 12 or fewer usable activated channels shall carry the signals of at least three local commercial television stations, except that if such a system has 300 or fewer subscribers, it shall not be subject to any requirements under this section so long as such system does not delete from carriage by that system any signal of a broadcast television station.

(B) A cable operator of a cable system with more than 12 usable activated channels shall carry the signals of local commercial television stations, up to one-third of the aggregate number of usable activated channels of such system.

(2) SELECTION OF SIGNALS

Whenever the number of local commercial television stations exceeds the maximum number of signals a cable system is required to carry under paragraph (1), the cable operator shall have discretion in selecting which such stations shall be carried on its cable system, except that:

(A) under no circumstances shall a cable operator carry a qualified low power station in lieu of a local commercial television station; and

(B) if the cable operator elects to carry an affiliate of a broadcast network (as such term is defined by the Commission by regulation), such cable operator shall carry the affiliate of such broadcast network whose city of license reference point, as defined in section 76.53 of title 47, Code of Federal Regulations (in effect on January 1, 1991), or any successor regulation thereto, is closest to the principal headend of the cable system.

(3) CONTENT TO BE CARRIED

(A) A cable operator shall carry in its entirety, on the cable system of that operator, the primary video, accompanying audio, and line 21 closed caption trans-

mission of each of the local commercial television stations carried on the cable system and, to the extent technically feasible, program-related material carried in the vertical blanking interval or on subcarriers. Retransmission of other material in the vertical blanking internal or other nonprogram-related material (including teletext and other subscription and advertiser-supported information services) shall be at the discretion of the cable operator. Where appropriate and feasible, operators may delete signal enhancements, such as ghost-canceling, from the broadcast signal and employ such enhancements at the system headend or headends.

(B) The cable operator shall carry the entirety of the program schedule of any television station carried on the cable system unless carriage of specific programming is prohibited, and other programming authorized to be substituted, under section 76.67 or subpart F of part 76 of title 47, Code of Federal Regulations (as in effect on January 1, 1991), or any successor regulations thereto.

(4) SIGNAL QUALITY

(A) NONDEGRADATION; TECHNICAL SPECIFICATIONS

The signals of local commercial television stations that a cable operator carries shall be carried without material degradation. The Commission shall adopt carriage standards to ensure that, to the extent technically feasible, the quality of signal processing and carriage provided by a cable system for the carriage of local commercial television stations will be no less than that provided by the system for carriage of any other type of signal.

(B) ADVANCEDTELEVISION

At such time as the Commission prescribes modifications of the standards for television broadcast signals, the Commission shall initiate a proceeding to establish any changes in the signal carriage requirements of cable television systems necessary to ensure cable carriage of such broadcast signals of local commercial television stations which have been changed to conform with such modified standards.

(5) DUPLICATION NOT REQUIRED

Notwithstanding paragraph (1), a cable operator shall not be required to carry the signal of any local commercial television station that substantially duplicates the signal of another local commercial television station which is carried on its cable system, or to carry the signals of more than one local commercial television station affiliated with a particular broadcast network (as such term is defined by regulation). If a cable operator elects to carry on its cable system a signal which substantially duplicates the signal of another local commercial television station carried on the cable system, or to carry on its system the signals of more than one local commercial television station affiliated with a particular broadcast network, all such signals shall be counted toward the number of signals the operator is required to carry under paragraph (1).

(6) CHANNEL POSITIONING

Each signal carried in fulfillment of the carriage obligations of a cable operator under this section shall be carried on the cable system channel number on which the local commercial television station is broadcast over the air, or on the

channel on which it was carried on July 19, 1985, or on the channel on which it was carried on January 1, 1992, at the election of the station, or on such other channel number as is mutually agreed upon by the station and the cable operator. Any dispute regarding the positioning of a local commercial television station shall be resolved by the Commission.

(7) SIGNAL AVAILABILITY

Signals carried in fulfillment of the requirements of this section shall be provided to every subscriber of a cable system. Such signals shall be viewable via cable on all television receivers of a subscriber which are connected to a cable system by a cable operator or for which a cable operator provides a connection. If a cable operator authorizes subscribers to install additional receiver connections, but does not provide the subscriber with such connections, or with the equipment and materials for such connections, the operator shall notify such subscribers of all broadcast stations carried on the cable system which cannot be viewed via cable without a converter box and shall offer to sell or lease such a converter box to such subscribers at rates in accordance with section 543(b)(3) of this title.

(10) COMPENSATION FOR CARRIAGE

A cable operator shall not accept or request monetary payment or other valuable consideration in exchange either for carriage of local commercial television stations in fulfillment of the requirements of this section or for the channel positioning rights provided to such stations under this section....

SEC. 615 [47 U.S.C. 535] CARRIAGE OF NONCOMMERCIAL TELEVISION STATIONS

(a) CARRIAGE OBLIGATIONS

In addition to the carriage requirements set forth in section 534 of this title, each cable operator of a cable system shall carry the signals of qualified noncommercial educational television stations in accordance with the provisions of this section.

(b) REQUIREMENTS TO CARRY QUALIFIED STATIONS

(1) GENERAL REQUIREMENT TO CARRY EACH QUALIFIED STATION

Subject to paragraphs (2) and (3) and subsection (e) of this section, each cable operator shall carry, on the cable system of that cable operator, any qualified local noncommercial educational television station requesting carriage.

(2) SYSTEMS WITH 12 OR FEWER CHANNELS

(A) Notwithstanding paragraph (1), a cable operator of a cable system with 12 or fewer usable activated channels shall be required to carry the signal of one qualified local noncommercial educational television station; except that a cable operator of such a system shall comply with subsection (c) of this section and may, in its discretion, carry the signals of other qualified noncommercial educational television stations.

(B) In the case of a cable system described in subparagraph (A) which operates beyond the presence of any qualified local noncommercial educational television station:

(i) the cable operator shall import and carry on that system the signal of one qualified noncommercial educational television station;

(ii) the selection for carriage of such a signal shall be at the election of the cable operator; and

(iii) in order to satisfy the requirements for carriage specified in this subsection, the cable operator of the system shall not be required to remove any other programming service actually provided to subscribers on March 29, 1990; except that such cable operator shall use the first channel available to satisfy the requirements of this subparagraph.

(3) SYSTEMS WITH 13 TO 36 CHANNELS

(A) Subject to subsection (c) of this section, a cable operator of a cable system with 13 to 36 usable activated channels:

(i) shall carry the signal of at least one qualified local noncommercial educational television station but shall not be required to carry the signals of more than three such stations, and

(ii) may, in its discretion, carry additional such stations.

(B) In the case of a cable system described in this paragraph which operates beyond the presence of any qualified local noncommercial educational television station, the cable operator shall import and carry on that system the signal of at least one qualified noncommercial educational television station to comply with subparagraph (A)(i).

(C) The cable operator of a cable system described in this paragraph which carries the signal of a qualified local noncommercial educational station affiliated with a State public television network shall not be required to carry the signal of any additional qualified local noncommercial educational television stations affiliated with the same network if the programming of such additional stations is substantially duplicated by the programming of the qualified local noncommercial educational television station receiving carriage.

(D) A cable operator of a system described in this paragraph which increases the usable activated channel capacity of the system to more than 36 channels on or after March 29, 1990, shall, in accordance with the other provisions of this section, carry the signal of each qualified local noncommercial educational television station requesting carriage, subject to subsection (e) of this section.

(e) SYSTEMS WITH MORE THAN 36 CHANNELS

A cable operator of a cable system with a capacity of more than 36 usable activated channels which is required to carry the signals of three qualified local noncommercial educational television stations shall not be required to carry the signals of additional such stations the programming of which substantially duplicates the programming broadcast by another qualified local noncommercial educational television station requesting carriage. Substantial duplication shall be defined by the Commission in a manner that promotes access to distinctive noncommercial educational television services.

PART III—FRANCHISING AND REGULATION

SEC. 621. [47 U.S.C. 541] GENERAL FRANCHISE REQUIREMENTS.

(a) (1) A franchising authority may award...one or more franchises within its jurisdiction; except that a franchising authority may not grant an exclusive franchise and may not unreasonably refuse to award an additional competitive franchise....

(2) Any franchise shall be construed to authorize the construction of a cable system over public rights-of-way, and through easements, which is within the area to be served by the cable system and which have been dedicated for compatible uses. . . .

(3) In awarding a franchise or franchises, a franchising authority shall assure that access to cable service is not denied to any group of potential residential cable subscribers because of the income of the residents of the local area in which such group resides.

(4) In awarding a franchise, the franchising authority—

(A) shall allow the applicant's cable system a reasonable period of time to become capable of providing cable service to all households in the franchise area;

(B) may require adequate assurance that the cable operator will provide adequate public, educational, and governmental access channel capacity, facilities, or financial support; and

(C) may require adequate assurance that the cable operator has the financial, technical, or legal qualifications to provide cable service.

(b) (1) [A] cable operator may not provide cable service without a franchise.

* * *

(c) Any cable system shall not be subject to regulation as a common carrier or utility by reason of providing any cable service.

SEC. 622. [47 U.S.C. 542] FRANCHISE FEES.

(a) Subject to the limitation of subsection (b), any cable operator may be required under the terms of any franchise to pay a franchise fee.

(b) For any twelve-month period, the franchise fees paid by a cable operator with respect to any cable system shall not exceed 5 percent of such cable operator's gross revenues derived in such period from the operation of the cable system. . . .

SEC. 623. [47 U.S.C. §543] REGULATION OF RATES.

(a) (1) No Federal agency or State may regulate the rates for the provision of cable service except to the extent provided under this section and section 612.

(2) If the Commission finds that a cable system is subject to effective competition, the rates for the provision of cable service by such system shall not be subject to regulation by the Commission or by a State or franchising authority under this section. If the Commission finds that a cable system is not subject to effective competition—

(A) the rates for the provision of basic cable service shall be subject to regulation by a franchising authority . . . and

(B) the rates for cable programming services shall be subject to regulation by the Commission under subsection (c).

(b) (1) The Commission shall, by regulation, ensure that the rates for the basic service tier are reasonable. Such regulations shall be designed to achieve the goal of

protecting subscribers of any cable system that is not subject to effective competition from rates for the basic service tier that exceed the rates that would be charged for the basic service tier if such cable system were subject to effective competition.

(2)   [T]he Commission shall prescribe, and periodically thereafter revise, regulations to carry out its obligations under paragraph (1). In prescribing such regulations, the Commission—

(A)   shall seek to reduce the administrative burdens on subscribers, cable operators, franchising authorities, and the Commission;

(B)   may adopt formulas or other mechanisms and procedures in complying with the requirements of subparagraph (A); and

(C) shall take into account the following factors:

(i)   the rates for cable systems, if any, that are subject to effective competition;

(ii)   the direct costs (if any) of obtaining, transmitting, and otherwise providing signals carried on the basic service tier, including signals and services carried on the basic service tier pursuant to paragraph (7)(B), and changes in such costs;

(iii)   only such portion of the joint and common costs (if any) of obtaining, transmitting, and otherwise providing such signals as is determined, in accordance with regulations prescribed by the Commission, to be reasonably and properly allocable to the basic service tier, and changes in such costs;

(iv)   the revenues (if any) received by a cable operator from advertising from programming that is carried as part of the basic service tier or from other consideration obtained in connection with the basic service tier;

(v)   the reasonably and properly allocable portion of any amount assessed as a franchise fee, tax, or charge of any kind imposed by any State or local authority on the transactions between cable operators and cable subscribers or any other fee, tax, or assessment of general applicability imposed by a governmental entity applied against cable operators or cable subscribers;

(vi)   any amount required, in accordance with paragraph (4), to satisfy franchise requirements to support public, educational, or governmental channels or the use of such channels or any other services required under the franchise; and

(vii) a reasonable profit, as defined by the Commission consistent with the Commission's obligations to subscribers under paragraph (1).

* * *

(7)   (A)   Each cable operator of a cable system shall provide its subscribers a separately available basic service tier to which subscription is required for access to any other tier of service. Such basic service tier shall, at a minimum, consist of the following:

(i)   All signals carried in fulfillment of the requirements of sections 614 and 615.

(ii)   Any public, educational, and governmental access programming required by the franchise of the cable system to be provided to subscribers.

(iii)   Any signal of any television broadcast station that is provided by the cable operator to any subscriber, except a signal which is secondarily transmitted by a satellite carrier beyond the local service area of such station.

(B) A cable operator may add additional video programming signals or services to the basic service tier. Any such additional signals or services provided on the basic service tier shall be provided to subscribers at rates determined under the regulations prescribed by the Commission under this subsection.

(8)   (A)   A cable operator may not require the subscription to any tier other than the basic service tier required by paragraph (7) as a condition of access to video programming offered on a per channel or per program basis. A cable operator may not discriminate between subscribers to the basic service tier and other subscribers with regard to the rates charged for video programming offered on a per channel or per program basis.

(c)   (1) [T]he Commission shall, by regulation, establish the following:

(A)   criteria prescribed in accordance with paragraph (2) for identifying, in individual cases, rates for cable programming services that are unreasonable;

(B)   fair and expeditious procedures for the receipt, consideration, and resolution of complaints from any subscriber, franchising authority, or other relevant State or local government entity alleging that a rate for cable programming services charged by a cable operator violates the criteria prescribed under subparagraph (A)...

(2)   In establishing the criteria for determining in individual cases whether rates for cable programming services are unreasonable under paragraph (1)(A), the Commission shall consider, among other factors—

(A)   the rates for similarly situated cable systems offering comparable cable programming services...

(B)   the rates for cable systems, if any, that are subject to effective competition;

(C)   the history of the rates for cable programming services of the system, including the relationship of such rates to changes in general consumer prices;

(D)   the rates, as a whole, for all the cable programming, cable equipment, and cable services provided by the system, other than programming provided on a per channel or per program basis;

(E)   capital and operating costs of the cable system, including the quality and costs of the customer service provided by the cable system; and

(F)   the revenues (if any) received by a cable operator from advertising from programming that is carried as part of the service for which a rate is being established...

(c) (4) SUNSET OF UPPER TIER RATE REGULATION—This subsection shall not apply to cable programming services provided after March 31, 1999.

* * *

(l) As used in this section—

(1) The term "effective competition" means that—

(A)   fewer than 30 percent of the households in the franchise area subscribe to the cable service of a cable system;

(B) the franchise area is—

(i)   served by at least two unaffiliated multichannel video programming distributors each of which offers comparable video programming to at least 50 percent of the households in the franchise area; and

(ii)   the number of households subscribing to programming services offered by multichannel video programming distributors other than the largest multichannel video programming distributor exceeds 15 percent of the households in the franchise area; or

(C)   a multichannel video programming distributor operated by the franchising authority for that franchise area offers video programming to at least 50 percent of the households in that franchise area.

(D)   a local exchange carrier or its affiliate (or any multichannel video programming distributor using the facilities of such carrier or its affiliate) offers video programming services directly to subscribers by any means (other than direct-to-home satellite services) in the franchise area of an unaffiliated cable operator which is providing cable service in that franchise area, but only if the video programming services so offered in that area are comparable to the video programming services provided by the unaffiliated cable operator in that area.

(2) The term "cable programming service" means any video programming provided over a cable system, regardless of service tier, including installation or rental of equipment used for the receipt of such video programming, other than (A) video programming carried on the basic service tier, and (B) video programming offered on a per channel or per program basis.

SEC. 624. [47 U.S.C. 544] REGULATION OF SERVICES, FACILITIES, AND EQUIPMENT.

(a) Any franchising authority may not regulate the services, facilities, and equipment provided by a cable operator except to the extent consistent with this title.

(b) In the case of any franchise granted after the effective date of this title, the franchising authority, to the extent related to the establishment or operation of a cable system—

(1)   in its request for proposals for a franchise (including requests for renewal proposals, subject to section 626), may establish

requirements for facilities and equipment, but may not, except as provided in subsection (h), establish requirements for video programming or other information services; and

(2)   subject to section 625, may enforce any requirements contained within the franchise —

(A) for facilities and equipment; and

(B) for broad categories of video programming or other services.

* * *

(d) (1)   Nothing in this title shall be construed as prohibiting a franchising authority and a cable operator from specifying...that certain cable services shall not be provided or shall be provided subject to conditions, if such cable services are obscene or are otherwise unprotected by the Constitution of the United States.

(2)   (A)   In order to restrict the viewing of programming which is obscene or indecent, upon the request of a subscriber, a cable operator shall provide (by sale or lease) a device by which the subscriber can prohibit viewing of a particular cable service during periods selected by that subscriber.

SEC. 626. [47 U.S.C. 546] RENEWAL.

(a) (1) A franchising authority may, on its own initiative during the 6-month period which begins with the 36th month before the franchise expiration, commence a proceeding which affords the public in the franchise area appropriate notice and participation for the purpose of (A) identifying the future cable-related community needs and interests, and (B) reviewing the performance of the cable operator under the franchise during the then current franchise term....

(b) (1) Upon completion of a proceeding under subsection (a), a cable operator seeking renewal of a franchise may, on its own initiative or at the request of a franchising authority, submit a proposal for renewal.

(c) (1) Upon submittal by a cable operator of a proposal to the franchising authority for the renewal of a franchise pursuant to subsection (b), the franchising authority shall provide prompt public notice of such proposal and, during the 4-month period which begins on the date of the submission of the cable operator's proposal pursuant to subsection (b), renew the franchise or, issue a preliminary assessment that the franchise should not be renewed and, at the request of the operator or on its own initiative, commence an administrative proceeding...

(2) To consider whether —

(A)   the cable operator has substantially complied with the material terms of the existing franchise and with applicable law;

(B)   the quality of the operator's service, including signal quality, response to consumer complaints, and billing practices, but without regard to the mix or quality of cable services or other services provided over the system, has been reasonable in light of community needs;

(C) the operator has the financial, legal, and technical ability to provide the services, facilities, and equipment as set forth in the operator's proposal; and

(D) the operator's proposal is reasonable to meet the future cable-related community needs and interests, taking into account the cost of meeting such needs and interests.

(d) Any denial of a proposal for renewal that has been submitted in compliance with subsection (b) shall be based on one or more adverse findings made with respect to the factors described in subparagraphs (A) through (D) of subsection (c)(1), pursuant to the record of the proceeding under subsection (c).

(e) (1) Any cable operator whose proposal for renewal has been denied by a final decision of a franchising authority made pursuant to this section, or has been adversely affected by a failure of the franchising authority to act in accordance with the procedural requirements of this section, may appeal such final decision or failure....

SEC. 628. [47 U.S.C. 548] DEVELOPMENT OF COMPETITION AND DIVERSITY IN VIDEO PROGRAMMING DISTRIBUTION.

(a) PURPOSE. The purpose of this section is to promote the public interest, convenience, and necessity by increasing competition and diversity in the multichannel video programming market, to increase the availability of satellite cable programming and satellite broadcast programming to persons in rural and other areas not currently able to receive such programming, and to spur the development of communications technologies.

(b) PROHIBITION. It shall be unlawful for a cable operator, a satellite cable programming vendor in which a cable operator has an attributable interest, or a satellite broadcast programming vendor to engage in unfair methods of competition or unfair or deceptive acts or practices, the purpose or effect of which is to hinder significantly or to prevent any multichannel video programming distributor from providing satellite cable programming or satellite broadcast programming to subscribers or consumers.

(c) REGULATIONS REQUIRED.

(2) MINIMUM CONTENTS OF REGULATIONS. The regulations to be promulgated under this section shall—

(A) establish effective safeguards to prevent a cable operator which has an attributable interest in a satellite cable programming vendor or a satellite broadcast programming vendor from unduly or improperly influencing the decision of such vendor to sell, or the prices, terms, and conditions of sale of, satellite cable programming or satellite broadcast programming to any unaffiliated multichannel video programming distributor;

(B) prohibit discrimination by a satellite cable programming vendor in which a cable operator has an attributable interest or by a satellite broadcast programming vendor in the prices, terms, and conditions of sale or delivery of satellite cable programming or satellite broadcast programming among or between cable systems, cable operators, or other multichannel video programming distributors, or their

agents or buying groups; except that such a satellite cable programming vendor in which a cable operator has an attributable interest or such a satellite broadcast programming vendor shall not be prohibited from—

imposing reasonable requirements for creditworthiness, offering of service, and financial stability and standards regarding character and technical quality;

(ii) establishing different prices, terms, and conditions to take into account actual and reasonable differences in the cost of creation, sale, delivery, or transmission of satellite cable programming or satellite broadcast programming;

(iii) establishing different prices, terms, and conditions which take into account economies of scale, cost savings, or other direct and legitimate economic benefits reasonably attributable to the number of subscribers served by the distributor; or

(iv) entering into an exclusive contract that is permitted under subparagraph (D);

(C) prohibit practices, understandings, arrangements, and activities, including exclusive contracts for satellite cable programming or satellite broadcast programming between a cable operator and a satellite cable programming vendor or satellite broadcast programming vendor, that prevent a multichannel video programming distributor from obtaining such programming from any satellite cable programming vendor in which a cable operator has an attributable interest or any satellite broadcast programming vendor in which a cable operator has an attributable interest for distribution to persons in areas not served by a cable operator as of the date of enactment of this section; and

(D) with respect to distribution to persons in areas served by a cable operator, prohibit exclusive contracts for satellite cable programming or satellite broadcast programming between a cable operator and a satellite cable programming vendor in which a cable operator has an attributable interest or a satellite broadcast programming vendor in which a cable operator has an attributable interest, unless the Commission determines (in accordance with paragraph (4)) that such contract is in the public interest.

(4) PUBLIC INTEREST DETERMINATIONS ON EXCLUSIVE CONTRACTS. In determining whether an exclusive contract is in the public interest for purposes of paragraph (2)(D), the Commission shall consider each of the following factors with respect to the effect of such contract on the distribution of video programming in areas that are served by a cable operator:

(A) the effect of such exclusive contract on the development of competition in local and national multichannel video programming distribution markets;

(B) the effect of such exclusive contract on competition from multichannel video programming distribution technologies other than cable;

(C)   the effect of such exclusive contract on the attraction of capital investment in the production and distribution of new satellite cable programming;

(D)   the effect of such exclusive contract on diversity of programming in the multichannel video programming distribution market; and

(E)   the duration of the exclusive contract.

(d) ADJUDICATORY PROCEEDING. Any multichannel video programming distributor aggrieved by conduct that it alleges constitutes a violation of subsection (b), or the regulations of the Commission under subsection (c), may commence an adjudicatory proceeding at the Commission.

(e) REMEDIES FOR VIOLATIONS.

(1)   REMEDIES AUTHORIZED. Upon completion of such adjudicatory proceeding, the Commission shall have the power to order appropriate remedies, including, if necessary, the power to establish prices, terms, and conditions of sale of programming to the aggrieved multichannel video programming distributor.

PART IV — MISCELLANEOUS PROVISIONS

SEC. 631. [47 U.S.C. 551] PROTECTION OF SUBSCRIBER PRIVACY.

(a) (1) At the time of entering into an agreement to provide any cable service or other service to a subscriber and at least once a year thereafter, a cable operator shall provide notice in the form of a separate, written statement to such subscriber which clearly and conspicuously informs the subscriber of —

(A)   the nature of personally identifiable information collected or to be collected with respect to the subscriber and the nature of the use of such information;

(B)   the nature, frequency, and purpose of any disclosure which may be made of such information, including an identification of the types of persons to whom the disclosure may be made;

(C)   the period during which such information will be maintained by the cable operator;

(D)   the times and place at which the subscriber may have access to such information in accordance with subsection (d); and

(E)   the limitations provided by this section with respect to the collection and disclosure of information by a cable operator and the right of the subscriber under subsections (f) and (h) to enforce such limitations.

(b) (1)   Except as provided in paragraph (2), a cable operator shall not use the cable system to collect personally identifiable information concerning any subscriber without the prior written or electronic consent of the subscriber concerned.

(2)   A cable operator may use the cable system to collect such information in order to —

(A)   obtain information necessary to render a cable service or other service provided by the cable operator to the subscriber; or

(B) detect unauthorized reception of cable communications.

(c) (1) Except as provided in paragraph (2), a cable operator shall not disclose personally identifiable information concerning any subscriber without the prior written or electronic consent of the subscriber concerned and shall take such actions as are necessary to prevent unauthorized access to such information by a person other than the subscriber or cable operator.

(2) A cable operator may disclose such information if the disclosure is—

(A) necessary to render, or conduct a legitimate business activity related to, a cable service or other service provided by the cable operator to the subscriber;

(B) subject to subsection (h), made pursuant to a court order authorizing such disclosure, if the subscriber is notified of such order by the person to whom the order is directed; or

(C) a disclosure of the names and addresses of subscribers to any cable service or other service, if—

(i) the cable operator has provided the subscriber the opportunity to prohibit or limit such disclosure, and

(ii) the disclosure does not reveal, directly or indirectly, the—

(I) extent of any viewing or other use by the subscriber of a cable service or other service provided by the cable operator, or

(II) the nature of any transaction made by the subscriber over the cable system of the cable operator.

(d) A cable subscriber shall be provided access to all personally identifiable information regarding that subscriber which is collected and maintained by a cable operator.

* * *

(h) A governmental entity may obtain personally identifiable information concerning a cable subscriber pursuant to a court order only if, in the court proceeding relevant to such court order—

(1) such entity offers clear and convincing evidence that the subject of the information is reasonably suspected of engaging in criminal activity and that the information sought would be material evidence in the case; and

(2) the subject of the information is afforded the opportunity to appear and contest such entity's claim.

SEC. 632. [47 U.S.C. 552] CONSUMER PROTECTION AND CUSTOMER SERVICE.

(a) A franchising authority may establish and enforce—

(1) customer service requirements of the cable operator; and

(2) construction schedules and other construction-related requirements, including construction-related performance requirements, of the cable operator.

(b) The Commission shall...establish standards by which cable operators may fulfill their customer service requirements. Such standards shall include, at a minimum, requirements governing—

    (1)   cable system office hours and telephone availability;

    (2)   installations, outages, and service calls; and

    (3)   communications between the cable operator and the subscriber (including standards governing bills and refunds).

SEC. 633. [47 U.S.C. 553] UNAUTHORIZED RECEPTION OF CABLE SERVICE.

(a) (1)   No person shall intercept or receive or assist in intercepting or receiving any communications service offered over a cable system, unless specifically authorized to do so by a cable operator or as may otherwise be specifically authorized by law.

    (2)   For the purpose of this section, the term "assist in intercepting or receiving" shall include the manufacture or distribution of equipment intended by the manufacturer or distributor (as the case may be) for unauthorized reception of any communications service offered over a cable system in violation of subparagraph (1).

SEC. 634. [47 U.S.C. 554] EQUAL EMPLOYMENT OPPORTUNITY.

(a) This section shall apply to any corporation, partnership, association, joint-stock company, or trust engaged primarily in the management or operation of any cable system.

(b) Equal opportunity in employment shall be afforded by each entity specified in subsection (a), and no person shall be discriminated against in employment by such entity because of race, color, religion, national origin, age, or sex.

(e) (2) The Commission shall, periodically, but not less frequently than every five years, investigate the employment practices of each entity described in subsection (a), in the aggregate, as well as in individual job categories, and determine whether such entity is in compliance with the requirements of subsections (b), (c), and (d), including whether such entity's employment practices deny or abridge women and minorities equal employment opportunities.

(f) (1) If the Commission finds after notice and hearing that the entity involved has willfully or repeatedly without good cause failed to comply with the requirements of this section, such failure shall constitute a substantial failure to comply with this title.

    (2)   Any person who is determined by the Commission, through an investigation pursuant to subsection (e) or otherwise, to have failed to meet or failed to make best efforts to meet the requirements of this section, or rules under this section, shall be liable to the United States for a forfeiture penalty of $500 for each violation....

SEC. 638. [47 U.S.C. 558] CRIMINAL AND CIVIL LIABILITY.

Nothing in this title shall be deemed to affect the criminal or civil liability of cable programmers or cable operators pursuant to the Federal, State, or local

law of libel, slander, obscenity, incitement, invasions of privacy, false or mis-leading advertising, or other similar laws, except that cable operators shall not incur any such liability for any program carried on any channel designated for public, educational, governmental use or on any other channel obtained under section 612 or under similar arrangements unless the program involves obscene material.

SEC. 639. [47 U.S.C. 559] OBSCENE PROGRAMMING.

Whoever transmits over any cable system any matter which is obscene or otherwise unprotected by the Constitution of the United States shall be fined not more than $10,000 or imprisoned not more than 2 years, or both.

SEC. 640. [47 U.S.C. 560] SCRAMBLING OF CABLE CHANNELS FOR NONSUBSCRIBERS.

(a) SUBSCRIBER REQUEST. Upon request by a cable service subscriber, a cable operator shall, without charge, fully scramble or otherwise fully block the audio and video programming of each channel carrying such programming so that one not a subscriber does not receive it.

SEC. 641. [47 U.S.C. 561] SCRAMBLING OF SEXUALLY EXPLICIT ADULT VIDEO SERVICE PROGRAMMING.

(a) REQUIREMENT. In providing sexually explicit adult programming or other programming that is indecent on any channel of its service primarily dedi-cated to sexually-oriented programming, a multichannel video programming dis-tributor shall fully scramble or otherwise fully block the video and audio portion of such channel so that one not a subscriber to such channel or programming does not receive it.

(b) IMPLEMENTATION. Until a multichannel video programming distribu-tor complies with the requirement set forth in subsection (a), the distributor shall limit the access of children to the programming referred to in that subsection by not providing such programming during the hours of the day (as determined by the Commission) when a significant number of children are likely to view it.

PART V—VIDEO PROGRAMMING SERVICES PROVIDED BY TELEPHONE COMPANIES

SEC. 651. [47 U.S.C. 571] REGULATORY TREATMENT OF VIDEO PRO-GRAMMING SERVICES.

(a) LIMITATIONS ON CABLE REGULATION.

(1) RADIO-BASED SYSTEMS. To the extent that a common carrier (or any other person) is providing video programming to sub-scribers using radio communication, such carrier (or other person) shall be subject to the requirements of title III and section 652, but shall not otherwise be subject to the requirements of this title.

(2) COMMON CARRIAGE OF VIDEO TRAFFIC. To the ex-tent that a common carrier is providing transmission of video pro-gramming on a common carrier basis, such carrier shall be subject to

the requirements of title II and section 652, but shall not otherwise be subject to the requirements of this title.

(3)   CABLE SYSTEMS AND OPEN VIDEO SYSTEMS. To the extent that a common carrier is providing video programming to its subscribers in any manner other than that described in paragraphs (1) and (2)—

(A)   such carrier shall be subject to the requirements of this title, unless such programming is provided by means of an open video system for which the Commission has approved a certification under section 653; or

(B)   if such programming is provided by means of an open video system for which the Commission has approved a certification under section 653, such carrier shall be subject to the requirements of this part, but shall be subject to parts I through IV of this title only as provided in 653(c).

(b) LIMITATIONS ON INTERCONNECTION OBLIGATIONS. A local exchange carrier that provides cable service through an open video system or a cable system shall not be required, pursuant to title II of this Act, to make capacity available on a nondiscriminatory basis to any other person for the provision of cable service directly to subscribers.

SEC. 652. [47 U.S.C. 572] PROHIBITION ON BUY OUTS.

(a) ACQUISITIONS BY CARRIERS. No local exchange carrier...may acquire more than a 10 percent financial interest, or any management interest, in any cable operator providing cable service within the local exchange carrier's telephone service area.

(b) ACQUISITIONS BY CABLE OPERATORS. No cable operator...may acquire more than a 10 percent financial interest, or any management interest, in any local exchange carrier providing telephone exchange service within such cable operator's franchise area.

(c) JOINT VENTURES. A local exchange carrier and a cable operator whose telephone service area and cable franchise area, respectively, are in the same market may not enter into any joint venture or partnership to provide video programming directly to subscribers or to provide telecommunications services within such market.

(d) EXCEPTIONS. [Several sub-sub-sections provide exemptions for certain rural systems, for certain competitive cable systems, and for certain small cable systems. The FCC is also granted limited authority to waive the requirements of (a), (b), and (c).]

SEC. 653. [47 U.S.C. 573] ESTABLISHMENT OF OPEN VIDEO SYSTEMS.

(a) OPEN VIDEO SYSTEMS.

(1)   CERTIFICATES OF COMPLIANCE. A local exchange carrier may provide cable service to its cable service subscribers in its telephone service area through an open video system that complies with this section. To the extent permitted by such regulations as the

Commission may prescribe consistent with the public interest, convenience, and necessity, an operator of a cable system or any other person may provide video programming through an open video system that complies with this section.

(b) COMMISSION ACTIONS.

(1)   REGULATIONS REQUIRED. [T]he Commission shall... prescribe regulations that—

(A)   except as required pursuant to section 611, 614, or 615, prohibit an operator of an open video system from discriminating among video programming providers with regard to carriage on its open video system, and ensure that the rates, terms, and conditions for such carriage are just and reasonable, and are not unjustly or unreasonably discriminatory;

(B)   if demand exceeds the channel capacity of the open video system, prohibit an operator of an open video system and its affiliates from selecting the video programming services for carriage on more than one-third of the activated channel capacity on such system, but nothing in this subparagraph shall be construed to limit the number of channels that the carrier and its affiliates may offer to provide directly to subscribers;

(D)   extend to the distribution of video programming over open video systems the Commission's regulations concerning sports exclusivity, network nonduplication, and syndicated exclusivity; and

(E)   (i) prohibit an operator of an open video system from unreasonably discriminating in favor of the operator or its affiliates with regard to material or information (including advertising) provided by the operator to subscribers for the purposes of selecting programming on the open video system, or in the way such material or information is presented to subscribers; [and]

(iv)   prohibit an operator of an open video system from omitting television broadcast stations or other unaffiliated video programming services carried on such system from any navigational device, guide, or menu.

(c) REDUCED REGULATORY BURDENS FOR OPEN VIDEO SYSTEMS.

(1)   IN GENERAL. Any provision that applies to a cable operator under—

(A)   sections 613 (other than subsection (a) thereof), 616, 623(f), 628, 631, and 634 of this title, shall apply,

(B)   sections 611, 614, and 615 of this title, and section 325 of title III, shall apply in accordance with the regulations prescribed under paragraph (2), and

(C)   sections 612 and 617, and parts III and IV (other than sections 623(f), 628, 631, and 634), of this title shall not apply, to any operator of an open video system for which the Commission has approved a certification under this section.

(B)　　FEES. An operator of an open video system under this part may be subject to the payment of fees on the gross revenues of the operator for the provision of cable service imposed by a local franchising authority or other governmental entity, in lieu of the franchise fees permitted under section 622. The rate at which such fees are imposed shall not exceed the rate at which franchise fees are imposed on any cable operator transmitting video programming in the franchise area.

(4)　　TREATMENT AS CABLE OPERATOR. Nothing in this Act precludes a video programming provider making use of an open video system from being treated as an operator of a cable system for purposes of section 111 of title 17, United States Code.

TITLE VII—MISCELLANEOUS PROVISIONS

SEC. 705. [47 U.S.C. 605] UNAUTHORIZED PUBLICATION OF COMMUNICATIONS.

(a) Except as authorized by chapter 119, title 18, United States Code, no person receiving, assisting in receiving, transmitting, or assisting in transmitting, any interstate or foreign communication by wire or radio shall divulge or publish the existence, contents, substance, purport, effect, or meaning thereof, except through authorized channels of transmission or reception, (1) to any person other than the addressee, his agent, or attorney, (2) to a person employed or authorized to forward such communication to its destination, (3) to proper accounting or distributing officers of the various communicating centers over which the communication may be passed, (4) to the master of a ship under whom he is serving, (5) in response to subpoena issued by a court of competent jurisdiction, or (6) on demand of other lawful authority. No person not being authorized by the sender shall intercept any radio communication and divulge or publish the existence, contents, substance, purport, effect, or meaning of such intercepted communication to any person. No person not being entitled thereto shall receive or assist in receiving any interstate or foreign communication by radio and use such communication (or any information therein contained) for his own benefit or for the benefit of another not entitled thereto. No person having received any intercepted radio communication or having become acquainted with the contents, substance, purport, effect, or meaning of such communication (or any part thereof) knowing that such communication was intercepted, shall divulge or publish the existence, contents, substance, purport, effect, or meaning of such communication (or any part thereof) or use such communication (or any information therein contained) for his own benefit or for the benefit of another not entitled thereto. This section shall not apply to the receiving, divulging, publishing, or utilizing the contents of any radio communication which is transmitted by any station for the use of the general public, which relates to ships in distress, or which is transmitted by an amateur radio station operator or by a citizens band radio operator.

(b) The provisions of subsection (a) shall not apply to the interception or receipt by any individual, or the assisting (including the manufacture or sale) of such interception or receipt, of any satellite cable programming for private viewing if—

(1) the programming involved is not encrypted; and

(2)　　(A)　　a marketing system is not established under which—

(i) an agent or agents have been lawfully designated for the purpose of authorizing private viewing by individuals, and

(ii) such authorization is available to the individual involved from the appropriate agent or agents; or

(B)   a marketing system described in subparagraph (A) is established and the individuals receiving such programming has obtained authorization for private viewing under that system.

CONCEPTUAL INDEX AND TELECOMMUNICATIONS GLOSSARY

1934 Act • An abbreviation for the Communications Act of 1934, the principal statute governing telecommunications regulation in the United States. Most other telecommunications statutes are actually just amendments to this Act. The Act is codified at 47 U.S.C., and it is discussed throughout this text.

1992 Cable Act • An abbreviation for the Cable Television Consumer Protection and Competition Act of 1992, a significant piece of legislation that amended the Communications Act of 1934 and also the Copyright Act of 1976. The 1992 Cable Act established many of the current rules governing cable service provision; it is discussed primarily in Chapters Ten, Eleven and Twelve.

1996 Act • An abbreviation for the Telecommunications Act of 1996. This statute amended the Communications Act of 1934 and, among other things, established most of the rules under which the telephone industry is today regulated. The 1996 Act is analyzed extensively in Chapter Eighteen, although provisions of the Act are discussed pervasively.

Access Charges • Charges that are paid by IXCs to LECs to compensate LECs for their costs of originating and terminating interexchange calls. These charges have to date overcompensated LECs for those costs and in that way forced IXCs to contribute to LEC universal service obligations. [Chapter Seventeen (pp. 712–714)] [Chapter Eighteen (pp. 768–791)].

Advanced Services • A term used by both Congress and the FCC to refer to a wide range of technologies and services capable of delivering large quantities of data at high speeds. Examples include digital subscriber line (DSL) service and cable modem technology. Advanced services are considered in Chapter Twenty-One.

Advanced Television (ATV) • A general term for any television technology that provides improved audio and video quality or otherwise enhances the current television broadcast system. *See also* DTV, HDTV, and NTSC. [Chapter Eight (pp. 332–360)].

Amplitude Modulation (AM) • A method of encoding information on a radio wave by varying the strength (voltage) of some agreed-upon baseline signal. To take a simple example: the baseline strength might be 2 volts, and all parties might understand that every time the signal increases to 5 volts the sender intends to tell the receiver that a customer has entered the building. AM is one of two common methods of encoding typically used for radio transmission. *See also* FM, Carrier Wave. [Chapter One (pp. 26–28)].

Analog • A signaling method that uses continuous changes in the amplitude or frequency of a radio transmission to convey information. *See also* Digital. [Chapter One (pp. 26–28)].

Asymmetric Digital Subscriber Line (ADSL) • *See* Digital Subscriber Line (DSL).

AT&T • An acronym for the American Telephone and Telegraph Company. The acronym is sometimes used to refer to the firm that ran most of the nation's telephone system prior to 1982 (what in this text we refer to as "Bell"); but it is more often used today to refer to the subsidiary of Bell that is today a large telecommunications conglomerate.

Baby Bell • One of several terms for the LECs that were once part of the Bell System. The phrase sometimes refers to a single LEC, but it is more often used to refer to the Regional Holding Companies of which the LECs were a part. *See also* LEC, RBOC, RHC.

Band Plan • A set of decisions regarding the allocation and assignment of radio spectrum. The band plan for a given block of spectrum typically establishes (1) how the spectrum may be used, (2) how it will be divided both across and within geographical areas, and (3) the rules for actually assigning the use of that spectrum to specific parties. [Chapter Three (pp. 62–79)].

Bandwidth • Transmission capacity of a communications channel.

Bell • The telecommunications firm built on Alexander Graham Bell's initial telephone patents. In this text, the word is used exclusively to refer to that company as it existed before divestiture. Bell is particularly discussed in Chapters Fifteen and Sixteen.

Bell Operating Company (BOC) • One of several terms for the LECs that were once part of the Bell System. The creation of the BOCs under the MFJ is discussed in Chapter Sixteen. *See also* Baby Bell, LEC, RHC.

Bill-and-Keep • An arrangement between two LECs where each agrees to terminate, at no charge, traffic that originates on the other's network. Each LEC *bills* its own customers and *keeps* those payments instead of sharing them with the other LEC. The concept is discussed as part of Chapter Eighteen's introduction to interconnection obligations and reciprocal compensation (pp. 749–755); it comes up again in Chapter Twenty-Two's discussion of reciprocal compensation for ISP-bound traffic (pp. 927–945).

Bit • A contraction of the term "binary digit" which refers to the smallest unit of information that a computer processes. A bit has a value of either zero or one. Digital information is transmitted as a string of bits. *See also* Digital.

Bottleneck • The point in a system or production process at which the traffic of competing providers must flow over facilities owned by a single provider. Bottlenecks raise concerns for competition policy because of the potential for the firm controlling the bottleneck to discriminate against competitors in access to the facility and thereby to exercise monopoly power over the good or service at issue.

Broadband • Broadband is a descriptive term for evolving technologies that provide consumers with access to high-speed services. Broadband services are usually integrated, meaning that they include some combination of voice, high-speed data service, video-demand services, and interactive delivery services. *See also* Advanced Services.

Carrier Wave • In situations where a radio wave is being modified for the purposes of encoding information on the wave, the "carrier wave" is the baseline, unmodified wave against which the modified waves are to be compared. [Chapter One (pp. 26–28)].

Cellular Telephony • Wireless telephone technology that divides spectrum into small geographic "cells" each of which contains its own transmitter and receiver. As a caller moves from cell to cell, her call is handed off from the equipment in one cell to the equipment in the next, allowing the first cell to handle other callers' signals. In this way callers moving about the same general area can use the same frequencies without interfering with one an-

other. We consider cellular telephony throughout the text, but we consider in particular spectrum allocation issues related to cellular telephony in Chapter Three (pp. 64–72) and interconnection obligations between wireline and cellular systems in Chapter Eighteen (pp. 749–755). *See also* CMRS, PCS.

Central Office • The primary place where a LEC houses its switches and other equipment for the routing and processing of telephone calls. *See also* Switch. [Chapter Fifteen (pp. 613–614)].

Circuit Switching • A circuit-switched network is one in which the path for a particular communication is kept open from the time the communication is initiated until the time transmission is complete. The major example is the telephone system, in which each voice call has a unique channel that is kept open for that call, even during pauses in the transmission when nothing is traveling along the voice path. In this way communications are not interrupted and flow smoothly from end to end as they are transmitted. *See also* Packet Switching.

Commercial Mobile Radio Service (CMRS) • The generic term for commercially available wireless services like cellular telephony, paging, and digital PCS. *See also* Cellular Telephony, PCS. [Chapter Three (pp. 64–72)].

Common Carrier • A firm that sells its services to the general public and serves all comers for a set fee. A telephone carrier, for example, serves anyone who wishes to subscribe and does so on non-discriminatory terms. [Chapter Fifteen (pp. 607–609)].

Comparative Hearing • The means by which the FCC long decided, and resolved disputes over, which among competing applicants should receive broadcasting licenses. This mechanism for assigning broadcast licenses is discussed and evaluated in Chapters Four and Five.

Competitive Local Exchange Carrier (CLEC) • Firms that provide local telephone service in competition with the incumbent local exchange carrier (ILEC) in a given area.

Cost-of-Service Regulation • *See* Rate-of-Return Regulation.

Cream Skimming • When a carrier seeks to serve only highly profitable customers, or to provide only highly profitable services, the strategy is called "cream skimming" or "cherry picking." Bell, and (after the 1996 Act) the ILECs, used the term to describe the strategies of new entrants into the telephone market and argued that such strategies interfere with the incumbents' abilities to meet their universal service obligations. Cream-skimming is discussed pervasively in Part Three of the text; the concept is introduced, however, in Chapter Fifteen (pp. 631–632).

Cross-Ownership Rules • Rules that restrict ownership across different telecommunications services. For example, in 1999, the Commission announced a radio/television cross-ownership rule that under certain circumstances allows a single party to own as many as one television station and seven radio stations in the same market. *See also* Multiple-Ownership Rules. [Chapter Seven (pp. 313–324)] [Chapter Twelve (pp. 499–524)].

Customer Premises Equipment (CPE) • Products like ordinary telephones, fax machines, modems, computers, answering machines, and even private branch exchange (PBX) equipment that connect to the telephone network at a customer's home or business. *See also* PBX. [Chapter Fifteen (pp. 613–614)].

Demand Variability • One of several factors that might create the conditions of natural monopoly. Systems that must maintain excess capacity to deal with periods of peak demand are expensive to operate because at least some of their resources sit idle some of the

time. The more customers a given system serves, however, the less expensive this factor might be; variance in customers' demand patterns will typically mean that some customers will use the shared resource while others do not, and vice versa, increasing the overall efficiency of the system as compared to a system with fewer customers. [Chapter Nine (pp. 374–380)] [Chapter Fifteen (pp. 614–621)].

Digital • A signal consisting of binary code (a stream of ones and zeroes) to represent voice, video or data.

Direct Broadcast Satellite (DBS) • High-powered satellite transmission or retransmission of signals intended for direct reception by the public. The signal is transmitted to a small earth station or dish (usually the size of a large pizza) mounted on homes or other buildings. The term DBS refers most often to satellite-based multichannel video services to which consumers can subscribe. Regulatory issues related to DBS are considered in Chapter Thirteen.

Digital Subscriber Line (DSL) • A high-speed data service provided over conventional telephone networks. DSL refers to the technology that allows telephone carriers to attach certain electronics to the telephone line that can transform the copper loop that already provides voice service into a conduit for high-speed data traffic. With most DSL technologies today, a high-speed signal is sent from the end-user's terminal over the local copper loop until it reaches a Digital Subscriber Line Access Multiplexer (DSLAM), usually located in the carrier's central office. There are numerous variants of DSL, the most common of which is "asymmetric" digital subscriber line (ADSL). DSL services are often referred to with the generic acronym "xDSL" where the "x" is simply a placeholder for a particular type of DSL. Regulatory issues related to DSL and other advanced services are considered in Chapter Twenty-One. *See also* Advanced Services.

Digital Television (DTV) • Television signals transmitted and received in digital format. DTV is a type of transmission, not a level of picture quality. Thus, DTV has several formats and varying degrees of resolution from standard definition to high definition (HDTV). Not all DTV is HDTV, because the bandwidth required for HDTV can be broken down to accommodate several DTV signals of lesser resolution. *See also* ATV, HDTV, NTSC. [Chapter Eight (pp. 332–360)].

Divestiture • From the verb "divest" which means to separate or take away, this term refers to the breakup of the Bell System that came as a result of the Department of Justice's 1974 antitrust prosecution. Divestiture is considered extensively in Chapter Sixteen.

Economy of Scale • An economy of scale is said to exist whenever the average cost of producing one unit of a good is constantly decreasing over the normal range of consumer demand for that good. The concept is important to telecommunications regulation because it can lead to natural monopoly conditions in the relevant market. *See also* Economy of Scope. [Chapter Nine (pp. 374–380)] [Chapter Fifteen (pp. 614–621)].

Economy of Scope • An economy of scope is said to exist whenever a single firm can produce a given quantity of two or more goods more cheaply than could multiple firms. Bell argued that economies of scope existed in the provision of local and long distance telephone service and, according to Bell, made it desirable to have a single national telephone company. *See also* Economy of Scale. [Chapter Fifteen (pp. 614–621)].

Facilities-Based Competition • Under the 1996 Act, this phrase refers to competition from CLECs that have built all or most of their own infrastructure.

Federal Communications Commission (FCC) • The federal agency in charge of telecommunications regulation, created by the 1934 Act. The FCC is also referred to as the Commission, and its actions are the core subjects of this text. *See also* FRC.

Federal Radio Commission (FRC) • The predecessor agency to the FCC, created by the Radio Act of 1927 and abolished by the 1934 Act. The history of the FRC is discussed in Chapter One (pp. 11–23).

Financial Interest and Syndication Rules (Finsyn Rules) • The now-repealed finsyn rules prohibited the major TV networks from exercising certain types of control over already-broadcast television content. The concern motivating these rules was that the major networks could use this control to deny independent stations access to high-quality syndicated reruns. [Chapter Seven (pp. 302–313)].

Frequency Modulation (FM) • A method of encoding information on a radio wave by varying the frequency of some agreed-upon baseline signal. To take a simple example: the baseline signal might reach its peak once every two seconds, and all parties might understand that every time the signal frequency drops below this level a customer has entered the building. FM is one of two common methods of encoding typically used for radio transmission. *See also* AM, Carrier Wave. [Chapter One (pp. 26–28)].

High Definition Television (HDTV) • An improved television standard which provides approximately twice the vertical and horizontal resolution of existing television standards. It also provides audio quality approaching that of compact discs. HDTV can be either analog or digital. *See also* ATV, DTV, NTSC. [Chapter Eight (pp. 332–360)].

Incumbent Local Exchange Carrier (ILEC) • The established provider of local telephone service in a given area, which until the 1996 Act usually had a monopoly franchise.

In-Region Long Distance • Provision of long distance service by a BOC to customers in the BOC's own local service territory, where the BOC controls the local exchange bottleneck; that is, a BOC's provision of long distance service to its own local exchange customers. Section 271 of the 1996 Act requires a BOC to meet certain market-opening conditions before it can offer in-region long distance service. *See also* Out-of-Region Long Distance. The legal implications of the in-region/out-of-region distinction are discussed in Chapter Eighteen (pp. 755–768); the policies motivating this legal distinction are discussed throughout Part Three of the text.

Interexchange Carrier (IXC) • An IXC is a long distance telephone company. The term comes from the fact that long distance carriers transport calls across the boundaries that separate one local exchange area from another. *See also* Local Access and Transport Area. [Chapter Fifteen (pp. 613–614)].

InterLATA Telephone Service • Long distance service that involves the transport of calls across LATA boundaries; this is another term for interexchange service, introduced by the MFJ. *See also* Local Access and Transport Area. [Chapter Sixteen (pp. 671–679)].

Internet • The Internet is a network of computer networks. It is in essence a decentralized, global information system that is linked together by addresses based on the Internet Protocol (IP), is able to support communications using the Transmission Control Protocol/Internet Protocol (TCP/IP) and/or other IP-compatible protocols; and provides, uses, or makes accessible, either publicly or privately, high-level services layered on the communications and related information infrastructure. [Chapter Twenty (pp. 827–837)].

Internet Backbone • Long-haul fiber optic networks that transport traffic among ISPs, content providers, online service companies, and other Internet customers. Each backbone

provider essentially creates a network over which customers and content providers can communicate. [Chapter Twenty (pp. 827–837)] [Chapter Twenty-One (pp. 915–925)].

Internet Service Provider (ISP) • ISPs provide customers with access to the Internet. An ISP is a firm that, at a minimum, receives and translates Internet-bound data. The ISP takes data in whatever form it arrives and translates it into a form consistent with the TCP/IP protocol of the Internet. Regulatory issues related to ISPs are considered in Chapters Twenty-One and Twenty-Two.

IntraLATA Telephone Service • Telephone service within a LATA. Much intraLATA service is just local exchange service, but some calls between distant points within a LATA have an additional toll charge. *See also* Local Access and Transport Area. [Chapter Sixteen (pp. 671–679)].

Last Mile • The segment of a telecommunications network that connects directly to a customer's premises. The term often refers to the twisted pair of copper wires that connects a customer to a LEC's switch and over which a telephone call begins and ends its journey. Many people believe the "last mile" to be a bottleneck, although that belief is today less strongly held than it once was. [Chapter Fifteen (pp. 613–614)] [Chapter Twenty-One (pp. 868–880)].

Local Access and Transport Area (LATA) • Geographic service areas created by the MFJ to define the boundaries between local and long distance calls. The MFJ authorized the divested Bell Operating Companies to transport calls within each LATA, but strictly prohibited them from carrying telephone calls across any LATA boundaries. LATAs were generally drawn to center around a metropolitan area or to incorporate a region comprising a community of common interest. There are 164 LATAs nationwide. *See also* InterLATA Telephone Service, IntraLATA Telephone Service. [Chapter Sixteen (pp. 671–679)].

Local Exchange • A geographical area in which customers receive service from a common central office or set of central offices. Sometimes an exchange is served by a single central office switch, in which case the switch itself is referred to as the "exchange." [Chapter Fifteen (pp. 613–614)].

Local Exchange Carrier (LEC) • A provider of local telephone services. The term includes the BOCs, independent telephone companies, and also the CLECs that entered the market primarily as a result of the 1996 Act. *See also* CLEC, ILEC, IXC.

Loop • The part of a local exchange network connecting the customer to the carrier's switch; in essence, the loop is the customer's telephone line. Sometimes an entire local exchange network is referred to as "the local loop" for a given area. [Chapter Fifteen (pp. 613–614)].

Low Power FM (LPFM) • A broadcast service that permits the licensing of 50–100 watt FM radio stations within a service radius of up to 3.5 miles and 1–10 watt FM radio stations within a service radius of 1 to 2 miles. [Chapter Eight (pp. 325–332)].

Modification of Final Judgment or Modified Final Judgment (MFJ) • The 1982 consent decree between Bell and the Department of Justice, which took effect on January 1, 1984, that broke up the Bell System into AT&T long distance and seven independent Regional Bell Operating Companies (RBOCs) that would provide local exchange service. The MFJ also imposed line of business restrictions on the local Bell operating companies. "Modification" here refers to the fact that the decree technically "modified" the 1956 consent decree entered against Bell's Western Electric manufacturing subsidiary. The MFJ is considered extensively in Chapter Sixteen.

Multichannel Video Programming Distributor (MVPD) • An entity engaged in the business of selling multiple channels of video programming to paying subscribers. Such entities include, but are not limited to, cable operators, multichannel multipoint distribution services (MMDS, often called "wireless cable"), and direct broadcast satellite (DBS) services.

Multiple-Ownership Rules • Rules that restrict ownership within the same service or closely connected services, designed to foster competition. These rules can apply nationally or locally, and they can set caps by stipulating a maximum number of licenses/franchises, a maximum percentage of the relevant audience, or both. So, for example, the "local television ownership rules" limit the number of broadcast licenses that a single entity can hold in a given market; and the "national television ownership rules" limit the percentage of the national audience that a single broadcaster can reach through stations it owns or controls. [Chapter Seven (pp. 313–324)] [Chapter Twelve (pp. 499–524)] [Chapter Twenty-One (pp. 893–894)].

Must-Carry Obligation • A 1992 Cable Act term referring to the statutory requirement that cable system carry the signals of a certain number of commercial and noncommercial television broadcast stations that are "local" to the area served by the cable system. The term was later used again in the context of DBS service. [Chapter Eleven (pp. 453–497)] [Chapter Thirteen (pp. 550–557)].

Natural Monopoly • A natural monopoly is said to exist in any market where the costs of production are such that it is less expensive for demand to be met by one firm than it would be for that same demand to be met by more than one firm. For example, this occurs when, over a sufficiently large range of output, the addition of each new customer lowers the average cost of serving every other customer. [Chapter Nine (pp. 374–380)].

Network Effect or Network Externality • A condition that causes the value a given consumer places on an item to increase as the number of other consumers of that product increases. There is a network effect or network externality at work in the telephone industry because, the more subscribers, the more people to call, and hence the more each subscriber values his or her own telephone subscription. [Chapter Fifteen (pp. 614–621)].

Network Nonduplication • Network nonduplication rules are companion rules to the syndicated exclusivity rules. They enable a local broadcaster to prevent a cable system from exhibiting that part of an imported distant broadcaster's signal that contains network programming for which the local broadcaster has obtained exclusive broadcast rights in that local area. The local broadcaster must acquire exclusive rights by contract with the network. Network nonduplication rules were later expanded to apply against retransmission by DBS providers as well. *See also* Syndicated Exclusivity. [Chapter Eleven (pp. 445–453)] [Chapter Thirteen (pp. 556–557)].

Notice of Inquiry (NOI) • The Commission releases an NOI for the purpose of gathering information about a broad subject or as a means of generating ideas on a specific issue. The Commission may issue an NOI *sua sponte*, or in response to an outside request. An NOI need not occur in order for a rulemaking to commence; that is, a rulemaking can begin with or without an NOI. *See also* NPRM, R&O. [Chapter Three (pp. 57–62)].

Notice of Proposed Rulemaking (NPRM) • A rulemaking proceeding ordinarily begins with a Notice of Proposed Rulemaking. An NPRM contains a discussion of the issues to be addressed and proposed regulations in response to those issues. Readers are invited to comment on both the issues and the proposed rules. After reviewing comments on the NPRM, the FCC might choose to issue a further Notice of Proposed Rulemaking—

thereby providing an opportunity for the public to comment further on a related or specific proposal—or the Commission might go ahead and release a final order (usually in the form of a Report and Order) that adopts some variant of the proposed rule, alters an existing rule, or decides not to take any action. *See also* NOI, R&O. [Chapter Three (pp. 57–62)].

NTSC Standard • The existing broadcasting standard is referred to as NTSC, after the National Television Systems Committee, an industry group established in 1940 to develop technical standards for television broadcasts. Specifically, the NTSC standard calls for generation, transmission, and reception of television communications at 525 lines per frame with 30 frames per second. HDTV (and, more generally, ATV) is aimed at improving the audio and visual quality of current broadcasts. *See also* ATV, DTV, HDTV. [Chapter Eight (pp. 332–360)].

Out-of-Region Long Distance • Long distance service provided by a BOC to customers outside the territory where the BOC provides local exchange service; *e.g.,* long distance service that one BOC might offer to the local exchange customers of another BOC. The MFJ prohibited such service, but the 1996 lifted that restriction. The legal implications of the in-region/out-of-region distinction are discussed in Chapter Eighteen (pp. 755–768); the policies motivating this legal distinction are discussed throughout Part Three of the text.

Packet Switching • In packet-switched networks, messages between network users are divided into units, commonly referred to as packets, frames, or cells. These individual units are then routed between network users. Unlike circuit switching, however, the path between network users is not kept open for any particular communication. This allows for more efficient use of the telecommunications infrastructure, but it also introduces the possibility of delays, often undetectable, in the movement of packets from end-to-end. The switches that route packets are called "packet switches," and the function of routing individual data packets based on address or other routing information contained in the packets is "packet switching." *See also* Circuit Switching. [Chapter Twenty (pp. 830–833)].

Personal Communications Service (PCS) • A wireless communications service similar to cellular telephony, but transmitted at lower power and generally using digital rather than analog signals. The FCC licensed PCS providers in the mid-1990s to compete with the two cellular providers originally licensed in each geographic market. *See also* Cellular Telephony, CMRS. [Chapter Three (pp. 64–72)].

Plain Old Telephone Service (POTS) • Basic, traditional telephone service without any enhanced features like call-waiting, caller-ID, integrated voice messaging, and so on. POTS is sometimes also referred to as basic dialtone service. [Chapter Fifteen (pp. 613–614)].

Point of Presence (POP) • The part of an interexchange (long-distance) carrier's network where that carrier connects to a local exchange network. The term more generally refers to any network connection point, so America Online has POPs—in that case, computers through which users can connect to AOL's network.

Price Cap Regulation • A method of rate regulation that has largely replaced rate-of-return regulation for telecommunications carriers. Price cap regulation limits the prices firms can charge rather than limiting the returns a firm can earn. The theory behind price caps is that they give regulated firms incentives to reduce costs and become more efficient because, for at least some period of time before regulators readjust the caps, firms can thereby increase their profits. Price caps are introduced in Chapter Nine (pp. 425–429) and discussed in

Chapters Fifteen (pp. 635–639) and Seventeen (pp. 682–691). *See also* Rate-of-Return Regulation.

Prime Time Access Rules (PTAR) • These rules limited ABC, CBS, and NBC to supplying their affiliates with only three hours of programing for use during the four-hour "prime-time" time block. The rules were designed to ensure that third-party program suppliers would have access to primetime audiences and also to help independent stations compete with network affiliates. The rules are no longer in effect. [Chapter Seven (pp. 302–303)].

Private Branch Exchange (PBX) • A switch that a customer, usually a business or institution with many internal lines, places on its premises to serve as a private exchange for routing internal calls. A PBX usually allows internal calls to be dialed in abbreviated form.

Program Clearance • This refers to the decision by a broadcast station to carry a particular program distributed by the network with which the station is affiliated. [Chapter Seven (pp. 297–302)].

Public Good • A term used to describe a product or service for which demand is "non-rivalrous." When one consumer's consumption of a good does not affect any other person's ability to consume that same good, then the thing being consumed has the properties of a public good. Broadcast television programming is a public good—a fact that has important implications for broadcast policy. [Chapter Two (pp. 49–52)].

Public Interest Standard • The standard that the Communications Act directs the FCC to apply in a variety of settings, ranging from licensing broadcasters to authorizing service operations by telecommunications carriers. The phrase—"public interest, convenience, and necessity"—appears throughout the 1934 Act.

Public Switched Telephone Network (PSTN) • Usually refers to the incumbent local exchange network that offers service to all customers in its operating area.

Public Trustee • This term is often attached to holders of broadcast licenses. It refers to their obligation to operate their stations in a manner that serves the interests of the viewing public. The term incorporates the idea that holders of scarce licenses have received a special benefit—use of the government's precious spectrum—in return for which they must serve the public's, and not just their own private, objectives. Many prominent public trustee obligations are surveyed in Chapter Six.

Public Utilities Commission (PUC) • A state regulatory authority that oversees the intrastate aspects of telephone (and usually other utility) services. Sometimes called a "public service commission" or other similar term.

Ramsey Pricing • Ramsey pricing is a method of setting prices applicable in many situations, including situations where a single firm or entity must recover fixed costs and can do so by manipulating prices on more than one good. Ramsey pricing suggests that the most efficient way to recover those fixed costs is to set price levels for the goods such that, when comparing the goods, the good for which consumers are less sensitive to price is priced such that there is a greater difference between price and marginal cost than there is for the good for which consumers are more sensitive to price. Serious equity concerns limit the applicability of Ramsey pricing in the telephone context, an issue considered in detail in Chapter Fifteen (pp. 621–623).

Rate-of-Return Regulation • A form of regulation under which firms are permitted to charge prices that both cover their total costs of providing a service and, in addition, pay a "reasonable" rate of return on their capital investments in providing the service. This form

of regulation, which was for decades the primary means of regulating telephone rates, requires the regulator to determine the regulated firm's costs and then to decide what rate of return is reasonable for the firm to earn. Rate-of-return regulation is introduced in Chapter Nine (pp. 425–429) and discussed again in Chapter Fifteen (pp. 635–639). *See also* Price Cap Regulation.

Reciprocal Compensation • Payment by one local exchange carrier to another for the additional, or marginal, costs of terminating calls that originated on the paying carrier's network. Reciprocal compensation is the general rule established by the Telecommunications Act of 1996 for interconnection among competing local exchange carriers. [Chapter Eighteen (pp. 749–755)] [Chapter Twenty-Two (pp. 927–945)].

Regional Bell Operating Company (RBOC) • Term for each of the seven regional local exchange carriers created by the MFJ. An RBOC (or RHC) was a holding company generally consisting of several LECs. Thus, for example, Pacific Telesis (now part of SBC) was an RBOC that in turn consisted of several subsidiaries, such as Nevada Bell and Pacific Bell (California), that served particular states. Pacific Bell, in turn, owned and operated local telephone companies throughout California. The word "regional" distinguishes these firms from the Bell Operating Companies of which they are comprised. A map showing the seven RBOCs can be found in Chapter Sixteen at page 673; broader discussion can be found at pages 671–673. *See also* Baby Bell, Bell Operating Company.

Regional Holding Company (RHC) • See Regional Bell Operating Company.

Regulation by Raised Eyebrow • A form of implicit regulation where an agency—here, the FCC—does not use the rulemaking process to announce its policies but, instead, indicates its desires less formally and then threatens to enforce those desires through the exercise of its discretion. One prominent example in this text: for many years, the Commission used its discretion in license renewal to encourage broadcast licensees to air diverse and also educational fare. [Chapter Four (pp. 111–122)].

Regulatory Capture • Phrase used to describe situations where a regulatory agency falls under the influence of a powerful interest group. The paradigmatic case of capture arises when an agency does the bidding of the very parties it was originally designed to regulate and therefore stops regulating in the public's interest and starts, instead, regulating for the benefit of the regulated parties. This is not an uncommon allegation, especially because regulators necessarily do work closely with the parties they regulate, for example gathering information from them, and so at least some form of a relationship is bound to form. Moreover, regulators and regulatees in some sense rely on one another for their survival: should the industry disappear or become fully competitive, the regulators might find themselves without work; should the regulators become too strict, the regulatees might find themselves losing considerable profits and freedoms. All this intuitively could cloud a regulator's judgment.

Regulatory Parity • The idea that competing or similar services and technologies should face equivalent or similar regulatory regimes.

Report and Order (R&O) • The title of the document that the FCC customarily uses to take final action on a proposed rule. After considering comments to a Notice of Proposed Rulemaking (or further Notice of Proposed Rulemaking), the FCC issues a Report and Order. The R&O might establish new rules, amend existing rules, or announce a decision not to make any changes. *See also* NOI and NPRM. [Chapter Three (pp. 57–62)].

Resale • One of the means by which Congress and the FCC have attempted to introduce competition into telecommunications markets. A key example is the 1996 Act's mandate

that ILECs make their services available at wholesale rates to new entrants such that those new entrants can, in turn, resell those services directly to consumers. [Chapter Eighteen (pp. 715–749)].

Retransmission Consent • A requirement of the 1992 Act that cable operators receive consent from the relevant broadcaster before retransmitting that broadcaster's signal to cable subscribers. A broadcaster has a choice between demanding carriage under the 1992 Act's must-carry provisions or demanding that a cable operator obtain its consent for carriage. DBS providers are subject to similar regulations. [Chapter Eleven (pp. 453–497)] [Chapter Thirteen (pp. 550–557)].

Satellite Home Viewer Act of 1988 (SHVA) • An Act that, among other things, granted satellite carriers a statutory license to retransmit network television programming to "unserved households" even without copyright permission from the relevant copyright holders. The act has since been significantly mooted by the Satellite Home Viewer Improvement Act of 1999 (SHVIA). [Chapter Thirteen (pp. 544–551)].

Satellite Home Viewer Improvement Act of 1999 (SHVIA) • An Act that established for DBS a regime of rules and licenses similar to that which governs retransmission of broadcast signals over cable television. For example, the Act establishes a retransmission consent requirement, must-carry obligations, and statutory licenses under which DBS providers can, in certain circumstances, retransmit copyrighted content without the relevant copyright holder's permission. [Chapter Thirteen (pp. 551–557)].

Separations • The regulatory division of facilities or costs between interstate and intrastate telecommunications services, usually for the purpose of drawing the line between state and federal regulatory jurisdiction. [Chapter Fifteen (pp. 610–613)].

Spectrum • The electromagnetic radio frequencies used in the transmission of television and other signals carrying video, sound, and data through the air. One of the Commission's major tasks is spectrum management. *See also* Band Plan, Comparative Hearings. [Chapter One (pp. 24–33)] [Chapter Three (pp. 64–79)].

Subscriber Line Charge (SLC) • The federally mandated flat charge that LECs pass along to customers. The SLC was first instituted as part of the access charge regime the FCC put in place in response to the MFJ. [Chapter Seventeen (pp. 712–714)].

Switch • The critical piece of telephone network equipment that routes calls among telephone subscribers. A switch is what enables a telephone network to operate efficiently: every customer need not have a line to every other customer, but instead need only have a single line to the switch, which then will connect a call from any customer's line to any other customer's line. [Chapter Fifteen (pp. 613–614)].

Syndication • The process of licensing television programming for re-broadcast after the program's primary network run has ended. [Chapter Seven (pp. 302–313)].

Syndicated Exclusivity • Syndicated exclusivity ("syndex") rules are companion regulations to the network nonduplication rules. Syndex rules enable a local broadcaster to prevent a cable system from exhibiting that part of an imported distant broadcaster's signal that contains programs (or episodes from a television series) for which the local broadcaster has obtained exclusive broadcast rights in that local area from the copyright holder. These rules were later applied against DBS providers as well. *See also* Network Nonduplication. [Chapter Eleven (pp. 445–453)] [Chapter Thirteen (pp. 536–537)].

Tariff • The document filed by a telecommunications provider (usually filed with a PUC) describing a particular service and the terms, including price, under which that service

will be offered. A "tariffed service" is one for which a service provider is required to file a tariff and, thus, one that is regulated by either state or federal authorities.

Taxation by Regulation • A phrase that refers to any situation where the government imposes a financial burden on a regulated party not directly, but instead by requiring a particular unprofitable behavior. The phrase is designed to remind policymakers to consider the explicit alternative—namely, actually taxing the regulated party in that same amount and then using the money to further the policy goal at issue. There are myriad examples of taxation by regulation in this text.

TCP/IP • A set of protocols that controls (1) the division of information into packets, (2) the addressing and identification of those packets, and (3) the transfer of those packets from host to host, on the Internet. [Chapter Twenty (pp. 827–837)].

Total Element Long-Run Incremental Cost (TELRIC) • The rule that the FCC adopted in 1996 for determining the price at which an ILEC must sell unbundled network elements to CLECs. [Chapter Eighteen (pp. 740–749)].

Ultra High Frequency (UHF) • A phrase that refers to television stations occupying frequencies above the 30 to 300 MHz bands used by VHF stations. Channels 60 to 69, for example, broadcast over the 700 MHz frequencies. UHF signals are weaker than VHF signals and can deliver a high-quality television picture only over a comparatively smaller geographic range. Broadcast stations thus for a long time preferred VHF licenses over UHF licenses, although because cable can retransmit VHF and UHF equally well, the "UHF handicap" is less important in modern times. *See also* VHF.

Unbundled Network Element (UNE) • A part ("element") of a telephone network, such as a switch or customer loop, that the 1996 Act requires ILECs to lease to CLECs at cost-based rates. *See also* TELRIC, Resale. [Chapter Eighteen (pp. 717–749)] [Chapter Twenty-One (pp. 880–892)].

Universal Service • A set of policies designed to keep rates for local telephone service affordable and reasonably homogenous for subscribers. At times, the phrase refers more broadly to any subsidy or program designed to assist low income or otherwise disadvantaged telecommunications consumers. [Chapter Fifteen (pp. 614–623)] [Chapter Seventeen (pp. 712–714)] [Chapter Eighteen (pp. 768–791)].

V-Chip • Device in a television that allows viewers to screen out unwanted television broadcasts. (The "V" stands for "violence.") The chip detects a rating and content-description signal embedded in the broadcast and blocks programs that meet criteria selected by the viewer. [Chapter Six (pp. 242–254)].

Very High Frequency (VHF) • A phrase that refers to the part of the radio spectrum from 30 to 300 MHz. These bands are used to broadcast (among other things) television channels 2 through 13. *See also* UHF.

Western Electric • The equipment manufacturing subsidiary of Bell before divestiture in 1984. After divestiture it was part of AT&T Network Systems and, in 1995, it was spun off and renamed Lucent Technologies.